THE JUDICIAL PROCESS

TEXT, MATERIALS AND CASES

Second Edition

By

Ruggero J. Aldisert

Senior U.S. Circuit Judge
Chief Judge Emeritus
U.S. Court of Appeals for the Third Circuit

AMERICAN CASEBOOK SERIES®

WEST PUBLISHING CO.
ST. PAUL, MINN., 1996

American Casebook Series, the key symbol appearing on the front
cover and the WP symbol are registered trademarks of West Publishing
Co. Registered in the U.S. Patent and Trademark Office.

COPYRIGHT © 1976 WEST PUBLISHING CO.

COPYRIGHT © 1996 By WEST PUBLISHING CO.
             610 Opperman Drive
             P.O. Box 64526
             St. Paul, MN 55164–0526
             1–800–328–9352

Library of Congress Cataloging-in-Publication Data

Aldisert, Ruggero J.
    The judicial process : text, materials, and cases / by Ruggero J.
Aldisert.
        p. cm. — (American casebook series)
    Includes index.
    ISBN 0–314–06776–0 (hardcover)
    1. Judicial process—United States—Cases. I. Title.
II. Series.
KF8700.A7A43   1996
347.73'1—dc20
[347.3071]   95–47145
                                    CIP

ISBN 0–314–06776–0

For my daughter, Lisa.

*

FOREWORD

Anyone who has seen Judge Ruggero J. Aldisert in action—whether in his practice, whether in his judging in the state trial court or on the federal appellate bench, whether in his teaching, or whether in his wide-ranging work as a member of the faculty of the Appellate Judges Seminar at New York University Law School, as a member of the Board of the Federal Judicial Center, as formulator of judicial study or other programs, or as a member and promoter of any number of civic endeavors—recognizes at once, with an assured conviction, various aspects of his legal personality: He loves the law. He yearns to know its history and its character or, to use the word he has employed effectively in this volume, its anatomy. He has a persistent but most refreshing curiosity about the law. He wants to know what it is, why it is what it is, and how all of us who labor in its vineyard use or misuse it.

This volume, with its broad approach, is the result of arduous and long, loving labor. How many judges have read seriously, if ever at all, what these pages contain, or, if they were read once, have remembered them, with the consequent rewards that that memory and its inherent guidance would bestow.

I venture to say that Judge Aldisert has learned much in assembling this material; has learned more in teaching it; and would be the first to concede that he is a better judge, because he perused it, thought about it, asked himself, as well as his students, the provocative questions that his notes contain, and grew in appreciation of what the law is or purports to be. It is a magnificent persuasion, this law of ours, as we perceive it. Efforts such as Judge Aldisert's help us to appreciate it—as we ought—and thereby to preserve it—as we must.

HARRY A. BLACKMUN
Retired Justice
Supreme Court of the United States

Washington, D.C.

*

V

PREFACE TO SECOND EDITION

Generations in the law are usually measured by 20 or 25 years, or in more ancestral terms, by a score of years or quarter century. One such generation has passed since the first edition of this book appeared in 1976. Similarly, that edition had surfaced two generations after Benjamin N. Cardozo authored *The Nature of the Judicial Process* (1921). The first edition was both an update and an expansion of Cardozo's insights; in it, we considered how Cardozo's novel ideas of the early Twenties were faring in the Seventies, particularly his concepts of how judges should decide cases.

These seminal concepts issued from a true revolution in legal philosophy that appeared around the turn of the century under the influence of three giants of the American legal tradition—Roscoe Pound, Oliver Wendell Holmes and Cardozo. These thinkers led us out of the discredited methodology of conceptual jurisprudence—the view that a legal precept should be followed to its dryly logical extreme, regardless of its effects on society. In its place emerged a new jural philosophy, one that Professor Harry W. Jones would describe in 1974, a half century after Cardozo had spoken his mighty words:

> A legal rule or a legal institution is a good rule or institution when—
> that is, to the extent that—it contributes to the establishment and
> preservation of a social environment in which the quality of human
> life can be spirited, improving and unimpaired.

Younger thinkers stepped into the shoes of this formidable triumvirate, casting long shadows of their own—Roger J. Traynor in California; Walter V. Schaefer in Chicago; Karl N. Llewellyn, first at Columbia University and later at the University of Chicago; Learned Hand, Jerome Frank and Henry J. Friendly of New York; Henry M. Hart of Harvard; Herbert Wechsler of Columbia University and the American Law Institute; and Justice William J. Brennan, Jr.

At the time we compiled the first edition, we had both the advantage of friendship and the privilege of exchanging ideas at seminars and programs with Roger Traynor, Wally Schaefer, Professor Bob Leflar of Arkansas, Dean Bob McKay of N.Y.U., longtime Harvard dean and Solicitor General Erwin N. Griswold, Charlie Wright and Bernie Ward of the University of Texas, Justice Bob Braucher of the Massachusetts Supreme Judicial Court, Sam Roberts of the Pennsylvania Supreme Court, Nat Heffernan of the Wisconsin Supreme Court, Lord Diplock and Master of the Rolls, Lord Denning, as well as Justice Brennan, Justice Harry Blackmun and Chief Justice Warren Burger. This rich intellectual exchange was a heady advantage indeed for one preparing a book on the judicial process.

As we prepare this edition, most of these friends are no longer with us, or have retired, but their writings endure and their brilliant insights still inspire. As unfortunate as the passing of these memorable legal minds is the virtual disappearance of the high quality judicial process discussions in seminars and workshops. Sadly, new jurisprudents, whether from the bench or the academy, have not taken center stage in these programs, which now seem primarily devoted to discrete substantive law subjects, with a heavy dose of contemporary Equal Protection and Due Process theory. In many respects, continuing legal education programs for judges seem to track current law school course offering: heavy on definitions of rights and remedies in areas of the law currently fashionable. Unfortunately, a sea change in Congress or a landmark decision of the U.S. Supreme Court easily exposes the fragility of such unbalanced scholarly concentrations.

In this volume we seek to achieve the same basic goal of the 1976 edition: a unique single volume that selects teachings of American masters in the law and supplies cases that illustrate techniques and approaches. It is a treatise-anthology-textbook-hornbook-casebook-reference book designed for three discrete readerships—law students, practicing lawyers and judges. As we emphasized in our original preface:

> The writings open doors of conference rooms and judges' chambers to identify and evaluate considerations which enter and explain decisions. But this book is not an informational anthology; its purpose is educational. Thus, the measures of its success will be two: The extent to which improves advocacy of lawyers, and the extent to which it provides method and incentive for more reasoned adjudications by judges.

From a pragmatic standpoint, this book gives law students, in one volume, a bread and butter exposure to the nuances of precedent, retroactivity, statutory construction, inductive and deductive reasoning, the exercise of discretion and standards of review in appellate courts. All this, plus a sampling of philosophy and jurisprudence sufficient to provide an understanding of fundamental theories but succinct enough to avoid overburdening the reader. And, to be sure, this will be the only lawbook students encounter that has been written by a judge explaining how judges decide cases today.

We regret that other judges are not writing about this important subject, and suggest two probable (and related) reasons for this. First, the caseload for judges, especially appellate judges, has reached explosive proportions. Permit a personal reference. In my first year as a U.S. Circuit Judge in 1968, the national average of cases assigned to each active judge was 93 fully briefed cases a year; in 1994 the figure had risen to 446. If you can stand another statistic, in 1975 when I prepared my first edition, 16,658 appeals were filed in the U.S. Courts of Appeals; in 1993 the figure had risen to 50,224. Filings in state courts tell the same unfortunate story. Such heavy calendar pressures reduce severely, if not totally eliminate, free time for scholarly research and writing. Hence today there is no quiet library time; instead, appellate judges find themselves laboring as though on treadmills, and the cases come to them in the midst of their gallop.

The other reason for the utter paucity of judicial scholarship on the judging process, while more difficult to identify, has nonetheless been hinted at by Harvard Professor Martha L. Minow:

> For the most part, people who engage in judging do not theorize about it, or when they do, they join the project of eternal theorizing already established by scholars. In this respect, I think we lack theories of the practice of judging . . . . [T]he actual practices and experiences involved in judgment remain largely unexamined.

Whether those "who engage in judging do not theorize about it" because they simply do not have the time, or because they lack the personal interest or the intellectual background, it is difficult to say. But in any case, the quality of the judicial process would surely improve with the increased scholarly attention of those who most directly give life to that process.

We are extremely satisfied with the success of the first edition. On the student level it was adopted by over 35 law schools, as well as by a number of political science faculties for graduate study, and institutions of higher learning from over ten countries have requested copies. In practical terms, the book's most impressive accolade came from then Solicitor General Erwin N. Griswold at the opening session of the Institute for Advocacy at the University of Cincinnati College of Law on October 25, 1979:

> The first step in good advocacy is to have Judge Aldisert's book on THE JUDICIAL PROCESS in your office. My copy is on the table behind my desk and I constantly turn to it as a resource.

Finally, the book served as the text for appellate judges attending the Intermediate and Senior Appellate Judge Seminars in New York and has been cited in a significant number of reported cases.

Notwithstanding our earlier success, we are content that the second edition constitutes an improvement. While we have maintained many of the original materials, we have also changed the book's structure and sequence and have added many new readings and cases. We now open with a chapter entitled "Philosophy and Jurisprudence," after which we proceed to the chapters "Creation of Legal Precepts," "The Doctrine of Precedent," "Decision Making Theory," "The Judging Process: Making the Decision," and "The Judging Process: Justifying the Decision and Exercising the Judicial Function." Although we have culled our materials from a profusion of legal lore and cases, our selection follows the same process used in the first edition—relying especially on my own judicial experience in making final judgments.

When I prepared the first edition, I had been a state and federal judge for 14 years; now I am in my 35th year as a judge. When first I wrote, my appellate experience was essentially limited to the U.S. Court of Appeals for the Third Circuit. Since taking senior status in 1987, I have been sitting regularly with the Third, Ninth and Tenth Circuits and intermittently with the Fifth, Seventh and Eleventh Circuits. I know the theory of judicial decision-making from the abundance of available literature, but more important, I have learned first hand how many, many judges, in the words of the Marine Hymn, "in every clime and place," decide cases and justify their decisions. In short, I truly know how judges *do* decide cases, and I have reflected much about how they *should* decide them. This is what the judicial process is all about.

I am indebted to many for assistance in preparing this volume and gratefully acknowledge the assistance of family and friends. My sons keep me close to the realities of the trial courtroom, by sharing insights of litigators who daily face the operation of the judicial process from the perspective of the counsel table. Rob is with Perkins Coie in Portland, Oregon, and Greg, with Kinsella, Boesch, Fujikawa and Towle in Los Angeles. They are always free with advice and I am quick to receive it.

I thank Mimi Hildbrand for her contagious vivacity and great skills in deciphering my handwritten revisions and inserts, Linda E. Schneider, Esq. of Pittsburgh, PA for her unique research skills; and to Gregory C. Pingree for scholarly editorial assistance.

I owe a profound debt to the loyalty, enthusiasm, professionalism and intelligence of Jason P. Baruch of the New York and California bars and Thomas O. Main of the Massachusetts bar. In Dean Acheson's words, "They Were Present at the Creation" when I wrote the first words in this edition and they gave valuable advice and counsel throughout the preparation to guarantee the integrity and accuracy of the manuscript.

Most of my gratitude, however, goes to Agatha, who as the wife of a senior federal judge, had the right to expect a somewhat normal life of quasi-retirement. Instead, she has had to endure six or seven-day work weeks, balancing extensive circuit-riding with preparing this book. Her love and inspiration of over four decades makes all of this possible. And every other good thing that I do.

RUGGERO J. ALDISERT

Santa Barbara, California
March, 1996

PREFACE TO FIRST EDITION

A study of the judicial process is a study of how courts decide cases. It is an analysis of decision making as it actually takes place and as it ought to take place. This collection of writings, chosen from a wealth of underlying materials, forms the basis for such an inquiry. Eclectic in purpose, the collection seeks to provide special insight into judicial decision making—allowing an examination that is both theoretical and pragmatic.

This volume was planned and executed for a law school course analyzing methods courts use to reach and justify decisions. It is designed to be comprehensive, but not exhaustive—to assist in isolating and examining components of the judicial process, and to demonstrate their interrelationships. It focuses on that final stage of the legal process when the judges take over after the brief writers and oral advocates complete their presentations. The writings open doors of conference rooms and judges' chambers to identify and evaluate considerations which enter and explain decisions. But this book is not an informational anthology; its purpose is educational. Thus, the measures of its success will be two: the extent to which it improves advocacy of lawyers, and the extent to which it provides method and incentive for more reasoned adjudications by judges.

The book takes as its beginning point elementary jurisprudential principles and relates them to separate elements of the judicial process. Examination of the judge's roles as a dispute settler and lawmaker precedes analyses of theoretical and practical decision-making methodologies, and the separate processes of reaching and justifying a decision. The study looks into judicial functions on both trial and appellate levels, emphasizing fact finding, exercise of discretion, and harmless and reversible error. The final chapter demonstrates the importance of understanding the various conceptions of law discussed in the first chapter as it details the doctrine of precedent and the related problems of retrospectivity.

The impetus to prepare this book came to me from teaching a variety of law school courses at the University of Pittsburgh and the University of Texas. I found a void, appalling at times, in student understanding and appreciation of judicial dispute settling, error correcting, law making —at trial and on appeal. I found too much dogmatism: at one extreme, fixed ideas that the law is only what freewheeling judges say it is; at the other, a naiveté that the written opinion represents not only a justification for the stated conclusion, but also a true account of the process by which that conclusion was reached. A source of special concern to me was that many students, perhaps the great bulk of them, candidly admitted having given no thought to many components of the judicial process—

even the more controversial ones—notwithstanding that their academic legal training derived principally from the case system. This book seeks to fill the void I found.

The book should serve first year law students well, delivering long range values and furnishing an early understanding of the processes that produced the cases contained in case books. When offered as a course to upper classes, the students' additional legal experience will give increased dimension and special value to the readings, materials and cases. A course covering these writings might be entitled simply "The Judicial Process", "Judicial Decision Making" or "Decision Process". The essence of advocacy is persuasion. In the context of a courtroom the essence of advocacy is to persuade courts to decide in one's favor. Thus the volume might serve as a source book for courses styled "Advocacy", "Trial Advocacy", "Appellate Advocacy" or "Advocacy and Adjudication".

This volume was prepared with the hope that it might be used in practice as well as in the classroom. Some selections are those I found when, as a very new judge, I sought guidance in the art, craft or business of judging. I then discovered that the gems of judicial process literature were not assembled in any one volume or set, but were tucked away, primarily in law reviews, and, more often than not, in older, less accessible publications. As one now in his fifteenth year as a judge, with a happy mix of state trial and federal appellate experience, I continue to enjoy and learn from the sparkling perceptions of the American legal tradition's masters. I admire, unabashedly, their incisive analyses of the myriad problems in advocacy and adjudication. I am confident that readers will experience similar feelings. My confidence is buttressed by the reactions of state and federal judges who have been exposed to portions of this book at the Senior Appellate Judges Seminars under the joint sponsorship of the New York University Law School and the Institute of Judicial Administration, and the directorship of Dean Robert A. Leflar.

Although I freely recommend these writings to any trial or appellate judge and to any law clerk, I do not view this book as a primer on how to judge. Rather, I look upon it as a source book into the elements of the process that decides our cases and controversies, that shapes our case law, that adds gloss to our statutes and that constantly gives new dimensions to our state and federal constitutions. These pages should be valuable to lawyers whose profession brings them within the ambit of the judicial process; to those whose professional lives will touch or be touched by it; to those who will be governed by its result and to those who, by advice and counsel, seek to predict that result. But especially there should be value here to those who see in the lawyer's noble role a primary responsibility to mold the product of the judicial process, law.

A book of excerpts is of necessity a book of severe editing. Much deliberation preceded this editing, in an effort to obtain maximum value for law school purposes. The reader who is interested in an unabridged text of a particular writing may go to the original source. Virtually all footnotes have been omitted; those retained are indicated by their original number; those added are identified by asterisks.

I am indebted to many. The authors of the writings are the actual authors of this book. I thank them first. I thank their publishers for permission to reprint excerpts.

I am indebted to my fellow faculty members at the NYU seminars for many valuable suggestions. I acknowledge a debt to the deans and faculty at the University of Pittsburgh School of Law where many of these materials were used in experimental courses in 1973–74, 1974–75, and 1975–76. And finally I acknowledge a profound and personal debt to Charles R. Ragan for his advice and counsel throughout the preparation and editing of these pages. I thank Roger L. Wise and Charles H. Cochran for many excellent suggestions and contributions, Jill Kremer and Judith E. Levinthal for research assistance, and Catherine Dorsch Wreath and Carol A. Ballock for dedicated secretarial support.

RUGGERO J. ALDISERT
United States Circuit Judge

Pittsburgh, Pennsylvania
February, 1976

*

SUMMARY OF CONTENTS

Page

TABLE OF CONTENTS

CHAPTER IV. DECISION MAKING THEORY

CHAPTER V. THE JUDGING PROCESS: MAKING THE DECISION

CHAPTER VI. JUSTIFYING THE DECISION

CHAPTER VII.   EXERCISING THE JUDICIAL FUNCTION

*

TABLE OF CASES

**Principal cases are in italic type. Non-principal cases
are in roman type. References are to Pages.**

TABLE OF AUTHORITIES

References are to Pages

INTRODUCTION

Our subject is the judicial process, a study of how our courts decide cases and how they should. It is an analysis of judicial decision making as it is and as it ought to be.

Basic to the study of government and law at any time, an analysis of the inner workings of the American judicial systems is especially pertinent today. More than ever in our history, the judicial branch of government has assumed an important, if not dominant, role in the governing schema. America has become a litigious society. This is evidenced not only by the tremendous number of case filings at the trial and appellate levels, in both the state and federal systems. Litigation is no longer concentrated in the traditional "lawyer's law" of the common law tradition seeking redress for private wrongs. More and more, the courts are called upon to decide questions of public law, the effect of which transcends the rights and obligation of the specific parties. Subjects of disputes are now polycentric problems, formerly adjusted in the private sector or by other branches of government.

American society is no longer content to accept decisions of its legislative and executive branches; it resorts to the judicial branch for the final word. This phenomenon offends orthodox notions of separation of powers, and disturbs the theoretical balance within the tripartite system of government; nevertheless, the trend is undiminished and there seems to be little public concern that it be slowed. Thus has come to fruition the 1850 prediction of de Tocqueville: "scarcely a political question arises in the United States that is not resolved sooner or later, into a judicial decision."[1]

Society's penchant for testing even the most mundane statute or administrative regulation in the courts brings to mind the story in which three baseball umpires argue about how they distinguish balls and strikes during the game. The first one says: "It's simple. I call 'em as I see 'em." The second snorts: "Huh! I call 'em as they are." And the third one ends the debate with: "They ain't nothin' 'til I call 'em."[2] American society today has opted for a jurisprudential philosophy that makes the third umpire the embodiment of our system of laws.

How the courts call these balls and strikes is the study of the judicial process, or, more precisely, part of it. As we shall examine in some detail when we embark on a study of permissible judicial law making, one may say that the courts not only determine when the ball comes within the

---

1. A. de Tocqueville, Democracy in America 28 (P. Bradley ed. 1945).

2. M. Rosenberg, *Judicial Discretion of the Trial Court, Viewed from Above,* 22 Syracuse L.Rev. 635, 640 (1971).

strike zone—one plate wide, between the knees and the shoulders—but they also reserve the right to modify the rules of the game from time to time in the middle of the game.

The importance of the judicial process product cannot be gainsaid. Court decisions have affected every class of persons in the United States as direct litigants, from the President to an impoverished alien. Notwithstanding its importance, however, the process and its components have been the subject of comparatively few tests for guidance in the law schools, departments of political science and government. Reasons are not clear for the paucity of such literature, but probably it is because the subject can be addressed with confidence only by those who have actual experience in the process. The view from within is probably the best perspective, although I cheerfully concede it is not the only one.

Those who operate within the process recognize the constraints and inhibitions in formulating an adequate description. There are so many dimensions of the subject that time limitations prevent an active judge from preparing a comprehensive treatise while conscientiously discharging the onerous duties of a judicial office. Added to these time limitations is an intimidation which stems from knowing that the previous authoritative work in this field has become a literary and legal classic, Benjamin N. Cardozo's *The Nature of the Judicial Process* (1921).

The passage of many decades since Cardozo, however, has accentuated the necessity for a re-examination of today's processes. It prompts this effort. The time has come to offer a fresh description of the stage of the legal process when the judges take over, after motions are made or petitions filed, arguments made or after witnesses have had their say.

Notwithstanding the all-pervasive interest in so many aspects of government and the legal profession, it is paradoxical that the mass media and professional journalists have neither satisfied, nor sought to satisfy, the obvious public interest in the decision making aspects of the American court systems, especially in the appellate courts. There is adequate coverage at the criminal court trial level, a coverage essentially emphasizing the factual accounts of witnesses, with the extent of coverage directly proportionate to the degree of sensationalism rather than the importance of the legal issues. Television programming such as Court TV has introduced more American households to the criminal justice system than any other type of law. There is also abundant coverage of the U.S. Supreme Court not only by the press, radio and television media, but by professional journalists and academics.

But in the courts where the bulk of judicial processes are at work— where trial judges struggle with difficult problems in summary judgment and other pre-trial motions, and appellate courts daily render decisions of extreme consequence—the public is not only denied reasonable coverage and analysis of a critical government activity, but it is appallingly unfamiliar with the methodologies of how courts decide cases. A veritable wasteland of public ignorance envelopes so many affected by the judicial process. There is more complete press coverage of a local town council meeting than a sitting of a state's supreme court, more coverage of a bail hearing before a magistrate judge than coverage of a U.S. Circuit Court's decision announcing a profound constitutional right. Thus, from the standpoint of the public interest alone, it should be essential to identify and evaluate the components of the judicial process.

Moreover, and equally important, an examination of course offerings in our institutions of higher learning, both in the law schools and the departments of political science, discloses only minimal academic treatment of the actual or theoretical methodologies of the judicial process, with one exception—the constitutional law cases of the U.S. Supreme Court which receive the fullest of academic exposure.

English legal philosopher H.L.A. Hart characterized "American jurisprudence, that is, American speculative thought about the general nature of law," as being obsessed with "the judicial process, that is, with what courts do and should do, how judges reason or should reason in deciding particular cases."[3] If Hart's reference is to the public's general inclination to become litigants it may be true that Americans form the most litigious society in the world. There is a stronger disposition to sue than to settle. The gentle admonition to turn the other cheek has been replaced by the more coarse philosophy, "sue the bastards." It is a great paradox that a society so infatuated with judicial resolution of a galaxy of disputes—both public and private, large and small, mundane and esoteric—can remain so woefully uninformed about the true workings of American judicial processes. This is so whether the cosmos of the public can be represented by editorial writers, journalists and political candidates, or by the local bartender, physician, mill-worker, clerk or the neighbor next door. General lay impressions run the gamut from impressions that judges never "make" law and only "interpret" it to notions that judges are free-wheeling officials endowed with unlimited autocratic power to affect the outcome of any factual or legal dispute.

There are basic tensions in the public perception of the American judiciary. One is a widely held view, the orthodox junior high school teaching, that government functions are separated neatly in watertight compartments; the legislature makes law, the executive administers it and the judiciary interprets it. Because the English experience has neither a written constitution to interpret nor the polyglot problems of 50 highly individualistic state sovereign court systems plus a separate federal system, the orthodox trichotomy of government powers is more real in England than it is in her former American colonies.

3. H.L.A. Hart, *American Jurisprudence Through English Eyes: The Nightmare and the Noble Dream,* 11 Ga.L.Rev. 969 (1977).

INTRODUCTION

There is a risk of oversimplification in any attempt to characterize the American system, probably because of divergent views within and without it. From within we have the views, and these have been with us now for almost three quarters of a century, of some true giants of the law. Thus, Oliver Wendell Holmes defined law to students in 1894: "The prophecies of what the courts will do in fact, and nothing more pretentious, is what I mean by the law."[4] His friend and early Harvard Law professor, John Chipman Gray, wrote at the turn of the century, "The law of the State or of any organized body of men is composed of the rules which the courts, that is, the judicial organs of that body, lay down for the determination of legal rights and duties."[5] A generation later, one of the most renowned legal scholars, Karl Llewellyn observed, "What these officials [judges] do about disputes, is, to my mind, the law itself."[6] To suggest that these views run counter to orthodox notions of separation of powers is to state the obvious, yet these views are commonplace in certain sectors of the community. If we judge by public attentiveness to the selection and confirmation process of U.S. Supreme Court nominees, there is widespread recognition of the lawmaking role of that Court. Perhaps this is because of the Court's national, rather than regional jurisdiction, and because of the cosmic effect of its constitutional law decisions. If, however, the public's attentiveness to other courts—state and federal, trial and appellate—measures its knowledge of their lawmaking potential, there is very little evidence of awareness.

Media coverage and civic interest in campaigns for state trial and appellate judges generally is subordinated to that of other municipal, county or state officials. Press coverage of state appellate court selections and inquiries into federal judicial nominations is limited, if not nonexistent. Presidential appointments of federal district and circuit judges rarely get front page attention unless local political tensions have been associated with the appointments. If we take as given that there should be, and is, great public interest in the conduct of our law makers, and if Holmes and Gray correctly characterize appellate judges as law makers, how many of us can name the judges on our state's highest court or on the U.S. Court of Appeals for the judicial circuit in which we live?

The book's aim is to provide deeper insight into the judicial process with the avowed purpose of increasing general awareness of its nuances and sophistication. Designed for those whose careers take them into the law, it is a mix of the abstract and the actual, of theory and experience. It recognizes that in every society there is a division between the rulers and the ruled, and asks whether judges rule the law or are ruled by law.

4. O.W. Holmes, *Path of the Law*, 10 Harv.L.Rev. 457 (1897).

5. J.C. Gray, The Nature and Sources of the Law 84 (2d ed. 1921).

6. K. Llewellyn, The Bramble Bush, 1x (2d ed. 1951).

If the former, we inquire by what warrant they do so; if the latter, we ask where they find it.

In this respect, we may possibly ask more questions than we answer, for we recognize, as Lord Devlin did, that the first mark of a free and ordered society is that the boundaries between rules and the ruled "should be guarded and trespasses from one side independently and impartially determined. The keepers of these boundaries cannot be among the outriders."[7] If we agree that judges are the keepers of the law, is it acceptable that they also be creators of the law? And if we deny them the right to create, do we not fly in the face of the common law tradition?

Beginning with an analysis of the common law tradition, our jurisprudential heritage, we inquire if Americans have breezed into uncharted jural waters more boldly than our English antecedents who proceeded "from case to case, like the ancient Mediterranean mariners, hugging the coast from point to point and avoiding the dangers of the open sea of system and science."[8] If we have chosen not to hug the shores, we ask what we have borrowed from the "system and science" of our civil law cousins on the European continent. To the extent we have borrowed from them, we have abandoned the lessons received from our English forbears.

Our study requires such inquiries, because by nature the American is more the rugged individualist than the traditionalist. At best, we have had only two centuries to build up a legal tradition, a comparatively short time when it is remembered that the beginning of English common law is generally attributed to be 1066, the date of the Norman Conquest, and that the common law is now only as old as was the Roman Law in 535 A.D. when Justinian published the *Corpus Juris Civilis* in Constantinople, after Roman Law first made its appearance in the Twelve Tables at Rome in 753 B.C. Should our inquiry reveal that contemporary American judicial process has also borrowed from civil law traditions of Continental Europe, this can be understood because not only are we young as a nation, we are also big. We are bigger than the English, big with a heterogeneous population and big and complicated mix of state and federal court systems.

If a study of the judicial process includes scrutiny of *how* we adjudicate, the study should also survey *what* we adjudicate. Perhaps the court's work is merely to choose, interpret and then apply a legal precept to the facts as found by the factfinder: If fact "A" were found, then rule "X" would apply; if fact "B," then rule "Y." If this were the case, then *what* is being adjudicated may not be important to a study of *how* it is being done. The current explosion of activity in the courts, with the concomitant astronomical increase of state and federal statutory law, is a

7. Lord Devlin, *Judges and Lawmakers,* 39 Mod.L.Rev. 1, 16 (1976).

8. C.A. Wright, *The Study of Law,* 54 L.Q.R. 185, 186 (1938).

force which a proper study of the judicial process cannot ignore. At the very least, it requires an inquiry into whether traditional common law methods of deciding cases have been changed by the gigantic legislative fallout.

Moreover, the legislative activity has also added great new dimensions to the executive branch. State and federal statutes have spawned a plethora of new administrative agencies, or have expanded the powers and jurisdiction of older ones. This proliferation of agencies has, in turn, caused a mushrooming of already voluminous administrative regulations which often have the force of law. It is no exaggeration that the life of the average American is controlled more intimately by administrative regulation than by specific statute or case law. Although there is now a movement to reverse the proliferation of the federal agencies and regulation, we are in the grip of a bureaucracy that possesses powers undreamed of a half century ago, prescribing regulations regarding the pharmaceuticals or the cigarettes we can purchase, the price for a bottle of wine and the personal details that must be revealed on a local, state or federal income tax return. The agencies themselves have created a layer of administrative courts. Hearing examiners or referees of yesteryear now bear the formidable titles of administrative law judges. Both rule making and adjudicating functions of administrative agencies serve as breeding grounds for much additional business for the courts. To the extent that these frenetic bursts of legislative and administrative energies affect the grist for the judicial mills, an understanding of the modern judicial process involves as much *what* the courts decide as *how* they do it.

If the mad rush to the courts has added to our mores a judicialization of relationships, and if the propagation of myriad governmental regulations has added an all-pervasive bureaucratization, yet another phenomenon may be detected in modern American judicial civilization. We may call it the "Constitutionalization" or "Fourteenth Amendmentization of our society—an aspect of the judicial process by which the most pedestrian of hiring and firing actions, court procedures and substantive law precepts are exposed to serious challenges under the Equal Protection and Due Process clauses. These provisions were created with the adoption of the Fourteenth Amendment, and for many, many decades they resembled a somnolent St. Bernard watchdog. The Warren Court revolution of the mid-1950's and 1960's replaced him with a Cerberus more akin to a Doberman, constantly vigilant against precepts and procedures offensive to the Great Clauses. If the Doberman is no longer necessary because of a heightened awareness of the Constitution's presence, at least a terrier is now on the jural premises, snapping and yelping whenever a law or practice is suspected of approaching the borderline of unconstitutionality.

Modern judicial processes, therefore, deal with far more intricate matters than in the halcyon days of Cardozo. Frightening caseloads, more sophisticated subjects, and cross-pollination of judicial precedent, statute, administrative regulation and constitutional provision more often being the rule than the exception, the process demands the highest professionalism from the bench and bar. Whether the judges and the lawyers meet these challenges adequately evokes much contemporary debate, and this is not the subject here. But there must be dimensions, if not standards, by which to measure judicial competence. This study of the judicial process is an inquiry into those dimensions, and it addresses the methodologies of the process more than its end product.

*

Chapter I

PHILOSOPHY OF LAW, JURISPRUDENCE AND ADJUDICATION

INTRODUCTION

What does a judge do when he or she decides a case?

Benjamin Cardozo posed this question in 1921, and answered it in what has become a classic of American legal literature, The Nature of the Judicial Process.[1] Drawing from his wealth of scholarship and his experience as Chief Judge of the New York Court of Appeals, he described the ingredients that enter "that strange compound which is brewed daily in the caldron of the courts."[2] His graceful description of the compound was both analytical and philosophical. He explained processes of the common law tradition and recommended new emphases within that tradition to accommodate the demands of a dynamic social order. Cardozo's analysis and philosophy examined the accepted definition of the judicial process: what courts do and should do, how judges reason and should reason in deciding particular cases.[3]

Who then should be interested in an understanding of the judicial process? The answer is obvious: Law students, lawyers and judges, or any person interested in judicial decision making as it actually takes place and as it ought to take place.

The starting point is recognition that the decisions judges make are based on law. But what is law? What may seem, on first reading, as so much academic, esoteric quibbling can eventually be seen as hard-boiled practical advice for the most pragmatic courtroom advocate. The statement of some law—a statute, a fact-driven legal rule contained in an appellate court decision, a broad legal principle emanating from a host of past court decisions or a clause of a state or federal constitution, or perhaps a highly accepted moral principle—is always the tool used to persuade the judge. It is what Oliver Wendell Holmes called an "implement of decision." These statements constitute the necessary theoretical foundation on how cases are decided.

Holmes cannot be accused of being obscure when he offered his definition of law: "The prophecies of what the courts will do in fact and nothing more pretentious, are what I mean by the law.[4] At bottom,

---

1. B. Cardozo, The Nature of the Judicial Process (1921) (Storrs lecture at Yale University).

2. Id. at 10.

3. H.L.A. Hart, *American Jurisprudence Through English Eyes: The Nightmare and the Noble Dream*, 11 Ga.L.Rev. 969 (1977).

4. O.W. Holmes, *Path of the Law*, 10 Harv.L.Rev. 457 (1897).

every time a lawyer gives advice to a client, he or she is prophesying as to what some tribunal "will do in fact." To make this prophecy, and thus to understand what is law, however, it is necessary to understand the terms "philosophy of law," "jurisprudence," and "adjudication," the subjects of this chapter.

Traditionally, these abstract terms, philosophy and jurisprudence, rate high in the "turn-me-off" department. The wails are familiar: "These subjects won't help me prepare for the bar exam!" "They won't help me writing a brief or making an argument in front of that hard-nosed judge." "As a trial judge, these are not my bread and butter subjects." But let us think about the laments that these subjects are academic exercises only and have no practical value for the lawyer and judge. To do this, we start with some definitions and basic understanding of these terms. It is first necessary to distinguish between philosophy of law and *a* philosophy of law.

PHILOSOPHY OF LAW

When we speak of philosophy, we are addressing a very broad inquiry into what the relationship between persons and between persons and government ought to be. In this context, problems of legal philosophy deal with the chief ideas that are common to rules and methods of law in the sense described by Roscoe Pound as "a body of philosophical, political and ethical ideas as to the end of law." [5] Legal philosophy is an inquiry into those elements which are common to all juridical systems, a search for the universal concept of law, a study that goes beyond the particularities of individual systems, past or present—in the various states of the United States, in the federal experience or in other countries. Legal philosophy deals with the various disciplines that bear directly on the solution of a galaxy of problems, inquiries into intricacies of terminology, legal methods, the role of precedent, statutory interpretation, underlying rationale, the use of different types of authority, the efficacy of various controls and their operation in diverse factual scenarios, and the basic issues concerning the values that are implemented.

When we speak of *a* legal philosophy, we address the specific answers to these queries. These answers come from respectable thinkers, both in academia and on the bench. Each thinker articulates, or at least demonstrates, some particular legal philosophy. Each of the various solutions to the myriad problems of judicial decision making, therefore, is what we call *a* legal philosophy, expressed in the form of a quest for justice, a need to declare the law as it *should* be. Giorgio Del Vecchio explains that "[p]hilosophy of Law seeks precisely that which *must* or *ought* to be in the Law, in contrast to that which *is*, bringing an ideal truth into comparison with an empirical reality (deontology—science of what ought to be)." [6]

5. R. Pound, I Jurisprudence 363 (1959).

6. G. Del Vecchio, Philosophy of Law 4 (8th ed. 1952, translated by Thomas Owen Martin 1953) ("Philosophy of law is the course of study which defines Law in its logical universality, seeks its origins and the general characteristics of its historical

Philosophers often offer ambitious programs to advance the cause of social progress, but these programs cannot succeed in the courts until and unless they take hold in the lawyers' imagination. Here the abstract must be married to the pragmatic. Dreams of philosophers are competitive. In academia, the alternatives can be set forth for unlimited discussion. In the courts, choices must be made. The philosopher recognizes that in the courts choices for change are much more circumscribed and immediate than those able to be the subjects of treatises or accepted by statesmen in high executive or legislative office.

JURISPRUDENCE

Jurisprudence is a concept separate from legal philosophy but, more often than not, writers use the terms interchangeably. Where legal philosophy considers law in the universal sense, jurisprudence in its "widest sense is the science of law," [7] what Del Vecchio describes as "the Science of Positive Law." [8] Philosophy deals with theoretical concepts of universal law; jurisprudence, with the actual law in place in particular jurisdictions, what Roscoe Pound described as "the comparative anatomy of developed systems of law." [9] So perceived, jurisprudence is indeed an important component of legal philosophy to the extent that research into elements of theoretical universal law requires a study of law as it exists or has existed. The terms "philosophy" and "jurisprudence" are often used interchangeably. Perhaps the concepts do overlap. And perhaps this is because "what is" and "what ought to be" sometimes coalesce. We prefer to proceed on the basis of a dichotomy, pinning the difference on what law should or ought to be in its universal or ideal state, and what statutes, and judicially created legal precepts suggest what the law really *is* in actual operation.

That we offer particular definitions here does not suggest a quarrel with other formulations. With a nod to Felix Cohen, a definition provided is either useful or useless. "It is not true or false, any more than a New Year's resolution or an insurance policy." [10] Jurisprudence thus is described as a body of law containing formal features. It is a system of rules, promulgated by those with power and authority, backed by sanctions and regulating behavior, what John Chipman Gray described as "the statement and systematic arrangement of the rules followed by the courts and of the principles involved in those rules." [11] So perceived, jurisprudence is a system of obligatory norms, both substantive and procedural, that shape and regulate the life of a people in a given governmental state.

development, and evaluates it according to the ideal of justice drawn from pure reason.").

7. R. Pound, I Jurisprudence 7.

8. G. Del Vecchio, Philosophy of Law 4, at 7.

9. R. Pound, I Jurisprudence 8 (1959).

10. F. Cohen, *Transcendental Nonsense and the Functional Approach,* 35 Colum.L.Rev. 809, 835 (1935).

11. J.C. Gray, The Nature and Sources of the Law 133 (1909).

ADJUDICATION

The study of the judicial process is a study of how judges actually decide cases and how they should decide them, a study of the methods of adjudication. To adjudicate is to "settle judicially" disputes and controversies, and to adjudicate is to become immersed in the venerable twin concepts of philosophy and jurisprudence.

In adjudication, philosophy forms the dream, the vision of what the law ought to be; jurisprudence is the engine that supplies both the methods to reach the dream as well as the justification for the court's acceptance of it, a justification respected only when legitimate reasoning is present to support its acceptance. It is not enough for the judge to agree with what the philosopher suggests, it is equally important to express acceptable grounds for embracing it.

There is a quick answer when the law student, lawyer or judge raises the question: "I am a busy person. Why should I pause in my pursuit of black letter law to read a smattering of philosophy and jurisprudence?" The truth is that you don't have to. You don't have to unless you are or want to be a litigator, a transaction, commercial, real estate or probate lawyer, government counsel, a sole practitioner, a member of a small or large firm, a professor or a trial or appellate judge.

Section 1

LEGAL PHILOSOPHY AND JURISPRUDENCE [1]

When members of the legal profession get together these days you don't hear much about tenets of legal philosophers. The writers are seldom, if ever, mentioned by name, and the creeds they expounded lay embalmed in some dusty hard cover book, and not on the latest CD–ROM. To be sure, names of judges are bandied about, especially those from our appellate courts, but what they do and what they say are usually couched in the guise of pronouncements as juridical officers rather than as legal philosophers. Moreover, when the judges are alluded to, mention is made only of the rulings they have made or results of opinions they have written and not the rational structure used to justify the conclusions. Yet these judges are legal philosophers—certainly federal judges on the Supreme Court or courts of appeals and judges on the state supreme courts and intermediate appellate courts. But don't tell them that, because they would probably deny it.

A good reason exists for both this lack of external perception and concomitant internal denial, a reason best described as the harried, badgered or harassed status of most members of the legal profession today. In the rarified appellate court atmosphere, judges are treading water constantly in an inundation of brutal case loads. Too many appellate judges are mere chambers managers, deciding only bottom

1. Adapted in part from R. Aldisert, *Philosophy, Jurisprudence and Jurispru-* *dential Temperament of Federal Judges,* 20 Ind.L.Rev. 453, 457–465 (1987).

lines and delegating the original writing of opinions to apple-cheeked law clerks after conveying broad-stroked instructions, and often serving only as editors of the published product. Not much time or room for a personal rationalized rumination of a legal philosophy here. Not much time, because boxes of cases for the next sitting have already arrived.

Meanwhile trial judges are on treadmills of their own, hampered by trials that are weeks and months unnecessarily too long, frustrated with procedural rules, and required by statutes or appellate courts to perform rituals akin to a Catholic Church solemn high mass prior to making the most simple ruling. Accordingly, seldom does the trial judge report to the spouse when coming home for dinner, "I came across some interesting statements by John Locke and Rene Descartes today." The lawyers are likewise buffeted from all fronts—insults from public opinion, costs of running a modern office, exposure to cranky clients and petulant judges. Today's lawyer seldom has time to ascertain the legal philosophies of members of the court that will consider their case. Rarely does a firm strategy session ponder whether the sitting judge is more inclined to follow Thomas Hobbes or Charles de Montesquieu on a clash between individual or societal rights. And forget the wretched law student who would like to take a course in legal philosophy or jurisprudence, but is not quite sure how the hiring committee would react to a transcript entry that may not contribute to the firm's bottom line billable hours.

Our purpose here is to answer the student's question. We defend the thesis that even a cursory introduction to basic legal philosophies can do wonders in understanding even the most fundamental "bread and butter courses" and will help even the most law-book-shy-street-smarts-lawyer learn something about what makes the people in the courthouse tick.

First, it is helpful to understand the categorical imperative of Immanuel Kant: "Act as if the maxim of your action were to become through your will a universal law of nature." [2] Two centuries later, an elaboration on the basic theme was forthcoming: "Judges must decide all the issues in a case on the basis of general principles that have legal relevance; the principles must be ones the judges would be willing to apply to the other situations that they reach; and the opinion justifying the decision should contain a full statement of those principles.[3]

It all comes back to Kant's imperative, the concept that undergirds the common law doctrine of precedent: The legal rule announced in a reported case of an appellate court will be applied in subsequent cases presenting the identical facts or materially similar ones. It is the whisper of Kant behind the voices of appellate judges at oral argument when they pose hypotheticals to the lawyers, inquiring how the rule urged upon them in argument would apply in future cases: How will the

---

2. I. Kant, Groundwork of the Metaphysics of Morals 89 (Paton trans. 1964) (1785).

3. K. Greenawalt, *The Enduring Significance of Neutral Principles,* 78 Co-

lum.L.Rev. 982, 990 (1978), commenting on H. Wechsler, *Toward Neutral Principles of Constitutional Law,* 73 Harv.L.Rev. 1 (1959).

rule work? What are the practical consequences? How far will the rule carry? How far will the law go? If we extend claims, demands or defenses, at what point can we draw the line before it conflicts with a competing legal precept? If we curtail claims, demands and defenses, will we now or in the immediate future be overruling settled case law? Would we be modifying it? If so, are there strong policy reasons for a change? Will it change current practice? Will it generate additional litigation?

The law now is much more complicated than it was in the 17th Century when Hugo Grotius published *De Jure Belli ac Pacis,* in which he set forth five supereminent principles of law:

Creating and protecting property interests.

Creating and protecting liberty interests.

Fulfilling promises.

Redressing losses caused by breach or fault.

Punishing those who wrong the public.[4]

Putting to one side those additions to substantive law occasioned by the development of written constitutions, the five supereminent principles of Grotius remain comprehensive. The law explosion—reflected by statute and case law, by the new causes of actions churned out by Congress, by the nuances of specialized government regulations, or by the geometric expansion of law school curricula—has not really spawned a corresponding increase in bedrock concepts upon which modern law and modern litigation rest. Fundamentals of law remain. They still loom large and foreboding, but are more easily seen once we blow away the mists that surround them.

Experienced appellate judges report that their work would be much easier and justice better served if written and oral arguments returned to more basic concepts in selecting major premises of syllogisms or prosyllogisms that constitute starting points of arguments. In many cases, a return to the basics articulated by Grotius may be more effective than starting the argument with the last reported case on the subject which may be neither relevant nor persuasive.

Legal Reasoning

Some critics have suggested that logic has no place in legal reasoning because logic is concerned with form and not truth, and because the same set of facts may yield any number of perfectly logical conclusions. But these are only superficial observations. No one is suggesting that briefs can be written, arguments made and cases decided solely by reference to the canons of logic. Were this so, the legal profession would simply move to analysis by computer, the paradigm of formal logic. Value judgments reflecting the views of advocates and judges form the

4. H. Grotius, De Jure Belli ac Pacis　(F. Kelsey trans. 1925).
(The Law of War and Peace) 12–13 (1646)

critical decisional points in the law. Rules of logic do not form these choices; they are simply means to implement them. After these preliminary judgments are made, the formal reasoning process sets in to test the validity of the propositions constituting the argument. Criticisms of fealty to logical order "are not designed in large measure to remove logic from legal reasoning but to remove bad logic from legal reasoning."[5]

Through the ages legal philosophers have emphasized the importance of reasoning. The deductive reasoning technique of the master Socrates is used in law schools as well as by judges in the courtrooms as they test the arguments offered by counsel. Today's categorical syllogism with two premises and a conclusion bears his name. Cicero put reason as the basis of law: "True law is right reason in agreement with nature; it is of universal application, unchanging and everlasting."[6] Thomas Aquinas said that "*Lex naturalis* is directly knowable to man [and woman] through reason."[7] Hugo Grotius emphasized: "Law is something which is presented by reason, not by revelation, something adapted to making possible a living together in society. It is that which right reason demonstrates to be in conformity with the social nature of man."[8]

In the 16th Century, Francis Bacon popularized the other prong of modern legal thinking—inductive reasoning. He explained that from experience, from the particulars of experiments in life, one can draw certain generalities, conclusions that may lack the logical force of deductions from true and valid premises, but inductive conclusions representing something probably more true than not. At the same time in Italy, Galileo Galilei was performing his experiments to reach the same results.

Yet Oliver Wendell Holmes is often quoted for his famous statement:

> The life of the law has not been logic; it has been experience. The felt necessities of the time, the prevalent moral and political theories, institutions of public policy, avowed or unconscious, even the prejudices which judges share with their fellowmen, have had a good deal more to do than the syllogism in determining the rules by which men should be governed.[9]

But in 1881 Holmes was speaking of only a type of deductive logic that has fixed premises. Over a century later, it is clear that by inductive logic we witness the drama of developing law to meet felt necessities of the times, current moral and political theories, intuitions of public policy, and the hopes, dreams and aspirations of an informed society. Moreover, when Holmes said this, he was not writing a brief. He was speaking as a legal philosopher. A lawyer's brief, however, is measured by its persuasive power, and persuasion depends upon the force of its formal logic.

5. S. Burton, An Introduction to Law and Legal Reasoning 1 (1985).

6. Cicero, De Republica, III, 2.

7. T. Aquinas, On Law and Justice (Summa Theologica) Q. 91. Art. 2, p t. 1–11.

8. H. Grotius, The Law of War and Peace (De Jure Belli ac Pacis (1646).

9. O.W. Holmes, The Common Law 1 (1881).

What Holmes was saying must always be considered in the context of his message: An appeal that the law adjust to changing social conditions, that we should not be bound by rigid legal precepts that were once justified by good reasons but are no longer viable in a changing society. His appeal did not go unnoticed. Aided by the writings of Roscoe Pound and Benjamin Cardozo, our jurisprudence moved away from a rigid German Begriffsjurisprudenz, which Rudolf von Jhering styled as a jurisprudence of concepts.[10] The current spirit was eloquently stated by Harry W. Jones, late Cardozo Professor of Jurisprudence at Columbia: "A legal rule or legal institution is a good rule or institution when—that is, to the extent that—it contributes to the establishment and preservation of a social environment in which the quality of human life can be spirited, improving and unimpaired." [11]

Although formal logic is not an end-in-view of law, it is one of the important means to the ends of law, perhaps the most important. Logical form and logical reasoning have never been subordinated in the judicial process. Upon his retirement after 23 years on the Supreme Court, Justice Felix Frankfurter stated: "[F]ragile as reason is and limited as law is as the expression of the institutionalized medium of reason, that's all we have standing between us and the tyranny of mere will and the cruelty of unbridled, undisciplined feeling." [12]

The test for a good written or oral argument, like the test of a "good judicial decision" was advanced by both Roscoe Pound and Harry W. Jones: "[H]ow thoughtfully and disinterestedly the Court weighed the conflicting social interest involved in the case and how fair and durable its adjustment of the interest-conflicts promised to be." [13] One cannot advocate or pronounce a position that is "fair and durable" unless formal rules of thought go into the process. Exhaustive string citation of cases is not enough. The formal order of deductive and inductive reasoning must show through—the logical order that has been preached by legal philosophers from the beginning of Western thought. We may not have decisions by judicial fiat alone, and without fealty to the formal rules of logic, that is all we will have.

Heraclitus Today

As early as 1930, a prescient Karl Llewellyn suggested that the future emphasis of litigation would not pit individual against individual, but the individual against the state.[14] This was long before the constitutionalization of our society, or as mentioned earlier, its Fourteenth Amendmentization. Ever since the Warren Court era, the dynamic area of American law has been the defining of individual rights, variously categorized as run-of-the-mill or fundamental, as superior to those

10. R. von Jhering, Der Geist Des Rominischen Rechts (1887).

11. H.W. Jones, *An Invitation to Jurisprudence,* 74 Colum.L.Rev. 1023, 1025 (1974).

12. As quoted in Time Magazine, Sept. 7, 1962 at 15.

13. H.W. Jones, *An Invitation to Jurisprudence,* 74 Colum.L.Rev. 1023, 1025 (1974).

14. K. Llewellyn, *A Realistic Jurisprudence—the Next Step,* 30 Colum.L.Rev. 431, 464 (1930).

possessed by society in general, or governments in particular. To be sure, there have been elemental developments in tort law that have wreaked profound changes—for example, comparative, instead of contributory, negligence, and the replacement of negligence by notions of strict products liability—but it is in the definition of constitutional rights where the most profound and dramatic activity in the courts has been taking place. In this animation and bustle, the varying precepts of legal philosophers, from ancient days on forward, have appeared in the caldron. They have been advocated and tested, accepted or rejected, but seldom have the lawyers or judges attributed authorship of competing precepts to the venerable persons of letters. This ignoring of authorship probably is a significant explanation of why the study of legal philosophy is relegated to academic enrichment instead of bread and butter priority status.

Drawing the line between individual liberties and rights, and society's rights reflected by government action for the larger good, is still the perpetual question of constitutional law. And about two thousand years before the Constitution, the same problem bothered an ancient social order which spoke through Heraclitus: "The major problem of human society is to combine that degree of liberty without which law is tyranny, with that degree of law without which liberty becomes license."

When individual rights spun off in countless dimensions, judges attempted to resolve the problem posed by Heraclitus. In so doing they often abandoned the "original intent of the Framers" theory and consciously or unconsciously adopted some theories of these competing rights as expounded by the ancients and the philosophers who followed. And with the adoption or rejection, there has been no credit to original authorship.

Some philosophers, for example, have argued that governments exist only to benefit their citizens—the classic utilitarian theory as urged by Jeremy Bentham [15] and refined by John Stuart Mill [16]—that any governmental action is justified only when, and to the extent that, it contributes to the general well-being. Others have argued for a limited form of government. They contend that persons are endowed with rights and that no action is justifiable if it interferes with these rights, and that governments exist to see that rights are protected and to promote well-being only when doing so does not involve infringement of rights. Most of these philosophers give primacy to the individual, but there are those, especially from ancient societies, as well as the modern fascists and nazis, who give primacy to the state as an end in itself.

Very few individuals today will accept Plato's notion that the State dominates all, or Herbert Spencer's theory—a theory rejected by Oliver Wendell Holmes in his Lochner v. New York dissent [17]—that it is the business of government to uphold and defend natural rights, but beyond

15. See J. Bentham, Principles of Morals & Legislation, (Haffner ed. 1970).

16. See J.S. Mill, On Liberty (1859) (Rev. ed. 1823).

17. 198 U.S. 45, 75 (1904) ("The Fourteenth Amendment does not enact Mr. Herbert Spencer's Social Statics.")

this, government should not interfere with the economic functioning of society at all. Nor will many accept the teachings of Jean Bodin that supreme power is vested in an absolute and perpetual sovereign which has the right to make laws, and that there is no right to rebel even against a tyrant because freedom is sacrificed to the authority of the State.[18] Nor has there been much modern infatuation with Thomas Hobbes' teachings that the State is an artificial creation, an omnipotent power over the individuals, that humankind is not sociable by nature, that by a social contract it surrendered its original rights, including liberty, to the State in order to prevent war among individuals.[19]

John Locke agreed with Hobbes on the existence of a social contract, but to the contrary contended that humankind is naturally sociable and endowed with the right to personal liberty, the right to work and consequently the right to property, and that the State is formed for the sole purpose of guaranteeing these rights. Locke said that the State was formed because in nature there was no guarantee to secure these rights.[20] Similarly, Jean–Jacques Rousseau believed that humankind was born good and was born happy.[21] He taught that the social contract was "a postulate of reason" and not an historical fact and explained how it came about: For an instant, the individuals confer all their rights (natural ones) to the State which thereafter gives them all back (civil rights) with the name changed; by this novation or transformation, the individuals have been assured by the State of those rights which they already possessed by nature.[22]

Thus, in the heroic Due Process and Fourteenth Amendment Revolution that succeeded in spinning off a galaxy of individual rights in both the criminal law and civil law disciplines, the philosophical justifications, although not substantially articulated or authenticated with the niceties of rational discourse, find legitimacy and verification in the tenets espoused some centuries past. Although Locke and Rousseau generally are cited most often to justify the form of government we adopted, their identification of natural rights and explanation of how they are protected by the State go a long way in supplying the philosophical justification for the new constitutional law jurisprudence.

Theories of "Liberal" and "Conservative"

One who is comfortable with the most familiar dichotomy—the division between so-called liberal and conservative judges—has a choice of a number of abstract theories. One can start with the clash between two renowned works of moral and political philosophy, John Rawls' A Theory of Justice (1971) and Robert Nozick's Anarchy, State, and Utopia (1974). Rawls expressed his conception of justice in the statement: "All

---

18. J. Bodin, De La Republique (1577).

19. T. Hobbes, Leviathan (1651).

20. J. Locke, Second Treatise on Civil Government (1690) (Everyman's ed. 1924).

21. J. Rousseau, Discours Sur L'Origine Et Les Fondements de L'Inegalité Parmi Les Hommes (1753) and Contrat Social (1762) ("He who first closed off a field and said 'This is mine' was the first creator of human unhappiness".).

22. Id.

social values—liberty and opportunity, income and wealth, and the bases of self respect—are to be distributed equally unless an unequal distribution of any, or all, of these values is to everyone's advantage." [23] Nozick defended a thesis of the "minimum state," and argued that state intervention is severely limited to the narrow function of protection against force, theft, and fraud, and to the enforcement of contracts. He contended: "The minimal state is the most extensive state that can be justified. Any state more extensive violates people's rights. Yet many persons have put forth reasons purporting to justify a more extensive state." [24] Perhaps liberal or activist judges will do what they can to enforce the egalitarian philosophy of Rawls, and that the conservatives will lay back with Nozick, content that the least government is the best government.

There is yet another method of separating the liberal sheep from the conservative goats by hearkening to the differences between Locke and Hobbes in reconstructing the state of nature. John Locke's Second Treatise on Civil Government [25] emphasized the natural rights of individuals as to "life, liberty and estate." [26] He built on English tradition as illustrated by Sir John Fortesque and Coke, the entire emphasis of which had always been on rights of the individual, rather than the rights of people considered en masse. Locke believed that the state of nature was an era of "peace, good will, mutual assistance, and preservation" in which the "free sovereign" individual is already in possession of all valuable rights. Yet the individual is not always able to make his rights good or to determine them accurately with respect to the like rights of his fellows.[27] Hobbes painted a far different picture of man's state before any government existed. He visualized it as one of "force and fraud" in which "every man is to every man a wolf." [28] From this, Hobbes traced all rights to government and regarded them simply as implements of public policy. On the other hand, Locke regarded government as creating no rights, as being strictly fiduciary in character, and as designed to make secure and more readily available rights that antedate government and that would survive it. Traces of labels of conservative and liberal peek through here.

Yet another option is available—the dichotomy suggested by Alexander M. Bickel in The Morality of Consent. He stated that the liberal and conservative traditions have competed, and still compete, for control of the democratic process and of our constitutional system, and that both have controlled the direction of our judicial policy at one time or another. Bickel, too, referred to John Locke in the context of the social contract theory. He described this tradition as contractarian, a tradition that rests on the vision of individual rights that have a clearly defined, independent existence predating society and that are derived from na-

---

23. J. Rawls, A Theory of Justice at 62.

24. R. Nozick, Anarchy, State, and Utopia at 149.

25. J. Locke, Second Treatise on Civil Government (1690).

26. Id. at 158–59.

27. Id. at 164–65.

28. T. Hobbes, Leviathan (1651) at c. 13.

ture and from a natural, if imagined, contract. Society must bend to these rights. Bickel named the other tradition the Whig tradition, one intimately associated with Edmund Burke. This model rests not on anything that existed prior to society but on flexible, slow-moving, highly political circumstances that emerge as values and society evolve. The task of government, according to this tradition, is to make a peaceable, good and improving society informed by the current state of values. In discussing Burke, Bickel stated:

> [The rights of man] do not preexist and condition civil society. They are in their totality the right to decent, wise, just, responsive, stable government in the circumstance of a given time and place. Under such a government, a partnership Burke calls it, "the restraints on men, as well as their liberties, are to be reckoned among their rights," and "all men have equal rights, but not to equal things," since a leveling egalitarianism, which does not reward merit and ability is harmful to all and is unjust as well.[29]

Because all these thoughtful analyses are couched in the abstract, to predict how a judge will decide a case based on a preconceived label is a risky enterprise. Yet the effort continues unabated, with the main journalistic effort taking the form of a track record tally. It is a quantitative analysis that proceeds by inductive reasoning from decisions made in specific cases that are then generalized into a conclusion. A judge is labeled a liberal, more or less, if inclined to favor claims in the following categories: criminal defendants or prisoners (excluding those accused of white collar crimes such as income tax evasion, fraud, embezzlement or antitrust violations); civil rights claims of women, minorities and aliens; labor unions and employees in labor-management cases; employees in Title VII employment discrimination claims; the insureds as against insurance companies; small businesses against big businesses; tenants in landlord-tenant cases; debtors or bankrupts; buyers of goods rather than sellers; stockholders in stockholder suits; civil antitrust plaintiffs; workers in compensation cases; Social Security disability claimants; the injured or the decedents' estates in automobile cases; patients or clients in professional malpractice cases; the injured in products liability or federal tort claims; section 1983 plaintiffs against local, county, or state government officials; and individuals or citizens' groups against government agencies, but in favor of the government agency in regulation of business cases. The judge is considered a conservative if inclined the other way.

Jurisprudence

As stated in the introduction, jurisprudence is distinct from legal philosophy. The principles of legal philosophy are the abstract moral and legal principles, or doctrines or conceptions, which we have called first or super-eminent principles. Standing by themselves, principles do not carry the horsepower of legal rules. They do not describe a detailed

29. Id. at 20.

legal consequence of a detailed set of facts. Jurisprudence is something else, best described as a body of law that has formal features. It is a system of rules, promulgated by those with power and authority, backed by sanctions, and regulating public behavior. The term "jurisprudence" is probably influenced by the expression currently in use in France to describe case law—*la jurisprudence*. Although case law in the French civil law tradition does not have the bite of precedent present in the common law countries, the name given to French case law nevertheless expresses at least part of what we comprehend. Our meaning goes much further. The term jurisprudence is used to describe a system of obligatory norms, both substantive and procedural, that shape and regulate the life of a people in a given State (used in both the international and American sense). Any valid legal rule is a norm if it is considered a command in the John Austin sense.[30] Yet, this binding quality may also spring from the "will" of parties to a transaction as well as from a legislator or it may emerge from the customs of a people or from a general belief that a norm is a rule expressing the notion that somebody ought to act in a certain way.[31]

A given jurisprudence may be in effect for a given people at a given period. For example, when we commonly refer to ancient Roman law, German law, Italian law, British law, Pennsylvania law, California law, Third Circuit law or federal law, we are referring to the jurisprudence of a particular system. Moreover, this jurisprudence takes the form of a body of legal precepts more or less defined, the element to which Jeremy Bentham referred when he said that law was an aggregate of legal precepts.[32] Jurisprudence may be viewed as the by-laws of a given society or rules that govern a given social order. Jurisprudence is law as it is, not as it ought to be. It is more properly a juridical science than a philosophy.

It is necessary to distinguish between "legal philosophy" and "jurisprudence." Although these are two important elements that go into the make-up of a judge's personality, this distinction is seldom made by those who evaluate judges and judging. To be sure, there are grey areas where the line of demarcation between the two concepts is evanescent, if it exists at all. Sometimes, when we think we are addressing substantive law, it may be more philosophy than jurisprudence, or maybe a little of both. The concepts are not mutually exclusive. Consider, for example, two dimensions of law articulated by Roscoe Pound. In addition to being a legal precept in the aggregate sense, law may be considered as "a body of traditional ideas as to how legal precepts should be interpreted and applied and causes decided, and a traditional technique of developing and applying legal precepts whereby these precepts are eked out, extended, restricted, and adapted to the exigencies of administration of jus-

---

30. "Every law or rule ... is a command. Or, rather, laws or rules, properly so called, are a species of command." J. Austin, Lectures on Jurisprudence 88 (5th ed. 1885).

31. See H. Kelsen, General Theory of Law and State 30–37 (1945).

32. J. Bentham, Principles of Morals & Legislation (1970) at 324.

tice." [33]   Moreover, law may be considered as "a body of philosophical, political, and ethical ideas as to the end of law, and as to what legal precepts should be in view thereof." [34]

If a judge truly is following "a body of traditional ideas," he or she is probably observing the law as it "is" and not as it "ought to be." If we talk about law as it should be, we are not dealing with juridical science, or what we have been calling jurisprudence. Instead, we have entered the world of philosophical generalities. Immanuel Kant suggested that the distinction existed in two simple Latin terms. When we ask *quid jus?* we are seeking what is included in general universal law. When we ask *quid juris?* we are seeking what the law of a certain system.[35] From this we can say that when we seek that which must or ought to be in the law, in contrast to that which is, we are in the realm of legal philosophy. This may be a subjective exercise with deontological overtones. When a judge resorts to legal philosophy for assistance, he or she looks at law in its logical universality, seeks its origins, notes the general characteristics of its historical development, and tests it according to personal ideals of justice, personal ideals that must be drawn from pure reason in order to avoid idiosyncratic arbitrariness.

Unfortunately, the line between what the law is and what it ought to be is not always bright. One legal precept, pushed to the limit of its logic, may point to one result; another precept, followed with like logic, may point with equal certainty to another result. For example, assume the presence of two contradictory legal precepts and that a choice must be made between the two. Where choice of two competing precepts is involved, are we faced with a case of what the law is or what it ought to be? Is the answer found in the jurisprudence, or is a resort to general philosophical principles necessary? Or take the questions posed by Cardozo:

> If a precedent is applicable, when do I refuse to follow it? If no precedent is applicable, how do I reach the rule that will make a precedent for the future? If I am seeking logical consistency, the symmetry of the legal structure, how far shall I seek it? At what point shall the quest be halted by some discrepant custom, by some consideration of the social welfare, by my own or the common standards of justice and morals? [36]

NOTE

In everyday trial and appellate practice, are the suggestions of legal philosophers and jurisprudents addressed very much? Consider the admonition of Cardozo in 1921:

33. R. Pound, *The Theory of Judicial Decision*, 36 Harv.L.Rev. 641, 645 (1923).

34. Id.

35. G. Del Vecchio, Philosophy of Law 2 (Martin Trans.1953). See I. Kant, The Phi-

losophy of Law 43–46 (Kelley ed. 1974) (Hastie trans. 1887) (2d ed. 1798).

36. B. Cardozo, The Nature of the Judicial Process 1 (1921).

Back of the precedent are the basic juridical conceptions which are the postulates of legal reasoning, and father back are the habits of life, the institutions of society, in which those conceptions had their origin, and which, by a process of interaction, they have modified in turn. None the less, in a system so highly developed as our own, precedents have so covered the ground that they fix the point of departure from which the labor of the judge begins. Almost invariably, his first step is to examine and compare them. If they are plain and to the point, there may be need of nothing more. *Stare decisis* is at least the everyday working rule of our law ... [T]he work of deciding cases in accordance with precedents that plainly fit them is a process similar in its nature to that of deciding cases in accordance with a statute. It is a process of search, comparison, and little more. Some judges seldom get beyond that process in any case. Their notion of their duty is to match the colors of the case at hand against the colors of many sample cases spread upon their desk. The sample nearest in shade supplies the applicable rule. But, of course, no system of living law can be evolved by such a process, and no judge of a high court, worthy of his office, views the function of his place so narrowly. If that we all there was to our calling, there would be little of intellectual interest about it.

B. Cardozo, The Nature of the Judicial Process 19–21 (1921). When you examine a modern appellate opinion, or the briefs submitted to the courts, how many truly contain the ingredients of legal philosophies and jurisprudence described as "basic juridical conceptions" and "postulates of legal reasoning"? How many briefs and opinions are simply exercises in color-matching precedents in the sense condemned by Cardozo?

During the first half of the nineteenth century, negligence began to gain recognition as a separate and independent basis of tort liability. It was greatly encouraged by the disappearance of the old forms of action, and the disappearance of the distinction between direct and indirect injuries found in trespass and case. It is defined as conduct which falls below the standard established by law for the protection of others against unreasonable risk of harm, or conduct below standards of a reasonable person of ordinary prudence. The application of the standard must be left to the fact finder—the jury or the court. The testimony for the fact finder is always fact specific.

In recent decades we have witnessed the astronomical increase of professional malpractice and product liability cases involving the accelerated use of expert witness testimony. Because juries composed of lay persons are normally incompetent to pass judgment of questions of medical or engineering science or technique, it has been held that in professional malpractice cases there can be no finding of negligence in the absence of expert testimony. Similarly, in strict product liability litigation it is necessary for an expert to testify that a product contained a manufacturing defect, is defective in design or is defective because of the inadequate instructions or warnings.

Is the replacement of fact evidence by opinion evidence a revolution in traditional jurisprudence? Are opinions of experts "facts"? If not, what is the jurisprudential basis of permitting opinion evidence in a search for the truth by presenting facts to a jury?

The philosophy stated for adopting strict products liability has been variously stated: Merchants and manufacturers have the capacity to distribute losses of the few among the many who purchase the products. Is this a "deep pocket" theory or a "risk bearing economic" theory? Can the manufacturers shift the cost of accidents to purchasers for use by charging higher prices for the costs of products? Do they? Does strict liability induce greater care than liability based on negligence? Does this inhibit the development of new products? In the small aircraft industry? The automobile industry? The pharmaceutical industry?

Compared to the gradual growth of negligence doctrine (over the centuries) and the explosion of strict product liability within a few years (from the seminal case, Greenman v. Yuba Power Prods., 59 Cal.2d 57, 27 Cal.Rptr. 697, 377 P.2d 897 (1963) to promulgation of Restatement (Second) of Torts § 402A (1965)), did the courts move too fast in creating a revolutionary jurisprudence of tort liability?

ROSCOE POUND, WHAT IS JURISPRUDENCE? *

Jurisprudence in its widest sense is the science of law. This is the original and etymological meaning and is in accord with the best usage. There are, however, three other uses of the term; two of them with some warrant, the third wholly unjustifiable.

1. The first is peculiar to England, British dominions, and the United States. As study of the science of law as such (i.e. apart from political science and political philosophy) dates in England and America from Austin's Province of Jurisprudence Determined (1832), and as Austin's method was exclusively analytical, a narrower meaning became current in English-speaking countries. It thinks of law as an aggregate of laws and of laws as rules, and this narrow definition of law gives a narrow limitation of the science of law. In this narrower sense in which the word has been used by many English writers, jurisprudence might be called *the comparative anatomy of developed systems of law.*

Holland uses the term in this sense when he defines Jurisprudence as the "formal science of positive law." This definition proceeds on the Aristotelian distinction between substance and form. To give an old-time illustration, a smith has in his hand the raw material, the substance, steel and wood. He has in his mind the idea, that is, the picture

* R. Pound, I Jurisprudence 7–11 (1959)
(West). Reprinted with permission.

of a saw. He fashions the substance to that mental picture and so gives to the substance the form of a saw. Hence the maxim *forma dat esse rei*. Accordingly, by saying that Jurisprudence is a formal science, Holland means that it has to do with systems of legal precepts but not with legal precepts, the substance given form in those systems. It does not criticize the content of a body of laws except for being out of line with the analytical system. It arranges and systematizes that content. By "positive law" he means the body of legal precepts which actually obtain as authoritative legal materials for decision and authoritative bases of predicting decisions in a given time and in given places; not the received ideals of legal systems, and not the ideal precepts which philosophical or economic or sociological considerations might dictate or indicate.

This is one side of the science of law. I shall call it *analytical jurisprudence*.

2. A second use of the term is French, and to some extent American. The French use the word *jurisprudence* to mean the course of decision in the courts, contrasting it with legislation and with "doctrine," i.e. the opinions of learned commentators. In the civilian's theory of forms of law, legislation alone had full authority; jurisprudence (i.e. case law) and doctrine (i.e. textbook law) were persuasive only. But this has undergone some change.

In America the word "jurisprudence" has been used to some extent in the French sense. Thus the phrase "equity jurisprudence" meaning the course of decision in Anglo–American courts of equity, has been fixed in good usage by the classical work of Judge Story.

3. By a not unnatural transition, the word has come to be used, chiefly in this country, as a polysyllabic synonym for "law."

"Medical jurisprudence" for the forensic applications of medicine or the law relating to or of interest to physicians, "dental jurisprudence" for the law of interest to dentists, "engineering jurisprudence" for the law of interest to engineers, and other phrases of the sort, are quite indefensible. But "medical jurisprudence" is more or less established in good usage.

I shall take it, then, that Jurisprudence means the science of law.

It should be noted, however, that the phrase "science of law" involves difficulties in that there is no agreement as to what constitutes a science, and the word "law" is used in juristic writing in more than one meaning.

Formerly jurisprudence was held to be a philosophy of law. Austin speaks of "General Jurisprudence, or the Philosophy of Positive Law." But we may very well distinguish philosophical jurisprudence from philosophy of law, as we may distinguish historical jurisprudence from legal history. Philosophical jurisprudence is one form or side of the science of law, organized by philosophical method and directed chiefly to the ideal element of law and to a philosophical critique of legal institutions, legal doctrines, and legal precepts. Philosophy of law is one side of practical philosophy; it is practical philosophy applied to the legal order and its problems, and to the body of authoritative legal materials whereby we seek to maintain that order.

Section 2

THE NATURE OF LAW

A study of the judicial process must begin with an analysis of the nature of law in the abstract. If the law is a "seamless web," so also is the process by which law is created. The various steps and components of that process are not discrete units each with independent existences; rather they are overlapping parts of an integrated whole. They exist solely in relation to each other. Upon close inspection, even the seemingly self-evident dichotomy often drawn between the legislative and judicial functions can be seen as highly artificial; both functions, it develops, are coordinate parts of a single law-making process.

Similarly, each part of the judicial process is defined largely in relation to other parts. The analyses and perceptions applied to one aspect of the process will have repercussions throughout the study of the entire process. Implications of choosing or preferring one definition of "law" over another extend to all phases of the legal process.

The question, "What is law?" is of primary importance throughout this study, and what may seem, on first reading, as so much academic, esoteric quibbling can eventually be seen as the necessary theoretical foundation of modern, functional jurisprudence. The writings show shifts from the conceptualism and definitionalism of the classical natural law theorists and the positivists, to the realism and functionalism of Holmes, Pound and Cardozo and the present-day "reasoned elaborationists". It is no longer necessary to "define" law. Indeed, Holmes' classic statement that "the prophecies of what the courts will do in fact, and nothing more pretentious, are what I mean by the law" is not a definition at all; it does not seek to isolate law's peculiar characteristics and distinguish it from other political, ethical and social phenomena. As Felix S. Cohen notes, a definition is not true or false, it is merely useful or useless.

Modern jurisprudence recognizes that the judge can, and indeed, must, make law, as well as apply it. Such recognition was impossible under natural law theory which held that law was only discovered in the operation of the universe and could not be created by any human institution. Similarly, under positivism, with its emphasis upon the command the legislature as the voice of the sovereign, inquiry into the judges' creative function was impossible. Only in this century has the judge been recognized, albeit grudgingly, as a lawmaker. A more than little nudge in this direction came from John Chapman Gray: "The Law, indeed, is identical with the rules laid down by the judges.... [R]ules for conduct which the courts do not apply are not Law; ... the fact that the courts apply rules is what makes them law."

Although the limits of judicial law making have not been finally articulated, the power undoubtedly is a broad one. Holmes and his followers propounded the "interstices" doctrine, but the cases show that judicial law making often exceeds the interstices. In practice, it might appear that the only proper limitations are those which are "functional"—such as inadequate facilities for extensive fact gathering, confinement to the facts of record, and the like. Ultimately the test of judge-made law, as with any law, is its effect on social welfare and its acceptance by society. The judge, therefore, must focus openly on policy considerations as he seeks to keep the law in tune with changing societal values.

The anatomy of the law still undergoes much analysis, if not dissection. H.L.A. Hart prefers to speak of law as a set of special rules which can be identified and distinguished by their validity or acceptability, not in the manner in which they were adopted or developed. Hart acknowledges the courts' right, "the discretion," to go beyond these special rules—indeed "beyond the law"—to decide a case and thus to fashion a fresh special rule. Professor Rolf Sartorius seems to agree with the basic Hart formulation, but disagrees that the materials used to fashion such "new law" are found "beyond the law."

Whatever the labels attached to its components, modern jurisprudence views law as a social process, the final aim of which is the society's welfare. Today law is no more (nor less) than one of many methods of ordering and channeling the energies of society; its only measure is its effect on society. Thus, the path seems clear for unabashed and open policy determinations by the courts: functional and result-oriented if the impression conveyed is of a new jurisprudence; doctrinaire and conceptual if, upon close analysis, certain elements of this new jurisprudence disclose a fealty to older, more orthodox concepts.

A. GENERAL

BLACKSTONE, OF THE NATURE OF LAWS IN GENERAL *

Law, in its most general and comprehensive sense, signifies a rule of action; and is applied indiscriminately to all kinds of action, whether animate or inanimate, rational or irrational. Thus we say, the laws of motion, of gravitation, of optics, or mechanics, as well as the laws of nature and of nations. And it is that rule of action, which is prescribed by some superior, and which the inferior is bound to obey.

. . .

* 1 W. Blackstone, Commentaries *38–41, 44–46.

This, then, is the general signification of law, a rule of action dictated by some superior being; and, in those creatures that have neither the power to think, nor to will, such laws must be invariably obeyed, so long as the creature itself subsists, for its existence depends on that obedience. But laws, in their more confined sense, and in which it is our present business to consider them, denote the rules, not of action in general, but of *human* action or conduct; that is, the precepts by which man, the noblest of all sublunary beings, a creature endowed with both reason and free-will, is commanded to make use of those faculties in the general regulation of his behavior.

. . .

Considering the Creator only as a being of infinite *power,* he was able unquestionably to have prescribed whatever laws he pleased to His creature, man, however unjust or severe. But, as he is also a being of infinite *wisdom,* he has laid down only such laws as were founded in those relations of justice that existed in the nature of things antecedent to any positive precept. These are the eternal immutable laws of good and evil, to which the Creator himself, in all his dispensations, conforms; and which he has enabled human reason to discover, so far as they are necessary for the conduct of human actions. Such, among others, are these principles: that we should live honestly, should hurt nobody, and should render to every one his due; to which three general precepts Justinian has reduced the whole doctrine of law.

... For he has so intimately connected, so inseparably interwoven the laws of eternal justice with the happiness of each individual, that the latter cannot be attained but by observing the former; and, if the former be punctually obeyed, it cannot but induce the latter. In consequence of which mutual connection of justice and human felicity, he has not perplexed the law of nature with a multitude of abstracted rules and precepts, referring merely to the fitness or unfitness of things, as some have vainly surmised, but has graciously reduced the rule of obedience to this one paternal precept, "that man should pursue his own happiness." This is the foundation of what we call ethics, or natural law. For the several articles, into which it is branched in our systems, amount to no more than demonstrating that this or that action tends to man's real happiness, and therefore very justly concluding that the performance of it is a part of the law of nature; or, on the other hand, that this or that action is destructive of man's real happiness, and therefore that the law of nature forbids it.

This law of nature, being coeval with mankind, and dictated by God himself, is of course superior in obligation to any other. It is binding over all the globe, in all countries, and at all times: no human laws are of any validity, if contrary to this; and such of them as are valid derive all their force, and all their authority, mediately or immediately, from this original.

. . .

Thus much I thought it necessary to premise concerning the law of nature, the revealed law, and the law of nations, before I proceeded to treat more fully of the principal subject of this section, municipal or civil law; that is, the rule by which particular districts, communities, or nations are governed; being thus defined by Justinian, "jus civile est quad quisque sibi populus constituit." I call it *municipal* law, in compliance with common speech; for, though strictly that expression denotes the particular customs of one single *municipium* or free town, yet it may with sufficient propriety be applied to any one state or nation, which is governed by the same laws and customs.

Municipal law, thus understood, is properly defined to be "a rule of civil conduct prescribed by the supreme power in a state, commanding what is right and prohibiting what is wrong." ...

. . .

It is ... "a rule *prescribed* " [b]ecause a bare resolution, confined in the breast of the legislator, without manifesting itself by some external sign, can never be properly a law. It is requisite that this resolution be notified to the people who are to obey it. But the manner in which this notification is to be made, is matter of very great indifference. It may be notified by universal tradition and long practice, which supposes a previous publication, and is the case of the common law of England. It may be notified, *viva voce,* by officers appointed for that purpose, as is done with regard to proclamations, and such acts of parliament as are appointed to be publicly read in churches and other assemblies. It may lastly be notified by writing, printing, or the like which is the general course taken with all our acts of parliament. Yet, whatever way is made use of, it is incumbent on the promulgators to do it in the most public and perspicuous manner; not like Caligula, who (according to Dio Cassius) wrote his laws in a very small character, and hung them up upon high pillars, the more effectually to ensnare the people. There is still a more unreasonable method than this, which is called making of laws *ex post facto;* when after an action (indifferent in itself) is committed, the legislator then for the first time declares it to have been a crime, and inflicts a punishment upon the person who has committed it. Here it is impossible that the party could foresee that an action, innocent when it was done, should be afterwards converted to guilt by a subsequent law; he had therefore no cause to abstain from it; and all punishment for not abstaining must of consequence be cruel and unjust. All laws should be therefore made to commence *in futuro,* and be notified before their commencement; which is implied in the term prescribed, it is then the subject's business to be thoroughly acquainted therewith; for if ignorance, of what he *might* know, were *"prescribed."* But when this rule is in the usual manner notified, or admitted as a legitimate excuse, the laws would be of no effect, but might always be eluded with impunity.

But farther: municipal law is "a rule of civil conduct prescribed *by the supreme power in a state.*" For legislature ... is the greatest act of superiority that can be exercised by one being over another. Wherefore it is requisite to the very essence of a law, that it be made by the supreme power. Sovereignty and legislature are indeed convertible terms; one cannot assist without the other.

NOTE

An instruction reads: "Answer this question in 25 words or less: What is Law?" It is directed to a nuclear physicist, a trial lawyer, a clergyman, a state legislator. Will the replies vary?

Using Blackstone's definition, how many courses of municipal law have you studied in law school?

When Blackstone speaks of "commanding what is right and prohibiting what is wrong," does he refer to morality? What makes it "right" or "wrong"?

Blackstone stated that the duty of the court was not to "pronounce a new law, but to maintain and expound the old one." 1 Blackstone, Commentaries *69. Is there any inconsistency between what he considers the duty of the court and the "unreasonable method" of *ex post facto* action by a legislator?

————

ROSCOE POUND, THREE MEANINGS OF LAW *

As to the term "law" as we use it in English, and the same is largely true of the corresponding word in other languages, we mean any of three things, or sometimes all three.

1. Historically, the oldest and longest continued use of "law" in juristic writing is to mean the aggregate of laws, the whole body of legal precepts which obtain in a given politically organized society. But in a wider phase of this sense it may mean the body of authoritative grounds of, or guides to, judicial and administrative action, and so of prediction of such action, established or recognized in such a society including precepts, technique, and received ideals. In this sense jurists speak of "systems of law" and "justice according to law." Usually also we use the word in this sense when we speak of "comparative law." We mean the body of received or established materials on which judicial and administrative determinations are to, and on the whole do, proceed. Hereafter, following a logical rather than a chronological order, I shall call this "law in the second sense."

2. In another sense the term "law" is used to mean the legal order (*ordre juridique, Rechtsordnung*). It is used to mean the regime of ordering human activities and adjusting human relations through the systematic application of the force of a politically organized society. Here again, however, there is a wider idea. The legal order is a

* R. Pound, I Jurisprudence 12–16 (1959)
(West). Reprinted with permission.

specialized phase of social control. It is from one standpoint a regime of ordering conduct through social pressure backed by the force of the political organization. If we go back a bit in legal history we come to regimes of social pressure without such backing. To unify the phenomena of developed societies with those of more primitive social orders, historical jurists have used "law" to mean the whole regime of social control. The word "law" is used in the sense of the legal order when we speak of "respect for law," or of "the end of law." Thus when we speak of respect for law we mean respect for the legal order. One might, for example, respect the legal order and yet object to some particular item of the body of legal precepts, such as a fugitive slave law, or the National Prohibition Act. Most of what is called philosophy of law is a philosophical consideration of the legal order. Also in recent years the science of law has come to be quite as much a science of the legal order as one of the authoritative materials of decision. Hereafter I shall speak of the legal order as "law in the first sense," using a logical rather than a historical sequence.

3. In still another sense, many who write of "law" mean what Mr. Justice Cardozo has taught us to call "the judicial process." In this sense law is used to mean the process of determining controversies whether as it actually takes place or as it is conceived it ought to take place. To this, today we shall have to add what may well be called the "administrative process," that is, the process of administrative determination, whether as it actually takes place or as it is conceived it ought to take place. The term "law" is used in this sense in most neo-realist writing of today, and in such pronouncements as that of Professor Llewellyn that he includes under "law" all that is done officially.

4. In addition, the term "law" may be used to mean all three of the foregoing as, for example, in much of the discussion of "law and morals," which may mean the relation of morals or morality, or both, to the legal order, or to the body of authoritative materials for the guidance of judicial and administrative action, or to the judicial process, or to all three. Similarly, when we speak of the "science of law" we may mean an organized body of knowledge as to the authoritative materials of judicial and administrative determination, as did the analytical jurists in the last century. In recent times, however, we are more likely to mean a body of knowledge or investigation in which the legal order, the authoritative materials for guidance of judges and officials, and the judicial and administrative processes are all taken into account as somehow making up one subject—the materials and processes of the systematic ordering of human relations by a politically organized society.

Can these three ideas, the legal order, the body of authoritative grounds of decision and bases of prediction, and the judicial and administrative processes be unified so as to make one subject of one science? They may be so unified by the idea of social control. I am not using that term here in the sense in which some economists have been using it, namely, to mean consciously planned guidance of economic processes through those who wield the force of politically organized society. I use it rather in the wider sense in which the term was first given currency by Professor Ross, whom it was my good fortune to have for a colleague at Nebraska, and to whom I owe my real start in the science of society. In that sense it means the control of each of us by the pressure of his fellow men, whether unconscious and involuntary or direct and purposive. It is this pressure, more and more organized and directed, which has established and maintains our mastery over human nature. All social control is not law in the lawyer's sense, nor achieved through law. Religion, ethical custom, the discipline of kin groups, of religious organizations, and of voluntary associations of all sorts, are also agencies of social control. The province of jurisprudence is social control through the systematic application of the force of politically organized society. That gives rise to the legal order, it requires a body of authoritative materials in which tribunals are to find the grounds of determinations, and in a developed legal order it requires a judicial and administrative process admitting of reasonable prediction.

Hence by the term "science of law" we mean an organized and critically controlled body of knowledge both of legal institutions and legal precepts and of the legal order, that is, of the legal ordering of society.

NOTE

More abstract definitions of law have been suggested:

Law is the ensemble of conditions whereby the will of each can coexist with the will of others, according to a universal law of liberty.

I. Kant, Groundwork of the Metaphysics of Morals (Paton Trans.1964) (1785).

Law is the objective coordination of possible actions between several subjects, according to an ethical principle which determines them, excluding the impediments thereto.... There are two kinds of ethical determinations, the subjective, or moral, and the objective, or juridical. There is a necessary coherence between the two. There are constant relationships between Morals and Law which can be determined *a priori* because they are logical necessities. The fundamental relationship is expressed in this maxim: *That which is a duty is always right, and that cannot be a duty which is not right.*

G. Del Vecchio, Philosophy of Law 270 (Martin Trans.1953) (8th ed. 1952).

Law in action involves legal institutions and procedures, legal values, and legal concepts and ways of thought, as well as legal rules. It involves what is sometimes called "the legal process," or what in German is called *Rechtsverwirklichung,* the "realizing" of law.

Lon L. Fuller has defined law as "the enterprise of subjecting human conduct to the governance of rules." This definition rightly stresses the primacy of legal activity over legal rules. Yet I would go further by adding to the purpose of the enterprise not just the making and applying of rules but also other modes of governance, including the casting of votes, the issuing of orders, the appointment of officials, and the handing down of judgments. Also the law has purposes other than governance, in the usual sense of that word: it is an enterprise for facilitating voluntary arrangements through the negotiation of transactions, the issuance of documents (for example, credit instruments or documents of title), and the performance of other acts of a legal nature. Law in action consists of people legislating, adjudicating, administering, negotiating, and carrying on other legal activities. It is a living process of allocating rights and duties and thereby resolving conflicts and creating channels of cooperation.

Harold J. Berman, Law and Revolution: The Formation of the Western Legal Tradition 4–5 (1983).

————

SOIA MENTSCHIKOFF AND IRWIN P. STOTZKY, LAW— THE LAST OF THE UNIVERSAL DISCIPLINES *

How can one define law? One way to approach that question is to discuss the functions that the law serves in any society, including our own.

There are at least three major functions of law: dispute settlement, channeling and rechanneling behavior, and allocating the final say. Lawyers play integral roles in each of these functions. Indeed, to understand the significance of lawyers and law in our broader civilization, one must understand the varying roles lawyers play in serving these functions.

The most basic function of law, and a fundamental aspect of any legal system, is dispute settlement. One of the prime requisites of a peaceful society or group is that the settlement of trouble cases be by processes which do not splinter the group in such a way as to destroy its groupness. In most groups, therefore, dispute resolution machinery requires processes that are non-violent in character.

Every legal system, if it is to survive, must create machinery for resolving disputes to a sufficient degree, with a sufficient regularity, and with a sufficient willingness by the group to abide by the result. Stated otherwise, the most basic function of law is to settle disputes well enough so that the society does not disintegrate, and so that the people whose law it is will follow its commands.

* S. Mentschikoff and I. Stotzky, *Law— The Last of the Universal Disciplines,* 54   U.Cin.L.Rev. 695, 705–708 (1986). Reprinted by permission.

The bare bones requirement of any legal system is to provide dispute settlement machinery of some kind that will perform that minimal function. Each individual, small group, and larger society also has aspirations, but they come later. The dispute settlement function, which is the bare bones function of any legal system, becomes the law of the group. Moreover, it is the way through which the law of the group can best be seen.

The second basic function of law—the channeling and rechanneling of behavior—is concerned with what we call the aspirational aspects of law. The aspirational aspects of law reflect the values we hold dear in our society, such as truth, freedom, and justice. These values are, in some sense, culturally derived. There are other aspirational aspects of law, however, that are biologically derived. They are also reflected in our legal culture. For example, almost from the time babies are born they are reaching out for something. It may be something as simple as love. Further, when human beings develop, they aspire for something beyond the minimal physical needs. One need not aspire to greatness but, at some point in life, everybody aspires to do something for oneself and for others. At some point, individuals within a group may have conflicting aspirations. Moreover, all of the conflicting aspirations may be acceptable. But, in terms of claims which have an arguable morality, an arguable need, and an arguable desirability, they cannot all be satisfied. There is not enough justice, for example, to satisfy everybody's felt need for some kind of satisfaction. The behavior conditioning function of law deals with attempting to work out a system that creates an image of "fairness" and recognizes that reasonable people differ in terms of their perceptions of the allocation. The fact that they differ is an aspirational aspect of law. Thus, to keep disputes at a minimum, to stop conflicting aspirations between individuals from bursting into a conflagration, law is created to get people to behave in certain ways. In sum, because of this aspirational quality, and because peace between individuals and groups is necessary to a society's own survival, one of the things law does is to channel and rechannel behavior.

Although this function of the law sounds like a very simplistic one, it is the most complex function that the law performs. It is also the most difficult function that the law performs and it is the least satisfactorily completed function that the law performs in anything other than bare bones character.

The third function that the law has in any kind of a complex society, and even in the small group, is to allocate the final say. That is, law determines who has the final power of decision. Somebody has to have that power. That somebody may be one person or a group of persons, but some identifiable somebody has to make the final say. The law is responsible for allocating that say and determining who the final decision maker will be.

The process of allocating the final say varies greatly among legal systems. In the United States, discussion of this function of law usually centers on whether the Federal government—the President or some administrative agency, the Congress, the Supreme Court—or the State government, in all its ramifications, shall have the final say. This focus on government results from our concern with Constitutional commands. In areas not covered by the structural restraints of the Constitution, however, there is a viable alternative to government: the particular private parties involved in the transaction.

On another level, it is important to understand that the power to decide finally, is also the power to decide incorrectly. Hence, to whom the legal system gives the power to decide issues both correctly and incorrectly is an issue with which one must be concerned. This has consequences as to, for example, whether members of the society even follow the dictates of the law.

HAROLD J. BERMAN, WHAT LAW IS *

Law is, in part, an instrument of class rule and an ideological reflection of the ruling class's interests. In every legal system examples may be found to illustrate that. But that is not all. Law in the West has also been a protection against the arbitrary power of the ruling class, and much in it that is derived from reason and morals, as well as much in it that is derived from earlier periods of history, does not necessarily reflect the interests of the ruling class.

Similarly, to say that Western law prior to the sixteenth century was an ideological reflection of feudalism is to point to only one aspect of that law. Other aspects—for example, the law of commercial credits to finance the wool trade or the spice trade in the thirteenth and fourteenth centuries—were a reflection of capitalism. Much of the law of the guilds was socialist in nature. A large part of the canon law of crimes, with its strong emphasis on retribution in the sense of vindication of the law, seems equally appropriate to any social-economic system.

Likewise, it is a serious oversimplification to categorize modern Western legal systems as ideological reflections of capitalism. Much modern law is more feudal in character than capitalist. Much defies any characterization in socioeconomic terms. A more complex system of categorization and characterization is needed, which will draw not only on types of economic and political formations but also on philosophical, religious, and other kinds of criteria.

To the question whether law is to be viewed as part of the material base or as part of the ideological superstructure, the answer is once again that in the West law is both—which is to say that Western law shows that the dichotomy itself is wrong. Law is as much a part of the mode of production of a society as farmland or machinery; the farmland

* H. Berman, Law and Revolution: The Formation of the Western Legal Tradition 556–558 (1983) Reprinted by permission of the President and Fellows of Harvard College.

or machinery is nothing unless it operates, and law is an integral part of its operation. Crops are not sown and harvested without duties and rights of work and of exchange. Machinery is not produced, moved from the producer to the user, and used, and the costs and benefits of its use are not valued, without some kind of legal ordering of these activities. Such legal ordering is itself a form of capital. Marx distinguished property as economic power from property as legal right, making the former a cause and the latter an effect, but this distinction rarely occurs in social-economic reality; generally, these are two interlocking ways of referring to the same thing.

Yet this is not to say that law is *only* social-economic fact or that legal right is *only* another way of saying economic power. Law is not only fact; it is also idea, or concept, and, in addition, it is a measure of value. It has, inevitably, an intellectual and a moral dimension. Unlike purely intellectual and moral standards, law is required to be practiced, but unlike purely material conditions it consists of ideas and values. Moreover, the ideas and values of law are supposed to have a certain degree of consistency with one another—and also with the nonlegal ideas and values of the community, that is, with its ideology as a whole.

The fact that law is, in its very nature, *both* material *and* ideological is connected with the fact that law *both* grows upward out of the structures and customs of the whole society and moves downward from the policies and values of the rulers of the society; Law helps to integrate the two. Thus theoretically at least, a conflict between social-economic conditions and political-moral ideology, which Marx saw as the primary cause of revolution, may be resolved by law. It was partly in order to avoid that—for him, unwelcome—theoretical result that Marx reduced law to ideology.

Finally, law in the West—ever since the Papal Revolution—has had a strong diachronic element, and more than that, a strong element of tradition. Tradition is more than historical continuity. A tradition is a blend of conscious and unconscious elements. In Octavio Paz's words, "It is a society's visible side—institutions, monuments, works, things,— but it is especially its submerged, invisible side: beliefs, desires, fears, repressions, dreams." Law is usually associated with the visible side, with works; but a study of the history of Western law, and especially its origins, reveals its rootedness in the deepest beliefs and emotions of a people. Without the fear of purgatory and the hope of the Last Judgment, the Western legal tradition could not have come into being.

It was also Octavio Paz who said, "Every time a society finds itself in crisis it instinctively turns its eyes towards its origins and looks there for a sign."

B.   NATURAL LAW

JOHN EDWARD LYNCH, NATURAL LAW *

Natural Law

Natural law [is] a set of principles, based on what are assumed to be the permanent characteristics of human nature, that can serve as a standard for evaluating conduct and civil laws. It is considered fundamentally unchanging and universally applicable. Because of the ambiguity of the word *nature,* the meaning of *natural* varies. Thus, natural law may be considered an ideal to which humanity aspires or a general fact, the way human beings usually act. Natural law is contrasted with positive law, the enactments of civil society.

Classical Theories

The ancient Greek philosophers were the first to elaborate a natural law doctrine. Heraclitus spoke in the 6th century b.c. of a common wisdom that pervades the whole universe, for all human laws are nourished by one, the divine. Aristotle distinguished between two kinds of justice: A rule of justice is natural that has the same validity everywhere, and does not depend on our accepting it or not; a rule is legal [conventional] that in the first instance may be settled in one way or the other indifferently. The Stoics, especially the philosopher Chrysippus of Soli (circa 280–206 b.c.), constructed a systematic natural law theory. According to *Stoicism,* the whole cosmos is rationally ordered by an active principle variously named God, mind or fate. Every individual nature is part of the cosmos. To live virtuously means to live in accord with one's nature, to live according to right reason. Because passion and emotion are considered irrational movements of the soul, the wise individual seeks to eradicate the passions and consciously embrace the rational life. This doctrine was popularized among the Romans by the 1st century b.c. orator Cicero, who gave a famous definition of natural law in his *De Republica:* True law is right reason in agreement with Nature; it is of universal application, unchanging and everlasting; it summons to duty by its commands, and averts from wrongdoing by its prohibitions.... There will not be different laws at Rome and at Athens, or different laws now and in the future, but one eternal and unchangeable law will be valid for all nations and for all times. * * *

Christian Conceptions

Christians found the natural law doctrine of the Stoics quite compatible with their beliefs. St. Paul spoke of Gentiles, who do not have the Mosaic law, doing by nature what the law requires (Romans 2:14). The 6th-century Spanish theologian St. Isidore of Seville affirmed that natural law is observed everywhere by natural instinct; he cited as illustrations the laws ordaining marriage and the procreation of children.

* Encarta Encyclopedia, Microsoft Corporation ©1993. Funk & Wagnall's Corporation ©1993. Reprinted with permission.

Texts from Isidore cited at the beginning of the Italian scholar Gratian's *Decretum* (circa 1140), the canon law textbook of the Middle Ages, stimulated extensive discussion among the Scholastics. The teaching of St. Thomas Aquinas on the natural law is the most widely known. In his *Summa Theologiae* (Summary Treatise of Theology, 1265–73), Aquinas called the rational guidance of creation by God the Eternal Law. The Eternal Law gives all beings the inclination to those actions and aims that are proper to them. Rational creatures, by directing their own actions and guiding the actions of others, share in divine reason itself. This participation in the Eternal Law by rational creatures is called the Natural Law. Its dictates correspond to the basic inclinations of human nature. Thus, according to Aquinas, it is possible to distinguish good from evil by the natural light of reason.

Modern Theories

The Dutch jurist Hugo Grotius is considered the founder of the modern theory of natural law. His break with Scholasticism is in methodology rather than content. His definition of natural law as that body of rules which can be discovered by the use of reason is traditional, but in raising the hypothetical argument that his law would have validity even if there were no God or if the affairs of human beings were of no concern to God, he effected a divorce from theological presuppositions and prepared the way for the purely rationalistic theories of the 17th and 18th centuries. A second innovation of Grotius was to view this law as deductive and independent of experience: "Just as the mathematicians treat their figures as abstracted from bodies, so in treating law I have withdrawn my mind from every particular fact." (*De Iure Belli ac Pacis;* On the Law of War and Peace, 1625).

The 17th-century English philosophers Thomas Hobbes and John Locke proposed an original state of nature from which a social contract arose and combined this theory with that of natural law. Locke's doctrine that nature had endowed human beings with certain inalienable rights that could not be violated by any governing authority was incorporated in the American Declaration of Independence.

In the 19th century a critical spirit dominated discussions of natural law. The existence of a natural law was generally regarded as unprovable, and it was largely replaced in legal theory by *utilitarianism,* formulated by the English philosopher Jeremy Bentham as the greatest happiness of the greatest number, and by legal positivism, according to which law is based simply on the command of the rule, in the phase of the English jurist John Austin (1790–1859).

The atrocities committed by Nazi Germany during World War II revived interest in a higher standard than positive law. The United Nations Charter declared the faith of that organization in human rights, and on December 10, 1948, the U.N. General Assembly adopted the Universal

Declaration of Human Rights, which, however, is more a moral pronouncement than a legally enforceable treaty.

———

CALVIN WOODARD, THOUGHTS ON THE INTERPLAY BETWEEN MORALITY AND LAW IN MODERN LEGAL THOUGHT *

I started this Article with the assertion that the relationship between law and morality is both complex and confusing. Some of the sources of confusion I have attributed to the variety of concepts of law. Thus (to restate the Paradigms ...)

A. *Law Reflects Morality*

PARADIGM I: *Law and morality are inseparable. Without morality, law is not law at all: it is naked power. Therefore the very idea of law implies morality.*

B. *Law and Morality are Different and Separate*

PARADIGM II: *Law, like morality, is a social sanction used to control human behavior; as such, it should be used to promote some moral purpose. In order to make law most effective for that (or any other) purpose, the task of Jurisprudence, as a science, is first to understand the nature of law itself in order to determine its basic attributes, the ways in which it differs from other social sanctions, and where and how it can be used most effectively. For this purpose, it is necessary to isolate law from all other social sanctions, including morality.*

C. *Law is Morally Neutral*

PARADIGM III: *The morality of law is found not in common notions of morality, and not in the just result reached in specific cases. It is found, rather, in the studied impartiality of the legal process itself.*

D. *The Morality of Law Depends Upon the Results It Reaches*

PARADIGM IV: *Law does not exist for its own sake. It is but a tool that exists to serve human-kind. Like hammers and laser beams, its only relationship with morality is in the uses to which it is put and the results it helps bring about in the real world.*

E. *Law is Based on, but Different From, Morality*

PARADIGM V: *Law and morality are integral parts of, but different stages in, a nation's own ever-developing form of civilization. They are organically linked together but the actual relationship between them, on any specific issue, depends on the*

* 64 Notre Dame L.Rev. 784, 803–804 (1989).

degree to which members of the nation share attitudes and beliefs with respect to that issue: the greater the consensus, the closer law and morality are to one another. Where there is no consensus, however, law must remain dormant and morality must do its work alone.

F. *Law is Institutionalized Immorality*

PARADIGM VI: *Law is institutionalized immorality.*

Other confusions arise from the fact that law is, in one sense, the voice of the government; and as the role of government changes, so the law's forms and functions must also change. Such changes bring about different relationships and conflicts with morality.

Then of course there is the question of the meaning of morality itself. Is it our consciences telling us intuitively what is right and wrong? Or is it some objective standard telling us which is right and wrong? Or is it our principled conclusions derived from the rational analysis of the dilemma we face in life and act upon in good faith? Or is it a system of values shared by, and in some senses peculiar to, the members of our society that find expression in the conscience of society?

Confusion abounds. Indeed, as Andre Breton long ago noted, we are lost in a forest of sign posts. But, to me, that observation confirms one of the dicta of old Legal Realists: where there is room for choice, there is not only indeterminacy—there is also the possibility of change for the better.

If that be true, the morality of our law, and indeed of our society, depends upon the choices we make, our motives, and the ways we act upon them. So put, the relationship between law and morality is, itself, a very personal moral problem for each of us. But it is also more. For the relationship between law and morality in the history of our times will be defined empirically, not philosophically, by those choices.

———

PARKER v. LEVY

Supreme Court of the United States, 1974.
417 U.S. 733, 94 S.Ct. 2547, 41 L.Ed.2d 439.

[The Court of Appeals had held that articles of the Uniform Code of Military Justice authorizing court-martial for conduct unbecoming an officer and a gentleman (Art. 133) and court-martial for disorders and neglects to prejudice of good order and discipline (Art. 134) were unconstitutionally vague and facially invalid for overbreadth. The Supreme Court reversed and emphasized the customs and usages of the military, holding that each article had been construed by the United States Court of Military Appeals or by other military authorities, such as the Manual for Courts–Martial, so as to limit its scope, thus narrowing the very broad reach of the literal language of the Articles, and at the same time supplying considerable specificity by way of examples of the conduct covered.]

MR. JUSTICE BLACKMUN, with whom THE CHIEF JUSTICE joins, concurring.

I wholly concur in the Court's opinion. I write only to state what for me is a crucial difference between the majority and dissenting views in this case. My Brother Stewart complains that men of common intelligence must necessarily speculate as to what "conduct unbecoming an officer and a gentleman" or conduct to the "prejudice of good order and discipline in the armed forces" or conduct "of a nature to bring discredit upon the armed forces" really mean. He implies that the average soldier or sailor would not reasonably expect, under the General Articles, to suffer military reprimand or punishment for engaging in sexual acts with a chicken, or window peeping in a trailer park, or cheating while calling bingo numbers, ... He argues that "times have changed" and that the Articles are "so vague and uncertain as to be incomprehensible to the servicemen who are to be governed by them."
. . .

These assertions are, of course, no less judicial fantasy than that which the dissent charges the majority of indulging. In actuality, what is at issue here are concepts of "right" and "wrong" and whether the civil law can accommodate, in special circumstances, a system of law which expects more of the individual in the context of a broader variety of relationships than one finds in civilian life.

In my judgment, times have not changed in the area of moral precepts. Fundamental concepts of right and wrong are the same now as they were under the Articles of the Earl of Essex (1642), or the British Articles of War of 1765, or the American Articles of War of 1775, or during the long line of precedents of this and other courts upholding the General Articles. And, however unfortunate it may be, it is still necessary to maintain a disciplined and obedient fighting force.

NOTE

Consider Justice Blackmun's 1974 statement of the issue in terms of the natural law theory.

NATURAL LAW AT THE CLARENCE THOMAS HEARING

At the September 10, 1991 opening of the Senate Judiciary Committee's hearing on the nomination of Clarence Thomas to the U.S. Supreme Court, Chairman Joseph Biden announced:

We are not seeking here to learn if you are a conservative—we expect no less.

Instead we must find out what sort of natural law philosophy you would employ as a justice of the Supreme Court.[1]

Judge Thomas explained his position:

> Yesterday as I spoke about the Framers and our Constitution and the higher law background—and it is background—is that our Framers had a view of the world. They subscribed to the notion of natural law, certainly the Framers of the 13th and 14th Amendments.
>
> My point has been that the Framers then reduced to positive law in the Constitution aspects of life principles that they believed in; for example, liberty. But when it is in the Constitution, it is not a natural right; it is a Constitutional right. And that is the important point. . . .
>
> At no time did I feel nor do I feel now that natural law is anything more than the background to our Constitution. It is not a method of interpreting or method of adjudicating in the constitutional law area.[2]

Various Senators expressed their views on natural law:

Senator Biden:

> There is good natural law, if you will, and bad natural law in terms of informing the Constitution, and there a whole new school of thought in America that would like very much to use natural law to lower the protections for individuals in the zone of personal privacy, . . . and who want to heighten the protection for businesses and corporations." [3]

Senator Patrick J. Leahy:

> Natural law, we all know, is an elastic concept. It can be used to defend but also to deny basic rights. In a case already alluded to at this hearing today, the famous case from the 1870's, one Supreme Court Justice would have upheld a law in Illinois that barred a Vermont woman from becoming a lawyer. And why would this Vermont woman be barred from becoming a lawyer? Because under the laws of nature, according to this Justice, women were granted the noble and benign offices of wife and mother, and that was it. He wanted to make certain we knew that natural law would never accept a woman as a lawyer.[4]

Senator Howard Metzenbaum:

> Judge Thomas has asserted that the Constitution must be interpreted in light of natural law. As has already been pointed out, natural law is a broad vague concept which means different things to different people. Over 50 years ago, conservative

1. Hearings before the Committee of the Judiciary, United States Senate One Hundred Second Congress. First Session. Part 1. 20.

2. Id. at 179–180.

3. Id. at 111.

4. Id. at 54.

judges used natural law to uphold anti-union practices by employers and strike down health and safety legislation.

Similarly, a 19th century Supreme Court decision relied upon natural law arguments about "the paramount destiny and mission of women" to justify an Illinois law which banned women from practicing law. Today, anti-abortion advocates have cited natural law as the basis for their argument that a fetus has a constitutionally protected right to life which overrides a women's right to choose. In 1987, Judge Thomas called one article which made that argument "a splendid example of applying natural law." [5]

Senator Herbert Kohl:

You have been an outspoken admirer of natural law, a doctrine largely dismissed for the past half-century. [6]

Senator Dennis DeConcini:

Judge Thomas, there has been much discussion already regarding reliance on natural law. Unfortunately, or maybe fortunately, depending on how you define it, natural law has been invoked historically, and goes back a long time.

For example, in 1873, in the Bradwell v. Illinois case, the Supreme Court denied a woman the right to practice law, arguing the following:

> Civil law, as well as nature herself, has always recognized a wide difference in the respective spheres and destinies of men and women. The natural and proper delicacy which belong to the female sex evidently unfits it for many of the occupations of civil life. The paramount destiny and mission of women is to fulfill the noble and benign office of wife and mother. This is the law of the Creator.

With the *Bradwell* case, we see that those justices applied natural law.

I know that you stated that your duty would be to uphold the Constitution and not a natural law philosophy, but I would just like to clarify for the record, do you disagree with the Justices' decision that were held back in 1873 in the *Bradwell* case?

Judge Thomas:

Senator I do. [7]

When Senator Leahy made mention of the *Bradwell* case, he stated that the views were those of one justice, but when it came to Senators Metzenbaum and DeConcini, (and also Judge Thomas) the quoted portion was attributed to the opinion of the court. The actual decision had nothing to do with comments on natural law, but on the Privileges and

5. Id. at 64. **7.** Id. at 202.
6. Id. at 81.

Immunities Clause, the Court holding that "the right to control and regulate the granting a license to practice law in the courts of a State is one of those powers which are not transferred to the Federal Government," citing the *Slaughter–House* cases. The excerpt quoted by Senator DeConcini was from the concurring opinion of Justice Bradley, in which Justices Swayne and Field joined.

NOTE

The Senators pushed Clarence Thomas into a corner to admit "[Natural law] is not a method of interpreting or method of adjudicating in the constitutional law area." Do you agree that it is improper to decide a case interpreting the Constitution on the basis of right reason and moral values? The Senators quoted one Supreme Court Justice in an 1872 case replete with politically-charged facts. Would you have been more comfortable if the Senators had made passing reference to Aristotle, Grotius or Aquinas?

Senator Leahy described natural law as an elastic concept, that "can be used to defend but also to deny basic rights." Are not all forms of law elastic? In any brief, are not competing legal precepts offered to support basic rights claimed by an individual or by society?

Can it be said that the piercing inquiry of Chief Justice Earl Warren at oral argument—"Is it fair?"—was devoid of natural law overtones? Recall the legal philosophy of Justices Brennan and Marshall and their unwavering view that the Constitution is a moral statement that must adjust to changing community moral values, and that we should not be content solely with the "original intent" of the framers. Were they apostles of natural law theories? Consider, for example, their opposition to the death penalty. Consider also the following excerpt from Justice Blackmun's dissent in Callins v. Collins, 114 S.Ct. 1127, 1130 (1994):

> From this day forward, I no longer shall tinker with the machinery of death.... Rather than continue to coddle the Court's delusion that the desired level of fairness has been achieved and the need for regulation eviscerated, I feel morally and intellectually obligated to concede that the death penalty experiment has failed.... The problem is that the inevitability of factual, legal and moral error gives us a system that we know must wrongly kill some defendants, a system that fails to deliver the fair, consistent, and reliable sentences of death required by the Constitution.

When Justice Blackmun said that he "was morally obligated" and distinguished between "legal and moral error," was he expressing a form of natural law philosophy in 1994?

Do you agree with the following statements of the Senators? "Natural law is a doctrine largely dismissed for the past half-century." "A judge's duty is to uphold the Constitution and not a natural law philosophy."

How is it possible to reconcile these statements with the observation of Professor Harold J. Berman:

> In the formative era of the Western legal tradition, natural-law theory predominated. It was generally believed that human law derived ultimately from, and was to be tested ultimately by, reason and conscience. According not only to the legal philosophy of the time but also to positive law itself, any positive law, whether enacted or customary, had to conform to natural law, or else it would lack validity as law and could be disregarded. This theory had a basis in Christian theology as well as in Aristotelian philosophy. But it also had a basis in the history of the struggle between ecclesiastical and secular authorities, and in the politics of pluralism. One may compare it with the theory that accompanies the law of the United States, under which any positive law must conform to the constitutional requirements of "due process," "equal protection," "freedom," "privacy," and the like, or lose its validity. "Due process of law" is, in fact, a fourteenth-century English phrase meaning natural law. Thus natural-law theory is written into the positive law of the United States. This does not, however, prevent one from giving a political ("positivist") explanation of it. It is easy enough to show that the state, or the powers that be, or the ruling class, benefits from the due process clause and "wills" it to be.

H. Berman, Law and Revolution: The Formation of the Western Legal Tradition 12 (1983).

C. POSITIVE LAW

JOHN AUSTIN, THE PROVINCE OF JURISPRUDENCE DETERMINED *

The matter of jurisprudence is positive law: law, simply and strictly so called: or law set by political superiors to political inferiors. But positive law (or law, simply and strictly so called) is often confounded with objects to which it is related by *resemblance,* and with objects to which it is related in the way of *analogy:* with objects which are *also* signified, *properly* and *improperly,* by the large and vague expression *law.* To obviate the difficulties springing from that confusion, I begin my projected Course with determining the province of jurisprudence, or with distinguishing the matter of jurisprudence from those various related objects....

---

* Reprinted from Volume I, John Austin, Lectures on Jurisprudence, *Analysis of Lec-* *tures* (5th ed. R. Campbell 1885).

A law, in the most general and comprehensive acceptation in which the term, in its literal meaning, is employed, may be said to be a rule laid down for the guidance of an intelligent being by an intelligent being having power over him.   Under this definition are concluded, and without impropriety, several species.   It is necessary to define accurately the line of demarcation which separates these species from one another, as much mistiness and intricacy has been infused into the science of jurisprudence by their being confounded or not clearly distinguished.   In the comprehensive sense above indicated, or in the largest meaning which it has, without extension by metaphor or analogy, the term *law* embraces the following objects:—Laws set by God to his human creatures, and laws set by men to men.

The whole or a portion of the laws set by God to men is frequently styled the law of nature, or natural law: being, in truth, the only natural law of which it is possible to speak without a metaphor, or without a blending of objects which ought to be distinguished broadly.   But, rejecting the appellation Law of Nature as ambiguous and misleading, I name those laws or rules, as considered collectively or in a mass, the *Divine law,* or the *law of God.*

Laws set by men to men are of two leading or principal classes: classes which are often blended, although they differ extremely; and which, for that reason, should be severed precisely, and opposed distinctly and conspicuously.

Of the laws or rules set by men to men, some are established by *political* superiors, sovereign and subject: by persons exercising supreme and subordinate *government,* in independent nations, or independent political societies.   The aggregate of the rules thus established, or some aggregate forming a portion of that aggregate, is the appropriate matter of jurisprudence, general or particular.   To the aggregate of the rules thus established, or to some aggregate forming a portion of that aggregate, the term *law,* as used simply and strictly, is exclusively applied. But, as contradistinguished to *natural* law, or to the law of *nature* (meaning, by those expressions, the law of God), the aggregate of the rules, established by political superiors, is frequently styled *positive* law, or law existing *by position . . . .*

Though *some* of the laws or rules, which are set by men to men, are established by political superiors, *others* are *not* established by political superiors, or are *not* established by political superiors, in that capacity or character.

Closely analogous to human laws of this second class, are a set of objects frequently but *improperly* termed *laws,* being rules set and enforced by *mere opinion,* that is, by the opinions or sentiments held or felt by an indeterminate body of men in regard to human conduct. Instances of such a use of the term *law* are the expressions—"The law of honour;" "The law set by fashion;" and rules of this species constitute much of what is usually termed "International law."

The aggregate of human laws properly so called belonging to the second of the classes above mentioned, with the aggregate of objects *improperly* but by *close analogy* termed laws, I place together in a common class, and denote them by the term *positive morality.* The name *morality* severs them from *positive law,* while the epithet *positive* disjoins them from the *law of God.* And to the end of obviating confusion, it is necessary or expedient that they *should* be disjoined from the latter by that distinguishing epithet. For the name *morality* (or *morals*), when standing unqualified or alone, denotes indifferently either of the following objects: namely, positive morality *as it is,* or without regard to its merits; and positive morality *as it would be,* if it conformed to the law of God, and were, therefore, deserving of *approbation.*

NOTE

RUPERT CROSS, *Precedent in English Law:* [*]

Subordinate legislation and judge-made law or "judiciary law", as Austin preferred to call it, come within his definition of law as the aggregate of the Sovereign's commands because they are set "circuitously" by the Sovereign to the members of the political society in question. But the same cannot be said of custom and juristic opinion....

In a famous passage he denied that laws originating in custom and laws originating in the opinions of private *juris consults* or institutional writers are properly speaking "distinct species of law in respect of their sources":

> A custom as such, independently of legislative sanction, is not a law, but a moral rule. When it has been embodied or promulgated in a statute, or made the ground of a judicial decision, it has the force of law; but then it is statute law built on an anterior custom, or law established by a judicial decision of which anterior custom was the basis or principle. The same reasoning applies to law originating in the opinion of private *juris consults.* The writings and opinions of *juris consults* are often causes of law by determining acts of legislation, and oftener by determining decisions of courts of justice. But the source or immediate author of the law is the legislator, sovereign or subordinate who legislates in pursuance of their opinions, or the judge, sovereign or subordinate, whose decisions their opinions determine.

Who promulgates "the aggregate of human laws" described by Austin as "positive morality"? Is it "promulgated" or does it merely "exist"? May "positive law" be promulgated by other than the sovereign?

"A law ... may be said to be a rule laid down for the guidance of an intelligent being by an intelligent being having power over him." Does justice play a role in the formation of law as so defined? Does it make a difference if the sovereign is represented by the legislature or the judiciary?

————

GEORGE C. CHRISTIE, A NOTE ON THE WORK OF H.L.A. HART *

Hart's greatest contribution to legal theory is probably his *The Concept of Law* (1961). In this work Hart undertook the ambitious task of "elucidating" the concept "law" and "legal system." The book starts out with a sympathetic yet penetrating criticism of John Austin's theory of law.... To meet the inability of the Austinian theory—with its core notion of a sovereign issuing coercive orders—to account adequately for what we mean by law, Hart, in Chapter V of *The Concept of Law*, proposes his own model for viewing the legal universe.

Hart contends that Austin failed because

the ideas of orders, obedience, habits, and threats, do not include, and cannot by their combination yield, the idea of a rule, without which we cannot hope to elucidate even the most elementary forms of law.

What makes the "idea of a rule" so important for Hart is his insistence that the essential characteristic of a functioning legal system is not so much that people generally obey the law but that they feel *bound* by the law. Hart wishes to distinguish between what he calls being *obliged* to obey the law—i.e. the idea of being forced to obey the law that is connoted in the command/sanction theory of law—and what he calls having an *obligation* to obey the law. He notes that a person's *being obliged* to do something is neither a sufficient nor a necessary condition for his *having an obligation* to obey the law. In order to derive the notion of obligation one must use the "idea of a rule." Rules not only prescribe what people are supposed to do, but, to those who accept the validity of a particular rule or system of rules, they provide a reason for acting in accordance with a particular rule over and above the unpleasant consequences that might result from a failure to observe or obey the rule. What Hart wishes to call attention to is the distinction between the *external* point of view of the outside observer and the *internal* point of view of someone, so-to-speak, "within" a system of rules who accepts the validity of the rules of that system.

* Christie, Jurisprudence 635–37 (1973).
Reprinted by permission.

Not all rules whose validity is accepted by an individual give rise, however, to an obligation. There is a difference between "He ought to have" and "He had an obligation to" which often makes it impossible to use them interchangeably. In order to give rise to obligations "the general demand for conformity [must be] ... insistent and the social pressure brought to bear upon those who deviate or threaten to deviate [must be] ... great." Law and morality share this element of *seriousness* which is essential to generate obligations. Rules of etiquette and of speech do not. Hart mentions two other characteristics that "go naturally together with this primary one" of seriousness. The serious pressure to conformity is imposed because the rules it supports are believed to be necessary for the maintenance of social life or of some valued features of social life *and* "it is generally recognized that the conduct required by these rules may, while benefiting others, conflict with what the person who owes the duty may wish to do."

Hart concedes that a primitive legal system might be able to exist and function satisfactorily with only what he calls basic or *primary* rules. Primary rules prescribe what people should or should not do, regardless of whether they wish to or not. Examples are rules prescribing that people should pay their taxes or should not murder one another or smoke in department stores. A legal system consisting merely of primary rules would, however, break down in a complex society. The need for *certainty* in the law, the necessity to accommodate *change,* and the requirements of *efficiency* require what Hart calls *secondary* rules. These are power-conferring rules and the more important ones are concerned with the allocation of basic political power in a society. The most important of these basic secondary rules Hart calls the "rule of recognition." It prescribes who is the ultimate lawmaker (or lawmaking body) and the conditions under which he (or it) can make law. The authority of all subordinate lawmakers must be traced back to the rule of recognition. Similarly, the validity of all other rules must be traced back to the rule of recognition in the sense that (1) they must be made by someone whose authority can be traced back to the ultimate lawmaker described in the rule of recognition and (2) their content must not contravene some prohibition contained in the rule of recognition that limits the content of the valid rules of a legal system. In short, the rule of recognition makes it possible to identify the individual rules of a legal system by specifying "some feature or features possession of which by a suggested rule is taken as a conclusive affirmative indication that it is a rule of the group to be supported by the social pressure it exerts." In addition to the "rule of recognition" there are two other types of fundamental secondary rules in mature legal systems. These are "rules of change," which allocate the power of "introducing new primary rules for the conduct of the life of the group ... and to eliminate old rules," *and,* in order to meet the needs of efficiency in the application of rules, "rules of adjudication" that allocate the power to adjudicate disputes about whether the primary rules have been broken. It is Hart's contention, at the end of his crucial Chapter V which we have just summarized, that:

> If we stand back and consider the structure which has resulted from the combination of primary rules of obligation with the secondary rules of recognition, change and adjudication, it is plain what we have here not only [is] the heart of a legal system but a most powerful tool for the analysis of much that has puzzled both the jurist and the political theorist.

NOTE

Ronald M. Dworkin, *The Model of Rules,* 35 U.Chi.L.Rev. 14, 17–22 (1967), emphasizes that H.L.A. Hart's view of positivism is more complex than Austin's. Hart described secondary rules as those "that stipulate how, and by whom such primary rules may be formed, recognized, modified or extinguished. The rules that stipulate how Congress is composed, how it enacts legislation, are examples of secondary rules" as are rules relating to the formulation of contracts and execution of wills. Dworkin also attributes to Hart two separate sources for a rule's authority: (1) acceptance by a group through practice in which the group accepts the rule as a standard for its conduct; (2) acceptance by adoption in conformity with some secondary rule stating that rules adopted in a certain way will be binding, e.g., a club by-law adopted in conformity with the club's constitution. Thus, a rule may be binding because it is (1) accepted or (2) valid. Hart would also emphasize that judges have and do exercise discretion in the adjudication process because often legal rules have "open texture".

In the Hart formulation, the pedigree of these rules is important because these rules are exhaustive of "the law". Therefore, if the case or controversy is not clearly covered by such a rule, then, according to Hart, it must be decided by a judge "exercising his discretion". By this, Dworkin continues, Hart meant that the judge had to reach "beyond the law for some other sort of standard to guide him in manufacturing a fresh legal rule or supplementing an old one."

Dworkin suggests that the reach of the judge under these circumstances is not "beyond the law", but that these other standards are part of the law itself.

––––––––

JEROME HALL, BENTHAM AND AUSTIN *

Subsequent moral and legal philosophy can be viewed as debates on the central themes of classical natural law philosophy, noted above. For the present purpose we may omit the intervening centuries and focus on

* J. Hall, Foundations of Jurisprudence 28–31 (1973). Reprinted with permission of Bobbs–Merrill Company.

Bentham. Among modern writers, it was Bentham who made it very clear not only that the natural law-legal positivism polemic is a debate in moral philosophy but also that the utilitarian theory of law occupies a distinctive place in that polemic. In his Principles of Morals and Legislation, Bentham said that the principle of utility encompasses "every action," especially every "measure of government" ("which is but a particular kind of action") to augment "the happiness of the community...."[26] Positive law was thus as important in Bentham's ethics as it was in classical and medieval moral philosophy. But there are important differences, and it is in his criticism of certain moral theories that the distinctive character of utilitarian legal philosophy is best revealed. Those theories, he said, "consist all of them in so many contrivances for avoiding the obligation of appealing to any external standard, and for prevailing upon the reader to accept of the author's sentiment or opinion as a reason ... for itself." Equal strictures were directed at the alleged moral sense "possessed by all mankind" of "the standard of right and wrong," at "an eternal and immutable Rule of Right" which in fact is only "his sentiments," at the "fitness of things," "the Law of Nature,"[27] the Law of Reason, right Reason, and Natural Justice. "[W]hen he ... talks of 'the nature of things,'" said Bentham, "I see him wrapped in clouds."[28]

Bentham, obviously, is criticizing earlier British moralists, especially Clarke, Price and Butler, who had revived the classical moral philosophy with emphasis, however, on the ethics of conscience[29] and on benevolence. Their moral philosophy was largely deontological, and intuition and common sense were the principal methods of discovering one's duties. Bentham had nothing but contempt for all of this. The expression of moral judgments in "such obscure terms as 'right' or 'fitting' ... serve only to express ... disapprobation and not the ground of it."[30] Of the central concept of deontological ethics, he said, "The talisman of arrogance, indolence, and ignorance, is to be found in a single word, an authoritative imposture.... It is the word 'ought'...."[31] There is only one sound principle, that of utility, and "duty" means only the production of happiness.[32] The foundation of it all is pain and pleasure:

26. 1 The Works of Jeremy Bentham 1, 2 (J. Bowring ed. 1838, reprinted 1962).

27. Id. 8 & nn. 1–4, 9 & nn. 5–7.

28. Bentham, A Comment on the Commentaries 105 (Everett ed. 1928). Yet, oddly, this did not keep Bentham from defending his own theory on the ground that "it grows out of the nature of things and the necessities of the case." 1 Bentham, Deontology 331 (Bowring ed. 1834).

29. British Moralists §§ 608, 612–21, 668, 672 (Selby–Bigge ed. 1897, 1964); see 1 Bentham, Deontology 71 (1834); D. Baumgardt, Bentham and the Ethics of Today 53 (1952).

30. 1 Bentham, supra note 29, at 279; D. Baumgardt, supra note 29, at 494.

31. 1 Bentham, id. 31–32; D. Baumgardt, id. 497.

32. "... the word [duty] itself has in it something disagreeable and repulsive." 1 Bentham, Deontology 10 (1834); "... veracity must be made subservient to prudence and benevolence...." Id. Vol. 2, at 66; "... those truths which are mischievous, truths which are creators of pain and destroyers of pleasure, let them be suppressed." Id. 67.

"take away *pleasures* and *pains,* not only *happiness,* but *justice,* and *duty,* and *obligation* and *virtue* ... are so many empty sounds." [33]

These views were repeated by Austin who was also very critical of the intuitionist school; he, too, rejected the thesis that man has a sense of justice which enables him instantaneously to recognize and approve the good and disapprove the bad.[34] This theory, he said, could not account for the frequent differences in valuation, the uncertainties felt in dealing with moral problems, and the length of time required to form moral judgments.[35] Without any discussion of the merits of this criticism, it may be pointed out that there is no necessary connection between the method of intuition and the deontological view of moral obligation; it is that which sharply separates utilitarianism (and its theory of law) from classical realism (and natural law philosophy).

One should, of course, distinguish some of Austin's views from those of Bentham, who was prone to attack a nonexistent theory of natural law. The version of natural law Austin opposed was that "right or justice ... is absolute, eternal, and immutable ... perfectly self-existent, to which ... law conforms, or to which ... law should conform." [36] As to this, Austin said, "I ... cannot understand it...." [37] But while Austin severely criticized this theory of the law of nature,[38] he recognized "the law of nature" in the *ius gentium* [39] and spoke of "the frequent coincidence of positive law and morality, and of positive law and the law of God ...," [40] and of "[t]he portion of positive law which is parcel of the *law of nature.*" [41] The *jus naturale,*" said Austin, "would be liable to little objection, if it were not supposed to be the offspring of a moral instinct or sense, or of innate practical principles." It is because "it is closely allied ... to that misleading and pernicious jargon, [that] it ought to be expelled ... from the sciences of jurisprudence and morality." [42]

NOTE

One need not be trained in the law to say with conviction: "I (he) (she) (they) ought to do this-and-so because it is 'right' or 'fitting.'" Without more, Bentham says that this is wrong. He says that the only sound principle is utility, that "'duty' means only the production of happiness, etc." Do you agree?

33. 1 Bentham, Works 206, b. no. 15; "Justice is of use no farther than as the handmaid of benevolence." 1 Bentham, Deontology 117; "The declaration that such and such an action ... is just or unjust, is mere declamatory pretense, unless, at the same time, the dependent pleasures and pains are brought into the calculation." 2 *id.* 58; *cf.* "... the balance of resulting good may be, and often is, not on the side of justice." Prichard, *Does Moral Philosophy Rest on a Mistake?,* 21 Mind NS 21 (1912).

34. 1 J. Austin, Lectures on Jurisprudence 107 (4th ed. 1879).

35. *Id.* 154.

36. Id. 310.

37. Id.

38. Id. 179.

39. Id. 216.

40. Id. 204.

41. Id. 205.

42. Id. 216.

It is often stated that positive law is the command of the sovereign, that law need not be grounded in morality. Here we learn that Austin referred to "the frequent coincidence of positive law and morality." Consider the positive law under Stalin and Hitler.

LINKLETTER v. WALKER

Supreme Court of the United States, 1965.
381 U.S. 618, 85 S.Ct. 1731, 14 L.Ed.2d 601.

The opinion of the Court was delivered by MR. JUSTICE CLARK.

At common law there was no authority for the proposition that judicial decisions made law only for the future. Blackstone stated the rule that the duty of the court was not to "pronounce a new law, but to maintain and expound the old one." 1 Blackstone, Commentaries 69 (15th ed. 1809). This Court followed that rule in Norton v. Shelby County, 118 U.S. 425, 6 S.Ct. 1121, 30 L.Ed. 178 (1886), holding that unconstitutional action "confers no rights; it imposes no duties; it affords no protection; it creates no office; it is, in legal contemplation, as inoperative as though it had never been passed." At 442, 6 S.Ct. at 1125. The judge rather than being the creator of the law was but its discoverer. Gray, Nature and Sources of the Law 222 (1st ed. 1909). In the case of the overruled decision, Wolf v. People of State of Colorado, supra, here, it was thought to be only a failure at true discovery and was consequently never the law; while the overruling one, Mapp, was not "new law but an application of what is, and theretofore had been, the true law." Shulman, Retroactive Legislation, 13 Encyclopaedia of the Social Sciences 355, 356 (1934).

On the other hand, Austin maintained that judges do in fact do something more than discover law; they make it interstitially by filling in with judicial interpretation the vague, indefinite, or generic statutory or common-law terms that alone are but the empty crevices of the law. Implicit in such an approach is the admission when a case is overruled that the earlier decision was wrongly decided. However, rather than being erased by the later overruling decision it is considered as an existing juridical fact until overruled, and intermediate cases finally decided under it are not to be disturbed.

The Blackstonian view ruled English jurisprudence and cast its shadow over our own as evidenced by Norton v. Shelby County, supra. However, some legal philosophers continued to insist that such a rule was out of tune with actuality largely because judicial repeal ofttime did "work hardship to those who [had] trusted to its existence." Cardozo, Address to the N.Y. Bar Assn., 55 Rep.N.Y.State Bar Assn. 263, 296–297 (1932). The Austinian view gained some acceptance over a hundred years ago when it was decided that although legislative divorces were illegal and void, those previously granted were immunized by a prospective application of the rule of the case. Bingham v. Miller, 17 Ohio 445 (1848). And as early as 1863 this Court drew on the same concept in Gelpcke v. City of Dubuque, 1 Wall. 175, 17 L.Ed. 520 (1863).

———

SWIFT v. TYSON

Supreme Court of the United States, 1842.
41 U.S. (16 Pet.) 1, 10 L.Ed. 865.

MR. JUSTICE STORY delivered the opinion of the Court.

But, admitting the doctrine [a pre-existing debt was not a sufficient consideration to shut out the equities of the original parties in favor of the holders] to be fully settled in New York, it remains to be considered, whether it is obligatory upon this court, if it differs from the principles established in the general commercial law. It is observable, that the courts of New York do not found their decisions upon this point, upon any local statute, or positive, fixed or ancient local usage; but they deduce the doctrine from the general principles of commercial law. It is, however, contended, that the 34th section of the judiciary act of 1789, ch. 20, furnishes a rule obligatory upon this court to follow the decisions of the state tribunals in all cases to which they apply. That section provides "that the laws of the several states, except where the constitution, treaties or statutes of the United States shall otherwise require or provide, shall be regarded as rules of decision, in trials at common law, in the courts of the United States, in cases where they apply." In order to maintain the argument, it is essential, therefore, to hold, that the word "laws," in this section, includes within the scope of its meaning, the decisions of the local tribunals. In the ordinary use of language, it will hardly be contended, that the decisions of courts constitute laws. They are, at most, only evidence of what the laws are, and are not, of themselves, laws. They are often reexamined, reversed and qualified by the courts themselves, whenever they are found to be either defective, or ill-founded, or otherwise incorrect. The laws of a state are more usually understood to mean the rules and enactments promulgated by the legislative authority thereof, or long-established local customs having the force of laws. In all the various cases, which have hitherto come before us for decision, this court have uniformly supposed, that the true interpretation of the 34th section limited its application to state laws, strictly local, that is to say, to the positive statutes of the state, and the construction thereof adopted by the local tribunals, and to rights and titles to things having a permanent locality, such as the rights and titles to real estate, and other matters immovable and intra-territorial in their nature and character. It never has been supposed by us, that the section did apply, or was designed to apply, to questions of a more general nature, not at all dependent upon local statutes or local usages of a fixed and permanent operation, as, for example, to the construction of ordinary contracts or other written instruments, and especially to questions of general commercial law, where the state tribunals are called upon to perform the like functions as ourselves, that is, to ascertain, upon general reasoning and legal analogies, what is the true exposition of the contract or instrument, or what is the just rule furnished by the principles of commercial law to govern the case. And we have not now the slightest difficulty in holding, that this section, upon its true intendment and construction, is strictly limited to local statutes and local usages of the character before stated, and does not extend to contracts and other instruments of a commercial nature, the true interpretation and effect whereof are to be sought, not in the decisions of the local tribunals, but in the general principles and doctrines of commercial jurisprudence. Undoubtedly, the decisions of the local tribunals upon such subjects are entitled to, and will receive, the most deliberate attention and respect of this court; but they cannot furnish positive rules, or conclusive authority, by which our own judgments are to be bound up and governed. The law respecting negotiable instruments may be truly declared in the languages of Cicero, adopted by Lord Mansfield in *Luke v. Lyde,* 2 Burr. 883, 887, to be in a great measure, not the law of a single country only, but of the commercial world. *Non erit alia lex Romae, alia Athenis; alia nunc, alia posthac; sed et apud omnes gentes, et omni tempore und eademque lex obtinebit.*

NOTE

For a background of this case and the active role played by Justice Story, see C. Swisher, V History of the Supreme Court of the United States 327–30 (1974).

The substantive holding in Swift v. Tyson was overruled in Erie Railroad Co. v. Tompkins, 304 U.S. 64 (1938). Although the parties assumed the continued validity of *Swift,* Justice Brandeis injected the question at oral argument and began the opinion of the court with the statement: "The question for decision is whether the oft-challenged doctrine of Swift v. Tyson shall now be disapproved." Id. at 69; see C. Wright, Law of Federal Courts 375 (5th ed. 1994). The central issue in Mapp v. Ohio, 367 U.S. 643 (1961), was apparently raised by the amicus curiae and not by the appellant or state of Ohio. Evaluate a judicial process where the appellate court turns the decision on an issue neither briefed nor raised by the parties. Does it make a difference whether the appellate court affirms or reverses? See Michelin Tire Corp. v. Wages, 423 U.S. 276, 302 (1976) (White, J., concurring in the judgment) ("I would affirm the judgment. There is little reason and no necessity at this time to overrule Low v. Austin. None of the parties has challenged that case here, and the issue of its overruling has not been briefed or argued.")

One of the serious problems leading to lack of uniformity in the law has been the practice in the federal courts of borrowing state statutes of limitations where Congress has not indicated a limitations period. This is especially acute where the federal courts have "invented" implied civil causes of action. Prior to the Third Circuit's action in 1988, the limitations in Securities Act cases presented a serious problem where different statutes of limitations could apply as to separate defendants depending on choice of law judgments, especially where the actors' conduct took place, i.e., a brokerage office in Chicago, an accountant's office in New York, or the Los Angeles office of the brokerage agent. The Third Circuit rejected the practice of borrowing state statutes and imposed a uniform limitations period found in other provisions of Securities Acts. The Supreme Court agreed in Lampf, Pleva, Lipkind, Prupis & Petigrow v. Gilbertson, 501 U.S. 350 (1991). See In re Data Access Systems Securities Litigation, 843 F.2d 1537, 1549 (3d Cir.1988):

> Again with a nod to Cicero [after quoting Swift v. Tyson] you simply should not have a different Securities limitations period for Rome, New York, and Athens, Georgia (*Non erit alia lex Romae, alia Athenis*). And since uniformity is not to be found in the diverse body of state tort limitations, we are impelled inexorably to look to federal limitations for borrowing purposes.

ILLINOIS v. CITY OF MILWAUKEE

Supreme Court of the United States, 1972.
406 U.S. 91, 92 S.Ct. 1385, 31 L.Ed.2d 712.

Mr. Justice Douglas delivered the opinion of the Court.

Mr. Justice Brennan, speaking for the four members of this Court in Romero v. International Terminal Operating Co., 358 U.S. 354, 393, 79 S.Ct. 468, 491, 3 L.Ed.2d 368 (dissenting and concurring), who reached the issue, concluded that "laws," within the meaning of § 1331(a), embraced claims founded on federal common law:

> "The contention cannot be accepted that since petitioner's rights are judicially defined, they are not created by 'the laws ... of the United States' within the meaning of § 1331.... In another context, that of state law, this Court has recognized that the statutory word 'laws' includes court decisions. The converse situation is presented here in that federal courts have an extensive responsibility of fashioning rules of substantive law.... These rules are as fully 'laws' of the United States as if they had been enacted by Congress." (Citations omitted.)

Lower courts have reached the same conclusion....

Judge Harvey M. Johnsen in Texas v. Pankey, 10 Cir., 441 F.2d 236, 240, stated the controlling principle:

> "As the field of federal common law has been given necessary expansion into matters of federal concern and relationship (where no applicable federal statute exists, as there does not here), the ecological rights of a State in the improper impairment of them from sources outside the State's own territory, now would and should, we think, be held to be a matter having

basis and standard in federal common law and so directly constituting a question arising under the laws of the United States."

Chief Judge Lumbard, speaking for the panel in Ivy Broadcasting Co. v. American Tel. & Tel. Co., 2 Cir., 391 F.2d 486, 492, expressed the same view as follows:

"We believe that a cause of action similarly 'arises under' federal law if the dispositive issues stated in the complaint require the application of federal common law.... The word 'laws' in § 1331 should be construed to include laws created by federal judicial decisions as well as by congressional legislation. The rationale of the 1875 grant of federal question jurisdiction—to insure the availability of a forum designed to minimize the danger of hostility toward, and specially suited to the vindication of, federally created rights—is as applicable to judicially created rights as to rights created by statute." (Citations omitted.)

We see no reason not to give "laws" its natural meaning, see Romero v. International Terminal Operating Co., supra, 358 U.S., at 393 n. 5, 79 S.Ct., at 490 (Brennan, J., dissenting and concurring), and therefore conclude that § 1331 jurisdiction will support claims founded upon federal common law as well as those of a statutory origin.

NOTE

How do you react to the news that it was not until 1972 that the U.S. Supreme Court would hold that federal question jurisdiction under 28 U.S.C.A. § 1331 would support claims "founded upon federal common law as well as those of a statutory origin"? Compare the 1842 statement in Swift v. Tyson that decisions of courts "are at most only evidence of what the laws are, and are not, of themselves, laws." Does this make sense?

How would you describe the centuries of English and American common law in the fields of torts, contracts and property law?

Section 3

DEVELOPMENT OF MODERN AMERICAN ADJUDICATION

OVERVIEW *

Cardozo explained that sometimes the source of the law to be embodied in a judgment is obvious, as when the Constitution or a statute applies.[1] In these situations, the judge simply obeys the constitutional or statutory rule. But when no constitutional or statutory mandate

---

* Adapted from R.J. Aldisert, *The Nature of the Judicial Process: Revisited,* 49 U.Cin. L.Rev. 1 (1980).

1. B. Cardozo, The Nature of the Judicial Process (1921).

controls, the judge must compare that case with the precedents, "whether stored in his mind or hidden in the books." [2] If the comparison yields a perfect fit, if both the law and its application are clear, the task is simple. If the law is unclear, it is necessary to "extract from the precedent the underlying principle" and then "determine the path or direction along which the principle is to move and develop, if it is not to wither and die." [3] Cardozo cautioned that decisions "do not unfold their principles for the asking. They yield up their kernel slowly and painfully." [4] He discussed what he called the "organons" of the judicial process—the instruments by which we fix the bounds and tendencies of that principle's development and growth. He also discussed the use of history and customs, and what in 1921 was considered a revolutionary technique of decision-making—the method of sociology.

By describing the elements at work in the caldron, Cardozo was performing the valued task of a traditional common law judicial analyst. That he ranks with Oliver Wendell Holmes, Jr. as one of our greatest common law judges is scarcely now debatable. But to the extent that he developed, persuasively and gracefully, a legitimation for result-oriented jurisprudence, he became more a legal philosopher than a common law judge. He sought what *ought* to be the law, in contrast with what *is*.

Although Cardozo is not generally listed as a member of the enthusiastic corps of American Realists, he must be ranked with Holmes, as an elder statesman of that exciting cadre of reformers. In the last quarter of the twentieth century critics are quick to recognize the legitimacy of decisions based on social welfare, but in 1921 Cardozo's arguments brought respectability to what theretofore had been condemned as blatant result-oriented jurisprudence. He was neither timid nor uncertain in espousing his self-styled method of sociology. To him it was "the power of social justice," and among all organons of the decision-making process, it was "the force which in our day and generation is becoming the greatest." [5] To him the preferred gap-filler in addressing novel questions of law was the social welfare, defined "as public policy, the good of the collective body," or "the social gain that is wrought by adherence to the standards of right conduct, which find expression in the *mores* of the community." [6]

Accustomed as we are today to lavish reliance by prestigious courts on judicial concepts of public policy, Cardozo's statements in the early nineteen twenties must be placed in the context of judicial process of that era. Judges then were disciples of what Rudolph von Ihering styled as *Begriffsjurisprudenz*, a jurisprudence of concepts, and as early as 1897 American courts were being chided for undue reliance on concepts. [7] In The Path of the Law, Holmes gently admonished:

2. Id. at 19.

3. Id. at 28.

4. Id. at 30–31.

5. Id. at 65–66.

6. Id. at 71–72.

7. R. von Ihering, Der Geist des Romischen Rechts (1907).

I think that the judges themselves have failed adequately to recognize their duty of weighing considerations of social advantage. The duty is inevitable, and the result of the often proclaimed judicial aversion to deal with such considerations is simply to leave the very ground and foundation of judgments inarticulate, and often unconscious.[8]

Within a decade Roscoe Pound was trumpeting the same theme: "The most important and most constant cause of dissatisfaction with all law at all times is to be found in the necessarily mechanical operation of legal rules."[9] Critics labeled this blind adherence to precedents, or to the rules and principles derived therefrom, "mechanical jurisprudence" and "slot machine justice." Pound called for a new look at what he described as "pragmatism as a philosophy of law," and stated vigorously: "The nadir of mechanical jurisprudence is reached when conceptions are used, not as premises from which to reason, but as ultimate solutions. So used, they cease to be conceptions and become empty words."[10]

Yet founders of the Sociological Method—Holmes, Pound and Cardozo—had early historical support for their advocacy. Professor Calvin Woodard suggests that their theory draws on Jeremy Bentham's utilitarian thesis:

[T]he advocates of Sociological Jurisprudence seized upon this aspect of Bentham's message. Like him, they insisted that law has a practical, real world moral purpose, though they defined that purpose more in terms of social justice, and the balancing of social interests, than [Bentham's] "the greatest good for the greatest number."[11]

Typical of judicial utterances that had disturbed Holmes, Pound, and Cardozo was one by the Maryland Court of Appeals in 1895: "Obviously a principle, if sound, ought to be applied wherever it logically leads, without reference to ulterior results."[12] In contrast, the same year that Cardozo delivered the Storrs Lecture at Yale, he seized the opportunity to put his new theory into practice by publicly rejecting blind conceptual jurisprudence in Hynes v. New York Central R. Co.[13] A sixteen-year-old boy had been injured while using a crude springboard to dive into the Harlem River. The trial court had ruled that if the youth had climbed on the springboard from the river before beginning his dive, the defendant landowner would have been held to the test of ordinary care, but because the boy had mounted from land owned by the defendant railroad company, the court held the defendant to the lower standard of care owed to a trespasser. Cardozo rejected this analysis,

8. O.W. Holmes, *The Path of the Law,* 10 Harv.L.Rev. 457, 467 (1897).

9. R. Pound, *The Causes of Popular Dissatisfaction with the Administration of Justice,* 40 Am.L.Rev. 729 (1906), *reprinted in* 8 Baylor L.Rev. 1 (1956).

10. R. Pound, *Mechanical Jurisprudence,* 8 Colum.L.Rev. 605, 608, 610 (1908).

11. C. Woodard, *Thoughts on the Interplay Between Morality and Law in Modern Legal Thought,* 64 Notre Dame L. Rev. 784, 795 (1989).

12. Gluck v. Baltimore, 81 Md. 315, 318, 32 A. 515, 517 (1895).

13. 231 N.Y. 229, 131 N.E. 898 (1921).

describing it as an "extension of a maxim or a definition with relentless disregard of consequences to 'a dryly logical extreme.' The approximate and relative became the definite and absolute." [14]

Cardozo's opinion in *Hynes* is a prototype, and his The Nature of the Judicial Process an apologia, for decision-making based on result-oriented judicial concepts of public policy. The philosophical underpinnings of what Cardozo described as the sociological method run counter to the widely held notion that the public policy should be formulated and promulgated only by the legislative branch of government. When judges rather than the legislators declare public policy, their declarations produce local and national tensions. When judges utilize this organon, laymen and lawyers label them "activists," "liberals," "loose constructionists," and a host of other epithets, gentle and otherwise.

But modern American jurisprudence is more than the sociological method, although its influence is strongly felt. The Legal Realists of the Thirties and Forties constantly worried about what they called "the social performance of law." Those same concerns are said to lie close to the heart of the Critical Studies Movement as well. To be sure, the Law and Economics school can be said to be result-oriented, but it stresses "economic efficiency" rather than social justice.

Modern American jurisprudence constantly seeks the answers to the serious questions presented by the theories of adjudication, theories both old and new, presented in the materials that follow. As the readings and cases are examined, keep in mind the central question put to us by the thoughtful Professor Woodard:

> What better measure is there of the value of a legal system, or indeed of the rule of law itself, than the quality of life of those subject to it? And if this approach stresses the morality of results, it also puts a huge moral burden on the hand that wields the tool of law.[15]

OLIVER WENDELL HOLMES, THE PATH OF THE LAW *

[With minor editing, this 1897 classic essay of Oliver Wendell Holmes is set forth in its entirety. It serves as an introduction to aspects of the judicial process which will command our attention in succeeding chapters. Written a century ago, his expressed concerns are not stale. For present purposes we emphasize his oft-quoted: "The prophecies of what the courts will do in fact, and nothing more pretentious, are what I mean by the law." But his statement cannot be understood *in vacuo*. It must be considered in the totality of his entire essay—his discussion of the limits of the law, the forces which determine

14. Id. at 231.
15. *Woodard,* ante note 11 at 796.
* Holmes, *The Path of the Law,* 10 Harvard Law Review 457 (1897). Copyright ©

1897 by The Harvard Law Review Association. Reprinted by permission.

its content and growth, and his analysis of American law at the turn of the century "as a subject for study, and the ideal for which it tends."]

When we study law we are not studying a mystery but a well known profession. We are studying what we shall want in order to appear before judges, or to advise people in such a way as to keep them out of court. The reason why it is a profession, why people will pay lawyers to argue for them or to advise them, is that in societies like ours the command of the public force is intrusted to the judges in certain cases, and the whole power of the state will be put forth, if necessary, to carry out their judgments and decrees. People want to know under what circumstances and how far they will run the risk of coming against what is so much stronger than themselves, and hence it becomes a business to find out when this danger is to be feared. The object of our study, then, is prediction, the prediction of the incidence of the public force through the instrumentality of the courts.

The means of the study are a body of reports, of treatises, and of statutes, in this country and in England, extending back for six hundred years, and now increasing annually by hundreds. In these sibylline leaves are gathered the scattered prophecies of the past upon the cases in which the axe will fall. These are what properly have been called the oracles of the law. Far the most important and pretty nearly the whole meaning of every new effort of legal thought is to make these prophecies more precise, and to generalize them into a thoroughly connected system. The process is one, from a lawyer's statement of a case, eliminating as it does all the dramatic elements with which his client's story has clothed it, and retaining only the facts of legal import, up to the final analyses and abstract universals of theoretic jurisprudence. The reason why a lawyer does not mention that his client wore a white hat when he made a contract, while Mrs. Quickly would be sure to dwell upon it along with the parcel gilt goblet and the sea-coal fire, is that he foresees that the public force will act in the same way whatever his client had upon his head. It is to make the prophecies easier to be remembered and to be understood that the teachings of the decisions of the past are put into general propositions and gathered into text-books, or that statutes are passed in a general form. The primary rights and duties with which jurisprudence busies itself again are nothing but prophecies. One of the many evil effects of the confusion between legal and moral ideas, about which I shall have something to say in a moment, is that theory is apt to get the cart before the horse, and to consider the right or the duty as something existing apart from and independent of the consequences of its breach, to which certain sanctions are added afterward. But, as I shall try to show, a legal duty so called is nothing but a prediction that if a man does or omits certain things he will be made to suffer in this or that way by judgment of the court;—and so of a legal right.

The number of our predictions when generalized and reduced to a system is not unmanageably large. They present themselves as a finite body of dogma which may be mastered within a reasonable time. It is a great mistake to be frightened by the ever increasing number of reports. The reports of a given jurisdiction in the course of a generation take up pretty much the whole body of the law, and restate it from the present point of view. We could reconstruct the corpus from them if all that went before were burned. The use of the earlier reports is mainly historical, a use about which I shall have something to say before I have finished.

I wish, if I can, to lay down some first principles for the study of this body of dogma or systematized prediction which we call the law, for men who want to use it as the instrument of their business to enable them to prophesy in their turn, and, as bearing upon the study, I wish to point out an ideal which as yet our law has not attained.

The first thing for a business-like understanding of the matter is to understand its limits, and therefore I think it desirable at once to point out and dispel a confusion between morality and law, which sometimes rises to the height of conscious theory, and more often and indeed constantly is making trouble in detail without reaching the point of consciousness. You can see very plainly that a bad man has as much reason as a good one for wishing to avoid an encounter with the public force, and therefore you can see the practical importance of the distinction between morality and law. A man who cares nothing for an ethical rule which is believed and practised by his neighbors is likely nevertheless to care a good deal to avoid being made to pay money, and will want to keep out of jail if he can.

I take it for granted that no hearer of mine will misinterpret what I have to say as the language of cynicism. The law is the witness and external deposit of our moral life. Its history is the history of the moral development of the race. The practice of it, in spite of popular jests, tends to make good citizens and good men. When I emphasize the difference between law and morals I do so with reference to a single end, that of learning and understanding the law. For that purpose you must definitely master its specific marks, and it is for that that I ask you for the moment to imagine yourselves indifferent to other and greater things.

I do not say that there is not a wider point of view from which the distinction between law and morals becomes of secondary or no importance, as all mathematical distinctions vanish in presence of the infinite. But I do say that that distinction is of the first importance for the object which we are here to consider,—a right study and mastery of the law as a business with well understood limits, a body of dogma enclosed within definite lines. I have just shown the practical reason for saying so. If you want to know the law and nothing else, you must look at it as a bad man, who cares only for the material consequences which such knowledge enables him to predict, not as a good one, who finds his reasons for conduct, whether inside the law or outside of it, in the vaguer sanctions of conscience. The theoretical importance of the distinction is no less, if you would reason on your subject aright. The law is full of phraseology drawn from morals, and by the mere force of language continually invites us to pass from one domain to the other without perceiving it, as we are sure to do unless we have the boundary constantly before our minds. The law talks about rights, and duties, and malice, and intent, and negligence, and so forth, and nothing is easier, or, I may say, more common in legal reasoning, than to take these words in their moral sense, at some stage of the argument, and so to drop into fallacy. For instance, when we speak of the rights of man in a moral sense, we mean to mark the limits of interference with individual freedom which we think are prescribed by conscience, or by our ideal, however reached. Yet it is certain that many laws have been enforced in the past, and it is likely that some are enforced now, which are condemned by the most enlightened opinion of the time, or which at all events pass the limit of interference as many consciences would draw it. Manifestly, therefore, nothing but confusion of thought can result from assuming that the rights of man in a moral sense are equally rights in the sense of the Constitution and the law. No doubt simple and extreme cases can be put of imaginable laws which the statute making power would not dare to enact, even in the absence of written constitutional prohibitions, because the community would rise in rebellion and fight; and this gives some plausibility to the proposition that the law, if not a part of morality, is limited by it. But this limit of power is not coextensive with any system of morals. For the most part it falls far within the lines of any such system, and in some cases may extend beyond them, for reasons drawn from the habits of a particular people at a particular time. I once heard the late Professor Agassiz say that a German population would rise if you added two cents to the price of a glass of beer. A statute in such a case would be empty words, not because it was wrong, but because it could not be enforced. No one will deny that wrong statutes can be and are enforced, and we should not all agree as to which were the wrong ones.

The confusion with which I am dealing besets confessedly legal conceptions. Take the fundamental question, What constitutes the law? You will find some text writers telling you that it is something different from what is decided by the courts of Massachusetts or England, that it is a system of reason, that it is a deduction from principles of ethics or admitted axioms or what not, which may or may not coincide with the decisions. But if we take the view of our friend the bad man we shall find that he does not care two straws for the axioms or deductions, but that he does want to know what the Massachusetts or English courts are likely to do in fact. I am much of his mind. The prophecies of what the courts will do in fact, and nothing more pretentious, are what I mean by the law.

Take again a notion which as popularly understood is the widest conception which the law contains;—the notion of legal duty, to which already I have referred. We fill the word with all the content which we draw from morals. But what does it mean to a bad man? Mainly, and in the first place, a prophecy that if he does certain things he will be

subjected to disagreeable consequences by way of imprisonment or compulsory payment of money. But from his point of view, what is the difference between being fined and being taxed a certain sum for doing a certain thing? That his point of view is the test of legal principles is shown by the many discussions which have arisen in the courts on the very question whether a given statutory liability is a penalty or a tax. On the answer to this question depends the decision whether conduct is legally wrong or right, and also whether a man is under compulsion or free. Leaving the criminal law on one side, what is the difference between the liability under the mill acts or statutes authorizing a taking by eminent domain and the liability for what we call a wrongful conversion of property where restoration is out of the question? In both cases the party taking another man's property has to pay its fair value as assessed by a jury, and no more. What significance is there in calling one taking right and another wrong from the point of view of the law? It does not matter, so far as the given consequence, the compulsory payment, is concerned, whether the act to which it is attached is described in terms of praise or in terms of blame, or whether the law purports to prohibit it or to allow it. If it matters at all, still speaking from the bad man's point of view, it must be because in one case and not in the other some further disadvantages, or at least some further consequences, are attached to the act by the law. The only other disadvantages thus attached to it which I ever have been able to think of are to be found in two somewhat insignificant legal doctrines, both of which might be abolished without much disturbance. One is, that a contract to do a prohibited act is unlawful, and the other, that, if one of two or more joint wrongdoers has to pay all the damages, he cannot recover contribution from his fellows. And that I believe is all. You see how the vague circumference of the notion of duty shrinks and at the same time grows more precise when we wash it with cynical acid and expel everything except the object of our study, the operations of the law.
* * *

In the law of contract the use of moral phraseology has led to equal confusion. Morals deal with the actual internal state of the individual's mind, what he actually intends. From the time of the Romans down to now, this mode of dealing has affected the language of the law as to contract, and the language used has reacted upon the thought. We talk about a contract as a meeting of the minds of the parties, and thence it is inferred in various cases that there is no contract because their minds have not met; that is, because they have intended different things or because one party has not known of the assent of the other. Yet nothing is more certain than that parties may be bound by a contract to things which neither of them intended, and when one does not know of the other's assent. Suppose a contract is executed in due form and in writing to deliver a lecture, mentioning no time. One of the parties thinks that the promise will be construed to mean at once, within a week. The other thinks that it means when he is ready. The court says that it means within a reasonable time. The parties are bound by the contract as it is interpreted by the court, yet neither of them meant what the court declares that they have said. In my opinion no one will understand the true theory of contract or be able even to discuss some fundamental questions intelligently until he has understood that all contracts are formal, that the making of a contract depends not on the agreement of two minds in one intention, but on the agreement of two sets of external signs,—not on the parties' having *meant* the same thing but on their having *said* the same thing. Furthermore, as the signs may be addressed to one sense or another,—to sight or to hearing,—on the nature of the sign will depend the moment when the contract is made. If the sign is tangible, for instance, a letter, the contract is made when the letter of acceptance is delivered. If it is necessary that the minds of the parties meet, there will be no contract until the acceptance can be read,—none, for example, if the acceptance be snatched from the hand of the offerer by a third person.

This is not the time to work out a theory in detail, or to answer many obvious doubts and questions which are suggested by these general views. I know of none which are not easy to answer, but what I am trying to do now is only by a series of hints to throw some light on the narrow path of legal doctrine, and upon two pitfalls which, as it seems to me, lie perilously near to it. Of the first of these I have said enough. I hope that my illustrations have shown the danger, both to speculation and to practice, of confounding morality with law, and the trap which legal language lays for us on that side of our way. For my own part, I often doubt whether it would not be a gain if every word of moral significance could be banished from the law altogether, and other words adopted which should convey legal ideas uncolored by anything outside the law. We should lose the fossil records of a good deal of history and the majesty got from ethical associations, but by ridding ourselves of an unnecessary confusion we should gain very much in the clearness of our thought.

So much for the limits of the law. The next thing which I wish to consider is what are the forces which determine its content and its growth. You may assume, with Hobbes and Bentham and Austin, that all law emanates from the sovereign, even when the first human beings to enunciate it are the judges, or you may think that law is the voice of the Zeitgeist, or what you like. It is all one to my present purpose. Even if every decision required the sanction of an emperor with despotic power and a whimsical turn of mind, we should be interested none the less, still with a view to prediction, in discovering some order, some rational explanation, and some principle of growth for the rules which he laid down. In every system there are such explanations and principles to be found. It is with regard to them that a second fallacy comes in, which I think it important to expose.

The fallacy to which I refer is the notion that the only force at work in the development of the law is logic. In the broadest sense, indeed, that notion would be true. The postulate on which we think about the universe is that there is a fixed quantitative relation between every phenomenon and its antecedents and consequents. If there is such a thing as a phenomenon without these fixed quantitative relations, it is a miracle. It is outside the law of cause and effect, and as such transcends our power of thought, or at least is something to or from which we cannot reason. The condition of our thinking about the universe is that it is capable of being thought about rationally, or, in other words, that every part of it is effect and cause in the same sense in which those parts are with which we are most familiar. So in the broadest sense it is true that the law is a logical development, like everything else. The danger of which I speak is not the admission that the principles governing other phenomena also govern the law, but the notion that a given system, ours, for instance, can be worked out like mathematics from some general axioms of conduct. This is the natural error of the schools, but it is not confined to them. I once heard a very eminent judge say that he never let a decision go until he was absolutely sure that it was right. So judicial dissent often is blamed, as if it meant simply that one side or the other were not doing their sums right, and, if they would take more trouble, agreement inevitably would come.

This mode of thinking is entirely natural. The training of lawyers is a training in logic. The processes of analogy, discrimination, and deduction are those in which they are most at home. The language of judicial decision is mainly the language of logic. And the logical method and form flatter that longing for certainty and for repose which is in every human mind. But certainty generally is illusion, and repose is not the destiny of man. Behind the logical form lies a judgment as to the relative worth and importance of competing legislative grounds, often an inarticulate and unconscious judgment, it is true, and yet the very root and nerve of the whole proceeding. You can give any conclusion a logical form. You always can imply a condition in a contract. But why do you imply it? It is because of some belief as to the practice of the community or of a class, or because of some opinion as to policy, or, in short, because of some attitude of yours upon a matter not capable of exact quantitative measurement, and therefore not capable of founding exact logical conclusions. Such matters really are battle grounds where the means do not exist for determinations that shall be good for all time, and where the decision can do no more than embody the preference of a given body in a given time and place. We do not realize how large a part of our law is open to reconsideration upon a slight change in the habit of the public mind. No concrete proposition is self evident, no matter how ready we may be to accept it, not even Mr. Herbert Spencer's Every man has a right to do what he wills, provided he interferes not with a like right on the part of his neighbors. * * *

Indeed, I think that even now our theory upon this matter is open to reconsideration, although I am not prepared to say how I should decide if a reconsideration were proposed. Our law of torts comes from the old days of isolated, ungeneralized wrongs, assaults, slanders, and the like, where the damages might be taken to lie where they fell by legal judgment. But the torts with which our courts are kept busy to-day are mainly the incidents of certain well known businesses. They are injuries to person or property by railroads, factories, and the like. The liability for them is estimated, and sooner or later goes into the price paid by the public. The public really pays the damages, and the question of liability, if pressed far enough, is really the question how far it is desirable that the public should insure the safety of those whose work it uses. It might be said that in such cases the chance of a jury finding for the defendant is merely a chance, once in a while rather arbitrarily interrupting the regular course of recovery, most likely in the case of an unusually conscientious plaintiff, and therefore better done away with. On the other hand, the economic value even of a life to the community can be estimated, and no recovery, it may be said, ought to go beyond that amount. It is conceivable that some day in certain cases we may find ourselves imitating, on a higher plane, the tariff for life and limb which we see in the Leges Barbarorum.

I think that the judges themselves have failed adequately to recognize their duty of weighing considerations of social advantage. The duty is inevitable, and the result of the often proclaimed judicial aversion to deal with such considerations is simply to leave the very ground and foundation of judgments inarticulate, and often unconscious, as I have said. When socialism first began to be talked about, the comfortable classes of the community were a good deal frightened. I suspect that this fear has influenced judicial action both here and in England, yet it is certain that it is not a conscious factor in the decisions to which I refer. I think that something similar has led people who no longer hope to control the legislatures to look to the courts as expounders of the Constitutions, and that in some courts new principles have been discovered outside the bodies of those instruments, which may be generalized into acceptance of the economic doctrines which prevailed about fifty years ago, and a wholesale prohibition of what a tribunal of lawyers does not think about right. I cannot but believe that if the training of lawyers led them habitually to consider more definitely and explicitly the social advantage on which the rule they lay down must be justified, they sometimes would hesitate where now they are confident, and see that really they were taking sides upon debatable and often burning questions.

So much for the fallacy of logical form. Now let us consider the present condition of the law as a subject for study, and the ideal toward which it tends. We still are far from the point of view which I desire to see reached. No one has reached it or can reach it as yet. We are only at the beginning of a philosophical reaction, and of a reconsideration of the worth of doctrines which for the most part still are taken for granted without any deliberate, conscious, and systematic questioning of their grounds. The development of our law has gone on for nearly a thousand years, like the development of a plant, each generation taking the inevitable next step, mind, like matter, simply obeying a law of spontaneous growth. It is perfectly natural and right that it should have been so. Imitation is a necessity of human nature, as has been illustrated by a remarkable French writer, M. Tarde, in an admirable book, "Les Lois de l'Imitation." Most of the things we do, we do for no better reason than that our fathers have done them or that our neighbors do them, and the same is true of a larger part than we suspect of what we think. The reason is a good one, because our short life gives us no time for a better, but it is not the best. It does not follow, because we all are compelled to take on faith at second hand most of the rules on which we base our action and our thought, that each of us may not try to set some corner of his world in the order of reason, or that all of us collectively should not aspire to carry reason as far as it will go throughout the whole domain. In regard to the law, it is true, no doubt, that an evolutionist will hesitate to affirm universal validity for his social ideals, or for the principles which he thinks should be embodied in legislation. He is content if he can prove them best for here and now. He may be ready to admit that he knows nothing about an absolute best in the cosmos, and even that he knows next to nothing about a permanent best for men. Still it is true that a body of law is more rational and more civilized when every rule it contains is referred articulately and definitely to an end which it subserves, and when the grounds for desiring that end are stated or are ready to be stated in words.

At present, in very many cases, if we want to know why a rule of law has taken its particular shape, and more or less if we want to know why it exists at all, we go to tradition. We follow it into the Year Books, and perhaps beyond them to the customs of the Salian Franks, and somewhere in the past, in the German forests, in the needs of Norman kings, in the assumptions of a dominant class, in the absence of generalized ideas, we find out the practical motive for what now best is justified by the mere fact of its acceptance and that men are accustomed to it. The rational study of law is still to a large extent the study of history. History must be a part of the study, because without it we cannot know the precise scope of rules which it is our business to know. It is a part of the rational study, because it is the first step toward an enlightened scepticism, that is, toward a deliberate reconsideration of the worth of those rules. When you get the dragon out of his cave on to the plain and in the daylight, you can count his teeth and claws, and see just what is his strength. But to get him out is only the first step. The next is either to kill him, or to tame him and make him a useful animal. For the rational study of the law the black-letter man may be the man of the present, but the man of the future is the man of statistics and the master of economics. It is revolting to have no better reason for a rule of law than that so it was laid down in the time of Henry IV. It is still more revolting if the grounds upon which it was laid down have vanished long since, and the rule simply persists from blind imitation of the past. I am thinking of the technical rule as to trespass *ab initio*, as it is called, which I attempted to explain in a recent Massachusetts case.

Let me take an illustration, which can be stated in a few words, to show how the social end which is aimed at by a rule of law is obscured and only partially attained in consequence of the fact that the rule owes its form to a gradual historical development, instead of being reshaped as a whole, with conscious articulate reference to the end in view. We think it desirable to prevent one man's property being misappropriated by another, and so we make larceny a crime. The evil is the same whether the misappropriation is made by a man into whose hands the owner has put the property, or by one who wrongfully takes it away. But primitive law in its weakness did not get much beyond an effort to prevent violence, and very naturally made a wrongful taking, a trespass, part of its definition of the crime. In modern times the judges enlarged the definition a little by holding that, if the wrongdoer gets possession by a trick or device, the crime is committed. This really was giving up the requirement of a trespass, and it would have been more logical, as well as truer to the present object of the law, to abandon the requirement altogether. That, however, would have seemed too bold, and was left to statute. Statutes were passed making embezzlement a crime. But the force of tradition caused the crime of embezzlement to be regarded as so far distinct from larceny that to this day, in some jurisdictions at least, a slip corner is kept open for thieves to contend, if indicted for larceny, that they should have been indicted for embezzlement, and if indicted for embezzlement, that they should have been indicted for larceny, and to escape on that ground.

Far more fundamental questions still await a better answer than that we do as our fathers have done. What have we better than a blind guess to show that the criminal law in its present form does more good than harm? I do not stop to refer to the effect which it has had in degrading prisoners and in plunging them further into crime, or to the question whether fine and imprisonment do not fall more heavily on a criminal's wife and children than on himself. I have in mind more far-reaching questions. Does punishment deter? Do we deal with criminals on proper principles? A modern school of Continental criminalists plumes itself on the formula, first suggested, it is said, by Gall, that we must consider the criminal rather than the crime. The formula does not carry us very far, but the inquiries which have been started look toward an answer of my questions based on science for the first time. If the typical criminal is a degenerate, bound to swindle or to murder by as deep seated an organic necessity as that which makes the rattlesnake bite, it is idle to talk of deterring him by the classical method of imprisonment. He must be got rid of; he cannot be improved, or frightened out of his structural reaction. If, on the other hand, crime, like normal human conduct, is mainly a matter of imitation, punishment fairly may be expected to help to keep it out of fashion. The study of criminals has been thought by some well known men of science to sustain the former hypothesis. The statistics of the relative increase of crime in crowded places like large cities, where example has the greatest chance to work, and in less populated parts, where the contagion spreads more slowly, have been used with great force in favor of the latter view. But there is weighty authority for the belief that, however this may be, "not the nature of the crime, but the dangerousness of the criminal" constitutes the only reasonable legal criterion to guide the inevitable social reaction against the criminal.

The impediments to rational generalization, which I illustrated from the law of larceny, are shown in the other branches of the law, as well as in that of crime. Take the law of tort or civil liability for damages apart from contract and the like. Is there any general theory of such liability, or are the cases in which it exists simply to be enumerated, and to be explained each on its special ground, as is easy to believe from the fact that the right of action for certain well known classes of wrongs like trespass or slander has its special history for each class? I think that there is a general theory to be discovered, although resting in tendency rather than established and accepted. I think that the law regards the infliction of temporal damage by a responsible person as actionable, if under the circumstances known to him the danger of his act is manifest according to common experience, or according to his own experience if it is more than common, except in cases where upon special grounds of policy the law refuses to protect the plaintiff or grants a privilege to the defendant. I think that commonly malice, intent, and negligence mean only that the danger was manifest to a greater or less degree, under the circumstances known to the actor, although in some cases of privilege malice may mean an actual malevolent motive, and such a motive may take away a permission knowingly to inflict harm, which otherwise would be granted on this or that ground of dominant public good. But when I stated my view to a very eminent English judge the other day, he said: "You are discussing what the law ought to be; as the law is, you must show a right. A man is not liable for negligence unless he is subject to a duty." If our difference was more than a difference in words, or with regard to the proportion between the exceptions and the rule, then, in his opinion, liability for an act cannot be referred to the manifest tendency of the act to cause temporal damage in general as a sufficient explanation, but must be referred to the special nature of the damage, or must be derived from some special circumstances outside of the tendency of the act, for which no generalized explanation exists. I think that such a view is wrong, but it is familiar, and I dare say generally is accepted in England.

Everywhere the basis of principle is tradition, to such an extent that we even are in danger of making the rôle of history more important than it is. ...

However, if we consider the law of contract, we find it full of history. The distinctions between debt, covenant, and assumpsit are merely historical. The classification of certain obligations to pay money, imposed by the law irrespective of any bargain as quasi contracts, is merely historical. The doctrine of consideration is merely historical. The effect given to a seal is to be explained by history alone.—Consideration is a mere form. Is it a useful form? If so, why should it not be required in all contracts? A seal is a mere form, and is vanishing in the scroll and in enactments that a consideration must be given, seal or no seal.—Why should any merely historical distinction be allowed to affect the rights and obligations of business men?

Since I wrote this discourse I have come on a very good example of the way in which tradition not only overrides rational policy, but overrides it after first having been misunderstood and having been given a new and broader scope than it had when it had a meaning. It is the settled law of England that a material alteration of a written contract by a party avoids it as against him. The doctrine is contrary to the general tendency of the law. We do not tell a jury that if a man ever has lied in one particular he is to be presumed to lie in all. Even if a man has tried to defraud, it seems no sufficient reason for preventing him from proving the truth. Objections of like nature in general go to the weight, not to the admissibility, of evidence. Moreover, this rule is irrespective of fraud, and is not confined to evidence. It is not merely that you cannot use the writing, but that the contract is at an end. What does this mean? The existence of a written contract depends on the fact that the offerer and offeree have interchanged their written expressions, not on the continued existence of those expressions. But in the case of a bond the primitive notion was different. The contract was inseparable from the parchment. If a stranger destroyed it, or tore off the seal, or altered it, the obligee could not recover, however free from fault, because the defendant's contract, that is, the actual tangible bond which he had sealed, could not be produced in the form in which it bound him. About a hundred years ago Lord Kenyon undertook to use his reason on this tradition, he sometimes did to the detriment of the law, and, not understanding it, said he could see no reason why what was true of a bond should not be true of other contracts. His decision happened to be right, as it concerned a promissory note, where again the common law regarded the contract as inseparable from the paper on which it was written, but the reasoning was general, and soon was extended to other written contracts, and various absurd and unreal grounds of policy were invented to account for the enlarged rule.

I trust that no one will understand me to be speaking with disrespect of the law, because I criticise it so freely. I venerate the law, and especially our system of law, as one of the vastest products of the human mind. No one knows better than I do the countless number of great intellects that have spent themselves in making some addition or improvement, the greatest of which is trifling when compared with the mighty whole. It has the final title to respect that it exists, that it is not a Hegelian dream, but a part of the lives of men. But one may criticise even what one reveres. Law is the business to which my life is devoted, and I should show less than devotion if I did not do what in me lies to improve it, and, when I perceive what seems to me the ideal of its future, if I hesitated to point it out and to press toward it with all my heart.

Perhaps I have said enough to show the part which the study of history necessarily plays in the intelligent study of the law as it is today. In the teaching of this school and at Cambridge it is in no danger of being undervalued. Mr. Bigelow here and Mr. Ames and Mr. Thayer there have made important contributions which will not be forgotten, and in England the recent history of early English law by Sir Frederick Pollock and Mr. Maitland has lent the subject an almost deceptive charm. We must beware of the pitfall of antiquarianism, and must remember that for our purposes our only interest in the past is for the light it throws upon the present. I look forward to a time when the part played by history in the explanation of dogma shall be very small, and instead of ingenious research we shall spend our energy on a study of the ends sought to be attained and the reasons for desiring them. As a step toward that ideal it seems to me that every lawyer ought to seek an understanding of economics. The present divorce between the schools of political economy and law seems to me an evidence of how much progress in philosophical study still remains to be made. In the present state of political economy, indeed, we come again upon history on a larger scale, but there we are called on to consider and weigh the ends of legislation, the means of attaining them, and the cost. We learn that for everything we have we give up something else, and we are taught to set the advantage we gain against the other advantage we lose, and to know what we are doing when we elect.

There is another study which sometimes is undervalued by the practical minded, for which I wish to say a good word, although I think a good deal of pretty poor stuff goes under that name. I mean the study of what is called jurisprudence. Jurisprudence, as I look at it, is simply law in its most generalized part. Every effort to reduce a case to a rule is an effort of jurisprudence, although the name as used in English is confined to the broadest rules and most fundamental conceptions. One mark of a great lawyer is that he sees the application of the broadest rules. There is a story of a Vermont justice of the peace before whom a suit was brought by one farmer against another for breaking a churn. The justice took time to consider, and then said that he had looked through the statutes and could find nothing about churns, and gave judgment for the defendant. The same state of mind is shown in all our common digests and text-books. Applications of rudimentary rules of contract or tort are tucked away under the head of Railroads or Telegraphs or go to swell treatises on historical subdivisions, such as Shipping or Equity, or are gathered under an arbitrary title which is thought likely to appeal to the practical mind, such as Mercantile Law. If a man goes into law it pays to be a master of it, and to be a master of it means to look straight through all the dramatic incidents and to discern the true basis for prophecy. Therefore, it is well to have an accurate notion of what you mean by law, by a right, by a duty, by malice, intent, and negligence, by ownership, by possession, and so forth. I have in my mind cases in which the highest courts seem to me to have floundered because they had no clear ideas on some of these themes. I have illustrated their importance already. If a further illustration is wished, it may be found by reading the Appendix to Sir James Stephen's Criminal Law on the subject of possession, and then turning to Pollock and Wright's enlightened book. Sir James Stephen is not the only writer whose attempts to analyze legal ideas have been confused by striving for a useless quintessence of all systems, instead of an accurate anatomy of one. The trouble with Austin was that he did not know enough English law. But still it is a practical advantage to master Austin, and his predecessors, Hobbes and Bentham, and his worthy successors, Holland and Pollock. Sir Frederick Pollock's recent little book is touched with the felicity which marks all his works, and is wholly free from the perverting influence of Roman models.

The advice of the elders to young men is very apt to be as unreal as a list of the hundred best books. At least in my day I had my share of such counsels, and high among the unrealities I place the recommendation to study the Roman law. I assume that such advice means more than collecting a few Latin maxims with which to ornament the discourse,—the purpose for which Lord Coke recommended Bracton. If that is all that is wanted, the title "De Regulis Juris Antiqui" can be read in an hour. I assume that, if it is well to study the Roman law, it is well to study it as a working system. That means mastering a set of technicalities more difficult and less understood than our own, and studying another course of history by which even more than our own the Roman law must be explained. If any one doubts me, let him read Keller's "Der Römische Civil Process und die Actionen," a treatise on the praetor's edict, Muirhead's most interesting "Historical Introduction to the Private Law of Rome," and, to give him the best chance possible, Sohm's admirable Institutes. No. The way to gain a liberal view of your subject is not to read something else, but to get to the bottom of the subject itself. The means of doing that are, in the first place, to follow the existing body of dogma into its highest generalizations by the help of jurisprudence; next, to discover from history how it has come to be what it is; and, finally, so far as you can, to consider the ends which the several rules seek to accomplish, the reasons why those ends are desired, what is given up to gain them, and whether they are worth the price.
* * *

I have been speaking about the study of the law, and I have said next to nothing of what commonly is talked about in that connection,—text-books and the case system, and all the machinery with which a student comes most immediately in contact. Nor shall I say anything about them. Theory is my subject, not practical details. The modes of teaching have been improved since my time, no doubt, but ability and industry will master the raw material with any mode. Theory is the most important part of the dogma of the law, as the architect is the most important man who takes part in the building of a house. The most important improvements of the last twenty-five years are improvements in theory. It is not to be feared as unpractical, for, to the competent, it simply means going to the bottom of the subject. For the incompetent, it sometimes is true, as has been said, that an interest in general ideas means an absence of particular knowledge. I remember in army days reading of a youth who, being examined for the lowest grade and being asked a question about squadron drill, answered that he never had considered the evolutions of less than ten thousand men. But the weak and foolish must be left to their folly. The danger is that the able and practical minded should look with indifference or distrust upon ideas the connection of which with their business is remote. I heard a story, the other day, of a man who had a valet to whom he paid high wages, subject to deduction for faults. One of his deductions was, "For lack of imagination, five dollars." The lack is not confined to valets. The object of ambition, power, generally presents itself nowadays in the form of money alone. Money is the most immediate form, and is a proper object of desire. "The fortune," said Rachel, "is the measure of the intelligence." That is a good text to waken people out of a fool's paradise. But, as Hegel says, "It is in the end not the appetite, but the opinion, which has to be satisfied." To an imagination of any scope the most far-reaching form of power is not money, it is the command of ideas. If you want great examples read Mr. Leslie Stephen's "History of English Thought in the Eighteenth Century," and see how a hundred years after his death the abstract speculations of Descartes had become a practical force controlling the conduct of men. Read the works of the great German jurists, and see how much more the world is governed to-day by Kant than by Bonaparte. We cannot all be Descartes or Kant, but we all want happiness. And happiness, I am sure from having known many successful men, cannot be won simply by being counsel for great corporations and having an income of fifty thousand dollars. An intellect great enough to win the prize needs other food beside success. The remoter and more general aspects of the law are those which give it universal interest. It is through them that you not only become a great master in your calling, but connect your subject with the universe and catch an echo of the infinite, a glimpse of its unfathomable process, a hint of the universal law.

NOTE

Consider Holmes' emphasis on "prophecies" in the law, his definition of law as "the prophecies of what the courts will do in fact"; "A legal duty so called is nothing but a prediction that if a man does or omits certain things he will be made to suffer in this or that by judgment of the court;—and so of a legal right." Does Holmes' definition of law assume law as something that "is" or "ought to be" or both?

"The number of our predictions when generalized and reduced to a system is not unmanageably large." Holmes made that statement in 1881. According to West Publishing Company, there were 27,527 published opinions in 1929 and 61,474 published opinions in 1994. Is this number still "not unmanageably large"? It reached an all-time high of 65,333 in 1991.

In view of the emphasis on ethics and the importance placed on morals by natural law precepts, consider Holmes' statements:

I think it desirable at once to point out and dispel a confusion between morality and law.

The law is the witness and external deposit of our moral life.

I often doubt that it would not be a gain if every word of moral significance could be banished from the law altogether, and other words adopted which could convey legal ideas uncolored by anything outside the law.

Consider his discussion of "malice" in the law and how it differs "from what it means in morals." Do you agree that it is "desirable . . . to point out and dispel a confusion between morality and law." Is there a difference between morality in justice and morality in law? Does your answer depend on your definition of law?

What did Holmes mean when he exposed as the second fallacy "the notion that the only force at work in the development of the law is logic." Keep in mind that an overarching thesis of his presentation is a criticism of a jurisprudence of conceptions and his call that judges should "weigh[ ] considerations of social advantage." To understand Holmes is to note that his criticism of the use of logic was limited to its use as "the only force at work."

Consider the comments of Mary Ann Glendon, Learned Hand Professor of Law at Harvard:

> Holmes wrote: "The life of the law has not been logic: it has been experience." In "The Path of the Law," he returned to that theme, declaring the need to expose the "fallacy" that logic is "the only force at work in the development of the law." The famous first line of The Common Law flows so majestically that a reader may not pause to wonder whether anyone had actually said that logic *was* the life of the law. The fact is that even at the height of nineteenth-century legal formalism, it would have been hard to find any American lawyer advancing such a proposition. That point was made by a commentator as soon as "The Path of the Law" appeared in 1897. Jabez Fox wrote that he could not believe "that this particular fallacy has taken a deep hold on the profession." Certainly Lord Coke himself had held no brief for logic. His passion was reason, "fined and refined" in the crucible of practical experience, a far different idea.
>
> Holmes's aphorism was perfectly aimed at the rigid conceptualism of the Germans who were trying to construct a code endowed with *logische Geschlossenheit* (a self-contained, logically closed system). But it was wildly inappropriate as applied to Coke and other writers on the judge-made, open-textured common law. And as to the weaker sort of formalism that prevailed in America in the 1870s, it fell beside the target. But it was a terrific line.

Holmes was a man on the move. With matchless verbal dexterity, he converted a living "tradition" into fossilized "history" and downgraded Coke's singing "reason" to dry "logic"— a collection, as he put it, of syllogisms, axioms, and deductions. That took the piano out of the *Emperor* Concerto.

There was more. Holmes announced, with all the fanfare of a discovery, what good lawyers have always known: that there are many times when the law is silent or unclear, and that part of a judge's role, therefore, includes a limited lawmaking function. With his flair for sensationalizing the obvious, Holmes mentioned some of the things that judges made law from. Expediency, opinion, and even prejudice, he said, had all played a greater part "than the syllogism" in fashioning the rules by which we are governed. In other words, a judge's mind operates much as everyone else's does.

In the blunt macho style that was his trademark, he told his young audience that the aim of legal study was simply the science of prediction, prediction of "where the axe will fall." And, in words that every lawyer still knows, he said that if you want to know the law, "you must look at it as a bad man, who cares only for the material consequences which such knowledge enables him to predict." He advised his listeners to use "cynical acid" to wash away all the moralizing language of right and wrong so that they could see the law as it truly is. "For my own part," he opined, "I often doubt whether it would not be a gain if every word of moral significance could be banished from the law altogether."

The "ideal" to be served by banishing the language of morality was, he said, to put the law on a truly scientific basis. That meant clear thinking about means and ends, costs and benefits—not Langdell's pseudoscience of extracting principles from scattered court decisions. Reason might be out, but what Holmes approvingly called "rationality" was in. He especially recommended that every lawyer should acquire a knowledge of economics, for the "man of the future is the man of statistics and the master of economics." A century later, lawyers all over the world are marching to the measure of those thoughts. Interdisciplinary law-and-economics scholarship is one of the most influential forces in legal studies today, the only indigenous American legal "school" to command a significant international following.

M. Glendon, A Nation Under Lawyers 188–190 (1994).

———

FELIX S. COHEN, THE DEFINITION OF LAW *

The starting point of functional analysis in American jurisprudence is found in Justice Holmes' definition of law as "prophecies of what the courts will do in fact." ...

A good deal of fruitless controversy has arisen out of attempts to show that this definition of law as the way courts actually decide cases is either true or false. A definition of law is *useful* or *useless*. It is not *true* or *false,* any more than a New Year's resolution or an insurance policy. A definition is in fact a type of insurance against certain risks of confusion. It cannot, any more than can a commercial insurance policy, eliminate all risks. Absolute certainty is as foreign to language as to life. There is no final insurance against an insurer's insolvency. And the words of a definition always carry their own aura of ambiguity. But a definition is useful if it insures against risks of confusion more serious than any that the definition itself contains.

"What courts do" is not entirely devoid of ambiguity. There is room for disagreement as to what a *court* is, whether, for instance, the Interstate Commerce Commission or the Hague Tribunal or the Council of Tesuque Pueblo is a court, and whether a judge acting in excess of those powers which the executive arm of the government will recognize acts as a court. There may even be disagreement as to the line of distinction between what courts *do* and what courts *say,* in view of the fact that most judicial behavior is verbal. But these sources of ambiguity in Holmes' definition of law are peripheral rather than central, and easily remedied. They are, therefore, far less dangerous sources of confusion than the basic ambiguity inherent in classical definitions of law which involve a confusion between what is and what ought to be.

The classical confusion against which realistic jurisprudence is a protest is exemplified in Blackstone's classical definition of law as "a rule of civil conduct, prescribed by the supreme power in a State, commanding what is right, and prohibiting what is wrong."

In this definition we have an attempt to unite two incompatible ideas which, in the tradition of English jurisprudence, are most closely associated with the names of Hobbes and Coke, respectively.

Hobbes, the grandfather of realistic jurisprudence, saw in law the commands of a body to whom private individuals have surrendered their force. In a state of nature there is war of all against all. In order to achieve peace and security, each individual gives up something of his freedom, something of his power, and the commands of the collective power, that is the state, constitute law.

Hobbes' theory of law has been very unpopular with respectable citizens, but I venture to think that most of the criticism directed against it, in the last two and a half centuries, has been based upon a

* 35 Colum.L.Rev. 809, 835–38, 844–45
(1935). Reprinted by permission.

misconception of what Hobbes meant by a state of nature. So far as I know, Hobbes never refers to the state of nature as an actual historical era, at the end of which men came together and signed a social contract. The state of nature is a stage in analysis rather than a stage of history. It exists today and has always existed, to a greater or lesser degree, in various realms of human affairs. To the extent that any social relationship is exempt from governmental control it presents what Hobbes calls a state of nature.

. . .

In all this conception of law, there is no appeal to reason or goodness. Law commands obedience not because of its goodness, or its justice, or its rationality, but because of the power behind it. While this power does rest to a real extent upon popular beliefs about the value of certain legal ideals, it remains true today, as Hobbes says in his Dialogue on the Common Law, "In matter of government, when nothing else is turned up, clubs are trump."

Quite different from this realistic conception of law is the theory made famous by Coke that law is only the perfection of reason. This is a notion which has had considerable force in American constitutional history, having served first as a basis for popular revolution against tyrannical violations of "natural law" and the "natural rights" of Englishmen, and serving more recently as a judicial ground for denying legality to statutes that judges consider "unreasonable." It would be absurd to deny the importance of this concept of natural law or justice as a standard by which to judge the acts of rulers, legislative, executive or judicial. It is clear, however, that the validity of this concept of law lies in a realm of values, which is not identical with the realm of social actualities.

The confusion and ambiguity which infest the classical conception of law, as formulated by Blackstone and implicitly accepted by most modern legal writers, arise from the attempt to throw together two inconsistent ideas. Blackstone attempts in effect to superimpose the picture of law drawn by the tender-minded hypocrite, Coke, upon the picture executed by the tough-minded cynic Hobbes, and to give us a composite photograph. Law, says Blackstone, is "a rule of civil conduct prescribed by the supreme power in a State (Hobbes speaking) commanding what is right and prohibiting what is wrong (Coke speaking)". Putting these two ideas together, we have a fertile source of confusion, which many important legal scholars since Blackstone have found about as useful in legal polemics as the ink with which a cuttlefish befuddles his enemies.

. . .

If the understanding of any decision involves us necessarily in prophecy (and thus in history), then the notion of law as something that exists completely and systematically at any given moment in time is false. Law is a social process, a complex of human activities, and an adequate legal science must deal with human activity, with cause and effect, with the past and the future. Legal science, as traditionally conceived, attempts to give an instantaneous snapshot of an existing and completed system of rights and duties. Within that system there are no temporal processes, no cause and no effect, no past and no future. A legal decision is thus conceived as a logical deduction from fixed principles. Its meaning is expressed only in terms of its logical consequences. A legal system, thus viewed, is as far removed from temporal activity as a system of pure geometry. In fact, jurisprudence is as much a part of pure mathematics as is algebra, unless it be conceived as a study of human behavior,—human behavior as it molds and is molded by judicial decisions. Legal systems, principles, rules, institutions, concepts, and decisions can be understood only as functions of human behavior.

Such a view of legal science reveals gaps in our legal knowledge to which, I think, legal research will give increasing attention.

————

ROSCOE POUND, MECHANICAL JURISPRUDENCE *

"I have known judges," said Chief Justice Erle, "bred in the world of legal studies, who delighted in nothing so much as in a strong decision. Now a strong decision is a decision opposed to common-sense and to common convenience. * * * A great part of the law made by judges consists of strong decisions, and as one strong decision is a precedent for another a little stronger, the law at last, on some matters, becomes such a nuisance that equity intervenes, or an Act of Parliament must be passed to sweep the whole away."

The instance suggested in the conversation from which the foregoing extract is taken illustrates very well the development of a mechanical legal doctrine. Successive decisions upon the construction of wills had passed upon the meaning of particular words and phrases in particular wills. These decisions were used as guides in the construction of other wills. Presently rules grew up whereby it was settled that particular words and phrases had prescribed hard and fast meanings, and the construction of wills became so artificial, so scientific, that it defeated the very end of construction and compelled a series of sections in the Wills Act of 1836.

I have referred to mechanical jurisprudence as scientific because those who administer it believe it such. But in truth it is not science at all. We no longer hold anything scientific merely because it exhibits a rigid scheme of deductions from *a priori* conceptions. In the philosophy of to-day, theories are "instruments, not answers to enigmas, in which we can rest." The idea of science as a system of deductions has become obsolete, and the revolution which has taken place in other sciences in this regard must take place and is taking place in jurisprudence also.

* R. Pound, *Mechanical Jurisprudence,* 8 Colum.L.Rev. 605, 608–612 (1908). Re-   printed with permission.

This revolution in science at large was achieved in the middle of the nineteenth century. In the first half of that century, scientific method in every department of learning was dominated by the classical German philosophy. Men conceived that by dialectics and deduction from controlling conceptions they could construe the whole content of knowledge. Even in the natural sciences this belief prevailed and had long dictated theories of nature and of natural phenomena. Linnaeus, for instance, lays down a proposition, *omne vivum ex ovo,* and from this fundamental conception deduces a theory of homologics between animal and vegetable organs.[13] He deemed no study of the organisms and the organs themselves necessary to reach or to sustain these conclusions. Yet, to-day, study of the organisms themselves has overthrown his fundamental proposition. The substitution of efficient for final causes as explanations of natural phenomena has been paralleled by a revolution in political thought. We do not base institutions upon deduction from assumed principles of human nature; we require them to exhibit practical utility, and we rest them upon a foundation of policy and established adaptation to human needs. It has been asserted that to no small extent the old mode of procedure was borrowed from the law. We are told that it involved a "fundamentally juristic conception of the world in which all kinds of action and every sort of judgment was expressed in legal phraseology."[14] We are told that "in the Middle Ages human welfare and even religion was conceived under the form of legality, and in the modern world this has given place to utility."[15] We have, then, the same task in jurisprudence that has been achieved in philosophy, in the natural sciences and in politics. We have to rid ourselves of this sort of legality and to attain a pragmatic, a sociological legal science.

"What is needed nowadays," it has been said, "is that as against an abstract and unreal theory of State omnipotence on the one hand, and an atomistic and artificial view of individual independence on the other, the facts of the world with its innumerable bonds of association and the naturalness of social authority should be generally recognized, and become the basis of our laws, as it is of our life."[16]

Herein is the task of the sociological jurist. Professor Small defines the sociological movement as "a frank endeavor to secure for the human factor in experience the central place which belongs to it in our whole scheme of thought and action."[17] The sociological movement in jurisprudence is a movement for pragmatism as a philosophy of law; for the adjustment of principles and doctrines to the human conditions they are to govern rather than to assumed first principles; for putting the human factor in the central place and relegating logic to its true position as an instrument.

13. Philosophia Botanica, aphorisms 134, *et seq.*

14. Figgis, From Gerson to Grotius, 152.

15. Ibid., 14.

16. Ibid., 206.

17. The Meaning of Sociology, 14 Am.Journ.Sociol. 13.

Jurisprudence is last in the march of the sciences away from the method of deduction from predetermined conceptions. On the continent of Europe, both the historical school of jurists and the philosophical school, which were dominant until at least the last quarter of the nineteenth century, proceeded in this way. The difference between them lay in the manner in which they arrived at their fundamental conceptions. The former derived them from the history of juristic speculation and the historical development of the Roman sources. The latter, through metaphysical inquiries, arrived at certain propositions as to human nature, and deduced a system from them. This was the philosophical theory behind the eighteenth-century movement for codification.[18] Ihering[19] was the pioneer in the work of superseding this jurisprudence of conceptions (*Begriffsjurisprudenz*) by a jurisprudence of results (*Wirklichkeitsjurisprudenz*).[20] He insisted that we should begin at the other end; that the first question should be, how will a rule or a decision operate in practice? For instance, if a rule of commercial law were in question, the search should be for the rule that best accords with and gives effect to sound business practice. In the Civil Law, the doctrine as to mistake in the formation of a contract affords an example of the working of the two methods. Savigny treated the subject according to the jurisprudence of conceptions. He worked out historically and analytically the conception of a contract and deduced therefrom the rules to govern cases of mistake. It followed, from his conception, that if *A* telegraphed *B* to *buy* shares and the telegram as delivered to *B* read *sell*, there was no contract between *A* and *B*, and hence no liability of *A* to *B;* and for a time it was so held. But this and some of the other resulting rules were so far from just in their practical operation that, following the lead of Ihering, they have been abandoned and the ordinary understanding of business men has been given effect.[21] And, in this same connection, the new German code has introduced, as a criterion of error in the content of an expression of the will, the question, what would be regarded as essential in the ordinary understanding of business.[22] Even better examples of the workings of a jurisprudence of conceptions, for our purposes, may be found in the manner in which common-law courts have dealt with points of mercantile law. For instance, the law of partnership is made difficult and often unjust by the insistence of the courts upon deducing its rules from a conception of joint ownership and joint obligation, instead of ascertaining and giving effect to the actual situation as understood and practiced by merchants. The legal theory does not affect the actual course of business an iota. But it leads to unfortunate results when that course of business, for some reason,

18. See Code of Frederick the Great, part I, Book I, tit. 2, §§ 3, 4.

19. Der Zweck im Recht (1878); Scherz und Ernst in der Jurisprudenz (1884) especially the two essays "Im juristischen Begriffshimmel" and "Wieder auf Erden."

20. Sternberg, Allegemeine Rechtslehre, I, 188. See Brütt, Die Kunst der Rechtsanwendung, § 5.

21. Bernhöft, Bürgerliches Recht (in Birkmeyer, Encyklopädie der Rechtswissenschaft) § 46. Cosack, Lehrbuch des Deutschen bügerlichen Rechts, I, § 64 (3 Ed. pp. 213–214), BGB, §§ 120, 122.

22. BGB, § 119, Saleilles, De la déclaration de la volonté, § 2, Leonhard, Der Irrtum als Ursache nichtiger Verträge (2 Ed.), II, 178.

comes before the courts.[23] Again, the refusal of Lord Holt to recognize the negotiability of promissory notes [24] proceeded upon a deduction from the conception of a chose in action. A jurisprudence of ends would have avoided each of these errors.

In periods of legal development through juristic speculation and judicial decision, we have a jurisprudence of ends in fact, even if in form it is a jurisprudence of conceptions.[25] The Roman *jus gentium* was worked out for concrete causes and the conceptions were later generalizations from its results. The *jus naturale* was a system of reaching reasonable ends by bringing philosophical theory into the scale against the hard and fast rules of antiquity. The development of equity in England was attained by a method of seeking results in concrete causes. The liberalizing of English law through the law merchant was brought about by substituting business practice for juridical conceptions. The development of the common law in America was a period of growth because the doctrine that the common law was received only so far as applicable led the courts, in adapting English caselaw to American conditions, to study the conditions of application as well as the conceptions and their logical consequences. Whenever such a period has come to an end, when its work has been done and its legal theories have come to maturity, the jurisprudence of conceptions tends to decay. Conceptions are fixed. The premises are no longer to be examined. Everything is reduced to simple deduction from them. Principles cease to have importance. The law becomes a body of rules. This is the condition against which sociologists now protest, and protest rightly.

NOTE

Pound's classic exposition in *Mechanical Jurisprudence* in 1908 must be considered in conjunction with Holmes' *The Path of the Law* in 1897 and Cardozo's The Nature of the Judicial Process in 1921. When Pound uses the expression "sociologists," he is referring to legal philosophers who advocate with him and Holmes "a study of the ends sought to be obtained and the reasons desiring them" instead of a mechanical jurisprudence of conceptions. Holmes said:

> I think that the judges themselves have failed adequately to recognize their duty of weighing considerations of social advantage. The duty is inevitable, and the result of the often proclaimed judicial aversion to deal with such considerations is simply to leave the very ground and foundation of judgments inarticulate, and often unconscious.

23. Lindley, Partnership (7 Ed.) 4.

24. Buller v. Crips (1703) 6 Mod. 29. Compare modern decisions as to presentment of checks through a clearing house. Holmes v. Roe (1886) 62 Mich. 199; Edmiston v. Herpolsheimer (1901) 66 Neb. 94. In the former case we are told gravely that "the clearing house and the method of doing business through it had no bearing" on the case!

25. See, for instance, Modestinus in Dig. I, 3, 25. As Stammler says: "It is notoriously a fundamental property of the classical Roman law to have shown itself exceedingly elastic in its substance, without thereby materially injuring the sharpness and certainty of its conceptions and rules." Wirthschaft und Recht (2 Ed.) 175.

And finally, Cardozo stated, "The final cause of the law is the welfare of society," and stressed the importance of ethical considerations in judicial decision making:

> Logic and history and custom have their place. We will shape the law to conform to them when we may; but only within bounds. The end which law serves will dominate them all.... I do not mean, of course, that judges are commissioned to set aside existing rules at pleasure in favor of any other set of rules which they may hold expedient or wise. I mean that when they are called upon to say how far existing rules are to be extended or restricted, they must let the welfare of society fix the path, its direction and its distance.

B. Cardozo, *The Nature of the Judicial Process* 66–67 (1921).

Thus, Holmes, Pound and Cardozo laid the basis for modern jurisprudence that considers the effect of judicial decisions on society and social welfare, instead of being restricted to a mechanical jurisprudence of conceptions only.

———

HYNES v. NEW YORK CENT. R. CO.

Court of Appeals of New York, 1921.
231 N.Y. 229, 131 N.E. 898.

CARDOZO, J. On July 8, 1916, Harvey Hynes, a lad of 16, swam with two companions from the Manhattan to the Bronx side of the Harlem River, or United States Ship Canal, a navigable stream. Along the Bronx side of the river was the right of way of the defendant, the New York Central Railroad, which operated its trains at that point by high-tension wires, strung on poles and cross-arms. Projecting from the defendant's bulkhead above the waters of the river was a plank or springboard, from which boys of the neighborhood used to dive. One end of the board had been placed under a rock on the defendant's land, and nails had been driven at its point of contact with the bulkhead. Measured from this point of contact the length behind was 5 feet; the length in front 11. The bulkhead itself was about 3½ feet back of the pier line as located by the government. From this it follows that for 7½ feet the springboard was beyond the line of the defendant's property and above the public waterway. Its height measured from the stream was 3 feet at the bulkhead, and 5 feet at its outermost extremity. For more than five years swimmers had used it as a diving board without protest or obstruction.

On this day Hynes and his companions climbed on top of the bulkhead, intending to leap into the water. One of them made the plunge in safety. Hynes followed to the front of the springboard, and stood poised for his dive. At that moment a cross-arm with electric wires fell from the defendant's pole. The wires struck the diver, flung him from the shattered board, and plunged him to his death below. His mother, suing as administratrix, brings this action for her damages. Thus far the courts have held that Hynes at the end of the springboard above the public waters was a trespasser on the defendant's land. They have thought it immaterial that the board itself was a trespass, an encroachment on the public ways. They have thought it of no significance that Hynes would have met the same fate if he had been below the board and not above it. The board, they have said, was annexed to the defendant's bulkhead. By force of such annexation, it was to be reckoned as a fixture, and thus constructively, if not actually, an extension of the land. The defendant was under a duty to use reasonable care that bathers swimming or standing in the water should not be electrocuted by wires falling from its right of way. But to bathers diving from the springboard, there was no duty, we are told, unless the injury was the product of mere willfulness or wantonness—no duty of active vigilance to safeguard the impending structure. Without wrong to them, cross-arms might be left to rot; wires highly charged with electricity might sweep them from their stand and bury them in the subjacent waters. In climbing on the board, they became trespassers and outlaws. The conclusion is defended with much subtlety of reasoning, with much insistence upon its inevitableness as a merely logical deduction. A majority of the court are unable to accept it as the conclusion of the law.

We assume, without deciding, that the springboard was a fixture, a permanent improvement of the defendant's right of way. Much might be said in favor of another view. We do not press the inquiry for we are persuaded that the rights of bathers do not depend upon these nice distinctions. Liability would not be doubtful, we are told, had the boy been diving from a pole, if the pole had been vertical. The diver in such a situation would have been separated from the defendant's freehold. Liability, it is said has been escaped because the pole was horizontal. The plank when projected lengthwise was an extension of the soil. We are to concentrate our gaze on the private ownership of the board. We are to ignore the public ownership of the circumambient spaces of water and of air. Jumping from a boat or a barrel, the boy would have been a bather in the river. Jumping from the end of a springboard, he was no longer, it is said, a bather, but a trespasser on a right of way.

Rights and duties in systems of living law are not built upon such quicksands.

. . .

This case is a striking instance of the dangers of "a jurisprudence of conceptions" (Pound, Mechanical Jurisprudence 8 Columbia Law Review, 605, 608, 610), the extension of a maxim or a definition with relentless disregard of consequences to "a dryly logical extreme." The approximate and relative become the definite and absolute. Landowners are not bound to regulate their conduct in contemplation of the presence of trespassers intruding upon private structures. Landowners are bound to regulate their conduct in contemplation of the presence of travelers upon the adjacent public ways. There are times when there is little trouble in marking off the field of exemption and immunity from that of liability and duty. Here structures and ways are so united and commingled, superimposed upon each other, that the fields are brought together. In such circumstances, there is little help in pursuing general maxims to ultimate conclusions. They have been framed *alio intuitu*. They must be reformulated and readapted to meet exceptional conditions. Rules appropriate to spheres which are conceived of as separate and distinct cannot both be enforced when the spheres become concentric. There must then be readjustment or collision. In one sense, and that a highly technical and artificial one, the diver at the end of the springboard is an intruder on the adjoining lands. In another sense, and one that realists will accept more readily, he is still on public waters in the exercise of public rights. The law must say whether it will subject him to the rule of the one field or of the other, of this sphere or of that. We think that considerations of analogy, of convenience, of policy, and of justice, exclude him from the field of the defendant's immunity and exemption, and place him in the field of liability and duty. . . .

The judgment of the Appellate Division and that of the Trial Term should be reversed, and a new trial granted, with costs to abide the event.

HOGAN, POUND, and CRANE, JJ., concur.

HISCOCK, C.J., and CHASE and McLAUGHLIN, JJ., dissent.

BENJAMIN N. CARDOZO, THE NATURE OF THE JUDICIAL PROCESS *

The final cause of law is the welfare of society. The rule that misses its aim cannot permanently justify its existence. "Ethical considerations can no more be excluded from the administration of justice which is the end and purpose of all civil laws than one can exclude the vital air from his room and live." Logic and history and custom have their place. We will shape the law to conform to them when we may; but only within bounds. The end which the law serves will dominate them all. There is an old legend that on one occasion God prayed, and his prayer was "Be it my will that my justice be ruled by my mercy." That is a prayer which we all need to utter at times when the demon of formalism tempts the intellect with the lure of scientific order. I do not mean, of course, that judges are commissioned to set aside existing rules at pleasure in favor of any other set of rules which they may hold to be expedient or wise. I mean that when they are called upon to say how far existing rules are to be extended or restricted, they must let the welfare of society fix the path, its direction and its distance. * * * So in this field, there may be a

* 66–67, 71–72 (1921). Reprinted by permission of Yale University Press from The Nature of the Judicial Process by Benjamin N. Cardozo. Copyright © 1921 by Yale University Press.

paramount public policy, one that will prevail over temporary inconvenience or occasional hardship, not lightly to sacrifice certainty and uniformity and order and coherence. All these elements must be considered. They are to be given such weight as sound judgment dictates. They are constituents of that social welfare which it is our business to discover. In a given instance we may find that they are constituents of preponderating value. In others, we may find that their value is subordinate. We must appraise them as best we can.

. . .

Social welfare is a broad term. I use it to cover many concepts more or less allied. It may mean what is commonly spoken of as public policy, the good of the collective body. In such cases, its demands are often those of mere expediency or prudence. It may mean on the other hand the social gain that is wrought by adherence to the standards of right conduct, which find expression in the *mores* of the community.

HARRY W. JONES, THE SOCIAL ENDS TO WHICH LAW IS MEANS *

When one has established, sufficiently and forcefully, that an existing rule of law is immoral, administratively unworkable or socially disadvantageous, he has done more than score a critical point; he has made it more likely than not that the immoral, unworkable or socially disadvantageous rule will be abolished, sooner or later, by legislative repeal or judicial overruling or emasculation. When you have read as many cases as I have in a probably misspent life, you will agree, I think, with what I make bold to call the Jones Hypothesis: the durability of a legal principle, its reliability as a source of guidance for the future, is determined far more by the principle's social utility, or lack of it, than by its verbal elegance or formal consistency with other legal precepts. And, mind you, this hypothesis applies in Contracts, Torts, Property and the like fully as much as in Constitutional Law. The only difference is that it is likely to take longer in the private law fields for the continuing process of reevaluation and overhaul to be accomplished.

... Law is not a form of art for art's sake; its ends-in-view are social, nothing more and nothing less than the establishment and maintenance of a social environment in which the quality of human life can be spirited, improving and unimpaired. Law serves these ends-in-view when—and to the extent that—its legislators, judges, practicing lawyers, and other decision-makers reach their judgments by way of a disinterested and informed evaluation of the probable consequences of their action, one way or the other, on the prevailing quality of human life in society....

. . .

* *An Invitation to Jurisprudence,* 74 Colum.L.Rev. 1023, 1024–26 (1974). Reprinted by permission.

A social environment would be intolerable without the existence of efficacious institutions for peace-keeping and dispute-settlement, but genuine "social tranquility" has further requirements and overtones. By almost anybody's definition, a good society is, among other things, a society in which creativity is unhobbled by constant apprehensions, diversity flourishes without group or class hostility, and inevitable social change is accepted not as something terrifying but as something to be planned for. We are brought, then, to three other of law's social ends-in-view: (1) the maintenance of a reasonable security of individual expectations, (2) the resolution of conflicting social interests, and (3) the channeling of social change. I am not suggesting for a moment that this is a complete tally of law's tasks in society.... Nonetheless, the three do go, as Contracts scholars used to say, "to the essence" of law in society and are items that must be taken into account in any serious attempt at evaluation of a questioned legal rule or legal institution.

CALVIN WOODARD, THOUGHTS ON THE INTERPLAY BETWEEN MORALITY AND LAW IN MODERN MODERN LEGAL THOUGHT *

A. *From Corrective to Distributive Justice*

A major difference between modern and pre-twentieth century law may be summarized, in Aristotelian terms, as follows: For generations, our law, like that of most societies, was used almost exclusively as a means of corrective justice, in the modern era, however, and especially from the 1930's down through the 1970's, it has been used, in addition, as the means by which society pursued various forms of distributive justice.

By "corrective justice," Aristotle meant making amends for wrongs arising out of private transactions (or what we would call tort and contract) and punishing criminal conduct. By "distributive justice" he meant establishing standards by which the goods of society are apportioned among and shared by its members. Law used in pursuit of corrective justice is silent with respect to the justice of existing patterns and standards of distribution; also it is largely reactive in form, responding to wrongs or alleged wrongs that have already occurred. Law used in pursuit of distributive justice is different, however, in that it may be anticipatory, being more concerned about establishing new values and relationships to prevail in the future.

Limiting the use of law to the pursuit of corrective justice is an attribute of a *laissez-faire* government: using law as a means of effectuating distributive justice is a characteristic, perhaps the most distinctive characteristic, of a welfare state. Of course each of the two forms of law, used in pursuit of different forms of justice, raise quite different types of moral issues.

* 64 Notre Dame L.Rev. 784, 799–801 (1989).

B. *The Relationship Between Corrective Justice–Law and Morality*

In nineteenth century America, the notion of corrective justice was hypostatized into a *laissez-faire* ideology that restricted the legitimate scope of governmental action to resolving private disputes, maintaining public order, and punishing criminal behavior. Paradoxically, however, this "hands off" ideology did not, as a matter of principle, deter the government from serving as a moral proctor.

Indeed the period during which *laissez-faire* was most dominant coincided to a remarkable degree with the Age of Victorian Morality. Innumerable nineteenth century reformers, legal and otherwise, dedicated themselves to bringing various aspects of life, including law, closer to morality. In keeping with the notion of corrective justice, they meant by "reform" the moral regeneration of "fallen" individuals or those at risk; and they had no scruples about enlisting law to help them accomplish that purpose. Thus, the great paradox of the nineteenth century: Though champions of *laissez-faire* governmental policy strictly limited the role of government to the pursuit of corrective justice, within that narrow range of activities, the government was given a virtually free hand to deal with immoral, criminal or wayward individuals or corrupting influences. Censorship and anti-smut crusades, as well as legal prohibition of the sale of alcohol and prostitution, were all among the great moral movements of a crusading age. Suspect groups of the poor were designated undeserving, and certain targeted persons assumed to be morally tainted, deserving few rights and less privacy. Moral proctors, like Inquisitors, do not normally worry about the niceties of procedure and privacy when hot on the trail of wickedness. Thus morality played a role in the *laissez-faire* world of corrective justice that would outrage civil libertarians of the twentieth century.

The same preoccupation with morality was infused more subtly in the Common Law itself, which was often used to pursue the aims of corrective justice with a vengeance. Thus, such staples as Contracts, Torts and Criminal Law were laced with moral overtones that legal scholars of a later time, especially during the period 1930–1970, have been at pains to remove. (For example, the jurisprudential critiques of "promise" as the key element of contract, of "fault" in tort, and of *mens rea* and the "right/wrong" (*M'Naghten*) rule in criminal law.)

As Dean James B. Ames of the Harvard Law School pointed out in 1900, the legal reformers during the nineteenth century had consciously inculcated moral concepts such as fault, intent and extenuating circumstances into both civil and criminal law. Law and morals had been drawn closer together so that legal accountability more accurately reflected moral culpability. But the triumphs of those reformers were in the context of corrective justice. As legal problems became more and more often seen as involving distributive justice, the morality of this system became subject to increasing criticism.

During the early years of the twentieth century, a powerful reaction and political protest, often vociferous, signaled the emergence of a new consensus that government should respond more positively to, and play a more active role in, dealing with social and economic problems. Implicit in those demands was the notion that the distribution of goods in our society had somehow become seriously unjust; and it was the responsibility of the Federal government to do more than pursue the ends of corrective justice. Specifically, acting through law, it should work to establish a new system of distributive justice.

During the New Deal era, advocates of the new ideology succeeded in significantly revamping the role of the Federal government in domestic affairs. The "night-watchman" state of the nineteenth century was transformed into a complex, multi-functional institution directly engaged in a wide range of activities, and providing a variety of social services previously left to private individuals or to other social institutions. Tax reform, including the Social Security Act, probably more than any other field of law, sought direct redistributions of economic wealth. But the goods of society Aristotle included in his discussion of distributive justice were not limited to money. And, in fact, much of the redistribution of goods in twentieth century America has involved non-economic goods such as the dignity and status of first-class (WASP) citizenship, better chances to become qualified to compete for more lucrative and prestigious careers, and access to the world of higher learning and the arts formerly restricted to a privileged few.

Innumerable Federal programs, now taken for granted, contributed to the twentieth century pursuit of distributive justice. The wealth of our society, ranging from public lands to government jobs, from access to public information to the private treasure troves of art on display in our museums and galleries, is in many subtle and not so subtle ways distributed differently today than it was a hundred years ago. And that redistribution was brought about through law, not bloodshed. That it is still not just in many respects does not diminish the value and effect of the change. Nor does it condone our brazen satisfaction with the glaring injustices that still abound.

HAROLD J. BERMAN, DANGERS OF DECLARING WHAT IS PUBLIC POLICY *

Almost all the nations of the West are threatened today by a cynicism about law, leading to a contempt for law, on the part of all classes of the population. The cities have become increasingly unsafe. The welfare system has almost broken down under unenforceable regulations. There is wholesale violation of the tax laws by the rich and the poor and those in between. There is hardly a profession that is not caught up in evasion of one or another form of governmental regulation.

* H. Berman, Law and Revolution: The   40–41 (1983).
Formation of the Western Legal Tradition

And the government itself, from bottom to top, is caught up in illegalities. But that is not the main point. The main point is that the only ones who seem to be conscience-stricken over this matter are those few whose crimes have been exposed.

Contempt for law and cynicism about law have been stimulated by the contemporary revolt against what is sometimes called legal formalism, which emphasizes the uniform application of general rules as the central element in legal reasoning and in the idea of justice. According to Roberto M. Unger, with the development of the welfare state, on the one hand, and of the corporate state, on the other, formalism is yielding to an emphasis on public policy both in legal reasoning and in the idea of justice. Policy-oriented legal reasoning, Unger writes, is characterized by emphasis upon broad standards of fairness and of social responsibility. He connects this shift in "post-liberal" Western legal thought with a change in beliefs concerning language. "Language is no longer credited with the fixity of categories and the transparent representation of the world that would make formalism plausible in legal reasoning or in ideas about justice," he writes. Thus described, the revolt against legal formalism seems both inevitable and benign. Yet what is to prevent discretionary justice from being an instrument of repression and even a pretext for barbarism and brutality, as it became in Nazi Germany? Unger argues that this is to be prevented by the development of a strong sense of community within the various groups that comprise a society. Unfortunately, however, the development of such group pluralism is itself frustrated by some of the same considerations that underlie the attack on legal formalism. Most communities of more than face-to-face size can hardly survive for long, much less interact with one another, without elaborate systems of rules, whether customary or enacted. To say this is not to deny that in the late nineteenth and early twentieth centuries, in many countries of the West, there was an excessive concern with logical consistency in the law, which still exists in some quarters; the reaction against it, however, loses its justification when it becomes an attack on rules per se, and on the Western tradition of legality which strikes a balance among rule, precedent, policy, and equity—all four.

The attack on any one of these four factors tends to diminish the others. In the name of antiformalism, "public policy" has come dangerously close to meaning the will of those who are currently in control: "social justice" and "substantive rationality" have become identified with pragmatism; "fairness" has lost its historical and philosophical roots and is blown about by every wind of fashionable doctrine. The language of law is viewed not only as necessarily complex, ambiguous, and rhetorical (which it is) but also wholly contingent, contemporary, and arbitrary (which it is not). These are harbingers not only of a "post-liberal" age but also of a "post-Western" age.

Cynicism about the law, and lawlessness, will not be overcome by adhering to a so-called realism which denies the autonomy, the integrity, and the ongoingness of our legal tradition. In the words of Edmund

Burke, those who do not look backward to their ancestry will not look forward to their posterity.

This certainly does not mean that the study of the past will save society. Society moves inevitably into the future. But it does so by walking backwards, so to speak, with its eyes on the past. Oliver Cromwell said, "Man never reaches so high an estate as when he knows not whither he is going." He understood the revolutionary significance of respect for tradition in a time of crisis.

NOTE

Professor Berman makes these comments several generations after Holmes, Pound and Cardozo trumpeted the virtue of deciding cases on the basis of public policy or social welfare. If these giants of American jurisprudence sounded a call against formalism, consider Berman's statement; "In the name of antiformalism, 'public policy' has become dangerously close to meaning the will of those who are currently in control ..." Consider also the enthusiastic endorsement of the activist Warren court and, to a limited extent, the Burger court, by academia and media commentators and their subsequent criticism of the Rehnquist majority of the mid-Nineties. What are they criticizing: the process or the product of judicial decision making? When formalism or conceptualism is abandoned is there a danger that the declaration of public policy will depend too much on the philosophical idiosyncracies of a given majority of a given court on a given issue at a given time? Does a constant balance of rule, precedent, policy and equity make for more stability or reckonability in the law? Is this good? Recall Roscoe Pound's aphorism, "The law must be stable, but it must not stand still."

In the early 20th Century, legal scholars condemned mechanical jurisprudence for its want of functional or pragmatic results. In the latter part of the Century, many legal scholars rebelled against what they deemed unbridled result-orientation; they argued that the trend detracted from predictability of and stability in the law. To what extent was *Hynes* result-oriented? Is reconciliation possible between the critics of mechanical jurisprudence and those of result-orientation? Is it desirable? Necessary?

———

RUPERT CROSS, *Precedent in English Law* 187–88 (2d ed. 1968):

So far as the United States is concerned, the twentieth-century case of Hynes v. New York Central Railway Co. is said to have been a welcome sign of the times because of the denunciation of "the jurisprudence of conceptions" by the New York Court of Appeals.

.   .   .

Another way of describing the vice against which Pound and Cardozo were protesting is to say that it is that of arguing on the following lines: "In the instant case the deceased was a trespasser. Previous cases show that no duty of care is owed to trespassers, therefore no duty of care was owed to the deceased although his trespass was incidental to the exercise of his rights as a bather in a public river in which capacity a duty of care was owed to him. A person cannot be in one legal category for the purpose of one branch of the law, e.g., that relating to the defendants' power to exclude trespassers, and in another category for the purpose of another branch of the law, e.g., that relating to the defendants' duty of care." This fallacy, if it is a fallacy, is one to which reasoning by analogy is prone because, if the instant case is compared first with previous cases concerning landowners' duties towards those exercising public rights, and next with those relating to landowners' duties to trespassers, the instant case must appear to bear a closer resemblance to cases of the second class than to those of the first. It is only when the consequences of the decision are considered that doubts about the wisdom of following cases of the second class are likely to arise. There would, for instance, be something quite unrealistic about a situation in which two bathers were struck by the same wire falling through the negligence of the occupier of land and one could recover because he was in the water at the time, while the other must fail because he was in the act of diving back into the water.

––––––

HERBERT MORRIS, Book Review: Dean Pound's Jurisprudence, 13 Stan.L.Rev. 185, 203–04 (1960) ***:

First, why does Dean Pound say that "there was usually no logical compulsion" [in cases decided by judges]? What types of cases does he have in mind in which there is in fact the logical compulsion to "take the starting point"? Must we not keep steadily before us a fundamental distinction between reasoning logically and regarding oneself as bound by one's duty as a judge? It is not logic that "binds" a judge to apply rules or to decide cases. It is his obligation as a judge to do so. He might fail in his duties as a judge without reasoning illogically. Next, Dean Pound holds that once we "take the starting point" we are logically compelled to reach a result. But it is not clear what is involved for Dean Pound in a judge's "taking a starting point" or in this "logically compelling a result."

Suppose a judge believes that a rule is clearly applicable to the facts of the case before him. Logic does not compel him to apply that rule. If he does not decide one way or the other he is an irresponsible judge, not illogical in his reasoning. If he should overrule a line of decisions, he is not illogical, though he may be, of course, unreasonable. It is not logic, but *stare decisis* that directs him and in such cases he may be disregarding that principle but not necessarily reasoning invalidly. The judge may agree with counsel that the rule is, for example, that two witnesses are required to the signing of the will; he may agree that there was only one witness to the signing of the will in the case before him, and he still need not be "logically compelled" to reach any result. It is always open to him to take any feature of the situation and treat it as a relevant difference. He may select any difference as relevant without being logically inconsistent. There is a difference between logical inconsistency, involving the holding of two contradictory views, and making unreasonable or absurd distinctions. This is why the expression "carrying concepts to their logical extreme" makes little sense. As far as logic is concerned a judge can stop anywhere. But suppose that he does not overrule nor does he distinguish, what role is then played by logic in the result reached? Judges may, indeed, set their opinions out in a form such that, given the rule and given an additional premise, the conclusion follows logically. But is this what Dean Pound means by "the starting point logically compelling a result"? The impression his language gives is that once a judge has selected a rule, he is compelled by logic to reach a certain conclusion, and that is not so. Logic does not compel that a valid conclusion be drawn, for logic does not tell people to do anything. A person who agreed that "all men are mortal and that Socrates is a man" would not be compelled by logic to do anything further. He can stop talking and he would not be inconsistent. But if he draws the conclusion that Socrates is immortal, then we may say that he is inconsistent. Neither "starting points" nor "logic" compels any decisions.

It is, then, still not clear from Dean Pound's presentation precisely what role is played by logic in mechanical jurisprudence. But there are other difficulties. If we characterize mechanical jurisprudence as a judge's selecting a rule or conception and deriving implications from it without considering the effects of so doing, the following question may remain: First, must the judge in fact believe that logic requires him to choose a certain rule or conception and derive certain implications? Or is it sufficient that in his written opinion he gives the impression that logic is directing the result? To be sure that we have an instance of mechanical jurisprudence, must we first interview a judge or have independent knowledge of the thought processes which led him to his result? When we charge some-one with mechanical jurisprudence are we objecting to the way he has written an opinion, setting forth his justification for a decision, or to the way we believe he has reached a particular result? Second, are judges who abide by *stare decisis,* and who apply rules without considering the social effects of so doing, guilty of mechanical jurisprudence? Third, suppose a judge concludes that justice in a particular case requires one kind of decision and the applicable rule another. Suppose, further, that he thinks it more important that a bad rule be applied and predictability furthered in the legal system than that a particu-lar case be decided on the equities. If he writes his opinion solely in conceptual terms, is he guilty of mechanical jurispru-dence? Fourth, suppose the judge believes the rule a desirable one but recognizes that in the case before him its application will not be in accord with the equities. Suppose he decides to apply the rule but does not mention in his opinion any consider-ations other than conceptual ones. Is this mechanical jurispru-dence?

We have all had occasion to object to mechanical jurispru-dence. We can pick out instances of it. What is rather more difficult to do is to pick out its essential characteristics so that we have a precise idea of what it is that we are objecting to.

. . .

Is the Morris criticism of Pound valid? Must not "Mechanical Jurisprudence" be considered in the light of Pound's overall approach to Jurisprudence? Especially in view of Pound's categorization of the three functions which may be involved in the decision of a case—finding the law (choice among competing legal precepts), interpretation of the pre-cept as chosen, application of the chosen precept as interpreted to the facts found by the fact finder. Is Pound not saying that if you follow the method of social welfare you should range broadly and choose the major premise which will lead to the desired result?

JEROME HALL, KELSEN'S PURE THEORY OF LAW *

Austin and Kelsen are usually regarded as the leaders of "legal positivism," but if their theories are compared in relation to their respective moral philosophies, it is evident that these legal philosophers should no longer be treated in that indiscriminate fashion. Kelsen rejects both natural law theory and utilitarianism. He has been called a "relativist," but what is prominent in his work are meta-ethical state-

* Reprinted from Foundations of Juris-prudence, 35–36 by Jerome Hall, copyright © 1973, by The Bobbs–Merrill Company Inc. Reprinted by permission. All rights reserved.

ments that represent the ethical subjectivism of the early logical positivists, the Vienna School, with which he was associated. For example (quite unlike Bentham and Austin), Kelsen states that ethical "questions cannot be answered by means of rational cognition. The decision of these questions is a judgment of value, determined by emotional factors, and is, therefore, subjective in character, valid only for the judging subject and therefore relative only.... [A] judgment of value ... [is always] determined by emotional factors.... Justice is an irrational ideal ... it is not subject to cognition." It is no accident, therefore, that unlike the utilitarians, Kelsen stands in uncompromising opposition to every one of the tenets of classical natural law. Far from being rationally justified by or grounded in facts and values (reality or utility) which validate them, "in the last instance, our feeling, our will, and not our reason ... decides...."

Kelsen's criticism of Austin (apart from that concerning utilitarian ethics) also reveals the gap between their legal philosophies. Kelsen states that "Austin ... pays no attention to the distinction between 'is' and 'ought' that is the basis of the concept of the norm"; indeed, Austin "does not employ ... the central concept of jurisprudence, the norm." For Kelsen, norms are pure ideas which must not be confused with the psychological process of thinking those ideas; norms are meanings formed and apprehended by cognition. What Kelsen is getting at is suggested by his criticism that, for Austin, laws are commands in a psychological sense, *i.e.,* they are expressions of the will of actual persons: "... commands, it is manifest, proceed not from abstractions, but from living and rational beings." Here, too, the Imperative Theory is fallacious, states Kelsen, because a command exists only so long as the will of the commander exists. But all the legislators may be dead and, in any case, a statute does not represent the actual will of the entire legislature since some of the legislators opposed it. Therefore "law cannot be the psychological will of the lawmakers...." It consists, instead, of norms "stating that an individual ought to behave in a certain way ...," and the subject matter of jurisprudence is therefore a system of ideas expressed as "hypothetical judgments," i.e., upon the commission of a delict, a sanction must be imposed.

NOTE

The American Law Institute publishes the various "Restatements of the Law". These works appear to originate as the joint work product of a reporter, who is a nationally-recognized professor of law, and the Council of ALI, which is a select group of distinguished professors, judges and attorneys. A tentative draft is then submitted to the general assembly of the ALI for final approval, rejection or amendment. Is Restatement "law" something that "is" or "ought to be" or both?

———

BENJAMIN N. CARDOZO, THE NATURE OF THE JUDICIAL PROCESS *

... I am not concerned to vindicate the accuracy of the nomenclature by which the dictates of reason and conscience which the judge is under a duty to obey, are given the name of law before he has embodied them in a judgment and set the *imprimatur* of the law upon them. I shall not be troubled if we say with Austin and Holland and Gray and many others that till then they are moral precepts, and nothing more. Such verbal disputations do not greatly interest me. What really matters is this, that the judge is under a duty, within the limits of his power of innovation, to maintain a relation between law and morals, between the precepts of jurisprudence and those of reason and good conscience. I suppose it is true in a certain sense that this duty was never doubted. One feels at times, however, that it was obscured by the analytical jurists, who, in stressing verbal niceties of definition, made a corresponding sacrifice of emphasis upon the deeper and finer realities of ends and aims and functions. The constant insistence that morality and justice are not law, has tended to breed distrust and contempt of law as something to which morality and justice are not merely alien, but hostile. The new development of "naturrecht" may be pardoned infelicities of phrase, if it introduces us to new felicities of methods and ideals. Not for us the barren logomachy that dwells upon the contrasts between law and justice, and forgets their deeper harmonies. For us rather the trumpet call of the French "code civil": "Le juge, qui refusera de juger, sous prétexte du silence, de l'obscurité ou de l'insuffisance de la loi, pourra être poursuivi comme coupable de déni de justice." [53] "It is the function of our courts," says an acute critic "to keep the doctrines up to date with the *mores* by continual restatement and by giving them a continually new content. This is judicial legislation, and the judge legislates at his peril. Nevertheless, it is the necessity and duty of such legislation that gives to judicial office its highest honor; and no brave and honest judge shirks the duty or fears the peril."

NOTE

Compare Holmes in *The Path of the Law, ante.* "For my own part, I often doubt whether it would not be a gain if every word of moral significance could be banished from the law altogether, and other words adopted which should convey legal ideas uncolored by anything outside the law", *with* Cardozo, "What really matters is this, that the judge is under a duty, within the limits of his power of innovation, to maintain a relation between law and morals between the precepts of jurisprudence and those of reason and good conscience."

53. "The judge who shall refuse to give judgment under pretext of the silence, of the obscurity, or of the inadequacy of the law, shall be subject to prosecution as guilty of a denial of justice."

Are Holmes, Cardozo, Austin and Gray proceeding from a common definition of "law"? Read Roscoe Pound's following article for some help.

———

ROSCOE POUND, THE THEORY OF JUDICIAL DECISION*

Bentham says that "law" is a collective term which can mean no more nor less than "the sum total of a number of individual laws taken together," and that "a law" is a command or the revocation of a command. But this is too simple for the actual phenomena for which we must frame our theory. In truth no fewer than three quite distinct things are included in the idea of law, even limited as the analytical jurists have limited it, namely to the apparatus by which tribunals actually decide controversies in modern societies. Sometimes the jurist has one of these before his mind, sometimes some two of them, sometimes all three. Much of the controversy as to the nature of law turns on which one of these is to be taken as the type and as standing for the whole. These three elements that make up the whole of what we call law are: (1) a number of legal precepts more or less defined, the element to which Bentham referred when he said that law was an aggregate of laws; (2) a body of traditional ideas as to how legal precepts should be interpreted and applied and causes decided, and a traditional technique of developing and applying legal precepts whereby these precepts are eked out, extended, restricted, and adapted to the exigencies of administration of justice; (3) a body of philosophical, political, and ethical ideas as to the end of law, and as to what legal precepts should be in view thereof, held consciously or subconsciously, with reference to which legal precepts and the traditional ideas of application and decision and the traditional technique are continually reshaped and given new content or new application.

———

FELIX S. COHEN, TRANSCENDENTAL NONSENSE AND THE FUNCTIONAL APPROACH **

That something is radically wrong with our traditional legal thought-ways has long been recognized. Holmes, Gray, Pound, Brooks Adams, M.R. Cohen, T.R. Powell, Cook, Oliphant, Moore, Radin, Llewellyn, Yntema, Frank, and other leaders of modern legal thought in America, are in fundamental agreement in their disrespect for "mechanical jurisprudence," for legal magic and word-jugglery. But mutual agreement is less apparent when we come to the question of what to do:

* 36 Harv.L.Rev. 641, 644–645 (1923) Copyright © by The Harvard Law Review Association. Reprinted by permission.

** 35 Colum.L.Rev. 809, 821–24 (1935). Reprinted by permission.

How are we going to get out of this tangle? How are we going to substitute a realistic, rational, scientific account of legal happenings for the classical theological jurisprudence of concepts?

Fundamentally there are only two significant questions in the field of law. One is, "How do courts actually decide cases of a given kind?" The other is, "How ought they to decide cases of a given kind?" Unless a legal "problem" can be subsumed under one of these forms, it is not a meaningful question and any answer to it must be nonsense.

ROSCOE POUND, THE THEORY OF JUDICIAL DECISION *

Let us put some examples of the second element that goes to make up the law[, *viz.*, a body of traditional ideas as to how legal precepts should be interpreted and applied and causes decided, and a traditional technique of developing and applying legal precepts]. In our legal system we have a good example in the doctrine as to the force of judicial decisions as affecting judicial decision of subsequent cases. It is almost impossible for the common-law lawyer and the civilian to understand each other in this connection. In fact our practice and the practice of the Roman-law world are not so far apart as legal theory makes them seem to be. We by no means attach as much force to a single decision as we purport to do in theory. Even the House of Lords, which purports never to overrule its decisions, on occasion deals with them so astutely as to deprive them of practical efficacy as a form of law.*** On the other hand, in Continental Europe a judicial decision tends to become the starting point of a settled course of decision, which in some countries is recognized as customary law having the force of a form of law, and in other countries is acquiring that effect in practice.**** But if the results are coming in their broader features to be much alike, the modes of thought are wholly unlike, and these modes of thought have decisive effect upon the administration of justice.

Another example may be seen in the attitude of legal systems toward specific and substituted redress. With us, substituted redress is the normal type; specific redress is exceptional and reserved for cases for which the former is not adequate. To the civilian, specific redress is the normal type; substituted redress is to be used only in cases in which specific redress is not practicable or would operate inequitably. Again,

* 36 Harv.L.Rev. 641, 646–48, 651–52, 654, 657–58 (1923). Copyright © 1923 by The Harvard Law Review Association. Reprinted by permission.

*** [Ed.: The House of Lords did an about face in 1966, announcing that thenceforth it would overrule precedents "when it appears right to do so."]

**** *But see* Von Mehren, post, p. ___ "In the United States, unity of judicial action within a given jurisdiction is ensured by the rule that a court has no right to deviate from precedents established by its hierarchical superior. Quite the contrary rule is found in France, and to a lesser degree in Germany. The French rule is still today that a previous decision, even by a hierarchically superior court, is never binding. Historically, the French rule is explained, at least in part, by a desire to prevent any systematic, judicial formulation and development of policy."

to us these two types of remedy are so distinct that we think of them commonly as calling for distinct types of proceeding. But the civilian conceives of the proceeding in terms of the right asserted, not of the remedy sought, and so thinks only of what is the practical means of giving effect to that right. In other words, we think procedurally in terms of the remedy; the civilian thinks in terms of the asserted right. . . .

NOTE

HARLAN F. STONE, *The Common Law in the United States,* 50 Harv.L.Rev. 4, 20 (1936): "I shall state succinctly what I think is the resulting tendency of our legal thinking. We are coming to realize more completely that law is not an end, but a means to an end—the adequate control and protection of those interests, social and economic, which are the special concern of government and hence of law; that that end is to be attained through the reasonable accommodation of law to changing economic and social needs, weighing them against the need of continuity of our legal system and the earlier experience out of which its precedents have grown; that within the limits lying between the command of statutes on the one hand and the restraints of precedents and doctrines, by common consent regarded as binding, on the other, the judge has liberty of choice of the rule which he applies, and that his choice will rightly depend upon the relative weights of the social and economic advantages which will finally turn the scales of judgment in favor of one rule rather than another. Within this area he performs essentially the function of the legislator, and in a real sense makes law."

* * *

How should present American jurisprudence be described?

How important a role does substituted redress play in current American jurisprudence? Is prison reform accomplished by making state prison guards answerable in money damages for violations of the Civil Rights Act, 42 U.S.C.A. § 1983? What percentage of the American population is individually judgment proof? Should this make any difference in evaluating ideas of substituted redress and specific redress?

Has there been a deleterious effect of the broadened use of substituted redress in medical malpractice cases? In malpractice claims against lawyers? Are there reasonable alternatives to substituted redress? Where specific redress is impossible or impractical, and where there are deleterious effects to substituted redress, must there be any redress? Should there? Why? *Cf.* Bell v. Hood, 327 U.S. 678, 684 (1946): "federal courts may use any available remedy to make good the wrong done."

Specific redress refers to injunctive or declaratory relief; substituted redress, compensatory or punitive monetary damages.

ALLAN C. HUTCHINSON AND PATRICK J. MONAHAN, LAW, POLITICS, AND THE CRITICAL LEGAL SCHOLARS *

The Critical Legal Studies (CLS) movement is mounting a full frontal assault on the edifice of modern jurisprudence. As in the celebrated dispute between Galileo and the Italian establishment, it is not merely the truth of nature that is at stake, but the nature of truth itself. The Critical scholars seek to reformulate the ground rules, to revise the criteria for valid legal theory. As is the case with many modern philosophers and sociologists, they are attempting to provide a new touchstone for distinguishing good knowledge from bad. Although traditional scholars purport to be engaged in "a continuing dialogue with reality," the Critical scholars reject the structure of that dialogue and the nature of that reality. Within the legal world, the confrontation between this "radical" movement and the traditional establishment is developing into a full-blown battle—always intense and heated, occasionally unsightly and vicious—over the establishment and enforcement of the entrenched clauses of the constitution of the republic of legal knowledge.

The CLS movement was formally founded in 1977 by a small group of scholars who had become dissatisfied with the intellectual mood and direction of the Law and Society Association. These scholars took the view that the Association had become too closely identified with the "empirico-behaviorist" wing of social science and that the road to jurisprudential enlightenment lay down a less data-oriented, more theoretical path. The lifeblood of the CLS movement was to be philosophy, not science. From this splinter group, the Movement has mushroomed.
* * *

The vast majority of American jurisprudential scholarship has, at bottom, been devoted to describing and justifying the role of the judiciary within a liberal democracy. America is a highly litigious society; as such, it places great confidence in the judiciary's ability to resolve its disputes. This state of affairs is problematic since the judiciary is, by and large, an unelected and unaccountable institution lacking any basic democratic mandate. The traditional response to this dilemma has been to posit adjudication as an objective and rationally-bounded process, in stark contrast to the nonrational, often arbitrary, character of political decisionmaking. By divorcing adjudication from the sphere of subjective, value-laden decisionmaking, this model makes judicial power seem less of an infringement on democratic values. Although many are critical of the present performance of the judiciary, most legal commentators (and lay people) cling to the belief that adjudication, suitably reformed and purified, can be carried out in conformity with the dictates

* A. Hutchinson and P. Monahan, *Law Politics, and the Critical Legal Scholars: The Unfolding Drama of American Legal*   *Thought,* 36 Stan.L.Rev. 199 (1984). Reprinted by permission.

of liberal democracy. There remains a very real commitment to the central and enduring assumption that a just compromise of competing interests can be effected through a resort to reason,[12] and that rational discourse can transcend the rhetoric of vulgar political debate.

Since 1800, America has experienced at least three different phases of legal thought, each of which has responded in some way to this need to regard adjudication as a rational process. Up to the mid-nineteenth century, there was wide acceptance of a broadly instrumental approach to law; judges decided cases by overt reference to policy considerations. Around 1860, there began a discernible, if tentative, shift away from this broad conception of the legal process. By the 1890's, this transformation was completed. The legal community had fallen victim to the classical contagion: Judges claimed to resolve disputes by the rigorous application of rules alone. This strain of legal thought—commonly known as conceptualism—flourished for a couple of decades or so, reaching its zenith by the mid–1920's. Its subsequent decline was swift and dramatic. * * *

Conceptualism gave way to Legal Realism, which flourished in several of the Eastern law schools in the 1920's and 30's. The Realists' critique of the legal process was profound and disturbing. The Realists demonstrated that the appeal of an objective, impartial system of legal thought was illusory: A set of precepts applied "objectively" to a given set of facts could result in a variety of equally plausible outcomes. The power of formal rationality was suspect; precedent could be manipulated to justify any decision at all. For instance, Fred Rodell, writing of the formalistic tendency to regard the Constitution as a source of explicit commands capable of direct implementation by a professional judiciary, opined that "the alleged logic of constitutional law is equally amorphous, equally unconvincing, equally silly whether the decisions the court is handing down are 'bad,' 'progressive' or 'reactionary,' 'liberal' or 'unliberal.' "

However, the thrust of Realist scholarship was essentially negative and iconoclastic; it lacked any unifying thread or positive political

---

12. The precise nature of this "reason" remains obscure. Kant argued that reason is simply a power of constructing norms; it is not "an arsenal of finished theoretical cognitions," but a dynamic for arriving at such ethical norms. See E. Pollack, Jurisprudence: Principles and Applications 47–48 (1979). However, the CLSers argue that rational discourse does not exist in a pure form, but inevitably embodies a deep structure of values.

Indeed, throughout the history of Western legal theory and practice, rationality has been equated with good, and irrationality and nonrationality with bad. See J. Rawls, A Theory of Justice 142–45 (1971); J.C. Smith & D. Weisstub, The Western Idea of Law (1981). Beginning with the Greco–Roman era, rationality has been seen

as the universal solvent of social conflict. See Berman, *The Origins of Western Legal Science,* 90 Harv.L.Rev. 894 (1977). Accordingly, law has always been portrayed and accepted as a rational structure and legal reasoning viewed as a rational process. This faith in the rational character of law has pervaded traditional Anglo–American legal thought. See, e.g., Galligan, Judicial Review and the Textbook Writers, 2 Oxford J. Legal Stud. 257, 271 (1982).

In this way, the dilemma of democratic decisionmaking is resolved; the law-making and law-applying functions are conveniently separated. Such an arrangement satisfies both the democratic demand for consensus, via the political process, and for rationality, via the legal process.

program. Thus, while the Realists accepted the indeterminacy of legal reasoning, they remained firmly committed to liberalism. The Realist response to the dismantling of the barrier between law and politics was a distrust of the authority of the judiciary and an attempt to augment the power of "expert" state agencies. The Realists were ideologically and practically wedded to the New Deal. Their underlying assumption could only have been that issues of public policy merely raised technical questions of the best means to achieve shared ends—questions that were amenable to the expertise of state staffers. As Felix Cohen suggested, "[l]aw reform must become rational and scientific." [22] It is possible, therefore, to detect in the Realist platform of the 1930's the seeds of the "consensus" and "end of ideology" theory of the 1950's.[23] Ironically, that generation of legal theorists insisted that a separation of law and morality was necessary if the judicial role were to be legitimated within a democracy. Thus, the Realist revolution was in fact nothing more than a palace revolution; it was an important, but simply evolutionary, phase in American legal thought.

The challenge for contemporary jurists has been to propose a theory of judicial decisionmaking that would satisfactorily resolve legal disputes, while displacing the Realist view that sound adjudication is a product of psychological maturity. The juristic response has been to acknowledge that law does not operate independently of morality. Yet, on the other hand, the judge is not viewed as simply "roam[ing] at will and impos[ing] upon the parties before him whatever decision seem[s] to him best to resolve their conflict." [26] Contemporary scholars have sought a theory of adjudication that would prescribe a structured judicial posture towards political morality. They have acknowledged an intimate and crucial relationship between law and morality: "[L]aw is a moral science and judges decide as moral agents." [27] Yet, mindful of the cogency of the Realist critique, scholars like Ronald Dworkin and Richard Posner have avoided the more obvious shortcomings of the conceptualist era and have instead attempted to uncover the morality that runs deep within the common law.[28]

22. Cohen, *Transcendental Nonsense and the Financial Approach*, 35 Colum.L.Rev. 809 (1935).

23. According to this jurisprudential theory, valid judicial decisionmaking proceeded on the basis of "neutral principles" that commanded widespread acceptance. See, e.g., Wechsler, *Toward Neutral Principles of Constitutional Law*, 73 Harv.L.Rev. 1 (1959).

26. Ackerman, Law and the Modern Mind, Daedalus, Winter 1974, at 123.

27. Fried, The Laws of Change: The Cunning of Reason in Moral and Legal History, 9 J.Legal Stud. 335, 336 (1980).

28. See R. Dworkin, Taking Rights Seriously (1977); R. Posner, Economic Analysis of Law (2d ed. 1977); R. Posner, The Economics of Justice (1981). In his most re-

cent contribution, Dworkin seems to leave himself open to the interpretation that objectivity exists only in the mind of the judge and not in the legal materials:

[A] judge cannot plausibly discover, in a long and unbroken string of prior judicial decisions in favor of the manufacturers of defective products, any principle establishing strong consumers' rights. For that discovery would not show the history of judicial practice in a better light; on the contrary it would show it as the history of cynicism and inconsistency, perhaps of incoherence. A naturalist judge must show the facts of history in the best light he can, and this means that he must not show that history as unprincipled chaos.

Dworkin, *"Natural" Law Revisited*, 34 U.Fla.L.Rev. 165, 169 (1982).

Like traditional jurists, the Critical scholars are obsessed with the judicial function and its alleged central importance for an understanding of law in society. Yet, while they share this infatuation, they adopt a radically different view of the judicial process: All the Critical scholars unite in denying the rational determinacy of legal reasoning. Their basic credo is that no distinctive mode of legal reasoning exists to be contrasted with political dialogue. Law is simply politics dressed in different garb; it neither operates in a historical vacuum nor does it exist independently of ideological struggles in society. Legal doctrine not only does not, but also cannot, generate determinant results in concrete cases. Law is not so much a rational enterprise as a vast exercise in rationalization. Legal doctrine can be manipulated to justify an almost infinite spectrum of possible outcomes. Moreover, a plausible argument can be made that any such outcome has been derived from the dominant legal conceptions. Legal doctrine is nothing more than a sophisticated vocabulary and repertoire of manipulative techniques for categorizing, describing, organizing, and comparing; it is not a methodology for reaching substantive outcomes. As psychiatrists create "a monologue of reason about madness,"[33] so, the CLSers claim, do lawyers establish a fake rationalistic discourse out of the chaos of political and social life.

The CLS critique should not be understood as simply an assault upon formalism—the notion that disputes can be resolved by the neutral application of objective rules; this naive faith in the dispositive power of rules is essentially moribund today. Indeed, contemporary legal thought is vigorously committed to a rejection of this discredited model of legal reasoning; "[b]ounded objectivity is the only kind of objectivity to which the law ... ever aspires and the only one about which we care."[36] Rather, the difference between Critical and mainstream legal thought is that, although the latter rejects formalism, it persists in the view that some viable distinction can be drawn between legal reasoning and vulgar political debate. CLSers, on the other hand, refuse to hedge on the indeterminacy of the legal order. They view the attempt to tread some middle path as a desperate, face-saving effort to conceal the irremediable crisis within the legal process and the breakdown of the social order.

Mainstream legal thought stakes its claim to this middle ground with the use of three major approaches. Some writers appeal to conventional morality.[38] They contend that, although American society is dynamic and pluralistic, different values interact and gel to form a coherent body of norms. The task of the judge is to ascertain and apply this societal consensus. Another group of writers seeks to identify and rely on a set of fundamental rights that are purported to exist indepen-

33. M. Foucault, Madness and Civilization at x (1967), quoted in Levinson, Law, 35 AM.Q. 191, 203 (1983).

36. Fiss, *Objectivity and Interpretation,* 34 Stan.L.Rev. 739, 745 (1982).

38. See, e.g., Wellington, Common Law Rules and Constitutional Double Standards: Some Notes on Adjudication, 83 Yale L.J. 221 (1973); see also G. Calabresi, A Common Law for the Age of Statutes (1982).

dently of conventional morality and to inhere within a liberal society.[39] Finally, a third approach claims that underlying the legal rhetoric of the courts is an economic thread that neatly ties together and justifies the seemingly illogical jumble of legal doctrine.[40] According to this school of thought, the criterion of allocative efficiency not only accounts for the development of the law, but also provides a neutral standard by which to evaluate judicial performance. Each of these three attempts to colonize and defend a middle ground claims that it alone has the answer to the democratic dilemma; each has a theory purportedly containing a defensible, ordered, and compelling agenda for the realization of liberal democracy.

The central thrust of the Critical critique is that all such efforts to reconstruct American legal thought in the wake of the Realists' challenge are doomed to failure, and that they simply offer more cogent evidence of the bankruptcy of mainstream legal thought. As Professor Schlegel puts it, "[L]egal analysis that gets relevant by gesturing outside law toward a pseudo-consensus morality or the technical abstraction of efficiency has already lost its own battle for autonomy...."[41] For the Critical scholars, no objectively correct results exist, regardless of whether presented in terms of legal doctrine or policy analysis, and no matter how skilled the advocate or judge is. Choosing between values is inescapable.

Furthermore, the Critical scholars see a ubiquitous contradiction between individual autonomy and communal force, between freedom and security. Although relations with others are necessary to achieve and protect real freedom, the creation of a communal entity restricts and threatens that freedom. Here is Duncan Kennedy's description of that "fundamental contradiction":

> [I]ndividual freedom is at the same time dependent on and incompatible with the communal coercive action that is necessary to achieve it. Others (family, friends, bureaucrats, cultural figures, the state) are necessary if we are to become persons at all—they provide us the stuff of our selves and protect us in crucial ways against destruction....

> But at the same time that it forms and protects us, the universe of others ... threatens us with annihilation and urges upon us forms of fusion that are quite plainly bad rather than good....

> Only collective force seems capable of destroying the attitudes and institutions that collective force has itself imposed.

---

39. See, e.g., L. Tribe, American Constitutional Law (1978); Karst, The Freedom of Intimate Association, 89 Yale L.J. 624 (1980). Ronald Dworkin's Taking Rights Seriously combines characteristics of both consensus and fundamental rights theory. See Mensch, The History of Mainstream Legal Thought, in The Politics of Law: A Progressive Critique 18 (D. Kairys ed. 1982).

40. See, e.g., R. Posner, The Economic Analysis of Law, supra note 28.

41. Schlegel, *Introduction*, 28 Buffalo L.Rev. 203 (1979).

Coercion of the individual by the group appears to be inextricably bound up with the liberation of that same individual....

Even this understates the difficulty. It is not just that the world of others is intractable. The very structures against which we rebel are necessary within us as well as outside of us. We are implicated in what we would transform, and it in us.[42]

Liberalism [43] and contemporary legal thought persist in treating this contradiction as a mere conflict of competing individual and communal interests which can be rationally compromised or mediated.[44] Moreover, they insist that the resulting solution is possessed of some objective moral force. Thus, contemporary legal theorists are obliged to argue that present societal arrangements are not only rational and just, but are also necessary and natural. This phenomenon leads Critical scholars to observe that contemporary legal thought, in all its different guises, reproduces rather than resolves the basic contradiction. In constructing elaborate schemes of legal rights and entitlements which are intended to permit individuals to interact with others without being obliterated by them, mainstream legal theorists simply justify the prevailing conditions of social life and erect formidable barriers to social change. According to the CLSers, liberals may believe that these contradictory values have been successfully accommodated, but, in reality, liberal society is riddled by domination and hierarchy. Class and managerial elites set the terms upon which others are to lead their lives.

The Critical scholars argue that the existence of hierarchy and contradiction in liberal society is masked by the ideal of the rule of law. Under this ideal, outcomes are said to be the product of impersonal, neutral methods of choice, rather than the imposed preferences of an illegitimate hierarchy. Moreover, the rule of law is presented as the only buttress against a descent into an anarchical world in which all moral claims would be equally subjective and therefore equally devoid of authority. By obscuring the value choices inherent in the application of rules, the liberal model of adjudication makes it possible to believe that existing social hierarchies are not just the result of interrupted fighting. In the process, a world of deals begins to be transformed into a world of rights.

As a simple illustration of CLS-style analysis, consider the Critical interpretation of the development of the law of products liability.[46]

---

42. Kennedy, *The Structure of Blackstone's Commentaries,* 28 Buffalo L.Rev. 205, 211–12 (1979).

43. The Critical scholars indiscriminately use the term "liberalism" to refer to any ideas outside the broad range of Marxism and Critical scholarship. For example, CLSers would characterize Rawls, Nozick, Dworkin, and Posner all as liberals.

44. It should be noted that this alleged error has the finest possible pedigree. See Plato, The Republic (I.A. Richards ed. 1966).

46. There has been a fairly recent avalanche of legal literature on the products liability issue. Beginning with the seminal opinion of Justice Traynor in Escola v. Coca Cola Bottling Co., 24 Cal.2d 453, 150 P.2d 436 (1944), there has been a definite trend from negligence to strict liability. See generally S. Waddams, Products Liability (2d ed. 1980); Prosser, *The Fall of the Citadel (Strict Liability to the Consumer),* 50 Minn. L.Rev. 791 (1966). In recent years, however, an intense debate has waged over the respective merits of negligence and strict

Although mainstream legal thought claims that a neutral legal calculus can generate a valid doctrine of products liability, CLSers argue that products liability law and theory is a replay of the hopelessness of the liberal enterprise in a microcosm; it is simply the basic contradiction writ small. The playing out of this small scene in the whole legal drama neatly serves to underline the continuity of legal analysis with ideological conflict. Products liability law chooses from a broad variety of options, the most extreme possibilities being no liability for product manufacturers except under contractual relationships, and absolute liability for all injuries caused by their products.[48] These extreme options reproduce the basic contradiction between individualism represented by the absence of liability, and community, represented by absolute liability. Insofar as liberal legal thought is premised on the realizable reconciliation of the competing interests of community and autonomy, opting for either extreme would be to negate its very raison d'etre. Yet neither legal logic nor policy analysis can provide any objective guidance as to where to locate liability on this spectrum. Under a consensus approach, any solution, by definition, merely reflects prevailing political preferences, which are arbitrary and non-rational. Moreover, conventional morality is such a manipulable concept that it can be used to support almost any position. The fundamental rights theorists rely on circular arguments. By insisting that human values are ultimately subjective, they concede that rights are the product of choice rather than its determinants. Finally, any resort to allocative efficiency is meaningful only within a given scheme of distribution. The determination of the most efficient solution to a problem cannot be divorced from the existing distribution of legal entitlements. Hence, allocative efficiency loses all claims to a supra- historical and objective legitimacy.

Accordingly, every doctrinal dispute is reducible to the contradictory claims of communal security and individual freedom. Any particular resolution of that conflict is simply an arbitrary choice. Through a series of historical and contemporary studies, the CLSers have sought to demonstrate that the legal process at large and its discrete doctrinal components, such as contract, tort, constitutional law, labor, criminal law, and the like, are fundamentally indeterminate and manipulable. In the blunt words of Duncan Kennedy:

> Teachers convince students that legal reasoning exists, and
> is different from policy analysis, by bullying them into accepting
> as valid in particular cases arguments about legal correctness

---

liability as appropriate bases of liability. See, e.g., Calabresi & Hirschoff, Toward a Test for Strict Liability Torts, 81 Yale L.J. 1055 (1972); Epstein, A Theory of Strict Liability, 2 J.Legal Stud. 151 (1973); Fletcher, *Fairness and Utility in Tort Theory*, 85 Harv.L.Rev. 537 (1972); Posner, Strict Liability. A Comment, 2 J.Legal Stud. 205 (1973). For an extensive survey of the different doctrinal and jurisprudential perspectives, see Hubbard, *Efficiency,*

Expectation, and Justice: A Jurisprudential Analysis of the Concept of Unreasonably Dangerous Product Defect, 28 S.C.L.Rev. 587 (1977).

48. It is unclear why the Critical scholars think absolute liability represents the value of community. A scheme of no-fault, comprehensive liability insurance would appear to be equally consistent with communal values.

that are circular, question-begging, incoherent, or so vague as to be meaningless.

Teachers teach nonsense when they persuade students that legal reasoning is distinct, as a method for reaching correct results, from ethical and political discourse in general.... Put another way, everything taught, except the formal rules themselves and the argumentative techniques for manipulating them, is policy and nothing more....

Legal thought can generate equally plausible ... justifications for almost any result.[56]

This rigorous commitment to exposing the indeterminacy of the legal order and the political quality of adjudication is not exclusive to the CLSers. There are certain writers within the mainstream tradition, albeit on its fringes, who also refuse to hedge on the law's indeterminacy. For instance, the late Arthur Leff viewed the legal order as nothing more than a chronological sequence of cases that represent particular solutions to problems arising at particular points in time; to Leff, law was an accumulation of ad hoc compromises. His basic message was that "the path of law leads not to the revelation of truth but to the progressive discovery of infinite complexity." [59] No mode of analysis or explanation has a stronger claim to acceptance than any other.

Yet, this final claim suggests a genuine difference between theorists such as Leff and the Critical scholars. The latter maintain that their work is contoured, colored, and conditioned by the belief that law is subordinate to social theory. According to the Critical scholars, there can be no fruitful legal theory without a social theory, and mainstream legal thought, even in its most enlightened form, has never possessed a social theory. Both the CLSers and neo-Realists, like Leff, tend toward a doctrinal nihilism. But the CLSers, unlike Leff, are not political nihilists; they passionately believe that some meaningful political theory can be created and defended. Legal thought must be both more theoretical and more sociologically concrete. It must relate theory to practice and expose the dysfunction between reason and reality.

NOTE

The Critical Legal Studies movement contends that mainstream legal thinking is not the objective reasoning process it appears to be. The argument is that value judgments are endemic to the reasoning process, and thus that there is no neutral ratiocination, only interest-oriented rationalization. Does anyone seriously disagree with the observation that no objectively perfect results exist in the real world of adjudication? Does it follow that there has been a "bankruptcy of mainstream legal thought"? And is there "objectively correct" reasoning to reach this conclusion?

56. Kennedy, Legal Education as Training for Hierarchy, in The Politics of Law, supra, at 40, 46–48.

59. Gilmore, For Arthur Leff, 91 Yale L.J. 217, 218 (1981).

Consider again the following excerpt from Law, Politics and the Critical Legal Scholars, ante:

> All the critical scholars unite in denying the rational determinacy of legal reasoning. Their basic credo is that no distinctive mode of legal reasoning exists to be contrasted with political dialogue. Law is simply politics dressed in different garb; it neither operates in a historical vacuum nor does it exist independently of ideological struggles in society. Legal doctrine not only does not, but it cannot, generate determinant results in concrete cases. Law is not so much a rational enterprise as a vast exercise in rationalization. Legal doctrine can be manipulated to justify an almost infinite spectrum of possible outcomes.

The CLS critique recognizes that in most litigation there can be two sides, with both sides more or less ably presented by competent counsel. It also recognizes that a value judgment *always* inheres in the judicial process, in (a) finding the law (whether choosing between rival principles, deciding if past cases create a legal principle by inductive generalization, or deciding if the resemblances and differences proffered in a given case constitute a proper analogy); (b) interpreting the precepts as found; or (c) applying the found and interpreted precept to facts found by the fact finder.

As the CLS argument demonstrates, not everything in the law is controlled unerringly by canons of logic. Yet if legal doctrine does not "identify, aid or determine the nature of something or fix, determine or condition an outcome or issue," where are we to turn to find a beginning point for legal reasoning? What, for example, is the beginning point of legal reasoning in the common law and civil law traditions? While selecting the "major premise" is indisputably a political decision in judicial reasoning, a principled selection must nonetheless be made if our system is to function. To what principles of judicial decision making would critics of the current system have us turn? Consider the following excerpt from Mary Ann Glendon, A Nation Under Lawyers 214 (1994):

> Many commentators, including several critical scholars themselves, see the crits as the direct descendants of the Realists. It is a big step, however, from observing, as Holmes and Llewellyn did, that there are certain leeways inherent in fact finding and rule application to asserting that there is no such thing as a fact and that all rules are radically indeterminate and manipulable. It is another major leap from being realistic about the difficulties of fair and impartial decision making to a condemnation of the entire legal system as fatally corrupted by racism, sexism, and exploitation. And there is a world of difference between the lawyerly reformism of the New Dealers and the view that law is nothing more than concentrated politics—between Felix Frankfurter and the Frankfurt School. Holmes, that archdebunker, enjoyed trashing legal traditions and conventional

pieties as much as any modern crit. But he was aware that it was a high-stakes game. "Experimenting in negations," he wrote, is "an amusing sport if it is remembered that while it takes but a few minutes to cut down a tree it takes a century for a tree to grow." Justice Oliver Wendell Holmes: His Book Notices and Uncollected Letters and Papers 139, Harry C. Shriver ed. (1936).

Section 4

HIERARCHY OF LEGAL PRECEPTS

Law must also be considered as a collection of legal precepts, the separate substantive courses to which the law student is exposed during his formal legal training. These precepts are, in part, in Roscoe Pound's phrase, "a body of authoritative guides to conduct," a compilation of regulations which govern society. But society is not governed completely by particularized by-laws of equal weight and specificity, such as the by-laws of the local fraternal lodge or college fraternity. The source of these guides to societal conduct occupies our attention in this section. We consider the composition of legal precepts and analyze, again in Pound's formulation, "the authoritative gradation of the materials, wherein judges are to find the grounds for decision, counsellors the basis of assured prediction as to the course of decision, and individuals reasonable guidance toward conducting themselves in accordance with the demands of the social order."

ROSCOE POUND, HIERARCHY OF SOURCES AND FORMS IN DIFFERENT SYSTEMS OF LAW *

... The question, what is law, has been compared aptly to Pilate's question, what is truth? This is not the place to discuss it at large. Yet we may well observe that the answer depends chiefly on who asks the question. It may be asked from the standpoint of the judge who is to decide a pending case or of an administrative official who is to take some course of action. Or it may be asked from the standpoint of the counsellor at law who is called upon to advise some client as to what he may or may not do with impunity or with assurance of the backing of courts or administrative officials in attaining desired results. Or, again, it may be put from the standpoint of the citizen who desires to walk in the path which comports with social ends and would have it charted for him. Or, again, it may be put from the standpoint of the teacher who seeks to put the materials presented as the basis of decision, or at hand for the counsellor, or provided for the guidance of the citizen, in the order of reason for the purposes of exposition. It should not be over-

* 7 Tul.L.Rev. 475, 475–76, 482–87
(1933). Reprinted by permission.

looked that if, from one standpoint, we may find the historical origin of much that we call law in precepts for guidance in decision, from another we may find it in formulas for the conduct of legal transactions quite as easily as in formulas for litigation, and from another in advice as to the conduct of individual life quite as easily as in either.

. . .

What we are talking about, then, is the body of authoritative materials, and the authoritative gradation of the materials, wherein judges are to find the grounds of decision, counsellors the basis of assured prediction as to the course of decision, and individuals reasonable guidance toward conducting themselves in accordance with the demands of the social order. This point of view assumes a developed social and economic order and a corresponding development of the legal order, with an organized judicial and administrative hierarchy, definite law giving and law declaring agencies, and above all a developed profession of advisers upon the legal conduct of affairs....

. . .

Even if we confine our idea of law to the precept element in the authoritative materials, excluding the authoritative technique and the authoritative ideals, it is not possible to maintain a set hierarchy of forms applicable for each type of precept. For reasons to be found in the history of juristic thought, a theory applicable to one type, which may be called rules in the narrower sense, has been assumed to apply to the whole. Let us think of five types in that part of the authoritative materials in which, by use of the received technique and on a background of the received ideals, the judges are to find the grounds of decision.

1. Rules (in the narrower sense). These are precepts attaching a definite detailed legal consequence to a definite, detailed state of facts. If one likes, they are definite threats of definite, detailed official action in case of a definite, detailed state of facts. Rules in this sense are the staple of ancient codes. One might take as the type such provisions as "if the father sell the son three times, let the son be free from the father," or the exactly prescribed tariff of compositions for exactly defined injuries in the code of Hammurabi, the Salic law, or the Anglo–Saxon laws. In modern law we find rules in this sense especially important in the law of property, in commercial law, and in criminal law. Rules in this sense determine the modes of acquiring and transferring property, the nature and incidents of interests in property, the duties of adjoining owners, the creation and effects of rights with respect to the property of others, and the like. They fix the mode of entering into the more common and significant relations of business life and of conducting the more common and significant business transactions. For example, they determine how negotiable instruments shall be drawn in order to have certain detailed and determinate legal effects. They fill our penal codes with detailed prescribings of definite penalties for definite detailed

acts or courses of action. Legal precepts of this type permit best of legislative expression. They tend everywhere to be codified. Also the gradation or hierarchy of forms of law (or sources in the third of the senses noted above) applies best here. Indeed it was set up with reference to this type of precept, assuming the law to be made up of them and of them only. When the precise facts called for by such a rule are squarely presented, the hierarchy of forms is fully regarded and the consequences called for by the rule, according to its place and precedence, is a matter of course. These rules have much more part in the legal order, in the advice of counsel, and even in the administration of justice in the courts than some recent thinking perceives. Cases within the four corners of such rules seldom come into court, especially the higher courts. Parties are advised in the assurance that the prescribed results will follow the prescribed facts, and resort to the courts over such questions is precluded. Thus they are the bone and sinew of the legal order. This is the kernel of truth in the idea that law is a body of laws and that laws are rules.

2. Principles. These are authoritative starting points for legal reasoning, employed continually and legitimately where cases are not covered or are not fully or obviously covered by rules in the narrower sense. Use of them is squared with the theory of law as a body of rules by assuming that they are used to discover the applicable rule. But it is the decision which is discovered. Very often these authoritative starting points compete. There is often a choice of such starting points from which to proceed and no precepts are at hand to determine which is to be chosen. Here usually choice is made by referring the result of the respective starting points to the received ideals and following the lines leading to decisions in accord therewith.

These principles do not attach any definite detailed legal results to any definite, detailed states of fact. They do not threaten any definite official action in case of any definitely described conduct. They do not provide any patterns for definite situations. They are starting points from which to proceed according to the received technique. As examples one may cite the proposition that liability is a corollary of fault, to which American courts and text writers sought vainly to make our law of torts conform in the nineteenth century, but by means of which they were able to accomplish much for better treatment of many cases; the proposition that one is not to be enriched unjustly at the expense of another, which in the hands of Lord Mansfield did so much for our law of quasi contract and has been used effectively in equity in such cases as constructive trust, subrogation, and merger; the principle that as between two persons equally innocent, one of whom must lose, a court of equity will not interfere; Lord Coke's proposition that estates in land begin in ceremony and end in ceremony, which is behind so many results in the Anglo–American law of real property. Any number of such propositions, from which legal reasoning continually proceeds, will occur to the Continental lawyer. Mostly they come from the Roman law or from the modern Roman law and are a common element in the law of all countries. They are not the work of lawmakers nor of courts. They come from lawyers, usually from writers and teachers, and are best formulated in doctrinal writing.

In practice the hierarchy of forms is less likely to be observed in case of principles. Where they come into play choice of starting points is the decisive consideration, and this choice is seldom authoritatively fixed. In Continental Europe and Latin America analogies are found in legislative formulas. In England, the British Dominions, and the United States, they are found in judicial decisions. But the difficulty of decision is apt to lie to the absence of any precept calling for one analogy rather than another. Reference to some principle, as formulated by some doctrinal writer, is one way out, and this principle is likely to be chosen, consciously or unconsciously to the measure of a received ideal.*

3. Conceptions. These are authoritative categories to which types of classes of transactions, cases, or situations are referred, in consequence of which a series of rules, principles, and standards become applicable. They are chiefly the work of law teachers and law writers. They are seldom formulated by legislation, and when so formulated the formulations are commonly taken over from doctrinal writing. Moreover, such legislative formulations are not notably effective. The doctrinal development of conceptions is in practice the significant basis of decision, no matter what the hierarchy of forms. This is quite as true in Anglo–American law, where such writings have no theoretical persuasive authority, as on the Continent, where, without having authority their persuasive force is recognized or they are even included in the formal lists of subsidia in some of the codes.**

* R. Pound, II Jurisprudence 126 (1959): "They come into the law with the advent of legal writing and juristic speculation, so that the presence of this element as a controlling factor is the mark of a developed legal system. Principles as such appear first at the end of the stage of strict law. But an earlier form in the shape of legal proverbs or maxims goes back to the beginnings of law.

"... Restitution (quasi contracts), constructive trusts, election, subrogation, contribution, title by judgment, and the doctrine of equity as to merger, to give but a few examples, have been worked out by reasoning from the principle as to unjust enrichment. Again, note how starting from a principle as to the duty of a common carrier, the precepts worked out for the carter were extended in one line to the stage coach, to the railroad, to the trolley car, to the auto truck, and to the airplane, as one type of carrier succeeded another. Note how in another line they were extended to telegraph, telephone, radio, gas, electric light, and power. Then note how lawyers later worked out a broader principle as to duties involved in a public service, which has enabled our law to deal with one after another of these rapidly developing agencies of public service by affording a starting point for reasoning."

** *Ibid.* at 127: "A legal conception is a legally defined category into which cases may be fitted so that, when certain situations of fact come within the category, a series of *rules* and *principles* and *standards* become applicable. Conceptions are the work of the systematizing and organizing activity of the maturity of law, and chiefly the work of teachers.

"Examples are: Bailment, trust, sale, partnership, public utility. In these cases there is no definite detailed legal consequence attached to a definite detailed state of facts. Nor is there a starting point for reasoning. There are instead defined categories into which cases may be put, with the result that certain rules and principles and standards applicable to the category are to be used to guide determination of a controversy. Principles and conceptions make it possible to get along with many fewer rules and to deal with assurance with new cases for which no rules are at hand."

4. Doctrines. These are systematic fittings together of rules, principles, and conceptions with respect to particular situations or types of case or fields of the legal order, in logically interdependent schemes, whereby reasoning may proceed on the basis of the scheme and its logical implications. Doctrines are sometimes more or less embedded in legislation and to some extent in the course of judicial decision. But they are the work of writers and teachers and in the end and on the whole their influence is exerted through the text books. As a rule, they have no formal authority. They are not enumerated in the express statements of the hierarchy of forms. Nevertheless, they may at times have controlling influence on the actual course of legal reasoning and judicial decision. In Anglo–American law the writings of Coke became authoritative, and although "books of authority" rank last in the theoretical gradation of authority, held a place far above what the hierarchy of forms conceded. One need only mention Pothier and Savigny and Story and Jhering to show how little relation there may be between the formal and the actual authority.

5. Standards. These are general limits of permissible conduct to be applied according to the circumstances of each case. They are the chief reliance of modern law for individualization of application and are coming to be applied to conduct and conduct of enterprises over a very wide domain. Examples are, in English law and its derivatives, the standard of fair conduct of a fiduciary, the standard of reasonable service and reasonable facilities in the law of public service companies. In the Roman and modern Roman law there are the standard of the good and diligent head of a family, the standard of proper use by a usufructuary, and the like. In these standards there is always a certain ethical quality and they are to be applied according to circumstances, much as in the case of purely moral precepts. It may be said that in each case there is a rule (in the narrower sense) prescribing adherence to the standard and imposing consequences if the standard is not lived up to. This is true. But no definite, detailed state of facts is provided for. No definite pattern is laid down. No threat is attached to any defined situation. The significant thing is the standard, to be applied, not absolutely as in case of a rule, but in view of the facts of each case. These standards are sometimes the work of legislation, as in the standard of fair competition set up by American legislation creating the Federal Trade Commission. Sometimes they are the creation of doctrinal writers. Sometimes they are the work of judicial decision. Here the hierarchy of forms might play a certain part. But it does not in practice because, if these standards are not precisely defined, yet their fields of application, so far, have been well limited and they do not come into competition. The effective check upon their application is to be found in the received ideals of the social and legal order by which the results of applying them are consciously or unconsciously measured.***

. . .

*** *Ibid.* at 127–28: "A standard is a measure of conduct prescribed by law from which one departs at his peril of answering for resulting damage or of legal invalidity of

What, then, are we to conclude from this consideration of the applicability of the hierarchy of forms of law to different types of the authoritative materials in and with which judges are to and do decide cases? Chiefly, as I see it, we must recognize that there is need of comparative historical and analytical study of the received technique of finding grounds of decision in the authoritative precepts, as it exists in different systems, and of the received ideals as they are authoritative in different systems. The work of the philosopher of law in uncovering, organizing, and criticizing this element is and ever will be of the first moment. But his work is not enough. We should not be leaving this part of our authoritative materials to the philosophers. They may tell us much of what it should be. We as lawyers and law teachers need to perceive what it is, how it has come to be what it is, and how it works in the different systems of today. Here is a great field for the comparative law of the future.

NOTE

RESTATEMENT OF RESTITUTION, Introductory Note at 11 (1937): "The rules stated in the Restatement of this Subject depend for their validity upon certain basic assumptions in regard to what is required by justice in the various situations. In this Topic, these are stated in the form of principles. They cannot be stated as rules since either they are too indefinite to be of value in a specific case or, for historical or other reasons, they are not universally applied. They are distinguished from rules in that they are intended only as general guides for the conduct of the courts and are not intended to express that universality of application to particular cases which is characteristic of the statements made in subsequent chapters."

RONALD M. DWORKIN, *The Model of Rules*, 35 U.Chi.L.Rev. 14, 25–28 (1967), makes the point that rules "are applicable on an all-or-nothing" basis. Because a rule is predicated on specific facts, a rule is either accepted or rejected. A rule may not conflict with another rule: "If two rules conflict, one of them cannot be a valid rule." It is here then that we usually resort to principles, because "[p]rinciples have a dimension that rules do not—the dimension of weight or importance. When principles intersect (the policy of protecting automobile consumers intersecting with principles of freedom of contract, for example), one who must resolve the conflict has to take into account the relative

what he does." Standards come in first in the stage of equity and natural law.

" . . . Note the element of fairness or reasonableness in standards. This is a source of difficulty. As has been said, there is no precept defining what is reasonable and it would not be reasonable to attempt to formulate one. In the end, reasonableness has to be referred to conformity to the authoritative ideal.

"Conduct requires standards. It is enough to instance one attempt to reduce conduct to rule, namely, the old 'stop, look, and listen' rule. Compare applying this rule to a horse and buggy crossing a single track railroad where trains ran thirty miles an hour with a heavy motor truck crossing a four-line track on which streamlined trains as like as not go one hundred miles an hour. By the time the driver has stopped, got off the truck, looked up and down the tracks, got back on his truck and started up again, the streamlined train may have come four miles."

weight of each." Dworkin also suggests that a legal system may regulate conflicts of rules by other rules, *viz.*, the rule that higher authority supercedes, the rule that a later case controls, etc.; or it may regulate conflicts by giving preference to the rule that is supported by the more important principles. Does our legal system use either or both techniques?

JOSEPH RAZ, *Legal Principles and the Limits of Law,* 81 Yale L.J. 823, 838 (1972), puts the distinction between rules and principles in a different perspective. Beginning with the thesis that both are legal norms guiding behavior, he says the distinction "turns on the character of the norm-act prescribed. Rules prescribe relatively specific acts; principles prescribe highly unspecific actions." Thus, smoking a pipe is a highly specific act, as are assault and speeding. In contrast are highly unspecific acts: "[p]romoting human happiness, respecting human dignity, increasing productivity, and behaving negligently or unjustly or unreasonably". Raz suggests that, based on this analysis, the difference between rules and principles is one of degree and that there is no bright line distinction between specific and unspecific acts. Thus, "there will be many borderline cases where it will be impossible to say that we definitely have a rule or definitely a principle."

ROBERT E. KEETON, COURTS AND LEGISLATURES AS AGENCIES OF ABRUPT CHANGE *

One way in which the contrast in acceptability of narrow and broad challenges to continuity may be expressed is to say that courts on occasion depart from continuity in rule but, even when so doing, preserve continuity in principle. The qualification must be added, however, that not even principles are immutable. Both their meaning and the scope of their influence are subject to change; even now the meaning and influence of the principle of liability based on fault are undergoing modification. The contrast between principles and rules that is relevant at this point concerns methods of change rather than susceptibility to change. The narrow propositions commonly called rules are on occasion changed abruptly; that is, precedents are overruled. The broadest propositions, to which the term "principle" is applied, are as near to immutability as anything in law. Because of their extreme degree of generality, however, they do not severely obstruct needed reform. They are imprecise, and rules or criticisms of rules cannot be derived from them merely by an exercise of logic. Indeed, a principle is not an accurate expression of the essence of many, if any, rules, because rules usually represent the product of interaction of more than one principle.

* Excerpted by permission of the author and publishers from pp. 15–19, 22–24 of Venturing to do Justice: Reforming Private Law by Robert E. Keeton, Cambridge, Mass.: Harvard University Press Copyright © 1969 by the President and Fellows of Harvard College.

Thus continuity in principle in the face of a change in rule may mean no more than that no principle speaks directly to the difference between the old and the new rule, and either rule can be reconciled with accepted principles.

But there is also continuity of principle in a more basic sense—in the sense of guiding decisions both by placing outside limits on the scope of choice and by influencing the choice within that scope. To the extent that principles are effective guides, they are amenable to judicial creativity, but change in such broadly generalized propositions as these comes about through a process not aptly described as an "overruling of precedent." A principle may be modified in consequence of an extended sequence of particular decisions, but even when an inventory discloses that a change has occurred, the opinion acknowledging the change is more likely to say merely that the old principle is no longer valid than to say that it is overruled. The choice of expression in this instance is more defensible than in those instances in which courts that are plainly overruling a more specific proposition decline to say so and insist upon leaving the reader to infer what has happened—as if hoping to soften criticism, even self-criticism, by obscuring the creative character of their action.

With respect to rules, as distinguished from principles, courts have both the power to overrule and the responsibility for exercising the power. Restraint in its exercise is essential to continuity, but as already observed, abstention defeats continuity. Even beyond such yielding to creativity to serve continuity itself, demands for continuity must on occasion be sacrificed in some degree to serve greater needs of creative re-examination of court-made law. Even when acting to serve these needs, however, a court may build its creative thought upon a foundation of established concepts in whose implications are found support for departing from the precedent under re-examination. The judicial method that invokes *stare decisis* even in challenging a particular application of it is characteristic of opinions overruling precedents in a legal system founded on the principle that grounds of decision shall be related in some reasoned way to established concepts. This form of judicial action exemplifies creative continuity not as an attempt to compromise between mutually negating ideals but as an integrated pursuit of values that in considerable measure are complementary.

The judiciary is, then, on the one hand a guardian of the law's continuity, stability, evenhandedness, and predictability and on the other hand a participant in creative evolution that keeps law contemporary and viable.

Superficially it may seem that the functions of changing the law and guarding its stability are mutually repugnant. But closer examination discloses that occasional legitimated changes in the law are essential to continuity itself. The aim of courts is to exercise their power of overruling precedents consistently with the principle that stability and change are to be not competitive but complementary values in the legal system.

————

Read the following cases with the view of identifying "rules" and "principles".

RIGGS v. PALMER

Court of Appeals of New York, 1889.
115 N.Y. 506, 22 N.E. 188.

[The testator had planned to make his 16–year old grandson the remainderman of a substantial portion of his estate. The Grandson] knew of the provisions made in his favor in the will, and, that he might prevent his grandfather from revoking such provisions, which he had manifested some intention to do, and to obtain the speedy enjoyment and immediate possession of his property, he willfully murdered him by poisoning him. He now claims the property, and the sole question for our determination is, can he have it?

The defendants say that the testator is dead; that his will was made in due form, and has been admitted to probate; and that therefore it must have effect according to the letter of the law. It is quite true that statutes regulating the making, proof, and effect of wills and the devolution of property, if literally construed, and if their force and effect can in no way and under no circumstances be controlled or modified, give this property to the murderer. The purpose of those statutes was to enable testators to dispose of their estates to the objects of their bounty at death, and to carry into effect their final wishes legally expressed; and in considering and giving effect to them this purpose must be kept in view. It was the intention of the law-makers that the donees in a will should have the property given to them. But it never could have been their intention that a donee who murdered the testator to make the will operative should have any benefit under it. If such a case had been present to their minds, and it had been supposed necessary to make some provision of law to meet it, it cannot be doubted that they would have provided for it.

. . .

What could be more unreasonable than to suppose that it was the legislative intention in the general laws passed for the orderly, peaceable, and just devolution of property that they should have operation in favor of one who murdered his ancestor that he might speedily come into the possession of his estate? Such an intention is inconceivable. We need not, therefore, be much troubled by the general language contained in the laws. Besides, all laws, as well as all contracts, may be controlled in their operation and effect by general, fundamental maxims of the common law. No one shall be permitted to profit by his own fraud, or to take advantage of his own wrong, or to found any claim upon his own iniquity, or to acquire property by his own crime. These maxims are dictated by public policy, have their foundation in universal law administered in all civilized countries, and have nowhere been superseded by statutes.

. . .

These maxims, without any statute giving them force or operation, frequently control the effect and nullify the language of wills. A will procured by fraud and deception, like any other instrument, may be decreed void, and set aside; and so a particular portion of a will may be excluded from probate, or held inoperative, if induced by the fraud or undue influence of the person in whose favor it is.... So a will may contain provisions which are immoral, irreligious, or against public policy, and they will be held void.

Here there was no certainty that this murderer would survive the testator, or that the testator would not change his will, and there was no certainty that he would get this property if nature was allowed to take its course. He therefore murdered the testator expressly to vest himself with an estate. Under such circumstances, what law, human or divine, will allow him to take the estate and enjoy the fruits of his crime? The will spoke and became operative at the death of the testator. He caused that death, and thus by his crime made it speak and have operation. Shall it speak and operate in his favor? If he had met the testator, and taken his property by force, he would have had no title to it. Shall he acquire title by murdering him? If he had gone to the testator's house, and by force compelled him, or by fraud or undue influence had induced him, to will him his property, the law would not allow him to hold it. But can he give effect and operation to a will by murder, and yet take the property? To answer these questions in the affirmative it seems to me would be a reproach to the jurisprudence of our state, and an offense against public policy. Under the civil law, evolved from the general principles of natural law and justice by many generations of jurisconsults, philosophers, and statesmen, one cannot take property by inheritance or will from an ancestor or benefactor whom he has murdered.... But, so far as I can find, in no country where the common law prevails has it been deemed important to enact a law to provide for such a case. Our revisers and law-makers were familiar with the civil law, and they did not deem it important to incorporate into our statutes its provisions upon this subject. This is not a *casus omissus*. It was evidently supposed that the maxims of the common law were sufficient to regulate such a case, and that a specific enactment for that purpose was not needed. For the same reasons the defendant Palmer cannot take any of this property as heir.

———

HENNINGSEN v. BLOOMFIELD MOTORS, INC.

Supreme Court of New Jersey, 1960.
32 N.J. 358, 161 A.2d 69.

[The question before the court was the extent to which an automobile manufacturer could limit liability on the sale of a defective automobile. In purchasing a car, Henningsen had signed a contract expressly limiting "warranties, express or implied made by either the dealer or manufacturer" except as therein stated. The language of contract then purported to limit responsibility to "making good" defective parts, "this warranty being expressly in lieu of all other warranties expressed or implied, and all other obligations or liabilities." After Henningsen's wife was injured while driving the car, Henningsen brought an action to recover damages on account of her injuries based on breach of implied warranty of merchantability. No statute and no previous case law had prevented defendant from relying on the express language of the sales contract. Nevertheless the New Jersey Supreme Court agreed with Henningsen.]

Putting aside for the time being the problem of the efficacy of the disclaimer provisions contained in the express warranty, a question of first importance to be decided is whether an implied warranty of merchantability by Chrysler Corporation accompanied the sale of the automobile to Claus Henningsen.

Preliminarily, it may be said that the express warranty against defective parts and workmanship is not inconsistent with an implied warranty of merchantability. Such warranty cannot be excluded for that reason. . . .

Chrysler points out that an implied warranty of merchantability is an incident of a contract of sale.

There is no doubt that under early common-law concepts of contractual liability only those persons who were parties to the bargain could sue for a breach of it. In more recent times a noticeable disposition has appeared in a number of jurisdictions to break through the narrow barrier of privity when dealing with sales of goods in order to give realistic recognition to a universally accepted fact. The fact is that the dealer and the ordinary buyer do not, and are not expected to, buy goods, whether they be foodstuffs or automobiles, exclusively for their own consumption or use. Makers and manufacturers know this and advertise and market their products on that assumption; witness, the "family" car, the baby foods, etc. The limitations of privity in contracts for the sale of goods developed their place in the law when marketing conditions were simple, when maker and buyer frequently met face to face on an equal bargaining plane and when many of the products were relatively uncomplicated and conducive to inspection by a buyer competent to evaluate their quality. See, Freezer, "Manufacturer's Liability for Injuries Caused by His Products," 37 Mich.L.Rev. 1 (1938). With the advent of mass marketing, the manufacturer became remote from the purchaser, sales were accomplished through intermediaries, and the demand for the product was created by advertising media. In such an economy it became obvious that the consumer was the person being cultivated. Manifestly, the connotation of "consumer" was broader than that of "buyer." He signified such a person who, in the reasonable contemplation of the parties to the sale, might be expected to use the product. Thus, where the commodities sold are such that if defectively manufactured they will be dangerous to life or limb, then society's interests can only be protected by eliminating the requirement of privity between the maker and his dealers and the reasonably expected ultimate consumer. In that way the burden of losses consequent upon use of defective articles is borne by those who are in a position to either control the danger or make an equitable distribution of the losses when they do occur. . . .

Although the courts, with few exceptions, have been most sensitive to problems presented by contracts resulting from gross disparity in buyer-seller bargaining positions, they have not articulated a general principle condemning, as opposed to public policy, the imposition on the buyer of a skeleton warranty as a means of limiting the responsibility of the manufacturer. They have endeavored thus far to avoid a drastic departure from age-old tenets of freedom of contract by adopting doctrines of strict construction, and notice and knowledgeable assent by the buyer to the attempted exculpation of the seller. Prosser, "Warranty of Merchantable Quality," 27 Minn.L.Rev. 117, 159 (1932). Accordingly to be found in the cases are statements that disclaimers and the consequent limitation of liability will not be given effect if "unfairly procured," . . . if not brought to the buyer's attention and he was not made understandingly aware of it. . . .

(Citing cases).

. . .

Under modern conditions the ordinary layman, on responding to the importuning of colorful advertising, has neither the opportunity nor the capacity to inspect or to determine the fitness of an automobile for use; he must rely on the manufacturer who has control of its construction, and to some degree on the dealer who, to the limited extent called for by the manufacturer's instructions, inspects and services it before delivery. In such a marketing milieu his remedies and those of persons who properly claim through him should not depend "upon the intricacies of the law of sales. The obligation of the manufacturer should not be based alone on privity of contract. It should rest, as was once said, upon 'the demands of social justice.' " Mazetti v. Armour & Co., 75 Wash. 622, 135 P. 633, 635, 48 L.R.A., N.S., 213 (Sup.Ct.1913).

Accordingly, we hold that under modern marketing conditions, when a manufacturer puts a new automobile in the stream of trade and promotes its purchase by the public, an implied warranty that it is reasonably suitable for use as such accompanies it into the hands of the ultimate purchaser. Absence of agency between the manufacturer and the dealer who makes the ultimate sale is immaterial.

. . .

In view of the cases in various jurisdictions suggesting the conclusion which we have now reached with respect to the implied warranty of merchantability, it becomes apparent that manufacturers who enter into promotional activities to stimulate consumer buying may incur warranty obligations of either or both the express or implied character. These developments in the law inevitably suggest the inference that the form of express warranty made part of the Henningsen purchase contract was devised for general use in the automobile industry as a possible means of avoiding the consequences of the growing judicial acceptance of the thesis that the described express or implied warranties run directly to the consumer.

In the light of these matters, what effect should be given to the express warranty in question which seeks to limit the manufacturer's liability to replacement of defective parts, and which disclaims all other warranties, express or implied? In assessing its significance we must keep in mind the general principle that, in the absence of fraud, one who does not choose to read a contract before signing it, cannot later relieve himself of its burdens. Fivey v. Pennsylvania R.R. Co., 67 N.J.L. 627, 52 A. 472, (E. & A.1902). And in applying that principle, the basic tenet of freedom of competent parties to contract is a factor of importance. But in the framework of modern commercial life and business practices, such rules cannot be applied on a strict, doctrinal basis. The conflicting interests of the buyer and seller must be evaluated realistically and justly, giving due weight to the social policy evinced by the Uniform Sales Act, the progressive decisions of the courts engaged in administering it, the mass production methods of manufacture and distribution to the public, and the bargaining position occupied by the ordinary consumer in such an economy. This history of the law shows that legal doctrines, as first expounded, often prove to be inadequate under the impact of later experience. In such case, the need for justice has stimulated the necessary qualifications or adjustments....

In these times, an automobile is almost as much a servant of convenience for the ordinary person as a household utensil. For a multitude of other persons it is a necessity. Crowded highways and filled parking lots are a commonplace of our existence. There is no need to look any farther than the daily newspaper to be convinced that when an automobile is defective, it has great potentiality for harm.

... In a society such as ours, where the automobile is a common and necessary adjunct of daily life, and where its use is so fraught with danger to the driver, passengers and the public, the manufacturer is under a special obligation in connection with the construction, promotion and sale of his cars. Consequently, the courts must examine purchase agreements closely to see if consumer and public interests are treated fairly.

What influence should these circumstances have on the restrictive effect of Chrysler's express warranty in the framework of the purchase contract? As we have said, warranties originated in the law to safeguard the buyer and not to limit the liability of the seller or manufacturer. It seems obvious in this instance that the motive was to avoid the warranty obligations which are normally incidental to such sales. The language gave little and withdrew much. In return for the delusive remedy of replacement of defective parts at the factory, the buyer is said to have accepted the exclusion of the maker's liability for personal injuries arising from the breach of the warranty, and to have agreed to the elimination of any other express or implied warranty. An instinctively felt sense of justice cries out against such a sharp bargain. But does the doctrine that a person is bound by his signed agreement, in the absence of fraud, stand in the way of any relief?

In the modern consideration of problems such as this, Corbin suggests that practically all judges are "chancellors" and cannot fail to be influenced by any equitable doctrines that are available. And he opines that "there is sufficient flexibility in the concepts of fraud, duress, misrepresentation and undue influence, not to mention differences in economic bargaining power" to enable the courts to avoid enforcement of unconscionable provisions in long printed standardized contracts. 1 Corbin on Contracts (1950) § 128, p. 188. Freedom of contract is not such an immutable doctrine as to admit of no qualification in the area in which we are concerned. As Chief Justice Hughes said in his dissent in Morehead v. People of State of New York ex rel. Tipaldo, 298 U.S. 587, 627, 56 S.Ct. 918, 930, 80 L.Ed. 1347, 1364 (1936):

> "We have had frequent occasion to consider the limitations on liberty of contract. While it is highly important to preserve that liberty from arbitrary and capricious interference, it is also necessary to prevent its abuse, as otherwise it could be used to override all public interests and thus in the end destroy the very freedom of opportunity which it is designed to safeguard."

That sentiment was echoed by Justice Frankfurter in his dissent in United States v. Bethlehem Steel Corp., 315 U.S. 289, 326, 62 S.Ct. 581, 599, 86 L.Ed. 855, 876 (1942):

> "It is said that familiar principles would be outraged if Bethlehem were denied recovery on these contracts. But is there any principle which is more familiar or more firmly embedded in the history of Anglo–American law than the basic doctrine that the courts will not permit themselves to be used as instruments of inequity and injustice? Does any principle in our law have more universal application than the doctrine that courts will not enforce transactions in which the relative positions of the parties are such that one has unconscionably taken advantage of the necessities of the other?

"These principles are not foreign to the law of contracts. Fraud and physical duress are not the only grounds upon which courts refuse to enforce contracts. The law is not so primitive that it sanctions every injustice except brute force and downright fraud. More specifically, the courts generally refuse to lend themselves to the enforcement of a 'bargain' in which one party has unjustly taken advantage of the economic necessities of the other...."

NOTE

Dworkin questions whether the rules of the *Riggs* and *Henningsen* cases fit traditional patterns for rule making. Rather, he suggests, their origin "lies not in a particular decision of some legislature or court, but in a sense of appropriateness developed in the profession and public over time. Their continued power depends upon this sense of appropriateness being sustained." If the profession and public find them unfair at some future time, the legal precepts "are eroded, not torpedoed."

－－－－－

KARL N. LLEWELLYN, PRECEPTS AS THE HEART AND CORE OF MOST THINKING ABOUT LAW *

... When men talk or think about law, they talk and think about *rules*. "Precepts" as used by Pound, for instance, I take to be roughly synonymous with rules and principles, the principles *being* wider in scope and proportionately vaguer in connotation, with a tendency toward idealization of some portion of the *status quo* at any given time. And I think you will find as you read Pound that the precepts are *central* to his thinking about law. Along with rules and principles—along with precepts proper, may I say?—he stresses for instance "standards" as a part of the subject matter of law. These standards seem to be those vague but useful pictures with which one approaches a wide and varied field of conduct to measure the rights of a particular situation: a conception of what a reasonable man would do in the circumstances, or of what good faith requires, and similar pictures. They differ from rules, though not from principles, partly in their vagueness; they differ from both in being not propositions in themselves, but normative approaches to working out the application of some one *term* in a major proposition. The principle, let us say, would read: a man must answer for what good faith requires. But a standard (like a concept; like any class-term loose or sharp) functions chiefly or exclusively as *part* of a precept. Consequently, it belongs in much the same world. It, too, *centers* on precepts. But Pound mentions more as law than precepts and standards. Along with the standards he stresses also ideals as to "the end" of law. These I

* A Realistic Jurisprudence—The Next Step, 30 Colum.L.Rev. 431, 434–35, 437–38, 464–65 (1930). Reprinted by permission.

take to be in substance standards on a peculiarly vague and majestic scale; standards perhaps, to be applied to rules rather than to individual transactions.   Finally, he stresses—and we meet here a very different order of phenomena—"the traditional techniques of developing and applying" precepts.   Only a man gifted with insight would have added to the verbal formulae and verbalized (though vague) conceptual pictures thus far catalogued, such an element *of practices,* of habits and techniques of action, of *behavior.*   But only a man partially caught in the traditional precept-thinking of an age that is passing would have focussed that behavior on, have given it a major reference to, have belittled its importance by dealing with it as a phase of, those merely verbal formulae: precepts.   I have no wish to argue the point.   It will appeal, or it will not, and argument will be of little service.   But not only this particular bit of phrasing (which might be accidental), but the use made in Pound's writings of the idea, brings out vigorously the limitations of rules, of precepts, of *words,* when made the focus, the *center of reference,* in thinking about law.

. . .

Substantive rights and rules are spoken of as prevailing between people, laymen: one has, *e.g.,* a right to the performance of a contract. It is a heresy when Coke or Holmes speaks of a man having liberty under the law to perform his contract, or pay damages, at his option.   It would likewise be a heresy to argue that the vital real evidence of this supposed "right" lies in an action for damages, and that the right could rather more accurately be phrased somewhat as follows: if the other party does not perform as agreed, you can sue, and *if* you have a fair lawyer, and nothing goes wrong with your witnesses or the jury, *and* you give up four or five days of time and some ten to thirty percent of the proceeds, and wait two to twenty months, you will *probably* get a judgment for a sum considerably less than what the performance would have been worth—which, if the other party is solvent and has not secreted his assets, you can in further due course collect with six percent interest for delay.   To argue thus would be to confuse the remedy (which you can see) with the substantive right (which you cannot see, but which you know is there—somewhere;   people tell you so).   The substantive right in this body of thought has a shape and scope independent of the accidents of remedies.   And herein lies the scientific advance involved in the concept.   You are freed of any necessity of observing what courts do, and of limiting your discussion to that.   You get back into the ultimate realities behind their doing.   Obviously you can think more clearly among those ultimate realities.   They are not so much obscured by inconsistency and divergence of detail.   They are not answerable to fact.

Most lay thinking, it may be noted in passing, is on this level today. Typical is the current acceptance of a paper rule or statute as meaning something simply because it has paper authority—indeed, as meaning all it says, or all it is supposed to have been intended to say, simply because it has paper authority.

Far be it from me to dispute that the concepts of substantive rights and of rules of substantive law have had great value.[7] They moved definitely and sharply toward fixing the attention of thinkers on the idea that procedure, remedies, existed not merely because they existed, nor because they had value in themselves, but because they had a purpose. From which follows immediate inquiry into what the purpose is, and criticism, if the means to its accomplishment be poor. They moved, moreover, to some extent, toward sizing up the law by situations, instead of under the categories of historically conditioned, often archaic remedy-law: a new base for a new synthesis; a base for law reform.

. . .

In conclusion, then, may I repeat that I have been concerned not at all with marking a periphery of law, with defining "it," with *excluding* anything at all from its field. I have argued that the trend of the most fruitful thinking about law has run steadily toward regarding law as an engine (a heterogenous multitude of engines) having purposes, not values in itself; and that the clearer visualization of the problems involved moves toward ever-decreasing emphasis on words, and ever-increasing emphasis on observable behavior (in which any demonstrably probable attitudes and thought-patterns should be included). Indeed that the focus of study, the point of reference for all things legal has been shifting, and should now be consciously shifted to the area of contact, of interaction, between official regulatory behavior and the behavior of those affecting or affected by official regulatory behavior; and that the rules and precepts and principles which have hitherto tended to keep the limelight should be displaced, and treated with severe reference to their bearing upon that area of contact—in order that paper rules may be revealed for what they are, and rules with real behavior correspondences come into due importance. That the complex phenomena which are lumped under the term "law" have been too broadly treated in the past, and that a realistic understanding, possible only in terms of observable behavior, is again possible only in terms of study of the way in which persons and institutions are organized in our society, and of the cross-bearings of any particular *part* of law and of any particular *part* of the social organization.

Included in the field of law under such an approach is everything currently included, and a vast deal more. At the very heart, I suspect, is the behavior of judges, peculiarly, that part of their behavior which marks them as judges—those practices which establish the continuity of their office with their predecessors and successors, and which make their official contacts with other persons; but that suspicion on my part may be a relic of the case law tradition in which we American lawyers have been raised. Close around it on the one hand lies the behavior of other government officials. On the other, the sets of accepted formulae which

7. Neither would I be understood to deny practical consequences to this mode of thinking, in our case results, in constitutional law, limitation of actions, etc., or to urge that describing the remedy describes the whole situation, today. It *does* describe the most important, and a much neglected aspect of the situation.

judges recite, seek light from, try to follow. Distinguishing here the formulae with close behavior-correspondences from others; those of frequent application from those of infrequent. Close around these again, lie various persons' ideas of what the law is; and especially their views of what it or some part of it ought to accomplish. At first hand contact with officials' behavior, from another angle, lies the social set-up where the official's acts impinge directly on it; and behind that the social set-up which resists or furthers or reflects the impingement of his acts. Farther from the center lies legal and social philosophy—approaching that center more directly in proportion as the materials with which it deals are taken directly from the center. Part of law, in many aspects, is all of society, and all of man in society. But that is a question of periphery and not of center, of the reach of a specific problem in hand, not of a general discussion. As to the overlapping of the field as thus sketched with that of other social sciences, I should be sorry if no overlapping were observable. The social sciences are not staked out like real estate. Even in law the sanctions for harmless trespass are not heavy.

NOTE

Is it "heresy when Coke or Holmes speaks of a man having liberty under the law to perform his contract, or pay damages, at his option"? If "law" resides in the common conscience of the people, or reflects the will of a majority in a democratic society, does the average layman appreciate the distinction between "paper rule" rights and actual remedies?

How valid is the observation that the "point of reference for all things legal has been shifting, and should not be shifted to the area of contract, of interaction between official regulatory behavior and the behavior of those affecting or affected by official regulatory behavior?" If valid, would you say this is more true of federal court litigation than state court litigation?

FELIX S. COHEN, THE NATURE OF LEGAL RULES AND CONCEPTS *

If the functionalists are correct, the meaning of a definition is found in its consequences. The definition of a general term like "law" is significant only because it affects all our definitions of specific legal concepts.

The consequence of defining law as a function of concrete judicial decisions is that we may proceed to define such concepts as "contract,"

* *Transcendental Nonsense and the Functional Approach,* 35 Colum.L.Rev. 809, 838– 40 (1935). Reprinted by permission.

"property," "title," "corporate personality," "right," and "duty," similarly as functions of concrete judicial decisions.

The consequence of defining law as a hodge-podge of political force and ethical value ambiguously amalgamated is that every legal concept, rule or question will present a similar ambiguity.

Consider the elementary legal question: "Is there a contract?"

When the realist asks this question, he is concerned with the actual behavior of courts. For the realist, the contractual relationship, like law in general, is a function of legal decisions. The question of what courts *ought* to do is irrelevant here. Where there is a promise that will be legally enforced there is a contract. So conceived, any answer to the question "Is there a contract" must be in the nature of a prophecy, based, like other prophecies, upon past and present facts. So conceived, the question "Is there a contract?" or for that matter any other legal question, may be broken up into a number of subordinate questions, each of which refers to the actual behavior of courts: (1) What courts are likely to pass upon a given transaction and its consequences? (2) What elements in this transaction will be viewed as relevant and important by these courts? (3) How have these courts dealt with transactions in the past which are *similar* to the given transaction, that is, *identical in those respects which the court will regard as important?* (4) What forces will tend to compel judicial conformity to the precedents that appear to be in point (*e.g.* inertia, conservatism, knowledge of the past, or intelligence sufficient to acquire such knowledge, respect for predecessors, superiors or brothers on the bench, a habit of deference to the established expectations of the bar or the public) and how strong are these forces? (5) What factors will tend to evoke new judicial treatment for the transaction in question (*e.g.* changing public opinion, judicial idiosyncrasies and prejudices, newly accepted theories of law, society or economics, or the changing social context of the case) and how powerful are these factors?

These are the questions which a successful practical lawyer faces and answers in any case. The law, as the realistic lawyer uses the term, is the body of answers to such questions. The task of prediction involves, in itself, no judgment of ethical value. Of course, even the most cynical practitioner will recognize that the positively existing ethical beliefs of judges are material facts in any case because they determine what facts the judge will view as important and what past rules he will regard as reasonable or unreasonable and worthy of being extended or restricted. But judicial beliefs about the values of life and the ideals of society are *facts,* just as the religious beliefs of the Andaman Islanders are facts, and the truth or falsity of such moral beliefs is a matter of complete unconcern to the practical lawyer, as to the scientific observer.

Washed in cynical acid, every legal problem can thus be interpreted as a question concerning the positive behavior of judges.

NOTE

Cohen suggests that his five subordinate questions to any legal question are those which a successful practical lawyer faces and answers in any case. May the "successful practical lawyer" find the answers in the reported opinions of the courts? If not, where may he or she find the "law ... the body of answers to such questions"?

Chapter II

CREATION OF LEGAL PRECEPTS

Section 1

THE JUDGE AS A LAWMAKER

INTRODUCTION

We can identify at least three theories of judicial law making:

- Judges do not create law. They do not "make" law. They merely discover and apply that which has always existed.

- Judges can and do make law on subjects not covered by previous decisions, but they cannot unmake old law. They cannot even change an existing rule of judge-made law.

- Judges can and do make new law, can and do unmake old law, i.e., law previously laid down by themselves or by their judicial predecessors.[1]

We will bear these basic conceptions in mind as we review the historical development of scholarly thought on the role of judge as lawmaker.

John Chipman Gray often quoted Bishop Hoadley's prescient observation about the close relationship between *making* law and *interpreting* law: "Nay, whoever hath an absolute authority to interpret any written or spoken laws, it is he who is truly the Law giver to all intents and purposes, and not the person who first wrote or spoke them." [2] Indeed, we might consider Francis Bacon's famous admonition that "[j]udges ought to remember that this office is *jus dicere,* and not *jus dare,* to interpret law, and not to make law, or give law." [3]

A judge's exercises of power as a lawmaker may challenge basic tenets regarding separation of power on local, state and national levels, and thereby raise fundamental questions of political authority. This may partially explain why judges and courts often are labeled as conservative or liberal, strict constructionist or activist. Yet even if a meaningful definition of these ambiguous terms were possible, a careful, specific evaluation of how a given judge perceives his or her role as a law maker would provide greater insight into his or her jurisprudential temperament than would resort to simplistic labels of questionable definitional

---

1. Smith, *Sequel to Workmen's Compensation Acts,* 27 Harv.L.Rev. 344, 365–66. (1914).

2. J.C. Gray, The Nature and Sources of Law 125 (2d ed. 1925).

3. F. Bacon, Of Judicature, in Essays Civil and Moral 58 (Murphy's ed. 1826) (1625).

121

value. In other words, a judge's actual jurisprudential temperament is usually more revealing than the more familiar characterizations of judicial temperament. For example, it would be useful to know that a judge's willingness to indulge in judicial law making will vary inversely with a personal psychology rooted in a sense of personal limitation or reflecting a hesitation to act originally or creatively.

Writing in the Eighteenth Century, Sir Matthew Hale said that decisions of courts cannot "*make* a law properly so called, for that only the King and Parliament can do; yet they have a great weight and authority in expounding, declaring, and publishing what the law of this Kingdom is." [4] Later, Blackstone wrote that decisions of courts are evidence of what is common law.[5] And as late as 1892, Lord Esher remarked that there was in fact "no such thing as judge-made law, for the judges do not make the law though they frequently have to apply existing law to circumstances as to which it has not previously been authoritatively laid down that such law is applicable."

Notwithstanding the formidable reputation of Blackstone, who proclaimed that judges did not create law but simply discovered something that was already there, it would have taken some persuasion to convince an active English practitioner that precepts related to offer and acceptance, liability through fault, contributory negligence, proximate cause, foreseeability and the like were not the law, for they clearly were created by the courts, not Parliament. Indeed, Blackstone's view would have to allow for the argument that a judgment of the House of Lords was not law if it conflicted with settled principles of the common law which were always out there, simply waiting to be discovered. Nevertheless, thoughtful observers have generally agreed that to claim that courts outright *make* law is to assert that courts habitually act unconstitutionally.[6]

The civil law tradition began with a "deification of statutes," a phrase used by European critics of their own systems. It is a tradition that contained, at least in France, the pre-revolutionary distrust of judicial law making. Basically, the position was that judges shall have no power to make law, for that kind of power was reserved to the legislature. The original 1790 legislative schema in France, which reorganized the judicial system, provided that judges "shall have recourse to the legislative body [only] whenever it appears desirable to interpret a law." However, by 1899, Francois Geny, the great French legal philosopher, was able to recite a large amount of nineteenth-century French judge-made law. Jurisprudentially speaking, this judicial innovation does not emerge from the power of the courts to promulgate rules of law, but from their power to interpret somewhat abstract provisions of the civil code. The principle of separation of powers, as

4. Sir Matthew Hale, The History of the Common Law of England 68 (4th ed. 1779) (1713).

5. 1 William Blackstone, Commentaries 70–71.

6. Zane, *German Legal Philosophy,* 16 Mich.L.Rev. 188, 337–38 (1918).

understood in France, prevents the formal creation of legal rules by the courts; hence a judicial decision in France can never be justified simply by stating that the rule of law has been applied previously by other judges.

In Germany, the issue is not free from doubt. Although rules established by opinions of the courts are not sources of law, in reality a kind of hierarchical discipline is imposed there, akin to our practice of *stare decisis,* in the sense that an inferior court may be bound by the view taken by a higher court on the *same* legal proceeding. Generally, however, the sources of German law are *Gesetz* (statute), *Rechtsverordnung* (administrative regulation), *Satzung* (internal administrative regulation), and *Gewohnheitsrecht* (customary law).

In theory, Italy maintains a strict separation of powers which calls for rejection of judicial decisions as a source of law. Italian doctrine claims that law making is one thing; interpretation and application of laws is quite another. The formal legislative statement on sources of law is Art. 1 of the Provisions of Law in General: "The following are sources of law: (1) *la legge* (statutes); (2) *regolamenti* (regulations); (3) *norme corporative* (corporative norms); (4) *usi* (usage)." Notwithstanding such apparently clear doctrine, what the Italians do in fact is another matter.

Whether the courts make law in the United States has been (until recently) a subject of interest only to legal philosophers. So long as the courts have dealt with lawyer's law, it has been fair game for the courts to develop the law on a case-by-case basis. Lawyers have understood this because they have not subscribed to "the lay attitude that the law is definite and certain. That is, the unchanging law is there to be found and followed if a jurist faithful to his oath will only look for it." [7]

Rather, American lawyers live with the reality that law always has been, and always will be,

> largely vague and variable. And how could this well be otherwise? The law deals with human relations in their most complicated aspects. The whole confused, shifting helter-skelter of life parades before it—more confused than ever, in our kaleidoscopic age.

> Even in a relatively static society, men have never been able to construct a comprehensive, eternized set of rules anticipating all possible legal disputes and settling them in advance. Even in such a social order no one could foresee all the future permutations and combinations of events; situations are bound to occur which were never contemplated when the original rules were made. How much less is such a frozen legal system possible in modern times.[8]

7. Day, *Why Judges Must Make Law,* 26 Case West.Res.L.Rev. 1, 2 (1976).

8. J. Frank, Law and the Modern Mind 6 (1963).

Only recently has the debate on judicial power moved from the philospher's essay and the professor's law review article to the newspaper and the political stump. Only when the courts gave new life to the Fourteenth Amendment—and thereby began to move from lawyer's law to public law—has the public become aware of catchwords like "separation of powers" and resurrected junior high school civic textbooks which, in simplistic style, instruct that the legislature makes law, the executive administers it, and the court simply interprets it. Starting in the 1960's, when the Supreme Court began the process of selective incorporation of the Bill of Rights by the Fourteenth Amendment, thus holding the states to higher standards of responsibility to their inhabitants, we began to experience heated public discussions on the jurisprudential temperaments of our judges. We began to classify them variously as activists, strict constructionists, liberals and conservatives.

Curiously, judicial intervention in the political process of the legislative and executive branches of government did not begin in the 1960s, but rather much earlier in the nation's history. Indeed, within fourteen years of the adoption of the Constitution, the judiciary's traditional role, as common law dispute settler, was enlarged. Resolving a conflict between a private citizen, one William Marbury, and James Madison, the Secretary of State, the Supreme Court set the precedential stage for a new judicial function—that of interpreter of a written constitution.[9] Thus, by declaring an act of a correlative branch of government unconstitutional, i.e. null and void, the Court allocated to itself a role that remains a much criticized aspect of the American judicial function today. In effect, the Court dictated what the executive could and could not do under the Constitution. So, it was early in our history that the judicial branch declared itself the overseer of the executive and legislative branches. Interestingly, the Supreme Court did not settle the dispute between Marbury and Madison in the sense of resolving the conflict between the two litigants (it dismissed Mr. Marbury's petition for lack of jurisdiction). Nonetheless, Marbury v. Madison marked a significant departure from the traditional dispute-settling role for the courts. Said Chief Justice Marshall in the landmark opinion: "It is emphatically the province and duty of the judicial department, to say what the law is. Those who apply the rule to particular cases, must of necessity expound and interpret that rule." [10]

Thirteen years later, the Supreme Court further enlarged the judicial function of interpreting the federal Constitution. Turning from the federal to the state level, the Court, in Martin v. Hunter's Lessee,[11] pronounced unconstitutional a decision of the highest court of the state of Virginia. The legal umbilical cord to mother England, severed in 1776, had now been replaced by another, linking the formerly—and formally—sovereign state courts with the Supreme Court of the United States, a court of technically "limited" jurisdiction sitting at the apex of

9. Marbury v. Madison, 5 U.S. (1 Cranch) 137 (1803).

10. 5 U.S. at 177.

11. 14 U.S. (1 Wheat.) 304 (1816).

the national legal system. Thus while the Constitution had defined the rights and obligations of the parties, state and federal, according to the system of dual sovereignty, one of the parties, the federal government, speaking through its Supreme Court, would retain the final authority to interpret the document.

Accordingly, modern American jurisprudence recognizes that the judge may, and indeed must, make law as well as apply it. Otherwise, there would be little room for the deployment of public policy as a tool in judicial decision making. Still, there are limits. In 1917, Holmes counseled

> I recognize without hesitation that judges do and must legislate, but they can do so only interstitially; they are confined from molar to molecular motions. A common law judge could not say I think the doctrine of consideration an act of historical nonsense and shall not enforce it in my court. No more could a judge exercising the limited jurisdiction of admiralty say I think well of the common law rules of master and servant and propose to introduce them here en bloc.[12]

The natural law had not admitted even to interstitial law making; it had held that law was only discovered by the operation of the universe and could not be created by any human institution. Similarly, under the tenets of early positivism, with its emphasis upon the command of the legislature as the voice of the sovereign, inquiry into the judge's creative function had been impermissible. Only in this century has the judge been recognized, albeit grudgingly, as a law maker.

In 1842, Swift v. Tyson [13] flatly stated that "it will hardly be contended that the decisions of courts constitute laws. They are, at most, only evidence of what the laws are, and are not, of themselves, laws." [14] Yet by 1972, Illinois v. City of Milwaukee [15] would reflect the metamorphosis of that earlier doctrine, emphasizing that in the context of state laws, court decisions were laws, and that, similarly, federal common law decisions were laws just as surely as those of statutory origin.[16]

Notwithstanding the bashfulness of judges and political scientists to admit it, the brute fact is, as Professor Robert A. Leflar has put it, that "[w]e know that courts make law, in fact, that they have made most of the law that we have. This is the way the common law has always been made." [17] Sir Rupert Cross, quoting Mellish, L.S., has suggested that it has not been otherwise in England: "The whole of the rules of equity and nine-tenths of the common law have in fact been made by judges." [18] And Lord Devlin has proposed that the judiciary may fashion new rights

12. Southern Pacific Co. v. Jensen, 244 U.S. 205, 221 (1917) (Holmes, J., dissenting).

13. 41 U.S. (16 Pet.) 1 (1842).

14. Id. at 17.

15. 406 U.S. 91 (1972).

16. Id. at 98–100.

17. R. Leflar, *Sources of Judge–Made Law*, 24 Okla.L.Rev. 319, 323–24 (1971).

18. R. Cross, Precedent in English Law 25 (2d ed. 1968).

if there is general community consensus as to the fundamental justice of such action.

Examples of judicial law making abound. Some are firmly grounded on considerations of public policy, while others rely on the Cardozan methods of philosophy or tradition. To identify but a few, in Moses v. MacPherlan,[19] a case of first impression in 1760, the Court of King's Bench allowed plaintiff to recover money obtained by the defendant in a deceitful manner; in 1905 the Supreme Court of Georgia permitted a new action for invasion of privacy,[20] although in 1902 New York had refused;[21] the Supreme Court has created a wrongful death action for maritime law;[22] and Massachusetts has announced a common law wrongful death action in tort.[23] In 1973, Florida abolished the contributory negligence rule, and replaced it with comparative negligence;[24] California followed suit in 1975.[25] The "Fall of the Citadel"[26] in products liability cases and the abrogation of hoary immunity rules[27] are likewise the products of judicial lawmaking. And in 1979, the Supreme Court reaffirmed its 1975 declaration that "[a]dmiralty law is judge-made law to a great extent."[28]

Although the precise limits of judicial law making have not been staked out, the power undoubtedly is a broad one. The cases illustrate that judicial law making often has exceeded the function of "filling interstices." In practice it might appear that the only limitations are functional—such as the inadequacy of facilities for extensive fact gathering, confinement to the facts of record, and the like. Ultimately, the test of judge-made law, as with any law, is its effect on social welfare and its acceptance by society. It behooves the judge who makes law, therefore, to focus *openly* on policy considerations as he or she seeks to keep the law in tune with changing societal values.

It may be argued that this approach pays mere lip service to the doctrine of separation of powers. The obvious response is that the federal and state constitutions must be read against the backdrop of the common law tradition—a tradition which has given to the courts the authority to interpret rules enacted by the legislature, and to fashion the

19. 2 Burr 1005, 96 Eng.Rep. 120 (1760).

20. Pasevich v. New England Life Insurance Co., 122 Ga. 190, 50 S.E. 68 (1905).

21. Roberson v. Rochester Folding Box Co., 171 N.Y. 538, 64 N.E. 442 (1902).

22. Moragne v. States Marine Lines, Inc., 398 U.S. 375 (1970).

23. Gaudette v. Webb, 362 Mass. 60, 284 N.E.2d 222 (1972).

24. Hoffman v. Jones, 280 So.2d 431 (Fla.1973).

25. Li v. Yellow Cab Co., 13 Cal.3d 804, 119 Cal.Rptr. 858, 532 P.2d 1226 (1975).

26. See Prosser, *The Fall of the Citadel (Strict Liability to the Consumer)*, 50 Minn. L.Rev. 791 (1966).

27. See, e.g., Muskopf v. Corning Hosp. Dist., 55 Cal.2d 211, 11 Cal.Rptr. 89, 359 P.2d 457 (1961) (governmental & charitable); Molitor v. Kaneland Community Unit Dist. No. 302, 18 Ill.2d 11, 163 N.E.2d 89 (1959), cert. denied, 362 U.S. 968 (1960) (governmental); Flagiello v. Pennsylvania Hosp., 417 Pa. 486, 208 A.2d 193 (1965) (charitable).

28. Edmonds v. Compagnie Generale Transatlantique, 443 U.S. 256 (1979) (citing United States v. Reliable Transfer Co., 421 U.S. 397, 409 (1975)).

aggregate of legal precepts that govern society.[29] Further, if legislative authority disagrees with judicial action, it can overrule that action by statute.[30] Ultimately, as John Chipman Gray observed, legislative acts are paramount to all other sources of law.[31]

RUPERT CROSS, THE DECLARATORY THEORY OF JUDICIAL DECISION *

Sir Matthew Hale, writing in the seventeenth century, stated the declaratory theory by asserting that the decisions of courts cannot

> make a law properly so called, for that only the King and Parliament can do; yet they have a great weight and authority in expounding, declaring, and publishing what the law of this Kingdom is, especially when such decisions hold a consonancy and congruity with resolutions and decisions of former times, and though such decisions are less than a law, yet they are a greater evidence thereof than the opinion of any private persons, as such whatsoever.

In the eighteenth century Blackstone said "the decisions of courts of justice are the evidence of what is common law". As late as 1892 Lord Esher said:

> There is in fact no such thing as judge-made law, for the judges do not make the law though they frequently have to apply existing law to circumstances as to which it has not previously been authoritatively laid down that such law is applicable.

The doctrine of Hale and Blackstone appears to have been that the common law consists of the usages and customary rules by which Englishmen have been governed since time immemorial supplemented by general principles of private justice and public convenience, and liable to be varied by Act of Parliament. This was the characteristic approach of the eighteenth-century judge towards the situation which was not covered by case-law. Thus, Willes J. said:

> Private justice, moral fitness and public convenience, when applied to a new subject, make common law without precedent, much more when received and approved by usage.

29. See generally, Pound, *Hierarchy of Sources and Forms in Different Systems of Law*, 7 Tul.L.Rev. 475 (1933).

30. See e.g., Molitor v. Kaneland Community Unit Dist. No. 302, 18 Ill.2d 11, 42, 163 N.E.2d 89, 104 (1959) (Davis, J., dissenting), cert. denied, 362 U.S. 968 (1960); cf. W. Friedmann, Legal Theory 501–03 (5th ed. 1967). See also, Breitel, *The Law-makers*, 65 Colum.L.Rev. 749, 767–72 (1965).

31. J.C. Gray, The Nature and Sources of the Law 124 (2d ed. 1921).

* From Precedent in English Law 23–25 (2d ed. 1968) by Rupert Cross. Copyright © by Oxford University Press 1968. Reprinted by permission of the Oxford University Press, Oxford.

It is difficult to be a great deal more explicit in the twentieth century about the basis of judicial reasoning when there is no precedent, but, when there is a precedent, orthodox theory has ceased to maintain that the precedent is no more than evidence of the moral fitness, public convenience, or conformity to usage of a rule derived from a previous decision or series of decisions. Such a rule is law "properly so called" and law because it was made by the judges, not because it originated in common usage, or the judges' idea of justice and public convenience. Holdsworth once wrote in a manner suggesting that the views of Hale and Blackstone represent twentieth-century judicial doctrine, but it is difficult not to share the skepticism of Dr. Goodhart who asked in reply whether it would be possible today for counsel to argue that a judgment of the House of Lords is not law because it conflicts with the settled principles of the common law.

So far as Lord Esher's statement is concerned, the application of existing law to new circumstances can never be clearly distinguished from the creation of a new rule of law. Moreover, if there is no such thing as judge-made law, it is impossible to account for the evolution of much legal doctrine. . . .

No one has ever denied that the rules of equity laid down by the Court of Chancery owe their authority to the fact that they are judge-made. Sir George Jessel said:

> It must not be forgotten that the rules of courts of equity are not, like the rules of the common law, supposed to have been established from time immemorial. It is perfectly well known that they have been established from time to time— altered, improved, and refined from time to time. In many cases we know the names of the chancellors who invented them.

Most modern lawyers would repudiate the remarks of Lord Esher and consider that Mellish L.J. came nearer to the truth when he said:

> The whole of the rules of equity and nine-tenths of the common law have in fact been made by judges.

ARTHUR T. VON MEHREN, THE JUDICIAL PROCESS *

There are basically four types of situations in which a court might be said to face the problem of whether it should "make law": First, where the court recognizes that the interests pressing for recognition in the case up for decision are authoritatively accommodated by the existing body of legal precepts, but disagrees, on policy grounds, with the consequences of this accommodation either for the instant case or in more general terms; Second, where historically the existing body of precepts authoritatively accommodated the interests now pressing for

* The Civil Law System, 836–37 (1957).   Boston: Little, Brown and Company, 1957. See Von Mehren, The Civil Law System.   Reprinted by permission.

recognition, but the court believes that political and ethical ideas about the proper accommodation have changed since these precepts were formulated; Third, where the patterns of interests accommodated by the existing body of precepts are similar to, but not identical with, the interests now before the court; Fourth, where no pattern of interests accommodated by the existing body of precepts can fairly be considered similar to the pattern of interests before the court.

In only the first of these situations can a court avoid deciding the case in terms of what is, empirically considered, new law. In the other three situations a court cannot—and judges having a non-mechanical conception of the judicial process recognize this fact—prevent changes in the law. As the material conditions of our social and economic life or the values held by society change, new patterns of interests arise, and old ones appear in a different context. A court, even one blinded to such changes in the law by a mechanical conception of the judicial process, either gives new meaning to an existing precept or formulates a new precept. It has no other choice. Applying "existing law" to accommodate interests to which that law was not addressed results, realistically speaking, in new law as inevitably as if a new precept had been formulated. As society changes, its law changes with it even if the law may appear to stand still.

"New law" thus necessarily results in all but the first of the situations in which a court faces the problem of whether to engage in judicial law making. However, neither the legal system as a whole nor the judges themselves consider that the court is making law when the precept historically addressed to the most nearly similar pattern of interests is applied to a novel pattern of interests. The court in such a case merely accepts and registers, as it were, changes in the law resulting from changed economic and social conditions. A court is ordinarily said to "make" new law only when it reacts to change by reformulating existing, or formulating new, policy. This action can take the form either of applying existing legal precepts in a modified form or of formulating and applying new ones.

————

ROBERT A. LEFLAR, SOURCES OF JUDGE–MADE LAW **

There has been a curious ambivalence among common law judges as to the law-making function of their courts. It used to be fashionable for judges to say that they never "made" law, but only "found" pre-existent law and applied it to new facts. Few appellate judges talk that way today, at least when they are talking with knowledgeable fellow-judges. Even the judges who talk that way will point, often proudly, to their own opinions as establishing the rules of law to be followed in the future.

** 24 Okla.L.Rev. 319, 323–28, 331–33,   Oklahoma Law Review © 1971.
335 (1971). Reprinted with permission of

We know that courts make law, in fact, that they have made most of the law that we have. That is the way that the common law has always been made, and it would be a sad day for our burgeoning economy and our developing civilization if our courts should cease to engage in the common law tradition of growth to make the law fit the ever-changing needs and demands of our ever-changing society. There is no indication today that such an unhappy state of stagnation in the law is likely to occur.

A part of the difficulty springs from a misconception about the materials from which the judges make the law. The misconception is that they build altogether from earlier announcements of the law, either judicial or legislative. These are used, of course. But much more is used.

The common law consists not only of judicial precedents (opinions in decided cases) but of principles, standards, doctrines, and traditions which in long-term effectiveness far outweigh the little rules that are derived from particular cases. These little rules come and go.

One of our good courts once held, on the issue of contributory negligence, that the driver of an automobile approaching a blind railroad crossing must not only stop, look, and listen but, if he could not see down the track, must get out of his car, go onto the track and look down it before driving upon it. This was silly, because an unseen train might reach the crossing while the driver walked back to his car and before he could restart it and drive upon the tracks. That decision was soon overruled, and the true common law rule, the standard of care which an ordinary prudent man would exercise under the same or similar circumstances, was reapplied. Little rules as to what constitutes reasonable care in this or that situation have been asserted in one case or another and then retracted in later cases, but the common law standard has remained. It is a standard that is sufficiently flexible to sustain one little judge-made rule today, and another little judge-made rule tomorrow, or ten years from now, as conditions change and as the conduct of ordinary prudent men changes along with the changed conditions.

Until quite recently caveat emptor was the rule of the marketplace, and the rule in the courts as well. It was a rule of dog eat dog, and even more of dog eat sheep. It is largely within my lifetime that the courts, motivated by changing social mores, have begun to develop the law of misrepresentation and to extend it to protect the mass of consumers under the pre-packaged economy that increasingly prevails in our modern society. Thus partially eaten sheep are beginning to receive compensation for the dog bites that have been taken out of them, and the new rules may even restrain the dogs somewhat in their sheep-eating tendencies. The changing ethical standards of the society themselves serve to change the law.

It would be wrong, however, to assume that the law keeps pace with the leaders in ethical improvement. It is more likely that courts will condemn old practices only after they have been long deplored by ethical laymen, after higher standards have already come to be accepted by the better element among those who do business in the marketplace. Yet it is the demands of the citizenry, buttressed by the ethics of the more conscientious business and professional men, rather than the precedents, that have caused the courts to move away from caveat emptor.

It would be easy to cite not merely scores but hundreds of areas in which our common law courts, as the interests and needs of the society changed, have moved the law away from old positions to newer ones that better fit society's new interests and needs.

. . .

Our common law started in the Middle Ages, from practically nothing. In its beginnings it dealt on the civil side with little more than assaults, batteries, and unpermitted entries upon the lands of others. The early common law of crimes was mostly concerned with protection of the interests of what we today call "the establishment." There was a long period when much of the new common law was lawyers' law, dealing with forms of action, pleading, and the like. Probably these preoccupations of the courts served the dominant interests of late medieval and early modern society, which was primarily concerned with maintaining things as they were, protection of the vested interests of landowners and royalty, with a minimum of change, and any change that was achieved to come as slowly as possible.

But change came, whether wanted or not. The merchant class came to be important, and law was needed to govern commercial transactions. When Lord Mansfield became Chief Justice of England, the common law courts knew nothing of business law. A wide variety of sales of goods, contracts, bills of lading, promissory notes, bills of exchange, and the like were employed by the merchants, but their interpretation and enforcement depended more upon the merchants' good faith and private sanctions than upon the law. Mansfield brought the law merchant, the customs of the merchants, into the law, made it part of the common law, with no help from Parliament. Also, during the same period, he created the common law of quasi-contract, derived partly from equity jurisprudence and partly from simple principles of ethics and morality.

What Mansfield's opinions brought into the common law of England was with little hesitation accepted by our judges as the common law of the American states as well. Yet it is notable that Mansfield was Chief Justice from 1756 to 1788, well past the dates fixed by most of our reception statutes for state adoption of England's common law. What happened was that the courts of England and of our states simply accepted as part of the common law a mass of materials whose time had come.

That is what common law courts have always done. The whole modern law of insurance, the law of corporations, the law of trusts, the law that governs new types of interests in land, oil and gas law, the law of aviation, the law of conflict of laws, and many other areas of today's law, have been created by our courts, with creation taking the form of judicial opinions, but with the demand for the new law coming from the extra-judicial society whose activities create the need for the new law.

We certainly cannot assert that the common law as announced by the courts is a body of rules that always keeps nicely abreast of the needs of society. That just is not true. Mr. Justice Holmes emphasized the slow and cumbersome character of the case-by-case approach of the common law method when he observed that it does no more than carry us from tuft to tuft across the morass.

The need for change must be felt before the change occurs. Even then, the cases that come into the courts, for which our growth-producing opinions must be written, seldom present whole problems, but little bits and pieces of problems only, so that the broad sweep of social needs in a given area can almost never be worked out according to a systematic and unified plan, if judicial pronouncements are restricted narrowly to the specific facts of the case before the court. The technique of deciding the narrow issue only, so that the *ratio decidendi* can be isolated from its supporting reasons and the case thereafter cited only for the precise point decided by it, is a principal barrier to intelligently planned progress in the common law. Decision-making directed to narrow issues does not encourage broad-gauge thinking, though it does not preclude it, either. Much of the progress in the law that we are proudest of has been achieved by great judges who refused to confine themselves to narrow issues, who were willing to seize upon relevant facts as a starting point for analysis of the larger issues that the facts suggested. Much of what their opinions covered might be classified as dictum, but it was dictum designed to light the path into the future. It was dictum fated to be followed.

That was true when Mansfield brought the law merchant and the law of quasi-contract into the common law. It was true of the great opinions of Chief Justice Doe of New Hampshire. Karl Llewellyn called it the "grand style of the common law," a technique that is recurring today. Our good courts are still willing, when there is need for it, to answer the principally litigated issue first, then to give answers to incidental questions that are apt to arise thereafter, thus avoiding the necessity for further litigation.

We can in a general way identify the types of situations, the areas, in which judicial lawmaking in the form of innovative appellate opinions is likely to occur, and those in which it is unlikely.

One of the easiest to identify is the Wisconsin experience . . . where a new statute was incomplete, and the courts had to fill in the gaps in order to make it meaningful and workable. Judges reluctant to admit that they make the law may call this statutory interpretation, but it achieves new law regardless of how it is labeled.

Clear and simple issues, not requiring a mass of distinctions and differentiations nor extensive implementation, are more apt candidates for judicial review and the making of new law than are complicated ones.

A court can come up with a new and desirable rule on the strict liability of manufacturers of defective products more effectively than it can formulate a system of no-fault liability for auto accidents.

A court is less likely to revise a common law rule that has recently been modified by legislation than it is to review one that the legislature has not worked on. The fact that a rule is altogether or primarily a judge-made one is itself a justification for judicial review of it.

Sometimes it is said that legislative noninterference with a long-lived judicially created rule is an indication of legislative confirmation of it, almost equivalent to legislative re-enactment of it. That is unsound reasoning. On such issues, it is more likely that legislators have simply regarded the matter as one that the courts have always taken care of, to be left for the courts to continue to take care of, through normal common law processes.

A common type of judicial innovation involves a sort of gnawing process. The courts may gradually eat away at the edges of a bad old rule until, after a generation or two, there is little or nothing left of it. That happened in New York with the charitable immunity rule as applied to hospitals, where the court-created distinction between "administrative" and "professional" activities finally became so cumbersome that the court of appeals swept the whole thing away. The judicial differentiation between "proprietary" and "governmental" activities has operated in the same way to cut down and in some states eventually eliminate sovereign immunity in tort.

Another sort of area in which courts feel free to act on their own is that in which a whole body of the law is substantially undeveloped, or underdeveloped. The conflict of laws area of choice of law is an illustration. Professor Joseph H. Beale almost single-handedly devised a new body of Conflicts law about a half-century ago, and secured some judicial acceptance of it, but courts which realized that they were in any event making new Conflicts law later decided to look beyond the Bealei-an conceptualism in order to base the new law more intelligently on true choice-influencing considerations.

Above all, the test for propriety of any judicial change in the law is the society's readiness for and probable approval of the change. Theoretically this is about the same as the test for legislative change in the law. Yet it requires a more delicate testing of, or guessing at, public attitudes, since legislators through their political contacts have readier means of measuring social pressures than judges have, and the pressures are likely to be more evident in legislative areas than in the less political areas where judicial revision of the law is indicated. Nevertheless, judges can be and quite often are aware of major surges in social attitudes. They may even be more aware of them than legislators are, with respect to problems that regularly come before the courts and do not come before legislatures. Also, good judges who keep abreast of new thinking in the law may have better ideas as to what the solutions should be than do most legislators.

. . .

Common law courts do make law, and they make it through their judicial opinions. Yet the sources of law, including new judge-made law, are for the most part neither the courts nor the judges themselves, but the society. The activities and interests and ethical attitudes of the citizenry, and especially of dominant groups within the citizenry, are the real sources of the common law. This was true in the Middle Ages when the common law had its beginnings, it has been true as the common law grew and developed in the intervening centuries, and it is true as the common law undergoes today the most rapid modernization in its entire history.

NOTE

Does Leflar disagree with Pound, *ante,* on the sources of law? Do Leflar and Pound use "sources of law" in the same sense? Is Leflar's interpretation as broad as Pound's?

True, "[t]he need for change must be felt before the change occurs," but by whom? The whole society? A majority of participating judges? In this respect, is the analogy to the development of mercantile law fair?

———

SOUTHERN PACIFIC CO. v. JENSEN

Supreme Court of the United States, 1917.
244 U.S. 205, 37 S.Ct. 524, 61 L.Ed. 1086.

Mr. Justice Holmes, dissenting.

... I recognize without hesitation that judges do and must legislate, but they can do so only interstitially; they are confined from molar to molecular motions. A common-law judge could not say I think the doctrine of consideration a bit of historical nonsense and shall not enforce it in my court. No more could a judge exercising the limited jurisdiction of admiralty say I think well of the common-law rules of master and servant and propose to introduce them here *en bloc.* Certainly he could not in that way enlarge the exclusive jurisdiction of the District Courts and cut down the power of the States. If admiralty adopts common-law rules without an act of Congress it cannot extend the maritime law as understood by the Constitution. It must take the rights of the parties from a different authority, just as it does when it enforces a lien created by a State. The only authority available is the common law or statutes of a State. For from the often repeated statement that there is no common law of the United States, ... the natural inference is that in the silence of Congress this court has believed the very limited law of the sea to be supplemented ... by the common law, ... here ... of the State.

. . .

The common law is not a brooding omnipresence in the sky but the articulate voice of some sovereign or quasi-sovereign that can be identified; although some decisions with which I have disagreed seem to me to have forgotten the fact. It always is the law of some State, and if the District Courts adopt the common law of torts, as they have shown a tendency to do, they thereby assume that a law not of maritime origin and deriving its authority in that territory only from some particular State of this Union also governs maritime torts in that territory—and if the common law, the statute law has at least equal force, as the discussion in The Osceola [189 U.S. 158, 23 S.Ct. 483, 47 L.Ed. 760] assumes. On the other hand the refusal of the District Courts to give remedies coextensive with the common law would prove no more than that they regarded their jurisdiction as limited by the ancient lines—not that they doubted that the common law might and would be enforced in the courts of the States as it always has been.

NOTE

Mr. Justice Douglas for the Court in Saxbe v. Bustos, 419 U.S. 65, 79–80 (1974):

> The changes suggested implicate so many policies and raise so many problems of a political, economic, and social nature that it is fit that the judiciary recuse itself. At times judges must legislate "interstitially" to resolve ambiguities in laws. But the problem of taking all or some alien commuters engaging in farm work out of the Act is not "interstitial" or as Mr. Justice Holmes once put it "molecular." It is a massive or "molar" action for which the judiciary is ill-equipped.

It is generally conceded that, within appropriate constitutional limitations, it is Congress that has the authority and the power to establish as well as withdraw jurisdiction of the inferior federal courts. Originally, 42 U.S.C.A. 1983 was part of the Civil Rights Act of 1871. The act was passed by the Reconstruction Congress in order to effectuate the fourteenth amendment which, in turn, was passed to insure protection of blacks in the southern states. The number of complaints filed under section 1983 after the post-war period was infinitesimal. See Justice Frankfurter's collection of cases, Monroe v. Pape, 365 U.S. 167, 214 n. 21 (1961). Monroe v. Pape was decided in 1961. Then the deluge began. In 1960 there were 280 cases brought under section 1983. In 1994 there were 29,636 civil rights cases filed out of a total of 190,981 private civil cases in the U.S. District Courts. From the standpoint of judicially legislating boundaries for the federal district courts, did the Supreme Court do so "interstitially," confining its motions "from molar to molecular"?

Where a socially desirable end is sought—e.g., the vindication of federal rights infringed by those acting under color of state law—does it make any difference that the expansion of statutory jurisdiction was created by the judiciary, and not by the legislature?

CHARLES D. BREITEL, THE LAWMAKERS *

It is now a commonplace that courts, not only of common-law jurisdictions but also those which have codified statutory law as their base, participate in the lawmaking process. The commonplace, for which the Holmeses and the Cardozos had to blaze a trail in the judicial realm, assumes the rightness of courts in making interstitial law, filling gaps in the statutory and decisional rules, and at a snail-like pace giving some forward movement to the developing law. Any law creation more drastic than this is often said and thought to be an invalid encroachment on the legislative branch.

. . .

It is well to consider some of the reasons why this happened. It will also be well then to consider the advantages and the marked disadvantages in this expanded process, especially in its effects upon the structure of a democratic political society.

Fundamentally, the very generality of rules of law, whether expressed in statutes or in the *rationes decidendi* of precedents, does not allow the intended precision for each case in the future. Predictable rules do not guarantee that the complexes of facts will be equally predictable. They rarely are. So, at the very start, as the modern jurists have made clear, there is inevitable judicial lawmaking in applying or refusing to apply the statutory or precedential rule. First, the very fact that there is no area of human conduct in which there is non-law also makes this inevitable. Second, bolstered by the common-law tradition, legislatures have encouraged the evolutionary elaboration of law by the courts through the deliberate enactment of highly generalized statutes or the refusal to enact any statutes. Third, the flexibility of constitutional interpretation has run over into the statutory field; once the technique of massive, or, in Holmes' word, molar, lawmaking has been learned and practiced, it moves of its own momentum beyond the narrower constitutional purview. These are generally the factors influential in the judicial process in the American scene. * * *

There is still another special reason why the judicial process, at least in this country, engenders an activist role in lawmaking. It is the failure or inability of the legislature to act where there is, nevertheless, a desperate need for creative lawmaking.... Whether it be deadlock or a refusal to face up to legislative or political hazards, there is often a deferral or refusal to act. Sometimes the reason is strongly based on the desire to permit the difficulties of the problem to be resolved judicially by

* 65 Colum.L.Rev. 749, 765, 767–72 (1965). Reprinted by permission.

an evolutionary case-by-case approach in the decisional process, at least for a time, until the question is ripe for legislative handling. Sometimes the reason is only the view that the common-law solution is best because of nice technical distinctions and because the need for harmony with other rules of law is deemed paramount. . . .

These are some of the reasons that make for a strong lawmaking function in the courts, far beyond the interstitial and the gap-filling. These reasons, however, do not mean that it is all to the good and that courts are best equipped to perform the function. On the contrary, there are grave limiting factors: the limitations of judicial procedure, political dependence upon other branches of government, and the isolated nature of the judicial office. . . .

. . . While in the particular case, the judge may come equipped to grasp the situation, in Llewellyn's term, by use of his situation-sense, this is no substitute for what is required for wise and broad legislating. For legislation, opportunities for unlimited external investigation are required and are substantially available. Moreover, in the nature of the judicial profession, and more so as the judge remains in his truly cloistered activity, disciplined by the etiquette and ethics that govern the conduct of a judge, and as importantly, the conduct of others toward him, the judge is ever removed more distantly from the maddening scene. This entails a loss of contact with the greater environment, and, for many men, a loss of sense of the movements of their time. For obvious reasons, it is no answer, in order to offset the cloister, to make the judicial career less than a lifetime commitment or opportunity or to require the judge to mingle to the full in the life-stream of his community, neither of which is desirable.

The greatness of the American and English judiciaries rests to a great extent in their relative independence from political vicissitudes and executive control. In the civil code countries we do not find their like. In the displacement of democratic regimes by tyrannies during this century there has been no need to subvert the judiciary; its members were easily removed or easily brought to heel. The same could not happen, at least I would like to think, in the Anglo–American jurisprudence. But a price is paid for this independence, namely, the separation from political involvement; it is an appropriate price to pay for a judiciary whose main function is law-application and interstitial lawmaking. When the judicial function expands beyond the molecular movements, in Holmes' figure, into the molar, the price paid in political independence and isolation produces disfunction.

By reason of relative judicial independence judges are not responsible to the electorate. Even with an elected judiciary it is a truism that the role of the electorate is all but an unconscious one without significant influence. The lifetime commitment or opportunity of the judicial career provides a guaranty of independence; it also becomes a denial of political responsibility expressed by standing for periodical re-election. A body of men thus chosen and thus responsible is not the proper organ for lawmaking on the molar scale in a democratically organized society. They may do well, to be sure; they may even do better, conceivably, than other available alternatives as Plato's philosopher-kings would. It should be recognized, however, that such a system does not produce or become a democratic structure.

.   .   .

There is another grave limiting factor affecting the courts. Their dependence upon the legislative and executive branches for their institutional strength is unlimited save for a few constitutional provisions and the support of public opinion. Their subject-matter jurisdiction to a large extent, the housing, financing, and staffing of the courts to a total extent, are dependent upon the legislature and executive. The appointing power, where judges are appointed, and the selection power, where judges are elected, reside where the political power rests. The specters of court-packing, jurisdiction limitation, and curtailment of financial support for judicial institutions have risen many times. The test of institutional strength is not in any condition extant at one time and place, but in the capacity of the institution to persist and survive through vicissitudes and even crises, at least until a major readjustment can be made.

Moreover, unlike the executive, the nature of the judicial office and the ethical standards with which the office is properly surrounded make it impossible for the courts to go over anyone's head to the people. Nor is there any direct mechanism for communication and transfers of support, as there is for the legislature and the executive, between the courts and the people, for the people to pass their strength on to the courts. There are only the opinions judges write. In short, a democratic society threatened from within is not likely to be saved between only a strong executive and a judicial presidium of nine, with subordinate judicial presidiums down to the base. It is the legislative branch, for good and for ill, which holds the key to democratic institutions.

NOTE

"It is the legislative branch, for good and for ill, which holds the key to democratic institutions." How valid is this statement with respect to the factual complexes underlying Brown v. Board of Education, 347 U.S. 483 (1954), and Baker v. Carr, 369 U.S. 186 (1962)? Consider the suggestion that because of their "cloistered", politically free life, judges do not constitute "proper organ[s] for lawmaking on the molar scale." Would this be true of academicians? Consider the input of judges and law professors to the American Law Institute's Restatements or the Uniform Commercial Code. Consider again Breitel's statement. Does a Congressman's parochial allegiance to the district which elects him qualify him for decisions on the "molar scale"? What qualifies the professional staffs of congressional committees to draft legislation and supervise legislative hearings to influence decisions on the "molar scale"?

RONALD M. DWORKIN, ARGUMENTS OF POLICIES, OF PRINCIPLES *

Theories of adjudication have become more sophisticated, but the most popular theories still put judging in the shade of legislation. The main outlines of this story are familiar. Judges should apply the law that other institutions have made; they should not make new law. That is the ideal, but for different reasons it cannot be realized fully in practice. Statutes and common law rules are often vague and must be interpreted before they can be applied to novel cases. Some cases, moreover, raise issues so novel that they cannot be decided even by stretching or reinterpreting existing rules. So judges must sometimes make new law, either covertly or explicitly. But when they do, they should act as deputy to the appropriate legislature, enacting the law that they suppose the legislature would enact if seized of the problem.

That is perfectly familiar, but there is buried in this common story a further level of subordination not always noticed. When judges make law, so the expectation runs, they will act not only as deputy to the legislature but as a deputy legislature. They will make law in response to evidence and arguments of the same character as would move the superior institution if it were acting on its own. This is a deeper level of subordination because it makes any understanding of what judges do in hard cases parasitic on a prior understanding of what legislators do all the time. This deeper subordination is therefore conceptual as well as political.

In fact, however, judges neither should be nor are deputy legislators, and the familiar assumption that when they go beyond political decisions already made by someone else they are legislating, is misleading. It misses the importance of a fundamental distinction within political theory, which I shall now introduce in a crude form. This is the distinction between arguments of principle on the one hand and arguments of policy on the other.

Arguments of policy justify a political decision by showing that the decision advances or protects some collective goal of the community as a whole. The argument in favor of a subsidy for aircraft manufacturers, that the subsidy will protect national defense, is an argument of policy. Arguments of principle justify a political decision by showing that the decision respects or secures some individual or group right. The argument in favor of anti-discrimination statutes, that a minority has a right to equal respect and concern, is an argument of principle. These two

* R. Dworkin, *Hard Cases,* 88 Harv. L.Rev. 1057, 1058–62 (1975). Copyright by Ronald Dworkin. Reprinted by permission of the author and publisher.

sorts of argument do not exhaust political argument. Sometimes, for example, a political decision, like the decision to allow extra income tax exemptions for the blind, may be defended as an act of public generosity or virtue rather than on grounds of either policy or principle. But principle and policy are the major grounds of political justification.

The justification of a legislative program of any complexity will ordinarily require both sorts of argument. Even a program that is chiefly a matter of policy, like a subsidy program for important industries, may require strands of principle to justify its particular design. It may be, for example, that the program provides equal subsidies for manufacturers of different capabilities, on the assumption that weaker aircraft manufacturers have some right not to be driven out of business by government intervention, even though the industry would be more efficient without them. On the other hand, a program that depends chiefly on principle, like an antidiscrimination program, may reflect a sense that rights are not absolute and do not hold when the consequences for policy are very serious. The program may provide, for example, that fair employment practice rules do not apply when they might prove especially disruptive or dangerous. In the subsidy case we might say that the rights conferred are generated by policy and qualified by principle; in the antidiscrimination case they are generated by principle and qualified by policy.

It is plainly competent for the legislature to pursue arguments of policy and to adopt programs that are generated by such arguments. If courts are deputy legislatures, then it must be competent for them to do the same. Of course, unoriginal judicial decisions that merely enforce the clear terms of some plainly valid statute are always justified on arguments of principle, even if the statute itself was generated by policy. Suppose an aircraft manufacturer sues to recover the subsidy that the statute provides. He argues his right to the subsidy; his argument is an argument of principle. He does not argue that the national defense would be improved by subsidizing him; he might even concede that the statute was wrong on policy grounds when it was adopted, or that it should have been repealed, on policy grounds, long ago. His right to a subsidy no longer depends on any argument of policy because the statute made it a matter of principle.

––––––

ROGER J. TRAYNOR, REASONING IN A CIRCLE OF LAW *

Unlike the legislator, whose lawmaking knows no bounds, the judge stays close to his house of the law in the bounds of stare decisis. He invariably takes precedent as his starting-point; he is constrained to arrive at a decision in the context of ancestral judicial experience: the given decisions, or lacking these, the given dicta, or lacking these, the given clues. Even if his search of the past yields nothing, so that he

* 56 Va.L.Rev. 739, 742–43, 749–50 (1970). Reprinted by permission.

confronts a truly unprecedented case, he still arrives at a decision in the context of judicial reasoning with recognizable ties to the past; by its kinship thereto it not only establishes the unprecedented case as a precedent for the future, but integrates it in the often rewoven but always unbroken line with the past.

Moreover, the judge is confined by the record in the case, which in turn is confined to legally relevant material, limited by evidentiary rules. So it happens that even a decision of far-reaching importance concludes with the words: "We hold today only that.... We do not reach the question whether...." Circumspectly the weaver stops, so as not to confuse the pattern of transition from yesterday to today. Tomorrow is time enough for new weaving, as the facts of tomorrow come due.

A decision that has not suffered untimely birth has a reduced risk of untimely death. Insofar as a court remains uncommitted to unduly wide implications of a decision, it gains time to inform itself further through succeeding cases. It is then better situated to retreat or advance with a minimum of shock to the evolutionary course of the law, and hence with a minimum of shock to those who act in reliance upon judicial decisions. The greatest judges of the common law have proceeded in this way, moving not by fits and starts, but at the pace of the tortoise that steadily makes advances though it carries the past on its back.

The very caution of the judicial process offers the best of reasons for confidence in the recurring reformation of judicial rules. A reasoning judge's painstaking exploration of place and his sense of pace, give reassurance that when he takes an occasional dramatic leap forward he is impelled to do so in the very interest of orderly progression. There are times when he encounters so much chaos on his long march that the most cautious thing he can do is to take the initiative in throwing chaos to the winds. The great Judge Mansfield did so when he broke the chaos of stalemated contractual relations with the concept of concurrent conditions. Holmes and Brandeis did so when they cleared the way for a liquidation of ancient interpretations of freedom of contract that had served to perpetuate child labor. Cardozo did so when he moved the rusting wheels of Winterbottom v. Wright [1] to one side to make way for MacPherson v. Buick Motor Co.[2] Chief Justice Stone did so, in the chaotic field of conflict of laws, when he noted the leeway in the United States Constitution between the mandate of the full faith and credit clause and the prohibition of the due process clause.[3]

. . .

In spelling out rules that form a Morse code common to statutes and judicial decisions, and in the United States common even to the Constitution of the country and the constitutions of the states, courts keep the law straight on its course. That high responsibility should not be

1. 152 Eng.Rep. 402 (Ex.1842).

2. 217 N.Y. 382, 111 N.E. 1050 (1916).

3. Yarborough v. Yarborough, 290 U.S. 202, 214 (1933) (dissenting opinion).

reduced to a mean task of keeping the law straight and narrow. It calls for literate, not literal, judges.

Hence we should not be misled by the half-truth that policy is a matter for the legislators to decide. Recurringly it is also for the courts to decide. There is always an area not covered by legislation in which they must revise old rules or formulate new ones, and in that process policy may be an appropriate and even a basic consideration. The briefs carry the first responsibility in stating the policy at stake and demonstrating its relevance; but if they fail or fall short, no conscientious judge will set bounds to his inquiry. If he finds no significant clues in the law books, he will not close his eyes to a pertinent study merely because it was written by an economist or perhaps an anthropologist or an engineer.

We need not distrust judicial scrutiny of such extralegal materials. The very independence of judges, fostered by judicial office even when not guaranteed by tenure, and their continuous adjustment of sight to varied problems tend to develop in the least of them some skill in the evaluation of massive data. They learn to detect latent quackery in medicine, to question doddered scientific findings, to edit the swarm spore of the social scientists, to add grains of salt to the fortune-telling statistics of the economists. Moreover, as with cases or legal theories not covered by the briefs, they are bound in fairness to direct the attention of counsel to such materials, if it appears that they may affect the outcome of the case, and to give them the opportunity to submit additional briefs. So the miter square of legal analysis, the marking blades for fitting and joining, reduce any host of materials to the gist of a legal construction.

NOTE

Is there a difference between the exercise of "policy" by the court and general judicial law making? Does it make any difference if the legislature has purported to codify all the law? Does it make a difference if one jurisdiction is purportedly a common law state augmented by statutes (Pennsylvania) and another jurisdiction (federal) promulgates its laws by statute and represents itself as having no general civil common law and no common law of crimes?

Does Traynor's use of the term "policy" resemble more closely that employed by Dworkin or that employed by Lord Denning?

Some states (see Alabama Code, Title 15, § 389 (1940)) have statutes requiring an appellate court to search the record ("to consider all questions apparent in the record") for error in criminal appeals, in addition to considering the contentions presented by brief and oral argument. Consider the propriety of a court's deciding a case on an issue neither briefed nor argued by the parties. Would it make a difference if the judgment of the trial court were affirmed or reversed?

WOLFGANG FRIEDMANN, LEGAL THEORY *

. . . It is a difficult question for a court to decide whether, in the face of continued legislative inaction, it should intervene to change a manifestly unjust and outdated legal principle, sometimes at the risk of stinging the legislator into retaliatory action, or remain passive. Certainly the answer cannot be given in terms of subject matter. The long overdue reform of the principles of liability of occupiers to visitors could easily have been carried out by the courts, by interpretations far less sweeping than those the House of Lords used in cases like Bonsor v. Musicians' Union [72] or Rookes v. Barnard.[73] In the end the law was changed by legislative reform. Such questions as the joint liability of tortfeasors, the immunity of public authorities (in the United States) from liability for negligence, or the rights of a married woman to occupancy of a matrimonial home could be and have been the subject of judicial as well as legislative reforms. In 1959 the Supreme Court of Illinois decided that it was time to do away with the absurd rule of immunity of local authorities from liability for negligence, in a typical case where a bus driver employed by a local school authority had negligently injured children riding to school in the bus.[75] But although the court applied its new doctrine only prospectively, the Illinois legislature was stirred into action and restored the old doctrine. The Supreme Court of California, which, in 1961, went even further by overruling the old immunity doctrine retroactively,[77] was somewhat luckier, in provoking a comprehensive study of the problem and an eventual legislative reform in 1963. There are those who would solve the dilemma by generally prescribing judicial inaction in the face of legislative inaction. This was propounded by Professor Henry M. Hart in a symposium on "Courts and Lawmaking" held in 1958 at the Columbia Law School:

> The Constitution of the United States and each of the state constitutions prescribe the ways in which bills shall become law. Failing to enact a bill is not one of these ways, even when a bill has been introduced and voted down. A fortiori, the failure to act is not an authorized way of making law when no bill on the subject was ever introduced in the first place. . . . A legislature is a deliberative body. It is an instrument for arriving at a consensus, not an instrument for recording a consensus previously arrived at, as if by some mysterious emanation from the electorate. To arrive at a consensus, the legislature follows an

---

* 501–03 (5th ed. 1967). Reprinted by permission of Columbia University Press.

72. [1956] A.C. 104.

73. [1964] A.C. 1129.

75. Molitor v. Kaneland Community Unit District No. 302, 18 Ill.2d 11, 163 N.E.2d 89 (1959). It should be noted that in the United States, the discredited doc-

trine of the sovereign's immunity from tort liability has, in application of the ancient decision of Russell v. Men of Devon (1788), 2 T.R. 667, been carried to much greater lengths than in England, where statutory public authorities, including school boards, have long been held subject to suit in tort.

77. Muskopf v. Corning Hospital District, 359 P.2d 457 (Cal.1961).

elaborate procedure of investigation and consideration eventuating in the approval of a particular form of words as law. For the courts to treat the legislature as making law by any other means is to treat this procedure and this agreement upon a particular form of words as mere froufrou—without any real function.

But two eminent judges are far less categorical: Judge Breitel, of the Court of Appeals of New York has observed:

> Legislative inaction, total or partial, in a troubled area, may indicate a rejection of proposals; or it may indicate a warrant to the courts to exercise the traditional common law responsibility of piercing out, case by case, the necessary legal innovations. Unfortunately there is no rule of thumb to distinguish these contradictory indications; the only course is examination of legislative purpose by investigation of surrounding circumstances and the available legislative history.

Chief Justice Traynor of the California Supreme Court writes:

> However timely an overruling seems, a judge may still be deterred from undertaking it if there are cogent reasons for leaving the task to the legislature. There are no ready lists of such reasons, and a judge has no absolute standards for testing his own. It is for him nevertheless to articulate the uneasiness he may feel about judicial liquidation of a precedent, however ripe it appears for displacement in the time and circumstances of the case that has brought it into question.

GIROUARD v. UNITED STATES

Supreme Court of the United States, 1946.
328 U.S. 61, 66 S.Ct. 826, 90 L.Ed. 1084.

[Presented was an appeal from a denial of naturalization, the appellant having refused to agree "to take up arms in defense of this country." In United States v. Schwimmer, 279 U.S. 644, 49 S.Ct. 448, 73 L.Ed. 889; United States v. Macintosh, 283 U.S. 605, 51 S.Ct. 570, 75 L.Ed. 1302, and United States v. Bland, 283 U.S. 636, 51 S.Ct. 569, 75 L.Ed. 1319, the Court had articulated "the same general rule—that an alien who refuses to bear arms will not be admitted to citizenship." The Girouard Court severely criticized these cases]:

Mr. Justice Douglas delivered the opinion of the Court.

We conclude that the Schwimmer, Macintosh and Bland cases do not state the correct rule of law.

We are met, however, with the argument that even though those cases were wrongly decided, Congress has adopted the rule which they announced. The argument runs as follows: Many efforts were made to amend the law so as to change the rule announced by those cases; but in every instance the bill died in committee. Moreover, in 1940 when the new Naturalization Act was passed, Congress reenacted the oath in its pre-existing form, though at the same time it made extensive changes in the requirements and procedure for naturalization. From this it is argued that Congress adopted and reenacted the rule of the Schwimmer, Macintosh, and Bland cases....

We stated in Helvering v. Hallock, 309 U.S. 106, 119, 60 S.Ct. 444, 451, 84 L.Ed. 604, 125 A.L.R. 1368, that "It would require very persuasive circumstances enveloping Congressional silence to debar this Court from re-examining its own doctrines." It is at best treacherous to find in Congressional silence alone the adoption of a controlling rule of law. We do not think under the circumstances of this legislative history that we can properly place on the shoulders of Congress the burden of the Court's own error. The history of the 1940 Act is at most equivocal. It contains no affirmative recognition of the rule of the Schwimmer, Macintosh and Bland cases. The silence of Congress and its inaction are as consistent with a desire to leave the problem fluid as they are with an adoption by silence of the rule of those cases. But for us, it is enough to say that since the date of those cases Congress never acted affirmatively on this question but once and that was in 1942. At that time, as we have noted, Congress specifically granted naturalization privileges to non-combatants who like petitioner were prevented from bearing arms by their religious scruples. That was affirmative recognition that one could be attached to the principles of our government and could support and defend it even though his religious convictions prevented him from bearing arms. And, as we have said, we cannot believe that the oath was designed to exact something more from one person than from another. Thus the affirmative action taken by Congress in 1942 negatives any inference that otherwise might be drawn from its silence when it reenacted the oath in 1940.

MR. CHIEF JUSTICE STONE dissenting.

I think the judgment should be affirmed, for the reason that the court below, in applying the controlling provisions of the naturalization statutes, correctly applied them as earlier construed by this Court, whose construction Congress has adopted and confirmed.

In three cases decided more than fifteen years ago, this Court denied citizenship to applicants for naturalization who had announced that they proposed to take the prescribed oath of allegiance with the reservation or qualification that they would not, as naturalized citizens, assist in the defense of this country by force of arms or give their moral support to the government in any war which they did not believe to be morally justified or in the best interests of the country....

. . .

With three other Justices of the Court I dissented in the Macintosh and Bland cases, for reasons which the Court now adopts as ground for overruling them. Since this Court in three considered earlier opinions has rejected the construction of the statute for which the dissenting Justices contended, the question, which for me is decisive of the present case, is whether Congress has likewise rejected that construction by its subsequent legislative action, and has adopted and confirmed the Court's earlier construction of the statutes in question. A study of Congressional action taken with respect to proposals for amendment of the naturalization laws since the decision in the Schwimmer case, leads me to conclude that Congress has adopted and confirmed this Court's earlier construction of the naturalization laws. For that reason alone I think that the judgment should be affirmed.

. . .

[F]or six successive Congresses, over a period of more than a decade, there were continuously pending before Congress in one form or another proposals to overturn the rulings in the three Supreme Court decisions in question. Congress declined to adopt these proposals after full hearings and after speeches on the floor advocating the change. 72 Cong.Rec. 6966–7; 75th Cong.Rec. 15354–7. In the meantime the decisions of this Court had been followed in Clarke's Case, 301 Pa. 321, 152 A. 92; Beale v. United States, 8 Cir., 71 F.2d 737; In re Warkentin, 7 Cir., 93 F.2d 42. In Beale v. United States, supra, [71 F.2d 739] the court pointed out that the proposed amendments affecting the provisions of the statutes relating to admission to citizenship had failed saying: "We must conclude, therefore, that these statutory requirements as construed by the Supreme Court have Congressional sanction and approval."

Any doubts that such were the purpose and will of Congress would seem to have been dissipated by the reenactment by Congress in 1940 of Paragraphs "Third" and "Fourth" of § 4 of the Naturalization Act of 1906, and by the incorporation in the Act of 1940 of the very form of oath which had been administratively prescribed for the applicants in the Schwimmer, Macintosh and Bland cases. See Rule 8(c), Naturalization Regulations of July 1, 1929.

The Nationality Act of 1940 was a comprehensive, slowly matured and carefully considered revision of the naturalization laws. The preparation of this measure was not only delegated to a Congressional Committee, but was considered by a committee of Cabinet members, one of whom was the Attorney General. Both were aware of our decisions in the Schwimmer and related cases and that no other question pertinent to the naturalization laws had been as persistently and continuously before Congress in the ten years following the decision in the Schwimmer case. The modifications in the provisions of Paragraphs "Third" and "Fourth" of § 4 of the 1906 Act show conclusively the careful attention which was given to them.

In the face of this legislative history the "failure of Congress to alter the Act after it had been judicially construed, and the enactment by Congress of legislation which implicitly recognizes the judicial construction as effective, is persuasive of legislative recognition that the judicial construction is the correct one. This is the more so where, as here, the application of the statute ... has brought forth sharply conflicting views both on the Court and in Congress, and where after the matter has been fully brought to the attention of the public and the Congress, the latter has not seen fit to change the statute." Apex Hosiery Co. v. Leader, 310 U.S. 469, 488, 489, 60 S.Ct. 982, 989, 84 L.Ed. 1311, 128 A.L.R. 1044.

LEARNED HAND, THE CONTRIBUTION OF AN INDEPENDENT JUDICIARY TO CIVILIZATION *

There are two ways in which the judges may forfeit their independence, if they do not abstain. If they are intransigent but honest, they will be curbed; but a worse fate will befall them if they learn to trim their sails to the prevailing winds. A society whose judges have taught it to expect complaisance will exact complaisance; and complaisance under the pretense of interpretation is rottenness. If judges are to kill this thing they love, let them do it, not like cowards with a kiss, but like brave men with a sword.

And so, ... I believe that for by far the greater part of their work it is a condition upon the success of our system that the judges should be independent; and I do not believe that their independence should be impaired because of their constitutional function. But the price of this immunity, I insist, is that they should not have the last word in those basic conflicts of "right and wrong—between whose endless jar justice resides." You may ask what then will become of the fundamental principles of equity and fair play which our constitutions enshrine; and whether I seriously believe that unsupported they will serve merely as counsels of moderation, I do not think that anyone can say what will be left of those principles; I do not not know whether they will serve only as counsels; but this much I think I do know—that a society so riven that the spirit of moderation is gone, no court can save; that a society where that spirit flourishes, no court need save; that in a society which evades its responsibility by thrusting upon the courts the nurture of that spirit, that spirit in the end will perish. What is the spirit of moderation? It is the temper which does not press a partisan advantage to its bitter end, which can understand and will respect the other side, which feels a unity between all citizens—real and not the factitious product of propaganda—which recognizes their common fate and their common aspirations—in a word, which has faith in the sacredness of the individual. If you ask me how such a temper and such a faith are bred and fostered, I cannot answer. They are the last flowers of civilization, delicate and easily overrun by the weeds of our sinful human nature; we may even now be witnessing their uprooting and disappearance until in

* The Supreme Court of Massachusetts 1692–1942 (1942). Reprinted with permission of the Massachusetts Bar Association.

the progress of the ages their seeds can once more find some friendly soil. But I am satisfied that they must have the vigor within themselves to withstand the winds and weather of an indifferent and ruthless world; and that it is idle to seek shelter for them in a courtroom. Men must take that temper and that faith with them into the field, into the marketplace, into the factory, into the council-room, into their homes; they cannot be imposed; they must be lived. Words will not express them; arguments will not clarify them; decisions will not maintain them. They are the fruit of the wisdom that comes of trial and a pure heart; no one can possess them who has not stood in awe before the spectacle of this mysterious Universe; no one can possess them whom that spectacle has not purged through pity and through fear—pity for the pride and folly which inexorably enmesh men in toils of their own contriving; fear, because that same pride and that same folly lie deep in the recesses of his own soul.

NOTE

Consider the phenomenon of the late Sixties and Seventies when so many societal problems were thrust upon the courts, especially the federal courts, in light of Hand's statement, "that in a society which evades its responsibility by thrusting upon the courts the nurture of that spirit [of moderation], that spirit in the end will perish." Is the phenomenon healthy?

ERWIN N. GRISWOLD, THE JUDICIAL PROCESS *

... [Cardozo] said: "The judge ... is to draw his inspiration from consecrated principles. He is not to yield to spasmodic sentiment, to vague and unregulated benevolence. He is to exercise a discretion informed by tradition, methodized by analogy, disciplined by system.... Wide enough in all conscience is the field of discretion which remains." In concluding this discussion he said: "So also the duty of a judge becomes itself a question of degree, and he is a useful judge or a poor one as he estimates the measure accurately or loosely." ...

Let me illustrate what I have in mind by reference to a field of current importance and interest. The First Amendment to the Constitution is one of our basic governmental provisions. Its language, with respect to freedom of speech and of the press, majestic and simple, is well known: "Congress shall make no law ... abridging the freedom of speech, or of the press; ...". There it is in its entirety. It is obviously of great importance, both symbolically and substantively. But what does it mean? What are its limits? How is it to be applied, especially at the fringes, in concrete cases?

There are two questions: (1) How far is it to be construed literally, so that it means everything that it says, and just what it says? In other

* 31 Fed.B.J. 309, 311, 315–16, 318–20 (1972). Reprinted by permission.

words, how far is it to be dealt with as a matter of "strict construction?" And the other question is, (2) How far is the Amendment to be extended to things that are not within its language, which can only be reached by extending the literal terms of the Amendment to new fields by the process of analogy designed to give effect to the spirit or broadly conceived purpose of the Amendment rather than its language? The evaluation and application of a proper scope on both of these matters fall within the proper function of the judge, and the test of the judge is or should be how he handles them. There is room for a good deal of judicial latitude in both directions....

Let us start with the application of the First Amendment to the States. This cannot be done by looking at the First Amendment itself, for, by its terms, it says that "Congress shall make no law...." It says nothing about the States at all. Of course we do have the due process clause of the Fourteenth Amendment. But it says nothing literally about freedom of speech or of the press. There is no doubt that the concept of "due process" requires interpretation and construction, but I fear that I am so unreconstructed, that I shall never understand how the First Amendment "is made obligatory on the States by the Fourteenth." [27] I have the feeling that this will go down as one of the greatest ipse dixits in Supreme Court history.[28] There are those of course who will say that this obtuseness on my part is due to my training at the feet of Felix Frankfurter. I do not think I was so dominated. Besides, I believe that Thomas Reed Powell was a greater influence on these matters....

It may well be a good idea to make the First Amendment applicable to the States in all its reaches. It tidies up a lot of things, and gives us a national unity that is appealing to some. On the other hand, applying the First Amendment and other provisions in the Bill of Rights in the same manner to the States as to the Federal Government may lead to a cutting back of protections that might not have occurred if the demand for flexibility from state-to-state were absent and if the provision fully applied only to the Federal Government, as was originally intended. The recent decisions allowing juries of less than twelve and permitting criminal convictions on less than a unanimous vote may be examples of this. In any event, my basic trouble on this score is not necessarily with the particular outcome, but rather that I cannot find this theory of incorporation, selective or otherwise, in the Constitution. If it is in the Constitution now it may be because the judges have put it there,[32] and I

27. Jacobellis v. Ohio, 378 U.S. 184, 196 (1964) (Black, J., concurring). Similarly, in Terry v. Ohio, 392 U.S. 1, 8 (1968), the Court referred to "the Fourth Amendment, made applicable to the States by the Fourteenth." See also Powell v. Texas, 392 U.S. 514, 531 (1968); Mancusi v. DeForte, 392 U.S. 364, 366 (1968); Board of Education v. Allen, 392 U.S. 236, 238 (1968).

28. See Henkin, "Selective Incorporation" in the Fourteenth Amendment, 73 Yale L.J. 74 (1963).

32. Compare Richard Harris, writing in the New Yorker, date unknown, but included in a current advertising circular for that magazine: "... Most Americans probably assume that they have always enjoyed the protection of the Bill of Rights by virtue of their citizenship. Until very recently, though, most of those protections were

wonder whether that is a proper exercise of the Judicial Process, at least as Benjamin Cardozo understood it.

There are other ways in which the First Amendment has grown under relatively recent judicial nurture. The First Amendment says nothing about a right of privacy. A right of privacy is essentially negative, or passive, a right to keep people or the government away, to prevent interference with one's own household or quiet—as Brandeis said, a "right to be let alone." But the right protected by the First Amendment is essentially active, the right to speak or to publish. How, then, can the First Amendment, even together with other provisions, be properly construed to provide a sweeping right of privacy?

Yet a good many steps have been taken in that direction although we are not all the way there. The invalidity of state laws against contraceptives—a practical result I find quite satisfactory—is rested on the First Amendment, or perhaps more accurately on the "penumbra" of the First Amendment. I do not know where these penumbras come from, nor do I know their extent or limitations. And I suspect that the true meaning of penumbra is that the Constitution does not cover the subject but ought to because it does so much else that is desirable. Of course if a litigant claims he has discovered a penumbra, determining whether it should be recognized is a judicial function. But I would maintain that the proper ambit of judicial judgment should be bounded by what can be found in the Constitution itself, not the surrounding space, which leads off into the blue yonder.

. . .

. . . As my former colleague, Professor Cox, has said, "constitutional adjudication presents an insoluble dilemma." Those who believe in strict construction, on the one hand, and those who believe in activism, on the other, are surely just as sincere and intelligent and conscientious and patriotic as those who see the importance of a different conception of the judicial function. In the words of Thoreau, "They march to a different drummer."

Speaking for myself alone, and I am not a judge, I feel that there are two stages to the problem. There is first the ambit within which it is appropriate to exercise judicial power. My own thought is that this must always be exercised, but that it should be kept within somewhat narrower limits than has sometimes been the case in our recent past. This is an extremely difficult question of judgment, for I am definitely not contending for a rigidly confined concept of judicial power. I do not like Baron Parke's approach any more than anyone else; neither do I like, for us, justice as administered by Harun al Raschid sitting under a tree. As Cardozo said, "That might result in a benevolent despotism if the Judges were benevolent men." When a judge's approach is that "I'd

theirs only in federal proceedings, and the states were more or less free to interpret them as they saw fit. The process of extending criminal-law procedures in the Bill of Rights to the states began only about thirty years ago, and it wasn't until the Warren Court applied the bulk of its provisions to the states that the average citizen got the rights that he had taken for granted all along. . . ."

rather create a precedent than find one," then I wonder if he might not be wrong. This was explained in these words: "... because the creation of a precedent in terms of the modern setting means the adjustment of the Constitution to the needs of the time." This is appealing until one recalls that such adjustment must be according to the judge's own predilection; and it is not surprising to find that many of those who urged the Court to make new law in the 1950's and 1960's are now urging the Court to follow precedent—and vice versa. Cardozo's view was rather different. "Judges have ... the power, though not the right," he wrote, "to travel beyond the walls of the interstices, the bounds set to judicial innovation by precedent and custom. Nonetheless, by that abuse of power, they violate the law."

It is not, as I see it, a question of strict construction or of activism. It is both. Construction is strict only to those who agree with the interpretation; to those who do not, it is simply wrong. Activism that carries us beyond the proper exercise of the judicial function is not legitimately called activism. The limits either way cannot be demonstrated. But there are limits. That is inherent in the idea of the judicial process. The supreme function of the judge is to recognize that there must be limits, both ways, avoiding undue literalism on the one hand, and too wide freedom of action on the other.

In nearly every case, in the Supreme Court, and to a lesser extent in other courts, there is an area of choice. How a judge marks out and determines that area largely determines the kind of judge he is. If a judge keeps this area too small, he is likely to be a poor judge, for he will be too hidebound by precedent, too much tied to the past, too unaware of variations in the situation now before him. On the other hand, if a judge allows this area to be too broad, he is not likely to be a good judge. He may run some risk of deciding according to his own personal choice rather than according to law as he is given light to understand the law; he may give too little weight to precedent, and make the law unsettled; he may arrogate to the courts a broader range for decision than it is appropriate for judges to exercise.

. . .

The judge must work out appropriate limits within which he can properly function, according to his conception of the Judicial Process. In Cardozo's words, "We must not throw to the winds the advantages of consistency and uniformity to do justice in the instance. We must keep within those interstitial limits which precedent and custom and the long and silent and almost indefinable practice of other judges through the centuries of the common law have set to judge-made innovations." And elsewhere he said, "The judge, even when he is free, is still not wholly free. He is not to innovate at pleasure."

———

LEARNED HAND, HOW FAR IS A JUDGE
FREE IN REACHING A DECISION *

In our country we have always been extremely jealous of mixing the different processes of government, especially that of making law, with that of saying what it is after it has been made. This distinction, if I am right, cannot be rigidly enforced; but like most of those ideas, which the men who made our constitutions believed in, it has a very sound basis as a guide, provided one does not try to make it into an absolute rule, like driving to the right. They wanted to have a government by the people, and they believed that the only way they could do it, was by giving the power to make laws to assemblies which the people chose, directly or at second hand. They believed that such assemblies would express the common will of the people who were to rule. Never mind what they thought that common will was; it is not so simple as it seems to learn just what they did mean by it, or what anybody can mean. It is enough that they did not mean by it what any one individual, whether or not he was a judge, should think right and proper. They might have made the judge the mouthpiece of the common will, finding it out by his contacts with people generally; but he would then have been ruler, like the Judges of Israel. Still, they had to leave him scope in which he in a limited sense does act as if he were the government, because, as we have seen, he cannot otherwise do what he is required to do. So far they had to confuse law-making with law-interpreting.

But the judge must always remember that he should go no further than he is sure the government would have gone, had it been faced with the case before him. If he is in doubt, he must stop, for he cannot tell that the conflicting interests in the society for which he speaks would have come to a just result, even though he is sure that he knows what the just result should be. He is not to substitute even his juster will for theirs; otherwise it would not be the common will which prevails, and to that extent the people would not govern.

So you will see that a judge is in a contradictory position; he is pulled by two opposite forces. On the one hand he must not enforce whatever he thinks best; he must leave that to the common will expressed by the government. On the other, he must try as best he can to put into concrete form what that will is, not by slavishly following the words, but by trying honestly to say what was the underlying purpose expressed. Nobody does this exactly right; great judges do it better than the rest of us. It is necessary that someone shall do it, if we are to realize the hope that we can collectively rule ourselves. And so, while it is proper that people should find fault when their judges fail, it is only reasonable that they should recognize the difficulties. Perhaps it is also fair to ask that before the judges are blamed they shall be given the credit of having tried to do their best. Let them be severely brought to

---

* Excerpted from transcript of a radio address presented May 14, 1933 over the Columbia Broadcasting System radio network.

book, when they go wrong, but by those who will take the trouble to understand.

NOTE

Consider the reality that most statutes are drafted by special legislative staffs, often from academia, and that in any given legislative session of, say, six months duration, legislators in a busy state such as New York may be required to pass upon as many as 10,000 bills. Can it be honestly asserted today that legislation derives from representatives elected by the people?

SOL WACHTLER, JUSTIFICATION FOR JUDICIAL LAWMAKING*

The evolution of judicial lawmaking is observable most clearly in the common law area, where the legislature's voice is paramount on the substance of the law and where the courts generate legal principles subject always to legislative modification or repeal. In the nineteenth and early twentieth centuries, the common law court dominated development of the law. But in the past fifty to eighty years, legislative activity in traditional common law areas has increased dramatically, with statutory law displacing, modifying, supplementing, and codifying the common law in infinite combinations and variations.[18] Consequently, today performance of what Cardozo described as interstitial lawmaking by filling in legislative gaps and forming a cohesive structure from new statutes and residual common law [19] is standard judicial practice. As Judge Traynor put it, "[t]he hydra headed problem is how to synchronize the unguided missiles launched by legislatures with a going system of common law." [20]

Despite the advent of the "age of the statute" and the understanding by the modern legislature that it is the final arbiter in classical common law areas, state legislatures generally, and most assuredly in New York, have not abandoned a significant lawmaking role for the judiciary. Instead, while enacting legislation to deal with problems needing immediate attention, the state legislatures continue to leave to the courts responsibility for development of the law in many traditional common law areas, along with opportunities for substantial interstitial lawmaking in the statutory area. Consequently, today, as a statistical matter, perhaps the amount of judicial lawmaking in the common law area has decreased. However, instead of displacement of the courts by the legislatures, the evolutionary process has formed what is an intimate

---

* S. Wachtler, *Judicial Lawmaking,* 65 N.Y.U.L.Rev. 1, 6–7, 17–20 (1990).

18. See G. Calabresi, A Common Law for the Age of Statutes 1 (1982).

19. B. Cardozo, The Nature of the Judicial Process 16–17, 113–115, 129 (1921).

20. Traynor, Statutes Revolving in Common–Law Orbits, 17 Cath.U.L.Rev. 401, 402 (1968).

lawmaking partnership—sometimes fluid, sometimes halting—between the legislature and the common law courts.

The lesson here is that the responsibility of the courts to form the common law is not a static power inherent in our governmental system. Taking a historical perspective, the amount of policymaking undertaken by the courts in this area is ultimately controlled by the legislature, and will fluctuate as the perceived needs of the times change.

The elemental justification for judicial lawmaking, I believe, is found in the recognition that " 'law springs from the relations of fact which exist between things.' "[56] Both the legislature and the judiciary are in a position to assess these relations and to make law based on their observations. Legislatures, however, view the world through a wide-angle lens, and, because their rules are by necessity designed for future and not present application, the lens through which it views the "relation of fact," while broad, also is clouded by prognostication.

It is the court, however, that applies law directly to real persons. It is in court where the collision between law and real-world events takes place. It is the judge who must, in every case, consider the discrete predicaments of specific persons, look these persons directly in the eye, and explain how the law affects them.

For a fair assessment of the facts and the social context, the court must be independent. The interests of continuity and stability, and the viability of judicial lawmaking, require a thorough understanding of the legal landscape followed by an exegesis of the basis for the judicial lawmaking act in an overtly reasoned opinion. Nevertheless, the heart of the judicial process, and what in the end justifies judicial lawmaking and explains the resilience and growth of the institution, is not limited to the legal expertise of judges and the reasoned step-by-step development of the caselaw; instead, its central ingredient is the constant bombardment, in the crucible of the lawsuit, of law as applied by the judge to specific factual real-world events and persons.[57] It is this function of the judiciary that distinguishes its lawmaking process from that of the legislature and renders its actions consistent with separation of powers principles.

With confidence I propose that this conclusion strongly justifies judicial common law formation. In this area, where judicial rules are subject to legislative revision, the courts' rational tradition, independence, and most of all its intimate view of existing real facts and the impact of law, make it a superb and legitimate lawmaking partner with the legislature.

---

56. B. Cardozo, supra note 19 at 122 (quoting P. Vander Eycken, Methode positive de l'Interprétation juridique 401 (1907)). Similarly, Montesquieu states that "[l]aws, in their most general signification, are the necessary relations arising from the nature of things."

57. See Kaye, The Human Dimension in Appellate Judging: A Brief Reflection on a Timeless Concern, 73 Cornell L.Rev. 1004, 1007 (1988).

Judicial lawmaking, therefore, is legitimate largely because of the nature of the judicial process; it is directly attributable to the courts' narrow but profound connection to the "relations of fact which exist between things," from which law springs. As the intimacy of this connection wanes, however, the legitimacy of judicial lawmaking necessarily diminishes. Thus the proximity of the courts to discrete real-world disputes, while providing a justification for lawmaking by the courts, also forms the perimeters outside of which the judiciary may not legitimately perform this function.

But what does it really mean to have a close view of a discrete problem ready for judicial resolution? What would be the harm, as opposed to the potential good, if a court announced a new rule of law that on its face seemed eminently fair, in a case in which the rule did not apply? What is wrong with judicial lawmaking founded solely upon logic, when the facts of the case at hand do not present the precise legal issue, if the new rule of law stated in the case seems obviously salutary and correct? When faced with even clear inequities, courts consistently have refused to evolve the law to create more fair relations between persons by relying on what appear to be "technicalities"—holding that the dispute is not "concrete" enough because the sword of Damocles, although in plain view, has not yet been placed over the plaintiff's head, or deciding that a plaintiff, who may have dedicated her life to rectifying a single injustice, lacks "standing" because the injustice does not befall her personally.

However, the requirements that there be a concrete dispute and that it be litigated by a personally affected party are not mere "technicalities." [59] Known variously as justiciability doctrines, or the bar against advisory opinions, these requirements are a measure of the proximity of the court to a real-world dispute. They form the "ancient bounds" of the judicial process, beyond which judicial lawmaking ceases to be judgment, and takes on the face of the exercise of raw lawmaking power. [60]

Much has been said and written, particularly recently, about "judicial legislation" and "judicial restraint." [61] To me, the former occurs when the courts forget that the judicial universe in reality is severely limited and that the judiciary is structurally incompetent to decide hypothetical disputes or to resolve cases in which the real-world facts necessary for there to be an actual dispute have not yet occurred, and may never come to pass. The courts, of course, have no resources to undertake independent inquiries aimed at appreciating general situations. Their understanding of general relationships must come in large part from the circumstances of the parties in a particular case. There-

59. A. Bickel, The Least Dangerous Branch 113 (1986).

60. See In re State Indust. Comm., 224 N.Y. 13, 17, 119 N.E. 1027, 1028 (1918) (Cardozo, J.); The Federalist No. 78 (A. Hamilton).

61. See Wachtler, Our Constitution—Alive and Well, 61 St. John's L.Rev. 381, 383–90 (1987) (discussing original intent).

fore, if a case lacks a concrete dispute, the court is without any means or context by which to appreciate a general situation and cannot, as a structural matter, reach a sound conclusion on how to assess fairly the rights and interests of persons.

It is the legislature and not the judiciary that is possessed of resources by which to understand general circumstances, and it is that body which is designed to make law in the abstract. Thus judicial lawmaking outside of the context of a concrete dispute not only risks erroneous determinations, it is nothing more than simple arrogation of legislative power, without the safeguards that allow a legislature to make law in the abstract. This is true "judicial legislation." As Holmes said, the life of the common law "has not been logic: it has been experience"; [62] but when a court renders a decision based on hypothetical facts, it relies solely upon logic, and from the perspective of the common law process the rule of law produced is stillborn.

Avoiding this problem, in my view, is the most important instance of "judicial restraint." The need for restraint by the judiciary is at its absolute highest when a longstanding problem, or an emotionally and perhaps politically charged issue, comes before the court, but the case is clouded by justiciability problems. At such times, armed with the power to effect what it feels to be a just result, the court surely feels the pull to dilute the principles of justiciability in what seems like a single case.

But there are no "single cases" in the common law system. Each judicial act is a building block, which, when performed, becomes set in place as part of the foundation of our legal structure. Thus each discrete instance of a weakened link between the court and a real-world event is a direct threat to the future of judge-made law.

ERWIN N. GRISWOLD, THE JUDICIAL PROCESS *

Let me interpolate here with reference to two cases not involving any constitutional question, and in a relatively unemotional field, for they seem to me to illustrate the question of judgment and degree which I am trying to develop. The first of these cases is Moragne v. States Marine Lines, Inc., decided by the Supreme Court in 1970. The question involved there was whether a right of action for wrongful death should be recognized in admiralty. Long ago, the Court had held that there was no such right of action. In the meantime Congress had passed various statutes, including one making state wrongful death actions applicable in certain situations. No generally applicable wrongful death statute had ever been passed. The *Moragne* case involved one of the omitted situations—a death on a ship within territorial waters where no state death act was applicable. The Court asked the Solicitor General

---

62. O.W. Holmes, The Common Law 1 (1881).

* 31 Fed.B.J. 309, 317–18 (1972). Reprinted by permission.

for his views, and I joined with others in the Department of Justice, in a brief urging the Court to overrule *The Harrisburg,* and to hold that the law had developed to the place where it was appropriate to recognize a generally applicable right of recovery for wrongful death in admiralty in situations not covered by the statutes Congress had enacted. The Court reached this result in the *Moragne* case, in a characteristically thorough opinion by Justice Harlan. With respect, it seems to me that this is a thoroughly appropriate exercise of judicial power, developing the law in the way that judges ought to develop it.

This decision led to a further development in Massachusetts which seems to me, again with great respect, to have gone beyond the appropriate bounds of judicial action. It is, indeed, an excellent illustration of the current judicial tendency to take the great leap forward. The case [was] Gaudette v. Webb,[40] decided ... by the Supreme Judicial Court of Massachusetts. In that case, the court held that there is now a common law action for wrongful death in Massachusetts, despite the facts that (1) the rule had been to the contrary for a century as evidenced by many decisions, and (2) acting on that rule, the legislature had enacted a comprehensive wrongful death statute which had been relied on and applied for many years. The result was to allow recovery under the newly found common law right although the suit was brought one year after expiration of the period of limitations for a wrongful death action, under the statute which had long been in effect and was applicable to the facts before the court.

This has been referred to as a "remarkable" and "drastic shift." [41] My own reaction is that it is an illustration of my suggestion that courts today sometimes exceed the proper bounds of the judicial function. The Supreme Court's decision in the *Moragne* case does not seem to me to warrant the conclusion reached by the Supreme Judicial Court. In the *Moragne* case, there was no statute covering the situation before the court; it was a casus omissus. It was wholly appropriate for the Court belatedly to fill the gap. The change in the admiralty law was quite in accordance with traditional common law principles where a field has been widely occupied by statutory change. This, it seems to me, is wholly inapplicable where a field has been fully occupied by statutory change. In such a situation, the proper function of the court is to apply the statute law. The addition of a common law right to a comprehensive statutory scheme is action taken in derogation of the legislative power. On the other hand, recognition of a right where haphazard and piecemeal legislation has left some gaps is an illustration of the appropriate function of courts to implement and support the legislative action.

---

40. 284 N.E.2d 222 (Mass.1972).   **41.** See *In the Supreme Judicial Court,* 57 Mass.L.Q. 293, 295, 296 (1972).

MORAGNE v. STATES MARINE LINES, INC.

Supreme Court of the United States, 1970.
398 U.S. 375, 90 S.Ct. 1772, 26 L.Ed.2d 339.

MR. JUSTICE HARLAN delivered the opinion of the Court.

We brought this case here to consider whether The Harrisburg, 119 U.S. 199, 7 S.Ct. 140, 30 L.Ed. 358, in which this Court held in 1886 that maritime law does not afford a cause of action for wrongful death, should any longer be regarded as acceptable law.

The complaint sets forth that Edward Moragne, a longshoreman, was killed while working aboard the vessel *Palmetto State* in navigable waters within the State of Florida. Petitioner, as his widow and representative of his estate, brought this suit in a state court against respondent States Marine Lines, Inc., the owner of the vessel, to recover damages for wrongful death and for the pain and suffering experienced by the decedent prior to his death. The claims were predicated upon both negligence and the unseaworthiness of the vessel.

. . .

The Court's opinion in *The Harrisburg* acknowledged that the result reached had little justification except in primitive English legal history—a history far removed from the American law of remedies for maritime deaths. That case, like this, was a suit on behalf of the family of a maritime worker for his death on the navigable waters of a State. Following several precedents in the lower federal courts, the trial court awarded damages against the ship causing the death, and the circuit court affirmed, ruling that death by maritime tort "may be complained of as an injury, and the wrong redressed under the general maritime law." 15 F. 610, 614 (1883). This Court, in reversing, relied primarily on its then-recent decision in Insurance Co. v. Brame, 95 U.S. 754, 24 L.Ed. 580 (1878), in which it had held that in American common law, as in English, "no civil action lies for an injury which results in . . . death." *Id.,* at 756. In *The Harrisburg,* as in *Brame,* the Court did not examine the justifications for this common-law rule; rather, it simply noted that "we know of no country that has adopted a different rule on this subject for the sea from that which it maintains on the land," and concluded, despite contrary decisions of the lower federal courts both before and after *Brame,* that the rule of *Brame* should apply equally to maritime deaths. 119 U.S., at 213, 7 S.Ct., at 146.

Our analysis of the history of the common-law rule indicates that it was based on a particular set of factors that had, when *The Harrisburg* was decided, long since been thrown into discard even in England, and that had never existed in this country at all. Further, regardless of the viability of the rule in 1886 as applied to American land-based affairs, it is difficult to discern an adequate reason for its extension to admiralty, a system of law then already differentiated in many respects from the common law.

One would expect, upon an inquiry into the sources of the common-law rule, to find a clear and compelling justification for what seems a striking departure from the result dictated by elementary principles in the law of remedies. Where existing law imposes a primary duty, violations of which are compensable if they cause injury, nothing in ordinary notions of justice suggests that a violation should be nonactionable simply because it was serious enough to cause death. On the contrary, that rule has been criticized ever since its inception, and described in such terms as "barbarous." *E.g.,* Osborn v. Gilliett, L.R. 8 Ex. 88, 94 (1873) (Lord Bramwell, dissenting); F. Pollock, Law of Torts 55 (Landon ed. 1951); 3 W. Holdsworth, History of English Law 676–677 (3d ed. 1927). Because the primary duty already exists, the decision whether to allow recovery for violations causing death is entirely a remedial matter. It is true that the harms to be assuaged are not identical in the two cases: in the case of mere injury, the person physically harmed is made whole for his harm, while in the case of death, those closest to him—usually spouse and children—seek to recover for their total loss of one on whom they depended. This difference, however, even when coupled with the practical difficulties of defining the class of beneficiaries who may recover for death, does not seem to account for the law's refusal to recognize a wrongful killing as an actionable tort. One expects, therefore, to find a persuasive, independent justification for this apparent legal anomaly.

Legal historians have concluded that the sole substantial basis for the rule at common law is a feature of the early English law that did not survive into this century—the felony-merger doctrine. See Pollock, *supra,* at 52–57; Holdsworth, The Origin of the Rule in Baker v. Bolton, 32 L.Q.Rev. 431 (1916). According to this doctrine, the common law did not allow civil recovery for an act that constituted both a tort and a felony. The tort was treated as less important than the offense against the Crown, and was merged into, or pre-empted by, the felony. Smith v. Sykes, 1 Freem. 224, 89 Eng.Rep. 160 (K.B.1677); Higgins v. Butcher, Yel. 89, 80 Eng.Rep. 61 (K.B.1606). The doctrine found practical justification in the fact that the punishment for the felony was the death of the felon and the forfeiture of his property to the Crown; thus, after the crime had been punished, nothing remained of the felon or his property on which to base a civil action. Since all intentional or negligent homicide was felonious, there could be no civil suit for wrongful death.

The first explicit statement of the common-law rule against recovery for wrongful death came in the opinion of Lord Ellenborough, sitting at *nisi prius,* in Baker v. Bolton, 1 Camp. 493, 170 Eng.Rep. 1033 (1808). That opinion did not cite authority, or give supporting reasoning, or refer to the felony-merger doctrine in announcing that "[i]n a Civil court, the death of a human being could not be complained of as an injury." *Ibid.* Nor had the felony-merger doctrine seemingly been cited as the basis for the denial of recovery in any of the other reported wrongful-death cases since the earliest ones, in the 17th century. *E.g.,* Smith v. Sykes, *supra;* Higgins v. Butcher, *supra.* However, it seems clear from those first cases that the rule of Baker v. Bolton did derive from the felony-merger doctrine, and that there was no other ground on which it might be supported even at the time of its inception. The

House of Lords in 1916 confirmed this historical derivation, and held that although the felony-merger doctrine was no longer part of the law, the rule against recovery for wrongful death should continue except as modified by statute. Admiralty Commissioners v. S.S. Amerika, [1917] A.C. 38. Lord Parker's opinion acknowledged that the rule was "anomalous ... to the scientific jurist," but concluded that because it had once found justification in the doctrine that "the trespass was drowned in the felony," it should continue as a rule "explicable on historical grounds" even after the disappearance of that justification....

The historical justification marshaled for the rule in England never existed in this country. In limited instances American law did adopt a vestige of the felony-merger doctrine, to the effect that a civil action was delayed until after the criminal trial. However, in this country the felony punishment did not include forfeiture of property; therefore, there was nothing, even in those limited instances, to bar a subsequent civil suit.... Nevertheless, despite some early cases in which the rule was rejected as "incapable of vindication," ... American courts generally adopted the English rule as the common law of this country as well. Throughout the period of this adoption, culminating in this Court's decision in *Brame,* the courts failed to produce any satisfactory justification for applying the rule in this country.

. . .

The most likely reason that the English rule was adopted in this country without much question is simply that it had the blessing of age. That was the thrust of this Court's opinion in *Brame,* as well as many of the lower court opinions.... Such nearly automatic adoption seems at odds with the general principle, widely accepted during the early years of our Nation, that while "[o]ur ancestors brought with them [the] general principles [of the common law] and claimed it as their birthright; ... they brought with them and adopted only that portion which was applicable to their situation." ... The American courts never made the inquiry whether this particular English rule, bitterly criticized in England, "was applicable to their situation," and it is difficult to imagine on what basis they might have concluded that it was.

. . .

We need not, however, pronounce a verdict on whether *The Harrisburg,* when decided, was a correct extrapolation of the principles of decisional law then in existence. A development of major significance has intervened, making clear that the rule against recovery for wrongful death is sharply out of keeping with the policies of modern American maritime law. This development is the wholesale abandonment of the rule in most of the areas where it once held sway, quite evidently prompted by the same sense of the rule's injustice that generated so much criticism of its original promulgation.

To some extent this rejection has been judicial. The English House of Lords in 1937 emasculated the rule without expressly overruling it.

Rose v. Ford, [1937] A.C. 826. Lord Atkin remarked about the decision in *S.S. Amerika* that "[t]he reasons given, whether historical or otherwise, may seem unsatisfactory," and that "if the rule is really based on the relevant death being due to felony, it should long ago have been relegated to a museum." ...

Much earlier, however, the legislatures both here and in England began to evidence unanimous disapproval of the rule against recovery for wrongful death. The first statute partially abrogating the rule was Lord Campbell's Act, 9 & 10 Vict., c. 93 (1846), which granted recovery to the families of persons killed by tortious conduct, "although the Death shall have been caused under such Circumstances as amount in Law to Felony."

In the United States, every State today has enacted a wrongful-death statute.

... The Congress has created actions for wrongful deaths of railroad employees, Federal Employers' Liability Act, 45 U.S.C.A. §§ 51–59; of merchant seamen, Jones Act, 46 U.S.C.A. § 688; and of persons on the high seas, Death on the High Seas Act, 46 U.S.C.A. §§ 761, 762. Congress has also, in the Federal Tort Claims Act, 28 U.S.C.A. § 1346(b), made the United States subject to liability in certain circumstances for negligently caused wrongful death to the same extent as a private person....

These numerous and broadly applicable statutes, taken as a whole, make it clear that there is no present public policy against allowing recovery for wrongful death. The statutes evidence a wide rejection by the legislatures of whatever justifications may once have existed for a general refusal to allow such recovery. This legislative establishment of policy carries significance beyond the particular scope of each of the statutes involved. The policy thus established has become itself a part of our law, to be given its appropriate weight not only in matters of statutory construction but also in those of decisional law. See Landis, Statutes and the Sources of Law, in Harvard Legal Essays 213, 226–227 (1934)....

. . .

... Both the Death on the High Seas Act and the numerous state wrongful-death acts have been implemented with success for decades. The experience thus built up counsels that a suit for wrongful death raises no problems unlike those that have long been grist for the judicial mill.

In sum, in contrast to the torrent of difficult litigation that has swirled about *The Harrisburg, The Tungus,* which followed upon it, and the problems of federal-state accommodation they occasioned, the recognition of a remedy for wrongful death under general maritime law can be expected to bring more placid waters. That prospect indeed makes for, and not against, the discarding of *The Harrisburg.*

We accordingly overrule *The Harrisburg,* and hold that an action does lie under general maritime law for death caused by violation of maritime duties.

———

GAUDETTE v. WEBB

Supreme Judicial Court of Massachusetts, 1972.
284 N.E.2d 222.

Before TAURO, C.J., and CUTTER, SPIEGEL, REARDON, QUIRICO, BRAUCHER and HENNESSEY, JJ.

QUIRICO, JUSTICE.

This is an action in tort seeking recovery from three defendants for the conscious suffering and death of the plaintiff's intestate, Joseph Francis Gaudette (Gaudette) as the result of a collision of two motor vehicles....

. . .

The question for our decision is whether, as matter of law, the statute of limitations had run against the causes of action for which this action was brought....

. . .

Wrongful Death. The wrongful death statute in effect at the time of Gaudette's death, ... provided, in pertinent part, that "[a]n action to recover damages under this section shall be commenced *within one year from the date of death or within such time thereafter as is provided by sections four,* four B, nine or ten of chapter two hundred and sixty" (emphasis added).... In this case the death occurred on April 15, 1967, and therefore the time for bringing the plaintiff's action for wrongful death would have expired on April 15, 1969, unless it was extended by the tolling provisions....

. . .

Despite the seeming hopelessness of the plaintiff's cause of action for death in the light of the formidable array of adverse judicial precedents reviewed above, she argues through counsel, more on the basis of common sense and fairness than on the basis of adherence to legal precedents, and perhaps despite the precedents, that the law should find some way to afford a remedy for redress of the legal wrongs of the defendants, even if the remedy is limited to the three minor children of the deceased. She urges that this court "release itself, *in the interest of justice,* from the thongs of mortmain which have bound for too long a time the law of torts in this Commonwealth." This, in effect, is a request that we depart from the doctrine of stare decisis to the extent necessary to afford relief in this and like cases.

As we view this case, there are several rules of law which stand as obstacles to the plaintiff's action for wrongful death. The first is the rule that there is no common law basis for a cause of action for death, and that such a cause of action in this Commonwealth is wholly a creature of our death statutes. The second is the rule that since the cause of action is a creature of the death statute, it exists only for the period limited by the death statute, after the expiration of which period there is not only no remedy to enforce the right but there is no right. The third is the rule that because the death statute places a limit on the existence of the right, the tolling provisions of the general statute of limitations are not available to the plaintiff in an action for wrongful death. We shall consider each of these three rules separately.

. . .

The statement that the common law did not permit recovery for death has since been repeated in many decisions of this court and in decisions of courts of other jurisdictions. Many of these decisions recognize Baker v. Bolton, 1 Campb. 493, decided in 1808, as the apparent basis for this doctrine. . . . [She urges that this court release itself,] in the principles governing survival of actions at common law. . . .

The lack of any discernible basis for the doctrine of Baker v. Bolton, and the harsh results it frequently produced, prompted bitter criticism of the decision in England. This criticism and the origin of the doctrine itself were recently reviewed in a scholarly opinion by Justice Harlan, speaking for the unanimous court in Moragne v. States Marine Lines, Inc. . . .

. . .

Upon consideration of the *Moragne* decision and the sound reasoning upon which it is based, we are convinced that the law in this Commonwealth has also evolved to the point where it may now be held that the right to recovery for wrongful death is of common law origin, and we so hold. To the extent that Carey v. Berkshire R.R., 1 Cush. 475, and any other prior decisions of this court conflict with our present holding, those decisions are no longer to be followed.

HARLAN F. STONE, THE COMMON LAW IN THE UNITED STATES *

The reception which the courts have accorded to statutes presents a curiously illogical chapter in the history of the common law. Notwithstanding their genius for the generation of new law from that already established, the common-law courts have given little recognition to statutes as starting points for judicial lawmaking comparable to judicial

* 50 Harv.L.Rev. 4, 12–15 (1936). Copyright © 1936 by The Harvard Law Review Association. Reprinted by permission.

decisions. They have long recognized the supremacy of statutes over judge-made law, but it has been the supremacy of a command to be obeyed according to its letter, to be treated as otherwise of little consequence. The fact that the command involves recognition of a policy by the supreme lawmaking body has seldom been regarded by courts as significant, either as a social datum or as a point of departure for the process of judicial reasoning by which the common law has been expanded.

The attitude of our courts toward statute law presents a contrast to that of the civilians who have been more ready to regard statutes in the light of the thesis of the civil law that its precepts are statements of general principles, to be used as guides to decision. Under that system a new statute may be viewed as an exemplification of a general principle which is to take its place beside other precepts, whether found in codes or accepted expositions of the jurists, as an integral part of the system, there to be extended to analogous situations not within its precise terms. With the modern practice of drawing a statute as a statement of a general rule, I can perceive no obstacle which need have precluded our adoption of a similar attitude except our unfamiliarity with the civilian habit of thought. The Scottish law, with its Roman law foundation, took this position, and the House of Lords, common-law learning and background notwithstanding, found no difficulty in approving it as applied to local statutes, in passing on appeals from the Scottish courts.

But quite apart from such a possibility, I can find in the history and principles of the common law no adequate reason for our failure to treat a statute much more as we treat a judicial precedent, as both a declaration and a source of law, and as a premise for legal reasoning. We have done practically that with our ancient statutes, such as the statutes of limitations, frauds and wills, readily molding them to fit new conditions within their spirit, though not their letter, possibly because their antiquity tends to make us forget or minimize their legislative origin. Professor Landis ... has recently pointed out in a valuable discussion of "Statutes and the Sources of Law", numerous examples in the Year Books of the application of the doctrine of the "equity of the statute" by which statutes were treated, in effect, as sources of law which by judicial decision could be extended to apply to situations analogous to those embraced within their terms. Apart from its command, the social policy and judgment, expressed in legislation by the lawmaking agency which is supreme, would seem to merit that judicial recognition which is freely accorded to the like expression in judicial precedent. But only to a limited extent do modern courts feel free, by resort to standards of conduct set up by legislation, to impose liability or attach consequences for the failure to maintain those or similar standards in similar but not identical situations, or to make the statutory recognition of a new type of right the basis for the judicial creation of rights in circumstances not dissimilar. Professor Landis and others have developed the subject with a detail unnecessary to consider now. It is enough for my purpose that they show that the legislative function has been reduced to mere rule making by the process of narrow judicial interpretation of statutes, and in consequence of the renunciation by the courts, where statutes are concerned, of some of their own lawmaking powers.

That such has been the course of the common law in the United States seems to be attributable to the fact that, long before its important legislative expansion, the theories of Coke and Blackstone of the self-sufficiency and ideal perfection of the common law, and the notion of the separation of powers and of judicial independence, had come to dominate our juristic thinking. The statute was looked upon as in the law but not of it, a formal rule to be obeyed, it is true, since it is the command of the sovereign, but to be obeyed grudgingly, by construing it narrowly and treating it as though it did not exist for any purpose other than that embraced within the strict construction of its words. It is difficult to appraise the consequences of the perpetuation of incongruities and injustices in the law by this habit of narrow construction of statutes and by the failure to recognize that, as recognitions of social policy, they are as significant and rightly as much a part of the law, as the rules declared by judges. A generation ago no feature of our law administration tended quite so much to discredit law and lawyers in the lay mind. A narrow literalism too often defeated the purpose of remedial legislation, while a seeming contest went on with the apparent purpose of ascertaining whether the legislatures would ultimately secure a desired reform or the courts would succeed in resisting it.

––––––

ROGER J. TRAYNOR, STATUTES REVOLVING IN COMMON–LAW ORBITS *

[Ed.: Consider Chief Justice Traynor's paper written 32 years after Chief Justice Stone's.]

Most [American] courts received English statutes, . . . hospitably. There was a disposition to receive English statutes enacted before 1776 as part of the common law, subject to such tests of relevance and propriety as were applicable to judge-made rules. . . .

The preponderant view was that indigenous law could not assimilate any English rule inconsistent with its own rules or repugnant to its tenor. That view found expression in varying constructions of what a reception statute encompassed by its reference to the common law of England. Sometimes judges construed it to extend to any English statute that had proved to have a beneficial effect upon the common law. . . .

Thus the statutes of England, like its judicial precedents, were frequently found wanting in their adaptability to new soil. At the same

* 17 Cath.U.L.Rev. 401, 410–11, 415–16, 422–23, 425 (1968). Reprinted by permission.

time there was no large fund of indigenous law upon which courts could draw. From the beginning, therefore, American judges were compelled to play a far more creative role in the law than their English contemporaries, and as time went on there would be no end to the creativity required to meet the novel problems of a rapidly growing economy. So it came about, often in the very process of examining English law, that the judges of this country, along with legislators and commentators, developed an American common law. In noting its substantial development in less than three quarters of a century, Dean Pound has commented that "[n]o other judicial and juristic achievement may be found to compare with this."

It has taken doing and redoing, but over the years judges have thus amplified the range and steadied the course of such legislative missiles as statutes of limitation and Married Women's Statutes. We come now to groups of statutes whose possibilities have yet to be fully explored. Among these are the penal or regulatory statutes constructed to specific standards of conduct. Given their built-in controls, judges have little difficulty in keeping them on course in cases involving direct violations of a statute. The problem of judicial guidance is not with the statutes themselves, but with all the unidentified flying objects that do not come strictly within their orbit. Judges have still to make optimum use of penal or regulatory statutes in civil cases on negligence, involving the very conduct forbidden by the statutes.

. . .

It is fair to ask why the statutory standard should govern civil liability when the statute prescribes criminal sanctions only. My answer is that it establishes a minimum standard of reasonableness, for a legislature responds to community experience in determining when conduct is likely to cause harm of such magnitude as to call for its prohibition in a penal statute. The rational course for a court is hence to adopt such a standard instead of delegating the formulation of one to a jury. It bears noting that "[t]he decision as to what should be the controlling standard is made by the court, whether it instructs the jury to determine what would have been due care of a man of ordinary prudence under the circumstances or to follow the standard formulated by a statute." If a judge gives the latter instruction, he thereby guides the flying objects of civil litigation on a course that can be rationally synchronized with that of the pilot penal statute.

. . .

It would be wasteful for courts not to utilize such statutory materials when they are so readily available for analogy as well as for adoption. The statutes that protect specified classes of people from specified risks in specified areas are rich sources of analogy.

. . .

The Uniform Commercial Code has become a major influence in the development of common law in the federal courts to govern cases involving government contracts and other commercial transactions. . . .

. . .

Only when a case is not governed by a statute is the court free to work out its own solution. Only then it is free to copy an appropriate model in a statute. A judicial rule that thus emerges signifies a discriminating choice of policy, in sharp contrast to the routine compliance with a legislative policy when the statute encompassing it governs.

The process of discriminating choice involves more than the usual deliberation characteristic of the judicial process. A judge may have to evaluate more than one policy and more than one model for a rule from whatever source, if they appear relevant, and in doing so he may decide to reject rather than accept one model or another. He is free to reject a statutory rule as a model, arriving instead at another or at a rule without benefit of any model that becomes itself a prototype, because the rule he rejects does not in any event govern the instant case. Its very rejection signifies a considered judgment that it is not appropriate to govern the case, just as its acceptance would signify a considered judgment that it is.

Once a court formulates a rule by analogy from a statutory rule, it creates a precedent of the same force as any other. Its continuing force, like that of any other precedent, depends on its continuing fitness to survive as it ages. It may endure for generations or succumb to rapid obsolescence.

It should not surprise us that such judicial rules analogized from statutes are at one with other judicial lawmaking. They always have been, despite the protestations of those who would have us believe that judicial rules and statutory rules are like set pieces of an automaton clock, springing from separate covertures to make wooden appearances at separate times.

HOFFMAN v. JONES

Supreme Court of Florida, 1973.
280 So.2d 431.

ADKINS, JUSTICE.

The question certified by the District Court of Appeal is:

"Whether or not the Court should replace the contributory negligence rule with the principles of comparative negligence?"

The District Court of Appeal answered the certified question in the affirmative and reversed the trial court in the case *sub judice* for following the precedent set down by this Court in Louisville and Nashville Railroad Co. v. Yniestra, 21 Fla. 700 (1886). This early case specifically held the contributory negligence rule to be the law of Florida, and it has uniformly been followed by the courts of the State ever since. . . .

. . .

Prior to answering the question certified, we must also consider our own power and authority to replace the rule of contributory negligence with that of comparative negligence. It has been suggested that such a change in the common law of Florida is properly within the province only of the Legislature, and not of the courts. We cannot agree.

The rule that contributory negligence is an absolute bar to recovery was—as most tort law—a judicial creation, and it was specifically judicially adopted in Florida in Louisville and Nashville Railroad Co. v. Yniestra, *supra*. Most scholars attribute the origin of this rule to the English case of Butterfield v. Forrester, 11 East 60, 103 Eng.Rep. 926 (K.B.1809). . . .

. . .

Even if it be said that the present bar of contributory negligence is a part of our common law by virtue of prior judicial decision, it is also true . . . that this Court may change the rule where great social upheaval dictates. It has been modified in many instances by judicial decision, such as those establishing the doctrines of "last clear chance," "appreciable degree" and others. . . . In a large measure the rule has been transfigured from any "statutory creation" by virtue of our adoption of the common law (if such it were) into decisional law by virtue of various court refinements. We have in the past, with hesitation, modified the common law in justified instances, and this is as it should be. Randolph v. Randolph, 146 Fla. 491, 1 So.2d 480 (1941), modified the common law doctrine that gave a father the superior right to the custody of a child; Banfield v. Addington, 104 Fla. 661, 140 So. 893 (1932), removed the common law exemption of a married woman from causes of action based on contract or mixed contracts in tort.

. . .

All rules of the common law are designed for application to new conditions and circumstances as they may be developed by enlightened commercial and business intercourse and are intended to be vitalized by practical application in advanced society. One of the most pressing social problems facing us today is the automobile accident problem, for the bulk of tort litigation involves the dangerous instrumentality known as the automobile. Our society must be concerned with accident prevention and compensation of victims of accidents. The Legislature of Florida has made great progress in legislation geared for accident prevention. The prevention of accidents, of course, is much more satisfying than the compensation of victims, but we must recognize the problem of determining a method of securing just and adequate compensation of accident victims who have a good cause of action.

The contemporary conditions must be met with contemporary standards which are realistic and better calculated to obtain justice among all of the parties involved, based upon the circumstances applying between them at the time in question. The rule of contributory negligence as a complete bar to recovery was imported into the law by judges. Whatever may have been the historical justification for it, today it is almost universally regarded as unjust and inequitable to vest an entire accidental loss on one of the parties whose negligent conduct combined with the negligence of the other party to produce the loss. If fault is to remain the test of liability, then the doctrine of comparative negligence which involves apportionment of the loss among those whose fault contributed to the occurrence is more consistent with liability based on a fault premise.

We are, therefore, of the opinion that we do have the power and authority to reexamine the position we have taken in regard to contributory negligence and to alter the rule we have adopted previously in light of current "social and economic customs" and modern "conceptions of right and justice."

. . .

The demise of the absolute-bar theory of contributory negligence has been urged by many American scholars in the law of torts. It has been abolished in almost every common law nation in the world, including England—its country of origin—and every one of the Canadian Provinces. Some form of comparative negligence now exists in Austria, France, Germany, Portugal, Switzerland, Italy, China, Japan, Persia, Poland, Russia, Siam and Turkey....

Also, our research reveals that sixteen states have so far adopted some form of the comparative negligence doctrine.

One reason for the abandonment of the contributory negligence theory is that the initial justification for establishing the complete defense is no longer valid. It is generally accepted that, historically, contributory negligence was adopted "to protect the essential growth of industries, particularly transportation." Institute of Judicial Administration, Comparative Negligence—1954 Supplement, at page 2. Modern economic and social customs, however, favor the individual, not industry.

We find that none of the justifications for denying any recovery to a plaintiff, who has contributed to his own injuries to any extent, has any validity in this age.

Perhaps the best argument in favor of the movement from contributory to comparative negligence is that the latter is simply a more equitable system of determining liability and a more socially desirable method of loss distribution. The injustice which occurs when a plaintiff suffers severe injuries as the result of an accident for which he is only slightly responsible, and is thereby denied any damages, is readily apparent. The rule of contributory negligence is a harsh one which either places the burden of a loss for which two are responsible upon only one party or relegates to Lady Luck the determination of the damages for which each of two negligent parties will be liable. When the negligence of more than one person contributes to the occurrence of an accident, each should pay the proportion of the total damages he has caused the other party.

Since we definitely consider the problem to be a judicial one, we feel the time has come for this Court to join what seems to be a trend toward almost universal adoption of comparative negligence. A primary function of a court is to see that legal conflicts are equitably resolved. In the field of tort law, the most equitable result that can ever be reached by a court is the equation of liability with fault. Comparative negligence does this more completely than contributory negligence, and we would be shirking our duty if we did not adopt the better doctrine.

Therefore, we now hold that a plaintiff in an action based on negligence will no longer be denied any recovery because of his contributory negligence.

ROBERTS, JUSTICE, Dissenting.

I most respectfully dissent from the majority opinion in this cause. My primary concern is whether this Court is empowered to reject and replace the established doctrine of contributory negligence by judicial decree.

The sovereign powers of the State are divided into three coordinate branches of government—legislative, judicial and executive—by the Constitution of Florida.... Our Constitution specifically prohibits a person belonging to one of such branches from exercising any powers appertaining to either of the other branches unless expressly provided herein. This Court has been diligent in preserving and maintaining the doctrine of separation of powers which doctrine was imbedded in both the state and federal constitutions at the threshold of constitutional democracy in this country, and under which doctrine the judiciary has no power to make statutory law....

In the case of Ponder v. Graham, 4 Fla. 23, 25 (1851), this Court ... stated, "... Montesquieu says there can be no liberty, where the judicial are not separated from the legislative powers. 1 Spirit of Laws, page 181. Mr. Madison says these departments should remain forever separate and distinct, and that there is no political truth of greater intrinsic value, and which is stamped with the authority or more enlightened patrons of liberty. Federalist, 270."

Applying this well established doctrine, we held that the matter of changing statutory law is not one to be indulged by the Court, but is a legislative function.... [T]his Court also reaffirmed the principle that the common law, if not abrogated by statute or constitutional provision, is in full force and effect in this state....

It is the statutory law of this state that,

>   "The common and statute laws of England which are of a general and not a local nature, with the exception hereinafter

mentioned, down to the fourth day of July, 1776, are declared to be of force in this state; provided, the said statutes and common law be not inconsistent with the constitution and laws of the United States and the acts of the legislature of this state." Florida Statutes, Section 2.01, F.S.A.

The doctrine of contributory negligence was a part of the common law of England prior to July 4, 1776, and therefore, is part of the common law of this state pursuant to Florida Statutes, ... and is secure from the desires of this Court to supplant it by the doctrine of comparative negligence, provided that it is not inconsistent with the Constitution and laws of the United States and the Constitution and acts of the Legislature of this state.... Furthermore, we have held that courts are bound by the rule of stare decisis to follow common law as it has been judicially declared in previously adjudicated cases....

. . .

Although the case of Butterfield v. Forrester, 11 East 60, 103 Eng.Rep. 926 (K.B.1809), is recognized as a leading case in the area of contributory negligence, such case was not the first pronouncement of the common law doctrine of contributory negligence.

. . .

Contributory negligence was adopted much earlier as a part of the common law. In Bayly v. Merrell, Cro.Jac. 386, 79 Eng.Rep. 331 (1606), the Court explicated,

> "[I]f he doubted of the weight thereof, he might have weighed it; and was not bound to give credence to another's speech; *and being his own negligence,* he is without remedy." (Emphasis supplied) Cro.Jac. 386, p. 387, 79 Eng.Rep. 331.

. . .

In fine, the primary question is not whether or not the law of contributory negligence should be changed, but rather, who should do the changing. Contributory negligence was recognized in the common law as far back as A.D. 1606 and made a part of the statute law of this State in A.D. 1829, and thus far not changed by statute. If such a fundamental change is to be made in the law, then such modification should be made by the legislature where proposed change will be considered by legislative committees in public hearing where the general public may have an opportunity to be heard and should not be made by judicial fiat. Such an excursion into the field of legislative jurisdiction weakens the concept of separation of powers and our tripartite system of government.

NOTE

See also Li v. Yellow Cab Company, 13 Cal.3d 804, 532 P.2d 1226, 119 Cal.Rptr. 858 (1975).

———

KIRKLAND v. GENERAL MOTORS CORPORATION

Supreme Court of Oklahoma, 1974.
521 P.2d 1353.

DOOLIN, JUSTICE.

The issue for us in this case is the present and the future of products liability litigation in Oklahoma. Much we do in this case may set the pattern of such litigation in Oklahoma and may determine whether this young, vigorous and progressive State shall now meet the challenge of the mass advertising of today, its hypnosis, and the pace and flow of the economics of the late twentieth century. Most of us were born in the waning days of the use of either animal or steam power and today we find ourselves anticipating the wonders of an age of jets, rockets, genetic science, and atomic energy. The law, likewise, finds itself confronted with the problems of change, not only in the field of torts, but probably in all of its many and broad areas.

. . .

It was Justice Traynor, who . . . gave this doctrine a label, "Strict Liability in Tort", . . . this theory or remedy we would adopt for Oklahoma, but would prefer to call it "Manufacturers' Products Liability", recognizing its origin in tort principles and its background of implied warranty liability and by so doing attempting to avoid the semantic confusion of and relationship of tort to common law negligence. We would include in the definition of manufacturer—processors, assemblers, and all other persons who are similarly situated in processing and distribution.

In order to avoid costly and multiplicious litigation . . . dealing with the pitfalls of negligence, warranties, and strict liability, . . . we turn to some of the practical applications raised by the adoption of strict liability in the areas of limitations, defenses, election of remedies, parties, proofs, etc. We recognize that in these areas we embark on judicial innovation and prospective overruling sometimes the source of criticism as dicta. Professor Leflar points out the vice of such a narrow approach in "Sources of Judge–Made Law", 24 Oklahoma Law Review 319. . . . As examples of such judicial innovation, Leflar reminds us that much of the modern law of insurance, corporations, trusts, oil and gas, aviation, and conflicts of law has been created by the courts from needs generated by society and accepted as a part of the common law "whose time has come." . . .

[Statute of Limitations]

We are persuaded that the limitation period to be applied in products liability actions is two (2) years, . . . for we recognize the tortious origin and nature of the single cause of action, Williams v. Ford Motor Company, Mo.App., 454 S.W.2d 611 (1970). The essential nature of an action based upon products liability is an action for injury to personal property or for injury to the rights of another. The action thus being primarily tortious in nature ... limitations should begin to run from the date of injury....

. . .

[Plaintiff's Burden]

By our adoption of manufacturers' products liability with its comparison to liability without fault in such areas as workmen's compensation, respondeat superior, the vicious or fractious animal, etc., we do not infer that the injury is of itself proof of the defect, or that proof of injury shifts the burden to the Defendant....

. . .

The practicing lawyer identified with the Plaintiff will seldom be able to produce actual or absolute proof of the defect so necessary in manufacturers' products liability since this information in the final analysis is usually within the peculiar possession of the Defendant. Carefully prepared interrogatories or depositions may be helpful to a Plaintiff, but more than likely Plaintiff may be forced to rely on circumstances and *proper* inferences drawn therefrom in making his proof. We note that in some accidents the surrounding circumstances and human experience should make Plaintiff's burden less arduous; he may be able to sustain his burden, but more than likely if the Defendant is a manufacturer or assembler of some highly complex product such as an automobile, human experience will play little or no part in reducing his burden, and he will be relying upon the inference drawn from circumstantial evidence.

. . .

Examination of the burden on the plaintiff reveals it to be a large and heavy one. Nor do we mean to say, by speaking of the burden of proof assigned to the plaintiff, that he is relieved from proof of causation, as that term is used and understood in the law of negligence, for he must prove that his injury has been caused not necessarily by the negligence of the Defendant but by reason of a defect "built in" and existing at the time of injury.

. . .

[Defenses]

... [C]ausation of the injury by the defective product beyond a mere possibility must be shown. If some act of the plaintiff *caused* the injury, rather than the defective product itself, causation is missing, and the plaintiff may not recover; e.g., the intoxication of the Plaintiff in the instant case. Although the act of the Plaintiff that did in fact cause the injury might have been negligent, it seems wise to avoid the semantic confusion of calling it contributory negligence, especially since the action itself is not based on negligence. It seems better to lump this defense in with the general causation requirement.

A second defense, well established in negligence cases, and applicable to manufacturers' products liability is the defense of abnormal use. If the plaintiff is using the product for some purpose for which it was not intended and is consequently injured, he should not recover....

Complicated semantic difficulties arise when the defense of assumption of risk is considered. In order to avoid abuse of this legitimate defense, or confusion of same with its common law counterpart of the same name, it should be narrowly defined as *voluntary assumption of the risk of a known defect.* This has been otherwise referred to as contributory fault ... [and] consists of voluntary and unreasonably encountering a known danger ... [which] will, in general, relieve the defendant of strict liability." Prosser, The Law of Torts, 3rd Ed., § 78.

The recent enactment of the comparative negligence statutes by the Oklahoma Legislature ... has no application to manufacturers' products liability, for its application is specifically limited to *negligence actions.* We have stated that manufacturers' products liability is not negligence, nor is it to be treated as a negligence action, but a new theory of recovery....

. . .

Because of the obvious impact of this decision and its effect on basic concepts of law, procedures and rules in Oklahoma, we specifically hold that the law hereby established will be applied prospectively to all cases for trial from and after the date the mandate issues herein; and may likewise be applied by the appellate courts in cases which have been tried and are for decision on appeal where it would not prejudice the rights of the litigants.

NOTE

Consider the basic authority of courts to revolutionize tort law by adopting Restatement (Second) of Torts § 402 A, as the Oklahoma supreme court did here. Was it proper for courts, rather than the legislature, to change the law so fundamentally. Are there any limits to enacting court-made law?

Both Holmes and Cardozo thought so. Recall Holmes: "I recognize without hesitation that judges do and must legislate, but they can do so only interstitially; they are confined from molar to molecular motions. A common-law judge could not say I think the doctrine of consideration a bit of historical nonsense and shall not enforce it in my court." Southern Pacific Co. v. Jensen, 244 U.S. 205 (1917) (Holmes, J. dissenting).

Cardozo explained:

[Judges] have the right to legislate within gaps, but often there are not gaps.... They have the power, though not the right, to travel beyond the walls of the interstices, the bounds set to judicial innovation by precedent and custom. None the less, by that abuse of power, they violate the law. If they violate it willfully, i.e. with guilty or evil mind, they commit a legal wrong, and may be removed or punished even though the judgments they have rendered stand.

B. Cardozo, The Nature of the Judicial Process 129 (1921)

Consider Cardozo's opinion in MacPherson v. Buick Motor Co., 217 N.Y. 382, 111 N.E. 1050 (1916). Did he "travel beyond the walls of the interstices?"

In the allocation of competence, is it appropriate for the judiciary and not the legislature to make policy determinations relating to the basis of strict product liability? Consider the stated reasons: the costs of damaging events due to defectively dangerous products can best be borne by the enterprises who make and sell these products; that they can pass on the additional costs (or insurance premiums) to the consumers; that it is understood that some may be unable to survive financially with a disastrous experience with a particular product; that strict liability may inhibit the development of new products; that even if fault or negligence were regarded as the primary justification for the imposition of liability on the manufacturer or other seller for the costs of accident attributable to defective products, it is often present but difficult to prove; and that for institutional reasons and because of the costs of litigation, proof of the existence of fault or negligence should no longer be required.

If court-made strict liability law is a legitimate exercise of judicial law-making, can we agree that there are now no restrictions or limitations whatsoever?

————

GUIDO CALABRESI, THE LEGITIMACY OF COURT–MADE LAW *

What, if anything, entitles judges to make law in a democracy? That they do is by now an accepted fact, but on what basis? The answer to this question has long been a source of concern among legal scholars and judges; I cannot do it justice in a few paragraphs. Yet without some discussion of the issue, it will be impossible to see whether the same basis applies where judges act in statutory areas as at common law.

There are several different grounds for the judicial power to make or evolve law. The first is that this power has been implicitly delegated to courts by majoritarian bodies. In purely formal terms such a justification suffices—a democracy can surely at times choose to act through agents. But this justification is neither very helpful nor very interesting. It immediately pushes us back one step to other questions. Has there in fact been any delegation—implicit or explicit—and if so, what is its scope? And, most important, why would the legislatures or the people in a democracy wish to make such a delegation of authority to courts?

* G. Calabresi, A Common Law for the Age of Statutes 92-97 (1982)

Since I am talking about judicial power to make or evolve ordinary laws—and not about the judicial power of constitutional nullification or review—these questions become almost identical to the original question I asked. If it makes sense in a democracy to give courts the power to evolve or to make the common law, then that very fact will go a long way toward legitimating the power, given the long history of legislative acquiescence in judicial making of the common law and the fact that any exercise of the power is subject to legislative revision. The trouble is, of course, that none of this tells us anything about why, whether, and when it makes sense to give such power to courts, and therefore can be of no use in analyzing the problems with which this book is concerned: Can or should this power extend to statutory areas?

The second ground is only slightly more interesting. It would justify judicial power to make law because such judge-made rules are all in a sense conditional, that is, they are subject to legislative or popular revision and hence are acceptable in a democracy. The trouble with this argument is that, taken literally, it can justify any law, however instituted or arrived at, so long as a legislature or other majoritarian body can reject it. It says lawmaking by any body, of any sort, is consistent with democratic theory if the people can have the last word.

There is of course something to this. Indeed, if there were no inertia and if it made no difference to anyone what the conditional or temporary rule was, because such a rule could immediately and at no cost to anyone be revised according to the popular will, the argument would be valid as well as tautological. Since there is inertia and since even conditional rules have enormous effect, the argument fails by itself. Despite inertia, however, the argument is not meaningless or foolish, for the amount of inertia does set a boundary on the "undemocratic" effect of allowing a nonmajoritarian body to make conditional rules. It allows us to restate the question of judicial power to make ordinary laws: What justifies court power to make temporary rules and thereby to assign the burden of overcoming inertia and of getting those rules revised? Or to put the issue in a slightly different way: What justifies courts in making law within the boundaries set by legislative inertia?

The answers to these questions necessarily depend on the way in which courts are constituted and the way in which they exercise the powers they have. As a result we are thrown back, as we were by the "implicit delegation" rationale, to the question of why one would in a democracy give courts the power to make conditional rules and to assign the burden of overcoming the inertial force that such rules have.

The third justification of judicial lawmaking power emphasizes the notion that courts do look at the election returns. Judges are, after all, either elected or appointed and ratified by elected officials. Their manner of selection suggests that they can both discern and respond to the popular will. The fact that their response is neither direct nor governed by immediate popular will is of little consequence in any democracy that rejects direct majoritarianism. The degree of independence accorded to judges—like the manner of their selection—leads them to follow longer-run majoritarian sentiments than, say, congressmen. But in the end, in a system in which senators have six-year terms, presidents four, congressmen two, and committee chairman indefinite ones, what is so disastrous or peculiar about having elected or appointed judges—with long or life terms—also shape our law, at least at the level of making conditional rules that can be revised by legislatures?

There is, again, something to this justification, but again not enough. Insofar as it says that judges are not immune from majoritarian pressures, it is surely correct. And insofar as it says that—apart from any judicial subservience to principles—the judiciary as a whole, *because* of the way it is chosen, tends to respond to a delayed majoritarianism, it is not only correct but significant. A democratic polity might well wish its conditional rules to reflect such delayed majoritarian trends. The argument is made more significant by the fact that judicial lawmaking takes place in case-by-case situations and therefore is of necessity accretional, incremental, and the product of many judges. Thus delayed majoritarianism is served even by judges who seek to respond to their own view of the immediate popular will because no one of them can make the common law and all of them together do represent (in a literal sense) our evolving majorities.

Why, though, do we want delayed majoritarian wishes to be the source of conditional rules? Conversely, if capacity to discern majoritarian wishes—current or delayed—is what we want, do we really believe that courts are suited for that task? Their capacity to figure out what current majorities wish is surely limited, and their memory of what was wanted when they were appointed or elected is bound to fade. Their terms are too long, their staffs are too limited, and their manner of selection too bizarre to give much support to the notion that judges work well as makers of the common law because they seek to follow the wishes of the majority; and end up doing so with a bias toward those majorities that dominated at the time they were selected.

If, in other words, we wanted the burden of inertia to be assigned primarily on the basis of a delayed majoritarianism, it seems unlikely that we would assign the job to judges. Other institutions, such as independent administrative agencies, less hampered by principles, with more limited terms, and supported by a staff that can be used to discern trends in popular desires, would seem more suitable. Still, the fact that courts are not divorced from political pressures, especially long-term ones, does form an outward boundary. Like the fact that the common law can be reversed by legislatures, it tends to limit the allegedly undemocratic effect of judicial lawmaking. For me, the limit is not sufficient.

The fourth justification of lawmaking by judges looks to their alleged capacity to "do what [is] right for the country." Under such a theory judges would be justified in following their own values in evolving the common law since it is their educated and disinterested sense of what is right that we are seeking. At first blush, this justification is distinctly antidemocratic; it seems to put lawmaking power in the hands of "wise people" because they are wise, and not because they represent current, delayed, or long-term majoritarian wishes. This first impression is rather too strong. We are not, after all, talking about final rules. We are talking about rules that are subject to legislative revisions and about allocating the burden of inertia. There is nothing in itself deeply inconsistent with democracy in the delegation to a group of wise people of the job of setting the starting points, so long as the polity can reject the decisions of its guardians which it dislikes. Such a "realistic" (and, without much refinement, false) view of judicial power may not be appropriate. But it cannot be dismissed out of hand. It is no more inconsistent with ultimate popular rule than is the appointment by an individual of an expert to make those preliminary decisions that the expert thinks best, subject to review by the individual.

Are judges, however, expert enough in what is right for society to justify even such temporary authority? That I trust my doctor or butcher to make preliminary suggestions on my behalf, which I sometimes do not have time to review adequately, does not mean that I would be wise to trust my doctor to make preliminary suggestions about a cut of beef or my butcher to prescribe a headache remedy. It is the qualifications of judges to decide society's wishes—even temporarily— that one properly questions.

Again, we should not exaggerate. There are many people less suited than judges to make decisions as to conditional rules based on their own values. The manner in which they are selected, their relative freedom from political pressures, the fact that they are required to be personally disinterested in the result, and most of all the fact that it takes so many of them to act effectively in shaping law, all combine to make them more suitable as temporary guardians than one might think. For me there is enough to be said for judges' disinterested values as a guide to policy that I am not shocked to read that one of France's leading scholars instructed judges to follow their own sense of right whenever the written law gave no directions. It is hard for me to believe, however, that judges' capacity to discern what is best for the country can justify more than this kind of very limited allocation of power. Like their responsiveness to a delayed popular will and the fact that they can be overruled by majoritarian bodies, their disinterested and occasionally wise sense of right and wrong does not justify the enormous power that judges came to exercise at common law.

Most classic justifications of judicial common law power do not, in fact, look to the previous rationales. Instead they emphasize the subservience of courts to principles, to rational decision making, and to the whole fabric of the law, as explaining and justifying judicial lawmaking power. As Chief Judge Charles Breitel put it: "The judicial process is based on reasoning and presupposes—all antirationalists to the contrary notwithstanding—that its determinations are justified only when explained or explainable in reason. No poll, no majority vote of the affected, no rule of expediency, and certainly no confessedly subjective or idiosyncratic view justifies a judicial determination. Emphatically, no claim of might, physical or political, justifies a judicial determination."

All this is well and good, but it leaves unanswered the crucial issue: what there is about principles of law, about the legal fabric, and about rational decision making which suggests that a body, selected for its capacity to discern these principles and to act rationally on them, should make the conditional rules for society and, at common law at least, set the starting points for legislative reaction. I will readily agree that courts are better than other institutions at discerning principles of law and at working out the demands of the ever changing legal topography. I will concede that the way judges are trained and selected, their relative independence, the limitations imposed on their staff, the fact that they make law incrementally in response to specific situations, and the requirement that they explain the grounds of their decisions, all seem designed to lead them to perform this job and not others. In other words, principled decision making within a legal landscape is the primary judicial task. But unless legal principles and the legal topography are sensible starting points for legislative reaction, reliance on judges to make the common law because of their skill at discerning the landscape is still misplaced.

Why does a democracy care about the rational application of legal principles? The answer must lie in the belief that the legal fabric, and the principles that form it, are good approximations of one aspect of the popular will, of what a majority in some sense desires. It cannot be an exact fit, but it must reflect enough of what is wanted so that it is a good starting point for lawmaking. Then it follows that those who by training and selection are relatively good at exploring and mapping the legal landscape can appropriately be given the task of evolving the law, and inevitably of allocating the burden of overcoming the inertia of that law.

It is, I think, this belief that characterizes most justifications of judicial common law power. Each judicial decision, at its best, is meant to represent a reasoned attempt to adapt a past set of decisions to a current problem. It tries to treat like cases alike when what is "alike" changes constantly because of ideological, technological, or even constitutional or statutory change. Common law rules become dominant slowly over time in response to many separate decisions in real cases by many disparate judges as to what has changed in the underlying framework. In seeking to apply that framework to new circumstances, each judge inevitably brings to the task some sense of the majority that selected him or her and some sense of what is right for the country, and this, together with the fact that what a "like" case is depends on the level of generality at which one asks the question, helps the fabric to change. But the judge does not directly seek to apply his or her sense of the popular will or of right and wrong except as it seems to fit in the fabric. As a result, the judge's lack of skill at guessing the popular will or the court's possibly bizarre sense of values becomes relatively unimportant. At any moment consistency with the fabric can be taken to be a reasonably accurate account of what has evolved from past popular desires, and the judge's task is to do what is needed to accommodate that account to present needs.

Note

Calabresi later suggests that for the purposes of his argument, it does not matter which of various theories of judicial interpretation is accepted, since some alternative mechanisms for updating statutes will always be necessary:

> The framework of original legislative intent permits widely different degrees of freedom in interpretation. Some courts apply a "plain-meaning test" and look only for legislative purpose if statutory words are not clear on their face. Other courts search for the original congressional purpose. A third group of courts adhere to the "last-resort" approach.

A Common Law For the Age of Statutes 214 n. 30 (1982)

Do Calabresi's "degrees of freedom in interpretation" resonate with the basic theories of judicial law making that were discussed at the beginning of this chapter?

Section 2

CREATING LAW IN THE COMMON LAW TRADITION *

OVERVIEW

Judge-made laws emerge as by-products of judicial decisions in specific cases or controversies. In the Poundian sense the law materializes as a legal rule—a definite legal consequence attached to a detailed set of facts. If the legal rule or principle has originated in case law, the development follows the "pure" common law tradition. During the Holmes–Pound–Cardozo era this was the major characteristic of the judicial process. The legal precept originated in a decided case and all subsequent refinements surfaced from succeeding cases.

As we will soon explain in detail, the common law tradition of adjudicating cases (with its consequent law-making by-products) still forms the heart of the judicial process. The same techniques that have been with us during generations of our legal history are still intact with maximum vitality. With one difference. The common law tradition has been used to make refinements in the law—expanding and contracting—as the courts have faced novel fact situations. But in most litigation today, the original source of the legal precept has come from a legislative body or a written constitution. In construing or interpreting statutes,

* Adapted in part from R. Aldisert, *The Judicial Process: Revisited,* 49 Univ.Cin-   ti.L.Rev. 1, 8–16 (1980).

resolutions, regulations, ordinances or clauses of constitutions, we use the common law tradition to add a judicial gloss to the original language.

The only difference, therefore, between the "pure" common law tradition where the original legal precept emerged from a case or controversy and the process we usually follow today lies in the origin of the seminal legal precept that forms the basis of adjudication. Whether the original precept has originated in a case or in a statute, we still follow the common law tradition in the adjudication process today. It therefore becomes important to understand how this tradition developed over the centuries.

The term "tradition" is deliberately used rather than an expression that would simply denote a body of legal precepts about torts, crimes, business associations, and contracts, although common law legal precepts will always reflect the common law tradition. A legal tradition is a set of deeply-rooted, historically-conditioned attitudes about the nature of law, about the role of law in the society and the polity, about the proper organization and operation of a legal system, and about the way law is or should be made, applied, perfected, studied, and taught. The common law owes its origin to the desire of early English kings to strengthen the royal, central power. It owes its capacity for growth to the inclination of the Tudors to adapt medieval institutions to changed conditions rather than to abandon those institutions altogether. It owes its flexibility to the Court of Chancery, which provided relief otherwise denied by the rigidity of complex and technical rules of procedure.

Starting in 1066, the Norman invasion brought to England a class of capable administrators in the service of a lord who claimed central political power by virtue of a single right, the right of conquest. In the twelfth century, Henry I began the practice of sending royal ministers throughout the country to hear cases in the local courts. By the end of the century, the king's court, composed of minister-judges who traveled the country resolving disputes, had become the most powerful political institution in the country.[29] Jenks explained the ascendancy of the royal court to its then current status as the body that declares the common law of England as a result of the absence of other judicial bodies with competing authority; by the time of Henry I, the old popular courts had already become antiquated.[30] Thus, through a slow and organic growth over the centuries, England achieved a truly common, unified law. This tradition is now in force in the United States, Great Britain, Ireland, Canada, Australia, and New Zealand.

While a unified common law was fast developing in England, the same was not true on the Continent. As the Normans were conquering England, "the revival of Roman law," as civil lawyers have called it, occurred at Bologna, Italy. There the first modern European university was founded, with law as the major subject of study. The law studied was Justinian's *Corpus Juris Civilis,* a compilation that first appeared in

29. A. von Mehren, The Civil Law System 10–11 (1957).

30. E. Jenks, Law and Politics in the Middle Ages 36 (2d ed. 1913).

the sixth century. From a purported 2,000 books with 3,000,000 lines, Justinian produced fifty books with 150,000 lines, and placed these sentences at the beginning: "Whoever wished to concern himself seriously with the law must first of all wish to know whence comes its name. Law (*ius*) is derived from justice (*iustitia*). For as Celsus has rightly said: Law is the art of the good and the fair (*bonum et aequum*)." [31] Justinian's monumental work became the basis for the civil law system in Europe. As Bologna became the center for legal study in Europe, a succession of schools of thought emerged, differing in their methods of scholarship and their explanations of the *Corpus Juris Civilis*. Of special prominence among these schools of thought were the Glossators and the Commentators, both of which prolifically produced legal literature. This literature was widely discussed and assumed great authority as a method of analyzing and teaching the *Corpus Juris Civilis*. [32] The nations of Europe based their law on the studies conducted at Bologna, and the *jus commune,* the common law of Europe, developed. [33]

The reception of the *jus commune* in European nations did not produce a uniformity equal to that achieved by the English common law. In northern France, for example, local customs, *pays de droit coutumier,* dominated the law; in southern France, Roman law, *pays de droit ecrit,* prevailed. Unification of French law did not occur until the Code Napoleon in 1804. Similarly, in Germany, the emphasis from the ninth century to the fifteenth century was on local, customary law. The disintegration of the Holy Roman Empire resulted in a loose confederation of states, and fragmented them into regional leagues of towns and provinces. [34] Before the emergence of the nation-state, every town, commune, dukedom, and principality had its own particular laws. Probably influenced by the need for some uniformity of law occasioned by the growth of trade, the German states gradually looked more and more to Roman law. The reception by the German courts of Roman law with the "gloss" of the Glossators and the Commentators continued until well into the eighteenth century.

In both France and Germany, Roman law was "received" and fused with native institutions. In contrast, although Roman law was brought to England, it was never "received" to the degree that it came to dominate. Rather, the English courts developed law from narrow rules emanating from cases and controversies. These rules were fashioned by the king's judges and developed by their successors in a manner in which, in contrast to the tendency on the continent, neither local nor customary law was decisive.

According to K.W. Ryan, [35] the common law was threatened in the sixteenth century by many influential advocates favoring reception of the

---

31. *Id.* at 38.

32. J. Hedemann, Die Flucht in die Generalklauseln 1 (1933).

33. J. Merryman & D. Clark, Comparative Law: Western European and Latin American Legal Systems 72 (1979).

34. K. Ryan, An Introduction to Civil Law 15–26 (1962).

35. *Id.*

Roman law system. The common law survived because of four influences. First, the Tudor sovereigns recognized the interrelationship of the common law and the constitution, and supported the common law as an institution to prevent what they perceived would be a revolutionary change. Second, the new courts, particularly the court of Chancery and the Court of Star Chamber, attended to the deficiencies of the common law and afforded relief denied by the strictures of rigid pleading rules. Third, Coke's restatement and modernization of common law principles at the beginning of the seventeenth century ensured its continuity. Finally, the Inns of Court played an important role in the preservation and propagation of the common law. These developments solidified the common law as part of the English political system. Holdsworth, noting the occasional reliance by English courts on Roman law, commented:

> We have received Roman law; but we have received it in small homeopathic doses, at different periods, and as and when required. It has acted as a tonic to our native legal system, and not as a drug or poison. When received it has never been continuously developed on Roman lines. It has been naturalized and assimilated; and with its assistance, our wholly independent system has, like the Roman law itself, been gradually and continuously built up, by the development of old and the creation of new rules to meet the needs of a changing civilisation and an expanding empire.[36]

Unity of law throughout the jurisdiction, and flexibility to incorporate useful precepts, thus began to characterize the common law tradition.

But more than unity and capacity to assimilate distinguish the common law tradition from the civil law tradition. Also at work is gradualness. At common law the sources of decision are rules of specific decisions, rules of law in the narrow sense, "precepts attaching a definite detailed legal consequence to a definite, detailed state of facts,"[37] or "fairly concrete guides for decision geared to narrow categories of behavior and prescribing narrow patterns of conduct."[38] The common law "creeps from point to point, testing each step"[39] and is most characteristically a system built by gradual accretion from the resolution of specific problems. Holmes noted that the great growth of the common law came about incrementally.[40] The courts fashioned *principles* from a number of *rules* of decision, in a process characterized by experimentation. Rules of case law are at common law treated not as final truths, "but as working hypotheses, continually retested in those great laboratories of the law, the courts of justice."[41] The common law has been described as "the byzantine beauty," a method "of reaching

36. *Id.* at 26 (quoting 4 W. Holdsworth, The History of English Law 293 (1903)).

37. Pound, *Hierarchy of Sources and Forms in Different Systems of Law,* 7 Tulane L.Rev. 475, 482 (1933).

38. Hughes, *Rules, Policy, and Decision Making,* 77 Yale L.J. 411, 419 (1968).

39. A. Whitehead, Adventures of Ideas ch. 2, § 6 (1967).

40. Holmes, *The Path of the Law,* 10 Harv.L.Rev. 457, 468 (1897).

41. M. Smith, Jurisprudence 21 (1909).

what instinctively seem[s] the right result in a series of cases, and only later (if at all) enunciating the principle that explains the pattern—a sort of connect the dots exercise." [42]

Principles, therefore, are judge-made, assembled from publicly stated reasons for publicly stated rules in cases previously decided. Formulation of a principle is a gradual process, shaped from actual incidents in social, economic, and political experience. It is a process in which countervailing rights are challenged, evaluated, synthesized, and adjudicated on a case-by-case basis in the context of an adversary proceeding before a factfinder in the law courts. For every rule at common law there is a publicly stated reason, the *ratio decidendi*. And for each principle that slowly emerges, there is a solid recorded experience from rules of law themselves and from the publicly stated reasons that support them.

The heart of the common law tradition is adjudication of specific cases.[43] Case-by-case development allows experimentation because each rule is reevaluated in subsequent cases to determine if it produces a fair result. If it operates unfairly, it can be modified. The modification does not occur at once, "for the attempt to do absolute justice in every single case would make the development and maintenance of general rules impossible; but if a rule continues to work injustice, it will eventually be reformulated." [44] The genius of the common law is that it has proceeded empirically and gradually, testing the ground at every step, and refusing, or at any rate evincing an extreme reluctance, to embrace broad theoretical principles.[45] This incremental development has produced a fundamental distinction between the American law student's approach to the study of law and that of his counterpart in civil law countries. The student of civil law views law not as a process for the perception and resolution of problems, but as a set of established rules and institutions. Instead of studying how judicial institutions perceive and resolve problems, or how they make, interpret, and apply the law, instruction focuses on the substantive content of existing rules.

Common law reasoning should not be characterized as merely inductive. It is more than a congeries of devised fact patterns converging to compel an induced conclusion. Rather, the reasoning process is both inductive and deductive. First, the principle is induced from a line of specific, reasoned decisions, and, once identified, the principle becomes the major premise in the cause at hand from which a conclusion may be

---

42. Ely, *The Supreme Court 1977 Term, Forward: On Discovering Fundamental Values,* 92 Harv.L.Rev. 5, 32 (1978) (citing Amsterdam, *Perspectives of the Fourth Amendment,* 58 Minn.L.Rev. 349, 351–52 (1974)). *See also* Arnold, *Professor Hart's Theology,* 73 Harv.L.Rev. 1298, 1311–12 (1960); Holmes, *Codes and the Arrangement of the Law,* 44 Harv.L.Rev. 725, 725 (1931).

43. Fuller, *The Forms and Limits of Adjudication,* 92 Harv.L.Rev. 353 (1978).

According to Fuller, adjudication is a device that gives formal and institutional expression to reasoned argument in human affairs. It assumes a burden of rationality not borne by other social processes. A decision that is the product of reasoned argument must be prepared to meet the test of reason.

44. M. Smith, *supra* note 41, at 21.

45. Lloyd, *Reason and Logic in the Common Law,* 64 L.Q.Rev. 468, 469 (1948).

deduced.[47] The problem of common law adjudication, in John Dewey's formulation, is that of finding statements of general principle and of particular fact that are worthy to serve as premises. The common law judge chooses these statements, by means of a value judgment, as the controlling legal precepts, and then structures the major premises that lead to conclusions in the case at hand. To do this, he uses a logic relative to consequences rather than to antecedents.[48] Use of this logic in the common law tradition facilitates the gradual development of legal principles for use in that tradition.

Another important characteristic of the common law tradition is that it is law fashioned by lawyers and judges from actual events that have raised issues for decision. It is law that emerges as a by-product of the major function of the courts—dispute settling, the adjustment of a specific conflict among the parties. Harlan Fiske Stone emphasized that a "[d]ecision [draws] its inspiration and its strength from the very facts which frame the issues for decisions." [49] By contrast, legislative law-making is not a subordinate effort. To a legislator, the law is not the by-product; it is the primary endeavor. Laws are enacted as general rules to control future conduct, not to settle a specific dispute from past experience.

Common law judicial process starts with the finding of facts in a dispute by a factfinder, a jury or judge. Once the facts are ascertained, the court compares them with fact patterns from previous cases. The process ends with a narrow decision confined to the facts before the court. Any portion of a judicial opinion that concerns an issue beyond the precise facts of the case is *obiter dictum*. Common law is case law of the specific instance—law that is reprinted in a galaxy of state and federal, trial and appellate law reports.

Explanations of the broad terms of the civil law codes are found primarily in treatises written by respected professors in respected universities, rather than in the published reports of common law judges. By contrast, the common law was, and is, judge-made. Harlan Fiske Stone called it "the law of the practitioner rather than the philosopher." It has been described "as a monument to the judicial activity of the common law judge. He, not the legislator or the scholar, created the common law." [55] The judge and the individual case are still central to the common law tradition. In contrast to the civil law, which conceives of law as "a logical framework" controlling directly or indirectly all human activity and relationships, the common law is more pragmatic, striving for workability and not requiring logic as an essential component.

Cardozo's observations about *The Nature of the Judicial Process* dealt with a common law tradition with six fundamental characteristics.

47. Nevertheless, a value judgment is involved in the choice of competing legal principles.

48. Dewey, *Logical Method and Law*, 10 Cornell L.Q. 17 (1924).

49. Stone, *The Common Law in the United States*, 50 Harv.L.Rev. 4, 6 (1936).

55. Stone, *supra* note 49 at 6.

First, the tradition sought and generally produced uniformity of law throughout the jurisdiction. Second, it produced decisions announcing a narrow rule of law covering a detailed and real fact situation. Third, principles developed gradually as the courts reconciled a series of narrow rules emanating from prior decisions. Fourth, the common law tradition produced judge-made law for the practitioner, not for the philosopher or academician. Fifth, lower courts operating in the tradition were bound by decisions of hierarchically superior courts. Finally, statutes in derogation of the common law were strictly construed and not extended by judicial construction. These then were the characteristics of the common law tradition at the time Cardozo delivered his classic essay in 1921.

————

Thousands of reported opinions reflect the "pure" common law tradition. They represent decisions from state and federal courts, as well as courts from the United Kingdom and the British Commonwealth. What may be considered a paradigm of the tradition was the speech (opinion) delivered by Lord Diplock in the following case in the House of Lords.

As you read this excerpt, contemplate the following: Where was the flash point of controversy between the parties—finding the law, that is, choosing between competing legal principles, or was it simply interpreting a single legal precept, or was it applying settled law to a set of facts? Did Lord Diplock state the issue succinctly? Without knowledge of the substantive law of the United Kingdom, are you able to follow the reasoning without difficulty? Other than the use of the first person, what do you perceive to be the basic difference between excerpts in this opinion and traditional state and federal high court opinions in the United States?

DORSET YACHT CO. v. HOME OFFICE

House of Lords, 1970.
1970 App.Cas. 1004.

[The Case was one of first impression in the Court of Appeal and the House of Lords. Seven Borstal boys (British juvenile detention residents) were working on an island under the control and supervision of three officers from the Home Office. During the night, the boys left the island, boarded, cast adrift, and damaged the plaintiffs' yacht, which was moored offshore. The plaintiffs brought an action for damages against the Home Office which charged negligence. In particular, they alleged that the officers, knowing of the boys' criminal records and records of previous escapes from Borstal institutions, and knowing that crafts such as the plaintiffs' yacht were moored offshore, had failed to exercise effective control and supervision of the boys. The Home Office conceded that they were vicariously liable for the torts of their servants (the officers), but denied that they, or their servants or agents, owed the plaintiffs any duty of care with respect to the detention, supervision, or control, of the boys.]

This is the first time that this specific question has been posed at a higher judicial level than that of a county court. Your Lordships in answering it will be performing [the] judicial function ... of deciding whether the English law of civil wrongs should be extended to impose legal liability to make reparation for the loss caused to another by conduct of a kind which has not hitherto been recognised by the courts as entailing any such liability.

This function, which judges hesitate to acknowledge as lawmaking, plays at most a minor role in the decision of the great majority of cases, and little conscious thought has been given to analysing its methodology. Outstanding exceptions are to be found in the speeches of Lord Atkin in Donoghue v. Stevenson and of Lord Devlin in Hedley Byrne & Co. Ltd. v. Heller & Partners Ltd. It was because the former was the first authoritative attempt at such an analysis that it has had so seminal an effect upon the modern development of the law of negligence.

It will be apparent that I agree with the Master of the Rolls that what we are concerned with in this appeal "is ... at bottom a matter of public policy which we as judges, must resolve." He cited in support Lord Pearce's dictum in Hedley Byrne & Co. Ltd. v. Heller & Partners Ltd. [1964] A.C. 465, 536: "How wide the sphere of the duty of care in negligence is to be laid depends ultimately upon the courts' assessment of the demands of society for protection from the carelessness of others."

The reference in this passage to "the courts" in the plural is significant, for as Lord Devlin in the Court of Appeals had put it: "As always in English law, the first step in such an inquiry is to see how far the authorities have gone, for new categories in the law do not spring into existence overnight."

[Ed. Note: In the next section, Lord Diplock combines the processes of inductive generalization by enumeration and inductive analogy to justify the House of Lords' use of public interest in a negligence case.]

The justification of the courts' role in giving the effect of law to the judges' conception of the public interest in the field of negligence is based upon the cumulative experience of the judiciary of the actual consequences of lack of care in particular instances. And the judicial development of the law of negligence rightly proceeds by seeking first to identify the relevant characteristics that are common to the kinds of conduct and relationships between the parties which are involved in the case for decision and the kinds of conduct and relationships which have been held in previous decisions of the courts to give rise to a duty of care.

The method adopted at this stage of the process is analytical and inductive. It starts with an analysis of the characteristics of the conduct and relationship involved in each of the decided cases. But the analyst must know what he is looking for, and this involves his approaching his analysis with some general conception of conduct and relationships which ought to give rise to a duty of care.

[Ed. Note: A generalization "based on the cumulative experience of the judiciary," is simply an elegant way of describing inductive generalization by an enumeration of instances. Just as "seeking ... to identify the relevant characteristics that are common [among cases]" is no more than analogy. You will also note that the process described in the second paragraph above is a classic description of inductive reasoning.

As we read on, Lord Diplock will carefully craft the logical form that the preliminary conclusion will take. This is very important because the conclusion from inductive reasoning will become the major premise of the subsequent deductive reasoning process.]

This analysis leads to a proposition which can be stated in the form: "In all the decisions that have been analyzed a duty of care has been held to exist wherever the conduct and the relationship possessed each of the characteristics A, B, C, D, etc., and has not so far been found to exist when any of these characteristics were absent."

For the second stage, which is deductive and analytical, that proposition is converted to: "In all cases where the conduct and relationship possess each of the characteristics A, B, C, D, etc., a duty of care arises." The conduct and relationship involved in the case for decision is then analysed to ascertain whether they possess each of these characteristics. If they do the conclusion follows that a duty of care does arise in the case for decision.

[Ed. Note: Note well the presence of the Socrates-is-a-man syllogism. The subject (middle term) of the proposition is distributed because it encompasses all. ("In all cases where the conduct, etc.") The proposition is affirmative. The major premise is thus both categorical and distributed.

In the next excerpt Lord Diplock explains that because the present case is lacking at least one of the characteristics, A, B, C, or D, etc., a reasoned judgment must be made by the House of Lords, a judgment that goes beyond the formal logical structure of any argument. It is a judgment influenced by the judges' concept of public policy: Do we hold the line on liability here, or, do we redefine the characteristics in more general terms, so as to extend the law of liability beyond what has gone before?

To preserve the logical form in the process of analogy, however, it is necessary to exclude those cases not relevant to the case at bar. You will note how the emphasis is now on relevant resemblances:]

But since ex hypothesi the kind of case which we are now considering offers a choice whether or not to extend the kinds of conduct or relationships which give rise to a duty of care, the conduct or relationship which is involved in it will lack at least one of the characteristics A, B, C or D, etc. And the choice is exercised by making a policy decision as to whether or not a duty of care ought to exist if the characteristic which is lacking were absent or redefined in terms broad enough to include the case under consideration. The policy decision will be influenced by the same general conception of what ought to give rise to a duty of care as was used in approaching the analysis. The choice to extend is given effect to by redefining the characteristics in more general terms so as to exclude the necessity to conform to limitations imposed by the former definition which are considered to be inessential. The cases which are landmarks in the common law, such as Lickbarrow v. Mason (1787) 2 Term Rep. 63, Rylands v. Fletcher (1868) L.R. 3 H.L. 330, Indermaur v. Dames (1866) L.R. 1 C.P. 274, Donoghue v. Stevenson [1932] A.C. 562, to mention but a few, are instances of cases where the cumulative experience of judges has led to a restatement in wide general terms of characteristics of conduct and relationships which give rise to legal liability.

Inherent in this methodology, however, is a practical limitation which is imposed by the sheer volume of reported cases. The initial selection of previous cases to be analysed will itself eliminate from the analysis those in which the conduct or relationship involved possessed characteristics which are obviously absent in the case for decision.

The proposition used in the deductive stage is not a true universal. It needs to be qualified so as to read: "In all cases where the conduct and relationship possess each of the characteristics A, B, C and D, etc., *but do not possess any of the characteristics Z, Y or X etc. which were present in the cases eliminated from the analysis,* a duty of care arises."

But this qualification, being irrelevant to the decision of the particular case, is generally left unexpressed.

The result of the survey of previous authorities can be summarised in the words of Dixon J. in Smith v. Leurs, 70 C.L.R. 256, 262: "The general rule is that one man is under no duty of controlling another man to prevent his doing damage to a third. There are, however, special relations which are the source of a duty of this nature."

From the previous decisions of the English courts, in particular those in Ellis v. Home Office [1953] 2 All E.R. 149 and D'Arcy v. Prison Commissioners, "The Times," November 17, 1955, which I accept as correct, it is possible to arrive by induction at an established proposition of law as respects one of those special relations, viz.: "A is responsible for damage caused to the person or property of B by the tortious act of C (a person responsible in law for his own acts) where the relationship between A and C has the characteristics (1) that A has the legal right to detain C in penal custody and to control his acts while in custody; (2) that A is actually exercising his legal right of custody of C at the time of C's tortious act and (3) that A if he had taken reasonable care in the exercise of his right of custody could have prevented C from doing the tortious act which caused damage to the person or property of B; and where also the relationship between A and B has the characteristics (4) that at the time of C's tortious act A has the legal right to control the situation of B or his property as respects physical proximity to C and (5) that A can reasonably foresee that B is likely to sustain damage to his person or property if A does not take reasonable care to prevent C from doing tortious acts of the kind which he did."

Upon the facts which your Lordships are required to assume for the purposes of the present appeal the relationship between the defendant, A, and the Borstal trainee, C, did possess characteristics (1) and (3) but did not possess characteristic (2), while the relationship between the defendant, A, and the plaintiff, B, did possess characteristic (5) but did not possess characteristic (4).

What your Lordships have to decide as respects each of the relationships is whether the missing characteristic is essential to the existence of the duty or whether the facts assumed for the purposes of this appeal disclose some other characteristic which if substituted for that which is missing would produce a new proposition of law which *ought* to be true.

I should therefore hold that any duty of a Borstal officer to use reasonable care to prevent a Borstal trainee from escaping from his custody was owed only to persons whom he could reasonably foresee had property situate in the vicinity of the place of detention of the detainee which the detainee was likely to steal or to appropriate and damage in the course of eluding immediate pursuit and recapture.

If, therefore, it can be established at the trial of this action (1) that the Borstal officers in failing to take precautions to prevent the trainees from escaping were acting in breach of their instructions and not in bona fide exercise of a discretion delegated to them by the Home Office as to the degree of control to be adopted and (2) that it was reasonably foreseeable by the officers that if these particular trainees did escape they would be likely to appropriate a boat moored in the vicinity of Brownsea Island for the purpose of eluding immediate pursuit and to cause damage to it, the Borstal officers would be in breach of a duty of care owed to the plaintiff and the plaintiff would, in my view, have a cause of action against the Home Office as vicariously liable for the "negligence" of the Borstal officers.

MARY ANN GLENDON, THE COMMON LAW TRADITION *

"A living tradition," in Alasdair MacIntyre's useful formulation, "is an historically extended, socially embodied argument, and an argument precisely about the goods which constitute that tradition. Within a tradition the pursuit of goods extends through generations, sometimes through many generations." The expression "common law tradition" refers to the type of law, and the mode of lawmaking, that historically distinguished the English legal system from the Romano–Germanic legal systems of continental Europe. The common law is an evolving body of

* M.A. Glendon, A Nation Under Lawyers
(1994), Reprinted by permission.

principles built by accretion from judicial decisions rendered in the context of countless individual disputes. Because those principles are embedded in concrete cases, they are highly fact-sensitive, and not too general. Until relatively recent times, the common law and the craft techniques associated with it were transmitted from one generation to the next chiefly by practitioners. Continental law, by contrast, always had the smell of the lamp—it was developed by Renaissance scholars of revived Roman law, and scholars again played leading roles when it was recast in comprehensive legislative codifications.

Another contrast with the legal systems of continental Europe is the common law's mode of evolution. Over centuries that saw the rise and fall of feudalism, the expansion of commerce, and the transition to constitutional monarchy and representative government, judges and lawyers adapted English law to each new circumstance, neither erasing prior arrangements completely nor becoming captives of them. Parliament made relatively few efforts to hasten or force the process. Its enactments, for the most part, were like patches here and there against the background of the judge-made law; and judges blended them, so far as possible, into the fabric of the case law. Thus, in 1894, the great English legal historian F.W. Maitland could look back on centuries of legal evolution and say, "When we speak of a body of law, we use a metaphor so apt that it is hardly a metaphor. We picture to ourselves a being that lives and grows, that preserves its identity while every atom of which it is composed is subject to a ceaseless process of change, decay, and renewal."

The key to the common law's ability to change and grow while maintaining its coherence and continuity was a distinctive set of habits and practices which its participants learned through doing and by observing and imitating others. To try to describe those methods is a bit like trying to describe swimming or bicycle riding. But the conventional understanding goes something like this: the common law judge is supposed to be a virtuoso of practical reason, weaving together the threads of fact and law, striving not only for a fair disposition of the dispute at hand but to decide each case with reference to a principle that transcends the facts of that case—all with a view toward maintaining continuity with past decisions, deciding like cases alike, and providing guidance for other parties similarly situated: and all in the spirit of caring for the good of the legal order itself and the polity it serves.

The best times were those marked by what Llewellyn called the "Grand Style." In such periods, he wrote, the outlook and manner of judges and lawyers were characterized by "an as-of-courseness in the constant questing for better and best law to guide the future, but the better and best law is to be built on and out of what the past can offer; the quest consists in a constant re-examination and reworking of a heritage, that the heritage may yield not only solidity but comfort for the new day and for the morrow.... It is a way of ongoing renovation of doctrine, but touch with the past is too close, the mood is too craft-conscious, the need for the clean line is too great, for the renovation to smell of revolution or, indeed, of campaigning reform." Judges in the Grand Style (John Marshall, Cardozo, Learned Hand), Llewellyn said, seek to fit rule and decision "with the feel of the body of our law," to assure "that they go with the grain rather than across or against it, that they fit into the net force-field and relieve instead of tautening the tensions and stresses."

Practicing lawyers, as participants in that tradition, framed their instruments and arguments with such habits and attitudes in view. It was that shared legal culture that stood behind Lord Coke's famous insistence: "Reason is the life of the law; nay, the common law itselfe is nothing else but reason." To Coke, "reason" did not mean deductive logic, or self-interested calculation, or any activity of an individual mind in isolation. It was, rather, an extended collaborative dialogue, a group achievement, "an artificial perfection of reason gotten by long studie, observation and experience ... fined and refined [over the ages] by an infinite number of grave and learned men.'

The most impressive accomplishments of the shared legal culture of English and American lawyers took the form of ingenious approaches to new political, social, and economic problems. Where Americans are concerned, the most important of these collective achievements was the American Founding, which gave this country's public law its own unique stamp and character. The Declaration of Independence, the Constitution, *The Federalist*, and the landmark early decisions of the Supreme Court could only have been produced by statesmen who were steeped in the common law tradition and supremely skilled at innovative extensions of established principles. In the very act of breaking with the mother country, the American colonists claimed their legal inheritance ("the rights of Englishmen"), transformed it, and made it into the basis of a new order that remains one of the wonders of the political world. What Ireland did for the English language, America did for English law. Seventy years after the Revolution, Daniel Webster described the process as "a sort of reverse hereditary transmission": "We have seen, in our generation, copious and salutary streams turning and running backward, replenishing their original fountains, and giving a fresher and a brighter green to the fields of English jurisprudence.'

Americans also enriched the common law tradition at the humbler everyday level where judges and practitioners, dealing with routine problems of social and business life, were adapting English law to the circumstances of the new continent. Office lawyers framed agreements, bylaws, contracts, deeds, leases, wills, and trusts that, at their best, aided citizens to live together with a minimum of friction, to make reliable plans for the future, and to avoid unnecessary disputes. For the occasions when preventive law failed, American judges and litigators fined and refined their procedures for fact finding and adjudication.

The history of the common law is a textbook example of what Alasdair MacIntyre calls a living tradition, one that is "historically extended" and "socially embodied," whose development constantly points beyond itself. To be a traditionalist in such a tradition is not to be frozen in the past, or mired in the status quo, but rather to participate in an intense ongoing conversation about what it is that gives the tradition its point and purpose. That discussion, carried on across generations, enabled the tradition's participants not only to make useful contributions to society through changing times but to recognize and correct for many of their own shortcomings. Unlike the Revolution in France, upheavals and civil strife in common law countries did not entail root-and-branch rejection of the legal past. The American revolutionaries stood on the ancient rights of Englishmen to shake off colonial oppression; feudal relations of protection and loyalty gradually evolved into rights and responsibilities in the modern state; the Civil War amendments brought the Declaration of Independence's promise of equality into the Constitution.

Section 3

STATUTORY CONSTRUCTION

OVERVIEW [1]

As construers of statutes, judges assume responsibilities akin to those in their role as an interpreters of judge-made law. As the Continental experience suggests,

> [C]odes and statutes do not render the judge superfluous, nor his work perfunctory and mechanical. There are gaps to be filled. There are doubts and ambiguities to be cleared. There are hardships and wrongs to be mitigated if not avoided. Interpretation is often spoken of as if it were nothing but the search and the discovery of a meaning which, however, obscure and latent, had none the less a real and ascertainable pre-existence in the legislator's mind. The process is, indeed, that at times, but it is often something more.[2]

To what extent, if any, do judicial processes differ when courts face the interpretation of statutory, as distinguished from judge-made rules?

This section examines the judicial process of statutory construction. A proliferation of federal and state statutes has revolutionized the task of courts. Although state courts have experienced a rise in the significance of statutory construction, in the federal judiciary nearly all of the cases and controversies implicating federal law rest on statutes or the Constitution. Various and conflicting methods of statutory construction now vie for the respect of judges and scholars. This chapter explores these techniques, as well as the strengths and weaknesses of each method of statutory construction.

1. Adapted in part from R. Aldisert, *Philosophy, Jurisprudence and Jurisprudential Temperament of Federal Judges,* 20 U. of Indiana L.Rev. 453, 489–510 (1987).

2. B. Cardozo, The Nature of the Judicial Process 14–15 (1921).

THE TASK OF COURTS

When the work of judges today is compared with the period when Benjamin Cardozo presented his classic lectures in 1921 on The Nature of the Judicial Process, one fundamental change stands out: Statutes have replaced case law as the major form of the American legal precept.

The common law tradition still controls the process of adjudication. It still persists, as a set of deeply-rooted, historically conditioned attitudes about the nature of law and about how law is or should be made, applied, perfected, studied and taught. The common law as a source of legal precepts emanating from judicial decisions, however, has given way to federal and state statutes and codes. By 1947, Felix Frankfurter noted:

> But even as late as 1875 more than 40% of the controversies before the [U.S. Supreme] Court were common law litigation, fifty years later only 5%, while today cases not resting on statutes are reduced almost to zero. It is therefore accurate to say that courts have ceased to be the primary makers of law in the sense in which they "legislated" the common law. It is certainly true of the Supreme Court that almost every case has a statute at its heart or close to it.[3]

Since 1947, this trend has only increased.

At times, the growth in statutory law—individual statutes as well as comprehensive codes—has seemed exponential. In addition to legislative enactments, the courts must interpret volumes of exasperatingly detailed regulations promulgated by the executive branch. Still further, even committees of the judicial branch have drafted and amended procedural rules with increasing frequency. And where the three branches of government have not acted, prestigious private organizations such as the American Bar Association and the American Law Institute have proposed voluminous codifications of substantive and procedural law.[4] Although not possessing the sanctions of positive law, these restatements and standards exert a potent, often persuasive, effect on state and federal judiciaries.

The proliferation of state and federal statutes has increased the burdens on the judiciary. Not all statutes contain the specificity of the

---

3. F. Frankfurter, *Some Reflections on the Readings of Statutes,* 47 Colum.L.Rev. 527 (1947).

4. See, e.g., ABA Standards for Criminal Justice (2d ed. 1986) (includes chapters on: Appellate Review of Sentences; Criminal Appeals; The Defense Function; Discovery & Procedure Before Trial; Electronic Surveillance; Fair Trial & Free Press; Joinder & Severance; Pleas of Guilty; Post-conviction Remedies; Pretrial Release; The Prosecution Function; Providing Defense Services; Sentencing Alternatives & Procedures; Special Functions of the Trial Judge; Trial by Jury; and the Urban Police Function). See also, Restatements of Agency; Conflicts of Law; Contracts; Foreign Relations; Judgments; Property; Restitution; Security; Torts and Trusts. See also Federal Securities Code (1978); Model Land Development Code (1975); Model Code of Pre–Arraignment Procedure (1975); Model Penal Code (1962).

Internal Revenue Code. Much statutory language is obscure, in part traceable to the desire that statutes speak in general terms, but which more often seems to be the result of legislative inability to reach meaningful compromises on detailed subjects. Frequently, for political reasons, the legislature abdicates the responsibility for making law to the courts. "The pattern taking shape appears to be that of a Congress intent upon bringing federal power to bear in an ever-widening range of human affairs, but having no better answer for the monitoring, supervision, and enforcement of that power than the employment of the federal courts to these ends".[5]

The general vagueness of many statutes and the wide scope allowed for their interpretation encourages an arbitrariness in reaching decisions that only an allegiance to justice can allay.

THE PROCESS OF STATUTORY CONSTRUCTION

A statute is a legal precept, the law's statement of a standard of conduct. In Roscoe Pound's formulation, legal precepts compose "the body of authoritative materials, and the authoritative gradation of the materials, wherein judges are to find the grounds of decision, counsellors the basis of assured prediction as to the course of decision, and individuals reasonable guidance toward conducting themselves in accordance with the demands of the social order." [6] Whether legal precepts emerge as by-products of court decisions or constitute deliberate products of the legislature, the courts should accord both types of precepts identical or similar treatment, whenever possible, in the twin processes of reaching and justifying a judicial decision.

Where the starting point of legal reasoning begins with a legal precept contained in a court's decision—generally a definite legal consequence attached to a detailed set of facts—the lawyer or judge charged with interpreting that precept has the advantage of two important components not found in statutes:

- The statement of facts contained in the opinion announcing the legal rule.

- The reasons set forth in the opinion announcing the rule.

Bereft of these backgrounds, the jurisprudence of statutory interpretation has led to less predictability or reckonability in construing statutory legal precepts than those originating in case law. Adding to the problem was the concept, fortunately now rejected, that statutes in derogation of the common law were to be strictly construed.

To solve the problems of no factual predicate for the legal rule, no form of reasons for it and the derogation concept, a series of "Canons of

---

5. See C. McGowan, "Congress and the Courts" 8–9 (1976) (University of Chicago Law School monograph of address given by Judge McGowan at University of Chicago Law School Annual Dinner, Apr. 17, 1975).

6. Pound, *Hierarchy of Sources and Forms in Different Systems of Law,* 7 Tul. L.Rev. 475, 476 (1933).

Construction" were fashioned. These canons provided the accepted conventional vocabulary to support a proposed construction of a statute in court.

————

KARL N. LLEWELLYN, CANONS OF CONSTRUCTION *

Statutory interpretation still speaks a diplomatic tongue. Here is some of the technical framework for maneuver.

THRUST	BUT	PARRY
1. A statute cannot go beyond its text.[9]		1. To effect its purpose a statute may be implemented beyond its text.[10]
. . .		. . .
7. A statute imposing a new penalty or forfeiture, or a new liability or disability, or creating a new right of action will not be construed as having a retroactive effect.[11]		7. Remedial statutes are to be liberally construed and if a retroactive interpretation will promote the ends of justice, they should receive such construction.[12]
8. Where design has been distinctly stated no place is left for construction.[13]		8. Courts have the power to inquire into real—as distinct from ostensible—purpose.[14]
9. Definitions and rules of construction contained in an interpretation clause are part of the law and binding.[15]		9. Definitions and rules of construction in a statute will not be extended beyond their necessary import nor allowed to defeat intention otherwise manifested.[16]
10. A statutory provision requiring liberal construction does not		10. Where a rule of construction is provided within the statute it-

* *Remarks on the Theory of Appellate Decision and the Rules or Canons About How Statutes Are to Be Construed,* 3 Vand.L.Rev. 395, 401–05 (1950). Reprinted by permission.

9. First National Bank of Webster Springs v. De Berriz, 87 W.Va. 477, 105 S.E. 900 (1921); Sutherland, Statutory Construction § 388 (2d ed. 1904); 59 C.J., Statutes § 575 (1932).

10. Dooley v. Penn. R.R., 250 Fed. 142 (D.Minn.1918); 59 C.J., Statutes § 575 (1932).

11. Keeley v. Great Northern Ry., 139 Wis. 448, 121 N.W. 167 (1909); Black, Construction and Interpretation of Laws § 119 (2d ed. 1911).

12. Falls v. Key, 278 S.W. 893 (Tex.Civ. App.1925); Black, Construction and Interpretation of Laws § 120 (2d ed. 1911).

13. Federoff v. Birks Bros., 75 Cal.App. 345, 242 Pac. 885 (1925); Sutherland, Statutory Construction § 358 (2d ed. 1904); 59 C.J., Statutes § 570 (1932).

14. Coulter v. Pool, 187 Cal. 181, 201 Pac. 120 (1921); 59 C.J., Statutes § 570 (1932).

15. Smith v. State, 28 Ind. 321 (1867); Black, Construction and Interpretation of Laws § 89 (2d ed. 1911); 59 C.J., Statutes § 567 (1932).

16. In re Bissell, 245 App.Div. 395, 282 N.Y.S. 983 (4th Dep't 1935); Black, Con-

THRUST	BUT	PARRY

mean disregard of unequivocal requirements of the statute.[17]

11. Titles do not control meaning; preambles do not expand scope; section headings do not change language.[19]

self the rule should be applied[18]

11. The title may be consulted as a guide when there is doubt or obscurity in the body; preambles may be consulted to determine rationale, and thus the true construction of terms; section headings may be looked upon as part of the statute itself.[20]

12. If language is plain and unambiguous it must be given effect.[21]

12. Not when literal interpretation would lead to absurd or mischievous consequences or thwart manifest purpose.[22]

. . .

15. Words are to be taken in their ordinary meaning unless they are technical terms or words of art.[23]

. . .

15. Popular words may bear a technical meaning and technical words may have a popular signification and they should be so construed as to agree with evident intention or to make the statute operative.[24]

16. Every word and clause must be given effect.[25]

16. If inadvertently inserted or if repugnant to the rest of the statute, they may be rejected as surplusage.[26]

struction and Interpretation of Laws § 89 (2d ed. 1911); 59 C.J., Statutes § 566 (1932).

17. Los Angeles County v. Payne, 82 Cal.App. 210, 255 Pac. 281 (1927); Sutherland, Statutory Construction § 360 (2d ed. 1904); 59 C.J., Statutes § 567 (1932).

18. State ex rel. Triay v. Burr, 79 Fla. 290, 84 So. 61 (1920); Sutherland, Statutory Construction § 360 (2d ed. 1904); 59 C.J., Statutes § 567 (1932).

19. Westbrook v. McDonald, 184 Ark. 740, 44 S.W.2d 331 (1931); Huntworth v. Tanner, 87 Wash. 670, 152 Pac. 523 (1915); Black, Construction and Interpretation of Laws §§ 83–85 (2d ed. 1911); Sutherland, Statutory Construction §§ 339–42 (2d ed. 1904); 59 C.J., Statutes § 599 (1932); 25 R.C.L., Statutes §§ 266–67 (1919).

20. Brown v. Robinson, 275 Mass. 55, 175 N.E. 269 (1931); Gulley v. Jackson International Co., 165 Miss. 103, 145 So. 905 (1933); Black, Construction and Interpretation of Laws §§ 83–85 (2d ed. 1911); Sutherland, Statutory Construction §§ 339–42 (2d ed. 1904); 59 C.J., Statutes §§ 598–99 (1932); 25 R.C.L., Statutes §§ 266, 267 (1919).

21. Newhall v. Sanger, 92 U.S. 761, 23 L.Ed. 769 (1875); Black, Construction and Interpretation of Laws § 51 (2d ed. 1911); 59 C.J., Statutes § 569 (1932); 25 R.C.L., Statutes §§ 213, 225 (1919).

22. Clark v. Murray, 141 Kan. 533, 41 P.2d 1042 (1935); Sutherland, Statutory Construction § 363 (2d ed. 1904); 59 C.J., Statutes § 573 (1932); 25 R.C.L., Statutes §§ 214, 257 (1919).

23. Hawley Coal Co. v. Bruce, 252 Ky. 455, 67 S.W.2d 703 (1934); Black, Construction and Interpretation of Laws § 63 (2d ed. 1911); Sutherland, Statutory Construction, §§ 390, 393 (2d ed. 1904); 59 C.J., Statutes, §§ 577, 578 (1932).

24. Robinson v. Varnell, 16 Tex. 382 (1856); Black, Construction and Interpretation of Laws § 63 (2d ed. 1911); Sutherland, Statutory Construction § 395 (2d ed. 1904); 59 C.J., Statutes §§ 577, 578 (1932).

25. In re Terry's Estate, 218 N.Y. 218, 112 N.E. 931 (1916); Black, Construction and Interpretation of Laws § 60 (2d ed. 1911); Sutherland, Statutory Construction § 380 (2d ed. 1904).

26. United States v. York, 131 Fed. 323 (C.C.S.D.N.Y.1904); Black, Construction and Interpretation of Laws § 60 (2d ed.

THRUST　　　　　　　BUT　　　　　　PARRY

. . .　　　　　　　　　　　　　　　　　　　. . .

18. Words are to be interpreted according to the proper grammatical effect of their arrangement within the statute.[27]

18. Rules of grammar will be disregarded where strict adherence would defeat purpose.[28]

19. Exceptions not made cannot be read.[29]

19. The letter is only the "bark." Whatever is within the reason of the law is within the law itself.[30]

20. Expression of one thing excludes another.[31]

20. The language may fairly comprehend many different cases where some only are expressly mentioned by way of example.[32]

. . .　　　　　　　　　　　　　　　　　　　. . .

22. It is a general rule of construction that where general words follow an enumeration they are to be held as applying only to persons and things of the same general kind or class specifically mentioned (*ejusdem generis*).[33]

22. General words must operate on something. Further, *ejusdem generis* is only an aid in getting the meaning and does not warrant confining the operations of a statute within narrower limits than were intended.[34]

Judge Richard Posner goes further: "I think Llewellyn's criticism is correct, but I also think that most of the canons are just plain wrong." [7] As Justice Felix Frankfurter was quick to caution, "even generalized restatements from time to time may not be wholly wasteful. Out of

1911); Sutherland, Statutory Construction § 384 (2d ed. 1904).

27. Harris v. Commonwealth, 142 Va. 620, 128 S.E. 578 (1925); Black, Construction and Interpretation of Laws § 55 (2d ed. 1911); Sutherland, Statutory Construction § 408 (2d ed. 1904).

28. Fisher v. Connard, 100 Pa. 63 (1882); Black, Construction and Interpretation of Laws § 55 (2d ed. 1911); Sutherland, Statutory Construction § 409 (2d ed. 1904).

29. Lima v. Cemetery Ass'n, 42 Ohio St. 128 (1884); 25 R.C.L., Statutes § 230 (1919).

30. Flynn v. Prudential Ins. Co., 207 N.Y. 315, 100 N.E. 794 (1913); 59 C.J., Statutes § 573 (1932).

31. Detroit v. Redford Twp., 253 Mich. 453, 235 N.W. 217 (1931); Black, Construction and Interpretation of Laws § 72 (2d ed. 1911); Sutherland, Statutory Construction §§ 491–94 (2d ed. 1904).

32. Springer v. Philippine Islands, 277 U.S. 189, 48 S.Ct. 480, 72 L.Ed. 845 (1928); Black, Construction and Interpretation of Laws § 72 (2d ed. 1911); Sutherland, Statutory Construction § 495 (2d ed. 1904).

33. Hull Hospital v. Wheeler, 216 Iowa 1394, 250 N.W. 637 (1933); Black, Construction and Interpretation of Laws § 71 (2d ed. 1911); Sutherland, Statutory Construction §§ 422–34 (2d ed. 1904); 59 C.J., Statutes § 581 (1932); 25 R.C.L., Statutes § 240 (1919).

34. Texas v. United States, 292 U.S. 522, 54 S.Ct. 819, 78 L.Ed. 1402 (1934); Grosjean v. American Paint Works, 160 So. 449 (La.App.1935); Black, Construction and Interpretation of Laws § 71 (2d ed. 1911); Sutherland, Statutory Construction, §§ 437–41 (2d ed. 1904); 59 C.J., Statutes § 581 (1932); 25 R.C.L., Statutes § 240 (1919).

7. *Statutory Interpretation—in the Classroom and in the Courtroom,* 50 U. of Chicago L.Rev. 800, 806 (1983).

them may come a sharper rephrasing of the conscious factors of interpretation; new instances may make them more vivid but also disclose more clearly their limitations." [8] Canons are no longer regarded as serviceable even though some states have codified them in statutory form, with case law eviscerating their literal words or the stated canons falling victim to desuetude.

Developing at the same time as the Canons of Construction was a series of four "Rules" of statutory construction emanating from England—the Mischief Rule of 1584, the "Golden" Rule of the late nineteenth century, and the Literal Rule of the early twentieth century.

REPLACING CANONS OF CONSTRUCTION

HART AND SACKS, NOTE ON SOME CONTRASTING APPROACHES *

A. *The Mischief Rule*

HEYDON'S CASE

Exchequer, 1584. 30 Co. 7a, 76 Eng.Rep. 637.

And it was resolved by them that for the sure and true interpretation of all statutes in general (be they penal or beneficial, restrictive or enlarging of the common law,) four things are to be discerned and considered:

1st.	What was the common law before the making of the Act.
2nd.	What was the mischief and defect for which the common law did not provide.
3rd.	What remedy the Parliament hath resolved and appointed to cure the disease of the commonwealth.
And 4th.	The true reason of the remedy; and then the office of all the Judges is always to make sure construction as shall suppress the mischief, and advance the remedy, and to suppress subtle inventions and evasions for continuance of the mischief, and *pro privato commodo,* and to add force and life to the cure and remedy, according to the true intent of the makers of the Act, *pro bono publico.*

B. *The "Golden" Rule*

"But it is to be borne in mind that the office of the judges is not to legislate, but to declare the expressed intention of the Legislature, even if that intention appears to the court injudicious; and I believe that it is

---

8. F. Frankfurter, *Some Reflections on the Readings of Statutes,* 47 Colum.L.Rev. 527, 545 (1947)

* H. Hart and A. Sacks, The Legal Process: Basic Problems in the Making and Application of Law 1144–46 (Cambridge Tent. ed. 1958). Reprinted by permission of Dean Albert M. Sacks.

not disputed that what Lord Wensleydale used to say is right, namely that we are to take the whole statute together, and construe it all together, giving the words their ordinary signification, unless when so applied they produce an inconsistency, or an absurdity or inconvenience so great as to convince the court that the intention could not have been to use them in their ordinary signification, and to justify the court in putting on them some other signification, which, though less proper, is one which the court thinks the words will bear." Lord Blackburn in River Wear Commissioners v. Adamson, 2 App.Cas. 742, 746 (House of Lords, 1877).

C. *The Literal Rule*

"If the language of a statute be plain, admitting of only one meaning, the Legislature must be taken to have meant and intended what it has plainly expressed, and whatever it has in clear terms enacted must be enforced though it should lead to absurd or mischievous results. If the language of this subsection be not controlled by some of the other provisions of the statute, it must, since its language is plain and unambiguous, be enforced, and your lordships' House sitting judicially is not concerned with the question whether the policy it embodies is wise or unwise, or whether it leads to consequences just or unjust, beneficial or mischievous." Lord Atkinson, in Vacher & Sons, Ltd. v. London Society of Compositers, [1913] A.C. 107, 121–22 (House of Lords).

"I should like to have a good definition of what is such an absurdity that you are to disregard the plain words of an Act of Parliament. It is to be remembered that what seems absurd to one man does not seem absurd to another ... I think it is infinitely better, although an absurdity or an injustice or other objectionable result may be evolved as the consequence of your construction, to adhere to the words of an Act of Parliament and leave the legislature to set it right than to, alter those words according to one's notion of an absurdity." Lord Bramwell, in Hill v. East and West India Dock Co., 9 A.C. 448, 464–65 (House of Lords, 1884).

THREE PROBLEMS OF STATUTORY INTERPRETATION

Evolving from the English Rules of statutory construction are numerous methods and techniques used by American courts to interpret statutes. The task of interpretation begins, however, only after recognizing three separate problems present in the analytical process.

    A. The problem of language analysis in the strict sense—the presence of an unclear norm;

    B. The problem of lacunae—the nonexistent norm; and

    C. The problem of evolution—the norm whose meaning changes while its text remains constant, thus bringing into tension the original intent and the ongoing history theories of interpretation.

A. THE UNCLEAR NORM

When it comes to statutory interpretation, no hard and fast rules apply, for the cumulative experience of the judiciary furnishes no absolute rules for guidance. Some judges seem always to favor certain techniques; others pick and choose the methods that will achieve a desired result.

Most methods of statutory construction come into play when the statutory norm is unclear. This approach assumes that the legislature intended to address the relevant factual scenario at issue, but did so in unclear language. It is then the necessary task of the court to construe the statute and clarify the norm. Undertaking this task, judges have played with the Mischief Rule of *Heydon's Case*,[9] the Golden Rule,[10] and the Literal Rule.[11] American jurisprudence also begot the "Plain Meaning Rule":

> It is elementary that the meaning of a statute must, in the first instance, be sought in the language in which the act is framed, and if that is plain, and if the law is within the constitutional authority of the law-making body which passed it, the sole function of the courts is to enforce it according to its terms. Where the language is plain and admits of no more than one meaning the duty of interpretation does not arise and the rules which are to aid doubtful meanings need no discussion.[12]

OLIVER WENDELL HOLMES, THE THEORY OF LEGAL INTERPRETATION *

It is true that in theory any document purporting to be serious and to have some legal effect has one meaning and no other, because the known object is to achieve some definite result. It is not true that in practice (and I know no reason why theory should disagree with the facts) a given word or even a given collocation of words has one meaning and no other. A word generally has several meanings, even in the dictionary. You have to consider the sentence in which it stands to decide which of those meanings it bears in the particular case, and very likely will see that it there has a shade of significance more refined than any given in the word-book. But in this first step, at least, you are not troubling yourself about the idiosyncrasies of the writer, you are considering simply the general usages of speech. So when you let whatever galvanic current may come from the rest of the instrument run through the particular sentence, you still are doing the same thing.

---

9. 30 Co. 7a, 76 Eng.Rep. 637 (Ex.1584).

10. See, e.g., River Wear Comm'rs v. Adamson, (1876–77) 2 A.C. 743, 764–65.

11. See, e.g., Vacher & Sons, Ltd. v. London Soc'y of Compositors, (1913) A.C. 107, 121–22 (Lord Atkinson).

12. Caminetti v. United States, 242 U.S. 470, 485 (1917) (Day, J.) (citations omitted); see Hamilton v. Rathbone, 175 U.S. 414, 419–21 (1899) (Brown, J.).

* 12 Harv.L.Rev. 417, 417–19 (1899). Reprinted by permission.

How is it when you admit evidence of circumstances and read the document in the light of them? Is this trying to discover the particular intent of the individual, to get into his mind and to bend what he said to what he wanted? No one would contend that such a process should be carried very far, but, as it seems to me, we do not take a step in that direction. It is not a question of tact in drawing a line. We are after a different thing. What happens is this. Even the whole document is found to have a certain play in the joints when its words are translated into things by parol evidence, as they have to be. It does not disclose one meaning conclusively according to the laws of language. Thereupon we ask, not what this man meant, but what those words would mean in the mouth of a normal speaker of English, using them in the circumstances in which they were used, and it is to the end of answering this last question that we let in evidence as to what the circumstances were. But the normal speaker of English is merely a special variety, a literary form, so to speak, of our old friend the prudent man. He is external to the particular writer, and a reference to him as the criterion is simply another instance of the externality of the law.

. . .

Different rules conceivably might be laid down for the construction of different kinds of writing. In the case of a statute, to turn from contracts to the opposite extreme, it would be possible to say that as we are dealing with the commands of the sovereign the only thing to do is to find out what the sovereign wants. If supreme power resided in the person of a despot who would cut off your hand or your head if you went wrong, probably one would take every available means to find out what was wanted. Yet in fact we do not deal differently with a statute from our way of dealing with a contract. We do not inquire what the legislature meant; we ask only what the statute means.

NOTE

Holmes also suggested that "[i]f language perfectly performed its function, as Bentham wanted to make it, it would point out the person or thing named in every case." In light of the modern American idiom, are we close to Bentham's ideal of the function of language? Is the English language becoming less precise? The "American" language? If meanings are being eroded, who are the chief eroders?

LEGISLATIVE INTENT

Other impressive authorities warned judges not to depend too much on the actual language of a statute. Cardozo wrote that "[w]hen things are called by the same name it is easy for the mind to slide into an assumption that the verbal identity is accompanied in all its sequences by identity of meaning." [13] Holmes told us: "A word is not a crystal, transparent and unchanged, it is the skin of a living thought and may

---

13. Lowden v. Northwestern Nat'l Bank & Trust Co., 298 U.S. 160, 165 (1936).

vary greatly in color and content according to the circumstances and the time in which it is used." [14]   Learned Hand said that "it is one of the surest indexes of a mature and developed jurisprudence not to make a fortress out of the dictionary; but to remember that statutes always have some purpose or object to accomplish, whose sympathetic and imaginative discovery is the surest guide to their meaning." [15]

These complaints would not be voiced today, for although contemporary courts are fond of stating that "[t]he starting point in every case involving the construction of a statute is the language itself," [16] most current approaches abjure a strictly semantic approach.

Influenced in large part by U.S. Supreme Court justices, federal judges often resort to the quest for legislative intent.[17]   Lord Denning described a transition from nineteenth century "strict constructionists" to twentieth century "intention" seekers: "The strict constructionists go by the letter of the document.   The 'intention seekers' go by the purpose or intent of the makers of it." [18]   Indeed, proper statutory construction, in the dominant modern view, requires recognition and implementation of the underlying legislative intention or purpose, and the judge, the theory holds, must accommodate the societal claims and demands reflected in that inquiry.[19]   To accomplish this task, as Justice Roger J. Traynor put it, we need "literate, not literal" judges,[20] lest a court make a construction within the statute's letter, but beyond its intent.

The difficulty lies in ascertaining what the legislature *intended* as distinguished from what it *said*.   The task is somewhat akin to pinpointing the intent of a testator or the intent of disputing parties to a contract—except that when we seek to ascertain the intent of over 500 members of Congress, it is, as one judge once said in another context, "like nailing a jellyfish to the wall." [21]   The endeavor ordinarily involves resort to legislative history.   The approach often is a combination of legal philosophy, jurisprudence and jurisprudential temperament.   In its

14.   Towne v. Eisner, 245 U.S. 418, 425 (1918).

15.   Cabell v. Markham, 148 F.2d 737, 739 (2d Cir.1945), aff'd, 326 U.S. 404 (1945).

16.   International Bhd. of Teamsters v. Daniel, 439 U.S. 551, 558 (1979) (quoting Blue Chip Stamps v. Manor Drug Stores, 421 U.S. 723, 756 (1975) (Powell, J., concurring)).

17.   See, e.g., Brown v. General Servs. Admin., 425 U.S. 820, 825 (1976) ("Congress simply failed explicitly to describe § 717's [of the Civil Rights Act of 1964] position in the constellation of anti-discrimination law.   We must, therefore, infer congressional intent in less obvious ways."); United States v. Bornstein, 423 U.S. 303, 309–10 (1976) ("There is no indication that Congress gave any thought to the question.... But the absence of specific legisla-

tive history in no way modifies the conventional judicial duty to give faithful meaning to the language Congress adopted in the light of the evident legislative purpose in enacting the law in question.").

18.   A. Denning, The Discipline of the Law 4 (1979).

19.   See Train v. Colorado Pub. Interest Research Group, Inc., 426 U.S. 1, 9–10 (1976); see also Levi, *An Introduction to Legal Reasoning*, 15 U.Chi.L.Rev. 501, 520–23 (1948); Murphy, *Old Maxims Never Die: The "Plain–Meaning Rule" and Statutory Interpretation in the "Modern" Federal Courts,* 75 Colum.L.Rev. 1299, 1316–17 (1975).

20.   Traynor, Reasoning in a Circle of Law, 56 Va.L.Rev. 739, 749 (1970).

21.   Rosanova v. Playboy Enterprises, 411 F.Supp. 440, 444 (S.D.Ga.1976).

most exaggerated form, the judge's temperament supplies the willpower and his or her subjective philosophy, the answer—with some fragment of legislative history exalted to justify a conclusion that the legislative intent was at odds with precise statutory language.

This approach demonstrates a fundamental difference in the process of statutory interpretation.

———

UNITED STEELWORKERS v. WEBER: THE PARADIGM CASE

The difference between the majority and dissenting opinions in the affirmative action case of United Steelworkers of America v. Weber [22] illustrates the clash between the majority's reliance on legislative intent and the dissent's reliance on the statutory text. The relevant statute, 42 U.S.C.A. § 2000–2(d), provided:

> It shall be an unlawful employment practice for any employer, labor organization, or joint labor-management committee controlling apprenticeship or other training or retraining, including on-the-job training programs to discriminate against any individual because of his race, color, religion, sex, or national origin in admission to, or employment in, any program established to provide apprenticeship or other training.

The majority reasoned:

> Respondent argues that Congress intended in Title VII to prohibit all race-conscious affirmative action plans. Respondent's argument rests upon a literal interpretation ... of the Act.
>
> Respondent's argument is not without force ... [B]ut respondent's reliance upon a literal construction ... is misplaced. It is a "familiar rule, that a thing may be within the letter of the statute and yet not within the statute, because not within its spirit, nor within the intention of its makers." ... The prohibition against racial discrimination in ... Title VII must therefore be read against the background of the legislative history of Title VII and the historical context from which the Act arose. [23]

Chief Justice Burger took a diametrically opposed view:

> When Congress enacted Title VII after long study and searching debate, it produced a statute of extraordinary clarity, which speaks directly to the issue we consider in this case....
>
> Often we have difficulty interpreting statutes either because of imprecise drafting or because legislative compromises

---

22. 443 U.S. 193 (1979).   **23.** 443 U.S. at 201.

have produced genuine ambiguities. But here there is no lack of clarity, no ambiguity. . . .

Oddly, the Court seizes upon the very clarity of the statute almost as a justification for evading the unavoidable impact of its language.[24]

CURRENT APPROACHES TO INTERPRETATION

The current approach to statutory application demonstrates a fundamental difference in the process employed today from the process of the 1920's. Today, many judges believe the language of the statute is not as important as what the legislature intended when enacting the statute. They seek ambiguities in the language in order to achieve a result deemed desirable, committed to the principle that the law "ought to be" somewhat different than that set forth in the plain statutory language.

One problem lies in the language of the statutes enacted by the legislative body. With the demise of the patronage system and the resulting lack of discipline in national political parties, and its replacement by high-pressure influence of special interest groups and political action committees, statutes frequently are enacted containing deliberate ambiguities. The eye of the Senator or Congressperson often is not focused on the national interest or a particular public policy so much as it is on the very pragmatic consideration: How will the statutory language affect my constituency? Will I be hurt or helped by it? Can I get away with an adequate explanation back home?

As a result, statutory language often is deliberately enigmatic and unintelligible. Hammered out in committee compromise, the language is designed to mean all things to all people, with Congress recognizing that in the end federal judges, with lifetime appointments, must interpret the statute. When the interpretation emerges from the courts, the legislator is then in the position to tell complaining constituents that the problem with the bill was not with the action of the legislature, but the action of judges in interpreting it. It's a "fault is in the stars" philosophy.[25]

---

24. Id. at 216–17 (Burger, C.J., dissenting).

25. Judge Richard Neely of the West Virginia Supreme Court, a former state legislator, is more blunt:

[A] legislature is designed to do nothing, with emphasis appropriately placed on the word "designed." The value of an institution whose primary attribute is inertia to politicians who wish to keep their jobs is that a majority of bills will die from inactivity; that then permits legislators to be "in favor" of a great deal of legislation without ever being required to vote on it. When constituents seek to hold a legislator responsible for the failure of a particular bill, he can say, plausibly, that it was assigned to a committee on which he did not serve and that he was unable to shake the bill out of that committee. If he has foreseen positive constituent interest, he can produce letters from the committee chairman in answer to his excited plea to report the legislation to the floor; correspondence of this sort is the stock in trade of legislators. Notwithstanding the earnest correspondence, it is quite possible that when the legislator and committee chairman

Whatever the reason, judicial statutory interpretation is much different today than it was fifty years ago. The words of a statute will be respected, it is true, but legislative intentions will be investigated and given equal, if not superior, respect. Less attention is now paid to the familiar teachings of a past era:

> "If the language be clear it is conclusive. There can be no construction where there is nothing to construe." [26]

> "If the words are plain, they give meaning to the act, and it is neither the duty nor the privilege of the courts to enter speculative fields in search of a different meaning." [27]

> "[T]he language being plain, and not leading to absurd or wholly impracticable consequences, it is the sole evidence of the ultimate legislative intent." [28]

A more apt mandate of statutory construction might be the cynical expression, "that only when legislative history is doubtful do you go to the statute." [29]

Perhaps, it is well that judges no longer follow the rigid semantic approach, because in the common law tradition a rule from case law is never considered *in vacuo*. The reason for the rule is always considered. No one said it better than Karl Llewellyn: "The rule follows where its reason leads; where the reason stops, there stops the rule." [30]

When all is said, however, it is difficult to lay down comprehensive guidelines of modern statutory construction. As the Supreme Court's 1982 statement advised:

> Generalities about statutory construction help us little. They are not rules of law but merely axioms of experience. They do not solve the special difficulties in construing a particular statute. The variables render every problem of statutory construction unique.[31]

Recourse to legislative history, a familiar source of inquiry into the intent of Congress, will continue to be an important aspect of statutory interpretation because (especially in federal cases) there is an abundance of materials in Congressional records. Judges of differing philosophies may find authority to justify conclusions they desire to reach; a statement of a representative or senator, or some excerpt from a committee report written by the congressional staff will serve as the necessary talisman. Such recourse may be truly validated only when it is recog-

were have a drink before dinner, the legislator indicated his personal desire to kill the bill in spite of the facade of excited correspondence.

R. Neely, How Courts Govern America 55 (1981).

26. United States v. Hartwell, 73 U.S. (6 Wall.) 385, 396 (1868).

27. Caminetti v. United States, 242 U.S. 470, 490 (1917).

28. Id.

29. Frankfurter, *Some Reflections on the Reading of Statutes,* 47 Colum.L.Rev. 527, 543 (1947).

30. K. Llewellyn, The Bramble Bush 157–58 (1960).

31. Weinberger v. Rossi, 456 U.S. 25, 28 (1982) (quoting United States v. Universal C.I.T. Credit Corp., 344 U.S. 218, 221 (1952) (citations omitted)).

nized that the history is used as a factor in inductive reasoning to reach a conclusion. Congressman A said so and Congresswoman B said so, and from these facts judges can conclude that the majority of the Senate and the House felt similarly. Obviously, such a generalization is valid only to the extent that the statements appeared in sufficient number or were cloaked with sufficient authority to permit the generalization. Otherwise, we are confronted with the material fallacy known as the Converse Fallacy of Accident. Also called the fallacy of selected instances or hasty generalization, this fallacy attempts to establish a generalization by the simple enumeration of instances without obtaining a representative number. A conclusion is derived before all the particular instances have been taken into consideration.

Irrespective of the use of legislative history to ascertain congressional intent, or of lengthy semantic excursions into the dictionary to reveal the statute's literal or plain meaning, the importance of statutory construction in today's judicial process cannot be overemphasized. The process is more sophisticated and complex, and requires the most careful attention of the legislature as well as the bench and bar.

Nevertheless, the purpose, the subject matter, the context, the legislative history and the executive interpretation of the statute appear to be important aids in considering statutory precepts today.[32] We refer again to the cynical expression "that only when legislative history is doubtful do you go to the statute." [33] Perhaps the reason for this aphorism is that recourse to legislative history has become a favorite pastime of federal courts. Federal judges may use this approach because they find it to be a useful technique, and because the Congressional Record and committee reports are usually readily available. The practice is, however, open to criticism. Professor Robert A. Leflar observed:

> I think that it was Chief Justice Hingham ... who said that the devil himself "knoweth not the mind of man." It is difficult to discover intent; and when you cannot discover with any authority the state of mind of one man, the process of discovering the states of mind, the intents of 535 men, who make up the Federal Congress, becomes an extremely difficult matter.[34]

Contemporary recourse to legislative history to divine the intent of the legislature is a relatively new development. Not practiced even a half century ago, this technique is a unique American methodology not followed in England.[35] As Lord Denning told us:

> But oddly enough the Judges cannot look at what the responsible Minister said to Parliament—at the object of the

---

32. See United States v. Cooper Corp., 312 U.S. 600, 605 (1941), cited in Pfizer, Inc. v. Government of India, 434 U.S. 308, 313 (1978).

33. F. Frankfurter, *Some Reflections on the Reading of Statutes*, 47 Colum.L.Rev. 527, 543 (1947).

34. Remarks by Robert A. Leflar to Federal Appellate Judges' Conference, Federal Judicial Center, Washington D.C. (May 13, 1975).

35. See, e.g., Assam Railways & Trading Co., Ltd. v. Comm'rs of Inland Revenue, [1935] A.C. 445; see also C. Allen, Law in the Making 479–504 (5th ed. 1951).

Statute as he explained it to the House—or to the meaning of the words as he understood them. Hansard [British version of the Congressional Record] is for the Judges as closed book. But not for you [lawyers]. You can read what was said in the House and adopt it as part of your argument—so long as you do not acknowledge the source. The writers of law books can go further. They can give thee very words from Hansard with chapter and verse. You can read the whole to the Judges.[36]

As early as 1769, the English said, "The sense and meaning of an Act of Parliament must be collected from what it says when passed into a law; and not from the history of changes it underwent in the house where it took its rise. That history is not known to the other house or to the sovereign."[37] Justice Frankfurter suggested that the recourse to reliance on legislative history was gradual.[38] Holmes gingerly approached this judicial technique, observing that "it is a delicate business to base speculations about the purposes or construction of a statute upon the vicissitudes of its passage,"[39] and he once referred to earlier bills relating to a statute under review with the reservation, "If it be legitimate to look at them."[40] A serious question exists as to whether the concerns expressed in 1953 by Mr. Justice Jackson have ever been answered:

> I should concur in this result more readily if the Court could reach it by analysis of the statute instead of by psychoanalysis of Congress. When we decide from legislative history, including statement of witnesses at hearings, what Congress probably had in mind, we must put ourselves in the place of a majority of Congressmen and act according to the impression we think this history should have made on them. Never having been a Congressman, I am handicapped in that weird endeavor. That process seems to me not interpretation of a statute but creation of a statute.[41]

B. THE LACUNAE OR NONEXISTENT NORM

A separate interpretive problem occurs when a legal issue arises in an area covered by the statute but in a context that clearly did not occur to the legislature at the time of the statute's enactment. This problem is not the problem of the unclear norm, but the problem of the lacunae, or a nonexistent norm.

36. A. Denning, The Discipline of the Law 10 (1979).

37. Frankfurter, *Some Reflections on the Reading of Statutes,* 47 Colum.L.Rev. 527, 541 (1947).

38. Id. at 542–43.

39. Pine Hill Coal Co. v. United States, 259 U.S. 191, 196 (1922).

40. Davis v. Pringle, 268 U.S. 315, 378 (1925).

41. United States v. Public Utilities Comm'n, 345 U.S. 295, 319 (1953) (Jackson, J., concurring); see also his opinion in Schwegmann Bros. v. Calvert Distillers Corp., 341 U.S. 384, 395–97 (1951).

In Plowden's note in Eyston v. Studd [42] in 1574, he made an observation that is in striking anticipation of modern principles of discerning the meaning or applicability of a statute:

> And in order to form a right judgment when the letter of a statute is restrained, and when enlarged, by equity, it is a good way, when you peruse a statute, to suppose that the lawmaker is present, and that you have asked him the question you want to know touching the equity; then you must give yourself an answer as you imagine he would have done, if he had been present ... And if the lawmaker would have followed the equity, notwithstanding the words of the law ... you may safely do the like. [43]

Referring to Plowden, Lord Denning wrote:

> Put into the homely metaphor it is this: A judge should ask himself the question: If the makers of the Act had themselves come across this muck in the texture of it, how would they have straightened it out? He must then do as they would have done. A judge must not alter the material of which it is woven but he can and should iron out the creases. [44]

Experience in civil law jurisdictions assumes situations will occur that were not contemplated by the legislative draftsmen, and that they made adequate provisions for these occurrences. Perhaps the most well known model is the Swiss Civil Code of 1907:

> Where no provision [in the Code] is applicable, the judge shall decide according to the existing Customary Law and, in default thereof, according to the rules which he would lay down if he had himself to act as legislator. Herein, he must be guided by approved legal doctrine and case law. [45]

Still another dimension of this problem is where the court finds the lacunae when there is no evidence that Congress left the matter open. An example of this may be found in the relatively new practice of inventing implied causes of action in statutes that make no mention of a right of recovery. This federal court innovation marks a drastic departure from the presumption that, on the topic a statute is dealing with, Congress said all that it wanted to say. The discovery, if not the fabrication, of implied federal causes of action represents activity by judges described by Lord Devlin as "moths outside a lighted window, ... irresistibly attracted by what they see within as the vast unused potentiality of judicial lawmaking." [46]

42. 2 Plowd, 463 (1574).

43. Quoted in W. Friedmann, Legal Theory 453 (5th ed. 1967).

44. A. Denning, supra note 18 at 12 (citing Seaford Court Estates Ltd. v. Asher, [1949] 2 K.B. 481).

45. Schweizerisches Zivilgesetzbuch (Code Civil Suisse) (Codice Civile Suizzero) § 1 (1907) (Williams trans. 1925). Similar provisions are found in the Austrian General Civil Code of 1811 (Algemeines Buergerliches Gesetzbuch § 7 (1811)); The Spanish Civil Code of 1899 (Codigo Civil Espanol § 6 (1899)); The Italian Civil Code (Codice Civile ch. 2, § 12 (1942)); and the Iraqi Civil Code of 1951 art. I, §§ 1–3 (1951).

46. P. Devlin, The Judge 8 (1974).

In Cort v. Ash,[47] the Supreme Court interpreted a federal criminal statute prohibiting corporations from making certain types of contributions in connection with a presidential election. The Court found that the language itself did not authorize, and Congress did not intend to so authorize, a shareholder to bring a private cause of action against a transgressing corporation. The Court developed factors to use in determining whether a statute authorizes such a cause of action.[48]

Therein lies the problem. The factors identified by the Court leave more than enough maneuvering room for a judge to decide the issue either way, and the courts have done just that. There has not been much predictability to the cases. Some decisions have found no implied cause of action.[49] Others have swung in the other direction.[50] Relying on legislative history as an indication of whether a private cause of action is permitted once again involves all the dangers of drawing conclusions from bits and pieces of legislative history. In doing so, courts often seem to ignore the reality that Congress knows when it wants to provide a cause of action and knows how to say it.[51]

Whether the problem arises in the unclear or nonexistent norm, at bottom always is the task of divining the intent of the legislature. "When a judge tries to find out what the government would have intended which it did not say, he puts into its mouth things which he thinks it ought to have said, and that is very close to substituting what he himself thinks right," [52] Learned Hand observed: "Nobody does this exactly right; great judges do it better than the rest of us. It is necessary that someone shall do it, if we are to realize the hope that we can collectively rule ourselves." [53]

---

47. 422 U.S. 66 (1975).

48. First, is the plaintiff "one of the class for whose especial benefit the statute was enacted," that is, does the statute create a federal right in favor of the plaintiff? Second, is there any indication of legislative intent, explicit or implicit, either to create such a remedy or to deny one? Third, is it consistent with the underlying purposes of the legislative scheme to imply such a remedy for the plaintiff? And finally, is the cause of action one traditionally relegated to state law, in an area basically the concern of the States, so that it would be inappropriate to infer a cause of action based solely on federal law?

49. See, e.g., Universities Research Ass'n v. Coutu, 450 U.S. 754 (1981); Touche Ross & Co. v. Redington, 442 U.S. 560 (1979); Santa Fe Indus. v. Green, 430 U.S. 462 (1977); Piper v. Chris–Craft Indus., 430 U.S. 1 (1977).

50. See e.g., Merrill Lynch, Pierce, Fenner & Smith, Inc. v. Curran, 456 U.S. 353 (1982); Cannon v. University of Chicago, 441 U.S. 677 (1979).

51. See, e.g., Right to Financial Privacy Act of 1978, 12 U.S.C.A. § 3417 (1982); Consumer Credit Protection Act of 1968, 15 U.S.C.A. § 1693m (1982); Surface Mining Control Reclamation Act of 1977, 30 U.S.C.A. § 1270 (1982); National Gas Pipeline Safety Act of 1968, 49 U.S.C.A. § 1686 (1982).

52. L. Hand, The Spirit of Liberty 108 (2d ed. 1954).

53. Id. at 109–10.

JOHN CHIPMAN GRAY, THE NATURE AND SOURCES OF THE LAW *

A fundamental misconception prevails, and pervades all the books as to the dealing of the courts with statutes. Interpretation is generally spoken of as if its chief function was to discover what the meaning of the Legislature really was. But when a Legislature has had a real intention, one way or another, on a point, it is not once in a hundred times that any doubt arises as to what its intention was. If that were all that a judge had to do with a statute, interpretation of statutes, instead of being one of the most difficult of a judge's duties, would be extremely easy. The fact is that the difficulties of so-called interpretation arise when the Legislature has had no meaning at all; when the question which is raised on the statute never occurred to it; when what the judges have to do is, not to determine what the Legislature did mean on a point which was present to its mind, but to guess what it would have intended on a point not present to its mind, if the point had been present. If there are any lawyers among those who honor me with their attention, let them consider any dozen cases of the interpretation of statutes, as they have occurred consecutively in their reading or practice, and they will, I venture to say, find that in almost all of them it is probable, and that in most of them it is perfectly evident, that the makers of the statutes had no real intention, one way or another, on the point in question; that if they had, they would have made their meaning clear; and that when the judges are professing to declare what the Legislature meant, they are in truth, themselves legislating to fill up *casus omissi.*[1]

THOMPSON v. THOMPSON

Supreme Court of the United States, 1988.
484 U.S. 174, 108 S.Ct. 513, 98 L.Ed.2d 512.

JUSTICE MARSHALL delivered the opinion of the Court.

We granted certiorari in this case to determine whether the Parental Kidnapping Prevention Act of 1980, 28 U.S.C. § 1738A, furnishes an implied cause of action in federal court to determine which of two conflicting state custody decisions is valid.

* 172–173 (2d ed. 1921) Reprinted by permission of Roland Gray, Jr., owner by inheritance, from J.C. Gray, The Nature and Sources of the Law (2d revised edition by R. Gray 1921), and by permission of Peter Smith Publishing, Inc.

1. "The intent of the Legislature is sometimes little more than a useful legal fiction, save as it describes in a general way certain outstanding purposes which no one disputes, but which are frequently of little aid in dealing with the precise points presented in litigation. Moreover, legislative ambiguity may at times not be wholly unintentional. It is not to be forgotten that important legislation sometimes shows the effect of compromises which have been induced by exigencies in its progress, and phrases with a convenient vagueness are referred to the courts for appropriate definition, each group interested in the measure claiming that the language adopted embodies its views." Mr. Justice Hughes, in 1 Mass.Law Quart. (No. 2), pp. 13, 15. On the point that the legislature sometimes deliberately leaves its intention doubtful, see Sir Courtenay Ilbert, Mechanics of Law Making, pp. 19–23.

I

The Parental Kidnapping Prevention Act (PKPA or Act) imposes a duty on the States to enforce a child custody determination entered by a court of a sister State if the determination is consistent with the provisions of the Act. In order for a state court's custody decree to be consistent with the provisions of the Act, the State must have jurisdiction under its own local law and one of five conditions set out in § 1738A(c)(2) must be met. Briefly put, these conditions authorize the state court to enter a custody decree if the child's home is or recently has been in the State, if the child has no home State and it would be in the child's best interest for the State to assume jurisdiction, or if the child is present in the State and has been abandoned or abused. Once a State exercises jurisdiction consistently with the provisions of the Act, no other State may exercise concurrent jurisdiction over the custody dispute, § 1738A(g), even if it would have been empowered to take jurisdiction in the first instance, and all States must accord full faith and credit to the first State's ensuing custody decree.

As the legislative scheme suggests, and as Congress explicitly specified, one of the chief purposes of the PKPA is to "avoid jurisdictional competition and conflict between State courts." Pub.L. 96–611, 94 Stat. 3569, § 7(c)(5), note following 28 U.S.C. § 1738A. This case arises out of a jurisdictional stalemate that came to pass notwithstanding the strictures of the Act. In July 1978, respondent Susan Clay (then Susan Thompson) filed a petition in Los Angeles Superior Court asking the court to dissolve her marriage to petitioner David Thompson and seeking custody of the couple's infant son, Matthew. The court initially awarded the parents joint custody of Matthew, but that arrangement became infeasible when respondent decided to move from California to Louisiana to take a job. The court then entered an order providing that respondent would have sole custody of Matthew once she left for Louisiana. This state of affairs was to remain in effect until the court investigator submitted a report on custody, after which the court intended to make a more studied custody determination. See App. 6.

Respondent and Matthew moved to Louisiana in December 1980. Three months later, respondent filed a petition in Louisiana state court for enforcement of the California custody decree, judgment of custody, and modification of petitioner's visitation privileges. By order dated April 7, 1981, the Louisiana court granted the petition and awarded sole custody of Matthew to respondent. Two months later, however, the California court, having received and reviewed its investigator's report, entered an order awarding sole custody of Matthew to petitioner. Thus arose the current impasse.

In August 1983, petitioner brought this action in the District Court for the Central District of California. Petitioner requested an order declaring the Louisiana decree invalid and the California decree valid, and enjoining the enforcement of the Louisiana decree. Petitioner did not attempt to enforce the California decree in a Louisiana state court before he filed suit in federal court. The District Court granted respondent's motion to dismiss the complaint for lack of subject-matter and personal jurisdiction. The Court of Appeals for the Ninth Circuit affirmed. Although it disagreed with the District Court's jurisdictional analyses, the Court of Appeals affirmed the dismissal of the complaint on the ground that petitioner had failed to state a claim upon which relief could be granted. 798 F.2d 1547 (CA9 1986). Canvassing the background, language, and legislative history of the PKPA, the Court of Appeals held that the Act does not create a private right of action in federal court to determine the validity of two conflicting custody decrees. *Id.*, at 1552–1559. We granted certiorari, 479 U.S. 1063 (1987), and we now affirm.

II

In determining whether to infer a private cause of action from a federal statute, our focal point is Congress' intent in enacting the statute. As guides to discerning that intent, we have relied on the four factors set out in Cort v. Ash, 422 U.S. 66, 78 (1975), along with other tools of statutory construction. See Daily Income Fund, Inc. v. Fox, 464 U.S. 523, 535–536 (1984); California v. Sierra Club, 451 U.S. 287, 293 (1981); Touche Ross & Co. v. Redington, 442 U.S. 560, 575–576 (1979). Our focus on congressional intent does not mean that we require evidence that Members of Congress, in enacting the statute, actually had in mind the creation of a private cause of action. The implied cause of action doctrine would be a virtual dead letter were it limited to correcting drafting errors when Congress simply forgot to codify its evident intention to provide a cause of action. Rather, as an *implied* cause of action doctrine suggests, "the legislative history of a statute that does not expressly create or deny a private remedy will typically be equally silent or ambiguous on the question." Cannon v. University of Chicago, 441 U.S. 677, 694 (1979). We therefore have recognized that Congress' "intent may appear implicitly in the language or structure of the statute, or in the circumstances of its enactment." Transamerica Mortgage Advisors, Inc. v. Lewis, 444 U.S. 11, 18 (1979). The intent of Congress remains the ultimate issue, however, and "unless this congressional intent can be inferred from the language of the statute, the statutory structure, or some other source, the essential predicate for implication of a private remedy simply does not exist." Northwest Airlines, Inc. v. Transport Workers, 451 U.S. 77, 94 (1981). In this case, the essential predicate for implication of a private remedy plainly does not exist. None of the factors that have guided our inquiry in this difficult area points in favor of inferring a private cause of action. Indeed, the context, language, and legislative history of the PKPA all point sharply away from the remedy petitioner urges us to infer.

C.   CHANGING MEANING OF THE NORM

From the unclear and nonexistent norm we turn now to the norm whose meaning changes. This became the subject of much public controversy in 1985, when Attorney General Edwin Meese III publicly criticized Supreme Court justices for failing to interpret the Constitution in accordance with the intent of the drafters and instead substituting the judges' idiosyncratic political science and moral philosophies.[54] Justices William J. Brennan, Jr., and John Paul Stevens leaped into public print arguing that judges were not required to rely on the original intent theory insofar as the Constitution was concerned.[55] Attorney General Meese put his finger on the serious question of how federal judges should determine public policy when it refuses to consider the intent of the framers. Perhaps he was correct in suggesting that many constitution law interpretations are at odds with the original intent of the drafters. The justices, however, were surely right in saying that insofar as interpreting the Constitution is concerned, unlike interpreting statutes and contracts, judges are not bound by the original intent theory of adjudication.

Because the Constitution is a moral statement more than a set of by-laws, conditions in the nation that have occurred since its ratification should be relevant to its interpretation. These changing conditions allow federal judges to reject the original intent theory of interpretation and use a continuing or ongoing historical approach, thus permitting the Constitution to reflect the prevailing temperament of the country. In Furman v. Georgia,[56] a widely-studied death penalty case, the various opinions relied on the ongoing history technique to demonstrate that the Eighth Amendment's proscription of cruel and unusual punishment "is not fastened to the obsolete but may acquire meaning as public opinion becomes enlightened by a humane justice," [57] and "must draw its meaning from the evolving standards of decency that mark the progress of a maturing society." [58] As Holmes stated:

> The life of the law has not been logic; it has been experience. The felt necessities of the times, the prevalent moral and political theories, intuitions of public policy, avowed or unconscious, even the prejudices which judges share with their fellow men, have had a good deal more to do than the syllogism in determining the rules by which men should be governed.[59]

TECHNIQUES AND METHODS OF STATUTORY CONSTRUCTION

We come now to the methods and techniques used by the judges or recommended by the scholars in solving the problems of the unclear

54. E. Meese, Speech to the American Bar Association (London, July 17, 1985), reported in N.Y. Times, July 18, 1985, at 7, col. 1.

55. W. Brennan, Speech before a Seminar at Georgetown University (Oct. 12, 1985), reported in N.Y. Times, Oct. 13, 1985, at 1, col. 1: J. Stevens, Remarks before a Luncheon of the Federal Bar Association (Chicago, Oct. 23, 1985), reported in N.Y. Times, Oct. 26, 1985, at 1, col. 1.

56. 408 U.S. 238 (1972).

57. Id. at 242 (quoting Weems v. United States, 217 U.S. 349, 378 (1910) (Douglas, J., concurring)).

58. Id. (quoting Trop v. Dulles, 356 U.S. 86, 101 (1958) (Douglas, J., concurring).

59. O.W. Holmes, The Common Law 1 (Howe ed. 1963) (1881).

norm, the nonexistent norm and the norm whose meaning changes while its text remains constant. The writings and cases that follow illustrate the diversity that abounds, including the American plain meaning rule, the modern "ism" concepts—Intentionalism, Literalism, Textualism and Purposivism—and finally, thoughtful descriptions of newer techniques offered by America's leading scholars in this field, concepts presented under the rubric, "Hybrid Dynamic Theories."

The following materials and cases discuss, or at least illustrate, these techniques. In introducing this subject, we recognize that the student, lawyer and judge encounter a "vast wasteland" of unpredictability as to what a given court will do in a specific case. Recall Holmes definition of law as "the prophecies of what the courts will do in fact, and nothing more pretentious." As long as the same judges on the same courts utilize different methods in interpreting statutory language in different cases, as illustrated by some of the examples from the U.S. Supreme Court, it remains a great challenge for the advocate to fashion or forge a proper prophecy in a given case.

As we noted earlier, when it comes to statutory interpretation the cumulative experience of the judiciary furnishes no absolute rules for guidance. Some judges seem always to favor certain techniques; others pick and choose the methods that will achieve a desired result. We are treated to abstract expressions: "If the statute is clear and unambiguous, that is the end of the matter, for the court must give effect to the unambiguously expressed intent of Congress," or, "in determining the scope of a statute, we first look at its language. In the case before us, the language is plain and unambiguous. We will apply it." But that is not always the end of the matter. The reports are filled with cases where "clear and unambiguous language" is shunted in a quest for legislative intention or purpose.

We introduce these many methods of statutory construction with an important caveat: Some of these techniques are mutually exclusive; others may be used in conjunction with one another. When the courts use a combination to reach a result, a greater authority attaches to that interpretation.

THE LITERAL RULE

OVERVIEW

Faithful adherents of this school believe that the interpreter should approach the statutory text as a reasonable intelligent reader would, and give the text its most common sense meaning. He or she will construe the language in the special sense the words had acquired at the time of enactment, consider the placement of the words in the sentence and the punctuation.

It is what Holmes described in 1899: "We do not inquire what the legislature meant; we ask only what the statute means." The statute must be literally enforced even though it should lead to absurd or mischievous results. In 1884 Lord Bramwell would say that "what seems absurd to one man does not seem absurd to another" and that we should "leave it to the legislature to set it right than to alter those words according to one's notion of an absurdity." [1]

CHUNG FOOK v. WHITE

Supreme Court of the United States, 1924.
264 U.S. 443, 44 S.Ct. 361, 68 L.Ed. 781.

MR. JUSTICE SUTHERLAND delivered the opinion of the Court.

Chung Fook is a native-born citizen of the United States. Lee Shee, his wife, is an alien Chinese woman, ineligible for naturalization. In 1922 she sought admission to the United States, but was refused and detained at the immigration station, on the ground that she was an alien, afflicted with a dangerous contagious disease. No question is raised as to her alienage or the effect and character of her disease; but the contention is that, nevertheless, she is entitled to admission under the proviso found in § 22 of the Immigration Act of February 5, 1917, c. 29, 39 Stat. 891. * * *

A petition for a writ of *habeas corpus* was denied by the Federal District Court for the Northern District of California, and upon appeal to the Circuit Court of Appeals, the judgment was affirmed. 287 Fed. 533.

The pertinent words of the proviso are: "That if the person sending for wife or minor children is naturalized, a wife to whom married or a minor child born subsequent to such husband or father's naturalization shall be admitted without detention for treatment in hospital, . . ." The measure of the exemption is plainly stated and, in terms, extends to the wife of a naturalized citizen only.

But it is argued that it cannot be supposed that Congress intended to accord to a naturalized citizen a right and preference beyond that enjoyed by a native-born citizen. The court below thought that the exemption from detention was meant to relate only to a wife who by marriage had acquired her husband's citizenship, and not to one who, notwithstanding she was married to a citizen, remained an alien under § 1994, Rev.Stats.: "Any woman who is now or may hereafter be married to a citizen of the United States, and who might herself be lawfully naturalized, shall be deemed a citizen." To the same effect, see *Ex parte Leong Shee,* 275 Fed. 364. We are inclined to agree with this view; but, in any event, the statute plainly relates only to the wife or children of a naturalized citizen and we cannot interpolate the words "native-born citizen" without usurping the legislative function. . . . The words of the statute being clear, if it unjustly discriminates against the native-born citizen, or is cruel and inhuman in its results, as forcefully

1. Hill v. East and West India Dock Co., 9 A.C. 448, 464–65 (House of Lords, 1884).

contended, the remedy lies with Congress and not with the courts. Their duty is simply to enforce the law as it is written, unless clearly unconstitutional.

NOTE

In Akers v. Sebren, 639 N.E.2d 370 (1994), the Indiana Court of Appeals was faced with the question: Does the word "sister" as included in the Indiana Guest Act apply to half sisters who have only one parent in common? The court answered in the negative, reasoning as follows:

> The use of the word "sister" in the Guest Act is clear and unambiguous and a search for legislative intent is unnecessary. The Court's inquiry should end here because no ambiguity exists as to the meaning of the word "sister." A search for legislative intent is required only when the language of the statute is unclear:
>
>> the threshold inquiry before the Court is whether the statute is ambiguous, for if no ambiguity exists the Court cannot interpret or substitute words to fit within a construction different from what the Legislature clearly and expressly intended.

Joseph v. Lake Ridge School Corporation (1991), Ind.App., 580 N.E.2d 316, 319:

> Judge Miller recently wrote about the Guest Act in Coplen v. Omni Restaurants, Inc. (1994), Ind.App., 636 N.E.2d 1285.
>
>> In construing our guest statute, we do not have the luxury of guidance from past decisions; however, we are cognizant of the cardinal rule of statutory construction that a statute clear and unambiguous on its face need not and cannot be interpreted by a court, which must hold it to its plain meaning. Grove v. Thomas (1983), Ind.App., 446 N.E.2d 641, 643.

Strict construction has been defined as "a close and conservative adherence to the literal or textual interpretation." Lagler v. Bye (1908), 42 Ind.App. 592, 85 N.E. 36, 37. Since the guest statute is in derogation of the common law it "must be strictly construed against limitations on a claimant's right to bring suit." Tittle v. Mahan (1991), Ind., 582 N.E.2d 796, 800. "Whenever the legislature adopts a statute that is in derogation of the common law, the appellate courts will presume that the legislature is aware of the common law and does not intend to make any change therein beyond what it declares, either in express terms or by unmistakable implication." Id. at 800. The court is prohibited from expanding the word "sister" to mean anything other than what is clearly expressed in the statute.

Akers's argument concerning the dictionary meaning of "sister" also fails because half sister is not included in the primary definition of the word. In order to include half sister as a primary definition of "sister" the court may also be forced to include stepsister in its definition. It is clear to this court that if the legislature had intended to include "half sister" or "stepsister" in the Guest Act, it would have simply listed that relationship as an additional party. The Guest Act does expressly include "stepchild" as a person included in the class under the Guest Act but it does not mention "stepsister" or "half sister." It is the duty of this court to strictly construe statutory language and this court must accept the primary meaning of sister which is "a female human being related to another person having the same parents as another."

BARHAUS v. CONKLIN

California Court of Appeal, 2d Dist., 6th Div. (1994) (Unpublished).

[Santa Barbara Superior Court Judge Ronald C. Stevens held that language in a 1990 referendum was unambiguous and ruled that the elected mayor was ineligible to serve. In proceedings prior to the election, Superior Court Judge William L. Gordon made a similar ruling but was reversed by the Court of Appeal on the ground that post-election challenge was an adequate remedy at law. The Mayor took office on November 23, 1993. On October 17, 1994, the Court of Appeal in an unpublished opinion removed him from office. Excerpts of this opinion follow.]

JUSTICE GILBERT delivered the Opinion of the Court.

[Section 500.1 of Santa Barbara's charter states that "No person shall be eligible to serve cumulatively as a member of the city Council and Mayor for more than four (4) consecutive four (4) year terms." Conklin became a candidate for mayor after the expiration of his fourth term as council member. He argues that the charter authorizes him to serve as mayor for four consecutive terms because the language "city council *and* mayor" is conjunctive rather than disjunctive. The court did not agree.]

Conklin spends much time on the section's legislative history in an effort to convince us that the section was not intended to bar his service as mayor. But we may resort to legislative history only if the terms of the measure are ambiguous; that is, only if there is more than one semantically permissible construction. Here the only semantically permissible construction of section 500.1 bars Conklin from serving his term as mayor.

Conklin points out that section 500.1 was enacted by the voters. He urges that we consider his election as extrinsic evidence that the voters did not intend to bar him from serving as mayor. But the meaning of section 500.1 must be found in its language; there can be no intent in a statute or charter not expressed in its words. Whatever the intent of the voters in electing Conklin may have been, we are bound by the language of section 500.1. That language unequivocally bars him from serving the term to which he was elected.

Finally, Conklin argues that his constitutional right to hold public office requires that we construe any ambiguity in section 500.1 in his favor. We agree, but in Conklin's case there is no ambiguity.

THE AMERICAN PLAIN MEANING RULE

OVERVIEW

At one time the Literal Rule was also called the "Plain Meaning Rule," but this concept has undergone a metamorphosis in America. By 1899, we were given the following understanding:

> When the act is clear upon its face, and when standing alone it is fairly susceptible of but one construction, that construction must be given to it.... Where the statute is of doubtful meaning and susceptible on its face of two constructions, the court may look into prior and contemporaneous acts, the reasons which induced the act in question, and the purpose intended to be accomplished by it to determine its proper construction.[1]

Plain meaning adherents avoid recourse to legislative history to ascertain intent: "In expounding this law, the judgment of this court cannot, in any degree, be influenced by the construction placed upon it by individual members of Congress in the debate which took place on its passage, nor by the motives or reasons assigned by them for supporting or opposing amendments that were offered. The law as it passed is the will of the majority of both houses, and the only mode in which that will is spoken is in the act itself; and we must gather their intention from the language there used."[2]

Most plain meaning proponents will turn to extrinsic sources where adherence to literalism would lead to absurd results:

> Where the language of an enactment is clear and construction according to its terms does not lead to absurd or impractical consequences, the words employed are to be taken as the final expression of the meaning intended.[3]

In 1993, the Court would make a modern statement of the plain meaning rule: "Our task is to give effect to the will of Congress, and

---

1. Hamilton v. Rathbone, 175 U.S. 414, 419, 421 (1899).

2. Aldridge v. Williams, 44 U.S. 9, 24 (1845); see also United States v. Union Pac. R.R., 91 U.S. 72, 79 (1875).

3. United States v. Missouri Pac. R.R., 278 U.S. 269, 278 (1929)

where its will has been expressed in reasonably plain terms, that language must ordinarily be regarded as conclusive.[4]

The plain meaning rule hit its dark age in the 1940's, during which time courts freely consulted any sources that might shed light on legislative intent, including lengthy congressional committee reports, transcripts from debates on the floor and other legislative history:

> When aid to construction of the meaning of words, as used in the statute, is available, there certainly can be no "rule of law" which forbids its use, however clear the words may appear on "superficial examination." [5]

And as recently as 1983, Judge Patricia Wald announced the "fall of the plain meaning rule." [6] The above views notwithstanding, in recent years the plain meaning rule has enjoyed a renaissance in the form of textualism.

MORENO v. STATE OF MISSISSIPPI

Supreme Court of Mississippi, 1994.
637 So.2d 200.

PRATHER, PRESIDING JUSTICE, for the Court:

This matter is before the Court on Moreno's pro se motion to appeal in forma pauperis. For the reasons stated in this opinion, we deny Moreno's motion to appeal in forma pauperis and dismiss this case with prejudice pursuant to Miss.Sup.Ct.R. 2(a)(2).

After Moreno's notice of appeal was received by this Court, no other action was taken by Moreno. Accordingly, the Clerk of this Court wrote Moreno a letter dated September 22, 1993, notifying him that the appeal costs should be paid and the Certificate of Compliance, required by Miss.Sup.Ct.R. 11(b)(1), should be filed with the trial court clerk and served on the court reporter.

The Clerk wrote the letter dated September 22, 1993, pursuant to Miss.Sup.Ct.R. 2(a)(2) which states as follows:

> (2) Discretionary Dismissal. An appeal may be dismissed upon motion of a party or on this Court's own motion, when a party fails to comply substantially with these rules.

Moreno failed to correct the deficiency by paying the appeal costs and, thereafter this Court, on October 26, 1993, ordered Moreno to show cause.

---

4. Negonsott v. Samuels, 113 S.Ct. 1119, 1122–23 (1993) (citing Griffin v. Oceanic Contractors, Inc., 458 U.S. 564, 570 (1982)).

5. United States v. American Trucking Assns., 310 U.S. 534, 543–44 (1940).

6. Patricia M. Wald, *Some Observations on the Use of Legislative History in the 1981 Supreme Court Term,* 68 Iowa L.Rev. 195, 196 (1983).

Moreno argues that he is not required to pay the appeal costs because he contends Miss.Code Ann. § 47–5–76 (1993) requires the Mississippi Department of Corrections to pay such costs:

> Department of Corrections to pay court costs for inmate filing pauper's affidavit in civil action against Department employee pertaining to condition of confinement.

> If an inmate plaintiff files a pauper's affidavit in a civil action and the defendant is an employee of the department and the civil action pertains to the inmate's condition of confinement, the department shall pay, out of any funds available for such purpose, all costs of court assessed against such inmate in such civil action.

The above statute is the only authority which Moreno cites in support of his argument that he is not required to pay the appeal costs. Moreno's appeal raises a point of first impression concerning the interpretation of Miss.Code Ann. § 47–5–76 (1993). After a thorough consideration of this issue, we hold that Miss.Code Ann. § 47–5–76 (1993) applies only to a trial and not to an appeal to this Court.

This Court has stated the following rule of statutory interpretation:

> In considering a statute passed by the legislature, ... the first question a court should decide is whether the statute is ambiguous. If it is not ambiguous, the court should simply apply the statute according to its plain meaning and should not use principles of statutory construction.

We hold that Miss.Code Ann. § 47–5–76 (1993), by its terms, limits the Mississippi Department of Corrections' responsibility to pay for inmate suits pertaining to conditions of confinement to actions in a trial court. The terms "plaintiff" and "defendant" are legal terms of art which are commonly understood to describe the parties to a civil suit in the trial of the action. In the same way, the term, "costs of court assessed," is commonly used in reference to the costs which a trial court may assess to the losing party. Had the legislature chosen, it could have extended the Mississippi Department of Corrections' responsibility to pay costs of appeal incurred by an appellant inmate, but Miss.Code Ann. § 47–5–76 (1993) does not so provide.

In summary, we are of the opinion that Miss.Code Ann. § 47–5–76 (1993) is unambiguous and that its plain meaning allows an inmate plaintiff only to proceed in forma pauperis at the trial level, if all of the statutory requirements are met, but not at the appellate level.

————

GRIFFIN v. OCEANIC CONTRACTORS, INC.

Supreme Court of the United States, 1982.
458 U.S. 564, 102 S.Ct. 3245, 73 L.Ed.2d 973.

[Griffin was injured while working aboard Oceanic's vessel in foreign waters. He brought suit under the Jones Act for the company's refusal to pay medical expenses and transportation back to the United States. He also made a claim for penalty wages for the company's failure to pay $412.50 in earned wages allegedly due upon discharge. The district court exercised discretion and assessed penalty wages at $6,881.60, reflecting the 34–day period from the date of discharge through the date when Griffin began work for another company. The Court of Appeals affirmed, but the Supreme Court reversed, holding that the sum recoverable as wages amounted to at least $302,790.40, reflecting the time between the date of discharge, April 1, 1976, and the date of judgment, May 6, 1980.]

JUSTICE REHNQUIST delivered the opinion of the Court.

This case concerns the application of 46 U.S.C. § 596, which requires certain masters and vessel owners to pay seamen promptly after their discharge and authorizes seamen to recover double wages for each day that payment is delayed without sufficient cause. The question is whether the district courts, in the exercise of discretion, may limit the period during which this wage penalty is assessed, or whether imposition of the penalty is mandatory for each day that payment is withheld in violation of the statute.

Respondent urges that the legislative purpose of the statute is best served by construing it to permit some choice in determining the length of the penalty period. In respondent's view, the purpose of the statute is essentially remedial and compensatory, and thus it should not be interpreted literally to produce a monetary award that is so far in excess of any equitable remedy as to be punitive.

Respondent, however, is unable to support this view of legislative purpose by reference to the terms of the statute. "There is, of course, no more persuasive evidence of the purpose of a statute than the words by which the legislature undertook to give expression to its wishes." United States v. American Trucking Assns., Inc., 310 U.S. 534, 543 (1940). See Caminetti v. United States, 242 U.S. 470, 490 (1917). Nevertheless, in rare cases the literal application of a statute will produce a result demonstrably at odds with the intentions of its drafters, and those intentions must be controlling. We have reserved "some 'scope for adopting a restricted rather than a literal or usual meaning of its words where acceptance of that meaning ... would thwart the obvious purpose of the statute.'" Commissioner v. Brown, 380 U.S. 563, 571 (1965) (quoting Helvering v. Hammel, 311 U.S. 504, 510–511 (1941)). This, however, is not the exceptional case.

As the Court recognized in Collie v. Fergusson, 281 U.S. 52 (1930), the "evident purpose" of the statute is "to secure prompt payment of seamen's wages ... and thus to protect them from the harsh consequences of arbitrary and unscrupulous action of their employers, to which, as a class, they are peculiarly exposed." *Id.,* at 55. This was to be accomplished "by the imposition of a liability which is not exclusively compensatory, but designed to prevent, by its coercive effect, arbitrary refusals to pay wages, and to induce prompt payment when payment is possible." *Id.,* at 55–56. Thus, although the sure purpose of the statute is remedial, Congress has chosen to secure that purpose through the use of potentially punitive sanctions designed to deter negligent or arbitrary delays in payment.

The legislative history of the statute leaves little if any doubt that this understanding is correct. The law owes its origins to the Act of July 20, 1790, ch. 29, § 6, 1 Stat. 133, passed by the the First Congress. Although the statute as originally enacted gave every seaman the right to collect the wages due under his contract "as soon as the voyage is ended," it did not provide for the recovery of additional sums to encourage compliance. Such a provision was added by the Shipping Commissioners Act of 1872, ch. 322, § 35, 17 Stat. 269, which provided for the payment of "a sum not exceeding the amount of two days' pay for each of the days, not exceeding ten days, during which payment is delayed." The Act of 1872 obviously established a ceiling of 10 days on the period during which the penalty could be assessed and, by use of the words "not exceeding," left the courts with discretion to choose an appropriate penalty within that period.

Congress amended the law again in 1898. As amended, it read in relevant part:

> "Every master or owner who refuses or neglects to make payment in manner hereinbefore mentioned without sufficient cause shall pay to the seaman a sum equal to one day's pay for each and every day during which payment is delayed beyond the respective period." Act of Dec. 21, 1898, ch. 28, § 4, 30 Stat. 756.

The amending legislation thus effected two changes: first, it removed the discretion theretofore existing by which courts might award less than an amount calculated on the basis of each day during which payment was delayed, and, second, it removed the 10–day ceiling which theretofore limited the number of days upon which an award might be calculated. The accompanying Committee Reports identify the purpose of the legislation as "the amelioration of the condition of the American seamen," and characterize the amended wage penalty in particular as "designed to secure the promptest possible payment of wages." ...

Nothing in the legislative history of the 1898 Act suggests that Congress intended to do anything other than what the Act's enacted language plainly demonstrates: to strengthen the deterrent effect of the statute by removing the courts' latitude in assessing the wage penalty.

The statute was amended for the last time in 1915 to increase further the severity of the penalty by doubling the wages due for each day during which payment of earned wages was delayed. Seamen's Act of 1915, ch. 153, § 3, 38 Stat. 1164. There is no suggestion in the Committee Reports or in the floor debates that, in so doing, Congress intended to reinvest the courts with the discretion it had removed in the Act of 1898. Resort to the legislative history, therefore, merely confirms that Congress intended the statute to mean exactly what its plain language says.

TEXTUALISM

OVERVIEW

Constant modifications of the plain meaning approach have given rise to what is now called "Textualism." The essential arguments of textualism are:

- Statutory language is of paramount importance.
- The text serves as the starting point, and in most cases the ending point, for statutory interpretation.
- Legislative history and various other extrinsic materials are inferior to the statutory text.

One of the more celebrated examples of this approach is United States v. Locke,[1] in which the Court interpreted a provision of the Federal Land Policy and Management Act of 1976 requiring holders of unpatented mining claims to re-register their claims annually "prior to December 31." Locke filed his registration on December 31, but the Bureau determined that he forfeited his claim by failing to register it prior to December 31; that is, on or before December 30. Writing for the majority, Justice Thurgood Marshall upheld the declaration of forfeiture, stating that although the Court would not allow a literal reading of the statute to produce absurd results:

> deference to the supremacy of the Legislature, as well as recognition that Congressmen typically vote on the language of a bill, generally required us to assume that "the legislative purpose is expressed by the ordinary meaning of the words used." ...
> The phrase 'prior to' may be clumsy, but its meaning is clear.[2]

Locke illustrates the point that textualists are not divorced from legislative intent, but part company with their intentionalist colleagues in a belief that the language of the statute in question should be the primary, and in most cases the only, source for determining the intent of the legislature.

Textualism marks both a return to the plain meaning rule and a refinement of it. The pure textualist, according to Professor William Eskridge, avoids sources beyond the actual text of the statute for realist

---

1. 471 U.S. 84 (1985).   **2.** 472 U.S. at 93, 95, 96.

reasons (the collective intent of the legislature is an unascertainable legal fiction), historicist reasons (even if collective intent were a coherent concept, an historically situated collective intent cannot be completely "reconstructed" by even the most "imaginative" jurist) and formalist reasons (democratic governance is threatened by judicial reliance on committee reports and individuals' comments not voted on and by broad judicial discretion to read into legislative enactments).[3]

If not a founding father of the "new textualism," Justice Scalia appears to have raised his sword against the traditional "soft" plain meaning adherents who would examine legislative history even after conceding that the language is clear: "Where the language of ... laws is clear, we are not free to replace it with an unenacted legislative intent." [4]

The approach seems more restrictive than the traditional "soft" plain meaning approach which allows for consultation to legislative history under certain circumstances when the specific statutory language in question is ambiguous or amenable to multiple interpretations. A pure textualist approach, however, actually marks a refinement and liberalization of the rule. To determine the plain meaning of the statute, Justice Scalia resorts to the whole of the statute, not merely the specific statutory language which is the subject of litigation:

> Statutory construction ... is a holistic endeavor. A provision that may seem ambiguous in isolation is often clarified by the remainder of the statutory scheme ... because the same terminology is used elsewhere in a context that makes its meaning clear, or because only one of the permissible meanings produces a substantive effect that is compatible with the rest of the law.[5]

Justice Scalia's textualist might also refer to dictionary definitions, and even other statutes enacted by the same legislature, to find clear meaning in the language of the section in question. It is only after resort to all of these textual aids, if statutory meaning is unclear or would lead to truly absurd results, that the textualist might reluctantly turn to legislative history for assistance, as Justice Scalia indicated in Green v. Bock Laundry Mach. Co.[6] Textualists argue that legislative history is not an accurate indicator of legislative intent but, when all else fails, even Justice Scalia would acknowledge that poor evidence is better than no evidence at all. Under no circumstances, however, do they believe that a court should examine legislative history in order to create an ambiguity or to lend support to its threshold conclusion that the statutory language is clear.

This approach shares two elements in common with the intentional and purposivist methods, discussed later in the chapter. First, it is

3. William N. Eskridge, Jr., *The New Textualism,* 37 U.C.L.A.L.Rev. 621 (1990).

4. I.N.S. v. Cardozo–Fonseca, 480 U.S. 421, 453 (1987) (Scalia, J., concurring).

5. United Savings Ass'n of Texas v. Timbers of Inwood Forrest Assocs., 484 U.S. 365, 371 (1988).

6. 490 U.S. 504 (1989) (Scalia, J., concurring).

static in that it attempts to capture the legislature's intent *at the time* the statute was enacted. Second, it examines the statutory language in the context of the *entire* statutory scheme in an effort to identify that intent. By viewing the entire statutory language in context, textualism marks a movement away from its plain meaning ancestor, which examines only the specific statutory language in question for guidance unless that language is ambiguous.

It would be inaccurate to suggest Justice Scalia invented this holistic approach. Judge Learned Hand stated over a half-century ago: "The meaning of a sentence may be more than that of the separate words, as a melody is more than the notes, and no degree of particularity can ever obviate recourse to the setting in which all appear, and which all collectively create." [7] Justice Cardozo agreed: "The meaning of a statute is to be looked for, not in any single section, but in all the parts together and in their relation to the end in view." [8] The following cases and materials exemplify the textualist approach, and the tension existing between its adherents and judges who favor legislative history as a method of ascertaining legislative intent.

IMMIGRATION AND NATURALIZATION SERV. v. CARDOZO–FONSECA

Supreme Court of the United States, 1986.
480 U.S. 421, 107 S.Ct. 1207, 94 L.Ed.2d 434.

JUSTICE STEVENS delivered the opinion of the Court.

Since 1980, the Immigration and Nationality Act has provided two methods through which an otherwise deportable alien who claims that he will be persecuted if deported can seek relief. Section 243(h) of the Act, 8 U.S.C. § 1253(h), requires the Attorney General to withhold deportation of an alien who demonstrates that his "life or freedom would be threatened" on account of one of the listed factors if he is deported. In INS v. Stevic, 467 U.S. 407 (1984), we held that to qualify for this entitlement to withholding of deportation, an alien must demonstrate that "it is more likely than not that the alien would be subject to persecution" in the country to which he would be returned. *Id.,* at 429–430. The Refugee Act of 1980, 94 Stat. 102, also established a second type of broader relief. Section 208(a) of the Act, 8 U.S.C. § 1158(a), authorizes the Attorney General, in his discretion, to grant asylum to an alien who is unable or unwilling to return to his home country "because of persecution or a well-founded fear of persecution on account of race, religion, nationality, membership in a particular social group, or political opinion." § 101(a)(42), 8 U.S.C. § 1101(a)(42).

In *Stevic*, we rejected an alien's contention that the § 208(a) "well-founded fear" standard governs applications for withholding of deportation under § 243(h). Similarly, today we reject the Government's con-

---

7. Helvering v. Gregory, 69 F.2d 809 (2d Cir.1934), aff'd, 293 U.S. 465 (1935).

8. Panama Refining Co. v. Ryan, 293 U.S. 388, 439 (1934).

tention that the § 243(h) standard, which requires an alien to show that he is more likely than not to be subject to persecution, governs applications for asylum under § 208(a). Congress used different, broader language to define the term "refugee" as used in § 208(a) than it used to describe the class of aliens who have a right to withholding of deportation under § 243(h). The Act's establishment of a broad class of refugees who are eligible for a discretionary grant of asylum, and a narrower class of aliens who are given a statutory right not to be deported to the country where they are in danger, mirrors the provisions of the United Nations Protocol Relating to the Status of Refugees, which provided the motivation for the enactment of the Refugee Act of 1980. In addition, the legislative history of the 1980 Act makes it perfectly clear that Congress did not intend the class of aliens who qualify as refugees to be coextensive with the class who qualify for § 243(h) relief.

JUSTICE SCALIA, concurring in the judgment.

I agree with the Court that the plain meaning of "well-founded fear" and the structure of the Immigration and Nationality Act (Act) clearly demonstrate that the "well-founded fear" standard and the "clear probability" standard are not equivalent. I concur in the judgment rather than join the Court's opinion, however, for two reasons. First, despite having reached the above conclusion, the Court undertakes an exhaustive investigation of the legislative history of the Act. It attempts to justify this inquiry by relying upon the doctrine that if the legislative history of an enactment reveals a " 'clearly expressed legislative intention' contrary to [the enactment's] language," the Court is required to "question the strong presumption that Congress expresses its intent through the language it chooses."

Although it is true that the Court in recent times has expressed approval of this doctrine, that is to my mind an ill-advised deviation from the venerable principle that if the language of a statute is clear, that language must be given effect—at least in the absence of a patent absurdity. Judges interpret laws rather than reconstruct legislators' intentions. Where the language of those laws is clear, we are not free to replace it with an unenacted legislative intent.

Even by its own lights, however, the Court's explication of the legislative history of the Act is excessive. The INS makes a number of specific arguments based upon the legislative history of the Act. It would have sufficed, it seems to me, for the Court to determine whether these specific arguments establish a "clearly expressed legislative intent" that the two standards be equivalent. I think it obvious that they do not, as apparently does the Court. That being so, there is simply no need for the lengthy effort to ascertain the import of the entire legislative history. And that effort is objectionable not only because it is gratuitous. I am concerned that it will be interpreted to suggest that similarly exhaustive analyses are generally appropriate (or, worse yet, required) in cases where the language of the enactment at issue is clear. I also fear that in this case the Court's conduct of that inquiry will be interpreted as a betrayal of its assurance that it does "not attempt to set forth a detailed description of how the well-founded fear test should be applied[.]"

NOTE

You will note that the concurrence quarrels only with the majority's resort to the legislative history to bolster its decision. Where two methods of statutory construction—plain meaning and legislative history—lead to the same result, is it sound judicial process to make an exhaustive inquiry into legislative history? If the meaning is clear and plain, is it necessary to go further?

CONROY v. ANISKOFF

Supreme Court of the United States, 1993.
___ U.S. ___, 113 S.Ct. 1562, 123 L.Ed.2d 229.

JUSTICE STEVENS delivered the opinion of the Court.

The Soldiers' and Sailors' Civil Relief Act of 1940, 54 Stat. 1178, as amended, 50 U.S.C.App. § 501 *et seq.* (Act), suspends various civil liabilities of persons in military service. At issue in this case is the provision in § 525 that the "period of military service shall not be included in computing any period ... provided by any law for the redemption of real property sold or forfeited to enforce any obligation, tax, or assessment." The question presented is whether a member of the Armed Services must show that his military service prejudiced his ability to redeem title to property before he can qualify for the statutory suspension of time.

II

The statutory command in § 525 is unambiguous, unequivocal, and unlimited. It states that the period of military service "shall not be included" in the computation of "any period now or hereafter provided by any law for the redemption of real property...." Respondents do not dispute the plain meaning of this text.

JUSTICE SCALIA, concurring in the judgment.

The Court begins its analysis with the observation: "The statutory command in § 525 is unambiguous, unequivocal, and unlimited." In my view, discussion of that point is where the remainder of the analysis should have ended. Instead, however, the Court feels compelled to demonstrate that its holding is consonant with legislative history, including some dating back to 1917—*a full quarter century* before the provision at issue was enacted. That is not merely a waste of research time and ink; it is a false and disruptive lesson in the law. It says to the bar that even an "unambiguous [and] unequivocal" statute can never be dispositive; that, presumably under penalty of malpractice liability, the oracles of legislative history, far into the dimmy past, must always be consulted. This undermines the clarity of law, and condemns litigants (who, unlike us, must pay for it out of their own pockets) to subsidizing historical research by lawyers.

The greatest defect of legislative history is its illegitimacy. We are governed by laws, not by the intentions of legislators. As the Court said in 1844: "The law as it passed is the will of the majority of both houses, *and the only mode in which that will is spoken is in the act itself....*" Aldridge v. Williams, 3 How. 9, 24 (emphasis added). But not the least of the defects of legislative history is its indeterminacy. If one were to search for an interpretive technique that, *on the whole,* was more likely to confuse than to clarify, one could hardly find a more promising candidate than legislative history. And the present case nicely proves that point.

Judge Harold Leventhal used to describe the use of legislative history as the equivalent of entering a crowded cocktail party and looking over the heads of the guests for one's friends. If I may pursue that metaphor: The legislative history of § 205 of the Soldiers' and Sailors' Civil Relief Act contains a variety of diverse personages, a selected few of whom—its "friends"—the Court has introduced to us in support of its result. But there are many other faces in the crowd, most of which, I think, are set against today's result.

[Justice Scalia then proceeded to analyze four statutes suggesting a legislative intent contrary to the majority view].

* * *

I confess that I have not personally investigated the entire legislative history—or even that portion of it which relates to the four statutes listed above. The excerpts I have examined and quoted were unearthed by a hapless law clerk to whom I assigned the task. The other Justices have, in the aggregate, many more law clerks than I, and it is quite possible that if they all were unleashed upon this enterprise they would discover, in the legislative materials dating back to 1917 *or earlier,* many faces friendly to the Court's holding. Whether they would or not makes no difference to me—and evidently makes no difference to the Court, which gives lip service to legislative history but does not trouble to set forth and discuss the foregoing material that others found so persuasive. In my view, that is as it should be, except for the lip service. The language of the statute is entirely clear, and if that is not what Congress meant then Congress has made a mistake and Congress will have to correct it. We should not pretend to care about legislative intent (as opposed to the meaning of the law), lest we impose upon the practicing bar and their clients obligations that we do not ourselves take seriously.

INTENTIONALISM

OVERVIEW

Justice Frankfurter once wrote that a court's "task is to construe not English but Congressional English." Acknowledging this difference between the two "languages," proponents of the interpretive technique of intentionalism attempt to obtain a more accurate "translation" by informing their construction of the words of a statute with evidence of the legislature's intent. They argue that, under principles of separation of powers, courts have an obligation to construe statutes so that they carry out the will—and not merely the words—of the law making branch of the government.

Although legislative intent has become a valuable method of statutory interpretation, it continues to be a subject of great debate where judges cut across clear words of a statute to find a meaning that is facially at odds with the literal language of the statutory provision, a meaning that is rationalized under the rubric of "legislative intent."

When legislative intent is employed as the criterion for interpretation, the primary emphasis is on what the statute meant to members of the legislature that enacted it. Much like textualism and literalism, the intent criterion is archeological in nature, orienting the judge to the time of enactment by the legislature. In many cases it is as if the court is trying to call up what mental images might have been entertained by the enacting legislators.

Study of intentionalism opens the door to discussion of the two categories of resource materials for statutory construction: "intrinsic" and "extrinsic" aids. These characterizations refer to the text of a statute. Intrinsic aids are those which derive a statute's meaning from the internal statutory schema, as well as from conventional or dictionary interpretation for textualists and literalists. But intentionalists go further than the text itself, reaching beyond it for additional assistance. They seek extrinsic aids, consisting of information that comprises the background of the text, most notably in federal matters, on legislative history. Proponents of intentionalism acknowledge that legislative intent often is difficult to discover or uncover, and therefore argue that not only is it legitimate, but it is also necessary to consult extrinsic aids to assist in interpretation.

Gaining the most favor with intentionalists is legislative history—the so-called "richest kind of evidence," revealing both the intent of the enacting legislature and the meaning of the statutory text. It is rich evidence from the standpoint of abundance, to be sure, but the ever present question persists when referring to snippets of legislative history—whether the informal converse fallacy of accident (hasty generalization) sets in when one attempts to generalize an intention purporting to reflect a majority of the lawmakers who voted for the legislation from a data base composed only of fragmented comments from a small number of legislators or statements drafted by committee staff.

———

EDWARD H. LEVI, AN INTRODUCTION
TO LEGAL REASONING *

... [I]n the application of a statute the intent of the legislature seems important. The rules of construction are ways of finding out the intent. The actual words used are important but insufficient. The report of congressional committees may give some clue. Prior drafts of the statute may show where meaning was intentionally changed. Bills presented but not passed may have some bearing. Words spoken in debate may now be looked at. Even the conduct of the litigants may be important in that the failure of the government to have acted over a period of time on what it now suggests as the proper interpretation throws light on the common meaning. But it is not easy to find the intent of the legislature.

Justice Reed has given us some Polonius-sounding advice on the matter:

> In the interpretation of statutes, the function of the court is easily stated. It is to construe the language so as to give effect to the intent of Congress. There is no invariable rule for the discovery of that intention....

The words of advice force one to reexamine whether there is any difference between case-law and statutory interpretation. It is not enough to show that the words used by the legislature have some meaning. Concepts created by case law also have some meaning, but the meaning is ambiguous. It is not clear how wide or narrow the scope is to be. Can it be said that the words used by the legislature have any more meaning than that, or is there the same ambiguity? One important difference can be noted immediately. Where case law is considered, there is a conscious realignment of cases; the problem is not the intention of the prior judge. But with a statute the reference is to the kind of things intended by the legislature. All concepts suggest, but case-law concepts can be re-worked. A statutory concept, however, is supposed to suggest what the legislature had in mind; the items to be included under it should be of the same order. We mean to accomplish what the legislature intended. This is what Justice Reed has said. The difficulty is that what the legislature intended is ambiguous. In a significant sense there is only a general intent which preserves as much ambiguity in the concept used as though it had been created by case law.

This is not the result of inadequate draftsmanship, as is so frequently urged. Matters are not decided until they have to be. For a legislature perhaps the pressures are such that a bill has to be passed

* 15 U.Chi.L.Rev. 501, 520–23 (1948).
Reprinted by permission.

dealing with a certain subject. But the precise effect of the bill is not something upon which the members have to reach agreement. If the legislature were a court, it would not decide the precise effect until a specific fact situation arose demanding an answer. Its first pronouncement would not be expected to fill in the gaps. But since it is not a court, this is even more true. It will not be required to make the determination in any event, but can wait for the court to do so. There is a related and an additional reason for ambiguity. As to what type of situation is the legislature to make a decision? Despite much gospel to the contrary, a legislature is not a fact-finding body. There is no mechanism, as there is with a court, to require the legislature to sift facts and to make a decision about specific situations. There need be no agreement about what the situation is. The members of the legislative body will be talking about different things; they cannot force each other to accept even a hypothetical set of facts. The result is that even in a non-controversial atmosphere just exactly what has been decided will not be clear.

Controversy does not help. Agreement is then possible only through escape to a higher level of discourse with greater ambiguity. This is one element which makes compromise possible. Moreover, from the standpoint of the individual member of the legislature there is reason to be deceptive. He must escape from pressures at home. Newspapers may have created an atmosphere in which some legislation must be passed. Perhaps the only chance to get legislation through is to have it mean something not understood by some colleagues. If the court in construing the legislation is going to look at committee reports and remarks during debates, words which would be voted down if included in the bill will be used on the floor or in a report as a kind of illicit and, it is hoped, effective legislation. And if all this were not sufficient, it cannot be forgotten that to speak of legislative intent is to talk of group action, where much of the group may be ignorant or misinformed. Yet the emphasis should not be on this fact, but on the necessity that there be ambiguity before there can be any agreement about how unknown cases will be handled.

But the court will search for the legislative intent, and this does make a difference. Its search results in an initial filling up of the gap. The first opinions may not definitely set the whole interpretation. A more decisive view may be edged toward, but finally there is likely to be an interpretation by the court which gives greater content to the words used. In building up this interpretation, the reference will be to the kind of examples that the words used, as commonly understood, would call to mind. Reasoning by example will then proceed from that point. There is a difference then from case law in that the legislature has compelled the use of one word. The word will not change verbally. It could change in meaning, however, and if frequent appeals as to what the legislature really intended are permitted, it may shift radically from time to time. When this is done, a court in interpreting legislation has really more discretion than it has with case law. For it can escape from prior cases by saying that they have ignored the legislative intent.

NOTE

How valid is the suggestion that legislatures are not fact-finding bodies?

Levi tells us that "rules of construction are ways of finding out the intent" of a legislature. Are they? Does his statement that legislatures "can wait for the courts" to fill gaps in legislation affect your answer? Reconsider your answer after reading Justice Frankfurter's observations which follow. Is Levi's asserted difference between case law and statutory construction a difference in form but not in substance?

In view of the tremendous recourse to legislative history by the United States Supreme Court and other federal courts, do Levi's observations give you pause? Consider his emphasis on legislative compromise and his statement that "from the standpoint of the individual member [of the legislature] there is reason to be deceptive." Can it be said that recorded remarks in legislative debates and committee reports truly reflect the intention of the Congress? Is there *any* intention of *Congress,* or are there only 535 intentions of Congresspersons? If the latter, what or how many should control?

UNITED STATES v. AMERICAN TRUCKING ASS'N

Supreme Court of the United States, 1940.
310 U.S. 534, 60 S.Ct. 1059, 84 L.Ed. 1345.

JUSTICE REED delivered the opinion of the Court.

[In the interpretation of statutes, the function of the court is easily stated. It is to construe the language so as to give effect to the intent of Congress. There is no invariable rule for the discovery of that intention. . . .]

There is, of course, no more persuasive evidence of the purpose of a statute than the words by which the legislature undertook to give expression to its wishes. Often these words are sufficient in and of themselves to determine the purpose of the legislature. In such cases we have followed their plain meaning. When that meaning had led to absurd or futile results, however, this Court has looked beyond the words to the purpose of the act. Frequently, however, even when the plain meaning did not produce absurd results but merely an unreasonable one "plainly at variance with the policy of legislation as a whole" this Court has followed that purpose rather than the literal words. When aid to construction of the meaning of words, as used in the statute, is available, there certainly can be no "rule of law" which forbids the use, however clear the words may appear on superficial examination. The interpretation of the meaning of statutes, as applied to justiciable controversies, is exclusively a judicial function. This duty requires one body of public servants, the judges, to construe the meaning of what another body, the legislators, has said. Obviously there is danger that the courts' conclusion as to legislative purpose will be unconsciously influenced by the judges' own views or by factors not considered by the enacting body. A lively appreciation of the danger is the best assurance of escape from its threat but hardly justifies an acceptance of a literal interpretation dogma which withholds from the courts available information for reaching a correct conclusion. Emphasis should be laid too upon the necessity for appraisal of the purposes as a whole of Congress in analyzing the meaning of clauses of sections of general acts. A few words of general connotation appearing in the text of statutes should not be given a wide meaning, contrary to settled policy, "except as a different purpose is plainly shown."

NOTE

" * * * While legislative history as well as the language of the statute may itself be used to interpret the meaning of statutory language ... the decisions of this court have established that some types of legislative history are substantially more reliable than others. The report of a joint conference committee of both Houses of Congress, for example, or the report of a Senate or House committee, is accorded a good deal more weight than the remarks even of the sponsor of a particular portion of the bill on the floor of the chamber."

Simpson v. United States, 435 U.S. 6 (1978) (Rehnquist, J., dissenting).

HIRSCHEY v. F.E.R.C.

United States Court of Appeals, D.C.Circuit, 1985.
777 F.2d 1.

SCALIA, CIRCUIT JUDGE, Concurring.

While not contesting that *Hirschey II,* 760 F.2d 305 (D.C.Cir.1985) is now the law of this circuit, I must nonetheless dissociate myself from the dictum of the court—which may be given effect in other circuits—that the legislative history of the 1985 EAJA amendments "ratifies the holding of the majority opinion in *Hirschey II.*" *Hirschey II* and the three decisions of other circuits reaching the same result (two of which, like *Hirschey II* itself, were accompanied by dissents), present a conflict with the contrary holding of the Ninth Circuit in Tulalip Tribes v. FERC, 749 F.2d 1367, 1369 (9th Cir.1984), rather than the sort of uniform judicial interpretation that Congress, by unamended reenactment of the subject provision, may be deemed to have approved. *See, e.g.,* Lorillard v. Pons, 434 U.S. 575, 580–81, 98 S.Ct. 866, 869–70, 55 L.Ed.2d 40 (1978). The entire case for the majority's asserted "ratification" of *Hirschey II* rests upon the following statement in the House Committee Report:

> The language of section 2412(d)(1)(A) expresses the view that prevailing parties shall be awarded attorney's fees and, when available, costs as well. This interpretation ratifies the approach taken by four circuits. [Citing, *inter alia*, *Hirschey II*.] ... Thus, the Committee rejects the interpretations of the statute by the 9th Circuit. See *Tulalip Tribes*....

H.R.Rep. No. 120, 99th Cong., 1st Sess. 17 (1985), 1985 U.S.Code Cong. & Ad.News 132, 145. It is most interesting that the House Committee rejected the interpretation of the Ninth Circuit, and perhaps that datum should be accorded the weight of an equivalently unreasoned law review article. But the authoritative, as opposed to the persuasive, weight of the Report depends entirely upon how reasonable it is to assume that that rejection was reflected in the law which *Congress* adopted. I frankly doubt that it is ever reasonable to assume that the details, as opposed to the broad outlines of purpose, set forth in a committee report come to the attention of, much less are approved by, the house which enacts the committee's bill.[1]

---

1. Several years ago, the following illuminating exchange occurred between members of the Senate, in the course of floor debate on a tax bill:

Mr. ARMSTRONG. ... My question, which may take [the chairman of the Committee on Finance] by surprise, is this: Is it the intention of the chairman that the Internal Revenue Service and the Tax Court and other courts take guidance as to the intention of Congress from the committee report which accompanies this bill?

Mr. DOLE. I would certainly hope so....

Mr. ARMSTRONG. Mr. President, will the Senator tell me whether or not he wrote the committee report?

Mr. DOLE. Did I write the committee report?

Mr. ARMSTRONG. Yes.

Mr. DOLE. No; the Senator from Kansas did not write the committee report.

Mr. ARMSTRONG. Did any Senator write the committee report?

Mr. DOLE. I have to check.

Mr. ARMSTRONG. Does the Senator know of any Senator who wrote the committee report?

Mr. DOLE. I might be able to identify one, but I would have to search. I was here all during the time it was written, I might say, and worked carefully with the staff as they worked....

Mr. ARMSTRONG. Mr. President, has the Senator from Kansas, the chairman of the Finance Committee, read the committee report in its entirety?

Mr. DOLE. I am working on it. It is not a bestseller, but I am working on it.

Mr. ARMSTRONG. Mr. President, did members of the Finance Committee vote on the committee report?

Mr. DOLE. No.

Mr. ARMSTRONG. Mr. President, the reason I raise the issue is not perhaps apparent on the surface, and let me just state it: .... The report itself is not considered by the Committee on Finance. It was not subject to amendment by the Committee on Finance. It is not subject to amendment now by the Senate.

* * *

... If there were matter within this report which was disagreed to by the Senator from Colorado or even by a majority of all Senators, there would be no way for us to change the report. I could not offer an amendment tonight to amend the committee report.

... [F]or any jurist, administrator, bureaucrat, tax practitioner, or others who might chance upon the written record of this proceeding, let me just make the point that this is not the law, it was not voted on, it is not subject to amendment, and we should discipline ourselves to the task of expressing congressional intent in the statute.

PURPOSIVISM

OVERVIEW

Considerations of the purpose that legislation purports to accomplish often are mentioned as grounds for the specific interpretation given to a statute. This method of statutory construction is unique in that it combines the liberal use of extrinsic aids with a dynamic approach of statutory construction.

Because many scholars and legal practitioners confuse purposivism and intentionalism, it is important to study the subtle distinctions. The legislature's intent in passing a particular statute does not ordinarily reflect consciousness of (new) factual contexts in which the statute may be applied. Intentionalism focuses on the individual author or authors' meaning which is given to statutory language; purposivism determines the goals of the statute as they are defined by the factual scenarios in which the statute is applied.

Karl Llewelyn suggested, "[i]f a statute is to make sense, it must be read in light of some assumed purpose. A statute merely declaring a rule, with no purpose or objective, is nonsense." Llewelyn's "assumed purpose" actually is the general understanding of the legislature regarding some actual or potential issue the statute is designed to address in the future. According to this mode of interpretation, a court should look back to the "legislative intent" and then define the purposes of the statute in the context of the instant case. Applications of this technique often allow statutes to address the non-existent or changing norm, otherwise excluded from the "legislative intent."

A challenged premise of purposivism's dynamic approach is that courts are implementing the actual or presumed public policy attributable to a rational, public-spirited legislature. Critics contend that the legislative process is much more complex, and that legislation is not necessarily accompanied by purpose. Proponents of purposivism counter that even if the benevolent assumptions of purpose are counterfactual in a given case, they nevertheless promote overall coherence and normative attractiveness of the law. In most cases, however, the methods of intentionalism are different only in style, not result.

––––––

HART AND SACKS, WHAT TO EXPECT FROM A THEORY OF STATUTORY INTERPRETATION*

Do not expect anybody's theory of a statutory interpretation, whether it is your own or somebody else's, to be an accurate statement of what courts actually do with statutes. The hard truth of the matter is that American courts have no intelligible, generally accepted, and consistently applied theory of statutory interpretation.

128 Cong.Rec. S8659 (daily ed. July 19, 1982).

* H. Hart and A. Sacks, The Legal Process: Basic Problems in the Making and

When an effort is made to formulate a sound and workable theory, therefore, the most that can be hoped for is that it will have some foundation in experience and in the best practice of the wisest judges, and that it will be well calculated to serve the ultimate purposes of law. * * * Consider the adequacy of the following tentative formulation:

In interpreting a statute a court should:

1. Decide what purpose ought to be attributed to the statute and to any subordinate provision of it which may be involved; and then

2. Interpret the words of the statute immediately in question so as to carry out the purpose as best it can, making sure, however, that it does not give the words either—

(a) a meaning they will not bear, or

(b) a meaning which would violate any established policy of clear statement.

FELIX FRANKFURTER, SOME REFLECTIONS ON THE READINGS OF STATUTES*

THE JUDGE'S TASK

Everyone has his own way of phrasing the task confronting judges when the meaning of a statute is in controversy. Judge Learned Hand speaks of the art of interpretation as "the proliferation of purpose." Who am I not to be satisfied with Learned Hand's felicities? And yet that phrase might mislead judges intellectually less disciplined than Judge Hand. It might justify interpretations by judicial libertines, not merely judicial libertarians. My own rephrasing of what we are driving at is probably no more helpful, and is much longer than Judge Hand's epigram. I should say that the troublesome phase of construction is the determination of the extent to which extraneous documentation and external circumstances may be allowed to infiltrate the text on the theory that they were part of it, written in ink discernible to the judicial eye.

. . .

And so I have examined the opinions of Holmes, Brandeis and Cardozo and sought to derive from their treatment of legislation what conclusions I could fairly draw, freed as much as I could be from impressions I had formed in the course of the years.

. . .

Application of Law 1200–1201 (Cambridge Tent. ed. 1958). Reprinted by permission of Dean Albert M. Sacks.

* 47 Colum.L.Rev. 527, 527–34, 338–45 (1947). Reprinted by permission.

If it be suggested that Mr. Justice Holmes is often swift, if not cavalier, in his treatment of statutes, there are those who level the same criticism against his opinions generally. It is merited in the sense that he wrote, as he said, for those learned in the art. I need hardly add that for him "learned" was not a formal term comprehending the whole legal fraternity. When dealing with problems of statutory construction also he illumined whole areas of doubt and darkness with insights enduringly expressed, however briefly. To say "We agree to all the generalities about not supplying criminal laws with what they omit, but there is no canon against using common sense in construing laws as saying what they obviously mean," is worth more than most of the dreary writing on how to construe penal legislation. Again when he said that "the meaning of a sentence is to be felt rather than to be proved," he expressed the wholesome truth that the final rendering of the meaning of a statute is an act of judgment. He would shudder at the thought that by such a statement he was giving comfort to the school of visceral jurisprudence. . . . One gets the impression that in interpreting statutes Mr. Justice Holmes reached meaning easily, as was true of most of his results, with emphasis on the language in the totality of the enactment and the felt reasonableness of the chosen construction. He had a lively awareness that a statute was expressive of purpose and policy, but in his reading of it he tended to hug the shores of the statute itself, without much re-enforcement from without.

Mr. Justice Brandeis, on the other hand, in dealing with these problems as with others, would elucidate the judgment he was exercising by proof or detailed argument. In such instances, especially when in dissent, his opinions would draw on the whole arsenal of aids to construction. More often than either Holmes or Cardozo, Brandeis would invoke the additional weight of some "rule" of construction. But he never lost sight of the limited scope and function of such "rules." Occasionally, however, perhaps because of the nature of a particular statute, the minor importance of its incidence, the pressure of judicial business or even the temperament of his law clerk, whom he always treated as a co-worker, Brandeis disposed of a statute even more dogmatically, with less explicit elucidation, than did Holmes.

For Cardozo, statutory construction was an acquired taste. He preferred common law subtleties, having great skill in bending them to modern uses. But he came to realize that problems of statutory construction had their own exciting subtleties and gave ample employment to philosophic and literary talents. Cardozo's elucidation of how meaning is drawn out of a statute gives proof of the wisdom and balance which, combined with his learning, made him a great judge. While the austere style of Brandeis seldom mitigated the dry aspect of so many problems of statutory construction, Cardozo managed to endow even these with the glow and softness of his writing. The differences in the tone and color of their style as well as in the moral intensity of Brandeis and Cardozo made itself felt when they wrote full-dress opinions on problems of statutory construction. Brandeis almost compels by demonstration; Cardozo woos by persuasion.

Words in statutes are not unlike words in a foreign language in that they too have "associations, echoes, and overtones." Judges must retain the associations, hear the echoes, and capture the overtones. In one of his very last opinions, dealing with legislation taxing the husband on the basis of the combined income of husband and wife, Holmes wrote: "The statutes are the outcome of a thousand years of history. . . . They form a system with echoes of different moments, none of which is entitled to prevail over the other."

> . . .

This duty of restraint, this humility of function as merely the translator of another's command, is a constant theme of our Justices. It is on the lips of all judges, but seldom, I venture to believe, has the restraint which it expresses, or the duty which it enjoins, been observed with so consistent a realization that its observance depends on self-conscious discipline. Cardozo put it this way: "We do not pause to consider whether a statute differently conceived and framed would yield results more consonant with fairness and reason. We take this statute as we find it." It was expressed more fully by Mr. Justice Brandeis when the temptation to give what might be called a more liberal interpretation could not have been wanting. "The particularization and detail with which the scope of each provision, the amount of the tax thereby imposed, and the incidence of the tax, were specified, preclude an extension of any provision by implication to any other subject. . . . What the Government asks is not a construction of a statute, but, in effect, an enlargement of it by the court, so that what was omitted, presumably by inadvertence, may be included within its scope." An omission at the time of enactment, whether careless or calculated, cannot be judicially supplied however much later wisdom may recommend the inclusion.

> . . .

PROLIFERATION OF PURPOSE

You may have observed that I have not yet used the word "intention." All these years I have avoided speaking of the "legislative intent" and I shall continue to be on my guard against using it. The objection to "intention" was indicated in a letter by Mr. Justice Holmes which the recipient kindly put at my disposal:

> "Only a day or two ago—when counsel talked of the intention of a legislature, I was indiscreet enough to say I don't care what their intention was. I only want to know what the words mean. Of course the phrase often is used to express a conviction not exactly thought out—that you construe a particular clause or expression by considering the whole instrument and any dominant purposes that it may express. In fact intention is a residuary clause intended to gather up whatever other aids

there may be to interpretation beside the particular words and the dictionary."

If that is what the term means, it is better to use a less beclouding characterization. Legislation has an aim; it seeks to obviate some mischief, to supply an inadequacy, to effect a change of policy, to formulate a plan of government. That aim, that policy is not drawn, like nitrogen, out of the air; it is evinced in the language of the statute, as read in the light of other external manifestations of purpose. That is what the judge must seek and effectuate, and he ought not to be led off the trail by tests that have overtones of subjective design. We are not concerned with anything subjective. We do not delve into the minds of legislators or their draftsmen, or committee members. Against what he believed to be such an attempt Cardozo once protested:

> "The judgment of the court, if I interpret the reasoning aright, does not rest upon a ruling that Congress would have gone beyond its power if the purpose that it professed was the purpose truly cherished. The judgment of the court rests upon the ruling that another purpose, not professed, may be read beneath the surface, and by the purpose so imputed the statute is destroyed. Thus the process of psychoanalysis has spread to unaccustomed fields. There is a wise and ancient doctrine that a court will not inquire into the motives of a legislative body...."[28]

. . .

SEARCH FOR PURPOSE

How then does the purpose which a statute expresses reveal itself, particularly when the path of purpose is not straight and narrow? The English courts say: look at the statute and look at nothing else.... "In Millar v. Taylor the principle of construction was laid down in words, which have never, so far as I know, been seriously challenged, by Willes J. as long ago as in 1769: 'The sense and meaning of an Act of Parliament must be collected from what it says when passed into a law; and not from the history of changes it underwent in the house where it took its rise. That history is not known to the other house or to the sovereign.'"

These current English rules of construction are simple. They are too simple. If the purpose of construction is the ascertainment of meaning, nothing that is logically relevant should be excluded. The rigidity of English courts in interpreting language merely by reading it disregards the fact that enactments are, as it were, organisms which exist in their environment. One wonders whether English judges are confined psychologically as they purport to be legally. The judges deem themselves limited to reading the words of a statute. But can they really escape placing the words in the context of their minds, which after all are not automata applying legal logic but repositories of all sorts of

28. United States v. Constantine, 296 U.S. 287, 298, 299 (1936) (dissenting).

assumptions and impressions? Such a modest if not mechanical view of the task of construction disregards legal history. In earlier centuries the judges recognized that the exercise of their judicial function to understand and apply legislative policy is not to be hindered by artificial canons and limitations. The well known resolutions in Heydon's Case, have the flavor of Elizabethan English but they express the substance of a current volume of U.S. Reports as to the considerations relevant to statutory interpretation....

At the beginning, the Supreme Court reflected the early English attitude. With characteristic hardheadedness Chief Justice Marshall struck at the core of the matter with the observation "Where the mind labours to discover the design of the legislature, it seizes everything from which aid can be derived." This commonsensical way of dealing with statutes fell into disuse, and more or less catchpenny canons of construction did service instead. To no small degree a more wooden treatment of legislation was due, I suspect, to the fact that the need for keeping vividly in mind the occasions for drawing on all aids in the process of distilling meaning from legislation was comparatively limited. As the area of regulation steadily widened, the impact of the legislative process upon the judicial brought into being, and compelled consideration of, all that convincingly illumines an enactment, instead of merely that which is called, with delusive simplicity, "the end result." Legislatures themselves provided illumination by general definitions, special definitions, explicit recitals of policy, and even directions of attitudes appropriate for judicial construction. Legislative reports were increasingly drawn upon, statements by those in charge of legislation, reports of investigating committees, recommendations of agencies entrusted with the enforcement of laws, etc. When Mr. Justice Holmes came to the Court, the U.S. Reports were practically barren of references to legislative materials. These swarm in current volumes. And let me say in passing that the importance that such materials play in Supreme Court litigation carry far-reaching implications for bench and bar.

The change I have summarized was gradual. Undue limitations were applied even after courts broke out of the mere language of a law. We find Mr. Justice Holmes saying, "It is a delicate business to base speculations about the purposes or construction of a statute upon the vicissitudes of its passage." And as late as 1925 he referred to earlier bills relating to a statute under review, with the reservation "If it be legitimate to look at them."

Such hesitations and restraints [into legislative history] are in limbo. Courts examine the forms rejected in favor of the words chosen. They look at later statutes "considered to throw a cross light" upon an earlier enactment. The consistent construction by an administrative agency charged with effectuating the policy of an enactment carries very considerable weight. While assertion of authority does not demonstrate its existence, long-continued, uncontested assertion is at least evidence that the legislature conveyed the authority. Similarly, while authority conferred does not atrophy by disuse, failure over an extended period to exercise it is some proof that it was not given. And since "a page of history is worth a volume of logic," courts have looked into the background of statutes, the mischief to be checked and the good that was designed, looking sometimes far afield and taking notice also as judges of what is generally known by men.

Unhappily, there is no table of logarithms for statutory construction. No item of evidence has a fixed or even average weight. One or another may be decisive in one set of circumstances, while of little value elsewhere. A painstaking, detailed report by a Senate Committee bearing directly on the immediate question may settle the matter. A loose statement even by a chairman of a committee, made impromptu in the heat of debate, less informing in cold type than when heard on the floor, will hardly be accorded the weight of an encyclical.

Spurious use of legislative history must not swallow the legislation so as to give point to the quip that only when legislative history is doubtful do you go to the statute. While courts are no longer confined to the language, they are still confined by it. Violence must not be done to the words chosen by the legislature. Unless indeed no doubt can be left that the legislature has in fact used a private code, so that what appears to be violence to language is merely respect to special usage. In the end, language and external aids, each accorded the authority deserved in the circumstances, must be weighed in the balance of judicial judgment. Only if its premises are emptied of their human variables, can the process of statutory construction have the precision of a syllogism. We cannot avoid what Mr. Justice Cardozo deemed inherent in the problem of construction, making "a choice between uncertainties. We must be content to choose the lesser." But to the careful and disinterested eye, the scales will hardly escape appearing to tip slightly on the side of a more probable meaning.

. . .

Insofar as canons of construction are generalizations of experience, they all have worth. In the abstract, they rarely arouse controversy. Difficulties emerge when canons compete in soliciting judgment, because they conflict rather than converge. For the demands of judgment underlying the art of interpretation, there is no vade mecum.

NOTE

Judge Charles E. Wyzanski, Jr., suggests that "[i]n two generations the law has moved in ways unforeseeable by any nineteenth-century lawyer. The center has shifted from the common law adjudged in the courts, to enacted law administered by executive agencies subject to limited judicial reviews. Statutory regulations became the bulk of the law; and judges used their remaining freedom to rewrite the constitution to effectuate what they conceived to be the unexpressed yet ultimate popular will." C. Wyzanski, Whereas—a Judge's Premises xi (1964).

Is there substance to the view that the statute itself is all-important and that resort to legislative history is improper? May an analogy be drawn to the rule admitting parol or extrinsic evidence for the purpose of aiding the construction of a contract? To explain an ambiguity in a written contract, evidence of conversations and circumstances attending the negotiations of the contract is generally admissible.

Consider Justice Frankfurter's aphorism, "In matters of statutory construction also it makes a great deal of difference whether you start with an answer or a problem." See also his expression in Roger's Estate v. Helvering, Commissioner, 320 U.S. 410, 413 (1943): "In law ... the right answer usually depends on putting the right question."

Consider the statement of the issue posed by Justice Fortas for the Court in United States v. Yazell, 382 U.S. 341, 342–43 (1966): "Specifically, the question presented is whether, in the circumstances of this case, the Federal Government, in its zealous pursuit of the balance due on a disaster loan made by the Small Business Administration, may obtain judgment against Ethel Mae Yazell of Lampasas, Texas." With the "question" so framed, could there be any doubt about the "answer"?

LEARNED HAND in Cabell v. Markham, 148 F.2d 737 (2d Cir.) aff'd, 326 U.S. 404 (1945): "[T]he decisions are legion in which [the courts] have refused to be bound by the letter [of the statute], when it frustrates the patent purpose of the whole statute.... As Holmes, J., said in a much-quoted passage from Johnson v. United States, 163 F. 30, 32, 18 L.R.A.,N.S., 1194: 'it is not an adequate discharge of duty for courts to say: We see what you are driving at, but you have not said it, and therefore we shall go on as before.' ... [I]t is one of the surest indexes of a mature and developed jurisprudence not to make a fortress out of the dictionary...."

HYBRID DYNAMIC THEORIES

OVERVIEW

The jurisprudence of statutory construction develops constantly. We have advanced from early theories that statutes in derogation of the common law must be strictly construed. We have moved from the Literal Rule to the American Plain Meaning Rule. We have emphasized legislative intent and legislative history in order to ascertain that intent. Recently, we have utilized new breeds of Textualism and Purposivism. Studies in statutory interpretation have attempted to rationalize, if not categorize, the wide range of methods used by judges. Their efforts have been met with varying degrees of success and an abundance of frustration.

Problems of statutory interpretation are exacerbated because neither the courts nor individual judges have been consistent in endorsing certain methods over others. Perhaps our academic scholars have been too generous with the judiciary and have refused to chronicle the inconsistencies that abound. In recent years, thoughtful commentators have contributed fresh observations which we now set forth under the general rubric, "Hybrid Dynamic Theories."

We call these theories "hybrid" because the scholars recognize that several methods of interpretation may be employed by a judge at one time, and different techniques may be appropriate in different cases. We call these theories "dynamic" because they are constantly developing but, more importantly, because they are not concerned with legislative intent at the time a given statute was enacted (an archeological, "static" approach). Rather, these theories emphasize how a statute should be interpreted in the context of a modern society, where the legislature either did not have—or could not have had—a specific intent at the time of enactment; i.e., in cases of the nonexistent norm or the norm whose meaning changes.

The materials that follow illustrate techniques that are being followed, as well as suggestions of techniques which ought to be. New theories are offered that critique and build upon traditional methods. These scholars reject reliance on any one specific approach and argue that courts should determine which mode of interpretation yields the best answer to the specific problem presented in the case.

————

ROBERT A. LEFLAR, STATUTORY CONSTRUCTION: THE SOUND LAW APPROACH *

There have been various approaches used down through the years through the process of statutory interpretation. The books on the construction of statutes and the articles that have been written in the field tend to list three major approaches to statutory construction. One of them is commonly called "the literalness test" involving rigid adherence to the letter of the law as written regardless of consequence. It probably has little to commend it today as an aid to carrying forward the enlightened—presumably enlightened—policies of the statutes involved. But, we still find courts or individual judges insisting that the judicial task is to accept the law as written, to find the words as they appear, look in the dictionary at what those words mean literally, and go on from there. Writers on statutory construction generally today condemn that approach, but we know it is still used. A second approach, which is much talked of in the books, has been called "the Golden Rule approach", and that makes it sound attractive if nothing else. It rejects the principle of purely literal interpretation, and suggests that the words of the statutes should be given their plain and natural meaning unless— unless manifest injustice or absurdity would result. The word "unless" is not very broad. Again, it leaves out the possibility of considering the true purposes of the statute. The emphasis under the so-called Golden Rule approach is on literalness unless extreme absurdity or injustice would result. Well, that's better than literalness alone, but it doesn't carry us very far beyond it.

* Remarks delivered to Federal Appellate Washington, D.C., May 13, 1975.
Judges Conference, Federal Judicial Center,

The third approach, sometimes called the modern approach, has been named from Chief Justice Edward Coke's famous Heydon's Case— the "mischief rule" to the effect that four things are to be looked for and considered in interpreting a statute. One, what was the common law before the making of the act? Second, what was the mischief and defect for which the common law did not provide? Third, what remedy the parliament had resolved and appointed to "cure the disease of the Commonwealth." And fourth, the true reason of the remedy. And then the office of all judges is always to make such construction as shall suppress the mischief and advance the remedy. And putting it in words more customary to this day, to advance the purpose of the statute. And if we give emphasis to that last point, that carries us substantially, I think, to our present situation.

What I would rather like to think in terms of is another approach— one that is not formally named, but I think it is representative of what judges in most courts do today. An approach which might be called "the proper judicial function", or "sound law approach".

I will pass those names or designations by for the moment in order to get to some illustrations, some ideas that might indicate what sort of thing we're talking about. Suppose that we have a statute enacted in 1910. How do we want to interpret that? Now if you look at a 1910 Webster's Dictionary or law dictionary you will find that a given word is likely to be shown with a different meaning in the 1910 dictionary than in a 1975 dictionary. You will find that time and time again. Do we interpret the 1910 statute, in 1975, in terms of the 1910 intent of the legislators? We talk at great length about legislative intent, maybe we will have some occasion to do so, but later on. Are we concerned more with the 1975 legislative attitudes or popular attitudes—the attitudes that would be, as best we can guess, taken by a legislature in 1975 if it were enacting the same statute—word for word. Should we interpret it in the light of a 1975 meaning for those very words, "legislative intent"? Of course, we know that the U.S. Supreme Court persistently does go back to legislative debates and legislative records to determine what legislators had in mind when they enacted a particular statute. But were they bound by what they said in 1910? Are we bound by the problems that they were thinking of in 1910 or, applying the statute in 1975, are we concerned with the different problems, the different social attitudes and the different wisdom that would characterize an initial consideration of the problem today? The literalness approach to the statute certainly would prevent us from using 1975 attitudes. [Citing examples.]

Well, I could go on with illustrations of that sort at great length. The books are full of them. But I am going just to refer to two or three other points. First, as to legislative intent. We say frequently that in interpreting a statute we want to discover the intent of the legislature. I think that it was Chief Justice Hingham, I'm not sure, who said that the devil himself "knoweth not the mind of man." It is difficult to discover intent; and when you cannot discover with any authority the state of mind of one man, the process of discovering the states of mind, the intent of 535 men, who make up the Federal Congress, becomes an extremely difficult matter. The United States Supreme Court, as I said a few moments ago, has time and again referred back to legislative debates to discussions in committee and to all other background sources. We could cite dozens of U.S. cases in which that has occurred. But if you have to work with state law few legislatures have transcripts of proceedings comparable to those that are available at the federal level. The problem of legislative intent as such seems to me to involve as much in the way of possibility of being misled as almost anything one can get into. There are bits of legislative record that are devised peculiarly by congressmen or senators for the purpose of misleading judges. And sometimes it is difficult to know which of those you are looking at. There are some types of legislative record that I think are truly useful. I think we can fairly say that if you have a record of what was done by the Commissioners on Uniform State Laws or by the members of the American Law Institute, you have a pretty authoritative and reliable key to legislative intent. But even there, provisions that were enacted or promulgated twenty years ago may not be applicable to current conditions, in the same way that they were applicable to conditions as they prevailed in the commercial world in 1955. True, the Commissioners on Uniform State Laws try to keep things of that sort up to date, but they sometimes don't quite do it, and sometimes the changes, the amendments, are not necessarily enacted.

The name of this fourth approach to interpretation of statutes, the name that I suggested a bit earlier, was in terms of "the proper judicial function" or "the sound law approach". That does not leave the judge or the court as free as a bird in terms of his interpretation of the statute. He has got to start with the words of the statute. But, assuming that there is argument about the words of any statute, what I am suggesting is, and what I think the recent history of judicial interpretation of statutes bears out, is that a sound law approach is what we are attempting to use today; that is, sound in terms of the new use and demands of society as related to the particular area of law to which the statute refers.

ROBERT E. KEETON, GUIDELINES FOR DECIDING MEANING*

C. Guidelines for Deciding Issues Regarding Statutory Meaning

I propose the following set of guidelines [1] for determining whether a statute has answered a particular question that is essential to deciding a

---

* Robert E. Keeton, Judging 151–154 (1990) Reprinted with permission of West Publishing Co.

1. For an earlier version of these guidelines, *see* R. Keeton, Venturing to Do Justice 94–95 (1969). Materials presenting varied views on this subject appear in R.

case before the court and, if not, how the court should go about deciding that case:

One. If the statute addressed the issue at hand and answered it, apply the mandate of the statute (absent unconstitutionality).

Two. If the issue at hand is one beyond that core area of issues that the statute addressed and answered, defer to the statute's manifestations of principle and policy as far as they can be ascertained and are relevant to the issue at hand.

Three. Subject to the first two propositions, aim for resolving the issue at hand so as to produce the best total set of rules, including those within the core area of the statute and other cognate rules of law, whatever their source. Defer to the statute's manifestations of principle and policy, as far as they can be ascertained. Accept the inapplicable statutory mandate as a datum. Accept inapplicable directives appearing in other statutes and judicial precedents as data. Aim for a decision on this issue that will produce an evenhanded system for this issue and all the cognate issues that are answered in statutes and precedents.

Four. In determining whether a statute addressed the issue at hand, dispense with contrary-to-fact presumptions about the legislative process; be realistic and be candid. Use legislative history as data; avoid proceeding as if legislative history were a statutory mandate. At most, declarations in legislative history are obiter dicta of the legislative process. If it is necessary to resort to legislative history, Guidelines Two and Three apply, not Guideline One. Also, do not treat failure to enact a mandate as if it were enacting a mandate. "Not speaking" to an issue is not "speaking" to that issue. Rarely, failure to enact legislation is a significant datum, and Guidelines Two and Three then apply. But never is it a mandate as in Guideline One.

D. The Contrast Between Intent and Objectively Manifested Meaning

If you have any doubts, or disagreement with me, about any of the four guidelines for determining the meaning of statutes and applying the statutes to particular cases, surely they are more likely to concern the second, third, or fourth. So, not only because the first precedes in logical order but also because I hope by discussing it to prepare you for what I wish to say on the others, I discuss it first.

In the title of this Section D, I have used the phrase "objectively manifested meaning." In explaining why, I will be reflecting some of the frustrations of my more recent experience—that is, experience as a trial judge—which came after the initial formulation of the four guidelines stated in Section C.

As a trial judge, I am constantly confronted with arguments of trial lawyers asserting, either expressly or impliedly, that we should be thinking about the intent—the state of mind—of "somebody" or "some

Aldisert, The Judicial Process 170–235
(1976).

body." That is, they argue we should be thinking about intent of some natural person—"somebody" in that sense—or intent of some legal entity, some legally constituted body that is not a natural person—such as a state legislature (or even a court that filed an opinion that is cited as precedent).

The first, fundamental difficulty with an argument about what the legislature intended is that, although a natural person may have a state of mind, such as intent, an entity that is not a natural person has no state of mind in any strictly factual sense. Thus, we have moved to legal fiction when we talk about a legislature's intent.

Distinguish "legislative intent" from "legislature's intent." Except for the risk of its being misunderstood to mean a state of mind, "legislative intent" is a less distracting usage. I have urged judges to use it cautiously in writing opinions, because of the risk of being misunderstood. Nevertheless, properly used and understood, "legislative intent" may be a synonym for objectively manifested meaning of the statute. Professor Lon Fuller, among others, made essentially this point in calling attention to the fact that when one reads a document such as a statute (or a contract, or a judicial opinion), one may sense in it not only explicit mandates (or agreements) but also an underlying objective or purpose that serves to inform the reader about how the different provisions fit together and why they were put together in one document.

Reading a document to determine "legislative intent" or "contractual intent" in this sense is synonymous with searching for objectively manifested meaning.

Coming back to the main point, then, and repeating it, I suggest that the first problem with speaking about a "legislature's intent" is that—unless it is meant to be a synonym for "objectively manifested meaning," and for "legislative intent" in the sense I have just explained—it is a legal fiction. Only a natural person can have a state of mind such as intent. No legal entity such as a legislature can have an "intent" in a strictly factual sense.

Second, arguments about what the legislature intended fail to take account of the governor's participation in the legislative process. A legislature does not ordinarily legislate alone, except by overriding a veto. The usual legislative entity consists of the legislature and the governor, acting together. Again, one may defensibly speak of "legislative intent" in the sense of objectively manifested meaning of what the legislature and governor do together. But it is fictional and misleading to speak of the "legislature's intent."

Third, even when in the legal system we are concerned with the meaning of something written, stated, or approved by a natural person, only very rarely are we concerned with that person's state of mind—that person's intent. The general rule is that we search for "objectively manifested intent"—an objective standard—not "intent," the subjective standard. Thus, the legal system with only the rarest exceptions, focuses not upon a writer's or speaker's intent but upon objectively manifested meaning. Indeed, the legal system often declines even to receive evidence of the person's secretly held state of mind, which may or may not be consistent with what the person said or did.

This fundamental characteristic of the way the law treats written documents—including statutes as well as contracts—helps to explain why Guideline Four cautions that statements in legislative history are the obiter dicta of the legislative process—more like obiter dicta in judicial opinions than like holdings. The issue is what is the *objectively manifested* meaning of the statute. What some individuals or even a legislative committee said in discussing the proposed legislation is not a part of the mandate. In search of the mandate we look first and foremost to the objectively manifested meaning of the statute itself.

CROKER v. BOEING CO.

United States Court of Appeals, Third Circuit, 1981.
662 F.2d 975.

ALDISERT, CIRCUIT JUDGE, concurring and dissenting, with whom A. LEON HIGGINBOTHAM, JR., CIRCUIT JUDGE, joins.

I join parts I, II, IV, and V of the majority opinion and dissent only from the majority's holding in part III that a plaintiff must prove a racially discriminatory purpose to establish a right to relief under 42 U.S.C. § 1981[1] for employment discrimination. I reach a contrary result for reasons of principle and policy; because of the desirability of clarity and understanding for the lay public, employees and employers alike; and because of the necessity for symmetry in the law of employment discrimination.

I.

The § 1981 issue that divides this court today is solely one of statutory construction. I agree completely with the majority's observation that "neither the language nor the legislative history provides certain guidance in interpreting section 1981."

The traditional approaches of statutory interpretation—the mischief rule, the golden rule, the literal rule, and the plain meaning rule[2]—also furnish little help with this troublesome problem. This is because the problem of statutory construction before us is not a problem of language

1. 42 U.S.C. § 1981 provides:

All persons within the jurisdiction of the United States shall have the same right in every State and Territory to make and enforce contracts, to sue, be parties, give evidence, and to the full and equal benefit of all laws and proceedings for the security of persons and property as is enjoyed by white citizens, and shall be subject to like punish-

ment, pains, penalties, taxes, licenses, and exactions of every kind, and to no other.

2. *See* H. Hart & A. Sacks, The Legal Process: Basic Problems in the Making and Application of Law 1144–46 (Cambridge Tent. ed. 1958), *reprinted in* R. Aldisert, The Judicial Process 175–77 (1976).

analysis in the strict sense, arising from the presence of an unclear norm, but a problem of a lacuna, a non-existent norm.[3]

This troublesome and recurring problem of statutory voids was recognized many decades ago by John Chipman Gray:

> The fact is that the difficulties of so-called interpretation arise when the legislation has had no meaning at all; when the question which is raised in the statute never occurred to it; when what the judges have to do is, not to determine what the Legislature did mean on a point which was present to its mind, but to guess what it would have intended on a point not present to its mind, if the point had been present.[4]

When this occurs, I am inclined to follow what Professor Robert A. Leflar has described as the "sound law" approach: "sound in terms of the new use and demands of society as related to the particular area of law to which the statute refers."[5] I am also attracted by the formulation of Professor (now U.S. District Judge) Robert E. Keeton, who has taught that under the circumstances presented here, we should

> aim for resolving the issue at hand so as to produce the best total set of rules, including those within the core area of the statute and other cognate rules of law, whatever their source. Defer to the statute's manifestations of principle and policy, as far as they can be ascertained. Accept the inapplicable statutory mandate as a datum. Accept other statutory directives and judicial precedents as data. Aim for a decision on this issue that will produce an evenhanded system for this issue and all the cognate issues that are answered in statutes and other precedents.[6]

I approach the solution to our immediate problem in the spirit of the Leflar and Keeton formulations.[7] This approach requires me to consider

---

3. *See* M. Cappelletti, J. Merryman & J. Perillo, The Italian Legal System 253 (1967).

4. J.C. Gray, Nature and Sources of Law 172–73 (2d ed. 1921). *See also* W. Friedmann, Legal Theory 453 (5th ed. 1967), *quoting Eyston v. Studd* (Eng.1574):

[I]t is a good way, when you peruse a statute, to suppose that the lawmaker is present; and that you have asked the question you want to know touching the equity; then you must give yourself an answer as you imagine he would have done, if he had been present.

5. *See* Leflar, *Statutory Construction: The Sound Law Approach*, in R. Aldisert, The Judicial Process 177, 180 (1976).

6. Keeton, *Statutes, Gaps, and Values in Tort Law*, 44 J. Air Law & Commerce 1, 9 (1978).

7. This approach is similar to that prescribed in several European Civil Codes,

which frankly and publicly recognize that situations will occur that were not within the contemplation of the legislative draftsmen. Perhaps the best known model is the Swiss Civil Code of 1907:

Art. 1: The Code governs all questions of law which come within the letter or the spirit of any of its provisions.

If the Code does not furnish an applicable provision, the judge shall decide in accordance with customary law, and failing that, according to the rule which he would establish as legislator.

In this he shall be guided by approved legal doctrine and judicial tradition.

The Austrian General Civil Code of 1811 provides:

Sec. 7: Where a case cannot be decided either according to the literal text or the plain meaning of a statute, regard

the field of employment discrimination law as a whole, and to consider § 1981 in conjunction with Title VII of the Civil Rights Act of 1964 and not separately or independently.

II.

Both statutes provide federal remedies for racial discrimination in private and public employment. Title VII, the later of the two statutes, was not enacted in a vacuum; it was adopted with a clear recognition that § 1981 was already available as a remedy. The legislative history of Title VII discloses Congress' understanding "that the remedies available to the individual under Title VII are co-extensive with the individual's right to sue under the provisions of the Civil Rights Act of 1866, 42 U.S.C. § 1981, and that the two procedures augment each other and are not mutually exclusive." H.R.Rep. No. 238, 92d Cong., 1st Sess. 19 (1971), *reprinted in* [1972] U.S.Code Cong. & Ad.News 2137, 2154.

Admittedly, the two remedies do not track each other precisely. "[A]lthough related, and although directed to most of the same ends, [they] are separate, distinct, and independent." Johnson v. Railway Express Agency, Inc., 421 U.S. 454, 461, 95 S.Ct. 1716, 1720, 44 L.Ed.2d 295 (1975). Section 1981 is more limited in that it prohibits only racial discrimination; Title VII encompasses discrimination because of sex, religion, and national origin. Section 1981 is not limited to employment discrimination; it has a much broader reach, not relevant for our purposes here. It does not exempt employers of fewer than fifteen persons, bona fide private membership clubs with less than twenty-five members, or religious groups employing workers in religion-oriented positions.[8] *See Johnson,* 421 U.S. at 460, 95 S.Ct. at 1720. It is not subject to the short limitations period of Title VII,[9] but is governed by the most closely analogous state statute of limitations. These are differences, to be sure, but I defend the thesis that these distinctions do not demand a difference in the elements of a claim for relief.

Recognizing that we are dealing with a lacuna, a void in the law, requiring us to divine somehow the legislative intent, we should candidly admit with Professor Gray that we are guessing what Congress would have intended "on a point not present to its mind." I believe it is entirely legitimate to regard our declared national policy of opposition to employment discrimination as a legitimate aid in solving this problem. With Roger J. Traynor I believe that dictates of public policy are legitimate tools in judicial decisionmaking when neither express statute

shall be had to the statutory provisions concerning similar cases and to the principles which underlie other laws regarding similar matters. If the case is still doubtful, it shall be decided according to the principles of natural justice, after careful research and consideration of all the individual circumstances.

See also Article 6, Spanish Civil Code of 1889; Chap. 2, Article 12 of the Italian Code, Provisions on the Laws in General; and Article I of the 1951 Civil Code of Iraq. For English translations *see* R. Schlesinger, Comparative Law 228, 317, 602–03 (4th ed. 1980).

8. *Compare* 42 U.S.C. §§ 2000e(b), 2000e–1.

9. *See* 42 U.S.C. §§ 2000e–5(e), 2000e–5(f)(1).

nor relevant precedent furnishes an answer.[10] I am persuaded that public policy as manifested by congressional activity is to expand, and not to contract, the reach of statutes dealing with employment discrimination. Congress enacted massive amendments to Title VII in 1972,[11] extending that statute's protection to public employees,[12] but it did not tinker with the judicially-created impact standard.[13] I have not discovered any federal legislation that suggests or demands a more exacting standard of proof in employment discrimination cases under § 1981.

I have emphasized the technical differences between the two statutes deliberately, because I must assume that in enacting Title VII Congress also recognized the circumstances where the two remedies are congruent. A mere glance at the annotations to the two statutes clearly indicates that in most actions where § 1981 will apply, Title VII will also apply. In terms of modern commercial and industrial activities, a qualified plaintiff may utilize either statute as a remedial vehicle except in cases affected by the different periods of limitation. Because Congress enacted the newer statute to augment the older in the field of employment discrimination, I must conclude that it deliberately designed the twin remedies to cover the entire field of employment discrimination based on race.

III.

I now turn to the mass of judicial decisions interpreting the legislative product. The fact is that the colossus of our employment discrimination law has not developed through judicial gloss being added to the language of § 1981, but rather to the text of Title VII. It has been Title VII, and not § 1981, that has served as the fountainhead of judicial lawmaking in the employment discrimination field. And like § 1981, Title VII contained lacunae.

The courts have already filled the Title VII lacunae. In an undeviating series of cases beginning with Griggs v. Duke Power Co., 401 U.S. 424, 91 S.Ct. 849, 28 L.Ed.2d 158 (1971), the courts—not Congress— have established a dichotomy that recognizes claims established by proof of disparate impact as well as disparate treatment. Having fashioned this dichotomy and having affirmed and reaffirmed that discriminatory intent is not a necessary element of a Title VII claim, the courts should not now unduly complicate this very difficult and sensitive area of the law by requiring proof of intent in overlapping actions under § 1981. The courts should not take two pieces of legislation, each containing serious and identical voids, and without good reason fabricate different standards for proof of a violation.

10. *See* Traynor, *Reasoning in a Circle of Law,* 56 Va.L.Rev. 739, 749–50 (1970).

11. Equal Employment Opportunity Act of 1972, Pub.L. No. 92–261, 86 Stat. 103.

12. *Id.* §§ 2(1), 11, *codified at* 42 U.S.C. §§ 2000e(a), 2000e–16.

13. Griggs v. Duke Power Co., 401 U.S. 424, 91 S.Ct. 849, 28 L.Ed.2d 158 (1971), the decision that recognized the disparate impact test, is discussed with approval in the legislative history of the 1972 Act. *See* H.R.Rep. No. 238, 92d Cong., 1st Sess.— (1971), *reprinted in* [1972] U.S.Code Cong. & Ad.News 2137, 2144.

I believe that there will be more predictability and reckonability to the law of employment discrimination, more understanding and societal acceptability by the lay public, including putative employees, employees, and employers alike, if there is consistency in the judicial interpretation of the two statutes. The interested lay public will not be able to understand that where a claim of discrimination antedates the limitation period of Title VII the employee must prove discriminatory intent for years one and two, but need only prove discriminatory impact for years three and four.

When the language of a statute is insufficient, the methods utilized by the courts to assist in the construction process are designed for one purpose—to ascertain the intent of Congress. Because I do not believe that Congress intended that § 1981 be interpreted in one way as to the standard of proof and Title VII in another, I would hold that the traditional wisdom that has emerged from the mass of judicial construction of Title VII should be applied to § 1981 cases as well. I believe that this is the sound approach, commensurate with the developing nuances of employment discrimination law, and sound in terms of societal claims, wants, and demands.

Racial discrimination can be the most virulent of strains that infect a society, and the illness in any society so infected can be quantified. Exposure to embarrassment, humiliation, and the denial of basic respect can and does cause psychological and physiological trauma to its victims. This disease must be recognized and vigorously eliminated wherever it occurs. But racial discrimination takes its most malevolent form when it occurs in employment, for prejudice here not only has an immediate economic effect, it has a fulminating integrant that perpetuates the pestilences of degraded housing, unsatisfactory neighborhood amenities, and unequal education.

Our profound national policy of opposition to racial discrimination must continuously and unstintingly concentrate on its eradication in employment. If the courts are to implement this policy in our functions of interpreting relevant statutes, our compass must be constantly jammed in that direction, for there we find the better rule of law. Professor Harry W. Jones has reminded us:

> A legal rule ... is a good rule ... when—that is, to the extent that—it contributes to the establishment and preservation of a social environment in which the quality of human life can be spirited, improving and unimpaired.[14]

The rule that I suggest meets this test. Accordingly, I would reverse the district court's judgment to the extent it held that the plaintiffs had to prove intentional discrimination in order to prevail in their § 1981 claims, and remand for further proceedings.

---

14. Jones, *An Invitation to Jurisprudence,* 74 Colum.L.Rev. 1023, 1030 (1974).

RICHARD A. POSNER,* IMAGINATIVE RECONSTRUCTION**

I suggest that the task for the judge called upon to interpret a statute is best described as one of imaginative reconstruction.[60] The judge should try to think his way as best he can into the minds of the enacting legislators and imagine how they would have wanted the statute applied to the case at bar.

Now it is easy to ridicule this approach by saying that judges do not have the requisite imagination and that what they will do in practice is assume that the legislators were people just like themselves, so that statutory construction will consist of the judge's voting his own preferences and ascribing them to the statute's draftsmen. But the irresponsible judge will twist any approach to yield the outcomes that he desires and the stupid judge will do the same thing unconsciously. If you assume a judge who will try with the aid of a reasonable intelligence to put himself in the place of the enacting legislators, then I believe he will do better if he follows my suggested approach than if he tries to apply the canons.

The judge who follows this approach will be looking at the usual things that the intelligent literature on statutory construction tells him to look at—such as the language and apparent purpose of the statute, its background and structure, its legislative history (especially the committee reports and the floor statements of the sponsors), and the bearing of related statutes. But he will also be looking at two slightly less obvious factors. One is the values and attitudes, so far as they are known today, of the period in which the legislation was enacted. It would be foolish to ascribe to legislators of the 1930's or the 1960's and early 1970's the skepticism regarding the size of government and the efficacy of regulation that is widespread today, or to impute to the Congress of the 1920's the current conception of conflicts of interest. It is not the judge's job to keep a statute up to date in the sense of making it reflect contemporary values; it is his job to imagine as best he can how the legislators who enacted the statute would have wanted it applied to situations that they did not foresee.

* Chief Judge, U.S. Court of Appeals, Seventh Circuit.

** *Statutory Interpretation—in the Classroom and in the Courtroom,* 50 U. of Chicago L.Rev. 800, 817–822 (1983). Reprinted by permission.

60. I associate this view primarily with Judge Learned Hand. *See* Lehigh Valley Coal Co. v. Yensavage, 218 F. 547, 553 (2d Cir.1914) (Hand, J.); Speech by Learned Hand, Opening Session of the National Conference on the Continuing Education of the Bar (Dec. 16, 1958), *reprinted in* Joint Committee on Continuing Legal Education of the American Law Institute and the American Bar Association, Continuing Legal Education for Professional Competence and Responsibility 116, 117–19 (1959), *also reprinted in* R. Aldisert, The Judicial Process: Readings, Materials and Cases 184, 184–85 (1976). But this view is clearly stated elsewhere, for example in J. Gray, The Nature and Sources of the Law 172–73 (2d ed. 1921), and has ancient antecedents, *see, e.g.,* Heydon's Case, 76 Eng.Rep. 637, 638 (Ex. 1584); 1 W. Blackstone, Commentaries *59–61; 3 *id.* *430–31.

Second, and in some tension with the first point, the judge will be alert to any sign of legislative intent regarding the freedom with which he should exercise his interpretive function. Sometimes a statute will state whether it is to be broadly or narrowly construed;[61] more often the structure and language of the statute will supply a clue. If the legislature enacts into statute law a common law concept, as Congress did when it forbade agreements in "restraint of trade" in the Sherman Act, that is a clue that the courts are to interpret the statute with the freedom with which they would construe and apply a common law principle—in which event the values of the framers may not be controlling after all.

The opposite extreme is a statute that sets out its requirements with some specificity, especially against a background of dissatisfaction with judicial handling of the same subject under a previous statute or the common law (much federal labor and regulatory legislation is of this character). Here it is probable that the legislature does not want the courts to paint with a broad brush in adapting the legislation to the unforeseeable future. The Constitution contains several such provisions—for example, the provision that the President must be thirty-five years old. This provision does not invite construction; it does not invite a court to recast the provision so that it reads, "the President must be either thirty-five or mature." There is nothing the court could point to that would justify such an interpretation as consistent with the framers' intent. It is not that the words are plain; it is that the words, read in context as words must always be read in order to yield meaning, do not authorize any interpretation except the obvious one.

The approach I have sketched—a word used advisedly—in this part of the paper has obvious affinities with the "attribution of purpose" approach of Hart and Sacks,[62] the antecedents of which go back almost 400 years.[63] But I should like to stress one difference between my approach and theirs. They say that in construing a statute a court "should assume, unless the contrary unmistakably appears, that the legislature was made up of reasonable persons pursuing reasonable purposes reasonably." [64] Coupled with their earlier statement that in trying to divine the legislative will the court should ignore "short-run currents of political expedience," Hart and Sacks appear to be suggesting that the judge should ignore interest groups, popular ignorance and prejudices, and other things that deflect legislators from the single-minded pursuit of the public interest as the judge would conceive it. But to ignore these things runs the risk of attributing to legislation not the purposes reasonably inferable from the legislation itself, but the judge's own conceptions of the public interest. Hart and Sacks were

---

61. *See, e.g.,* Racketeer Influenced and Corrupt Organizations Act (RICO) § 904(a), *printed at* 18 U.S.C. § 1961 note (1976).

62. See 2 H. Hart & A. Sacks. The Legal Process, Basic Problems in the Making and Application of Law 1413–17.

63. See Heydon's Case, 76 Eng.Rep. 637, 638 (Ex. 1584). 2 H. Hart & A. Sacks, *supra* note 62 at 1415.

64. *Id.* at 1414.

writing in the wake of the New Deal, when the legislative process was widely regarded as progressive and public spirited. There is less agreement today that the motives behind most legislation are benign. That should be of no significance to the judge except to make him wary about too easily assuming a congruence between his concept of the public interest and the latent purposes of the statutes he is called on to interpret. He must not automatically assume that the legislators had the same purpose that he thinks he would have had if he had been in their shoes.

A related characteristic of the passages I have quoted from Hart and Sacks is a reluctance to recognize that many statutes are the product of compromise between opposing groups and that a compromise is quite likely not to embody a single consistent purpose. Of course there are difficulties for the judge, limited as he is to the formal materials of the legislative process—the statutory text, committee reports, hearings, floor debates, earlier bills, and so forth—in identifying compromise. A court should not just assume that a statute's apparent purpose is not its real purpose. But where the lines of compromise are discernible, the judge's duty is to follow them,[66] to implement not the purposes of one group of legislators, but the compromise itself.[67]

But what if the lines of compromise are not clear? More fundamentally, what if the judge's scrupulous search for the legislative will turns up nothing? There are of course such cases, and they have to be decided some way. It is inevitable, and therefore legitimate, for the judge in such a case to be moved by considerations that cannot be referred back to legislative purpose. These might be considerations of judicial administrability—what interpretation of the statute will provide greater predictability, require less judicial factfinding, and otherwise reduce the cost and frequency of litigation under the statute—or considerations drawn from some broadly based conception of the public interest. It is always possible, of course, to refer these considerations back to Congress—to say that Congress would have wanted the courts, in cases where they could not figure out what interpretation would advance the substantive objectives of the statute, to adopt the "better" one, or to say à la Hart and Sacks that congressmen ought to be presumed reasonable until shown otherwise. But these methods of imputing congressional intent are artificial; and as I argued earlier, it is not healthy for the judge to conceal from himself that he is being creative when he is, as sometimes he has to be even when applying statutes.

I want to end by contrasting my suggested approach with the positions in the contemporary debate over interpretation, a debate I have thus far ignored. The debate is mostly over constitutional rather than

66. *See, e.g.,* NLRB v. Rockaway News Supply Co., 197 F.2d 111, 115–16 (2d Cir. 1952) (Clark, J., dissenting), *aff'd on other grounds,* 345 U.S. 71 (1953).

67. Compare United States v. Armour & Co., 402 U.S. 673, 681–83 (1971), where the Court interpreted the Meat Packers Consent Decree of 1920 not with reference to the intent of the parties to the decree but rather with reference to the compromise between the parties embodied in the decree.

statutory interpretation, but Professor Calabresi's recent book carries it into the statutory arena.[68] He argues that courts ought to be given, and maybe ought to take without being given, the power to update statutes; he flirts with judicial "misreading" of statutes as a second-best route to this end,[69] remarks that "[t]he limits of honest interpretation are too constricting," [70] and expresses at least qualified approval of judicial amendment of statutes where legislative amendment is blocked by interest-group pressures.[71]

Professor Calabresi has done us a service by bringing out into the open what are after all the secret thoughts not only of many modern legal academics but of some modern judges. Since one extreme begets another he has also helped us understand why there is today a revival of "strict constructionism,".

But contrary to a widespread impression, strict—that is, narrow—construction, if perhaps a useful antidote to the school of no construction, is not a formula for ensuring fidelity to legislative intent. It is almost the opposite. It is the lineal descendant of the canon that statutes in derogation of the common law are to be strictly construed and, like that canon, was used in nineteenth-century England to emasculate social welfare legislation.[73]

To construe a statute strictly is to limit its scope and its life span—to make Congress work twice as hard to produce the same effect.[74] The letter killeth but the spirit giveth life.

There is a story of a Vermont justice of the peace before whom a suit was brought by one farmer against another for breaking a churn. The justice took time to consider, and then said that he had looked through the statutes and could find nothing about churns, and gave judgment to the defendant.[75]

It is not an accident that most "loose constructionists" are political liberals and most "strict constructionists" are political conservatives. The former think that modern legislation does not go far enough, the latter that it goes too far. Each school has developed interpretive techniques appropriate to its political ends. But as I said earlier, I know

68. G. Calabresi, A Common Law for the Age of Statutes (1982).

69. *Id.* at 34.

70. *Id.* at 38.

71. *Id.* at 34.

73. *See* Jones, *Should Judges be Politicians? The English Experience,* 57 Ind.L.J. 211, 213 (1982).

74. *See* Easterbrook, *Statutes' Domains,* 50 U.Chi.L.Rev. 533, 548–49 (1983), where a theory of strict construction is explicitly defended as a limitation on the power of legislatures to legislate with future effect.

In speaking of the effect of strict construction on the effectiveness of the legislative process, I emphasize that I am speaking only of strict construction of statutes. If one construes the Constitution strictly, one will reduce the effectiveness of constitutional enactments; but of course one will increase the effectiveness of the legislative process by reducing the limitations that the Constitution places on that process. This is easily seen by thinking back to the discussion of the canon that statutes should be interpreted wherever possible to avoid being held unconstitutional. To construe the Constitution narrowly and statutes broadly would maximize the effectiveness of that process. But the analysis of these and other interesting permutations must await another day.

75. Holmes, *The Path of the Law,* 10 Harv.L.Rev. 457, 474–75 (1897).

of no principled, nonpolitical basis for a court to adopt the view that Congress is legislating too much and ought therefore to be reined in by having its statutes construed strictly. I add now that such a view would be a form of judicial activism because it would cut down the power of the legislative branch; and at this moment in history, we do not need more judicial activism.

———

FISHGOLD v. SULLIVAN DRYDOCK & REPAIR CORP.

United States Court of Appeals, Second Circuit, 1946.
154 F.2d 785.

Before L. HAND, CHASE, and FRANK, CIRCUIT JUDGES.

Local 13 of the Industrial Union of Marine and Shipbuilding Workers of America appeals from a judgment awarding damages to the plaintiff for his loss of wages because of two lay-offs by his employer, the Sullivan Drydock and Repair Corporation, against which alone the action was brought. The union intervened, and charged itself with the defence; the United States, the Railway Labor Executives Association and the Congress of Industrial Organizations have filed briefs, as amici. The appeal raises only the proper interpretation of subdivision (b) and (c) of Sec. 8 of the Selective Training and Service Act of 1940, as amended in 1944 (Sec. 308(b) and Sec. 308(c)).

When we consider the situation at the time that the Act was passed—September, 1940—it is extremely improbable that Congress should have meant any broader privilege than as we are measuring it. It is true that the nation had become deeply disturbed at its defenseless position, and had begun to make ready; but it was not at war, and the issue still hung in the balance whether it ever would be at war. If we carry ourselves back to that summer and autumn, we shall recall that the presidential campaigns of both parties avoided commitment upon that question, and that each candidate particularly insisted that no troops should be sent overseas. The original act limited service to one year, and it was most improbable that within that time we should be called upon to fight upon our own soil; as indeed the event proved, for we were still at peace in September, 1941. Congress was calling young men to the colors to give them an adequate preparation for our defence, but with no forecast of the appalling experiences which they were later to undergo. Against that background it is not likely that a proposal would then have been accepted which gave industrial priority, regardless of their length of employment, to unmarried men—for the most part under thirty—over men in the thirties, forties or fifties, who had wives and children dependent upon them. Today, in the light of what has happened, the privilege then granted has happened, the privilege then granted may appear an altogether inadequate equivalent for their services; but we have not to decide what is now proper; we are to reconstruct, as best we may, what was the purpose of Congress when it used the words in which Sec. 8(b) and Sec. 8(c) were cast.

NOTE

The *Fishgold* case illustrates Judge Posner's reference to "values and attitudes, so far as they are known today, of the period in which the legislation was enacted." In emphasizing the same point, other judges and commentators remind us that to interpret words correctly we should use the dictionary definitions in use at the time of legislative enactment.

ST. FRANCIS COLLEGE v. AL–KHAZAJI (MAJID GHADEN)

Supreme Court of the United States, 1987.
481 U.S. 604, 107 S.Ct. 2022, 95 L.Ed.2d 582.

JUSTICE WHITE delivered the opinion of the Court.

Section 1981 provides:

"All persons within the jurisdiction of the United States shall have the same right in every State and Territory to make and enforce contracts, to sue, be parties, give evidence, and to the full and equal benefit of all laws and proceedings for the security of persons and property as is enjoyed by white citizens, and shall be subject to like punishment, pains, penalties, taxes, licenses, and exactions of every kind, and to no other."

Although § 1981 does not itself use the word "race," the Court has construed the section to forbid all "racial" discrimination in the making of private as well as public contracts. Runyon v. McCrary, 427 U.S. 160, 168, 174–175 (1976). Petitioner college, although a private institution, was therefore subject to this statutory command. There is no disagreement among the parties on these propositions. The issue is whether respondent has alleged *racial* discrimination within the meaning of § 1981.

Petitioners contend that respondent is a Caucasian and cannot allege the kind of discrimination § 1981 forbids. Concededly, McDonald v. Santa Fe Trail Transportation Co., 427 U.S. 273 (1976), held that white persons could maintain a § 1981 suit; but that suit involved alleged discrimination against a white person in favor of a black, and petitioner submits that the section does not encompass claims of discrimination by one Caucasian against another. We are quite sure that the Court of Appeals properly rejected this position.

Petitioner's submission rests on the assumption that all those who might be deemed Caucasians today were thought to be of the same race when § 1981 became law in the 19th century; and it may be that a variety of ethnic groups, including Arabs, are now considered to be within the Caucasian race. The understanding of "race" in the 19th century, however, was different. Plainly, all those who might be deemed Caucasian today were not thought to be of the same race at the time § 1981 became law.

In the middle years of the 19th century, dictionaries commonly referred to race as a "continued series of descendants from a parent who is called the *stock*," N. Webster, An American Dictionary of the English Language 666 (New York 1830) (emphasis in original), "[t]he lineage of a family," 2 N. Webster, A Dictionary of the English Language 411 (New Haven 1841), or "descendants of a common ancestor," J. Donald, Chambers' Etymological Dictionary of the English Language 415 (London 1871). The 1887 edition of Webster's expanded the definition somewhat: "The descendants of a common ancestor; a family, tribe, people or nation, believed or presumed to belong to the same stock." N. Webster, Dictionary of the English Language 589 (W. Wheeler ed. 1887). It was not until the 20th century that dictionaries began referring to the Caucasian, Mongolian, and Negro races, 8 The Century Dictionary and Cyclopedia 4926 (1911), or to race as involving divisions of mankind based upon different physical characteristics. Webster's Collegiate Dictionary 794 (3d ed. 1916). Even so, modern dictionaries still include among the definitions of race "a family, tribe, people, or nation belonging to the same stock." Webster's Third New International Dictionary 1870 (1971); Webster's Ninth New Collegiate Dictionary 969 (1986).

Encyclopedias of the 19th century also described race in terms of ethnic groups, which is a narrower concept of race than petitioners urge. Encyclopedia Americana in 1858, for example, referred to various races such as Finns, vol. 5, p. 123, gypsies, 6 *id.*, at 123, Basques, 1 *id.*, at 602, and Hebrews, 6 *id.*, at 209. The 1863 version of the New American Cyclopaedia divided the Arabs into a number of subsidiary races, vol. 1, p. 739; represented the Hebrews as of the Semitic race, 9 *id.*, at 27, and identified numerous other groups as constituting races, including Swedes, 15 *id.*, at 216, Norwegians, 12 *id.*, at 410, Germans, 8 *id.*, at 200, Greeks, 8 *id.*, at 438, Finns, 7 *id.*, at 513, Italians, 9 *id.*, at 644–645 (referring to mixture of different races), Spanish, 14 *id.*, at 804, Mongolians, 11 *id.*, at 651, Russians, 14 *id.*, at 226, and the like. The Ninth edition of the Encyclopedia Britannica also referred to Arabs, vol. 2, p. 245 (1878), Jews, 13 *id.*, at 685 (1881), and other ethnic groups such as Germans, 10 *id.*, at 473 (1879), Hungarians, 12 *id.*, at 365 (1880), and Greeks, 11 *id.*, at 83 (1880), as separate races.

These dictionary and encyclopedic sources are somewhat diverse, but it is clear that they do not support the claim that for the purposes of § 1981, Arabs, Englishmen, Germans, and certain other ethnic groups are to be considered a single race. We would expect the legislative history of § 1981, which the Court held in Runyon v. McCrary had its source in the Civil Rights Act of 1866, 14 Stat. 27, as well as the Voting Rights Act of 1870, 16 Stat. 140, 144, to reflect this common understanding, which it surely does. The debates are replete with references to the Scandinavian races, Cong. Globe, 39th Cong., 1st Sess., 499 (1866) (remarks of Sen. Cowan), as well as the Chinese, *id.*, at 523 (remarks of

Sen. Davis), Latin, *id.*, at 238 (remarks of Rep. Kasson during debate of home rule for the District of Columbia), Spanish, *id.*, at 251 (remarks of Sen. Davis during debate of District of Columbia suffrage), and Anglo–Saxon races, *id.*, at 542 (remarks of Rep. Dawson). Jews, *ibid.*, Mexicans, see *ibid.* (remarks of Rep. Dawson), blacks, *passim*, and Mongolians, *id.*, at 498 (remarks of Sen. Cowan), were similarly categorized. Gypsies were referred to as a race. *Ibid.* (remarks of Sen. Cowan). Likewise, the Germans:

> "Who will say that Ohio can pass a law enacting that no man of the German race ... shall ever own any property in Ohio, or shall ever make a contract in Ohio, or ever inherit property in Ohio, or ever come into Ohio to live, or even to work? If Ohio may pass such a law, and exclude a German citizen ... because he is of the German nationality or race, then may every other State do so." *Id.*, at 1294 (remarks of Sen. Shellabarger).

There was a reference to the Caucasian race, but it appears to have been referring to people of European ancestry. *Id.*, at 523 (remarks of Sen. Davis).

The history of the 1870 Act reflects similar understanding of what groups Congress intended to protect from intentional discrimination. It is clear, for example, that the civil rights sections of the 1870 Act provided protection for immigrant groups such as the Chinese. This view was expressed in the Senate. Cong. Globe, 41st Cong., 2d Sess., 1536, 3658, 3808 (1870). In the House, Representative Bingham described § 16 of the Act, part of the authority for § 1981, as declaring "that the States shall not hereafter discriminate against the immigrant from China and in favor of the immigrant from Prussia, nor against the immigrant from France and in favor of the immigrant from Ireland." *Id.*, at 3871.

Based on the history of § 1981, we have little trouble in concluding that Congress intended to protect from discrimination identifiable classes of persons who are subjected to intentional discrimination solely because of their ancestry or ethnic characteristics. Such discrimination is racial discrimination that Congress intended § 1981 to forbid, whether or not it would be classified as racial in terms of modern scientific theory.

NOTE

St. Francis College exemplifies a court's failure to start at the beginning point of statutory construction: the language of the statute. The statute states that all persons shall have the rights "enjoyed by white citizens." The statute does not mention race, as conceded by the Court, yet the entire opinion describes the dictionary meaning of "race" and various views of the word in place at the time of the adoption of the Ku Klux Klan Acts of which Section 1981 was part. The Pulitzer-prize winning historian Arthur M. Schlesinger, Jr. has noted:

The word *race* as used in the eighteenth and nineteenth centuries meant what we mean by nationality today; thus people spoke of "the English race," "the German race," and so on.

The Disuniting of America 12 (1991).

Consider the logical validity of a judicial opinion that intermingles the 1987 meaning of the word with a completely different meaning used in the "middle of the nineteenth century." Can it seriously be argued that the members of the 1866 Congress considered the protection of any group other than African–Americans when it enacted the Ku Klux Klan Acts?

Putting aside the nineteenth century dictionaries, in the formulation of Judge Posner, "what were the values and attitudes, so far as they are known today, of the period in which the legislation was enacted?"

———

SHAARE TEFILA CONGREGATION v. COBB

Supreme Court of the United States, 1987.
481 U.S. 615, 107 S.Ct. 2019, 95 L.Ed.2d 594.

JUSTICE WHITE delivered the opinion of the Court.

On November 2, 1982, the outside walls of the synagogue of the Shaare Tefila Congregation in Silver Spring, Maryland, were sprayed with red and black paint and with large anti-Semitic slogans, phrases, and symbols. A few months later, the Congregation and some individual members brought this suit in the Federal District Court, alleging that defendants' desecration of the synagogue had violated 42 U.S.C. §§ 1981, 1982, 1985(3) and the Maryland common law of trespass, nuisance, and intentional infliction of emotional distress.

Section 1982 guarantees all citizens of the United States, "the same right ... as is enjoyed by white citizens ... to inherit, purchase, lease, sell, hold, and convey real and personal property." The section forbids both official and private racially discriminatory interference with property rights, Jones v. Alfred H. Mayer Co., 392 U.S. 409 (1968). Petitioners' allegation was that they were deprived of the right to hold property in violation of § 1982 because the defendants were motivated by racial prejudice.

We agree with petitioners, however, that the Court of Appeals erred in holding that Jews cannot state a § 1982 claim against other white defendants. That view rested on the notion that because Jews today are not thought to be members of a separate race, they cannot make out a claim of racial discrimination within the meaning of § 1982. That construction of the section we have today rejected in Saint Francis College v. Al–Khazraji, ante. Our opinion in that case observed that definitions of race when § 1982 was passed were not the same as they are today, and concluded that the section was "intended to protect from discrimination identifiable classes of persons who are subjected to intentional discrimination solely because of their ancestry or ethnic characteristics."   As *Saint Francis* makes clear, the question before us is not whether Jews are considered to be a separate race by today's standards, but whether, at the time § 1982 was adopted, Jews constituted a group of people that Congress intended to protect.   It is evident from the legislative history of the section reviewed in *Saint Francis College,* a review that we need not repeat here, that Jews and Arabs were among the peoples then considered to be distinct races and hence within the protection of the statute.   Jews are not foreclosed from stating a cause of action against other members of what today is considered to be part of the Caucasian race.

The judgment of the Court of Appeals is therefore reversed, and the case is remanded for further proceedings consistent with this opinion.

NOTE

What methodology was used by the Court in interpreting the statute at issue?   As its beginning point, did the Court start with the language of the statute?   Does Section 1982 use the word "race"?   As a matter of statutory interpretation, is not the precise reasoning of this case: American members of the Jewish faith have "the same right . . . as is enjoyed by white citizens.   42 U.S.C.A. § 1982"?   Do you have any problem with the necessary factual predicate of the reasoning that American Jews are not "white citizens" but are entitled to the "same right[s] . . . as [are] enjoyed by white citizens"?

LEARNED HAND, A PERSONAL CONFESSION *

I have often said to myself: "What do you mean by interpreting?" Here are the words used; but they have all kinds of fringes, as James used to call it.   The occasion that has arisen wasn't actually provided for; the "terms" are inevitably equivocal and ambiguous.   What do you mean by "what they were intended for"?   Perhaps you won't agree, but the best I can make of it is that, as far as you can, you are to try to put yourself—imaginatively to project yourself—into the position (resuscitate, you might say) of the authors of those words at the time they uttered them.   What would they have said had they been faced with this present occasion?   Well, I know people who say that this is a fantastic unreality, yet certainly in the case of statutes (I am not going to get into the Constitution) you really must ask what they would have said.   There are, indeed, occasions when a statute which I like to call an open-ended statute will say to you: "You do what you think best about that," just as we do with juries in the case of negligence.   We say to them: "What do

* Continuing Legal Education for Professional Competence and Responsibility, the Report on the Arden House Conference, December 16–19, 1958, pp. 116–23.   Copyright © 1959.   Reprinted by permission of the American Law Institute.

you think is fair? What do you think is reasonable?" We call it a question of fact, but we have to close our eyes when we say it, for obviously it isn't. But in other cases, when the legislators have not handed over the authority to us to make our own choices, we have to assume that they did mean to impose some choice of their own.

As time goes on we shall be faced more and more with necessity for this kind of determination, for I think you will agree that, if you look forward fifty years or more, we are going into an era of increasing detailed regulation. In our court we recently happened to have a case before us about the Farm Excess Quota Act. When I read the statute I had to go over it over and over; the words danced before me, and I didn't know what they meant; and, yet, although everything was detailed, there remained a measure of the kind of interpretation I have been speaking of. Somehow we have to find out what are the implications of these congeries of words.

But that isn't all. What are you to do when the meaning remains uncertain? Then, if the situation is not too bad, we say that we make a "just" interpretation. Remember what Justice Holmes said about "justice." I don't know what you think about him, but on the whole he was to me the master craftsman certainly of our time; and he said: "I hate justice," which he didn't quite mean. What he did mean was this. I remember once I was with him; it was a Saturday when the Court was to confer. It was before we had a motor car, and we jogged along in an old coupé. When we got down to the Capitol, I wanted to provoke a response, so as he walked off, I said to him: "Well, sir, goodbye. Do justice!" He turned quite sharply and he said: "Come here. Come here." I answered: "Oh, I know, I know." He replied: "That is not my job. My job is to play the game according to the rules." I have never forgotten that. I have tried to follow, though oftentimes I found that I didn't know what the rules were. Ulpian, as you remember, said that justice is to insure to "each one his own." Well, what is "his own"? How are you going to tell what "his own" is? Does anybody know? As they say in English, "My submission, my Lord, is that you can't measure values." Values are incommensurables. You can get a solution only by a compromise, or call it what you will. It must be one that people won't complain of too much; but you cannot expect any more objective measure.

WILLIAM N. ESKRIDGE, JR. AND PHILIP P. FRICKEY, STATUTORY INTERPRETATION AS PRACTICAL REASONING *

Our model holds that an interpreter will look at a broad range of evidence—text, historical evidence, and the text's evolution—and thus form a preliminary view of the statute. The interpreter then develops

* 42 Stanford L.Rev. 321, 383–384, 352 (1990) Reprinted by permission.

that preliminary view by testing various possible interpretations against the multiple criteria of fidelity to the text, historical accuracy, and conformity to contemporary circumstances and values. Each criterion is relevant, yet none necessarily trumps the others. Thus while an apparently clear text, for example, will create insuperable doubts for a contrary interpretation if the other evidence reinforces it (*Griffin*), an apparently clear text may yield if other considerations cut against it (*Bob Jones* and *Weber*). As the interpreter comes to accept an interpretation (perhaps a confirmation of her preliminary view), she considers a congeries of supporting arguments, which may buttress her view much "like the legs of a chair and unlike the links of a chain."

We do believe that the Court's approach to resolving issues of statutory interpretation is largely grounded in practical reasoning, and thus that the Court's technique is consistent with other twentieth century trends, such as pragmatism. To be sure, the Court could substantially improve its performance if it more candidly reflected this reasoning process in its opinions. The Court ought to acknowledge that, standing alone, textualist and archeological approaches to statutory interpretation are overly simplistic techniques that provide only a chimera of the legitimacy the Court seeks. In contrast, by bringing all the relevant factors and all of our problem-solving skills to bear on difficult questions of statutory interpretation through deliberation and candor. The legitimation is by no means ironclad, and in particular instances even sensitive efforts in practical reasoning may misfire. But, a candid explication of the reasoning process promises to narrow and highlight the elements in dispute and fosters a deliberative dialogue about statutory meaning in a concrete circumstance.

In the last analysis, statutory interpretation is neither mechanical foundationalism nor unbounded, unpredictable, and unprincipled decisionmaking. It is, therefore, fundamentally similar to judicial lawmaking in the areas of constitutional law and common law. In each area of judicial decisionmaking, deliberation and candor are necessary but not sufficient conditions for legitimating outcomes. For, as Richard Bernstein has noted, practical reasoning "presuppose[s] the existence of a sense of community and solidarity." Even many of those who agree with us that dialogical practical reason might perform a substantial legitimating role may question whether there is an American legal interpretive community in which such a communal dialogue may flourish, or whether the interpretive community should be limited to the legal community. We find much to commend about this point of view, and our descriptive model offers a framework for making this criticism. That is, if statutory interpretation is a fusion of horizons—those of the past text and the present interpreter—it makes a difference who the interpreter is. If judges are inevitably making political choices, their own political preunderstandings will make a difference in at least some cases, especially those where there is no political consensus.

One answer to this challenge that hermeneutics and modern pragmatism suggest is the potentially reconstructive nature of interpretation.

Even without apparent consensus in society or in the legal community, the interpreter can often create some kind of agreement in the context of the narrow case, and through the case enlighten attitudes in the larger community.

We have usually been impressed with the ability of most Justices to rise above their personal prejudgments. Legislative history, precedent, reasoned commentary, and other constraining factors do not completely close off avenues of judicial discretion, but the Justices do seem to learn from those links between past and present and often are able to apply those lessons to solve concrete cases in narrow, practical ways. In turn, these decisions teach the legal interpretive community something about the dynamic nature of statutes and the process of interpretation itself. That the dialogue between Court and community is imperfect is not so much a reason to reject the dialogic enterprise as it is to describe its shortcomings and expand its possibilities.

NOTE

Professors Eskridge and Frickey describe Griffin v. Oceanic Contractors, Inc., *ante* at 222, as a case "where an apparently clear text will create insuperable doubts for a contrary interpretation if other evidence reinforces it." What are these commentators talking about? They also describe Bob Jones University v. United States, *post* at 273, and United Steelworkers v. Weber, *ante* at 204, as examples where "an apparently clear text may yield if other considerations cut against it". How does one decide when other considerations "cut against" the text? Consider again Professor Leflar, *ante* at 244, and Judge Keeton, *ante* at 244, for assistance.

———

GUIDO CALABRESI, THE ROLE OF THE COURTS IN AN AGE OF STATUTES *

What, then, is the common law function to be exercised by courts today? *It is no more and no less than the critical task of deciding when a retentionist or a revisionist bias is appropriately applied to an existing statutory or common law rule.* It is the judgmental function (which cannot successfully be accomplished by sunset laws or automatic updatings) of deciding when a rule has come to be sufficiently out of phase with the whole legal framework so that, whatever its age, it can only stand if a current majoritarian or representative body reaffirms it. It is to be the allocator of that burden of inertia which our system of separation of powers and checks and balances mandates. It is to assign the task of overcoming inertia to that interest, whose desires do not conform with the fabric of the law, and hence whose wishes can only be recognized if current and clear majoritarian support exists for them. It

* G. Calabresi, A Common Law for the Age of Statutes 164–166 (1982).

is this task (so like that exercised by courts in updating the common law) which desperately needs doing in a checked and balanced statutory world like ours, and it can be done by courts using traditional judicial methods and modes of reasoning.

The task can be accomplished by courts regardless of whether they are capable of carrying out the updating on their own by promulgating new rules or whether they must use techniques designed to influence the legislative and even the administrative agendas, and induce these bodies to act and to write new, or reaffirm old, rules. It can be achieved without in any way depriving popular or representative bodies of their last say, of their right to assert and impose new distinctions that do not fit the fabric of the law and that do not, merely on this account, violate constitutional guarantees. Indeed, it encourages the legislatures to act responsibly to affirm precisely such distinctions when, despite the fact that in the courts' judgments they do not fit in the legal landscape, the distinctions are nonetheless wanted. As a result, this judicial function—like its common law equivalent—can ask for consistency among what scholars call policies as well as among principles. Or it can ask for firm, current majoritarian support for such "inconsistent" policies, rather than allowing them to remain in force simply on the basis of an inappropriate retentionist bias. It can do all this without confusing this job with that of constitutional adjudication which our system also assigns to the courts, and without ignoring the relevance that must be given to the fact that a rule—even if in the end it is constitutionally valid—is entitled to little or no retentionist bias when it comes close to violating constitutional guarantees.

In carrying out this task the courts would, as I have said, be doing little different from what they have traditionally done. Their main job would still be to give us continuity and change by applying the great vague principle of treating like cases alike. They would exercise the same capacity to define what are "like" cases at different levels of generality, in terms of different sources of law (statutory, jurisprudential, case, scholarly comment) and in response to technological, societal, and even ideological changes. Some courts would presumably be aggressive and even willful in their use of such data: others would not. But that has always been the case with the common law function, and whether the aggressive or the passive mode is preferable is not really germane to this book. What is relevant is that in carrying out this task, passively or actively according to their own judicial philosophies, the courts would be establishing a modern version of the traditional American judicial-legislative balance.

To establish such a modern balance, two principal changes would be needed. First, the courts would not be bound to declare or promulgate the new in order to find that the old fails to fit. To some extent that has always been the case, for often an old rule was destroyed at common law while the new one was only hinted at by the courts. In a statutory world, that may occasionally be appropriate. Often, however, the appropriate technique will be to enter into a dialogue, to ask, cajole, or force another body (usually the legislature but sometimes the agencies) to define the new rule or reaffirm the old. Second, and this is the change with which I have been most concerned, the judicial common law would attach to statutory rules that are out of phase just as much as to common law precedents or doctrines. This last may be less of an innovation than it seems, for courts through subterfuges, fictions, and willful use of inappropriate doctrines have already been anything but reluctant to deal with obsolete statutes.

The first change may, in fact, be more significant because it entails a separation of functions that were united in the old common law judicial roles. The role of maker of new law was intimately tied to the job of deciding when the old rule no longer deserved the benefit of a retentionist bias. To abandon the old the courts had to be willing at least to start making the new. The same reasons that have made our system statutory tend to make the lawmaking role much harder for courts to perform. This fact (rather than the existence of statutes as such) calls for new judicial techniques designed to bring forth legislative and administrative revisions in old rules, and would call for them whether the old rules are statutory or court-made. It in no way diminishes the capacity of courts to tell when old rules are out of phase, however. And the same fact, since it has led to the existence of a multitude of statutes, makes the need to employ this judicial capacity all the greater if we are to preserve a system that can, at the same time, give us continuity and change.

If the courts and legislatures openly accept this common law function as appropriate to the age of statutes, they will be recognizing some significant changes in our legal-political system. But they will only be recognizing the changes, not making them. The statutorification and the concomitant tendency toward obsolescence of American law have already occurred. So have the judicial reactions to these changes. What remains to be done is only the taking of the last step, the seeing of the world as it is, and the giving of a name to what is already happening in indirect and often careless ways. But such a last step is by no means insignificant, and also by no means necessarily desirable. Candor gives benefits, but it surely entails risks. Are they justified?

ORE IN PUBLISHED OPINIONS

Read the following cases and ascertain the methodology(ies) embraced by the courts. Are the courts concerned with the intent of the legislature? The purpose of the statute? Are they confining themselves to the plain meaning of the text? Does their approach differ where a literal reading would lead to absurd results? Finally, can you identify any of the dynamic theories in the cases that follow?

BOSTON SAND & GRAVEL CO. v. UNITED STATES

Supreme Court of the United States, 1928.
278 U.S. 41, 49 S.Ct. 52, 73 L.Ed. 170.

Mr. Justice Holmes delivered the opinion of the Court.

This is a libel in admiralty brought by the petitioner to recover for damages done to its steam lighter *Cornelia* by a collision with the United States destroyer *Bell*. It is brought against the United States by authority of a special Act of May 15, 1922, c. 192, 42 Stat. 1590. There has been a trial in which both vessels ultimately were found to have been in fault and it was ordered that the damages should be divided. Thereafter the damages were ascertained and the petitioner sought to be allowed interest upon its share. (There was no cross libel.) The Circuit Court of Appeals, going on the words of the statute, parallel legislation, and the general understanding with regard to the United States, held that no interest could be allowed.

The material words of the Act are that the District Court "shall have jurisdiction to hear and determine the whole controversy and to enter a judgment or decree for the amount of the legal damages sustained by reason of said collision, if any shall be found to be due either for or against the United States, upon the same principle and measure of liability with costs as in like cases in admiralty between private parties with the same rights of appeal." On a hasty reading one might be led to believe that Congress had put the United States on the footing of a private person in all respects. But we are of opinion that a scrutiny leads to a different result. It is at least possible that the words fixing the extent of the Government's liability were carefully chosen, and we are of opinion that they were.

Mr. Justice Sutherland, dissenting.

By the statute under consideration the United States is made liable for "legal damages" upon the same principle and measure of liability as in like cases between private parties. The authorities above reviewed put the meaning of these words beyond all reasonable doubt; and it is not permissible to attempt to vary that meaning by construction. The rule announced by Chief Justice Marshall in United States v. Wiltberger, 5 Wheat. 76, 95–96—"Where there is no ambiguity in the words, there is no room for construction. The case must be a strong one indeed, which would justify a court in departing from the plain meaning of words, especially in a penal act, in search of an intention which the words themselves did not suggest."—has, ever since, been followed by this Court.

In Hamilton v. Rathbone, 175 U.S. 414, 419, it is said: "The general rule is perfectly well settled that, where a statute is of doubtful meaning and susceptible upon its face of two constructions, the court may look into prior and contemporaneous acts, the reasons which induced the act in question, the mischiefs intended to be remedied, the extraneous circumstances, and the purpose intended to be accomplished by it, to determine its proper construction. But where the act is clear upon its face, and when standing alone it is fairly susceptible of but one construction, that construction must be given to it." (Citing cases.)

And the Court added (p. 421): "Indeed, the cases are so numerous in this court to the effect that the province of construction lies wholly within the domain of ambiguity, that an extended review of them is quite unnecessary. The whole doctrine applicable to the subject may be summed up in the single observation that prior acts may be resorted to, to *solve,* but not to *create* an ambiguity."

It was further said that if the section of law there under consideration were an original act there would be no room for construction, and that only by calling in the aid of a prior act was it possible to throw a doubt upon its proper interpretation.

The rule was tersely stated in United States v. Hartwell, 6 Wall. 385, 396: "If the language be clear it is conclusive. There can be no construction where there is nothing to construe."

This is also the recognized rule of the English courts. In one of the English decisions Lord Denman said the court was bound to look to the language employed and construe it in its natural and obvious sense, even though that was to give the words of the act an effect probably never contemplated by those who obtained the act and very probably not intended by the legislature which enacted it.

The enforcement of the statute according to its plain terms results in no absurdity or injustice, for, as this Court recently said, in holding the United States liable for damages including interest in a collision case where the Government had come into court to assert a claim on its own behalf: "The absence of legal liability in a case where but for its sovereignty it would be liable does not destroy the justice of the claim against it." United States v. The Thekla, 266 U.S. 328, 340.

To refuse interest in this case, in my opinion, is completely to change the clear meaning of the words employed by Congress by invoking the aid of extrinsic circumstances to import into the statute an ambiguity which otherwise does not exist and thereby to set at naught the prior decisions of this Court and long established canons of statutory construction.

CHURCH OF THE HOLY TRINITY v. UNITED STATES

Supreme Court of the United States, 1892.
143 U.S. 457, 12 S.Ct. 511, 36 L.Ed. 226.

Mr. Justice Brewer delivered the opinion of the court.

Plaintiff in error is a corporation duly organized and incorporated as a religious society under the laws of the state of New York. E. Walpole

Warren was, prior to September, 1887, an alien residing in England. In that month the plaintiff in error made a contract with him, by which he was to remove to the city of New York, and enter into its service as rector and pastor; and, in pursuance of such contract, Warren did so remove and enter upon such service. It is claimed by the United States that this contract on the part of the plaintiff in error was forbidden by chapter 164, 23 St. p. 332; and an action was commenced to recover the penalty prescribed by that act. The circuit court held that the contract was within the prohibition of the statute, and rendered judgment accordingly, and the single question presented for our determination is whether it erred in that conclusion.

The first section describes the act forbidden, and is in these words:

"Be it enacted by the senate and house of representatives of the United States of America, in congress assembled, that from and after the passage of this act it shall be unlawful for any person, company, partnership, or corporation, in any manner whatsoever, to prepay the transportation, or in any way assist or encourage the importation or migration, of any alien or aliens, any foreigner or foreigners, into the United States, its territories, or the District of Columbia, under contract or agreement, parol or special, express or implied, made previous to the importation or migration of such alien or aliens, foreigner or foreigners, to perform labor or service of any kind in the United States, its territories, or the District of Columbia."

It must be conceded that the act of the corporation is within the letter of this section, for the relation of rector to his church is one of service, and implies labor on the one side with compensation on the other. Not only are the general words "labor" and "service" both used, but also, as it were to guard against any narrow interpretation and emphasize a breadth of meaning, to them is added "of any kind;" and, further, as noticed by the circuit judge in his opinion, the fifth section, which makes specific exceptions, among them professional actors, artists, lecturers, singers, and domestic servants, strengthens the idea that every other kind of labor and service was intended to be reached by the first section. While there is great force to this reasoning, we cannot think congress intended to denounce with penalties a transaction like that in the present case. It is a familiar rule that a thing may be within the letter of the statute and yet not within the statute, because not within its spirit nor within the intention of its makers. This has been often asserted, and the Reports are full of cases illustrating its application. This is not the substitution of the will of the judge for that of the legislator; for frequently words of general meaning are used in a statute, words broad enough to include an act in question, and yet a consideration of the whole legislation, or of the circumstances surrounding its enactment, or of the absurd results which follow from giving such broad meaning to the words, makes it unreasonable to believe that the legislator intended to include the particular act. As said in Stradling v. Morgan, Plow. 205: "From which cases it appears that the sages of the law heretofore have construed statutes quite contrary to the letter in some appearance, and those statutes which comprehend all things in the letter they have expounded to extend to but some things, and those which generally prohibit all people from doing such an act they have interpreted to permit some people to do it, and those which include every person in the letter they have adjudged to reach to some persons only, which expositions have always been founded upon the intent of the legislature, which they have collected sometimes by considering the cause and necessity of making the act, sometimes by comparing one part of the act with another, and sometimes by foreign circumstances."

In Pier Co. v. Hannam, 3 Barn. & Ald. 266, Abbott, C.J., quotes from Lord Coke as follows: "Acts of parliament are to be so construed as no man that is innocent or free from injury or wrong be, by a literal construction, punished or endangered."

"All laws should receive a sensible construction. General terms should be so limited in their application as not to lead to injustice, oppression, or an absurd consequence. It will always, therefore, be presumed that the legislature intended exceptions to its language which would avoid results of this character. The reason of the law in such cases should prevail over its letter. The common sense of man approves the judgment mentioned by Puffendorf, that the Bolognian law which enacted 'that whoever drew blood in the streets should be punished with the utmost severity,' did not extend to the surgeon who opened the vein of a person that fell down in the street in a fit. The same common sense accepts the ruling, cited by Plowden, that the statute of 1 Edw. II., which enacts that a prisoner who breaks prison shall be guilty of felony, does not extend to a prisoner who breaks out when the prison is on fire, 'for he is not to be hanged because he would not stay to be burnt.' And we think that a like common sense will sanction the ruling we make, that the act of congress which punishes the obstruction or retarding of the passage of the mail, or of its carrier, does not apply to a case of temporary detention of the mail caused by the arrest of the carrier upon an indictment for murder."

Among other things which may be considered in determining the intent of the legislature is the title of the act. We do not mean that it may be used to add to or take from the body of the statute, (Hadden v. Collector, 5 Wall. 107,) but it may help to interpret its meaning.

Again, another guide to the meaning of a statute is found in the evil which it is designed to remedy; and for this the court properly looks at contemporaneous events, the situation as it existed, and as it was pressed upon the attention of the legislative body. U.S. v. Railroad Co., 91 U.S. 72, 79. The situation which called for this statute was briefly but fully stated by Mr. Justice Brown when, as district judge, he decided the case of U.S. v. Craig, 28 Fed.Rep. 795, 798: "The motives and history of the act are matters of common knowledge. It had become the practice for large capitalists in this country to contract with their agents abroad for the shipment of great numbers of an ignorant and servile class of foreign laborers, under contracts by which the employer agreed, upon the one hand, to prepay their passage, while, upon the other hand, the laborers agreed to work after their arrival for a certain time at a low rate of wages. The effect of this was to break down the labor market, and to reduce other laborers engaged in like occupations to the level of the assisted immigrant. The evil finally became so flagrant that an appeal was made to congress for relief by the passage of the act in question, the design of which was to raise the standard of foreign immigrants, and to discountenance the migration of those who had not sufficient means in their own hands, or those of their friends, to pay their passage."

The construction invoked cannot be accepted as correct. It is a case where there was presented a definite evil, in view of which the legislature used general terms with the purpose of reaching all phases of that evil; and thereafter, unexpectedly, it is developed that the general language thus employed is broad enough to reach cases and acts which the whole history and life of the country affirm could not have been intentionally legislated against. It is the duty of the courts, under those circumstances, to say that, however broad the language of the statute may be, the act, although within the letter, is not within the intention of the legislature, and therefore cannot be within the statute.

BOB JONES UNIVERSITY v. UNITED STATES

Supreme Court of the United States, 1983.
461 U.S. 574, 103 S.Ct. 2017, 76 L.Ed.2d 157.

CHIEF JUSTICE BURGER delivered the opinion of the Court.

We granted certiorari to decide whether petitioners, nonprofit private schools that prescribe and enforce racially discriminatory admissions standards on the basis of religious doctrine, qualify as tax-exempt organizations under § 501(c)(3) of the Internal Revenue Code of 1954.

In Revenue Ruling 71–447, the IRS formalized the policy, first announced in 1970, that § 170 and § 501(c)(3) embrace the common-law "charity" concept. Under that view, to qualify for a tax exemption pursuant to § 501(c)(3), an institution must show, first, that it falls within one of the eight categories expressly set forth in that section, and second, that its activity is not contrary to settled public policy.

Section 501(c)(3) provides that "[c]orporations ... organized and operated exclusively for religious, charitable ... or educational purposes" are entitled to tax exemption. Petitioners argue that the plain language of the statute guarantees them tax-exempt status. They emphasize the absence of any language in the statute expressly requiring all exempt organizations to be "charitable" in the common-law sense, and they contend that the disjunctive "or" separating the categories in § 501(c)(3) precludes such a reading. Instead, they argue that if an institution falls within one or more of the specified categories it is automatically entitled to exemption, without regard to whether it also qualifies as "charitable." The Court of Appeals rejected that contention and concluded that petitioners' interpretation of the statute "tears section 501(c)(3) from its roots." 639 F.2d, at 151.

It is a well-established canon of statutory construction that a court should go beyond the literal language of a statute if reliance on that language would defeat the plain purpose of the statute:

> "The general words used in the clause ..., taken by themselves, and literally construed, without regard to the object in view, would seem to sanction the claim of the plaintiff. But this mode of expounding a statute has never been adopted by any enlightened tribunal—because it is evident that in many cases it would defeat the object which the Legislature intended to accomplish. And it is well settled that, in interpreting a statute, the court will not look merely to a particular clause in which general words may be used, *but will take in connection with it the whole statute ... and the objects and policy of the law....*"
> Brown v. Duchesne, 19 How. 183, 194 (1857) (emphasis added).

Section 501(c)(3) therefore must be analyzed and construed within the framework of the Internal Revenue Code and against the background of the congressional purposes. Such an examination reveals unmistakable evidence that, underlying all relevant parts of the Code, is the intent that entitlement to tax exemption depends on meeting certain common-law standards of charity—namely, that an institution seeking tax-exempt status must serve a public purpose and not be contrary to established public policy.

PEOPLES DRUG STORES v. DISTRICT OF COLUMBIA [1]

District of Columbia Court of Appeals, 1983.
470 A.2d 751.

Before NEWMAN, CHIEF JUDGE, and KERN, NEBEKER, MACK, FERREN, PRYOR and TERRY, ASSOCIATE JUDGES.

FERREN, ASSOCIATE JUDGE:

The trial court dismissed appellant's petition challenging a District of Columbia use tax assessment, concluding that the court lacked jurisdiction because the petition was not timely filed pursuant to D.C.Code § 47–2403 (1978). A division of this court, in an unpublished memorandum opinion and judgment issued July 19, 1983, concluded that it was

---

1. D.C.Code § 47–2403 (1973) provides:

Any person aggrieved by any assessment by the District of any personal property, inheritance, estate, business privilege, gross receipts, gross earnings, insurance premiums, or motor vehicle fuel tax or taxes, or penalties thereon, may within six months after payment of the tax together with penalties and interest assessed thereon, appeal from the assessment to the Superior Court of the District of Columbia. The mailing to the taxpayer of a statement of taxes due shall be considered notice of assessment with respect to the taxes.

"constrained to affirm the trial court's dismissal" in light of the interpretation given § 47–2408 in Donahue v. District of Columbia, 368 A.2d 1147 (D.C.1977) (per curiam). Upon consideration by the full court, we now overrule *Donahue* (except to the extent necessary to address the particular facts of that case) and reverse the trial court's order dismissing appellant's petition.

I.

On August 18, 1977, appellee District of Columbia mailed to appellant taxpayer a Notice of D.C. Tax Due. The notice included a use tax assessment of $50,309.33, plus interest, for advertising supplements paid for by taxpayer and distributed in the District of Columbia. Taxpayer paid the tax on September 14, 1977, but filed a petition for refund in the Tax Division of Superior Court on March 14, 1978.

The only issue in this case is whether taxpayer's petition was timely filed. The District of Columbia concedes that, under Sears, Roebuck and Co. v. District of Columbia, Tax Div. Docket No. 2468 (D.C.Super.Ct. May 13, 1981), the use tax paid by taxpayer with respect to advertising supplements was assessed in error; thus, if taxpayer's petition was timely filed, taxpayer is entitled to a refund. The District maintains, however, that pursuant to D.C.Code § 47–2403 (1973), an appeal from an assessment must be taken within six months of the assessment, and thus taxpayer's petition—filed nearly seven months after the assessment—was untimely. Taxpayer argues, to the contrary, that the plain wording of § 47–2403 permits appeals "within six months after payment of the tax," and that its petition, filed exactly six months after payment, complied with this statutory requirement.

We agree with the earlier memorandum opinion and judgment of the division in this case that, if *Donahue, supra,* is good law, it controls this case and the District of Columbia must prevail. Although the factual scenario in *Donahue* can be distinguished from the facts here, the *Donahue* holding clearly purports to extend to cases such as the one now before the court:

> We previously suggested, and now hold, "that the period for *all* appeals under § 47–2403 runs from the mailing of the assessment, the clause 'after payment ...' to be read as 'provided payment has been made.' "

368 A.2d at 1148 (emphasis in original) (quoting National Graduate University v. District of Columbia, 846 A.2d 740, 743 n. 7 (D.C.1975)). Moreover, the *Donahue* court expressly "reject[ed] [the] argument that the six-month period for filing an appeal does not commence until after payment of the tax." *Id.*

II.

In reviewing this court's interpretation of § 47–2403 in *Donahue,* "[w]e must first look at the language of the statute by itself to see if the language is plain and admits of no more than one meaning." Davis v.

United States, 397 A.2d 951, 956 (D.C.1979). "The primary and general rule of statutory construction is that the intent of the law-maker is to be found in the language that he has used." Varela v. Hi–Lo Powered Stirrups, Inc., 424 A.2d 61, 64 (D.C.1980) (en banc) (quoting United States v. Goldenberg, 168 U.S. 95, 102–03, 18 S.Ct. 3, 4, 42 L.Ed. 394 (1897)). Moreover, in examining the statutory language, it is axiomatic that "[t]he words of the statute should be construed according to their ordinary sense and with the meaning commonly attributed to them." *Davis, supra,* 397 A.2d at 956.

The critical language of § 47–2403 provides: "Any person aggrieved by any assessment ... may within six months after payment of the tax together with penalties and interest assessed thereon, appeal from the assessment to the Superior Court." These words, given their ordinary meaning, plainly indicate that the six-month period for filing an appeal does not begin to run until after the taxpayer has paid the assessment.

The *Donahue* decision did not, however, simply rely on the statutory language for its reading of § 47–2403. The court based its conclusion on a reading of the legislative history of the statute.

This resort to the legislative history was not, in and of itself, improper. Both the Supreme Court and this court have recognized that "words are inexact tools at best, and for that reason there is wisely no rule of law forbidding resort to explanatory legislative history no matter how 'clear the words may appear on superficial examination.'" Harrison v. Northern Trust Co., 317 U.S. 476, 63 S.Ct. 361, 87 L.Ed. 407 (1943) (citations omitted).

Lynch v. Overholser, 369 U.S. 705, 710, 82 S.Ct. 1063, 1067, 8 L.Ed.2d 211 (1962) ("The decisions of this Court have repeatedly warned against the dangers of an approach to statutory construction which confines itself to the bare words of a statute, ... for 'literalness may strangle meaning.' ")

Nor should *Donahue* necessarily be overruled simply because its reading of § 47–2403 does not comport with the meaning most readily derived from the words of the statute. Although the "plain meaning" rule is certainly the first step in statutory interpretation, it is not always the last or the most illuminating step. This court has found it appropriate to look beyond the plain meaning of statutory language in several different situations.

First, even where the words of a statute have a "superficial clarity," a review of the legislative history or an in-depth consideration of alternative constructions that could be ascribed to statutory language may reveal ambiguities that the court must resolve. Barbee v. United States, 392 F.2d 532, 535 n. 4 (5th Cir.), *cert. denied,* 391 U.S. 935, 88 S.Ct. 1849, 20 L.Ed.2d 855 (1968) (" 'Whether or not the words of a statute are clear is itself not always clear' ").

Second, " 'the literal meaning of a statute will not be followed when it produces absurd results.' " District of Columbia National Bank v. District of Columbia, 121 U.S.App.D.C. 196, 198, 348 F.2d 808, 810 (1965); *Berkley v. United States,* 370 A.2d 1331, 1332 (D.C.1977) (per curiam) ("statutes are to be construed in a manner which assumes that Congress acted logically and rationally"). Third, whenever possible, the words of a statute are to be construed to avoid "obvious injustice." Metzler v. Edwards, 53 A.2d 42, 44 (D.C.Mun.App.1947); *see* Center for National Policy Review on Race & Urban Issues v. Weinberger, 163 U.S.App.D.C. 368, 372, 502 F.2d 370, 374 (1974) ("[a] court may qualify the plain meaning of a statute" to avoid consequences that would be "plainly ... inequitable").

Finally, a court may refuse to adhere strictly to the plain wording of a statute in order "to effectuate the legislative purpose," Mulky v. United States, 451 A.2d 855, 857 (D.C.1982), as determined by a reading of the legislative history or by an examination of the statute as a whole. Floyd E. Davis Mortgage Corp. v. District of Columbia, 455 A.2d 910, 911 (D.C.1983) (per curiam) ("a statute is to be construed in the context of the entire legislative scheme"); Dyer v. D.C. Department of Housing and Community Development, 452 A.2d 968, 969–70 (D.C.1982) ("[t]he use of legislative history as an aid in interpretation is proper when the literal words of the statute would bring about a result completely at variance with the purpose of the Act"); District of Columbia v. Orleans, 132 U.S.App.D.C. 139, 141, 406 F.2d 957, 959 (1968) ("the 'plain meaning' doctrine has always been subservient to a truly discernible legislative purpose however discerned, by equitable construction or recourse to legislative history").[4]

These exceptions to the plain meaning rule should not, however, be understood to swallow the rule completely. There are strong policy reasons for maintaining the certainty, fairness, and respect for the legal system that the plain meaning rule engenders in most instances. Unless the meaning of statutes can be readily ascertained by a reading of

---

4. There has been, at least since 1930, a debate as to how willing courts should be to deviate from the plain meaning rule when engaging in statutory interpretation. *Compare* Landis, *A Note on "Statutory Interpretation"*, 43 HARV.L.REV. 886, 888 (1930) (advocating that courts limit themselves to seeking legislative intent on specific matters and claiming that judicial resort to general legislative purposes or policies leads to "spurious interpretation") *with* Radin, *Statutory Interpretation*, 43 HARV.L.REV. 863, 871 (1930) (arguing that a search for actual legislative intent is unrealistic and recommending "purposive interpretation" of statutory language). When a court is confronted with a question of statutory interpretation, the "legislative intent" model, described by Landis, *supra,* prescribes an essentially historical inquiry to determine how the enacting legislature would have answered the specific question before the court. "Purposive interpretation," on the other hand, recognizes that courts most often confront questions of statutory interpretation that never occurred to the enacting legislature. Under this model, a court

will attempt to discern the general purpose or policy that motivated the legislature to pass a statute, and then construe the statute in the manner most consistent with that purpose. *See generally,* Note, *Intent, Clear Statements, And the Common Law,* 95 HARV.L.REV. 892 (1982); Lehman, *How to Interpret a Difficult Statute,* 1979 WISC. L.REV. 489.

Most commentators agree that, despite the fact that many courts use the terms "intent" and "purpose" interchangeably, purpose-based analysis has dominated judicial decision making for the past twenty-five years. G. Calabresi, A COMMON LAW FOR THE AGE OF STATUTES 30 (1982); *see* H. Hart & A. Sacks, The Legal Process 1410 (tent. ed. 1958) (unpublished manuscript); *but see* Note, *Intent, Clear Statements, And the Common Law, supra* (recognizing general predominance of "purposive interpretation," but suggesting that recent Supreme Court cases reflect a return to stricter legislative intent analysis).

statutory language, the ability of citizens to comply with statutory standards is diminished and the administration of such standards may be unmanageable or even erratic. For these reasons, a court should look beyond the ordinary meaning of the words of a statute only where there are "persuasive reasons" for doing so. *Tuten v. United States,* 440 A.2d 1008, 1013 (D.C.1982), *aff'd* 460 U.S. 660, 103 S.Ct. 1412, 75 L.Ed.2d 359 (1983).

We find no such "persuasive reasons" to support the *Donahue* holding. The legislative history relied on by the court in *Donahue,* as well as by both parties in this case, is ambiguous and conflicting on the issue before the court.[5] Where legislative materials are " 'without probative value, or contradictory, or ambiguous,' [they] should not be permitted to control the customary meaning of words." NLRB v. Plasterers' Local Union No. 79, Operative Plasterers' & Cement Masons' Int'l Ass'n, 404 U.S. 116, 129 n. 24, 92 S.Ct. 360, 369 n. 24, 30 L.Ed.2d 312 (1971) (quoting United States v. Dickerson, 310 U.S. 554, 562, 60 S.Ct. 1034, 1038, 84 L.Ed. 1356 (1940)).

Moreover, an in-depth consideration of the wording of § 47–2403, "within six months after payment of the tax," does not reveal any hidden ambiguity. Nor does reading this language according to its ordinary meaning produce absurd or inequitable results, or undermine the purposes or policies that underlie the District of Columbia Tax Code. Indeed, it is not uncommon for a tax statute to use the date of payment to mark the commencement of the filing period for a refund claim. *See* D.C.Code § 47–2020 (Supp.1983) (sales tax refunds); *see also* 26 U.S.C. § 6511 (1954 & Supp.1983) (period of limitation for filing claim with the Internal Revenue Service for refund of overpayment of federal income tax).

D.C.Code § 47–2403 (1973) governed the right to appeal from a wide range of tax assessments, including taxes applicable to individual taxpayers. Statutes of this type should generally be construed to protect a taxpayer's reliance on statutory language and to preserve a taxpayer's right to challenge an assessment. *See, e.g., Public Service Co. of New Hampshire v. Assessors of Barwick,* 158 Me. 285, 188 A.2d 205 (1962). A taxpayer should not be forced to achieve familiarity with the intricacies of case law or to retain legal counsel simply to determine the extent of the right to question the size of a tax payment. The court in *Donahue* read § 47–2403 in a manner which rendered the otherwise plain language of that section misleading. Accordingly, we overrule the holding

5. The court in *Donahue,* and the District of Columbia here, rely on a single sentence from a House of Representatives Committee Report to support their reading of § 47–2403. *See* H.R.Rep. No. 907, 91st Cong., 2d Sess. 165 (1970). Taxpayer, on the other hand, points to the technical manner in which § 47–2403 was reworded by the District of Columbia Court Reform and Criminal Procedure Act of 1970 in support of its argument. While both pieces of legislative history provide some minimal support for their proponents' respective positions, neither represents conclusive evidence of legislative intent or purpose.

of *Donahue,* except as applied to its specific facts reverse the trial court's dismissal of taxpayer's petition, and remand for further proceedings.

————

GREEN v. BOCK LAUNDRY MACHINE CO.

Supreme Court of the United States, 1989.
490 U.S. 504, 109 S.Ct. 1981, 104 L.Ed.2d 557.

[A previous version of Rule 609(a)(1) Federal Rules of Evidence describing circumstances under which a criminal record could be introduced at trial to attack the credibility of a witness required the trial court to determine "that the probative value of admitting this evidence outweighs its prejudicial effect to the *defendant.*" The question for decision was whether the rule could be applied to allow a civil litigant to impeach the credibility of its *plaintiff* adversary. The Court held that an interpretation that would deny a civil plaintiff the same right to impeach an adversary's testimony that it grants a civil defendant is unacceptable; therefore, the Rule cannot mean what it says as far as civil trials are concerned. The Court stated: "The Rule's plain language commands weighing of prejudice to a defendant in a civil trial as well as in a criminal trial. But that literal reading would compel an odd result in a case like this."]

Justice Scalia, concurring in the judgment.

We are confronted here with a statute which, if interpreted literally, produces an absurd, and perhaps unconstitutional, result. Our task is to give some alternative meaning to the word "defendant" in Federal Rule of Evidence 609(a)(1) that avoids this consequence; and then to determine whether Rule 609(a)(1) excludes the operation of Federal Rule of Evidence 403.

I think it entirely appropriate to consult all public materials, including the background of Rule 609(a)(1) and the legislative history of its adoption, to verify that what seems to us an unthinkable disposition (civil defendants but not civil plaintiffs receive the benefit of weighing prejudice) was indeed unthought of, and thus to justify a departure from the ordinary meaning of the word "defendant" in the Rule. For that purpose, however, it would suffice to observe that counsel have not provided, nor have we discovered, a shred of evidence that anyone has ever proposed or assumed such a bizarre disposition. The Court's opinion, however, goes well beyond this. Approximately four-fifths of its substantive analysis is devoted to examining the evolution of Federal Rule of Evidence 609, from the 1942 Model Code of Evidence, to the 1953 Uniform Rules of Evidence, to the 1965 *Luck* case and the 1970 statute overruling it, to the Subcommittee, Committee, and Conference Committee Reports, and to the so-called floor debates on Rule 609—all with the evident purpose, not merely of confirming that the word "defendant" cannot have been meant literally, but of determining what, precisely, the Rule does mean.

I find no reason to believe that any more than a handful of the Members of Congress who enacted Rule 609 were aware of its interesting evolution from the 1942 Model Code; or that any more than a handful of them (if any) voted, with respect to their understanding of the word "defendant" and the relationship between Rule 609 and Rule 403, on the basis of the referenced statements in the Subcommittee, Committee, or Conference Committee Reports, or floor debates—statements so marginally relevant, to such minute details, in such relatively inconsequential legislation. The meaning of terms on the statute books ought to be determined, not on the basis of which meaning can be shown to have been understood by a larger handful of the Members of Congress; but rather on the basis of which meaning is (1) most in accord with context and ordinary usage, and thus most likely to have been understood by the *whole* Congress which voted on the words of the statute (not to mention the citizens subject to it), and (2) most compatible with the surrounding body of law into which the provision must be integrated—a compatibility which, by a benign fiction, we assume Congress always has in mind. I would not permit any of the historical and legislative material discussed by the Court, or all of it combined, to lead me to a result different from the one that these factors suggest.

I am frankly not sure that, despite its lengthy discussion of ideological evolution and legislative history, the Court's reasons for both aspects of its decision are much different from mine. I respectfully decline to join that discussion, however, because it is natural for the bar to believe that the juridical importance of such material matches its prominence in our opinions—thus producing a legal culture in which, when counsel arguing before us assert that "Congress has said" something, they now frequently mean, by "Congress," a committee report; and in which it was not beyond the pale for a recent brief to say the following: "Unfortunately, the legislative debates are not helpful. Thus, we turn to the other guidepost in this difficult area, statutory language."

PUBLIC CITIZEN v. U.S. DEPARTMENT OF JUSTICE

Supreme Court of the United States, 1989.
491 U.S. 440, 109 S.Ct. 2558, 105 L.Ed.2d 377.

JUSTICE BRENNAN delivered the opinion of the Court.

The Department of Justice regularly seeks advice from the American Bar Association's Standing Committee on Federal Judiciary regarding potential nominees for federal judgeships. The question before us is whether the Federal Advisory Committee Act (FACA), 86 Stat. 770, as amended, 5 U.S.C.App. § 1 *et seq.* (1982 ed. and Supp. V), applies to these consultations and, if it does, whether its application interferes unconstitutionally with the President's prerogative under Article II to nominate and appoint officers of the United States; violates the doctrine of separation of powers; or unduly infringes the First Amendment right of members of the American Bar Association to freedom of association and expression. We hold that FACA does not apply to this special advisory relationship. We therefore do not reach the constitutional questions presented.

I

A

The Constitution provides that the President "shall nominate, and by and with the Advice and Consent of the Senate, shall appoint" Supreme Court Justices and, as established by Congress, other federal judges. Art. II, § 2, cl. 2. Since 1952 the President, through the Department of Justice, has requested advice from the American Bar Association's Standing Committee on Federal Judiciary (ABA Committee) in making such nominations.

The American Bar Association is a private voluntary professional association of approximately 343,000 attorneys. It has several working committees, among them the advisory body whose work is at issue here. The ABA Committee consists of 14 persons belonging to, and chosen by, the American Bar Association. Each of the 12 federal judicial Circuits (not including the Federal Circuit) has one representative on the ABA Committee, except for the Ninth Circuit, which has two; in addition, one member is chosen at large. The ABA Committee receives no federal funds. It does not recommend persons for appointment to the federal bench of its own initiative.

III

Section 3(2) of FACA, as set forth in 5 U.S.C.App. § 3(2), defines "advisory committee" as follows:

"For the purpose of this Act—

. . .

"(2) The term 'advisory committee' means any committee, board, commission, council, conference, panel, task force, or other similar group, or any subcommittee or other subgroup thereof (hereafter in this paragraph referred to as 'committee'), which is—

"(A) established by statute or reorganization plan, or

"(B) established or utilized by the President, or

"(C) established or utilized by one or more agencies, in the interest of obtaining advice or recommendations for the President or one or more agencies or officers of the Federal Government, except that such term excludes (i) the Advisory Commission on Intergovernmental Relations, (ii) the Commission on Government Procurement, and (iii) any committee which is composed wholly of full-time officers or employees of the Federal Government."

Appellants agree that the ABA Committee was not "established" by the President or the Justice Department.

Equally plainly, the ABA Committee is a committee that furnishes "advice or recommendations" to the President via the Justice Department. Whether the ABA Committee constitutes an "advisory committee" for purposes of FACA therefore depends upon whether it is "utilized" by the President or the Justice Department as Congress intended that term to be understood.

A

There is no doubt that the Executive makes use of the ABA Committee, and thus "utilizes" it in one common sense of the term. As the District Court recognized, however, "reliance on the plain language of FACA alone is not entirely satisfactory." "Utilize" is a woolly verb, its contours left undefined by the statute itself. Read unqualifiedly, it would extend FACA's requirements to any group of two or more persons, or at least any formal organization, from which the President or an Executive agency seeks advice. We are convinced that Congress did not intend that result. A nodding acquaintance with FACA's purposes, as manifested by its legislative history and as recited in § 2 of the Act, reveals that it cannot have been Congress' intention, for example, to require the filing of a charter, the presence of a controlling federal official, and detailed minutes any time the President seeks the views of the National Association for the Advancement of Colored People (NAACP) before nominating Commissioners to the Equal Employment Opportunity Commission, or asks the leaders of an American Legion Post he is visiting for the organization's opinion on some aspect of military policy.

Nor can Congress have meant—as a straightforward reading of "utilize" would appear to require—that all of FACA's restrictions apply if a President consults with his own political party before picking his Cabinet. It was unmistakably not Congress' intention to intrude on a political party's freedom to conduct its affairs as it chooses, cf. Eu v. San Francisco County Democratic Central Comm., 489 U.S. 214, 230 (1989), or its ability to advise elected officials who belong to that party, by placing a federal employee in charge of each advisory group meeting and making its minutes public property. FACA was enacted to cure specific ills, above all the wasteful expenditure of public funds for worthless committee meetings and biased proposals; although its reach is extensive, we cannot believe that it was intended to cover every formal and informal consultation between the President or an Executive agency and a group rendering advice. As we said in Church of the Holy Trinity v. United States, 143 U.S. 457, 459 (1892): "[F]requently words of general meaning are used in a statute, words broad enough to include an act in question, and yet a consideration of the whole legislation, or of the circumstances surrounding its enactment, or of the absurd results which follow from giving such broad meaning to the words, makes it unreasonable to believe that the legislator intended to include the particular act."

Where the literal reading of a statutory term would "compel an odd result," Green v. Bock Laundry Machine Co., 490 U.S. 504, 509 (1989), we must search for other evidence of congressional intent to lend the term its proper scope. See also, *e.g., Church of the Holy Trinity, supra,* at 472; FDIC v. Philadelphia Gear Corp., 476 U.S. 426, 432 (1986). "The circumstances of the enactment of particular legislation," for example, "may persuade a court that Congress did not intend words of common meaning to have their literal effect." Walt v. Alaska, 451 U.S. 259, 266 (1981). Even though, as Judge Learned Hand said, "the words used, even in their literal sense, are the primary, and ordinarily the most reliable, source of interpreting the meaning of any writing," nevertheless "it is one of the surest indexes of a mature and developed jurisprudence not to make a fortress out of the dictionary; but to remember that statutes always have some purpose or object to accomplish, whose sympathetic and imaginative discovery is the surest guide to their meaning." Cabell v. Markham, 148 F.2d 737, 739 (CA2), aff'd, 326 U.S. 404 (1945). Looking beyond the naked text for guidance is perfectly proper when the result it apparently decrees is difficult to fathom or where it seems inconsistent with Congress' intention, since the plain-meaning rule is "rather an axiom of experience than a rule of law, and does not preclude consideration of persuasive evidence if it exists." Boston Sand & Gravel Co. v. United States, 278 U.S. 41, 48 (1928) (Holmes, J.). See also United States v. American Trucking Assns., Inc., 310 U.S. 534, 543–544 (1940) ("When aid to construction of the meaning of words, as used in the statute, is available, there certainly can be no 'rule of law' which forbids its use, however clear the words may appear on 'superficial examination'") (citations omitted).

Consideration of FACA's purposes and origins in determining whether the term "utilized" was meant to apply to the Justice Department's use of the ABA Committee is particularly appropriate here, given the importance we have consistently attached to interpreting statutes to avoid deciding difficult constitutional questions where the text fairly admits of a less problematic construction. It is therefore imperative that we consider indicators of congressional intent in addition to the statutory language before concluding that FACA was meant to cover the ABA Committee's provision of advice to the Justice Department in connection with judicial nominations.

JUSTICE KENNEDY, with whom THE CHIEF JUSTICE and JUSTICE O'CONNOR join, concurring in the judgment.

Although I believe the Court's result is quite sensible, I cannot go along with the unhealthy process of amending the statute by judicial interpretation. Where the language of a statute is clear in its application, the normal rule is that we are bound by it. There is, of course, a legitimate exception to this rule, which the Court invokes, citing Church of the Holy Trinity v. United States, 143 U.S. 457, 459 (1892), and with which I have no quarrel. Where the plain language of the statute would lead to "patently absurd consequences," United States v. Brown, 333 U.S. 18, 27 (1948), that "Congress could not *possibly* have intended,"

FBI v. Abramson, 456 U.S. 615, 640 (1982) (O'Connor, J., dissenting) (emphasis added), we need not apply the language in such a fashion. When used in a proper manner, this narrow exception to our normal rule of statutory construction does not intrude upon the lawmaking powers of Congress, but rather demonstrates a respect for the coequal Legislative Branch, which we assume would not act in an absurd way.

This exception remains a legitimate tool of the Judiciary, however, only as long as the Court acts with self-discipline by limiting the exception to situations where the result of applying the plain language would be, in a genuine sense, absurd, *i.e.,* where it is quite impossible that Congress could have intended the result, and where the alleged absurdity is so clear as to be obvious to most anyone. A few examples of true absurdity are given in the *Holy Trinity* decision cited by the Court, such as where a sheriff was prosecuted for obstructing the mails even though he was executing a warrant to arrest the mail carrier for murder, or where a medieval law against drawing blood in the streets was to be applied against a physician who came to the aid of a man who had fallen down in a fit. In today's opinion, however, the Court disregards the plain language of the statute not because its application would be patently absurd, but rather because, on the basis of its view of the legislative history, the Court is "fairly confident" that "FACA should [not] be construed to apply to the ABA Committee." I believe the Court's loose invocation of the "absurd result" canon of statutory construction creates too great a risk that the Court is exercising its own "WILL instead of JUDGMENT," with the consequence of "substituti[ng] [its own] pleasure to that of the legislative body." The Federalist No. 78, p. 469 (C. Rossiter ed. 1961) (A. Hamilton).

Unable to show that an application of FACA according the plain meaning of its terms would be absurd, the Court turns instead to the task of demonstrating that a straightforward reading of the statute would be inconsistent with the congressional purposes that lay behind its passage. To the student of statutory construction, this move is a familiar one. It is, as the Court identifies it, the classic *Holy Trinity* argument. "[A] thing may be within the letter of the statute and yet not within the statute, because not within its spirit, nor within the intention of its makers." *Holy Trinity, supra,* at 459. I cannot embrace this principle. Where it is clear that the unambiguous language of a statute embraces certain conduct, and it would not be patently absurd to apply the statute to such conduct, it does not foster a democratic exegesis for this Court to rummage through unauthoritative materials to consult the spirit of the legislation in order to discover an alternative interpretation of the statute with which the Court is more comfortable. It comes as a surprise to no one that the result of the Court's lengthy journey through the legislative history is the discovery of a congressional intent not to include the activities of the ABA Committee within the coverage of FACA. The problem with spirits is that they tend to reflect less the views of the world whence they come than the views of those who seek their advice.

Even if I were inclined to disregard the unambiguous language of FACA, I could not join the Court's conclusions with regard to Congress' purposes. I find the Court's treatment of the legislative history one sided.

In sum, it is quite desirable not to apply FACA to the ABA Committee. I cannot, however, reach this conclusion as a matter of fair statutory construction. The plain and ordinary meaning of the language passed by Congress governs, and its application does not lead to any absurd results. An unnecessary recourse to the legislative history only confirms this conclusion. And the reasonable and controlling interpretation of the statute adopted by the agency charged with its implementation is also in accord.

PEOPLE ex rel. FYFE v. BARNETT

Supreme Court of Illinois, 1925.
319 Ill. 403, 150 N.E. 290.

[At issue was the effect of women's suffrage on the construction of an 1887 statute authorizing voters to serve on juries. Because only men could vote at the time of the statute's enactment, the court assumed that the members of the legislature had not intended to extend the right of jury service to women.]

The legislative intent that controls in the construction of a statute has reference to the Legislature which passed the given act. * * * Applying the rules of construction herein mentioned, it is evident that when the Legislature enacted the law in question, which provided for the appointment of jury commissioners in counties having more than 250,-000 inhabitants and imposing upon them the duty of making a jury list, using the words "shall prepare a list of all electors between the ages of twenty-one and sixty years, possessing the necessary legal qualifications for jury duty, to be known as the jury list," it was intended to use the words "electors" and "elector" as the same were then defined by the Constitution and laws of the state of Illinois. At that time the Legislature did not intend that the name of any women should be placed on the jury list, and must be held to have intended that the list should be composed of the names of male persons, only.

In interpreting a statute, the question is what the words used therein meant to those using them. * * * The word "electors," in the statute here in question, meant male persons, only, to the legislators who used it. We must therefore hold that the word "electors," as used in the statute, means male persons, only, and that the petitioner was not entitled to have her name replaced upon the jury list of Cook county.

NOTE

Compare this case with Commonwealth v. Maxwell, 271 Pa. 378, 114 A. 825 (1921).

————

COMMONWEALTH v. MAXWELL

Supreme Court of Pennsylvania, 1921.
271 Pa. 378, 114 A. 825.

[The Pennsylvania Supreme Court interpreted a statute regarding women voters and jury service identical in all relevant respects to that interpreted by the Illinois Supreme Court in People ex rel. Fyfe v. Barnett, supra at ——. Unlike the Illinois Court which sought to ascertain the legislature's intent, the Pennsylvania court focused on the purpose of the statute. Although the legislature never *intended* women to be included on the list, the *purpose* of the statute was merely to ensure a jury list consisting of competent voters. Because the Nineteenth Amendment gave women the right to vote, the purpose of the statute would be furthered by construing the statute to include women on the jury list. It is noteworthy that the Pennsylvania court never mentions legislative *intent* in this opinion.]

* * * We then have the act of 1867, constitutionally providing that the jury commissioners are required to select "from the whole qualified electors of the respective county * * * persons, to serve as jurors in the several courts of such county," and the Nineteenth Amendment to the federal Constitution, putting women in the body of electors.

"The term 'elector' is a technical, generic term, descriptive of a citizen having constitutional and statutory qualifications that enable him to vote, and including not only those who vote, but also those who are qualified, yet fail to exercise the right of franchise." 20 Corpus Juris, 58.

If the act of 1867 is prospective in operation, and takes in new classes of electors as they come to the voting privilege from time to time, then, necessarily, women, being electors, are eligible to jury service. That the act of 1867 does cover those who at any time shall come within the designation of electors there can be no question.

"Statutes framed in general terms apply to new cases that arise, and to new subjects that are created from time to time, and which come within their general scope and policy. It is a rule of statutory construction that legislative enactments in general and comprehensive terms, prospective in operation, apply alike to all persons, subjects, and business within their general purview and scope coming into existence subsequent to their passage." 25 Ruling Case Law, 778.

* * *

————

REGENTS OF THE UNIVERSITY
OF CALIFORNIA v. BAKKE

Supreme Court of the United States, 1978.
438 U.S. 265, 98 S.Ct. 2733, 57 L.Ed.2d 750.

Opinion of JUSTICE POWELL.

The language of § 601, 78 Stat. 252, like that of the Equal Protection Clause, is majestic in its sweep:

> "No person in the United States shall, on the ground of race, color, or national origin, be excluded from participation in, be denied the benefits of, or be subjected to discrimination under any program or activity receiving Federal financial assistance."

The concept of "discrimination," like the phrase "equal protection of the laws," is susceptible of varying interpretations, for as Mr. Justice Holmes declared, "[a] word is not a crystal, transparent and unchanged, it is the skin of a living thought and may vary greatly in color and content according to the circumstances and the time in which it is used." Towne v. Eisner, 245 U.S. 418, 425 (1918). We must, therefore, seek whatever aid is available in determining the precise meaning of the statute before us. Train v. Colorado Public Interest Research Group, 426 U.S. 1, 10 (1976), quoting United States v. American Trucking Assns., 310 U.S. 534, 543–544 (1940). Examination of the voluminous legislative history of Title VI reveals a congressional intent to halt federal funding of entities that violate a prohibition of racial discrimination similar to that of the Constitution. Although isolated statements of various legislators, taken out of context, can be marshaled in support of the proposition that § 601 enacted a purely colorblind scheme,[19] without regard to the reach of the Equal Protection Clause, these comments must be read against the background of both the problem that Congress was addressing and the broader view of the statute that emerges from a full examination of the legislative debates.

The problem confronting Congress was discrimination against Negro citizens at the hands of recipients of federal moneys. Indeed, the color blindness pronouncements generally occur in the midst of extended remarks dealing with the evils of segregation in federally funded programs. Over and over again, proponents of the bill detailed the plight of Negroes seeking equal treatment in such programs. There simply was no reason for Congress to consider the validity of hypothetical preferences that might be accorded minority citizens; the legislators were dealing with the real and pressing problem of how to guarantee those citizens equal treatment.

19. For example, Senator Humphrey stated as follows:

"Racial discrimination or segregation in the administration of disaster relief is particularly shocking; and offensive to our sense of justice and fair play. Human suffering draws no color lines, and the administration of help to the sufferers should not." *Id.*, at 6547.

In addressing that problem, supporters of Title VI repeatedly declared that the bill enacted constitutional principles. For example, Representative Celler, the Chairman of the House Judiciary Committee and floor manager of the legislation in the House, emphasized this in introducing the bill:

> "The bill would offer assurance that hospitals financed by Federal money would not deny adequate care to Negroes. It would prevent abuse of food distribution programs whereby Negroes have been known to be denied food surplus supplies when white persons were given such food. It would assure Negroes the benefits now accorded only white students in programs of high[er] education financed by Federal funds. It would, in short, *assure the existing right to equal treatment* in the enjoyment of Federal funds. It would not destroy any rights of private property or freedom of association." (emphasis added).

Other sponsors shared Representative Celler's view that Title VI embodied constitutional principles.

In the Senate, Senator Humphrey declared that the purpose of Title VI was "to insure that Federal funds are spent in accordance with the Constitution and the moral sense of the Nation." Senator Ribicoff agreed that Title VI embraced the constitutional standard: "Basically, there is a constitutional restriction against discrimination in the use of federal funds; and title VI simply spells out the procedure to be used in enforcing that restriction." Other Senators expressed similar views.

Further evidence of the incorporation of a constitutional standard into Title VI appears in the repeated refusals of the legislation's supporters precisely to define the term "discrimination." Opponents sharply criticized this failure, but proponents of the bill merely replied that the meaning of "discrimination" would be made clear by reference to the Constitution or other existing law. For example, Senator Humphrey noted the relevance of the Constitution:

> "As I have said, the bill has a simple purpose. That purpose is to give fellow citizens—Negroes—the same rights and opportunities that white people take for granted. This is no more than what was preached by the prophets, and by Christ Himself. It is no more than what our Constitution guarantees." Id., at 6553.

In view of the clear legislative intent, Title VI must be held to proscribe only those racial classifications that would violate the Equal Protection Clause or the Fifth Amendment.

Opinion of JUSTICES BRENNAN, WHITE, MARSHALL and BLACKMUN.

The Chief Justice and our Brothers Stewart, Rehnquist, and Stevens have concluded that Title VI of the Civil Rights Act of 1964, 78 Stat. 252, as amended, 42 U.S.C. § 2000d et seq., prohibits programs such as that at the Davis Medical School. On this statutory theory alone, they would hold that respondent Allan Bakke's rights have been violated and that he must, therefore, be admitted to the Medical School. Our Brother Powell, reaching the Constitution, concludes that, although race may be taken into account in university admissions, the particular special admissions program used by petitioner, which resulted in the exclusion of respondent Bakke, was not shown to be necessary to achieve petitioner's stated goals. Accordingly, these Members of the Court form a majority of five affirming the judgment of the Supreme Court of California insofar as it holds that respondent Bakke "is entitled to an order that he be admitted to the University."

We agree with Mr. Justice Powell that, as applied to the case before us, Title VI goes no further in prohibiting the use of race than the Equal Protection Clause of the Fourteenth Amendment itself. We also agree that the effect of the California Supreme Court's affirmance of the judgment of the Superior Court of California would be to prohibit the University from establishing in the future affirmative-action programs that take race into account. Since we conclude that the affirmative admissions program at the Davis Medical School is constitutional, we would reverse the judgment below in all respects. Mr. Justice Powell agrees that some uses of race in university admissions are permissible and, therefore, he joins with us to make five votes reversing the judgment below insofar as it prohibits the University from establishing race-conscious programs in the future.

Mr. Justice Stevens, with whom The Chief Justice, Mr. Justice Stewart, and Mr. Justice Rehnquist join, concurring in the judgment in part and dissenting in part.

It is always important at the outset to focus precisely on the controversy before the Court.[1] It is particularly important to do so in this case because correct identification of the issues will determine whether it is necessary or appropriate to express any opinion about the legal status of any admissions program other than petitioner's.

The University, through its special admissions policy, excluded Bakke from participation in its program of medical education because of his race. The University also acknowledges that it was, and still is, receiving federal financial assistance. The plain language of the statute therefore requires affirmance of the judgment below. A different result cannot be justified unless that language misstates the actual intent of the Congress that enacted the statute or the statute is not enforceable in a private action. Neither conclusion is warranted.

Title VI is an integral part of the far-reaching Civil Rights Act of 1964. No doubt, when this legislation was being debated, Congress was not directly concerned with the legality of "reverse discrimination" or "affirmative action" programs. Its attention was focused on the prob-

---

1. Four Members of the Court have undertaken to announce the legal and constitutional effect of this Court's judgment. See opinion of Justices Brennan, White, Marshall, and Blackmun. It is hardly nec- essary to state that only a majority can speak for the Court or determine what is the "central meaning" of any judgment of the Court.

lem at hand, the "glaring ... discrimination against Negroes which exists throughout our Nation," and, with respect to Title VI, the federal funding of segregated facilities. The genesis of the legislation, however, did not limit the breadth of the solution adopted. Just as Congress responded to the problem of employment discrimination by enacting a provision that protects all races, see McDonald v. Santa Fe Trail Transp. Co., 427 U.S. 273, 279, so, too, its answer to the problem of federal funding of segregated facilities stands as a broad prohibition against the exclusion of *any* individual from a federally funded program "on the ground of race." In the words of the House Report, Title VI stands for "the general principle that *no person* ... be excluded from participation ... on the ground of race, color, or national origin under any program or activity receiving Federal financial assistance." This same broad view of Title VI and § 601 was echoed throughout the congressional debate and was stressed by every one of the major spokesmen for the Act.

Petitioner contends, however, that exclusion of applicants on the basis of race does not violate Title VI if the exclusion carries with it no racial stigma. No such qualification or limitation of § 601's categorical prohibition of "exclusion" is justified by the statute or its history. The language of the entire section is perfectly clear; the words that follow "excluded from" do not modify or qualify the explicit outlawing of any exclusion on the stated grounds.

The legislative history reinforces this reading. The only suggestion that § 601 would allow exclusion of nonminority applicants came from opponents of the legislation and then only by way of a discussion of the meaning of the word "discrimination." The opponents feared that the term "discrimination" would be read as mandating racial quotas and "racially balanced" colleges and universities, and they pressed for a specific definition of the term in order to avoid this possibility. In response, the proponents of the legislation gave repeated assurances that the Act would be "colorblind" in its application.

UNITED STATES v. MONSANTO

Supreme Court of the United States, 1989.
491 U.S. 600, 109 S.Ct. 2657, 105 L.Ed.2d 512.

JUSTICE WHITE delivered the opinion of the Court.

The questions presented here are whether the federal drug forfeiture statute authorizes a District Court to enter a pretrial order freezing assets in a defendant's possession, even where the defendant seeks to use those assets to pay an attorney; if so, we must decide whether such an order is permissible under the Constitution. We answer both of these questions in the affirmative.

"In determining the scope of a statute, we look first to its language." United States v. Turkette, 452 U.S. 576, 580 (1981). In the case before us, the language of § 853 is plain and unambiguous: all assets falling within its scope are to be forfeited upon conviction, with no exception existing for the assets used to pay attorney's fees—or anything else, for that matter.

As observed above, § 853(a) provides that a person convicted of the offenses charged in respondent's indictment "shall forfeit ... any property" that was derived from the commission of these offenses. After setting out this rule, § 853(a) repeats later in its text that upon conviction a sentencing court "shall order" forfeiture of *all* property described in § 853(a). Congress could not have chosen stronger words to express its intent that forfeiture be mandatory in cases where the statute applied, or broader words to define the scope of what was to be forfeited. Likewise, the statute provides a broad definition of "property," when describing what types of assets are within the section's scope: "real property ... tangible and intangible personal property, including rights, privileges, interests, claims, and securities." 21 U.S.C. § 853(b) (1982 ed., Supp. V). Nothing in this all-inclusive listing even hints at the idea that assets to be used to pay an attorney are not "property" within the statute's meaning.

Respondent urges us, nonetheless, to interpret the statute to exclude such property for several reasons. Principally, respondent contends that we should create such an exemption because the statute does not expressly include property to be used for attorneys' fees, and/or because Congress simply did not consider the prospect that forfeiture would reach assets that could be used to pay for an attorney. In support, respondent observes that the legislative history is "silent" on this question, and that the House and Senate debates fail to discuss this prospect. But this proves nothing: the legislative history and congressional debates are similarly silent on the use of forfeitable assets to pay stock-broker's fees, laundry bills, or country club memberships; no one could credibly argue that, as a result, assets to be used for these purposes are similarly exempt from the statute's definition of forfeitable property. The fact that the forfeiture provision reaches assets that could be used to pay attorney's fees, even though it contains no express provisions to this effect, " 'does not demonstrate ambiguity' " in the statute: " 'It demonstrates breadth.' " Sedima, S.P.R.L. v. Imrex Co., 473 U.S. 479, 499 (1985) (quoting Haroco, Inc. v. American Nat. Bank & Trust Co. of Chicago, 747 F.2d 384, 398 (CA7 1984)). The statutory provision at issue here is broad and unambiguous, and Congress' failure to supplement § 853(a)'s comprehensive phrase—"*any* property"—with an exclamatory "and we even mean assets to be used to pay an attorney" does not lessen the force of the statute's plain language.

We also find unavailing respondent's reliance on the comments of several legislators—made following enactment—to the effect that Congress did not anticipate the use of the forfeiture law to seize assets that would be used to pay attorneys.

As we have noted before, such postenactment views "form a hazard-ous basis for inferring the intent" behind a statute, United States v. Price, 361 U.S. 304, 313 (1960); instead, Congress' intent is "best determined by [looking to] the statutory language that it chooses," Sedima, S.P.R.L., supra, at 495, n. 13.   Moreover, we observe that these comments are further subject to question because Congress has refused to act on repeated suggestions by the defense bar for the sort of exemption respondent urges here, even though it has amended § 853 in other respects since these entreaties were first heard.

CHISOM v. ROEMER

Supreme Court of the United States, 1991.
501 U.S. 380, 111 S.Ct. 2354, 115 L.Ed.2d 348.

JUSTICE STEVENS delivered the opinion of the Court.

The preamble to the Voting Rights Act of 1965 establishes that the central purpose of the Act is "[t]o enforce the fifteenth amendment to the Constitution of the United States."   The Fifteenth Amendment provides:

"The right of citizens of the United States to vote shall not be denied or abridged by the United States or by any State on account of race, color, or previous condition of servitude."   U.S. Const., Amdt. 15, § 1.

In 1982, Congress amended § 2 of the Voting Rights Act to make clear that certain practices and procedures that result in the denial or abridg-ment of the right to vote are forbidden even though the absence of proof of discriminatory intent protects them from constitutional challenge. The question presented by these cases is whether this "results test" protects the right to vote in state judicial elections.   We hold that the coverage provided by the 1982 amendment is coextensive with the coverage provided by the Act prior to 1982 and that judicial elections are embraced within that coverage.

I

Petitioners in No. 90–757 represent a class of approximately 135,000 black registered voters in Orleans Parish, Louisiana.

The Louisiana Supreme Court consists of seven justices, five of whom are elected from five single-member Supreme Court Districts, and two of whom are elected from one multimember Supreme Court District. Each of the seven members of the court must be a resident of the district from which he or she is elected and must have resided there for at least two years prior to election.   Each of the justices on the Louisiana Supreme Court serves a term of 10 years.   The one multimember district, the First Supreme Court District, consists of the parishes of Orleans, St. Bernard, Plaquemines, and Jefferson.   Orleans Parish contains about half of the population of the First Supreme Court District and about half of the registered voters in that district.

More than one-half of the registered voters of Orleans Parish are black, whereas more than three-fourths of the registered voters in the other three parishes are white.

Petitioners allege that "the present method of electing two Justices to the Louisiana Supreme Court at-large from the New Orleans area impermissibly dilutes minority voting strength" in violation of § 2 of the Voting Rights Act.

The full text of § 2 as amended in 1982 reads as follows:

"Sec. 2. (a) No voting qualification or prerequisite to voting or standard, practice, or procedure shall be imposed or applied by any State or political subdivision in a manner which results in a denial or abridgement of the right of any citizen of the United States to vote on account of race or color, or in contravention of the guarantees set forth in section 4(f)(2), as provided in subsection (b).

"(b) A violation of subsection (a) is established if, based on the totality of circumstances, it is shown that the political processes leading to nomination or election in the State or political subdivision are not equally open to participation by members of a class of citizens protected by subsection (a) in that its members have less opportunity than other members of the electorate to participate in the political process and to elect representatives of their choice. The extent to which members of a protected class have been elected to office in the State or political subdivision is one circumstance which may be considered: *Provided,* That nothing in this section establishes a right to have members of a protected class elected in numbers equal to their proportion in the population." 96 Stat. 134.

Respondents contend and the [League of United Latin American Citizens Council No. 4434 v. Clements, 914 F.2d 620 (5th Cir.(1990) "LULAC")] majority agreed that Congress' choice of the word "representatives" in the phrase "have less opportunity than other members of the electorate to participate in the political process and to elect representatives of their choice" in subsection (b) is evidence of congressional intent to exclude vote dilution claims involving judicial elections from the coverage of § 2. We reject that construction because we are convinced that if Congress had such an intent, Congress would have made it explicit in the statute, or at least some of the Members would have identified or mentioned it at some point in the unusually extensive legislative history of the 1982 amendment.

Both respondents and the *LULAC* majority place their principal reliance on Congress' use of the word "representatives" instead of "legislators" in the phrase "to participate in the political process and to elect representatives of their choice." 42 U.S.C. § 1973. When Congress borrowed the phrase from White v. Regester, it replaced "legislators" with "representatives." This substitution indicates, at the very least, that Congress intended the amendment to cover more than legislative elections. Respondents argue, and the majority agreed, that the term "representatives" was used to extend § 2 coverage to executive officials, but not to judges. We think, however, that the better reading of the word "representatives" describes the winners of representative, popular elections. If executive officers, such as prosecutors, sheriffs, state attorneys general, and state treasurers, can be considered "representatives" simply because they are chosen by popular election, then the same reasoning should apply to elected judges.

Respondents suggest that if Congress had intended to have the statute's prohibition against vote dilution apply to the election of judges, it would have used the word "candidates" instead of "representatives." But that confuses the ordinary meaning of the words. The word "representative" refers to someone who has prevailed in a popular election, whereas the word "candidate" refers to someone who is seeking an office. Thus, a candidate is nominated, not elected. When Congress used "candidate" in other parts of the statute, it did so precisely because it was referring to people who were aspirants for an office. See, e.g., 42 U.S.C. §§ 1971(b) ("any candidate for the office of President"), 1971(e) ("candidates for public office"), 1973i(c) ("any candidate for the office of President"), 1973i(e)(2) ("any candidate for the office of President"), 1973l(c) ("candidates for public or party office"), 1973ff–2 ("In the case of the offices of President and Vice President, a vote for a named candidate"), 1974 ("candidates for the office of President"), 1974e ("candidates for the office of President").

The fundamental tension between the ideal character of the judicial office and the real world of electoral politics cannot be resolved by crediting judges with total indifference to the popular will while simultaneously requiring them to run for elected office. When each of several members of a court must be a resident of a separate district, and must be elected by the voters of that district, it seems both reasonable and realistic to characterize the winners as representatives of that district. Indeed, at one time the Louisiana Bar Association characterized the members of the Louisiana Supreme Court as representatives for that reason: "Each justice and judge now in office shall be considered as a representative of the judicial district within which is situated the parish of his residence at the time of his election." Louisiana could, of course, exclude its judiciary from the coverage of the Voting Rights Act by changing to a system in which judges are appointed, and in that way, it could enable its judges to be indifferent to popular opinion. The reasons why Louisiana has chosen otherwise are precisely the reasons why it is appropriate for § 2, as well as § 5, of the Voting Rights Act to continue to apply to its judicial elections.

Justice Scalia, with whom The Chief Justice and Justice Kennedy join, dissenting.

Section 2 of the Voting Rights Act of 1965 is not some all-purpose weapon for well-intentioned judges to wield as they please in the battle against discrimination. It is a statute. I thought we had adopted a regular method for interpreting the meaning of language in a statute: first, find the ordinary meaning of the language in its textual context; and second, using established canons of construction, ask whether there is any clear indication that some permissible meaning other than the ordinary one applies. If not—and especially if a good reason for the ordinary meaning appears plain—we apply that ordinary meaning.

Today, however, the Court adopts a method quite out of accord with that usual practice. It begins not with what the statute says, but with an expectation about what the statute must mean absent particular phenomena (*"[W]e are convinced* that if Congress had ... an intent [to exclude judges] Congress would have made it explicit in the statute, or at least some of the Members would have identified or mentioned it at some point in the unusually extensive legislative history," (emphasis added)); and the Court then interprets the words of the statute to fulfill its expectation. Finding nothing in the legislative history affirming that judges were excluded from the coverage of § 2, the Court gives the phrase "to elect representatives" the quite extraordinary meaning that covers the election of judges.

As method, this is just backwards, and however much we may be attracted by the result it produces in a particular case, we should in every case resist it. Our job begins with a text that Congress has passed and the President has signed. We are to read the words of that text as any ordinary Member of Congress would have read them, see Holmes, The Theory of Legal Interpretation, 12 Harv.L.Rev. 417 (1899), and apply the meaning so determined. In my view, that reading reveals that § 2 extends to vote dilution claims for the elections of representatives only, and judges are not representatives.

These cases are about method. The Court transforms the meaning of § 2, not because the ordinary meaning is irrational, or inconsistent with other parts of the statute, see, *e.g.,* Green v. Bock Laundry Machine Co., 490 U.S. 504, 510–511 (1989); Public Citizen v. Department of Justice, 491 U.S., at 470 (Kennedy, J., concurring in judgment), but because it does not fit the Court's conception of what Congress must have had in mind. When we adopt a method that psychoanalyzes Congress rather than reads its laws, when we employ a tinkerer's toolbox, we do great harm. Not only do we reach the wrong result with respect to the statute at hand, but we poison the well of future legislation, depriving legislators of the assurance that ordinary terms, used in an ordinary context, will be given a predictable meaning. Our highest responsibility in the field of statutory construction is to read the laws in a consistent way, giving Congress a sure means by which it may work the people's will. We have ignored that responsibility today. I respectfully dissent.

CORNING GLASS WORKS v. BRENNAN

[Two cases arose out of the Equal Pay Act of 1963, 29 U.S.C.A. § 206(d)(1) which added to the Fair Labor Standards Act the principle of equal pay for equal work regardless of sex: one in the Second Circuit, 474 F.2d 226 (1973); the other in the Third Circuit, 480 F.2d 1254 (1973). The principal question in each case was whether Corning violated the Act by paying a higher base wage to male night shift inspectors than it paid to female inspectors performing the same tasks on the day shift, where the higher wage was paid in addition to a separate night shift differential paid to all employees for night work. The Second Circuit held that the practice violated the Act, basing its decision essentially on an examination of the legislative history of the Act. Interpreting that same history, the Third Circuit reached the opposite conclusion. To resolve "this unusually direct conflict between two circuits," the Supreme Court granted certiorari. The Supreme Court majority of five justices agreed with the Second Circuit; three justices agreed with the Third Circuit; one justice did not participate. Excerpts from the various opinions follow:]

HODGSON v. CORNING GLASS WORKS

United States Court of Appeals, Second Circuit, 1973.
474 F.2d 226.

Before FRIENDLY, CHIEF JUDGE, KAUFMAN, CIRCUIT JUDGE, and HOLDEN, DISTRICT JUDGE.

FRIENDLY, CHIEF JUDGE:

Corning's most basic contention—one which if sustained, would immediately end the case—is that work on a steady night shift is not performed under "working conditions" similar to work on day or afternoon shifts. To those uninitiated in the language of industrial relations, that would indeed seem to be true, and the District Court for the Middle District of Pennsylvania has so held.... But, as said in one of Mr. Justice Frankfurter's early opinions, "[t]he recognized practices of an industry give life to the dead words of a statute dealing with it." United States v. Maher, 307 U.S. 148, 155, 59 S.Ct. 768, 771, 83 L.Ed. 1162 (1939). Statutory language addressed to experts must be read in the way the experts would understand it. See NLRB v. Highland Park Mfg. Co., 341 U.S. 322, 326–327, 71 S.Ct. 758, 95 L.Ed. 969 (1951) (Frankfurter, J., dissenting).

The legislative history of the Equal Pay Act supports the construction that the time at which work is performed was not regarded as a "working condition" but rather as a proper subject for "a differential based on any other factor other than sex." The equal pay bills, H.R. 3861, 88th Cong., 1st Sess. (1963); S. 910, 88th Cong., 1st Sess. (1963), as originally introduced in Congress, would have required equal pay for "equal work on jobs the performance of which requires equal skills." Ezra G. Hester, then Corning's Director of Industrial Relations Research, testified before both House and Senate Committees in opposition to this formulation. He pointed out that most of industry was by then using formal job evaluation systems in order to establish equitable wage structures in their plants, and that most of these job classification systems considered three factors in addition to "skill," to wit, effort, responsibility, and working conditions. As an example, he cited his own company's plan, which was introduced into the record. Under "working conditions" the plan and the accompanying job evaluation sheets listed two factors: "surroundings" (requiring evaluation of exposure to elements, intensity, and frequency) and "hazards" (requiring evaluation of frequency of exposure to hazard, frequency of injury, and seriousness of injury); nothing was said about time of day worked or differences in shift. Mr. Hester testified that "Other companies use similar job evaluation sheets," and urged the committees to amend the proposed legislation to conform to these industry practices. See Hearings on H.R. 3861 and Related Bills Before the Special Subcommittee on Labor of the House Committee on Education and Labor, 88th Cong., 1st Sess. 232–40 (1963); Hearings on S. 882 and S. 910 Before the Subcommittee on Labor of the Senate Committee on Labor and Public Welfare, 88th Cong., 1st Sess. 96–104 (1963).

In response to this, the bill was rewritten in committee and placed in its present form. Five House Committee members thus explained the change, H.R.Rep. No. 309, 88th Cong., 1st Sess. 8 (1963), U.S.Code Cong. & Admin.News, p. 690:

> The concept of equal pay for jobs demanding equal skill has been expanded to require equal effort, responsibility, and similar working conditions as well. These factors are the core of all job classification systems and the basis for legitimate differentials in pay.

Earlier in the Report, at p. 3, U.S.Code Cong. & Admin.News p. 689, the Committee had indicated where it thought shift differentials would fit into the statute:

> Three specific exceptions and one broad general exception are also listed.... As it is impossible to list each and every exception, the broad general exclusion ["differentials based on any other factor other than sex"] has also been included. Thus, among other things, shift differentials, restrictions on or differences based on time of day worked, hours of work, lifting or moving heavy objects, differences based on experience, training, or ability would also be excluded.

This persuasive explanation of how the bill took shape, and the evident understanding of the Committee, consistent with this explanation, of the structure of the amended bill, outweigh the point, strongly pressed by Corning, that Representative Goodell, who introduced the bill and had a hand in redrafting it, remarked during the course of an explanation of its provisions that "hours of work, difference in shift ... would logically fall within the working condition factor." 109 Cong.Rec. 9209 (1963). Corning also relies upon a statement by Representative Thompson, chairman of the Subcommittee:

> Thus, among other things, shift differentials, restrictions on or differences based on time of day worked, hours of work, lifting or moving heavy objects, differences based on experience, training, or ability would also be exempted under this act.

109 Cong.Rec. 9196. But this does not assist Corning; indeed, since it is apparent that Representative Thompson was only paraphrasing his Committee's Report, this rather supports the construction that time of day differentials were covered under the catch-all exception rather than by the term "working conditions."

BRENNAN v. CORNING GLASS WORKS

United States Court of Appeals, Third Circuit, 1973.
480 F.2d 1254.

Before KALODNER, ALDISERT, and ADAMS, CIRCUIT JUDGES.

ADAMS, CIRCUIT JUDGE.

Of course, our interpretation of the Committee Report—that the examples set forth are not *all* "factor[s] other than sex"—does not by itself suggest the converse—that they are all examples of "skill, effort, and responsibility, and ... working conditions." Thus, the listing made by the Committee Report may in fact be not simply a set of black-or-white illustrations taken exclusively from the Act's requisites (i.e., effort, skill, responsibility, and working conditions) or solely from one of its defenses ("factor[s] other than sex"), but rather a chiaroscuro picture painted with brushes dabbed in both groups. The question, therefore, remains whether time of day worked is a "working condition" or a "factor other than sex."

The only clear and unambiguous evidence concerning this point is the following statement made during the course of an explanation of the Act by Congressman Goodell, who sponsored the bill and participated in redrafting it:

> "Ninth. Although only the factors, skill, effort, responsibility, and working conditions are listed, such things as experience, ability, and training may be considered under the broad heading of skill. The usual factors of push, pull, lift, and carry come under effort. Direction of others as well as value of commodity worked upon and overall importance of assignment may be considered as part of an employee's job responsibility. Finally, standing as opposed to sitting, pleasantness or unpleasantness of surroundings, periodic rest periods, hours of work, difference

in shift, all would logically fall within the working condition factor." (Emphasis supplied)

Because of its interpretation of the Committee Report, the Second Circuit discounted this explanation by Congressman Goodell, although it was made by the bill's sponsor immediately before reading the Committee Report into the Congressional Record. In addition, it was proclaimed by Congressman Goodell as an example and guideline as to the intent of Congress. Whatever may be the merits of minimizing the views of a bill's sponsor when a Committee Report is thought to be clear and contrary to the statements of individual legislators, this Court's interpretation of the Committee Reports suggests no basic conflict between the Report and Congressman Goodell's statements. A comparison of the two demonstrates this:

Committee Report:	Congressman Goodell:
"Thus, among other things, shift differentials, restrictions on or differences based on time of day worked ... would also be excluded ..."	"Ninth ... Finally ... hours of work, differences in shift all would logically fall within the working condition factor." (emphasis supplied)
"Thus, among other things ... lifting or moving heavy objects ... would also be excluded."	"Ninth ... The usual factors of push, pull, lift, and carry come under effort ..." (emphasis supplied)
"Thus, among other things ... differences based on experience, training or ability would also be excluded."	"Ninth ... such things as experience, ability, and training may be considered under the broad heading of skill...."

Under these circumstances, where the ambiguous Committee Report and the statements by the sponsor of the legislation may reasonably be read not as conflicting but as complimentary and harmonious, giving emphasis to Congressman Goodell's explanation would not appear inappropriate. Indeed, a sponsor's views are entitled to great weight in any event. As this Court stated in Gartner v. Soloner [384 F.2d 348, 353 (3d Cir.1967)]:

"In attempting to extract the legislative purpose primary concern should always be given to the views expressed by the sponsors of the bill and in this respect the statements of Senator McClellan and Rep. Elliott should be looked to as representing the true spirit of Section 102."

We conclude, then, that time of day worked is a "working condition" within the meaning of the Equal Pay Act and not merely a "factor other than sex" to be used by an employer as a matter of defense.

―――――

CORNING GLASS WORKS v. BRENNAN

(Brennan v. Corning Glass Works)
Supreme Court of the United States, 1974.
417 U.S. 188, 94 S.Ct. 2223, 41 L.Ed.2d 1.

MR. JUSTICE MARSHALL delivered the opinion of the Court.

The courts below relied in part on conflicting statements in the legislative history having some bearing on this question of statutory construction. The Third Circuit found particularly significant a statement of Congressman Goodell, a sponsor of the Equal Pay bill, who, in the course of explaining the bill on the floor of the House, commented that "standing as opposed to sitting, pleasantness or unpleasantness of surroundings, periodic rest periods, hours of work, *differences in shift,* all would logically fall within the working conditions factor." 109 Cong. Rec. 9209 (1973) (emphasis added). The Second Circuit, in contrast, relied on a statement from the House Committee Report which, in describing the broad general exception for differentials "based on any other factor other than sex," stated: "Thus, among other things, shift differentials ... would also be excluded...." H.R.Rep. No. 309, 88th Cong., 1st Sess. (1963), at 3, U.S.Code Cong. & Admin.News, 1963, pp. 687, 689.

We agree with Judge Friendly, however, that in this case a better understanding of the phrase "performed under similar working conditions" can be obtained from a consideration of the way in which Congress arrived at the statutory language than from trying to reconcile or establish preferences between the conflicting interpretations of the Act by individual legislators or the committee reports. As Mr. Justice Frankfurter remarked in an earlier case involving interpretation of the Fair Labor Standards Act, "regard for the specific history of the legislative process that culminated in the Act now before us affords more solid ground for giving it appropriate meaning." United States v. Universal C.I.T. Credit Corp., 344 U.S. 218, 222, 73 S.Ct. 227, 230, 97 L.Ed. 260 (1952).

The most notable feature of the history of the Equal Pay Act is that Congress recognized early in the legislative process that the concept of equal pay for equal work was more readily stated in principle than reduced to statutory language which would be meaningful to employers and workable across the broad range of industries covered by the Act. As originally introduced, the Equal Pay bills required equal pay for "equal work on jobs the performance of which requires equal skills." There were only two exceptions—for differentials "made pursuant to a seniority or merit increase system which does not discriminate on the basis of sex...."

Congress' intent, as manifested in this history, was to use these terms to incorporate into the new federal act the well-defined and well-accepted principles of job evaluation so as to ensure that wage differentials based upon bona fide job evaluation plans would be outside the purview of the Act. The House Report emphasized:

> "This language recognizes there are many factors which may be used to measure the relationships between jobs and which establish a valid basis for a difference in pay. These factors will be found in a majority of the job classification systems. Thus, it is anticipated that a bona fide job classification program that does not discriminate on the basis of sex will serve as a valid defense to a charge of discrimination." H.R.Rep., *supra,* at 3, U.S.Code Cong. & Admin.News, 1963, pp. 688, 689.

MR. JUSTICE STEWART took no part in the consideration or decision of these cases.

THE CHIEF JUSTICE, MR. JUSTICE BLACKMUN, and MR. JUSTICE REHNQUIST dissent and would affirm the judgment of the Court of Appeals for the Third Circuit and reverse the judgment of the Court of Appeals for the Second Circuit for the reasons stated by Judge Adams in his opinion for the Court of Appeals in Brennan v. Corning Glass Works, 480 F.2d 1254 (3d Cir.).

———

DE MARTINEZ v. LAMAGNO

Supreme Court of the United States, 1995.
—— U.S. ——, 115 S.Ct. 2227, 132 L.Ed.2d 375.

JUSTICE GINSBURG delivered the opinion of the Court.

When a federal employee is sued for a wrongful or negligent act, the Federal Employees Liability Reform and Tort Compensation Act of 1988 (commonly known as the Westfall Act) empowers the Attorney General to certify that the employee "was acting within the scope of his office or employment at the time of the incident out of which the claim arose...." 28 U.S.C. § 2679(d)(1). Upon certification, the employee is dismissed from the action and the United States is substituted as defendant. The case then falls under the governance of the Federal Tort Claims Act (FTCA), ch. 753, 60 Stat. 812, 842. Generally, such cases unfold much as cases do against other employers who concede respondeat superior liability. If, however, an exception to the FTCA shields the United States from suit, the plaintiff may be left without a tort action against any party.

This case is illustrative. The Attorney General certified that an allegedly negligent employee "was acting within the scope of his ... employment" at the time of the episode in suit. Once brought into the case as a defendant, however, the United States asserted immunity, because the incident giving rise to the claim occurred abroad and the FTCA excepts "[a]ny claim arising in a foreign country." 28 U.S.C. § 2680(k). Endeavoring to redeem their lawsuit, plaintiffs (petitioners here) sought court review of the Attorney General's scope-of-employment certification, for if the employee was acting outside the scope of his employment, the plaintiffs' tort action could proceed against him. The lower courts held the certification unreviewable. We reverse that determination and hold that the scope-of-employment certification is reviewable in court.

I

Shortly before midnight on January 18, 1991, in Barranquilla, Colombia, a car driven by respondent Dirk A. Lamagno, a special agent of the United States Drug Enforcement Administration (DEA), collided with petitioners' car. Petitioners, who are citizens of Colombia, allege that Lamagno was intoxicated and that his passenger, an unidentified woman, was not a federal employee.

Informed that diplomatic immunity shielded Lamagno from suit in Colombia, petitioners filed a diversity action against him in the United States District Court for the Eastern District of Virginia, the district where Lamagno resided. Alleging that Lamagno's negligent driving caused the accident, petitioners sought compensation for physical injuries and property damage. In response, the local United States Attorney, acting pursuant to the Westfall Act, certified on behalf of the Attorney General that Lamagno was acting within the scope of his employment at the time of the accident. The certification, as is customary, stated no reasons for the U.S. Attorney's scope-of-employment determination.

[Section 2679(d) provides in pertinent part:

(1) Upon certification by the Attorney General that the defendant employee was acting within the scope of his office or employment at the time of the incident out of which the claim arose, any civil action or proceeding commenced upon such claim in a United States district court shall be deemed an action against the United States under the provisions of this title and all references thereto, and the United States shall be substituted as the party defendant.

(2) Upon certification by the Attorney General that the defendant employee was acting within the scope of his office or employment at the time of the incident out of which the claim arose, any civil action or proceeding commenced upon such claim in a State court shall be removed without bond at any time before trial by the Attorney General to the district court of the United States for the district and division embracing the place in which the action or proceeding is pending. Such action or proceeding shall be deemed to be an action or proceeding brought against the United States under the provisions of this title and all references thereto, and the United States shall be substituted as the party defendant. This certification of the Attorney General shall conclusively establish scope of office or employment for purposes of removal.

(3) In the event that the Attorney General has refused to certify scope of office or employment under this section, the employee may at any time before trial petition the court to find and certify that the employee was acting within the scope of his office or employment. Upon such certification by the court, such action or proceeding shall be deemed to be an action or proceeding brought against the United States under the provisions of this title and all references thereto, and the United States shall be substituted as the party defendant.]

Thus, absent judicial review and court rejection of the certification, Lamagno would be released from the litigation; furthermore, he could not again be pursued in any damages action arising from the "same subject matter." § 2679(b)(1). Replacing Lamagno, the United States would become sole defendant.

Ordinarily, scope-of-employment certifications occasion no contest. While the certification relieves the employee of responsibility, plaintiffs will confront instead a financially reliable defendant. But in this case, substitution of the United States would cause the demise of the action: petitioners' claims "ar[ose] in a foreign country," FTCA, 28 U.S.C. § 2680(k), and thus fell within an exception to the FTCA's waiver of the United States' sovereign immunity. See § 2679(d)(4) (upon certification, the action "shall proceed in the same manner as any action against the United States ... and shall be subject to the limitations and exceptions applicable to those actions"). Nor would the immunity of the United States allow petitioners to bring Lamagno back into the action.

To keep their action against Lamagno alive, and to avoid the fatal consequences of unrecallable substitution of the United States as the party defendant, petitioners asked the District Court to review the certification. Petitioners maintained that Lamagno was acting outside the scope of his employment at the time of the accident; certification to the contrary, they argued, was groundless and untrustworthy. Following Circuit precedent, ..., the District Court held the certification unreviewable, substituted the United States for Lamagno, and dismissed petitioners' suit. App. 7–9. In an unadorned order, the Fourth Circuit affirmed. 23 F.3d 402 (1994).

The Circuits divide sharply on this issue. Parting from the Fourth Circuit, most of the Courts of Appeals have held certification by the Attorney General or her delegate amenable to court review. We granted certiorari to resolve the conflict, ..., and we now reverse the Fourth Circuit's judgment.

II

We encounter in this case the familiar questions: where is the line to be drawn; and who decides. Congress has firmly answered the first question. "Scope of employment" sets the line. See § 2679(b)(1); United States v. Smith, 499 U.S. 160, 111 S.Ct. 1180, 113 L.Ed.2d 134 (1991). If Lamagno is inside that line, he is not subject to petitioners' suit; if he is outside the line, he is personally answerable. The sole question, then, is who decides on which side of the line the case falls: the local U.S. Attorney, unreviewably or, when that official's decision is contested, the court. Congress did not address this precise issue unambiguously, if at all. As the division in the lower courts and in this Court shows, the Westfall Act is, on the "who decides" question we confront, open to divergent interpretation.

Two considerations weigh heavily in our analysis, and we state them at the outset. First, the Attorney General herself urges review, mindful that in cases of the kind petitioners present, the incentive of her delegate to certify is marked. Second, when a government official's determination of a fact or circumstance—for example, "scope of employment"—is dispositive of a court controversy, federal courts generally do not hold the determination unreviewable. Instead, federal judges traditionally proceed from the "strong presumption that Congress intends judicial review." Bowen v. Michigan Academy of Family Physicians, 476 U.S. 667, 670, 106 S.Ct. 2133, 2136, 90 L.Ed.2d 623 (1986); see id., at 670–673, 106 S.Ct., at 2135–37; Abbott Laboratories v. Gardner, 387 U.S. 136, 140, 87 S.Ct. 1507, 1511, 18 L.Ed.2d 681 (1967). Chief Justice Marshall long ago captured the essential idea:

> "It would excite some surprise if, in a government of laws and of principle, furnished with a department whose appropriate duty it is to decide questions of right, not only between individuals, but between the government and individuals; a ministerial officer might, at his discretion, issue this powerful process ... leaving to [the claimant] no remedy, no appeal to the laws of his country, if he should believe the claim to be unjust. But this anomaly does not exist; this imputation cannot be cast on the legislature of the United States." United States v. Nourse, 34 U.S. (9 Pet.) 8, 28–29, 9 L.Ed. 31 (1835).

Accordingly, we have stated time and again that judicial review of executive action "will not be cut off unless there is persuasive reason to believe that such was the purpose of Congress." Abbott Laboratories, 387 U.S., at 140, 87 S.Ct., at 1511 (citing cases). No persuasive reason for restricting access to judicial review is discernible from the statutory fog we confront here.

III

We return now, in more detail, to the statutory language, to determine whether it overcomes the presumption favoring judicial review, the tradition of court review of scope certifications, and the anomalies attending foreclosure of review.

The certification, removal, and substitution provisions of the Westfall Act, 28 U.S.C. § 2679(d)(1)–(3), work together to assure that, when scope of employment is in controversy, that matter, key to the application of the FTCA, may be resolved in federal court. To that end, the Act specifically allows employees whose certification requests have been denied by the Attorney General, to contest the denial in court. § 2679(d)(3). If the action was initiated by the tort plaintiff in state court, the Attorney General, on the defendant-employee's petition, is to enter the case and may remove it to the federal court so that the scope determination can be made in the federal forum. Ibid.

When the Attorney General has granted certification, if the case is already in federal court (as is this case, because of the parties' diverse citizenship), the United States will be substituted as the party defendant. § 2679(d)(1). If the case was initiated by the tort plaintiff in state court, the Attorney General is to remove it to the federal court, where, as in a case that originated in the federal forum, the United States will be substituted as the party defendant. § 2679(d)(2).

The statute next instructs that the "certification of the Attorney General shall conclusively establish scope of office or employment for purposes of removal." Ibid. (emphasis added). The meaning of that instruction, in the view of petitioners and the Attorney General, is just what the emphasized words import. Congress spoke in discrete sentences in § 2679(d)(2) first of removal, then of substitution. Next, Congress made the Attorney General's certificate conclusive solely for purposes of removal, and notably not for purposes of substitution. It follows, petitioners and the Attorney General conclude, that the scope-of-employment judgment determinative of substitution can and properly should be checked by the court, i.e., the Attorney General's scarcely disinterested certification on that matter is by statute made the first, but not the final word.

Lamagno's construction does not draw on the "certification . . . shall [be conclusive] . . . for purposes of removal" language of § 2679(d)(2). Instead, Lamagno emphasizes the word "shall" in the statement: "Upon certification by the Attorney General . . . any civil action or proceeding . . . shall be deemed an action against the United States . . ., and the United States shall be substituted as the party defendant." § 2679(d)(1) (emphasis added). Any doubt as to the commanding force of the word "shall," [9] Lamagno urges, is dispelled by this further feature: the Westfall Act's predecessor, the Federal Drivers Act, provided for court review of "scope-of-employment" certifications at the tort plaintiff's behest. Not only does the Westfall Act fail to provide for certification challenges by tort plaintiffs, Lamagno underscores, but the Act prominently provides for court review of refusals to certify at the behest of

---

9. Though "shall" generally means "must," legal writers sometimes use, or misuse, "shall" to mean "should," "will," or even "may." See D. Mellinkoff, Mellinkoff's Dictionary of American Legal Usage 402–403 (1992) ("shall" and "may" are "frequently treated as synonyms" and their meaning depends on context); B. Garner, Dictionary of Modern Legal Usage—(to be published, 2d ed. 1995) ("[C]ourts in virtually every English-speaking jurisdiction have held—by necessity—that shall may mean may in some contexts, and vice versa."). For example, certain of the Federal Rules use the word "shall" to authorize, but not to require, judicial action. See, e.g., Fed.Rule Civ.Proc. 16(e) ("The order following a final pretrial conference shall be modified only to prevent manifest injustice.") (emphasis added); Fed.Rule Crim. Proc. 11(b) (A nolo contendere plea "shall be accepted by the court only after due consideration of the views of the parties and the interest of the public in the effective administration of justice.") (emphasis added).

defending employees. See § 2679(d)(3). Congress, in Lamagno's view, thus plainly intended the one-sided review, i.e., a court check at the call of the defending employee, but no check at the tort plaintiff's call.

We recognize that both sides have tendered plausible constructions of a text most interpreters have found far from clear. * * * Indeed, the United States initially took the position that the local U.S. Attorney's scope-of-employment certifications are conclusive and unreviewable but, on further consideration, changed its position. See Brief for United States 14, n. 4. Because the statute is reasonably susceptible to divergent interpretation, we adopt the reading that accords with traditional understandings and basic principles: that executive determinations generally are subject to judicial review and that mechanical judgments are not the kind federal courts are set up to render. Under our reading, the Attorney General's certification that a federal employee was acting within the scope of his employment—a certification the executive official, in cases of the kind at issue, has a compelling interest to grant—does not conclusively establish as correct the substitution of the United States as defendant in place of the employee. * * *

For the reasons stated, the judgment of the United States Court of Appeals for the Fourth Circuit is reversed, and the case is remanded for proceedings consistent with this opinion.

It is so ordered.

Justice Souter, with whom The Chief Justice, Justice Scalia and Justice Thomas join, dissenting.

One does not instinctively except to a statutory construction that opens the door of judicial review to an individual who complains of a decision of the Attorney General, when the Attorney General herself is ready to open the door. But however much the Court and the Attorney General may claim their reading of the Westfall Act to be within the bounds of reasonable policy, the great weight of interpretive evidence shows that they misread Congress's policy. And so I respectfully dissent.

The two principal textual statements under examination today are perfectly straightforward. "Upon certification by the Attorney General . . . any civil action or proceeding . . . shall be deemed an action against the United States . . ., and the United States shall be substituted as the party defendant." 28 U.S.C. § 2679(d)(1); see also § 2679(d)(4) ("[u]pon certification, any action or proceeding . . . shall proceed in the same manner as any action against the United States filed pursuant to [the FTCA]. . . ."). Notwithstanding the Court's observation that some contexts can leave the word "shall" a bit slippery, ante, at 2235, n. 9, we have repeatedly recognized the normally uncompromising directive that it carries. See United States v. Monsanto, 491 U.S. 600, 607, 109 S.Ct. 2657, 2662, 105 L.Ed.2d 512 (1989); Anderson v. Yungkau, 329 U.S. 482, 485, 67 S.Ct. 428, 430, 91 L.Ed. 436 (1947); see also Griggs v. Provident Consumer Discount Co., 459 U.S. 56, 61, 103 S.Ct. 400, 403, 74 L.Ed.2d 225 (1982) (per curiam); Association of Civilian Technicians v. FLRA, 22

F.3d 1150, 1153 (CADC 1994) ("The word 'shall' generally indicates a command that admits of no discretion on the part of the person instructed to carry out the directive"); Black's Law Dictionary 1375 (6th ed. 1990) ("As used in statutes ... this word is generally imperative or mandatory"). There is no hint of wobbling in the quoted language, and the normal meaning of its plain provisions that substitution is mandatory on certification is the best evidence of the congressional intent that the Court finds elusive. That normal meaning and manifest intent is confirmed by additional textual evidence and by its consonance with normal jurisdictional assumptions.

We would not, of course, read "shall" as so uncompromising if the Act also included some express provision for review at the behest of the tort plaintiff when the Attorney General certifies that the acts charged were inside the scope of a defendant employee's official duties. But the Westfall Act has no provision to that effect, and the very fact that its predecessor, the Federal Drivers Act, Pub.L. 87–258, 75 Stat. 539 (1961), combined "shall" with just such authorization for review at the will of a disappointed tort plaintiff, ibid. (previously codified at 28 U.S.C. § 2679(d) (1982 ed.)), makes the absence of a like provision from the Westfall Act especially good evidence that Congress meant to drop this feature from the system, leaving "shall" to carry its usual unconditional message. See Brewster v. Gage, 280 U.S. 327, 337, 50 S.Ct. 115, 118, 74 L.Ed. 457 (1930) ("The deliberate selection of language so differing from that used in ... earlier Acts indicates that a change of law was intended"); 2A N. Singer, Sutherland on Statutory Construction § 51.02, p. 454 (4th ed. 1984). That conclusion gains further force from the presence in the Westfall Act of an express provision for judicial review at the behest of a defending employee, when the Attorney General refuses to certify that the acts fell within the scope of government employment. See 28 U.S.C. § 2679(d)(3) ("[i]n the event that the Attorney General has refused to certify scope of office or employment under this section, the employee may at any time before trial petition the court to find and certify that the employee was acting within the scope of his office or employment"). Providing authority in one circumstance but not another implies an absence of authority in the statute's silence. See Russello v. United States, 464 U.S. 16, 23, 104 S.Ct. 296, 300, 78 L.Ed.2d 17 (1983) ("Where Congress includes particular language in one section of a statute but omits it in another section of the same Act, it is generally presumed that Congress acts intentionally and purposely in the disparate inclusion or exclusion"); see also United States v. Naftalin, 441 U.S. 768, 773–774, 99 S.Ct. 2077, 2081–2082, 60 L.Ed.2d 624 (1979). * * *

The Court's final counterpoint to plain reading relies heavily on "the strong presumption that Congress intends judicial review of administrative action," citing a line of cases involving judicial challenges to regulations claimed to be outside the statutory authority of the administrative agencies that promulgated them. See ante, at 2231, citing Bowen v. Michigan Academy of Family Physicians, 476 U.S. 667, 670–673, 106

S.Ct. 2133, 2136–2137, 90 L.Ed.2d 623 (1986); Abbott Laboratories v. Gardner, 387 U.S. 136, 140, 87 S.Ct. 1507, 1511, 18 L.Ed.2d 681 (1967). It is, however, a fair question whether this presumption, usually applied to permit review of agency regulations carrying the force and effect of law, should apply with equal force to a Westfall Act certification. The very narrow factual determination committed to the Attorney General's discretion is related only tangentially, if at all, to her primary executive duties; she determines only whether a federal employee, who will probably not even be affiliated with the Justice Department, acted within the scope of his employment on a particular occasion. This function is far removed from the agency action that gave rise to the presumption of reviewability in Bowen, supra, at 668–669, 106 S.Ct., at 2134–2135, in which the Court considered whether Congress provided the Secretary of Health and Human Services with non-reviewable authority to promulgate certain Medicare distribution regulations, and in Abbott Laboratories, supra, at 138–139, 87 S.Ct., at 1510, in which the Court considered whether Congress provided the Secretary of Health, Education and Welfare with non-reviewable authority to promulgate certain prescription drug labeling regulations.

The Court's answer that the presumption of reviewability should control this case rests on the invocation of a different, but powerful principle, that no person may be a judge in his own cause. But this principle is not apt here. The Attorney General (who has delegated her Westfall Act responsibilities to the United States Attorneys, 28 CFR § 15.3(a) (1994)) is authorized to determine when any one of nearly three million federal employees was acting within the scope of authority at an allegedly tortious moment. She will characteristically have no perceptible interest in the effect of her certification decision, except in the work it may visit on her employees or the liability it may ultimately place on the National Government (each of which considerations could only influence her to deny certification subject to the employee's right to challenge her). And even where she certifies under circumstances of the Government's immunity, as here, she does not save her employer, the United States, from any liability it would face in the absence of certification; if she refused to certify, the Government would remain as free of exposure as if she issued a certification. The most that can be claimed is that when the Government would enjoy immunity it would be easy to do a favor for a federal employee by issuing a certification. But at this point the possibility of institutional self interest has simply become de minimis, and the likelihood of improper influence has become too attenuated to analogize to the case in which the interested party would protect himself by judging his own cause or otherwise take the law into his own hands in disregard of established legal process. * * *

In any event, even when this presumption is applicable, it is still no more than a presumption, to be given controlling effect only if reference to "specific language or specific legislative history" and "inferences of intent drawn from the statutory scheme as a whole," Block v. Community Nutrition Institute, 467 U.S. 340, 349, 104 S.Ct. 2450, 2455–2456, 81

L.Ed.2d 270 (1984), leave the Court with "substantial doubt" as to Congress's design, id., at 351, 104 S.Ct., at 2456. There is no substantial doubt here. The presumption has no work to do.

I would affirm.

VINCENT v. PABST BREWING CO.

Supreme Court of Wisconsin, 1970.
47 Wis.2d 120, 177 N.W.2d 513.

HANLEY, JUSTICE.

Two related questions are presented on this appeal:

(1) Should the doctrine of pure comparative negligence be adopted in Wisconsin; and, if so.

(2) Should such adoption be accomplished by this court rather than by the legislature?

Under the current law in Wisconsin, the appellant can recover nothing from the respondents because his negligence exceeded that of the respondent Nye. Under pure comparative negligence, however, appellant would recover 40 percent of his damages, for pure comparative negligence never bars recovery. Instead, it merely reduces the recoverable amount of one's damages by the percentage of his negligence. In considering the appellant's contention that a doctrine of pure comparative negligence should be adopted, the Wisconsin history of both contributory negligence and comparative negligence should be briefly noted.

The doctrine of contributory negligence as a complete bar to recovery was originally adopted by the English courts in Butterfield v. Forrester (1809), 11 East. 60, 103 Eng.Rep. 926. This doctrine then spread to this country and was adopted by this court in Chamberlain v. Milwaukee & Mississippi R.R. Co. (1858), 7 Wis. 425, 431, and in Dressler v. Davis (1958), 7 Wis. 527, 531. In order to avoid the harshness of the doctrine of contributory negligence, which had its origin in an era of economic individualism, the Wisconsin legislature in 1875 created what exists in our present statutes as sec. 192.50, Stats. This section, however, is limited in its application to railroads and their employees. It was not until 1931 that our legislature passed, for general application, what is now sec. 895.045, Stats.

In its present form sec. 895.045, Stats., reads:

"Contributory negligence; when bars recovery. Contributory negligence shall not bar recovery in an action by any person or his legal representative to recover damages for negligence resulting in death or in injury to person or property if such negligence was not as great as the negligence of the person against whom recovery is sought, but any damages allowed shall be diminished in the proportion to the amount of negligence attributable to the person recovering.''

Noting that contributory negligence is a court-adopted doctrine, the appellant contends that such doctrine has only been partially eliminated by sec. 895.045, Stats. In other words, the appellant contends that the statute eliminates the doctrine where the negligence of the defendant exceeds that of the plaintiff, but that the court-adopted doctrine remains in effect where the negligence of the plaintiff equals or exceeds that of the defendant. Thus, according to the appellant, it is not sec. 895.045, Stats., but the common law doctrine of contributory negligence (to the extent it was left unchanged by the statute) which bars his recovery. If, in fact, such were the case, this court, of course, would have authority to change the common law.

Although considerable disagreement exists as to whether a doctrine of pure comparative negligence should be adopted in Wisconsin, there has been considerable agreement as to the ability or propriety of this court's initiating such adoption.

In short, the legislature should consider whether fairness is preserved by applying the comparative negligence doctrine as we now know it or by applying a doctrine of pure comparative negligence.

Without passing judgment upon the merits of pure comparative negligence as opposed to comparative negligence as it is presently applied in this jurisdiction, we think that the legislature is the body best equipped to adopt the change advocated by the appellant. Such was also the decision of the Illinois Supreme Court in Maki v. Frelk (1968), 40 Ill.2d 193, 239 N.E.2d 445, when it was asked to adopt for general application the doctrine of comparative negligence.

HEFFERNAN, JUSTICE (concurring).

I concur in the result and agree that, in view of the legislature's present study of comparative negligence problems, this court should abstain from considering the question raised by the plaintiff-appellant.

I do not agree, however, that the passage of the comparative negligence act has divested this court of its inherent common-law prerogative of reconsidering matters that stem from judicial decision.

WILKIE, JUSTICE (concurring).

I believe there is a need for changing the rule under the Wisconsin comparative negligence system which prohibits a plaintiff from recovering a portion of his damages where his negligence is equal to or greater than the defendant's who is at least partially responsible for his injuries.

Although, in my opinion, the court has the authority to make these changes in the rule, and the legislature has not preempted the entire subject, at this time I would defer to the legislature as the proper body to make a complete study of the subject and to adopt changes it concludes appropriate. Therefore, I concur.

I have been authorized to state that Mr. Justice Beilfuss joins in this concurrence.

Hallows, Chief Justice (dissenting).

The doctrine of pure comparative negligence should be adopted and the unjust doctrine of contributory negligence repudiated; this can and should be done by this court exercising its inherent power.

I see the justice of the cause and read history differently than does the majority opinion. The doctrine of contributory negligence came into the common law rather late in the development of the fault principle in torts.

In 1913 by ch. 644 of the laws of that year, there was added a comparison of negligence in terms of proportion of negligence in order to mitigate the amount of recovery. From analogy mainly to this statute and to the FELA (45 U.S.C.A. sec. 53), the legislature adopted in 1931 what is now sec. 895.045. This section related to personal-injury actions and was expressly addressed, not to comparative negligence, but to the proposition that "contributory negligence shall not bar a recovery * * *." This escape from the bar of contributory negligence was in terms of whether the negligence was not as great as the negligence of the person against whom recovery is "sought" and in such cases damages would be "diminished in proportion to the amount of negligence attributable to the person recovering." This statute had two effects: (1) It used the comparison of negligence to determine when contributory negligence was not a bar; and (2) it used comparison of negligence to determine the amount of damages when recovery was allowed.

While the so-called limited-comparative-negligence doctrine was an advance step and other states have some form of it, it is almost 40 years old and its limitation is not now in accord with modern concepts of social justice. Justice demands a person be held responsible for his acts and to the full extent which they cause injury even though the negligence of other persons may contribute to the same injury. If A, B, and C all cause an injury to the extent of 20, 30, and 50 percent, respectively, they should all pay that portion of the damages. If A, B, and C were defendants or if A was a plaintiff, that is what would happen under the Wisconsin rule. A, as a plaintiff, contributes by assuming his own negligence and only recovering 80 percent of his damages. However, the Wisconsin law works an injustice because if B is the plaintiff, A is let out entirely because B's contributory negligence is greater than A's; and C, although 50 percent negligent, must bear A's 20 percent or a total of 70 percent. If C is not financially responsible, B collects nothing. There is no rhyme or reason in justice why A, being 20 percent at fault, ought not to pay his just proportionate share or why C should pay it without a right to recover in contribution.

The majority of the court states if there is to be any change it should be done by the legislature. This court has never construed sec. 895.045. Stats., to pre-empt the contributory negligence field of the common law. All this court has done was to decide cases under that section and to interpret what its language meant. This is not the same as holding the section preempted the field by legislative action or by silence. The doctrine of acquiescence by silence at best is a scapegoat doctrine, and it has no application here. The legislature does not read our advance sheets; and if a few lawyer legislators do, it is not with a supervisory eye. Nor is the use of lay language to describe the results flowing from the application of the section or to loosely characterize it a holding or a decision for pre-emption.

This court has a duty of leadership to advance the jurisprudence of this state and when an injustice is found in a doctrine of the common law, the court should not have reluctance to correct it. In this case we are asked to do so and we should respond.

NOTE

In his book, A Common Law for the Age of Statutes 36 (1982), U.S. Circuit Judge (former Dean and Professor of Law at Yale) Guido Calabresi analyzed the various opinions of the court and commented:

> In this way, the Wisconsin legislature was informed (blackmailed if you will) that failure to revise the law would lead to judicial revision, but it was left in the dark as to what that revision would be.

In Lupie v. Hartzheim, 54 Wis.2d 415, 195 N.W.2d 461, 462 (1972) the court furnished the subsequent history:

> After the mandate of *Vincent* ... the legislature enacted ch. 47 of the Laws of 1971, published on June 22, 1971. That statutory modification struck from the statute the words "as great as" and substituted therefore the words "greater than." Under this statutory modification, plaintiffs found to be 50 percent negligent will be able to recover 50 percent of their damages from a defendant who is found to be equally at fault. The point at which a plaintiff is barred from recovering has been raised by one percentile point.

Chapter III

THE DOCTRINE OF PRECEDENT

Section 1

INTRODUCTION TO PRECEDENT

RUGGERO J. ALDISERT, PRECEDENT: WHAT IT IS AND WHAT IT ISN'T; WHEN DO WE KISS IT AND WHEN DO WE KILL IT *

The title of this offering is inspired by Holmes' sparkling apothegm:

> When you get the dragon out of his cave on to the plain and in the daylight, you can count his teeth and claws, and see just what is his strength. But to get him out is only the first step. The next is either to kill him, or to tame him and make him a useful animal.[1]

The doctrine of precedent is everyone's dragon. If facts in the putative precedent are identical with or reasonably similar to those in the compared case, the precedent is recognized as legitimate, and it is applied. In such cases, all of us—student and professor, lawyer and judge, commentator and philosopher—consider it merely, as the Italians say, *un dragonetto* (a small dragon). But if the material facts in the compared case do not run on all fours with the putative precedent, the doctrine becomes *un dragone* or, to give equal time, *una dragonessa* (a full grown, ferocious dragon). Wrestling with such a dragon can be the most difficult and controversial job in the judging business.

I realize that literature on how to deal with this dragon abounds. To borrow Rabelais' Judge Bridlegoose,

> The subject has been well and exactly seen, surveyed, over-looked, reviewed, recognized, read and read over again, tossed and turned about, seriously perused and [we have] examined the preparatories, productions, evidences, proofs, allegations, depositions, cross-speeches, contradictions ... and other such like confects and spiceries.[2]

Undeterred, I make bold to mount my charger, draw my lance, and gallop into the lists to volunteer some advice on how to tweak the

---

* R.J. Aldisert, *Precedent: What It Is and What It Isn't; When Do We Kiss It and When Do We Kill It,* 17 Pepperdine L.Rev. 605 (1990). The article expands remarks delivered at the Mid–Winter Meeting of the Conference of State Chief Justices, Orlando, Florida, January 25, 1989.

1. Holmes, *The Path of the Law,* 10 Harv.L.Rev. 457, 469 (1897).

2. Rabelais, Bk III, at 39.

dragon's tail. Perhaps the dragon will prove too elusive, or I too bold or too meek, but ever persistent I will press on, hoping to tame this dragon. I bring with me experience, not only as a judge, to be sure, but also as one who has explored and meandered in the judicial process thicket, seeking trails to understand what it is all about.

I.

Let's take a moment to review some basics. Precedent is an often misunderstood concept. Some believe it is more understandable than explainable. I tried my hand at a definition in Allegheny County General Hospital v. NLRB in 1979:

> A judicial precedent attaches a specific legal consequence to a detailed set of facts in an adjudged case or judicial decision, which is then considered as furnishing the rule for the determination of a subsequent case involving identical or similar material facts and arising in the same court or a lower court in the judicial hierarchy.[4]

Chief Justice Marshall expressed the reason for this definition in 1821:

> It is a maxim not to be disregarded, that general expressions, in every opinion, are to be taken in connection with the case in which those expressions are used. If they go beyond the case, they may be respected, but ought not to control the judgment in a subsequent suit when the very point is presented for decision. The reason of this maxim is obvious. The question actually before the Court is investigated with care, and considered in its full extent. Other principles which may serve to illustrate it, are considered in their relation to the case decided, but their possible bearing on all other cases is seldom completely investigated.[5]

Stare decisis is the policy of the courts to stand by precedent.[6] The expression *stare decisis* is but an abbreviation of *stare decisis et non quieta movere* (to stand by or adhere to decisions and not disturb that which is settled). Consider these words. First, *decisis*. This word means literally, and legally, the decision. The doctrine is not *stare dictis*. It is not "to stand by or keep to what was said." The doctrine is not *stare rationibus decidendi* or "keep to the *rationes decidendi* of past cases." Rather, a case is important only for what it decides: for "the what," not for "the why," and not for "the how." It is important only for the decision, for the detailed legal consequence following a detailed set of facts. Thus, *stare decisis* means what the court *did,* not what it *said.*

4. Allegheny County Gen. Hosp. v. NLRB, 608 F.2d 965, 969–70 (3d Cir.1979) (footnote omitted).

5. Cohens v. Virginia, 19 U.S. (6 Wheat.) 264, 399–400 (1821).

6. Black's Law Dictionary 1261 (5th ed. 1979).

Strictly speaking, the later court is not bound by the statement of reasons, or *dictis,* set forth in the rationale. We know this because a decision may still be vital although the original reasons for supporting it may have changed drastically or been proved terribly fallacious. In a large number of cases, both ancient and modern, one or more of the reasons given for the decision can be proved to be wrong, but the cases have retained vitality.

Priestly v. Fowler,[7] announcing the common law fellow-servant rule, is one such case. The court based the holding on the alleged consent of a servant to run the risk. Yet there was no evidence that such consent was ever requested of, or given by, fellow servants. Of this case, it has been said that Lord Abinger planted it, Baron Alderson watered it, and the devil gave it increase.[8] The concept, however, was almost immediately adopted in the United States in Farwell v. Boston & Worcester Railroad.[9] Chief Justice Shaw reasoned that an employee consented to assume the risk of negligence by a fellow servant upon accepting employment. Again, there were no facts to support the assertion that the employee actually consented to anything. This was a concept built out of thin air. Yet, the fellow-servant rule remained the law in the United States for many years.[10]

II.

Our understanding is furthered by setting forth in symbolic logic the canonical formula which to me expresses the entire philosophy of the common-law tradition. The "material implication" formula is the essence of precedent: if antecedent fact P is present, then legal consequence Q will follow. This is indicated: P⊃Q. Precedent thus is embodied in the following formula:

$$P \supset Q$$
$$R \cdot P$$
$$\therefore R \supset Q$$

The key to logic and the law is correctly deciding when R is equal to P. If R's material facts are similar or the same as P's, then the previous case, P⊃Q, controls. The essence of common-law precedent is, therefore, two-fold:

+ The rule or holding of the case has the force of law.

+ The decision constitutes the rule in subsequent cases containing material facts similar to or identical with those in the case.

---

7. 3 M. & W. 1, 150 Eng.Rep. 1030 (1838).

8. C. Kenny, Law of Tort 90 (5th ed. 1928).

9. 45 Mass. (4 Met.) 49 (1842).

10. *See* W. Keeton, D. Dobbs, R. Keeton, D. Owen, Prosser and Keeton on Torts § 80 (5th ed. 1984).

This doctrine is central to legal reasoning, briefs, arguments, decision-making, and opinion writing. Yet precedent is but one aspect of the doctrine of stare decisis. Precedent means simply that like cases should be treated alike. Stare decisis requires that the holding of a similar case with sufficiently similar facts to the case at issue, be applied to courts of equal or lesser hierarchy within the same jurisdiction.[11]

Precedent and stare decisis, as discussed above, are peculiar to common-law countries. Neither Roman law nor civil-law traditions that built on it affords to a court decision the dignity and legal efficacy of this Anglo–American notion. In theory at least, precedent in its pristine elegance is not followed on the European continent, in Latin America or in the Socialist countries. In actual practice, however, civil-law courts are today borrowing our concepts of precedent as shortcut interpretations of codes and statutes, while theoretically speaking, each case must be an ab initio interpretation of a legislative act.[12]

III.

Precedent can be discussed in the context of four common types of opinions:

1. The textbook common-law model. Here the opinion discusses only the adjudicative facts. Facts are carefully and meticulously set forth so that the reader may quickly become acquainted with the material facts that form the subject of the holding. The court does not suggest how it would decide another case based on a change in the material facts. The fabric is tightly woven. There is no room, there is no give, to stretch the holding beyond the stated facts.[13]

2. A variation of this purist model exists when, in addition to the adjudicative (or material) facts, the court also discusses narrow and specific facts not in the record and gratuitously suggests how it would decide a case based on those non-record facts. Such a discussion is easily recognized as *obiter dictum*. Consider this example: Operating his car at an improperly high rate of speed, the driver-defendant attempts a turn and whips across the centerline and crashes into oncoming traffic. The court decides the case in favor of the plaintiff and says by way of *dictum*, "Of course, although the facts are not present here, if the steering wheel suddenly becomes defective, we would have a products liability case and the defendant would not have been liable."

3. A third model occurs when the court suggests how it would decide an entire series of cases based on a broad array of facts not in the record. So long as this discussion does not implicate the adjudicative facts at bar, it also is recognized as *obiter dictum*. Consider the same

---

11. Black's Law Dictionary 1261 (5th ed. 1979).

12. *See generally Continental Legal Systems, supra* note 3, at 935–93 (discussion of civil law in theory and in practice).

13. *See, e.g.,* Strotman v. K.C. Summers Buick, Inc., 141 Ill.App.3d 8, 11–12, 489 N.E.2d 1148, 1151 (1986) (upholding the dismissal of a complaint alleging strict products liability for a car accident, because the complaint lacked specificity as to what was defective).

operative facts presented in our second model. This time the court says, "If the manufacturer designed a defective brake, a sticking accelerator, a poorly designed steering mechanism, the plaintiff would have a valid cause of action against the car dealer and manufacturer." This is only dictum. The facts of the case do not discuss defective steering.

4. A fourth model is an opinion in which the court's statement of its conclusion is broad enough to cover not only record facts but also additional facts not in the record. Here, the court's decision is not *obiter dictum*. It is truly the decision of the case, arrived at in the common-law tradition, but couched in a holding that is beyond a rule of law in the narrow sense.[14] The decision takes the form of a general principle instead of a narrow rule of law.

Each of the foregoing variations announce decisions of the court and can be components of the doctrine of *stare decisis*. As precedents, however, they are not currency of equal value. Clearly, the first one, the classic common-law model, possesses the strongest bite of precedent. As we go down the list of examples, numbers two and three are not precedent, and yet they are authority that can be considered by a court in a subsequent decision. The fourth variation meets the definition's technical niceties, but does not possess maximum strength, and therefore, does not achieve the reliability of a decision limited to the record material facts. An able advocate may convince a subsequent court that its original holding, although technically precedent, was only "a little bit precedent."

This fourth model causes the courts more trouble than any aspect of adjudication. It occurs when a court does not announce a narrow rule based solely on record facts, but embarks on an intellectual frolic of its own. Two examples of the fourth variation, decided in the same year, are illustrative.

In Webb v. Zern,[15] Charles Webb purchased a keg of beer from a distributor, John Zern. Webb's son, Nelson, was injured when the keg exploded. The Pennsylvania Supreme Court held that section 402A of the *Restatement (Second) of Torts* was controlling and then stated: "We hereby adopt the foregoing language as the law of Pennsylvania." The court should have held: Nelson, the son, could recover in tort from the brewer, beer distributor and keg manufacturer on the theory of strict products liability, for the reasons set forth in the *Restatement (Second) of Torts,* section 402A. This holding would have met the strictures of the pure common-law model. In holding as they did, the judges galloped out of the courtroom, up the hill to the legislature, and proceeded to legislate. The decision was not limited to the material facts, but rather announced a broad principle of law that could be applied to cases with materially different facts.

---

14. *See, e.g.,* Finberg v. Sullivan, 634 F.2d 50 (3d Cir.1980). Although the facts before the court in *Finberg* were limited to Philadelphia County, and only that county's procedural rules were interpreted, the court announced a decision governing the entire State of Pennsylvania.

15. 422 Pa. 424, 220 A.2d 853 (1966).

Another example of this type of judicial legislation can be seen in Miranda v. Arizona.[16] *Miranda* was decided in 1966 and promulgated a broad legal principle, the so-called *"Miranda* Rule." For the past twenty years, courts and police departments across the country have been forced to decide what does and what does not implicate *Miranda.* The common-law tradition requires starting with a narrow holding and then, depending upon the collective experience of the judiciary, either applying it or not applying it to subsequent facts. The Court did the opposite in *Miranda.*

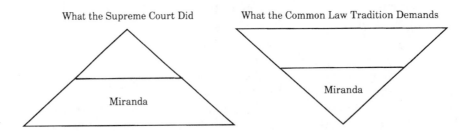

What the Supreme Court Did   What the Common Law Tradition Demands

Miranda   Miranda

Because the usual model was inverted in this case, the Court has spent the last twenty years chipping away at its holding.

Miranda says that a prisoner must be advised that he or she has a right to remain silent, a right to have an attorney present during questioning, and a right to the appointment of an attorney if the prisoner cannot afford one. In 1971, the Court said that *Miranda*'s proscription did not apply if the statement was used only to impeach a witness.[17] The Court subsequently held that although it was necessary to cut off questioning in a robbery case when the defendant invoked his right to remain silent, it was permissible to question about an unrelated murder if fresh warnings were given "after the passage of a significant period of time."[18] In Beckwith v. United States,[19] the Court held that the questioning of a person suspected of criminal tax fraud by Internal Revenue agents did not give rise to *Miranda.* Later the Court held that *Miranda* was not violated when a defendant who initially invoked *Miranda* waived his rights before seeing an attorney, even though his attorney attempted to see her client but was assured that he would not be questioned until the following day.[20] In Duckworth v. Eagan,[21] the Court held that informing a suspect that an attorney would be appointed for him "if and when you go to court" did not render the warnings inadequate.

The end result is that the broad legal principle announced in Miranda v. Arizona has been consistently chipped away in the 23 years

16. 384 U.S. 436 (1966).

17. Harris v. New York, 401 U.S. 222, 226 (1971).

18. Michigan v. Mosley, 423 U.S. 96, 106 (1975).

19. 425 U.S. 341, 344 (1976).

20. Moran v. Burbine, 475 U.S. 412, 420 (1986).

21. 109 S.Ct. 2875, 2876 (1989).

since the decision was filed. Perhaps the same results would have been forthcoming if the traditional application of precedent had been followed. For our purposes, the important point is that *Miranda* was a drastic departure from the common-law tradition of incremental and gradual accretion of an original narrow rule. It was the exact opposite. We saw a broad structure erected in one case that has been subsequently subject to do-it-yourself remodeling. . . .

V.

Precedent then, is a doctrine with two jurisprudential concepts in tension:

- The notion that the reasoning supporting the past decision may be wrong, but the decision itself may be right. We have mentioned this concept before. The logic of the argument, the analysis of the historical background and the legislative history may all be demonstrably incorrect.

- The countervailing notion is that expressed by Karl Llewellyn: "Where stops the reason, there stops the rule." [23]

All of us will continue to struggle with these countervailing considerations. I suggest, however, that these problems which I freely admit do exist do not go to the precedent's definition; rather, they go to the precedent's vitality. I express these tensions now solely to emphasize that for definitional purposes, *stare decisis* means no more and no less than that precedent is simply a fact-specific concept, pure and simple. The doctrine refers only to a detailed legal consequence that follows a detailed statement of material facts.

VI.

Yet another view of precedent is the perception of the doctrine as a method of classification. In this view, precedent covers the fact situation of the instant case and at least one other. It decides one case and classifies another.

Any classification is an abstraction. The art of legal advocacy is to expand or contract an abstraction to the extent it is either desirable or undesirable. If contracted, the original case retains only the highly constructive confines of a legal rule. If expanded, the precept develops from a narrow rule of law into a full-fledged legal principle. The precepts may form the basis of what Herman Oliphant once called "a mounting and widening structure, each proposition including all that has gone before and becoming more general by embracing new states of fact." [24]

When we expand, we indulge in the process of classification. We have two fact situations. The first has a definite legal result. We see one or two elements common to the two fact situations. We then put the two fact situations in one class, and, using the combined elements as

---

23. K. Llewellyn, The Bramble Bush 158 (7th printing 1981).

24. Oliphant, *A Return to Stare Decisis,* 14 A.B.A. J. 71, 72–73 (1928).

one enlarged antecedent fact situation, we apply the legal consequence of the first case. Such a class may include multitudes of fact situations so long as a single common attribute exists.

These classes of fact situations give us a parallel series of corresponding propositions of law, each more and more generalized as we recede farther and farther from the original state of facts and include more and more fact situations in the successive classes. It becomes a mounting and widening structure, each proposition including all that has gone before and becoming more general by embracing new states of facts.

For example:

1. "An employee in an Executive agency [of the federal government] or an individual employed by the government of the District of Columbia may not ... take an active part in political management or in political campaigns." [25]

2. Any employee of any agency, office or department of the federal government may not take an active part in political management or political campaigns.

3. The spouse of a federal government employee may not take an active part in political management or political campaigns.

4. The parents and children of a federal government employee may not take an active part in political management or political campaigns.

5. Acquaintances, friends or business associates of federal government employees may not take an active part in political management or political campaigns.

6. No one may take an active part in political management or political campaigns.

Clearly, gradation six is far removed from the basic case and it is clearly illegitimate as classic *reductio ad absurdum*. Yet the tendency to build a gradation of generalization upon the basic case is the centerpiece of the art of advocacy; it is external as seen in the arguments of counsel, and internal, insofar as the value judgments of individual judges are concerned.

Another example is a presently-developing concept of tort law—the tort of negligent infliction of emotional distress. At common law, there was no recovery for the negligent infliction of emotional distress.[26] Consider this developing law in the context of a gradation of widening propositions:

1. A mother may recover for the negligent infliction of emotional distress if she watches her child suffer harm, provided the mother, herself, is in the zone-of-danger, the area of possible physical peril.[27]

25. 5 U.S.C. § 7324(a)(2) (1982).

26. *See generally* Restatement (Second) of Torts §§ 313, 436, 436A (1966).

27. Dillon v. Legg, 68 Cal.2d 728, 741, 441 P.2d 912, 921, 69 Cal.Rptr. 72, 81 (1968).

2. A child who watches his step-grandmother run down and killed may recover for the negligent infliction of emotional distress, even though he was not within the zone-of-danger.[28]

3. A friend may recover for emotional harm if he or she witnesses another friend being harmed.

4. Bystanders may recover for emotional harm whenever they witness an accident.

Examine another example that is more typical in the judicial process. It is taken from Donoghue v. Stevenson,[29] the House of Lords case that is similar to our MacPherson v. Buick Motor Co.:[30] A Scottish widow bought a bottle of beer containing a snail. The court held:

> The presence of a dead snail in an opaque bottle of beverage caused by the negligence of the defendant who is a manufacturer whose goods are distributed to a wide and dispersed public by retailers that caused physical injury to a Scots woman will render the defendant liable.

This can be stated more generally:

> Whether the manufacturer of an article of drink sold by it in circumstances that prevent the distributor or the ultimate purchaser or consumer from discerning by inspection any defect is under a legal duty to the ultimate purchaser or consumer to take reasonable care that the article is free from defect likely to cause injury to health.

To extend a rule to cover a novel fact pattern is a technique that lies at the heart of the common-law tradition. It is accomplished through the use of analogy or generalization. If it suits the purpose of an advocate to limit application of the precept to the original facts, the argument will be designed accordingly, and the opponent will take the contrary view.

The question for the judge is critical. Where on that gradation of propositions do we take our stand and say: "This proposition is the decision of this case within the meaning of the doctrine of *stare decisis* and we go no further?" To hold tight or to expand is a question of line-drawing. Classification, then, is simply line-drawing.

Classification is also a process of abstraction. We can visualize it as an inverted pyramid:

28. Leong v. Takasaki, 55 Haw. 398, 402–07, 520 P.2d 758, 762–64 (1974).

29. 1932 App.Cas. 562.

30. 217 N.Y. 382, 111 N.E. 1050 (1916).

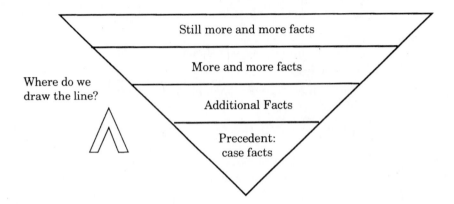

Our problem as judges is obvious: as the French General Robert Nivelle told the Germans under General de Castelnau in World War I, *"Ils ne passeront pas!"* [31] When do we say, "You go this far and no farther"?

Professor Oliphant suggested another view of classification. Imagine standing in the middle of the field in a stadium and looking at the seats. If you focus on one seat on the lower level, the angle between you and the seat is rather slight; if you look at a seat in the upper level, it's a larger angle.[32] The smaller the angle, the closer the classified case to the original precedent.

Karl Llewellyn put it another way. He said that precedent can be viewed as having a minimum or maximum effect.[33] The minimum would be a strict view or small angle; the maximum, a loose view, or large angle. The problem facing judges is how to treat the precedent. Strict or loose. Lower seat or higher seat. Minimum or maximum. We must remember that this is a value judgment, depending upon the individual judge's notion of correct public policy. If we want to expand the holding, we will do so. If we want to hold tight, we will. As Llewellyn suggests, you can find that the putative precedent "holds only of redheaded Walpoles in pale magenta Buick cars." [34]

Is the process of classification strictly subjective? Is it simply a roll of the dice? I do not think so. There are certain guidelines to help us. And it is to that subject that I now turn.

VII.

How do we determine where to draw the line? Is there some guidance to know when the precedential force of one case must stop? Or is it purely personal intuition? At what level in the model classification

---

31. The phrase translated means, "They shall not pass!" It has been attributed to Petain but actually was uttered by General Nivelle at Verdun on January 23, 1916.

32. Oliphant, *supra* note 24, at 73.

33. K. Llewellyn, *supra* note 23, at 56–69.

34. *Id.* at 66–67.

do we say that the rule must stop? Cardozo raised the same sort of question 75 years ago:

> What is it that I do when I decide a case? To what sources of information do I appeal for guidance? In what proportions do I permit them to contribute to the result? In what proportions ought they to contribute? If a precedent is applicable, when do I refuse to follow it? If no precedent is applicable, how do I reach the rule that will make a precedent for the future?

We judges seek answers to these questions throughout our judicial careers. I do not purport to give you answers; however, I make bold to suggest a *method* to find those answers. I emphasize that I will be talking about methods, not answers....

VIII.

The questions that face the judges of the highest courts go much further than a mere determination of when to apply a putative precedent to the case at hand. We also must decide whether to *overrule* the holding of the case. Do we bite the bullet and say so? Or do we make meaningless distinctions and, in Karl Llewellyn's expression, decide if it were a loose or strict precedent? [51] It is essential to study the anatomy of a precedent—what it is, how it is created, how long it should endure, and whether it should be left to wither or should be nourished and strengthened.

We have repeatedly recognized that the principle of *stare decisis* should not be a "confining phenomenon." We are mindful of the observation of Justice Schaefer of the Supreme Court of Illinois. "Precedent speaks for the past; policy for the present and the future. The goal which we seek is a blend which takes into account in due proportion the wisdom of the past and the needs of the present." [52] The doctrine of *stare decisis* is not a vehicle for perpetuating error, but rather a legal concept which responds to the demands of justice and, thus, permits the orderly growth processes of the law to flourish.

As said before, *stare decisis,* or, in its complete form, *stare decisis et non quieta movere,* is usually translated "[t]o adhere to precedents, and not to unsettle things which are established." [53] The classic English statement is attributed to Coke: "[T]hose things which have been so often adjudged, ought to rest in peace." [54] Blackstone's statement was more detailed:

> For it is an established rule to abide by former precedents, where the same points come again in litigation: as well to keep the scale of justice even and steady, and not liable to waver with every new judge's opinion; as also because the law in that case being solemnly declared and determined, what before was un-

---

51. *See* K. Llewellyn, *supra* note 23, at 67–68.

52. Schaefer, *Precedent and Policy,* 34 U.Chi.L.Rev. 3, 24 (1966).

53. Black's Law Dictionary 1261 (5th ed. 1979).

54. Spicer v. Spicer, Cro.Jac. 527, 79 Eng.Rep. 451 (K.B. 1620).

certain, and perhaps indifferent, is now become a permanent rule which it is not in the breast of any subsequent judge to alter or vary from according to his private sentiments.[55]

My dear friend and colleague of happy memory, Roger Traynor, noted:

> *Stare decisis,* to stand by decided cases, conjures up another phrase dear to Latin lovers—*stare super antiquas vias,* to stand on the old paths. One might feel easier about that word *stare* if itself it stood by one fixed star of meaning. In modern Italian *stare* means to stay, to stand, to lie, or to sit, to remain, to keep, to stop, or to wait. With delightful flexibility it also means to depend, to fit or to suit, to live and, of course, to be.[56]

Why do we adhere to precedent? To a considerable extent rules are grounded in factors of habit, tradition, historical accident, and sheer intellectual inertia. We can also go back to the predictability factor in law, recalling Holmes' definition, "The prophecies of what the courts will do in fact, and nothing more pretentious, are what I mean by the law." [57] In addition to these social and psychological roots, precedent also appears to rest in the following values:

(1) *Stability.* It is clearly socially desirable that social relations should have a reasonable degree of continuity and cohesion, held together by a framework of reasonably stable institutional arrangements. . . .

(2) *Protection of Reliance. . . .* [P]rotection of persons who have ordered their affairs in reliance upon contemporaneously announced law [is a value to be safe-guarded]. . . .

(3) *Efficiency in the Administration of Justice.* If every case coming before the courts had to be decided as an original proposition, without reference to precedent, the judicial work-load would obviously be intolerable. Judges must be able to ease this burden [of the judicial work-load] by seeking guidance from what other judges have done in similar cases.

(4) *Equality.* [Persons similarly situated should be equally treated.] It is a fundamental ethical requirement that like cases should receive like treatment, that there should be no discrimination between one litigant and another except by reference to some relevant differentiating factor. . . .

(5) *The Image of Justice.* [This phrase does] not mean that any judicial decision ought to be made on the basis of its likely impact upon the court's public relations, in the Madison Avenue sense, but merely that it is important not only that the court provide equal treatment to persons similarly situ-

55. 1 W. Blackstone, Commentaries *69–70.

56. Traynor, *Reasoning in a Circle of Law,* 56 Va.L.Rev. 739, 744–45 (1970).

57. Holmes, *supra* note 1, at 461.

ated, but that, insofar as possible, the court should appear to do so.[58]

In 1970, Justice Harlan set forth similar values in Moragne v. States Marine Lines, Inc.,

> Very weighty considerations underlie the principle that courts should not lightly overrule past decisions. Among these are the desirability that the law furnish a clear guide for the conduct of individuals, to enable them to plan their affairs with assurance against untoward surprise; the importance of furthering fair and expeditious adjudication by eliminating the need to relitigate every relevant proposition in every case; and the necessity of maintaining public faith in the judiciary as a source of impersonal and reasoned judgments. The reasons for rejecting any established rule must always be weighed against these factors.[59]

IX.

When do we overrule? We start with Roscoe Pound's warning that the law must be stable, yet it cannot stand still.[60] No black letter guidelines determine when to follow precedent. Weighty considerations underlie the principle that courts should not lightly overrule past decisions. Yet, Roger J. Traynor reminds us, "a bad precedent is easier said than undone." [61] Thus, the decision whether to stand still often requires a balancing of hardships. We should not fall into the trap confronted by Gulliver in his Travels:

> It is a maxim among these men, that whatever has been done before may legally be done again; and therefore they take special care to record all the decisions formerly made, even those which have through ignorance or corruption contradicted the rule of common justice and the general reason of mankind. These under the name of precedents, they produce as authorities and thereby endeavor to justify the most iniquitous opinions. . . .[62]

The court may be inclined to overrule "if the hardships it would impose upon those who have relied upon the precedent appear not so great as the hardships that would inure to those who would remain saddled with a bad precedent." [63] Again, Roger Traynor stated:

> Legal minds at work on this word might well conjecture that to *stare* or not to *stare* depends on whether *decisis* is dead or alive. We might inquire into the life of what we are asked to stand by. In the language of *stare decisers: Primo,* should it ever have

58. Currier, *Time and Change in Judge–Made Law: Prospective Overruling,* 51 Va.L.Rev. 201, 235–37 (1965).

59. Moragne v. States Marine Lines, Inc., 398 U.S. 375, 403 (1970).

60. Pound, *The Theory of Judicial Decision II,* 36 Harv.L.Rev. 802, 825 (1923).

61. Traynor, *La Rude Vita, La Dolce Giustizia; Or Hard Cases Can Make Good Law,* 29 U.Chi.L.Rev. 223, 231 (1962).

62. R. Kluger, Simple Justice 541 (1975) (citing J. Swift, Gulliver's Travels (1726)).

63. Traynor, *supra* note 61, at 231.

been born? *Secondo,* is it still alive? *Terzio* does it now deserve to live? [64]

As to be expected, the United States Supreme Court has written extensively on the question of *stare decisis.* "[I]t is indisputable that *stare decisis* is a basic self-governing principle within the Judicial Branch, which is entrusted with the sensitive and difficult task of fashioning and preserving a jurisprudential system that is not based upon 'an arbitrary discretion.' " [65] *Stare decisis* ensures that the law will not change erratically and "permits society to presume that bedrock principles are founded in the law rather than in the proclivities of individuals...." [66]

The Court is fond of saying that it is difficult to overrule statutory interpretations because theoretically Congress will correct the ruling if dissatisfied. But with the Court it is sometimes a case of "do as I say, not as I do." The deed occasionally speaks louder than the word. Many statutory precedents have been explicitly overruled in the past two decades.[67] Yet the Court seems to justify its action by suggesting categories that inform its occasional inclination to overrule. Because most state and federal cases involve statutory construction, it may be useful to summarize the reasons the Court gives for departing from its stated "general rule" that disfavors overruling statutory precedents:

- Intervening development of the law, either through the growth of judicial doctrine or further action taken by Congress.

- A precedent may be a positive detriment to coherence and consistency on the law, either because of inherent confusion created by an unworkable decision, or because the decision poses a direct obstacle to the realization of important objectives embodied in other laws.

- A precedent becomes more vulnerable as it becomes outdated and after being, in Cardozo's words, "tested by experience, has been found to be inconsistent with the sense of justice or

64. Traynor, *supra* note 56, at 745.

65. Patterson v. McClean Credit Union, 109 S.Ct. 2363, 2370 (1989) (citing The Federalist No. 78, at 490 (A. Hamilton) (H. Lodge ed. 1888)).

66. Vasquez v. Hillery, 474 U.S. 254, 265 (1986).

67. *See, e.g.,* Monell v. New York City Dept. of Social Servs., 436 U.S. 658 (1978) (overruling Monroe v. Pape, 365 U.S. 167 (1961)); Continental T.V., Inc. v. GTE Sylvania, Inc., 433 U.S. 36 (1977) (overruling United States v. Arnold, Schwinn & Co., 388 U.S. 365 (1967)); Lodge 76, Int'l Ass'n of Machinists v. Wisconsin Employment Relations Comm'n, 427 U.S. 132 (1976) (over-

ruling International Union v. Wisconsin Employment Relations Bd., 336 U.S. 245 (1949)); Braden v. 30th Judicial Circuit Court of Ky., 410 U.S. 484 (1973) (overruling Ahrens v. Clark, 335 U.S. 188 (1948)); Andrews v. Louisville & N.R.R., 406 U.S. 320 (1972) (overruling Moore v. Illinois Cent. R.R., 312 U.S. 630 (1941)); Boys Markets, Inc. v. Retail Clerks Union Local 770, 398 U.S. 235 (1970) (overruling Sinclair Refining Co. v. Atkinson, 370 U.S. 195 (1962)); Peyton v. Rowe, 391 U.S. 54 (1968) (overruling McNally v. Hill, 293 U.S. 131 (1934)); *see also* Burnet v. Coronado Oil & Gas Co., 285 U.S. 393, 405–13 (1931) (Brandeis, J., dissenting) (collecting cases overruled by the Court prior to 1931).

with the social welfare." [68]

It must be remembered that a judicial precedent may reflect as little as 51 percent of the opinion writer's point of view at the time of authorship. Depending upon the interest in the case by the non-writing judges at the time of the decision, their conviction certainly cannot be guaranteed to be any higher. Too many appellate lawyers operate on the assumption that the opinion of a unanimous court reflects 100 percent conviction and endorsement by all members of the court. Often, the minimum of effective persuasion could effectively move a court to a position desired by an advocate if it is realized that, at best, the case holding is but a narrow rule limited to a particular set of facts, and that the slightest change of facts could possibly bring about a different result.

Another factor that must be reckoned with is that we judges do change our minds. What do we say when we do this? I admire what Justice Potter Stewart said, concurring in Boys Markets, Inc. v. Retail Clerks Union, Local 770, where the Court reversed itself in a prior decision rendered only eight years before:

> When Sinclair Refining Co. v. Atkinson ... was decided in 1962, I subscribed to the opinion of the Court. Before six years had passed I had reached the conclusion that the *Sinclair* holding should be reconsidered, and said so.... Today I join the Court in concluding "that *Sinclair* was erroneously decided and that subsequent events have undermined its continuing validity...."
>
> In these circumstances the temptation is strong to embark upon a lengthy personal *apologia*. But since Mr. Justice Brennan has so clearly stated my present views in his opinion for the Court today, I simply join in that opinion and in the Court's judgment. An aphorism of Mr. Justice Frankfurter provides me refuge: "Wisdom too often never comes, and so one ought not to reject it merely because it comes late." [69]

I also admire the opinion of Justice Jackson, concurring in *McGrath v. Kristensen:*

> And Mr. Justice Story, accounting for his contradiction of his own former opinion, quite properly put the matter: "My own error, however, can furnish no ground for its being adopted by this Court...." [A]n escape ... was taken by Lord Westbury, who, it is said, rebuffed a barrister's reliance upon an earlier opinion of his Lordship: "I can only say that I am amazed that a man of my intelligence should have been guilty of giving such an opinion." If there are other ways of gracefully and good-

---

68. B. Cardozo, *supra* note 35, at 150. *See generally Patterson,* 109 S.Ct. at 2370.

69. Boy's Markets, Inc. v. Retail Clerks Union, Local 770, 398 U.S. 235, 255 (1970)

(Stewart, J., concurring) (citations omitted) (quoting Henslee v. Union Planters Bank, 335 U.S. 595, 600 (1949)).

naturedly surrendering former views to a better considered position, I invoke them all.[70]

Or Baron Bramwell's simple statement, in Andrews v. Styrap: "The matter does not appear to me now as it appears to have appeared to me then." [71]

Too many advocates and commentators assume that all precedents are equivalent, that all are precedents *fortissimo*. As Judge Walter V. Schaefer has cogently observed, "To the working profession there is no such thing as an opinion which is just 'a little bit' precedent or a precedent *pianissimo*. All of them carry the same weight." [72] This, however, is simply not so. There are precedents, and there are precedents. All are not currency of equal value.

A limitation upon the binding authority of precedent may be noted by the statement of the Court of Appeals of the State of New York: "But the doctrine of *stare decisis* ... does not apply to a case where it can be shown that the law has been misunderstood or misapplied, or where the former determination is evidently contrary to reason." [73] From this we can say that one ground for departing from what would otherwise be precedent is an error in the logical argument in the opinion of the prior case. The other ground is that a case should not be followed if it is based upon principles enshrining social or economic conceptions which have been legislatively abandoned or otherwise by-passed. Chancellor Kent wrote:

> A solemn decision upon a point of law arising in any given case, becomes an authority in a like case, because it is the highest evidence which we can have of the law applicable to the subject, and the judges are bound to follow that decision so long as it stands unreversed, unless it can be shown that the law was misunderstood or misapplied in that particular *case*.[74]

X.

As explained, all precedents do not have the same bite. Some are less powerful than others. Notable commentators have addressed certain aspects of this phenomenon. For example, Henry Campbell Black observed:

> A decision is not authority as to any questions of law which were not raised or presented to the court, and were not considered and decided by it, even though they were logically present in the case and might have been argued, and even though such questions, if considered by the court, would have caused a

---

70. McGrath v. Kristensen, 340 U.S. 162, 178 (1950) (Jackson, J., concurring) (citations omitted).

71. Andrews v. Styrap, 26 L.T.R. (N.S.) 704, 706 (Ex.1872).

72. Schaefer, *supra* note 52, at 7.

73. Rumsey v. New York & N.E.R.R., 133 N.Y. 79, 85, 30 N.E. 654, 655 (1892).

74. Kent's Commentaries 475 (12th ed. 1896).

different judgment to be given.[75]

Black has highlighted the importance of examining carefully the opinion, if not the briefs, in the prior case.[76] Were the issues presented, considered and decided? If not, even though they could have been, the prior decision should not be considered a binding precedent on unaddressed points. If so, the prior decision is to be considered binding precedent.

To be sure, issues raised in a case stem from the facts presented. *Facts,* therefore, are of controlling importance, as explained by Professor Brumbaugh:

> Decisions are not primarily made that they may serve the future in the form of precedents, but rather to settle issues between litigants.

> Their use in after cases is an incidental aftermath. A decision, therefore, draws its peculiar quality of justice, soundness and profoundness from the particular facts and conditions of the case which it has presumed to adjudicate. In order, therefore, that this quality may be rendered with the highest measure of accuracy, it sometimes becomes necessary to expressly limit its application to the peculiar set of circumstances out of which it springs.[77]

As emphasized, the use of the precedent's authority depends upon, and is limited to "the particular facts and conditions of the case which it has presumed to adjudicate." [78] We should not apply precedents blindly. The putative precedent must be analyzed carefully to ascertain the actual holding of the court to determine whether a similarity of facts and issues exists. It must be studied to determine whether the precept emerging therefrom is the case's true holding or merely *dictum.*

Is the principle or precept deduced from the prior case contained in a thorough, well-reasoned opinion which was, itself, based upon clear and binding precedents? Is the prior case one that is seriously weakened by a trenchant dissent, or by a concurring opinion which casts doubt upon the wisdom of the majority's reasoning? Is the applicable precept found in a single case, or has it been restated and applied in several cases which have reaffirmed its value and social desirability? Clearly, the currency value of precedents varies widely. At one extreme are those that are rock-bound, the precedents *fortissimo;* at the other extreme are those that must be subject to question.

It is important to note again here that only the holding is entitled to recognition and respect as binding authority. *Dictum* is merely persuasive, although in varying degrees. Factors that affect or determine the degree of persuasiveness accorded to *dicta* are many and varied. How pertinent or relevant is the *dictum* to the decision wherein it was uttered? Does the court or judge who authored the *dictum* enjoy a

---

75. H. Black, Law of Judicial Precedents 37 (1912).

76. *Id.*

77. J. Brumbaugh, Legal Reasoning and Briefing 171–72 (1917).

78. *Id.* at 172.

special respect for scholarship and wisdom? Is the *dictum* reasonable?
Although prior cases have precedential and persuasive value, their
relative value as precedents and as persuasions may differ radically.

A. *Precedent and Persuasive Authority*

Absent formal overruling, judges must follow a precedent whether
they approve of it or not. It binds them and excludes judicial discretion
for the future. On the other hand, judges are under no obligation to
follow persuasive authority that lacks the force of a true precedent.
They will consider it, but will attach to it only the weight such authority
seems to deserve.

Persuasive authority can be considered merely historical comment.
It depends for its influence upon its own merits, not upon any legal claim
which it has to recognition, as opposed to precedent, which is considered
a legal source of law. For example, different types of cases are more
properly classified as persuasive authority than as binding precedent:

+ + Dictum.

+ + Decisions of courts of other jurisdictions.

+ + Plurality, concurring and dissenting opinions.

+ + The summary affirmance by the U.S. Supreme Court: a hybrid
type that both is and is not precedent.

+ + The denial of a writ of certiorari.

1.   Courts of Other Jurisdictions

A decision of a superior court is an authoritative precedent for all
inferior courts in the same judicial hierarchy. There is a bit of provin-
cialism or parochialism here. A decision of the New York Court of
Appeals is authoritative precedent for all New York trial courts, but it is
only a persuasive authority for courts in Pennsylvania because those
courts are in another judicial hierarchy.

2.   Plurality Opinions

In the American tradition, a full-fledged precedent must be pronounced by a majority of the court. An opinion emanating from a court
that reflects only a plurality view does not have the power of a majority
opinion. Reasons given by the plurality are only persuasive authority.
Here we must be careful to distinguish between the specific holding of a
case and the reasons that support it. When concurrences are added to a
plurality opinion, a true holding of the court has been established: a
detailed legal consequence has accompanied a detailed set of facts. But,
because the holding is not supported by a majority reasoning, the power
and vitality of the holding is diluted.

In Berkebile v. Brantly Helicopter Corp.,[79] for example, the plurality
and concurring judges agreed that the trial judge's jury charge on
abnormal use in a product liability case improperly directed a verdict for
the manufacturer by removing from the jury one of the plaintiff's

---

79. 462 Pa. 83, 337 A.2d 893 (1975)
(plurality opinion).

theories that the helicopter was defectively designed. However, the opinions contained different reasons for this decision. The plurality opinion stated that the requirement that a product be "unreasonably dangerous" should be purged from Pennsylvania strict liability law, the court having previously adopted in *ipsissimis verbis* the entire text of section 401A of the *Restatement (Second) of Torts* as "the law of Pennsylvania." [80] But only one other justice joined in the writer's opinion; three justices concurred only in the result; and two justices concurred specially, each filing a short opinion.

Later in Bair v. American Motors Corp.,[81] a diversity case, the Court of Appeals for the Third Circuit refused to recognize as Pennsylvania law the court's opinion in *Berkebile,* that proof of "unreasonably dangerous" was not necessary in a products liability case because it had originated in a plurality opinion. In so holding, the federal court followed Commonwealth v. Little,[82] in which the Pennsylvania State Supreme Court declined to follow a prior opinion representing the views of only two of its justices, the court being of the view that an opinion "joined by only one other member of this Court, has no binding precedential value."[83]
* * *

3. Summary Affirmance by the United States Supreme Court

Another circumstance that does not have the fullest bite of precedent is a summary affirmance by the United States Supreme Court. In Illinois Elections Board v. Socialist Workers Party, the Court explained: "[We] note ... that summary affirmances have considerably less precedential value than an opinion on the merits.... '[U]pon fuller consideration of an issue under plenary review, the Court has not hesitated to discard a rule which a line of summary affirmances may appear to have established.' " [87]

4. The Denial of a Writ of Certiorari

It is hornbook law that "[t]he denial of a writ of certiorari imports no expression of opinion upon the merits of the case, as the bar has been told many times." [88]

XI.

Well, there it is. I do not know whether I have helped or made a confusing subject even more so. I have tried to suggest guidelines to help you decide whether to kiss or kill the precedential dragon. In either event you must go back to its very definition. In so doing, you recognize that a case holding in the common-law tradition is fact specific. When you compare a putative precedent with the case at bar, you compare facts and not the reasons stated. Yet, I freely admit that my

---

80. *Id.* at 90–91, 337 A.2d at 900 (plurality opinion).

81. 535 F.2d 249, 250 (3d Cir.1976).

82. 432 Pa. 256, 248 A.2d 32 (1968).

83. *Id.* at 260, 248 A.2d at 35.

87. Illinois Elections Bd. v. Socialist Workers Party, 440 U.S. 173, 180–81 (1979) (citations omitted).

88. United States v. Carver, 260 U.S. 482, 490 (1923).

emphasis on facts for definitional purposes is not shared by those who seem to say that the reasons given in the holding are also the precedent.[91]

I have tried to show that reasons go only to support a decision, and when original reasons are later proved to be faulty, or when social, economic, or political conditions have changed, it is legitimate not to follow the holding because the reasoning is no longer valid. This is the theory that "where stops the reason, there stops the rule." But all is not that quick and easy. There are times when the rule must be held valid for reasons other than those stated in the original opinion.

Judges will continue to struggle with what is and is not precedent. The source of the struggle may be an uneasiness with what are and are not material facts in the compared cases, or it may be a struggle on where to hold the line in the expansion of facts from the specific to the abstract. There are guidelines, to be sure, but often it is a question of a value judgment, what Max Weber described as " 'practical' evaluations of a phenomenon which is capable of being ... worthy of either condemnation or approval."[92] He distinguished between "logically demonstrable or empirically observable facts" and "the value judgments which are derived from practical standards, ethical standards or world views."[93] Then too, as Justice Walter V. Schaefer explained, the personality of a given judge may be the decisive factor:

> If I were to attempt to generalize, as indeed I should not, I should say that most depends upon the judge's unspoken notion as to the function of his court. If he views the role of the court as a passive one, he will be willing to delegate the responsibility for change, and he will not greatly care whether the delegated authority is exercised or not. If he views the court as an instrument of society designed to reflect in its decisions the morality of the community, he will be more likely to look precedent in the teeth and to measure it against the ideals and the aspirations of his time.[94]

Tail-tweaking of dragons is not a task for the faint-hearted. But, you know that. You can still hear echoes of law school's first year when professors warned about and demonstrated the very difficult problems in the practice of law. I can only suggest you learn from the experience of dragon-slayers:

> "Kiss me!" cried the dragon, which had already devoured many gallant knights for declining to kiss it. "Give you a kiss,"

91. *See* Goodhart, *Determining the Ratio Decidendi of a Case*, 40 Yale L.J. 161 (1930). Professor Goodhart's method is summarized in G. Christie, Jurisprudence 921–44 (1973); R. Cross, *supra* note 22, at 67–76; *see also id.* at 35–40, 104–05.

92. M. Weber, *Value Judgments in Social Science,* in Max Weber Selections in Translation 69 (W. Runciman ed. 1987).

93. *Id.*

94. Schaefer, *supra* note 52, at 23.

murmured the prince; "Oh, certainly, if that's all! Anything for a quiet life."

So saying, he kissed the dragon, which instantly became a most beautiful princess; for she had lain enchanted as a dragon by a wicked magician, till somebody should be bold enough to kiss her.[95]

Section 2

Anatomy of Precedent

––––

BLACKSTONE, COMMENTARIES*

For it is an established rule to abide by former precedents, where the same points come again in litigation: as well to keep the scale of justice even and steady, and not liable to waver with every new judge's opinion; as also because the law in that case being solemnly declared and determined, what before was uncertain, and perhaps indifferent, is now become a permanent rule, which it is not in the breast of any subsequent judge to alter or vary from according to his private sentiments: he being sworn to determine, not according to his own private judgment, but according to the known laws and customs of the land; not delegated to pronounce a new law, but to maintain and expound the old one. Yet this rule admits of exception, where the former determination is most evidently contrary to reason; much more if it be clearly contrary to the divine law. But even in such cases the subsequent judges do not pretend to make a new law, but to vindicate the old one from misrepresentation. For if it be found that the former decision is manifestly absurd or unjust, it is declared, not that such a sentence was *bad law,* but that it was *not law;* that is, that it is not the established custom of the realm, as has been erroneously determined. And hence it is that our lawyers are with justice so copious in their encomiums on the reason of the common law; that they tell us, that the law is the perfection of reason, that it always intends to conform thereto, and that what is not reason is not law. Not that the particular reason of every rule in the law can at this distance of time be always precisely assigned; but it is sufficient that there be nothing in the rule flatly contradictory to reason, and then the law will presume it to be well founded.

––––

95. A. Lang, *The Lady Dragonissa,* in A Cavalcade of Dragons (R. Green ed. 1970).　　* 1 W. Blackstone, Commentaries *69–70.

BENJAMIN N. CARDOZO, THE NATURE OF THE JUDICIAL PROCESS*

The first thing [the judge] does is to compare the case before him with the precedents, whether stored in his mind or hidden in the books. I do not mean that precedents are ultimate sources of the law, supplying the sole equipment that is needed for the legal armory, the sole tools, to borrow Maitland's phrase, "in the legal smithy." Back of precedents are the basic juridical conceptions which are the postulates of judicial reasoning, and farther back are the habits of life, the institutions of society, in which those conceptions had their origin, and which, by a process of interaction, they have modified in turn. Nonetheless, in a system so highly developed as our own, precedents have so covered the ground that they fix the point of departure from which the labor of the judge begins. Almost invariably, his first step is to examine and compare them. If they are plain and to the point, there may be need of nothing more. *Stare decisis* is at least the everyday working rule of our law.... [U]nless [exceptional] conditions are present, the work of deciding cases in accordance with precedents that plainly fit them is a process similar in its nature to that of deciding cases in accordance with a statute. It is a process of search, comparison, and little more. Some judges seldom get beyond that process in any case. Their notion of their duty is to match the colors of the case at hand against the colors of many sample cases spread out upon their desk. The sample nearest in shade supplies the applicable rule. But, of course, no system of living law can be evolved by such a process, and no judge of a high court, worthy of his office, views the function of his place so narrowly. If that were all there was to our calling, there would be little of intellectual interest about it. The man who had the best card index of the cases would also be the wisest judge. It is when the colors do not match, when the references in the index fail, when there is no decisive precedent, that the serious business of the judge begins. He must then fashion law for the litigants before him. In fashioning it for them, he will be fashioning it for others. The classic statement is Bacon's: "For many times, the things deduced to judgment may be meum and tuum, when the reason and consequence thereof may trench to point of estate." The sentence of today will make the right and wrong of tomorrow. If the judge is to pronounce it wisely, some principles of selection there must be to guide him among all the potential judgments that compete for recognition.

NOTE

In the next ten cases of contemporary courts that you read, consider Cardozo's 1921 criticism of color-matching judges. How many are guilty of adhering to "a process of search, comparison, and little more." If many, is this caused by the methods of brief writing? If so, are the brief

* 19–21 (1921). Reprinted by permission of Yale University Press from The Nature of the Judicial Process by Benjamin N. Car-dozo. Copyright © 1921 by Yale University Press.

writers influenced by the opinion writers?　If so, can the vicious circle be broken?

ROSCOE POUND, REMARKS ON STATUS OF THE RULE OF JUDICIAL PRECEDENT*

One of the means by which we achieve that, or seek to achieve it, is to require the judicial process to be carried on by applying to an authoritative body of materials of decision an authoritative technique. This doctrine of *stare decisis,* as was said over and over again this morning, very truly, is a part of the technique which has developed in the courts in the English speaking world.　It represents experience developed by reason and reason tried and tested by experience.

Now, a great deal of the trouble that the layman finds with the doctrine of precedent grows out of, as I see it, an entire misunderstanding of what we are doing.　The layman seems to think a certain number of cases were decided back in the time of the Plantagenets and were laid down in a fossilized state in the Middle Ages and from time to time are dug up and are used as the measure of decision in controversies of Twentieth Century America.

Now, the fact is, as far as rules are concerned, the life of a rule of law in the strict sense is relatively short.　I had occasion in 1924, at the request of a committee of the American Bar Association, to investigate the reports beginning in 1774, at intervals of fifty years, down to 1924, and the thing that struck me as I went on with that, and could be shown conclusively as I had finished it, was that the general run of rules of law,—what I mean by that I will explain in a moment,—the general run of rules of law had a life of simply one generation.　Fifty years is a long life for a rule, that is, a legal precept that attaches a definite detailed legal consequence to a definite detailed state of facts.　And it is with rules, very largely, that this doctrine of *stare decisis* has its immediate application.

Now, these rules of law are the earliest development of the law in the way of furnishing authoritative grounds of decision.　Ancient codes are made up entirely of rules.　In the law of Hammarabi, if a man strike a freeman he shall pay ten shekels of silver; in the law of the Salian Franks, if a man call another a fox, let him pay three shillings; in the law of the twelve tables, if a father sells a son three times, let the son be free from the father—a definite detailed statement of fact with a definite legal consequence attached.

It doesn't take the law very long to get beyond that.　It is true much of the law comes to be made up of these rules; you have to have many of

* *Survey of the Conference Problems,* 14　　ed by permission.
U.Cin.L.Rev. 324, 328–32 (1940).　Reprint-

them. But principles are a very different thing, for a principle doesn't lay down any definite detailed state of facts and doesn't attach any definite legal consequence. It is an authoritative starting point for legal reasoning.

For example, a principle that is very far reaching in the Roman law, Lord Mansfield took it over and made it a far reaching principle behind our law of quasi contract, that one person is not to be unjustly enriched at the expense of another. There is no definite, detailed statement of fact, no definite legal consequence attached to it, but you have a starting point there for legal reasoning when you have a case, and such cases arise continually, to which no rule is exactly applicable.

Our common law technique is that when you have a decision on a particular point and in order to decide that particular point it becomes necessary to lay down a rule, that that rule then is binding; it points out what a court ought to do upon that state of facts. If the court is inferior to or is subject to review by the court laying it down, it must conform its decisions to that rule. Also, the court which lays down the rule is not as a general proposition at liberty to depart from it, but must be consistent in its holdings and apply the same legal consequence to the same state of fact when it arises again.

KARL N. LLEWELLYN, THIS CASE SYSTEM: PRECEDENT*

We turn first to what I may call the orthodox doctrine of precedent, with which, in its essence, you are already familiar. Every case lays down a rule, the rule of the case. The express ratio decidendi is prima facie the rule of the case, since it is the ground upon which the court chose to rest its decision. But a later court can reexamine the case and can invoke the canon that no judge has power to decide what is not before him, can, through examination of the facts or of the procedural issue, narrow the picture of what was actually before the court and can hold that the ruling made requires to be understood as thus restricted. In the extreme form this results in what is known as expressly "confining the case to its particular facts." This rule holds only of redheaded Walpoles in pale magenta Buick cars. And when you find this said of a past case you know that in effect it has been overruled. Only a convention, a somewhat absurd convention, prevents flat overruling in such instances. It seems to be felt as definitely improper to state that the court in a prior case was wrong, peculiarly so if that case was in the same court which is speaking now. It seems to be felt that this would undermine the dogma of the infallibility of courts. So lip service is done to that dogma, while the rule which the prior court laid down is disembowelled. The execution proceeds with due respect, with mandarin courtesy.

* The Bramble Bush 66–69 (1960). Reprinted by permission of Oceana Publications, Inc., and Soia Mentschikoff Llewellyn.

Now this orthodox view of the authority of precedent—which I shall call the *strict* view—is but *one of two views* which seem to me wholly contradictory to each other. It is in practice the dogma which is applied to *unwelcome* precedents. It is the recognized, legitimate, honorable technique for whittling precedents away, for making the lawyer, in his argument, and the court, in its decision, free of them. It is a surgeon's knife. * * *

For when you turn to the actual operations of the courts, or, indeed, to the arguments of lawyers, you will find a totally different view of precedent at work beside this first one. That I call, to give it a name, the *loose view* of precedent. That is the view that a court has decided, and decided authoritatively, *any* point or all points on which it chose to rest a case, or on which it chose, after due argument, to pass. No matter how broad the statement, no matter how unnecessary on the facts or the procedural issues, if that was the rule the court laid down, then that the court has held. Indeed, this view carries over often into dicta, and even into dicta which are grandly obiter. In its extreme form this results in thinking and arguing exclusively from *language* that is found in past opinions, and in citing and working with that language wholly without reference to the facts of the case which called the language forth.

Now it is obvious that this is a device not for cutting past opinions away from judges' feet, but for using them as a springboard when they are found convenient. This is a device for *capitalizing welcome precedents*. And both the lawyers and the judges use it so. And judged by the *practice* of the most respected courts, as of the courts of ordinary stature, this doctrine of precedent is like the other, recognized, legitimate, honorable.

What I wish to sink deep into your minds about the doctrine of precedent, therefore, is that it is two-headed. It is Janus-faced. That it is not one doctrine, nor one line of doctrine, but two, and two which, *applied at the same time to the same precedent, are contradictory of each other*. That there is one doctrine for getting rid of precedents deemed troublesome and one doctrine for making use of precedents that seem helpful. That these two doctrines exist side by side. That the same lawyer in the same brief, the same judge in the same opinion, may be using the one doctrine, the technically strict one, to cut down half the older cases that he deals with, and using the other doctrine, the loose one, for building with the other half. Until you realize this you do not see how it is possible for law to change and to develop, and yet to stand on the past. You do not see how it is possible to avoid the past mistakes of courts, and yet to make use of every happy insight for which a judge in writing may have found expression. Indeed it seems to me that here we may have part of the answer to the problem as to whether precedent is not as bad as good—supporting a weak judge with the labors of strong predecessors, but binding a strong judge by the errors of the weak. For look again at this matter of the *difficulty* of the doctrine. The strict view—that view that cuts the past away—is *hard* to use. An ignorant, an unskilful judge will find it hard to use: the past will bind him. But the skilful judge—he whom we would make free—*is* thus made free. He has the knife in hand; and he can free himself.

Nor, until you see this double aspect of the doctrine-in-action, do you appreciate how little, in detail, you can predict *out of the rules alone;* how much you must turn, for purposes of prediction, to the reactions of the judges to the facts and to the life around them. Think again in this connection of an English court, all the judges unanimous upon the conclusion, all the judges in disagreement as to what rule the outcome should be rested on.

Applying this two-faced doctrine of precedent to your work in a case class you get, it seems to me, some such result as this: You read each case from the angle of its *maximum* value as a precedent, at least from the angle of its maximum value as a precedent *of the first water.* You will recall that I recommended taking down the ratio decidendi in substantially the court's own words. You see now what I had in mind. Contrariwise, you will also read each case for its *minimum* value as a precedent, to set against the maximum. In doing this you have your eyes out for the narrow issue in the case, the narrower the better. The first question is, how much can this case fairly be made to stand for by a later court to whom the precedent is welcome? You may well add— though this will be slightly flawed authority—the dicta which appear to have been well considered. The second question is, how much is there in this case that cannot be got around, even by a later court that wishes to avoid it?

You have now the tools for arguing from that case as counsel on *either* side of a new case. You turn them to the problem of prediction. Which view will this same court, on a later case on slightly different facts, take: will it choose the narrow or the loose? Which use will be made of this case by one of the other courts whose opinions are before you? Here you will call to your aid the matter of attitude that I have been discussing. Here you will use all that you know of individual judges, or of the trends in specific courts, or, indeed, of the trend in the line of business, or in the situation, or in the times at large—in anything which you may expect to become apparent and important to the court in later cases. But always and always, you will bear in mind that each precedent has not one value, but two, and that the two are wide apart, and that whichever value a later court assigns to it, such assignment will be respectable, traditionally sound, dogmatically correct. Above all, as you turn this information to your own training you will, I hope, come to see that in most doubtful cases the precedents *must* speak ambiguously until the court has made up its mind whether each one of them is welcome or unwelcome. And that the job of persuasion which falls upon you will call, therefore, not only for providing a technical ladder to reach on authority the result that you contend for, but even more, if you are to have *your* use of the precedents made as *you* propose it, the job calls for you, on the facts, to persuade the court your case is sound.

People—and they are curiously many—who think that precedent produces or ever did produce a certainty that did not involve matters of judgment and of persuasion, or who think that what I have described involves improper equivocation by the courts or departure from the court-ways of some golden age—such people simply do not know our system of precedent in which they live.

NOTE

Do you begin to see the inner workings of the law? Consider Holmes' basic definition, Pound's classifications of legal precepts and Llewellyn's statement that "until you see this double aspect of the doctrine [of precedent]-in-action, [you do not] appreciate how little, in detail, you can predict *out of the rules alone....*" *Compare* Cardozo's statement that there must be principles of selection to guide judges in the choice of precedent, *with* Schaefer's assertion, that "[e]ach judge will have his individual reaction to the value of a particular precedent."

Consider Llewellyn's Janus-faced doctrine of precedents in terms of the law expression "strict constructionist" usually bandied about by the same observers who label judges as "liberal" or "conservative". Are individual judges capable of being categorized as generally devotees of either the "strict" or "loose" view of precedents? When reference is made to the "reactions of the judges to the facts and to the life around them", is this a reference to whether the individual judge will employ the "strict" or "loose" view in a given case?

May there be a type of judge, seemingly preferred by Cardozo and Traynor, who would settle disputes without matching "the colors of the case at hand", who would make decisions on the facts at hand and then write opinions distinguishing precedents on the "loose" or "strict" view, as necessary, to justify the result? Is such result-oriented jurisprudence to be criticized? Would it make a difference if the judge entered the decision-making process with an open mind and gave careful consideration to countervailing arguments?

———

WALTER V. SCHAEFER, PRECEDENT AND POLICY*

I shall be mainly concerned with those cases that "count for the future." Statistics are lacking, but it is undoubtedly true that the great bulk of all litigation is disposed of upon the facts, that is, by a determination that the facts do or do not fall within an established legal principle. Only a minute fraction of all cases reach reviewing courts, and it is there, in the main, that legal doctrines are shaped and formulated. Of the cases which are determined by reviewing courts, it is again only a small percentage which "count for the future."

The dimensions of the area of my concern do not measure its significance. For it is here that the law grows, that existing doctrines

* 34 U.Chi.L.Rev. 3 (1966). Reprinted by permission.

are tested, and that new doctrines are developed. It is here that the tone of a judicial system is set. And if the number of litigants immediately affected is small, the number which may be indirectly affected is great indeed, for each decision in this area is the potential progenitor of a long line.

. . .

Some writers have ... suggested that the ordinary judicial opinion is a fraud, in that it purports to be derived by impeccable and inevitable logic from what has already been decided, and that the judge who wrote it is either a fool for thinking the process so simple or a knave for pretending that it is. I do not think we need to go so far. It may be conceded that judicial opinions are something less than mirrors of the thinking behind the decision and that a judge has more freedom than the mustering of precedents makes it appear. But precedents, for the judge as well as the lawyer, are the starting point of decision; more often than not they are in practice the concluding point as well. When and to what extent they should prevail is the intriguing question.

. . .

In the main, lawyers tend to treat all judicial opinions as currency of equal value. Exceptions must be made, of course, for the opinions of the acknowledged masters and for those opinions which carry dissents or special concurrences. But the masters are quickly numbered, and the discounted value of the opinion which carries a dissent or concurrence shows upon its face. When allowance has been made for the exceptions, there emerges the working thesis of the bar and perhaps even of the courts: "A case is a case is a case." To the working profession there is no such thing as an opinion which is just "a little bit" precedent or a precedent *pianissimo*. All of them carry the same weight.

Yet, when the judicial process is viewed from the inside, nothing is clearer than that all decisions are not of equivalent value to the court which renders them. There are hidden factors of unreliability in judicial opinions, whether or not there is dissent or special concurrence. Many an opinion, fair upon its face and ringing in its phrases, fails by a wide margin to reflect accurately the state of mind of the court which delivered it.

Several ingredients combine against complete certainty, even at the moment of decision. For a reviewing court the common denominator of all cases is that they must be decided, and must be disposed of, ordinarily by opinion. There are no intermediates. Judgment must go for one party or for the other. There are many cases in which complete conviction comes rather quickly. But there are many others in which conviction to a degree comes hard, and complete conviction never. Uncertainty, however, will not justify a failure to dispose of the case. So some opinions get written because the case must be disposed of rather than because the judge is satisfied with the abiding truth of what he writes.

That process is repeated with the other members of the court who are not directly charged with the preparation of the opinion. Indeed, with them it is likely to be aggravated. As a renowned jurist once said, or should have said, the judge who writes an opinion must be at least 51 per cent convinced in the direction of the result he reaches. But with the other judges of the court conviction may be less than 50 per cent, and the doubt will still go without expression. For that statement I can vouchsafe high authority to support my own observation. The constitutionality of the Adamson Law, which provided an eight-hour day for railroad employees, was sustained by a divided Court. Chief Justice White wrote the opinion of the Court. Justice McKenna wrote a concurring opinion, and Justice Van Devanter concurred in Justice Pitney's dissent.[8] One might assume that this array of opinions fully expressed the views of members of the Court. But then we find Mr. Justice Holmes, who filed no opinion, writing this to Laski: "I send the Adamson opinions by this mail. They are all together. I thought Day's dissent wrong but the most rational. My own opinion goes the whole hog with none of the C.J.'s squeams."[9] And on another occasion Holmes tells Laski of an opinion he wrote "at high pressure in a short time, and with our Court very evenly balanced, though only Pitney and Clarke dissented."[10]

There is more unexpressed doubt of that sort than the bar is aware of. Dissents do not remove these lurking doubts, for dissents are born not of doubt but of firm convictions. The fighting spirit which spells dissent appears in another letter from Justice Holmes to Laski:

> I had last Monday the recrudescence of an old problem. Whether to dissent as to the judge's salaries being included in the income tax, was the occasion and the problem whether to allow other considerations than those of the detached intellect to count. The subject didn't interest me particularly. I wasn't at all in love with what I had written and I hadn't got the blood of controversy in my neck.[11]

And on another occasion:

> After all I succumbed and have written a short dissent in a case which still hangs fire. I do not expect to convince anyone as it is rather a statement of my convictions than an argument, although it indicates my grounds. Brandeis is with me, but I had written a note to him saying that I did not intend to write when the opinion came and stirred my fighting blood.[12]

Here is the stuff dissents are made of. Here, too, is additional evidence that there may be disagreement without dissent. Whether or not to express publicly his disagreement with the prevailing opinion by a dissent is not a novel problem to Holmes but an old, familiar one.

---

8. Wilson v. New, 243 U.S. 332 (1917).

9. 1 Holmes–Laski Letters 68 (Howe ed. 1953).

10. *Id.* at 85.

11. *Id.* at 266.

12. *Id.* at 560.

Writing of Brandeis, Paul Freund says:

Not infrequently the preparation of a dissenting opinion was foregone because the demands of other items of work prevented an adequate treatment, but with the promise to himself that another occasion would be taken when circumstances were more propitious.[13]

The case of the specially concurring opinion is not quite so clear. Typically it would rest the result upon grounds other than those asserted in the prevailing opinion. Sometimes the choice of grounds may be the result of doubt as to that chosen by the majority. More often, I suspect, it, too, is the result of fighting conviction on the part of the concurring judge as to the ground which he selects.

The older practice of filing separate opinions helped considerably to eliminate the inherent element of unreliability in judicial decisions. But the working bar does not like multiple opinions. Paradoxically, the dislike seems to be based upon a desire for certainty. Moreover, only those courts whose jurisdiction is largely discretionary, or whose volume of work is small for other reasons, can indulge in the luxury of separate opinions in every case. With most of the state courts, that practice is out of the question. In our own court, the number of formal opinions handed down in the course of a year is now around 250 to 275. With Sundays and holidays excluded, and even without consideration of the large part of the work of the court which is not reflected in formal opinions, that works out perilously close to an opinion per day.

It seems to me that the style of judicial opinion contributes its share to their latent uncertainties. Although an opinion may be born only after deep travail and may be the result of a very modest degree of conviction, it is usually written in terms of ultimate certainty. Learned Hand has referred to the tendency of some judges to reach their result by sweeping "all the chessmen off the board." [14] The contentions which caused deep concern at one stage have a way of becoming "clearly applicable" or "completely unsound" when they do not prevail. Perhaps opinions are written in that positive vein so that they may carry conviction, both within the court and within the profession; I suspect, however, that the positive style is more apt to be due to the psychological fact that when the judge has made up his mind and begins to write an opinion, he becomes an advocate.

The fact that reviewing courts are multijudge courts influences the reliability of precedent in ways too numerous to mention. Opinions are read under the microscope. Particularly in the more esoteric reaches of property law, they are read with an eye to subtle nuances of meaning. The subtleties may, and often do, express the meaning of the judge who wrote the opinion. They do not in any realistic sense express the view of the court as a whole. On a multijudge court no man can or should have every opinion expressed in words which he chooses. Of course every

13. Freund, on Understanding the Supreme Court 71 (1950).

14. Hand, The Spirit of Liberty 131 (1952).

judge can and should make suggestions to his colleagues. But the relationship among the judges is a personal one and a continuing one, and effectiveness can be blunted by excessive suggestions. The balance between complacent acquiescence and overassertiveness is delicate indeed.

The late Mr. Justice Jackson, speaking of decisional law and stare decisis some years ago, made an observation upon which I should like to comment. He said:

> The first essential of a lasting precedent is that the court or the majority that promulgates it be fully committed to its principle. That means such individual study of its background and antecedents, its draftsmanship and effects that at least when it is announced it represents not a mere acquiescence but a conviction of those who support it. When that thoroughness and conviction are lacking, a new case, presenting a different aspect or throwing new light, results in overruling or in some other escape from it that is equally unsettling to the law.

With the ideal that doubt should be eliminated and with the suggestion that every opinion should express, so far as conscientious effort can make it possible, the conviction of every member of the court, I agree wholeheartedly. But I venture to doubt that the ideal of full commitment of every member of the court can be realized in every case, regardless of the amount of effort expended.

At this point I can hear the practicing lawyers say, somewhat irritably: "What you say is all very well, but it is the published opinion of the court with which we must deal. For our purposes a hidden reservation is unimportant." I am certainly not proposing that they poll the court, if that were possible. What I have said perhaps has practical value only as a counsel of caution.

There are additional respects, and more perceptible ones, however, in which opinions, and hence precedents, differ.

The intrinsic quality of the precedent relied upon is significant in determining its fate. Judges in the act of overruling a prior decision have often reconciled their action with the general requirements of stare decisis by stating that there is no duty to follow decisions which are absurd or manifestly in error. That formula may obscure the fact that a decision is often overruled, not because of inherent error, but because it has become obsolete. Yet it remains true that an opinion which does not within its own confines exhibit an awareness of relevant considerations, whose premises are concealed, or whose logic is faulty is not likely to enjoy either a long life or the capacity to generate offspring. There are exceptions. The decision that a corporation could claim equal protection of the laws was made by a court which simply announced from the bench that it did not wish to hear argument on the point inasmuch as all the members of the court were agreed on it.[16] The point so decided has successfully resisted attack. But, by and large, the appearance of full

---

16. Santa Clara County v. Southern Pacific R.R., 118 U.S. 394, 396 (1886).

consideration is important. Beyond the appearance there lies the question of actual consideration. Hardly a term of court goes by but that we send for and examine the briefs in an earlier case which is relied upon as decisive to see just what was argued in the earlier case and the quality of the argument made. And I may say parenthetically that the results of our examination make it clear to me that the advocates who present the cases to us do not follow the same practice.

Dissenting and specially concurring opinions have their weight at this point, for they detract from the intrinsic value of the precedent. The therapeutic value of a dissenting opinion is important to the dissenting judge, but that is not its only value. Consider what our constitutional law might be today had there been no dissents. Nor is their value restricted to the field of public law.[17]

Along with quality, quantity too is significant. A settled course of decision is more compelling than an isolated precedent, particularly when the latter, though never formally expelled from the books, has been vigorously ignored by the court which brought it into being.

This is not to say that a great volume of decisions upon a point of law necessarily commands respect. In some areas of the law decisions have proliferated without forming recognizable patterns. As examples I would cite the federal decisions on state taxation of interstate commerce or our own decisions in will-contest cases and zoning cases. The result is that although general principles are always stated in the opinions, decision actually turns on the court's subjective appraisal of the facts. Under such circumstances a court, unless it is bold enough to wipe the slate clean, is forced, despite Holmes's injunction, to join the lawyers in a search for cases on a pots-and-pans basis.[18]

So much, then, for the reported decisions and opinions on their face. What use will be made of them? Baldly stated, I suppose that whether a precedent will be modified depends on whether the policies which underlie the proposed rule are strong enough to outweigh both the policies which support the existing rule and the disadvantages of making a change. The problem is not different in kind from that which is involved in the decisions of other regulatory organs, private or public. In the case of any one decision we may be able to explain why this or that consideration has prevailed, but it is hardly possible to state a general formula which will describe the process in its totality.

A court does not select the materials with which it works. It is not self-starting. It must be moved to action by the record and the advocate. The role of the advocate is more significant, I think, than has been suspected. The record must be adequate to raise the issue. But even a record which is technically correct may not cast light on all the aspects of the problem. It was to supply this kind of deficiency that the

---

17. For an example of a dissent which profoundly affected the future growth of the law see that of Justice Boggs in Allaire v. St. Luke's Hospital, 184 Ill. 359, 368, 56 N.E. 638, 640 (1900).

18. Holmes, *The Path of the Law,* in Collected Legal Papers 195–96 (1920). [*See ante,* p. 27 *et seq.*]

technique of the Brandeis brief was evolved. More recently, I think, the kind of information contained in the Brandeis brief has been finding its way into the actual record before the court.

Much depends upon the extent to which the court feels sure that it can see the ultimate results which will flow from a departure from precedent. Its willingness to depart will, I think, vary in inverse ratio to the complexity of the problem. Mr. Justice Brandeis expressed the thought in the *Associated Press* case:[19]

> The unwritten law possesses capacity for growth; and has often satisfied new demands for justice by invoking analogies or by expanding a rule or principle. This process has been in the main wisely applied and should not be discontinued. Where the problem is relatively simple, as it is apt to be when private interests only are involved, it generally proves adequate.... Courts are ill-equipped to make the investigations which should precede a determination of the limitations which should be set upon any property right in news or of the circumstances under which news gathered by a private agency should be deemed affected with a public interest. Courts would be powerless to prescribe the detailed regulations essential to full enjoyment of the rights conferred or to introduce the machinery required for enforcement of such regulations. Considerations such as these should lead us to decline to establish a new rule of law in the effort to redress a newly-disclosed wrong, although the propriety of some remedy appears to be clear.

. . .

It remains to consider the factor of change itself. In part this involves matters of a tactical quality. In deciding whether to translate its dissatisfaction with a former decision into action, a court takes into account the likelihood of cure from some other source. So there is general agreement, I think, that, because constitutions are difficult to change, courts exercise a greater freedom in dealing with constitutional precedents than with others. The expectation of prompt legislative action militates against judicial change.

The frequency with which the court will have an opportunity to deal with the problem has a bearing. If the problem is recurrent, a more suitable case may soon come. The countering consideration, of course, is that with each repetition the unsatisfactory ruling becomes more firmly riveted.

. . .

More basic, of course, than tactical considerations is the magnitude of the change involved. Courts may legislate, said Holmes, but they do

19. International News Service v. Associated Press, 248 U.S. 215[, 262, 267] (1918).

so interstitially. They are restricted from movement of the mass and confined to movement of the particles....

In another, and perhaps deeper sense, this factor is expressed in another remark of Holmes:

> As law embodies beliefs that have triumphed in the battle of ideas and then have translated themselves into action, while there still is doubt, while opposite convictions still keep a battle-front against each other, the time for law has not come; the notion destined to prevail is not yet entitled to the field.

The merit and magnitude of a particular change are not determined by a court on the basis of its own subjective appraisal. It does not measure competing doctrines solely on its own determination of their intrinsic value without reference to the status of those doctrines among those who are informed on the subject and who are particularly affected. One informed class whose opinion carries weight is the legal profession. Its comments, expressed in treatises, law reviews, and other legal publications, always affect the attitude of a court toward a precedent. Of course the class of persons who are informed and who are concerned with the question can vary widely. When it becomes so large as to include the public generally, its attitude becomes more difficult to ascertain and, I think, less significant. But where the class is small, and its informed status apparent, as with Lord Mansfield's reliance upon special juries and the extra-judicial statements of merchants in the development of commercial law, informed opinion becomes significant. The state of medical knowledge as to the capacity of an unborn child to sustain life apart from its mother influences the right to recover for injuries suffered *en ventre sa mère*.[29] And the attitude of psychiatrists toward the rule in the *M'Naghten* case goes far to determine whether the common law test for determining sanity in criminal cases will be reconsidered.[30]

In addition to the state of mind and the expectancy of the informed public is the state of mind and the expectancy of the parties immediately concerned. The most frequent, and perhaps the most substantial, argument made against a court's departure from precedent is that a sudden shift in the law will frustrate past transactions made in reliance on existing law. It is easy to overstate the objection, for in many fields of human action there is no reliance on past decisions and in many others no knowledge of the existing law.

> The picture of the bewildered litigant lured into a course of action by the false light of a decision, only to meet ruin when the light is extinguished and the decision overruled, is for the most part a figment of excited brains.

29. See Amann v. Faidy, 415 Ill. 422, 114 N.E.2d 412 (1953).

30. See Durham v. United States, 214 F.2d 862 (D.C.Cir.1954).

But some reliance there undoubtedly is, and how much a court can only guess, so it is a consideration which cannot properly be disregarded.

. . .

I have spoken of precedents and of some of the factors which move a court to adhere to a precedent or to depart from it. Having gone so far, I am unable to go further and indicate what weight is to be assigned to each of these factors in a particular case. Not only that—I must mention another pervasive ingredient which further complicates the problem.

The forces and factors which I have mentioned are not weighed in objective scales. Each judge will have his individual reaction to the value of a particular precedent. Each will respond in his own degree to the pressure of the facts of the case. And each will make his own appraisal of the weight to be given to the other considerations I have mentioned.

There is nothing new in the notion that the personality of the judge plays a part in the decision of cases. Cardozo pointed out that on the Court of Appeals in his day there were ten judges, of whom only seven at a time. "It happens again and again," he says, "where the question is a close one, that a case which one week is decided one way might be decided another way the next if it were then heard for the first time." [58] And, again, in speaking of the subconscious forces that shape judgments, he says: "There has been a certain lack of candor in much of the discussion of the theme, or rather perhaps in the refusal to discuss it, as if judges must lose respect and confidence by the reminder that they are subject to human limitations." [59]

Perhaps there has been a lack of candor. I do not think so. Rather it seems to me that we lack the ability to describe what happens. I have tried to analyze my own reactions to particular cases. When I have tried in retrospect, I have doubted somewhat the result, for the tendency is strong to reconstruct along the lines of an assumed ideal process. William James said, "When the conclusion is there we have already forgotten most of the steps preceding its attainment." And, when I have tried to carry on simultaneously the process of decision and of self-analysis, the process of decision has not been natural. I suspect that what is lacking is not candor but techniques and tools which are sensitive enough to explore the mind of man and report accurately its conscious and subconscious operations.

So far as I am aware, decision with me has not turned upon the state of my digestion. And, if I have reached decision by means of a hunch, it has been a hunch with a long-delayed fuse, for often I have started confidently toward one conclusion, only to be checked and turned

58. Cardozo, The Nature of the Judicial Process 150 (1921).

59. *Id.* at 167–68.

about by further study. Cardozo has described an experience which I think is familiar to every judge:

> I have gone through periods of uncertainty so great, that I have sometimes said to myself, "I shall never be able to vote in this case either one way or the other." Then, suddenly the fog has lifted. I have reached a stage of mental peace. I know in a vague way that there is doubt whether my conclusion is right. I must needs admit the doubt in view of the travail that I suffered before landing at the haven. I cannot quarrel with anyone who refuses to go along with me; and yet, for me, however it may be for others, the judgment reached with so much pain has become the only possible conclusion, the antecedent doubts merged, and finally extinguished, in the calmness of conviction.[61]

It was actually this experience, I am confident, that was intended to be compressed into the phrase "judicial hunch."

If I were to attempt to generalize, as indeed I should not, I should say that most depends upon the judge's unspoken notion as to the function of his court. If he views the role of the court as a passive one, he will be willing to delegate the responsibility for change, and he will not greatly care whether the delegated authority is exercised or not. If he views the court as an instrument of society designed to reflect in its decisions the morality of the community, he will be more likely to look precedent in the teeth and to measure it against the ideals and the aspirations of his time.

I do not feel that because it is impossible to place a precise value upon each of the elements which enter into the process of decision it is therefore futile to attempt to enumerate them. It is important that advocates be aware of them, so that cases can be brought more sharply into focus. And it is even more important that judges be conscious of them. If it is true, as I think it is, that in many cases the law stands at a crossroad, the men who choose the path for the future should make the choice, so far as they can, with an awareness of the elements that determine their decision.

Precedent speaks for the past; policy for the present and the future. The goal which we seek is a blend which takes into account in due proportion the wisdom of the past and the needs of the present. Two agencies of government are responsible for the proper blend, but each has other responsibilities as well. The legislature must deal with the ever increasing details of governmental operations. It has little time and little taste for the job of keeping the common law current. The courts are busy with the adjudication of individual controversies. Inertia and the innate conservatism of lawyers and the law work against judicial change.

---

61. Cardozo, Paradoxes of Legal Science 80–81 (1928).

NOTE

Apropos the lawyer's lament, "... but it is the published opinion of the court with which we must deal", how can a law firm or a law school researcher attempt to ascertain whether a given case is a precedent *pianissimo* or a precedent *fortissimo?*

Is the law, in its various disciplines, developing sufficiently to justify the thousands of published opinions emanating each year? If a case has no precedential or institutional value, is there justification for publication? Is there justification for committing court energies to the writing of an opinion? *See* Winslow, *The Courts and the Papermills,* 10 Ill. L.Rev. 157 (1915). The former chief justice of Wisconsin, John B. Winslow, therein contended that no opinion should ever be written upon affirmance where (1) questions of fact are involved, (2) the case is determined by following well-established legal principles, or (3) the matter involves settled rules of practice and procedure. "In cases of affirmance generally no opinion should be written unless in the judgment of the court the question is of such exceptional importance as to demand treatment in an opinion." Id. at 161.

Look for a moment at the paper storm that has descended upon West Publishing Company, publishers of this book:

Cases Received for Publication, 1895–1994

Year	Number of Cases
1895	19,476
1929	27,527
1942	23,283
1950	21,450
1964	27,336
1970	36,892
1977	46,983
1981	54,104[1]
1985	63,508
1989	61,901
1990	62,637
1991	65,333
1992	66,500
1993	62,911
1994	61,474[2]

In 1983, Justice Charles G. Douglas III, of the New Hampshire Supreme Court, observed:

The number of opinions received by West in 1929 was the same number it received in 1964—some 35 years later. Yet the number has [almost] doubled to 54,104 in 1981 in just half that time![3]

1. *Reprinted in* Douglas, How to Write A Concise Opinion, 22 Judges' J. 4 (Spring 1983).

2. Statistics on the Number of Opinions Received for Publication 1982–1994 (West 1995).

3. Douglas, *ante,* note 1.

Is case law churning and developing at the rate reflected by the number of the opinions submitted for publication? Of course not. Our common-law tradition requires unity of law throughout a jurisdiction and requires also the flexibility to incorporate legal precepts as they develop. Within this tradition is the concept of gradualness, with case law that creeps from point to point, testing each step, in a system built by accretion from the resolution of specific problems. Nevertheless, no one, not even the most fervent supporter of publication in every case, can seriously suggest that every one of these cases submitted for publication refines or defines the law or has precedential or institutional value. The reason for the avalanche is not only the expansion of trial and appellate litigation, but also the fact that there is today no institutional inhibition against the paper storm.

Section 3

Precedential Vitality

———

KARL N. LLEWELLYN, THE LEEWAYS OF PRECEDENT*

The following classification of standard techniques is rough-hewn. It is above all incomplete. The finer shadings are hard to communicate, perhaps hard to agree upon, and the going diversity even of the coarser approaches is too large to warrant the effort needed to exhaust it. It is enough if one can demonstrate a true multiplicity, each aspect in active use, with variation in direction and degree and with different results if the varying procedures should be applied to the same precedent on the same point in any single pending cause.

The multiplicity is real, and it is vital. It disposes of all question of "control" or dictation by precedent. But it does not, of course, ... impair the importance of the rule of law as a tool of law, or the importance of guidance suggestion, even pressure, which falls short of absolute control; nor, and especially, does it touch the differential effects and the differential values of clean tools as against clumsy or bad tools.

Meanwhile, to the judge or court each individual precedent technique speaks thus: As you search for the right rule of law to govern the case in hand, *I* am *one* of the things which, respectably, honorably, and in full accordance with the common law tradition as inherited and as currently practiced among your brethren of the high bench—I am *one* of the things you are *formally* entitled in and by your office to do to and with any prior relevant judicial language or holding as it comes before

* The Common Law Tradition 76–91 (1960). Boston: Little, Brown and Company, 1960. Reprinted by permission.

you. To the advocate or counselor the technique talks in slightly different terms: *I* am what the court *may* do (and be within its office and tradition) *to* any prior judicial language or holding *you* may bring forward, however relevant, and/or *with or without* any prior relevant judicial language or holding presented by your adversary or discovered by the court itself.

A SELECTION OF AVAILABLE IMPECCABLE PRECEDENT TECHNIQUES

I. FOLLOWING PRECEDENT

A. *Illustrating Some Conscious Controlling or Even Constricting Effects of Standing or Following*

1. The rule is too firmly established to disturb.

2. Even though doubts are felt or policy disapproved, the rule is still too firmly established to disturb.

3. The wide rule on which the court chose to rest bears out what might have been an appealing distinction.

4. The state of precedent overrides a broader principle otherwise applicable.

5. The constellation of prior decisions has frozen the meaning of the rule.

6. The constellation of prior decisions has frozen the number and nature of legal concepts available to hold new states of fact.

7. The fair implications or tendencies of the cases require stasis.

8. (Anticipatory): Care is taken to defend existing precedent against imputation from the present decision.

B. *Illustrating the Range of Choice Open via Simple "Standing" On or by "Things Decided"*

9. A *rule* previously phrased and held is applied as such and without change.

10. A rule is taken as firmly established—yet movement either occurs or is presaged.

11. The *exact language of the ground* on which the court chose to rest the case is applied without reference to anything more than that language.

12. A *holding* not put by the prior case into rule form or language at all is pulled out, phrased, and followed.

13. The *explicit reason or theory,* rather than either the rule or the holding, is accepted and followed.

14. An established *concept-label* is applied, and some corollary rule follows without more.

15. A *practice of judicial action,* previously unaccompanied by discussion, is noted, stated, and followed.

16. The *hole* in the authorities is followed: no positive precedent, *therefore* no positive right.

C. *Illustrating a Variety of the Simpler Types of Creation, Mostly Conscious, While Following Authority*

17. The prior holding is followed, though it is seen to be distinguishable, because its reason applies.

18. The prior rule is consciously applied or extended to a new fact-situation.

19. The prior rule or distinction is kept from application because its reason does not fit.

20. The authorities are re-examined and their reason and rule approved and applied. (The suspicion being that nonapproval might have led to some different course.)

21. A simple positive rule (or concept) has a negative twin attributed to it which is then duly "applied" as if the negative implication had been considered, announced, and held.

22. *Filling the hole* by the following: there is *no* precedent *against* a remedy; *therefore* a "right" calls one forth.

23. The point which has been explicitly reserved as possibly or probably significant is ruled significant, indeed, and is applied.

24. (Anticipatory): Care is taken in the present opinion to lay out guidance on a point considered but not ruled, and to lay a foundation for a ruling later.

D. *Illustrating Importantly Expansive or Redirected Use of the Precedent–Material*

25. An unnecessarily broad basis for decision is applied to the edge of its language, in uncharted territory.

26. An unnecessarily broad basis for decision is applied via language *and reason* to a bold new area.

27. The whole theory of a complex situation announced in a prior case is accepted, and used beyond the actual holding.

28. A principle theretofore unphrased is extracted from the decisions and applied.

29. "The tendency of the decisions" is stated, consecrated, and founds the ruling.

30. A pure dictum is quoted and consecrated as the authoritative rule, and applied. (How frequent and indeed standard this technique is, the precedent-discussions very rarely suggest....)

31. An unnecessary ruling is accepted as a principle and applied or even extended. (This seems, today, to account for more than a fifth of the simple citations. . . .)

32. A dictum about the reason of a situation is quoted, elevated into the foundation of a principle, and applied.

II. Avoidance of "The Decided"

A. *Avoidance Without Accepting Responsibility to the Future: Legitimate Techniques*

33. "The rule (or principle) was there recognized, the only difficulty being in its application."

34. "Each case of this kind must be dealt with on its own facts."

35. "This case, in any event, falls outside [or inside] the rule."

36. "Distinguishable," without more.

B. *Avoidance Without Acceptance of Responsibility: Illegitimate Techniques*

37. A distinction is taken, but without a difference (dubiously legitimate, except in a system which will not face up to overruling).

38. The older case, though significantly parallel in real facts, is brushed off because of the "facts" (arti-facts often "constructed") there, while a completely different manner of interpretation and classification is used on the raw facts of the case in hand. (Rarely, barely legitimate.)

39. The older case is knowingly disregarded without mention. (Flatly illegitimate.)

40. The facts in the pending case—or of the "precedent"—are misrepresented or misclassified so as to evade the application of the older case and rule. (Flatly illegitimate in either or any branch.)

C. *Limiting or Narrowing, Explicitly*

41. Kill off a dictum, as such and without more.

42. Distinguish on the facts; especially if the reason is discussed.

43. Undercut and distinguish or disregard via the authorities used in the older case.

44. "We here limit that rule," or other whittling "explanation."

D. *Killing the Precedent*

45. "Must be confined to its exact facts."

46. "Can no longer be regarded as authority, since Younger v. Older." (Means: Younger v. Older itself was illegitimate, if consciously silent about its effect on prior authority.)

47. "Involves a misapplication of the true principle" (or rule.)

48. "Is (explicitly) overruled."

III.   SOME CORRECT BUT LESS USUAL USES OF MATERIALS OR TECHNIQUES, ESPECIALLY FOR EXPANSION, REDIRECTION, OR FRESH START

A.   *Fresh Starts from Old Materials*

49.   Capitalization of the mere squint.

50.   The spirit of some statute or body of law takes on rule-form.

51.   Deliberate and important redirection of a rule.

52.   Introducing or establishing a new method of construction of the facts.

53.   Material enlargement or subdivision of a concept.

54.   Introducing or establishing a new concept.

55.   Unchaining a new principle to substitute order for conflict or confusion.

56.   (Contrast): Introducing a new pseudo principle to continue conflict or confusion *sub rosa:* Words which do not guide.

B.   *Enlarging the Standard Set of Sources or Techniques*

57.   Tapping the lower courts, the administrative agency, the attorney general, etc.

58.   Resort to the briefs or the record or court's unpublished notes, etc., in regard to the prior case.

59.   Enlisting the rule's reason to carry the rule into novel territory.

60.   Basing decision and rule on common knowledge and sense.

61.   Announcing new principle ex cathedra.

62.   Introducing rule or principle from the critical literature.

63.   (Anticipatory): The deliberate forward-prophecy.

64.   (Anticipatory): The deliberate hedge via an alternative which can, on call, render the main ruling "mere dictum."

––––––

MacPHERSON v. BUICK MOTOR CO.

Court of Appeals of New York, 1916.
217 N.Y. 382, 111 N.E. 1050.

CARDOZO, J.

The defendant is a manufacturer of automobiles. It sold an automobile to a retail dealer. The retail dealer resold to the plaintiff. While the plaintiff was in the car, it suddenly collapsed. He was thrown out and injured. One of the wheels was made of defective wood, and its spokes crumbled into fragments. The wheel was not made by the defendant; it was bought from another manufacturer. There is evidence, however, that its defects could have been discovered by reasonable inspection, and that inspection was omitted. There is no claim that the defendant knew of the defect and willfully concealed it. The case, in other words, is not brought within the rule of Kuelling v. Lean Mfg. Co., 183 N.Y. 78, 75 N.E. 1098, 2 L.R.A. (N.S.) 303, 111 Am.St.Rep. 691, 5 Ann.Cas. 124. The charge is one, not of fraud, but of negligence. The question to be determined is whether the defendant owed a duty of care and vigilance to any one but the immediate purchaser.

The foundations of this branch of the law, at least in this state, were laid in Thomas v. Winchester (6 N.Y. 397). A poison was falsely labeled. The sale was made to a druggist, who in turn sold to a customer. The customer recovered damages from the seller who affixed the label. "The defendant's negligence," it was said, "put human life in imminent danger." A poison falsely labeled is likely to injure any one who gets it. Because the danger is to be foreseen, there is a duty to avoid the injury. Cases were cited by way of illustration in which manufacturers were not subject to any duty irrespective of contract. The distinction was said to be that their conduct, though negligent, was not likely to result in injury to any one except the purchaser. We are not required to say whether the chance of injury was always as remote as the distinction assumes. Some of the illustrations might be rejected to-day. The *principle* of the distinction is for present purposes the important thing.

Thomas v. Winchester became quickly a landmark of the law. In the application of its principle there may at times have been uncertainty or even error. There has never in this state been doubt or disavowal of the principle itself. . . .

These early cases suggest a narrow construction of the rule. Later cases, however, evince a more liberal spirit. . . .

. . .

We hold, then, that the principle of Thomas v. Winchester is not limited to poisons, explosives, and things of like nature, to things which in their normal operation are implements of destruction. If the nature of a thing is such that it is reasonably certain to place life and limb in peril when negligently made, it is then a thing of danger. Its nature gives warning of the consequences to be expected. If to the element of danger there is added knowledge that the thing will be used by persons other than the purchaser, and used without new tests, then, irrespective of contract, the manufacturer of this thing of danger is under a duty to make it carefully. That is as far as we are required to go for the decision of this case. There must be knowledge of a danger, not merely possible, but probable. . . .

. . .

. . . Precedents drawn from the days of travel by stage coach do not fit the conditions of travel to-day. The principle that the danger must be imminent does not change, but the things subject to the principle do change. They are whatever the needs of life in a developing civilization require them to be.

BARTLETT, CH. J. dissenting.

I do not see how we can uphold the judgment in the present case without overruling what has been so often said by this court and other courts of like authority in reference to the absence of any liability for negligence on the part of the original vendor of an ordinary carriage to any one except his immediate vendee. The absence of such liability was the very point actually decided in the English case of Winterbottom v. Wright [10 M. & W. 109, 152 Eng.Rep. 402 (1842)], and the illustration quoted from the opinion of Chief Judge Ruggles in Thomas v. Winchester *(supra)* assumes that the law on the subject was so plain that the statement would be accepted almost as a matter of course. In the case at bar the defective wheel on an automobile moving only eight miles an hour was not any more dangerous to the occupants of the car than a similarly defective wheel would be to the occupants of a carriage drawn by a horse at the same speed; and yet unless the courts have been all wrong on this question up to the present time there would be no liability to strangers to the original sale in the case of the horse-drawn carriage.

NOTE

Did the principal case represent the application of a legal precept to the facts at hand? Or was it the formulation of a new legal precept? Is the precept implicated a "rule" or "principle" of law? Does your answer to the last question make a difference in deciding whether precedents were overruled in the principal case?

———

REIMANN v. MONMOUTH CONSOLIDATED WATER CO.

Supreme Court of New Jersey, 1952.
9 N.J. 134, 87 A.2d 325.

CASE, JUSTICE.

Plaintiff suffered a fire loss said to have been due to lack of water and pressure at fire hydrants served by the defendant water company. He instituted action by a complaint which defendant attacked upon the ground that it did not state a claim upon which relief could be granted. On motion the court rendered judgment for the defendant. This appeal brings up that judgment.

The complaint alleges that plaintiff owned and operated a recreation center in the Township of Ocean, Monmouth County. Near the said premises were two fire hydrants, located respectively at distances of 100 feet and 200 feet. On July 11, 1949, a fire broke out on the premises and the township volunteer fire department responded with its equipment. The water volume and pressure were insufficient, even with the "boost" from the fire apparatus to combat the fire. As a result the building and contents were completely destroyed. The defendant company was a public utility engaged in the supply and distribution of water.

It exercised exclusive control over the fire hydrants and the exclusive function of furnishing water thereat for the inhabitants and property owners of the township and for the fire department, and it had knowledge of the existence of plaintiff's building and of the business conducted there. Such is the substance of the allegations.

. . .

Before there can be either nonfeasance or misfeasance there must be a duty. Had there been a contract between the company and the owner whereby the company undertook to furnish water to the owner with a pressure sufficient for fire purposes, followed by a breach, liability would have been according to the terms of the contract.... There was no contract, therefore no duty imposed by contract. There is no applicable statute and therefore no statutory duty. Plaintiff argues for a common law duty, but the Court of Errors and Appeals held in Baum v. Somerville Water Company, 84 N.J.L. 611, 87 A. 140, 46 L.R.A.,N.S., 966 (1913), upon facts that bear a striking resemblance to the facts of the present case, that the common law does not impose a duty upon a company serving a municipality with water to provide a sufficient supply of water at sufficient pressure at fire hydrants to extinguish a fire which is destroying an individual's property. Very plainly it holds that in the absence of contract no liability exists....

. . .

The law in this State as heretofore pronounced is entirely clear. Appellant, although arguing to the contrary, apparently anticipates that such may be the holding and thereupon asks that the old law be discarded and a modern principle adopted—a prayer which could more properly be addressed to the Legislature. The Baum case was decided nearly 40 years ago and has never been attacked or weakened. Water companies sell a commodity and their rates have been established and approved by the Board of Public Utility Commissioners upon that basis, not upon the assumption that, without an undertaking to that end, they are responsible for fire losses. A way of business has grown up on that understanding. There are many companies whose function is to insure against fire, and the property owner may protect himself fully against fire loss by contract with those companies. In the making of such a contract the premium varies with the risk and with the character of the property insured, and the insurer may limit its liability. Water rates are uniform; they do not rise or fall with the inherent danger. If the principle for which appellant contends were the law there would be no predetermined limit of liability....

If such a broad liability as that sought by the plaintiff were established, the ensuing litigation would doubtless be great. Fire insurance companies, entitled to subrogation to their insureds' claims, could, if they would, sue, whether successfully or not, upon settling a fire loss with their insureds in accordance with their contract liability. No one can foretell the degree of confusion which would follow so revolutionary a decision; a decision which would work backward as well as forward; it would unsettle the past as well as be effective in the future.

We conclude that if our law is to be overturned, the result should be effected by the Legislature, vested with the lawmaking power. Statutory changes are accompanied by publicity and an opportunity for all interested persons to be heard; incidents which are quite impossible in a suit between parties.

The majority rule in this country appears to be consistent with our New Jersey holdings. . . .

VANDERBILT, CHIEF JUSTICE dissenting.

Under Baum v. Somerville Water Co., . . . the defendant water company, in the absence of an express contract with a property owner and a breach thereof, has no obligation to furnish water with sufficient pressure and in sufficient quantity for fire fighting purposes. Because I am of the opinion that the rule in the Baum case is repugnant not only to fundamental concepts of substantial justice but to modern principles of tort liability, I am constrained to dissent from the opinion of the majority and to state the reasons why I think the rule should be discarded in favor of one in keeping with the needs of the times.

The question is whether, assuming that the rule in Baum v. Somerville Water Co. needs to be changed, the courts should refuse to act and leave it to the Legislature to correct the injustice. In my dissenting opinion in the case of Fox v. Snow, 6 N.J. 12, 21, 76 A.2d 877 (1950), I had occasion to discuss this very question at some length and so I shall not here presume to traverse the same ground in detail again. . . . The courts are under as great an obligation to revise an outmoded rule of the common law as the legislatures are to abolish or modernize an archaic statute. The common law is not merely a conglomeration of rules to be gleaned from decisions of the ancient past; it is a living and growing body of legal principles. It derives its life and growth from judicial decisions which alter an existing rule, or abandon an old rule and substitute in its place a new one in order to meet new conditions. It is because of this gradual but continuous process of change that the body of our common law today is as different from that of mediaeval England as our physical surroundings are from those of that era. And it is absolutely essential that this be so, for it would be an impossible situation indeed if we attempted to determine twentieth century disputes by means of rules of law applicable to 15th Century facts.

. . .

True it is that when a rule has been established by legislation, however undesirable it may be, it is for the Legislature alone to remedy the situation, see Martin v. Curran, 303 N.Y. 276, 101 N.E.2d 683, 686 (N.Y.1951). . . . But when the rule is one of common law established by the courts the remedy lies with either the Legislature or the courts, and inaction by one does not preclude action by the other.

BOYS MARKETS v. RETAIL CLERKS UNION

Supreme Court of the United States, 1970.
398 U.S. 235, 90 S.Ct. 1583, 26 L.Ed.2d 199.

Mr. Justice Brennan delivered the opinion of the Court.

In this case we re-examine the holding of Sinclair Refining Co. v. Atkinson, 370 U.S. 195, 82 S.Ct. 1328, 8 L.Ed.2d 440 (1962), that the anti-injunction provisions of the Norris–LaGuardia Act preclude a federal district court from enjoining a strike in breach of a no-strike obligation under a collective bargaining agreement, even though that agreement contains provisions, enforceable under § 301(a) of the Labor Management Relations Act, 1947, for binding arbitration of the grievance dispute concerning which the strike was called. The Court of Appeals for the Ninth Circuit, considering itself bound by *Sinclair* reversed the grant by the District Court for the Central District of California of petitioner's prayer for injunctive relief.... Having concluded that *Sinclair* was erroneously decided and that subsequent events have undermined its continuing validity, we overrule that decision and reverse the judgment of the Court of Appeals.

. . .

At the outset, we are met with respondent's contention that *Sinclair* ought not to be disturbed because the decision turned on a question of statutory construction which Congress can alter at any time. Since Congress has not modified our conclusions in *Sinclair*, even though it has been urged to do so, respondent argues that principles of *stare decisis* should govern the present case.

We do not agree that the doctrine of *stare decisis* bars a re-examination of *Sinclair* in the circumstances of this case. We fully recognize that important policy considerations militate in favor of continuity and predictability in the law. Nevertheless, as Mr. Justice Frankfurter wrote for the Court, "[S]tare decisis *is a principle of policy and not a mechanical formula of adherence to the latest decision, however recent and questionable, when such adherence involves collision with a prior doctrine more embracing in its scope, intrinsically sounder, and verified by experience." Helvering v. Hallock, 309 U.S. 106, 119, 60 S.Ct. 444, 451, 84 L.Ed. 604 (1940). See Swift & Co. v. Wickham, 382 U.S. 111, 116, 86 S.Ct. 258, 261, 15 L.Ed.2d 194 (1965). It is precisely because* Sinclair *stands as a significant departure from our otherwise consistent emphasis upon the congressional policy to promote the peaceful settlement of labor disputes through arbitration and our efforts to accommodate and harmonize this policy with those underlying the anti-injunction provisions of the Norris–LaGuardia Act that we believe* Sinclair *should be reconsidered. Furthermore, in light of developments subsequent to* Sinclair, *in particular our decision in Avco Corp. v. Aero Lodge 735, 390 U.S. 557, 88 S.Ct. 1235, 20 L.Ed.2d 126 (1968), it has become clear that the* Sinclair *decision does not further but rather frustrates realization of an important goal of our national labor policy.*

Nor can we agree that conclusive weight should be accorded to the failure of Congress to respond to *Sinclair* on the theory that congressional silence should be interpreted as acceptance of the decision. The Court has cautioned that "[i]t is at best treacherous to find in congressional silence alone the adoption of a controlling rule of law." Girouard v. United States, 328 U.S. 61, 69, 66 S.Ct. 826, 830, 90 L.Ed. 1084 (1946). Therefore, in the absence of any persuasive circumstances evidencing a clear design that congressional inaction be taken as acceptance of *Sinclair,* the mere silence of Congress is not a sufficient reason for refusing to reconsider the decision. . . .

. . .

Subsequent to the decision in *Sinclair,* we held in Avco Corp. v. Aero Lodge 735, *supra,* that § 301(a) suits initially brought in state courts may be removed to the designated federal forum under the federal question removal jurisdiction delineated in 28 U.S.C.A. § 1441. In so holding, however, the Court expressly left open the questions whether state courts are bound by the anti-injunction proscriptions of the Norris–LaGuardia Act and whether federal courts, after removal of a § 301(a) action, are required to dissolve any injunctive relief previously granted by the state courts. . . . Three Justices who concurred expressed the view that *Sinclair* should be reconsidered "upon an appropriate future occasion." 390 U.S., at 562, 88 S.Ct. at 1238. Stewart, J., concurring.

The decision in *Avco,* viewed in the context of [Textile Workers Union v.] *Lincoln Mills* [353 U.S. 448, 77 S.Ct. 912, 11 L.Ed.2d 972 (1957)] and its progeny, has produced an anomalous situation which, in our view, makes urgent the reconsideration of *Sinclair.* The principal practical effect of *Avco* and *Sinclair* taken together is nothing less than to oust state courts of jurisdiction in § 301(a) suits where injunctive relief is sought for breach of a no-strike obligation. Union defendants can, as a matter of course, obtain removal to a federal court, and there is obviously a compelling incentive for them to do so in order to gain the advantage of the strictures upon injunctive relief which *Sinclair* imposes on federal courts. The sanctioning of this practice, however, is wholly inconsistent with our conclusion in [Charles Dowd Box Co. v. Courtney, 368 U.S. 502, 82 S.Ct. 519, 7 L.Ed.2d 483 (1962)] that the congressional purpose embodied in § 301(a) was to *supplement,* and not to encroach upon, the pre-existing jurisdiction of the state courts. It is ironic indeed that the very provision that Congress clearly intended to provide additional remedies for breach of collective-bargaining agreements has been employed to displace previously existing state remedies.

PATTERSON v. McLEAN CREDIT UNION

Supreme Court of the United States, 1989.
491 U.S. 164, 109 S.Ct. 2363, 105 L.Ed.2d 132.

JUSTICE KENNEDY delivered the opinion of the Court.

In this case, we consider important issues respecting the meaning and coverage of one of our oldest civil rights statutes, 42 U.S.C. § 1981.

We granted certiorari to decide whether petitioner's claim of racial harassment in her employment is actionable under § 1981, and whether the jury instruction given by the District Court on petitioner's § 1981 promotion claim was error. 484 U.S. 814 (1987). After oral argument on these issues, we requested the parties to brief and argue an additional question:

> "Whether or not the interpretation of 42 U.S.C. § 1981 adopted by this Court in Runyon v. McCrary, 427 U.S. 160 (1976), should be reconsidered." Patterson v. McLean Credit Union, 485 U.S. 617 (1988).

We now decline to overrule our decision in Runyon v. McCrary, 427 U.S. 160 (1976).

The Court has said often and with great emphasis that "the doctrine of *stare decisis* is of fundamental importance to the rule of law." Welch v. Texas Dept. of Highways and Public Transportation, 483 U.S. 468, 494 (1987). Although we have cautioned that "*stare decisis* is a principle of policy and not a mechanical formula of adherence to the latest decision," Boys Markets, Inc. v. Retail Clerks, 398 U.S. 235, 241 (1970), it is indisputable that *stare decisis* is a basic self-governing principle within the Judicial Branch, which is entrusted with the sensitive and difficult task of fashioning and preserving a jurisprudential system that is not based upon "an arbitrary discretion." The Federalist, No. 78, p. 490 (H. Lodge ed. 1888) (A. Hamilton). See also Vasquez v. Hillery, 474 U.S. 254, 265 (1986) (*stare decisis* ensures that "the law will not merely change erratically" and "permits society to presume that bedrock principles are founded in the law rather than in the proclivities of individuals").

Our precedents are not sacrosanct, for we have overruled prior decisions where the necessity and propriety of doing so has been established. See Patterson v. McLean Credit Union, *supra*, at 617–618 (citing cases). Nonetheless, we have held that "any departure from the doctrine of *stare decisis* demands special justification." Arizona v. Rumsey, 467 U.S. 203, 212 (1984). We have said also that the burden borne by the party advocating the abandonment of an established precedent is greater where the Court is asked to overrule a point of statutory construction. Considerations of *stare decisis* have special force in the area of statutory interpretation, for here, unlike in the context of constitutional interpretation, the legislative power is implicated, and

Congress remains free to alter what we have done. See, *e.g.*, Square D Co. v. Niagara Frontier Tariff Bureau, Inc., 476 U.S. 409, 424 (1986); Illinois Brick Co. v. Illinois, 431 U.S. 720, 736 (1977).

We conclude, upon direct consideration of the issue, that no special justification has been shown for overruling *Runyon*. In cases where statutory precedents have been overruled, the primary reason for the Court's shift in position has been the intervening development of the law, through either the growth of judicial doctrine or further action taken by Congress. Where such changes have removed or weakened the conceptual underpinnings from the prior decision, see, *e.g.*, Rodriguez de Quijas v. Shearson/American Express, Inc., 490 U.S. 477, 480–481 (1989); Andrews v. Louisville & Nashville R. Co., 406 U.S. 320, 322–323 (1972), or where the later law has rendered the decision irreconcilable with competing legal doctrines or policies, see, *e.g.*, Braden v. 30th Judicial Circuit Ct. of Ky., 410 U.S. 484, 497–499 (1973); Construction Laborers v. Curry, 371 U.S. 542, 552 (1963), the Court has not hesitated to overrule an earlier decision. Our decision in *Runyon* has not been undermined by subsequent changes or development in the law.

Another traditional justification for overruling a prior case is that a precedent may be a positive detriment to coherence and consistency in the law, either because of inherent confusion created by an unworkable decision, see, *e.g.*, Continental T. V., Inc. v. GTE Sylvania, Inc., 433 U.S. 36, 47–48 (1977); Swift & Co. v. Wickham, 382 U.S. 111, 124–125 (1965), or because the decision poses a direct obstacle to the realization of important objectives embodied in other laws, see, *e.g.*, *Rodriguez de Quijas, supra,* at 484; Boys Markets, Inc. v. Retail Clerks, *supra,* at 240–241. In this regard, we do not find *Runyon* to be unworkable or confusing. Respondent and various *amici* have urged that *Runyon's* interpretation of § 1981, as applied to contracts of employment, frustrates the objectives of Title VII. The argument is that a substantial overlap in coverage between the two statutes, given the considerable differences in their remedial schemes, undermines Congress' detailed efforts in Title VII to resolve disputes about racial discrimination in private employment through conciliation rather than litigation as an initial matter. After examining the point with care, however, we believe that a sound construction of the language of § 1981 yields an interpretation which does not frustrate the congressional objectives in Title VII to any significant degree. See Part III, *infra*.

Finally, it has sometimes been said that a precedent becomes more vulnerable as it becomes outdated and after being " 'tested by experience, has been found to be inconsistent with the sense of justice or with the social welfare.' " *Runyon*, 427 U.S., at 191 (Stevens, J., concurring), quoting B. Cardozo, The Nature of the Judicial Process 149 (1921). Whatever the effect of this consideration may be in statutory cases, it offers no support for overruling *Runyon*. In recent decades, state and federal legislation has been enacted to prohibit private racial discrimination in many aspects of our society. Whether *Runyon's* interpretation of § 1981 as prohibiting racial discrimination in the making and enforcement of private contracts is right or wrong as an original matter, it is certain that it is not inconsistent with the prevailing sense of justice in this country.　To the contrary, *Runyon* is entirely consistent with our society's deep commitment to the eradication of discrimination based on a person's race or the color of his or her skin.　See Bob Jones University v. United States, 461 U.S. 574, 593 (1983) ("[E]very pronouncement of this Court and myriad Acts of Congress and Executive Orders attest a firm national policy to prohibit racial segregation and discrimination"); see also Brown v. Board of Education, 347 U.S. 483 (1954);　Plessy v. Ferguson, 163 U.S. 537, 559 (1896) (Harlan, J., dissenting) ("The law regards man as man, and takes no account of his ... color when his civil rights as guaranteed by the supreme law of the land are involved").

We decline to overrule *Runyon* and acknowledge that its holding remains the governing law in this area.

NOTE

Anent the Court's statement:

Considerations of *stare decisis* have special force in the area of statutory interpretation, for here, unlike in the context of constitutional interpretation, the legislative power is implicated, and Congress remains free to alter what we have done.

Congress did just that.　The Civil Rights Act of 1991, Pub.L. No. 102–166, § 101(2)(b), 105 Stat. 1071, 1072 added a subsection that defined the "make and enforce contracts" language broadly to include "the making, performance, modification, and termination of contracts, and the enjoyment of all benefits, privileges, terms and conditions of the contractual relationship."

ADARAND CONSTRUCTORS, INC. v. PENA

Supreme Court of the United States, 1995.
___ U.S. ___, 115 S.Ct. 2097, 132 L.Ed.2d 158.

JUSTICE O'CONNOR delivered the opinion of the Court.

"Although adherence to precedent is not rigidly required in constitutional cases, any departure from the doctrine of stare decisis demands special justification."　Arizona v. Rumsey, 467 U.S. 203, 212, 104 S.Ct. 2305, 2311, 81 L.Ed.2d 164 (1984).　In deciding whether this case presents such justification, we recall Justice Frankfurter's admonition that "stare decisis is a principle of policy and not a mechanical formula of adherence to the latest decision, however recent and questionable, when such adherence involves collision with a prior doctrine more embracing in its scope, intrinsically sounder, and verified by experience."　Helvering v. Hallock, 309 U.S. 106, 119, 60 S.Ct. 444, 451, 84 L.Ed. 604 (1940).　Remaining true to an "intrinsically sounder" doctrine established in prior cases better serves the values of stare decisis than would following a more recently decided case inconsistent with the decisions that came before it; the latter course would simply compound the recent error and would likely make the unjustified break from previously established doctrine complete. In such a situation, "special justification" exists to depart from the recently decided case.

Metro Broadcasting v. FCC [497 U.S. 547, 110 S.Ct. 2997, 111 L.Ed.2d 445 (1990)] undermined important principles of this Court's equal protection jurisprudence, established in a line of cases stretching back over fifty years.... Those principles together stood for an "embracing" and "intrinsically soun[d]" understanding of equal protection "verified by experience," namely, that the Constitution imposes upon federal, state, and local governmental actors the same obligation to respect the personal right to equal protection of the laws. This case therefore presents precisely the situation described by Justice Frankfurter in Helvering: we cannot adhere to our most recent decision without colliding with an accepted and established doctrine. We also note that Metro Broadcasting's application of different standards of review to federal and state racial classifications has been consistently criticized by commentators. *See, e.g.,* Fried, Metro Broadcasting, Inc. v. FCC: Two Concepts of Equality, 104 Harv.L.Rev. 107, 113–117 (1990) (arguing that Metro Broadcasting's adoption of different standards of review for federal and state racial classifications placed the law in an "unstable condition," and advocating strict scrutiny across the board); Devins, Metro Broadcasting, Inc. v. FCC: *Requiem for a Heavyweight,* 69 Texas L.Rev. 125, 145–146 (1990) (same); Linder, Review of Affirmative Action After Metro Broadcasting v. FCC: The Solution Almost Nobody Wanted, 59 UMKC L.Rev. 293, 297, 316–317 (1991) (criticizing "anomalous results as exemplified by the two different standards of review"); Katz, *Public Affirmative Action and the Fourteenth Amendment: The Fragmentation of Theory After* Richmond v. J.A. Croson Co. *and* Metro Broadcasting, Inc. v. Federal Communications Commission, 17 T. Marshall L.Rev. 317, 319, 354–355, 357 (1992) (arguing that "the current fragmentation of doctrine must be seen as a dangerous and seriously flawed approach to constitutional interpretation," and advocating intermediate scrutiny across the board).

Our past practice in similar situations supports our action today. In United States v. Dixon, 509 U.S. ___, 113 S.Ct. 2849, 125 L.Ed.2d 556 (1993), we overruled the recent case of Grady v. Corbin, 495 U.S. 508, 110 S.Ct. 2084, 109 L.Ed.2d 548 (1990), because *Grady* "lack[ed] constitutional roots" and was "wholly inconsistent with earlier Supreme Court precedent." *Dixon, supra,* at ___, ___, 113 S.Ct., at 2852, 2860. In Solorio v. United States, 483 U.S. 435, 107 S.Ct. 2924, 97 L.Ed.2d 364 (1987), we overruled O'Callahan v. Parker, 395 U.S. 258, 89 S.Ct. 1683, 23 L.Ed.2d 291 (1969), which had caused "confusion" and had rejected "an unbroken line of decisions from 1866 to 1960." *Solorio, supra,* at 439–441, 450–451, 107 S.Ct., at 2926–2928, 2932–2933. And in Continental T.V., Inc. v. GTE Sylvania Inc., 433 U.S. 36, 97 S.Ct. 2549, 53

L.Ed.2d 568 (1977), we overruled United States v. Arnold, Schwinn & Co., 388 U.S. 365, 87 S.Ct. 1856, 18 L.Ed.2d 1249 (1967), which was "an abrupt and largely unexplained departure" from precedent, and of which "[t]he great weight of scholarly opinion ha[d] been critical." *Continental T.V., supra,* at 47–48, 58, 97 S.Ct., at 2556, 2561. *See also, e.g.,* Payne v. Tennessee, 501 U.S. 808, 830, 111 S.Ct. 2597, 2611, 115 L.Ed.2d 720 (1991) (overruling Booth v. Maryland, 482 U.S. 496, 107 S.Ct. 2529, 96 L.Ed.2d 440 (1987), and South Carolina v. Gathers, 490 U.S. 805, 109 S.Ct. 2207, 104 L.Ed.2d 876 (1989)); Monell v. New York City Dept. of Social Services, 436 U.S. 658, 695–701, 98 S.Ct. 2018, 2038–2041, 56 L.Ed.2d 611 (1978) (partially overruling Monroe v. Pape, 365 U.S. 167, 81 S.Ct. 473, 5 L.Ed.2d 492 (1961), because *Monroe* was a "departure from prior practice" that had not engendered substantial reliance); Swift & Co. v. Wickham, 382 U.S. 111, 128–129, 86 S.Ct. 258, 267–268, 15 L.Ed.2d 194 (1965) (overruling Kesler v. Department of Public Safety of Utah, 369 U.S. 153, 82 S.Ct. 807, 7 L.Ed.2d 641 (1962), to reaffirm "pre-*Kesler* precedent" and restore the law to the "view ... which this Court has traditionally taken" in older cases).

It is worth pointing out the difference between the applications of stare decisis in this case and in Planned Parenthood of Southeastern Pa. v. Casey, 505 U.S. ___, 112 S.Ct. 2791, 120 L.Ed.2d 674 (1992). *Casey* explained how considerations of stare decisis inform the decision whether to overrule a long-established precedent that has become integrated into the fabric of the law. Overruling precedent of that kind naturally may have consequences for "the ideal of the rule of law," *id.,* at ___, 112 S.Ct., at 2797. In addition, such precedent is likely to have engendered substantial reliance, as was true in *Casey* itself, *id.,* at ___, 112 S.Ct., at 2809 ("[F]or two decades of economic and social developments, people have organized intimate relationships and made choices that define their views of themselves and their places in society, in reliance on the availability of abortion in the event that contraception should fail"). But in this case, as we have explained, we do not face a precedent of that kind, because *Metro Broadcasting* itself departed from our prior cases— and did so quite recently. By refusing to follow *Metro Broadcasting,* then, we do not depart from the fabric of the law; we restore it. We also note that reliance on a case that has recently departed from precedent is likely to be minimal, particularly where, as here, the rule set forth in that case is unlikely to affect primary conduct in any event. *Cf.* Allied–Bruce Terminix Cos. v. Dobson, 513 U.S. ___, ___, 115 S.Ct. 834, 838–839, 130 L.Ed.2d 753 (1995) (declining to overrule Southland Corp. v. Keating, 465 U.S. 1, 104 S.Ct. 852, 79 L.Ed.2d 1 (1984), where "private parties have likely written contracts relying upon *Southland* as authority" in the ten years since *Southland* was decided).

ALLIED–BRUCE TERMINIX COS. v. DOBSON

Supreme Court of the United States, 1995.
___ U.S. ___, 115 S.Ct. 834, 130 L.Ed.2d 753.

JUSTICE BREYER delivered the opinion of the Court.

This case concerns the reach of § 2 of the Federal Arbitration Act. That section makes enforceable a written arbitration provision in "a contract *evidencing* a transaction *involving* commerce." 9 U.S.C. § 2 (emphasis added). Should we read this phrase broadly, extending the Act's reach to the limits of Congress' Commerce Clause power? Or, do the two underscored words—"involving" and "evidencing"—significantly restrict the Act's application? We conclude that the broader reading of the Act is the correct one; and we reverse a State Supreme Court judgment to the contrary.

I

In August 1987 Steven Gwin, a respondent, who owned a house in Birmingham, Alabama, bought a lifetime "Termite Protection Plan" (Plan) from the local office of Allied–Bruce Terminix Companies, a franchise of Terminix International Company. In the Plan, Allied–Bruce promised "to protect" Gwin's house "against the attack of subterranean termites," to reinspect periodically, to provide any "further treatment found necessary," and to repair, up to $100,000, damage caused by new termite infestations. App. 69. Terminix International "guarantee[d] the fulfillment of the terms" of the Plan. *Ibid.* The Plan's contract document provided in writing that

> "*any controversy or claim* ... arising out of or relating to the interpretation, performance or breach of any provision of this agreement *shall be settled exclusively by arbitration.*" *Id.*, at 70 (emphasis added).

In the Spring of 1991 Mr. and Mrs. Gwin, wishing to sell their house to Mr. and Mrs. Dobson, had Allied–Bruce reinspect the house. They obtained a clean bill of health. But, no sooner had they sold the house and transferred the Termite Protection Plan to Mr. and Mrs. Dobson than the Dobsons found the house swarming with termites. Allied–Bruce attempted to treat and repair the house, but the Dobsons found Allied–Bruce's efforts inadequate. They therefore sued the Gwins, and (along with the Gwins, who cross-claimed) also sued Allied–Bruce and Terminix in Alabama state court. Allied–Bruce and Terminix, pointing to the Plan's arbitration clause and § 2 of the Federal Arbitration Act, immediately asked the court for a stay, to allow arbitration to proceed. The court denied the stay. Allied–Bruce and Terminix appealed.

The Supreme Court of Alabama upheld the denial of the stay on the basis of a state statute, Ala.Code § 8–1–41(3) (1993), making written, predispute arbitration agreements invalid and "unenforceable." 628 So.2d 354, 355 (Ala.1993). To reach this conclusion, the court had to find that the federal Arbitration Act, which pre-empts conflicting state law, did not apply to the termite contract. It made just that finding. The court considered the federal Act inapplicable because the connection between the termite contract and interstate commerce was too slight. Some initially assumed that the Federal Arbitration Act represented an exercise of Congress' Article III power to "ordain and establish" federal courts, U.S. Const., Art. III, § 1. See Southland Corp. v. Keating, 465 U.S. 1, 28, n. 16 (1984) (O'Connor, J., dissenting) (collecting cases). In 1967, however, this Court held that the Act "is based upon and confined to the incontestable federal foundations of 'control over interstate commerce and over admiralty.'" Prima Paint Corp. v. Flood & Conklin Mfg. Co., 388 U.S. 395, 405 (1967) (quoting H.R.Rep. No. 96, 68th Cong., 1st Sess., 1 (1924)). In Southland Corp. v. Keating, supra, this Court decided that Congress would not have wanted state and federal courts to reach different outcomes about the validity of arbitration in similar cases. The Court concluded that the Federal Arbitration Act pre-empts state law; and it held that state courts cannot apply state statutes that invalidate arbitration agreements. *Id.,* at 15–16.

We have set forth this background because respondents, supported by 20 state attorneys general, now ask us to overrule *Southland* and thereby to permit Alabama to apply its antiarbitration statute in this case irrespective of the proper interpretation of § 2. The *Southland* Court, however, recognized that the pre-emption issue was a difficult one, and it considered the basic arguments that respondents and *amici* now raise (even though those issues were not thoroughly briefed at the time). Nothing significant has changed in the 10 years subsequent to *Southland;* no later cases have eroded *Southland*'s authority; and, no unforeseen practical problems have arisen. Moreover, in the interim, private parties have likely written contracts relying upon *Southland* as authority. Further, Congress, both before and after *Southland,* has enacted legislation extending, not retracting, the scope of arbitration. See, *e.g.,* 9 U.S.C. § 15 (eliminating the Act of State doctrine as a bar to arbitration); 9 U.S.C. §§ 201–208 (international arbitration). For these reasons, we find it inappropriate to reconsider what is by now well-established law.

Justice O'Connor, concurring.

Were we writing on a clean slate, I would adhere to that view and affirm the Alabama court's decision. But, as the Court points out, more than 10 years have passed since *Southland,* several subsequent cases have built upon its reasoning, and parties have undoubtedly made contracts in reliance on the Court's interpretation of the Act in the interim. After reflection, I am persuaded by considerations of *stare decisis,* which we have said "have special force in the area of statutory interpretation," Patterson v. McLean Credit Union, 491 U.S. 164, 172–173 (1989), to acquiesce in today's judgment. Though wrong, *Southland* has not proved unworkable, and, as always, "Congress remains free to alter what we have done." *Ibid.*

Today's decision caps this Court's effort to expand the Federal Arbitration Act. Although each decision has built logically upon the decisions preceding it, the initial building block in *Southland* laid a faulty foundation. I acquiesce in today's judgment because there is no "special justification" to overrule *Southland*. Arizona v. Rumsey, 467 U.S. 203, 212 (1984). It remains now for Congress to correct this interpretation if it wishes to preserve state autonomy in state courts.

JUSTICE SCALIA, dissenting.

I have previously joined two judgments of this Court which rested upon the holding of Southland Corp. v. Keating, 465 U.S. 1 (1984). See Volt Information Sciences, Inc. v. Board of Trustees of Leland Stanford Junior Univ., 489 U.S. 468 (1989); Perry v. Thomas, 482 U.S. 483 (1987). In neither of those cases, however, did any party ask that *Southland* be overruled, and it was therefore not necessary to consider the question. In the present case, by contrast, one of respondents' central arguments is that *Southland* was wrongly decided, and their request for its overruling has been supported by an *amicus* brief signed by the attorneys general of 20 States. For the reasons set forth in Justice Thomas' opinion, which I join, I agree with the respondents (and belatedly with Justice O'Conner) that *Southland* clearly misconstrued the Federal Arbitration Act.

JUSTICE THOMAS, with whom JUSTICE SCALIA joins, dissenting.

I disagree with the majority at the threshold of this case, and so I do not reach the question that it decides. In my view, the Federal Arbitration Act (FAA) does not apply in state courts. I respectfully dissent.

In Southland Corp. v. Keating, 465 U.S. 1 (1984), this Court concluded that § 2 of the FAA "appl[ies] in state as well as federal courts," *id.*, at 12, and "withdr[aws] the power of the states to require a judicial forum for the resolution of claims which the contracting parties agreed to resolve by arbitration," *id.*, at 10. In my view, both aspects of *Southland* are wrong.

The majority and Justice O'Connor properly focus on whether overruling *Southland* would frustrate the legitimate expectations of people who have drafted and executed contracts in the belief that even state courts will strictly enforce arbitration clauses. I do not doubt that innumerable contracts containing arbitration clauses have been written since 1984, or that arbitrable disputes might yet arise out of a large proportion of these contracts. Some of these contracts might well have been written differently in the absence of *Southland*. Still, I see no reason to think that the costs of overruling *Southland* are unacceptably high. Certainly no reliance interests are involved in cases like the present one, where the applicability of the FAA was not within the contemplation of the parties at the time of contracting. In many other cases, moreover, the parties will simply comply with their arbitration agreement, either on the theory that they should live up to their promises or on the theory that arbitration is the cheapest and best way of resolving their dispute. In a fair number of the remaining cases, the party seeking to enforce an arbitration agreement will be able to get into federal court, where the FAA will apply. And even if access to federal court is impossible (because § 2 creates no independent basis for federal-question jurisdiction), many cases will arise in States whose own law largely parallels the FAA. Only Alabama, Mississippi, and Nebraska still hold all executory arbitration agreements to be unenforceable, though some other States refuse to enforce particular classes of such agreements. See Strickland, The Federal Arbitration Act's Interstate Commerce Requirement: What's Left for State Arbitration Law?, 21 Hofstra L.Rev. 385, 401–403, and n. 93 (1992).

Quoting Arizona v. Rumsey, 467 U.S. 203, 212 (1984), Justice O'Conner nonetheless acquiesces in the majority's judgment "because there is no 'special justification' to overrule *Southland.*" *Ante,* at 3. Even under this approach, the necessity of "preserv[ing] state autonomy in state courts," *ibid.,* seems sufficient to me.

PAYNE v. TENNESSEE

Supreme Court of the United States, 1991.
501 U.S. 808, 111 S.Ct. 2597, 115 L.Ed.2d 720.

JUSTICE MARSHALL, with whom JUSTICE BLACKMUN joins, dissenting.

[In Booth v. Maryland, 482 U.S. 496 (1987) and South Carolina v. Gathers, 490 U.S. 805 (1989), the Court held that the Eighth Amendment bars the admission of victim impact evidence during the penalty phase of a capital trial. Victim impact evidence relates to the personal characteristics of the victim and the emotional impact of the crimes on the victim's family. In this case, the majority decided that these cases "were wrongly decided and should be, and now are, overruled."]

The overruling of one of this Court's precedents ought to be a matter of great moment and consequence. Although the doctrine of *stare decisis* is not an "inexorable command," Burnet v. Coronado Oil & Gas Co., 285 U.S. 393, 405 (1932) (Brandeis, J., dissenting), this Court has repeatedly stressed that fidelity to precedent is fundamental to "a society governed by the rule of law," Akron v. Akron Center for Reproductive Health, Inc., 462 U.S. 416, 420 (1983). See generally Patterson v. McLean Credit Union, 491 U.S. 164, 172 (1989) ("[I]t is indisputable that *stare decisis* is a basic self-governing principle within the Judicial Branch, which is entrusted with the sensitive and difficult task of fashioning and preserving a jurisprudential system that is not based upon 'an arbitrary discretion.' The Federalist, No. 78, p. 490 (H. Lodge ed. 1888) (A. Hamilton)"); Appeal of Concerned Corporators of Portsmouth Savings Bank, 129 N.H. 183, 227, 525 A.2d 671, 701 (1987) (Souter, J., dissenting) ("*[S]tare decisis* . . . 'is essential if case-by-case judicial decision-making is to be reconciled with the principle of the rule of law, for when governing legal standards are open to revision in every case, deciding cases becomes a mere exercise of judicial will, with arbitrary and unpredictable results,'" quoting Thornburgh v. American College of Obstetricians and Gynecologists, 476 U.S. 747, 786–787 (1986) (WHITE, J., dissenting)).

Consequently, this Court has never departed from precedent without "special justification." Arizona v. Rumsey, 467 U.S. 203, 212 (1984). Such justifications include the advent of "subsequent changes or development in the law" that undermine a decision's rationale, Patterson v. McLean Credit Union, supra, at 173; the need "to bring [a decision] into agreement with experience and with facts newly ascertained," Burnet v. Coronado Oil & Gas Co., *supra,* at 412 (Brandeis, J., dissenting); and a showing that a particular precedent has become a "detriment to coherence and consistency in the law," Patterson v. McLean Credit Union, *supra,* at 173.

The majority cannot seriously claim that *any* of these traditional bases for overruling a precedent applies to *Booth* or *Gathers.* The majority does not suggest that the legal rationale of these decisions has been undercut by changes or developments in doctrine during the last two years. Nor does the majority claim that experience over that period of time has discredited the principle that "any decision to impose the death sentence be, and appear to be, based on reason rather than caprice or emotion," Gardner v. Florida, 430 U.S. 349, 358 (1977) (plurality opinion), the larger postulate of political morality on which *Booth* and *Gathers* rest.

The majority does assert that *Booth* and *Gathers* "have defied consistent application by the lower courts." But the evidenc that the majority proffers is so feeble that the majority cannot sincerely expect anyone to believe this claim. To support its contention, the majority points to Justice O'Connor's dissent in *Gathers,* which noted a division among lower courts over whether *Booth* prohibited prosecutorial arguments relating to the victim's personal characteristics. See 490 U.S., at 813. That, of course, was the issue expressly considered and resolved in *Gathers.* The majority also cites The Chief Justice's dissent in Mills v. Maryland, 486 U.S. 367, 395–398 (1988). That opinion does not contain a *single word* about any supposed "[in]consistent application" of *Booth* in the lower courts. Finally, the majority refers to a divided Ohio Supreme Court decision disposing of an issue concerning victim-impact evidence. See State v. Huertas, 51 Ohio St.3d 22, 553 N.E.2d 1058 (1990), cert. dism'd as improvidently granted, 498 U.S. 336 (1991). Obviously, if a division among the members of a single lower court in a single case were sufficient to demonstrate that a particular precedent was a "detriment to coherence and consistency in the law," Patterson v. McLean Credit Union, *supra,* at 173, there would hardly be a decision in United States Reports that we would not be obliged to reconsider.

It takes little real detective work to discern just what *has* changed since this Court decided *Booth* and *Gathers:* this Court's own personnel. Indeed, the majority candidly explains why this particular contingency, which until now has been almost universally understood *not* to be sufficient to warrant overruling a precedent, see, *e.g.,* Florida Dept. of Health and Rehabilitative Services v. Florida Nursing Home Assn., 450 U.S. 147, 153 (1981) (Stevens, J., concurring); Mitchell v. W.T. Grant Co., 416 U.S. 600, 636 (1974) (Stewart, J., dissenting); Mapp v. Ohio, 367 U.S. 643, 677 (1961) (Harlan, J., dissenting); but see South Carolina v. Gathers, *supra,* at 824 (Scalia, J., dissenting), *is* sufficient to justify overruling *Booth* and *Gathers*. "Considerations in favor of *stare decisis* are at their acme," the majority explains, "in cases involving property and contract rights, where reliance interests are involved[;] the opposite is true in cases such as the present one involving procedural and evidentiary rules." *Ante,* at 828 (citations omitted). In addition, the majority points out, "*Booth* and *Gathers* were decided by the narrowest of margins, over spirited dissents" and thereafter were "questioned by Members of the Court." *Ante,* at 828–829. Taken together, these considerations make it legitimate, in the majority's view, to elevate the position of the *Booth* and *Gathers* dissenters into the law of the land.

This truncation of the Court's duty to stand by its own precedents is astonishing. By limiting full protection of the doctrine of *stare decisis* to "cases involving property and contract rights," *ante,* at 828, the majority sends a clear signal that essentially *all* decisions implementing the personal liberties protected by the Bill of Rights and the Fourteenth Amendment are open to reexamination. Taking into account the majority's additional criterion for overruling—that a case either was decided or reaffirmed by a 5–4 margin "over spirited dissen[t],"—the continued vitality of literally scores of decisions must be understood to depend on nothing more than the proclivities of the individuals who *now* comprise a majority of this Court. See, *e.g.,* Metro Broadcasting v. FCC, 497 U.S. 547 (1990) (authority of Federal government to set aside broadcast licenses for minority applicants); Grady v. Corbin, 495 U.S. 508 (1990) (right under Double Jeopardy Clause not to be subjected twice to prosecution for same criminal conduct); Mills v. Maryland, *supra,* (Eighth Amendment right to jury instructions that do not preclude consideration of nonunanimous mitigating factors in capital sentencing); United States v. Paradise, 480 U.S. 149 (1987) (right to promotions as remedy for racial discrimination in government hiring); Ford v. Wainwright, 477 U.S. 399 (1986) (Eighth Amendment right not to be executed if insane); Thornburgh v. American College of Obstetricians and Gynecologists, 476 U.S. 747 (1986) (reaffirming right to abortion recognized in Roe v. Wade, 410 U.S. 113 (1973)); Aguilar v. Felton, 473 U.S. 402 (1985) (Establishment Clause bar on governmental financial assistance to parochial schools).[2]

---

2. Based on the majority's new criteria for overruling, these decisions, too, must be included on the "endangered precedents" list: Rutan v. Republican Party of Illinois, 497 U.S. 62 (1990) (First Amendment right not to be denied public employment on the basis of party affiliation); Peel v. Attorney Registration and Disciplinary Comm'n of Ill., 496 U.S. 91 (1990) (First Amendment right to advertise legal specialization); Zinermon v. Burch, 494 U.S. 113 (1990) (due process right to procedural safeguards aimed at assuring voluntariness of decision to commit oneself to mental hospital);

In my view, this impoverished conception of *stare decisis* cannot possibly be reconciled with the values that inform the proper judicial function. Contrary to what the majority suggests, *stare decisis* is important not merely because individuals rely on precedent to structure their commercial activity but because fidelity to precedent is part and parcel of a conception of "the judiciary as a source of impersonal and reasoned judgments." Moragne v. States Marine Lines, 398 U.S., at 403. Indeed, this function of *stare decisis* is in many respects even *more* critical in adjudication involving constitutional liberties than in adjudication involving commercial entitlements. Because enforcement of the Bill of Rights and the Fourteenth Amendment frequently requires this Court to rein in the forces of democratic politics, this Court can legitimately lay claim to compliance with its directives only if the public understands the Court to be implementing "principles ... founded in the law rather than in the proclivities of individuals." Vasquez v. Hillery, 474 U.S. 254, 265 (1986).[3] Thus, as Justice Stevens has explained, the "stron[g] presumption of validity" to which "recently decided cases" are entitled "is an essential thread in the mantle of protection that the law affords the individual.... It is the unpopular or beleaguered individual—not the man in power—who has the greatest stake in the integrity of the law." Florida Dept. of Health and Rehabilitative Services v. Florida Nursing Home Assn., 450 U.S., at 153–154 (concurring opinion).

Carried to its logical conclusion, the majority's debilitated conception of *stare decisis* would destroy the Court's very capacity to resolve authoritatively the abiding conflicts between those with power and those without. If this Court shows so little respect for its own precedents, it can hardly expect them to be treated more respectfully by the state

---

James v. Illinois, 493 U.S. 307 (1990) (Fourth Amendment right to exclusion of illegally obtained evidence introduced for impeachment of defense witness); Rankin v. McPherson, 483 U.S. 378 (1987) (First Amendment right of public employee to express views on matter of public importance); Rock v. Arkansas, 483 U.S. 44 (1987) (Fifth Amendment and Sixth Amendment right of criminal defendant to provide hypnotically refreshed testimony on his own behalf); Gray v. Mississippi, 481 U.S. 648 (1987) (rejecting applicability of harmless error analysis to Eighth Amendment right not to be sentenced to death by "death qualified" jury); Maine v. Moulton, 474 U.S. 159 (1985) (Sixth Amendment right to counsel violated by introduction of statements made to government informant-codefendant in course of preparing defense strategy); Garcia v. San Antonio Metropolitan Transit Authority, 469 U.S. 528 (1985) (rejecting theory that Tenth Amendment provides immunity to states from federal regulation); Pulliam v. Allen, 466 U.S. 522 (1984) (right to obtain injunctive relief from constitutional violations committed by judicial officials).

3. It does not answer this concern to suggest that Justices owe fidelity to the text of the Constitution rather than to the case law of this Court interpreting the Constitution. See, *e.g.,* South Carolina v. Gathers, 490 U.S., at 825. (Scalia, J., dissenting). The text of the Constitution is rarely so plain as to be self-executing; invariably, this Court must develop mediating principles and doctrines in order to bring the text of constitutional provisions to bear on particular facts. Thus, to rebut the charge of personal lawmaking, Justices who would discard the mediating principles embodied in precedent must do more than state that they are following the "text" of the Constitution; they must explain why they are entitled to substitute *their* mediating principles for those that are already settled in the law. And such an explanation will be sufficient to legitimize the departure from precedent only if it measures up to the extraordinary standard necessary to justify overruling one of this Court's precedents. See generally Note, 103 Harv.L.Rev. 1344, 1351–1354 (1990).

actors whom these decisions are supposed to bind. See Mitchell v. W.T. Grant Co., 416 U.S., at 634 (Stewart, J., dissenting). By signaling its willingness to give fresh consideration to any constitutional liberty recognized by a 5–4 vote "over spirited dissen[t]," the majority invites state actors to renew the very policies deemed unconstitutional in the hope that this Court may now reverse course, even if it has only recently reaffirmed the constitutional liberty in question.

Indeed, the majority's disposition of this case nicely illustrates the rewards of such a strategy of defiance. The Tennessee Supreme Court did nothing in this case to disguise its contempt for this Court's decisions in *Booth* and *Gathers*. Summing up its reaction to those cases, it concluded:

> "It is an affront to the civilized members of the human race to say that at sentencing in a capital case, a parade of witnesses may praise the background, character and good deeds of Defendant (as was done in this case), without limitation as to relevancy, but nothing may be said that bears upon the character of, or harm imposed, upon the victims." 791 S.W.2d 10, 19 (1990).

Offering no explanation for how this case could possibly be distinguished from *Booth* and *Gathers*—for obviously, there is none to offer—the court perfunctorily declared that the victim-impact evidence and the prosecutor's argument based on this evidence "did not violate either [of those decisions]." *Ibid.* It cannot be clearer that the court simply declined to be bound by this Court's precedents.

Far from condemning this blatant disregard for the rule of law, the majority applauds it. In the Tennessee Supreme Court's denigration of *Booth* and *Gathers* as " 'an affront to the civilized members of the human race,' " the majority finds only confirmation of "the unfairness of the rule pronounced by" the majorities in those cases. It is hard to imagine a more complete abdication of this Court's historic commitment to defending the supremacy of its own pronouncements on issues of constitutional liberty. See Cooper v. Aaron, 358 U.S. 1 (1958); see also Hutto v. Davis, 454 U.S. 370, 375 (1982) (per curiam) ("[U]nless we wish anarchy to prevail within the federal judicial system, a precedent of this Court must be followed by the lower federal courts no matter how misguided the judges of those courts may think it to be"). In light of the cost that such abdication exacts on the authoritativeness of *all* of this Court's pronouncements, it is also hard to imagine a more short-sighted strategy for effecting change in our constitutional order.

Today's decision charts an unmistakable course. If the majority's radical reconstruction of the rules for overturning this Court's decisions is to be taken at face value—and the majority offers us no reason why it should not—then the overruling of *Booth* and *Gathers* is but a preview of an even broader and more far-reaching assault upon this Court's precedents. Cast aside today are those condemned to face society's ultimate penalty. Tomorrow's victims may be minorities, women, or the indigent. Inevitably, this campaign to resurrect yesterday's "spirited dissents" will squander the authority and the legitimacy of this Court as a protector of the powerless.

I dissent.

NOTE

Monroe v. Pape, 365 U.S. 167 (1961), Justice Frankfurter, dissenting:

> "The rule of *stare decisis,* though one tending to consistency and uniformity of decision, is not inflexible." ... It is true, of course, that the reason for the rule is more compelling in cases involving inferior law, law capable of change by Congress, than in constitutional cases, where this Court—although even in such cases a wise consciousness of the limitations of individual vision has impelled it always to give great weight to prior decisions—nevertheless bears the ultimate obligation for the development of the law as institutions develop.... But the Court has not always declined to re-examine cases whose outcome Congress might have changed. See Mr. Justice Brandeis, dissenting, in Burnet v. Coronado Oil & Gas Co., 285 U.S. 393, 406–407, note 1, 52 S.Ct. 443, 447, 76 L.Ed. 815. Decisions involving statutory construction, even decisions which Congress has persuasively declined to overrule, have been overruled here. See Girouard v. United States, 328 U.S. 61, 66 S.Ct. 826, 90 L.Ed. 1084, overruling United States v. Schwimmer, 279 U.S. 644, 49 S.Ct. 448, 73 L.Ed. 889, United States v. Macintosh, 283 U.S. 605, 51 S.Ct. 570, 75 L.Ed. 1302, and United States v. Bland, 283 U.S. 636, 51 S.Ct. 569, 75 L.Ed. 1319; see also Commissioner of Internal Revenue v. Estate of Church, 335 U.S. 632, 69 S.Ct. 322, 337, 93 L.Ed. 288, overruling May v. Heiner, 281 U.S. 238, 50 S.Ct. 286, 74 L.Ed. 826.

Flagiello v. Pennsylvania Hospital, 417 Pa. 486, 208 A.2d 193 (1965), Justice Michael A. Musmanno, speaking for the court:

> *Stare Decisis* channels the law. It erects lighthouses and flys the signals of safety. The ships of jurisprudence must follow that well-defined channel which, over the years, has been proved to be secure and trustworthy. But it would not comport with wisdom to insist that, should shoals rise in a heretofore safe course and rocks emerge to encumber the passage, the ship should nonetheless pursue the original course, merely because it presented no hazard in the past. The principle of *stare decisis* does not demand that we follow precedents which shipwreck justice.
>
> *Stare decisis* is not an iron mold into which every utterance by a Court—regardless of circumstances, parties, economic ba-

rometer and sociological climate—must be poured, and, where, like wet concrete, it must acquire an unyielding rigidity which nothing later can change.

The history of law through the ages records numerous inequities pronounced by courts because the society of the day sanctioned them. Reason revolts, humanity shudders, and justice recoils before much of what was done in the past under the name of law. Yet, we are urged to retain a forbidding incongruity in the law simply because it is old. That kind of reasoning would have retained prosecution for witchcraft, imprisonment for debt and hanging for minor offenses which today are hardly regarded misdemeanors.

There is nothing in the records of the courts, the biographies of great jurists, or the writings of eminent legal authorities which offers the slightest encouragement to the notion that time petrifies into unchanging jurisprudence a palpable fallacy. As years can give no sturdiness to a decayed tree, so the passing decades can add no convincing flavor to the withered apple of sophistry clinging to the limb of demonstrated wrong. There are, of course, principles and precepts sanctified by age, and no one would think of changing them, but their inviolability derives not from longevity but from their universal appeal to the reason, the conscience and the experience of mankind....

. . .

The charitable immunity rule proves itself an instrument of injustice and nothing presented by the defendant or by *amicus curiae* shows it to be otherwise. In fact, the longer the argument for its preservation the more convincing is the proof that it long ago outlived its purpose if, indeed, it ever had a purpose consonant with sound law. "Ordinarily, when a court decides to modify or abandon a court-made rule of long standing, it starts out by saying that 'the reason for the rule no longer exists.' In this case, it is correct to say that the 'reason' originally given for the rule of immunity never did exist." (Pierce v. Yakima Valley Hospital Ass'n, supra, 260 P.2d 768.)

Section 4

OBITER DICTUM

Obiter dictum is where the precedential dragon often reposes. Gratuitous statements in an opinion which do not implicate the adjudicative facts of the case's specific holding do not have the bite of precedent. They bind neither coordinate nor inferior courts in the judicial hierarchy. They are classic *obiter dicta:* "statement[s] of law in the opinion which could not logically be a major premise of the selected facts of the decision." [1]

We do not accept the cynic's wail that *dictum* is merely a label pasted on a case that a subsequent court simply does not want to follow. We suggest two ways to identify *dicta:*

- First, *dictum* is the express or implied description of a factual scenario that does not appear in the case record.

- Second, *dictum* is any statement of facts that does not appear in the minor premise of the court's syllogistic reasoning.

For example, using the familiar categorical syllogism in deductive logic as used in the law:

Major Premise: All men are mortal.

Minor Premise: Socrates is a man.

Conclusion: Therefore, Socrates is mortal.

This syllogism is legitimate only to the extent that Socrates appears in the record and legitimately belongs both in the minor premise and also the conclusion. We cannot properly say that a cyborg is also a man, is qualified to be in the minor premise, and is therefore, mortal. The fact of a cyborg's mortality is simply not a matter of record. *Dictum* is the antithesis of precedent.

ROBERT E. KEETON, PROSPECTIVE JUDICIAL LAWMAKING *

It is sometimes argued that broad statements of reasons for decision ... are obiter dicta rather than holdings. Even if one insists upon such a definition of the distinction between holding and dictum, however, the prospectively creative character of these broad pronouncements remains.

They give notice of the way in which the court is likely to resolve the issue with which they deal when it is squarely presented, and they tend to be self-fulfilling prophecies, even if not binding as precedents, because they have some weight as considered expressions. Moreover, whether or not so intended, obiter dicta, insofar as they express views not fully developed in existing precedents, are primarily prospective in influence. Indeed, it is more likely than not in routine situations that they will be exclusively prospective in application. It is true that such a dictum might have retroactive application to previous transactions brought into issue thereafter, but it is more likely that even the first judicial application of the dictum will concern a transaction occurring after the dictum

1. R. Cross, Precedent in English Law 80 (2d ed. 1968) (citing E. Patterson, Jurisprudence: Man and Ideas of the Law 313 (1953)).

* Excerpted by permission of the author and publishers from pp. 25–27, 29–31, 33–

34, 36–38 of Venturing To Do Justice: Reforming Private Law by Robert E. Keeton, Cambridge, Mass.: Harvard University Press, Copyright © 1969 by the President and Fellows of Harvard College.

was published. The common practice of including dicta of this type in opinions suggests a consensus that this is permissible judicial behavior— a consensus that undermines the notion that the prospective effect of judicial opinions is supposed to be wholly incidental to retroactive decisional application.

... As already observed, dicta have long served a function of notice about the way the court is likely to respond to an issue when it is squarely presented. Ordinarily the function of giving notice has not been a declared objective, but occasionally an explicit statement of this intention appears in a judicial opinion. Such a statement increases the force of the prospective pronouncement by declaring it to be purposive and legitimate rather than merely a coincidental by-product of the court's legitimate work.

Section 5

THE UNITED KINGDOM AND CONTINENTAL LEGAL SYSTEMS

HAROLD F. BIRNBAUM, STARE DECISIS VS. JUDICIAL ACTIVISM: NOTHING SUCCEEDS LIKE SUCCESS *

Article I—Separation of Powers

Section 1. The powers of government are divided among the legislature, executive and judiciary.

Section 2. The legislature shall enact statutes of general application, subject to any overriding provisions of this Constitution or of any treaty made in conformity with it.

Section 3. The executive shall enforce the laws.

Section 4. The judiciary shall apply the laws, by decisions in litigated controversies. Decisions shall involve any necessary interpretation of an applicable statute, constitutional provision or treaty. On matters not covered by the express terms of a statute, constitutional provision or treaty, the judiciary shall state what the applicable law is. Every such interpretation or statement shall continue effective until changed by subsequent legislation, constitutional amendment or treaty.

American lawyers, brought up on written constitutions, would recognize, without substantial dissent, that such an article on separation of powers as that above speaks in constitutional language, within the dictionary definition of a "constitution": "The fundamental organic law or principles of a nation, state, society or other organized body of men...."—Webster's New International Dictionary (Second Edition).

---

* 54 A.B.A.J. 482, 482–83 (1968). Reprinted by permission.

All of the articles on separation of powers set forth above is based on the United States Constitution except the last sentence of Section 4. That sentence is derived from the British rule which was expounded by the Earl of Halsbury, Lord Chancellor, in London Street Tramways Company v. London County Council, [1898] A.C. 375, 379, 381.

> ... that a decision of this House upon a question of law is conclusive, and that nothing but an Act of Parliament can set right that which is alleged to be wrong in a judgment of this House.

The opinion, concurred in by the other judges, declared that this rule had been established for "some centuries".... [At least] from 1898 until 1966 the rule was accepted as the undoubted law of England.

Ultimately, on July 26, 1966, the present Lord Chancellor and all nine Lords of Appeal in Ordinary assembled in the chamber of the House of Lords, together with the Bishop of Chester as Lord Spiritual. Before judgments in any pending cases were given, the Lord Chancellor made the following statement on behalf of himself and the Lords of Appeal in Ordinary:

Practice Statement

(Judicial Precedent)

> Their Lordships regard the use of precedent as an indispensable foundation upon which to decide what is the law and its application to individual cases. It provides at least some degree of certainty upon which individuals can rely in the conduct of their affairs as well as a basis for orderly development of legal rules.

> Their Lordships nevertheless recognize that too rigid adherence to precedent may lead to injustice in a particular case and also unduly restrict the proper development of the law. They propose therefore to modify their present practice and, while treating former decisions of this House as normally binding, to depart from a previous decision when it appears right to do so.

> In this connection they will bear in mind the danger of disturbing retrospectively the basis on which contracts, settlements of property and fiscal arrangements have been entered into and also the especial need for certainty as to the criminal law.

> This announcement is not intended to affect the use of precedent elsewhere than in this House.

Thus, the statement in *London Street Tramways,* "Nothing but an Act of Parliament can set right that which is alleged to be wrong in a judgment of this House" has been changed, not by an act of Parliament, but by an announcement that the judges of the highest court of England "propose to modify their present practice and ... to depart from a previous decision when it appears right to do so".

The first, or at least the second, thought which comes to mind is, "Can such a change be effected in this manner?" An American lawyer is not presumptuous in asking this question, for it was immediately raised on behalf of both branches of the legal profession in Britain. In the London *Times* of July 27, 1966, page 10, directly following the text of the Practice Statement, there appears the comment of the vice chairman of the General Council of the Bar, starting as follows:

> It is a little difficult to see how the House of Lords can now depart from the law of the land as so stated. It might be thought that only an Act of Parliament can give them the power to reverse their own decisions.

This was followed by a comment on behalf of the Law Society, of the concluding paragraph reads: "The only doubt in our mind is this alteration can be effected without legislation."

BEAMISH v. BEAMISH

House of Lords, 1861.
9 H.L.C. 274.

[In The Queen v. Millis, 10 Cl. & F. 534 (1844), without much previous authority, the House of Lords adopted the rule that the presence of an Episcopalian ordained priest is essential at common law to a valid marriage in England and Ireland and held as void an Irish Presbyterian marriage. In this case the priest was present, not as a celebrant, but as a party to the ceremony. As stated by Lord Campbell: "Assuming the law to be settled, that to constitute a valid marriage by the common law of *England,* there must have been present a clergyman in orders conferred by a bishop, the question now to be determined is, 'Whether, the bridegroom being such a clergyman, and there being no other clergyman present, a valid marriage was contracted?' " Although Lord Campbell disapproved of the *Millis* decision, he said:]

My Lords, the decision in The Queen v. Millis, that unless a priest, especially ordained, was present at the marriage ceremony, the marriage was null and void for all civil purposes, and the children of the marriage were illegitimate, seemed to me so unsatisfactory, that I deemed it my duty to resort to the extraordinary proceeding of entering a protest against it on your Lordships' Journals.

. . .

If it were competent to me, I would now ask your Lordships to reconsider the doctrine laid down in The Queen v. Millis [10 Cl. and F. 534], particularly as the judges who were then consulted, complained of being hurried into giving an opinion without due time for deliberation, and the Members of this House who heard the argument, and voted on the question, "That the judgment appealed against be reversed," were equally divided; so that the judgment which decided the marriage by a Presbyterian clergyman of a man and woman, who both belonged to his religious persuasion, who both believed that they were contracting lawful matrimony, who had lived together as husband and wife, and who had procreated children while so living together as husband and wife, to be a nullity, was only pronounced on the technical rule of your Lordships' House, that where, upon a division, the numbers are equal, *semper praesumitur pro negante.*

But it is my duty to say that your Lordships are bound by this decision as much as if it had been pronounced *nemine dissentiente,* and that the rule of law which your Lordships lay down as the ground of your judgment, sitting judicially, as the last and supreme Court of Appeal for this empire, must be taken for law till altered by an Act of Parliament, agreed to by the Commons and the Crown, as well as by your Lordships. The law laid down as your *ratio decidendi,* being clearly binding on all inferior tribunals, and on all the rest of the Queen's subjects, if it were not considered as equally binding upon your Lordships, this House would be arrogating to itself the right of altering the law, and legislating by its own separate authority.

[The question for decision was answered in the negative.]

LONDON STREET TRAMWAYS COMPANY v. LONDON COUNTY COUNCIL

House of Lords, 1898.
[1898] A.C. 375.

[At issue was the amount of compensation to be paid to the appellant company on being taken over by the London County Council. In previous cases the House of Lords had previously decided on the method of calculating damages. The question for decision was whether the House of Lords was bound by its earlier decisions. This case explains that the House of Lords could not depart from precedent.]

Of course I do not deny that cases of individual hardship may arise, and there may be a current of opinion in the profession that such and such a judgment was erroneous; but what is that occasional interference with what is perhaps abstract justice, as compared with the inconvenience—the disastrous inconvenience—of having each question subject to being re-argued and the dealings of mankind rendered doubtful by reason of different decisions, so that in truth and in fact there would be no real final court of appeal. My lords, "interest reipublicae" that there should be "finis litium" sometime and there could be no "finis litium" if it were possible to suggest in each case that it might be reargued because it is "not an ordinary case" whatever that may mean.

... that a decision of this House once given upon a point of law is conclusive upon this House afterwards, and that it is impossible to raise that question again as if it was res integra and could be reargued, and so the House be asked to reverse its own decision.

... that a decision of this House upon a question of law is conclusive, and that nothing but an Act of Parliament can set right that which is alleged to be wrong in a judgment of this House.

ARTHUR T. VON MEHREN, THE JUDICIAL PROCESS: A COMPARATIVE ANALYSIS *

In a system of case law such as is found in the United States, the degree of particularity with which interests are authoritatively accommodated does not vary as much [as in France or Germany]. A mature case law system contains a vast body of precepts authoritatively accommodating fairly specific patterns of interests. In such a system, a court is not likely to start its reasoning with a proposition as abstract and general as are some of the provisions of the French and German Civil Codes. Thus, an American judge puzzled by some problem of tort law does not usually begin his reasoning with a broad principle; he is more likely to start with a rather specific proposition of the type exemplified by most of the 951 sections of the Restatement of Torts. In dealing with a problem of delictual obligation (tort law), the French judge calls upon five articles of his Civil Code that purport to cover the entire field. A German judge, faced with the same problem, looks (unless the matter is covered by special legislation) to the thirty pertinent articles of the German Civil Code. So far as this element in the total situation is concerned, French and German judges are more likely than their American colleagues to engage in judicial law making.

Moreover, a case law system tends, by its very nature and through the operation of the principle of *stare decisis,* to make its precepts continually more detailed and more precise. These characteristics progressively reduce the likelihood of judicial law making, a trend that is reversed only when a court announces a new principle that can form a fresh and less specific starting point for the judicial treatment of future cases. Particularity is often still more marked when an American court finds its authoritative precept in a statutory provision because of the more rigid application in this area of the principle of *stare decisis.*

In a code system, on the other hand, the body of legal precepts remains, at least in theory, uninfluenced by the body of decided cases. A legal precept in a code system thus tends to retain longer its initial level of generality or particularity. This tendency should not be exaggerated. It is, of course, true that a pattern of judicial interpretation emerges in connection with code provisions. A court is always, however, on good theoretical ground when it goes back to the pristine provision. The

* The Civil Law System 845–50 (1957).   printed by permission. Boston: Little, Brown and Company. Re-

provisions in their unglossed form thus remain available as starting points for legal reasoning. Moreover, when legislative revisions are relatively infrequent, as tends to be the case, the authoritative accommodations of interests contained in the more detailed code provisions acquire in practice a greater degree of generality as changes in social and economic conditions or social values emphasize the need to consider such provisions as drafted not only for the needs of the moment but also for the future.

. . .

... In general, common-law courts have perhaps greater possibilities than French or German courts for rationalizing judicial law making in terms of the existing body of legal precepts. This condition results from the rich fabric of common-law decisions, which can be analyzed on a variety of levels and in several ways, thus potentially supporting a wider range of reasonable implications than code provisions ordinarily permit. On the other hand, "general clauses," such as the requirement of good faith found in the German Civil Code, have most spacious implications once the court is prepared to rationalize its results in terms of a fairly broad, and hence overtly policy-oriented, premise.

. . .

... In American law the body of legal precepts is continually expanded and, in a sense, modernized. New decisions introduce new bases for the rationalization of future results. This change also occurs to a degree in French and German law. But, as already pointed out, the authoritative starting points for reasoning in these systems are largely contained in legislatively given materials that tend to retain their pristine state until legislatively revised.

. . .

If judicial reconsideration and reformulation of policy is to be effective, innovations must in practice be accepted by the whole judiciary. In the United States, unity of judicial action within a given jurisdiction is ensured by the rule that a court has no right to deviate from precedents established by its hierarchical superior. Quite the contrary rule is found in France, and to a lesser degree in Germany. The French rule is still today that a previous decision, even by a hierarchically superior court, is never binding. Historically, the French rule is explained, at least in part, by a desire to prevent any systematic, judicial formulation and development of policy.

In practice, a lower French or German court is today under strong pressure to conform to the views of its hierarchical superior. A court that does not accept the lines laid down by the decisions of courts superior to it faces probable reversal. This is not only expensive for the parties but also unpleasant for the lower court, especially when, as in France and Germany, advancement within the judicial hierarchy depends to a certain extent upon an evaluation of a judge's work. Today in these three systems no marked difference exists with respect to this potential limitation on judicial law making.

RUGGERO J. ALDISERT, RAMBLING THROUGH CONTINENTAL LEGAL SYSTEMS *

In France and the civil law countries, only the code and statutes are the source of law. Each adjudication is but an application of some interpretation of the code to a particular set of facts. Continental appellate decisions, although respected, cited, and generally followed, do not have the force of law. There are exceptions, however. Decisions of the constitutional courts of the German Federal Republic, Italy, and Yugoslavia and its republics have some precedential value. Also, the Swiss Federal Court binds lower courts when it declares a law unconstitutional, as do some decisions by the full bench of the highest court in Portugal.[3] The common law tradition is, of course, otherwise. Although in 1842 Justice Story would say that decisions of courts "are, at most, only evidence of what the laws are, and are not of themselves laws," [4] we have gone a long way since then and it can no longer be doubted that in the United States laws are created by "judicial decisions as well as by congressional legislation." [5]

The French emphasis on the exclusivity of parliamentary law making is rooted in its revolutionary tradition. In prerevolutionary France, the judges were the objects of hatred because they were seen as tools of the crown. The highest royal courts, called *parlements,* combined both legislative and judicial functions. Post-revolutionary dogma dictated that there be strict division of duties to dilute the power of judges and thereby prevent a return of autocratic power to the royal courts. It was proclaimed that only the legislature could make law and that questions about the justice, utility, or appropriateness of statutes were questions removed from the judiciary and vested solely in the legislative organ. Although Germany, Italy, Austria, and the other Continental countries did not have this historical experience, they accepted both the idea of the French code and the rationalist dogma of how it was to be properly interpreted, and they similarly deprived their judiciaries of lawmaking powers. The French pattern still serves as the model on the Continent.

The review of judgments in the first instance is by way of appeal (*appel*) to the *cours d'appel,* of which there are thirty in France. Most courts of appeals have several multi-judge chambers; Paris, the largest, has twenty-five. For purposes of a decision, a chambers consists of three judges. The *appel* may bring up questions of fact as well as law.

---

* Adapted from 43 Univ.Pitt.L.Rev. 935 (1982).

3. *See generally* R. David & J. Brierly, Major Legal Systems in the World Today 132 (2d ed. 1978).

4. Swift v. Tyson, 41 U.S. (16 Pet.) 166, 170 (1842).

5. Illinois v. City of Milwaukee, 406 U.S. 91, 100 (1972) (quoting Ivy Broadcasting Co. v. American Tel. & Tel. Co., 391 F.2d 486, 492 (2d Cir.1968)).

At the apex of the ordinary court hierarchy is the *cour de cassation,* the prototype of Continental high courts. It sits in Paris and today is staffed with 106 judges—of whom 22 are *conseillers référendaires,* simi- lar to the supreme court commissioners in many of our states, possessing judicial powers but no right to vote on cases. The court sits in one criminal chambers and six civil chambers including one designated as *chambre civil, section commerciale et financière.* For a chambers to sit, at least seven judges must be present.

The French appellate mold, which is followed in most Continental jurisdictions, does not give to the highest court the power to pronounce judgment. It has the power solely to reject the appeal (a *pourvoi en cassation*) or to quash the decision of the court of appeal and refer the case back to it (*renvoi*). (The court takes its name from the act of quashing, *casser,* to break or crack.) The French high court, as its progeny in other Continental jurisdictions, does not have the power to affirm or reverse the judgments of the lower courts. There is a histori- cal reason for this in France: a deliberate intention that the high courts will never be vested with the powers possessed by the royal pre- revolutionary courts, the *parlements.*

When the *pourvoi en cassation* is unsuccessful, the proceedings are terminated. If successful, the decision below is quashed but the proceed- ings do not end. The case is remanded to the *cour d'appel* (usually drawn from judges from other chambers), and this five judge court reconsiders the matter. But unlike the common law tradition, it is not bound by the highest court's determination of the law. It is free to accept or reject it. Indeed, it is also free to adduce new facts. If a second appeal is brought to the *cour de cassation,* an ordinary chamber does not hear the case upon the second *pourvoi.* This time it is heard by an *assemblée plenière* of twenty-five judges consisting of the first presi- dent, the president and senior judge of each of the six chambers, and two other judges from each chambers. If the appeal is allowed and the decision quashed, the proceedings are again remanded to the *cour d'appel,* but on this second remand the intermediate court is bound by the plenary assembly's decision on points of law.

An immediate comparison springs to mind. The United States Supreme Court consists of only nine judges, most state supreme courts have only seven judges. Yet these American courts, with relatively few judges, determine the course of the law, binding the lower courts. With less power than our highest courts, the *cour de cassation* requires twenty-five judges to make its decision binding, and this only after a chambers of at least seven judges has heard the appeal at a prior time.

NOTE

"[An important difference between the Civil Law and Common Law Worlds] is the absence in most civil law countries of anything analogous to a formal doctrine of *stare decisis.* To be sure, this absence is far from being, as it was described in 1934 by a distinguished comparative law scholar, the 'fundamental' difference between the civil law and the common law methods to make and develop the law. On the one hand, everyone knows that the doctrine can be, and usually is, applied in a very flexible manner, especially in the United States, and that modern developments, including the famous 1966 statement by the British Lord Chancellor speaking for a unanimous House of Lords, have lessened its rigidity even in Great Britain. On the other hand, *de facto* an *auctoritas rerum similiter judicatarum*—the authority of precedents—has always been recognized even in the civil law tradition.

"The difference, in fact, is essentially one of degree, and has to be seen in connection with what was said before: the more diluted structure of the courts, the flood of irrelevant decisions submerging the few significant ones, the more anonymous and routine-oriented judicial personnel—all these characteristics conspire to make that *auctoritas* less pronounced, less visible, and less dramatic than the authority of precedents in the areas where the common law tradition prevails."

Mauro Cappelletti, The Judicial Process in Comparative Perspective 52–53 (1989).

SOL WACHTLER, THE FRENCH TRADITION *

The fathers of the French revolution, such as Le Chaplier and Robespierre, were convinced that written law alone must dominate and that "the judge-made law was the most detestable of institutions, and should be destroyed." [8] Indeed, Robespierre went so far as ordering that the word "jurisprudence" ("case-law" in English)—the heart of the common law system—be banished from the French language. Consistent with this view, legislative codes eventually were enacted which promulgated the substantive law largely developed by the judiciary in this country.

The zeal with which this doctrine was at first articulated was no doubt the product of the revolutionary desire to cast out the traditional law and remake the law consistent with the will of all the people.[10] Nevertheless, today the structure of the French courts, and their source of law, at its root retains this aversion to judge-made doctrine. Thus, in France every judicial decision must be based upon the written law.[11]

* S. Wachtler, *Judicial Lawmaking,* 65 N.Y.U.L.Rev. 1, 4–5 (1990).

8. 1 M. Planiol, Traité Elémentaire de Droit Civil, §§ 153 n. 8, 155 (1939) [Treatise on Civil Law] (Louisiana State Law Institute trans. 1959) (citing Archives Parlementaires 1st series, at 516–17).

10. Stated Voltaire, "Voulez-vous avoir des bonnes lois? Brûlez les vôtres, et faites-en des nouvelles." [Do you want good laws? Burn yours and make new ones!] See Friedrich, The Ideological and

Philosophical Background, in The Code of Napoleon and the Common–Law World 1, 1 (B. Schwartz ed. 1956) (quoting Voltaire); see also F. Ridley & J. Blondel, Public Administration in France 127 (1965) ("laws were no longer to evolve through the centuries; they were to be *made* in accordance with the will of the people.").

11. See Sereni, The Code and the Case Law, in The Code of Napoleon and the Common–Law World 55, 62 (B. Schwartz ed. 1956).

General pronouncements of legal rules, or "arrêts de règlement" [12]—a central characteristic of the common law court—are expressly prohibited by the French Civil Code.[13]   Likewise, French judges "are forbidden, when giving judgment in the cases which are brought before them, . . . to decide a case by holding it was governed by a previous decision." [14]

Consequently, as Planiol put it, in France

[t]he regulation-making power is today reserved exclusively to representatives of the executive power.   The judicial authorities do not enjoy it.   The effect of their decisions is purely relative. Their rulings, in other words, bind only the parties before the court.   Courts have thus lost the right which they had under the old regime of rendering obligatory decisions having a binding effect upon the future and applying to all persons within their jurisdiction.[15]

Also in dramatic contrast to what has become the American tradition, in neither France nor the common law system of England are the courts the final expositors of constitutional-type doctrine, either in the area of individual rights or concerning relationships between governmental branches.[16]   Consequently, our closest political relatives do not employ the courts as the ultimate protectors of fundamental rights, nor, in these countries, are the courts the final arbiters of governmental power.

Section 6

RETROACTIVITY OR PROSPECTIVITY

All learning associated with the nature of the judicial process coalesces in considering the retroactivity vel non of the rule of a case. Whether a court will accord retroactivity may depend on whether the court thinks it merely discovers or actually creates the law.   The court making the retroactivity decision must also consider the development of modern American adjudication.

If a court recognizes that the rule of law must change to reflect new social values, it will have to consider views beyond the orthodox legal disciplines.   Moreover, this question always will require a consideration of the desiderata of equality, stability and certainty, generally considered to be the advantages of stare decisis.   And more often than not, whether a court departs from stare decisis may depend on whether the court feels

---

12. M. Planiol, supra note 8, at 120–21.

13. Code Civil [C.Civ.] art. 5 (Fr.).

14. The French Civil Code art. 5(c)2 (E. Wright trans. 1908).   It has been noted, however, that some informal yet important use of precedent does exist in France. See R. Cross, Precedent in English Law 8–11 (1961); Tunc, The Grand Outlines of the Code. The Code of Napoleon and the Common Law World 19, 26–27 (B. Schwartz ed. 1956).

15. M. Planiol, supra note 8, at 120.

16. See id. at 121; Cappelletti, Fundamental Guarantees of the Parties in Civil Litigation: Comparative Constitutional, International, and Social Trends, 25 Stan. L.Rev. 651, 655, 657 (1973).

the departure should be effective from some date in the future, from the date of the decision forward, or in a manner truly Blackstonian: fully retroactive, not on the theory that what was changed was "bad law," rather that "it was not law."

There are degrees of retroactive and prospective applications of newly announced legal precepts. As the following materials make clear, the gradations of retroactive effect may include:

- Full retroactivity.
- Retroactive to some event or trial.
- Retroactive to criminal cases on direct appeal, but not to cases on collateral review.
- Applicable to the case announcing the new rule and prospectively.
- Prospective-prospective. Not applicable to the case announcing the new rule, but only to some specific future time and thereafter.

The effect of a given precept depends on its source—whether statute or case law, and whether civil or criminal.

Congressional enactments and administrative rules have no retroactive effect unless their language requires this result. There is, however, one caveat: a presumption against retroactivity attaches to substantive statutory enactments; and a presumption in favor of retroactivity attaches to procedural statutory enactments.

In civil cases, the Supreme Court declared that when the Court "applies a rule of federal law to the parties before it, that rule is the controlling interpretation of federal law and must be given full retroactive effect in all cases still open on direct review and as to all events, regardless of whether such events predate or postdate our announcement of the rule." [1]

In constitutional law matters relating to criminal procedures, criminal cases are retroactive to cases on direct appeal which have not reached final judgment, but are prospective only as to cases on collateral review.

The evolution of the law of retroactivity of statutes, and civil and criminal cases has been long and torturous. Their development is summarized in the following timelines:

FEDERAL RETROACTIVITY: DECISIONAL LAW

1932   Gt. Northern Ry. v. Sunburst Co., 287 U.S. 358, 364. "A state in defining the limits of adherence to precedent may make a choice for itself between the principle of forward operation [prospectivity] and that of relation backward [retroactivity].

---

1. Harper v. Va. Dept. of Taxation, 113 S.Ct. 2510 (1993).

1965   Linkletter v. Walker, 381 U.S. 618, 636. Rule of selective prospectivity announced with respect to pending criminal cases. Court may deny retroactive effect to a newly announced rule of criminal law after taking into consideration the purpose of the new rule, the reliance placed upon the previous view of the law and "the effect on the administration of justice of a retroactive application of the new rule."

1971   Mackey v. U.S., 401 U.S. 667, 675. Justice Harlan, concurring in judgments in part and dissenting in part, challenges *Linkletter* holding and argues that new rules of criminal law should always be applied retroactively to cases on direct review, but generally not to criminal cases on collateral review, unless they place "certain kinds of primary, private conduct beyond the power of the criminal law-making authority to proscribe," or unless they require the observance of "those procedures that ... are 'implicit in the concept of ordered liberty.'" 401 U.S. at 693, 693. *See also* Desist v. U.S., 394 U.S. 244, 256 (1969) (Harlan, J., dissenting).

1971   Chevron Oil Co. v. Huson, 404 U.S. 97, 106–107. Rule of selective prospectivity announced in civil context. Three factors to be considered. The decision to be applied non-retroactively must establish a new principle of law. Look to history of rule in question, its purpose and effort, and decide if retrospective operation will further or retard its operation. Avoid "injustice or hardship" of a holding of non-retroactivity.

1973   Robinson v. Neil, 409 U.S. 505, 507. Foreshadowing things to come, the Court writes: "[B]oth the common law and our own decisions" have "recognized a general rule of retrospective effect for the Constitutional decisions of this Court."

1987   Griffith v. Kentucky, 479 U.S. 314, 322. Court overrules Linkletter in criminal context and adopts Justice Harlan's approach in Mackey with respect to direct review. Limits on retroactivity now eliminated in criminal cases pending on direct review. All "newly declared ... rule[s]" must be applied retroactively to all "criminal cases pending on direct review." [Dicta at n. 8: civil case retroactivity "continues to be governed by the standard announced in *Chevron Oil Co.*"]

1989   Teague v. Lane, 489 U.S. 288, 310. Court adopts remainder of Justice Harlan's approach in *Mackey* with respect to collateral review. Unless cases on *collateral review* fall within an exception to the general rule, "new constitutional rules of criminal procedure will not be applicable to those cases which have become final before the new rules are announced." The law appeared settled in the context of pending criminal cases but unsettled in the context of pending civil cases.

1990   American Trucking Assn. v. Smith, 496 U.S. 167. Three opinions written in this civil case, none garnering a majority. Although

Court remains divided over meaning of dicta in *Griffith,* case shows movement away from *Chevron Oil* test in civil context. Although four-justice plurality applies *Chevron,* Justice Stevens (dissenting, with three other justices) writes: "The Court has no more constitutional authority in civil cases than in criminal cases to disregard current law or to treat similarly situated litigants differently."

1991   Jim Beam v. Georgia, 501 U.S. 529. Five opinions written, no single one carrying more than three votes. However, majority of justices agree that a rule of federal law, once announced and applied to the parties to the controversy, must be given full retroactive effect by all courts adjudicating federal law. Justice Souter's view of retroactivity is interpreted to supersede "any claim based on a *Chevron Oil* analysis."

1991   Lampf v. Gilbertson, 501 U.S. 350. Announced on same day as *Jim Beam,* Court holds statute of limitations for private right of action under Rule 10b–5 is limitations period found in § 9(e) of the 1934 Act (one year from discovery of fraud or three years from commission of fraud). Lower courts begin applying *Jim Beam* to *Lampf* and dismiss pending 10b–5 cases. In response, Congress enacts § 27A of 1934 Act overruling retroactive application of *Lampf* decision. To this date, most courts of appeals held that § 27A is a valid exercise of Congressional power.

1993   Harper v. Va. Dept. of Taxation, 113 S.Ct. 2510. Majority embraces *Griffith* rationale in civil context, the final move away from *Chevron Oil:* When Court "applies a rule of federal law to the parties before it, that rule is the controlling interpretation of federal law and must be given full retroactive effect in all cases still open on direct review and as to all events, regardless of whether such events predate or postdate our announcement of the rule." Four justices find "no reason to abandon" the longstanding precedent of *Chevron Oil* retroactivity analysis.

1995   Plaut v. Spendthrift Farm, Inc., 115 S.Ct. 1447. Court holds that § 27A violated constitutional separation of powers principles by instructing federal courts to reopen final judgments.

FEDERAL RETROACTIVITY: STATUTORY LAW

1974   Bradley v. Richmond School Bd., 416 U.S. 696, 711. "[A] court is to apply the law in effect at the time it renders its decision, unless doing so would result in manifest injustice or there is statutory or legislative history to the contrary. Case creates a presumption in favor of retroactive application of statutes.

1988   Bowen v. Georgetown Univ. Hosp., 488 U.S. 204. Decision constitutes a sea change in the law. Legislation will not have a retroactive effect unless the language specifically provides for it, as retroactivity is not favored in the law. Case creates a presumption against retroactive application of statutes.

1994   Landgraf v. USI Film Prods., 114 S.Ct. 1483, 1500. "Congressional enactments and administrative rules will not be construed to have retroactive effect unless their language requires this result.... [P]rospectivity remains the appropriate default rule" absent "clear intent" by Congress. "The presumption against statutory retroactivity is founded upon sound considerations of general policy and practice, and accords with long held and widely shared expectations about the usual operation of legislators."

GRIFFITH v. KENTUCKY

Supreme Court of the United States, 1987.
479 U.S. 314, 107 S.Ct. 708, 93 L.Ed.2d 649.

Justice Blackmun delivered the opinion of the Court.

These cases, one state and one federal, concern the retrospective application of Batson v. Kentucky, 476 U.S. 79 (1986).

In *Batson*, 476 U.S., at 96–98, this Court ruled that a defendant in a state criminal trial could establish a prima facie case of racial discrimination violative of the Fourteenth Amendment, based on the prosecution's use of peremptory challenges to strike members of the defendant's race from the jury venire, and that, once the defendant had made the prima facie showing, the burden shifted to the prosecution to come forward with a neutral explanation for those challenges. In the present cases we consider whether that ruling is applicable to litigation pending on direct state or federal review or not yet final when *Batson* was decided. We answer that question in the affirmative.

Twenty-one years ago, this Court adopted a three-pronged analysis for claims of retroactivity of new constitutional rules of criminal procedure. See Linkletter v. Walker, 381 U.S. 618 (1965). In *Linkletter,* the Court held that Mapp v. Ohio, 367 U.S. 643 (1961), which extended the Fourth Amendment exclusionary rule to the States, would not be applied retroactively to a state conviction that had become final before *Mapp* was decided. The Court explained that "the Constitution neither prohibits nor requires retrospective effect" of a new constitutional rule, and that a determination of retroactivity must depend on "weigh[ing] the merits and demerits in each case." 381 U.S., at 629. The Court's decision not to apply *Mapp* retroactively was based on "the purpose of the *Mapp* rule; the reliance placed upon the [previous] doctrine; and the effect on the administration of justice of a retrospective application of *Mapp.*" 381 U.S., at 636. See also Stovall v. Denno, 388 U.S. 293, 297 (1967) (retroactivity depends on "(a) the purpose to be served by the new standards, (b) the extent of the reliance by law enforcement authorities on the old standards, and (c) the effect on the administration of justice of a retroactive application of the new standards'').

Shortly after the decision in *Linkletter,* the Court held that the three-pronged analysis applied both to convictions that were final and to convictions pending on direct review. See Johnson v. New Jersey, 384 U.S. 719, 732 (1966); Stovall v. Denno, 388 U.S., at 300. In the latter case, the Court concluded that, for purposes of applying the three factors of the analysis, ''no distinction is justified between convictions now final . . . and convictions at various stages of trial and direct review.'' *Ibid.* Thus, a number of new rules of criminal procedure were held not to apply retroactively either to final cases or to cases pending on direct review. See, *e.g.,* Stovall v. Denno, *supra;* DeStefano v. Woods, 392 U.S. 631, 635, n. 2 (1968); Desist v. United States, 394 U.S. 244, 253–254 (1969); Daniel v. Louisiana, 420 U.S. 31 (1975) (*per curiam*).

In United States v. Johnson, 457 U.S. 537 (1982), however, the Court shifted course. In that case, we reviewed at some length the history of the Court's decisions in the area of retroactivity and concluded, in the words of Justice Harlan: '' ' ''[R]etroactivity'' must be rethought.' '' *Id.,* at 548 (quoting Desist v. United States, 394 U.S., at 258 (dissenting opinion)). Specifically, we concluded that the retroactivity analysis for convictions that have become final must be different from the analysis for convictions that are not final at the time the new decision is issued. We observed that, in a number of separate opinions since *Linkletter,* various Members of the Court ''have asserted that, at a minimum, all defendants whose cases were still pending on direct appeal at the time of the law-changing decision should be entitled to invoke the new rule.'' 457 U.S., at 545, and n. 9 (collecting opinions). The rationale for distinguishing between cases that have become final and those that have not, and for applying new rules retroactively to cases in the latter category, was explained at length by Justice Harlan in Desist v. United States, 394 U.S., at 256 (dissenting opinion), and in Mackey v. United States, 401 U.S. 667, 675 (1971) (opinion concurring in judgment). In United States v. Johnson, we embraced to a significant extent the comprehensive analysis presented by Justice Harlan in those opinions.

In Justice Harlan's view, and now in ours, failure to apply a newly declared constitutional rule to criminal cases pending on direct review violates basic norms of constitutional adjudication. First, it is a settled principle that this Court adjudicates only ''cases'' and ''controversies.'' See U.S. Const., Art. III, § 2. Unlike a legislature, we do not promulgate new rules of constitutional criminal procedure on a broad basis. Rather, the nature of judicial review requires that we adjudicate specific cases, and each case usually becomes the vehicle for announcement of a new rule. But after we have decided a new rule in the case selected, the integrity of judicial review requires that we apply that rule to all similar cases pending on direct review. Justice Harlan observed:

"If we do not resolve all cases before us on direct review in light of our best understanding of governing constitutional principles, it is difficult to see why we should so adjudicate any case at all. . . . In truth, the Court's assertion of power to disregard current law in adjudicating cases before us that have not already run the full course of appellate review, is quite simply an assertion that our constitutional function is not one of adjudication but in effect of legislation." Mackey v. United States, 401 U.S., at 679 (opinion concurring in judgment).

As a practical matter, of course, we cannot hear each case pending on direct review and apply the new rule. But we fulfill our judicial responsibility by instructing the lower courts to apply the new rule retroactively to cases not yet final. Thus, it is the nature of judicial review that precludes us from "[s]imply fishing one case from the stream of appellate review, using it as a vehicle for pronouncing new constitutional standards, and then permitting a stream of similar cases subsequently to flow by unaffected by that new rule." *Ibid.* See United States v. Johnson, 457 U.S., at 546–547, 555.

Second, selective application of new rules violates the principle of treating similarly situated defendants the same. See Desist v. United States, 394 U.S., at 258–259 (Harlan, J., dissenting). As we pointed out in United States v. Johnson, the problem with not applying new rules to cases pending on direct review is "the *actual inequity* that results when the Court chooses which of many similarly situated defendants should be the chance beneficiary" of a new rule. 457 U.S., at 556, n. 16 (emphasis in original). Although the Court had tolerated this inequity for a time by not applying new rules retroactively to cases on direct review, we noted: "The time for toleration has come to an end." *Ibid.*

In United States v. Johnson, our acceptance of Justice Harlan's views led to the holding that "subject to [certain exceptions], a decision of this Court construing the Fourth Amendment is to be applied retroactively to all convictions that were not yet final at the time the decision was rendered." *Id.,* at 562. The exceptions to which we referred related to three categories in which we concluded that existing precedent established threshold tests for the retroactivity analysis. In two of these categories, the new rule already was retroactively applied: (1) when a decision of this Court did nothing more than apply settled precedent to different factual situations, see *id.,* at 549, and (2) when the new ruling was that a trial court lacked authority to convict a criminal defendant in the first place. See *id.,* at 550.

The third category—where a new rule is a "clear break" with past precedent—is the one at issue in these cases.

[W]e recognized what may be termed a "clear break exception." Under this exception, a new constitutional rule was not applied retroactively, even to cases on direct review, if the new rule explicitly overruled a past precedent of this Court, or disapproved a practice this Court had arguably sanctioned in prior cases, or overturned a longstanding practice that lower courts had uniformly approved. *Id.*, at 551. The Fourth Amendment ruling in Payton v. New York, 445 U.S. 573 (1980), with which United States v. Johnson was concerned, was not a clear break in any of these senses, and thus its retroactivity status was not "effectively preordained" by falling within the "clear break" exception. 457 U.S., at 553–554.

The question whether a different retroactivity rule should apply when a new rule is a "clear break" with the past, however, is squarely before us in the present cases. In Allen v. Hardy, 478 U.S. 255 (1986), a case which was here on federal habeas, we said that the rule in *Batson* "is an explicit and substantial break with prior precedent" because it "overruled [a] portion of *Swain.*" 478 U.S., at 258. We therefore now reexamine the rationale for maintaining a "clear break" exception to the general proposition that new rules governing criminal procedure should be retroactive to cases pending on direct review. For the same reasons that persuaded us in United States v. Johnson to adopt different conclusions as to convictions on direct review from those that already had become final, we conclude that an engrafted exception based solely upon the particular characteristics of the new rule adopted by the Court is inappropriate.

We therefore hold that a new rule for the conduct of criminal prosecutions is to be applied retroactively to all cases, state or federal, pending on direct review or not yet final, with no exception for cases in which the new rule constitutes a "clear break" with the past.

TEAGUE v. LANE

Supreme Court of the United States, 1989.
489 U.S. 288, 109 S.Ct. 1060, 103 L.Ed.2d 334.

JUSTICE O'CONNOR announced the judgment of the Court and delivered the opinion of the Court with respect to Parts I, II, and III, and an opinion with respect to Parts IV and V, in which THE CHIEF JUSTICE, JUSTICE SCALIA, and JUSTICE KENNEDY join.

In Taylor v. Louisiana, 419 U.S. 522 (1975), this Court held that the Sixth Amendment required that the jury venire be drawn from a fair cross section of the community. The Court stated, however, that "in holding that petit juries must be drawn from a source fairly representative of the community we impose no requirement that petit juries actually chosen must mirror the community and reflect the various distinctive groups in the population. Defendants are not entitled to a jury of any particular composition." *Id.*, at 538. The principal question presented in this case is whether the Sixth Amendment's fair cross section requirement should now be extended to the petit jury. Because we adopt Justice Harlan's approach to retroactivity for cases on collateral review, we leave the resolution of that question for another day.

I

Petitioner, a black man, was convicted by an all-white Illinois jury of three counts of attempted murder, two counts of armed robbery, and one count of aggravated battery. During jury selection for petitioner's trial, the prosecutor used all 10 of his peremptory challenges to exclude blacks. Petitioner's counsel used one of his 10 peremptory challenges to exclude a black woman who was married to a police officer. After the prosecutor had struck six blacks, petitioner's counsel moved for a mistrial. The trial court denied the motion.

On appeal, petitioner argued that the prosecutor's use of peremptory challenges denied him the right to be tried by a jury that was representative of the community. The Illinois Appellate Court rejected petitioner's fair cross section claim. The Illinois Supreme Court denied leave to appeal, and we denied certiorari.

Petitioner then filed a petition for a writ of habeas corpus in the United States District Court for the Northern District of Illinois.

II

Petitioner's first contention is that he should receive the benefit of our decision in Batson v. Kentucky, 476 U.S. 79 (1986) even though his conviction became final before Batson was decided.

In Allen v. Hardy, the Court held that *Batson* constituted an "explicit and substantial break with prior precedent" because it overruled a portion of *Swain*. 478 U.S., at 258. Employing the retroactivity standard of Linkletter v. Walker, 381 U.S. 618, 636 (1965), the Court concluded that the rule announced in *Batson* should not be applied retroactively on collateral review of convictions that became final before *Batson* was announced. The Court defined final to mean a case " 'where the judgment of conviction was rendered, the availability of appeal exhausted, and the time for petition for certiorari had elapsed before our decision in' *Batson*...." 478 U.S., at 258, n. 1 (citation omitted).

Petitioner's conviction became final 2½ years prior to *Batson,* thus depriving petitioner of any benefit from the rule announced in that case.

We reject the basic premise of petitioner's argument. As we have often stated, the "denial of a writ of certiorari imports no expression of opinion upon the merits of the case." United States v. Carver, 260 U.S. 482, 490 (1923) (Holmes, J.). Accord, Hughes Tool Co. v. Trans World Airlines, Inc., 409 U.S. 363, 366, n. 1 (1973); Brown v. Allen, 344 U.S. 443, 489–497 (1953). The "variety of considerations [that] underlie denials of the writ," Maryland v. Baltimore Radio Show, 338 U.S. 912, 917 (1950) (opinion of Frankfurter, J.), counsels against according denials of certiorari any precedential value. Concomitantly, opinions accompanying the denial of certiorari cannot have the same effect as decisions on the merits. We find that Allen v. Hardy is dispositive, and that petitioner cannot benefit from the rule announced in *Batson*.

V

Petitioner's conviction became final in 1983. As a result, the rule petitioner urges would not be applicable to this case, which is on collateral review, unless it would fall within an exception.

The first exception suggested by Justice Harlan—that a new rule should be applied retroactively if it places "certain kinds of primary, private individual conduct beyond the power of the criminal law-making authority to proscribe," Mackey v. United States, 401 U.S. 667, 692 (1971) (opinion concurring in judgments in part and dissenting in part)—is not relevant here. Application of the fair cross section requirement to the petit jury would not accord constitutional protection to any primary activity whatsoever.

The second exception suggested by Justice Harlan—that a new rule should be applied retroactively if it requires the observance of "those procedures that ... are 'implicit in the concept of ordered liberty.' " *id.*, at 693 (quoting Palko v. United States, 302 U.S. 319, 325 (1937))—we apply with a modification. The language used by Justice Harlan in *Mackey* leaves no doubt that he meant the second exception to be reserved for watershed rules of criminal procedure:

> "Typically, it should be the case that any conviction free from federal constitutional error at the time it became final, will be found, upon reflection, to have been fundamentally fair and conducted under those procedures essential to the substance of a full hearing. However, in some situations it might be that time and growth in social capacity, as well as judicial perceptions of what we can rightly demand of the adjudicatory process, will properly alter our understanding of the *bedrock procedural elements* that must be found to vitiate the fairness of a particular conviction. For example, such, in my view, is the case with the right to counsel at trial now held a necessary condition precedent to any conviction for a serious crime." 401 U.S., at 693–694 (emphasis added).

In *Desist,* Justice Harlan had reasoned that one of the two principal functions of habeas corpus was "to assure that no man has been incarcerated under a procedure which creates an impermissibly large risk that the innocent will be convicted," and concluded "from this that all 'new' constitutional rules which significantly improve the pre-existing fact-finding procedures are to be retroactively applied on habeas." 394 U.S., at 262. In *Mackey*, Justice Harlan gave three reasons for shifting to the less defined *Palko* approach. First, he observed that recent precedent, particularly Kaufman v. United States, 394 U.S. 217 (1969) (permitting Fourth Amendment claims to be raised on collateral review), led "ineluctably ... to the conclusion that it is not a principal purpose of the writ to inquire whether a criminal convict did in fact commit the deed alleged." 401 U.S., at 694. Second, he noted that cases such as Coleman v. Alabama, 399 U.S. 1 (1970) (invalidating lineup procedures in the absence of counsel), gave him reason to doubt the marginal effectiveness of claimed improvements in factfinding. 401 U.S., at 694–695. Third, he found "inherently intractable the purported distinction between those new rules that are designed to improve the factfinding process and those designed principally to further other values." *Id.*, at 695.

We believe it desirable to combine the accuracy element of the *Desist* version of the second exception with the *Mackey* requirement that the procedure at issue must implicate the fundamental fairness of the trial. Were we to employ the *Palko* test without more, we would be doing little more than importing into a very different context the terms of the debate over incorporation. Compare Duncan v. Louisiana, 391 U.S. 145, 171–193 (1968) (Harlan, J., dissenting), with Adamson v. California, 332 U.S. 46, 68–92 (1947) (Black, J., dissenting). Reviving the *Palko* test now, in this area of law, would be unnecessarily anachronistic.

We therefore hold that, implicit in the retroactivity approach we adopt today, is the principle that habeas corpus cannot be used as a vehicle to create new constitutional rules of criminal procedure unless those rules would be applied retroactively to *all* defendants on collateral review through one of the two exceptions we have articulated. Because a decision extending the fair cross section requirement to the petit jury would not be applied retroactively to cases on collateral review under the approach we adopt today, we do not address petitioner's claim.

For the reasons set forth above, the judgment of the Court of Appeals is affirmed.

———

HARPER v. VIRGINIA DEP'T OF TAXATION

Supreme Court of the United States, 1993.
___ U.S. ___, 113 S.Ct. 2510, 125 L.Ed.2d 74.

JUSTICE THOMAS delivered the opinion of the Court.

In Davis v. Michigan Dept. of Treasury, 489 U.S. 803 (1989), we held that a State violates the constitutional doctrine of intergovernmental tax immunity when it taxes retirement benefits paid by the Federal Government but exempts from taxation all retirement benefits paid by the State or its political subdivisions. Relying on the retroactivity analysis of Chevron Oil Co. v. Huson, 404 U.S. 97 (1971), the Supreme Court of Virginia twice refused to apply *Davis* to taxes imposed before *Davis* was decided. In accord with Griffith v. Kentucky, 479 U.S. 314 (1987), and James B. Beam Distilling Co. v. Georgia, 501 U.S. ___ (1991), we hold that this Court's application of a rule of federal law to the parties before the Court requires every court to give retroactive effect to that decision. We therefore reverse.

I

The Michigan tax scheme at issue in *Davis* "exempt[ed] from taxation all retirement benefits paid by the State or its political subdivisions, but levie[d] an income tax on retirement benefits paid by ... the Federal Government." 489 U.S., at 805. We held that the United States had not consented under 4 U.S.C. § 111 to this discriminatory imposition of a heavier tax burden on federal benefits than on state and local benefits. *Id.,* at 808–817. Because Michigan "conceded that a refund [was] appropriate," we recognized that federal retirees were entitled to a refund of taxes "paid ... pursuant to this invalid tax scheme." *Id.,* at 817.

Like Michigan, Virginia exempted state and local employees' retirement benefits from state income taxation while taxing federal retirement benefits. Va.Code Ann. § 58.1–322(c)(3) (Supp.1988). In response to *Davis,* Virginia repealed its exemption for state and local government employees. 1989 Va.Acts, Special Sess. II, ch. 3. It also enacted a special statute of limitations for refund claims made in light of *Davis.* Under this statute, taxpayers may seek a refund of state taxes imposed on federal retirement benefits in 1985, 1986, 1987, and 1988 for up to one year from the date of the final judicial resolution of whether Virginia must refund these taxes. Va.Code Ann. § 58.1–1823(b) (Supp.1992).

Petitioners, 421 federal civil service and military retirees, sought a refund of taxes "erroneously or improperly assessed" in violation of *Davis'* nondiscrimination principle. Va.Code Ann. § 58.1–1826 (1991). The trial court denied relief. Law No. CL891080 (Va.Cir.Ct., Mar. 12, 1990). Applying the factors set forth in Chevron Oil Co. v. Huson, *supra,* at 106–107, the court reasoned that "*Davis* decided an issue of first impression whose resolution was not clearly foreshadowed," that "prospective application of *Davis* will not retard its operation," and that "retroactive application would result in inequity, injustice and hardship."

The Supreme Court of Virginia affirmed. 241 Va. 232, 401 S.E.2d 868 (1991). It too concluded, after consulting *Chevron* and the plurality opinion in American Trucking Assns., Inc. v. Smith, 496 U.S. 167 (1990), that "the *Davis* decision is not to be applied retroactively." 241 Va., at 240, 401 S.E.2d, at 873.

II

"[B]oth the common law and our own decisions" have "recognized a general rule of retrospective effect for the constitutional decisions of this Court." Robinson v. Neil, 409 U.S. 505, 507 (1973). Nothing in the Constitution alters the fundamental rule of "retrospective operation" that has governed "[j]udicial decisions ... for near a thousand years." Kuhn v. Fairmont Coal Co., 215 U.S. 349, 372 (1910) (Holmes, J., dissenting). In Linkletter v. Walker, 381 U.S. 618 (1965), however, we developed a doctrine under which we could deny retroactive effect to a newly announced rule of criminal law. Under *Linkletter,* a decision to confine a new rule to prospective application rested on the purpose of the new rule, the reliance placed upon the previous view of the law, and "the effect on the administration of justice of a retrospective application" of the new rule. *Id.,* at 636 (limiting Mapp v. Ohio, 367 U.S. 643 (1961)).

In the civil context, we similarly permitted the denial of retroactive effect to "a new principle of law" if such a limitation would avoid " 'injustice or hardship' " without unduly undermining the "purpose and effect" of the new rule. Chevron Oil Co. v. Huson, 404 U.S., at 106–107 (quoting Cipriano v. City of Houma, 395 U.S. 701, 706 (1969)).

We subsequently overruled *Linkletter* in Griffith v. Kentucky, 479 U.S. 314 (1987), and eliminated limits on retroactivity in the criminal context by holding that all "newly declared ... rule[s]" must be applied retroactively to all "criminal cases pending on direct review." *Id.*, at 322. This holding rested on two "basic norms of constitutional adjudication." *Ibid.* First, we reasoned that "the nature of judicial review" strips us of the quintessentially "legislat[ive]" prerogative to make rules of law retroactive or prospective as we see fit. *Ibid.* Second, we concluded that "selective application of new rules violates the principle of treating similarly situated [parties] the same." *Id.*, at 323.

Dicta in *Griffith,* however, stated that "civil retroactivity.... continue[d] to be governed by the standard announced in *Chevron Oil.*" *Id.*, at 322, n. 8. We divided over the meaning of this dicta in American Trucking Assns., Inc. v. Smith, 496 U.S. 167 (1990). The four Justices in the plurality used "the *Chevron Oil* test" to consider whether to confine "the application of [American Trucking Assns., Inc. v. Scheiner, 483 U.S. 266 (1987)] to taxation of highway use prior to June 23, 1987, the date we decided *Scheiner.*" *Id.*, at 179 (opinion of O'Connor, J., joined by Rehnquist, C.J., and White and Kennedy, JJ.). Four other Justices rejected the plurality's "anomalous approach" to retroactivity and declined to hold that "the law applicable to a particular case is the law which the parties believe in good faith to be applicable to the case." *Id.*, at 219 (Stevens, J., dissenting, joined by Brennan, Marshall, and Blackmun, JJ.). Finally, despite concurring in the judgment, Justice Scalia "share[d]" the dissent's "perception that prospective decisionmaking is incompatible with the judicial role." *Id.*, at 201 (Scalia, J., concurring in judgment).

Griffith and *American Trucking* thus left unresolved the precise extent to which the presumptively retroactive effect of this Court's decisions may be altered in civil cases. But we have since adopted a rule requiring the retroactive application of a civil decision such as *Davis.* Although James B. Beam Distilling Co. v. Georgia, 501 U.S. 529 (1991), did not produce a unified opinion for the Court, a majority of Justices agreed that a rule of federal law, once announced and applied to the parties to the controversy, must be given full retroactive effect by all courts adjudicating federal law. In announcing the judgment of the Court, Justice Souter laid down a rule for determining the retroactive effect of a civil decision: After the case announcing any rule of federal law has "appl[ied] that rule with respect to the litigants" before the court, no court may "refuse to apply [that] rule ... retroactively." (Opinion of Souter, J., joined by Stevens, J.). Justice Souter's view of retroactivity superseded "any claim based on a *Chevron Oil* analysis."

Ibid. Justice White likewise concluded that a decision "extending the benefit of the judgment" to the winning party "is to be applied to other litigants whose cases were not final at the time of the [first] decision." *Id.,* at 544 (opinion concurring in judgment). Three other Justices agreed that "our judicial responsibility ... requir[es] retroactive application of each ... rule we announce." (Blackmun, J., joined by Marshall and Scalia, JJ., concurring in judgment). See also *id.,* at 548. (Scalia, J., joined by Marshall and Blackmun, JJ., concurring in judgment).

    Beam controls this case, and we accordingly adopt a rule that fairly reflects the position of a majority of Justices in *Beam:* When this Court applies a rule of federal law to the parties before it, that rule is the controlling interpretation of federal law and must be given full retroactive effect in all cases still open on direct review and as to all events, regardless of whether such events predate or postdate our announcement of the rule. This rule extends *Griffith* 's ban against "selective application of new rules." 479 U.S., at 323. Mindful of the "basic norms of constitutional adjudication" that animated our view of retroactivity in the criminal context, *id.,* at 322, we now prohibit the erection of selective temporal barriers to the application of federal law in noncriminal cases. In both civil and criminal cases, we can scarcely permit "the substantive law [to] shift and spring" according to "the particular equities of [individual parties'] claims" of actual reliance on an old rule and of harm from a retroactive application of the new rule. *Beam, supra,* at 543 (opinion of Souter, J.). Our approach to retroactivity heeds the admonition that "[t]he Court has no more constitutional authority in civil cases than in criminal cases to disregard current law or to treat similarly situated litigants differently." *American Trucking, supra,* at 214 (Stevens, J., dissenting).

NOTE

    In *Harper,* the Court acknowledged the freedom that state courts enjoy to limit the retroactive operation of their own interpretations of *state* law. Accordingly, state courts are not in lockstep with the federal case law of retroactivity. Indeed, the full range of formulations persist in the state courts.

    New Mexico courts, for example, still employ the three-factor analysis introduced in *Chevron Oil.* In Beavers v. Johnson Controls, 118 N.M. 391, 881 P.2d 1376 (1994), the New Mexico Supreme Court considered whether an earlier opinion recognizing the tort of intentional infliction of emotional distress should be applied retroactively. In retaining the *Chevron Oil* test, the court expressly declined to follow the federal court's *Harper* analysis. *Harper* did persuade the court, however, that there should be at least a presumption in favor of retroactivity in civil cases: "Because of the compelling force of the desirability of treating similarly situated parties alike, we adopt a presumption of retroactivity for a new rule imposed by a judicial decision in a civil case, in lieu of the hard-and-fast rule prescribed for federal cases in *Harper.*" In *Beavers,* the "presumption of retroactivity" was not overcome.

New York has disavowed the U.S. Supreme Court's retreat from *Linkletter,* and reaffirmed the principle of prospective application of decisional law by holding that "a new rule of State law need not automatically be applied to all cases currently in the direct appellate pipeline." Accordingly, when confronted with a direct appeal that implicates a newly announced State rule of law, appellate courts must consider the threshold question of retroactivity, weighing the three basic factors: (1) the purpose to be served by the new rule; (2) the extent of reliance on the old rule; and (3) the effect on the administration of justice of retroactive application. At the same time, however, the court is reluctant to apply the *Linkletter* rule. In People v. Favor, 82 N.Y.2d 254, 604 N.Y.S.2d 494, 624 N.E.2d 631 (1993), the New York Court of Appeals had to determine the retroactive effect to be given an earlier decision establishing a defendant's right to be present during a pre-trial hearing. After setting the stage with a recitation of the *Linkletter* factors, the court found that the earlier decision was not "really a 'new' rule of law at all" and was "clearly foreshadowed" by earlier cases, and thus should be applied retroactively regardless of the *Linkletter* factors.

Yet another standard prevails in North Carolina where "*Harper* is inapplicable." City of New Bern v. New Bern–Craven Cty. Board of Educ., 338 N.C. 430, 443, 450 S.E.2d 735, 743 (1994). "[A] test of reasonableness and good faith is to be applied in determining the effect." *Id.* at 442, 450 S.E.2d at 743.

Finally, Pennsylvania has "several approaches" it uses to determine the retroactive application of new decisions: (1) the common law approach (new decisions always have retrospective application to cases pending at the time of the decision); (2) a modified form of the common law approach (recognizing an exception to the rule where there is a "clear break with the past"); and (3) selective application (the *Linkletter* approach). Pennsylvania courts continue to utilize alternately all three approaches. *See* Commonwealth v. McCormick, 359 Pa.Super. 461, 519 A.2d 442 (1986).

LANDGRAF v. USI FILM PRODUCTS

Supreme Court of the United States, 1994.
___ U.S. ___, 114 S.Ct. 1483, 128 L.Ed.2d 229.

JUSTICE STEVENS delivered the opinion of the Court.

The Civil Rights Act of 1991 (1991 Act or Act) creates a right to recover compensatory and punitive damages for certain violations of Title VII of the Civil Rights Act of 1964. See Rev.Stat. § 1977A(a), 42 U.S.C. § 1981a(a), as added by § 102 of the 1991 Act, Pub.L. 102–166, 105 Stat. 1071. The Act further provides that any party may demand a trial by jury if such damages are sought. We granted certiorari to decide whether these provisions apply to a Title VII case that was pending on appeal when the statute was enacted. We hold that they do not.

Petitioner's primary submission is that the text of the 1991 Act requires that it be applied to cases pending on its enactment. Her argument, if accepted, would make the entire Act (with two narrow exceptions) applicable to conduct that occurred, and to cases that were filed, before the Act's effective date.

It is not uncommon to find "apparent tension" between different canons of statutory construction. As Professor Llewellyn famously illustrated, many of the traditional canons have equal opposites.[16] In order to resolve the question left open by the 1991 Act, federal courts have labored to reconcile two seemingly contradictory statements found in our decisions concerning the effect of intervening changes in the law. Each statement is framed as a generally applicable rule for interpreting statutes that do not specify their temporal reach. The first is the rule that "a court is to apply the law in effect at the time it renders its decision," *Bradley,* 416 U.S., at 711. The second is the axiom that "[r]etroactivity is not favored in the law," and its interpretive corollary that "congressional enactments and administrative rules will not be construed to have retroactive effect unless their language requires this result." *Bowen,* 488 U.S., at 208.

As Justice Scalia has demonstrated, the presumption against retroactive legislation is deeply rooted in our jurisprudence, and embodies a legal doctrine centuries older than our Republic.[17] Elementary considerations of fairness dictate that individuals should have an opportunity to know what the law is and to conform their conduct accordingly; settled expectations should not be lightly disrupted.[18] For that reason, the "principle that the legal effect of conduct should ordinarily be assessed under the law that existed when the conduct took place has timeless and universal appeal." *Kaiser,* 494 U.S., at 855 (Scalia, J., concurring). In a free, dynamic society, creativity in both commercial and artistic endeavors is fostered by a rule of law that gives people confidence about the legal consequences of their actions.

---

16. See Llewellyn, Remarks on the Theory of Appellate Decision and the Rules or Canons about How Statutes are to be Construed, 3 Vand.L.Rev. 395 (1950). Llewellan's article identified the apparent conflict between the canon that

"[a] statute imposing a new penalty or forfeiture, or a new liability or disability, or creating a new right of action will not be construed as having a retroactive effect" and the countervailing rule that

"[r]emedial statutes are to be liberally construed and if a retroactive interpretation will promote the ends of justice, they should receive such construction." *Id.,* at 402 (citations omitted).

17. See Kaiser Aluminum & Chemical Corp. v. Bonjourno, 494 U.S. 827, 842–844, 855–856 (1990) (Scalia, J., concurring). See also, *e.g.,* Dash v. Van Kleeck, 7 Johns. *477, *503 (N.Y.1811) ("It is a principle of the *English* common law, as ancient as the law itself, that a statute, even of its omnipotent parliament, is not to have a retrospective effect") (Kent, C.J.); Smead, *The Rule Against Retroactive Legislation: A Basic Principle of Jurisprudence,* 20 Minn.L.Rev. 775 (1936).

18. See General Motors Corp. v. Romein, 503 U.S. ___, ___ (1992) ("Retroactive legislation presents problems of unfairness that are more serious than those posed by prospective legislation, because it can deprive citizens of legitimate expectations and upset settled transactions"); Munzer, *A Theory of Retroactive Legislation,* 61 Texas L.Rev. 425, 471 (1982) ("The rule of law ... is a defeasible entitlement of persons to have their behavior governed by rules publicly fixed in advance"). See also L. Fuller, The Morality of Law 51–62 (1964) (hereinafter Fuller).

Our statement in *Bowen* that "congressional enactments and administrative rules will not be construed to have retroactive effect unless their language requires this result," 488 U.S., at 208, was in step with this long line of cases. *Bowen* itself was a paradigmatic case of retroactivity in which a federal agency sought to recoup, under cost limit regulations issued in 1984, funds that had been paid to hospitals for services rendered earlier, see *id.*, at 207; our search for clear congressional intent authorizing retroactivity was consistent with the approach taken in decisions spanning two centuries.

The presumption against statutory retroactivity had special force in the era in which courts tended to view legislative interference with property and contract rights circumspectly. In this century, legislation has come to supply the dominant means of legal ordering, and circumspection has given way to greater deference to legislative judgments. See *Usery v. Turner Elkhorn Mining Co.*, 428 U.S., at 15–16; *Home Bldg. & Loan Assn. v. Blaisdell*, 290 U.S. 398, 436–444 (1934). But while the *constitutional* impediments to retroactive civil legislation are now modest, prospectivity remains the appropriate default rule. Because it accords with widely held intuitions about how statutes ordinarily operate, a presumption against retroactivity will generally coincide with legislative and public expectations. Requiring clear intent assures that Congress itself has affirmatively considered the potential unfairness of retroactive application and determined that it is an acceptable price to pay for the countervailing benefits. Such a requirement allocates to Congress responsibility for fundamental policy judgments concerning the proper temporal reach of statutes, and has the additional virtue of giving legislators a predictable background rule against which to legislate.

Changes in procedural rules may often be applied in suits arising before their enactment without raising concerns about retroactivity. For example, in *Ex parte Collett*, 337 U.S. 55, 71 (1949), we held that 28 U.S.C. § 1404(a) governed the transfer of an action instituted prior to that statute's enactment. We noted the diminished reliance interests in matters of procedure. *Id.*, at 71. Because rules of procedure regulate secondary rather than primary conduct, the fact that a new procedural rule was instituted after the conduct giving rise to the suit does not make application of the rule at trial retroactive. Cf. *McBurney v. Carson*, 99 U.S. 567, 569 (1879).

When a case implicates a federal statute enacted after the events in suit, the court's first task is to determine whether Congress has expressly prescribed the statute's proper reach. If Congress has done so, of course, there is no need to resort to judicial default rules. When, however, the statute contains no such express command, the court must determine whether the new statute would have retroactive effect, *i.e.*, whether it would impair rights a party possessed when he acted, increase a party's liability for past conduct, or impose new duties with respect to transactions already completed. If the statute would operate retroactively, our traditional presumption teaches that it does not govern absent clear congressional intent favoring such a result.

The presumption against statutory retroactivity is founded upon sound considerations of general policy and practice, and accords with long held and widely shared expectations about the usual operation of legislation. We are satisfied that it applies to § 102. Because we have found no clear evidence of congressional intent that § 102 of the Civil Rights Act of 1991 should apply to cases arising before its enactment, we conclude that the judgment of the Court of Appeals must be affirmed.

THOMAS S. CURRIER, TIME AND CHANGE IN JUDGE–MADE LAW: PROSPECTIVE OVERRULING *

PROSPECTIVE LIMITATION IN FEDERAL COURTS: JUSTICIABILITY AND SEPARATION OF POWERS

Arguments have been made that the prospective limitation technique is beyond the scope of the federal judicial power authorized by article III of the Constitution, because it results in judicial pronouncements on the law that are not dispositive of the case or controversy before the court; and that use of the technique by federal courts violates the constitutional requirement of separation of powers. Each argument has a certain appeal, but neither seems to survive a close analysis. The two arguments have been separated for the discussion and analysis that follow.

A. Prospective Limitation Under Article III

Critics of the prospective effect approach maintain that, if an overruling decision is prospectively limited, the overruling language is dicta; and, further, that it is an advisory opinion beyond the scope of the federal judicial power enumerated in article III of the Constitution and may not be given by a court established under that article. Similarly it is suggested that if the newly announced rule is applied to the case at bar, then any language indicating that the overruling decision is to have only prospective effect in other cases is also dicta, and constitutes advisory opinion beyond the constitutional power of federal courts.

The argument confuses appraisal of what an article III court may properly do in exercising the federal judicial power with the weight that may properly be attributed to its decisions as stare decisis. The former is the constitutional restriction imposed by article III that "the jurisdiction of the federal courts can be invoked only under circumstances which to the expert feel of lawyers constitute a 'case or controversy.'" There is an ample body of Supreme Court decisions placing cases to one side of the line or the other, but there is no serious suggestion that, in a dispute which would otherwise present a case or controversy, justiciability is destroyed by the contention that precedent should be overruled—or that

* 51 Va.L.Rev. 201, 211–18, 220–25, 231–32, 234–35, 240–41, 252–58 (1965). Re-   printed by permission.

the overruling should be limited to prospective effect. The argument against federal use of the prospective overruling technique is rather that the constitutional restriction of federal judicial power to determination of cases or controversies prevents a federal court from considering contentions that are not dispositive of an admitted case or controversy properly before it.

It is true that the limitations imposed by article III should and do influence federal courts to restrict their consideration to issues that are potentially dispositive of pending litigation. But there is an important difference between an issue that is potentially dispositive and one that ultimately turns out to be dispositive in fact; and, because of this difference, what a federal court does in disposing of a case or controversy is generally subject only to influence, and not to command, by article III. It frequently is not possible at the outset, or even midway through the course of litigation, to ascertain which issues will in fact be dispositive of the case.

An example may be in order. At conclusion of trial, a court may find all facts as alleged by the plaintiff, but conclude as a matter of law that the facts alleged and proved entitle him to no relief. It might have been possible for the court to reach this conclusion of law prior to trial of the factual issues, and there are procedural devices available for this purpose. But the defendant need not utilize these devices, and, even if he does, the court may postpone decision of the issue of law, for one reason or another, until the factual issues have been tried and determined. Thus a determination of the plaintiff's factual contentions will be necessary. They are potentially dispositive, and the court may hope to avoid a difficult question of law in the event plaintiff fails to prove his propositions of fact. In the end, the plaintiff having proved his facts, it may turn out that the law is with the defendant, so that these issues of fact are not ultimately dispositive, though they were potentially so. The example is surely homely and familiar enough; no one would urge that the procedure followed is beyond the power of a federal court, or even improper, under article III.

Cases and controversies also frequently involve two or more issues of law or mixed law and fact that are potentially dispositive, even though, in the end, only one may dispose of the case. When this is true, it is a proper exercise of judicial power to determine both issues. In the end, perhaps both adjudications will support the judgment rendered, and hence be dispositive; or possibly one issue will be adjudicated adversely to the winning litigant, but judgment will be rendered in his favor on the basis of a favorable adjudication of the other. Both results are commonplace, and neither is subject to query under article III.

. . .

The situation is the same when the two issues are, first, whether a precedent ought to be overruled and, second, whether the overruling decision ought to be limited to prospective effect. A defendant relying on the precedent may prevail if the court either decides to retain the precedent or, having rejected it, decides to limit the new rule to prospective effect. Both issues are justiciable, even though the decision of one of them may, in the end, not be dispositive in the collateral estoppel or stare decisis sense.

B. The Separation-of-Powers Argument

Even though prospective limitation fits neatly enough into the traditional framework of article III judicial power—in that it merely adds a potentially nondispositive issue, perhaps one of several such, to a justiciable case or controversy—the separation-of-powers argument remains. It is basically that prospective limitation is a technique suited primarily to law-making, or law-changing, and that its use by courts invites, or perhaps even constitutes, invasion by the judiciary of areas relegated to other institutions of government—in the case of the federal government, to Congress and to the constitutional amendment processes.

Since the Supreme Court has never expressly considered whether it is proper for federal courts to use the prospective limitation technique, it has never directly considered the separation-of-powers argument. Mr. Justice Black, however, urged the argument in a dissenting opinion in James v. United States:

> In our judgment one of the great inherent restraints upon this Court's departure from the field of interpretation to enter that of lawmaking has been the fact that its judgments could not be limited to prospective application. This Court and in fact all departments of the Government have always heretofore realized that prospective lawmaking is the function of Congress rather than of the courts. We continue to think that this function should be exercised only by Congress under our constitutional system.[62]

Chief Justice von Moschzisker [of Pennsylvania] in 1924 had urged similarly, but more broadly, that prospective limitation of overruling decisions was "plain and outright legislation by the courts," and arguments have since been made that the pliability of the prospective limitation approach might promote judicial legislation to an undesirable extent, and that normally legislation is a more suitable tool for bringing about desired changes in the law.

Mr. Justice Black's language brings these objections to bear upon the federal courts, and in particular, of course, the Supreme Court of the United States.

The bearing of the doctrine of separation of powers on the availability of prospective limitation as a technique for exercising the federal judicial power appears to raise problems of constitutional proportions, even though the technique does not violate the justiciability requirement imposed by article III. Although measured to some extent by article III, the separation doctrine is more broadly based, and is rooted in various

---

62. 366 U.S. 213, 225 (1961).

other provisions of the Constitution, as well as in the organizational structure of the first three articles.

In the absence of any obviously relevant specific constitutional language or precedent, it might be reasonable to hope that the constitutional aspect of the separation-of-powers problem could be resolved by an appeal to history. Both Mr. Justice Frankfurter and the first Mr. Justice Harlan suggested that the key to the question of justiciability under the "case or controversy" language of article III was to be found in the *modus operandi* of the courts of Westminster at the time the article was drafted and adopted. Given the apparent hegemony of the Blackstonian declaratory-retroactive view of judge-made law at that time, it would appear that the phrase "judicial power" in article III could not have been understood by eighteenth century lawyers to give to the federal judiciary any law-making power in the sense generally recognized today; and hence one might conclude that the separation of powers contemplated by those who drafted, and those who accepted, the Constitution would be violated by adoption of a broader judicial technique that frankly recognizes, and is designed specifically to facilitate, the judicial law-making function. But one might more accurately surmise that since the drafters had not even imagined prospective limitation, they did not contemplate its possible impact upon the separation of powers, and that the creation of the federal judicial power thus does not imply any judgment at all on the question. If this view is taken, the propriety of prospective limitation with reference to the separation of powers remains open for consideration on its merits. But even if the former view is taken, the historical approach does not compel rejection of the prospective limitation technique by federal courts.

The historical argument, in its more ambitious form, attaches to the "judicial power" language of the Constitution and thus would appear to be equally applicable, if valid, to any case that might come before a federal court at least on a question of federal law. Thus if the question is one of federal common law, not requiring interpretation of a federal statute or of the Constitution, the original understanding of "judicial power" indicates that federal common law does not change, but rather that the Supreme Court's appreciation of it becomes more acute. Changing the law is a function intended to be left to the legislative branch. Similarly, judicial reinterpretation of statutory language is proper only if understood as an altered judgment as to the original meaning of the statute, and violates the historically contemplated separation of powers if engaged in for the purpose of change, which is a power given only to the legislative branch. If the question is one of constitutional interpretation, "judicial power" cannot be regarded as having any additional meaning; reinterpretation is a judicial function only when its purpose is better to ascertain original meaning. Change here is left not to Congress, but to the constitutional amending processes. In short, if the original understanding of "judicial power" were accepted as the sole determinant, it would appear to draw the same line in all of these areas: the federal courts invade fields left by the

Constitution to other institutions of government if they reverse precedent for any reason other than recognition of a result that has always been correct; facilitation of judicial law-making as such is encouragement to the federal judiciary to make such invasions.

Adherence to this historical evaluation of "judicial power" would certainly be embarrassing in a number of areas. The constitutional basis for the Erie [Railroad v. Tompkins, 304 U.S. 64 (1938)] decision, for instance, would be destroyed, or at least rendered precarious, and a lot else besides. But there is no need to dwell on the consequences of making the Blackstonian declaratory theory constitutional dogma, because no one would seriously suggest that this be done. It having long since been generally accepted that the Constitution is a living document, one must be cautious in pushing historical interpretations of its meaning.

. . .

Consider, for example, the potential impact of retroactive application of Brown v. Board of Education. While it has not been discussed in those terms, it seems clear that the rule derived in *Brown* was limited to prospective effect, else how explain the Court's order the following fall that the rule be complied with only with "deliberate speed?" Given the normal retroactive application, ought not all state officials responsible for registration of pupils in public schools to have complied immediately? Indeed, might not a state official who had, in reliance upon Plessy v. Ferguson, denied a Negro child admission to an all-white school on the basis of race be rendered civilly liable for this intentional deprivation of a constitutional right? Yet this appears to be a clear case for protection of those who act in reliance upon contemporaneous law. In the case of *Brown,* analysis of the problem of retroactive application was apparently forestalled by the announcement, in the Court's original opinion, that the newly recognized principle would require conscious, planned implementation, but the result seems sound on the basis of the values discussed in the following section. . . .

. . .

ROBERT E. KEETON, PROSPECTIVE
JUDICIAL LAWMAKING *

That blend of retroactive and prospective overruling in which the new rule is applied retroactively only to the case at hand illustrates the point that more than one technique of partly prospective overruling can be devised. In fact, a congeries of possibilities exists, representing

* Excerpted by permission of the author and publishers from pp. 25–27, 29–31, 33–34, 36–38 of Venturing To Do Justice: Reforming Private Law by Robert E. Keeton, Cambridge, Mass.: Harvard University Press, Copyright © 1969 by the President and Fellows of Harvard College.

differing blends of retroactive and prospective effect to the court's newly fashioned rule. One may also see these as various ways of limiting the scope of application of the decision. From this perspective a determination that the new rule shall apply only to specified classes of future transactions is a prospective limitation—that is, a limitation of the new rule to prospective application—rather than a prospective overruling.

Definitions of the future transactions to which a new rule applies may vary in detail. For example, it may be determined that the new rule will apply to all cases based on incidents occurring after the opinion is filed; or, in order to provide reasonable notice to parties whose interests might be affected or to provide reasonable opportunity for the state's legislature to consider the issue, the new rule may be applied only to cases based on incidents occurring after a specified interval.

Definitions of past transactions to which a new rule applies may also vary in detail. [S]ome courts have chosen to apply a new rule only to the case at hand or to that case and a very limited number of others closely associated with it. Another body of cases has defined past transactions affected by the new rule in a way distinctively associated with liability insurance.

. . .

These illustrations are sufficient to demonstrate that the methods of overruling are numerous and diverse. One who puts together the various blends of retroactive and prospective application suggested even by this brief discussion discovers many possible combinations. The judicial and other writings on this subject have as yet proceeded only a little way toward exposition of the standards for choosing among the many available blends.

Prospective overruling, then, is a new and relatively undeveloped judicial technique in a sense. But various methods of prospective judicial lawmaking are within our legal tradition. Prospective overruling of decisional law is not a departure from the traditional function of courts, but a new way of discharging a function courts have been performing since the dawn of the common-law tradition. There will be occasions, of course, when prospective lawmaking by courts is less appropriate than either retroactive lawmaking or staunch adherence to precedent. But total rejection of prospective overruling would be a crippling limitation of judicial method.

———

GREAT NORTHERN RAILWAY CO. v. SUNBURST OIL & REFINING CO.

Supreme Court of the United States, 1932.
287 U.S. 358, 53 S.Ct. 145, 77 L.Ed. 360.

[The Montana Supreme Court had ruled that Sunburst could recover excessive rates which had been charged by the railroad. By a second decision it ruled that (1) Sunburst could not recover and (2) its second ruling was prospective only, thus permitting Sunburst to recover under the first decision. The railroad sought relief in the U.S. Supreme Court, contending that the Montana court's failure to give retroactive effect to its second ruling contravened the federal Constitution.]

Mr. Justice Cardozo delivered the opinion of the Court.

We have no occasion to consider whether this division in time of the effects of a decision is a sound or an unsound application of the doctrine of stare decisis as known to the common law. Sound or unsound, there is involved in it no denial of a right protected by the Federal Constitution. This is not a case where a court, in overruling an earlier decision, has given to the new ruling a retroactive bearing, and thereby has made invalid what was valid in the doing. Even that may often be done, though litigants not infrequently have argued to the contrary. Tidal Oil Co. v. Flanagan, 263 U.S. 444, 450, 44 S.Ct. 197, 68 L.Ed. 382; Fleming v. Fleming, 264 U.S. 29, 44 S.Ct. 246, 68 L.Ed. 547; Brinkerhoff–Faris Co. v. Hill, 281 U.S. 673, 680, 50 S.Ct. 451, 74 L.Ed. 1107; cf. Montana Bank v. Yellowstone County, 276 U.S. 499, 503, 48 S.Ct. 331, 72 L.Ed. 673. This is a case where a court has refused to make its ruling retroactive, and the novel stand is taken that the Constitution of the United States is infringed by the refusal.

We think the Federal Constitution has no voice upon the subject. A state in defining the limits of adherence to precedent may make a choice for itself between the principle of forward operation and that of relation backward. It may say that decisions of its highest court, though later overruled, are law none the less for intermediate transactions. Indeed, there are cases intimating, too broadly (cf. Tidal Oil Co. v. Flanagan, supra), that it *must* give them that effect; but never has doubt been expressed that it *may* so treat them if it pleases, whenever injustice or hardship will thereby be averted. Gelpcke v. Dubuque, 1 Wall. 175, 17 L.Ed. 520.... On the other hand, it may hold to the ancient dogma that the law declared by its courts had a Platonic or ideal existence before the act of declaration, in which event the discredited declaration will be viewed as if it had never been, and the reconsidered declaration as law from the beginning. Tidal Oil Co. v. Flanagan, supra; Fleming v. Fleming, supra; Central Land Co. v. Laidley, 159 U.S. 103, 112, 16 S.Ct. 80, 40 L.Ed. 91; see, however, Montana Bank v. Yellowstone County, supra. The alternative is the same whether the subject of the new decision is common law (Tidal Oil Co. v. Flanagan, supra) or statute. Gelpcke v. Dubuque, supra; Fleming v. Fleming, supra. The choice for any state may be determined by the juristic philosophy of the judges of her courts, their conceptions of law, its origin and nature. We review, not the wisdom of their philosophies, but the legality of their acts. The state of Montana has told us by the voice of her highest court that, with these alternative methods open to her, her preference is for the first. In making this choice, she is declaring common law for those within her borders. The common law as administered by her judges ascribes to the decisions of her highest court a power to bind and loose that is unextinguished, for intermediate transactions, by a decision overruling them. As applied to such transactions, we may say of the earlier decision that it has not been overruled at all. It has been translated into a judgment of affirmance and recognized as law anew. Accompanying the recognition is a prophecy, which may or may not be realized in conduct, that transactions arising in the future will be governed by a different rule. If this is the common-law doctrine of adherence to precedent as understood and enforced by the courts of Montana, we are not at liberty, for anything contained in the Constitution of the United States, to thrust upon those courts a different conception either of the binding force of precedent or of the meaning of the judicial process.

NOTE

See also Walter v. Schaefer, *The Control of "Sunbursts": Techniques of Prospective Overruling,* 42 N.Y.U.L.Rev. 631, 637–39 (1967): * "The type of overruling with which Mr. Justice Cardozo was concerned is now called 'purely prospective,' to distinguish it from two variations that have rather recently been introduced. Purely prospective overruling has been characterized as dictum, and courts have not always adhered to their predictions. It has also been suggested that since the litigant whose efforts brought about the change in judicial doctrine receives no reward, other individual litigants would not be encouraged to attempt to reform the law through judicial decisions. The latter criticism is closely related to the objection, advanced in due process terms by the Great Northern Railroad in the *Sunburst* case, that the party who brings about the change in law may not properly be deprived of the fruits of his victory, whatever may be the situation as to others. The first innovation is designed to meet these objections by applying the new doctrine to the litigants immediately before the court while at the same time announcing that the court will limit the application of the new rule to events that occur after the date of its decision. This technique meets the objections to which it was addressed, but its fairness has been questioned. As T.S. Eliot said, in a somewhat different context: 'Here is a place of disaffection—Time before and time after—In a dim light.' I shall not be able to 'turn the shadow into transient beauty,' but there are some considerations I can put before you.

. . .

"The second innovation has been termed 'prospective-prospective' overruling. It was used by the Supreme Court of Minnesota in a case involving municipal immunity from tort liability. Both on historical grounds and on contemporary considerations the court found immunity unwarranted, but refused to allow the plaintiff to recover:

> We recognize that by denying recovery in the case at bar the remainder of the decision becomes dictum. However, the court is unanimous in expressing its intention to overrule the doctrine of sovereign tort immunity as a defense with respect to tort

* Reprinted by permission.

claims against school districts, municipal corporations, and other subdivisions of government on whom immunity has been conferred by judicial decision arising after the next Minnesota Legislature adjourns....[30]

The same technique was used again by the Minnesota court in determining the effectiveness of a Totten trust in Minnesota. The court announced its preference for the rule stated in the Restatement of Trusts, but said: '[W]e do not feel free to adopt the Restatement rule without first giving the legislature an opportunity to provide for it by statute' " [31]

Both the Congress and the states are forbidden to pass ex post facto laws; in general, this applies only to statutes imposing criminal penalties. Calder v. Bull, 3 U.S. (3 Dall.) 386, 390 (1798). Only the states, and not Congress, are in terms forbidden to "pass any ... Law impairing the Obligation of Contracts". Do these constitutional provisions seem to place more restrictions on legislative, as distinguished from judicial, lawmakers? Is there any restriction that prevents a court from giving full retroactivity to a new decision on the Blackstonian theory that the old was "not law"?

Prospective overruling is familiarly described as "sunbursting," a name derived from the seminal case Great N. Ry. Co. v. Sunburst Oil. Thus, in Harmann v. Hadley, 128 Wis.2d 371, 382 N.W.2d 673 (1986), Justice Shirley S. Abrahamson explained:

> This court generally adheres to the "Blackstonian Doctrine" that a decision which overrules or repudiates an earlier decision is retrospective in operation. This court has ... recognized exceptions to the "Blackstone" doctrine and has used the device of prospective overruling, sometimes dubbed "sunbursting" to limit the effect of a newly announced rule.

The *Harmann* case presents an interesting example of the problems related to sunbursting. In a case prior to *Harmann*, the Wisconsin Supreme Court had announced a new rule of social host liability, but said it would apply only "when the conduct which cause[d] injury occur[red] on or after September 1, 1985." The lower courts accordingly dismissed Harmann's complaint, because the relevant conduct occurred in June of 1982, more than three years before the sunburst date. Because of the "equities," however, the Supreme Court reversed and allowed retroactive application. The "equities" were that the plaintiffs in the earlier case and in this case were pursuing the same claims in the trial court, the court of appeals and the Supreme Court at the same time; it was merely "chance" that the Supreme Court did not hear the *Harmann* case first. Because it allowed the plaintiffs in the earlier

---

30. Spanel v. Mounds View School Dist., 264 Minn. 279, 292, 118 N.W.2d 795, 803 (1962).

31. In re Jeruzal, 269 Minn. 183, 195, 130 N.W.2d 473, 481 (1964). This degree of judicial restraint seems questionable.

litigation to recover, it made an exception to its "sunburst" rule and allowed the *Harmann* plaintiffs also to recover.

MOLITOR v. KANELAND COMMUNITY UNIT DISTRICT

Supreme Court of Illinois 1959.
188 Ill. 11, 163 N.E.2d 89.

KLINGBIEL, JUSTICE.

Plaintiff, Thomas Molitor, a minor, by Peter his father and next friend, brought this action against Kaneland Community Unit School District for personal injuries sustained by plaintiff when the school bus in which he was riding left the road, allegedly as a result of the driver's negligence, hit a culvert, exploded and burned.

Defendant's motion to dismiss the complaint on the ground that a school district is immune from liability for tort was sustained by the trial court, and a judgment was entered in favor of defendant. Plaintiff elected to stand on his complaint and sought a direct appeal to this court on the ground that the dismissal of his action would violate his constitutional rights. At that time we held that no fairly debatable constitutional question was presented so as to give this court jurisdiction on direct appeal, and accordingly the cause was transferred to the Appellate Court for the Second District. The Appellate Court affirmed the decision of the trial court and the case is now before us again on a certificate of importance.

In his brief, plaintiff recognizes the rule, established by this court in 1898, that a school district is immune from tort liability, and frankly asks this court to abolish the rule in toto.

We conclude that the rule of school district tort immunity is unjust, unsupported by any valid reason, and has no rightful place in modern day society.

In here departing from stare decisis because we believe justice and policy require such departure, we are nonetheless cognizant of the fact that retrospective application of our decision may result in great hardship to school districts which have relied on prior decisions upholding the doctrine of tort immunity of school districts. For this reason we feel justice will best be served by holding that, except as to the plaintiff in the instant case, the rule herein established shall apply only to cases arising out of future occurrences. This result is in accord with a substantial line of authority embodying the theory that an overruling decision should be given only prospective operation whenever injustice or hardship due to reliance on the overruled decisions would thereby be averted. Gelpcke v. City of Dubuque, 1 Wall. 175, 68 U.S. 175, 17 L.Ed. 520; Harmon v. Auditor of Public Accounts, 123 Ill. 122, 13 N.E. 161 (where decision sustaining validity of statute authorizing bond issue is, subsequent to the issue, overruled, overruling decision operates prospectively); Davies Warehouse Co. v. Bowles, 321 U.S. 144, 64 S.Ct. 474, 88 L.Ed. 635; People ex rel. Attorney General v. Salomon, 54 Ill. 39 (where public officers have relied on statutes subsequently held unconstitutional, decision given only prospective operation); State v. Jones, 44 N.M. 623, 107 P.2d 324 (prospective operation given decision overruling precedent as to what constitutes a lottery); Continental Supply Co. v. Abell, 95 Mont. 148, 24 P.2d 133 (prospective operation given decision overruling prior cases as to corporate directors' liability to stockholders); Hare v. General Con. Purchase Corp., 220 Ark. 601, 249 S.W.2d 973 (prospective operation given decision changing prior rule as to what constitutes usury.) See also: Snyder, Retrospective Operation of Overruling Decisions, 35 Ill.L.Rev. 121; Kocourek, Retrospective Decisions and Stare Decisis, 17 A.B.A.J. 180; Freeman, The Protection Afforded Against the Retroactive Operation of an Overruling Decision, 18 Col.L.Rev. 230; Carpenter, Court Decisions and the Common Law, 17 Col.L.Rev. 593; Note, Prospective Operation of Decisions Holding Statutes Unconstitutional or Overruling Prior Decisions, 60 Harv.L.Rev. 437.

Likewise there is substantial authority in support of our position that the new rule shall apply to the instant case. Dooling v. Overholser, 100 U.S.App.D.C. 247, 243 F.2d 825; Shioutakon v. District of Columbia, 98 U.S.App.D.C. 371, 236 F.2d 666, 60 A.L.R.2d 686; Durham v. United States, 94 U.S.App.D.C. 228, 214 F.2d 862, 45 A.L.R.2d 1430; Barker v. St. Louis County, 340 Mo. 986, 104 S.W.2d 371; Farrior v. New England Mortgage Security Co., 92 Ala. 176, 9 So. 532, 12 L.R.A. 856; Haskett v. Maxey, 134 Ind. 182, 33 N.E. 358, 19 L.R.A. 379; Dauchey Co. v. Farney, 105 Misc. 470, 173 N.Y.S. 530. At least two compelling reasons exist for applying the new rule to the instant case while otherwise limiting its application to cases arising in the future. First, if we were to merely announce the new rule without applying it here, such announcement would amount to mere dictum. Second, and more important, to refuse to apply the new rule here would deprive appellant of any benefit from his effort and expense in challenging the old rule which we now declare erroneous. Thus there would be no incentive to appeal the upholding of precedent since appellant could not in any event benefit from a reversal invalidating it.

It is within our inherent power as the highest court of this State to give a decision prospective or retrospective application without offending constitutional principles. Great Northern Railway Co. v. Sunburst Oil & Refining Co., 287 U.S. 358, 53 S.Ct. 145, 77 L.Ed. 360.

———————

DOMERACKI v. HUMBLE OIL & REFINING CO.

United States Court of Appeals, Third Circuit, 1971.
443 F.2d 1245.

[The court held that in personal injuries actions, trial courts must, upon request of counsel, instruct the jury that any award will not be subject to federal income taxes and that the jury should not add or subtract taxes in fixing the amount of any award.]

We decline, however, to reverse the judgment of the court below. Two important considerations influence this determination. First, the purpose of the rule which we promulgate for prospective application [14] in this Circuit is to remove the possibility that juries will increase awards based on mistaken considerations of tax consequences. In the case at bar, however, there is no evidence that the jury was in fact so motivated, and because of the settled rule, heretofore discussed, that the sanctity of jury deliberations may not be invaded subsequent to the rendition of the verdict, any inquiry is now foreclosed.

Secondly, we recognize that our approach to this problem represents a new view in this judicial circuit as well as in other Circuits. Indeed, the position we adopt has been accepted by only a handful of state jurisdictions. In this situation, it cannot be said that the trial court erred in refusing the instruction at the time it was proffered. Paying even the most scrupulous attention to the sometimes subtle shifting of appellate winds, the district court could not have been expected to forecast the decision we reach here.

14. The Supreme Court of Missouri in Dempsey v. Thompson, 363 Mo. 339, 251 S.W.2d 42 (1952), made prospective only its overruling of the refusal to give a requested cautionary instruction. Our action in giving prospective effect to our ruling is based on our general supervisory power over the district courts in this Circuit. See McNabb v. United States, 318 U.S. 332, 63 S.Ct. 608, 87 L.Ed. 819 (1943); United States v. Fioravanti, 412 F.2d 407, 420 (3 Cir.1969).

Chapter IV

DECISION MAKING THEORY

Section 1

GENERAL

It is helpful to separate and isolate the functions of decision making and law making. "Law making" is the legal consequence of judicial "decision making." Although every instance of law making requires simultaneous decision making, the converse is not always true: not every instance of decision making requires rule making. Therefore, decision making must be considered both absolutely and relatively. Its techniques and methodologies are applicable, in varying degrees, to all cases on the trial and appellate levels.

Once a factual dispute is resolved by a fact finder or by stipulation, most cases unerringly are controlled by unambiguous statutory or regulatory language, or by precedent; these ultimate dispositions should be predictable, reckonable and truly foreordained. The major portion of the calendar in any court is comprised of such cases where the controlling legal precepts are brightly visible and a wealth of tried and tested reasoning is available for application.

In a small minority of cases the law is not clear, and perforce, its application to the facts is not plain. Cardozo described these cases as the "serious business" of the courts, where "the courts work for the future." The American judicial system functions well only because such cases constitute a small portion of its dockets. In studying elements of the decision making process, one must remain mindful that although some techniques and methodologies are applicable absolutely in all cases, only a few cases will require the full panoply of methodologies.

Cardozo estimated that at least nine-tenths of appellate cases in 1924 "could not, with semblance of reason, be decided in any way but one," since the law and its application alike are plain"; or "the rule of law is certain, and the application alone doubtful."[1] In 1961, Judge Henry Friendly wrote: "Indeed, Cardozo's nine-tenths estimate probably should be read as referring to the first category alone. Thus reading it, Professor Harry W. Jones finds it 'surprising' on the high side.[2] So would I. If it includes both categories, I would not."[3] The U.S. Court

---

1. B. Cardozo, The Nature of the Judicial Process 164 (1921)

2. See H.W. Jones, *Law and Morality in the Perspective of Legal Realism,* 61 Colum.L.Rev. 799, 803 n. 16 (1961).

3. H. Friendly, *Reactions of a Lawyer— Newly Become Judge,* 71 Yale L.J. 218, 222 n. 23 (1961).

of Appeals for the Third Circuit provides by internal operating procedure that no opinion need be written where (1) there is an affirmance and (2) the case has no institutional or precedential value. In the 1994 court year, of 1840 fully briefed cases decided on the merits, 1413 were terminated without an opinion (published or unpublished). These statistics indicate that at least 77% percent of that court's affirmances fit into both categories or possibly the first alone.[4]

We now discuss the sources of rules used by courts when they decide cases. John Chipman Gray reminds us that "[t]he State requires that the acts of its legislative organ shall bind the courts, and so far as they go, shall be paramount to all other sources."[5] Even the most free-wheeling judge must concede the validity of this first principle as a necessary consequence from the very conception of an organized community. Gray also suggested that:

> The other sources from which courts may draw their general rules are fourfold—judicial precedents, opinions of experts, customs, and principles of morality (using morality as including public policy). Whether there is any precedent, expert opinion, custom or principle from which a rule can be drawn, and whether a rule shall be drawn accordingly, are questions which, in most communities, are left to the courts themselves; and yet there are probably in every community limits within or beyond which courts may, or, on the other hand, cannot, seek for rules from the sources mentioned, although the limits are not precisely defined.[6]

Civil law practice starts out with the same major premises—the source of law is that of the legislative organ, in France, *loi* ; in Germany, *Gesetz* ; in Italy, *legge* ; in Spanish speaking countries, *ley*. None of the civil law codes, however, provides that court decisions, in and of themselves, can officially be utilized as a source of law. Officially, they may not; in actual practice, as previously observed, they are being used to justify decisions.

---

4. The total figure has to be higher because a number of signed opinion affirmances come within the first two categories. In a speech before the American Law Institute on May 18, 1994, the author commented: "In 1986, in an article, I wrote that 90 percent of the cases coming before my court came within Cardozo's first two categories.... Eight years later, I alter my position.... I am prepared to say that nine out of ten federal appeals fall within the first category alone: 'The law and its application alike are plain.'" The American Law Institute, Remarks and Addresses, 71st Annual Meeting 23–24 (1994).

5. J.C. Gray, The Nature and Sources of the Law 124–25

6. Id.

BENJAMIN N. CARDOZO, THE NATURE OF THE JUDICIAL PROCESS *

What is it that I do when I decide a case? To what sources of information do I appeal for guidance? In what proportions do I permit them to contribute to the result? In what proportions ought they to contribute? If a precedent is applicable, when do I refuse to follow it? If no precedent is applicable, how do I reach the rule that will make a precedent for the future? If I am seeking logical consistency, the symmetry of the legal structure, how far shall I seek it? At what point shall the quest be halted by some discrepant custom, by some consideration of the social welfare, by my own or the common standards of justice and morals? Into that strange compound which is brewed daily in the caldron of the courts, all these ingredients enter in varying proportions. I am not concerned to inquire whether judges ought to be allowed to brew such a compound at all. I take judge-made law as one of the existing realities of life. There, before us, is the brew. Not a judge on the bench but has had a hand in the making. The elements have not come together by chance. *Some* principle, however unavowed and inarticulate and subconscious, has regulated the infusion. It may not have been the same principle for all judges at any time, nor the same principle for any judge at all times. But a choice there has been, not a submission to the decree of Fate; and the considerations and motives determining the choice, even if often obscure, do not utterly resist analysis. In such attempt at analysis as I shall make, there will be need to distinguish between the conscious and the subconscious. I do not mean that even those considerations and motives which I shall class under the first head are always in consciousness distinctly, so that they will be recognized and named at sight. Not infrequently they hover near the surface. They may, however, with comparative readiness be isolated and tagged, and when thus labeled, are quickly acknowledged as guiding principles of conduct. More subtle are the forces so far beneath the surface that they cannot reasonably be classified as other than subconscious. It is often through these subconscious forces that judges are kept consistent with themselves, and inconsistent with one another. We are reminded by William James in a telling page of his lectures on Pragmatism that every one of us has in truth an underlying philosophy of life, even those of us to whom the names and the notions of philosophy are unknown or anathema. There is in each of us a stream of tendency, whether you choose to call it philosophy or not, which gives coherence and direction to thought and action. Judges cannot escape that current any more than other mortals. All their lives, forces which they do not recognize and cannot name, have been tugging at them— inherited instincts, traditional beliefs, acquired convictions; and the resultant is an outlook on life, a conception of social needs, a sense in James's phrase of "the total push and pressure of the cosmos," which, when reasons are nicely balanced, must determine where choice shall

* 10–14, 28–31 (1921). Reprinted by permission of Yale University Press from The Nature of the Judicial Process by Benjamin N. Cardozo. Copyright © 1921 by Yale University Press.

fall. In this mental background every problem finds its setting. We may try to see things as objectively as we please. None the less, we can never see them with any eyes except our own. To that test they are all brought—a form of pleading or an act of parliament, the wrongs of paupers or the rights of princes, a village ordinance or a nation's charter.

. . .

Before we can determine the proportions of a blend, we must know the ingredients to be blended. Our first inquiry should therefore be: Where does the judge find the law which he embodies in his judgment? There are times when the source is obvious. The rule that fits the case may be supplied by the constitution or by statute. If that is so, the judge looks no farther. The correspondence ascertained, his duty is to obey. The constitution overrides a statute, but a statute, if consistent with the constitution, overrides the law of judges. In this sense, judge-made law is secondary and subordinate to the law that is made by legislators. . . .

. . .

. . . For every tendency, one seems to see a counter-tendency; for every rule its antinomy. . . . Doubtless in the last three centuries, some lines, once wavering, have become rigid. We leave more to legislatures today, and less perhaps to judges. Yet even now there is change from decade to decade. The glacier still moves.

In this perpetual flux, the problem which confronts the judge is in reality a twofold one: he must first extract from the precedents the underlying principle, the *ratio decidendi* ; he must then determine the path or direction along which the principle is to move and develop, if it is not to wither and die.

The first branch of the problem is the one to which we are accustomed to address ourselves more consciously than to the other. Cases do not unfold their principles for the asking. They yield up their kernel slowly and painfully. The instance cannot lead to a generalization till we know it as it is. That in itself is no easy task. For the thing adjudged comes to us oftentimes swathed in obscuring dicta, which must be stripped off and cast aside. . . .

But dicta are not always ticketed as such, and one does not recognize them always at a glance. There is the constant need, as every law student knows, to separate the accidental and the non-essential from the essential and inherent. Let us assume, however, that this task has been achieved, and that the precedent is known as it really is. Let us assume too that the principle, latent within it, has been skillfully extracted and accurately stated. Only half or less than half of the work has yet been done. The problem remains to fix the bounds and the tendencies of development and growth, to set the directive force in motion along the right path at the parting of the ways.

The directive force of a principle may be exerted along the line of logical progression; this I will call the rule of analogy or the method of philosophy; along the line of historical development; this I will call the method of evolution; along the line of the customs of the community; this I will call the method of tradition; along the lines of justice, morals and social welfare, the *mores* of the day; and this I will call the method of sociology.

RUGGERO J. ALDISERT, JURISPRUDENTIAL TEMPERAMENT *

It is here where that quality which I call jurisprudential temperament, or the judge's intuition, comes into play.[44] This temperament invariably influences the decision. It inclines the decision one way or another. It is a major determinant of whether the case is controlled by precedent or settled law. That is to say, this temperament determines whether the result is found in the jurisprudence, or whether the result requires a choice between two competing precepts, also in the jurisprudence, or whether the case requires movement to square one—recourse to first principles.[45] In the federal courts, especially in constitutional law spinoffs in actions brought under 42 U.S.C. § 1983, the judge's view of the role of the court is all-important. There is probably more subjectivity brought into play in these cases, more activity on the intuition scale, than in any other aspect of the law. Much of this problem can be laid at the door of the Supreme Court because it has served up a mishmash that furnishes no identifiable criteria as to what are garden variety common law torts dressed in the tinsel and glitter of fourteenth amendment deprivations and what are truly important and,

* R. Aldisert, *Philosophy, Jurisprudence and Jurisprudential Temperament of Federal Judges,* 20 Ind.L.Rev. 453, 465–68 (1987).

44. Jurisprudential temperament is not to be confused with the more familiar judicial temperament, the lawyer's evaluation of the judge's demeanor in open court. The lawyer's universal perception of the judge with ideal judicial temperament is the one described by West Virginia Justice Richard Neely: "colorless, odorless, and tasteless." R. Neely, *How Courts Govern America* 213 (1981). It is a judge who is always patient and courteous, who never interrupts a lawyer, never asks a question, never raises his voice, never frowns, and always smiles. Under these criteria, Oliver Wendell Holmes, Learned Hand, and Roger J. Traynor would have passed into oblivion. *See* Aldisert, *What Makes a Good Appellate Judge,* Judges J., Spring 1983, at 14 (appellate judges should strive to attain the qualities of: fairness, justness, impartiality; de-

votion and decisiveness; clear thought and expression; professional literacy; institutional fidelity; and political responsibility).

45. What Judge Walter V. Schaefer said in a related context closely approximates the judge's intuition thermometer, or what I am describing as jurisprudential temperament:

> [M]ost depends upon the judge's unspoken notion as to the function of his court. If he views the role of the court as a passive one, he will be willing to delegate the responsibility for change, and he will not greatly care whether the delegated authority is exercised or not. If he views the court as an instrument of society designed to reflect in its decisions the morality of the community, he will be more likely to look precedent in the teeth and to measure it against the ideals and the aspirations of his time.

Schaefer, *Precedent and Policy* 34 U.Chi. L.Rev. 3 (1966).

to use a favorite word, "fundamental" rights. To federal circuit and district judges, this may be what Winston Churchill is reported to have said of a pudding someone served him: it seems to lack a theme.[46]

Yet I hasten to add that federal court decisionmaking is not subjectivity run rampant. In terms of numbers, quite the contrary is true.

Most tasks, perhaps eighty to ninety percent, involve a kind of mechanical process: the law and its application alike are clear; or the law is clear and the sole question is its application to the facts. The results in these cases are often predetermined, some, from the instant the complaint is filed. But where the result is not predetermined and the law is not clear, the courts are faced with what Hart called the "penumbral" cases, where the language of the legislation or the Constitution is intentionally general.

For now we must recognize that some statutory language is inevitably vague because the legislator who can anticipate and decide all the particular cases that will fall under a given statute has yet to be born.

Whether judges must, in certain cases, resort to a penumbral area of the law reflects a value judgment and is indicative of the judge's jurisprudential temperament. Some judges have lower thresholds than others, and are more inclined to find solace in shades and fringes rather than the black letter law. But when they so function, it means that they have exhausted the guidance that hefty, hearty precedents can give and they feel that they must turn to other resources. These resources are found in the body of first or supereminent principles, legal or moral, that form the body of legal philosophy. Dworkin suggested that when this occurs, the decision depends "on the judge's own preferences among a sea of respectable extralegal standards, any one in principle eligible, because if that were the case we could not say that any rules were binding."[51] In this respect, the nature of the temperament may be reflected by the particular choice of moral values offered by diverse philosophers. Those whom we may call the naturalists will claim that law is best explained by reference to natural moral principles, principles inherent in the notion of an ideal society and the moral potentiality of persons. Yet Austinian positivists will claim that law is best understood formally as a system of orders, commands, or rules enforced by power. Moreover, although consistency is required of a legal system, that is to say, stated reasons in the cases must be consistent with legal or moral principles, the collection of private moral decisions by judges need not necessarily be consistent. The judge may pick and choose in various cases among the various philosophies expressed by our writers and

46. *Quoted in* Fried, *Correspondence: Author's Reply*, 86 Yale L.J. 573, 584 (1977). A dimension of the jurisprudential temperament encountered in our judges can be illustrated by a playwright's attribution to Saint Thomas More: "The law, Roper, the law. I know what's legal, not what's right.... I'm not God. The currents and eddies of right and wrong, which you find such plain-sailing, I can't navigate, I'm no voyager." R. Bolt, A Man for All Seasons (1966).

51. R. Dworkin, Taking Rights Seriously (1977).

judges, one time following a rights theorist, another time, a garden variety Benthamite.

But to understand jurisprudential temperament is to recognize that the judge's initial reaction as to whether a case is controlled by precedent (or by unambiguous statutory language) or comes within what Hart called the penumbral area is itself a gauge of that temperament.[52] As I said before, we judges have different thresholds, or as Emerson said, "We boil at different degrees."[53] What makes a case controversial or difficult at times is precisely this difference. It makes the difference whether a utilitarian weighing of material benefits is preempted by a right. Dworkin offers some advice here. A useful definition of a hard case is one in which existing case law and statutes, the presence of precedents and other immediately relevant rules of decision, tend to generate or fit a result that offends the judge's intuitions about benefit and harm. These are the intuitions that constitute his temperament. Yet these reactions should not be mechanical, as the label-tossers of "liberal" and "conservative" would have us believe. Nor should they be unpredictable. Our legal system is both a system and a history of reasons; reasons that judges have given for past determinations and reasons that embody many conceptions of human nature. The judge's matured decision must be informed by this history. His own determination of benefit and harm will be informed by consulting the justifications offered by other judges in other relevant opinions. Dworkin described this task as an ideal, and stated that it demands a judicial Hercules.

But alas, we are not all Hercules. Judges are merely human beings. The inflow from the cumulative experience of the judiciary mixes with what is already in the judge's mind. What is already there is an accumulation of personal experience including tendencies, prejudices, and maybe biases. I don't mean conscious biases, but the unconscious ones that any person may have and which the judge cannot eradicate because he does not know they are there. One of these may be a bias in favor of the justice or equity of the particular case and against any precedent or law that seems to deny it. This is an example of temperament. When such a feeling dominates, the judge's mental notes may emphasize those facts that he deems to be significant; the insignificant, being omitted, will disappear from his memory. The facts will be molded to fit the justice of the case, what Lord Devlin calls "the aequum et bonum,"[56] and the law will be stretched. Yet another judge may possess the same intensity of justice for the case, but will refuse to stretch the law, and instead state, "We are constrained to hold...." In

52. Lord Denning, a British cousin, tells us exactly where his temperament stands on the gauge:

What is the argument on the other side? Only this, that no case has been found in which it has been done before. That argument does not appeal to me in the least. If we never do anything which is not done before, we shall never get any-

where. The law will stand still whilst the rest of the world goes on: and that will be bad for both.

Packer v. Packer [1953] All E.R. 127, 129.

53. R.W. Emerson, Society and Solitude 92 (1870).

56. Devlin, The Judge 84–116 (1974).

these two cases, the feelings of justice are the same. But disparate jurisprudential temperaments command different results.

ROSCOE POUND, THE THEORY OF JUDICIAL DECISION *

Dividing our process of decision, as apart from the duty of providing a well considered precedent, into the three steps, finding the law, interpreting the legal material selected, and applying the resulting legal precept to the cause, let us look into the first of these, the process of finding or selection, and ask what it involves, as the process actually goes on. It may involve nothing more than a selection from among fixed precepts of determined content calling only for a mechanical ascertainment of whether the facts fit the rule. Such is the case when a tribunal looks to an instrument to see whether it contains the words of negotiability required by the Negotiable Instruments Law or by the law merchant, or when it looks to a conveyance to see whether it contains the formal covenant of warranty without which at common law one may not hold his grantor. Or it may involve selection from competing analogies, urged by the respective parties as the ground of decision. Here, as it were, there is to be an inductive selection. Or it may involve selection by logical development of conceptions or principles. Here, as it were, there is a deductive selection. If these fail, it calls for selection from outside of the legal system in whole or in part—from custom, from comparative law, from morals, or from economics.

KENNETH CULP DAVIS, THE FUTURE OF JUDGE–MADE PUBLIC LAW IN ENGLAND: A PROBLEM OF PRACTICAL JURISPRUDENCE *

On most matters of private law, it may be more important that the law be settled than that it be settled correctly. Therefore, governing most matters of private law by the ideas of men long dead is usually not only satisfactory but may sometimes be affirmatively desirable. But on problems of public law, which at any given time are especially difficult, creating law that will benefit living people is far more important than that the law be settled. Therefore, on most matters of public law, being governed by the ideas of men long dead is unsatisfactory and may be even abominable.

All judge-made law is made up of two major ingredients—application of logic to the authoritative materials (precedents and statutes) and considerations of policy. The relative effect of each of the two major

* 36 Harv.L.Rev. 940, 947–49 (1923). Copyright © 1923 by The Harvard Law Review Association. Reprinted by permission.

* 61 Colum.L.Rev. 201, 211–15 (1961). Reprinted by permission.

ingredients should be a variable and should not be allowed to become fixed. In property law, the weight given precedents and logic should be relatively large. In many matters of public law, the weight given considerations of policy should be relatively large. The determination of how much weight to give to each of the two major elements in any case is itself a question of policy to be determined by the court.

NOTE

Does Davis define "private" and "public" law? Is the division easy of demarcation? Consider a class action by prisoners against a warden asking injunctive relief from living conditions brought under the Civil Rights Act, 42 U.S.C.A. § 1983. Is this "private" or "public" law?

Do you agree that "[i]n most matters of private law, it may be more important that law be settled than settled correctly?" Consider Fuentes v. Shevin, 407 U.S. 67 (1972), Mitchell v. W.T. Grant Co., 416 U.S. 600 (1974), and North Georgia Finishing Inc. v. Di–Chem, Inc., 419 U.S. 601 (1975).

HARLAN F. STONE, THE COMMON LAW IN THE UNITED STATES *

Distinguishing characteristics [of the common law] are its development of law by a system of judicial precedent, its use of the jury to decide issues of fact, and its all-pervading doctrine of the supremacy of law— that the agencies of government are no more free than the private individual to act according to their own arbitrary will or whim, but must conform to legal rules developed and applied by courts....

... [P]erhaps the most significant feature of the common law, past and present, and the essential element in its historic growth, the fact that it is preëminently a system built up by gradual accretion of special instances.

With the common law, unlike the civil law and its Roman law precursor, the formulation of general principles has not preceded decision. In its origin it is the law of the practitioner rather than the philosopher. Decision has drawn its inspiration and its strength from the very facts which frame the issues for decision. Once made, the decision controls the future judgments of courts in like or analogous cases. General rules, underlying principles, and finally legal doctrine, have successively emerged only as the precedents, accumulated through the centuries, have been seen to follow a pattern, characteristically not without distortion and occasional broken threads, and seldom conforming consistently to principle.

* 50 Harv.L.Rev. 4, 5–7 (1936). Copyright © 1936 by The Harvard Law Review Association. Reprinted by permission.

Lord Macmillan, in a recent address at Cambridge University on "Two Ways of Thinking", classifies civilized peoples of the Western World, as the two great systems of law have substantially divided them, into those who think inductively and those who think deductively, a difference which, he holds, has pervaded the history of all human thought and activity. We will not be inclined to challenge his conclusion that the habit of mind which is content to make a workable decision suitable to the case in hand, without bothering too much about principle, or pressing matters to a logical extreme, has exercised a profound influence on law, politics and government in the common-law countries, and has given to these institutions a certain stability and continuity, not without adaptability, of great practical worth. But there are some, even among those trained in the common law, who may share the doubts, which he suggests, whether a rigid adherence to the doctrine of *stare decisis* is needful in order to attain these ends, and, in any case, whether continuity of legal doctrine is worth the price which, in some periods of our legal history, we have paid for it. The Continental lawyer, when told that a judicial decision reported in the Year Books is not only sufficient for the purpose, but actually controls decision upon like events in the present year of our Lord, is openly skeptical of a system by which the living are thus ruled by the dead, and he is ready to echo the pungent remark of Mr. Justice Holmes that "It is revolting to have no better reason for a rule of law than that so it was laid down in the time of Henry IV."

I do not propose to enter the lists in the never-ending debate on the merits of a system which, to some extent, places precedent above principle, as compared with another in which formulated principle is the controlling guide to decision. It is enough, for present purposes, if we recognize that its strength is derived from the manner in which it has been forged from actual experience by the hammer and anvil of litigation, and that the source of its weakness lies in the fact that law guided by precedent which has grown out of one type of experience can only slowly and with difficulty be adapted to new types which the changing scene may bring. Whatever its defects, the system, deep rooted in our tradition and habit of mind, after serving us for some six centuries, will not be discarded. In the rôle of critics and prophets we will do well to accept that as the probable verdict of history....

CHARLES A. MILLER, PRINCIPLES OF ADJUDICATION *

"If you have the decision," a judge is quoted as saying, "reasons will

* Charles A. Miller, The Supreme Court and The Uses of History 14–18 (1969). Excerpted by permission of the author and publishers from pp. 14–18 of The Supreme Court and the Uses of History by Charles A. Miller, Cambridge, Mass.: The Belknap Press of Harvard University Press, Copyright © 1969 by the President and Fellows of Harvard College.

be found to be as plentiful as blackberries." [18] The judge is as correct as his analogy: blackberries, even when plentiful, may be unripe or over-ripe, and they are always surrounded by thorns. In constructing a judicial opinion, in other words, one must be careful to pluck only the appropriate reasons and to go about it in the least painful manner. As Justice Holmes once warned: "Every question of construction is unique, and an argument that would prevail in one case may be inadequate in another." [19]

Although the judicial opinion is written with a foregone conclusion in mind, it is written in a carefully arranged order so that its arguments, separately and together, support the conclusion in a way that is natural to our ways of thinking about law. This "naturalness" is primarily a matter of social and legal conditioning. But it also contains elements of an informal logic, a logic of presentation. The logic of presentation resembles only faintly a sequence of "if-then" statements; it is perhaps nearer the classical study of rhetoric. This logic is a pattern of argument, usually including several separate lines of reasoning, that leads to a single conclusion. Each of the paths may be considered as a principle of adjudication in the sense of being a vehicle for deciding cases. Principles of adjudication as vehicles in constitutional law include the constitutional text, constitutional and other legal doctrines, precedent, social facts, and history. In view of the purpose of this study the first four of these will be given relatively brief treatment.

Constitutional text. The first step in the construction of written documents, whether literary or legal, is to consult the document itself. If a legal document is supposed to control the outcome of a case and its unadorned text is perfectly plain, then legal interpretation stops right there. It is difficult to disagree with Justice Noah Swayne's remark a century ago: "If the language be clear it is conclusive. There can be no construction where there is nothing to construe." [21] But as Justice Holmes stated, this is "rather an axiom of experience than a rule of law," and very few cases have come to a conclusion in as short order as the axiom suggests.[22] Although some causes of the Constitution are perfectly clear today, most have required considerable interpretation. The constitutional text continues as the touchstone of interpretation, but it is not by itself sufficient as a principle of adjudication.

Doctrine. Constitutional doctrines are formulas extracted from a combination of the constitutional text and a series of related cases. Typically stated in shorthand fashion, they may be used almost as an emendation on the constitutional text. A good example of a constitutional doctrine developed in the nineteenth century is the "Cooley doctrine," which set at rest the pendulum swings of Supreme Court

18. The judge is quoted in J. Walter Jones, *Historical Introduction to the Theory of Law* (Oxford: Clarendon Press, 1965), p. 195.

19. United States v. Jin Fuey Moy, 241 U.S. 394, 402 (1916).

21. United States v. Hartwell, 6 Wall. 385, 396 (1868). [*ante,* p. 216]

22. Boston Sand and Gravel Co. v. United States, 278 U.S. 41, 48 (1928).

opinion on the extent to which states could exercise control over interstate commerce in the absence of congressional legislation. The Cooley doctrine forbids states to legislate on subjects that are "in their nature national, or admit only of one uniform system, or plan of regulation." An example of a twentieth-century doctrine is that of "one person, one vote," the simplest expression of the meaning of the fourteenth amendment with respect to legislative apportionment.

Neither the Cooley doctrine nor the apportionment rule is self-interpreting. But as doctrines they are intermediaries between the Constitution and a case that may come before the Court. Once established they may be resorted to as principles of adjudication with high authority. Because their purpose is to relate the abstractions, generalizations, or obscurities of the Constitution to the concreteness of a case, constitutional doctrines are subject to some flexibility and adaptability without becoming either verbal ornament (as the text of the Constitution may appear to be) or dead-end conclusions (as the outcome of a single case often is).

Precedent. One of the distinctive features of the common law system is the use of precedent, or previously decided cases, in the determination of later cases. Precedents may be used as examples or as sources of insight into particular legal problems. But they may also become binding legal authority for later cases which a court considers similar. When this happens, the court is following the doctrine of stare decisis. In constitutional law stare decisis has been applied with much less rigor than in other fields of law, on the theoretical ground that it is the Constitution which is the basic standard and not the previous decisions of the Court. The practical justification for the ease with which precedent, as stare decisis, is ignored in constitutional law is that constitutional cases deal with momentous social and political issues that only temporarily take the form of litigation, and these issues cannot be dealt with on the same terms as other legal problems. Constitutional law has great need for the continuity and certainty that the doctrine of stare decisis can provide, and precedents have been dispensed with only over strong dissent. But since constitutional law depends even more on its soundness than its firmness, in a conflict between precedent and progress, precedent will, more quickly than in other fields of law, yield to progress.

Social evidence. Since its earliest days the Supreme Court has taken notice of social facts in its opinions and has used them as a principle of constitutional adjudication. But only in the twentieth century has the principle become generally recognized and, at the same time, the subject of controversy.

Social and economic legislation of both state and federal governments, beginning in the late nineteenth century, has provided the chief test of the Supreme Court's willingness to recognize the significance of factual situations in constitutional adjudication. In the *Lochner* case the Court declared invalid a New York law limiting the working hours of bakers, with the assertion that the legislation involved "neither the safety, the morals, nor the welfare of the public." [30] To overcome such an outlook on welfare legislation, Louis Brandeis presented a brief (in a case decided three years later) which contained more than a hundred pages of statistics and other documentary material in support of the reasonableness of a state labor law affecting women. The Brandeis brief succeeded. The Court agreed that the mass of evidence was persuasive in determining "the extent to which a special constitutional limitation" would go, even though "technically speaking" the evidence was not constitutional authority.[31]

The Brandeis brief did not assume that all constitutional limitations could be overcome by evidence from the social world. This, indeed, offers theoretical justification for the failure of the technique in many cases where it has been applied. It did succeed, however, in the watershed decision between the "old" and "new" Courts in 1937, and this victory was its undoing.[32] In the new era, when the Court assumed that social legislation was constitutional rather than unconstitutional, the Brandeis brief was no longer necessary. When the burden of argument fell to those who had to prove a negative (that a statute was invalid on the grounds of factual evidence), the task became almost impossible.

NOTE

Is Miller using "principles of adjudication" in the same sense as Pound? "Doctrine"?

Apropos the statement, "In constitutional law stare decisis has been applied with much less rigor than in other fields of law, on the theoretical ground that it is the Constitution which is the basic standard and not the previous decisions of the Court," see Justice Rehnquist's dissenting opinion in Fry v. United States, 421 U.S. 542, 559 (1975):

> The overruling of a case such as Maryland v. Wirtz [392 U.S. 183 (1968)] quite obviously should not be lightly undertaken. But we have the authority of Chief Justice Taney in The Passenger Cases, 7 How. 283, 470, of Mr. Justice Brandeis in Burnet v. Coronado Oil & Gas Co., 285 U.S. 393, 406–411 (1932), and Mr. Justice Douglas in New York v. United States, [326 U.S. 572 (1946)] at 590–591, for the proposition that important decisions of constitutional law are not subject to the same command of *stare decisis* as are decisions of statutory questions. Surely there can be

---

30. Lochner v. New York, 198 U.S. 45, 57 (1905).

31. Muller v. Oregon, 208 U.S. 412, 420–21 (1908).

32. For five members of the Court, Chief Justice Hughes wrote: "We may take judicial notice of the unparalleled demands for relief which arose during the recent period of depression and still continue to an alarming extent despite the degree of economic recovery which has been achieved." West Coast Hotel Co. v. Parrish, 300 U.S. 379, 399 (1937). The conservative minority succinctly but unavailingly replied: "The meaning of the Constitution does not change with the ebb and flow of economic events." 300 U.S. at 402.

no more fundamental constitutional question than that of the intention of the Framers of the Constitution as to how authority should be allocated between the National and State Governments. I believe that re-examination of the issue decided in Maryland v. Wirtz would lead us to the conclusion that the judgment of the Temporary Emergency Court of Appeals in this case should be reversed.

Consider Miller's assertion that in constructing a judicial opinion, one must be careful to pluck only the appropriate reasons. Is this an intellectually honest way of judging? Is it necessary?

Section 2

USE OF LOGIC *

"Fragile as reason is and limited as law is as the expression of the institutionalized medium of reason, that's all we have standing between us and the tyranny of mere will and the cruelty of unbridled, unprincipled, undisciplined feeling."
Felix Frankfurter [1]

To state that a decision is based on logic or is logical may be ambiguous. Canons of logic are essentially concerned with the conditions of formal correctness as distinguished from desirability or preference. It concerns the relations between propositions rather than the content of the propositions themselves. Logic so described refers to an instrumental use, a structured, syllogistic form, or what Professor Dewey labels a "logic of rigid demonstration" or "formal consistence, consistency of concepts with one another." [2] Logic, as an instrument, structures the exposition and is utilized with other jurisprudential tools—history, custom, or sociology—as a device to relate selected premises to a conclusion. In the judicial process logic is what Cardozo described as the rule of analogy. It utilizes analogy to extend application of a legal precept to a different set of facts, including the extension of a precedent to sets of facts in which the social implications may be quite different from any which the precedents have considered. Thus, it becomes important to understand separate meanings of logic in the law. What is meant in Holmes' classic statement, "The life of the law has not been logic; it has been experience", must be distinguished from what Cardozo described as the "line of logical progression; . . . the rule of analogy or the method of philosophy."

Clearly, value judgments affect the resolution of the three flashpoints of legal conflicts: finding the law to formulate the major premise,

---

* Adapted from R.J. Aldisert, Logic For Lawyers: A Guide to Clear Legal Thinking (1989) and *Precedent: What It Is and What It Isn't; When Do We Kiss It and When Do We Kill It,* 17 Pepperdine L.Rev. 605 (1990).

1. On his retirement after 23 years on the U.S. Supreme Court, as quoted in Time Magazine, September 7, 1962 at 15.

2. J. Dewey, *Logical Method and Law* 10 Cornell L. Quarterly 17, 20–21 (1924).

interpreting the precept as chosen, and applying the chosen and interpreted precept to facts found by the fact finder.

Involved here is an interrelationship between terms that sound alike, but whose meanings diverge in the decisional process: "reasonable" and "reasoning." A judge's decision on the choice, interpretation, and application of a legal precept involves a value judgment justifiable in his or her mind because the decision is "reasonable," in the sense that it is fair, just, sound, and sensible. One judge may believe that it is "reasonable" to maintain the law in harmony with existing circumstances and precedents, and accede to the magnetic appeal of consistency in the law; another may assert that the issue should be considered pragmatically, and will respond only to its practical consequences. What is "reasonable" in given circumstances may permit endless differences of opinion, and this is how it should be. The inevitably varying views found in multi-judge courts is one of the most vitalizing traditions animating the growth of common law.

Determining what is "reasonable" is closely related to the overarching process called "reasoning," or solving a problem by pondering a given set of facts to perceive their relationship and reach a logical conclusion. The application of "reasonableness" to "reasoning" is an ever-recurring scenario: If A has been found to be liable in set of circumstances B, we have to decide, often without an exact precedent to guide us, whether A is also liable if B obtains plus or minus circumstances C. To do this we must determine which facts are material. Given the situation that A is liable if set of circumstances B applies, we must decide if plus or minus circumstances C is material or immaterial.

Thus, it is critically important to use logical, reflective thinking in the law, for the logical process is the cement that binds the determination of "reasonableness" with the statement of "reasons." "Reasons" merely are the explanation or justification of an act. Judges and lawyers give "reasons" to prove that their conclusion reflects "reasonableness." "Reasons" are the "how" in the process; "reasonableness" is the "why." "Reasons" are the logical premises that justify the desired conclusion of "reasonableness." What is used to coalesce "reasons" and "reasonableness" is "reasoning," which we know as the "logical process."

It is necessary to remember that logical order in the law is an instrumentality, not an end. John Dewey wrote that it is "a means of improving, facilitating, clarifying the inquiry that leads up to concrete decisions; primarily that particular inquiry which has just been engaged in, but secondarily, and of greater ultimate importance, other inquiries directed at making other decisions in similar fields. We have emphasized that, unlike in mathematics and science, there are few immutable major premises in the law." [3]

In the common law tradition, as we have seen, the logic of the law is neither all deductive nor all inductive. It is a circular process. First, as

---

3. J. Dewey, How We Think 19 (2d ed. 1933).

cases are compared, that is, as resemblances and differences are noted, a legal precept is created. Next there is a period when the precept becomes more or less fixed. A further stage takes place when the "new" precept becomes "old" and breaks down, or evolves, as new cases are decided. Inductive reasoning figures in the first stage—the creation of the precept; deductive reasoning is used in refining the created precept and in applying it to the facts before the court; inductive reasoning appears again at a later stage, when efforts are made in subsequent cases to break down the precept.

This being so, what form of reasoning do we discuss first? As we have explained, the common law develops from specific narrow rules to broader precepts, a classic process of inductive reasoning. Yet, to understand induction, it is best first to learn deduction. Hence we put the deductive cart before the inductive horse with some introductory observations on deductive reasoning.

Deductive Reasoning

Deductive reasoning is a mental operation that a law student, lawyer, or judge must employ every working day of his or her life. Formal deductive logic is an act of the mind in which, from the relation of two propositions to each other, we infer, that is, we understand and affirm, a third proposition. In deductive reasoning, the two propositions which imply the third proposition, the conclusion, are called premises. The broad proposition that forms the starting point of deduction is called the major premise; the second proposition is called the minor premise. They have these titles because the major premise represents the all; the minor premise, something or someone included in the all.

Logical argument is a means of determining the truth or falsity of a purported conclusion. We do this by following well-established canons of logical order in a deliberate and intentional fashion. In law we simply must think and reason logically. We must follow a thought process that emancipates us from impulsively jumping to conclusions, or from argument supported only by strongly felt emotions or superstitions. That which John Dewey said for the benefit of teachers in generations past is still vital and important today: Reflective thought "converts action that is merely appetitive, blind, and impulsive into intelligent action." [4]

The classic means of deductive reasoning is the syllogism. Aristotle, who first formulated its theory, offered this definition: "A syllogism is discourse in which, certain things being stated, something other than what is stated follows of necessity from their being so." [5] He continued: "I mean by the last phrase that they produce the consequence, and by this, that no further term is required from without to make the consequence necessary." [6] From this definition we can say that a syllogism is

---

4. J. Dewey, How We Think 17 (2d ed. 1933).

5. L. Stebbing, A Modern Introduction to Logic 81 (6th ed. 1948) (quoting Anal. Priora at 24b).

6. Id. (quoting Anal. Priora at 18).

a form of implication in which two propositions jointly imply a third.[7]

Special rules of the syllogism serve to inform exactly under what circumstances one proposition can be inferred from two other propositions. Consider the classic syllogism:

All men are mortal.

Socrates is a man.

Therefore, Socrates is mortal.

This is a *categorical syllogism,* an argument having three propositions—two premises and a conclusion. A categorical syllogism contains exactly three terms or class names, each of which occurs in two of the three constituent propositions. A few definitions such as these propositions and terms appear in the judicial process: [8]

- The *major term* is the predicate term of the conclusion, and of the major premise.
- The *minor term* is the subject term of the conclusion, and of the minor premise.
- The *middle term* does not appear in the conclusion, but must appear in each of the two other propositions.
- The *major premise* is the premise containing the major term.
- The *minor premise* is the premise containing the minor term.

Because the first proposition contains the major, or larger, term, it is called the *major premise.* Because the second contains the minor, or smaller, term, it is called the *minor premise,* the lesser statement laid down. Because it follows from the major and minor premises the third proposition is called the *conclusion.* In the standard form categorical syllogism as used in the law, the major premise is stated first, the minor premise second, and finally the conclusion. Returning to our classic syllogism:

Major premise:	All men are mortal
Major term:	Mortal
Middle term:	All men
Minor premise:	Socrates is a man
Minor term:	Socrates
Middle term:	Man
Conclusion:	Therefore, Socrates is mortal
Minor term:	Socrates
Major term:	Mortal

Let us parse this syllogism identifying its parts:

Major premise: The subject, "all men" (the middle term); the predicate "are mortal" (the major term).

---

7. Id.

8. To be sure, other forms of the categorical syllogism appear in variations of subjects and predicates, but this form illustrates the general appearance for an understanding of fundamentals.

Minor premise: The subject, "Socrates" (the minor term); the predicate "is a man" (the middle term).

Conclusion: Therefore "Socrates" (the minor term) "is a man" (the major term).

Some helpful hints derive from the foregoing rules: the middle term ("all men") may always be known by the fact that it does not occur in the conclusion. The major term ("mortal") is always the predicate of the conclusion. The minor term ("Socrates") is always the subject of the conclusion.

A universal proposition (e.g., "all offers in contract law") is described as containing a "distributed subject term." A particular proposition (e.g., "some offers in contract law") has an "undistributed subject term." Thus, logicians say that whatever is predicated of a distributed term (all men are mortal), whether affirmatively or negatively, may be predicated in like manner of everything contained under it (*Socrates* is mortal). For purposes of law, we say that what is incorporated in a general proposition (conveyances of land must be in writing) is also true in a specific of that proposition (this conveyance of land must be in writing). To put it simply, what pertains to the higher class pertains also to the lower one.

Logicians refer to six rules for categorical syllogisms.[9] We will use the formulations of Professor Copi:

Rule 1: A valid categorical syllogism must contain exactly three terms, each of which is used in the same sense throughout the argument.

Rule 2: In a valid categorical syllogism, the middle term must be distributed in at least one premise.

Rule 3: In a valid categorical syllogism, no term can be distributed in the conclusion which is not distributed in the premise.

Rule 4: No categorical syllogism is valid which has two negative premises.

Rule 5: If either premise of a valid categorical syllogism is negative, the conclusion must be negative.

Rule 6: No valid categorical syllogism with a particular conclusion can have two universal premises.

A departure from these rules results in a fallacy of form, or formal fallacy. Unfortunately, such fallacies occur frequently in oral arguments, written briefs and judges' opinions. For a syllogism to be effective, however, more is necessary than proper logical form. The major premise must be correct. If, under analysis, the major premise falls, so does the conclusion.

9. See Copi, Introduction to Logic 217–222 (7th ed. 1986); W. Jevons, Elementary Lessons in Logic: Deductive and Inductive 127–29 (1870); L. Stebbing, A Modern Introduction to Logic 87–88 (6th ed. 1948); J. Creighton, An Introductory Logic 139 (1898); R. Eaton, General Logic, An Introductory Survey 95–100 (1931); J. Cooley, A Primer of Formal Logic 306 (1942).

Consider, the following syllogism:

All federal judges have green blood.

Judge X is a federal judge.

Therefore, Judge X has green blood.

Does this syllogism contain logical order or logical validity or cogency? Before responding, consider the following:

- We can always appraise a specific argument from the sole vantage of its reasoning to determine whether or not it is valid (or cogent), without at the same time troubling ourselves over the truth and falsity of its premise.

- We can always appraise a specific argument from the sole vantage of the truth and falsity of its premises, without troubling ourselves over the validity or cogency of its reasoning.

- Whenever we appraise an argument to determine whether we ought to accept it and its conclusion, we must do both of these things. Arguments that have both valid or cogent reasoning and true premises, are sound arguments.

- Thus, an argument fails to be sound, and we ought not to accept its conclusion, if either, (i) the reasoning it employs from premises to conclusion is not acceptable, or (ii) one or more of its premises is false.

The "All federal judges have green blood" syllogism is an example of a valid cogent argument that contains false premises.

Inductive Reasoning

Deductive reasoning and adherence to the Socrates-is-a-man type of syllogism is only one of the major components of the common law logic tradition. Inductive reasoning is equally important. In legal logic, it is very often used to fashion either the major or the minor premises of the deductive syllogism.

In legal analysis, often a statute or specific constitutional provision qualifies as the controlling major premise. It is the law of the case, with which the facts (minor term) will be compared, so as to reach a decision (conclusion). Where no clear rule is present, however, it is necessary to draw upon the experience of the judiciary to fashion a proper major premise from existing legal rules, and specific holdings of other cases. This is done by inductive reasoning. Deductive reasoning moves by inference from the more general, to the less general, to the particular. Inductive reasoning moves from the particular to the general, or from the particular to the particular. In law, as in general logic, there is a fundamental difference between the deductive and inductive reasoning.

- In deduction, the connection between a given piece of information and another piece of information concluded from it is a necessary connection.

- In a valid deductive argument, if the premises are true, the conclusion *must* be true.

- In induction, the connection between given pieces of information and another piece inferred from them is *not* a logically necessary connection.

- In a valid inductive argument, the conclusion is not necessarily an absolute truth; by induction, we reach a conclusion that is *more probably* true than not.

In the law, the method of arriving at a general or, in the logician's language, a universal proposition (a principle or doctrine) from the particular facts of experience (legal rules or holdings of cases) is called *inductive generalization*. This is reasoning from the particular to the general.

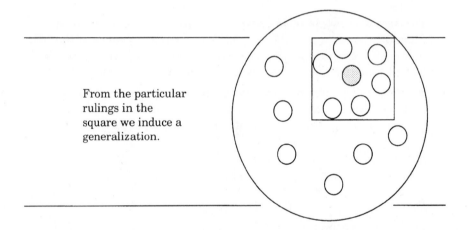

From the particular rulings in the square we induce a generalization.

We borrow this process from the certainty of scientific laboratory experiments. If nine particular pieces of blue litmus paper turn red when dipped in acid, we may draw a general conclusion about what happens to all blue litmus paper dipped in acid. We use the technique of *enumeration* to reach an inductive generalization. Unlike in science, however, in law we do not assert that our conclusion is true, only that it is more probably true than not.[10]

---

10. But see K. Popper, Conjectures and Refutations: The Growth of Scientific Knowledge vii (1962) ("The way in which knowledge progresses, and especially our scientific knowledge, is by unjustified (and unjustifiable) anticipations, by guesses, by tentative solutions to our problems, by con-*jectures*. These conjectures are controlled by criticism; that is, by attempted *refutations,* which include severely critical tests. They may survive these tests; but they can never be positively justified: they can neither be established as certainly true nor even as 'probable.' ")

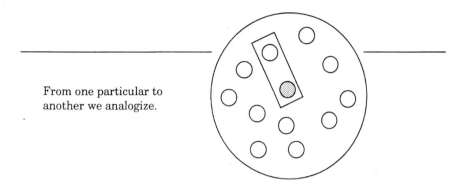

From one particular to
another we analogize.

The structure of these two types of inductive arguments—induced generalization and analogy—is similar. There is, however, a basic difference, extremely important in the law, when the premises contain a number of instances in which the certain attributes occur together.

- By inductive generalization we may infer that every instance of the one attribute will also be an instance of the other.

- By analogy we may infer that a difference particular instance of one attribute will also exhibit the other attribute.

Let us examine *inductive generalization* in the law;

A's oral conveyance of real estate is invalid.

B's oral conveyance of real estate is invalid.

C's oral conveyance of real estate is invalid.

Z's oral conveyance of real estate is invalid.

Therefore, all oral conveyances of real estate are invalid.

Inferences proceed on the assumption that the new instances will resemble the old one in all material circumstances. This is purely hypothetical, and sometimes we discover we are mistaken. Thus, for years we proceeded along the following induction:

A is a swan and it is white.

B is a swan and it is white.

C is a swan and it is white.

  . . .

Z is a swan and it is white.

Therefore, all swans are white.

But then explorers discovered Australia and it was learned that there are swans that are black. Inductive generalization underlies the development of the common law. From many specific case holdings, we reach a generalized proposition.

From the rules we create principles:

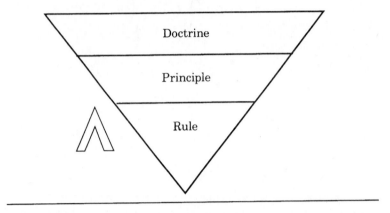

From many cases deciding that individual oral conveyances of real estate were invalid, we reached the conclusion that all such conveyances were invalid. We arrived at that point by what Lord Diplock described as "the cumulative experience of the judiciary." [11] In generalization by enumeration, we can say that the larger the number of specific instances, the more certain the resulting generalization. This simply bodes fealty to the concept of probability. It is the common law tradition of creating a principle by connecting the dots.

The process of *analogy* is a little different. Analogy does not seek proof of an identity of one thing with another, but only a comparison of resemblances. Unlike the technique of enumeration, analogy does not depend upon the *quantity* of instances, but upon the *quality* of resemblances between things. J.S. Mill reduced it to a formula: Two things resemble each other in one or more respects; a certain proposition is true of one; therefore, it is true of the other.[12] In legal analogies, we may have two cases which resemble each other in a great many properties, and we infer that some additional property in one will be found in the other. The process of analogy is used on a case-by-case basis. It is used to compare the resemblance of prior cases to the case at bar. Reaching a conclusion by enumeration has the benefit of experience. Reaching a conclusion by analogy has the benefit of the high degree of similarity of the compared data.

The degree of similarity is always the crucial inquiry in analogies. Clearly, one cannot conclude that a partial resemblance between two entities is equal to an entire and exact correspondence. Here the skill of the advocate will often be the determining factor. The plaintiff's lawyer

11. Home Office v. Dorset Yacht Co., 1970 App.Cas. 1004, 1058 (Lord Diplock).

12. See J. Mill, A System of Logic Ratiocinative and Inductive 98–142 (8th ed. 1916).

may argue that the historical event or entity in the putative precedent, Alpha, bears many resemblances to the case at bar, Beta. The defense will argue that although the facts in Alpha and Beta are similar in some respects, this does not mean that those similarities are material and, therefore, relevant, or argue that the cases are dissimilar in other respects. He or she will argue that a false analogy is present.

What is one attorney's material and relevant fact in analogical comparisons is another attorney's immaterial and irrelevant fact. Often the art of advocacy resolves itself into convincing the court which facts in previous cases are indeed positive analogies and which are not. The judge is required to draw this distinction. The successful lawyer is one who is able to convince the judge to draw the distinction in the manner most favorable to his or her client.

Fallacies

Logicians and members of the legal profession generally use the term "fallacy" in a narrow sense, to describe a type of incorrect argument, rather than use the word in the lay sense as a false or erroneous statement. It is used to describe a flaw in the purported relations between several statements. There are several types of fallacies. One type of fallacy occurs when we neglect the rules of logic and fall into erroneous reasoning, often from true factual premises. Other fallacies, generally called informal or material fallacies, meticulously follow logical form but suffer from improper content or emphasis. A fallacy, then, is not merely an error, but a way of falling into an error. The name comes from the Latin, "fallax," which suggests a deliberate deception. But most fallacies are not intentional. Fallacies are dangerous, however, because they are false conclusions or interpretations resulting from processes of thinking that claim or appear to be valid, but fail to conform to the requirements of logic.[13] A fallacy can be defined as a form of argument that seems to be correct but which proves upon examination not to be so. They have been identified as such ever since Aristotle described these arguments: "That some reasonings are genuine, while others seem to be so but are not, is evident. This happens with arguments, as also elsewhere, through a certain likeness between the genuine and the sham."[14]

Although there often is agreement as to the existence of a fallacious argument, the method of labelling or characterizing them is up for grabs. Each logician seems to have his or her own method of classification. Common fallacies abound in all writings—speeches, commentaries, legislative debates, political oratory, television editorials, columns, articles, household and family discussions, and personal conversations. One commentator has indicated that over 120 different types of fallacies may

13. J. Creighton, An Introductory Logic 198 (1898).

14. DeSophisticis Elenchis in The Works of Aristotle (W.D. Ross trans. 1928).

be identified.[15]   Our discussion here is limited to the violation of formal rules of inference.   The discussion divides into two subtopics:

- Fallacies of logical form, or formal fallacies, and
- Fallacies based on factual content, known as material or informal fallacies.

We use this method of distinguishing the two groupings—formal fallacies and material fallacies—acknowledging that the labels "runneth over," and what we and the reported cases may describe as a particular type, may very well properly bear another name.   Labels and names aside, the importance is to avoid fallacious reasoning, whatever its classification.

The following definitions should be useful to the legal profession: Formal fallacies occur when one does not follow the rules of the syllogism.   Formal fallacies can be discovered without any knowledge of the subject matter with which the argument is concerned.   Factual or material fallacies involve the subject of the argument and cannot be set right except by those acquainted with the subject.   They do not violate specific logical rules.   They are said to exist not in the *form,* but in the *matter,* hence the label, material.

It is necessary to add a caveat at this time.   We are outlining logical processes in the law.   This is not an attempt to discuss all fallacies in existence.   Rather, we will concentrate on those fallacies that usually find expression in the law.

Formal Fallacies

Formal fallacies arise when there is an error in the logic of the argument.   The discussion will categorize the fallacies according to the type of syllogism asserted.

Fallacies in Categorical Syllogisms

In categorical arguments there are at least six possible fallacies:

1. Four terms instead of three.
2. Undistributed middle.
3. Illicit major term.
4. Illicit minor term.
5. Negative premises.
6. Particular premises.

Fallacies in Hypothetical Syllogisms

In hypothetical arguments there are at least two possible fallacies:

1. Denying the antecedent.
2. Affirming the consequent.

---

15.   Landau, Logic for Lawyers, 13 Pacific L.J. 59, 89 (1981).

Fallacies in Disjunctive Syllogisms

In disjunctive arguments the fallacy consists of the imperfect disjunctive.

Material (Informal) Fallacies

Material fallacies can sneak up on us as do fallacies of form. Logicians, scientists and other careful scholars are especially adept at detecting and avoiding these. Professors William and Mabel Sahakian describe them as "numerous, deceptive and elusive—so elusive that a person untrained in detecting them can easily be misled into accepting them as valid." [16] Logicians may differ as to their precise categorization because some resemble, or relate to, a type of argument rather than a type of logic. For this brief summary we follow, in major part, the classification set forth by the Sahakians.

Fallacies of Irrelevant Evidence

Fallacies of Irrelevant Evidence are arguments that miss the central point at issue and rely principally upon emotions, feelings, and ignorance, *inter alia,* to defend a thesis.

1. Fallacy of irrelevance, often referred to as irrelevant conclusions or ignoratio elenchi.
2. Fallacies of distraction.
   a. Argumentum ad misericordium, or the appeal to pity.
   b. Argumentum ad verecundiam, or the appeal to prestige.
   c. Argumentum ad hominem, or the appeal to personal ridicule.
   d. Argumentum ad populum, or the appeal to the masses.
   e. Argumentum ad antiquitam, or the appeal to age.
   f. Argumentum ad terrorem, or the appeal to terror.

Miscellaneous Material Fallacies

1. Fallacy of accident, or dicto simpliciter.

2. Converse fallacy of accident, or the fallacy of selective instances or hasty generalizations.

3. False cause, or post hoc ergo propter hoc.

4. Conclusion that does not follow from the premise, or non sequitur.

5. Compound questions. The fallacy of multiple questions, or poisoning the wells.

6. Begging the question, petitio principii.

7. Tu Quoque, or you yourself do it so it must be right.

16. W. & M. Shakian, Ideas of the Great
Philosophers 11 (1966).

Linguistic Fallacies

1. Fallacy of equivocation.

2. Fallacy of amphibology.

3. Fallacy of composition.

4. Fallacy of division.

5. Fallacy of vicious abstraction.

6. Argumentum ad nauseum.

Cardozo's Rule of Analogy

Reasoning by analogy is the process by which legal precepts found applicable to one set of fact patterns are extended to other fact patterns that are similar in relevant and material respects. In general, legal reasoning is the process with which one infers from a general "primary authority" the precepts applicable to a particular situation. Primary authority includes case law from judicial opinions, statutes, administrative regulations, treaties and constitutions. The central focus of American legal reasoning is the choice, interpretation, and application of case law. Cardozo's rule of analogy simply commands the judge to apply reason in the most primitive of the basic common law formulae: As stated before, if it is conceded that D is liable in a set of circumstances A, the judge must decide, without an exact precedent to guide him or her, whether D is also liable if A obtains, plus or minus circumstances B. If one has a penchant for graphic display, the rule of analogy has been compared to a moving line. Thus, deciding whether a defendant was entitled to counsel in a petty offense, the Supreme Court evaluated the precedent on the basis of "whether one considers that opinion to be a point on a moving line or a holding that the States are required to go only so far in furnishing counsel to indigent defendants." [17] In "holding the line," the court said it was "less willing to extrapolate an already extended line when, although the general nature of the principle sought to be applied is clear, its precise limits and their ramifications become less so." [18]

To state that the rule of analogies, even if the compared facts are materially similar, always requires a given result risks a double fallacy: that the general legal proposition on which the deduction is based is of complete and unqualified generality, and that in any case there is some legal compulsion inherent in the rules of logic. Numerous cases may no doubt be found where courts, faced with unanswerable arguments in formidable briefs based on logical deduction from existing precepts, have in effect declined to accept the deduction. In so doing they choose to reject the major premise that has been constructed individually either by induced generalization or analogy. But the virtue of the process is not to achieve a universal, for that is not an objective of the common law tradition. Rather, as David Richards has written: "[T]he principle of

17. Scott v. Illinois, 440 U.S. 367 (1979).   **18.** *Id.*

reasoning by analogy preserves the values of uniformity and stability of legal doctrine in a manner compatible with the flexible development of legal doctrine. In the absence of binding precedents, courts may develop legal doctrine, but they must do so by a publicly articulated process of reasoning that shows how this development is compatible with the reasons underlying existing precedent." [19]

In extending a precept to a new set of facts, value judgments regulate the process at least as forcefully as the rote application of rules of logical consistency. Cardozo recognized this, candidly admitting that one precedent, pushed to the limit of its logic, may point to one conclusion; another, followed with like logic, may point with equal certainty to another, and that accordingly, "we must choose between two paths, selecting one or another, or perhaps striking out upon a third." [20] Professor Paul Freund has made the same point: "In this respect judicial decision tends to resemble efforts at decision by maxims: when we remember that the early bird catches the worm . . ., we are at once reminded that haste makes waste." [21] It must be emphasized, therefore, that Cardozo's line of logical progression and the rule of analogy must be kept in proper perspective. The process of legal argument is not a chain of demonstrative reasoning. The reasons are like the legs of a chair, John Wisdom reminds us, not the links of a chain: "the process of deciding the issue becomes the matter of weighing the cumulative effect of one group of several inconclusive items, and thus lends itself to description in terms of conflicting 'probabilities.' " [22] In this sense, therefore, the judicial process is reduced, in the case of the judge, to the highly refined art of drawing distinctions, and, in the case of the lawyer, to the equally highly refined art of anticipating the distinctions the judge is likely to draw. There should be no need, therefore, to accept without qualification "[t]he tendency of a principle to expand itself to the limit of its logic," as Cardozo put the underlying problem.[23] All law, including constitutional law, involves the resolution of competing claims. The living world cannot be reduced to a mere "ballet of bloodless categories." [24] Professor Freund has referred to "the great antinomies of our aspirations: liberty and order; privacy and knowledge; stability and change; security and responsibility." [25] In the classic phrasing of the Supreme Court, "All rights tend to declare themselves absolute to their logical extreme. Yet all in fact are limited by the neighborhood of principles of policy which are other than those on which the particular

19. D. Richards, *Rules, Policies, and Neutral Principles: The Search for Legitimacy in Common Law and Constitutional Adjudication,* 11 Ga.L.Rev. 1069, 1078 (1977).

20. B. Cardozo, The Judicial Process 40 (1921).

21. P. Freund, Rational Decision: Nomos VIII, Rationality in Judicial Decisions 111–13 (1967).

22. J. Wisdom, Philosophy and Psycho–Analysis 157–58 (1953).

23. B. Cardozo, The Judicial Process 51 (1921).

24. Lloyd, *Reason and Logic in Common Law* 64 Law Q.Rev. 468, 482 n. 68 (1948) (Quoting F.H. Bradley).

25. P. Freund, On Law and Justice (1968).

right is founded, and which become strong enough to hold their own when a certain point is reached." [26]

At bottom then, the limit to the expansion of a precedent is the relevancy of the reasons for that precedent to the facts at bar. The double maxim says it all: *cessante ratione, cessat ipsa lex,* the rule follows where its reason leads; where the reason stops, there stops the rule. This is probably attributable to Bentham: "Good laws are such laws for which good reasons can be given."

KARL N. LLEWELLYN, SHIPS AND SHOES AND SEALING WAX**

[W]e have looked at the relation of logic to the law from the angle of the observer, or adviser, and from the angle of the advocate. We have seen how the counsellor must add to his logic his understanding of the attitude of the judge; and how the advocate must add not only that, but also the wherewithal to persuade the judge to accept a major premise from which the advocate's conclusion flows. *What now of the judge himself?* Is he a machine, merely with a set, an attitude, which goes on mechanically, and which an observer requires only to discover? Is he a weather-vane which the advocate can blow this way or that? Is he a despot, free of all control, thanks to the leeway offered by the ambiguities of his material, and able at will, or as a favor, or in caprice, or for a price, to throw the decision this way or that? As to this last question, within limits, yes; but much more truly, no. He *can* throw the decision this way or that. *But not freely.* For to him the logical ladder, or the several logical ladders, are ways of keeping himself in touch with the decisions of the past. This, as a judge, he wishes to do. This, as a judge, he would have to do even if he did not wish. This is the public's check upon his work. This is his own check on his own work. For while it is possible to build a number of divergent logical ladders up out of the same cases and down again to the same dispute, *there are not so many that can be built defensibly.* And of these few there are some, or there is one, toward which the prior cases pretty definitely press. Already you see the walls closing in around the judge. Finally, when all is done, he does remain free to choose—in a sense. But not free in another—for he is a judge. As a human being, his "attitude"—the resultant of his life—conditions him. As a judge—and a potent factor in his attitude—his conscience conditions him. It is his job to decide which ladder leads to the *just* conclusion, or to the *wise* conclusion—when he sees two clear possibilities. He does that job, and in the main he does it well. Often indeed he will not get that far. Often the prior cases push so strongly toward one line-up that he will not even see the chance we here point

26. Hudson County Water Co. v. McCarter, 209 U.S. 349, 355 (1908).

** The Bramble Bush 73–75 (1960). Reprinted by permission of Oceana Publications, Inc., and Soia Mentschikoff Llewellyn.

out to line them up differently. Then, unless the result raises the hair (*his* hair, not yours!), and forces a different outcome so to speak at the muzzle of a gun, the judge will never get as far as inquiring into justice. He will decide "by law" and let it go at that. Particularly, to come back to a point made earlier, will this be true of the weaker, the less skillful judge. Advance upon him with a ladder sound in logic, and he grows uncomfortable: his duty calls for application of the law; his skill does not suffice to find the alternative ladder which a more able or sophisticated mind might find. Again we see wisdom made institutional, caught up and crystallized into a working system: by way of logic the weak judge is penned within the walls his predecessors built; by way of logic the strong judge can scale those walls when in his judgment that is needed. And either phase, and both, promote the common weal.

Now this ad hoc approach to logic, this building of major premises out of a group of cases not so much to find what is in them as to decide a case in hand—this is of the essence of our case-law system. It is not so of every legal system, even of every system built on case law. The classical jurists of Rome seem, though they worked case by case, to have built up a strangely systematic whole; the French and German writers before the Codes had gone a great distance further on that road. *Elegantia juris* is the Latin for it: *form* in the law, in whole and in each part. Our sin is lack of elegance and even taste; our virtue is a sturdy, earthy common-sense.

From this angle I think you will understand the attitude of some of your instructors. They show so little interest in the deductive consequences of a proposition. They show no patience in following deductive reasoning through. Put them an inconvenient case within their rule; there is no thrill of battle. The minute they see the inconvenience they will junk the rule, restate it to avoid the bother, and go on. They do not seem depressed. Students who have had rigorous deductive training are amazed—and often are disgusted, I think, with no great reason. Here is a man whose training is ad hoc, who knows our courts to work as he is working. His search is not for a rule which holds, at large, but for a rule which holds good *for the matter in hand*. His interest is in *forming premises* in consonance with the authorities, and premises which decide according to need the case before him. One is as good as another, ad hoc—apart from the question of persuasion. That he is there to teach you. And one thing he can teach you which is worth learning. That is, resilience in *choosing* major premises. This is a pragmatic world. Most major premises still are dictated by a conclusion needed and already fixed.

Not that I would have your training stop at this. You must have exercise in deduction as well. Fortunately, you have other instructors who lay down major premises and work with them, though they tend to be as weak in logic as the others. They, too, are products of their training ground, our law. And our law has had no love for definitions— except ad hoc. The more careful of our statutes do include some definitions. But for the law at large? Not at all. "In this act", is as far as they purport to go. And even there, they lack (and lack for reason) the touch of Puritan courage of conviction. The definitions follow weasel words: "except when the context or subject-matter otherwise requires" *x* shall mean *a* or *b* or *c*. Now deduction without definition of terms is a game of cop and robber: you can have anything you catch. You will find, too, in this academic deductive exercise—as with the legal writers—that what we have seen as a most difficult, ambiguous task is regularly slurred over: to wit, the allocation of the raw facts among the generalized "significant" categories of the law.

In short, on the side of logic, our law has much to learn, and we, your instructors, not a little. But, as I hope I have indicated, that does not mean that *you* can get along without it. It means that you have a chance to improve on the techniques now current—if you will season your logic *at each end* with knowledge of the cases, and with common sense.

From this angle, moreover, you will observe another value in the study of the cases. Each opinion is an example of legal reasoning—with and from prior cases. Each opinion is an example of what some court has thought persuasive. Both as to the legal use of logic and as to persuasion there is something here to learn. And please note that there is as much, almost, to learn from the poor reasoning as from the good. A fine opinion is a model piece of work. But an execrable opinion gives an example of a type of mind you have to deal with, too.

In this connection, too, I should like to ask you to observe the difference between logical argument and argumentative statement, between showing a given logical relation between two matters, and *persuading* someone else that it exists by *attributing* the relationship to them in your discussion or description. This appears nowhere more strikingly than in the presentation of the facts with an eye to the rule you are trying to bring them under. Allied in technique, but different logically, is the use of *emotive* words in your argument, which are designed to induce the attitude toward the result your argument requires. The crass case, as you already must have seen, is in old-fashioned pleadings. Watch for these things in the judges' opinions. Not always, but often, they mean that defective logic is being covered up.

NOTE

How does one tell whether a judge is a "strong judge" or a "less skillful judge"? Llewellyn observes that "an execrable opinion gives an example of a type of mind you have to deal with, too." Is this to suggest that, when dealing with an author of execrable opinions one should cater to his or her idiosyncrasies? If so, is this to bankrupt the law?

In making a decision does the average person utilize an account of the procedures followed in reaching decisions which then are "the outcome of inquiry, comparison of alternatives, weighing of facts"? Can it be said that the process takes place "without any conscious thought of logic"? Does an all-pro quarterback employ this process during the few seconds when he is dropping back to pass and the blitz is on? How do you define "good sense" or "common sense"? Are these terms synonyms for one's ability to exercise good judgment in making a decision? Is it possible to write an opinion using a precedent without utilizing the standard syllogism?

When you say that a decision was "right" or "wrong" are you saying anything more than that you agree with it? Does it make a difference if you couch your evaluation in terms of "correct" or "incorrect"? Consider a case in which you feel the court reached the right result even though it used the "wrong" reasons. Does an intuition of the "correctness" of a decision qualify in itself as a "right" reason?

EDWARD H. LEVI, AN INTRODUCTION TO LEGAL REASONING *

The basic pattern of legal reasoning is reasoning by example.[2] It is reasoning from case to case. It is a three-step process described by the doctrine of precedent in which a proposition descriptive of the first case is made into a rule of law and then applied to a next similar situation. The steps are these: similarity is seen between cases; next the rule of law inherent in the first case is announced; then the rule of law is made applicable to the second case. This is a method of reasoning necessary for the law, but it has characteristics which under other circumstances might be considered imperfections.

These characteristics become evident if the legal process is approached as though it were a method of applying general rules of law to diverse facts—in short, as though the doctrine of precedent meant that general rules, once properly determined, remained unchanged, and then were applied, albeit imperfectly, in later cases. If this were the doctrine, it would be disturbing to find that the rules change from case to case and are remade with each case. Yet this change in the rules is the indispensable dynamic quality of law. It occurs because the scope of a rule of law, and therefore its meaning, depends upon a determination of what facts will be considered similar to those present when the rule was first announced. The finding of similarity or difference is the key step in the legal process.

---

* 15 U.Chi.L.Rev. 501, 501–04, 506 (1948). Reprinted by permission.

2. "Clearly then to argue by example is neither like reasoning from part to whole, nor like reasoning from whole to part, but rather reasoning from part to part, when both particulars are subordinate to the same term and one of them is known. It differs from induction, because induction starting from all the particular cases proves . . . that the major term belongs to the middle and does not apply the syllogistic conclusion to the minor term, whereas argument by example does make this application and does not draw its proof from all the particular cases." Aristotle, Analytica Priora 69a (McKeon ed., 1941).

The determination of similarity or difference is the function of each judge. Where case law is considered, and there is no statute, he is not bound by the statement of the rule of law made by the prior judge even in the controlling case. The statement is mere dictum, and this means that the judge in the present case may find irrelevant the existence or absence of facts which prior judges thought important. It is not what the prior judge intended that is of any importance; rather it is what the present judge, attempting to see the law as a fairly consistent whole, thinks should be the determining classification. In arriving at his result he will ignore what the past thought important; he will emphasize facts which prior judges would have thought made no difference. It is not alone that he could not see the law through the eyes of another, for he could at least try to do so. It is rather that the doctrine of dictum forces him to make his own decision.

Thus it cannot be said that the legal process is the application of known rules to diverse facts. Yet it is a system of rules; the rules are discovered in the process of determining similarity or difference. But if attention is directed toward the finding of similarity or difference, other peculiarities appear. The problem for the law is: When will it be just to treat different cases as though they were the same? A working legal system must therefore be willing to pick out key similarities and to reason from them to the justice of applying a common classification. The existence of some facts in common brings into play the general rule. If this is really reasoning, then by common standards, thought of in terms of closed systems, it is imperfect unless some overall rule has announced that this common and ascertainable similarity is to be decisive. But no such fixed prior rule exists. It could be suggested that reasoning is not involved at all; that is, that no new insight is arrived at through a comparison of cases. But reasoning appears to be involved; the conclusion is arrived at through a process and was not immediately apparent. It seems better to say there is reasoning, but it is imperfect.[5]

Therefore it appears that the kind of reasoning involved in the legal process is one in which the classification changes as the classification is made. The rules change as the rules are applied. More important, the rules arise out of a process which, while comparing fact situations, creates the rules and then applies them. But this kind of reasoning is open to the charge that it is classifying things as equal when they are somewhat different, justifying the classification by rules made up as the reasoning or classification proceeds. In a sense all reasoning is of this type, but there is an additional requirement which compels the legal process to be this way. Not only do new situations arise, but in addition peoples' wants change. The categories used in the legal process must be left ambiguous in order to permit the infusion of new ideas....

5. The logical fallacy is the fallacy of the undistributed middle or the fallacy of as- suming the antecedent is true because the consequent has been affirmed.

Section 3

USE OF HISTORY

Past thoughts dominate the common law. If the past is truly prologue, historical considerations inhere in the doctrine of precedent. Blackstone said that "it is an established rule to abide by former precedents, where the same points come again in litigation ... because the law in that case being solemnly declared is now become a permanent rule." [1] But precedent, per se, is more properly related to an internal judicial history of legal precepts.

Courts often deal with another form of history which we may describe as external history, an account of historical events which helped decide a previous case or which may have assisted in the decision at hand. We must evaluate history's true role, for an aura of authenticity seems to radiate from the lawyer's brief or judge's opinion which recites history extensively. We must examine that aura for the reality.

One who looks to history for a scaling of values is confronted with the problem of "differentiating history from the historians," or in Yeats' words, the dancers from the dance, or in Santayana's, looking over a crowd to find one's friends.

Pulitzer-prize winning historian Arthur M. Schlesinger, Jr. comments in the Disuniting of America 46–47 (1991):

> Historians do their damnedest to maintain the standards of their trade. Heaven knows how dismally we fall short of our ideals, how sadly our interpretations are dominated and distorted by unconscious preconceptions, how obsessions of race and nation blind us to our own bias. We remain creatures of our times, prisoners of our own experience, swayed hither and yon, like all sinful mortals, by partisanship, prejudice, dogma, by fear and by hope.
>
> The spotlight we flash into the darkness of the past is guided by our own concerns in the present. When new preoccupations arise in our own times and lives, the spotlight shifts, throwing into sharp relief things that were always there but that earlier historians had casually excised from the collective memory. In this sense, the present may be said to re-create the past.
>
> Historians must always strive toward the unattainable ideal of objectivity. But as we respond to contemporary urgencies, we sometimes exploit the past for nonhistorical purposes, taking from the past, or projecting upon it, what suits our own society or ideology. History thus manipulated becomes an instrument less of disinterested intellectual inquiry than of social cohesion and political purpose.
>
> People live by their myths, and some may argue that the facts can be justifiably embroidered if embroiderment serves a higher good, such as the nurture of a nation or the elevation of

---

1. W. Blackstone, Commentaries *69.

a race. It may seem more important to maintain a beneficial fiction than to keep history pure—especially when there is no such thing as pure history anyway. This may have been what Plato had in mind when he proposed the idea of the "noble lie" in *The Republic*.

We must distinguish the *fact* of history from what they *believe* to be the fact. We are also admonished to be alert for distinctions between an original understanding or intent theory, and an ongoing history theory which reflects currents and lessons of experience. This distinction does not demean history's importance in the judicial process so much as it alerts one to differences in historical methods at work within the judiciary. To know what law is, "we must know what it has been, and what it tends to become." In law, as in communications, there are times when the medium is the message. The *Dred Scott* majority opinion drew its authority from history and, so doing, altered the course of that history.

The contrasting opinions in *Dred Scott* demonstrate the different interpretations of colonial history at the time of the Constitution's adoption. Chief Justice Taney declared that a "negro of the African race was regarded by them as an article of property, and held, and bought and sold as such, in *every one* of the thirteen colonies which united in the Declaration of Independence, and afterwards formed the Constitution of the United States." His interpretation of history formed the factual basis of the major premise of his opinion. Justice Curtis in dissent had the more accurate recollection of history and noted:

> At the time of the ratification of the Articles of Confederation, all free native-born inhabitants of the States of New Hampshire, Massachusetts, New York, New Jersey, and North Carolina, although descended form African slaves, were not only citizens of those states, but such of them as had the other necessary qualifications possessed the franchise of electors, on equal terms with other citizens.

Putting aside the emotional and political overtones of the day, Chief Justice Taney's misinterpretation of history destroyed the logical validity of his legal argument and forced him into the formal fallacy of the "undistributed middle term" of his major premise. When he said that "every one" of the Colonies regarded African Americans as chattel, he erred grievously and erroneously formulated an "undistributed term" to make a "general proposition." Because contents of his major premise were false and did not form a universal proposition, his majority opinion lacked both valid reasoning and true premises.

DRED SCOTT v. SANFORD

Supreme Court of the United States, 1857.
60 U.S. (19 How.) 393, 15 L.Ed. 691.

Mr. Chief Justice Taney delivered the opinion of the Court:

The question is simply this: can a negro whose ancestors were imported into this country and sold as slaves, become a member of the political community formed and brought into existence by the Constitution of the United States, and as such become entitled to all the rights, and privileges, and immunities, guaranteed by that instrument to the citizen. One of these rights is the privilege of suing in a court of the United States in the cases specified in the Constitution.

It becomes necessary, therefore, to determine who were citizens of the several States when the Constitution was adopted. And in order to do this, we must recur to the governments and institutions of the thirteen Colonies, when they separated from Great Britain and formed new sovereignties, and took their places in the family of independent nations. We must inquire who, at that time, were recognized as the people or citizens of a State, whose rights and liberties had been outraged by the English Government; and who declared their independence, and assumed the powers of government to defend their rights by force of arms.

In the opinion of the court, the legislation and histories of the times, and the language used in the Declaration of Independence, show, that neither the class of persons who had been imported as slaves, nor their descendants, whether they had become free or not, were then acknowledged as a part of the people, nor intended to be included in the general words used in that memorable instrument.

The opinion thus entertained and acted upon in England was naturally impressed upon the colonies they founded on this side of the Atlantic. And, accordingly, a negro of the African race was regarded by them as an article of property, and held, and bought and sold as such, in every one of the thirteen Colonies which united in the Declaration of Independence, and afterwards formed the Constitution of the United States. The slaves were more or less numerous in the different Colonies, as slave labor was found more or less profitable. But no one seems to have doubted the correctness of the prevailing opinion of the time.

The legislation of the different Colonies furnishes positive and indisputable proof of this fact.

The legislation of the States therefore shows, in a manner not to be mistaken, the inferior and subject condition of that race at the time the Constitution was adopted, and long afterwards, throughout the thirteen States by which that instrument was framed; and it is hardly consistent with the respect due to these States to suppose that they regarded at that time, as fellow citizens and members of the sovereignty, a class of beings whom they had thus stigmatized; whom, as we are bound, out of respect to the State sovereignties, to assume they had deemed it just and necessary thus to stigmatize, and upon whom they had impressed such deep and enduring marks of inferiority and degradation; or that when they met in convention to form the Constitution, they looked upon them as a portion of their constituents, or designed to include them in the provisions so carefully inserted for the security and protection of the liberties and rights of their citizens. It cannot be supposed that they intended to secure to them rights, and privileges, and rank, in the new political body throughout the Union which every one of them denied within the limits of its own dominion. More especially, it cannot be believed that the large slaveholding States regarded them as included in the word "citizens," or would have consented to a constitution which might compel them to receive them in that character from another State. For if they were so received, and entitled to the privileges and immunities of citizens, it would exempt them from the operation of the special laws and from the police regulations which they considered to be necessary for their own safety. It would give to persons of the negro race, who were recognized as citizens in any one State of the Union, the right to enter every other State whenever they pleased, singly or in companies, without pass or passport, and without obstruction, to sojourn there as long as they pleased, to go where they pleased at every hour of the day or night without molestation, unless they committed some violation of law for which a white man would be punished; and it would give them the full liberty of speech in public and in private upon all subjects upon which its own citizens might speak; to hold public meetings upon political affairs, and to keep and carry arms wherever they went. And all of this would be done in the face of the subject race of the same color, both free and slaves, inevitably producing discontent and insubordination among them and endangering the peace and safety of the State.

. . .

What the construction was at that time, we think can hardly admit of doubt. We have the language of the Declaration of Independence and of the Articles of Confederation, in addition to the plain words of the Constitution itself; we have the legislation of the different States, before, about the time, and since the Constitution was adopted; we have the legislation of Congress, from the time of its adoption to a recent period; and we have the constant and uniform action of the Executive Department, all concurring together, and leading to the same result. And if anything in relation to the construction of the Constitution can be regarded as settled, it is that which we now give to the word "citizen" and the word "people."

... Upon the whole, therefore, it is the judgment of this court, that it appears by the record before us that the plaintiff in error is not a citizen of Missouri, in the sense in which that word is used in the

Constitution; and that the Circuit Court of the United States, for that reason, had no jurisdiction in the case, and could give no judgment in it.

Mr. Justice Curtis, dissenting.

To determine whether any free persons, descended from Africans held in slavery, were citizens of the United States under the Confederation, and consequently at the time of the adoption of the Constitution of the United States, it is only necessary to know whether any such persons were citizens of either of the States under the Confederation, at the time of the adoption of the Constitution.

Of this there can be no doubt. At the time of the ratification of the Articles of Confederation, all free native-born inhabitants of the States of New Hampshire, Massachusetts, New York, New Jersey, and North Carolina, though descended from African slaves, were not only citizens of those states, but such of them as had the other necessary qualifications possessed the franchise of electors, on equal terms with other citizens.

. . .

I can find nothing in the Constitution which, *proprio vigore,* deprives of their citizenship any class of persons who were citizens of the United States at the time of its adoption, or who should be native-born citizens of any state after its adoption; nor any power enabling Congress to disfranchise persons born on the soil of any state, who is a citizen of that state by force of its Constitution or laws, is also a citizen of the United States.

. . .

It has been often asserted that the Constitution was made exclusively by and for the white race. It has already been shown that in five of the thirteen original states, colored persons then possessed the elective franchise, and were among those by whom the Constitution was ordained and established. If so, it is not true, in point of fact, that the Constitution was of those persons who were qualified by its laws to act thereon, in behalf of themselves and all other citizens of that state. In some of the states, as we have seen, colored persons were among those qualified by law to act on this subject. These colored persons were not only included in the body of "the people of the United States," by whom the Constitution was ordained and established, but in at least five of the states they had the power to act, and doubtless did act, by their suffrages, upon the question of its adoption. It would be strange, if we were to find in that instrument anything which deprived of their citizenship any part of the people of the United States who were among those by whom it was established.

NOTE

Carl B. Swisher, V History of the Supreme Court of the United States, 622, 628–30 (1974): *

* *The Taney Period,* 1835–64 (History of the Supreme Court, Volume V) (Copyright © 1974 Macmillan Publishing Co., Inc.) Reprinted by permission.

"On March 5 it was reported that Chief Justice Taney had remained at home to work on his opinion in the Dred Scott case. On Friday, March 6, 'in a tone of voice almost inaudible,' which brought derisive comment from the *Tribune,* he read his opinion in Court, taking about two hours, and Nelson and Catron read their concurring opinions. On the following day, Saturday, Justices McLean and Curtis read their dissenting opinions, taking some five hours. It was said that Justices Campbell and Daniel had withheld their concurring opinions until after the dissenting opinions were read, 'with the view of rebutting their arguments.' but when McLean and Curtis had finished it was as if everybody had had enough of Dred Scott and his case, and Justices Wayne, Grier, Campbell, and Daniel submitted their opinions without reading them in Court.

. . .

"Justice Curtis delivered a dissenting opinion of sixty-seven pages which bore throughout the stamp of the disciplined jurist. Avoiding plays to the political galleries and jabs at his colleagues, he produced a document which as a work of legal craftsmanship was enormously persuasive, and impressive to those who refused to be persuaded. While pursuing his own line of argument, he took the position taken by Taney that the plea in abatement was before the Supreme Court. But he rejected the grounds of the plea, and adduced an enormous amount of evidence to show that at the time of the adoption of the Constitution Negroes had been regarded as citizens in a number of the states. It was this devastating display of evidence, derived largely from state court decisions and statutes, that goaded Chief Justice Taney to make the additions to the opinion of the Court.... While considering citizenship oftentimes in terms of voting, he emphasized that citizenship under the Constitution was 'not dependent on the possession of any particular political or even of all civil rights.' As he saw it, 'citizens' as referred to in the Constitution were to be identified with 'free inhabitants.' Free colored people were citizens in some of the states, were therefore citizens of the United States, and were therefore entitled to sue and be sued in federal courts. The plea to the jurisdiction was therefore bad, and the Circuit Court had correctly overruled it.

"Justice Benjamin Cardozo encouraged those who now read the Curtis dissenting opinion to 'feel after the cooling time of the better part of a century the glow and fire of a faith that was content to bide its hour. The prophet and the martyr do not see the hooting throng. Their eyes are fixed on the eternities.' If this encomium was deserved it was because the opinion was written out of the warp and woof of the law itself and not because it was intended to ignite a crusade for freedom. As a performance in juristic art it resembled that of the Chief Justice himself, who, recognizing the artist in his specialized field, reacted strongly to the probing of his own vulnerability. In terms of judicial craftsmanship the performances of Taney and Curtis, among the nine highly diverse performances, were outstanding. The clash of judicial strategists had its repercussions through much of the aftermath of the decision."

———

CHARLES A. MILLER, PRINCIPLES OF ADJUDICATION *

History. The final vehicle used to decide cases in constitutional law is history. For purposes of this study history may be defined as that which, in the opinions of the Supreme Court, is believed to be true about the past—about past facts and past thoughts.[37] From the Supreme Court's first terms to the present, history has played a large role in constitutional adjudication. It is perhaps too much to claim, as Justice Horace Gray did in 1895, that the "question [in this case], like all questions of constitutional construction, is largely a historical question," but concerning no other principle could such a claim even be proposed. Indeed, each of the previously discussed principles of adjudication ** may be seen under the aspect of history: the constitutional text because it is an eighteenth-century document; constitutional doctrine because it is a distillation of the Court's past decisions and practices; precedent because it is judicial history; and social facts because they are, in effect, the materials of contemporary history. More generally, the nature of law, particularly constitutional law, and the function of the Supreme Court in American society both contain a large element of viewing the present in terms of the past. They both have the historical question built into them.

The most restricted form of history used in constitutional law is that which is internal to a particular case, its factual background. All other history used by the Court is external to the case. By the time a case reaches the Supreme Court the facts are seldom in dispute, yet the opposing briefs and majority and minority opinions almost always present this internal history in different ways.[39] The Court has said that its

* The Supreme Court and the Uses of History 20–27 (1969). Excerpted by permission of the author and publishers from pp. 20–27 of The Supreme Court and the Uses of History by Charles A. Miller, Cambridge, Mass.: The Belknap Press of Harvard University Press, Copyright © 1969 by the President and Fellows of Harvard College.

37. History is also, of course, what is actually true about the past, what happened at the time regardless of what anyone later believes about it. Among historians this is a common distinction, and it is one sometimes necessary to observe in analyzing the Court's uses of history. But the Court itself does not make the distinction ... the Court's uses of the past are primarily a function of its own beliefs.

The reason for distinguishing facts (physical events) from thoughts (mental events) is that, while the historical sources giving evidence of either are largely the same, the first is almost always agreed upon by the Court, but the second, especially in the form of the contemporaneous significance of facts, is often not.

** *Ante.*

39. ... "In my experience in the conference room of the Supreme Court of the United States, which consists of nine judges," declared Justice Samuel Miller in the late nineteenth century, "I have been surprised to find how readily those judges come to an agreement upon questions of law, and how often they disagree in regard to questions of fact." Quoted in Barbara

duty "is not limited to the elaboration of constitutional principles; we must also in proper cases review the evidence to make certain that those principles have been constitutionally applied." This means that the Court may sometimes review issues of fact, by which it means "basic, primary, or historical facts."

Once outside the background of an individual case, history is immensely varied. For purposes of analysis it may again be divided into two categories: history internal to the law and history external to the law. This distinction, like many distinctions, is blurred at the boundaries but clear at the center. History internal to the law consists of precedents, which have already been discussed, and legal history. Legal history pertains to the history of legal terms and doctrine, legal systems, and judicial practices.

In American history the most important broad topic in legal history dealt with by the courts has been the extent to which the English common law was "received" as the law of the colonies and, later, of the states. Like many issues in legal history, the nineteenth-century argument over the reception of the common law was not a legal issue alone but was embroiled in politics. Like other legal receptions it was conditioned by cultural attitudes towards the home country of the system—in the American case the attitude towards England—but the issue was argued in terms of law. At one point, indeed, the opposition to British law was so great that several states enacted legislation forbidding the courts from even citing prerevolutionary British cases. Ultimately the country succumbed to the Anglo–Saxon heritage, but with the qualification that the law adopted would have to measure up to the "civil and political condition" of America.

Recent cases in which the Supreme Court has used legal history to decide constitutional issues have been no less enmeshed in politics, and the result, quite naturally, has been to make legal history the subject of political manipulation in briefs and in court opinions. One example will indicate the close relationship between politics and legal history in constitutional law. In 1964 the Supreme Court decided a case in which the Governor of Mississippi, when cited for criminal contempt by a federal court for disobeying injunctions relating to the desegregation of the state university, had insisted that he was guaranteed a jury trial by the Constitution.[44] His expectation was that a jury of fellow Mississippians would not convict him but independent federal judges probably would. This is the political context of the case. But half of the Supreme Court's opinion, plus a twenty-three page appendix of "statutes and cases relevant to the punishment for contempt imposed by colonial courts," is devoted to legal history. In the end, the Court denied the official's claim. The major dissenting opinion in the case relied largely on the same authorities cited in the majority's appendix but concluded

Frank Kristein (ed.), *A Man's Reach: The Philosophy of Judge Jerome Frank* (New York: Macmillan, 1965), p. 208.

44. United States v. Barnett, 376 U.S. 681 (1964).

that legal history supported the claim of a constitutional right to a jury trial in these circumstances.

. . .

The final form of history to be considered as a principle of constitutional adjudication is general history. General history, which is external to the law, includes political, social, economic, and cultural history. It has been an accepted guide to constitutional interpretation since the establishment of the nation. The distinguishing feature of general history is the scope it gives the Supreme Court for policy choices. General history not only takes the justices into fields where their training and knowledge may be limited, but it also invites the avoidance of the more strictly legal principles of decision. The use of general history may seem to confess the inadequacy of the traditional tools of law for deciding cases. More than this, the political authority of the Court often endows it with a certain intellectual authority. By writing history into its opinions the Court contributes to the public's view of the American past as much as, and sometimes even more than, professional historians and other historical writers do. When the Supreme Court has the chance to tell us what American history is, history becomes more than a tool of decision. It affirms or denies the significance of past events for the activities of the present. While this may be of little consequence in the field of legal history, it is not so in general history. With the increased scope and power granted the Court by the use of history goes the increased responsibility in the handling of historical materials.

In terms of its use by the Supreme Court, general history may be seen as both the history which serves to explicate the meaning of the original Constitution (and the amendments) as drafted and ratified and the history which serves to reveal conditions in the nation since the ratification, conditions that the justices believe have a bearing on later interpretation of the Constitution. Typically, the history concerned with the formation and ratification of the Constitution serves to restrain the Court in its decisions. It shares this feature with two other principles of adjudication: the constitutional text and precedent. In contrast, the use of continuing or "ongoing" history allows the Constitution to move with the prevailing temper of the country and may therefore be considered forward-looking. The evidence of ongoing history merges into contemporary observation at no clearly definable date. It eventually yields to the use of social evidence as a principle of adjudication.

The difference between the two types of general history can be expressed in another way. The history that searches for the "original understanding" of a constitutional clause is a history that recognizes and places a high value on the "intent theory" of documentary interpretation. The intent theory holds that a document, such as the Constitution, should be construed in agreement with the intentions of the person or persons who wrote it. To discover these intentions for the Constitution one must turn to the history of the late eighteenth century. Since it is the Constitution that commands the Supreme Court to decide one way or another, since the Constitution should mean what it was intended to mean, and since intent is ascertainable only by resort to historical material, history as intent is essentially history as command. The other history, ongoing history, is not to be viewed as determining the command of the Constitution but as demonstrating the currents and lessons of experience. Ongoing history does not say "this is what was expected," but "this is what the nation has become."

The Supreme Court has availed itself liberally of both "intent history" and ongoing history since its first sessions, changing the techniques only as new perspectives, documents, and professional standards have influenced opinion-writing. For two reasons an essential identity between intent history and ongoing political history existed during the early years of the Court. First, there was a relative absence of source material concerning the Constitutional Convention. Second, the events surrounding the adoption of the Constitution were merged in the minds and experience of the justices with the early history of the national period.[54] But when memory could no longer serve to explicate the original understanding of the Constitution and when ongoing history— the political, economic, and social changes since 1789—pressed increasingly for recognition in constitutional law, the two types of history diverged permanently.

NOTE

Various opinions in Furman v. Georgia, 408 U.S. 238 (1972), held that the death penalty, as then implemented, constituted cruel and unusual punishment in violation of the Eighth and Fourteenth Amendments. Justice Douglas relied on Weems v. United States, 217 U.S. 349, 378 (1910), holding that the proscription of cruel and unusual punishment "is not fastened to the obsolete but may acquire meaning as public opinion becomes enlightened by a humane justice." A like statement was made in Trop v. Dulles, 356 U.S. 86, 101 (1958), that the Eighth Amendment "must draw its meaning from the evolving standards of decency that mark the progress of a maturing society." (Chief Justice Warren). Evaluate Part I of Justice Brennan's opinion in Furman, 408 U.S. at 258–69, as to the intent of the framers. *See also* the opinion of

---

54. John Marshall is the best example of this. His devotion to George Washington and the cause of American nationalism was the result of his experience during the Revolution. He argued for the adoption of the Constitution at the Virginia ratification convention. He was envoy to Paris, member of Congress, and Secretary of State before becoming Chief Justice. And in a five-volume *Life of Washington* he wrote a general political history of the country since the time of settlement. In short, the text of the Constitution was the distillation of a history that Marshall knew well; and his opinions on the Court, which contain abun-

dant evidence of his historical interests, firmly established the validity of history as a principle of adjudication in constitutional law. See Marie Carolyn Klinkhamer, *The Use of History in the Supreme Court,* 1789–1835, University of Detroit Law Journal, 36 (1959), 553–78; Klinkhamer, *John Marshall's Use of History,* Catholic University Law Review, 6 (1956), 78–96; Albert J. Beveridge, *The Life of John Marshall* (4 vols.; Boston: Houghton Mifflin, 1916–19), esp. III, 223–73; William A. Foran, *John Marshall as a Historian,* American Historical Review, 43 (1937), 51–64.

Justice Marshall, 408 U.S. at 329: "Perhaps the most important principle in analyzing 'cruel and unusual' punishment questions is one that is reiterated again and again in the prior opinions of the Court: *i.e.,* the cruel and unusual language 'must draw its meaning from the evolving standards of decency that mark the progress of a maturing society.' Thus, a penalty that was permissible at one time in our Nation's history is not necessarily permissible today."

Recall the discussion of statutory construction and the propriety of considering legislative intent. In a similar context, consider the legitimacy of "intent history".

————

BROWN v. BOARD OF EDUCATION

Supreme Court of the United States, 1954.
347 U.S. 483, 74 S.Ct. 686, 98 L.Ed. 873.

Mr. Chief Justice Warren delivered the opinion of the Court.

In each of the cases, minors of the Negro race, through their legal representatives, seek the aid of the courts in obtaining admission to the public schools of their community on a nonsegregated basis. In each instance, they had been denied admission to schools attended by white children under laws requiring or permitting segregation according to race. This segregation was alleged to deprive the plaintiffs of the equal protection of the laws under the Fourteenth Amendment. In each of the cases other than the Delaware case, a three-judge federal district court denied relief to the plaintiffs on the so-called "separate but equal" doctrine announced by this Court in Plessy v. Ferguson, 163 U.S. 537, 16 S.Ct. 1138, 41 L.Ed. 256. Under that doctrine, equality of treatment is accorded when the races are provided substantially equal facilities, even though these facilities be separate. In the Delaware case, the Supreme Court of Delaware adhered to that doctrine, but ordered that the plaintiffs be admitted to the white schools because of their superiority to the Negro schools.

The plaintiffs contend that segregated public schools are not "equal" and cannot be made "equal," and that hence they are deprived of the equal protection of the laws....

. . .

In approaching this problem, we cannot turn the clock back to 1868 when the amendment was adopted, or even to 1896 when Plessy v. Ferguson was written. We must consider public education in the light of its full development and its present place in American life throughout the Nation. Only in this way can it be determined if segregation in public schools deprives these plaintiffs of the equal protection of the laws.

Today, education is perhaps the most important function of state and local governments. Compulsory school attendance laws and the great expenditures for education both demonstrate our recognition of the importance of education to our democratic society. It is required in the performance of our most basic public responsibilities, even service in the armed forces. It is the very foundation of good citizenship. Today it is a principal instrument in awakening the child to cultural values, in preparing him for later professional training, and in helping him to adjust normally to his environment. In these days, it is doubtful that any child may reasonably be expected to succeed in life if he is denied the opportunity of an education. Such an opportunity, where the state has undertaken to provide it, is a right which must be made available to all on equal terms.

We come then to the question presented: Does segregation of children in public schools solely on the basis of race, even though the physical facilities and other "tangible" factors may be equal, deprive the children of the minority group of equal educational opportunities? We believe that it does.

In Sweatt v. Painter, [339 U.S. 629, 70 S.Ct. 848, 94 L.Ed. 1114] in finding that a segregated law school for Negroes could not provide them equal educational opportunities, this Court relied in large part on "those qualities which are incapable of objective measurement but which make for greatness in a law school." In McLaurin v. Oklahoma State Regents, 339 U.S. 637, 70 S.Ct. 853, 94 L.Ed. 1149, the Court in requiring that a Negro admitted to a white graduate school be treated like all other students, again resorted to intangible considerations: ". . . his ability to study, to engage in discussions and exchange views with other students, and, in general, to learn his profession." Such considerations apply with added force to children in grade and high schools. To separate them from others of similar age and qualifications solely because of their race generates a feeling of inferiority as to their status in the community that may affect their hearts and minds in a way unlikely ever to be undone. The effect of this separation on their educational opportunities was well stated by a finding in the Kansas case by a court which nevertheless felt compelled to rule against the Negro plaintiffs:

> "Segregation of white and colored children in public schools has a detrimental effect upon the colored children. The impact is greater when it has the sanction of the law; for the policy of separating the races is usually interpreted as denoting the inferiority of the negro group. A sense of inferiority affects the motivation of a child to learn. Segregation with the sanction of law, therefore, has a tendency to [retard] the educational and mental development of negro children and to deprive them of some of the benefits they would receive in a racial[ly] integrated school system."

Whatever may have been the extent of psychological knowledge at the time of Plessy v. Ferguson, this finding is amply supported by modern authority.[11] Any language in Plessy v. Ferguson contrary to this finding is rejected.

————

NOTE

In Brown v. Board of Education,[1] the Court addressed circumstance *B*, black children in segregated schools. It decided that under the doctrine of "separate but equal," no black school could be considered "equal." In Mayor of Baltimore v. Dawson,[2] the Court was again presented with a segregation issue—this time minus circumstance *C* (i.e., not in the context of segregated schools). The Court affirmed the Fourth Circuit's ruling that the *Brown* decision would nevertheless apply to end segregation in public beaches and bathhouses. Segregation minus circumstance *C* led to the same result in Holmes v. Atlanta[3] (municipal golf course) and Gayle v. Browder[4] (buses). When *Browder* came down, it was recognized that, as a matter of law, the entire doctrine of separate but equal was overruled without being limited to the reasons stated in *Brown*: the special and particular problems of segregated education. Changing social and judicial perspectives had rendered that circumstance immaterial.

From this, we can learn something about the process of analogy, which lies at the heart of the system of evaluating precedents. In analogizing, it is mandatory to determine which facts in the previous case are to be deemed material. The decision in a subsequent case depends as much on the exclusion of "immaterial" facts as it does on the inclusion of "material" ones.

Section 4

USE OF CUSTOMS

The energy of customs, both general and particular, was recognized in early common law expressions. The body of English law assimilated the trade usage of the law merchant from the Italian city states, Amalfi, Genoa, Pisa, and Venice. Unlike Roman law which was dominated by scholars, the law merchant was the pragmatic creation of the practical men of commerce. It was an account of market place custom.

Yet it is difficult to answer the question: Does custom create law? If so, how do the positivists rationalize it? Is it more proper to say that

11. K.B. Clark, Effect of Prejudice and Discrimination on Personality Development (Midcentury White House Conference on Children and Youth, 1950); Witmer and Kotinsky, Personality in the Making (1952), c. VI; Deutscher and Chein, The Psychological Effects of Enforced Segregation: A Survey of Social Science Opinion, 26 J.Psychol. 259 (1948); Chein, What are the Psychological Effects of Segregation Under Conditions of Equal Facilities?, 3 Int.J.Opinion and Attitude Res. 229 (1949); Brameld, Educational Costs, in Discrimination and National Welfare (MacIver, ed., 1949), 44–48; Frazier, The Negro in the United States (1949), 674–681. And see generally Myrdal, An American Dilemma (1944).

1. 347 U.S. 483 (1954).

2. 350 U.S. 877 (1955).

3. 350 U.S. 879 (1955).

4. 352 U.S. 903 (1956).

custom is merely a moral rule or a ground for judicial decision, or is it evidence of existing law, separately promulgated? In public and private organizations, especially those with long histories, unwritten codes of conduct are as rigidly enforced as written or formally promulgated bylaws or ordinances.

Custom played an important role in the early formulation of the common law. Blackstone has recorded:

> The municipal law of England, or the rule of civil conduct prescribed to the inhabitants of this kingdom, may with sufficient propriety be divided into two kinds: the *lex non scripta,* the unwritten, or common law,; and the *lex scripta,* the written, or statute law.

> The *lex non scripta,* or unwritten law, includes not only *general customs,* or the common law properly so called; but also the *particular customs* of certain parts of the kingdom; and likewise those *particular law,* that are by custom observed only in certain courts and jurisdictions.[1]

English courts have allowed a proven custom or usage to modify legal rights when certain requirements have been satisfied, including legality, antiquity, continuance, peaceable enjoyment, obligatoriness, certainty and reasonableness. Generally speaking, for a custom to be given legal effect there must be some societal value that will be served directly and the custom must have been in use for a considerable length of time. Except for mercantile and labor cases, few American courts have treated this problem, probably because fifty state sovereignties can enact local custom into law by statute or court decision.

Within the last two centuries an entire field of law arising out of mercantile customs has been made part of our law through its recognition as such by the judges and by the legislatures in the various Sales Acts and now the Uniform Commercial Code. Judge Arlin M. Adams thoughtfully observed: "Where a language is capable of two reasonable meanings, a court, in the commercial field, should choose that interpretation which comports with current universal practice in the business world." [2]

Observant European lawyers have recently lamented that in the Common Market countries, the law has not kept pace with business practice.

The Supreme Court announced in 1960 that by means of our national labor policy the collective bargaining institution had introduced a new common law—the common law of a particular industry or particular plant.[3] It has become known as the law of the shop and in general implement defines the context of labor agreements.[4] Because judicial

---

1. Blackstone, Commentaries at 63.

2. In the Matter of Bristol Associates, Inc., 505 F.2d 1056, 1062–63 (3d Cir.1974).

3. United Steelworkers of America v. Warrior and Gulf Navigation Co., 363 U.S. 574 (1960).

4. Cox, *Reflections Upon Labor Arbitration,* 72 Harv.L.Rev. 1482, 1498–99 (1959).

review of labor arbitration awards is extremely restricted, the American labor arbitrator is highly conversant with the interface of customs and the law. A prominent arbitrator has described the role of custom:

> A custom or practice is not something which arises simply because a given course of conduct has been pursued by Management or the employees on one or more occasions. A custom or a practice is a usage evolved by men as a normal reaction to a recurring type situation. It must be shown to be the accepted course of conduct characteristically repeated in response to the given set of underlying circumstances. This is not to say that the course of conduct must be accepted in the sense of both parties having agreed to it, but rather that it must be accepted in the sense of being regarded by the men involved as the normal and proper response to the underlying circumstances presented.[5]

If, then, custom does not occupy the commanding role for creating new rules of law as it did in the formative years of the common law, we must not overlook the importance of custom on the everyday life external to the judicial process. Most aspects of social business life never reach the courts in the form of a case or controversy. Without the stringency of statute, regulation or decisional law, these behavioral aspects of society exert an informal regulation of their own, with a predictability and reckonability and various accouterments of formal law. Many of these behavioral patters or habits are customs.

In the heightened use of expert witnesses in personal injury, products liability and criminal cases, the use of customs in the judicial process has become extremely important. The expert is permitted to express an opinion, rather than give eye witness or ear witness testimony as to a narrative or historical fact. This is because in qualifying for the exalted status of expert, the witness vouches for a familiarity with the "acceptable expected standards" of medical care, engineering design or some scientific specialty. In this respect, the "acceptable expected standards" of a particular specialty are nothing more than a statement of the recognized customs of that profession. Usually put to expert physician witnesses in personal injuries and criminal cases is the familiar "Can you state with reasonable medical certainty" that such and such was the cause of the trauma.

In Frye v. United States, the court explained that the testimony is accepted because "the thing from which the deduction is made must be sufficiently established to have gained acceptance in the particular field in which it belongs."[6]

Rule 702 of Federal Evidence Rules provides:

5. Sylvester Garrett quoted in Block, Customs and Usages as Factors in Arbitration Disputes, Proceedings of New York University 15th Annual Conference on Labor 312–13 (1962).

6. 293 Fed. 1013, 1014 (App.D.C.1923).

If scientific, technical, or otherwise specialized knowledge will assist the trier of fact to understand the evidence or to determine a fact in issue, a witness qualified as an expert by knowledge, skill, experience, training, or education, may testify thereto in the form of an opinion or otherwise.

In Daubert v. Merrell Dow Pharmaceuticals, Inc.,[7] the Court considered the *Frye* ruling that scientific expert opinion evidence is admissible only if the principle upon which it is based is "sufficiently established to have general acceptance in the field to which it belongs." The Court concluded that "general acceptance" is not a necessary precondition to the admissibility of scientific evidence, but that Federal Rules of Evidence, including Rule 702, assign to the trial judge the task of ensuring that an expert's testimony both rests on a reliable foundation and is relevant to the task at hand.

In other countries, especially Spain and Africa, customs still constitute a formal source of judicial decision. Thus Article 6 of the Spanish Civil Code of 1889 provides: "When there is no statute (*ley*) exactly applicable to the issue in question, one shall apply the custom of the place (*la costumbre del lugar*) and, in default, the general principles of the law (*los principios generales de derecito*)."

Professors Merryman and Clark have described the importance of customs in the emerging countries of Africa:

> African law is a cauldron of tribal custom and of Christian, Moslem, and colonial influences. Independence upset the pot, and one can make only the most tentative generalizations about the shape of the law in Africa. Customary law differs radically from tribe to tribe. It is often unwritten. Like Moslem and Hindu law it orders social, religious and legal life, and it functions conservatively to preserve traditional forms of family and society. The colonial power superimposed another layer of law on African culture, an influence still felt strongly in the court systems and elsewhere, but tribal custom has persisted and in some cases has even grown more important as a consequence of post-independence nationalism. Customary law, however, is inadequate as a vehicle for modernization or economic progress, and legislators in the new nations struggle to reconcile the heritage of African law with the African future. Internal diversity of customary laws is an additional complication. Nigeria, for example, must contend with 200 tribes and, not surprisingly, favors internal unification over custom. Increasingly, law is used not to serve existing preferences and institutions but to remake them. Land law has been reformed to meet the exigencies of market economics and family law has been rewritten to improve the status of women and to eliminate polygamy, dowry

---

7. 113 S.Ct. 2786 (1993).

and other practices. The future of customary law in Africa is uncertain." [8]

FRYE v. UNITED STATES

United States Court of Appeals, District of Columbia, 1923.
293 Fed. 1013.

VAN ORSDEL, ASSOCIATE JUSTICE.

Appellant, defendant below, was convicted of the crime of murder in the second degree, and from the judgment prosecutes this appeal.

A single assignment of error is presented for our consideration. In the course of the trial counsel for defendant offered an expert witness to testify to the result of a deception test made upon defendant. The test is described as the systolic blood pressure deception test. It is asserted that blood pressure is influenced by change in the emotions of the witness, and that the systolic blood pressure rises are brought about by nervous impulses sent to the sympathetic branch of the autonomic nervous system. Scientific experiments, it is claimed, have demonstrated that fear, rage, and pain always produce a rise of systolic blood pressure, and that conscious deception or falsehood, concealment of facts, or guilt of crime, accompanied by fear of detection when the person is under examination, raises the systolic blood pressure in a curve, which corresponds exactly to the struggle going on in the subject's mind, between fear and attempted control of that fear, as the examination touches the vital points in respect of which he is attempting to deceive the examiner.

In other words, the theory seems to be that truth is spontaneous, and comes without conscious effort, while the utterance of a falsehood requires a conscious effort, which is reflected in the blood pressure. The rise thus produced is easily detected and distinguished from the rise produced by mere fear of the examination itself. In the former instance, the pressure rises higher than in the latter, and is more pronounced as the examination proceeds, while in the latter case, if the subject is telling the truth, the pressure registers highest at the beginning of the examination, and gradually diminishes as the examination proceeds.

Prior to the trial defendant was subjected to this deception test, and counsel offered the scientist who conducted the test as an expert to testify to the results obtained. The offer was objected to by counsel for the government, and the court sustained the objection. Counsel for defendant then offered to have the proffered witness conduct a test in the presence of the jury. This also was denied.

8. J. Merryman & D. Clark, Comparative Law: Western European and Latin American Legal Systems 9 (1979).

Counsel for defendant, in their able presentation of the novel question involved, correctly state in their brief that no cases directly in point have been found. The broad ground, however, upon which they plant their case, is succinctly stated in their brief as follows:

The rule is that the opinions of experts or skilled witnesses are admissible in evidence in those cases in which the matter of inquiry is such that inexperienced persons are unlikely to prove capable of forming a correct judgment upon it, for the reason that the subject-matter so far partakes of a science, art, or trade as to require a previous habit or experience or study in it, in order to acquire a knowledge of it. When the question involved does not lie within the range of common experience or common knowledge, but requires special experience or special knowledge, then the opinions of witnesses skilled in that particular science, art, or trade to which the question relates are admissible in evidence.

Numerous cases are cited in support of this rule. Just when a scientific principle or discovery crosses the line between the experimental and demonstrable stages is difficult to define. Somewhere in this twilight zone the evidential force of the principle must be recognized, and while courts will go a long way in admitting expert testimony deduced from a well-recognized scientific principle or discovery, the thing from which the deduction is made must be sufficiently established to have gained general acceptance in the particular field in which it belongs.

We think the systolic blood pressure deception test has not yet gained such standing and scientific recognition among physiological and psychological authorities as would justify the courts in admitting expert testimony deduced from the discovery, development, and experiments thus far made.

The judgment is affirmed.

DAUBERT v. MERRELL DOW PHARMACEUTICALS, INC.

Supreme Court of the United States, 1993.
___ U.S. ___, 113 S.Ct. 2786, 125 L.Ed.2d 469.

JUSTICE BLACKMUN delivered the opinion of the Court.

In this case we are called upon to determine the standard for admitting expert scientific testimony in a federal trial.

I

Petitioners Jason Daubert and Eric Schuller are minor children born with serious birth defects. They and their parents sued respondent in California state court, alleging that the birth defects had been caused by the mothers' ingestion of Bendectin, a prescription anti-nausea drug marketed by respondent. Respondent removed the suits to federal court on diversity grounds.

After extensive discovery, respondent moved for summary judgment, contending that Bendectin does not cause birth defects in humans and that petitioners would be unable to come forward with any admissible evidence that it does. In support of its motion, respondent submitted an affidavit of Steven H. Lamm, physician and epidemiologist, who is a well-credentialed expert on the risks from exposure to various chemical substances. Doctor Lamm stated that he had reviewed all the literature on Bendectin and human birth defects—more than 30 published studies involving over 130,000 patients. No study had found Bendectin to be a human teratogen (*i.e.,* a substance capable of causing malformations in fetuses). On the basis of this review, Doctor Lamm concluded that maternal use of Bendectin during the first trimester of pregnancy has not been shown to be a risk factor for human birth defects.

Petitioners did not (and do not) contest this characterization of the published record regarding Bendectin. Instead, they responded to respondent's motion with the testimony of eight experts of their own, each of whom also possessed impressive credentials. These experts had concluded that Bendectin can cause birth defects. Their conclusions were based upon "in vitro" (test tube) and "in vivo" (live) animal studies that found a link between Bendectin and malformations; pharmacological studies of the chemical structure of Bendectin that purported to show similarities between the structure of the drug and that of other substances known to cause birth defects; and the "reanalysis" of previously published epidemiological (human statistical) studies.

The District Court granted respondent's motion for summary judgment. The court stated that scientific evidence is admissible only if the principle upon which it is based is " 'sufficiently established to have general acceptance in the field to which it belongs.' " 727 F.Supp. 570, 572 (S.D. Cal.1989), quoting United States v. Kilgus, 571 F.2d 508, 510 (CA9 1978). The court concluded that petitioners' evidence did not meet this standard. Given the vast body of epidemiological data concerning Bendectin, the court held, expert opinion which is not based on epidemiological evidence is not admissible to establish causation. Thus, the animal-cell studies, live-animal studies, and chemical-structure analyses on which petitioners had relied could not raise by themselves a reasonably disputable jury issue regarding causation. Petitioners' epidemiological analyses, based as they were on recalculations of data in previously published studies that had found no causal link between the drug and birth defects, were ruled to be inadmissible because they had not been published or subjected to peer review.

The United States Court of Appeals for the Ninth Circuit affirmed. 951 F.2d 1128 (1991). Citing Frye v. United States, 54 App.D.C. 46, 47, 293 F. 1013, 1014 (1923), the court stated that expert opinion based on a scientific technique is inadmissible unless the technique is "generally accepted" as reliable in the relevant scientific community. 951 F.2d, at 1129–1130. The court declared that expert opinion based on a methodology that diverges "significantly from the procedures accepted by recognized authorities in the field ... cannot be shown to be 'generally accepted as a reliable technique.'" *Id.,* at 1130, quoting United States v. Solomon, 753 F.2d 1522, 1526 (CA9 1985).

In the 70 years since its formulation in the *Frye* case, the "general acceptance" test has been the dominant standard for determining the admissibility of novel scientific evidence at trial. See E. Green & C. Nesson, Problems, Cases, and Materials on Evidence 649 (1983). Although under increasing attack of late, the rule continues to be followed by a majority of courts, including the Ninth Circuit.

The *Frye* test has its origin in a short and citation-free 1923 decision concerning the admissibility of evidence derived from a systolic blood pressure deception test, a crude precursor to the polygraph machine. In what has become a famous (perhaps infamous) passage, the then Court of Appeals for the District of Columbia described the device and its operation and declared:

> "Just when a scientific principle or discovery crosses the line between the experimental and demonstrable stages is difficult to define. Somewhere in this twilight zone the evidential force of the principle must be recognized, and while courts will go a long way in admitting expert testimony deduced from a well-recognized scientific principle or discovery, *the thing from which the deduction is made must be sufficiently established to have gained general acceptance in the particular field in which it belongs.*" 54 App.D.C., at 47, 293 F., at 1014 (emphasis added).

Because the deception test had "not yet gained such standing and scientific recognition among physiological and psychological authorities as would justify the courts in admitting expert testimony deduced from the discovery, development, and experiments thus far made," evidence of its results was ruled inadmissible. *Ibid.*

The merits of the *Frye* test have been much debated, and scholarship on its proper scope and application is legion. Petitioners' primary attack, however, is not on the content but on the continuing authority of the rule. They contend that the *Frye* test was superseded by the adoption of the Federal Rules of Evidence. We agree.

We interpret the legislatively-enacted Federal Rules of Evidence as we would any statute. Beech Aircraft Corp. v. Rainey, 488 U.S. 153, 163 (1988). Rule 402 provides the baseline:

> "All relevant evidence is admissible, except as otherwise provided by the Constitution of the United States, by Act of Congress, by these rules, or by other rules prescribed by the Supreme Court pursuant to statutory authority. Evidence which is not relevant is not admissible."

"Relevant evidence" is defined as that which has "any tendency to make the existence of any fact that is of consequence to the determination of the action more probable or less probable than it would be without the evidence." Rule 401. The Rule's basic standard of relevance thus is a liberal one.

Frye, of course, predated the Rules by half a century. In United States v. Abel, 469 U.S. 45 (1984), we considered the pertinence of background common law in interpreting the Rules of Evidence. We noted that the Rules occupy the field, *id.,* at 49, but, quoting Professor Cleary, the Reporter, explained that the common law nevertheless could serve as an aid to their application:

> "In principle, under the Federal Rules no common law of evidence remains. 'All relevant evidence is admissible, except as otherwise provided....' In reality, of course, the body of common law knowledge continues to exist, though in the somewhat altered form of a source of guidance in the exercise of delegated powers." *Id.,* at 51–52.

We found the common-law precept at issue in the *Abel* case entirely consistent with Rule 402's general requirement of admissibility, and considered it unlikely that the drafters had intended to change the rule. *Id.,* at 50–51. In Bourjaily v. United States, 483 U.S. 171 (1987), on the other hand, the Court was unable to find a particular common-law doctrine in the Rules, and so held it superseded.

Here there is a specific Rule that speaks to the contested issue. Rule 702, governing expert testimony, provides:

> "If scientific, technical, or other specialized knowledge will assist the trier of fact to understand the evidence or to determine a fact in issue, a witness qualified as an expert by knowledge, skill, experience, training, or education, may testify thereto in the form of an opinion or otherwise."

Nothing in the text of this Rule establishes "general acceptance" as an absolute prerequisite to admissibility. Nor does respondent present any clear indication that Rule 702 or the Rules as a whole were intended to incorporate a "general acceptance" standard. The drafting history makes no mention of *Frye,* and a rigid "general acceptance" requirement would be at odds with the "liberal thrust" of the Federal Rules and their "general approach of relaxing the traditional barriers to 'opinion' testimony." Beech Aircraft Corp. v. Rainey, 488 U.S., at 169 (citing Rules 701 to 705). See also Weinstein, Rule 702 of the Federal Rules of Evidence is Sound; It Should Not Be Amended, 138 F.R.D. 631, 631 (1991) ("The Rules were designed to depend primarily upon lawyer-adversaries and sensible triers of fact to evaluate conflicts"). Given the Rules' permissive backdrop and their inclusion of a specific rule on expert testimony that does not mention "general acceptance," the assertion that the Rules somehow assimilated *Frye* is unconvincing. *Frye* made "general acceptance" the exclusive test for admitting expert scientific testimony. That austere standard, absent from and incompatible with the Federal Rules of Evidence, should not be applied in federal trials.

That the *Frye* test was displaced by the Rules of Evidence does not mean, however, that the Rules themselves place no limits on the admissibility of purportedly scientific evidence. Nor is the trial judge disabled from screening such evidence. To the contrary, under the Rules the trial judge must ensure that any and all scientific testimony or evidence admitted is not only relevant, but reliable.

BENJAMIN N. CARDOZO, THE NATURE OF THE JUDICIAL PROCESS *

If history and philosophy do not serve to fix the direction of a principle, custom may step in. When we speak of custom, we may mean more things than one. "Consuetudo," says Coke, "is one of the maine triangles of the lawes of England; these lawes being divided into common law, statute law and customs." Here common law and custom are thought of as distinct. Not so, however, Blackstone: "This unwritten or Common Law is properly distinguishable into three kinds: (1) General customs, which are the universal rule of the whole Kingdom, and form the Common Law, in its stricter and more usual signification. (2) Particular customs, which for the most part affect only the inhabitants of particular districts. (3) Certain particular laws, which by custom are adopted and used by some particular courts of pretty general and extensive jurisdiction."

Undoubtedly the creative energy of custom in the development of common law is less today than it was in bygone times. Even in bygone times, its energy was very likely exaggerated by Blackstone and his followers. "Today we recognize," in the words of Pound, "that the custom is a custom of judicial decision, not of popular action." It is "doubtful," says Gray, "whether at all stages of legal history, rules laid down by judges have not generated custom, rather than custom generated the rules." In these days, at all events, we look to custom, not so much for the creation of new rules, but for the tests and standards that are to determine how established rules shall be applied. When custom seeks to do more than this, there is a growing tendency in the law to leave development to legislation. Judges do not feel the same need of putting the *imprimatur* of law upon customs of recent growth, knocking for entrance into the legal system, and viewed askance because of some novel aspect of form or feature, as they would if legislatures were not in frequent session, capable of establishing a title that will be unimpeached and unimpeachable. But the power is not lost because it is exercised with caution. "The law merchant," says an English judge, "is not fixed and stereotyped, it has not yet been arrested in its growth by being moulded into a code; it is, to use the words of Lord Chief Justice Cockburn in Goodwin v. Roberts, L.R. 10 Exch. 346, capable of being expanded and enlarged to meet the wants of trade." In the absence of inconsistent statute, new classes of negotiable instruments may be created by mercantile practice. The obligations of public and private

* 58–62 (1921). Reprinted by permission of Yale University Press from The Nature of the Judicial Process by Benjamin N. Cardozo. Copyright © 1921 by Yale University Press.

corporations may retain the quality of negotiability, despite the presence of a seal, which at common law would destroy it. "There is nothing immoral or contrary to good policy in making them negotiable if the necessities of commerce require that they should be so. A mere technical dogma of the courts or the common law cannot prohibit the commercial world from inventing or issuing any species of security not known in the last century." So, in the memory of men yet living, the great inventions that embodied the power of steam and electricity, the railroad and the steamship, the telegraph and the telephone, have built up new customs and new law. Already there is a body of legal literature that deals with the legal problems of the air.

NOTE

Compare Cardozo's observations with those of Friedrich Von Savigny: "The foundation of the Law has its existence, its reality in the common consciousness of the people. This existence is invisible. How can we become acquainted with it? We become acquainted with it as it manifests itself in external acts, as it appears in practice, manners, and custom: by the uniformity of a continuous and continuing mode of action, we recognize that the belief of the people is its common root, and not mere chance. Thus custom is the sign of positive law, not its foundation." [1] Heut. rom. Recht. § 12 p. 35.

Gray wondered whether law generates custom or custom, law. The Autobiography of Miss Jane Pittman chronicled the life of a black woman, born on a pre-Civil War plantation in the south and who capped a courageous career by drinking from a "whites-only" public fountain during the height of the civil rights movement in the 1960's. How do you think she would have responded to Gray's query?

Consider Justice Brennan's statement:

When the common law flourished greatly, law was merged ... with the other disciplines and sources of human value. Custom, for example, was the cherished source of the common law of that time. What was declared custom but the accumulated wisdom of social problems of society itself? The function of law was to formalize and preserve this wisdom, but it certainly did not purport to originate it.

Brennan, *How Goes the Supreme Court*, 36 Mercer L.Rev. 781, 786 (1985).

––––––––

MOORE v. GANIM

Supreme Court of Connecticut, 1995.
233 Conn. 557, 660 A.2d 742.

BERDON, J., dissenting. * * * These cases are about the state government's obligation to provide the minimal subsistence necessary for humane survival to those of its population who are utterly impoverished.

Connecticut has recognized, from the time the colony first came into existence in the middle of the seventeenth century, that the government must provide these survival needs for the indigent. This history demonstrates that the collective conscience of our people requires that these provisions be made for the poor. Furthermore, it is clear that this historic right of the poor, which equates to the right to humane survival, is absolutely fundamental and is implicit under our state constitution. Therefore, any legislative act that restricts the right to the minimal subsistence necessary for such survival must withstand constitutional scrutiny. * * *

The state constitution, which was first formally adopted in 1818, does not explicitly provide for the right of the poor to receive subsistence from the towns. Nevertheless, we have previously recognized that there are some rights that are so fundamental they need not be explicitly set forth in the state constitution.

The preamble and article first, s 10, of the Connecticut constitution provide the textual framework for the implicit right of the poor to minimal subsistence and its enforcement. The preamble provides: "The People of Connecticut acknowledging with gratitude, the good providence of God, in having permitted them to enjoy a free government; do, in order more effectually to define, secure, and perpetuate the liberties, rights and privileges which they have derived from their ancestors; hereby, after a careful consideration and revision, ordain and establish the following constitution and form of civil government." Section 10 of article first of the Declaration of Rights provides: "All courts shall be open, and every person, for an injury done to him in his person, property or reputation, shall have remedy by due course of law, and right and justice administered without sale, denial or delay."

The plain language of the preamble makes clear that the framers intended our constitution to perpetuate and protect the rights and privileges of the people that were firmly rooted in the law and customs of Connecticut prior to the adoption of the state's first formal charter of liberty. The framers provided in article first, s 10, that the court will be open to enforce these rights. In order to determine the scope of the rights and privileges encompassed in these open-ended constitutional provisions, therefore, we must begin by examining the state of the law as it existed prior to 1818. See State v. Ross, supra, 230 Conn. 46–47. Indeed, this is the crucial step in our state constitutional analysis.

We look primarily at two sources in order to determine the state of the law as it existed in 1818 and prior thereto: law codified in statutory form and the common law.

Statutory Law

As a source of Connecticut legal history, our colonial statutes are perhaps a more accurate and complete statement of colonial law than the law stated in the written decisions of our early courts. As one commentator pointed out, Connecticut eschewed the idea that rules of law should be developed through a process of judicial decisions. L. Lewis, "The Development of a Common Law System in Connecticut," 27 Conn.B.J. 419, 421 (1953). Fearful that such a system might harken back to the common law injustices of England, and desiring to express their laws in explicit terms, the colonists exhibited "complete reliance on statute law." Id. Indeed, of all the colonies, Connecticut most clearly rejected the common law system. Id., 419. These early statutes, therefore, are an important and reliable source for understanding our legal tradition in Connecticut. W. Horton, The Connecticut State Constitution (1993) p. 4. We have consistently stated that rights established by statute prior to 1818 are an important source of rights recognized as implicit under our 1818 constitution. See, e.g., Kelley Property Development, Inc., v. Lebanon, supra, 226 Conn. 331–33; Dubay v. Irish, supra, 207 Conn. 529; Ecker v. West Hartford, supra, 205 Conn. 234; Gentile v. Altermatt, supra, 169 Conn. 286.

The first codification of Connecticut statutes occurred in 1650, when the General Court of the colony of Connecticut adopted a systematic body of laws prepared by attorney Roger Ludlow. This body of laws became known as the Ludlow Code. Significantly, that Code included a provision for governmental assistance to the poor. This provision stated in pertinent part: "POORE. It is ordered by this courte and authority thereof, That the court of magistrates shall have power to determine all differences about lawfull settling, and providing for pore persons, and shall have power to dispose of all unsettled persons, into such townes as they shall judge to bee most fitt, for the maintenance and imployment of such persons and familyes, for the ease of the countrye." The Code of 1650 of the General Court of Connecticut (S. Andrus pub. 1822) p. 80.
* * *

In sum, from the colony's first code adopted in 1650 through the adoption of the first formal constitution in 1818—a period of 168 years— the statutory law of the state was clear: the towns were required to provide for the basic needs of the poor. * * *

These early statutes are striking proof of our tradition in Connecticut, and of the obligation of the towns, to provide minimal subsistence to our poor and needy. The fundamental importance of these statutes is underscored by the statutory requirement during the early colonial period that each family purchase a copy of the code. Indeed, these early statutes reveal that "[w]e have a continuous unbroken tradition in Connecticut dating back from the middle of the seventeenth century right down to the present that the public will be responsible for all the medical care and other needs of [the] poor in the State of Connecticut...." Doe v. Maher, supra, 40 Conn.Sup. 412–13.

Common Law

Although our early statutes are very instructive in interpreting the legal traditions of Connecticut that are incorporated as rights in our state constitution, they are not the only source of these implied rights. "In Connecticut constitutional law, it is well established that several rights now denominated as constitutional law had well-recognized common law antecedents." E. Peters, "Common Law Antecedents of Constitutional Law in Connecticut," 53 Albany L.Rev. 259, 261 (1989). To gain a complete understanding of the meaning of our constitutional history, therefore, we must also examine the early common law of Connecticut. * * *

Superior Court Judge Jesse Root, a prominent member of the judiciary in the eighteenth and early nineteenth centuries, defined the common law in his introduction to the first of two volumes of court reports, which covered decisions rendered by the Superior Court and the Supreme Court of Errors between July, 1789, and June, 1793. Judge Root defined the common law of this state to include (1) "the adjudication of the courts of justice and rules of practice"; (2) "usages and customs, universally assented to"; and (3) what could be loosely summarized as "natural law." 1 J. Root, supra, pp. ix-xiii. Judge Root's understanding of our early common law is particularly instructive on the issue of the incorporation of the common law into the open-ended preamble of the constitution of 1818. Not only was Judge Root one of the outstanding legal scholars of his day, but he was also a prominent delegate to the constitutional convention. W. Horton, The Connecticut State Constitution, supra, p. 12. Each of Judge Root's three identified sources of common law reveals the tradition of this state of providing minimal subsistence to its destitute inhabitants.

1. *Adjudication of the Courts*

Judge Root recognized the difficulty of identifying the common law as it had developed in decisions of Connecticut courts. He pointed out that "we have no treatises upon the subject, and but one small volume of reports containing a period of about two years only, and a treatise lately wrote by Mr. [Zephaniah] Swift, containing a commentary on the government and laws of this state...." 1 J. Root, supra, p. xiii.

Notwithstanding the small number of published opinions of the courts, the only two legal scholars who wrote on the subject prior to 1818 clearly indicated that the poor had a right to minimal subsistence. Chief Justice Swift defined the law of Connecticut with respect to the rights of poor people in his 1795 treatise. His words are illuminating: "[E]ach town [is] obliged to take care of and maintain their own poor, [and] this [is] a principal part of the duty of the selectmen. The selectmen are bound to provide necessaries for all the inhabitants of the town, who are incapable of supporting themselves. Towns are obliged to support their respective inhabitants, whether living in the town to which they belong, or any other town, either with or without a certificate, who may need relief." 1 Z. Swift, A System of the Laws of the State of Connecticut (1795) p. 119.

Although Judge Root was a conservative member of the judiciary, he, unlike the majority in this case, recognized government's obligation to the poor. In his introduction to the published cases of 1789 through 1793, Judge Root wrote that "[i]t is the duty of every government to protect and to provide for the poor; the laws of the state ... ordain ... that every town shall take care of, provide for and maintain, its own poor." (Internal quotation marks omitted.) 1 J. Root, supra, p. xxviii. Judge Root explained that "[t]he poor and indigent in all countries, call not only for private charity, but for support and assistance from the government, and to give scope to the exercise of benevolence, the most noble and godlike virtue...." Id. * * *

2. Usages and Customs

A second component of the common law, according to Judge Root, was the "usages and customs, universally assented to and adopted in practice by the citizens at large." 1 J. Root, supra, p. xi. Judge Root wrote: "So these unwritten customs and regulations which are reasonable and beneficial, and which have the sanction of universal consent and adoption in practice, amongst the citizens at large or particular classes of them, have the force of laws under the authority of the people, and the courts of justice will recognize and declare them to be such, and to be obligatory upon the citizens as necessary rules of construction and of justice. The reasonableness and utility of their operation, and the universality of their adoption, are the better evidence of their existence and of their having the general consent and approbation, than the circumstance of its being forgotten when they began to exist." Id., pp. xii-xiii.

The practice of government to provide for the poor in this state is well documented in recorded history. "During the early colonial period [the principle that poor relief was a town matter] was so fully carried out in both the Connecticut and the New Haven colony, that in the town records are the earliest statements regarding poor relief. Thus in March, 1640 ... the town of Hartford voted to set aside twenty acres on the east side of the Connecticut river 'for the accommodating of several poor men that the town shall think meet to accommodate there.'" E. Capen, supra, pp. 22–23. Indeed, the practice of this state of caring for the poor was documented for a period of at least 175 years before the adoption of the constitution of 1818.

Christopher Collier, the Connecticut state historian and a professor of history at the University of Connecticut, testified in the Hilton case with respect to our history of supporting the poor. According to Professor Collier, Connecticut was unique in placing this obligation on government. While other colonies and states allowed private charities to fulfill the basic needs of their poor, Connecticut did so as a matter of governmental responsibility and obligation. The history, usage and customs of Connecticut, therefore, imparted into our 1818 constitution an affirmative obligation on the part of the state and its towns to provide minimal subsistence for the poor.

3. *Natural Law*

Finally, it is important to consider the third component recognized by Judge Root as a source of our early common law: the legal and philosophical theory known today as natural law. Although this theory has fallen into disfavor since the era of Judge Root, we nevertheless must examine its tenets in order to determine what legal notions were in the minds and hearts of the drafters of our first formal constitution.

Natural law occupied a prominent position in our colonial jurisprudence. The Fundamental Orders were premised on natural law, as were the laws of the colony of Connecticut of 1672. According to Professor Collier, "to Connecticut jurists, common law meant more than judicial precedent and case law; it included the natural law as well." C. Collier, "The Connecticut Declaration of Rights Before the Constitution of 1818: A Victim of Revolutionary Redefinition," 15 Conn.L.Rev. 87, 94 (1982); see also Doe v. Maher, supra, 40 Conn.Sup. 423. Indeed, many of our early decisions supported the legal principle that the government must be guided by fundamental notions of what is morally right. See, e.g., Booth v. Woodbury, 32 Conn. 118, 127 (1864) ("principles of natural justice"); Welch v. Wadsworth, 30 Conn. 149, 155 (1861) ("But the power of the legislature in this respect is not unlimited. They can not entirely disregard the fundamental principles of the social compact. Those principles underlie all legislation, irrespective of constitutional restraints, and if the act in question is a clear violation of them, it is our duty to hold it abortive and void."); Goshen v. Stonington, 4 Conn. 209, 225 (1822) ("vested rights").

Judge Root addressed the natural law obligation of the government to provide for the poor: "[T]he highest character given of any ruler on earth is, that he judgeth the people in his righteousness, and the poor with judgment; that he delivereth the needy when they cry, and the poor that hath no helper; that he dealeth bread to the hungry, and delivereth him that is ready to perish." 1 J. Root, supra, p. xxviii. Furthermore, in Judge Root's view, natural law of the late eighteenth and early nineteenth centuries "define[d] the obligations and duties between husbands and wives, parents and children, brothers and sisters, between the rulers and the people, and the people or citizens towards each other: This is the Magna Charta of all our natural and religious rights and liberties, and the only solid basis of our civil constitution and privileges—in short, it supports, pervades and enlightens all the ways of man, to the noblest ends by the happiest means, when and wherever its precepts and instructions are observed and followed—the usages and customs of men and the decisions of the courts of justice serve to declare and illustrate the principles of this law...." (Emphasis added.) 1 J. Root, supra, pp. x-xi.

Indeed, the framers of our 1818 constitution incorporated this concept directly into that document. Article first, s 1, provides that "[a]ll men when they form a social compact, are equal in rights; and no man or set of men are entitled to exclusive government emoluments or privileges from the community.'' This social compact is deeply entrenched in this state's history. It first was articulated in the Fundamental Orders of 1639, and was repeated in the Declaration of Rights of 1650.

Professor Collier discussed the significance of this theory during his testimony in the Hilton case. He explained that the social compact not only establishes government, but defines and limits the authority of government. It is a contract, in fact, between the people and their government. The substance of this contract today, which has been carried forward from the Declaration of Rights in 1650, is set forth in article first, s 1, of the state constitution. According to Professor Collier, the affirmative obligation of the state to provide subsistence to the poor was part of the fabric of the social compact in Connecticut.

Section 5

VALUE JUDGMENTS *

To understand the role of value judgments, we must first identify the types of conflicts facing the courts. Cardozo taught that there are three:

- Where the rule of law is clear and its application to the facts is equally clear.

- Where the rule of law is clear and the sole question is its application to the facts at bar.

- Where neither the rule is clear, nor, a fortiori, its application is clear.

Cardozo described the third category as the "serious business" of judges, "where a decision one way or another, will count for the future, will advance and retard, sometimes much, sometimes little, the development of the law." [34] If the controversy is in the third category, it is imperative to recognize with specificity where lies the conflict between the litigants. Here, too, I suggest three categories:

- Finding the law. This may involve inductive generalization or analogy. It may also involve choosing among competing precepts. The choice becomes the major premise of the deductive reasoning syllogism.

- Interpretation of the legal precept. Here there are no competing precepts. The parties agree on the controlling major premise. They differ only as to what it means.

- Application of the chosen legal precept, as interpreted, to the facts found or to be found by the fact finder. The facts found

---

* Adapted from R. Aldisert, Logic for Lawyers: A Guide to Clear Legal Thinking (1989).

34. B. Cardozo, The Nature of the Judicial Process 168–170 (1921).

>comprise the minor premise; here is where many sparks fly
>in the pleading or trial stages.

Early recognition of the specific conflict can immediately sharpen the issues. If it's a category-one case, the lawyer and the judge must also proceed into a consideration of categories two and three; in a category-two case, it is necessary to consider category three as well.

We emphasize this aspect of the judicial process here because, at this stage, formal rules of logic do not inform the choice for the judge. Judges constantly strive to seek an accommodation between competing sets of principles. There are times, however, when the scales seem evenly balanced, and it is difficult to determine exactly where the weight does lie. At these times, the jural philosophy of the individual judge comes into play, consciously or otherwise, by means of a value judgment that places a greater weight on one competing principle than another. "Indeed, the most important attributes of a judge are his value system and his capacity for evaluative judgment," writes Professor Robert S. Summers. "Only through the mediating phenomena of reasons, especially substantive reasons, can a judge articulately bring his values to bear." [35]

>Consider the observations of Professor Paul Freund:

>Much of law is designed to avoid the necessity for the judge to reach what Holmes called his "can't helps," his ultimate convictions or values. The force of precedent, the close applicability of statute law, the separation of powers, legal preemptions, statutes of limitations, rules of pleading and evidence, and above all the pragmatic assessments of fact that point to one result whichever ultimate values be assumed, all enable the judge in most cases to stop short of a resort to his personal standards. When these prove unavailing, as is more likely in the case of courts of last resort at the frontiers of the law, and most likely in a supreme constitutional court, the judge necessarily resorts to his own scheme of values. It may therefore be said that the most important thing about a judge is his philosophy; and if it be dangerous for him to have one, it is at all events less dangerous than the self-deception of having none.[36]

From counsel's trial memorandum or brief, or from experience and independent research, the judge recognizes that a weighing process or assigning of priorities precedes his or her embarkation on a journey of legal reasoning. The judge thus begins by choosing from among competing legal precepts or competing analogies. Often there is no choice. Often the judge must formulate a rule of law because no rule or principle appears visible for the choosing. In either event, this formulation must be fortified by persuasive reasoning. Two guidelines aid both the choice

35. Summers, *Two Types of Substantive Reasons: The Core of a Theory of Common-Law Justification,* 63 Cornell L.Rev. 707, 710 (1978).

36. Freund, "Social Justice and the Law," in Social Justice 93, 110 (R. Brandt ed. 1962).

or formulation and its ultimate acceptance: first, the judge should avoid arbitrary or aleatory choices; second, the judge has a duty of "reasoned elaboration in law-finding." Julius Stone says this is necessary so that the choice seems, to the entire legal profession, "if not right, then as right as possible. The *duty* of elaboration indicates that reasons cannot be *merely* ritualistic formulae or diversionary sleight of hand." [37]

Max Weber, the important European social theorist, suggested that the term "value judgment" refers "to practical evaluation of a phenomenon which is capable of being ... worthy of either condemnation or approval." He distinguished between "logically determinable or empirically observable facts" and "the value judgments which are derived from practical standards, ethical standards or ... views." [38] We draw the same distinction here. We judges each have our own preferences among a sea of legal standards, any one in principle respectable, and we make our selections. Sometimes we select extralegal standards, making a choice from ethical, moral, social, political, or economic concepts offered by diverse teachers or philosophers. Because a value judgment figures in the choice of competing precepts, interpretations and applications, how can a judge arrive at this decision without being arbitrary?

Roger J. Traynor reminded us that "one entrusted with decision, traditionally above base prejudices, must also rise above the vanity of stubborn preconceptions, sometimes euphemistically called the courage of one's convictions. He knows well enough that he must severely discount his own predilections, of however high grade he regards them, which is to say he must bring to his intellectual labors a cleansing doubt of his omniscience, indeed even of his perception." [39]

In the law, as well as in life itself, judging is the act of selecting and weighing facts and suggestions as they present themselves, as well as deciding whether the alleged facts are really facts and whether an idea suggested is a sound idea or merely a fancy. A good judge, dealing with relative values, can estimate, appraise, and evaluate with discernment. No hard-and-fast rules can be given for this operation of selecting and rejecting, or fixing upon significant evidentiary facts. It all comes down to the good judgment, and the good sense, of the one judging. To be a good judge is to perceive the relevant indicative or signifying values of the various features of a perplexing situation. It is to know what to eliminate as irrelevant and what to retain as relevant. In ordinary matters, we call this power knack, tact, or cleverness. In the law, as in other important affairs, we call it insight or discernment.

What we should expect from our judges, at a minimum, is a willingness to consider alternative solutions to a problem. A "result-oriented" judge, in the sense condemned, is one who consistently resists

37. Stone, *Man and Machine in the Search for Justice,* 16 Stan.L.Rev. 515, 530, 536–37 (1964).

38. Weber, "Value Judgments in Social Science," in Weber Selections 69 (W. Runciman, ed. 1987).

39. Traynor, *Reasoning in a Circle of Law,* 56 Va.L.Rev. 739, 751 (1970).

considering arguments contrary to an initial impression or preexisting inclination. We cannot expect judicial minds to be untainted by their first impressions of a case. What we can expect is that the initial impression will be fluid enough to yield to later impressions. We can also expect that judges will be intellectually interested in an outcome based on sound reason. What we can demand is that judges employ logically sound techniques of intellectual inquiry and reflection when making value judgments, and then explain both their premises and their conclusions to us in clear language evidencing impeccable logical form.

Section 6

PUBLIC POLICY AND SOCIAL WELFARE

A. GENERAL CONSIDERATIONS

In retrospect, Cardozo chose an unfortunate label to describe a decisional process along lines of justice, morals and social welfare as the "method of sociology." [1] The name not only did not stick, but it has also created confusion, primarily because process sometimes is mistaken for data used to decide cases. For example, use of a Brandeis brief to emphasize social data in a case is confused with methodologies of reaching or justifying a decision. What Cardozo meant in 1921 was probably what Harry W. Jones, Cardozo Professor of Jurisprudence at Columbia, had in mind in 1974: "Law is not a form of art for art's sake; its ends-in-view are social, nothing more and nothing less than the establishment and maintenance of a social environment in which the quality of human life can be spirited, improving and unimpaired." [2] A proper shorthand version probably would be "the method of public policy and social welfare."

The heart of Cardozo's essay, The Nature of the Judicial Process, was an appeal for an end-in-view in decision making, an appeal for a process in which the court should not concern itself exclusively with the logical symmetry of legal precepts in reaching a decision. A stirring argument was sounded that it was legitimate, and often preferable, for the court to consider the effect of a given decision on society. Cardozo's plea must be considered in terms of the juridical environment in which it was made, America in the early 1920's. A brief repetition of this era's history is now helpful.

At the end of the previous century, Roscoe Pound had identified excessive rigidity in American decision making processes. He described our system as conceptual jurisprudence, a slavish adherence to *elegantia juris*, the symmetry of law, and suggested that we resembled too much

---

1. Similarly, there is some difficulty in reconciling his label "method of philosophy" with his description of extending a legal precept by what he called the rules of analogy. Perhaps, it would have been more comfortable to describe the "method of philosophy" as Inductive and Deductive Reasoning.

2. Jones, *An Invitation to Jurisprudence*, 74 Colum.L.Rev. 1023, 1024–26 (1974).

the rigid German *Begriffsjurisprudenz.* In his classic The Causes of Popular Dissatisfaction with the Administration of Justice,[3] Pound called for the end of mechanical jurisprudence: "The most important and most constant cause of dissatisfaction with all law at all times is to be found in the necessarily mechanical operation of legal rules."[4] He attacked blind adherence to precedents, to the rules and principles derived therefrom, as mechanical jurisprudence and slot machine justice. He advocated pragmatism as a philosophy of law.[5]

Pound's theme had been played more softly by Oliver Wendell Holmes a decade earlier—that the social consequences of a court's decision were legitimate considerations in decision making.[6] The lament was not limited to the time nor the place. A half century later Italy's great legal scholar Calamendrei passionately explained that juridical logic is the most valuable instrument of justice only so long as it remains an instrument, but it becomes its own most dangerous enemy when allowed to dominate. He contended that at present formal logic has got the upper hand, and that this is perhaps a secular legacy of the scholastic tradition, "not yet exhausted in our university education, in which jurisprudence was nothing but a chapter of logic, understood as the art of language. ... I confess to you ... my diffidence, which sometimes approaches terror" of juridical logic. "I have the suspicion that in general we jurists ... abuse the logic: even in the field of justice we have inherited, perhaps from medieval scholasticism more than the Roman *aequitas,* a tendency toward systematic architecture: we build castles of concepts to provide a dignified dwelling for justice, and we do not notice that little by little they are transformed into barred prisons from which she is unable to free herself."[7]

If Roscoe Pound's 1908 warning against mechanical decision making did not create a new American school of jurisprudence, at least it spawned widespread respectability for social utilitarianism. It added a new dimension to law's traditional objectives of consistency, certainty and predictability: a concern for society's welfare. A few years after Pound's warning, Cardozo delivered the Storrs lectures at Yale, stating: "The final cause of law is the welfare of society. The rule that misses its aim cannot permanently justify its existence."[8]

Holmes, Pound and Cardozo thus became America's leading exponents of a decision making school that traced its origin to the Franco–German movement of the late nineteenth century. Herman Kantorowicz summarized that which was known in Europe as the free law doctrine:

3. *Address by Roscoe Pound to the American Bar Association,* Aug. 29, 1906, in 40 American L.Rev. 729 (1906), reprinted in 8 Baylor L.Rev. 1 (1956).

4. *Id.* at 31; *see* 8 Baylor L.Rev. at 8.

5. *See generally* Pound, *Mechanical Jurisprudence,* 8 Colum.L.Rev. 605 (1908).

6. Holmes, *The Path of the Law,* 10 Harv.L.Rev. 457, 468–74 (1897).

7. P. Calamandrei *La funzione della giurisprudenza nel temp presente* (1955), in 6 Studi Sul Processo Civile 89 (1957).

8. Cardozo, The Nature of the Judicial Process 66.

The free law doctrine teaches (if we may sum up an elaborate system in a few words): The traditional sources of the law, the "formal" law, statutes and precedents, have gaps which must be filled up, must be filled up with law if the decision is to be a judicial decision, and this law must have a general character if equality before the law is to be maintained; the gap-filling material must therefore consist of rules, rules of law. These are "free" law in the sense that they are not formal law: they have not been formalized but are still in a state of transition like bills, principles of policy, business customs, inarticulate convictions, emotional preferences. Many of them are formulated for the purpose of a concrete judicial decision by the courts, acting within their discretion, through acts of will and value-judgments, and constitute therefore judge-made law. Their validity is far less than that of the formal law and sometimes nil, but their practical importance is even greater, because, where the formal law is clear and complete, litigation is not likely to occur.[9]

Today it can be said that in many legal disciplines, the objective of *elegantia juris* in legal precepts, institutions and procedures has become subordinate. In all but a few areas of static law, mechanical jurisprudence has become more historical than operational. As we have seen, by 1974 Professor Harry W. Jones was able to state elegantly that the new spirit of the law's purpose was to "establish and preserve a social environment in which the quality of human life can be spirited, improving and unimpaired."[10]

Achieving law's utilitarian purpose within a framework of reasonable predictability and stability is thus the ultimate, if sometimes elusive, objective. For the "sociological jurisprudent," the task is a most difficult one, because "public policy" and "social welfare" are not easily defined.

Notwithstanding lack of precise definition, contemporary American courts are resorting more and more to this method as a primary decisional tool. As we have earlier indicated, they are considering the pragmatic effects of alternative courses of decision. They are attempting to vindicate social needs of those who would be affected by their decision, irrespective of whether those ultimately affected are the precise litigants before them. They are looking to the general state of contemporary legislative policy and the felt needs of an increasingly pluralistic society insofar as they can be discerned. The courts are considering economic forces, scientific developments and identifiable expressions of public opinion.[11] This decisional process has deontological as well as teleologi-

9. Kantorowicz, *Some Rationalism About Realism*, 43 Yale L.J. 1240, 1241 (1934).

10. Jones, *An Invitation to Jurisprudence*, 74 Colum.L.Rev. 1023, 1030 (1974).

11. *See* Friedmann, *Legal Philosophy and Judicial Lawmaking*, 61 Colum.L.Rev. 821, 842–45 (1961).

cal overtones, and bears a remarkable resemblance to classical natural law.[12]

Cardozo's sociological method is now in full flower in the two important and dynamic disciplines of constitutional law and tort law. Contemporary American courts, state and federal alike, are very busy formulating public policy. Written opinions articulating the decisions become primary organons of the decisional process[13] and, as such, qualify as "performative utterances." So as not to be accused of deciding by magisterial caprice, personal bias, idiosyncracy or unstructured opinion, and to avoid criticism of *ipse dixit* declarations of public policy, the courts have taken to setting forth reasoned elaborations for their interest-conflicts resolutions.

ROSCOE POUND, MECHANICAL JURISPRUDENCE *

We are told that "in the Middle Ages human welfare and even religion was conceived under the form of legality, and in the modern world this has given place to utility." We have, then, the same task in jurisprudence that has been achieved in philosophy, in the natural sciences and in politics. We have to rid ourselves of this sort of legality and to attain a pragmatic, a sociological legal science.

> "What is needed nowadays," it has been said, "is that as against an abstract and unreal theory of State omnipotence on the one hand, and an atomistic and artificial view of individual independence on the other, the facts of the world with its innumerable bonds of association and the naturalness of social authority should be generally recognized, and become the basis of our laws, as it is of our life."

Herein is the task of the sociological jurist. Professor Small defines the sociological movement as "a frank endeavor to secure for the human factor in experience the central place which belongs to it in our whole scheme of thought and action." The sociological movement in jurisprudence is a movement for pragmatism as a philosophy of law; for the adjustment of principles and doctrines to the human conditions they are to govern rather than to assumed first principles; for putting the human factor in the central place and relegating logic to its true position as an instrument.

Jurisprudence is last in the march of the sciences away from the method of deduction from predetermined conceptions.

---

12. *See* J. Hall, Foundations of Jurisprudence 24–25 (1973).

13. *See* Keeton, *Judicial Law Reform— A Perspective on the Performance of Appellate Courts,* 44 Texas L.Rev. 1254 (1966).

* 8 Colum.L.Rev. 605, 609–10 (1908). Reprinted by permission.

BENJAMIN N. CARDOZO, THE NATURE
OF THE JUDICIAL PROCESS*

From history and philosophy and custom, we pass, therefore, to the force which in our day and generation is becoming the greatest of them all, the power of social justice which finds its outlet and expression in the method of sociology.

The final cause of law is the welfare of society. The rule that misses its aim cannot permanently justify its existence. "Ethical considerations can no more be excluded from the administration of justice which is the end and purpose of all civil laws than one can exclude the vital air from his room and live." [21] Logic and history and custom have their place. We will shape the law to conform to them when we may; but only within bounds. The end which the law serves will dominate them all....

The fissures in the common law are wider than the fissures in a statute, at least in the form of statute common in England and the United States. In countries where statutes are oftener confined to the announcement of general principles, and there is no attempt to deal with details or particulars, legislation has less tendency to limit the freedom of the judge. That is why in our own law there is often greater freedom of choice in the construction of constitutions than in that of ordinary statutes. Constitutions are more likely to enunciate general principles, which must be worked out and applied thereafter to particular conditions. What concerns us now, however, is not the size of the gaps. It is rather the principle that shall determine how they are to be filled, whether their size be great or small. The method of sociology in filling the gaps, puts its emphasis on the social welfare.

Social welfare is a broad term. I use it to cover many concepts more or less allied. It may mean what is commonly spoken of as public policy, the good of the collective body. In such cases, its demands are often those of mere expediency or prudence. It may mean on the other hand the social gain that is wrought by adherence to the standards of right conduct, which find expression in the *mores* of the community. In such cases, its demands are those of religion or of ethics or of the social sense of justice, whether formulated in creed or system, or immanent in the common mind....

It is true, I think, today in every department of the law that the social value of a rule has become a test of growing power and importance. This truth is powerfully driven home to the lawyers of this country in the writings of Dean Pound. "Perhaps the most significant advance in the modern science of law is the change from the analytical to the functional attitude." "The emphasis has changed from the content

* 65–66, 71–76 (1921). Reprinted by permission of Yale University Press from The Nature of the Judicial Process by Benjamin N. Cardozo. Copyright © 1921 by Yale University Press.

21. Dillon, Laws and Jurisprudence of England and America, p. 18, quoted by Pound, 27 Harvard L.R. 731, 733.

of the precept and the existence of the remedy to the effect of the precept in action and the availability and efficiency of the remedy to attain the ends for which the precept was devised." Foreign jurists have the same thought: "The whole of the judicial function," says Gmelin, "has ... been shifted. The will of the State, expressed in decision and judgment is to bring about a just determination by means of the subjective sense of justice inherent in the judge, guided by an effective weighing of the interests of the parties in the light of the opinions generally prevailing among the community regarding transactions like those in question. The determination should under all circumstances be in harmony with the requirements of good faith in business intercourse and the needs of practical life, unless a positive statute prevents it; and in weighing conflicting interests, the interest that is better founded in reason and more worthy of protection should be helped to achieve victory." "On the one hand," says Gény, "we are to interrogate reason and conscience, to discover in our inmost nature, the very basis of justice; on the other, we are to address ourselves to social phenomena, to ascertain the laws of their harmony and the principles of order which they exact." And again: "Justice and general utility, such will be the two objectives that will direct our course."

... A few broad areas may ... be roughly marked as those in which the method of sociology has fruitful application. ... [I]n the field of constitutional law ... the primacy of this method is, I think, undoubted. ...

NOTE

Pound and Cardozo were on the cutting edge of sociological jurisprudence in the early 1920's. Were they prophets or voices crying in the wilderness?

Does a court have more freedom in filling the gaps between fissures of common law than between those of statutes? Is the difference only in the size of the gaps?

Is there any similarity between, on the one hand, decisions based on social welfare, "public policy, the good of the collective body ... [expressed in] demands ... of religion or of ethics or of the social sense of justice ... [or in the] subjective sense of justice inherent in the judge" and, on the other, classic deontological natural law?

How does the court ascertain "the *mores* of the community" or "the opinions generally prevailing among the community regarding transactions like those in question"? By judicial notice? From evidence in the record? By a Brandeis brief?

In applying this method to constitutional law, would the "subjective sense of justice" inherent in a North Carolina appellate judge elected for a term differ from that inherent in a federal appellate judge holding a lifetime appointment? Should there be a difference in the utilization of the method of sociology by a judge elected for a term and one appointed for life? Is there? Would an elected judge reflect "the mores of the community" to a greater or lesser extent than an appointed one?

As you read the materials on the method of sociology, reflect upon Justice Holmes' assertion that his job was not to "do justice", but "to play the game according to the rules." Recall too, Cardozo's statement, "The rule that misses its aim cannot permanently justify its existence."

Evaluate the propriety of an appellate court's consideration of "legislative facts" set forth in a Brandeis brief which was not presented to the trial court. Consider Rupert Cross' observation: "The 'Brandeis brief' has much to be said for it, but to an Englishman it may well seem that a court would be considering matters that are best considered as a prelude to parliamentary legislation if it were to do much more than act on the personal notion of its members with regard to such questions." R. Cross, Precedent in English Law 195 (2d ed. 1968). How should these "facts"—tables, surveys, expert opinions—properly be presented in the judicial process? To what extent should there be communication between the judge and "the social sciences"? Consider ABA Code of Judicial Conduct Canon 3(7):

> A judge shall accord to every person who has a legal interest in a proceeding, or that person's lawyer, the right to be heard according to law. A judge shall not initiate, permit, or consider ex parte communications, or consider other communications made to the judge outside the presence of the parties concerning a pending or impending proceeding except that:
>
> (a) Where circumstances require, ex parte communications for scheduling, administrative purposes or emergencies that do not deal with substantive matters or issues on the merits are authorized; provided:
>
> (i) the judge reasonably believes that no party will gain a procedural or tactical advantage as a result of the ex parte communication, and
>
> (ii) the judge makes provision promptly to notify all other parties of the substance of the ex parte communication and allows an opportunity to respond.
>
> (b) A judge may obtain the advice of a disinterested expert on the law applicable to a proceeding before the judge if the judge gives notice to the parties of the person consulted and the substance of the advice, and affords the parties reasonable opportunity to respond.
>
> (c) A judge may consult with court personnel whose function is to aid the judge in carrying out the judge's adjudicative responsibilities or with other judges.
>
> (d) A judge may, with the consent of the parties, confer separately with the parties and their lawyers in an effort to mediate or settle matters pending before the judge.

(e) A judge may initiate or consider any ex parte communications when expressly authorized by law to do so.

Commentary:

The proscription against communications concerning a proceeding includes communications from lawyers, law teachers, and other persons who are not participants in the proceeding, except to the limited extent permitted.

* * *

An appropriate and often desirable procedure for a court to obtain the advice of a disinterested expert on legal issues is to invite them to file a brief *amicus curiae.* Should this also extend to communications with professors? What is the difference between consulting a book written by a professor and having correspondence or a conversation with him? Does the availability of the book to the litigants and the non-availability of the private correspondence or conversation make a difference?

Rolf Sartorius, The Justification of the Judicial Decision, 78 Ethics 171, 180 (1968): "[I]t is not *any* social policy but only those policies and principles which are established in prior judicial obligations, or which may be derived from those which are so established, which provide good reasons for judicial decisions."

HARRY W. JONES, THE CHANNELING OF SOCIAL CHANGE *

A legal rule or a legal institution is a *good* rule or institution when—that is, to the extent that—it contributes to the establishment and preservation of a social environment in which the quality of human life can be spirited, improving and unimpaired. If this be granted, it follows that any account of the social ends to which law is means must proceed from a view or concept of the social world as it is and can reasonably be expected to become.

I have no credentials as a social prophet, but there is one thing we can be quite sure about: tomorrow's society will be different from today's in its material conditions and moral attitudes, just as today's society is far different from that of fifty or even twenty-five years ago. "Nothing steadfastly *is,*" said Heraclitus, "Everything is becoming," and these words express a truth that lawyers, no less than philosophers and theologians, must understand and learn to live with. This is not to say that change is always and necessarily progress; history records about as

* *An Invitation to Jurisprudence,* 74 Co-   ed by permission.
lum.L.Rev. 1023, 1030–31 (1974). Reprint-

many social changes for the worse as for the better. Change is simply predictable, inevitable and ceaseless as the basic social fact. In the words of the old song, "We don't know where we're going, but we're on our way."

This sets one of law's most important ends-in-view. Law, thought of merely as a body of doctrine and aggregate of institutions, is neither for social change nor against it. What law does—or can do when its legislators, judges and practicing lawyers are socially aware and professionally resourceful—is to provide institutions and procedures for the channeling of inevitable social change in ways that make sought reforms effective with the minimum possible impairment of law's other ends-in-view: the public peace, just dispute-settlement, reasonable security of expectations and tolerable adjustment of conflicting social interests. Law's principles, institutions and procedures are there to be drawn on for the social task at hand, but they have to be used. The channeling of social change can be accomplished only through continuing acts of creative and informed intuition by men and women who combine genuine mastery of legal techniques with equally profound understanding of social forces.

It has become a truism that law must be kept up to date, responsive to the continuing processes of social change. Present-day judges are very much aware that concepts and categories received from law's past— privity of contract, sovereign immunity, "fault" in divorce actions and many more—may not order contemporary phenomena effectively and justly. It is not that these concepts were necessarily wrong when they were handed down; we are, I think, too quick to assume that. It is simply that, whatever their original justification, they offer the wrong answers for today's problems. One hates, in a way, to see old friends like negligence, consideration and "state action" withering away in vitality and influence, but, to borrow a phrase from Justice Roger Traynor, "the number they have called is no longer in service."

To say that law must be kept responsive to changing social conditions and social attitudes is, however, to state only half of the equation. The relation between law and social change is reciprocal, for law, in its turn, can have a molding effect on social development. The imperatives of the legal order carry at least prima facie rightness for most members of society. More often than not, a legal principle, if soundly conceived and resolutely enforced, becomes a kind of self-fulfilling prophecy and creates the social climate necessary for its acceptance. When wisely and imaginatively employed, law is far more than an instrument of command; it is organized society's principal resource for the engineering of that widespread and supportive public assent—the true consent of the governed—without which great social initiatives never really get off the ground. I have been wondering lately if this is not the most important way in which law operates—or can be drawn on—for the sound and effective channeling of social change.

NOTE

Is it realistic to expect a "minimum possible impairment" of "reasonable security of expectations" and decision making patterned on Jones' definition of a good legal rule or institution? How do lawyers and judges acquire a "profound understanding of social forces"?

Professor Jones' test of a good rule or institution necessarily implicates a law-making function in the judiciary's role as a dispute settler. Evaluate this test if the judiciary simply settled disputes and neither made nor followed precedents.

———

HARLAN F. STONE, THE COMMON LAW IN THE UNITED STATES *

It is just here, within the limited area where the judge has freedom of choice of the rule which he is to adopt, and in his comparison of the experiences of the past with those of the present, that occurs the most critical and delicate operation in the process of judicial lawmaking. Strictly speaking, he is often engaged not so much in extracting a rule of law from the precedents, as we were once accustomed to believe, as in making an appraisal and comparison of social values, the result of which may be of decisive weight in determining what rule he is to apply. The law itself is on trial, quite as much as the cause which is to be decided, for the product of the decision of the common-law judge is always law, as well as the particular judgment which he gives for the plaintiff or defendant. The skill, resourcefulness and insight with which judges and lawyers weigh competing demands of social advantage, not unmindful that continuity and symmetry of the law are themselves such advantages, and with which they make choices among them in determining whether precedents shall be extended or restricted, chiefly give the measure of the vitality of the common-law system and its capacity for growth.

———

B. BALANCING INTERESTS

More often than not, the distillation of public policy derives from a component of the judicial process popularly known as "balancing interests."[1] Competing interests are identified and categorized as individual, public or social interests. They are variously compared, evaluated, accepted, rejected, tailored, adjusted, and, in general, subjected to the

* 50 Harv.L.Rev. 4, 10 (1936). Copyright © 1936 by The Harvard Law Review Association. Reprinted by permission.

1. First so described by Justice Hugo Black: See C. Fried, *Two Concepts of Interest: Some Reflections on the Supreme Court's Balancing Test,* 76 Harv.L.Rev. 755, 757 n. 3 (1963).

political contrivance or compromise. The result is what Professor Jones calls "a reasoned accommodation" of opposing interests.[2] With public policy playing such a prominent role in contemporary adjudication, and with a seemingly inexhaustible inventory of social interests pressing upon judges and jurists for attention, Dean Pound's A Survey of Social Interests[3] should be mandatory reading for today's law student and the subject of refresher courses for lawyers, legislators and judges.

Pound recognized that "[i]n the common law we have been wont to speak of social interests under the name of 'public policy.' "[4] But he emphasized that the extent to which this technique may be considered valid depends, in the first instance, on whether all relevant identifiable interests are placed on the scale. The validity of the technique requires that all the interests be identified. Although the expression "balancing interests" may be useful, it also is misleading, suggesting that the subject matter of the judicial process is somehow quantifiable. It is not. The best that can be hoped for is that all the interests at stake in a case are identifiable. Having identified the interests at stake, judges can at least consider them; it is doubtful that they are ever able to "balance" them. The judge's accommodation of the competing interests, his or her priorities in resolving the interests conflicts, will be durable and acceptable to the extent that it is regarded and accepted as fair. Before the accommodation takes place, however, like types of interests must be identified. As there are apples and oranges, so there are interests and interests.

"[T]he whole of the judicial function [involves] the subjective sense of justice inherent in the judge, guided by an effective weighing of the interests of the parties ... and in weighing conflicting interests, the interest that is better founded in reason and more worthy of protection should be helped to achieve victory."[5] We then get to a definition of an interest. Many questions abound: How do judges identify the desired "groupings of behavior" other than by exercising a threshold value judgment on certain factual phenomena either in the record or part of cosmic experience? At the time this value judgment is made, do not judges actually identify or denominate a grouping of behavioral phenomena which they call an interest? Do they not then decide whether this should be protected? Do they not then make a further value judgment, whether this interest deserves magisterial concern? If judges get to this point—if they designate an interest and decide it merits protection—do judges not then summon for consideration some applicable rule of law commanding some definite, detailed, desired legal result? And if the rules of law are found wanting, do they not range further and find a sweeping generalization, which we call a principle? Or if they cannot locate a principle, do they not resort to a broader legal or moral conception? Or if rules of law, principles or legal conceptions fail to

2. H.W. Jones, *An Invitation to Jurisprudence,* 74 Colum.L.Rev. 1023, 1029 (1974).

3. 57 Harv.L.Rev. 1 (1943).

4. Id. at 4.

5. B. Cardozo, The Nature of the Judicial Process 73–74.

answer, do they not rely on a community standard and make a judgment as to what is fair and reasonable based on the experience of ordinary prudent members of the community? Having found a satisfactory rule, principle, conception or standard, do they not then wrap legal protection around certain behavioral phenomena in the guise of designating certain social facts or factors as "interests," the protection of which is the purpose of substantive legal precepts? Perhaps the answers to these questions accurately describe the anatomy of the judicial process. Perhaps also a critical component of the process is the interest identified or favored by a given judge in a given court reaching a given result in a given case.

We are now prepared to define an interest. An interest is a social fact, factor or phenomenon reflected by a claim or demand or desire which human beings, either individually or as groups or associations or relations, seek to satisfy and which has been recognized as socially valid by authoritative decision makers in society.[6]

What are the interests identified by the federal and state courts in their opinions today? To identify these interests is the task of the advocate. The good advocate, and the lay or professional commentator, is not permitted to be simplistic and merely say that interests involve only the rights of the individual person against the rights of society. What individual person is meant? An underprivileged migrant worker, or Exxon Corporation? Both may be persons in the eyes of the law.

Effective advocates must learn more about interests which are favored or neglected or ignored by the courts in which they practice. They must study the individual opinion writers of a court and learn which interests attract them and command their attention in reaching the result. Suppose that Judge X and Judge Y agree on the same result. To say that they are philosophical comrades merely because they agree on a common result is unwise. Yet observers of the judicial process often make this mistake in affixing labels to judges. That two appellate judges join a decision is no definitive clue as to the value judgments each has placed on the interests that predicate the *ratio decidendi*.

Let us hypothesize an example of countervailing interests. In Milltown, Pennsylvania, Bigbucks Corporation operates a steel mill that belches smoke into the Monongahela Valley. Superficially, identification of the countervailing interests is simple. The steel mill is owned by a big corporation. In Brandeisian philosophy, big is bad. But Bigbucks has a right to use private property. Opposing this right is the right of the individual to physical well-being, the right to breathe clean air; if not a common law right, it has now been so defined by legislative fiat. It is immaterial whether we consider county ordinances, state or federal statutes, or the common law to determine those rights. The same

---

6. See K. Llewellyn, *A Realistic Jurisprudence—The Next Step*, 30 Colum.L.Rev. 431, 441 (1930) ("One starts with the interest. That is a social fact or factor of some kind, existing independent of the law. And it has value independent of the law.").

methodology is utilized in the judicial process. A judge identifies social facts, groups them into interests, puts them on the scale, weighs them, applies some law and decides the case.

Let us change certain of the sociological phenomena and ask whether different interests are identifiable. Would it make a difference that the steel mill has recently reopened after falling victim to the deterioration of the steel manufacturing industry in Western Pennsylvania? That it is the only mill operating following the closure of gigantic mills and blast furnaces throughout the valley, when Homestead, Duquesne, McKeesport, Clairton and Glassport have become almost ghost towns? That in the late 1970's and 1980's some 250,000 steelworkers lost their jobs and the new mill is an attempt to rejuvenate the valley through public and private grants to Bigbucks Corporation? Why does this make a difference if the legal issue is the right of the individual against the right of a private property owner? Would it make any difference if the individuals were members of an underprivileged class who work in the mill and would be unemployed if the mill shut down? If so, why? Let us assume that the individuals are African–Americans. Would that make a difference? Why? Suppose the mill is a federally financed, black capital project, designed as the first black-owned steel mill in the United States. Does it make any difference that in one case the mill is owned by a giant corporation and in the other it is a government-subsidized minority project?

In weighing the various interests identifiable in different cases Pound's survey is always helpful, for he has analyzed and classified individual, public and social interests. There is an interest in general security—the interest of society in being secure against actions that threaten its existence. An interest in the security of social institutions—domestic, including marriage and the family, as well as religious, political, commercial and industrial institutions. An interest in general morals—the claim or demand of a civilized society to be secure against conduct offensive to the moral sentiments of the general populace prevalent at a given time. An interest in general progress—development of human powers and human control over nature for the satisfaction of human wants in economic, political and cultural progress. An interest in the individual human life for free self-assertion in physical, mental, religious and political belief and full individual opportunity.

Referring to this survey, in a magnificent abstraction of the nature and ends of law, Pound said: "Looked at functionally, the law is an attempt to satisfy, to reconcile, to harmonize, to adjust these overlapping and often conflicting claims and demands, either through securing them directly and immediately, or through securing certain individual interests, so as to give effect to the greatest total of interests or to the interests that weigh most in our civilization, with the least sacrifice of the scheme of interests as a whole." [7]

7. R. Pound, ante.

The process derives from the German jurist, Rudolf von Jhering [8] who designated the method as *Interessenjurisprudenz*, a jurisprudence of interests. Under this method of dispute resolution, according to Chester James Antieau, the court *identifies* the opposed societal interests, *reconciles* them if possible, and, if reconciliation is not possible, *rules* that one societal interest under the circumstances must prevail over another, with an explanation of why this is so.[9] The process is very much at work today in many aspects of adjudication, especially in tort and constitutional law. Interpretation of constitutional principles play a dominate role in contemporary state and federal courts, at trial and appellate levels, in both criminal and civil law. The use of *Interessenjurisprudenz* in constitutional law stems from two starting points: Cardozo's recognition that "the content of constitutional immunities is not constant, but varies from age to age" [10] and Edward Levi's observation that "[e]ach major concept written in the document embodies a number of conflicting ideals. . . . The major words written in the document are too ambiguous; the ideals are too conflicting, and no interpretation can be decisive." [11] Although Felix Frankfurter assured us that "[t]he ultimate touchstone of constitutionality is the Constitution itself, and not what we have said about it," [12] Charles Evan Hughes' words probably ring truer: "We are under a Constitution, but the Constitution is what the judges say it is." [13]

Dred Scott and *Plessy* demonstrate that traditional common law judicial processes are not practical in constitutional adjudication. To search for the intent of the framers and drafters or to adhere slavishly to precedents of past generations, be they from the legislature, the executive or the judiciary, simply will not work. As long ago as 1908, Pound was preaching that *Begriffsjurisprudenz*, a jurisprudence of conceptions, was not meeting the challenges of American political, social, cultural and economic development. And in 1881 Holmes emphasized, "Every important principle which is developed by litigation is in fact and at bottom the result of more or less definitely understood views of public policy; most generally, to be sure, under our practices and traditions, the unconscious result of instinctive preferences and inarticulate convictions, but nonetheless traceable to views of public policy in the last analysis." [14]

We have yet to receive a satisfactory explanation of how to decide cases on the basis of public policy without identifying the competing societal interests, reconciling them if possible, and if not, selecting a preference with a reasoned explanation for the choice. As Professor

---

8. R. von Jhering, Der Zweck Im Recht (Law as Means to an End) (1904).

9. C.J. Antieau, *The Jurisprudence of Interests as a Method of Constitutional Adjudication*, 27 Case West.Res.L.Rev. 823, 829 (1977).

10. B. Cardozo, The Nature of the Judicial Process 82–83 (1921).

11. E. Levi, *An Introduction to Legal Reasoning*, 15 U.Chi.L.Rev. 501, 541–43 (1948).

12. Graves v. New York, 306 U.S. 466, 491 (1939).

13. C.E. Hughes, Speeches before Elmira Chamber of Commerce in 1907, in Addresses and Papers, 133, 139 (1908).

14. O.W. Holmes, The Common Law 35–36 (1881).

Antieau puts it, "Nothing is to be gained by attempts of balancing principles; rather, courts ... must confine their evaluations and adjustments to societal interests." [15] Even if public policy is a prevalent basis for decision in tort and constitutional law,[16] critics of the process abound. Although these critics aver that judges typically do not have the means nor the competence to weigh and adjust competing interests, their major contention is that this process permits judges to impose their own values upon society, a task properly reserved for the legislature. Suffice it to say that the exercise of value judgment inheres throughout the judicial process. The judge makes a value judgment when choosing between competing legal precepts as the beginning point for legal reasoning. This choice becomes the major premise in the syllogism that will lead the judge to a logical conclusion. The judge also makes a value judgment when interpreting the chosen precept, be it statutory or judge-made. And the judge also makes a value judgment in applying the chosen precept and interpreting it to the facts at hand. When judges decide whether these facts are or are not similar to a putative precedent clamoring for recognition, they make as many value judgments as often as they rely on rigid rules of logic.

But more important, the judicial process admits to few absolutes. The same decisional process does not, and should not, be used in all disciplines of the law. It should come as no surprise that in certain areas it is better that the law be settled than that it be decided "correctly." The importance of maintaining a reasonable security of individual expectations in matters of property, private contract, estates and trusts, securities, chattels, banking, payment and credit cannot be questioned. In these areas it is desirable that there be maximum predictability and reckonability. Here, although certainty in the law is not an absolute, the governing precepts should be more stable than fluid, and if this means more *Begriffsjurisprudenz* than *Interessenjurisprudenz,* so be it.

But the process cannot be compartmentalized neatly. Controversies as to the best methodologies will not end, nor should the debates end because a certain amount of name-calling always has been a part of the legal tradition, no matter how euphemistically phrased. Often it will depend upon whose ox is being gored. If we agree with a certain decision, we may be tempted to describe the effort as "principled" in the sense that it follows venerable and time-tested legal precepts. Another may refer to the same efforts as "mechanical jurisprudence" or "slot

15. C.J. Antieau, *The Jurisprudence of Interests as a Method of Constitutional Adjudication,* 27 Case West.Res.L.Rev. 823, 843 (1977).

16. The Supreme Court has applied the interest test to a large number of constitutional law cases. Typical is Mathews v. Eldridge, 424 U.S. 319, 334–35 (1976) ("[I]dentification of the specific dictates of due process generally requires consideration of three distinct facts: First, the pri-

vate interest that will be affected by the official action; second, the risk of an erroneous deprivation of such interest through the procedures used, and the probable value, if any, of additional or substitute procedural safeguards; and finally, the government's interest, including the function involved and the fiscal and administrative burdens that the additional or substitute procedural requirement would entail.").

machine justice." Some of us may agree with a decision, on the cutting edge of social reform, and describe it as the method of sociology in the true Holmes–Pound–Cardozo tradition; others may look at it with disdain, casting it off as "result-oriented" jurisprudence.

Devotees of sociological jurisprudence must be prepared to answer the charge of result-orientation. There is no acceptable answer if the offense is the one described by Judge Henry J. Friendly as "a judge's personal belief in what is desirable, formed before study of the case at hand and resistant to contrary argument." [17] Yet a result-oriented decision may be a good one if it satisfies what we have been calling the Jones–Pound test, emanating from an anecdote related by Professor Harry W. Jones:

> When one asked Pound whether a recent Supreme Court decision was a "good" decision or a "bad" one, the old gentleman ... had a way of answering not in terms of the correctness or incorrectness of the Court's application of constitutional precedents or doctrine but in terms of how thoughtfully and disinterestedly the Court had weighed the conflicting social interests involved in the case and how fair and durable its adjustment of the interest-conflicts promised to be.[18]

To put Cardozo's method of sociology in the proper perspective, therefore, it is necessary to recall some jurisprudential history. We start with the early liberalism of Chief Justice John Marshall:

> Judicial power, as contradistinguished from the power of the laws, has no existence. Courts are the mere instruments of law, and can will nothing. When they are said to exercise a discretion, it is a mere legal discretion, a discretion to be exercised in discerning the course prescribed by law; and, when that is discerned, it is the duty of the court to follow it. Judicial power is never exercised for the purpose of giving effect to the will of the judge; always for the purpose of giving effect to the will of the legislature; or, in other words, to the will of the law.[19]

For years law was characterized as an objective body of rules, principles, conceptions, doctrines or maxims. Beginning with Holmes, continuing with Pound and later with Cardozo, the effort was made to show that law was more than a network of legal precepts which could be used by any judge to get a precise result. Dependence upon history alone, customs alone, made for stability in the law. It gave us *elegantia juris.* Then began the movement decrying a process in which rules were often applied mechanically without regard to justice or sound results. Reasoning by analogy was given a new dimension in the new movement.

17. H. Friendly, *Reactions of a Lawyer—Newly Become Judge,* 71 Yale L.J. 218, 230–232 (1961).

18. H.W. Jones, *An Invitation to Jurisprudence,* 74 Colum.L.Rev. 1023, 1028–30 (1974).

19. Osborn v. Bank of U.S., 22 U.S. (9 Wheat.) 738, 866 (1824).

The dimension centered on a logical process that evaluated the soundness of the result, rather than emphasizing the beauty of the syllogism.

At that time law was beginning to be perceived as more than a "brooding omnipresence" in the sky, as more than an aggregate of legal precepts that formed by-laws of society. The ends of law were expanded to include what we now accept as the Harry W. Jones formulation, a formulation by which we can understand Brown v. Board of Education: whether the decision establishes or preserves "a social environment in which the quality of human life can be spirited, improving, and unimpaired." [20] Thus, deciding a case on the basis of policy or social welfare calls for "adjustment of principles and doctrines to human conditions they are to govern rather than to assumed first principles." [21] And it calls for more than an understanding of orthodox lawyer's law.

"What is it that I do when I decide a case?," Cardozo asked in 1921. Whatever is involved in the process today, the methods of logic, history and custom are still decisively important. What Cardozo called the method of philosophy emphasizes logical extension of rules by way of principles to reach new fact situations. The historical method can be considered as internal to the law, the doctrine of precedent, a source of decision making that still persists as the mightiest force in the common law tradition. External history is resorted to in order to explain, to form reasons and to eliminate ambiguity. Customs, from which we created the rudimentary common law, are still with us; they provide powerful force and majestic effect in business and labor law and in qualifying expert witnesses.

Where, then, do we place Cardozo's method of sociology today? To answer this is to emphasize much that has gone before. It is to recognize the distinction between rules and principles; that rules are detailed legal consequences to a detailed set of facts; that principles are broader legal precepts that form the beginning points of legal reasoning. Rules prescribe relatively specific acts, principles cover general situations. Principles have a dimension that rules do not have, the dimension of weight or importance. Rules may not conflict, principles may and do.

When principles compete, one who must decide the case must take into account the relative weight of the conflicting interests. This weighing of interests lies at the heart of the judicial process, for the process involves a choice that becomes the major premise in the reasoning process, by which the use of logic compels the ultimate conclusion.

The sociological jurisprudents contributed much to discussion of the judicial process. They argued that a rule of law may be developed by considering the consequences which it may involve, rather than simply identifying wider principles that the rule presupposes. They contended that consideration of that ultimate conclusion was valid and legitimate,

20. H.W. Jones, *An Invitation to Jurisprudence,* 74 Colum.L.Rev. 1023, 1030 (1974).

21. R. Pound, *Mechanical Jurisprudence,* 8 Colum.L.Rev. 695, 609–10 (1908).

because it is the conclusion of the judicial process, the ultimate decision, which has the effect on society; that therefore the result of a decision should be considered in the initial process of weighing the competing interests.

Where several principles command the identical conclusion, the judicial opinion is strengthened. Where a single principle is chosen over those that would command different results, it must be a decision based on persuasive reason, based on recognized legal principles or upon reasoning based on some justificatory principle of morality, justice, social policy or common sense; it must be genuinely principled, on analysis and reason transcending the immediate result that is achieved; it must be reasonably calculated to find acceptance in the social groups intimately affected by claim, or demand or desire which forms the basis of the litigation before the court. And the result should meet the test of the ends of law: the Jones test that the decision should contribute to the establishment and preservation of a social environment in which the quality of human life can be spirited, improving and unimpaired. At the same time the result must also respect the other ends-in-view of law: the public peace, just dispute-settlement, reasonable security of expectations and tolerable adjustment of conflicting social interests.

ROSCOE POUND, A SURVEY OF SOCIAL INTERESTS *

There has been a notable shift throughout the world from thinking of the task of the legal order as one of adjusting the exercise of free wills to one of satisfying wants, of which free exercise of the will is but one. Accordingly, we must start today from a theory of interests, that is, of the claims or demands or desires which human beings, either individually or in groups or associations or relations, seek to satisfy, of which, therefore, the adjustment of relations and ordering of conduct through the force of politically organized society must take account.... It is enough to say here that the classification into individual interests, public interests, and social interests was suggested by Jhering. As I should put it, individual interests are claims or demands or desires involved immediately in the individual life and asserted in title of that life. Public interests are claims or demands or desires involved in life in a politically organized society and asserted in title of that organization. They are commonly treated as the claims of a politically organized society thought of as a legal entity. Social interests are claims or demands or desires involved in social life in civilized society and asserted in title of that life. It is not uncommon to treat them as the claims of the whole social group as such.

But this does not mean that every claim or demand or desire which human beings assert must be put once and for all for every purpose into

* 57 Harv.L.Rev. 1, 1–3 (1943). Copyright © 1943 by The Harvard Law Review Association. Reprinted by permission.

one of these three categories. For some purposes and in some connections it is convenient to look at a given claim or demand or desire from one standpoint. For other purposes or in other connections it is convenient to look at the same claim or demand or the same type of claims or demands from one of the other standpoints. When it comes to weighing or valuing claims or demands with respect to other claims or demands, we must be careful to compare them on the same plane. If we put one as an individual interest and the other as a social interest we may decide the question in advance in our very way of putting it.... If we think of either in terms of a policy we must think of the other in the same terms. If we think of the employee's claim in terms of a policy of assuring a minimum or a standard of human life, we must think of the employer's claim in terms of a policy of upholding and enforcing contracts. If the one is thought of as a right and the other as a policy, or if the one is thought of as an individual interest and the other as a social interest, our way of stating the question may leave nothing to decide.

In general, but not always, it is expedient to put claims or demands in their most generalized form, *i.e.,* as social interests, in order to compare them. But where the problems are relatively simple, it is sometimes possible to take account of all the factors sufficiently by comparing individual interests put directly as such. It must be borne in mind that often we have here different ways of looking at the same claims or same type of claims as they are asserted in different titles. Thus, individual interests of personality may be asserted in title of or subsumed under the social interest in the general security, or the social interest in the individual life, or sometimes from different standpoints or in different aspects, both of them. Again, individual interests in the domestic relations may be subsumed under the social interest in the security of social institutions of which domestic institutions are the oldest and by no means the least important. Again, the public interest in the integrity of the state personality may be thought of as the social interest in the security of social institutions of which political institutions are one form. When we have recognized and legally delimited and secured an interest, it is important to identify the generalized individual interest behind and giving significance and definition to the legal right. When we are considering what claims or demands to recognize and within what limits, and when we are seeking to adjust conflicting and overlapping claims and demands in some new aspect or new situation, it is important to subsume the individual interests under social interests and to weigh them as such.

NOTE

Applying Pound's definitions of individual, public and social interests, describe the clash of interests involved in Roe v. Wade, 410 U.S. 113 (1973); Bowers v. Hardwick, 478 U.S. 186 (1986); Richmond v. J.A. Crosson Co., 488 U.S. 469 (1989). Were the flash points of controversy between various categories of interests, or separate interests with a specific category?

KARL N. LLEWELLYN, INTERESTS *

The term *interests,* ... comes in to focus attention on the presence of social factors, and to urge that substantive rights themselves, like remedies, exists only for a purpose. Their purpose is now perceived to be the protection of the interests. To be sure, we do not know what interests are. Hence, behind substantive rights (which we need not check against anything courts *do*) we now have interests (which we need not check against anything at all, and about whose presence, extent, nature and importance, whether the interests be taken absolutely or taken relatively one to another, no two of us seem to be able to agree). The scientific advance should again be obvious. Complete subjectivity has been achieved.

At this stage of the development, then, one arrives at a double chain of purposes. One starts with the interest. That is a social fact or factor of some kind, existing [in]dependent of the law.[9b] And it has value independent of the law. Indeed, its protection is the purpose of substantive legal rights, of legal rules, of precepts of substantive law. "Security of transactions" is such an interest. The rules and rights of contract law exist to protect and effectuate it. The rules and rights are not ends, but means. But they are means which in another aspect (like most means) themselves become ends: remedies exist as means to effectuate the substantive rights, to realize the substantive rules. Obviously the means may be inadequate, badly chosen, wasteful, even self-defeating, at either stage. They may be so, cumulatively, at both stages. The rule that consideration is necessary to make an offer irrevocable for three days, even when the offer is fully intended, business like, signed, in writing, and expressed to be irrevocable for three days, may be thought not adapted to further security of transactions.... The means, I say, may be inadequate; but the analysis invites discovery of the inadequacy. Hence, whatever one thinks of the sufficiency in the large of the analysis in the threefold terms of interests, substantive rights and rules, and remedies, one can but pay homage to the sureness with which it forces law on the attention as something man-made, something capable of criticism, of change, of reform—and capable of criticism, change, and reform not only according to standards found inside law itself (inner harmony, logical consistence of rules, parts and tendencies, *elegantia juris*) but also according to standards vastly more vital found *outside* law itself, in the society law purports both to govern *and to serve.*

---

* *A Realistic Jurisprudence—The Next Step,* 30 Colum.L.Rev. 431, 441–42 (1930). Reprinted by permission.

9b. This is an overstatement. Past law may have contributed much to the present existence of an interest, and to its shape and extent.

ROSCOE POUND, A SURVEY OF SOCIAL INTERESTS *

The body of the common law is made up of adjustments or compromises of conflicting individual interests in which we turn to some social interest, frequently under the name of public policy, to determine the limits of a reasonable adjustment.

In the common law we have been wont to speak of social interests under the name of "public policy." ...

In truth, the nineteenth-century attitude toward public policy was itself only the expression of a public policy. It resulted from a weighing of the social interest in the general security against other social interests which men had sought to secure through an overwide magisterial discretion in the stage of equity and natural law.

Thus, the conception of public policy was never clearly worked out, nor were the several policies recognized by the common law defined as were the individual interests to which the juristic thought of the last century gave substantially its whole attention....

If legal phenomena are social phenomena, observation and study of them as such may well bear fruit for social science in general, as well as for jurisprudence. Why should not the lawyer make a survey of legal systems in order to ascertain just what claims or demands or desires have pressed or are now pressing for recognition and satisfaction and how far they have been or are now recognized and secured? ... The first step in such an investigation is a mere survey of the legal order and an inventory of the social interests which have pressed upon lawmakers and judges and jurists for recognition.

In such a survey and inventory, first place must be given to the social interest in the general security—the claim or want or demand, asserted in title of social life in civilized society and through the social group, to be secure against those forms of action and courses of conduct which threaten its existence. Even if we accept Durkheim's view that it is what shocks the general conscience, not what threatens the general security, that is repressed, I suspect that the general conscience reflects experience or superstition as to the general safety. A common-law judge observed that there would be no safety for human life if it were to be considered as law that drunkenness could be shown to negative the intent element of crime where a drunk man kills while intoxicated though he would never do such a thing when sober. It should be noted how the exigencies of the general security outweighed the traditional theory of the criminal law.

This paramount social interest takes many forms. In its simplest form it is an interest in the general safety, long recognized in the legal order in the maxim that the safety of the people is the highest law. It

* 57 Harv.L.Rev. 1, 4, 6–7, 16–18, 20–27,   Harvard Law Review Association. Reprint-
30–39 (1943). Copyright © 1943 by The   ed by permission.

was recognized in American constitutional law in the nineteenth century by putting the general safety along with the general health and general morals in the "police power" as a ground of reasonable restraint to which natural rights must give way. In another form, quite as obvious today but not so apparent in the past, before the nature and causes of disease were understood, it is an interest in the general health. In another form, recognized from the very beginnings of law, it is an interest in peace and public order. In an economically developed society it takes on two other closely related forms, namely, a social interest in the security of acquisitions and a social interest in the security of transactions. The two last came to be well understood in the nineteenth century, in which they were more or less identified with individual interests of substance and individual interests in freedom of contract....

Other examples of recognition of the security of transactions may be seen in the presumption as to transactions of a corporation through its acting officers, the stress which the courts put upon *stare decisis* in cases involving commercial law, and the doctrine allowing only the sovereign to challenge *ultra vires* conveyances of corporations. As to recognition of the social interest in the security of acquisitions, note the insistence of the courts upon *stare decisis* where rules of property are involved. In such cases it is an established proposition that it is better that the law be settled than that it be settled right.

Second, we may put the social interest in the security of social institutions—the claim or want or demand involved in life in civilized society that its fundamental institutions be secure from those forms of action and courses of conduct which threaten their existence or impair their efficient functioning. Looking at them in chronological order, this interest appears in three forms.

The first is an interest in the security of domestic institutions, long recognized in the form of a policy against acts affecting the security of domestic relations or in restraint of marriage. Legislation intended to promote the family as a social institution has been common. There is a policy against actions by members of the family against each other. Today, although the law is becoming much relaxed, this social interest is still weighed heavily against the individual claims of married persons in most divorce legislation. It still weighs heavily against individual claims in the law as to illegitimate children. At times this has been carried so far that great and numerous disabilities have attached to such children lest recognition of their individual interests should weaken a fundamental social institution. The movement to give independence to married women has had collateral effects of impairing the security of this interest, and the balance is not easy to make nor to maintain....

A second form is an interest in the security of religious institutions. In the beginning this is closely connected with the general security. A chief point of origin of the criminal law, of that part of the law by which social interests as such are directly and immediately secured, is in religion. Sacrifice of the impious offender who has affronted the gods, and exclusion from society of the impious offender whose presence threatens to bring upon his fellows the wrath of the gods, are, in part at least, the originals of capital punishment and of outlawry. Religious organization was long a stronger and more active agency of social control than political organization. In the Anglo–Saxon laws the appeals or exhortations addressed to the people as Christians are at least as important as the threats addressed to them as subjects. One of the great English statutes of the thirteenth century recites that Parliament had met to make laws "for the common Profit of holy Church, and of the Realm." It is only in relatively recent times that we have come to think of blasphemy as involving no more than a social interest in the general morals, of Sunday laws only in terms of a social interest in the general health, of heresy as less dangerous socially than radical views upon economics or politics, or of preaching or teaching of atheism as involved in a guaranteed liberty. Today what was formerly referred to this interest is usually referred to the social interest in the general morals. Questions as to the interest in the security of religious institutions have been debated in all lands.

In a third form the interest is one in the security of political institutions. This interest has weighed heavily in much twentieth-century legislation too familiar to require more than mention. When the public called for such legislation for the security of political institutions, absolute constitutional guarantees of free speech and natural rights of individual self-assertion, which in other times had moved courts to refuse to enjoin repeated and undoubted libels, lest liberty be infringed, were not suffered to stand in the way. If the individual interests involved had been conceived less absolutely and had been looked at in another light, as identified with a social interest in the general progress, they might have fared better.

Perhaps a fourth form of the interest in the security of social institutions should be added, namely, an interest in the security of economic institutions. Formerly, these were chiefly commercial. Today industrial institutions also must be taken into account. Judicial recognitions of a social interest in the security of commercial institutions are numerous. . . .

Third, we may put the social interest in the general morals, the claim or want or demand involved in social life in civilized society to be secured against acts or courses of conduct offensive to the moral sentiments of the general body of individuals therein for the time being. This interest is recognized in Roman law in the protection of *boni mores*. It is recognized in our law by policies against dishonesty, corruption, gambling, and things of immoral tendency; by treating continuing menaces to the general morals as nuisances; and by the common-law doctrine that acts contrary to good morals and subversive of general morals are misdemeanors. It is recognized in equity in the maxim that he who comes into equity must come with clean hands. Similar provisions are to be found in the private law and in the criminal law in other lands. Obstinately held ideas of morality may in time come in conflict with ideas arising from changed social and economic conditions or newer religious and philosophical views. In such cases we must reach a balance between the social interest in the general morals, and the social interest in general progress, taking form in a policy of free discussion. What was said above as to free speech and writing and the social interest in security of social institutions applies here also.

Fourth, there is the social interest in conservation of social resources, that is, the claim or want or demand involved in social life in civilized society that the goods of existence shall not be wasted; that where all human claims or wants or desires may not be satisfied, in view of infinite individual desires and limited natural means of satisfying them, the latter be made to go as far as possible; and, to that end, that acts or courses of conduct which tend needlessly to destroy or impair these goods shall be restrained. In its simplest form this is an interest in the use and conservation of natural resources, and is recognized in the doctrines as to *res communes,* which may be used but not owned, by the common law as to riparian rights and constitutional and statutory provisions where irrigation is practiced, by modern game laws, by the recent doctrines as to percolating water and surface water, and by laws as to waste of natural gas and oil. There has been a progressive tendency to restrict the *ius abutendi* which the maturity of law attributed to owners. A crowded and hungry world may yet weigh this interest against individual claims to free action still further by preventing destruction of commodities in order to keep up prices, or even cutting off the common-law liberty of the owner of land to sow it to salt if he so desires. At times overproduction of agricultural products has led to proposals for restriction of the owner's *ius utendi* by regulation of what crops he may raise. At other times there are projects for administrative appointment of receivers of agricultural land cultivated or managed by the owner "in such a manner as to prejudice materially the production of food thereon...." Restrictions with respect to housing proceed on another aspect of this same social interest.

. . .

Fifth there is the social interest in general progress, that is, the claim or want or demand involved in social life in civilized society, that the development of human powers and of human control over nature for the satisfaction of human wants go forward; the demand that social engineering be increasingly and continuously improved; as it were, the self-assertion of the social group toward higher and more complete development of human powers. This interest appears in three main forms, an interest in economic progress, an interest in political progress, and an interest in cultural progress. The social interest in economic progress has long been recognized in law and has been secured in many ways. In the common law it is expressed in four policies: the policy as to freedom of property from restrictions upon sale or use, the policy as to free trade and consequent policy against monopoly, the policy as to free industry, which has had to give much ground in recent legislation and judicial decision, and the policy as to encouragement of invention, which is behind patent legislation and there comes in conflict with the policy as to free trade. All of these policies have important consequences in everyday law. It may be thought that some of them should be classified rather as forms of a social interest in the security of economic institutions. As I read the cases, however, these demands have pressed upon courts and jurists from the standpoint of their relation to economic progress. If that relation fails, they are not likely to maintain themselves. Likewise the law has long recognized a social interest in political progress. In American bills of rights, and in written constitutions generally, a policy of free criticism, of public men, public acts, and public officers, and a policy of free formation, free holding, and free expression of political opinion are guaranteed as identified with individual rights. Moreover, at common law, the privilege of fair comment upon public men and public affairs recognizes and secures the same interest. But the third form, the social interest in cultural progress, has not been recognized in the law so clearly. It may be said to involve four policies: a policy of free science, a policy of free letters, a policy of encouragement of arts and letters, and a policy of promotion of education and learning. The last two have been recognized to some extent in copyright laws and in American constitutional provisions for the promotion of higher learning. The first two have made their way more slowly because of conflict or supposed conflict with the security of religious and political institutions.

Closely connected with the interest in cultural progress is a social interest in aesthetic surroundings, which recently has been pressing for legal recognition.... In the United States, courts and legislatures were long engaged in a sharp struggle over billboard laws and laws against hideous forms of outdoor advertising. For a time also the interest pressed in another way in connection with town planning legislation. It is significant that the courts are now ready to admit a policy in favor of the aesthetic as reasonable and constitutionally permissible.

Last, and in some ways most important of all, as we now are coming to think, there is the social interest in the individual life. One might call it the social interest in the individual moral and social life, or in the individual human life. It is the claim or want or demand involved in social life in civilized society that each individual be able to live a human life therein according to the standards of the society. It is the claim or want or demand that, if all individual wants may not be satisfied, they be satisfied at least so far as is reasonably possible and to the extent of a human minimum. Three forms of this social interest have been recognized in common law or in legislation: individual self-assertion, individual opportunity, and individual conditions of life. The first, the interest in free self-assertion, includes physical, mental, and economic activity. In Spencer's scheme of natural rights, they appear as a "right of free motion and locomotion," a "right of free exchange and free contract," deduced as a sort of free economic motion and locomotion, a "right of free industry," deduced expressly as a modern outgrowth of free motion and locomotion, as a right of free economic activity, a "right of free religious belief and opinion" and a right of free political belief and opinion, the two last being deduced also as modern developments of the same natural right of free motion and locomotion. These are deduced from a "law of equal freedom" which is taken to have been discovered by observation of social phenomena and verified by further observation. Without the aid of his "law of equal freedom" he might have found them by observation of the policies set forth in the law books. The old common-law policy in favor of freedom, the doctrine that one may justify by his natural liberty of action, except where his action takes the form of aggression and so threatens the general security, and in part the policy of free industry, are examples of recognition of a social interest in individual physical self-assertion. The policy in favor of free speech and free belief and opinion, although related also to the social interest in political progress, must be referred in part to a social interest in individual mental self-assertion. Policies favoring free trade and free industry are in part referable to a social interest in free economic self-assertion.

But the most important phase of the social interest in individual self-assertion, from the standpoint of modern law, is what might be called the social interest in freedom of the individual will—the claim or interest, or policy recognizing it, that the individual will shall not be subjected arbitrarily to the will of others. This interest is recognized in an old common-law policy which is declared in the Fifth and Fourteenth Amendments. If one will is to be subjected to the will of another through the force of politically organized society, it is not to be done arbitrarily, but is to be done upon some rational basis, which the person coerced, if reasonable, could appreciate. It is to be done upon a reasoned weighing of the interests involved and a reasoned attempt to reconcile them or adjust them. This policy obviously expresses political and juristic experience of what modern psychology has discovered as to the ill effects of repression. For example, it is more and more recognized today in our penal legislation and in our treatment of offenders. It has come to be recognized particularly of late as a result of pressure upon courts and lawmakers for security in the relation of employer and employee. It is coming to be recognized also in juristic thought in another connection as sociological theories of property replace metaphysical theories. There are many signs of a growing feeling that complete exclusion of all but him whom the law pronounces owner from objects which are the natural media of human existence or means of human activity, must be measured and justified by a reasoned weighing of the interests on both sides and a reasoned attempt to harmonize them or to save as much as we may with the sacrifice of as little on the part of the excluded, no less than on the part of the owner, as we may.

I have called a second form the social interest in individual opportunity. It is the claim or want or demand involved in social life in civilized society that all individuals shall have fair or reasonable (perhaps, as we are coming to think, we must say equal) opportunities—political, physical, cultural, social, and economic. In American thinking we have insisted chiefly on equal political opportunities, since in the pioneer conditions in which our institutions were formative other opportunities, so far as men demanded them, were at hand everywhere. But a claim to fair physical opportunities is recognized in public provision of parks and playgrounds and in public provisions for recreation; the claim to fair cultural opportunities is recognized by laws as to compulsory education of children (although the social interests in general progress and in dependents are also recognized here) as well as by state provisions for universities and for adult education; the claim to fair social opportunities is recognized by civil rights laws; and the claim to fair economic opportunities is recognized, for example, in the legal right to "freedom of the market," and in the so-called "right to pursue a lawful calling," which is weighed with other social interests in regulating training for and admission to professions.

In a third form, an interest in individual conditions of life, the social interest in the individual life appears as a claim that each individual shall have assured to him the conditions of at least a minimum human life under the circumstances of life in the time and place. I have said minimum, which certainly was all that was recognized until relatively recent times. But perhaps we should now say reasonable or even equal. A claim for equal conditions of life is pressing and we can't put the matter as to what is recognized with assurance as we could have done a generation ago. Moreover, the scope of generally asserted demands with respect to the individual life is obviously growing. The Roman law recognized a policy of this sort, and it has long been recognized in American legislation. In weighing individual interests in view of the social interest in security of acquisitions and security of transactions, we must also take account of the social interest in the human life of each individual, and so must restrict the legal enforcement of demands to what is consistent with a human existence on the part of the person subjected thereto. The Roman law imposed such a limitation in a number of cases in what is called the *beneficium competentiae*. At common law there were restrictions on what could be taken in distress for rent, and the thirteenth-century statute providing for execution by writ of *elegit* exempts the debtor's oxen and beasts of the plow and half of his land. In the United States and recently in continental Europe, this policy is given effect in homestead laws and in exemptions from execution. In the latter, the social interest in the family as a social institution is also a factor. But nineteenth-century opposition to homestead and exemption laws, and in Europe to the *beneficium competentiae*, is significant. The nineteenth century sought to treat such cases as if they involved nothing more than the individual interests of the parties to the debtor-creditor relation, or, if a social interest was considered, sought to think only of the general security, which here takes the form of security of transactions. Other recognitions of this interest may be seen in restrictions on the power of debtors or contractors to saddle themselves with oppressive burdens, as in the doctrines of equity heretofore referred to, as in usury laws, and more recently in "loan shark" legislation. A notable instance in recent judicial decision may be seen in the English doctrine as to covenants not to exercise the calling for which one has trained himself. Statutes forbidding contracts by laborers to take their pay in orders on company stores, and as to conditions and hours of labor, minimum wage laws, child labor laws, and housing laws, are recognitions of the same interest.

Again, when the law confers or exercises a power of control, we feel that the legal order should safeguard the human existence of the person controlled. Thus the old-time sea law, with its absolute power of the master over the sailor, the old-time ignominious punishments, that treated the human offender like a brute, that did not save his human dignity—all such things are disappearing as the circle of recognized interests widens and we come to take account of the social interest in the individual life and to weigh that interest with the social interest in the general security, on which the last century insisted so exclusively.

Such in outline are the social interests which are recognized or are coming to be recognized in modern law. Looked at functionally, the law is an attempt to satisfy, to reconcile, to harmonize, to adjust these overlapping and often conflicting claims and demands, either through securing them directly and immediately, or through securing certain individual interests, or through delimitations or compromises of individual interests, so as to give effect to the greatest total of interests or to the interests that weigh most in our civilization, with the least sacrifice of the scheme of interests as a whole.

NOTE

By examining the decisions of an appellate court and considering the contemporary interplay of Pound's social interests, may one develop a comprehensive picture of the jural public policy inclinations of individual judges and the court as a collegial body? Does the multi-member nature of appellate benches render such a study infeasible? Is the adjustment of conflicting interests or claims capable of systemization? If so, is it on the basis of individual opinion writers? Majority or concurring or dissenting groupings? Or by courts? Does it make a difference if the opinion writer is "weak" or "sterile", or "strong"?

CHESTER JAMES ANTIEAU, THE JURISPRUDENCE OF INTERESTS *

The Interests Presently Identified by the Supreme Court as Deserving

In almost two centuries of existence the United States Supreme Court has identified most of the substantial interests of our society deserving constitutional protection, and worthy of being placed on the judicial scales in opposition to other societal interests with which they at

---

* Antieau, *The Jurisprudence of Interests*   27 Case Western L.Rev. 823, 856–857
as a Method of Constitutional Adjudication,   (1977).

times clash. The interests of our society, already identified by the Court as values worthy of protection under the Constitution, include:

(a)   the interest in freedom of communication and religion,[182]
(b)   the interest in the liberty of the individual, embracing many particulars, such as
   (1)   the interest that no person be held in slavery or peonage,[183]
   (2)   the interest in freedom of the individual to travel,[184]
   (3)   the interest in freedom of enterprise and contract,[185]
   (4)   the interest in giving breathing space to individuals in the expression of their personalities,[186] and
   (5)   the interest in freedom from an establishment of religion,[187]
(c)   the interest in equality of law and opportunity,[188]
(d)   the interest in protecting private property,[189]
(e)   the interest in peace, safety, and good order,[190]
(f)   the interest in protecting private reputation,[191]
(g)   the interest in protecting the privacy of the individual,[192]
(h)   the interest in protecting the public health,[193]
(i)   the interest in protecting public morality,[194]
(j)   the interest in protecting the security of the state,[195]
(k)   the interest in the fair and effective administration of justice,[196]
(*l*)   the interest in an effective educational process,[197]
(m)   the interest in protecting the legislative process,[198]
(n)   the interest in the integrity of the electoral process,[199]
(*o*)   the interest in the continued availability of political opportunity,[200] and
(p)   the interest in safeguarding the security of transactions.[201]

While some of these have been identified as individual rather than

182. "The fundamental law declares the interest of the United States that the free exercise of religion be not prohibited and that freedom to communicate information and opinion be not abridged" Cantwell v. Connecticut, 310 U.S. 296, 307 (1940).

183. U.S. CONST. amend. XIII.

184. Griffin v. Breckenridge, 403 U.S. 88 (1971).

185. Allgeyer v. Louisiana, 165 U.S. 578 (1897).

186. Liberty includes "the autonomous control over the development and expression of one's intellect, interests, tastes and personality." Roe v. Wade, 410 U.S. 113, 211 (1973) (Douglas, J., concurring in *Roe* and Doe v. Bolton, 410 U.S. 179 (1973)). *But see* Doe v. Commonwealth's Attorney, 403 F.Supp. 1199 (E.D.Va.1975), *aff'd mem.*, 425 U.S. 901 (1976).

187. Lemon v. Kurtzman, 403 U.S. 602 (1971).

188. Shapiro v. Thompson, 394 U.S. 618 (1969).

189. Central Hardware Co. v. NLRB, 407 U.S. 539 (1972).

190. Feiner v. New York, 340 U.S. 315 (1951).

191. Rosenblatt v. Baer, 383 U.S. 75 (1966). *But see* Paul v. Davis, 424 U.S. 693 (1976).

192. Griswold v. Connecticut, 381 U.S. 479 (1965).

193. Huron Portland Cement Co. v. Detroit, 362 U.S. 440 (1960).

194. Roth v. United States, 354 U.S. 476 (1957).

195. Dennis v. United States, 341 U.S. 494 (1951).

196. Cox v. Louisiana, 379 U.S. 559 (1965).

197. Grayned v. City of Rockford, 408 U.S. 104 (1972).

198. Watkins v. United States, 354 U.S. 178 (1957).

199. United States v. UAW, 352 U.S. 567 (1957).

200. Lubin v. Panish, 415 U.S. 709 (1974).

201. Columbia Ry., Gas & Elec. Co. v. South Carolina, 261 U.S. 236 (1923).

societal interests by the Court, they are, in fact, societal concerns to be balanced in applying the method of *interessenjurisprudenz* advocated here. Each one reflects a value of a free society, necessary for the survival of our way of life. Nevertheless, each interest assumes a greater or lesser importance when it comes into conflict with another societal interest depending upon the state of contemporary culture. When the Court correctly identifies these interests and acknowledges in its opinions that it is balancing one against another, it is applying a jurisprudence of interests.

Section 7

ORE IN PUBLISHED OPINIONS

Analyze the following cases from the standpoint of materials previously set forth in this chapter. Which decision making theory(ies) were used by the opinion writer? Was more than one method used? Analyze the logic and identify the deductive syllogisms used. If inductive logic was used, determine whether it was inductive generalization or the method of analogy.

NEW YORK TIMES CO. v. SULLIVAN

Supreme Court of the United States, 1964.
376 U.S. 254, 84 S.Ct. 710, 11 L.Ed.2d 686.

Mr. Justice Brennan delivered the opinion of the Court.

We are required in this case to determine for the first time the extent to which the constitutional protections for speech and press limit a State's power to award damages in a libel action brought by a public official against critics of his official conduct.

Respondent L.B. Sullivan is one of the three elected Commissioners of the City of Montgomery, Alabama. He testified that he was "Commissioner of Public Affairs and the duties are supervision of the Police Department, Fire Department, Department of Cemetery and Department of Scales." He brought this civil libel action against the four individual petitioners, who are Negroes and Alabama clergymen, and against petitioner the New York Times Company, a New York corporation which publishes the New York Times, a daily newspaper. A jury in the Circuit Court of Montgomery County awarded him damages of $500,000, the full amount claimed, against all the petitioners, and the Supreme Court of Alabama affirmed.

The question before us is whether this rule of liability, as applied to an action brought by a public official against critics of his official conduct, abridges the freedom of speech and of the press that is guaranteed by the First and Fourteenth Amendments.

Respondent relies heavily, as did the Alabama courts, on statements of this Court to the effect that the Constitution does not protect libelous publications. Those statements do not foreclose our inquiry here. None of the cases sustained the use of libel laws to impose sanctions upon expression critical of the official conduct of public officials.... In deciding the question now, we are compelled by neither precedent nor policy to give any more weight to the epithet "libel" than we have to other "mere labels" of state law. N.A.A.C.P. v. Button, 371 U.S. 415, 429, 83 S.Ct. 328, 9 L.Ed.2d 405. Like insurrection, contempt, advocacy of unlawful acts, breach of the peace, obscenity, solicitation of legal business, and the various other formulae for the repression of expression that have been challenged in this Court, libel can claim no talismanic immunity from constitutional limitations. It must be measured by standards that satisfy the First Amendment.

The general proposition that freedom of expression upon public questions is secured by the First Amendment has long been settled by our decisions. The constitutional safeguard, we have said, "was fashioned to assure unfettered interchange of ideas for the bringing about of political and social changes desired by the people." Roth v. United States, 354 U.S. 476, 484, 77 S.Ct. 1304, 1308, 1 L.Ed.2d 1498. "The maintenance of the opportunity for free political discussion to the end that government may be responsive to the will of the people and that changes may be obtained by lawful means, an opportunity essential to the security of the Republic, is a fundamental principle of our constitutional system." Stromberg v. California, 283 U.S. 359, 369, 51 S.Ct. 532, 536, 75 L.Ed. 1117. "[I]t is a prized American privilege to speak one's mind, although not always with perfect good taste, on all public institutions," Bridges v. California, 314 U.S. 252, 270, 62 S.Ct. 190, 197, 86 L.Ed. 192, and this opportunity is to be afforded for "vigorous advocacy" no less than "abstract discussion." N.A.A.C.P. v. Button, 371 U.S. 415, 429, 83 S.Ct. 328, 9 L.Ed.2d 405. The First Amendment, said Judge Learned Hand, "presupposes that right conclusions are more likely to be gathered out of a multitude of tongues, than through any kind of authoritative selection. To many this is, and always will be, folly; but we have staked upon it our all." United States v. Associated Press, 52 F.Supp. 362, 372 (D.C.S.D.N.Y.1943)....

Thus we consider this case against the background of a profound national commitment to the principle that debate on public issues should be uninhibited, robust, and wide-open, and that it may well include vehement, caustic, and sometimes unpleasantly sharp attacks on government and public officials. See Terminiello v. Chicago, 337 U.S. 1, 4, 69 S.Ct. 894, 93 L.Ed. 1131; De Jonge v. Oregon, 299 U.S. 353, 365, 57 S.Ct. 255, 81 L.Ed. 278....

. . .

The constitutional guarantees require, we think, a federal rule that prohibits a public official from recovering damages for a defamatory falsehood relating to his official conduct unless he proves that the statement was made with "actual malice"—that is, with knowledge that it was false or with reckless disregard of whether it was false or not.

MOTION TO ADMIT MISS LAVINIA GOODELL
TO THE BAR OF THIS COURT

Supreme Court of Wisconsin, 1875.
39 Wis. 232.

RYAN, C.J.

So we find no statutory authority for the admission of females to the bar of any court of this state. And, with all the respect and sympathy for this lady which all men owe to all good women, we cannot regret that we do not. We cannot but think the common law wise in excluding women from the profession of the law. The profession enters largely into the well being of society; and, to be honorably filled and safely to society, exacts the devotion of life. The law of nature destines and qualifies the female sex for the bearing and nurture of the children of our race and for the custody of the homes of the world and their maintenance in love and honor. And all life-long callings of women, inconsistent with these radical and sacred duties of their sex, as is the profession of the law, are departures from the order of nature; and when voluntary, treason against it. The cruel chances of life sometimes baffle both sexes, and may leave women free from the peculiar duties of their sex. These may need employment, and should be welcome to any not derogatory to their sex and its proprieties, or inconsistent with the good order of society. But it is public policy to provide for the sex, not for its superfluous members; and not to tempt women from the proper duties of their sex by opening to them duties peculiar to ours. There are many employments in life not unfit for female character. The profession of the law is surely not one of these. The peculiar qualities of womanhood, its gentle graces, its quick sensibility, its tender susceptibility, its purity, its delicacy, its emotional impulses, its subordination of hard reason to sympathetic feeling, are surely not qualifications for forensic strife. Nature has tempered woman as little for the judicial conflicts of the court room, as for the physical conflicts of the battle field. Womanhood is moulded for gentler and better things. And it is not the saints of the world who chiefly give employment to our profession. It has essentially and habitually to do with all that is selfish and malicious, knavish and criminal, coarse and brutal, repulsive and obscene, in human life. It would be revolting to all female sense of the innocence and sanctity of their sex, shocking to man's reverence for womanhood and faith in woman, on which hinge all the better affections and humanities of life, that woman should be permitted to mix professionally in all the nastiness of the world which finds its way into courts of justice; all the unclean issues, all the collateral questions of sodomy, incest, rape, seduction, fornication, adultery, pregnancy, bastardy, legitimacy, prostitution, lascivious cohabitation, abortion, infanticide, obscene publications, libel and slander of sex, impotence, divorce: all the nameless catalogue of indecencies, *la chronique scandaleuse* of all the vices and all the infirmities of all society, with which the profession has to deal, and which go towards filling judicial reports which must be read for accurate knowledge of the law. This is bad enough for men. We hold in too high reverence the sex without which, as is truly and beautifully written, *le commencement de la vie est sans secours, le milieu sans plaisir, et le fin sans consolation,* voluntarily to commit it to such studies and such occupations. *Non tali auxilio nec defensoribus istis,* should juridical contests be upheld. Reverence for all womanhood would suffer in the public spectacle of woman so instructed and so engaged. This motion gives appropriate evidence of this truth. No modest woman could read without pain and self abasement, no woman could so overcome the instincts of sex as publicly to discuss, the case which we had occasion to cite *supra,* King v. Wiseman. And when counsel was arguing for this lady that the word, person, in sec. 32, ch. 119, necessarily includes females, her presence made it impossible to suggest to him as *reductio ad absurdum* of his position, that the same construction of the same word in sec. 1, ch. 37, would subject woman to prosecution for the paternity of a bastard, and in secs. 39, 40, ch. 164, to prosecution for rape. Discussions are habitually necessary in courts of justice, which are unfit for female ears. The habitual presence of women at these would tend to relax the public sense of decency and propriety. If, as counsel threatened, these things are to come, we will take no voluntary part in bringing them about.

By the Court.—The motion is denied.

LUBIN v. IOWA CITY

Supreme Court of Iowa, 1964.
257 Iowa, 383, 131 N.W.2d 765.

STUART, JUSTICE.

Plaintiffs brought this action in three counts against the city seeking damages for injuries sustained when a city water main broke, flooding the basement of plaintiffs' store and damaging merchandise stored there. Count I was based on the doctrine of liability without fault announced in Rylands v. Fletcher, L.R.I.Exch. 265 (1866) L.R. 3HL 330 (1868). Count II was founded upon the doctrine of res ipsa loquitur. Count III contained allegations of specific acts of negligence. The trial court submitted to the jury only res ipsa loquitur and the specific charge of failing to act promptly in turning off the water. The jury returned a defendant's verdict on both counts. The trial court, on plaintiffs' motion, granted a new trial on the ground that the verdict failed to do substantial justice. Defendant has appealed from the trial court's ruling on the motion for new trial.

. . .

The trial court ... invited us to reverse his refusal to submit the case on the theory of absolute liability, saying: "I am satisfied that the only protection that a property owner may, with some degree of certainty, have, is the absolute liability rule, and it should be adopted by the courts of this country. I respectfully ask the Supreme Court of Iowa to reverse me in this case for failure to submit said rule, and to give to the people of this state a genuinely true rule in this type of case, to provide for substantial justice."

As "we will affirm the ruling on any sufficient ground shown by the record even though the ruling was placed upon different reasons", McMaster v. Hutchins, Iowa, 120 N.W.2d 509, 514, we have examined the record to determine if the motion for new trial should have been granted for one of the specific errors claimed in the motion. We agree with the trial court that there was insufficient evidence to submit the three other allegations of specific negligence to the jury. We did not find anything in the record to justify a reversal on the other grounds urged, except for the failure of the trial court to submit the case on the theory of strict liability.

. . .

We have not been asked, prior to this case, to apply strict liability to broken water mains. We have, however, applied strict liability in other instances. The doctrine of Ryland v. Fletcher, supra, was discussed and approved in the case of percolating water or water seepage in Healey v. Citizens Gas and Electric Company, 199 Iowa 82, 201 N.W. 118, 38 A.L.R. 1226. Strict liability has also been imposed on the theory of nuisance ... and trespass....

. . .

Whether we say the invasion of plaintiffs' property by water escaping from defendant's broken water main constitutes a trespass or nuisance or results from an extra-hazardous activity as defined in the Restatement of Torts, Section 520, or is an application of the doctrine of Rylands v. Fletcher, or that the practice of leaving pipes in place until they break is negligence per se, we believe the facts in this case disclose a situation in which liability should be imposed upon the city without a showing of negligent conduct.

It is neither just nor reasonable that the city engaged in a proprietary activity can deliberately and intentionally plan to leave a water main underground beyond inspection and maintenance until a break occurs and escape liability. A city or corporation so operating knows that eventually a break will occur, water will escape and in all probability flow onto the premises of another with resulting damage. We do not ordinarily think of water mains as being extra-hazardous but when such a practice is followed, they become "inherently dangerous and likely to damage the neighbor's property".... The risks from such a method of operation should be borne by the water supplier who is in a position to spread the cost among the consumers who are in fact the true beneficiaries of this practice and of the resulting savings in inspection and maintenance costs. When the expected and inevitable occurs, they should bear the loss and not the unfortunate individual whose property is damaged without fault of his own.

. . .

The reasons stated by the Supreme Court of Minnesota in adhering to the doctrine of Ryland v. Fletcher in Bridgeman–Russell, supra, are appropriate here.

"Congestion of population in large cities is on the increase. This calls for water systems on a vast scale either by the cities themselves or by strong corporations. Water in immense quantities must be accumulated and held where none of it existed before. If a break occurs in the reservoir itself, or in the principal mains, the flood may utterly ruin an individual financially. In such a case, even though negligence be absent, natural justice would seem to demand that the enterprise, or what really is the same thing, the whole community benefitted by the enterprise, should stand the loss rather than the individual. It is too heavy a burden upon one. The trend of modern legislation is to relieve the individual from the mischance of business or industry without regard to its being caused by negligence." ... We see no logical distinction between mains leading from a reservoir and other mains. Damage may utterly ruin an individual financially in either case.

If the city accepts the advantages of lower maintenance costs and other benefits which result from its practice of burying long lasting cast iron pipe six feet underground beyond any reasonable opportunity to inspect and intentionally leaves them there until breaks began to occur, it should also expect to pay for the damages resulting from such practice as a cost of its doing business in this manner.

The result reached here seems to be in line with modern trends. Legal scholars, with justification, accuse the courts of tending to fix tort liability, not by determining which party is at fault but by deciding which party can best stand the loss. 1963 Annual Survey of American Law, p. 363. While we cannot accept such a basis for determining liability in most tort cases, it seems to be appropriate here. Most jurisdictions which rejected Rylands v. Fletcher did so during that period of time when our country was still young and expanding. "Dangerous enterprises, involving a high degree of risk to others, were clearly indispensable to the industrial and commercial development of a new country and it was considered that the interests of those in the vicinity of such enterprises must give way to them, and that too great a burden must not be placed upon them. With the disappearance of the frontier, and the development of the country's resources, it was to be expected that the force of this objection would be weakened, and that it would be replaced in time by the view that the hazardous enterprise, even though it be socially valuable, must pay its way, and make good the damage inflicted. After a long period during which Rylands v. Fletcher was rejected by the large majority of the American courts which considered it, the pendulum has swung to acceptance of the case and its doctrine in the United States." Prosser, Law of Torts, p. 332, see also Bohlen, Studies in the Law of Torts, pp. 367–370.

ROWLAND v. CHRISTIAN

Supreme Court of California, 1968.
69 Cal.2d 108, 70 Cal.Rptr. 97, 443 P.2d 561.

PETERS, JUSTICE.

Plaintiff appeals from a summary judgment for defendant Nancy Christian in this personal injury action.

In his complaint plaintiff alleged that about November 1, 1963, Miss Christian told the lessors of her apartment that the knob of the cold water faucet on the bathroom basin was cracked and should be replaced; that on November 30, 1963, plaintiff entered the apartment at the invitation of Miss Christian; that he was injured while using the bathroom fixtures, suffering severed tendons and nerves of his right hand; and that he has incurred medical and hospital expenses. He further alleged that the bathroom fixtures were dangerous, that Miss Christian was aware of the dangerous condition, and that his injuries were proximately caused by the negligence of Miss Christian. Plaintiff sought recovery of his medical and hospital expenses, loss of wages, damage to his clothing, and $100,000 general damages. It does not appear from the complaint whether the crack in the faucet handle was obvious to an ordinary inspection or was concealed.

. . .

Section 1714 of the Civil Code provides: "Every one is responsible, not only for the result of his willful acts, but also for an injury occasioned to another by his want of ordinary care or skill in the management of his property or person, except so far as the latter has, willfully or by want of ordinary care, brought the injury upon himself. . . ." This code section, which has been unchanged in our law since 1872, states a civil law and not a common law principle. . . .

. . .

. . . Although it is true that some exceptions have been made to the general principle that a person is liable for injuries caused by his failure to exercise reasonable care in the circumstances it is clear that in the absence of statutory provision declaring an exception to the fundamental principle enunciated by section 1714 of the Civil Code, no such exception should be made unless clearly supported by public policy. . . .

A departure from this fundamental principle involves the balancing of a number of considerations; the major ones are the foreseeability of harm to the plaintiff, the degree of certainty that the plaintiff suffered injury, the closeness of the connection between the defendant's conduct and the injury suffered, the moral blame attached to the defendant's conduct, the policy of preventing future harm, the extent of the burden to the defendant and consequences to the community of imposing a duty to exercise care with resulting liability for breach, and the availability, cost, and prevalence of insurance for the risk involved. . . .

One of the areas where this court and other courts have departed from the fundamental concept that a man is liable for injuries caused by his carelessness is with regard to the liability of a possessor of land for injuries to persons who have entered upon that land. It has been suggested that the special rules regarding liability of the possessor of land are due to historical considerations stemming from the high place which land has traditionally held in English and American thought, the dominance and prestige of the landowning class in England during the formative period of the rules governing the possessor's liability, and the heritage of feudalism. . . .

The departure from the fundamental rule of liability for negligence has been accomplished by classifying the plaintiff either as a trespasser, licensee, or invitee and then adopting special rules as to the duty owed by the possessor to each of the classifications. Generally speaking a trespasser is a person who enters or remains upon land of another without a privilege to do so; a licensee is a person like a social guest who is not an invitee and who is privileged to enter or remain upon land by virtue of the possessor's consent, and an invitee is a business visitor who is invited or permitted to enter or remain on the land for a purpose directly or indirectly connected with business dealings between them. . . .

Although the invitor owes the invitee a duty to exercise ordinary care to avoid injuring him . . . the general rule is that a trespasser and licensee or social guest are obliged to take the premises as they find them insofar as any alleged defective condition thereon may exist, and that the possessor of the land owes them only the duty of refraining from wanton or willful injury. . . . The ordinary justification for the general rule severely restricting the occupier's liability to social guests is based on the theory that the guest should not expect special precautions to be made on his account and that if the host does not inspect and maintain his property the guest should not expect this to be done on his account. . . .

An increasing regard for human safety has led to a retreat from this position, and an exception to the general rule limiting liability has been made as to active operations where an obligation to exercise reasonable care for the protection of the licensee has been imposed on the occupier of land. . . . In an apparent attempt to avoid the general rule limiting liability, courts have broadly defined active operations, sometimes giving the term a strained construction in cases involving dangers known to the occupier.

. . .

... Whatever may have been the historical justifications for the common law distinctions, it is clear that those distinctions are not justified in the light of our modern society and that the complexity and confusion which has arisen is not due to difficulty in applying the original common law rules—they are all too easy to apply in their original formulation—but is due to the attempts to apply just rules in our modern society within the ancient terminology.

[I]t is apparent that the classifications of trespasser, licensee, and invitee, the immunities from liability predicated upon those classifications, and the exceptions to those immunities, often do not reflect the major factors which should determine whether immunity should be conferred upon the possessor of land. Some of those factors, including the closeness of the connection between the injury and the defendant's conduct, the moral blame attached to the defendant's conduct, the policy of preventing future harm, and the prevalence and availability of insurance, bear little, if any, relationship to the classifications of trespasser, licensee and invitee and the existing rules conferring immunity.

Although in general there may be a relationship between the remaining factors and the classifications of trespasser, licensee, and invitee, there are many cases in which no such relationship may exist.... The last of the major factors, the cost of insurance, will, of course, vary depending upon the rules of liability adopted, but there is no persuasive evidence that applying ordinary principles of negligence law to the land occupier's liability will materially reduce the prevalence of insurance due to increased cost or even substantially increase the cost.

. . .

A man's life or limb does not become less worthy of protection by the law nor a loss less worthy of compensation under the law because he has come upon the land of another without permission or with permission but without a business purpose. Reasonable people do not ordinarily vary their conduct depending upon such matters, and to focus upon the status of the injured party as a trespasser, licensee, or invitee in order to determine the question whether the landowner has a duty of care, is contrary to our modern social mores and humanitarian values. The common law rules obscure rather than illuminate the proper considerations which should govern determination of the question of duty.

It bears repetition that the basic policy of this state set forth by the Legislature in section 1714 of the Civil Code is that everyone is responsible for an injury caused to another by his want of ordinary care or skill in the management of his property. The factors which may in particular cases warrant departure from this fundamental principle do not warrant the wholesale immunities resulting from the common law classifications, and we are satisfied that continued adherence to the common law distinctions can only lead to injustice or, if we are to avoid injustice, further fictions with the resulting complexity and confusion. We decline to follow and perpetuate such rigid classifications. The proper test to be applied to the liability of the possessor of land in accordance with section

1714 of the Civil Code is whether in the management of his property he has acted as a reasonable man in view of the probability of injury to others, and, although the plaintiff's status as a trespasser, licensee, or invitee may in the light of the facts giving rise to such status have some bearing on the question of liability, the status is not determinative.

TRAYNOR, C.J., and TOBRINER, MOSK and SULLIVAN, JJ., concur.

BURKE, JUSTICE, dissenting.

I dissent. In determining the liability of the occupier or owner of land for injuries, the distinctions between trespassers, licensees and invitees have been developed and applied by the courts over a period of many years. They supply a reasonable and workable approach to the problems involved, and one which provides the degree of stability and predictability so highly prized in the law. The unfortunate alternative, it appears to me, is the route taken by the majority in their opinion in this case; that such issues are to be decided on a case by case basis under the application of the basic law of negligence, bereft of the guiding principles and precedent which the law has heretofore attached by virtue of the relationship of the parties to one another.

Liability for negligence turns upon whether a duty of care is owed, and if so, the extent thereof. Who can doubt that the corner grocery, the large department store, or the financial institution owes a greater duty of care to one whom it has invited to enter its premises as a prospective customer of its wares or services than it owes to a trespasser seeking to enter after the close of business hours and for a nonbusiness or even an antagonistic purpose? I do not think it unreasonable or unfair that a social guest (classified by the law as a licensee, as was plaintiff here) should be obliged to take the premises in the same condition as his host finds them or permits them to be. Surely a homeowner should not be obliged to hover over his guests with warnings of possible dangers to be found in the condition of the home (*e.g.,* waxed floors, slipping rugs, toys in unexpected places, etc., etc.). Yet today's decision appears to open the door to potentially unlimited liability despite the purpose and circumstances motivating the plaintiff in entering the premises of another, and despite the caveat of the majority that the status of the parties may "have some bearing on the question of liability ....," whatever the future may show that language to mean.

In my view, it is not a proper function of this court to overturn the learning, wisdom and experience of the past in this field. Sweeping modifications of tort liability law fall more suitably within the domain of the Legislature, before which all affected interests can be heard and which can enact statutes providing uniform standards and guidelines for the future.

McCOMB, J., concurs.

———

DILLON v. LEGG

Supreme Court of California, 1968.
68 Cal.2d 728, 69 Cal.Rptr. 72, 441 P.2d 912.

TOBRINER, JUSTICE.

That the courts should allow recovery to a mother who suffers emotional trauma and physical injury from witnessing the infliction of death or injury to her child for which the tort-feasor is liable in negligence would appear to be a compelling proposition. As Prosser points out, "All ordinary human feelings are in favor of her [the mother's] action against the negligent defendant. If a duty to her requires that she herself be in some recognizable danger, then it has properly been said that when a child is endangered, it is not beyond contemplation that its mother will be somewhere in the vicinity, and will suffer serious shock." (Prosser, Law of Torts (3d ed. 1964) p. 353.)

Nevertheless, past American decisions have barred the mother's recovery. Refusing the mother the right to take her case to the jury, these courts ground their position on an alleged absence of a required "duty" of due care of the tortfeasor to the mother. Duty, in turn, they state, must express public policy; the imposition of duty here would work disaster because it would invite fraudulent claims and it would involve the courts in the hopeless task of defining the extent of the tortfeasor's liability. In substance, they say, definition of liability being impossible, denial of liability is the only realistic alternative.

We have concluded that neither of the feared dangers excuses the frustration of the natural justice upon which the mother's claim rests. We shall point out that in the past we have rejected the argument that we should deny recovery upon a legitimate claim because other fraudulent ones may be urged. . . .

. . .

The denial of "duty" in the instant situation rests upon the prime hypothesis that allowance of such an action would lead to successful assertion of fraudulent claims. . . . The rationale apparently assumes that juries, confronted by irreconcilable expert medical testimony, will be unable to distinguish the deceitful from the bona fide. The argument concludes that only a per se rule denying the entire class of claims that potentially raises this administrative problem can avoid this danger.

In the first instance, the argument proceeds from a doubtful factual assumption. Whatever the possibilities of fraudulent claims of physical injury by disinterested spectators of an accident, a question not in issue in this case, we certainly cannot doubt that a mother who sees her child killed will suffer physical injury from shock. "It seems sufficiently obvious that the shock of a mother at danger or harm to her child may be both a real and a serious injury." (Prosser, Law of Torts, supra, at p. 353.)

. . .

In sum, the application of tort law can never be a matter of mathematical precision. In terms of characterizing conduct as tortious and matching a money award to the injury suffered as well as in fixing the extent of injury, the process cannot be perfect. Undoubtedly, ever since the ancient case of the tavern-keeper's wife who successfully avoided the hatchet cast by an irate customer (I de S et ux v. W de S, Y.B. 22 Edw. iii, f. 99, pl. 60 (1348)), defendants have argued that plaintiffs' claims of injury from emotional trauma might well be fraudulent. Yet we cannot let the difficulties of adjudication frustrate the principle that there be a remedy for every substantial wrong.

VEGELAHN v. GUNTNER

Supreme Judicial Court of Massachusetts, 1896.
167 Mass. 92, 44 N.E. 1077.

ALLEN, J.

The principal question in this case is whether the defendants should be enjoined against maintaining the patrol. The report shows that, following upon a strike of the plaintiff's workmen, the defendants conspired to prevent him from getting workmen, and thereby to prevent him from carrying on his business, unless and until he should adopt a certain schedule of prices. The means adopted were persuasion and social pressure, threats of personal injury or unlawful harm conveyed to persons employed or seeking employment, and a patrol of two men in front of the plaintiff's factory, maintained from half past 6 in the morning till half past 5 in the afternoon, on one of the busiest streets of Boston.... Such an act is an unlawful interference with the rights both of employer and of employed. An employer has a right to engage all persons who are willing to work for him, at such prices as may be mutually agreed upon, and persons employed or seeking employment have a corresponding right to enter into or remain in the employment of any person or corporation willing to employ them. These rights are secured by the constitution itself.... No one can lawfully interfere by force or intimidation to prevent employers or persons employed or wishing to be employed from the exercise of these rights. It is in Massachusetts, as in some other states, even made a criminal offense for one, by intimidation or force, to prevent, or seek to prevent, a person from entering into or continuing in the employment of a person or corporation.... Intimidation is not limited to threats of violence or of physical injury to person or property. It has a broader signification, and there also may be a moral intimidation which is illegal. Patrolling or picketing, under the circumstances stated in the report, has elements of intimidation.... The patrol was an unlawful interference both with the plaintiff and with the workmen, within the principle of many cases; and, when instituted for the purpose of interfering with his business, it became a private nuisance....

The defendants contend that these acts were justifiable, because they were only seeking to secure better wages for themselves, by compelling the plaintiff to accept their schedule of wages. This motive or purpose does not justify maintaining a patrol in front of the plaintiff's premises, as a means of carrying out their conspiracy. A combination among persons merely to regulate their own conduct is within allowable competition, and is lawful, although others may be indirectly affected thereby. But a combination to do injurious acts expressly directed to another, by way of intimidation or constraint, either of himself or of persons employed or seeking to be employed by him, is outside of allowable competition, and is unlawful....

HOLMES, J., dissenting.

In a case like the present, it seems to me that, whatever the true result may be, it will be of advantage to sound thinking to have the less popular view of the law stated....

. . .

I agree, whatever may be the law in the case of a single defendant ... that when a plaintiff proves that several persons have combined and conspired to injure his business, and have done acts producing that effect, he shows temporal damage and a cause of action, unless the facts disclose or the defendants prove some ground of excuse or justification; and I take it to be settled, and rightly settled, that doing that damage by combined persuasion is actionable, as well as doing it by falsehood or by force....

Nevertheless, in numberless instances the law warrants the intentional infliction of temporal damage, because it regards it as justified. It is on the question of what shall amount to a justification, and more especially on the nature of the considerations which really determine or ought to determine the answer to that question, that judicial reasoning seems to me often to be inadequate. The true grounds of decision are considerations of policy and of social advantage, and it is vain to suppose that solutions can be attained merely by logic and general propositions of law which nobody disputes. Propositions as to public policy rarely are unanimously accepted, and still more rarely, if ever, are capable of unanswerable proof. They require a special training to enable any one even to form an intelligent opinion about them.

In the early stages of law, at least, they generally are acted on rather as inarticulate instincts than as definite ideas, for which a rational defense is ready.

To illustrate what I have said in the last paragraph: It has been the law for centuries that a man may set up a business in a small country town, too small to support more than one, although thereby he expects and intends to ruin some one already there, and succeeds in his intent. In such a case he is not held to act "unlawfully and without justifiable cause".... The reason, of course, is that the doctrine generally has been accepted that free competition is worth more to society than it costs, and that on this ground the infliction of the damage is privileged.... Yet even this proposition nowadays is disputed by a considerable body of persons, including many whose intelligence is not to be denied, little as we may agree with them.

I have chosen this illustration partly with reference to what I have to say next. It shows without the need of further authority that the policy of allowing free competition justifies the intentional inflicting of temporal damage, including the damage of interference with a man's business by some means, when the damage is done, not for its own sake, but as an instrumentality in reaching the end of victory in the battle of trade. In such a case it cannot matter whether the plaintiff is the only rival of the defendant, and so is aimed at specially, or is one of a class all of whom are hit. The only debatable ground is the nature of the means by which such damage may be inflicted. We all agree that it cannot be done by force or threats of force. We all agree, I presume, that it may be done by persuasion to leave a rival's shop, and come to the defendant's. It may be done by the refusal or withdrawal of various pecuniary advantages, which, apart from this consequence, are within the defendant's lawful control. It may be done by the withdrawal of, or threat to withdraw, such advantages from third persons who have a right to deal or not to deal with the plaintiff, as a means of inducing them not to deal with him either as customers or servants.... I have seen the suggestion made that the conflict between employers and employed was not competition. But I venture to assume that none of my brethren would rely on that suggestion. If the policy on which our law is founded is too narrowly expressed in the term "free competition," we may substitute "free struggle for life." Certainly, the policy is not limited to struggles between persons of the same class, competing for the same end. It applies to all conflicts of temporal interests.

. . .

One of the eternal conflicts out of which life is made up is that between the effort of every man to get the most he can for his services, and that of society, disguised under the name of capital, to get his services for the least possible return. Combination on the one side is patent and powerful. Combination on the other is the necessary and desirable counterpart, if the battle is to be carried on in a fair and equal way....

If it be true that workingmen may combine with a view, among other things, to getting as much as they can for their labor, just as capital may combine with a view to getting the greatest possible return, it must be true that, when combined, they have the same liberty that combined capital has, to support their interests by argument, persuasion, and the bestowal or refusal of those advantages which they otherwise lawfully control. I can remember when many people thought that, apart from violence or breach of contract, strikes were wicked, as organized refusals to work. I suppose that intelligent economists and legislators have given up that notion today. I feel pretty confident that they equally will abandon the idea that an organized refusal by workmen of social intercourse with a man who shall enter their antagonist's employ is unlawful, if it is dissociated from any threat of violence, and is made for the sole object of prevailing, if possible, in a contest with their employer about the rate of wages. The fact that the immediate object of the act by which the benefit to themselves is to be gained is to injure their antagonist does not necessarily make it unlawful, any more than when a great house lowers the price of goods for the purpose and with the effect of driving a smaller antagonist from the business.

ESCOLA v. COCA COLA BOTTLING CO.

Supreme Court of California, 1944.
24 Cal.2d 453, 150 P.2d 436.

TRAYNOR, JUSTICE, concurring.

I concur in the judgment, but I believe the manufacturer's negligence should no longer be singled out as the basis of a plaintiff's right to recover in cases like the present one. In my opinion it should now be recognized that a manufacturer incurs an absolute liability when an article that he has placed on the market, knowing that it is to be used without inspection, proves to have a defect that causes injury to human beings. MacPherson v. Buick Motor Co., 217 N.Y. 382, 111 N.E. 1050, L.R.A.1916F, 696, Ann.Cas.1916C, 440 established the principle, recognized by this court, that irrespective of privity of contract, the manufacturer is responsible for an injury caused by such an article to any person who comes in lawful contact with it. Sheward v. Virtue, 20 Cal.2d 410, 126 P.2d 345; Kalash v. Los Angeles Ladder Co., 1 Cal.2d 229, 34 P.2d 481. In these cases the source of the manufacturer's liability was his negligence in the manufacturing process or in the inspection of component parts supplied by others. Even if there is no negligence, however, public policy demands that responsibility be fixed wherever it will most effectively reduce the hazards to life and health inherent in defective products that reach the market. It is evident that the manufacturer can anticipate some hazards and guard against the recurrence of others, as the public cannot. Those who suffer injury from defective products are unprepared to meet its consequences. The cost of an injury and the loss of time or health may be an overwhelming misfortune to the person injured, and a needless one, for the risk of injury can be insured by the manufacturer and distributed among the public as a cost of doing business. It is to the public interest to discourage the marketing of products having defects that are a menace to the public. If such products nevertheless find their way into the market it is to the public interest to place the responsibility for whatever injury they may cause upon the manufacturer, who, even if he is not negligent in the manufacture of the product, is responsible for its reaching the market. However intermittently such injuries may occur and however haphazardly they may strike, the risk of their occurrence is a constant risk and a general one. Against such a risk there should be general and constant protection and the manufacturer is best situated to afford such protection.

GREENMAN v. YUBA POWER PRODUCTS, INC.

Supreme Court of California, 1963.
59 Cal.2d 57, 27 Cal.Rptr. 697, 377 P.2d 897.

OPINION OF THE COURT

TRAYNOR, JUSTICE.

Plaintiff brought this action for damages against the retailer and the manufacturer of a Shopsmith, a combination power tool that could be used as a saw, drill, and wood lathe. He saw a Shopsmith demonstrated by the retailer and studied a brochure prepared by the manufacturer. He decided he wanted a Shopsmith for his home workshop, and his wife bought and gave him one for Christmas in 1955. In 1957 he bought the necessary attachments to use the Shopsmith as a lathe for turning a large piece of wood he wished to make into a chalice. After he had worked on the piece of wood several times without difficulty, it suddenly flew out of the machine and struck him on the forehead, inflicting serious injuries. About ten and a half months later, he gave the retailer and the manufacturer written notice of claimed breaches of warranties and filed a complaint against them alleging such breaches and negligence.

After a trial before a jury, the court ruled that there was no evidence that the retailer was negligent or had breached any express warranty and that the manufacturer was not liable for the breach of any implied warranty. Accordingly, it submitted to the jury only the cause of action alleging breach of implied warranties against the retailer and the causes of action alleging negligence and breach of express warranties against the manufacturer. The jury returned a verdict for the retailer against plaintiff and for plaintiff against the manufacturer in the amount of $65,000. The trial court denied the manufacturer's motion for a new trial and entered judgment on the verdict. The manufacturer and plaintiff appeal. Plaintiff seeks a reversal of the part of the judgment in favor of the retailer, however, only in the event that the part of the judgment against the manufacturer is reversed.

. . .

. . . A manufacturer is strictly liable in tort when an article he places on the market, knowing that it is to be used without inspection for defects, proves to have a defect that causes injury to a human being. Recognized first in the case of unwholesome food products, such liability has now been extended to a variety of other products that create as great or greater hazards if defective.

Although in these cases strict liability has usually been based on the theory of an express or implied warranty running from the manufacturer to the plaintiff, the abandonment of the requirement of a contract between them, the recognition that the liability is not assumed by agreement but imposed by law ... and the refusal to permit the manufacturer to define the scope of its own responsibility for defective products ... make clear that the liability is not one governed by the law of contract warranties but by the law of strict liability in tort. Accordingly, rules defining and governing warranties that were developed to meet the needs of commercial transactions cannot properly be invoked to govern the manufacturer's liability to those injured by their defective products unless those rules also serve the purposes for which such liability is imposed.

... The purpose of such liability is to insure that the costs of injuries resulting from defective products are borne by the manufacturers that put such products on the market rather than by the injured persons who are powerless to protect themselves. Sales warranties serve this purpose fitfully at best.... In the present case, for example, plaintiff was able to plead and prove an express warranty only because he read and relied on the representations of the Shopsmith's ruggedness contained in the manufacturer's brochure. Implicit in the machine's presence on the market, however, was a representation that it would safely do the jobs for which it was built. Under these circumstances, it should not be controlling whether plaintiff selected the machine because of the statements in the brochure, or because of the machine's own appearance of excellence that belied the defect lurking beneath the surface, or because he merely assumed that it would safely do the jobs it was built to do.

It should not be controlling whether the details of the sales from manufacturer to retailer and from retailer to plaintiff's wife were such that one or more of the implied warranties of the sales act arose.... "The remedies of injured consumers ought not to be made to depend upon the intricacies of the law of sales." ... To establish the manufacturer's liability it was sufficient that plaintiff proved that he was injured while using the Shopsmith in a way it was intended to be used as a result of a defect in design and manufacture of which plaintiff was not aware that made the Shopsmith unsafe for its intended use.

NOTE

See also Goldberg v. Kollsman Instrument Corp., 12 N.Y.2d 432, 240 N.Y.S.2d 592, 191 N.E.2d 81 (1963). Note that it was 18 years before the legal precept in Justice Traynor's *Escola* concurring opinion of 1944 became the majority opinion of the court in *Greenman* in 1962.

Chapter V

THE JUDGING PROCESS: MAKING
THE DECISION

Section 1

REALISTS, HUNCHERS AND REFLECTIVE THINKERS

OVERVIEW

During the heyday of conceptual jurisprudence it was assumed, somewhat naively, that judges simply compared the facts of the case before them to a pre-existing, clearly defined set of legal rules, and that the judge's decisions flowed directly, with no range of free choice for the judge. In the late 1920's and 1930's, Realism struck at the heart of this assumption. The more extreme Realists asserted that the decisions ultimately depended on extra-legal, personal phenomena, such as the judges' experiences, or the state of their digestion the day they heard a case. If, in retrospect, the Realists were excessive in some of their claims, at least they deserve credit for clarifying that the judge's role in framing a decision involves a free choice among competing legal precepts, a free choice in interpreting a precept and a free choice in applying settled law to what they considered as material facts. They showed that there were many value judgments used in the judicial process and that judges wielded a creative hand in law making.

Judge Hutcheson asserted that decisions may emerge from any of four separate processes: "first, the cogitative, of and by reflection and logomachy; second, aleatory, of and by the dice; third, intuitive, of and by feeling or 'hunching'; and fourth, asinine, of and by an ass." [1] Because judges are not automatons, and because they are given more authority than administrators to refine and define law, it should come as no surprise that a degree of subjectivity, if not emotion, is alive and kicking in the judicial process. This is particularly true in that aspect of the judicial process referred to as decision making. Neither viable rules of law nor precedents which seem to be on all fours command a particular decision in an individual case. Often the sole source of a decision is a judge's intuition or hunch about the right result.

Hunching may be an emotive experience in which principles and logic play a secondary role. It was Thomas Carlyle who said, "The healthy understanding, we should say, is not the logical argumentative, but the intuitive; for the end of understanding is not to prove and find

---

1. J.C. Hutcheson, Jr., *The Judgment Intuitive: The Function of the "Hunch" in* *Judicial Decision,* 14 Cornell L.Q. 274 (1919.)

reasons, but to know and believe." [2] Yet hunching may be far more respectable than it appears initially, for it embodies something not easily defined, a quality found in certain experienced judges who are said to possess a "trained intuition" for the right result: What Karl Llewellyn calls, "good hunching power.... a resultant of good sense, imagination, and much knowledge." [3] Perhaps this was what Oliver Wendell Holmes, a master of the epigram, had in mind in his historic dissent in Lochner v. New York: "General propositions do not decide concrete cases. The decision will depend on a judgment or intuition more subtle than any articulate major premise." [4] But some are quick to disagree with any suggestion that seeks to separate logical reasoning from knowledge, as did Carlyle. What is knowledge but hard information or facts and the inferences logically drawn therefrom? An assertion that a person is intuitive is often taken as a back-handed compliment. It is a suggestion that the intuitive one does not have the capacity for reaching judgments through principle and logic.

If the result of a decision is just, may we not agree with Judge Henry J. Friendly that "the conclusion which flashes before the shaving mirror in the morning does not differ in intellectual quality from that matured from study in chambers in night before"? [5] If so, that which often passes as intuition may be an extremely swift reasoning process, a lightning human computer operation.

Judge Hutcheson confessed that "when the case is difficult or involved, and turns upon a hairsbreadth of law or of fact, ... I, after canvassing all the available material at my command, and duly cogitating upon it, give my imagination play, and brooding over the case, wait for the feeling, the hunch—that intuitive flash of understanding which makes the jump-spark connection between question and decision, and at the point where the path is darkest for the judicial feet, sheds its light along the way." [6] But there are hunches and there are hunches. A decision based on an impression without any evaluation of the evidence may be little more than a guess. What is it to bet on a horse, say No. 5, solely because you felt his number would win? If he loses, it's a guess. If he wins, it's a hunch. But if you study track records of the No. 5 horse, his thoroughbred pedigree, the reputation of the jockey and posted odds, then make a similar examination of the competing horses, and then say, "I have a hunch that No. 5 will win," the decision to bet on No. 5 really is not a hunch at all. It is a rational judgment, based on careful examination of the data and a thoughtful evaluation, couched in the expression "hunch."

We must learn to distinguish a real hunch from an ersatz one. Often so-called devotees of intuition are in truth superbly endowed

2. T. Carlyle, On History.

3. K. Llewellyn, The Bramble Bush 98–99 (1960).

4. 198 U.S. 45, 76 (1905) (Holmes, J. dissenting).

5. H. Friendly, *Reactions of a Lawyer—Newly Became a Judge* 71 Yale L.J. 218, 229 (1961).

6. J.C. Hutcheson, Jr., *The Judgment Intuitive: The Function of the "Hunch" in Judicial Decision*, 14 Cornell L.Q. 274, 282 (1929).

analysts capable of seeing the big picture, recognizing all the reasonable alternatives, evaluating them, predicting consequences and seizing upon the solution—all in one fell swoop. If asked why a particular decision was made, a shrug of the shoulders and "just a hunch" might be the response. But do not believe it. In reality, Judge Hutcheson is discussing an "educated" hunch when he states that according to the judge's "training, his experience, and his general point of view, [the decision] strikes him as the jural consequence that ought to flow from the facts.... This hunch, sweeping aside hesitancy and doubt, takes the judge vigorously on to his decision; and yet, the case decided, the way thither, which was for the blinding moment a blazing trail, becomes wholly lost to view." [7]

Cardozo put it this way: "The doctrine of the hunch, if viewed as an attempt at psychological analysis, embodies an important truth; it is a vivid and arresting description of one of the stages in the art of thought. The hunch is the divination of the scientist, ... the apocalyptic insight, that is back of his experiments.... The intuitive flash of inspiration is at the root of all science, of all art, and even of all conduct." [8] Cardozo feared that the word "hunch," with its ambiguity, would cause problems. He, too, would recognize that most so-called hunches are in fact the product of reflective thought. He, too, would deplore any practice that "might tend to establish the empire of mere feeling or emotion, of arbitrary preference, and by the same token to disprove the value of conceptions, rules and principles, the value of all logic, till we are driven like the sophist in the Greek comedy, to proclaim that Whirl is King." [9]

But there is another side to the "mere feeling or emotion" coin. Sigmund Freud reported: "When making a decision of minor importance I have always found it advantageous to consider all the pros and cons. In vital matters, however, such as the choice of a mate or a profession, the decision should come from the unconscious, from somewhere within ourselves. In the important decisions of our personal life, we should be governed, I think, by the deeper inner needs of our nature." This may raise the question of how important questions are decided in court. Do the decisions "come from the unconscious, from somewhere within" the judges? If we are willing to acknowledge that judges are not judicial slot machines and that environmental, experiential, and emotional factors do play a part in the decision making process, we must also acknowledge an accommodation between impersonal, theoretical decision making and the subjectivity of the actual practice. But those who wear black robes are not the only judges in this land. Every rational being makes decisions daily, variously utilizing forms of instant intuition or lengthy reasoning, either quickly summoning very personal and wishful thoughts or carefully evaluating dispassionate considerations. One might wish the decision making process to take the form of Missouri detachment, as described in Max Radin's charming anecdote: "You remember the Missouri mountai-

7. Id.
9. Id. at 26.
8. B. Cardozo, Selected Writings 27–28 (Hall ed. 1967).

neer woman who watched a fight between her husband and a bear and remarked as she inhaled smoke through her clay pipe that this was the first fight she ever saw in which she did not care who won." Whether this is an appropriate ideal is debatable. Whether it often manifests itself in reality is also a matter of doubt.

The American Legal Realists were responsible for raising public consciousness that courts are not judicial slot machines and that certainly subjective factors do play a part in the decision making process. The advocate must recognize this and, when possible, identify those factors which are most likely to influence a particular judge or court, and then use this knowledge to maximum advantage in persuasive argument. But it must be quickly emphasized that some of the Realists overstated the case. It must also be emphasized the Legal Realism was not a systematic philosophy of law to which all the so-called Realists subscribed. The hero figure of the clan was Holmes. Llewellyn was one of its most prolific writers. Others included Jerome Frank, Joseph Bingham, Walter Cook, Herman Oliphant, Max Radin and Felix Cohen.

At the risk of oversimplification, it can be said that Legal Realism was simply a way of looking at legal rules and legal processes. In points of stress and details of belief, the Realists differed widely, often passionately, from one another. The constant inquiry seems to have been: We are not interested in what the rules of law say as to the problem. We want to know what happens in life—in the law offices, courtrooms and prosecutors' conferences? What are the actual materials with which the judge and practicing lawyer work? Where is the power, the discretion, the actual responsibility center for decision? George C. Christie has indicated that Legal Realism was a basic approach towards the law which is characterized by one or more of the following: a desire to separate legal from moral elements in legal analysis, a distrust of the judicial technique of seeming to deduce legal conclusions from "so-called" rules of law, a suspicion of all generalizations and a belief that legal progress was only possible by breaking down the legal universe into smaller and smaller components that were easier to analyze and comprehend, a belief in the instrumental value of law. Law was not something that existed in and of itself but to some certain social ends, and a marked preference for behavioral explanations of legal phenomena.[12] Distilled to its essence, this approach to law was the approach of the hard-boiled practitioner: One who defined law, with Holmes, as the predictions of what the courts and officials will do in fact. This practitioner constantly made factor analyses, constructed predictive models on the basis of how different judges have responded to given facts of record in different cases.

Whatever deficiencies the Realists had as legal philosophers, they nevertheless set the framework for the modern courtroom and appellate advocate. Perhaps knowing the legal precept today, and knowing that a judge will embrace the precept may not be as important as knowing why he does. The advocate must construct a predictive model that contains

12. G. Christie, Jurisprudence 641–44 (1968).

those interests to which judges have reacted in the past. We have previously defined an interest as a social fact, factor or phenomenon reflected in a claim or demand or desire which human beings, either individually or as groups or associates or relations, seek to satisfy and which has been recognized as socially valid by authoritative decision makers in society. The effective advocate must identify these interests, classify them variously as individual, public or societal, and then determine how particular judges have reacted to them in the past. The skilled advocate must understand what diverse segments of the populace seek to satisfy: the union member or corporate president, the war veteran or protester, the products manufacturer or consumer, the teenager or senior citizen, the welfare recipient or white collar worker, the myriad racial and ethnic groups.

Understanding past responses of given judges to identified interests is important to the modern advocate in any field of law, but especially in the emotionally charged areas of constitutional law where the values, judgments and attitudes of judges are important ingredients in the decision making processes. Llewellyn believed this had to be a constant process of predicting before the judicial event, and analyzing thereafter: "If you were right, were your bases those the court displays? If you were wrong, wherein did you go wrong? The bad with the good you want, the blind with the keen, the stupid with the wise. For you will have to hunch as to *all* kinds of judges." [13]

JOSEPH C. HUTCHESON, JR., THE JUDGMENT INTUITIVE: THE FUNCTION OF THE "HUNCH" [1] IN JUDICIAL DECISION *

Many years ago, at the conclusion of a particularly difficult case both in point of law and of fact, tried to a court without a jury, the judge, a man of great learning and ability, announced from the Bench that since the narrow and prejudiced modern view of the obligations of a judge in the decision of causes prevented his resort to the judgment aleatory by the use of his "little, small dice" he would take the case under advisement, and, brooding over it, wait for his hunch.

To me, a young, indeed a very young lawyer, picked, while yet the dew was on me and I had just begun to sprout, from the classic gardens of a University, where I had been trained to regard the law as a system of rules and precedents, of categories and concepts, and the judge had been spoken of as an administrator, austere, remote, "his intellect a cold logic engine," who, in that rarified atmosphere in which he lived coldly

13. K. Llewellyn, The Bramble Bush 98 (1960).

1. "A strong, intuitive impression that something is about to happen." Webster International Dictionary.

* 14 Cornell L.Q. 274, 274–80, 282, 284–87 (1929). Copyright © 1929 by Cornell University.

and logically determined the relation of the facts of a particular case to some of these established precedents, it appeared that the judge was making a jest, and a very poor one, at that.

I had been trained to expect inexactitude from juries, but from the judge quite the reverse. I exalted in the law its tendency to formulize. I had a slot machine mind. I searched out categories and concepts and, having found them, worshiped them.

I paid homage to the law's supposed logical rigidity and exactitude. A logomachist, I believe in and practiced logomachy. I felt a sense of real pain when some legal concept in which I had put my faith as permanent, constructive and all-embracing opened like a broken net, allowing my fish to fall back into the legal sea. Paraphrasing Huxley, I believed that the great tragedy of the law was the slaying of a beautiful concept by an ugly fact. Always I looked for perfect formulas, fact proof, concepts so general, so flexible, that in their terms the jural relations of mankind could be stated, and I rejected most vigorously the suggestion that there was, or should be, anything fortuitous or by chance in the law. Like Jurgen I had been to the Master Philologist and with words he had conquered me.

I had studied the law in fragments and segments, in sections and compartments, and in my mind each compartment was nicely and logically arranged so that every case presented to me only the problem of arranging and re-arranging its facts until I could slip it into the compartment to which it belonged. The relation of landlord and tenant, of principal and agent, of bailor and bailee, of master and servant, these and a hundred others controlled my thinking and directed its processes.

Perceiving the law as a thing fullgrown, I believed that all of its processes were embraced in established categories, and I rejected most vigorously the suggestion that it still had life and growth, and if anyone had suggested that the judge had a right to feel, or hunch out a new category into which to place relations under his investigation, I should have repudiated the suggestion as unscientific and unsound, while as to the judge who dared to do it, I should have cried "Away with him! Away with him!"

I was too much influenced by the codifiers, by John Austin and Bentham, and by their passion for exactitude. I knew that in times past the law had grown through judicial action; that rights and processes had been invented by the judges, and that under their creative hand new remedies and new rights had flowered.

I knew that judges "are the depositories of the laws like the oracles, who must decide in all cases of doubt and are bound by an oath to decide according to the law of the land," but I believed that creation and evolution were at an end, that in modern law only deduction had place, and that the judges must decide "through being long personally accustomed to and acquainted with the judicial decisions of their predecessors."

I recognized, of course, that in the preparation of the facts of a case there was room for intuition, for feeling; that there was a sixth sense which must be employed in searching out the evidence for clues, in order to assemble facts and more facts, but all of this before the evidence was in. I regarded the solution of the problem when the evidence was all in as a matter for determination by the judge by pure reason and reflection, and while I knew that juries might and did arrive at their verdicts by feeling, I repudiated as impossible the idea that good judges did the same.

I knew, of course, that some judges did follow "hunches,"—"guesses" I indignantly called them. I knew my Rabelais, and had laughed over without catching the true philosophy of old Judge Bridlegoose's trial, and roughly, in my youthful, scornful way, I recognized four kinds of judgments; first the cogitative, of and by reflection and logomachy; second, aleatory, of and by the dice; third, intuitive, of and by feeling or "hunching;" and fourth, asinine, of and by an ass; and in that same youthful, scornful way I regarded the last three as only variants of each other, the results of processes all alien to good judges.

As I grew older, however, and knew and understood better the judge to whom I have in this opening referred; as I associated more with real lawyers, whose intuitive faculties were developed and made acute by the use of a trained and cultivated imagination; as I read more after and came more under the spell of those great lawyers and judges whose thesis is that "modification is the life of the law," I came to see that "as long as the matter to be considered is debated in artificial terms, there is danger of being led by a technical definition to apply a certain name and then to deduce consequences which have no relation to the grounds on which the name was applied;" that "the process of inclusion and exclusion so often applied in developing a rule, cannot end with its first enunciation. The rule announced must be deemed tentative. For the many and varying facts to which it will be applied cannot be foreseen."

I came to see that "every opinion tends to become a law." That "regulations, the wisdom, necessity and validity of which as applied to, existing conditions, are so apparent that they are now uniformly sustained, a century ago, or even half a century ago, would probably have been rejected as arbitrary and oppressive, . . . and that in a changing world it is impossible that it should be otherwise."

I came to see that "resort to first principles is, in the last analysis, the only safe way to a solution of litigated matters."

I came to see that instinct in the very nature of law itself is change, adaptation, conformity, and that the instrument for all of this change, this adaptation, this conformity, for the making and the nurturing of the law as a thing of life, is the power of the brooding mind, which in its very brooding makes, creates and changes jural relations, establishes philosophy, and drawing away from the outworn past, here a little, there a little, line upon line, precept upon precept, safely and firmly, bridges for the judicial mind to pass the abysses between that past and the new future.

. . .

I knew that "general propositions do not decide concrete cases. The decision will depend on a judgment or intuition more subtle than any articulate major premise."

And so, after eleven years on the Bench following eighteen at the Bar, I being well advised by observation and experience of what I am about to set down, have thought it both wise and decorous to now boldly affirm that "having well and exactly seen, surveyed, overlooked, reviewed, recognized, read and read over again, turned and tossed about, seriously perused and examined the preparatories, productions, evidences, proofs, allegations, depositions, cross speeches, contradictions . . . and other such like confects and spiceries, both at the one and the other side, as a good judge ought to do, I posit on the end of the table in my closet all the pokes and bags of the defendants—that being done I thereafter lay down upon the other end of the same table the bags and satchels of the plaintiff."

Thereafter I proceed "to understand and resolve the obscurities of these various and seeming contrary passages in the law, which are laid claim to by the suitors and pleading parties," even just as Judge Bridlegoose did, with one difference only. "That when the matter is more plain, clear and liquid, that is to say, when there are fewer bags," and he would have used his "other large, great dice, fair and goodly ones," I decide the case more or less off hand and by rule of thumb. While when the case is difficult or involved, and turns upon a hairsbreadth of law or of fact, that is to say, "when there are many bags on the one side and on the other" and Judge Bridlegoose would have used his "little small dice," I, after canvassing all the available material at my command, and duly cogitating upon it, give my imagination play, and brooding over the cause, wait for the feeling, the hunch—that intuitive flash of understanding which makes the jump-spark connection between question and decision, and at the point where the path is darkest for the judicial feet, sheds its light along the way.

And more, "lest I be stoned in the street" for this admission, let me hasten to say to my brothers of the Bench and of the Bar, "my practice is therein the same with that of your other worships."

For let me premise here, that in feeling or "hunching" out his decisions, the judge acts not differently from, but precisely as the lawyers do in working on their cases, with only this exception; that the lawyer, having a predetermined destination in view,—to win his law suit for his client—looks for and regards only those hunches which keep him in the path that he has chosen, while the judge, being merely on his way with a roving commission to find the just solution, will follow his hunch wherever it leads him, and when, following it, he meets the right solution face to face, he can cease his labors and blithely say to his troubled mind—"Trip no farther, pretty, sweeting, journeys end in lovers meeting, as every wise man's son doth know."

. . .

And not only do I set down boldly that I, "even as your other worships do," invoke and employ hunches in decisions, but I do affirm, and will presently show, that it is that tiptoe faculty of the mind which can fell and follow a hunch which makes not only the best gamblers, the best detectives, the best lawyers, the best judges, the materials of whose trades are the most chancey because most human, and the results of whose activities are for the same cause the most subject to uncertainty and the best attained by approximation, but it is that same faculty which has guided and will continue to guide the great scientists of the world, and even those august dealers in certitude, the mathematicians themselves, to their most difficult solutions, which have opened and will continue to open hidden doors; which have widened and will ever widen man's horizon.

"For facts are sterile until there are minds capable of choosing between them and discerning those which conceal something, and recognizing that which is concealed. Minds which under the bare fact see the soul of the fact."

. . .

Now, what is this faculty? What are its springs, what its uses? Many men have spoken of it most beautifully. Some call it "intuition"—some, "imagination," this sensitiveness to new ideas, this power to range when the track is cold, this power to cast in ever widening circles to find a fresh scent, instead of standing baying where the track was lost.... Cardozo expresses it most beautifully....

. . .

" 'When I once asked the best administrator whom I knew,' writes Mr. Wallas, 'how he formed his decisions, he laughed, and with the air of letting out for the first time a guilty secret, said: 'Oh, I always decide by feeling. So and so always decides by calculation, and that is no good.' When again I asked an American judge, who is widely admired both for his skill and for his impartiality, how he and his fellows formed their conclusions, he also laughed, and said that he would be stoned in the street if it were known that, after listening with full consciousness to all the evidence, and following as carefully as he could all the arguments, he waited until he "felt" one way or the other. He had elided the preparation and the brooding, or at least had come to think of them as processes of faint kinship with the state of mind that followed.' 'When the conclusion is there', says William James, 'we have already forgotten most of the steps preceding its attainment.' "

. . .

Time was when judges, lawyers, law writers and teachers of the law refused to recognize in the judge this right and power of intuitive decision. It is true that the trial judge was always supposed to have superior facilities for decision, but these were objectivized in formulas, such as—the trial judge has the best opportunity of observing the witnesses, their demeanor,—the trial judge can see the play and inter-play of forces as they operate in the actual clash of the trial.

Under the influence of this kind of logomachy, this sticking in the "skin" of thought, the trial judge's superior opportunity was granted, but the real reason for that superior position, that the trial creates an atmosphere springing from but more than the facts themselves, in which and out of which the judge may get the feeling which takes him to the desired end, was deliberately suppressed.

. . .

[Max Radin] tells us, first, that the judge is a human being; that therefore he does not decide causes by the abstract application of rules of justice or of right, but having heard the cause and determined that the decision ought to go this way or that way, he then takes up his search for some category of the law into which the case will fit.

He tells us that the judge really feels or thinks that a certain result seems desirable, and he then tries to make his decision accomplish that result. "What makes certain results seem desirable to a judge?" he asks, and answers his question that that seems desirable to the judge which, according to his training, his experience, and his general point of view, strikes him as the jural consequence that ought to flow from the facts, and he advises us that what gives the judge the struggle in the case is the effort so to state the reasons for his judgment that they will pass muster.

Now what is he saying except that the judge really decides by feeling, and not by judgment; by "hunching" and not by ratiocination, and that the ratiocination appears only in the opinion?

Now what is he saying but that the vital, motivating impulse for the decision is an intuitive sense of what is right or wrong for that cause, and that the astute judge, having so decided, enlists his every faculty and belabors his laggard mind, not only to justify that intuition to himself, but to make it pass muster with his critics?

There is nothing unreal or untrue about this picture of the judge, nor is there anything in it from which a just judge should turn away. It is true, and right that it is true, that judges really do try to select categories or concepts into which to place a particular case so as to produce what the judge regards as a righteous result, or, to avoid any confusion in the matter of morals, I will say a "proper result."

This is true. I think we should go further, and say it ought to be true. No reasoning applied to practical matters is ever really effective unless motivated by some impulse.

Occasionally and frequently, the exercise of the judgment ought to end in absolute reservation. We are not infallible, so we ought to be cautious. "Sometimes," however, "if we would guide by the light of reason, we must let our minds be bold."

. . .

If the judge sat upon the Bench in a purely abstract relation to the cause, his opinion in difficult cases would be worth nothing. He must have some motive to fire his brains, to "let his mind be bold."

By the nature of his occupation he cannot have advocacy for either side of the case as such, so he becomes an advocate, an earnest one, for the—in a way—abstract solution. Having become such advocate, his mind reaches and strains and feels for that result. He says with Elihu, the son of Barachel, the Buzite, of the family of Ram—"There is a spirit in man, and the breath of the Almighty giveth him understanding. It is not the great that are wise, nor the aged that understand justice.— Hearken to me; I also will show mine opinion. For I am full of matter; the spirit within me constraineth me. Behold my belly is as wine which hath no vent. Like new wineskins it is ready to burst."

And having travailed and reached his judgment, he struggles to bring up and pass in review before his eager mind all of the categories and concepts which he may find useful directly or by analogy, so as to select from them that which in his opinion will support his desired result.

For while the judge may be, he cannot appear to be, arbitrary. He must at least appear reasonable, and unless he can find a category which will at least "semblably" support his view, he will feel uncomfortable.

Sometimes he must almost invent a category, but he can never do quite that thing ... the growth of the law is interstitial, and the new category cannot be new enough wholly to avoid contact and placement in the midst of prior related categories.

But whether or not the judge is able in his opinion to present reasons for his hunch which will pass jural muster, he does and should decide difficult and complicated cases only when he has the feeling of the decision, which accounts for the beauty and the fire of some, and the labored dullness of many dissenting opinions.

All of us have known judges who can make the soundest judgments and write the dullest opinions on them; whose decisions were hardly ever affirmed for the reasons which they gave. Their difficulty was that while they had the flash, the intuitive power of judgment, they could not show it forth. While they could by an intuitive flash leap to a conclusion, just as an inventor can leap to his invention, just as often as an inventor cannot explain the result or fully understand it, so cannot and do not they.

There is not one among us but knows that while too often cases must be decided without that "feeling" which is the triumphant precursor of the just judgment, that just as "sometimes a light surprises the Christian while he sings," so sometimes, after long travail and struggle of the mind, there does come to the dullest of us, flooding the brain with the vigorous blood of decision, the hunch that there is, or is not invention; that there is or is not, anticipation; that the plaintiff should be protected by a decree, or should be denied protection. This hunch, sweeping aside hesitancy and doubt, takes the judge vigorously on to his decision; and yet, the cause decided, the way thither, which was for the blinding moment a blazing trail, becomes wholly lost to view.

NOTE

To put Judge Hutcheson's charming observations in proper perspective one must agree that, in discussing the judicial "hunch", he is addressing the deciding process only. He states as much when he says that the judge really decides "by 'hunching' and not by ratiocination, and that the ratiocination appears only in the opinion."

Is there any relationship between decision by intuition and any particular theory discussed in the previous chapter? Would "Mechanical Jurisprudence" encourage or discourage decision by intuition? When called upon to express a judgment on a set of objective facts, do you ever rely on "hunches"?

ROSCOE POUND, *The Theory of Judicial Decision*, 36 Harv.L.Rev. 940, 951–52 (1923) *:

> Nor need we be ashamed to confess that much that goes on in the administration of justice is intuitive. Bergson tells us that intelligence, which frames and applies rules, is more adapted to the inorganic, while intuition is more adapted to life. In the same way rules of law and legal conceptions which are applied mechanically are more adapted to property and to business transactions; standards where application proceeds upon intuition are more adapted to human conduct and to the conduct of enterprises. Bergson tells us that what characterizes intelligence as opposed to instinct is "its power of grasping the general element in a situation and relating it to past situations." But, he points out, this power is acquired by loss of "that perfect mastery of a special situation in which instinct rules." Standards, applied intuitively by court or jury or administrative officer, are devised for situations in which we are compelled to take circumstances into account; for classes of cases in which each case is to a large degree unique. For such cases we must rely on the common sense of the common man as to common things and the trained common sense of the expert as to uncommon things.

RICHARD WASSERSTROM, *The Judicial Decision* 89 (1961) **:

Throughout this chapter the word "intuition" is used in a special sense, one that admittedly is broader than ordinary philosophical usage. For I employ "intuition" to denote any process by which truth or correctness is *directly apprehended*. In this sense it includes both intuition in the more usual philosophic sense and also such things as *emotional apprehension*. In other words, I do not distinguish between an epistemology based upon an intuition of justice and one based upon knowledge directly acquired by the "sense of justice" or the "sense of injustice." There may be differences between the two approaches, but for my purposes they can be treated as being essentially similar.

HENRY J. FRIENDLY, REACTIONS OF A LAWYER— NEWLY BECOME JUDGE *

[W]e are a long way from some of the more excessive realist outbursts, such as the characterization of decision as "an emotive experience in which principles and logic play a secondary part." Few would now accept even the testimony, given many years ago by a most distinguished judge, that cases are decided by a "hunch," if that means only "an intuitive sense of what is right or wrong for that cause" or by a flash of romantic imagination "in which the meagre stale forbidding ways of custom, law and statute ..." are happily cast aside. This is not to assert that all judges or any one judge will inevitably follow the identical or, indeed, any describable logical process, or to deny that on occasions a night's sleep or a morning's walk will suddenly produce what seems clarity where all was confusion before. Ultimately some conclusion must emerge, for it is "a judge's duty to decide, not to debate." The point is that the conclusion which flashes before the shaving-mirror in the morning does not differ in intellectual quality from that matured from study in chambers the night before; each represents a synthesis of the ways "of custom, law and statute"—not "stale" and "forbidding" but fresh and inviting—with the judge's years of experience and days of reflection. An important ingredient omitted from what Judge Hutcheson wrote, although doubtless included in what he meant, is that what he called intuition is not free but trained; Dean Pound put it more accurately when he said: "The trained intuition of the judge continually

** Reprinted from The Judicial Decision: Toward a Theory of Legal Justification by Richard A. Wasserstrom with the permission of the publishers, Stanford University Press © 1961 by the Board of Trustees of the Leland Stanford Junior University.

* 71 Yale L.J. 218, 229–30 (1961). Reprinted by permission of The Yale Law Journal Company and Fred B. Rothman & Company.

leads him to right results for which he is puzzled to give unimpeachable legal reasons.''

NOTE

What do you understand by an intuition that ''is not free but trained''? Are Dean Pound and Judge Friendly talking about a distinct method of decision-making or a shorthand expression for rapid use of the theoretical methods discussed in the previous chapter?

In ''Epilogue'', written thirty-two years later, 71 Yale L.J. 277 (1961) *, Judge Hutcheson would say that ''it was [Judge Cardozo's] friendly and understanding reception of that article, particularly of its striking and, to the uninitiated, misleading title [2] which enabled it to pass muster without being attacked and torn to pieces.''

''In my article, *Judgment Intuitive,* I undertook, in a personal sort of way to make the point that, while a judge may not completely reject settled, that is established, law merely because he does not like the results of its application to a particular case, he has the right, indeed the duty to make use of all lawful expedients supporting him in the result he desires to reach and announce, and I drew heavily on Mr. Justice Cardozo and quoted copiously from him. I did not mean to espouse, just as he did not espouse, the right of a judge completely to disregard or reject all the applicable precedents in favor of a solution merely because in his opinion abstract justice supported his desired result. A reading of his leading opinions, *McPherson, Palsgraf,* and others shows how far this was from his mind and thinking.''

See also Schaefer, *Precedent and Policy,* 34 U.Chi.L.Rev. 3 (1966).

---

* Reprinted by permission of The Yale Law Journal Company and Fred B. Rothman & Company.

2. ''Justice Cardozo correctly apprehended and explained the meaning intended by me when he wrote of the key word 'Hunch':

The doctrine of the hunch, if viewed as an attempt at psychological analysis, embodies an important truth; it is a vivid and arresting description of one of the stages in the art of thought. The hunch is the divination of the scientist, ... the apocalyptic insight, that is back of his experiments.... The intuitive flash of inspiration is at the root of all science, of all art, and even of all conduct.

''Cardozo, Selected Writings 27–28 (Hall ed. 1947), adding, however:

I do not mean that there was any such misapprehension in the mind of the distinguished judge and author by whom the hunch may be said to have been given its card of admission into the polite society of juristic methodology. I am fearful, however, that the newcomer's importance, even if justly rated by its sponsor, has been exaggerated by others.

''*Ibid.* at 26.

''Cardozo expressed the fear that the nomenclature might tend to 'establish the empire of mere feeling or emotion, of arbitrary preference, and by the same token to disprove the value of conceptions, rules and principles, the value of all logic, till we are driven, like the sophist in the Greek comedy, to proclaim that Whirl is King.' *Ibid.*

. . .''

KARL N. LLEWELLYN, GOOD HUNCHING POWER *

One thing, however, I must touch upon: the schooling of your *hunching-power* as to the outcome of a case, as to the way a court will jump. If I am right in what I have argued as to the uncertainty of the law in *any one detail,* if I am right about the leeway open to the court on facts and precedent, if I am right about the huge importance of court-attitude—then hunching must be vital to your practice. Your client pays you to hunch right. Of course, he pays you too, if you hunch wrong. Once.

Now this hunching is not a matter of mere guesswork. Haul Johnson off the street: his hunch is worthless. Good hunching-power is a resultant of good sense, imagination, and *much* knowledge. The *more* knowledge of what courts have done, the more skilful the hunch. The *better quality* the knowledge has, the more open-eyed the reading of the cases, the more skilful will be the hunch. So that your casework here builds a foundation in another way, for all your practice. Only this: that the foundation from the classes is *not broad enough.* You need more cases, more cases, more and more and more. It is not so important that you remember their details, their holdings, where they can be found again. What is important is their constant, careful reading—seeing and following and *understanding* court's reactions, over and over again. As you get the facts in the case, hunch first, *before* you meet the outcome. Then go back over. If you were right, were your bases those the court displays? If you were wrong, wherein did you go wrong? The bad with the good you want, the blind with the keen, the stupid with the wise. For you will have to hunch as to *all* kinds of judges. Now in the main your casebooks give you better cases rather than worse. For a fair sampling you must turn to the advance sheets. Moreover, in the main your casebooks give you doubtful cases rather than the better settled. Again, for perspective you must turn to the current grist of the advance sheets. And I say once more, it does not make so very much difference whether you remember the specific rules. Good, if you do. But even if you do not, there remains a deposit, formless, curious—but one which informs your hunches in the future. *Authorities* can in the main be found. An outcome that will go, a theory that will *carry*—these are the goal.

NOTE

Does Llewellyn use "hunching" in the same context as Judge Hutcheson? As Roscoe Pound?

Reconsider Holmes' definition of law: "The prophecies of what the courts will do in fact, and nothing more pretentious, are what I mean by the law." Consider this definition again in conjunction with Llewellyn's reference to "hunching-power as to the outcome of a case, as to the way

---

* The Bramble Bush 98–99 (1960). Reprinted by permission of Oceana Publications, Inc., and Soia Mentschikoff Llewellyn.

a court will jump." May the bar and the litigants truly prophesy or give a reasoned prediction "as to the way a court will jump" if the court does not publicly disclose the true process of discovering the conclusion, the true motivation for the decision-making?

CHARLES M. YABLON, JUSTIFYING THE JUDGE'S HUNCH: AN ESSAY ON DISCRETION [1]

A major theme in Legal Realist literature is the importance of the intuition on "hunch." [2] For the Realists, it was the judge's "hunch," more than any body of precedent, codes, or learned treatises, that represented and preserved the great traditions of the common law. Joseph C. Hutcheson, a Realist as well as an accomplished judge, describes the judicial hunch with a mixture of mystery and reverence:

> I, after canvassing all the available material at my command, and duly cogitating upon it, give my imagination play, and brooding over the cause, wait for the feeling, the hunch—that intuitive flash of understanding which makes the jump spark connection between question and decision, and at the point where the path is darkest for the judicial feet, sheds its light along the way.[4]

This quotation typifies the vague and often metaphorical descriptions of judicial decision making that characterized much of the Realist work. Legal thought always has had difficulty developing a satisfactory criterion for distinguishing rule bound judicial actions from discretionary ones and, in turn, distinguishing appropriate exercises of discretion from "abuses." The singular achievement of the Realists was successfully attacking formalism and deductive method in law, which managed to muddy these distinctions still further.

1. 41 Hastings Law Journal 231 (1990) Reprinted by permission.

2. See, e.g., Frank, *What Courts Do in Fact*, 26 Ill.L.Rev. 645 (1932) (recognizing that the "judicial hunch" cannot be described in terms of legal rules and principles); Haines, *General Observations on the Effects of Personal, Political and Economic Influences in the Decisions of Judges*, 17 Ill.L.Rev. 96 (1922) (examining the effect of extra-legal influences on judges' decisions); Hutcheson, *Lawyer's Law and the Little Small Dice*, 7 Tul.L.Rev. 1 (1932) (judges attempt to follow precedents and give reasons for them); Hutcheson, *The Judgment Intuitive: The Function of the "Hunch" in Judicial Decision*, 14 Cornell L.Q. 274 (1929) (recognizing the presence of intuition in judicial decisions); Llewellyn, *A Realistic Jurisprudence—The Next Step*, 30 Colum.L.Rev. 431 (1930) (recognizing shift in study of law to interaction between behavior and rules); Radin, *The Theory of Judicial Decision: Or How Judges Think*, 11 A.B.A.J. 357 (1925) (priority given to decisions leading to "desirable results"). Forerunners of this work, who had substantial influence on it, are B. Cardozo, The Nature of the Judicial Process, (1921) (exploring judges' decision making process);

B. Cardozo, The Paradoxes of Legal Science 59–61 (1928) (discussing the role of "feelings" in a judge's decision); and Kocourek, *Formal Relation Between Law and Discretion*, 9 Ill.L.Rev. 225 (1914) (recognizing that discretion is not a defect but rather an integral characteristic of law).

4. Hutcheson, *The Judgment Intuitive: The Function of the "Hunch" in Judicial Decision*, supra note 2, at 278.

Since the Realists, a major project of American jurisprudential thought has been providing a coherent and accurate account of judicial decision making that recognizes the discretionary character of the process yet provides a rational basis for evaluating or justifying decisions. Accordingly, jurisprudes have argued over whether legal decisions can or should be justified as applications of a preexisting body of legal norms, as a process calling for particular psychological attributes, or as manifestations of shared interpretative strategies. Others have extended the Realist critique to conclude that no rational criteria exist for justifying judicial decisions.

While this debate has continued, discretion has also been a major theme in legal proceduralist writing, which examines decision making of public officials in specific institutional contexts. In much of this literature, often focusing on administrative law or civil or criminal procedure, discretion appears relatively unproblematic. It is assumed that decision makers can operate with various degrees of freedom or constraint on their decision making powers. The goal of much of this work is to determine the appropriate degree of discretion to exercise in particular decisions such as sentencing, arrest, or granting injunctions. While skirting philosophical issues, such writing is often wonderfully sophisticated about the institutional and structural aspects of decision making— recognizing that discretion appropriately may be thought of as a description of the power relationships among decision makers, rather than a description of a particular category of an individual judge's thought processes.

I. The Problem of Discretion in American Legal Thought

The Realists' fascination with judicial intuition grew out of their rejection of legal formalism. Relying in part on American pragmatism, and in part on German theorists like Eugene Ehrlich and Rudolph von Jhering, they launched a full scale attack on what they called "mechanical jurisprudence." [15] The Realists rejected the notion that legal reasoning involved a deductive process. They denied that the actions of legal decision makers were the determinate results of applying general legal rules found in statutes or appellate cases. Rather, the Realists asserted that in virtually every case the legal decision maker, in the paradigmatic case the trial judge, was free to decide the case in directly contradictory ways (for example, either for plaintiff or defendant) and then find adequate grounds for justifying either result.

---

15. Pound, *Mechanical Jurisprudence*, 8 Colum.L.Rev. 605 (1908). The relation between Pound and the Legal Realists was ambivalent and troubled. While recognizing his important role in debunking the notion of law as a formal science of rules, particularly in the article cited above, the Realists found much of Pound's other work to present an overly determinate picture of the functioning of the legal system. Jerome Frank stated his ambivalence this way: Notably Dean Pound was among the leaders of those who combated the naive notion that the work of lawyers and judges ends with legal rules. But he adopted the Holmes idea in a strange way. While brilliantly elaborating it in some directions, he nevertheless repressed it, obstructed its full growth. Frank, *Are Judges Human?*, 80 U.Pa.L.Rev. 17, 18 (1931). See also Llewellyn, supra note 2, at 435 n. 3 (criticizing the limitations of Pound's writing).

Whether or not this is an accurate picture of legal decision making (and I believe that in most respects it is), the rejection of authoritative legal rules as a sufficient basis for judicial decisions left two other major possibilities. One possibility is that judicial decision making is random or arbitrary. This does not necessarily mean that the judicial decision is unintentional or accidental, but rather that the causal agents are personal, or individual, and not necessarily tied to broader legal or social norms. Opponents of the Realists often took this as their position, reducing it to the derogatory slogan that legal decisions are determined by "what the judge ate for breakfast." [16]

The second possibility is that judges apply legal norms appropriately—to give answers that are "correct" and make sense within the existing legal and social context—even though those answers cannot be deduced or determined by authoritative legal rules or principles. But if the legal rules themselves did not produce such "correct" judicial responses, then they had to be the result of some other looser interaction between societal norms and values and the thought processes of the individual judge. Thus, the stage was set for the serious study of the judicial hunch.

A. The Jurisprudential Debate

Jerome Frank's 1932 article, What the Courts Do in Fact, provides a good example of the centrality of the judicial hunch in the jurisprudence of the Realists. As its title indicates, Frank's article is intended as an objective empirical description of the activities of trial court judges from the point of view of the practicing lawyer or litigant. From this perspective, Frank derides the notion that lawyers, merely because of their knowledge of legal rules, can predict judicial actions with any degree of certainty. He argues that the legal rules are of marginal importance in most trials, particularly jury trials. When judges act as fact finders, Frank argues, they have much the same discretion as jurors to decide the case for either the plaintiff or defendant with little concern for legal rules.

Thus, Frank concludes, the primary determinant of the judicial decision is not the legal rule structure but the "personality of the judge" or the "judicial intuition," that is, the whole set of characteristics that lead the judge to perceive the world, including the plaintiffs, the defen-

---

16. R. Dworkin, Law's Empire 36 (1986). While this is perhaps the most popular formulation of the strong rule-skeptical position, and is still widely used, I have not been able to locate its precise origins. I suspect, however, that it may derive from a statement by Pound in which he contrasts a system of law to the arbitrariness of "cadi" justice. Pound refers to "the oriental cadi administering justice at the city gate by the light of nature tempered by the state of his digestion...." Pound, *The Decadence of*

Equity, 5 Colum.L.Rev. 20, 21 (1905). Twenty-five years later, seeking to refute the notion that non-rule based decision making necessarily involved arbitrariness, Jerome Frank made reference to Pound's comment and answered, "no more than in France, Germany, England or the United States, is the judge in Mohammedan countries supposed to decide cases according to his passing whim or the temporary state of his digestion." Frank, supra note 15, at 24.

dants, and the witnesses, in a particular way. Frank is quite aware of the vagueness of this concept. As he says:

> "The personality of the judge" is a phrase which too glibly describes an exquisitely complicated mass of phenomena. The phrase "judicial hunch" is likewise beautifully vague. But those phrases will do for present purposes. Be it noted then that "the personality of the judge" and the "judicial hunch" are not and cannot be described in terms of legal rules and principles.

For Frank and for other Legal Realists, the vagueness of the "judicial hunch" concept was part of its appeal. It helped shake lawyers out of a mind set in which every legal problem had a deductively demonstrable "right answer." This notion that legal certainty could be achieved by careful study of legal rules and concepts was the prime focus of the Realist attack.

The next generation of legal theorists, responded to the Realists' rejection of legal rules as the basis for judicial action. While acknowledging the existence of a certain amount of "discretion" in judicial decision making, that is, the judicial ability to decide a case either way consistently with the preexisting rule structure, such discretion was seen as existing at the margin of the legal system, in the extreme or "hard" cases. These theorists insisted that judges, in their ordinary endeavors, were in fact limited and constrained in significant ways by legal rules.

The primary exponent of this view was H.L.A. Hart, who devotes considerable energy to refuting "rule-skepticism," which he views as the claim that application of preexisting legal rules are never the source of judicial decisions. Hart stresses the binding or obligatory quality of rules, and offers an "internal perspective" on the way rules affect decision makers. For Hart, the distinguishing feature of laws (unlike the orders of an armed bandit) is that people feel obliged to obey them even when the likelihood of sanctions is small or nonexistent. Thus, Hart is not overly disturbed by the Realists' claim that knowledge of authoritative legal rules is not particularly useful in predicting judicial decisions. He recognizes that rules cannot always be written so as to determine actions precisely, but may often be loose or "open textured." For Hart, the fact that judges still feel bound to apply these loosely written rules (or at least to act within their scope in areas where they apply) indicates that the rules, however "loosely" applied, are still determining judicial decisions.

Hart thus divides the judge's role into two kinds of decision making—those in which the decision clearly is constrained by a preexisting rule or precedent (the clear or paradigmatic case) and those in which it is not. Hart calls these latter cases "indeterminate" or "discretionary." The judge's role in such cases is a legislative or lawmaking one, choosing between possible outcomes on various policy or equitable grounds, and thereby creating new legal rules for subsequent cases.[27] For Hart, there

---

27. On this point, Hart substantially agrees with Cardozo, who argued that in cases where no precedent was applicable, the judge, like the legislator, was essential-is no uniquely discretionary form of decision making, no magical judicial hunch. Rather, discretion is simply what occurs when the guidance of authoritative legal rules run out. The judge then has the authority and role of a legislator. Hart does not take very seriously the Realist insight that judges decide cases by intuition rather than by applying authoritative rules. Viewing this as simply a statement about the psychological behavior of judges (and not about the nature of legal rules) Hart replies, rather off-handedly, that one need not think about a rule in order to follow it. For example, when a driver sees a red light and steps on the brake, she is following a rule even though the action appears intuitive. For Hart, this is rule-following behavior because, if questioned, she would cite the rule as a justification for her action. Judges, he points out, behave similarly when they cite legal rules in support of their decisions.

Hart refutes the argument that judicial decisions that are unreviewable (such as those of a highest court) are therefore not determined by legal rules. He cites the example of a group of individuals playing a game (perhaps cricket or baseball) who, after keeping score themselves for some time, decide to appoint an official scorer. The scorer's decisions are final and not subject to appeal. Hart argues that the scorer must follow the rules of the game, but also can exercise judgment in close calls. If the scorer began to drastically depart from the rules, the game would no longer be cricket or baseball, but an entirely different game, which Hart calls "scorer's discretion." In the same way, Hart argues, it is perfectly appropriate to describe a high court judge as acting unlawfully when she does not conform her decisions to legal rules.

This argument, which has received great attention from subsequent legal scholars, was a turning point in the jurisprudential debate we have been following. Hart's argument divorces the question of the judge's internal thought processes from the judge's position in a bureaucratic structure. In Hart's model, the judge's internal apprehension of preexisting legal rules constrains her independently of any power relationships, simply because the judge perceives rules as creating legitimate legal obligations. The effect of authoritative rules on a Supreme Court Justice, a trial court judge, and a game scorer are presumed to be similar.

For Hart, understanding the law meant understanding the way legal rules could create constraints and obligations on individuals, including judges, while still permitting flexibility and judgment. Since the effect of the legal rules on the judge's internal deliberations was the key jurisprudential issue for Hart, he, and the writers who followed him,

ly free to make the law: Each indeed is legislating within the limits of his competence. No doubt the limits for the judge are narrower. He legislates only between gaps. He fills the open spaces in the law.... Nonetheless, within the confines of these open spaces and those of precedent and tradition, choice moves with a freedom which stamps its action as creative. The law which is the resulting product is not found, but made. The process, being legislative, demands the legislator's wisdom. B. Cardozo, The Nature of the Judicial Process, supra note 2, at 113–15.

tended to separate consideration of the judge as individual decision maker from considerations of: (1) the judge's role in a bureaucratic hierarchy; (2) the allocation of decision making power within that hierarchy; and, (3) the relation between a judge's internal deliberations and the external constraints on her behavior. This tended to exacerbate the dichotomy between the jurisprudential debate over discretion and the more institutional, procedural perspective.

Hart's analysis also involves a subtle change in its approach toward the judge. Frank's perspective is of a practicing lawyer or litigant, and he asks the question most relevant from such a perspective: How can I predict what the judge will do, and with what degree of certainty? Hart's question, however, is quite different. It considers when we can say that a judge is acting lawfully. (The payoff of the "scorer's discretion" argument, after all, is that if the scorer departs too drastically from the rules we must change the name of the game.) This is not the perspective of the lawyer, or even the litigator (who may frequently accuse judges of acting unlawfully, to little effect), but that of the legal theorist. It is a form of empiricism—Hart is trying to explain observed phenomena (like the fact that Supreme Court decisions are, and can be, critiqued). Hart, however, is concerned with explaining such empirical phenomena qualitatively as conforming to a generalized and highly abstract concept of law. The result is to lose some of the practitioner oriented perspective of Frank's analysis and to move toward a description of an ideal theory of judging.

[Ed. Note: As we later explain in Chapter VII, Sec. 3, Discretion, it is unfortunate that jurisprudents have attached several meanings to the term, discretion. Some use it to describe the choice of a legal norm when principles of law compete, others refer to discretion as natural justice, or equity or good conscience. Some of these meanings are what Dworkin describes as "discretion in the strong sense." As we later set forth in detail, in this book our use of the term tracks the Hart and Sacks definition as "the power to choose between two or more courses of action each of which is thought of as permissible" :]

Ronald Dworkin continued and extended Hart's attack on discretion as the source of judicial decisions.[33] Unlike Hart, Dworkin denies that a judge is ever without authoritative legal norms for deciding a case. Accordingly, Dworkin denies that discretion in any "strong sense," ever enters into judicial decision making. Dworkin's "strong sense" of discretion appears equivalent to the freedom a legislator has to promulgate new laws on any basis he deems appropriate. Dworkin carefully notes that exercises of strong discretion can be criticized as unwise or ill considered, but he does not think the term "abuse of discretion" can be applied appropriately to such actions.

We have seen that the theoretical debate concerning discretion began with the Realist insight that, as a matter of actual practice, judges did not decide cases in accordance with preexisting legal rules, but with

---

33. Dworkin, *The Model of Rules,* 35 U.Chi.L.Rev. 14, 32 (1967).

some looser, discretionary form of intuition. This insight was recognized and incorporated into new theories of judging by Hart and Dworkin, who attempted to show that judges, even though not bound by determinate rules, nonetheless could act in normatively appropriate ways within a system of law. But in seeking to show that certain forms of discretion might be theoretically justified within a particular jurisprudential theory, these theorists gave little attention to whether discretionary decision making, as practiced by actual judges, bore any resemblance to the normatively justifiable discretion posited by their theories. Rather, the attempt to describe the actual process of discretionary decision making was the subject of a separate body of work among legal scholars, which I have chosen to call the proceduralist debate.

B. The Proceduralist Debate

The jurisprudential or theoretical debate is not the only legal literature dealing with discretion. Describing a decision as "discretionary" has important practical implications for how that decision is made, constrained, and reviewed. A decision maker with discretion has power to decide either way, without fear that the decision will be nullified or reversed, unless the discretion is "abused." It is not surprising, therefore, that some legal scholars have chosen to analyze discretion as a characteristic of power relationships in certain institutional arrangements.

These scholars generally share three characteristics: (1) concern with discretion as a matter of power, often focusing on the institutional arrangements, if any, that constrain or limit that power; (2) greater emphasis on the practical problems of decision making (proceduralists tend to analyze and cite actual cases more frequently than the jurisprudes who are often content with a few paradigmatic examples or thought experiments); and, (3) constant awareness of (and often great frustration with) the desire for predictable and general rules of conduct and its inevitable conflict with the needs of individual justice in particular cases.

Proceduralist works do not take the form of a debate like that of the jurisprudes, with each writer expressly responding to the position of a predecessor. Some of the work is categorized in particular subject matter areas, primarily administrative law, criminal procedure, and civil procedure. Yet a common perspective on discretion unites them and a debate of sorts can be created by looking at different writers' responses to the same types of issues.

Once again, Legal Realism posed the question and set the terms of the debate. Thurman Arnold's article, The Role of Substantive Law and Procedure in the Legal Process,[47] was contemporaneous with Jerome Frank's piece and shared many of its assumptions. Arnold also believed that legal rules do not determine the actions of decision makers. In

47. Arnold, *The Role of Substantive Law and Procedure in the Legal Process,* 45   Harv.L.Rev. 617 (1932).

considering the implications of that central Realist insight, however, Arnold looked at more than the paradigmatic case of the trial court judge rendering final judgment. He was aware that judges "sometimes sit as 'courts', sometimes as 'commissions' and sometimes as 'bureaus.'" Once judges are seen as independent decision makers unconstrained by formal rules, the distinction between judges and other governmental decision makers (such as bureaucrats) seems rather artificial. Indeed, judges seem to be bureaucrats who have somehow managed to avoid the obloquy of their colleagues.[49]

Proceeding from the assumption that discretion as exercised by courts is not fundamentally different from that exercised by bureaucrats, Arnold argues for a discretion that is publicly recognized and acknowledged, exercised by those with expertise in the subject, open to public criticism, and subject to modification if subsequent conditions warrant. One does not find any reverence in Arnold for the magical judicial hunch. Rather, he argues that courts simply do covertly, with little understanding, what bureaucrats do openly and often with greater expertise. Arnold, in short, argues for the creation of the bureaucratic state.

Even as he derides popular misconceptions about the different roles of courts and bureaucrats, Arnold is aware of the importance of that public perception. He feels that any reform movement that attacks directly that perception is doomed to fail.[51] Arnold does believe, however, that judicial reform is possible, if that reform is through revisions of procedure rather than substantive law.

Arnold does not believe that "procedure" and "substantive law" denominate different kinds of legal rules. Rather, calling a rule "procedural" is a rhetorical strategy, one that makes use of the flexibility and malleability of the rule structure to bring about changed attitudes on the part of judges. The very usefulness of the strategy, however, indicates that decision makers respond differently when an action is described as "substantive" or "procedural." Arnold describes this as simply a difference in "attitude." But attitude, after all, is the prime determinant of judicial response from a Realist point of view. Thus, Arnold, as a jurisprude, may deny any fundamental difference between decisions on constitutional issues, procedural rulings, and administrative determinations. As a practical political reformer, however, Arnold recognizes that

49. As Arnold notes (somewhat tongue in cheek): The distinction between bureaus and courts is important. Courts are bound by precedent, and bureaus are bound by red tape. Of course courts are forced to follow precedent even when it leads to absurd results because of their solemn obligation not to do anything in the future very much different from what they have done in the past. But bureaus, in allowing themselves to be bound by red tape, do so out of pure malice and lack of regard for the fundamentals of freedom. They have taken no oath not to violate the rules and analogies of the past. Therefore, they are much worse than courts because courts only act unreasonably when they can help it, and bureaus act unreasonably when it is in their power to do differently. Id. at 624–25.

51. As he says: "Our judicial system, objectively examined, seems to be founded on so many imponderable psychological factors that it can never be molded by a direct attack upon its ideals without impairing its prestige."

the institutional response to these categories of decisions may be quite different, and that courts may be more flexible and more willing to exercise discretion in procedural matters. Arnold does not face the problem of reconciling this notion of discretion in a process sense with the strong Realist position that all decisions are discretionary. He simply indicates that the attitudes (the type of "hunch" the judge obtains) will differ in the various cases.

Arnold's political agenda was extremely successful. The New Deal vastly expanded the power and number of administrative decision makers. The adoption of the Federal Rules of Civil Procedure was also a victory for his reform program, incorporating and institutionalizing discretion in various parts of the judicial process.

Judith Resnick's article, Tiers,[84] presents an extremely careful and sophisticated theory of institutional competence, while eschewing any position on the existence or nonexistence of "right answers" in law. In this sense, Resnick's work represents the polar opposite of Dworkin's, which, while providing a theory of right answers for the individual and unconstrained judge, eschews discussions of institutional power relationships.

Although Resnick is unwilling to describe certain legal outcomes as "correct" in light of a larger normative theory, she recognizes that the process of adjudication itself incorporates various "values." The first rule of the Federal Rules of Civil Procedure, which calls for "just, speedy, and inexpensive" determination of every civil action, aptly illustrates that we want many things from the litigative process. Some, like speed, may conflict with others, like justice. Resnick carefully delineates a series of such process values and shows how various forms of judicial review enhance certain values at the expense of others. For example, a single judge whose decisions are final may be optimal for increasing speed and reducing expense. At the same time, a provision for limited review at the appellate level may promote other values, such as greater autonomy by litigants who may choose, at some expense, to pursue their case on appeal, and the added formality and ritual of a "higher" court examining the "correctness" of the lower courts' decisions.

Resnick shows how various types of proceedings utilize each of these models of judicial review and implicitly invites us to decide what process values are most important and to what degree. She criticizes recent Supreme Court opinions on review of habeas corpus proceedings because, she believes, the Court gave too much weight to certain process values and none at all to others. She makes it clear that her criticism is based not on some jurisprudential theory of correct answers, but on her belief that most Americans disagree with the Court's concern with speed and reduction of expense over other process values.

The proceduralist debate has provided a number of important insights into the relationship among institutional structure, rules, and

84. Resnick, *Tiers,* 57 S.Cal.L.Rev. 837 (1984).

discretionary decision making. Arnold first pointed out that both society's attitude toward legal decisions, and the attitudes of legal decision makers themselves, were the result of certain preconceptions about institutional categories. Describing decision makers as "judges" applying "substantive law" made for a far more rigid, formalized decision structure than one in which "administrators" determined matters of "process." Davis, Rosenberg, and Resnick each sharpened and expanded this insight pointing out how different rule structures and systems of review can promote or discourage discretionary decision making and other systemic values. But just as the theoretical debate slowly lost its empirical grounding, the proceduralist debate has slowly lost its normative grounding. The proceduralists can demonstrate different ways in which discretion can be encouraged, checked, or channeled to different institutional levels, but increasingly have become reluctant to justify any particular structure as providing better, fairer, or normatively preferable results.

Section 2

"THE WHY" AND "THE HOW"

OVERVIEW

If courts are not judicial slot machines, some accommodation must be sought between the objectivity of theoretical decision making and the subjectivity that is prevalent in the actual process. To do this, it is important to recognize that the judicial resolution of a legal dispute implicates two separate processes: (1) deciding, or the process of discovering the conclusion, and (2) justifying, or the process of public exposition of that conclusion.

The anatomy of the decision making process reveals the acquisition of an initial tentative disposition, followed by testing or retesting of that disposition to determine whether it should prevail. Thus, even with the most objective of decision makers, lay and juridical, there is always a risk that an initially acquired disposition will prevail over a later view. H.H. Price characterized this phenomenon as the "preferential character" of the "initial assent." Implicated in the initial disposition and its subsequent testing processes are the judge's personal sympathies and antipathies, his or her political, economic, moral and social prejudices. To recognize this is not to exaggerate its importance because, in the words of Felix Cohen, "actual experience does reveal a significant body of predictable uniformity in the behavior of courts. Law is not a mass of unrelated decisions nor a product of judicial bellyaches." [1]

Nevertheless, if we are to have a complete and accurate understanding of the judicial process, we must be acquainted with personality

1. F. Cohen, *Transcendental Nonsense and the Functional Approach,* 35 Co- lum.L.Rev. 809 (1935).

profiles of those who judge in order to ascertain the "maturity of the motive," to discern "the intellectual method," and to probe "behind the decision of the forces which it reflects." This more searching analysis may be as important as knowing the naked holding of the case or its supporting rationale. The lawyer who discovers "why" the decision was made is the consummate investigator and will probably be the successful advocate. The lawyer who understands at least that a distinction does exist between "how" a decision was reached and "why" it was reached is on his or her way to becoming a good lawyer. That lawyer has learned that two processes abide within the judicial process—first, discovering the decision and second, justifying it.

Putting aside the judge's biography and the external stimuli which contributed to fashioning his or her total personality, a valuable study of the court may be gleaned scientifically from the written opinions themselves. The substantive law set forth in the *ratio decidendi* constitutes the "how" of the conclusion, or the reasoning supporting it. Publicly stated procedures of inquiry constitute the "performative utterances" of a court. If properly analyzed, however, the methodologies that opinion writers use may reveal much more. As we have emphasized, an identification of the interests that have affected the opinion writer, positively or negatively, may provide insight into the motivation for the conclusion, or the "why" of the case. Such study, then, is the earnest work of accomplished advocates, who become true legal scientists. They identify and isolate, one by one, the tools of decision making used by a given judge, or by the judges of a multi-member court before which they practice. Having identified, isolated and collated, the advocates relate their findings to the cause at hand. They translate forensic data into arguments that reflect the methodologies to which the court is hospitable and that will, therefore, be effective and probably persuasive.

On the other side of the bench, judges who epitomize intellectual honesty always will equate the publicly stated reasons for their decisions with their true motivation in reaching them. Yet even as to such judges, Herman Oliphant reassures us that "[a] study with more stress on their *non-vocal behavior, i.e.,* what the judges actually do when stimulated by the facts of the case before them, is the approach indispensable to exploiting scientifically the wealth of material in the cases." [2] A classic example of a Supreme Court case that did not publicly express the process of discovery, the motivation for the decision, is Fay v. Noia.[3] The unexpressed motivation, "the why," for the case: a distrust of state court fact-finding and a lack of confidence that state courts would vindicate the constitutional rights of unpopular litigants, to-wit, those convicted of crime. Fourteen years were to pass until the Court made an oblique reference to the true reason for *Fay.* In Stone v. Powell,[4] the majority inserted a very significant footnote:

2. H. Oliphant, *A Return to Stare Deci-*   **4.** 428 U.S. 465 (1976).
sis, 14 A.B.A.J. 71, 161–62 (1928).

3. 372 U.S. 391 (1963).

The policy arguments that respondents marshal in support of the view that federal habeas corpus review is necessary to effectuate the Fourth Amendment stem from a basic mistrust of the state courts as fair and competent forums for the adjudication of federal constitutional rights. The argument is that state courts cannot be trusted to effectuate Fourth Amendment values through fair application of the rule, and the oversight jurisdiction of this Court on certiorari is an inadequate safeguard. The principal rationale for this view emphasizes the broad differences in the respective institutional settings within which federal judges and state judges operate. Despite differences in institutional environment and the unsympathetic attitude to federal constitutional claims of some state judges in years past, we are unwilling to assume that there now exists a general lack of appropriate sensitivity to constitutional rights in the trial and appellate courts of the several States. State courts, like federal courts, have a constitutional obligation to safeguard personal liberties and to uphold federal law. Martin v. Hunter's Lessee, 1 Wheat. 304, 341–344 (1816). Moreover, the argument that federal judges are more expert in applying federal constitutional law is especially unpersuasive in the context of search-and-seizure claims, since they are dealt with on a daily basis by trial level judges in both systems. In sum, there is "no intrinsic reason why the fact that a man is a federal judge should make him more competent, or conscientious, or learned with respect to the [consideration of Fourth Amendment claims] than his neighbor in the state courthouse." [5]

Mr. Justice Brennan, author of Fay v. Noia, responded in dissent:

Enforcement of federal constitutional rights that redress constitutional violations directed against the "guilty" is a particular function of federal habeas review, lest judges trying the "morally unworthy" be tempted not to execute the supreme law of the land. State judges popularly elected may have difficulty resisting popular pressures not experienced by federal judges given lifetime tenure designed to immunize them from such influences, and the federal habeas statutes reflect the congressional judgment that such detached federal review is a salutary safeguard against any detention of an individual "in violation of the Constitution or laws ... of the United States." [6]

Considering Holmes' definition of law as "the prophecies of what the courts will do in fact and nothing more pretentious," how can lawyers "predict" if publicly stated reasons given to justify a court's decision do not square with the true reasons for reaching it?

––––––––

5.   428 U.S. at 493, n. 35.

6.   428 U.S. at 525 (Brennan, J., dissenting).

RICHARD A. WASSERSTROM, THE JUDICIAL DECISION *

[T]he question "What is the nature of the judicial decision process?" might be ambiguous, since it is not clear whether a descriptive or a prescriptive reply is being requested, nor whether this is a demand for a single monolithic response that must adequately describe all decisions, or only a request for an answer that can account for the most important or significant ones. . . . [I]t is necessary to ask whether there may not be still a third kind of ambiguity contained within or implied by the question. For the phrase "judicial decision process" is, I submit, capable in itself of denoting two quite different procedures, neither of which has as yet been carefully isolated or described. And until this is done, intelligent inquiry into the nature of the judicial decision process cannot be effected, nor can the issue of the correctness of the deductive theory be resolved.

Placing the problem within the broader context of decision procedures in general, there are two quite distinctive procedures that might be followed before any particular decision is made or accepted. This is as true in science or ethics as it is in law. The way in which these two procedures operate can be indicated by reference to two types of questions that may be asked about any decision. One kind of question asks about the manner in which a decision or conclusion was reached; the other inquires whether a given decision or conclusion is justifiable. That is to say, a person who examines a decision process may want to know about the factors that led to or produced the conclusion; he may also be interested in the manner in which the conclusion was to be justified.

.   .   .

. . . Just as these two kinds of questions can be roughly distinguished, so the factors that led to the "discovery" of the conclusion can be differentiated from the process by which it is to be justified. I will refer to the procedure by which a conclusion is reached as the *process of discovery,* and to the procedure by which a conclusion is justified as the *process of justification.*

Having succeeded in establishing a rigid dichotomy between these two procedures, we must indicate three ways in which they may be related in actual practice. In the first place it should be evident that there is nothing immutable about any particular process of discovery or justification. Various procedures of discovery are possible; so too are various processes of justification. In both instances the procedure may be highly ordered or formalized, or it may be quite unsystematic and haphazard. When the procedure has a regular pattern that is systemat-

* 25–29 (1961). Reprinted from The Judicial Decision: Toward a Theory of Legal Justification by Richard A. Wasserstrom with the permission of the publishers, Stanford University Press © 1961 by the Board of Trustees of the Leland Stanford Junior University.

ically employed in each instance of discovery or justification, it might be called a "logic of discovery" or a "logic of justification," the word logic denoting precisely that attribute of order of procedure.

In the second place, for any given conjunction of a process of discovery and a process of justification an asymmetrical relationship obtains between them. That is to say, a procedure of discovery may be adopted if it succeeds in "generating" more conclusions that can be justified within the accepted logic of justification than any other discovery procedure. In a real sense the logic of justification provides the criteria by which both particular conclusions and the procedures of discovery may be evaluated; it is not easy to see how the converse could be true for any logic of discovery.

And finally, it would be a mistake to conclude that because two separable procedures are involved, they are not usually performed by the same individual. Indeed, although it is not always true, it is generally assumed that one should not put forward a conclusion or act upon a decision until one has subjected it to, and substantiated it by, one's logic of justification. This is perhaps what is meant by *rational behavior.*

I have labored this point both because it is one that is seldom appreciated by legal philosophers and because it is directly relevant to many of the theories that concern themselves with the nature of legal reasoning. For if someone talks about the legal decision process, he might be seeking to ask the kinds of questions that are relevant to an understanding of what I have called the process of discovery. But he might also be endeavoring to pose questions which relate to the procedure of justification that was employed. I think that at least some of the legal philosophers ... have tended to ask plausible questions about discovery. Those who have stressed the inadequacies of the deductive theory and who have sought to substitute some other description in its place have perhaps shed much light upon the discovery procedures used by the courts. By equating the process of discovery with the process of decision they have argued quite persuasively that the judge's *opinion* is surely not an accurate report of the decision process. And indeed, if the decision process is coextensive with the process of discovery, it is probable that they are correct.[25]

But it is, I think, chimerical to suppose that most judicial opinions purport to describe the process of discovery. Surely the kind of reasoning process that is evidenced by the usual judicial opinion is more suggestive of a typical justificatory procedure. Turning by way of

---

25. I know of only two legal philosophers who have attempted to make a comparable distinction. One is Hermann Kantorowicz, *Some Rationalism about Realism,* 43 Yale Law Journal 1240 (1934): "The question chiefly interesting the judge is whether the decision he wants to give can be justified as a consequence of the particular statute, or at least as being compatible with its consequences.

... Genetic explanation and normative justification must be kept apart—this is one of the most important lessons of modern epistemology" (*ibid.,* p. 1249). The other is Max Radin, whose article entitled *The Method of Law,* Washington University Law Quarterly 471 (1950), is a systematic analysis of several different processes of judicial justification.

analogy to the example of the scientist—it is one thing to read a judicial opinion as a report of why or how the judge "hit upon" the decision and quite another thing to read the opinion as an account of the procedure he employed in "testing" it. To insist—as many legal philosophers appear to have done—that a judicial opinion is an accurate description of the decision process there employed if and only if it faithfully describes the procedure of discovery is to help to *guarantee* that the opinion will be found wanting. But if the opinion is construed to be a report of the justificatory procedure employed by the judge, then the not infrequent reliance upon such things as rules of law and rules of logic seems more plausible. For conceivably, at least, some judges have felt that before they render a decision in a case they must be able to justify that decision. They may have had a hunch that a particular decision would be "right," they may have had a grudge against a particular defendant or plaintiff, but they might also have felt that considerations of this kind do not count as justifications for rendering a binding judicial decision, and that unless they could justify the decision "they would like to give" by appealing to certain other criteria, the decision ought not to be handed down as binding upon the litigants. And it may just be that some judges have thought they must be able to establish a formally valid relationship between the decision and certain more general premises, and able also to give good reasons for the premises so selected. If this is so, then the attacks upon the deductive theory are not wrong; they are simply irrelevant.

CHARLES A. MILLER, PRINCIPLES OF ADJUDICATION *

The "complete education of the mind" does not stop at a complete legal education. It refers to an entire system of social and political principles and values. It is these values, plus the rules of the judicial process to which Justice Holmes referred, plus the facts of a case before the judge, which form the materials or sources of decision. The three sources of decision—values, rules, and facts—combine to focus on the mysterious "act of deciding." While the sources of decision are rationally comprehensible, the act of deciding is not. But after that act, adjudication becomes understandable once more when the opinion of the court, the explanation of decision, is handed down.

---

* The Supreme Court and the Uses of History 10–11 (1969). Excerpted by permission of the author and publishers from pp. 10–11 of The Supreme Court and the Uses of History by Charles A. Miller, Cambridge, Mass.: The Belknap Press of Harvard University Press, Copyright © 1969 by

ANTHONY G. AMSTERDAM, PERSPECTIVES ON THE FOURTH AMENDMENT*

The Court cannot always state openly all of the considerations that affect its decisions. For example, I am convinced that the major force shaping the evolution of Supreme Court confession cases from Brown v. Mississippi through *Haynes* and *Escobedo* to *Miranda* was distrust of the fact-finding propensities of state trial courts. Doubtless, the same distrust accounts for the unexplained and intellectually unsatisfactory "discretion" that Townsend v. Sain allowed to federal habeas corpus courts to conduct new evidentiary hearings notwithstanding prior state-court hearings meeting every objective test of fairness. Yet obviously the Supreme Court could not talk about its distrust of state-court factfinding in these cases. Both decorum and the necessity of encouraging better performance by state judges in the enforcement of federal rights forbade the Supreme Court Justices "to put their brethren of the state judiciary on trial."

Instead, the Court responded to perverse factfinding by expanding constitutionally protective legal rules in a manner that made the suspect facts irrelevant. It did not announce outright that its reason for disregarding the facts was their susceptibility to manipulation by triers of fact who were not to be trusted. It simply treated apparently relevant facts as irrelevant. In so doing, of course, it exposed itself to the scourges of critics forearmed with Henry Friendly's lashing quip about "the domino method of constitutional adjudication ... wherein every explanatory statement in a previous opinion is made the basis for extension to a wholly different situation." The quip is a masterful metaphor but betrays a certain lack of appreciation of the art of dominoes. Skillful domino players have a prescient purpose in the moves they make, however arbitrary these may seem to an observer lacking knowledge of their hidden pieces or their game plan.

NOTE

It has been suggested that the intellectually honest judicial opinion is one in which the motive for the decision approximates the publicly stated reasons supporting it. Consider the following hypothetical advice directed to the "realistic" lawyer or advocate: "For a lawyer who is trying to prophesy what the courts will do in fact, it is more important for him to understand *why* the courts picked up Roger Traynor's concurring opinion in Escola v. Coca Cola, *ante,* p. 369, the precusor to 402A, and adopted strict liability in products liability cases. It is more important to understand what motivated the courts to change proof procedures in medical malpractice cases than simply to know that they did do it.

the President and Fellows of Harvard College.

* 58 Minn.L.Rev. 349, 350–52 (1974). Reprinted by permission of the author and the Minnesota Law Review.

"Knowing *why* a court does what it does is the first step in truly learning the law, in Holmes' phrase, in prophesying what the courts will do in fact."

Section 3

FACTORS THAT ALTER REFLECTIVE THINKING

OVERVIEW

In 1922, Charles C. Haines set forth certain categories of factors likely to influence decisions. In the category of remote and indirect factors, Haines listed general and legal education, family and personal associates, wealth and social position. For direct factors, he listed legal and political experience, political affiliation and opinions, and intellectual and temperamental traits.[1] These factors do affect judicial thinking to some extent. Judges inevitably come to their robes with the stigmata of their past experience. The difficult question is the degree to which any one experiential factor exerts a meaningful influence. For attorneys who appear before the judges, the important consideration is to what extent a given judge's decision will be predictable on the basis of these factors.

A judge's track record on the bench is more likely to furnish indicia to predictability than pre- or extra-judicial experience. New judges from certain geographical and psychological environments that might have suggested the judge would decide social and civil rights matters one way, have adjudicated those cases in a different manner. Court-watching disciplines of journalism, political science and sociology often prove to be wrong. Former prosecutors have become staunch defenders of individual rights in criminal cases. Former plaintiff lawyers in personal injuries actions have become extremely defense-oriented on the bench. Former criminal defense lawyers have become prosecution-oriented. And minority judges and justices who may have benefitted from affirmative action prove themselves opposed to it once installed on the bench.

With sufficient bench experience, especially on a court that requires opinion writing, a judge's jurisprudential personality may be detected. Moreover, after proper analysis, a certain predictability of approach may be ascertained. More often than not, this requires an identification of the individual, public and societal interests implicated in the litigation, as previously discussed in Chapter IV, Section 6, and a determination of the circumstances in which an identifiable interest receives approbation or reprobation.

The media's favorite labels of "liberal" and "conservative" are of little value. Sheldon Goldman suggests that a more accurate analysis would be an understanding of a judge's position in (1) criminal cases: for the claims of criminal defendants or prisoners, excluding white collar

---

1. C. Haines, *General Observations on the Effects of Personal, Political and Eco-* *nomic Influences on the Decision of Judges,* 17 Ill.L.Rev. 96, 115–16 (1922).

crimes; (2) civil rights cases: for the claims of blacks, women, and identifiable minority groups who lack political clout in a given context; (3) labor: for the claims of employees and unions in labor-management cases; (4) private economic cases: for the claims of the insured as opposed to the insurance company, for small businesses when opposed by a large business; for the tenant in landlord-tenant cases; for the debtor or bankrupt; for the buyer as opposed to the seller; for the stockholder in stockholder suits; against alleged antitrust violators; (5) injured persons: for the claims of injured workers'; for the injured or deceased's estate in automobile or other accidents; for the injured in federal tort cases. Professor Goldman intimates that one voting in favor of the foregoing positions is a "political liberal" or an "economic liberal," and that one who votes in favor of the governmental agency in regulation of business cases is also an "economic liberal." [2]

A quality of relative anonymity generally is associated with a judge's activity notwithstanding the fragility of tenure due to political selection processes. State judges who seek reelection, who have either received the approval of the bar or, more important, have not incurred its wrath, usually have no difficulty in being re-elected. Where a volatile political climate is present, the judge is more inclined to conduct him or herself in a manner that seeks the approbation of the bar and the media than to placate identifiable political elements. Where the political climate is more stable, where the judge's political party dominates or where the jurisdiction has a modified Missouri plan in which one runs against no opponent but only against one's record, political considerations are minimized.

"The process of judging, so the psychologists tell us, seldom begins with a premise from which a conclusion is subsequently worked out," Jerome Frank noted. "Judging begins rather the other way around— with a conclusion more or less vaguely formed; a man ordinarily starts with such a conclusion and afterwards tries to find premises which will substantiate it. If he cannot, to his satisfaction, find proper arguments to link up his conclusion with premises which he finds acceptable, he will, unless he is arbitrary or mad, reject the conclusion and seek another." [3] John Dewey instructed that reflective thinking "involves (1) a state of doubt, hesitation, perplexity, mental difficulty, in which thinking originates, and (2) an act of searching, hunting, inquiry, to find material that will resolve the doubt, settle and dispose of the perplexity." [4]

The conscientious judicial decision maker will recognize this and understand that forming tentative conclusions is all part of the reflective thinking process. Experienced appellate judges begin with some general conclusion, or at least alternative conclusions, and then look around for principles and data which will substantiate it or which will enable them

2. S. Goldman, *Conflicts in the U.S. Courts of Appeals, 1965–1971: A Quantitative Analysis,* 42 U.Cinti.L.Rev. 635 (1973).

3. J. Frank, Law and the Modern Mind 100–06 (1930).

4. J. Dewey, How We Think 12 (1933).

to choose intelligently between rival conclusions.[5] But being aware that appellate judges form tentative impressions is not enough. We must be careful not to fall in love with initial conclusions. H.H. Price has explained the danger of the initial assent to any proposition:

> Believing a proposition is, I think, a disposition and not an occurrence or "mental act," though the disposition is not necessarily a very long-lived one and may last only a few seconds.... There is a characteristic sort of mental occurrence which we sometime notice when we are in the process of *acquiring* such a disposition. I am going to call this occurrence "assenting" to the proposition.... When our belief is a reasonable one, this assenting, and especially the initial assent, has a *preferential* character.
>
> Now because of this preferential element in it, assent may look like voluntary choice. But the appearance is deceptive. It is not a free choice at all, but a forced one. If you are in a reasonable frame of mind ... you cannot help preferring the proposition which *your* evidence favors, the evidence *you* are at the moment attending to, though the evidence which other people have may of course be different.... It just is not in your power to avoid assenting to the proposition which the evidence [your evidence] favors, or to assent instead to some other proposition when the evidence [your evidence] is manifestly unfavorable to it.[6]

Human experience has demonstrated that when there is a lack of disinterestedness there is not likely to be independence of judgment. Lord Chancellor Birkenhead said that the judge "must purge his mind not only of partiality to persons, but partiality to arguments, a much more subtle matter, for every legal mind is apt to have an innate susceptibility to particular classes of argument. Hume Brown used to say that 'a man cannot jump off his own shadow, but the judge must try his best to do so.' "[7] Intellectual disinterestedness in a judge "is a price, achieved only by continual care and striving."[8]

SCOTT v. COMMANDING OFFICER

United States Court of Appeals, Third Circuit, 1970.
431 F.2d 1132.

Aldisert, Circuit Judge, concurring.

My major disagreement with the majority is the adoption by this court of the minority rule of the circuits—the Second and Tenth—that

---

5. J. Dewey, *Logical Method and Law,* 10 Cornell L.Q. 17, 23–27 (1924).

6. H.H. Price, Relief and Will, Proceedings of the Aristotelian Society, Vol. 28., pp. 14–15 (1954).

7. Macmillan, Lord Chancellor Birkenhead, Law and Other Things 218 (1937).

8. E. Griswold, *Foreword: Of Time and Attitudes—Professor Hart and Judge Arnold,* 74 Harv.L.Rev. 81, 91 (1960).

the crystallization of one's conscientious objector belief is always beyond one's control. The Fourth, Fifth, Sixth, Seventh and Ninth Circuits have held that it is a circumstance over which he has control. To resolve this conflict the Supreme Court has accepted certiorari, 397 U.S. 1074, 90 S.Ct. 1525, 25 L.Ed.2d 808, in Ehlert v. United States, 422 F.2d 332 (9th Cir.1970). And my specific quarrel with the majority action is their promulgation of a sweeping rule deciding the question of control over circumstances in all applications for reopening of classification.

In adopting this new rule for the circuit, the majority states:

> This question, of course, is one upon which psychologists and philosophers may differ. Nevertheless, it is our duty to supply an answer which the local boards can apply. At the risk of being simplistic, we think that we must again deal with the ordinary usage of the words in the regulation. By common definition beliefs of conscience are always beyond one's control.

I do not choose to enter the lists to decide whether it is the function of the judiciary, or that of Congress or the Executive to supply answers "which the local boards can apply." But I cannot bring myself to concur in an approach which, while recognizing the complexity and sophistication of a behavioral science problem, nonetheless, formulates a conclusion, under the aegis of "common definition," without discussing the specifics of a problem which has perplexed so many courts, and led to divergent conclusions.

As a starting point, it has been suggested that if the acquisition of the conscientious objector belief resulted from deliberate action, then it must follow that the crystallization resulted from circumstances within the registrant's control. William James described deliberate action as that which results when the mind has many objects before it, related to each other in antagonistic or favorable ways, creating a feeling of inward unrest known as indecision. He suggested that as long as this process lasts, with the various considerations competing for attention, we are said to deliberate. When the original suggestion either prevails and causes the movement to take place, or becomes definitely quashed by its antagonists, we are said to decide in favor of one or another course, and the reinforcing or inhibiting objects which have competed for attention are termed the reasons or motives by which the decision is brought about.[3] All deliberations, according to James, do not involve the same methodologies or cerebral intensities, but do have the common characteristic of a constant conflict of arguments for and against a given course.[4]

John Dewey and Bertrand Russell both emphasized the use of the deliberative process in making decisions. Dewey said that "[w]hile a man lives, he never is called upon to judge whether he shall act, but simply *how* he shall act. A decision not to act is a decision to act in a

---

3. William James, Psychology (Briefer Course), Collier Books, 1969 Edition, 426.

4. *Id.* at 427–31. For a categorization of the chief types of decisions, see *id.* at 376–81.

certain way; it is never a judgment not to act, unqualifiedly. It is a judgment to do something else—to wait, for example." And Russell has asserted: "[F]ew beliefs, if any, are *wholly* spontaneous in an educated man. The more a man has organized this knowledge, the more his beliefs will be interdependent, and the more will obvious truths be reinforced by their connection with other obvious truths."

But to test the crystallization of conscientious objector beliefs by the presence of deliberate thought-action is not enough. Considering the evidence—the various objects competing for attention—is a deliberate, rational, intellectual activity. As an activity, it is within one's control, and this fact is reflected in numerous phrases in ordinary language, as when we say that someone willfully refused to look at the facts. Once one has decided to consider the evidence, however, it is not clear that reaching a conclusion is to the same extent an activity within one's control. We speak of "being forced to conclude," or "being compelled by the facts" to a certain conclusion. One may be driven by the evidence or led against one's will to a conclusion. If we are rational, and honest, then we let the evidence decide for us and do not control the conclusion we will reach.

Putting aside the deliberative process in its classical sense, and turning to the broader concept of "belief", we find that formidable authorities have posed the questions: Can one really make oneself believe something, or make oneself go on believing it, just by an effort of will? Are our beliefs really under voluntary control at all? [7]

David Hume thought it quite obvious that they are not. H.H. Price seemed to agree, at least to the extent of saying:

> Believing a proposition is, I think, a disposition and not an occurrence or "mental act", though the disposition is not necessarily a very long-lived one and may last only a few seconds.... There is a characteristic sort of mental occurrence which we sometimes notice when we are in the process of *acquiring* such a disposition. I am going to call this occurrence "assenting" to the proposition.... When our belief is a reasonable one, this assenting, and especially the initial assent, has a *preferential* character....
>
> Now because of this preferential element in it, assent may look like voluntary choice. But the appearance is deceptive. It is not a free choice at all, but a forced one. If you are in a reasonable frame of mind ... you cannot help preferring the proposition which *your* evidence favours, the evidence *you* are at the moment attending to, though the evidence which other people have may of course be different.... It just is not in your power to avoid assenting to the proposition which the evidence [your evidence] favours, or to assent instead to some

7. H.H. Price, "Belief and Will," Pro-   pp. 14, 15 (1954).
ceedings of the Aristotelian Society, Vol. 28

other proposition when the evidence [your evidence] is manifestly unfavourable to it.[9]

. . .

I have limited this analysis thus far to decision-making processes
which involve the weighing of evidence, pro and con, in varying degrees
of personal control. Not all decisions, however, are reached by an
evidence-weighing procedure.

Professor James included as "movement consequent upon cerebro-
mental change" expressions of emotions and instinctive and implusive
performances. "An emotion," he said, "is a tendency to feel, an instinct
is a tendency to act, characteristically, when in the presence of a certain
object in the environment."[11] Instinct to him was "the faculty of acting
in such a way as to produce certain ends without foresight of the ends,
and without previous education in the performance," and he declared
that every instinct is an impulse. Bertrand Russell believed it possible
for there to be a spontaneous belief. C.J. Adcock suggests that it is
sometimes difficult to decide whether behavior based on emotionality
results because "the immediate drive strength is overvalued and so
difficult to control. The same result will obtain if the control function
itself is too weak. It is very important to notice that while low ego
control and high emotionality have similar effects they are functionally
very different." And no discussion of a comparison between reason and
uncontrolled action would be considered complete without a reference to
Freud's analysis: "The ego represents what may be called reason and
common sense, in contrast to the *id,* which contains the passions."

Based on the views heretofore rehearsed, I am convinced that the
acquisition or maturation of conscientious objector beliefs may arise
from circumstances beyond one's control: when one reaches the decision
by a rational process of weighing countervailing arguments in a purely
objective fashion, to the end that he is compelled to a conclusion, such
decision is not controlled by his will but is determined by the evidence;
when one engages in an apparently rational process of evaluating the
evidence but, in fact, "prefers" certain evidence favorable to an "acquired disposition," the development of a belief is, at least in part, not

9. Price, *supra,* note [7], at 15, 16.

11. He conceded that there may be
purely cerebral emotion, *i.e.,* the so-called
subtler emotions:

> Such feelings as moral satisfactions,
> thankfulness, curiosity, relief at getting a
> problem solved, may be of this sort. But
> the thinness and paleness of these feel-
> ings, when unmixed with bodily effects, is
> in very striking contrast to the coarser
> emotions. In all sentimental and impres-
> sionable people the bodily effects mix in:
> the voice breaks and the eyes moisten
> when the moral truth is felt, etc. Wher-
> ever there is anything like *rapture,* how-

> ever intellectual its ground, we find these
> secondary processes ensue. Unless we
> actually laugh at the neatness of the dem-
> onstration or witticism; unless we thrill
> at the case of justice, or tingle at the act
> of magnanimity, our state of mind can
> hardly be called emotional at all. It is in
> fact a mere intellectual perception of how
> certain things are to be called—need,
> right, witty, generous, and the like. Such
> a judicial state of mind as this is to be
> classed among cognitive rather than
> among emotional acts. James, *supra,*
> note 3, at 392.

controlled by will; when the acquisition of belief results from emotion, instinct, or impulse, it cannot be characterized as voluntary.

On the other side, there can be little doubt that a belief may come about through the exercise of one's will and thus arise from circumstances within one's control. If one enters upon an objective process of weighing and evaluating conflicting views, scrupulously avoiding the assigning of preferential regard for certain evidence, but in the end opts for a belief without being "driven" by the evidence, or in spite of the evidence, certainly this belief cannot be characterized as involuntarily acquired.

. . .

Accordingly, I would abjure the promulgation of a hard-and-fast rule on the "control" issue for the governance of all cases of this kind. I would hold that the crystallization of conscientious objector beliefs may be within the control or beyond the control of the registrant, depending upon the specific circumstances of his case. Each case, then, should be evaluated on its own facts.

NOTE

The Supreme Court declined to enter the debate among psychologists:

> That those whose views are late in crystallizing can be required to wait, however, does not mean they can be deprived of a full and fair opportunity to present the merits of their conscientious objector claims for consideration under the same substantive criteria that must guide the Selective Service System. . . . The very assertion of crystallization just before induction might cast doubt upon the genuineness of some claims, but there is no reason to suppose that such claims could not be every bit as bona fide and substantial as the claims of those whose conscientious objection ripens before notice or after induction. It would be wholly arbitrary to deny the late crystallizer a full opportunity to obtain a determination on the merits of his claim to exemption from combatant training and service just because his conscientious scruples took shape during a brief period in legal limbo. A system in which such persons could present their claims after induction, with the assurance of no combatant training or service before opportunity for a ruling on the merits, would be wholly consistent with the conscientious objector statute.

> . . .

> We need not take sides in the somewhat theological debates about the nature of "control" over one's own conscience that the phrasing of this regulation has forced upon so many federal courts. Rather, since the meaning of the language is not free from doubt, we are obligated to regard as controlling a reason-

able, consistently applied administrative interpretation if the Government's be such. . . .

The Government argues for an interpretation identical in effect with the unambiguous rule hypothecated above, which, we have said, would clearly be a reasonable timeliness rule, consistent with the conscientious objector statute. . . .

. . . We are assured . . . by a letter included in the briefs in this case from the General Counsel of the Department of the Army to the Department of Justice, that present practice allows presentation of such claims, and that there thus exists no possibility that late crystallizers will find themselves without a forum in which to press their claims. Our conclusion in this case is based upon that assurance. . . .

Given the prevailing interpretation of the Army regulation, we hold that the Court of Appeals did not misconstrue the Selective Service regulation in holding that it barred presentation to the local board of a claim that allegedly arose between mailing of a notice of induction and the scheduled induction date. . . .

Ehlert v. United States, 402 U.S. 99, 103–105, 107–108 (1971) (footnotes omitted).

Do you agree with the Court that one's acquisition of belief, thought-action, decision-making processes, exercise of will, emotion, acquiring an original disposition as to result, or weighing evidence, constitute part of "somewhat theological debates about the nature of 'control' over one's own conscience"?

———

JEROME FRANK, THE JUDGING PROCESS *

Daily, judges, in connection with their decisions, deliver so-called opinions in which they purport to set forth the bases of their conclusions. Yet you will study these opinions in vain to discover anything remotely resembling a statement of the actual judging process. They are written in conformity with the time-honored theory. They picture the judge applying rules and principles to the facts, that is, taking some rule or principle (usually derived from opinions in earlier cases) as his major premise, employing the facts of the case as the minor premise, and then coming to his judgment by processes of pure reasoning.

Now and again some judge, more clear-witted and outspoken than his fellows, describes (when off the bench) his methods in more homely terms.... Judge Hutcheson essayed such an honest report of the judicial process....

We may accept [his] as an approximately correct description of how all judges do their thinking. But see the consequences. If the law consists of the decisions of the judges and if those decisions are based on the judge's hunches, then the way in which the judge gets his hunches is the key to the judicial process. Whatever produces the judge's hunches makes the law.

What, then, are the hunch-producers? What are the stimuli which make a judge feel that he should try to justify one conclusion rather than another?

The rules and principles of law are one class of such stimuli. But there are many others, concealed or unrevealed, not frequently considered in discussions of the character or nature of law. To the infrequent extent that these other stimuli have been considered at all, they have been usually referred to as "the political, economic and moral prejudices" of the judge. A moment's reflection would, indeed, induce any open-minded person to admit that factors of such character must be operating in the mind of the judge.

But are not those categories—political, economic and moral biases—too gross, too crude, too wide? Since judges are not a distinct race and since their judging processes must be substantially of like kind with those of other men, an analysis of the way in which judges reach their conclusions will be aided by answering the question, What are the hidden factors in the inferences and opinions of ordinary men? The answer surely is that those factors are multitudinous and complicated, depending often on peculiarly individual traits of the persons whose inferences and opinions are to be explained. These uniquely individual factors often are more important causes of judgments than anything which could be described as political, economic, or moral biases.

In the first place, all other biases express themselves in connection with, and as modified by, these idiosyncratic biases. A man's political or economic prejudices are frequently cut across by his affection for or animosity to some particular individual or group, due to some unique experience he has had; or a racial antagonism which he entertains may be deflected in a particular case by a desire to be admired by some one who is devoid of such antagonism.

Second (and in the case of the judge more important), is the consideration that in learning the facts with reference to which one forms an opinion, and often long before the time when a hunch arises with reference to the situation as a whole, these more minute and distinctly personal biases are operating constantly. So the judge's sympathies and antipathies are likely to be active with respect to the persons of the witness, the attorneys and the parties to the suit. His own past may have created plus or minus reactions to women, or blonde women, or men with beards, or Southerners, or Italians, or Englishmen, or plumbers, or ministers, or college graduates, or Democrats. A certain

twang or cough or gesture may start up memories painful or pleasant in
the main.   Those memories of the judge, while he is listening to a
witness with such a twang or cough or gesture, may affect the judge's
initial hearing of, or subsequent recollection of, what the witness said, or
the weight or credibility which the judge will attach to the witness's
testimony.

. . .

It is ... a legal commonplace that a witness cannot mechanically
reproduce the facts, but is reporting his judgment of the facts and may
err in the making of this judgment.

Strangely enough, it has been little observed that, while the witness
is in this sense a judge, *the judge, in a like sense, is a witness.* He is a
witness of what is occurring in his court-room.   He must determine
what are the facts of the case from what he sees and hears; that is, from
the words and gestures and other conduct of the witnesses.   And like
those who are testifying before him, the judge's determination of the
facts is no mechanical act.   If the witnesses are subject to lapses of
memory or imaginative reconstruction of events, in the same manner the
judge is subject to defects in his apprehension of the testimony; so that
long before he has come to the point in the case where he must decide
what is right or wrong, just or unjust, with reference to the facts of the
case as a whole, the trial judge has been engaged in making numerous
judgments or inferences as the testimony dribbles in.   His beliefs as to
what was said by the witnesses and with what truthfulness the witnesses
said it, will determine what he believes to be the "facts of the case."   If
his final decision is based upon a hunch and that hunch is a function of
the "facts," then of course what, as a fallible witness of what went on in
his courtroom, he believes to be the "facts," will often be of controlling
importance.   So that the judge's innumerable unique traits, dispositions
and habits often get in their work in shaping his decisions not only in his
determination of what he thinks fair or just with reference to a given set
of facts, but in the very processes by which he becomes convinced what
those facts are.

. . .

If [Theodore] Schroeder * were right, the discovery of the hidden
causes of decisions would be fairly simple.   But the job is not so easy.
The directing impulses of judges will not so readily appear from analyses
of their rationalizing words.   We shall not learn how judges think until
the judges are able and ready to engage in ventures of self-discovery.

Which is not to say that, as a preliminary, it will not be valuable to
make studies, from the outside, of the motives and biases of judges—
studies based on their biographies and on shrewd surmises as to the
buried meanings obliquely expressed in their language....

Now, such investigations might prove of immense value if they
would stimulate judges to engage in searching self-analysis.   For the

---

* Schroeder, *The Psychologic Study of Judicial Opinions,* 6 Calif.L.Rev. 89 (1918).

ultimately important influences in the decisions of any judge are the most obscure, and are the least easily discoverable—by any one but the judge himself. They are tied up with intimate experiences which no biographer, however sedulous, is likely to ferret out, and the emotional significance of which no one but the judge, or a psychologist in the closest contact with him, could comprehend. What we may hope some day to get from our judges are detailed autobiographies containing the sort of material that is recounted in the autobiographical novel; or opinions annotated, by the judge who writes them, with elaborate explorations of the background factors in his personal experience which swayed him in reaching his conclusions. For in the last push, a judge's decisions are the outcome of his entire life-history. . . .

NOTE

When Judge Frank addresses the "weight or credibility which the judge will attach to the witness's testimony" in the discussion of "minute and distinctly personal biases", should not this have been addressed to all fact-finders, to juries as well as judges?

Compare Frank's discussion of the tentative judgments of judges with Price's analysis of a "disposition" or "initial assent" to a proposition described in Scott v. Commanding Officer, *ante.*

––––––

JEROME FRANK, LAW AND THE MODERN MIND *

The following is from the reminiscences of a man who has served both as prosecuting attorney and as judge:

"The jockeying for a judge is sometimes almost humorous. Lawyers recognize the peculiarities, previous opinions, leanings, strength and weakness, and likes or dislikes of a particular judge in a particular case. Some years ago one of the bright lawyers of Chicago conferred with me as an assistant state's attorney, to agree on a judge for the trial of a series of cases. We proceeded to go over the list. For the state's attorney, I objected to but one judge of all the twenty-eight Cook County judges, and as I went through the list I would ask him about one or another, 'How about this one?' As to the first one I named he said 'No, he decided a case a couple of weeks ago in a way that I didn't like, and I don't want him to use my client as a means to get back to a state of virtue.' As to another, he said, 'No, he is not very clear-headed; he is likely to read an editorial by the man who put him on the ticket, and get confused on the law.' Of another he said, 'No, he might sneer at my witnesses, and I can't get the sneer in the record.' To another he objected that 'If my clients were found guilty this judge would give them the limit.' To still another he said, 'No, you can't get him to make a ruling in a case without creating a disturbance in the court room, he is so careful of the Supreme Court.' Again he replied to one, 'No, if the state's attorney should happen to sit in the court room I won't get a favorable ruling in the entire case.' And so we went along."

————

KARL N. LLEWELLYN, WHAT LAW IS ABOUT *

In any event, and whether I am right or whether I am wrong in this analysis, it is certain that you will spend much of your time attempting to discover and to study and to remember and to see the meaning of these so-called *rules of law* which judges say they are bound by, which judges say they have to apply. If I am wrong you can perhaps rest content when you have found out what the judges say. If I am wrong, you can believe what they say and be happy. But if I am right, finding out what the judges *say* is but the beginning of your task. You will have to take what they say and compare it with what they *do*. You will have to see whether what they say matches with what they do. You will have to be distrustful of whether they themselves know (any better than other men) the ways of their own doing, and of whether they describe it accurately, even if they know it. Nor is this all. If I am right you will also have to look into the question of what difference what the judges do is going to make to you, or to your client, or to any other person who may be affected by the judges' rulings on disputes. And even that will not be all. For when you find out what difference the judges' acts will make, you will then be confronted with the task of figuring what you, or your client, are to do about it. . . . If I am right, in a word, the action of the judges past and prospective becomes a piece of your environment, a condition of your living—like the use of money—with which you must reckon if you want to get where you would go to. And you cannot then rest content upon their *words*. It will be their *action* and the available means of influencing their action or of arranging your affairs with reference to their action which make up the "law" you have to study. And *rules*, in all of this, are important to you so far as they help you see or predict what the judges will do or so far as they help you get judges to do something. That is their importance.

NOTE

G. EDWARD WHITE, *The Evolution of Reasoned Elaboration: Jurisprudential Criticism and Social Change*, 59 Va.L.Rev. 279, 286 (1973): "To assert, as some Realists had, that '[i]t is not what the judges say which is important but what they do' was to arrive, Henry Hart wrote in

* The Bramble Bush 14 (1960). Reprint-   Inc., and Soia Mentschikoff Llewellyn.
ed by permission of Oceana Publications,

1951, at the 'monstrous conclusion that reason and argument, the conscious search for justice, are in vain.' "

EICHMANN v. ATTORNEY GENERAL OF ISRAEL
Supreme Court of Israel, 1962.

Briefly to the contention of counsel for the appellant that the judges of the District Court—and he advanced the same contention with reference to the judges of this Court—were psychologically incapable of judging the case of his client objectively.

Like the District Court, we too reject this contention, and the reply it gave in so doing is also our reply:

> As to the fears of the accused on the score of the background to the hearing of this case, we can do no more than reiterate the views that hold good with respect to every system of law worthy of its name: that the judge, when dispensing justice in a court of law, does not cease to be a human being, with human passions and human emotions. Yet he is enjoined by the law to restrain and control such passions and emotions, else there will never be a judge qualified to try a criminal case which evokes deep feelings and revulsion, such as a case of treason or murder or any other grave crime. It is true that the memory of the Nazi holocaust stirs every Jew to the depths of his being, but once this case has been brought before us it becomes our duty to control even these emotions when we sit in judgment, and this duty we shall honour.

JOHN DEWEY, A LOGIC RELATIVE TO CONSEQUENCES RATHER THAN TO ANTECEDENTS *

As a matter of fact, men do not begin thinking with premises. They begin with some complicated and confused case, apparently admitting of alternative modes of treatment and solution. Premises only gradually emerge from analysis of the total situation. The problem is not to draw a conclusion from given premises; that can best be done by a piece of inanimate machinery by fingering a keyboard. The problem is to *find* statements, of general principle and of particular fact, which are worthy to serve as premises. As matter of actual fact, we generally begin with some vague anticipation of a conclusion (or at least of alternative conclusions), and then we look around for principles and data which will

---

* *Logical Method and Law,* 10 Cornell   permission.
L.Q. 17, 18–19, 23–27 (1924). Reprinted by

substantiate it or which will enable us to choose intelligently between rival conclusions. No lawyer ever thought out the case of a client in terms of the syllogism. He begins with a conclusion which he intends to reach, favorable to his client of course, and then analyzes the facts of the situation to find material out of which to construct a favorable statement of facts, to *form* a minor premise. At the same time he goes over recorded cases to find rules of law employed in cases which can be presented as similar, rules which will substantiate a certain way of looking at and interpreting the facts. And as his acquaintance with rules of law judged applicable widens, he probably alters perspective and emphasis in selection of the facts which are to form his evidential data. And as he learns more of the facts of the case he may modify his selection of rules of law upon which he bases his case.

I do not for a moment set up this procedure as a model of scientific method; it is too precommitted to the establishment of a particular and partisan conclusion to serve as such a model. But it does illustrate, in spite of this deficiency, the particular point which is being made here: namely, that thinking actually sets out from a more or less confused situation, which is vague and ambiguous with respect to the conclusion it indicates, and that the formation of both major premise and minor proceed tentatively and correlatively in the course of analysis of this situation and of prior rules. As soon as acceptable premises are given and of course the judge and jury have eventually to do with their becoming accepted—and the conclusion is also given. In strict logic, the conclusion does not follow from premises; conclusions and premises are two ways of stating the same thing. Thinking may be defined either as a development of premises or development of a conclusion; as far as it is one operation it is the other.

Courts not only reach decisions; they expound them, and the exposition must state justifying reasons. The mental operations therein involved are somewhat different from those involved in arriving at a conclusion. The logic of exposition is different from that of search and inquiry. In the latter, the situation as it exists is more or less doubtful, indeterminate, and problematic with respect to what it signifies. It unfolds itself gradually and is susceptible of dramatic surprise; at all events it has, for the time being, two sides. Exposition implies that a definitive solution is reached, that the situation is now determinate with respect to its legal implication. Its purpose is to set forth grounds for the decision reached so that it will not appear as an arbitrary dictum, and so that it will indicate a rule for dealing with similar cases in the future. It is highly probable that the need of justifying to others conclusions reached and decisions made has been the chief cause of the origin and development of logical operations in the precise sense; of abstraction, generalization, regard for consistency of implications. It is quite conceivable that if no one had ever had to account to others for his decisions, logical operations would never have developed, but men would use exclusively methods of inarticulate intuition and impression, feeling; so that only after considerable experience in accounting for their decisions to others who demanded a reason, or exculpation, and were not satisfied till they got it, did men begin to give an account to themselves of the process of reaching a conclusion in a justified way. However this may be, it is certain that in judicial decisions the only alternative to arbitrary dicta, accepted by the parties to a controversy only because of the authority or prestige of the judge, is a rational statement which formulates grounds and exposes connecting or logical links.

It is at this point that the chief stimulus and temptation to mechanical logic and abstract use of formal concepts come in. Just because the personal element cannot be wholly excluded, while at the same time the decision must assume as nearly as possible an impersonal, objective, rational form, the temptation is to surrender the vital logic which has actually yielded the conclusion and to substitute for it forms of speech which are rigorous in appearance and which give an illusion of certitude.

Another moving force is the undoubted need for the maximum possible of stability and regularity of expectation in determining courses of conduct. Men need to know the legal consequences which society through the courts will attach to their specific transactions, the liabilities they are assuming, the fruits they may count upon in entering upon a given course of action.

The facts involved in this discussion are commonplace and they are not offered as presenting anything original or novel. What we are concerned with is their bearing upon the logic of judicial decisions. For the implications are more revolutionary than they might at first seem to be. They indicate either that logic must be abandoned or that it must be a logic *relative to consequences rather than to antecedents,* a logic of prediction of probabilities rather than one of deduction of certainties. For the purposes of a logic of inquiry into probable consequences, general principles can only be tools justified by the work they do. They are means of intellectual survey, analysis, and insight into the factors of the situation to be dealt with. Like other tools they must be modified when they are applied to new conditions and new results have to be achieved. Here is where the great practical evil of the doctrine of immutable and necessary antecedent rules comes in. It sanctifies the old; adherence to it in practise constantly widens the gap between current social conditions and the principles used by the courts. The effect is to breed irritation, disrespect for law, together with virtual alliance between the judiciary and entrenched interests that correspond most nearly to the conditions under which the rules of law were previously laid down.

Failure to recognize that general legal rules and principles are working hypotheses, needing to be constantly tested by the way in which they work out in application to concrete situations, explains the otherwise paradoxical fact that the slogans of the liberalism of one period often become the bulwarks of reaction in a subsequent era.

––––––––

HENRY J. FRIENDLY, REACTIONS OF A LAWYER— NEWLY BECOME JUDGE *

How far are appellate decisions "result-oriented"? How far may they permissibly be? A passage from a recent comment by Dean Griswold furnishes a useful springboard for discussion:

> Intellectual disinterestedness in a judge is a pearl of very great price, achieved only by continual care and striving. Even the greatest sometimes succumb. For example, Willing v. Chicago Auditorium Ass'n, and Erie R.R. v. Tompkins, both opinions by Justice Brandeis, have always seemed to me to be strongly result-oriented decisions. But to say that shaping the opinion to the result is hard to avoid, and that it has been done by the best, is only to emphasize the difficulties involved and the importance of constant effort to see that decisions are really reached, as far as humanly possible, on intellectually valid and disinterested grounds.

I assume that when Dean Griswold used the phrase "result-orientation" in this pejorative sense, he did not mean merely some consideration of the relative desirability of the result of one decision or another. That is Cardozo's "method of sociology," and no one to my knowledge, and surely not Dean Griswold, has ever questioned Cardozo's disinterestedness. "Result-orientation" in the sense condemned must thus refer to a judge's personal belief in what is desirable, formed before study of the case at hand and resistant to contrary argument.

Bad as all this may sound, to condemn it *semper et ubique* is to put the criticism on the wrong ground. The way to handle this kind of "result-orientation" is to require that a judge keep his personal beliefs as to desirability in their appropriate subordinate place in the judicial process—not to insist on his pretending to an intellectual equilibrium on great policy matters that cannot be expected or, in many instances, desired. No one recognized the impracticability of the latter more clearly than Cardozo. Although the judge ought to "disengage himself, so far as possible, of every influence that comes from the particular situation which is presented to him, and base his judicial decision on elements of an objective nature," nevertheless the judges "do not stand aloof on ... chill and distant heights; and we shall not help the cause of truth by acting and speaking as if they do." Centuries earlier, Hobbes required that the judge "diveste himself of all feare, anger, hatred, love and compassion" but not of all conviction. To this limited extent I agree with some of the thoughts Judge Arnold has so strongly expressed; his error is in making it appear that the judge will probably, and may permissibly, hold the same deep-seated personal faith about the reorganization sections of the Internal Revenue Code as about the First

* 71 Yale L.J. 218, 230–32, 234 (1961). Reprinted by permission of The Yale Law Journal Company and Fred B. Rothman & Company.

Amendment. Even as to questions of the latter sort the judge should try to make sure he is interpreting the long term convictions of the community rather than his own evanescent ones; but we may as well recognize this goal will not always be realized even "by the best." Sometimes the judge will fail of this because the community has no true convictions—the people of the United States scarcely entertained any common will as to Swift v. Tyson—on other occasions because it is asking too much that a judge suppress the basic beliefs by which he lives. What seems to me important is not to insist on a degree of detachment that often is unattainable and sometimes is undesirable, but to limit severely the cases in which a judge may consult his views on such matters, to define the stage in the judicial process when such considerations may enter and to what degree. . . .

. . .

. . . The cases where an appellate judge may properly be affected by consideration of the desirability of the result are a fraction of the category, itself a relatively small fraction of the decisions he will have to make, where a new rule of law must be forged. The rule must be the desirable one for the situation, not for the idiosyncracies of the particular parties. Even after all this he should do his level best to eliminate purely personal views of the desirable. But in some cases the best of judges will not succeed in that and in a few, a very few, it is wrong to expect them to try. I would not altogether ban this medicine of personal belief—indeed, we could not effectively ban it if we would, so long as the bench is occupied by human beings rather than Univacs—but it must be prescribed rarely and then with restraint. In those few cases where the prescription is appropriate, it betrays no lack of disinterestedness that the judge does not go through the form of reexamining the efficacy of every element in the pharmacopoeia.

NOTE

Do you agree that, as to the First Amendment, "the judge should try to make sure he is interpreting the long term convictions of the community"? Did the Supreme Court decisions in Engel v. Vitale, 370 U.S. 421 (1962), and School District of Abington Tp. v. Schempp, 374 U.S. 203 (1963) (school prayer cases), reflect these "long term convictions"? West Virginia State Board v. Barnette, 319 U.S. 624 (1943) (flag salute)?

Consider: "Sometimes . . . the community has no true convictions." Does the community have true convictions in most matters that are the subject of judicial resolutions? A majority of such matters? Relatively few such matters? Does it depend upon the discipline of law—tort, contract, property, decedent's estate, business, constitutional law?

Section 4

SUBTLE EXTRA JUDICIAL FACTORS

Additional and subtle extra-judicial factors affecting judicial decision makers include a lack of "judicial confidence," slothful work habits, and psychological barriers to decision making not present in other professions or other aspects of the legal profession. These factors undermine the quality of the judicial process and, regrettably, there has been little exposure of this problem to public analysis.

Some judges simply lack judicial confidence, stemming from either an actual lack of basic intelligence or intellectual strength or a strongly held feeling that they lack these basic qualities. This lack is manifested in several ways. One is to adjudicate strictly on the basis of precedent, to articulate no original or reasoned elaboration for a given decision, but simply to note the existence of conflicting precedents, to select one with the unreflective justification that "this is the better reasoned view" without adequate explanation of why it is better. To this judge there is nothing new in the law; decisions must be based on cases that have been pre-digested and pre-packaged by other judges in earlier cases. This is the process condemned by Cardozo in 1921 when he stated that some judges decide cases in accordance with precedents that plainly fit, in a process of search, comparison, and little more: "Their notion of their duty is to match the colors of many sample cases spread out upon their desk. The sample nearest in shade supplies the applicable rule."[1]

Another manifestation of lack of judicial confidence is a relatively new phenomenon: an undue reliance on law clerks for the actual decisional process. Over-awed by impressive credentials of law review editors and members of the Order of the Coif, some judges yield too much responsibility to these judicial assistants. Often this is illustrated by a change in the judge's jural philosophy as law clerks come and go, or at least a change in the judge's opinion writing style which makes it difficult for students of the opinion to identify the societal, individual or public interests which really have influenced the judge. Undue reliance upon law clerks by appellate judges, especially in the highest federal and state appellate levels, is a more serious problem than legal literature and public discussions reveal. It is one thing for a judge to use the clerk as a research and writing assistant; it is quite another thing to abdicate to the clerk the dominating role in both the decision making and opinion writing process.

Another aspect of lack of judicial confidence relates to a felt awareness of personal unworthiness to make final evaluations. To recognize the awesome responsibility in meeting the challenge of "crisis" cases is one thing; to run and to duck the issue to be decided is quite another. Often a judge simply cannot explain "why" a decision is reached, as is

1. B. Cardozo, The Nature of the Judicial Process 20 (1921).

evidenced by Holmes "can't help" formulation: "When I say a thing is true, I mean that I can't help believing it."[2]   To decide, and to acknowledge that the responsibility goes with the robe, requires a steadfastness of spirit described by Harry W. Jones as "attributes of judicial greatness fully as important as the attributes of reason."[3] Professor Jones makes these thoughtful observations:

> Is there any reason for jurisprudence to suppress or underplay the known fact that moral courage and integrity are as important as intelligence as qualifications for judicial office? This is not to abandon one's faith in law's rationality but to insist that intellect and character are factors of equal significance in legal decision making. Marshall, Holmes, or Cardozo could, I think, have written the following:
>
>> Certainly the relation of faith is no book of rules which can be looked up to discover what is to be done now, in this very hour. . . .   I give the word of my answer by accomplishing among the actions possible that which seems to my devoted insight to be the right one. With my choice and decision and action—committing or omitting, acting or preserving—I answer the word, however inadequately, yet properly: I answer for my hour.[4]

Another factor generally ignored in the writings is, bluntly speaking, the lazy judge. Judging today is hard work. It often is intensive, demanding and taxing, requiring the judge to be a self-starter, to face up to the rigors of a calendar and not to put off until tomorrow what can be done today. Or, unfortunately, not to put off until next month or six months hence what should be done today. Often members of the bar complain, with justification, that judicial sloth is more to be disdained than incorrect decisions. Work habits of individual judges constitute a more important factor in the decisional process than the writings and studies reveal.

Herbert Simon describes management decisions in industry: "Making non-programmed decisions depends upon psychological processes, that, until recently, have not been understood at all. Because we have not understood them, our theories about non-programmed decision making have been rather empty and our practical advice only moderately helpful."[5]   Often we hear that these non-programmed decisions are made by good judgment, insight and experience. But saying this is not saying much. Simon refers to a scene in *La Malade Imaginaire* in which the physician is asked why opium puts people to sleep. "Because it possesses a dormitive faculty," he replies triumphantly. Saying that good personal decisions are made by exercising good judgment names the

2. O.W. Holmes, *Ideas and Doubts,* 10 Ill.L.Rev. 1, 2 (1915).

3. H.W. Jones, *Law and Morality in the Perspective of Legal Realism,* 61 Colum.L.Rev. 799, 804–05 (1961).

4. Id. at 804 n. 20, quoting M. Buber, Between Man and Man 68 (Beacon ed. 1955).

5. H. Simon, The New Science of Management Decision 11 (1960).

phenomenon, but does not explain it. It does not help one who does not make decisions well but does not know why.

A possible reason why we may have difficulty in understanding this problem may be that no single educational discipline, no single college or university department, treats all dimensions of the decisional process. Mathematicians, psychologists, political scientists, military strategists and management analysts approach the subject from different perspectives. Decisional theory also attracts the attention of philosophers, economists, anthropologists and psychiatrists, and these specialists, too, have addressed the problem from specialized points of view. Leon Festinger pointedly observes that, after much theorizing, experimenting and studying, much of the psychology of decision making is still not well understood:

> How do human beings make decisions? This seemingly simple question has been a major concern of psychologists for many decades and of philosophers for centuries. In the eighteenth century, for example, an argument raged as to whether or not the fact that human beings could, and did, make choices implied a free will which contradicted the idea of determinism. If a human being could voluntarily decide which of several possible courses of action he would pursue, then clearly he had free will and a deterministic philosophy was untenable. The success of this argument, of course, depended upon the assumption that the process of making a choice, of making a decision, was inevitably surrounded with mystery.[6]

Knowing it is desirable in judicial decision making that careful thought should precede every choice selection, the problem is that ordinary problems present sophisticated nuances. In the words of one commentator:

> The answer is very simple if the choice is merely between something the person likes and something he dislikes. Some doubts arise when the choice is more difficult, as when it is between two things which the individual likes and his preference is very slight. The question becomes difficult and interesting when the alternatives offered are complex, each involving some pleasant and some unpleasant aspects, or where the person chooses without being certain as to the outcome he will receive.[7]

But any help to a judge with pre-decision jitters must start by eradicating a threshold barrier—the emotional trauma generated by the mere prospect of making the decision. Often, it is not the choosing itself that causes the problem; it is the specter that the prospective decider sees down the road. To this judge it is a lion roaring in the distance. That at decision time it turns out to be a pussycat makes no difference. The afflicted judge already has suffered. His or her pre-decision jitters,

6. L. Festinger, Conflict, Decision and Dissonance 1 (1964).

7. Id. at 2.

in most instances, are unnecessary. What causes the fear is the judge's unfamiliarity with the rudiments of the decisional process. In the words of President Franklin D. Roosevelt, "The only thing we have to fear is fear itself."

The common verbalization "I just don't know where to begin!" is real and signifies actual anguish. This distress then feeds on itself, causes frustrations to multiply in intensity, often climaxing in anger and aggression or withdrawal, but always causing a deterioration of performance. Pre-decision jitters magnify the dimensions of the actual problem and create mental clutter at the very time when the judge should be making up his or her mind effectively and efficiently. Heilbroner perceptively observes that, faced with a choice, we often *allow* our thought to fly around and our emotional generators to overheat rather than try to bring our energies to bear as systematically as we can.[8] The problem is not new. The French schoolman, Buridan, posed the problem five centuries ago. He argued that a hungry ass placed equidistant from two bales of hay would starve to death. Why? Because the attraction of the two bales being equal and opposite, the ass would never make a choice. But Festinger suggests that the problem is not which pile of food is chosen. "The real problem concerns the process by which the organism evaluates the alternatives and does make a choice." [9]

But whatever be the idiosyncratic aspects of judicial decision making—be they hunching or pre- and extra-judicial subjective factors— actual experience reveals a significant body of predictable uniformity in the behavior of a court. The great majority of cases are adjudicated in accordance with time-tested precepts of substantive and procedural law, applied fairly and justly in orthodox and professional form. The exceptional case which is decided because of the state of a judge's digestion is just that—exceptional. Notwithstanding the excitement of a large body of lay and professional literature that attempts to "psyche out" a court and to show how many extra-judicial factors go into decision making, one must not forget the high percentage of cases which could not, with semblance of reason, be decided in any way but one.

Section 5

STABILIZING AND UNIFYING FACTORS

OVERVIEW

Notwithstanding the potential for widespread variations in the decision making process, most law is institutionalized in the sense that it is predictable and reckonable. Given the possibility for decision by hunch, environment or personality, and given the reality that many subjective value judgments inhere in the process of choosing, interpreting and applying legal precepts, the judicial process nevertheless contains stabi-

8. R. Heilbroner, How to Make an Intelligent Decision, Think Magazine 2–4 (1960).

9. L. Festinger, Conflict, Decision and Dissonance 2 (1964).

lizing or unifying factors. These jurisprudential fail-safe mechanisms attach, especially to multi-judge reviewing courts which are the ultimate decision makers and dispute settlers, and the promulgators and interpreters of most legal precepts.

The American tradition of writing majority opinions—opinions of the court—as distinguished from the English practice of separate opinions, is one important factor lending predictability and reckonability to the law. Experience on any multi-judge court demonstrates that judges often compromise some portion of personal views for the sake of a unitary opinion. Because no two judges will have precisely the same views on deep issues of the judicial role in legal interpretation, the likelihood of some difference is great. But in most cases the interaction of mutual concessions is present. Judge Walter Schaefer described the collegial interaction: "Of course every judge can and should make suggestions to his colleagues. But the relationship among the judges is a personal one and a continuing one, and effectiveness can be blunted by excessive suggestion. The balance between complacent acquiescence and overassertiveness is delicate indeed." [1] Karl Llewellyn prepared a list of major steadying factors in our appellate courts, placing a great emphasis on the factor of "law-conditioned officials":

> Few judges make the American appellate bench without twenty and more years of other work in some aspect of law, in addition to their schooling. The judges are therefore not mere Americans. They have been law-conditioned. They *see* things, they see *significance,* both through law-spectacles in terms of torts and trusts and corporation and due process and motions to dismiss; and this is the way they sort and size up any welter of facts. Moreover, they *think* like lawyers, not like laymen; and more particularly like *American* lawyers, not like German lawyers or Brazilian lawyers. [2]

Llewellyn listed other factors that suggested that judicial decision making is predictable and reckonable: legal doctrine, known doctrinal techniques, responsibility for justice, the tradition of one single right answer, an opinion of the court, a frozen record from below, issues that are limited, sharpened and phrased; adversary argument by counsel, group decision, judicial security and honesty, and the professional judicial office.

The very institution of the multi-judge court is the best means to achieve the twin, seemingly contradictory, objectives of the law: the law must be stable, yet it must not stand still. So long as each judge on the court is conscious of a duty in every case, whether that judge be the opinion writer or one concurring therein, these objectives can be achieved. It is a duty eloquently described by Dean Erwin N. Griswold:

> It is on the whole fairly easy to cut through to a decision that seems pleasing and in accordance with one's predilections, and

---

1. W. Schaefer, *Precedent and Policy,* 34 U.Chi.L.Rev. 3, 10 (1966).

2. K. Llewellyn, The Common Law Tradition 59–60 (1960).

then to compose a workmanlike form of words to justify it. It is far more difficult to start without any conclusion, to analyze issues, dissect and assemble facts, explore hypotheses, consider competing arguments, and finally come to a resolution which, in terms of the law as it has been received and understood, and with as little personal admixture as possible, seems to be sound. This is a time-consuming, soul-searching, deeply intellectual task, requiring great humility, a tentative approach, and an inquiring and probing rather than a determined mind. It is a task, be it said, on which, in the experience of many people, consultation, discussion, drafting, circulation of drafts and re-drafting, and collective deliberation are often very helpful.[3]

We should demand no less from our judges than that their publicly stated reasons for decision be the true motivations that impelled it. Professor Edward Levi has said that "the function of articulated judicial reasoning is to help protect the court's moral power by giving some assurance that private views are not masquerading behind public views."[4] There can be little of Holmes' predictability or Llewellyn's reckonability in the law if the judge who utters the reasons for decision speaks with forked tongue. If a judge decides as well as explains on the basis of neutral principles, this "can make him as disinterested as possible and can signal the reflective evaluation that will more nearly bring congruence of particular outcomes and broad principles."[5] And, as Alexander Bickel put it, "[t]he restraints of reason tend to ensure also the independence of the judge, to liberate him from the demands and fears—dogmatic, arbitrary, irrational, self-or group-centered—that so often enchain other public officials."[6] "[N]o formal method of reasoning from axioms will answer questions of moral philosophy and political theory plainly and definitively, but it will help answer them differently than a process open to trials of strength, and to the free play of interest, predilection, and prejudice."[7]

Making a decision can be described in terms of acknowledged duty. As Karl Llewellyn expressed it, "It is ABC stuff that our appellate courts *are* interested in and *do* feel a duty to the production of a result which satisfies, placed upon a ground which also satisfies. One can indicate this crudely as the presence of a felt duty to Justice, a felt duty to The Law, and a felt duty to satisfy both of the first two at once, if that be possible."[8]

3. E. Griswold, *Foreword: Of Time and Attitudes* Professor Hart and Judge Arnold, 74 Harv.L.Rev. 81, 91–92 (1960).

4. E. Levi, The Nature of Legal Reasoning, in Law and Philosophy, 263, 281 (S. Hook ed. 1964).

5. K. Greenawalt, *The Enduring Significance of Neutral Principles*, 78 Colum.L.Rev. 982, 998 (1978).

6. A. Bickel, The Supreme Court and the Idea of Progress 82 (1970).

7. Id. at 87.

8. K. Llewellyn, The Common Law Tradition 59 (1960).

NOTE: PREDICTABLE UNIFORMITY IN APPELLATE COURTS

The layperson's perception that an appellant has a 50–50 chance of prevailing on appeal is unsupported by the raw statistics. When a lawyer responds to the client when asked: "If I take an appeal, what are my chances of winning?" the numbers are there to make book. If you take a direct appeal of right to the U.S. Court of Appeals, the odds of getting a reversal are as follows:

REVERSALS

U.S. Court of Appeals—National Average [1]

Nature of Proceeding	1990	1991	1992	1993	1994
All Appeals	12.4%	11.1%	11.0%	9.8%	10.4%
Criminal	8.0	7.4	7.6	7.4	7.8
U.S. prisoner petitions	5.6	5.6	5.8	4.8	3.9
Other U.S. civil	17.9	17.5	16.8	13.2	14.1
Private prisoner petitions	9.8	9.3	7.5	7.5	8.2
Other private civil	15.6	14.5	15.2	13.9	14.8
Bankruptcy	18.4	17.2	15.7	16.5	14.7
Administrative appeals	15.1	10.9	11.6	9.1	9.4

From this, what may we conclude as to odds of an appellant winning in a federal appeal? From 1990 to 1994, the reversal rate for all appeals averaged 10.94 percent. This means that the odds were less than one in nine, generally; in direct criminal appeals, approximately one in thirteen; and in collateral appeals in criminal cases, about one in seventeen. In the much discussed federal habeas corpus cases which constitute federal review of state criminal convictions, of 3,748 appeals terminated there were only 150 reversals of district court judgments.[2] In the state court systems, the following table reflects the chances of obtaining a reversal before a sample group of state intermediate courts where appeals generally may be taken of right. The percentages are for 1990 unless otherwise indicated.

1. Statistics on federal court filings and terminations are published annually in Director of the Administrative Office of the United States Courts, Annual Report. See Reports for years 1990 through 1994.

2. Special analysis Table B–5 of state habeas cases only prepared by Director of Administrative Office of the United States Courts FY 1994. Of 3,748 state habeas appeals terminated, 1,483 reached decisions on the merits with only 150 reversed. This includes appeals taken by both petitioners and respondent states.

State Intermediate Courts [3]

State	Reversal Percentage
Arkansas	9.0%
California	11.6%
Connecticut	24.2%
Hawaii	28.0%
Illinois *	18.6%
Iowa	13.7%
Kansas	24.0%
Maryland	17.3%
Missouri	20.0%
New Jersey *	18.3%
New Mexico	27.8%
North Carolina	24.8%
Pennsylvania *	15.0%
Texas	13.3%
Virginia	21.2%
Wisconsin	30.3%

* Statistics are for the 1989 fiscal or court year.

Certiorari Appellate Courts

When the highest court of the jurisdiction grants a petition for review (also known as a petition for writ of certiorari), the odds of prevailing generally increase. The real trick is to get the court to grant the petition. During the 1994 court year, the U.S. Supreme Court granted only 98, or 1.8 percent, of the 5,450 petitions it received from litigants attempting to appeal from judgments of the U.S. Courts of Appeals.[4] The following table reflects the chances of having a petition for review granted by the highest court of several representative states, if applicable, as well as the odds for obtaining a reversal. The statistics are for 1990 unless otherwise indicated.

State Highest Courts

State	Petitions Considered	Number Granted	Percentage Granted	Total Cases Decided [5]	Percentage Reversed
Arizona	762	80	10.5%	54	24.1%
Arkansas	—	—	—	448	21.2%

3. The state court statistics in this chapter were obtained directly from the administrative offices of the individual state courts, some in published reports and some in private correspondence with the author.

4. Director of the Administrative Office of the United States Courts, Annual Report, Table B–2 (1994).

5. Including direct appeals and other types of cases, where applicable.

State	Petitions Considered	Number Granted	Percentage Granted	Total Cases Decided [5]	Percentage Reversed
California	3402	150	4.4%	—	—
Colorado	759	98	12.9%	75	58.6%
Connecticut	190	31	16.3%	227	30.0%
Delaware	—	—	—	515	7.6%
Hawaii	—	—	—	311	31.2%
Illinois *	1321	109	8.3%	—	—
Iowa	—	—	—	411	21.0%
Kansas	390	34	8.7%	200	29.0%
Louisiana	2571	563	21.9%	—	—
Maryland	608	113	18.6%	165	49.7%
Mississippi	—	—	—	779	30.0%
Missouri	612	56	9.2%	31	41.9%
Nebraska	—	—	—	421	21.1%
New Jersey	1200	111	9.3%	205	40.0%
New Mexico	315	28	8.9%	166	38.0%
North Carolina	601	106	17.6%	141	36.9%
North Dakota	—	—	—	—	38.0%
Ohio *	1686	161	9.5%	—	—
Oklahoma [6]	—	—	—	415	15.9%
Oregon *	733	101	13.8%	—	—
Pennsylvania *	2227	230	10.3%	—	—
Rhode Island	121	1	0.8%	660	11.2%
South Carolina	27	7	25.9%	—	—
South Dakota	—	—	—	273	26.4%
Tennessee	772	60	7.8%	—	—
Texas [7]	876	84	9.6%	154	77.3%
Texas [8]	1352	202	14.9%	457	46.2%
Utah	80	14	17.5%	—	—
Vermont	—	—	—	207	27.1%
Virginia	1135	194	17.1%	164	54.9%
West Virginia	—	—	37.2%	—	—
Wisconsin	674	77	11.4%	—	—
Wyoming	—	—	—	161	27.3%

* Statistics are for the 1989 fiscal or court year.

6. Statistics are for the Oklahoma Court of Criminal Appeals, which is the court of last resort for the state's criminal cases.

7. Statistics are for the Supreme Court of Texas, which is the court of last resort for the state's civil appeals.

8. Statistics are for the Texas Court of Criminal Appeals, which is the court of last resort for the state's criminal appeals.

FELIX S. COHEN, TRANSCENDENTAL NONSENSE AND THE FUNCTIONAL APPROACH *

The "hunch" theory of law, by magnifying the personal and accidental factors in judicial behavior, implicitly denies the relevance of significant, predictable, social determinants that govern the course of judicial decision. Those who have advanced this viewpoint have performed a real service in indicating the large realm of uncertainty in the actual law. But actual experience does reveal a significant body of predictable uniformity in the behavior of courts. Law is not a mass of unrelated decisions nor a product of judicial bellyaches. Judges are human, but they are a peculiar breed of humans, selected to a type and held to service under a potent system of governmental controls. Their acts are "judicial" only within a system which provides for appeals, rehearings, impeachments, and legislation. The decision that is "peculiar" suffers erosion—unless it represents the first salient manifestation of a new social force, in which case it soon ceases to be peculiar. It is more useful to analyze a judicial "hunch" in terms of the continued impact of a judge's study of precedents, his conversations with associates, his reading of newspapers, and his recollections of college courses, than in strictly physiological terms.

A truly realistic theory of judicial decisions must conceive every decision as something more than an expression of individual personality, as concomitantly and even more importantly a function of social forces, that is to say, as a product of social determinants and an index of social consequences. A judicial decision is a social event. Like the enactment of a Federal statute, or the equipping of police cars with radios, a judicial decision is an intersection of social forces: Behind the decision are social forces that play upon it to give it a resultant momentum and direction; beyond the decision are human activities affected by it. The decision is without significant social dimensions when it is viewed simply at the moment in which it is rendered. Only by probing behind the decision to the forces which it reflects, or projecting beyond the decision the lines of its force upon the future, do we come to an understanding of the meaning of the decision itself.

* 35 Colum.L.Rev. 809, 843 (1935). Reprinted by permission.

Section 6

ORE IN PUBLISHED OPINIONS

KARL N. LLEWELLYN, ORE IN THE
PUBLISHED OPINION *

Of course, only by happenstance will an opinion accurately report the process of deciding. Indeed, I urge flatly that such report is not really a function of the opinion at all, though if the court so chooses there is no impropriety in recording such significant portions of the work as doubt, long pondering, independent research, any published source of illumination, division within the college, and the like. And one has ever to bear in mind as among the possibilities of deflection the type of thing which infatuated the cynics of the '20's and '30's: If the opinion is a justification, nay, a "mere rationalization" of a decision already reached, a justification intended "only" for public consumption, its "light" can be contrived delusion. Vital factors may go unmentioned; pseudo factors may be put forward; emphasis and weighing of factors may be hugely skewed; any statements of policy may be not for revelation but merely for consumption; the very alleged statement of "the facts" may be only a lawyer's argumentative arranged selection, omission, emphasis, distortion, all flavored to make the result tolerable or toothsome. That something of this does occur is demonstrated by that occasional dissenting opinion which, for instance, pounds home facts or authorities the majority has found it convenient to ignore. In such a maze, to reach for signs of actual motivation and process by watching say tone of language or manner of stress and arrangement or the like is surely, urges the skeptic, to do blind amateur pseudopsychoanalytical guesswork on data so intangible and scanty as to make a professional lose his lunch—the very kind of guesswork which many (this present writer included) sneer at as lightheaded and unwarranted when it is practiced by jejune or jaundiced jibers at the courts. No, says the skeptic, the only safe course is to follow the lawyers' ancient practice. Confine study of the opinion to what the opinion really offers: official authoritative light not on the birth-pangs of the decision, but on that very different something: what, on the relevant points, is the resultant actually prevailing state of correct legal doctrine—provided always, scoffs our dear skeptic, that *that* means anything, in life.

. . .

[B]y the early '30's there had been a fair beginning of what may be called critical study of certain documents known as opinions of the court. Some individual decisions had been subjected to deep and careful study of context, of legal and other background, of argument and personnel, so that the opinion came both to take on and to give new light about its genesis. Some judicial biographers had brought insight into the deciding process by exploring the sequence of a given appellate judge's life, times,

* The Common Law Tradition 56–58 (1960). Boston: Little Brown and Company. Reprinted by permission.

and product. Holmes, while still on the Supreme Judicial Court of Massachusetts, had suggested one piece of a large picture, one "outside" factor, "fear of socialism," as having heavily affected one whole group of untoward decisions. Cardozo had again and again drawn on his own experience in efforts to articulate various processes of conscious shift and conscious refusal to shift doctrine when troublesome case law problems had come before his court.

But to me much more significant is that by 1925 there had come to be a top bracket of the bar all over the country—not too many by percentage or even by nose count, but enough to be a bracket, not isolated poets, geniuses, or freaks—a top bracket who had begun to read any current case of interest not only for what it had laid down in words as doctrine or principle, nor only further (or in contrast) for what it had actually and narrowly decided, but for the "flavor" that could indicate how far that court, tomorrow, would stand to today's decision, or would expand it.

Now such reading, though addressed in intention to the future, is addressed in fact even more to the past: it reaches into the opinion for light on what has most strongly moved the court into the actual deciding. It presupposes that when taken in conjunction with, say, the times and what is known of the judges concerned, and read with sensitivity, the *opinion* yields such light. More, it presupposes that there are processes of deciding which remain constant enough to be reckoned with, at least by an artist. Still more, nay, most: this approach to opinions proved to work out in the practical life of law. It made for safer counseling. It won cases on appeal. It brought its practitioners into the top bracket and it kept them there. Here was the *best* practice, ready to feed theory. What remained to be done was to turn into a standard and sustained procedure for anybody's practice (and also for observation inquiry) an approach which had already become familiar for particular persons, particular cases, and particular occasions.

NOTE

Do you have a problem with Llewellyn's notion that a report on the process of deciding "is really not a function of the opinion at all"? How can a litigant prophesy what the courts will do in fact? How can there be, in Llewellyn's favorite expression, "reckonability" in the law?

Is not Llewellyn's real thesis that the "ore" found in the opinions, the "flavor", is a clue to the methodology of the decision-making process? Is he not advising us to ascertain what the courts "do" as much as what they "say"? Is not his developed thesis—try to find "the flavor"—another way of saying "try to find what is motivating the court"? And if this is so, would it not be preferable that the court's opinion state directly what Llewellyn asks you to discover indirectly?

The cases that follow represent decisions in the sensitive area of federal-state relations. Read each case "not only for what it had laid down in words as doctrine

or principle ... or for what it had actually and narrowly decided," but for what Llewellyn called the "flavor" for the future and "for light on what has most strongly moved the court into the actual deciding."

EX PARTE YOUNG

Supreme Court of the United States, 1908.
209 U.S. 123, 28 S.Ct. 441, 52 L.Ed. 714.

MR. JUSTICE PECKHAM delivered the opinion of the court.

We recognize and appreciate to the fullest extent the very great importance of this case, not only to the parties now before the court, but also to the great mass of the citizens of this country, all of whom are interested in the practical working of the courts of justice throughout the land, both Federal and state, and in the proper exercise of the jurisdiction of the Federal courts, as limited and controlled by the Federal Constitution and the laws of Congress.

That there has been room for difference of opinion with regard to such limitations the reported cases in this court bear conclusive testimony. It cannot be stated that the case before us is entirely free from any possible doubt nor that intelligent men may not differ as to the correct answer to the question we are called upon to decide.

The question of jurisdiction, whether of the Circuit Court or of this court, is frequently a delicate matter to deal with, and it is especially so in this case, where the material and most important objection to the jurisdiction of the Circuit Court is the assertion that the suit is in effect against one of the States of the Union. It is a question, however, which we are called upon, and which it is our duty, to decide....

[This was an original application for leave to file a petition for habeas corpus and certiorari in behalf of Edward T. Young, as Attorney General of Minnesota. The Minnesota legislature enacted legislation reducing railroad rates and providing for serious criminal penalties for any railroad, or its representative, that failed to comply. Before the act was to take effect stockholders of nine railroads brought suit in federal court to enjoin their companies from complying with the law, contending that the rates were confiscatory and would deprive the property holders of due process of law. They also joined state Attorney General Young, asking that he be restrained from seeking to enforce the law. An injunction was issued. Young then sued in the state court for a writ of mandamus against the railroads, compelling them to comply with the new law. The federal court adjudged him guilty of contempt for this action. He was ordered to jail until he dismissed the state mandamus proceeding.]

We have, therefore, upon this record the case of an unconstitutional act of the state legislature and an intention by the Attorney General of the State to endeavor to enforce its provisions, to the injury of the company, in compelling it, at great expense, to defend legal proceedings of a complicated and unusual character and involving questions of vast importance to all employes and officers of the company, as well as to the company itself. The question that arises is whether there is a remedy that the parties interested may resort to, by going into a Federal court of equity, in a case involving a violation of the Federal Constitution....

This inquiry necessitates an examination of the most material and important objection made to the jurisdiction of the Circuit Court, the objection being that the suit is, in effect, one against the State of Minnesota, and that the injunction issued against the Attorney General illegally prohibits state action, either criminal or civil, to enforce obedience to the statutes of the State. This objection is to be considered with reference to the Eleventh and Fourteenth Amendments to the Federal Constitution. The Eleventh Amendment prohibits the commencement or prosecution of any suit against one of the United States by citizens of another State or citizens or subjects of any foreign State. The Fourteenth Amendment provides that no State shall deprive any person of life, liberty or property without due process of law, nor shall it deny to any person within its jurisdiction the equal protection of the laws.

The case before the Circuit Court proceeded upon the theory that the orders and acts heretofore mentioned would, if enforced, violate rights of the complainants protected by the latter Amendment. We think that whatever the rights of complainants may be, they are largely founded upon that Amendment, but a decision of this case does not require an examination or decision of the question whether its adoption in any way altered or limited the effect of the earlier Amendment. We may assume that each exists in full force, and that we must give to the Eleventh Amendment all the effect it naturally would have, without cutting it down or rendering its meaning any more narrow than the language, fairly interpreted, would warrant. It applies to a suit brought against a State by one of its own citizens as well as to a suit brought by a citizen of another State. Hans v. Louisiana, 134 U.S. 1. It was adopted after the decision of this court in Chisholm v. Georgia (1793), 2 Dall. 419 where it was held that a State might be sued by a citizen of another State. Since that time there have been many cases decided in this court involving the Eleventh Amendment, among them being Osborn v. United States Bank (1824), 9 Wheat. 738, 846, 857, which held that the Amendment applied only to those suits in which the State was a party on the record. In the subsequent case of Governor of Georgia v. Madrazo (1828), 1 Pet. 110, 122, 123, that holding was somewhat enlarged, and Chief Justice Marshall, delivering the opinion of the court, while citing Osborn v. United States Bank, *supra,* said that where the claim was made, as in the case then before the court, against the Governor of Georgia as governor, and the demand was made upon him, not personally, but officially (for moneys in the treasury of the State and for slaves in possession of the state government), the State might be considered as the party on the record (page 123), and therefore the suit could not be maintained.

Davis v. Gray, 16 Wall. 203, 220, reiterates the rule of Osborn v. United States Bank, so far as concerns the right to enjoin a state officer from executing a state law in conflict with the Constitution or a statute of the United States, when such execution will violate the rights of the complainant.

. . .

The various authorities we have referred to furnish ample justification for the assertion that individuals, who, as officers of the State, are clothed with some duty in regard to the enforcement of the laws of the State, and who threaten and are about to commence proceedings, either of a civil or criminal nature, to enforce against parties affected an unconstitutional act, violating the Federal Constitution, may be enjoined by a Federal court of equity from such action.

. . .

In making an officer of the State a party defendant in a suit to enjoin the enforcement of an act alleged to be unconstitutional it is plain that such officer must have some connection with the enforcement of the act, or else it is merely making him a party as a representative of the State, and thereby attempting to make the State a party.

It has not, however, been held that it was necessary that such duty should be declared in the same act which is to be enforced. In some cases, it is true, the duty of enforcement has been so imposed (154 U.S. 362, 366, 14 S.Ct. 1047, 38 L.Ed. 1014, § 19 of the act), but that may possibly make the duty more clear; if it otherwise exists it is equally efficacious. The fact that the state officer by virtue of his office has some connection with the enforcement of the act is the important and material fact, and whether it arises out of the general law, or is specially created by the act itself, is not material so long as it exists.

. . .

. . . It is contended that the complainants do not complain and they care nothing about any action which Mr. Young might take or bring as an ordinary individual, but that he was complained of as an officer, to whose discretion is confided the use of the name of the State of Minnesota so far as litigation is concerned, and that when or how he shall use it is a matter resting in his discretion and cannot be controlled by any court.

The answer to all this is the same as made in every case where an official claims to be acting under the authority of the State. The act to be enforced is alleged to be unconstitutional, and if it be so, the use of the name of the State to enforce an unconstitutional act to the injury of complainants is a proceeding without the authority of and one which does not affect the State in its sovereign or governmental capacity. It is simply an illegal act upon the part of a state official in attempting by the use of the name of the State to enforce a legislative enactment which is void because unconstitutional. If the act which the state Attorney

General seeks to enforce be a violation of the Federal Constitution, the officer in proceeding under such enactment comes into conflict with the superior authority of that Constitution, and he is in that case stripped of his official or representative character and is subjected in his person to the consequences of his individual conduct. The State has no power to impart to him any immunity from responsibility to the supreme authority of the United States. . . .

. . .

It is further objected (and the objection really forms part of the contention that the State cannot be sued) that a court of equity has no jurisdiction to enjoin criminal proceedings, by indictment or otherwise, under the state law. This, as a general rule, is true. But there are exceptions. When such indictment or proceeding is brought to enforce an alleged unconstitutional statute, which is the subject matter of inquiry in a suit already pending in a Federal court, the latter court having first obtained jurisdiction over the subject matter, has the right, in both civil and criminal cases, to hold and maintain such jurisdiction, to the exclusion of all other courts, until its duty is fully performed. Prout v. Starr, 188 U.S. 537, 544, 23 S.Ct. 398, 47 L.Ed. 584. But the Federal court cannot, of course, interfere in a case where the proceedings were already pending in a state court. Taylor v. Taintor, 16 Wall. 366, 370; Harkrader v. Wadley, 172 U.S. 148.

Where one commences a criminal proceeding who is already party to a suit then pending in a court of equity, if the criminal proceedings are brought to enforce the same right that is in issue before that court, the latter may enjoin such criminal proceedings. Davis & Co. v. Los Angeles, 189 U.S. 207. In Dobbins v. Los Angeles, 195 U.S. 223–241, it is remarked by Mr. Justice Day, in delivering the opinion of the court, that "it is well settled that where property rights will be destroyed, unlawful interference by criminal proceedings under a void law or ordinance may be reached and controlled by a court of equity." . . .

Mr. Justice Harlan, dissenting.

Let it be observed that the suit instituted by Perkins and Shepard in the Circuit Court of the United States was, as to the defendant Young, one against him *as, and only because he was,* Attorney General of Minnesota. No relief was sought against him individually but only in his capacity *as* Attorney General. And the manifest, indeed the avowed and admitted, object of seeking such relief was *to tie the hands* of the *State* so that it could not in any manner or by any mode of proceeding, *in its own courts,* test the validity of the statutes and orders in question. It would therefore seem clear that within the true meaning of the Eleventh Amendment the suit brought in the Federal court was one, in legal effect, against the State—as much so as if the State had been formally named on the record as a party—and therefore it was a suit to which, under the Amendment, so far as the State or its Attorney General was concerned, the judicial power of the United States did not and could not extend. If this proposition be sound it will follow—indeed, it is conceded that if, so far as relief is sought against the Attorney General of Minnesota, this be a suit against the State—then the order of the Federal court enjoining that officer from taking any action, suit, step or proceeding to compel the railway company to obey the Minnesota statute was beyond the jurisdiction of that court and wholly void; in which case, that officer was at liberty to proceed in the discharge of his official duties as defined by the laws of the State, and the order adjudging him to be in contempt for bringing the mandamus proceeding in the state court was a nullity.

The fact that the Federal Circuit Court had, prior to the institution of the mandamus suit in the state court, preliminarily (but not finally) held the statutes of Minnesota and the orders of its Railroad and Warehouse Commission in question to be in violation of the Constitution of the United States, was no reason why that court should have laid violent hands upon the Attorney General of Minnesota and by its orders have deprived the State of the services of its constitutional law officer in its own courts. Yet that is what was done by the Federal Circuit Court; for, the intangible thing, called a State, however extensive its powers, can never appear or be represented or known in any court in a litigated case, except by and through its officers. When, therefore, the Federal court forbade the defendant Young, as Attorney General of Minnesota, from taking any action, suit, step or proceeding whatever looking to the enforcement of the statutes in question, it said in effect to the State of Minnesota: "It is true that the powers not delegated to the United States by the Constitution, nor prohibited by it to the States, are reserved to the States respectively or to its people, and it is true that under the Constitution the judicial power of the United States does not extend to any suit brought against a State by a citizen of another State or by a citizen or subject of a foreign State, yet the Federal court adjudges that you, the State, although a sovereign for many important governmental purposes, shall not appear in your own courts, by your law officer, with the view of enforcing, or even for determining the validity of the state enactments which the Federal court has, upon a preliminary hearing, declared to be in violation of the Constitution of the United States."

This principle, if firmly established, would work a radical change in our governmental system. It would inaugurate a new era in the American judicial system and in the relations of the National and state governments. It would enable the subordinate Federal courts to supervise and control the official action of the States as if they were "dependencies" or provinces. It would place the States of the Union in a condition of inferiority never dreamed of when the Constitution was adopted or when the Eleventh Amendment was made a part of the Supreme Law of the Land. I cannot suppose that the great men who framed the Constitution ever thought the time would come when a subordinate Federal court, having no power to compel a State, in its corporate capacity, to appear before it as a litigant, would yet assume to deprive a State of the right to be represented in its own courts by its regular law officer. That is what the court below did, as to Minnesota, when it adjudged that the appearance of the defendant Young *in the state court,* as the Attorney General of Minnesota, representing his State as its chief law officer, was a contempt of the authority of the Federal court, punishable by fine and imprisonment. Too little consequence has been attached to the fact that the courts of the States are under an obligation equally strong with that resting upon the courts of the Union to respect and enforce the provisions of the Federal Constitution as the Supreme Law of the Land, and to guard rights secured or guaranteed by that instrument. We must assume—a decent respect for the States requires us to assume—that the state courts will enforce every right secured by the Constitution. If they fail to do so, the party complaining has a clear remedy for the protection of his rights; for, he can come by writ of error, in an orderly, judicial way, from the highest court of the State to this tribunal for redress in respect of every right granted or secured by that instrument and denied by the state court....

NOTE

The authors of McCormick, Chadbourn and Wright, Cases On Federal Courts, suggest that this is one of the three most important cases decided by the Supreme Court, along with Marbury v. Madison, 5 U.S. (1 Cranch) 137 (1803), and Martin v. Hunter's Lessee, 14 U.S. (1 Wheat.) 304 (1816). Thousands of cases against officials acting under color of state law and brought under the Civil Rights Acts of 1871, 42 U.S.C.A. § 1983, trace their authority to it. Do you have any difficulty with the reasoning that the state attorney general was an "individual" for Eleventh Amendment purposes and thus the suit was not barred as one against the state, but his action was "state action" for Fourteenth Amendment purposes, thus conferring federal court jurisdiction? The seed of this controversy was an attempt by a state to reduce railroad rates. Keeping in mind that the case was decided in 1908, do you believe that the subject matter of the litigation had any influence on the result? Recall from Llewellyn. "Holmes, while still on the Supreme Judicial Court of Massachusetts, had suggested one piece of a large picture, one 'outside' factor, 'fear of socialism,' as having heavily affected one whole group of untoward decisions."

EDELMAN v. JORDAN

Supreme Court of the United States, 1974.
415 U.S. 651, 94 S.Ct. 1347, 39 L.Ed.2d 662.

Mr. Justice Rehnquist delivered the opinion of the Court.

Respondent John Jordan filed a complaint in the United States District Court for the Northern District of Illinois, individually and as a representative of a class, seeking declaratory and injunctive relief against two former directors of the Illinois Department of Public Aid, the director of the Cook County Department of Public Aid, and the comptroller of Cook County. Respondent alleged that these state officials were administering the federal-state programs of Aid to the Aged, Blind and Disabled (AABD) in a manner inconsistent with various federal regulations and with the Fourteenth Amendment to the Constitution.

. . .

On appeal to the United States Court of Appeals for the Seventh Circuit, the Illinois' officials contended, *inter alia,* that the Eleventh Amendment barred the award of retroactive benefits, that the judgment of inconsistency between the federal regulations and the provisions of the Illinois Categorical Assistance Manual could be given prospective effect only, and that the federal regulations in question were inconsistent with the Social Security Act itself. The Court of Appeals rejected these contentions and affirmed the judgment of the District Court. . . . The petition for certiorari raised the same contentions urged by the petitioner in the Court of Appeals. Because we believe the Court of Appeals erred in its disposition of the Eleventh Amendment claim, we reverse that portion of the Court of Appeals decision which affirmed the District Court's order that retroactive benefits be paid by the Illinois state officials.

The historical basis of the Eleventh Amendment has been oft-stated, and it represents one of the more dramatic examples of this Court's effort to derive meaning from the document given to the Nation by the Framers nearly 200 years ago. . . .

. . .

While the Amendment by its terms does not bar suits against a State by its own citizens, this Court has consistently held that an unconsenting State is immune from suits brought in federal courts by her own citizens as well as by citizens of another State. Hans v. Louisiana, 134 U.S. 1, 10 S.Ct. 504, 33 L.Ed. 842 (1890); . . . It is also well established that even though a State is not named a party to the action, the suit may nonetheless be barred by the Eleventh Amendment. . . . Thus the rule has evolved that a suit by private parties seeking to impose a liability which must be paid from public funds in the state treasury is barred by the Eleventh Amendment. . . .

The Court of Appeals in this case, while recognizing that the *Hans* line of cases permitted the State to raise the Eleventh Amendment as a defense to suit by its own citizens, nevertheless concluded that the Amendment did not bar the award of retroactive payments of the statutory benefits found to have been wrongfully withheld. The Court of Appeals held that the above cited cases, when read in light of the Court's landmark decision in Ex parte Young, 209 U.S. 123, 28 S.Ct. 441, 52 L.Ed. 714 (1908), do not preclude the grant of such a monetary award in the nature of equitable restitution.

Petitioner concedes that Ex parte Young, *supra,* is no bar to that part of the District Court's judgment that prospectively enjoined petitioner's predecessors from failing to process applications within the time limits established by the federal regulations. Petitioner argues, however, that Ex parte Young does not extend so far as to permit a suit which seeks the award of an accrued monetary liability which must be met from the general revenues of a State, absent consent or waiver by the State of its Eleventh Amendment immunity, and that therefore the award of retroactive benefits by the District Court was improper.

Ex parte Young was a watershed case in which this Court held that the Eleventh Amendment did not bar an action in the federal courts seeking to enjoin the Attorney General of Minnesota from enforcing a statute claimed to violate the Fourteenth Amendment of the United States Constitution. This holding has permitted the Civil War Amendments to the Constitution to serve as a sword, rather than merely as a shield, for those whom they were designed to protect. But the relief awarded in Ex parte Young was prospective only; the Attorney General of Minnesota was enjoined to conform his future conduct of that office to the requirement of the Fourteenth Amendment. Such relief is analogous to that awarded by the District Court in the prospective portion of its order under review in this case.

But the retroactive position of the District Court's order here, which requires the payment of a very substantial amount of money which that court held should have been paid, but was not, stands on quite a different footing. These funds will obviously not be paid out of the pocket of petitioner Edelman....

... The funds to satisfy the award in this case must inevitably come from the general revenues of the State of Illinois, and thus the award resembles far more closely the monetary award against the State itself, Ford Motor Co. v. Department of Treasury, [323 U.S. 459 (1945)] than it does the prospective injunctive relief awarded in Ex parte Young.

The Court of Appeals, in upholding the award in this case, held that it was permissible because it was in the form of "equitable restitution" instead of damages, and therefore capable of being tailored in such a way as to minimize disruptions of the state program of categorical assistance. But we must judge the award actually made in this case, and not one which might have been differently tailored in a different case, and we must judge it in the context of the important constitutional principle embodied in the Eleventh Amendment.

We do not read Ex parte Young or subsequent holdings of this Court to indicate that any form of relief may be awarded against a state officer, no matter how closely it may in practice resemble a money judgment payable out of the state treasury, so long as the relief may be labeled "equitable" in nature. The Court's opinion in Ex parte Young hewed to no such line. Its citation of Hagood v. Southern, 117 U.S. 52, 6 S.Ct. 608, 29 L.Ed. 805 (1886), and In re Ayers, 123 U.S. 443, 8 S.Ct. 164, 31 L.Ed. 216 (1887), which were both actions against state officers for specific performance of a contract to which the State was a party, demonstrate that equitable relief may be barred by the Eleventh Amendment.

As in most areas of the law, the difference between the type of relief barred by the Eleventh Amendment and that permitted under Ex parte Young will not in many instances be that between day and night. The injunction issued in Ex parte Young was not totally without effect on the State's revenues, since the state law which the Attorney General was enjoined from enforcing provided substantial monetary penalties against railroads which did not conform to its provisions. Later cases from this Court have authorized equitable relief which has probably had greater impact on state treasuries than did that awarded in Ex parte Young. . . . But the fiscal consequences to state treasuries in these cases were the necessary result of compliance with decrees which by their terms were prospective in nature. State officials, in order to shape their official conduct to the mandate of the Court's decrees, would more likely have to spend money from the state treasury than if they had been left free to pursue their previous course of conduct. Such an ancillary effect on the state treasury is a permissible and often an inevitable consequence of the principle announced in Ex parte Young, *supra*.

But that portion of the District Court's decree which petitioners challenge on Eleventh Amendment grounds goes much further than any of the cases cited. It requires payment of state funds, not as a necessary consequence of compliance in the future with a substantive federal question determination, but as a form of compensation to those whose applications were processed on the slower time schedule at a time when petitioners were under no court-imposed obligation to conform to a different standard. While the Court of Appeals described this retroactive award of monetary relief as a form of "equitable restitution," it is in practical effect indistinguishable in many aspects from an award of damages against the State. It will to a virtual certainty be paid from state funds, and not from the pocket of the individual state official who was the defendant in the action. It is measured in terms of a monetary loss resulting from a past breach of a legal duty on the part of the defendant state officials.

NOTE

Do you find indication in this opinion of how the majority of the 1974 Supreme Court would have decided *Ex parte Young?*

What inviolate concept of state's rights did this opinion seek to protect? As a matter of contemporary political science, could this decision have gone any other way?

PENNHURST STATE SCHOOL v. HALDERMAN

Supreme Court of the United States, 1984.
465 U.S. 89, 104 S.Ct. 900, 79 L.Ed.2d 67.

JUSTICE POWELL delivered the opinion of the Court.

When the suit is brought only against state officials, a question arises as to whether that suit is a suit against the State itself. Although prior decisions of this Court have not been entirely consistent on this issue, certain principles are well established. The Eleventh Amendment bars a suit against state officials when "the state is the real, substantial party in interest." Ford Motor Co. v. Department of Treasury of Indiana, 323 U.S. 459, 464 (1945). See, *e.g., In re Ayers,* 123 U.S. 443, 487–492 (1887); Louisiana v. Jumel, 107 U.S. 711, 720–723, 727–728 (1883). Thus, "[t]he general rule is that relief sought nominally against an officer is in fact against the sovereign if the decree would operate against the latter." Hawaii v. Gordon, 373 U.S. 57, 58 (1963) (*per curiam*). And, as when the State itself is named as the defendant, a suit against state officials that is in fact a suit against a State is barred regardless of whether it seeks damages or injunctive relief. See Cory v. White, 457 U.S. 85, 91 (1982).

The Court has recognized an important exception to this general rule: a suit challenging the constitutionality of a state official's action is not one against the State. This was the holding in *Ex parte Young,* 209 U.S. 123 (1908), in which a federal court enjoined the Attorney General of the State of Minnesota from bringing suit to enforce a state statute that allegedly violated the Fourteenth Amendment. This Court held that the Eleventh Amendment did not prohibit issuance of this injunction. The theory of the case was that an unconstitutional enactment is "void" and therefore does not "impart to [the officer] any immunity from responsibility to the supreme authority of the United States." *Id.,* at 160. Since the State could not authorize the action, the officer was "stripped of his official or representative character and [was] subjected in his person to the consequences of his individual conduct." *Ibid.*

While the rule permitting suits alleging conduct contrary to "the supreme authority of the United States" has survived, the theory of *Young* has not been provided an expansive interpretation. Thus, in Edelman v. Jordan, 415 U.S. 651 (1974), the Court emphasized that the Eleventh Amendment bars some forms of injunctive relief against state officials for violation of federal law. *Id.,* at 666–667. In particular, *Edelman* held that when a plaintiff sues a state official alleging a violation of federal law, the federal court may award an injunction that governs the official's future conduct, but not one that awards retroactive monetary relief. Under the theory of *Young,* such a suit would not be one against the State since the federal-law allegation would strip the state officer of his official authority. Nevertheless, retroactive relief was barred by the Eleventh Amendment.

With these principles in mind, we now turn to the question whether the claim that petitioners violated *state law* in carrying out their official duties at Pennhurst is one against the State and therefore barred by the Eleventh Amendment. Respondents advance two principal arguments in support of the judgment below. First, they contend that under the doctrine of Edelman v. Jordan, *supra*, the suit is not against the State because the courts below ordered only prospective injunctive relief. Second, they assert that the state-law claim properly was decided under the doctrine of pendent jurisdiction. Respondents rely on decisions of this Court awarding relief against state officials on the basis of a pendent state-law claim. See, *e.g.*, Siler v. Louisville & Nashville R. Co., 213 U.S., at 193.

We first address the contention that respondents' state-law claim is not barred by the Eleventh Amendment because it seeks only prospective relief as defined in Edelman v. Jordan, *supra*. The Court of Appeals held that if the judgment below rested on federal law, it could be entered against petitioner state officials under the doctrine established in *Edelman* and *Young* even though the prospective financial burden was substantial and ongoing. The court assumed, and respondents assert, that this reasoning applies as well when the official acts in violation of state law. This argument misconstrues the basis of the doctrine established in *Young* and *Edelman*.

As discussed above, the injunction in *Young* was justified, notwithstanding the obvious impact on the State itself, on the view that sovereign immunity does not apply because an official who acts unconstitutionally is "stripped of his official or representative character," *Young*, 209 U.S., at 160. This rationale, of course, created the "well-recognized irony" that an official's unconstitutional conduct constitutes state action under the Fourteenth Amendment but not the Eleventh Amendment. Florida Dept. of State v. Treasure Salvors, Inc., 458 U.S. 670, 685 (1982) (opinion of STEVENS, J.). Nonetheless, the *Young* doctrine has been accepted as necessary to permit the federal courts to vindicate federal rights and hold state officials responsible to "the supreme authority of the United States." *Young, supra*, at 160. As Justice Brennan has observed, "*Ex parte Young* was the culmination of efforts by this Court to harmonize the principles of the Eleventh Amendment with the effective supremacy of rights and powers secured elsewhere in the Constitution." Perez v. Ledesma, 401 U.S. 82, 106 (1971) (concurring in part and dissenting in part). Our decisions repeatedly have emphasized that the *Young* doctrine rests on the need to promote the vindication of federal rights. See, *e.g.*, Quern v. Jordan, 440 U.S., at 337; Scheuer v. Rhodes, 416 U.S. 232, 237 (1974); Georgia Railroad & Banking Co. v. Redwine, 342 U.S. 299, 304 (1952).

The Court also has recognized, however, that the need to promote the supremacy of federal law must be accommodated to the constitutional immunity of the States. This is the significance of Edelman v. Jordan, *supra*. We recognized that the prospective relief authorized by *Young* "has permitted the Civil War Amendments to the Constitution to serve as a sword, rather than merely a shield, for those whom they were designed to protect." 415 U.S., at 664. But we declined to extend the fiction of *Young* to encompass retroactive relief, for to do so would effectively eliminate the constitutional immunity of the States. Accordingly, we concluded that although the difference between permissible and impermissible relief "will not in many instances be that between day and night," 415 U.S., at 667, an award of retroactive relief necessarily " 'fall[s] afoul of the Eleventh Amendment if that basic constitutional provision is to be conceived of as having any present force.' " Id., at 665 (quoting Rothstein v. Wyman, 467 F.2d 226, 237 (CA2 1972) (McGowan, J., sitting by designation), cert. denied, 411 U.S. 921 (1973)). In sum, *Edelman* 's distinction between prospective and retroactive relief fulfills the underlying purpose of *Ex parte Young* while at the same time preserving to an important degree the constitutional immunity of the States.

This need to reconcile competing interests is wholly absent, however, when a plaintiff alleges that a state official has violated *state* law. In such a case the entire basis for the doctrine of *Young* and *Edelman* disappears. A federal court's grant of relief against state officials on the basis of state law, whether prospective or retroactive, does not vindicate the supreme authority of federal law. On the contrary, it is difficult to think of a greater intrusion on state sovereignty than when a federal court instructs state officials on how to conform their conduct to state law. Such a result conflicts directly with the principles of federalism that underlie the Eleventh Amendment. We conclude that *Young* and *Edelman* are inapplicable in a suit against state officials on the basis of state law. . . .

The reasoning of our recent decisions on sovereign immunity thus leads to the conclusion that a federal suit against state officials on the basis of state law contravenes the Eleventh Amendment when—as here—the relief sought and ordered has an impact directly on the State itself. In reaching a contrary conclusion, the Court of Appeals relied principally on a separate line of cases dealing with pendent jurisdiction. The crucial point for the Court of Appeals was that this Court has granted relief against state officials on the basis of a pendent state-law claim. See 673 F.2d, at 657–658. We therefore must consider the relationship between pendent jurisdiction and the Eleventh Amendment.

This Court long has held generally that when a federal court obtains jurisdiction over a federal claim, it may adjudicate other related claims over which the court otherwise would not have jurisdiction. See, *e.g.,* Mine Workers v. Gibbs, 383 U.S. 715, 726 (1966); Osborn v. Bank of United States, 9 Wheat. 738, 819–823 (1824). The Court also has held that a federal court may resolve a case solely on the basis of a pendent state-law claim, see *Siler,* 213 U.S., at 192–193, and that in fact the court usually should do so in order to avoid federal constitutional questions, see *id.,* at 193; Ashwander v. TVA, 297 U.S. 288, 347 (1936) (Brandeis, J., concurring) ("[I]f a case can be decided on either of two grounds, one involving a constitutional question, the other a question of statutory construction or general law, the Court will decide only the latter"). But pendent jurisdiction is a judge-made doctrine inferred from the general language of Art. III. The question presented is whether this doctrine may be viewed as displacing the explicit limitation on federal jurisdiction contained in the Eleventh Amendment. "The Eleventh Amendment is an explicit limitation of the judicial power of the United States." Missouri v. Fiske, 290 U.S., at 25. It deprives a federal court of power to decide certain claims against States that otherwise would be within the scope of Art. III's grant of jurisdiction. For example, if a lawsuit against state officials under 42 U.S.C. § 1983 alleges a constitutional claim, the federal court is barred from awarding damages against the state treasury even though the claim arises under the Constitution. See Quern v. Jordan, 440 U.S. 332 (1979). Similarly, if a § 1983 action alleging a constitutional claim is brought directly against a State, the Eleventh Amendment bars a federal court from granting any relief on that claim. See Alabama v. Pugh, 438 U.S. 781 (1978) (*per curiam*). The Amendment thus is a specific constitutional bar against hearing even *federal* claims that otherwise would be within the jurisdiction of the federal courts. Edelman v. Jordan makes clear that pendent jurisdiction does not permit such an evasion of the immunity guaranteed by the Eleventh Amendment. We there held that "the District Court was correct in exercising pendent jurisdiction over [plaintiffs'] statutory claim," 415 U.S., at 653, n. 1, but then concluded that the Eleventh Amendment barred an award of retroactive relief on the basis of that pendent claim. *Id.,* at 678.

In sum, contrary to the view implicit in decisions such as *Greene v. Louisville & Interurban R. Co.,* 244 U.S. 499 (1917), neither pendent jurisdiction nor any other basis of jurisdiction may override the Eleventh Amendment. A federal court must examine each claim in a case to see if the court's jurisdiction over that claim is barred by the Eleventh Amendment. We concluded above that a claim that state officials violated state law in carrying out their official responsibilities is a claim against the State that is protected by the Eleventh Amendment. We now hold that this principle applies as well to state-law claims brought into federal court under pendent jurisdiction.

MONROE v. PAPE

Supreme Court of the United States, 1961.
365 U.S. 167, 81 S.Ct. 473, 5 L.Ed.2d 492.

Mr. Justice Douglas delivered the opinion of the Court.

This case presents important questions concerning the construction of R.S. § 1979, 42 U.S.C.A. § 1983, which reads as follows:

"Every person who, under color of any statute, ordinance, regulation, custom, or usage, of any State or Territory, subjects, or causes to be subjected, any citizen of the United States or other person within the jurisdiction thereof to the deprivation of any rights, privileges, or immunities secured by the Constitution and laws, shall be liable to the party injured in an action at law, suit in equity, or other proper proceeding for redress."

The complaint alleges that 13 Chicago police officers broke into petitioners' home in the early morning, routed them from bed, made them stand naked in the living room, and ransacked every room, emptying drawers and ripping mattress covers. It further alleges that Mr. Monroe was then taken to the police station and detained on "open" charges for 10 hours, while he was interrogated about a two-day-old murder, that he was not taken before a magistrate, though one was accessible, that he was not permitted to call his family or attorney, that he was subsequently released without criminal charges being preferred against him. It is alleged that the officers had no search warrant and no arrest warrant and that they acted "under color of the statutes, ordinances, regulations, customs and usages" of Illinois and of the City of Chicago. Federal jurisdiction was asserted under R.S. § 1979, which we have set out above, and 28 U.S.C.A. § 1343 and 28 U.S.C.A. § 1331.

. . .

Petitioners claim that the invasion of their home and the subsequent search without a warrant and the arrest and detention of Mr. Monroe without a warrant and without arraignment constituted a deprivation of their "rights, privileges, or immunities secured by the Constitution" within the meaning of R.S. § 1979. It has been said that when 18 U.S.C.A. § 241 made criminal a conspiracy "to injure, oppress, threaten, or intimidate any citizen in the free exercise or enjoyment of any right or privilege secured to him by the Constitution," it embraced only rights that an individual has by reason of his relation to the central government, not to state governments.... But the history of the section of the Civil Rights Act presently involved does not permit such a narrow interpretation.

. . .

The Ku Klux Act grew out of a message sent to Congress by President Grant on March 23, 1871, reading:

"A condition of affairs now exists in some States of the Union rendering life and property insecure and the carrying of the mails and the collection of the revenue dangerous. The proof that such a condition of affairs exists in some localities is now before the Senate. That the power to correct these evils is beyond the control of State authorities I do not doubt; that the power of the Executive of the United States, acting within the limits of existing laws, is sufficient for present emergencies is not clear. Therefore, I urgently recommend such legislation as in the judgment of Congress shall effectually secure life, liberty, and property, and the enforcement of law in all parts of the United States...."

The legislation—in particular the section with which we are now concerned—had several purposes. There are threads of many thoughts running through the debates. One who reads them in their entirety sees that the present section had three main aims.

First, it might, of course, override certain kinds of state laws. Mr. Sloss of Alabama, in opposition, spoke of that object and emphasized that it was irrelevant because there were no such laws.

> "The first section of this bill prohibits any invidious legislation by States against the rights or privileges of citizens of the United States. The object of this section is not very clear, as it is not pretended by its advocates on this floor that any State has passed any laws endangering the rights or privileges of the colored people."

Second, it provided a remedy where state law was inadequate. That aspect of the legislation was summed up as follows by Senator Sherman of Ohio:

> "... it is said the reason is that any offense may be committed upon a negro by a white man, and a negro cannot testify in any case against a white man, so that the only way by which any conviction can be had in Kentucky in those cases is in the United States courts, because the United States courts enforce the United States laws by which negroes may testify."

. . .

But the purposes were much broader. The *third* aim was to provide a federal remedy where the state remedy, though adequate in theory, was not available in practice. The opposition to the measure complained that "It overrides the reserved powers of the States," just as they argued that the second section of the bill "absorb[ed] the entire jurisdiction of the States over their local and domestic affairs."

. . .

The debates were long and extensive. It is abundantly clear that one reason the legislation was passed was to afford a federal right in federal courts because, by reason of prejudice, passion, neglect, intolerance or otherwise, state laws might not be enforced and the claims of citizens to the enjoyment of rights, privileges, and immunities guaranteed by the Fourteenth Amendment might be denied by the state agencies.

. . .

... In [United States v. Classic, 313 U.S. 299, 61 S.Ct. 1031, 85 L.Ed. 1368 (1941),] an opinion written by Mr. Justice (later Chief Justice) Stone, in which Mr. Justice Roberts, Mr. Justice Reed, and Mr. Justice Frankfurter joined, the Court ruled, "Misuse of power, possessed by virtue of state law and made possible only because the wrongdoer is clothed with the authority of state law, is action taken 'under color of' state law." *Id.,* 326. There was a dissenting opinion; but the ruling as to the meaning of "under color of" state law was not questioned.

. . .

If the results of our construction of "under color of" law were as horrendous as now claimed, if they were as disruptive of our federal scheme as now urged, if they were such as unwarranted invasion of States' rights as pretended, surely the voice of the opposition would have been heard in those Committee reports. Their silence and the new uses to which "under color of" law have recently been given reinforce our conclusion that our prior decisions were correct on this matter of construction.

We conclude that the meaning given "under color of" law in the Classic case and in the Screws v. United States, 325 U.S. 91, 65 S.Ct. 1031, 89 L.Ed. 1495 (1945) and Williams v. United States, 341 U.S. 97, 71 S.Ct. 576, 95 L.Ed. 774 (1951) cases was the correct one; and we adhere to it.

In the Screws case we dealt with a statute that imposed criminal penalties for acts "wilfully" done. We construed that word in its setting to mean the doing of an act with "a specific intent to deprive a person of a federal right." 325 U.S. at page 103, 65 S.Ct. at page 1036. We do not think that gloss should be placed on § 1979 which we have here. The word "wilfully" does not appear in § 1979. Moreover, § 1979 provides a civil remedy, while in the Screws case we dealt with a criminal law challenged on the ground of vagueness. Section 1979 should be read against the background of tort liability that makes a man responsible for the natural consequences of his actions.

Mr. Justice Frankfurter, dissenting [in part].

This case presents the question of the sufficiency of petitioners' complaint in a civil action for damages brought under the Civil Rights Act, R.S. § 1979, 42 U.S.C.A. § 1983. The complaint alleges that on October 29, 1958, at 5:45 a.m., thirteen Chicago police officers, led by Deputy Chief of Detectives Pape, broke through two doors of the Monroe apartment, woke the Monroe couple with flashlights, and forced them at gunpoint to leave their bed and stand naked in the center of the living room; that the officers roused the six Monroe children and herded them into the living room; that Detective Pape struck Mr. Monroe several times with his flashlight, calling him "nigger" and "black boy"; that another officer pushed Mrs. Monroe; that other officers hit and kicked several of the children and pushed them to the floor; that the police ransacked every room, throwing clothing from closets to the floor, dumping drawers, ripping mattress covers; that Mr. Monroe was then taken to the police station and detained on "open" charges for ten hours, during which time he was interrogated about a murder and exhibited in line-ups; that he was not brought before a magistrate ... and that it is the custom of the Department to arrest and confine individuals for prolonged periods on "open" charges for interrogation, with the purpose of inducing incriminating statements, exhibiting its prisoners for identification, holding them *incommunicado* while police officers investigate their activities, and punishing them by imprisonment without judicial trial. On the basis of these allegations various members of the Monroe family seek damages against the individual police officers and against the City of Chicago. The District Court dismissed the complaint for failure to state a claim and the Court of Appeals for the Seventh Circuit affirmed. . . .

Petitioners base their claim to relief in the federal courts on what was enacted as § 1 of the "Ku Klux Act" of April 20, 1871, "An Act to enforce the Provisions of the Fourteenth Amendment to the Constitution of the United States, and for other Purposes." . . .

. . . .

. . . Petitioners' allegations that respondents in fact did the acts which constituted violations of constitutional rights are sufficient.

. . . .

. . . Still, in this supposed case we would arrive at the question of what Congress could do only after we had determined what it was that Congress had done. So, in the case before us now, we must ask what Congress did in 1871. We must determine what Congress meant by "under color" of enumerated state authority.

Congress used that phrase not only in R.S. § 1979, but also in the criminal provisions of § 2 of the First Civil Rights Act of April 9, 1866, 14 Stat. 27, from which is derived the present 18 U.S.C.A. § 242, and in both cases used it with the same purpose. During the seventy years which followed these enactments, cases in this Court in which the "under color" provisions were invoked uniformly involved action taken either in strict pursuance of some specific command of state law or within the scope of executive discretion in the administration of state laws. [Justice Frankfurter then discussed certain cases.]

A sharp change from this uniform application of seventy years was made in 1941, but without acknowledgment or indication of awareness of the revolutionary turnabout from what had been established practice. The opinion in United States v. Classic, 313 U.S. 299, 61 S.Ct. 1031, 85 L.Ed. 1368, accomplished this. The case presented an indictment under § 242 charging certain local Commissioners of Elections with altering ballots cast in a primary held to nominate candidates for Congress. Sustaining the sufficiency of the indictment in an extensive opinion concerned principally with the question whether the right to vote in such a primary was a right secured by the Constitution, Mr. Justice Stone wrote that the alteration of the ballots was "under color" of state law. This holding was summarily announced without exposition; it had been only passingly argued. Of the three authorities cited to support it, two did not involve the "under color" statutes, and the third, Hague v.

C.I.O., 307 U.S. 496, 59 S.Ct. 954, 83 L.Ed. 1423, was a case in which high-ranking municipal officials claimed authorization for their actions under municipal ordinances (here held unconstitutional) and under the general police powers of the State. All three of these cases had dealt with "State action" problems, and it is "State action," not the very different question of the "under color" clause, that Mr. Justice Stone appears to have considered. (I joined in this opinion without having made an independent examination of the legislative history of the relevant legislation or of the authorities drawn upon for the Classic construction. Acquiescence so founded does not preclude the responsible recognition of error disclosed by subsequent study.) . . .

. . .

This case squarely presents the question whether the intrusion of a city policeman for which that policeman can show no such authority at state law as could be successfully interposed in defense to a state-law action against him, is nonetheless to be regarded as "under color" of state authority within the meaning of R.S. § 1979. Respondents, in breaking into the Monroe apartment, violated the laws of the State of Illinois. Illinois law appears to offer a civil remedy for unlawful searches; petitioners do not claim that none is available. Rather they assert that they have been deprived of due process of law and of equal protection of the laws under color of state law, although from all that appears the courts of Illinois are available to give them the fullest redress which the common law affords for the violence done them, nor does any "statute, ordinance, regulation, custom, or usage" of the State of Illinois bar that redress. Did the enactment by Congress of § 1 of the Ku Klux Act of 1871 encompass such a situation?

. . .

The Court now says . . . that "It was not the unavailability of state remedies but the failure of certain States to enforce the laws with an equal hand that furnished the powerful momentum behind this 'force bill.'" . . . The question is, *what* class of cases other than those involving state statute law were meant to be reached. And, with respect to this question, the Court's conclusion is undermined by the very portions of the legislative debates which it cites. For surely the misconduct of individual municipal police officers, subject to the effective oversight of appropriate state administrative and judicial authorities, presents a situation which differs *toto coelo* from one in which "Immunity is given to crime, and the records of the public tribunals are searched in vain for any evidence of effective redress," or in which murder rages while a State makes "no successful effort to bring the guilty to punishment or afford protection of redress," or in which the "State courts . . . [are] unable to enforce the criminal laws . . . or to suppress the disorders existing," or in which, in a State's "judicial tribunals one class is unable to secure that enforcement of their rights and punishment for their infraction which is accorded to another," or "of . . . hundreds of outrages . . . not one [is] punished," or "the courts of the . . . States fail and refuse to do their duty in the punishment of offenders against the law," or in which a "class of officers charged under the laws with their administration permanently and as a rule refuse to extend [their] protection." These statements indicate that Congress—made keenly aware by the post-bellum conditions in the South that States through their authorities could sanction offenses against the individual by settled practice which established state law as truly as written codes—designed § 1979 to reach, as well, official conduct which, because engaged in "permanently and as a rule," or "systematically," came through acceptance by law-administering officers to constitute "custom, or usage" having the cast of law.... They do not indicate an attempt to reach, nor does the statute by its terms include, instances of acts in defiance of state law and which no settled state practice, no systematic pattern of official action or inaction, no "custom, or usage, of any State," insulates from effective and adequate reparation by the State's authorities.

Rather, all the evidence converges to the conclusion that Congress by § 1979 created a civil liability enforceable in the federal courts only in instances of injury for which redress was barred in the state courts because some "statute, ordinance, regulation, custom, or usage" sanctioned the grievance complained of. This purpose, manifested even by the so-called "Radical" Reconstruction Congress in 1871, accords with the presuppositions of our federal system. The jurisdiction which Article III of the Constitution conferred on the national judiciary reflected the assumption that the state courts, not the federal courts, would remain the primary guardians of that fundamental security of person and property which the long evolution of the common law had secured to one individual as against other individuals. The Fourteenth Amendment did not alter this basic aspect of our federalism.

It commands were addressed to the States. Only when the States, through their responsible organs for the formulation and administration of local policy, sought to deny or impede access by the individual to the central government in connection with those enumerated functions assigned to it, or to deprive the individual of a certain minimal fairness in the exercise of the coercive forces of the State, or without reasonable justification to treat him differently than other persons subject to their jurisdiction, was an overriding federal sanction imposed. As between individuals, no corpus of substantive rights was guaranteed by the Fourteenth Amendment, but only "due process of law" in the ascertainment and enforcement of rights and equality in the enjoyment of rights and safeguards that the States afford. This was the base of the distinction between federal citizenship and state citizenship drawn by the Slaughter–House Cases, 16 Wall. 36 [21 L.Ed. 394 (1873)]. This conception begot the "State action" principle on which, from the time of the Civil Rights Cases, 109 U.S. 3 [3 S.Ct. 18, 27 L.Ed. 835 (1883)] this Court has relied in its application of Fourteenth Amendment guarantees. As between individuals, that body of mutual rights and duties which constitute the civil personality of a man remains essentially the creature of the legal institutions of the States.

. . .

The unwisdom of extending federal criminal jurisdiction into areas of conduct conventionally punished by state penal law is perhaps more obvious than that of extending federal civil jurisdiction into the traditional realm of state tort law. But the latter, too, presents its problems of policy appropriately left to Congress. Suppose that a state legislature or the highest court of a state should determine that within its territorial limits no damages should be recovered in tort for pain and suffering, or for mental anguish, or that no punitive damages should be recoverable. Since the federal courts went out of the business of making "general law," Erie R. Co. v. Tompkins, 304 U.S. 64 [58 S.Ct. 817, 82 L.Ed. 1188 (1938)] such decisions of local policy have admittedly been the exclusive province of state lawmakers.

NOTE

Would this decision have been the same if Mr. Monroe had been a White Anglo–Saxon Protestant millionaire? An American of Italian descent? An American of Mexican descent? An American of Polish descent? Compare the facts deemed material by the majority with those recited by the dissent.

Evaluate Justice Frankfurter's parenthetical concession, *ante,* pp. ___. *See also* Boys Markets v. Retail Clerk's Union, 398 U.S. 235, 255 (1970) (Stewart, J., concurring). How often do most judges admit such aspects of prior decisions so as to avoid the binds of stare decisis? Should they do so more often?

Implementing Section 1983 in Monroe v. Pape did more than move state cases to the federal arena. The effect has been to remove brutality from our police and prisons, naked arbitrariness from public officials' decisions, reduce discrimination in hiring, promoting and firing, and require advanced professionalism in discharge of duties from public officials. In this sense Monroe v. Pape has to be considered one of the most important decisions ever handed down by the U.S. Supreme Court.

In the century after its enactment, only a smattering of decisions involved Section 1983. In 1960, 280 civil rights cases were filed. Then came the landmark case of Monroe v. Pape. From that day in February, 1961 forward, the federal judiciary at all levels—district court, court of appeals and Supreme Court—has added new strength and increased vigor to the Act in the form of thousands of judicial decisions. Of a total of 190,981 civil actions there were 29,636 general civil rights actions filed and 37,929 prisoner civil actions during 1994. Taken together, all categories of civil rights actions comprised 35.42 percent of the pending federal civil caseload.

Chapter VI

JUSTIFYING THE DECISION

Section 1

THE ANATOMY OF THE OPINION

"When one asked Pound whether a recent Supreme Court decision was a "good" decision or a "bad" one, the old gentleman—for so I remember him with gratitude and considerable awe—had a way of answering not in terms of the correctness or incorrectness of the Court's application of constitutional precedents or doctrine but in terms of how thoughtfully and disinterestedly the Court had weighed the conflicting social interests involved in the case and how fair and durable its adjustment of the interest-conflicts promised to be."—Professor Harry W. Jones [1]

As we reach another vantage point from which to view the judicial process, it is well to review what has been seen already. This pause to examine the panorama is important because we have not only seen separate methodologies at work, but we have also viewed the same components from different perspectives and thereby acquired different impressions. At times our approach has been dichotomous. Thus, we examined functions and differentiated decision making from law making. Then, we learned that two processes inhere in the judicial function: first, reaching the decision and second, justifying it. It is to the second part of this analysis that we now turn.

Some judges will deny that such a dichotomy exists, insisting that decisions are the results only of their stated reasons. Sometimes this contention is true, often it is not. Surely the most desirable jurisprudential climate occurs when the motivation of the decision—the "why"—coincides with the public exposition justifying it—the "how." That reasons given in justification may coincide with reasons leading to the decision does not disprove the existence of two separate processes. Rather, the reality that the public justification often does not coincide with the actual motivation tends to prove that there is a dichotomy.

William James succinctly articulated why many judges fail to recognize the distinction: "The completed decision wipes off memory's slate most of the process of its attainment." [2] When judges read their public exposition (the court's opinion) a year or so after decision, they may incorrectly but honestly believe that what was stated coincides precisely with that which went into the making of the decision. Another reason

1. H.W. Jones, *An Invitation to Jurisprudence,* 74 Colum.L.Rev. 1023, 1029 (1974).

2. W. James, Principles of Psychology 260 (1890).

for not recognizing the distinction is a reluctance to admit publicly that decisions are made sometimes for extra-legal, even political, populist or pro- or anti-business reasons. Sometimes, they are made for purely personal, if not petty, motivations. Sometimes, they are made for overriding considerations which cannot, or so it is felt, be publicly stated. For purposes of our study, many of the previous observations relating to the process of decision making apply as well to the process of justification. Similarly, what follows relates primarily to the justifying process, although it may also be considered in the context of decision making. In this chapter we focus on justification—a public explanation for the decision, a statement of norms which contains an exposition of stated rules and principles of law, a statement that originates with the judge's choice of a legal precept, through the interpretation of that choice, and finally to its application to the cause at hand.

The several phases of the process are intimately interrelated and no doubt often occur simultaneously. With this qualification in mind, and also recognizing that value judgments inhere throughout, we must accord this aspect of the judicial process careful attention and analysis. If a sufficient number of a given court's opinions are scrutinized, some guidance is available, in Holmes' words, in predicting "what the court will do in fact."

It is critical, however, that the private reasons for the decision be the same as those publicly stated justifying it. This is most critical because those to be affected by the decision must have the benefit of the true motivation and explanation in order for there to be "predictability" in the Holmes formulation or in Karl Llewellyn's words "reckonability".

Piero Calamadrei, the Italian jurisprudent, explains in *Procedura e Democrazia (Process and Democracy)*:

> Naturally, if in the actual process of judging, the reasoning follows the decision and is an explanation of it rather than a preparation for it, the reasoning may become a screen to hide the real factors on which the judgment is based, covering with plausible reasoning the true motives for the decision, which cannot be admitted. Once a German jurist made a painstaking analysis of many decisions to show that the reasons alleged in the opinion were not the real motives that had actually led to the decision. This was a subtle study of psychology and of judicial logic, the purpose of which was to reveal the true motives beneath the apparent ones. The legal scholar with little experience in the courtroom reading the intricate reasoning of a decision as reported in a law review may often suspect, from the dialectical contortions and subtleties that the judge uses to justify his decision, that not even he was fully convinced by what he was writing, and that those arguments, couched in legal language, serve merely as a façade to hide from view the

intrigue or partiality that was the true motivating factor of the decision.

In order to obtain the desirable fusion between the intuition that suggests the decision and the reasoning that verifies it (and consequently to make certain that the reasoned opinion be a true explanation and not a fallacious travesty of the decision), it is necessary that the judge's "feeling" and reasoning faculties be "in unison".

Although the process of discovery—making or reaching the decision—is locked in the thought processes of the judge, the process of justification is public and discernible; it manifests itself in the opinion of the court. Perhaps some elementary definitions from Professor John Dewey are in order for a basic understanding of the process of justification:

Considerations which have weight in reaching the conclusion as to what is to be done, or which are to be employed to justify it when it is questioned are called "reasons." If they are stated in sufficiently general terms they are "principles." When the operation is formulated in a compact way the decision is called a conclusion, and the considerations which led up to it are called the premises.[3]

These "considerations" form the anatomy of a judicial opinion. A judicial opinion may be defined as a reasoned elaboration, publicly stated, that justifies the court's conclusion or decision. Its purpose is to set forth an explanation for a decision that adjudicates a live case or a controversy that has been presented before a court. This explanatory function of the opinion is paramount. In the common law tradition, the court's ability to develop case law finds legitimacy and acceptance only because the decision is accompanied by a publicly recorded statement of reasons.

Announcing a rule of law of the case is solely a by-product of the court's adjudicative function. It is acceptable only because the public explanation sets forth the grounds for the decision. Without this explanation, the court's decision would merely resolve that particular dispute presented by parties to the court. Thus, in our tradition the critical by-product of the decision survives long after the dispute between the litigants has been resolved. That by-product promulgates a legal rule describing the legal consequence that flows from the adjudicative facts set forth in the opinion. It forms the bedrock of the common law doctrine of *stare decisis* because the consequence attached to the relevant or material facts becomes case law, which is binding on all future cases that come before the court containing identical or similar material facts. Case law possesses the same power and force as a legislative act

3. J. Dewey, *Logical Method and Law,*
10 Cornell L.Q. 17 (1929).

until or unless subsequently changed by the court or modified by the legislature.

The judicial opinion is much more than a naked utterance. To use J.L. Austin's phrase, it becomes a "performative utterance" [4] because the *decision* that it explains performs as a declaration of law. We have chosen the word "decision" deliberately. It is not the "opinion" that performs; it is the "decision." Only the decision declared in the opinion has the force of law. The doctrine we respect is *stare decisis;* it is not *stare rationibus decidendi* or *stare rationes dictis.* Our tradition, elegantly stated, is *stare decisis et non quieta movere* (to stand by the decisions and not to disturb that which is settled).

Because courts tend to overwrite opinions (and this is particularly true in the U.S. Supreme Court), it often may be said that the "discussion outran the decision." [5] It should be understood, therefore, that the decision of the case will be measured by the precise adjudicative facts that give rise to the rule of the case. "Two cases or decisions which are alike in all material aspects and precisely similar in all the circumstances affecting their determination, are said to be or run on all fours with each other, or, in the more ancient language of the law, the one is said to 'run upon four feet' with the other." [6] To be sure, case law may survive and endure when the decision reflects desirable current public opinion or is congruent with contemporary community moral standards even though, upon analysis, the case's stated reasons may prove to have been fallacious or the reasons prove to be valid because societal changes have intervened. Even recognizing this, it is necessary to emphasize that the acceptability and vitality of the decision are usually measured by the quality of the reasons that originally supported it.

The stated reasons constitute the critical support for the decision. The quality of a decision is commensurate with the quality and logical force of the reasons that support it. Even so, two other necessary ingredients go into the mix: (a) the narration of adjudicative facts and (b) the statement of the issue or issues framing the case for decision.

Adjudicative facts are those selected from the gross facts found by the fact-finder from the congeries of record evidence. They are facts deemed necessary, relevant and material to the particular issue(s) presented for decision. There is an important reason why the facts set forth in an opinion should be selected with care, a reason that goes to the heart of *stare decisis:* like cases should be treated alike. And because our tradition is fact-specific, it is critical that the concept of "like cases" should refer to cases that contain like material or relevant facts. The decision that emanates from the opinion, the law of the case, is used to inform, guide and govern future private and public transactions. This future use of the decision is absolutely necessary if we accept Holmes's definition that law is nothing more pretentious than a

---

4. J.L. Austin, Philosophical Papers 233–41 (1961).

5. See, e.g., Wells v. Garbutt, 132 N.Y. 430, 435, 30 N.E. 978, 979 (1892).

prediction of what the courts will do in fact.[7] Thus perceived, a quality opinion will predict how similar factual scenarios will be treated.

The opinion is usually published in the law reports, although more often than not today it is prepared only for the litigants and the court record. Generally, it takes the form of a signed opinion in which the opinion of the court goes out over the name of its author. At times it takes the form of an anonymous, or per curiam opinion. A signed, published opinion has institutional or precedential value and lays down a new rule of law, or alters or modifies an existing rule, or involves a legal issue of continuing public interest, or criticizes existing law, or resolves an apparent conflict of authority. A legal essay expressing a judgment, it is designed to induce the audience to accept the judgment. A published *per curiam* is written when a case does not warrant a signed published opinion. It fits somewhere between an unpublished or memorandum opinion and the full-blown signed published opinion. A *per curiam* is used when the rule of law and its application to relatively simple facts are clear, or when the law has been made clear by a higher court's appellate decision subsequent to the court's judgment. It may be used to reverse the trial court or deny the requested relief from or enforcement of administrative agency action. It may be used also to affirm the trial court or grant relief from or enforcement of administrative action under circumstances where a signed opinion is unnecessary but there remains a need for some published statement of the court's reasons. A *per curiam* may be as brief as one or two sentences that cite a controlling precedent or that adopt the published opinion of a lower court. The United States Supreme Court has often used a truncated one- or two-sentence *per curiam* with citations.[8]

The purpose of a judicial opinion is to tell the participants in the lawsuit why the court acted the way it did. Drawing upon an analogy to marketing strategy, the opinion should first address a primary market. There are two discrete sectors of the primary market for appellate opinions. One sector consists of the actual participants before the appellate court—the appellant or petitioner, the appellee or respondent, and the tribunal of the first instance whose judgment or order is being criticized or upheld. These participants have an all-pervasive interest in the case, an interest in the error-correcting activity of the appellate court. The other sector is the appellate court as an institution. Although always concerned with error-correcting, the reviewing court must at all times consider the effect the opinion will have on itself as an institution charged with responsibilities for setting precedent and for defining law. These two sectors—one, the litigants and the trial court, the other, the appellate court itself—form the audience in the primary market. Writing should be directed to them. The opinion writer must

6. H. Black, The Law of Judicial Precedents 61 (1912).

7. O.W. Holmes, *The Path of the Law,* 10 Harv.L.Rev. 457, 460–61 (1890).

8. See the cases following the landmark decision in Brown v. Board of Education,
including Mayor of Baltimore v. Dawson, 350 U.S. 877 (1955); Holmes v. Atlanta, 350 U.S. 879 (1955); Gayle v. Browder, 352 U.S. 903 (1956).

focus on these mutually interested primary readers at all times in order to make as certain as possible that they understand the contents of the written communication precisely as the writer intends. What the receiver receives should be exactly what the sender has sent.

The lay parties to the lawsuit should understand what is being said. "Lay parties" do not mean the public at large. The broad spectrum of society may often be unfamiliar with the context, the terms of art, usages or customs of the transaction that gave rise to the litigation. The lay parties to the litigation, however, understand those elements. They will understand the decision if the explanation is clear and logical. All is lost if the parties do not know why the court did what it did. It is one thing to lose a case; not to understand why compounds the loss. Mehler summed it up: "[T]he gulf that often separates sender and receiver [of communications], spanned at best by a bridge of signs and symbols, is sought to be narrowed yet further so that ultimately the intended communication may have the same meaning, or approximately the same meaning, for those on the left bank as those on the right." [9] If the explanation is clear to "lay parties," it should be clear to all members of the court.

Important secondary markets also exist for judicial opinions. Although they ought not be ignored, their interests are subordinate to those of primary market consumers. These markets may be far removed in space and time from the instant case, but if the opinion is written well enough for the primary consumers, the secondary ones will also reap the same cognitive benefits. These secondary consumers vary. Some are institutions in the same judicial hierarchy, some at a higher rung, some lower. The highest court of the jurisdiction may be called upon to examine carefully the explanations of trial and intermediate court decisions. The court or agency in which the litigation originates studies them for future direction and seeks materials that will form the grounds for future decisions. Other secondary markets include lawyers, who generally look for prediction as to the course of future decisions. Still others represent the persons and institutions in the court's jurisdiction who seek reasonable guidance for conducting themselves in accordance with the demands of the social, political and economic order.

Law school faculties and students seek the opinions as study tools and research materials. Depending on the subject matter, so do state legislators and academics, among them, political scientists, philosophers, sociologists, behaviorists and historians. In addition, representatives of the print and electronic media are among the instant readers. When the media does report opinions, the courts' statements are subject to merciless editing or compressed to 60–second TV or radio sound bites. Ultimate consumers also may be the bench and bar of other jurisdictions, the committees, the council and assembly of the American Law Institute, committees of federal and state legislators and authors of popular and professional commentary.

9. M. Mehler, Effective Legal Communication 3 (1975).

We can say that a court's public performance in reaching a conclusion is at least as important as the conclusion. If we evaluate a decision in terms not of "right" or "wrong," nor of subjective agreement or disagreement with the result, but rather in terms of thoughtful and disinterested weighing of conflicting social interests, it becomes critical that the "performative utterance" include a socially acceptable explanation.

Earlier, we warned that although reasoned exposition traditionally takes the form of a logical syllogism, there is much more to the judicial process than dry logical progression. We have recognized that judges do not necessarily use formal logic to select or formulate legal premises. Professor John Wisdom suggests that this selection process "becomes a matter of weighing the cumulative effect of one group of severally inconclusive items against the cumulative effect of another group of severally inclusive items." [10]   In exercising this choice, courts do not necessarily appeal to any rational or objective criteria; essentially they exercise a value judgment and should be recognized flatly as doing so. Moreover, because courts have the power to alter the content of rules, no immutability attaches to their major or beginning premises. The desirability of *elegantia juris,* with its concomitant of stability and reckonability, is often subordinate to the desirability of rule revision in the light of claims, demands or desires asserted in the public interest. Once the controlling rule or principle has been selected or modified, however, there is an insistence, as we have observed previously in Chapter IV, that the public exposition—the process of justification—follow the canons of logic with respect to formal correctness. The process requires formal consistency of concepts with one another. The logic of justification is concerned with the relations between propositions rather than the content of the propositions themselves.[11]   Thus, the reasoning process dictates formal correctness, rather than material desirability.

Section 2

WHAT IS EXPECTED FROM OUR JUDGES

What we should expect from our judges, at a minimum, is a willingness to *consider* alternative solutions to a problem. A "result-oriented" judge, in the sense condemned, is one who consistently resists the act of considering arguments that may be contrary to an initial impression, to the conscious or unconscious initial assent to a given proposition. We cannot expect judicial minds, just as we cannot expect any reflective thinker, to be completely divorced from an initial assent to a proposition in the evaluating process.

What we can expect, however, is that the initial assent to a proposition, giving it a preferential character, will be fluid enough to yield to

10. J. Wisdom, Philosophy and Psycho–Analysis, 157–58 (1953).

11. R. Wasserstrom, The Judicial Decision 4 (1961).

later impressions. What we can expect is that a judge be sufficiently intellectually interested to respect and consider competing arguments and arrive at an outcome based on sound reason. We can demand that judges channel their interest by means of inquiry and reflection to reach a value judgment as to what the law ought to be, and then to tell us why in clearly understood language.

People do take judicial reasoning seriously, Professor Charles H. Miller observes, and "they are not fools nor being fooled in doing so, at least no more than in other forms of communication or with respect to other strands that form the web of a political culture."[1] Legal reasoning must not be esoteric or artificial. It must be capable of public comprehension and not a ritual understandable only to an elite legal priesthood.

At bottom, we ask our judges to have wisdom, and to have had an education or experience in history, letters, poetry, philosophy, science and the arts. Responding to a young man who had requested advice as to how he should prepare for a law career, Justice Frankfurter once wrote: "No one can be a truly competent lawyer unless he is a cultivated man.... The best way to prepare for the law is to come to the study of the law as a well-read person."[2] He recommended a "truly liberal education" in order to acquire "habits of good thinking" and "the capacity to use the English language on paper and in speech."[3] He also wrote: "No less important for a lawyer is the cultivation of the imaginative faculties by reading poetry, seeing great paintings, in the original or in easily available reproductions, and listening to great music. Stock your mind with the deposit of much good reading, and widen and deepen your feelings by experiencing vicariously as much as possible the wonderful mysteries of the universe."[4] Learned Hand also fashioned a statement of inspiration:

> I venture to believe that it is as important to a judge called upon to pass on a question of constitutional law, to have a bowing acquaintance with Acton and Maitland, with Thucydides, Gibbon and Carlyle, with Homer, Dante, Shakespeare and Milton, with Machiavelli, Montaigne, and Rabelais, with Plato, Bacon, Hume, and Kant as with books which have been specifically written on the subject. For in such matters everything turns upon the spirit in which he approaches the questions before him. The words he must construe are empty vessels into which he can pour nearly everything he will. Men do not gather figs of thistles, nor supply institutions from judges whose outlook is limited by parish or class. They must be aware that there are before them more than verbal problems; more than final solutions cast in generalizations of universal applicability. They must be aware of the changing social tensions in every

1. C. Miller, The Supreme Court and the Uses of History 12 (1969).

2. L. Blom–Cooper, The Language of the Law 357 (1965).

3. Id.

4. Id.

society which make it an organism; which demand new schemata of adaptation; which will disrupt it, if rigidly confined.[5]

But assuming wisdom in our judges, we are brought to what Harry W. Jones calls the final and showdown question: If judges are to reach their decisions by way of a genuinely informed evaluation of the probable consequences on the quality of human life in society, where do they get the data they need to accomplish that design?[6] We addressed a kindred question in Chapter IV, Section 6, in order to determine the source of the judicial determination of public policy. Certainly in the traditional fields of law, the judge may turn to sources of legal scholarship such as treatises, studies, case books and law reviews where a thoughtful answer may be readily available. At other times, only a vague hint is discernible to form the proper guidepost; at still other times, there simply is no answer.

But even the great Cardozo, when pressed with the question of where a judge is to get the social data he or she needs to know when one interest outweighs another, gave an answer that at once said it all, and still said nothing: "[H]e must get his knowledge ... from experience and study and reflection; in brief, from life itself."[7] Professor White noted:

> As legal scholars of the 1950's grew increasingly convinced of the importance of judicial rationalization, they came to criticize its contemporary manifestations and to formulate a new set of ideals and standards for judicial decision making. Reasoned Elaboration, a catch phrase coined by Henry Hart and Albert Sacks in 1958, came to summarize those ideals and standards. The phrase, as applied to the U.S. Supreme Court, demanded first, that judges give reasons for their decisions; second, that the reasons be set forth in a detailed and coherent manner; third, that they exemplify what Hart called 'the maturing of collective thought'; and fourth, that the Court adequately demonstrate that its decisions, in the area of constitutional law, were vehicles for the expression of the ultimate social preferences of contemporary society.[8]

The public explanation for the decision is the public's insurance policy against decision by judicial fiat. As Justice Frankfurter once observed, a court is "not a tribunal unbounded by rules. We do not sit like a kadi under a tree dispensing justice according to considerations of individual expediency."[9] Courts are justifiably criticized when they act without stating a reason or utter cryptic non-reasons such as "reasons

5. As quoted in The New York Times Magazine, November 28, 1954, p. 14.

6. H.W. Jones, *An Invitation to Jurisprudence*, 74 Colum.L.Rev. 1023, 1041–43 (1974).

7. B. Cardozo, The Nature of the Judicial Process 113 (1921).

8. White, *The Evolution of Reasoned Elaboration: Jurisprudential Criticism and Social Change*, 50 Va.L.Rev. 279, 286 (1973).

9. Teminiello v. Chicago, 337 U.S. 1, 11 (1949).

and authority support the decision" or "utility and justice require this result."

Public expression of judicial reasoning is a necessary concomitant of what is generally conceded to be the dual function of any appellate court—settling the dispute between the parties and institutionalizing the law. Dispute-settling can be described as reviewing the trial record for the errors asserted in a particular case; it is a review for correctness. The review process may also serve as a vehicle for stating and applying constitutional principles, for authoritatively interpreting statutes, for formulating and expressing policy on legal issues, for developing the common law, and for supervising the levels of the judicial hierarchy below the appellate courts. This set of tasks is called the institutional function of the court.[10]

Finally, what is expected from our judges is to protect the solemnity and importance of the judicial process. This is especially important in high profile trials. The trial judge must never become a prisoner of the media and permit extra-judicial versions of the litigation to be described in sidewalk press conferences. A trial is a search for the truth, and the dog of undue controversial advocacy, especially outside the courtroom in an era of sound-bite journalism, must never wag the high noble purpose of a court's quest for the true facts in the cause. The judge is the public's trustee and by his or her oath is sworn to preserve respect for court traditions; the judge must never permit a circus-like peripheral atmosphere to deface or disfigure the public's perception of our judicial system. At a minimum the trial judge must possess an expert's knowledge of the law of evidence and at the end of pre-trial proceedings must be totally familiar with the substantive law of the particular case to avoid delays in the conduct of the trial. Judges and attorneys are officers of the court, but they are not of equal rank. Judges are superior commissioned officers and possess broad discretionary powers to preserve the propriety and decorum of the judicial process.

Section 3

FINDING THE LAW

OVERVIEW

Once the facts are established by the fact finder, the general judicial function follows a three-step procedure: (1) finding, selecting or choosing the legal precept, (2) interpreting it, and then (3) applying it, as interpreted, to the facts. At the onset, a judge will evaluate the facts to determine which are material to settlement of a dispute. Selection of the relevant law then envelops these facts in a particular arena of competing legal precepts or competing analogies. The next step, inter-

---

10. Hufstedler, *New Blocks for Old Pyr-*   S.Cal.L.Rev. 901, 906–07 (1971).
amids: Reshaping the Judicial System, 44

pretation, may be clear-cut, as with some precepts of property, contract or tort law, or it may involve broad principles subject to disparate analyses. Reasoned elaboration should support the application of the precepts, so found and so interpreted, to the facts at hand. It may be useful to recall what Jerome Frank has observed:

> It is sometimes said that part of the judge's function is to pick out the relevant facts. Not infrequently this means that in writing his opinion he stresses (to himself as well as to those who will read the opinion) those facts which are relevant to his conclusion—in other words, he unconsciously selects those facts which, in combination with the rules of law which he considers to be pertinent, will make "logical" his decision. A judge, eager to give a decision which will square with his sense of what is fair, but unwilling to break with the traditional rules, will often view the evidence in such a way that the "facts reported by him," combined with those traditional rules, will justify the result which he announces.
>
> If this were done deliberately, one might call it dishonest, but one should remember that with judges this process is usually unconscious and that, however unwise it may be, upright men in other fields employ it, and sometimes knowingly.[1]

The judicial function may be viewed also from the perspective of the relations between logical propositions. Thus, steps one and two, selecting and interpreting the legal precept, become the major premise of the logical categorical syllogism. Step three, applying the selected and interpreted legal precept, appears as the minor premise. Accordingly, if one accepts the value judgment inherent in the major premise and if the minor premise is valid, then, theoretically, one should accept the conclusion. But we know that it is not always that neat, for the reverse process often takes place. One may accept a conclusion as a valid legal norm and seek to use it as a precedent, and purposely omit the major and minor premises (the logicians call such omissions "enthymemes"). This conclusion may be considered as a precedent but, lacking logical support, it is merely judicial fiat and will not be considered as a precedent with a strong bite. In the words of Karl Llewellyn, "Where stops the reason, there stops the rule," the old common law maxim of *cessante ratione legis, cessat et ipsa legit.*

Legal reasoning is subject to more scrutiny than any aspect of the judicial process. Forming the very fiber of argument and persuasion, it is the heart of the written brief, the essence of the process of justification. It constitutes the foundation of the case system by which law students are trained. Criticism of the "reasoning" of courts seems, at times, to form the *raison d'etre* for many law review publications. Yet in these publications there is little analysis of reasoning *qua* reasoning. Often an alleged attack on the "reasoning" of a court is really a disagreement with the value judgment implicit in the court's choice of a

---

1. J. Frank, Law and the Modern Mind 134–35 (1930).

major premise—a disagreement with the selection and interpretation of the legal precept. This difference is actually a quarrel with the value judgment that accepted a particular legal norm rather than a disaffection with the reasoning process. Criticism of court opinions would be more professional, briefs more clear, points of friction between litigants earlier identified and accommodated with more fairness and durability, if resort to the cosmos of "reasoning" were minimized, and attention directed instead to the precise components of that cosmos. It is not too much to ask whether one disagrees with the choice of the "authoritative starting point" and, if so, why; or whether the quarrel is with formal correctness of the syllogism used and, if so, where. It is not too much to ask if it is contended that facts in the minor premise are not properly subsumed in the major, or the conclusion lacks elements common to the major and minor premises.

From the trial memoranda or briefs submitted by counsel, or from experience and independent research, judges begin the process of justification by making a value judgment in the form of a choice. They select from competing legal precepts or competing analogies or a putative inductive generalization as presented by counsel in the adversary process. Often, however, these suggestions offered by counsel are inadequate or inappropriate. Professor Herbert Wechsler warns that often there is no choice. Often it is for the judge to formulate a rule of law because no rule or principle appears visible for the choosing. Moreover, he cautions that this formulation must be fortified by persuasive reasoning.[2]

Two guidelines may aid both the choice or the formulation and its ultimate acceptance: the judge should avoid arbitrary or aleatory choices and the judge has a duty of "reasoned elaboration in law-finding." Julius Stone says this is necessary so that the choice seems to the entire legal profession, "if not right, then as right as possible. The duty of elaboration indicates that reasons cannot be merely ritualistic formulae or diversionary sleight of hand." [3]

Because a value judgment inheres in finding the law, how can a judge arrive at this threshold decision yet avoid being arbitrary? Sometimes the exercise of the value judgment involves forthright line-drawing. The Supreme Court acknowledged this in 1979 in deciding that although a six-person jury satisfied the Sixth and Fourteenth Amendments, a jury of five did not: "[W]e do not pretend the ability to discern *a priori* a bright line below which the number of jurors participating in the trial or in the verdict would not permit the jury to function in the manner required by our prior cases ... [, but] it is inevitable that lines must be drawn somewhere.... This line-drawing process, 'although essential, cannot be wholly satisfactory, for it requires attaching different consequences to events which, when they lie near the line, actually

2. H. Wechsler, Toward Neutral Principles of Constitutional Law: Principles, Politics and Fundamental Law 10 (1961).

3. J. Stone, *Man and Machine in the Search for Justice,* 16 Stan.L.Rev. 515 (1964).

differ very little.' " [4]   Roger Traynor reminded us that "one entrusted with decision, traditionally above base prejudices, must also rise above the vanity of stubborn preconceptions, sometimes euphemistically called the courage of one's convictions. He knows well enough that he must severely discount his own predilections, of however high grade he regards them, which is to say he must bring to his intellectual labors a cleansing doubt of his omniscience, indeed even of his perception." [5]

ROSCOE POUND, THE JUDICIAL PROCESS IN ACTION

* Analysis of the judicial process ... distinguishes as the functions which are involved in the decision of a case according to law: (1) Finding the facts, i.e. ascertaining the state of facts to which legal precepts are to be applied in order to reach a determination; (2) finding the law, i.e. ascertaining the legal precept or precepts applicable to the facts found; (3) interpreting the precept or precepts to be applied, i.e. ascertaining their meaning by genuine interpretation, and (4) applying the precept or precepts so found and interpreted to the case in hand.

† Supposing the facts to have been ascertained, decision of a controversy according to law involves (1) selection of the legal material on which to ground the decision, or as we commonly say, finding the law; (2) development of the grounds of decision from the material selected, or interpretation in the stricter sense of that term; (3) application of the abstract grounds of decision to the facts of the case. The first may consist merely in laying hold of a prescribed text of code or statute, or of a definite, prescribed, traditional rule; in which case it remains only to determine the meaning of the legal precept,** with reference to the state of facts in hand, and to apply it to those facts. It is the strength of judicial administration of justice today that in the general run of causes that have to do with our economic life this is all that is called for, or so nearly all, that the main course of judicial decision may be predicted with substantial accuracy. But it happens frequently that the first process involves choice among competing texts or choice from among competing analogies so that the texts or rules must be interpreted—that is, must be developed tentatively with reference to the facts before the court—in order that intelligent selection may be made. Often such

---

4. Burch v. Louisiana, 441 U.S. 130, 137–38 (1979) (quoting Duncan v. Louisiana, 391 U.S. 145, 161 (1968)).

5. R. Traynor, *Reasoning in a Circle of Law,* 56 Va.L.Rev. 739, 750–51 (1970).

* 4 R. Pound, Jurisprudence 5 (1959). Reprinted by permission.

† Pound, *The Theory of Judicial Decision,* 36 Harv.L.Rev. 940, 945–46, 951 (1923). Copyright © 1923 by The Harvard Law Review Association. Reprinted by permission.

** Categorizing "legal precepts", Pound refers to "five types [of precepts] in that part of the authoritative materials in which, by use of the received technique and on a background of the received ideals, the judges are to find the grounds of decision." His five types are: (1) rules (in the narrower sense), (2) principles, (3) conceptions, (4) doctrines, and (5) standards. Pound, *Hierarchy of Sources and Forms in Different Systems of Law,* 7 Tul.L.Rev. 475, 482 (1933).

interpretation shows that no existing rule is adequate to a just decision and it becomes necessary to formulate the ground of decision for the given facts for the first time. The proposition so formulated may, as with us, or may not, as with the civilian, become binding for like cases in the future. In any event this process has gone on and still goes on in all systems of law, no matter what their form, and no matter how completely in their juristic theory they limit the function of adjudication to mechanical application of authoritatively given precepts.

. . . .

. . . Frequently application of the legal precept, as found and interpreted, is intuitive. This is conspicuous when a court of equity judges the conduct of a fiduciary, or exercises its discretion in enforcing specific performance, or passes upon a hard bargain, or where a court sitting without a jury determines a question of negligence. However repugnant to our nineteenth century notions it may be to think of anything anywhere in the judicial administration of justice as proceeding otherwise than on rule and logic, we cannot conceal from ourselves that in at least three respects the trained intuition of the judge does play an important role in the judicial process. One is in the selection of grounds of decision—in finding the legal materials that may be made both to furnish a legal ground of decision and to achieve justice in the concrete case. It is an everyday experience of those who study judicial decisions that the results are usually sound, whether the reasoning from which the results purport to flow is sound or not. The trained intuition of the judge continually leads him to right results for which he is puzzled to give unimpeachable legal reasons. Another place where the judge's intuition comes into play is in development of the grounds of decision, or interpretation. This is especially marked when it becomes necessary to apply the criterion of the intrinsic merit of the possible interpretations. A third is in application of the developed grounds of decision to the facts.

HARRY W. JONES, THE CONSTRUCTION OF LAW– MAKING JUDGMENTS: WHAT THE COURTS NEED MOST AND HOW THEY ARE TO GET IT *

Why is it so hard to tell, on a first reading of the court's opinion in a "serious business" case, that the controversy was originally a stand-off, as concerns formal legal doctrine, and was decided as it was chiefly in accordance with the court's views—informed judgment, intuitive impression or largely unconscious predilection, depending on judge or judges involved—of what is sound public policy? The source of the analytical difficulty is in the syllogistic form characteristic of judicial opinions, which operates, as often as not, to obscure policy decision in a wrapping

* H. Jones, *An Invitation to Jurisprudence,* 74 Colum.L.Rev. 1023, 1041–43 (1974). Reprinted by permission.

of essentially secondary doctrinal explanations. For courts must not only reach decisions, they also have to justify them, and, as John Dewey wrote a long time ago, there is always danger that the logic of justification will overpower and conceal the logic of search and inquiry by which a decision was actually arrived at.

.   .   .

So we are brought to the final and show-down question. If judges are to reach their decisions by way of a genuinely informed evaluation of the probable consequences of their action on the quality of human life in society, where do they get the data they need to accomplish that design? Courts, unlike legislative committees, hold no investigative hearings and have miniscule research staffs—a law clerk or two per judge, and these largely occupied with library research. If considerations of social advantage or disadvantage are to be brought clearly to judicial attention, it must be through the adversary system, yet the adversary system, in most cases, works far less effectively to present the social consequences dimension of a controversy than its more purely "legal," or legalistic, side.

.   .   .

One who would appraise the soundness of the social policy judgments that are, and have to be, made in the courts must consider also the actual and potential usefulness, to this end, of legal scholarship: the treatises, studies, casebooks and law reviews. Legal scholarship is less doctrine-bound, more nearly "law in society" oriented, than it was when I began law teaching in the late 1930's, but it is still not as helpful as it should be on "social consequences" issues. This is partly due to out-of-date but surviving notions that law is somehow an autonomous and self-contained discipline, partly due to the circumstance that what I call "efficacy research"—field studies of how legal precepts are actually working out in society—takes longer and costs incomparably more than analytical work in a law library.

Perhaps a new generation of legal scholars will come to the aid of the law and the courts in this respect. But somehow I doubt it. My impression, which again may be unfair, is that our younger, more "activist," law scholars are fully as infatuated with doctrines and concepts as we were in my day. The only visible change is that the concepts are different. When entirely new and quite prickly issues of public policy demand authoritative decision, the typical young law scholar, like most of us years ago, can find more final answers, more certain and revealed truth, in an obscure text from the Constitution than Rabbi Joshua ben Perahya could find in a passage from the Torah. Surely it is not that easy. The urgent need of the courts is for social facts, not super-refined doctrinal exegesis. Picasso could say *"Je ne cherche pas, je trouve,"* but lawyers and legal scholars are in a very different line of business.

When pressed with the question of where a judge is to get the social data he needs for instrumentally sound decisions, Judge Cardozo had only this answer: "[H]e must get his knowledge . . . from experience and study and reflection; in brief, from life itself." We smile at this, perhaps, yet there is great truth in the answer, because it underlines the vast importance of wise and disinterested judicial selection; the judge-made law can never be much better than the judges who make it. But a more socially imaginative style of appellate advocacy and a legal scholarship better balanced between the law library and the social out-of-doors could help make good judges better at weighing social alternatives and the inevitable poor judges a little better at it than they would otherwise be. That is the only way of insuring, in the long run of things, that the courts—stumbling occasionally, as we all do—will make their full potential contribution towards realization of law's social ends-in-view.

NOTE

Do you understand Professor Jones to be saying that those who announced the dawn of the Age of Realism turned out to be heralding simply a neo-mechanical jurisprudence?

OLIVER RUNDELL, *The Judge as Legislator*, 26 U.Kan.City L.Rev. 1, 7–9 (1958) *: "The judge then is never free, but rarely without choice. Within the range of choice where shall he find the solutions to his problems? The answer must be, where he may. There is no field of learning, no mode of reasoning closed to him. To perform at the highest level he must have them all at his command. To perform at an acceptable level he must be receptive to all sources of learning and modes of thought available to him. Judges have been wise with little learning, and foolish with much; none has been wise without learning, and none has been among the wisest with little."

. . .

ALBERT TATE, JR., "POLICY" IN JUDICIAL DECISIONS **

Although a great preponderance of an appellate judge's caseload—perhaps 90 or 95% or more—involves routine application of precedent and word-logic, fairly soon in the life of the new judge the moment comes when he realizes that there are some cases in which he (or no one) can find "the" law—that is, legislative enactments or sufficiently related decisions by his own or other courts that definitely indicate which of two

* Reprinted by permission.   ** 20 La.L.Rev. 62, 62–63, 69–71 (1959).
Reprinted by permission.

contrary reasonable positions should have favorable judgment upon the facts found to be correct. It is then for this new judge an interesting experience to have policy arguments re-emerge as a factor in the resolution of some legal controversies.

Suppose, for instance, he finds that his own court or the reported decisions of the other courts of his state have never considered the question now before him, but that in other jurisdictions the various lines of jurisprudence provide two or more opposing but equally logical resolutions of the issue. What should the judge do then? Should he follow the decisions of the states closest to him? Of the greater number of states? Does he flip a coin? Should he count the number of cases or of pages in the opposing briefs, and decide in favor of the party with the more numerous citations or pages? Should he instead rest his decision on some apt excerpt from some decision, even though in the context of its own facts it is completely inappropriate to the present legal question?

No. I think he properly should decide on the basis of what is best for the community as a precedent and of what impresses him as the fair solution of the question for the parties concerned: that is, on the basis of policy considerations.

NOTE

In difficult cases, Tate says the judge "should decide on the basis of what is best for the community as a precedent and of what impresses him as the fair solution of the question for the parties concerned...." If these factors compete, which should control? Why? Does it make a difference if the issue is one of private or public law?

HARRY W. JONES, "REASON IS BUT CHOOSING" *

"Reason is but choosing." These key words in Milton's *Areopagitica* have particular force in relation to those decisional situations in which the judge or the practicing lawyer finds little guidance in established legal doctrine and yet must choose between alternative courses of action that will affect profoundly the lives of other people. Does someone ask, at this point, whether that area of inescapable choice is not closely bounded in a mature legal system? Does a judge really decide major questions in a government that is "of laws and not of men?" Is it not more accurate to say that the authoritative rules of law, for which the judge is spokesman, decide his problems for him?

Legal realism's answer is that the syllogistic form characteristic of judicial opinions operates, in many instances, to obscure policy decisions in a wrapping of formal and essentially secondary explanations. A statement of Holmes is again the classic one:

* Harry W. Jones, *Law and Morality in the Perspective of Legal Realism*, 61 Colum.L.Rev. 799, 802–803 (1961). Reprinted by permission.

> Behind the logical form lies a judgment as to the relative worth
> and importance of competing legislative grounds, often an inar-
> ticulate and unconscious judgment, it is true, and yet the very
> root and nerve of the whole proceeding. You can give any
> conclusion a logical form. You always can imply a condition in
> a contract. But why do you imply it? [15]

Every lawyer of competence knows this; he is a legal realist in his
practice, however passionately he may disapprove of legal realism as an
explicit legal philosophy.

To limit the range of possible disagreement, I will not take an
extreme realist position in this brief but necessary analysis of the
common law judicial process. I am not saying that the judge is undirect-
ed, uncontrolled by the precedents and statutes, in all the cases before
him, or even in most of them. Many, perhaps most, of the controversies
that reach the courts can be decided without much more than a reference to existing rules. Some judges and lawyers of experience will say
that at least three-fourths of the cases that come to court leave the judge
no room, no leeway, for alternative decision.[16] I would set the figure far
lower, but that is not relevant to our present inquiry. On any account of
the judicial process, there is a substantial incidence of cases that can be
decided, and justified with all traditional common law proprieties, either
way. Whatever the incidence may be—a fifth, a fourth, a third—it is
indisputable that the work of the judge involves the inescapability of
choice and so of responsibility for externally uncontrolled decisions.

Great judges have been peculiarly sensitive to the demand of decisional responsibility in the hard or unprovided-for case. Cardozo,
Holmes's only equal as an American common law judge, had this to say:

> It is when the colors do not match, when the references in the
> index fail, when there is no decisive precedent, that the serious
> business of the judge begins.[17]

Is it not manifest that the area of the judge's serious business is the area
most worth studying to reveal the moral dimension of judicial action? If
the judge, whatever his metaphysical views, takes his moral convictions
seriously, they will be relevant, above all, to his serious business.

ORE IN PUBLISHED OPINIONS

**Dividing our process of decision, in the Poundian formula-
tion, into the three steps—finding the law, interpreting the legal
material selected, and applying the resulting legal precept to the**

15. *Path of the Law,* 10 Harv.L.Rev.
457, 466 (1897); in Holmes, Collected Legal
Papers at 181.

16. Cardozo's estimate is surprising.
"Nine tenths, perhaps more, of the cases
that come before a court are predetermined—predetermined in the sense that
they are predestined—their fate preestab-

lished by inevitable laws that follow them
from birth to death." The Growth of the
Law 60 (1924). But, to Cardozo, the unpre-
determined tenth make up the judge's "serious business." The Nature of the Judicial
Process 21 (1921).

17. *Ibid.*

facts—we now look to a sample of excerpts from recorded opinions. It bears emphasis that the following cases involve a choice between rival legal precepts, succinctly stated by the opinion writer. These are the easier examples, because the inventory of choices are limited and are uncomplicated to describe. But "finding the law" often involves more than merely choosing. It may involve nothing more than a selection among fixed precepts to see if the facts make a fit, like determining if the requirements of a conveyance have been met. Often it involves selection from competing analogies, urged by the respective parties as the proper ground for decision. Or it may involve selection by logical development of principles by inductive generalization. Or, as we have seen in vigorous extensions of constitutional law, it may call for selection from outside the legal systems—from contemporary community moral values, from comparative law or from economics.

Note also that these excerpts are culled from orientation paragraphs of the several opinions. By setting forth early in the opinion the precise issue to be decided, the skilled opinion writer immediate furnishes the reader with a statement of the main topic of the statement of reasons.

———

This appeal requires us to decide if a sufficient quantum of admissible evidence was presented at trial to establish a prima facie case of negligence. We determine that plaintiff-appellee Aloe Coal Company did not present sufficient evidence of causation to submit its negligence claim to the jury.

We also visit again the issue that was before us in Pennsylvania Glass Sand Corp. v. Caterpillar Tractor Co., 652 F.2d 1165 (3d Cir.1981): whether Pennsylvania courts would permit a purchaser of industrial equipment to bring a tort action against the manufacturer for damages to the product caused by a sudden fire.

When the damages issue was here before we recognized that Pennsylvania had not yet settled the question of whether injury to an allegedly defective product itself was compensable in tort. We identified the majority rule, set forth in Seely v. White Motor Co., 63 Cal.2d 9, 45 Cal.Rptr. 17, 403 P.2d 145 (1965), which seeks to preserve a proper role for the law of warranty by precluding tort liability if a defective product injures only itself, causing purely economic loss. The decision in Santor v. A. & M. Karagheusian, Inc., 44 N.J. 52, 207 A.2d 305 (1965), embodies the minority approach. That case held that a manufacturer's duty to make nondefective products encompasses injury to the product itself, whether or not the defect creates an unreasonable risk of harm. In *Pennsylvania Glass Sand,* our court fashioned an intermediate position by declaring that whether product damages are classified as economic loss, and therefore not recoverable in tort but only under contract precepts, depends on the nature of the defect, the type of risk, and the manner in which the injury arose.

In the context of admiralty law, the Supreme Court in East River S.S. Corp. v. Transamerica Delaval, Inc., 476 U.S. 858, 106 S.Ct. 2295, 90 L.Ed.2d 865 (1986), specifically rejected our *Pennsylvania Glass Sand* position. We now predict that Pennsylvania courts, although not bound to do so, would nevertheless adopt as state law the Supreme Court's reasoning in *East River*.

––––––

The Commonwealth of Pennsylvania finds itself between a rock and a hard place. A consent decree entered in August 1978 by the federal court commands it to implement a vehicle emission inspection and maintenance program. At the same time, its own state court system by an order dated January 9, 1984, enjoins it from carrying out the federal decree. The January Pennsylvania court order implemented a decision by that state's supreme court determining that the parties to the federal consent decree lacked the authority to consent to establishing and implementing an auto emissions inspection program and ordered that "an injunction should issue enjoining [the state] from performing the terms and conditions of the consent decree." Scanlon v. Commonwealth of Pennsylvania, 502 Pa. 577, 590, 467 A.2d 1108, 1115 (1983).

––––––

Thus we face a difficult *Erie*-doctrine choice. We must choose between maintaining important internal administrative and equitable powers of our courts at the cost of disuniformity of result between state and federal diversity courts, or uniformity at the cost of giving up part of our self-regulatory powers. It is fashionable to call a difficult choice between important objectives a "balancing" test, but we decline to resort to this metaphor. It is simply a matter of choice, and choose we must.

We hold that the interests of the federal forum in self-regulation, in administrative independence, and in self-management are more important than the disruption of uniformity created by applying federal *forum non conveniens* in diversity cases. We are far down this road already, having made a series of similar choices in cases such as Boeing Co. v. Shipman and its progeny. We think those choices were correct. We therefore hold that a federal court sitting in a diversity action is required to apply the federal law of *forum non conveniens* when addressing motions to dismiss a plaintiff's case to a foreign forum.

––––––

The question for decision is whether the captain of a merchant ship violated applicable maritime law when he buried at sea a seaman who died of a heart attack on the return trip of the vessel eight days from its next port-of-call. After seaman James Floyd died, the captain conducted a burial-at-sea ritual. Maria Floyd, the seaman's daughter, for herself, as executrix of her father's estate, and for the next-of-kin, sued the vessel's owner for improperly disposing of her father's body. The district court granted summary judgment in favor of Lykes Bros. Steamship Company. Maria Floyd has appealed. We will affirm.

. . .

On appeal, Floyd contends that state tort law has established that the spouse or next-of-kin is entitled to possession of a body for the purpose of arranging for final disposition of the remains, *see, e.g.,* Blanchard v. Brawley, 75 So.2d 891, 893 (La.Ct.App.1954), and that violation of the right of possession and burial is an actionable tort. *See, e.g.,* Papieves v. Lawrence, 437 Pa. 373, 263 A.2d 118, 120 (1970). She argues that this state law tort precept should be incorporated into general maritime law. She says that currently recognized maritime authority deems burial at sea anachronistic and improper when the next-of-kin are not notified in advance.

Lykes responds that this case is not governed by state tort concepts, but by federal maritime law. Relying on Brambir v. Cunard White Star Ltd., 37 F.Supp. 906 (S.D.N.Y.1940), *aff'd mem.,* 119 F.2d 419 (2d Cir.1941), Lykes argues that maritime law does not provide a cause of action for burial at sea.

———

We are called upon here to resolve a conflict of law that lays upon the probate of an estate. The conflict is between the law of this Commonwealth and that of our sister, the garden state of New Jersey. The controversy is directly stated: until 1978, the state of New Jersey denied an attesting witness to a will any benefit under that will. Pennsylvania did not. Nancy M. Janney, a Pennsylvania domiciliary, executed a will leaving her entire estate to her sister, Carolyn Case. Ms. Case was named executrix and subscribed as one of two attesting witnesses. The estate consisted of various assets situated in Pennsylvania, and realty located in New Jersey. During the course of administration, the property was sold. Distribution of the proceeds of the sale of that real property, the subject matter here, was excepted to by intestate heirs in the Orphans Court of Monroe County, Pennsylvania. They excepted alleging that since the testatrix died in 1974, the law then extant in the state of New Jersey denied an attesting witness benefit under the will.

The exceptions were sustained, and an intestacy as to the proceeds of the New Jersey property was declared. Ms. Case, executrix and beneficiary, appeals. We reverse.

Section 4

INTERPRETING THE LEGAL PRECEPT

OVERVIEW

As value judgments inhere in finding or choosing the law, so do they also loom large in interpreting the legal precept selected. Interpretation may occur after choosing the precept or simultaneously with the choice. Some rules or principles—particularly in orthodox fields of static law, such as contract or property law and most statutes—admit to but one, clear interpretation. In other sectors of the law, such as constitutional law, principles are "rubbery," possessed of what H.L.A. Hart calls "open texture," and subject to disparate interpretations.

As with the choice of a precept, the interpreting process can be intellectually disinterested. Usually, however, some degree of orientation is present that leads to a desired result, albeit a rational and respectable one. As with the choice or formulation, reasoned elaboration, not naked conclusion, should support judicial justifications of interpretations. Absent such elaboration, determining whether the ultimate decision is "as right as possible" or "good" is a difficult, if not impossible, task.

Statutory construction is a chief example of the interpreting process, and various techniques have evolved and continue to evolve to assist in the interpreting process. We have detailed this in Chapter II, Section 3, Statutory Construction.

As in statutes, however, interpreting case law and legal documents is the subject of various methodologies. Comparison of the material facts of the cases must be made to determine controlling precedents—as discussed in Chapter III, The Doctrine of Precedent—and the presence of proper analogies under the teachings of inductive reasoning—as set forth in Chapter IV, Section 2, Use of Logic.

The meaning of legal instruments, especially contracts, brings into play two related but distinct concepts, with different standards of appellate review: "contract interpretation" and "contract construction." [1] The distinction between interpretation and construction is not always easy. Professor Corbin described the distinction:

> By "interpretation of language" we determine what ideas that language induces in other persons. By "construction of the contract," as that term will be used here, we determine its legal operation—its effect upon the action of courts and administrative officials. If we make this distinction, then the construction of a contract starts with the interpretation of its language but does not end with it; while the process of interpretation stops wholly short of a determination of the legal relations of the

---

1. See John F. Harkins Co., Inc. v. Waldinger Corp., 796 F.2d 657 (3d Cir.1986).

parties. When a court gives a construction to the contract as that is affected by events subsequent to its making and not foreseen by the parties, it is departing very far from mere interpretation of their symbols of expression, although even then it may claim somewhat erroneously to be giving effect to the "intention" of the parties.[2]

Professor Patterson makes the same point:

Construction, which may be usefully distinguished from interpretation, is a process by which legal consequences are made to follow from the terms of the contract and its more or less immediate context, and from a legal policy or policies that are applicable to the situation.[3]

Thus we often are presented with the question of "interpreting the fact" of language and the related question of "interpreting law," or as the nice distinction appears in the law of contracts, "construction," of the legal aspects of the instrument. This brings into play Pound's definition of legal rules: "These are precepts attaching a definite detailed legal consequence to a definite, detailed state of facts." In construing, explaining or comprehending case law, it does make a difference whether one is describing the factual or legal component of the legal precept.

———

ERWIN N. GRISWOLD, THE JUDICIAL PROCESS *

If the meaning of the First Amendment cannot be defined from the language itself, how far is it appropriate to extend its reach by a broad interpretation? When one frees himself from literalism, the question, of course, is where to stop. And this is the area where the problem of activism arises.

. . .

Other extensions can be found. There is an opinion in a case that says—though I am not sure that it decides—that the First Amendment protects the right to possess printed materials, and thus protects the right of a man to keep pornography in his own home. Again, I do not mind the practical result; I just cannot find it in the Constitution. Now it is being contended in a current case that if a man can keep pornography in his home, then he must be able to bring it to his home, with the consequence that a long-standing Act of Congress forbidding the importation of obscene material is unconstitutional as long as the importer says that he is bringing it in for his personal use. We will have to wait

---

2. 3 Corbin, Corbin on Contracts § 534 at 9 (1960).

3. Patterson, *The Interpretation and Construction of Contracts,* 64 Colum.L.Rev. 833, 835 (1964).

* 31 Fed.B.J. 309, 315, 317 (1972). Reprinted by permission.

for the answer on that.** Whatever the decision, it still remains extremely difficult to see how the question can be brought within a rational and judicially appropriate construction of anything that is written in the Constitution. The danger here, as elsewhere, is that a sort of decisional leapfrogging takes over as a principle expands: the first decision is distilled from the language of the Constitution, but the next expansion begins from the reasoning of the last decision, and so on down the line until we reach a point where the words of the Constitution are so far in the background that they are virtually ignored. In the end we may be left with a rationale that comes to little more than, "Well, it really is a good idea. We want a free society where all of these things can be done and we want to keep the Government off the backs of the people." There are governmental processes for bringing such results about, but it is hard to think that such adumbrations of the Constitution are an appropriate exercise of judicial power.

NOTE

In the same vein, Judge Henry J. Friendly has warned against "the domino method of constitutional adjudication ... wherein every explanatory statement in a previous opinion is made the basis for extension to a wholly different situation." Friendly, *The Bill of Rights as a Code of Criminal Procedure,* 53 Calif.L.Rev. 929, 950 (1965).

But see Amsterdam, *Perspectives on the Fourth Amendment,* 58 Minn.L.Rev. 349, 351 (1974).

ROSCOE POUND, THE THEORY OF JUDICIAL DECISION *

In the second step in decision, namely, development of the grounds of decision from the material selected, [or interpretation in the stricter sense of the term,] the usual process is one of traditional legal reasoning, scholastic down to the seventeenth century, rationalist more and more in the seventeenth and eighteenth centuries, and tending to be deductive on a metaphysical basis in the nineteenth century. But in new and difficult cases this merges in, and in all cases is influenced by, current moral, political and social ideas, especially fixed pictures of the end of law and of an ideal legal and social order, by reference to which, consciously or subconsciously, the tribunal determines how far possible interpretations will yield a just result in the individual cause and judges of the intrinsic merit of the different developments of the legal materials potentially applicable which are urged by the contending parties. Along with these we must put an intuition of what will achieve justice in action and what will not, expressing the experience of the magistrate both as

** [Ed.: The answer was that the statute is constitutional. United States v. Thirty–Seven Photographs, 402 U.S. 363 (1971).]

* 36 Harv.L.Rev. 940, 949–50 (1923). Copyright © 1923 by The Harvard Law Review Association. Reprinted by permission.

lawyer and as judge. The traditional legal reasoning represents the experience of generations of judges in the past. It is in some sort a traditionally transmitted judicial intuition founded in experience. But it has been given shape by philosophy. In our stage of strict law it was cast in a mold of scholasticism which gave it permanent shape. Rationalism in the seventeenth and eighteenth centuries and the metaphysical jurisprudence of the nineteenth century affected its substance more than its form. It is at its best as a technique of developing the grounds of judicial decision from materials selected from reported judgments of the past. It is usually at its worst, except in simple cases, in developing the grounds of judicial decision on the basis of materials found in legislation. A theory of "the will of the lawmaker" taken over from the civilian who thought of a text of the Digest as the declared will of Justinian, and a traditional attitude toward legislation ... make judicial handling of statutes the least satisfactory part of the work of American tribunals.

HERBERT WECHSLER, TOWARD NEUTRAL PRINCIPLES OF CONSTITUTIONAL LAW *

Does not the special duty of the courts to judge by neutral principles addressed to all the issues make it inapposite to contend, as Judge Hand does, that no court can review the legislative choice—by any standard other than a fixed "historical meaning" of constitutional provisions—without becoming "a third legislative chamber"? Is there not, in short, a vital difference between legislative freedom to appraise the gains and losses in projected measures and the kind of principled appraisal, in respect of values that can reasonably be asserted to have constitutional dimension, that alone is in the province of the courts? Does not the difference yield a middle ground between a judicial House of Lords and the abandonment of any limitation on the other branches—a middle ground consisting of judicial action that embodies what are surely the main qualities of law, its generality and its neutrality? This must, it seems to me, have been in Mr. Justice Jackson's mind when in his chapter on the Supreme Court "as a political institution" he wrote in words that I find stirring, "Liberty is not the mere absence of restraint, it is not a spontaneous product of majority rule, it is not achieved merely by lifting underprivileged classes to power, nor is it the inevitable by-product of technological expansion. It is achieved only by a rule of law." Is it not also what Mr. Justice Frankfurter must mean in calling upon judges for "allegiance to nothing except the effort, amid tangled words and limited insights, to find the path through precedent, through policy, through history, to the best judgment that fallible creatures can reach in that most difficult of all tasks: the achievement of justice between man and man, between man and state, through reason called law"?

* Principles, Politics and Fundamental Law 10, 15–28, 43–47 (1961). Excerpted by permission of the author and publishers of Principles, Politics and Fundamental Law by Herbert Wechsler, Cambridge, Mass.: Harvard University Press, Copyright © 1961 by the President and Fellows of Harvard College.

You will not understand my emphasis upon the role of reason and of principle in the judicial, as distinguished from the legislative or executive, appraisal of conflicting values to imply that I depreciate the duty of fidelity to the text of the Constitution, when its words may be decisive—though I would certainly remind you of the caution stated by Chief Justice Hughes: "Behind the words of the constitutional provisions are postulates which limit and control." Nor will you take me to deny that history has weight in the elucidation of the text, though it is surely subtle business to appraise it as a guide. Nor will you even think that I deem precedent without importance, for we surely must agree with Holmes that "imitation of the past, until we have a clear reason for change, no more needs justification than appetite." But after all, it was Chief Justice Taney who declared his willingness "that it be regarded hereafter as the law of this court, that its opinion upon the construction of the Constitution is always open to discussion when it is supposed to have been founded in error, and that its judicial authority should hereafter depend altogether on the force of the reasoning by which it is supported." Would any of us have it otherwise, given the nature of the problems that confront the courts?

Let me repeat what I have thus far tried to say. The courts have both the title and the duty when a case is properly before them to review the actions of the other branches in the light of constitutional provisions, even though the action involves value choices, as invariably action does. In doing so, however, they are bound to function otherwise than as a naked power organ; they participate as courts of law. This calls for facing how determinations of this kind can be asserted to have any legal quality. The answer, I suggest, inheres primarily in that they are—or are obliged to be—entirely principled. A principled decision, in the sense I have in mind, is one that rests on reasons with respect to all the issues in the case, reasons that in their generality and their neutrality transcend any immediate result that is involved. When no sufficient reasons of this kind can be assigned for overturning value choices of the other branches of the Government or of a state, those choices must, of course, survive. Otherwise as Holmes said in his first opinion for the Court, "a constitution, instead of embodying only relatively fundamental rules of right, as generally understood by all English-speaking communities, would become the partisan of a particular set of ethical or economical opinions ...".

The virtue or demerit of a judgment turns, therefore, entirely on the reasons that support it and their adequacy to maintain any choice of values it decrees, or, it is vital that we add, to maintain the rejection of a claim that any given choice should be decreed. The critic's role, as T.R. Powell showed throughout so many fruitful years, is the sustained, disinterested, merciless examination of the reasons that the courts advance, measured by standards of the kind I have attempted to describe. I wish that more of us today could imitate his dedication to that task.

HERBERT WECHSLER, TOWARD NEUTRAL
PRINCIPLES: REVISITED (1975) *

[Professor Wechsler appeared on a panel before a conference of federal appellate judges at the Federal Judicial Center, Washington, D.C. on March 12, 1975. He was asked to comment on his paper, *Toward Neutral Principles of Constitutional Law,* which had been delivered on April 7, 1959 as the Oliver Wendell Holmes Lecture at the Harvard Law School. Part of his response follows.]

Well, I'm older now, and I hope I may be slightly wiser, but I must say that restatement of the thesis that I had taken does not lead me to repent at all. I do recognize that there are problems, as there are bound to be in any such delineation. How general must supporting reasons be to a decision to be adequately principled? What does "neutral" add to "general" or, indeed, "general" to "principle" as a description of the governing criteria?

The only answer I can honestly make is that I am not entirely sure. I used the words that I hoped would convey an attitude, a mood. I did not think that I was drafting an invention. The central thought is surely that the principle once formulated must be tested by the adequacy of its derivation from its sources and its implications with respect to other situations that the principle, if evenly applied, will comprehend. Unless those implications are acceptable the principle surely must be reformulated or withdrawn. How many other situations, you may ask, must be considered? At least those, I would insist, that we can now imagine or foresee, granting, of course, that all of us, including even the courts, wear blinkers of some kind.

Does this mean anything concrete? This, I suppose is where I got into my troubles because I did fail an obligation to give some illustrations of judicial action that I considered to be questionable in the terms that I was trying to put forth. The easiest case—in a sense, to challenge, easy, because from my point of view it preceded the Warren court, because it was the unanimous opinion and because it laid down a rule with which I myself was very deeply sympathetic and that I hoped the state courts, having general authority over the law of contracts in their jurisdiction or the state legislature similarly empowered, would adopt— was the restrictive covenant case [Shelley v. Kraemer, 334 U.S. 1 (1948).] There, you may remember, all the opinion said was that this was a judgment of the state court, the court was an organ of the state, the covenant embodied a racial discrimination, therefore, its enforcement by the state court was racial discrimination by the state, patently and unquestionably forbidden by the Equal Protection Clause. The only difficulty with the principle is, of course, that it would abrogate a good part of the law of property, the law of wills, most private law which has good purpose if you permit individuals to make discriminations of all

* Transcript of Proceedings, March 12, 1975.

kinds with respect to the acquisition or distribution of property. And none of those other cases is dealt with in the opinion. And that of course is why it is an enigmatic judgment in the books as efforts to extend it had been made in the sit-in cases before the Act of Congress and in many other situations as well.

Another illustration on the state action problem comes from Justice Douglas who frequently reiterates the proposition that any licensed activity, licensed by the state, should be considered action of the state, or the action of any licensed body should be considered action of the state for purposes of the Fourteenth Amendment. The barber shop where you get your hair cut is functioning as an organ of the state authority when it cuts your hair. This is so patently an absurdity in relation to the Constitutional language, purpose, or conceivably desirable interpretation that one can hardly believe that it was put forth seriously—except for the number of instances in which it was repeated by the justice, but happily never embraced by the Court.

Pressure, however, is plainly there as one would speedily find if you went through the state action cases, as I suppose you must constantly be doing, as imagination conjures up new causes of action under [42 U.S.C.A. §] 1983. That's why the state action problem is both currently of great importance as well as delightfully challenging.

A philosopher summed the matter up for me in one short sentence. It goes this way: "Just as a factual composition is shown to be false if it implies a false statement, so also is a practical principle shown to be unacceptable if it leads to pragmatic inconsistencies or when it would require treating some given case in a way in which ex-hypothesis it may not be treated." This is, I suppose, the underlying type of logic which is full of moral philosophy, isn't it? One doesn't have to be a Kantian and as strict about it as that, if you recognize that this is the way we usually go about testing the rightness of actions when we undertake to test them seriously.

A court, in my submission, acts by fiat not by law unless its judgments meet this minimal criterion. But it is a minimal criterion and this is the final point which I'm going to make in explanation. If a judgment meets this minimal criterion, then one must face the harder question of its wisdom and its justice. A decision may, in short, be wholly principled and wrong. All I was saying is that it cannot be unprincipled and right.

THE RIGHTS' STUFF

A. Fundamental Rights

From 1887 to 1937, the Supreme Court used the equal protection and due process clauses to invalidate those forms of economic or social welfare legislation with which the justices were in fundamental disagreement.   Lochner v. New York[1] was the classic example.   The case concerned a New York law limiting bakery employees to a 60–hour work week.   The state legislature wanted to improve the lot of bakery workers by giving them shorter hours but the court would have none of it, concerned instead with "freedom of contract," an economic theory that was then fashionable among conservative intellectuals.   The state's restriction on working hours interfered with the precious liberty of workers to sell their labor to employers, although the fact was that it was employers, not workers, who were complaining about the law. Bakery workers probably felt that cutting back to 10 hours a day, six days a week increased their liberty, if anything.   But the Court did more than apply conservative economics.   It read them into the Constitution, and for this, Justice Oliver Wendell Holmes, Jr., took them to task in a famous dissent: "Some of these laws embody convictions or prejudices which judges are likely to share.   Some may not.   But a constitution is not intended to embody a particular economic theory. . . .   It is made for people of fundamentally differing views.[2]

Attempts to regulate working conditions for the improvement of public health and welfare were a prominent feature of President Franklin D. Roosevelt's New Deal.   The Court, however, stuck by its freedom-of-contract position.   By 1937, the practice of declaring New Deal legislation unconstitutional had become so rampant that Roosevelt launched a campaign to add seats to the Court, intending to appoint sympathetic justices until he had a majority that would leave his laws alone.   The court-packing plan failed, but the justices got the word. They backed down, a change of position sometimes referred to as "the switch in time that saved nine."[3]

From 1937 until the modern era, few statutes were declared unconstitutional.   From 1937 to the 1960's, the Court apparently discarded the concept that our constitution gave it legitimate power to invalidate legislative enactments simply because the justices believed the legislature acted unwisely.   But cracks in this philosophy began to appear. For example, in Griswold v. Connecticut, the Court said: "We do not sit as a super-legislature to determine the wisdom, need, and propriety of laws that touch economic problems, business affairs, or social conditions. This law [prohibiting physicians from prescribing contraceptive devices to married women] however, operates directly on an intimate relation of husband and wife, and their physician's role in one aspect of that relation.[4]   *Griswold* exemplified the era of using the equal protection clause, and to a more limited extent the due process clause, as the basis of declaring state and federal statutes null and void.

1.   198 U.S. 45 (1905).

2.   Id. at 75 (Holmes, J., dissenting).

3.   Chief Justice Charles Evans Hughes has another version suggesting that two older, more conservative justices had wanted to retire, but Congress had not provided for retirement benefits for Supreme Court justices like those possessed by other federal judges.   When Congress enacted the legislation in 1937 affecting such benefits, Justices Van Devanter and Sutherland resigned, thus giving Roosevelt two immediate vacancies to fill.   D.J. Danelski & J.S. Tulchin, The Autobiographical Notes of Charles Evans Hughes 302, 303 (1973).

4.   381 U.S. 479, 482 (1965).

In the post–1937 period, we have seen a dichotomy in the way the Court treats laws that are challenged on constitutional grounds. In the first category are legislative enactments pertaining to economic and social welfare. In the second category are enactments that either touch upon what the Court describes as "fundamental rights" or that classify people in a way deemed offensive to the equal protection clause in that they affront the notion that all people are equal before the law. The economic and social welfare legislative enactments in the first category will be upheld so long as they arguably relate to a legitimate function of government. Legislative enactments in the second category, however, will be subjected to "strict scrutiny" (those are the magic words) and upheld only if they are necessary to promote an extremely important or "compelling" end of government.

Although we have emphasized the necessity for "reasoned elaboration" to support court decisions, in these cases there is a maximum of value judgment if not judicial fact, and a minimum of ratiocination. This is an anomaly in the decisional process. Once the label is posted in the case, the issue is decided. The Court manufactured a "tool," a kind of judicial microscope with adjustable powers of magnification. Depending on the strength of the lens, the statute is either approved or rejected.

In our private lives, when we decide whether certain conduct is good or bad, we usually use the same test. We use the same tool, the same lens, the same magnification all the time. We do not like naughty children. We do not like drunken drivers. We do not like loud, vulgar people. We do not like people who steal our cars or break our windows or swipe our televisions, VCRs or car radios. To evaluate all of this, we use some kind of socially devised standard of conduct. We use an informal code of community morality to measure conduct that we do not like. The standard of conduct—give or take a little—tends to be uniform among average, law-abiding men and women. Whether it be wide-scale socialization or an innate sense, we seem to have a feel for what is right and wrong.

But when it comes to declaring acts of the legislature unconstitutional—when courts make the decision as to whether a particular statute is good or bad—a uniform measuring rod is not used. Courts do not use a lens of the same power to make the examination. Instead, they have fashioned separate methods to measure the statute in deciding whether it is constitutional. They use different tools to decide whether it is a go or a no-go, and one can not even begin to understand a court's decisions in affirmative action and abortion cases until one understands these different tools.

Depending upon the U.S. Supreme Court's preliminary evaluation of a certain constitutional right, the test that a given statute must pass is easy, moderate, or extremely hard. The Court uses three different tests. Put this in the context of any examination given in any university's law school or political science department. Imagine a system of grading, where the student writes an examination on the material covered in the course. The professors start to grade the papers, but they do not use a uniform grading system based on the correctness of the answer describing materials covered in the course. They do not grade A, B, or C depending on the accuracy or logical development of the answer, nor do they use a curve to grade on the relative class performance. Instead, the professors use a different measure depending on how important they think the subject matter is, question by question. The graders do not consider the difficulty of the question, but only their own notion of how important they think that particular area is. And on those questions that the professors classify as seriously important, the student will not get an "A." He or she will get an "F," no matter what the answer. This sounds strange, but that is what the Court has done with statutes that affect what it calls "fundamental" constitutional rights (or "suspect classifications") as we will describe in the following section. Let us turn to these three lenses that judges use to examine statutes. This is important, because unless one understands this, one cannot begin to understand the Court's decisions in certain important constitutional areas such as abortion and affirmative action.

The most intense test—the most powerful lens—is called strict scrutiny. Strict scrutiny means that the statute will be upheld only if it is necessary to promote a "compelling state interest" and is "narrowly tailored" to promote that interest. The critical point is that once the Court decides to use the test of strict scrutiny the statute rarely, if ever, passes constitutional muster. Nothing looks good when examined this closely. Hidden blemishes become visible and ugly. In this case, the test used almost always commands the answer: The statute flunks. This is the test used by the professor that automatically results in an "F." The second test is the rational basis test. The statute is upheld if it bears a reasonable relationship to a legitimate governmental interest. The rational basis test is used in examining the vast majority of the cases and almost always results in the statute being upheld. When the Court picks the weakest lens, almost everything looks good. The Court consequently finds that the statute rests upon some rational basis within the knowledge and experience of the legislators. The third test involves scrutiny that is somewhere between strict scrutiny and rational basis, and is called intermediate scrutiny or the middle-tier test: a statute viewed under this lens is upheld if it is substantially related to an important governmental objective. The cases in this area are a mixed bag.

This is all well and good, but how do the courts decide which test to use? They have said that all rights in the Constitution are not currency of equal value. There are ordinary rights and there are fundamental rights, and a right becomes fundamental only when it is so anointed by a majority of the Court.[5]

5. See, e.g., Dunn v. Blumstein, 405 U.S. 330 (1972) (voting); Shapiro v. Thompson, 394 U.S. 618 (1969) (interstate travel); San Antonio Independent School District v. Rodriguez, 411 U.S. 1, 35, n. 78 (1973) ("[T]he right to vote, *per se,* is not a constitutionally protected right, ... references to that right are simply shorthand

But here's the clincher: once the Court calls it fundamental, in the vast majority of cases we know in advance what the result will be. If the courts use strict scrutiny, the statute will fall, and down will come preamble, clauses and all. The standard of review is "strict" in theory and usually "fatal" in fact. The rights involved in Roe v. Wade, 410 U.S. 113 (1973) (abortion) were described as fundamental and state legislation did not survive. The rights in Bowers v. Hardwick, 478 U.S. 186 (1986) (Homosexual acts between consenting adults) were not described as fundamental. "Prescriptions against that conduct have ancient roots.... Sodomy was a criminal offense at common law and was forbidden by the laws of the original thirteen States when they ratified the Bill of Rights. In 1868, when the Fourteenth Amendment was ratified, all but five of the 37 in the Union had criminal sodomy laws. In fact until 1961, all 50 states outlawed sodomy ...") Measured by the rational basis test, the Georgia statute survived.

B.   Suspect Classifications

"The law in its majestic equality, forbids the rich as well as the poor to sleep under bridges, to beg in the streets, and to steal bread." Anatole France, The Red Lily.

"Once loose, the idea of Equality is not cabined."[1] "At the beginning of the 1960's, judicial intervention under the banner of equal protection was virtually unknown outside racial discrimination cases."[2] In the following years the "idea" has been given broad judicial expansion in matters affecting criminal trials, voting, interstate travel, alienage, and a host of social, economic and political interests. As the good genie has escaped from the bottle, the courts have made attempts at control, often giving specific orders for conduct, but more frequently, simply emitting imperative commands with explanations, often vague and sometimes reasoned, as to what the genie can and cannot do.

An instrument of control, unabashedly a method of the decisional process, (and similar to the separation of constitutional rights into fundamental and ordinary) has been devised by the Supreme Court—categorization. In all equal protection cases some classification has occurred. In some cases, the classification itself is designated as "suspect."[3] If the case involves fundamental rights or suspect classifications, state activity will be subject to strict judicial scrutiny, and will prevail only if justified by "compelling state interests."[4] State regula-

references to the protected right, implicit in our constitutional system, to participate in state elections on an equal basis with other qualified voters whenever the State has adopted an elective process.").

1. A. Cox, The Warren Court 6 (1968)

2. G. Gunther, The Supreme Court, 1971 Term—*Foreword: In Search of Evolving Doctrine on a Changing Court: A Model*

for a Newer Equal Protection, 86 Harv. L.Rev. 1, 8 (1972).

3. See, e.g., Graham v. Richardson, 403 U.S. 365 (1971) (alienage); Loving v. Virginia, 388 U.S. 1 (1967) (race); McLaughlin v. Florida, 379 U.S. 184 (1964) (race).

4. American Party of Texas v. White, 415 U.S. 767, 780 (1974) (primary elections).

tions bearing upon rights and classifications not so denominated are subject to less rigorous judicial scrutiny, and will pass muster if the purpose of the classification "has a fair and substantial relation to the object of the legislation, so that all persons similarly circumstanced shall be treated alike".[5]

Between these extremes of rational basis review and strict scrutiny lies a level of intermediate scrutiny, which generally has been applied to discriminatory classifications based on gender or illegitimacy.[6] To withstand intermediate scrutiny, a statutory classification must be substantially related to an important governmental objective. A deceptive simplicity envelops the major dichotomy between the rational basis test and strict scrutiny. The litmus test depends upon whether the right is or is not "fundamental" or whether the classification is or is not "suspect." Unfortunately, the preliminary determination—of what is or is not—must be made in a jurisprudential demilitarized zone. Because the various rights claimed to be infringed emanate from a sophisticated complex of sociology, philosophy, anthropology, history, biology, psychology, economics and politics, a set of objective standards for this critical determination is difficult to formulate.

In San Antonio Independent School District v. Rodriguez[7] the Court indicated that a fundamental right exists only if "explicitly or implicitly guaranteed by the Constitution." This formula helps, but leaves the difficulty of ascertaining implied "fundamental" rights. Similarly, the Court in *San Antonio* provided some guidance as to what are suspect classifications by referring to "the traditional indicia of suspectness: [a] class ... saddled with such disabilities, or subjected to such a history of purposeful unequal treatment or relegated to such a position of political powerlessness as to command extraordinary protection from the majoritarian political process."[8]

The developing law of equal protection also raises an ancillary problem. In formulating new definitions of constitutional infringements, the courts constitute the arbiters of the roles they play, the U.S. Supreme Court being the final arbiter. Thus, as Professor Charles Fried advises:

> The question inevitably arises—especially in the mind of one who disagrees: by what authority is this judgment made and imposed? And that question is a question of role, of limited competence against a systematic background. A court cannot avoid, therefore, justifying its judgment not only in terms of its inherent validity ..., but also in terms of its authority to decide finally this sort of case, in terms of a system which entrusts the

---

5. F.S. Royster Guano Co. v. Virginia, 253 U.S. 412, 415 (1920) (taxation of corporations.)

6. See Clark v. Jeter, 486 U.S. 456, 461 (1988) (collecting cases).

7. 411 U.S. 1, 33–34 (1973).

8. Id. at 18–25.

final though not the infallible decision of this dispute to this body.[9]

In making threshold value judgments in equal protection cases, the courts in effect address themselves to notions of competencies and allocation of decisional power. This is a necessary concomitant to the judicial resolution of conflicts between levels and branches of government.

Role allocation—that is, a conscious preliminary attention to the question whether the court is or is not the most appropriate decision maker for the particular issue—is probably the safest and fairest approach to a determination whether a challenged classification should be deemed "suspect," or a right infringed should be considered "fundamental." If the axe so falls, theoretically state action is still permitted and not absolutely proscribed; the practical effect in most cases, however, is to dislodge the state political and social hierarchy from making a value judgment on the classification. In the exercise of "strict judicial scrutiny" the Court seldom finds state action "necessary to promote a compelling state interest"; or that the legislative enactments have been sufficiently narrowly drawn.[10] As a result of the Supreme Court decisions, therefore, the state is virtually preempted from decisional roles in classification matters related to race,[11] speech,[12] voting,[13] privacy,[14] interstate travel,[15] and alienage or national origin [16] *unless* the state can prove that the classifications "are necessary to further *compelling* state interests." [17]

The strict scrutiny test legitimized substantive due process methodologies previously discredited in Lochner v. New York, because the reality was that the test was "strict in theory, but fatal in fact" [18] and, where the test was employed, few, if any, statutes or regulations passed constitutional muster. When affirmative action jurisprudence had run its course by the 1990's [19] the test had run its full circle. "Suspect

9. C. Fried, *Two Concepts of Interests: Some Reflection on the Supreme Court's Balancing Test,* 76 Harv.L.Rev. 755, 761 (1963).

10. Justice Douglas observed that "... [the Supreme] Court has not sustained a racial classification since the wartime cases of Korematsu v. United States, 323 U.S. 214 (1944), and Hirabayashi v. United States, 320 U.S. 81 (1943), involving curfews and relocations imposed upon Japanese–Americans." DeFunis v. Odegaard, 416 U.S. 312, 339 (1974) (Douglas, J., dissenting) (footnote omitted). Likewise, since the decision in Takahashi v. Fish and Game Comm'n, 334 U.S. 410 (1948), the Court has consistently struck down state classifications based upon alienage. See Sugarman v. Dougall, 413 U.S. 634 (1973); Graham v. Richardson, 403 U.S. 365 (1971).

11. Where the classification adversely affects a member of a racial group. See

Loving v. Virginia, supra; McLaughlin v. Florida; Bolling v. Sharpe, 347 U.S. 497 (1954).

12. Police Dep't of Chicago v. Mosely, 408 U.S. 92 (1972).

13. See Bullock v. Carter, 405 U.S. 134 (1972).

14. Skinner v. Oklahoma, 316 U.S. 535 (1942).

15. Memorial Hospital v. Maricopa County, 415 U.S. 250 (1974).

16. Graham v. Richardson, supra.

17. American Party of Texas v. White, 415 U.S. 767, 780 (1974) (emphasis supplied).

18. Gunther n. 2., at 8.

19. See Richmond v. J.A. Croson Co., 488 U.S. 469 (1989); Adarand Constructors, Inc. v. Pena, 115 S.Ct. 2097 (1995).

classification" now will be subject to strict scrutiny regardless of whether the purpose of the classification is benign or not.

Absent suspect classification or impingement of a fundamental right, the state is free to exercise a decisional role in matters relating to education,[20] housing,[21] welfare benefits,[22] taxation,[23] and economic regulation.[24] The only caveat is that the classification "must be reasonable, not arbitrary, and must rest upon some ground of difference having a fair and substantial relation to the object of the legislation, so that all persons similarly circumstanced shall be treated alike."[25]

Where a fundamental right or a suspect classification is not involved, the statute has the advantage of "the usual presumption of validity,"[26] In terms of allocation of burdens of proof, "[u]nder 'traditional' equal protection analysis, a legislative classification must be sustained unless it is 'patently arbitrary' and bears no rational relationship to a legitimate governmental interest."[27] These teachings reiterate the burden of proof allocation enunciated in Lindsley v. Natural Carbonic Gas Co.: "One who assails the classification in such a law must carry the burden of showing that it does not rest upon any reasonable basis, but is essentially arbitrary."[28]

C. Affirmative Action: The Full Circle

The fate of government-sponsored affirmative action legislation tested in the Supreme Court depended on the magnification power of the judicial microscope the Court used to examine it. Until 1995, a majority of the Court was content to use the rational basis or intermediate scrutiny test for so-called benign violations of the equal protection clause.

The beginning point of any inquiry into affirmative action is the equal protection clause of the Fourteenth Amendment: "No State shall ... deny to any person within its jurisdiction the equal protection of the laws." Thus, it is a violation of the Constitution to discriminate. Yet until 1994, in affirmative action cases, the same constitutional clause that demanded "thou shalt not discriminate" was interpreted to mean "discriminate if the discrimination is benign, that is, if a minority group is helped in the process." Justice O'Connor described the concept: "[A] public employer, consistent with the Constitution, may undertake an

20. San Antonio Independent School District v. Rodriguez, ante n. 7.

21. Lindsey v. Normet, 405 U.S. 56 (1972).

22. Jefferson v. Hackney, 406 U.S. 353 (1972); Dandridge v. Williams, 397 U.S. 471 (1970).

23. Lehnhausen v. Lake Shore Auto Parts Co., 410 U.S. 356 (1973).

24. McGowan v. Maryland, 366 U.S. 420 (1961).

25. F.S. Royster Guano Co. v. Virginia, 253 U.S. 412, 415 (1920).

26. San Antonio Independent School District v. Rodriguez, 411 U.S. at 16. See also McGowan v. Maryland, 366 U.S. 420, 425 (1961) ("State legislatures are presumed to have acted within their constitutional power.").

27. Frontiero v. Richardson, 411 U.S. 677, 683 (1973).

28. 220 U.S. 61, 78–79 (1911).

affirmative action program which is designed to further a legitimate remedial purpose and which implements that purpose by means that do not impose disproportionate harms on the interests, or unnecessarily trammel the rights, of innocent individuals directly and adversely affected by a plan's racial preference".[1]

The law had been in flux since the passage of the 1964 Civil Rights Acts, but it leaped to the headlines in Regents of University of California v. Bakke in 1978.[2] It had been in flux because the Supreme Court justices could not agree on what magnifying lens to use when testing the constitutionality of an affirmative action plan. The *Bakke* case involved a medical school admissions program that gave preference to minority students. Mr. Bakke was a white college student with the 3.4 G.P.A. and exceptionally high scores on the medical school boards. He was turned down. The school did admit minority students with 2.4 G.P.A.'s and lower board scores. In examining whether Mr. Bakke's constitutional rights had been violated, different justices used different tests and arrived at different conclusions.

Four justices—Burger, Stevens, Stewart and Rehnquist—thought the program was invalid but chose not to reach the constitutional issue. Four others—Brennan, Marshall, Blackmun and White—said that although this was a racial classification, and racial classifications ordinarily called for strict scrutiny, this program was designed to help minorities, so the Court should lower the power of the examining lens and use intermediate scrutiny—substantially related to an important governmental interest. Under this test, they found the program valid. The ninth and deciding vote was cast by Justice Powell, who said that a racial classification is a racial classification no matter whom it helps, so strict scrutiny was the appropriate test. And if strict scrutiny was used, that meant the plan had to fail, and the Board of Regents had to find another way of encouraging minority enrollment.

Two years later, in Fullilove v. Klutznick[3], the Court considered a federal statute providing that 10 percent of federally funded public works contracts had to go to minority-owned businesses. Admittedly this was a classification involving race, Justice Powell used the strict scrutiny test and determined that it passed muster, one of the few exceptions to the strict-in-theory-fatal-in-fact rule. Justices Rehnquist and Stewart also applied strict scrutiny, but said that the statute failed. Justices Brennan, Marshall and Blackmun used intermediate scrutiny and agreed with Justice Powell's result. Justices Burger and White joined this group, but for other reasons. Justice Stevens voted the other way for still other reasons. In case you lost count, the final vote was 6–3 in favor of constitutionality. This case illustrates that even when a majority of the justices agree, they still may disagree.

Six years later, in Wygant v. Jackson Board of Education, the Court examined a collective bargaining agreement that provided for teacher

---

1. Wygant v. Jackson Bd. of Educ., 476 U.S. 267, 287 (1986).

2. 438 U.S. 265 (1978).

3. 448 U.S. 448 (1980).

layoffs. Although layoffs usually follow the last-hired-first-fired rule (teachers with seniority keep their jobs), this particular agreement demanded that the school board retain minority teachers and fire white teachers regardless of seniority. The agreement was found to violate the equal protection clause. Justices Burger, Powell, Rehnquist and O'Connor applied strict scrutiny, and Justice White went along for reasons of his own. Then came the modern era.

In City of Richmond v. J.A. Croson [4], the Court had before it a city ordinance requiring that 30 percent of city construction projects be subcontracted to minority-owned businesses, and held that the ordinance violated the equal protection clause. In *Croson,* a majority held that an affirmative action plan must be subjected to strict scrutiny: Justices Rehnquist, White, O'Connor, Kennedy and Scalia. Justices Brennan, Marshall and Blackmun stuck by the intermediate scrutiny and dissented.

In the following year the Court would change directions again. In Metro Broadcasting v. Federal Communications Commission [5], the Court had before it the FCC policy that gave minorities preference in the ownership of radio and television licenses. Five members of the Court, led by Justice Brennan and joined by Justices Marshall, Blackmun, White and Stevens, applied the intermediate scrutiny test and held that the policy did not violate the equal protection clause. Justice White had voted in *Croson* to apply strict scrutiny, but here defected and applied the intermediate test. The other four justices—Rehnquist, O'Connor, Kennedy and Scalia—would apply strict scrutiny and concluded that the program violated the equal protection clause.

By 1995, Justices Brennan, Marshall and White were no longer on the Court and new members Souter, Thomas, Ginsburg and Breyer had joined. In Adarand Constructors, Inc. v. Pena [6], the Court had a federal set-aside minority preference contracting provision. Justice O'Connor, with whom Justices Rehnquist, Scalia, Kennedy and Thomas joined, announced an overruling of *Metro Broadcasting* and determined that whether the affirmative action program was state or federal, the same test applied. And the test was strict scrutiny.

The state of flux that characterized the review of affirmative action programs from the 1978 Bakke case seems to have been settled in 1995. At least to the date of publication of this book.

———

MILLER v. JOHNSON

Supreme Court of the United States, 1995.
___ U.S. ___, 115 S.Ct. 2475, 132 L.Ed.2d 762.

JUSTICE KENNEDY delivered the opinion of the Court.

4. 488 U.S. 469 (1989).   **6.** 115 S.Ct. 2097 (1995).

5. 497 U.S. 547 (1990).

The constitutionality of Georgia's congressional redistricting plan is at issue here. In Shaw v. Reno, 509 U.S. ___ (1993), we held that a plaintiff states a claim under the Equal Protection Clause by alleging that a state redistricting plan, on its face, has no rational explanation save as an effort to separate voters on the basis of race. The question we now decide is whether Georgia's new Eleventh District gives rise to a valid equal protection claim under the principles announced in *Shaw*, and, if so, whether it can be sustained nonetheless as narrowly tailored to serve a compelling governmental interest.

I
A

The Equal Protection Clause of the Fourteenth Amendment provides that no State shall "deny to any person within its jurisdiction the equal protection of the laws." U.S. Const., Amdt. 14, § 1. Its central mandate is racial neutrality in governmental decisionmaking. See, *e.g.,* Loving v. Virginia, 388 U.S. 1, 11 (1967); McLaughlin v. Florida, 379 U.S. 184, 191–192 (1964); see also Brown v. Board of Education, 347 U.S. 483 (1954). Though application of this imperative raises difficult questions, the basic principle is straightforward: "Racial and ethnic distinctions of any sort are inherently suspect and thus call for the most exacting judicial examination.... This perception of racial and ethnic distinctions is rooted in our Nation's constitutional and demographic history." Regents of Univ. of California v. Bakke, 438 U.S. 265, 291 (1978) (opinion of Powell, J.). This rule obtains with equal force regardless of "the race of those burdened or benefited by a particular classification." Richmond v. J.A. Croson Co., 488 U.S. 469, 494 (1989) (plurality opinion) (citations omitted); *id.,* at 520 (SCALIA, J., concurring in judgment) ("I agree ... with JUSTICE O'CONNOR's conclusion that strict scrutiny must be applied to all governmental classification by race"); see also Adarand Constructors, Inc. v. Pena, ___ U.S. ___, ___ (1995) (*slip op.,* at 21); *Bakke, supra,* at 289–291 (opinion of Powell, J.). Laws classifying citizens on the basis of race cannot be upheld unless they are narrowly tailored to achieving a compelling state interest. See, *e.g., Adarand, supra,* at ___ (*slip op.,* at 29); *Croson, supra,* at 494 (plurality opinion); Wygant v. Jackson Bd. of Ed., 476 U.S. 267, 274, 280, and n. 6 (1986) (plurality opinion).

In Shaw v. Reno, *supra,* we recognized that these equal protection principles govern a State's drawing of congressional districts, though, as our cautious approach there discloses, application of these principles to electoral districting is a most delicate task. Our analysis began from the premise that "[l]aws that explicitly distinguish between individuals on racial grounds fall within the core of [the Equal Protection Clause's] prohibition." *Id.,* at ___ (slip op., at 10). This prohibition extends not just to explicit racial classifications, but also to laws neutral on their face but "'unexplainable on grounds other than race.'" *Id.,* at ___ (slip op., at 12) (quoting Arlington Heights v. Metropolitan Housing Development Corp., 429 U.S. 252, 266 (1977)). Applying this basic Equal Protection analysis in the voting rights context, we held that "redistricting legislation that is so bizarre on its face that it is 'unexplainable on grounds other than race,' ... demands the same close scrutiny that we give other state laws that classify citizens by race." 509 U.S., at ___ (slip op., at 12) (quoting *Arlington Heights, supra,* at 266).

This case requires us to apply the principles articulated in *Shaw* to the most recent congressional redistricting plan enacted by the State of Georgia.

A special session opened in August 1991, and the General Assembly submitted a congressional redistricting plan to the Attorney General for preclearance on October 1, 1991. The legislature's plan contained two majority-minority districts, the Fifth and Eleventh, and an additional district, the Second, in which blacks comprised just over 35% of the voting age population. Despite the plan's increase in the number of majority-black districts from one to two and the absence of any evidence of an intent to discriminate against minority voters, 864 F.Supp. 1354, 1363, and n. 7 (SD Ga.1994), the Department of Justice refused preclearance on January 21, 1992. App. 99–107. The Department's objection letter noted a concern that Georgia had created only two majority-minority districts, and that the proposed plan did not "recognize" certain minority populations by placing them in a majority-black district. *Id.,* at 105, 105–106.

The General Assembly returned to the drawing board. A new plan was enacted and submitted for preclearance. This second attempt assigned the black population in Central Georgia's Baldwin County to the Eleventh District and increased the black populations in the Eleventh, Fifth and Second Districts. The Justice Department refused preclearance again, relying on alternative plans proposing three majority-minority districts.

Twice spurned, the General Assembly set out to create three majority-minority districts to gain preclearance. *Id.,* at 1366. Using the ACLU's "max-black" plan as its benchmark, *id.,* at 1366–1367, the General Assembly enacted a plan that

> "bore all the signs of [the Justice Department's] involvement:
> The black population of Meriwether County was gouged out of
> the Third District and attached to the Second District by the
> narrowest of land bridges; Effingham and Chatham Counties
> were split to make way for the Savannah extension, which itself
> split the City of Savannah; and the plan as a whole split 26
> counties, 23 more than the existing congressional districts."
> *Id.,* at 1367; see Appendix A (attached).

The new plan also enacted the Macon/Savannah swap necessary to create a third majority-black district. The Eleventh District lost the black population of Macon, but picked up Savannah, thereby connecting the black neighborhoods of metropolitan Atlanta and the poor black populace of coastal Chatham County, though 260 miles apart in distance and worlds apart in culture. In short, the social, political and economic makeup of the Eleventh District tells a tale of disparity, not community. See *id.*, at 1376–1377, 1389–1390; Plaintiff's Exh. No. 85, pp. 10–27 (report of Timothy G. O'Rourke, Ph.D.). As the attached appendices attest,

> "[t]he populations of the Eleventh are centered around four discrete, widely spaced urban centers that have absolutely nothing to do with each other, and stretch the district hundreds of miles across rural counties and narrow swamp corridors." 864 F.Supp., at 1389 (footnote omitted).

> "The dense population centers of the approved Eleventh District were all majority-black, all at the periphery of the district, and in the case of Atlanta, Augusta and Savannah, all tied to a sparsely populated rural core by even less populated land bridges. Extending from Atlanta to the Atlantic, the Eleventh covered 6,784.2 square miles, splitting eight counties and five municipalities along the way." *Id.*, at 1367 (footnote omitted).

The Almanac of American Politics has this to say about the Eleventh District: "Geographically, it is a monstrosity, stretching from Atlanta to Savannah. Its core is the plantation country in the center of the state, lightly populated, but heavily black. It links by narrow corridors the black neighborhoods in Augusta, Savannah and southern DeKalb County." M. Barone & G. Ujifusa, Almanac of American Politics 356 (1994). Georgia's plan included three majority-black districts, though, and received Justice Department preclearance on April 2, 1992. Plaintiff's Exh. No. 6; see 864 F.Supp., at 1367.

Elections were held under the new congressional redistricting plan on November 4, 1992, and black candidates were elected to Congress from all three majority-black districts.

II

A

Finding that the "evidence of the General Assembly's intent to racially gerrymander the Eleventh District is overwhelming, and practically stipulated by the parties involved," the District Court held that race was the predominant, overriding factor in drawing the Eleventh District. 864 F.Supp., at 1374; see *id.*, at 1374–1378. Appellants do not take issue with the court's factual finding of this racial motivation. Rather, they contend that evidence of a legislature's deliberate classification of voters on the basis of race cannot alone suffice to state a claim under *Shaw*. They argue that, regardless of the legislature's purposes, a plaintiff must demonstrate that a district's shape is so bizarre that it is unexplainable other than on the basis of race, and that appellees failed to make that showing here. Appellants' conception of the constitutional violation misapprehends our holding in *Shaw* and the Equal Protection precedent upon which *Shaw* relied.

Shaw recognized a claim "analytically distinct" from a vote dilution claim. 509 U.S., at ___ (slip op., at 21); see *id.,* at ___ (slip op., at 18). Whereas a vote dilution claim alleges that the State has enacted a particular voting scheme as a purposeful device "to minimize or cancel out the voting potential of racial or ethnic minorities," Mobile v. Bolden, 446 U.S. 55, 66 (1980) (citing cases), an action disadvantaging voters of a particular race, the essence of the equal protection claim recognized in *Shaw* is that the State has used race as a basis for separating voters into districts.   Just as the State may not, absent extraordinary justification, segregate citizens on the basis of race in its public parks, New Orleans City Park Improvement Assn. v. Detiege, 358 U.S. 54 (1958) *(per curiam),* buses, Gayle v. Browder, 352 U.S. 903 (1956) *(per curiam),* golf courses, Holmes v. Atlanta, 350 U.S. 879 (1955) *(per curiam),* beaches, Mayor and City Council of Baltimore v. Dawson, 350 U.S. 877 (1955) *(per curiam),* and schools, *Brown, supra,* so did we recognize in *Shaw* that it may not separate its citizens into different voting districts on the basis of race.   The idea is a simple one: "At the heart of the Constitution's guarantee of equal protection lies the simple command that the Government must treat citizens 'as individuals, not "as simply components of a racial, religious, sexual or national class." ' "   Metro Broadcasting, Inc. v. FCC, 497 U.S. 547, 602 (1990) (O'Connor, J., dissenting) (quoting Arizona Governing Comm. for Tax Deferred Annuity and Deferred Compensation Plans v. Norris, 463 U.S. 1073, 1083 (1983)); cf. Northeastern Fla. Chapter, Associated Gen. Contractors of America v. Jacksonville, 508 U.S. ___, ___ (1993) (slip op., at 9) (" 'injury in fact' " was "denial of equal treatment ... not the ultimate inability to obtain the benefit").   When the State assigns voters on the basis of race, it engages in the offensive and demeaning assumption that voters of a particular race, because of their race, "think alike, share the same political interests, and will prefer the same candidates at the polls."   *Shaw, supra,* at ___ (slip op., at 16); see *Metro Broadcasting, supra,* at 636 (Kennedy, J., dissenting).   Race-based assignments "embody stereotypes that treat individuals as the product of their race, evaluating their thoughts and efforts—their very worth as citizens—according to a criterion barred to the Government by history and the Constitution."   *Metro Broadcasting, supra,* at 604 (O'Connor, J., dissenting) (citation omitted); see Powers v. Ohio, 499 U.S. 400, 410 (1991) ("Race cannot be a proxy for determining juror bias or competence"); Palmore v. Sidoti, 466 U.S. 429, 432 (1984) ("Classifying persons according to their race is more likely to reflect racial prejudice than legitimate public concerns; the race, not the person, dictates the category").   They also cause society serious harm. As we concluded in *Shaw:*

> "Racial classifications with respect to voting carry particular dangers.   Racial gerrymandering, even for remedial purposes, may balkanize us into competing racial factions; it threatens to carry us further from the goal of a political system in which race no longer matters—a goal that the Fourteenth and Fifteenth Amendments embody, and to which the Nation continues to

aspire. It is for these reasons that race-based districting by our state legislatures demands close judicial scrutiny." *Shaw, supra,* at ___ (slip op., at 26). * * *

Race was, as the District Court found, the predominant, overriding factor explaining the General Assembly's decision to attach to the Eleventh District various appendages containing dense majority-black populations. 864 F.Supp., at 1372, 1378. As a result, Georgia's congressional redistricting plan cannot be upheld unless it satisfies strict scrutiny, our most rigorous and exacting standard of constitutional review.

III

To satisfy strict scrutiny, the State must demonstrate that its districting legislation is narrowly tailored to achieve a compelling interest. *Shaw, supra,* at ___ (slip op., at 21–26); see also *Croson,* 488 U.S., at 494 (plurality opinion); *Wygant,* 476 U.S., at 274, 280, and n. 6 (plurality opinion); cf. *Adarand,* ___ U.S., at ___ (slip op., at 29). There is a "significant state interest in eradicating the effects of past racial discrimination." *Shaw, supra,* at ___ (slip op., at 25). The State does not argue, however, that it created the Eleventh District to remedy past discrimination, and with good reason: there is little doubt that the State's true interest in designing the Eleventh District was creating a third majority-black district to satisfy the Justice Department's preclearance demands. 864 F.Supp., at 1378 ("the only interest the General Assembly had in mind when drafting the current congressional plan was satisfying [the Justice Department's] preclearance requirements"); *id.,* at 1366; compare *Wygant, supra,* at 277 (plurality opinion) (under strict scrutiny, state must have convincing evidence that remedial action is necessary before implementing affirmative action), with Heller v. Doe, 509 U.S. ___, ___ (1993) (slip op., at 6) (under rational basis review, legislature need not " 'actually articulate at any time the purpose or rationale supporting its classification' ") (quoting Nordlinger v. Hahn, 505 U.S. 1, 15 (1992)). Whether or not in some cases compliance with the Voting Rights Act, standing alone, can provide a compelling interest independent of any interest in remedying past discrimination, it cannot do so here. As we suggested in *Shaw,* compliance with federal antidiscrimination laws cannot justify race-based districting where the challenged district was not reasonably necessary under a constitutional reading and application of those laws. See 509 U.S., at ___ (slip op., at 23–24). The congressional plan challenged here was not required by the Voting Rights Act under a correct reading of the statute. * * *

IV

The Voting Rights Act, and its grant of authority to the federal courts to uncover official efforts to abridge minorities' right to vote, has been of vital importance in eradicating invidious discrimination from the electoral process and enhancing the legitimacy of our political institutions. Only if our political system and our society cleanse themselves of that discrimination will all members of the polity share an equal opportunity to gain public office regardless of race. As a Nation we share both the obligation and the aspiration of working toward this end. The end is neither assured nor well served, however, by carving electorates into racial blocs.

"If our society is to continue to progress as a multiracial democracy, it must recognize that the automatic invocation of race stereotypes retards that progress and causes continued hurt and injury." Edmondson v. Leesville Concrete Co., 500 U.S. 614, 630–631 (1991). It takes a shortsighted and unauthorized view of the Voting Rights Act to invoke that statute, which has played a decisive role in redressing some of our worst forms of discrimination, to demand the very racial stereotyping the Fourteenth Amendment forbids.

ADARAND CONSTRUCTORS, INC. v. PENA

Supreme Court of the United States, 1995.
___ U.S. ___, 115 S.Ct. 2097, 132 L.Ed.2d 158.

JUSTICE O'CONNOR delivered the Opinion of the Court.

Petitioner Adarand Constructors, Inc., claims that the Federal Government's practice of giving general contractors on government projects a financial incentive to hire subcontractors controlled by "socially and economically disadvantaged individuals," and in particular, the Government's use of race-based presumptions in identifying such individuals, violates the equal protection component of the Fifth Amendment's Due Process Clause. The Court of Appeals rejected Adarand's claim. We conclude, however, that courts should analyze cases of this kind under a different standard of review than the one the Court of Appeals applied. We therefore vacate the Court of Appeals' judgment and remand the case for further proceedings.

In 1989, the Central Federal Lands Highway Division (CFLHD), which is part of the United States Department of Transportation (DOT), awarded the prime contract for a highway construction project in Colorado to Mountain Gravel & Construction Company. Mountain Gravel then solicited bids from subcontractors for the guardrail portion of the contract. Adarand, a Colorado-based highway construction company specializing in guardrail work, submitted the low bid. Gonzales Construction Company also submitted a bid.

The prime contract's terms provide that Mountain Gravel would receive additional compensation if it hired subcontractors certified as small businesses controlled by "socially and economically disadvantaged individuals," App. 24. Gonzales is certified as such a business; Adarand is not. Mountain Gravel awarded the subcontract to Gonzales, despite Adarand's low bid, and Mountain Gravel's Chief Estimator has submitted an affidavit stating that Mountain Gravel would have accepted Adarand's bid, had it not been for the additional payment it received by hiring Gonzales instead. *Id.*, at 28–31. Federal law requires that a subcontracting clause similar to the one used here must appear in most federal agency contracts, and it also requires the clause to state that "[t]he contractor shall presume that socially and economically disadvantaged individuals include Black Americans, Hispanic Americans, Native Americans, Asian Pacific Americans, and other minorities, or any other individual found to be disadvantaged by the [Small Business] Administration pursuant to section 8(a) of the Small Business Act." 15 U.S.C. §§ 637(d)(2), (3). Adarand claims that the presumption set forth in that statute discriminates on the basis of race in violation of the Federal Government's Fifth Amendment obligation not to deny anyone equal protection of the laws.

Adarand's claim arises under the Fifth Amendment to the Constitution, which provides that "No person shall ... be deprived of life, liberty, or property, without due process of law." Although this Court has always understood that Clause to provide some measure of protection against *arbitrary* treatment by the Federal Government, it is not as explicit a guarantee of *equal* treatment as the Fourteenth Amendment, which provides that "No *State* shall ... deny to any person within its jurisdiction the equal protection of the laws" (emphasis added). Our cases have accorded varying degrees of significance to the difference in the language of those two Clauses. We think it necessary to revisit the issue here.

Cases continued to treat the equal protection obligations imposed by the Fifth and the Fourteenth Amendments as indistinguishable; one commentator observed that "[i]n case after case, fifth amendment equal protection problems are discussed on the assumption that fourteenth amendment precedents are controlling." Karst, The Fifth Amendment's Guarantee of Equal Protection, 55 N.C.L.Rev. 541, 554 (1977). Loving v. Virginia, which struck down a race-based state law, cited *Korematsu* for the proposition that "the Equal Protection Clause demands that racial classifications ... be subjected to the 'most rigid scrutiny.'" 388 U.S. 1, 11 (1967). The various opinions in Frontiero v. Richardson, 411 U.S. 677 (1973), which concerned sex discrimination by the Federal Government, took their equal protection standard of review from Reed v. Reed, 404 U.S. 71 (1971), a case that invalidated sex discrimination by a State, without mentioning any possibility of a difference between the standards applicable to state and federal action. *Frontiero,* 411 U.S., at 682–684 (plurality opinion of Brennan, J.); *id.,* at 691 (Stewart, J., concurring in judgment); *id.,* at 692 (Powell, J., concurring in judgment). Thus, in 1975, the Court stated explicitly that "[t]his Court's approach to Fifth Amendment equal protection claims has always been precisely the same as to equal protection claims under the Fourteenth Amendment." Weinberger v. Wiesenfeld, 420 U.S. 636, 638, n. 2 (1975); see also Buckley v. Valeo, 424 U.S. 1, 93 (1976) ("Equal protection analysis in the Fifth Amendment area is the same as that under the Fourteenth Amendment"); United States v. Paradise, 480 U.S. 149, 166, n. 16 (1987) (plurality opinion of Brennan, J.) ("[T]he reach of the equal protection guarantee of the Fifth Amendment is coextensive with that of the Fourteenth"). We do not understand a few contrary suggestions appearing in cases in which we found special deference to the political branches of the Federal Government to be appropriate, *e.g.,* Hampton v. Mow Sun Wong, 426 U.S. 88, 100, 101–102, n. 21 (1976) (federal power over immigration), to detract from this general rule.

The Court resolved the issue, at least in part, in 1989. Richmond v. J.A. Croson Co., 488 U.S. 469 (1989), concerned a city's determination that 30% of its contracting work should go to minority-owned businesses. A majority of the Court in *Croson* held that "the standard of review under the Equal Protection Clause is not dependent on the race of those burdened or benefited by a particular classification," and that the single standard of review for racial classifications should be "strict scrutiny." *Id.,* at 493–494 (opinion of O'Connor, J., joined by Rehnquist, C.J., White, and Kennedy, JJ.); *id.,* at 520 (Scalia, J., concurring in judgment) ("I agree ... with Justice O'Connor's conclusion that strict scrutiny must be applied to all governmental classification by race"). As to the classification before the Court, the plurality agreed that "a state or local subdivision ... has the authority to eradicate the effects of private discrimination within its own legislative jurisdiction," *id.,* at 491–492, but the Court thought that the city had not acted with "a 'strong basis in evidence for its conclusion that remedial action was necessary,' " *id.,* at 500 (majority opinion) (quoting *Wygant, supra,* at 277 (plurality opinion)). The Court also thought it "obvious that [the] program is not narrowly tailored to remedy the effects of prior discrimination." 488 U.S., at 508.

With *Croson,* the Court finally agreed that the Fourteenth Amendment requires strict scrutiny of all race-based action by state and local governments. But *Croson* of course had no occasion to declare what standard of review the Fifth Amendment requires for such action taken by the Federal Government. *Croson* observed simply that the Court's "treatment of an exercise of congressional power in *Fullilove* cannot be dispositive here," because *Croson*'s facts did not implicate Congress' broad power under § 5 of the Fourteenth Amendment. *Croson,* 488 U.S., at 491 (plurality opinion); see also *id.,* at 522 (Scalia, J., concurring in judgment).

Our action today makes explicit what Justice Powell thought implicit in the *Fullilove* lead opinion: federal racial classifications, like those of a State, must serve a compelling governmental interest, and must be narrowly tailored to further that interest.

NOTE

Essayist Richard Rodriguez has observed in *Unilingual, Not Unilateral:*

The era that began with integration ended up with scorn for assimilation.

Draw upon your own experience as an undergraduate and a law student. To what extent were minority students admitted under affirmative action integrated into the campus community? At lunch? In extra-curricular activities like clubs and publications? Dances? Parties? Study groups?

WILLIAM A. HENRY, ELITISM AND EGALITARIANISM*

[S]ince modern America took shape at the end of World War II . . . nearly every great domestic policy debate has revolved around the poles of elitism and egalitarianism—and that egalitarianism has been winning far too thoroughly. This debate underlies the thorniest social issues of our era, from feminism, multiculturalism, and proposed bans on hate speech to affirmative action, racial quotas, the erosion of political parties, and the re-enshrinement of the more aggressive forms of "progressive" taxation. * * *

We have foolishly embraced the unexamined notions that everyone is pretty much alike (and, worse, should be), that self-fulfillment is more important than objective achievement, that the common man is always right, that he needs no interpreters or intermediaries to guide his thinking, that a good and just society should be far more concerned with succoring its losers than with honoring and encouraging its winners to achieve more and thereby benefit everyone. At times—indeed, at almost all times when educational policy is involved—we are as silly as the people in Garrison Keillor's fictional heartland, where *all* the children are claimed to be "above average." We have devoted our rhetoric and our resources to the concept of entitlement, the notion that citizens are not to ask what they can do for their country, but rather to demand what it can do for them. The list of what people are said to be "entitled" to has exploded exponentially as we have redefined our economy, in defiance of everyday reality, as a collective possession—a myth of communal splendor rather than simultaneous individual achievements. * * *

In the pursuit of egalitarianism, an ideal wrenched far beyond what the founding fathers took it to mean, we have willfully blinded ourselves to home truths those solons well understood, not least the simple fact that some people are better than others—smarter, harder working, more learned, more productive, harder to replace. Some ideas are better than others, some values more enduring, some works of art more universal. Some cultures, though we dare not say it, are more accomplished than others and therefore more worthy of study. Every corner of the human race may have something to contribute. That does not mean that all contributions are equal. We may find romantic appeal, esthetic power, and even political insight in cultures that never achieved modern technological sophistication. That does not mean we should equate them with our own. * * *

Looking for equality of outcomes rather than equality of opportunity means relinquishing responsibility and control. Obsessing about justice

* W. Henry, In Defense of Elitism, 11–12, 13, 210–212 (1994). Reprinted by permission.

and fairness too readily leads to succoring the disadvantaged instead of urging them to make the best of their circumstances. Individualism maximizes human potential and ultimately propels the whole human race forward, albeit admittedly at different rates of progress. The expectation that our leaders will represent us literally, that they will be nice guys in the same way that we fancy ourselves to be, deprives us of leadership that can inspire and challenge and demand, and replaces it instead with leadership that simply smooths out the bumps of a static life. * * *

We cannot, of course, put the genie back into the bottle. Serene confidence about everything in the American experiment, from the civilizing value of Columbus's voyages to the conquest of the plains and mountains to the rough-and-tumble process of assimilation in the melting pot, has given way to an edgy relativism that insists on viewing things from all sides without embracing any of them. The historic and in some cases present grievances of women and blacks and Hispanics and Asians and gays and so many others are real, and the urge toward recompense among the alleged oppressors is reinforced by righteous indignation from the downtrodden.

But we can draw comfort from a few undeniable facts. The rest of the world wants to come here because America is better—not just economically better but politically better, intellectually better, culturally better. Ours is a superior culture, and it is so precisely because of its individualism. More than any other world power, in fact, we gave to global consciousness the very idea of the individual as the focal point of social relations—not the king, not the army, not the church, and not the tribe. Just when the world is rushing toward us and our ways, let us not slide toward embracing theirs.

The past that made our culture is a seamless web. The attitudes one may lament in the present are inextricable from the attitudes that spawned a desirable modern world. And the past need not be ashamed of itself, nor we for it, that it included racism and sexism and homophobia and other offenses against modern notions of human rights. Human beings are an evolving species, morally as well as biologically. To get to where we are, we had to come from somewhere less humane. An imperfect world is not the same thing as a worthless one.

Accepting that people have varying gifts and abilities and will arrive at varying outcomes is not diminishing their humanity. Rather, it is more demeaning to engage in the egalitarian deceit of equating achievements and outright charity.

Above all, fairness is not the same thing as equality. It is unfair to the able to deny them special programs for the gifted, to impinge on their attainments, to take a larger share of their money away in taxes simply to deprive them rather than to raise revenue. It is unfair to men and whites and children of privilege to hold their achievements suspect. It is unfair to women and blacks and the poor to create compensatory programs so pervasive that they can never know with full confidence the joy of having achieved something entirely on their own. A fair society is one in which some people fail—and they may fail in something other than precise, demographically representative proportions.

NOTE

To what extent do you accept Henry's observations? Has the extension of equal protection concepts led to egalitarianism? Is this bad? The 1990 declaration of principles at the Democratic Leadership Conference (William Jefferson Clinton, Chair) stated:

> "We believe the promise of America is equal opportunity, not equal outcomes."

Is egalitarianism the philosophical underpinning of affirmative action? Can it be justified? Is affirmative action predicated on equal opportunity or equal outcome? Does it make a difference when the action refers to college admissions, as opposed to set-aside construction contracts? If one accepts the notion that affirmative action is justified to atone for past discrimination, is there a time limit for the requirement of these programs? If so, what standards should be used to set time limits?

ORE IN PUBLISHED OPINIONS

The second step in the decisional process is interpretation or construction of legal precepts. We now look to a sample of excerpts from recorded opinions. As explained in detail in Chapter II, interpreting statutes play a dominating role in judicial decision making today. In addition to the excerpts set forth below, it will be helpful to refer again to cases set forth in that chapter, also listed under the caption "ORE IN PUBLISHED OPINIONS." Roscoe Pound suggested that in interpreting a legal precept, a court "is influenced by current moral, political and social ideas, especially fixed pictures of the end of law and of an ideal legal and social order, by reference to which, consciously or subconsciously, the tribunal determines how far possible interpretations will yield a just result in the individual cause." [1]

In this appeal by two coal producing companies from summary judgment in favor of the government, we must decide what is meant by the expression "coal produced by surface mining" under the Surface Mining Control and Reclamation Act (SMCRA or the Act), 30 U.S.C.A. §§ 1201–1328. This is not mere semantic exercise, because upon our decision depends the extent of tonnage upon which a reclamation fee of 35 cents per ton may be levied by the Secretary of the Interior. The government argues, and the district court found, that tonnage of "coal produced" includes the weight of rock, clay, dirt and other debris mined with the "coal" that was delivered by the companies to a coal washing

---

1. R. Pound, *The Theory of Judicial Decision*, 36 Harv.L.Rev. 940, 949 (1923).

and sizing plant. The companies seem to borrow from Gertrude Stein's "a rose is a rose is a rose" and argue that coal is coal and it means a mineral that is combustible. We conclude that we have jurisdiction to hear this appeal, and that the district court erred in determining that all the material mined by appellants was subject to the reclamation fee. Accordingly, we reverse the judgment of the district court.

———

The major question for decision is one of first impression in the United States Courts of Appeals. We must decide whether a claim deemed filed in a Chapter 11 (reorganization) proceeding remains effective when the debtor converts the Chapter 11 case into one under Chapter 7 (liquidation). The issue requires that we construe relevant statutes and the rules of practice and procedure in bankruptcy. The bankruptcy judge, 43 B.R. 937, and, after appeal, the district court, 52 B.R. 960, held that listing the claim on the debtor's schedule, which was filed under Chapter 11, did not preserve the claim under Chapter 7. We disagree and reverse.

———

There are other questions, but the principal issue presented for decision is whether a private cause of action for damages against corporate directors is to be implied in favor of a corporate stockholder under 18 U.S.C.A. § 610, a criminal statute prohibiting corporations from making "a contribution or expenditure in connection with any election at which Presidential and Vice Presidential electors ... are to be voted for." We conclude that implication of such a federal cause of action is not suggested by the legislative context of § 610 or required to accomplish Congress' purposes in enacting the statute. We therefore have no occasion to address the questions whether § 610, properly construed, proscribes the expenditures alleged in this case, or whether the statute is unconstitutional as violative of the First Amendment or of the equal protection component of the Due Process Clause of the Fifth Amendment.

———

In this appeal we are required to construe Section 25(a) of the Act of July 9, 1976, P.L. 586, No. 142, effective June 27, 1978, and determine whether it was intended to reduce the two year limitation established by the Judicial Code, 42 Pa.C.S.A. § 5524, for the commencement of an action for trespass to real estate. The trial court held that the statute of limitations had been so reduced and granted a motion for summary judgment which dismissed an action for blasting damages which had occurred less than 23 months prior to commencement of the action. We reverse.

———

In this appeal from a dismissal of plaintiff-appellants' complaint under Rule 12(b)(6) of the Federal Rules of Civil Procedure, we are asked to decide whether the complaint made out a sufficient claim for relief against *Time, Inc.* under New Jersey defamation law. Because we conclude that the district court erred in determining that New Jersey's fair report privilege barred plaintiff-appellants' claim as a matter of law, we reverse the judgment of the district court, and remand for further factual proceedings.

Section 5

APPLYING THE LAW TO THE FACTS

OVERVIEW

From choosing the law and interpreting it, we come now to applying the law to the facts found by the fact finder. This is the third of the methodologies described under this chapter's general rubric, "Justifying the Decision." It also is the third of the flash points of controversy between the litigants.

In the typical difficult case, usually one of first impression, the courts will have expended much thought in the earlier processes: finding the law, or making a choice among competing legal precepts. After the choice is made, efforts must then be directed toward interpreting the law. Once the law is chosen and then interpreted, courts are ready for the final process—applying the law to the facts. Because all three processes have been utilized, this is the paradigm case that uses all three methodologies.

Often, however, the first step is not involved because there is no question of choice, but instead the question is one of interpretation, usually in the form of statutory construction. After the question of interpretation is resolved, the court then must apply the law as interpreted to the facts.

Most cases, however, do not involve the questions of choice or interpretation. The issue in what have been estimated to be 90% of the cases is solely the application of settled law to the facts found by the fact-finder. In the overwhelming percentage of litigation the law is settled and its interpretation equally clear, and the sole issue for the decision is the application of the law to the facts. Here the court may be faced with a "slam dunk" case, where the law and its application alike are plain, or alternatively, a dispute in which the law is plain and the sole issue is its application to the facts.

Clearly, the process of justification always requires application of a legal precept to a fact situation. The application may be, and usually is, purely mechanical. If the material facts at hand are substantially similar to those present in an earlier case announcing a rule of law, the doctrine of precedent becomes operative and the case is quickly decided and easily justified. Where there is no quarrel over the choice or interpretation of the legal precept, the root controversy, as we have emphasized in the discussion of precedents, is traced to the value judgment of whether there is similarity between the fact situations under comparison. Professor Levi explains that "the scope of a rule of law, and therefore its meaning, depends upon a determination of what facts will be considered similar to those present when the rule was first announced. The finding of similarity or difference is the key step in the legal process." [1] Predicting a court's action in a precept-application controversy, therefore, requires a prediction of which facts in the compared cases a given court at a given time will deem either material or insignificant. The facts considered material are "adjudicative" facts, or "facts relevant in deciding whether a given general proposition is or is not applicable to a particular situation." [2]

HADLEY v. BAXENDALE

9 Ex.Ch. 341, 156 Eng.Rep. 145 (Ex.1854).

[Baron Alderson laid down a rule by which damages for breach of contract were to be measured. This rule has since been followed almost universally both in England and in America.]

ALDERSON, B.

We think that there ought to be a new trial in this case; but, in so doing, we deem it to be expedient and necessary to state explicitly the rule which the Judge, at the next trial, ought, in our opinion, to direct the jury to be governed by when they estimate the damages.

. . .

Now we think the proper rule in such a case as the present is this:— Where two parties have made a contract which one of them has broken, the damages which the other party ought to receive in respect to such breach of contract should be such as may fairly and reasonably be considered either arising naturally, i.e., according to the usual course of things, from such breach of contract itself, or such as may reasonably be supposed to have been in the contemplation of both parties, at the time they made the contract, as the probable result of the breach of it. Now, if the special circumstances under which the contract was actually made were communicated by the plaintiffs to the defendants, and thus known to both parties, the damages resulting from the breach of such a contract, which they would reasonably contemplate, would be the amount of injury which would ordinarily follow from a breach of contract under these special circumstances so known and communicated. But, on the other hand, if these special circumstances were wholly unknown to

----

1. E. Levi, *An Introduction to Legal Reasoning,* 15 U.Chi.L.Rev. 501 (1948).

2. H. Hart and A. Sacks, The Legal Process: Basic Problems in the Making and Application of Law 384.

the party breaking the contract, he, at the most, could only be supposed to have had in his contemplation the amount of injury which would arise generally, and in the great multitude of cases not affected by any special circumstances, from such a breach of contract. For, had the special circumstances been known, the parties might have specially provided for the breach of contract by special terms as to the damages in that case; and of this advantage it would be very unjust to deprive them.... Now, in the present case, if we are to apply the principles above laid down, we find that the only circumstances here communicated by the plaintiffs to the defendants at the time the contract was made, were, that the article to be carried was the broken shaft of a mill, and that the plaintiffs were the millers of that mill. But how do these circumstances show reasonably that the profits of the mill must be stopped by an unreasonable delay in the delivery of the broken shaft by the carrier to the third person? Suppose the plaintiffs had another shaft in their possession put up or putting up at the time, and that they only wished to send back the broken shaft to the engineer who made it; it is clear that this would be quite consistent with the above circumstances, and yet the unreasonable delay in the delivery would have no effect upon the intermediate profits of the mill. Or, again, suppose that, at the time of the delivery to the carrier, the machinery of the mill had been in other respects defective, then, also, the same results would follow. Here it is true that the shaft was actually sent back to serve as a model for a new one, and that the want of a new one was the only cause of the stoppage of the mill, and that the loss of profits really arose from not sending down the new shaft in proper time, and that this arose from the delay in delivering the broken one to serve as a model. But it is obvious that, in the great multitude of cases of millers sending off broken shafts to third persons by a carrier under ordinary circumstances, such consequences would not, in all probability, have occurred; and these special circumstances were here never communicated by the plaintiffs to the defendants. It follows, therefore, that the loss of profits here cannot reasonably be considered such a consequence of the breach of contract as could have been fairly and reasonably contemplated by both the parties when they made this contract. For such loss would neither have flowed naturally from the breach of this contract in the great multitude of such cases occurring under ordinary circumstances, nor were the special circumstances, which, perhaps, would have made it a reasonable and natural consequence of such breach of contract, communicated to or known by the defendants.

NOTE

Can it be argued that Baron Alderson misapplied his rule to the facts before him?

Consider the many cases and controversies you have read. Putting aside disputed fact situations, at what point did the litigants part ways on the legal question? Selecting or choosing the governing legal precept? Interpreting the found or chosen precept? Or applying the found or chosen precept as interpreted to the cause at hand? As you proceed to read cases, examine the contentions of the parties, or, in the case of a divided court, the separate opinions, to ascertain the precise point of conflict.

Is there justification for writing a dissenting opinion when the facts are undisputed by the parties and the sole difference is the third step of the foregoing analysis? When there is a difference in the third step as to which facts are material? If so, is there justification for a lengthy opinion? Does it make a difference if the appeal is from a jury or a bench trial?

BENJAMIN N. CARDOZO, THE LAW AND ITS APPLICATION *

Of the cases that come before the court in which I sit, a majority, I think, could not, with semblance of reason, be decided in any way but one. The law and its application alike are plain. Such cases are predestined, so to speak, to affirmance without opinion. In another and considerable percentage, the rule of law is certain, and the application alone doubtful. A complicated record must be dissected, the narratives of witnesses, more or less incoherent and unintelligible, must be analyzed, to determine whether a given situation comes within one district or another upon the chart of rights and wrongs. The traveler who knows that a railroad crosses his path must look for approaching trains. That is at least the general rule. In numberless litigations the description of the landscape must be studied to see whether vision has been obstructed, whether something has been done or omitted to put the traveler off his guard. Often these cases and others like them provoke difference of opinion among judges. Jurisprudence remains untouched, however, regardless of the outcome. Finally there remains a percentage, not large indeed, and yet not so small as to be negligible, where a decision one way or the other, will count for the future, will advance or retard, sometimes much, sometimes little, the development of the law. These are the cases where the creative element in the judicial process finds its opportunity and power. It is with these cases that I have chiefly concerned myself in all that I have said to you. In a sense it is true of many of them that they might be decided either way. By that I mean that reasons plausible and fairly persuasive might be found for one conclusion as for another. Here come into play that balancing of judgment, that testing and sorting of considerations of analogy and logic and utility and fairness, which I have been trying to describe. Here it is that the judge assumes the function of a lawgiver.

* Benjamin N. Cardozo, The Nature of the Judicial Process, 164–165 (1921). Reprinted by permission of Yale University Press. Copyright © 1921 by Yale University Press.

NOTE

Cardozo estimated that at least nine-tenths of appellate cases in 1924 "could not, with semblance of reason, be decided in any way but one." B. Cardozo, Growth of the Law 60 (1924). In 1961, Judge Henry Friendly wrote: "Indeed, Cardozo's nine-tenths estimate probably should be read as referring to the first category alone. Thus reading it, Professor Harry W. Jones finds it 'surprising' on the high side.... So would I. If it includes both categories, I would not." Friendly, *Reactions of a Lawyer—Newly Become Judge,* 71 Yale L.J. 218, 222–23 (1961) (quoting Jones, *Law and Morality in the Perspective of Legal Realism,* 61 Colum.L.Rev. 799, 803 n. 16 (1961)).

DOES THE LEGAL PRECEPT APPLY TO THE FACTS FOUND? *

Analogy does not seek proof of an identity of one thing with another, but only a comparison of resemblances. Unlike the technique of enumeration, analogy does not depend upon the quantity of instances but upon the quality of resemblances between things. J.S. Mill reduced it to a formula: Two things resemble each other in one or more respects; a certain proposition is true of one; therefore it is true of the other.[1] In legal analogies, we may have two cases which resemble each other in a great many properties, and we infer that some additional property in one will be found in the other. Moreover, the process of analogy is used on a case-by-case basis. It is used to compare the resemblance of prior cases to the case at bar reaching a conclusion as to cases other than the one at bar.

If reaching a conclusion by enumeration has the benefit of experience, reaching a conclusion by analogy has the benefit of the high degree of similarity of the compared data. The degree of similarity is always the crucial inquiry in analogies. Clearly, you cannot conclude that a partial resemblance between two entities is equal to an entire and exact correspondence. Here the skill of the advocate will often be the determining factor. Plaintiff's lawyer may argue that the historical event or entity *A*—in law, a precedent—bears many resemblances to the case at bar, *B*. The opponent will argue that although the facts in *A* and *B* are similar in some respects, this does not mean that those similarities are material and therefore relevant, or that the cases are similar in other respects; he or she will argue that a false analogy is present.

What is one person's meat is another person's poison. What is one attorney's material and relevant fact in analogical comparisons is the other attorney's immaterial and irrelevant fact. Often the art of advocacy resolves itself into convincing the court which facts in previous cases are indeed positive analogies, and which are not. The judge is required to draw this distinction. The successful lawyer is one who is able to

---

* Adapted from Ruggero J. Aldisert, Logic for Lawyers: a Guide to Clear Legal Thinking (1989).

1. *See* J.S. Mill, A System of Logic Ratiocinactive and Inductive 98–142 (8th ed. 1916).

have the judge draw the distinction in the manner most favorable to the advocate.

But effective advocacy in determining positive/negative analogies must at all times be kept within the perimeters of objectivity. Students and lawyers must not fall in love with pet theories by opening their eyes only to instances that corroborate a favorite belief more readily than those that contradict it. In the process of analogy you must always have a full view of all that relates to the question. Do not be the type of person who sincerely believes that only your thoughts are reason. In the words of John Locke: "They converse but with one sort of man, they read but one set of books, they will not come in the hearing but of one set of motions.... They have a pretty traffic with known correspondents in some little creek ... but will not venture out in the great ocean of knowledge." [2]

Thus, it should now be understood that points of unlikeness are as important as likeness in the cases examined. Comparison without contrast is not an ideal to be followed. In examining the cases, as does a scientist in a laboratory, the lawyer should not look for the rigid fixity of facts. Seldom are there perfectly identical experiences in human affairs. The lawyer must recognize also the problems of those facts, which when compared, prove to be the rare experience in human affairs. And in order to understand completely what is being compared, always be aware of subtleties and minuteness.

Whether using enumerated instances to reach a generalized conclusion to frame a broad legal precept, or selected instances to bring about a convenient analogy, it is well to keep in mind the object of bringing into consideration a multitude of cases. It is to facilitate the selection of the evidential or significant features upon which to base inferences in some single case.

To do this effectively, you will be well served to: (1) jettison any pet beliefs or theories if the research is not supportive—do not be dogmatic; (2) not hesitate to confront the novel situation; and (3) remember that the study and practice of law has no room for mental inertia and laziness. Be aware always that the analysis you have failed to pursue will often be performed by your adversary, and if not by him or her, by the judge or the chambers' law clerks.

We repeat again for emphasis that the conclusion reached by inductive reasoning is not considered a truth; rather, it is a proposition that is more probably true than not. We must also understand that often in inductive reasoning the two processes of enumeration and analogy are used simultaneously. From this it follows that, if the conclusion is reached by simultaneously using the twin processes, there is a greater probability that truth will lie in the conclusion. Jevons described this process: "The things usually resemble each other only in two or three

---

2. J. Dewey, How We Think 26 (1933) (citing J. Locke, The Conduct of Under-   standing Ch. 3 (1690)).

properties, and we require to have more instances to assure us that what is true of these is probably true of all similar instances. The less, in short, the intention of the resemblance the greater must be the extension of our inquiries." [3]

Other commentators have made perceptive observations relating to inductive reasoning. Jeffrey G. Murphy observes:

> Most of us, in claiming analogies between various things, rely on perception. That is, we "just see" that Mary is mighty like a rose. And, if pressed to give reasons for making such a claim, we will direct our questioner to certain features of the case that he too can "just see." But there are no decision procedures for "just seeing." There is no logic of perception. However, the legal use of analogy is more like the scientific use than the ordinary use in the following sense: that the claim that X and Y are analogous is made with respect to some theoretical basis. The appeal is not (at least wholly) to perception. Rather the theoretical basis (in law, certain conventional rules of relevance established as precedents) gives us a decision procedure for determining whether or not cases X and Y are indeed analogous. [4]

Yet we must be very careful to make sure that "Mary is mighty like a rose." We must look at Mary with all her warts and blemishes. There must be open-mindedness, whole-heartedness, and responsibility. [5] From my own experiences as a lawyer, with juices running fast because of intense sympathy for my client's cause—yes, a cause, not a case—I know how strong the tendency is to be closed-minded. This is a mistake. The consummate advocate must look at things free from bias, partisanship, traits, and habits that close the mind and make it unwilling to consider new problems and entertain new ideas. In analyzing previous cases for resemblances and differences in the facts, give full attention to facts from whatever source they come; give full attention to alternative propositions. It is difficult, to be sure, to abandon a pet notion and recognize the possibility of error. But the true advocate realizes that self-conceit is not always the best attitude and that to do your job properly for your client you must be prepared to undergo troublesome hours to alter beliefs that are strongly held at the beginning of research, but that, upon analysis, find little or no support in the law.

To do this there must be whole-heartedness, the ability to work long hours to test both old and new theories. Remember, your responsibility is to advance your client's interest, even if it means dumping the client's original theories and embarking upon fresh consideration of new points of view and new ideas.

3. W. Jevons, Elementary Lessons in Logic: Deductive and Inductive 208 (1870).

4. Murphy, "Law Logic," 77 Ethics 193, 197 (1966).

5. *See, e.g.,* J. Dewey, ante note 2 at 30–33.

Analogies can be considered the most important aspect of the study and practice of law. It is the method by which putative precedents are subjected to the acid test of searching analysis. It is the method to determine whether factual differences contained in the case at bar and those of the case compared are material or irrelevant. This requires counsel to be intellectually responsible at all times, to consider the consequences of projected steps when they reasonably follow from any position taken or about to be taken. Intellectual responsibility means integrity; it means recognizing the true consequences of any proposition or belief. It is irresponsible to cling to a proposition without acknowledging those consequences that will logically flow from it. If it is necessary to "kill the baby," do it, then move to another theory. If you don't, your opponent will kill it for you.

Arthur L. Goodhart has written:

Having established the material and immaterial facts of the case as seen by the court, we can then proceed to state the principle of the case. It is to be found in the conclusion reached by the judge on the basis of the material facts and on the exclusion of the immaterial ones. In a certain case the court finds that A, B and C exist. It then excludes fact A as immaterial, and on facts B and C it reaches conclusion X. What is the *ratio decidendi* of this case? There are two principles: (1) In any future case in which the facts are A, B and C, the court must reach conclusion X, and (2) in any future case in which the facts are B and C the court must reach conclusion X. In the second case the absence of fact A does not affect the result, for fact A has been held to be immaterial. The court, therefore, creates a principle [makes a value judgment?] when it determines which are the material and which are the immaterial facts on which it bases its decision.[6]

The importance of legal reasoning by analogy cannot be overstated. It is the heart of the study of law; it lies at the heart of the Socratic method. It is important for professors to use the Socratic method, because the method of analogy goes to the fundamentals of the common law tradition. Cardozo has taught us that "[t]he common law does not work from pre-established truths of universal and inflexible validity to conclusions derived from them deductively. Its method is inductive and it draws its generalizations from particulars."[7]

One must always appraise an analogical argument very carefully. Several criteria may be used:

- The acceptability of the analogy will vary proportionally with the number of circumstances that have been analyzed.

6. Goodhart, *Determining the Ratio Decidendi of a Case,* 40 Yale L.J. 161, 179 (1930).

7. B. Cardozo, The Nature of the Judicial Process 22–23 (1921).

- The acceptability will depend upon the number of positive resemblances (similarities) and negative resemblances (dissimilarities).

- The acceptability will be influenced by the relevance of the purported analogies. An argument based on a single relevant analogy connected with a single instance will be more cogent than one which points out a dozen irrelevant resemblances.

ORE IN PUBLISHED OPINIONS

Applying the law to the facts, or application of the abstract grounds for decision to the facts of the particular case, is in most cases purely mechanical. Certainly, the law is plain and its application to the facts equally clear in approximately 90 percent of the cases. Where it is not purely mechanical, as evidenced by the excerpts in the following recorded cases, much depends on the court's feelings as to what is right between the parties before it, and the institutional or precedential considerations that will be influenced by the decision. It is here that a value judgment will be made whether to expand or constrict the law on the basis of the facts. If the controlling legal precept involves facts A, B and C, the court will have to decide if the same rule will apply when fact C is not before it, or, in another case, whether it will apply when additional fact D is present. Justice Walter V. Schaefer suggested:

> **[M]ost depends upon the judge's unspoken notion as to the function of his court. If he views the role of the court as a passive one, he will be willing to delegate the responsibility for change, and he will not greatly care whether the delegated authority is exercised or not. If he views the court as an instrument of society designed to reflect in its decisions the morality of the community, he will be more likely to look precedent in the teeth and to measure it against the ideals and the aspirations of his time.[1]**

Although the contents of a document may not be privileged under the fifth amendment, the act of producing or authenticating the document may be privileged. This terse summary of the law originated with Fisher v. United States, 425 U.S. 391, 410, 96 S.Ct. 1569, 1581, 48 L.Ed.2d 39 (1976), and was confirmed in United States v. Doe, 465 U.S. 605, 104 S.Ct. 1237, 79 L.Ed.2d 552 (1984). Application of this precept may produce profound consequences when an individual is the target of an Internal Revenue Service (IRS) investigation and the IRS directs a summons to a corporation solely owned by the individual. We have been asked to address such consequences in this case.

---

1. W. Schaefer, *Precedent and Policy,* 34 U.Chi.L.Rev. 3 (1966).

The major question for decision raised by these two appeals from a judgment in favor of plaintiff in a diversity action brought under Pennsylvania law is the extent to which delay damages may be awarded under Rule 238, Pa.R.Civ.P. Here, defendant obtained a directed verdict at the close of the first trial, but, after a retrial was ordered by this court, ultimately lost on the merits. Because defendant lost and because he never made a settlement offer, plaintiff was awarded Rule 238 delay damages totaling $247,500. This award included damages for the time the case was on appeal from the directed verdict, but, because of plaintiff's mathematical miscalculation, did not include damages for the 17 days immediately preceding the final verdict. For these reasons, the defendant, at No. 82–5711, argues that the delay damages award was excessive and the plaintiff, at No. 82–5836, contends that it was insufficient.

This appeal requires us to decide whether Blue Shield's prepaid dental service program in Pennsylvania violates the antitrust laws. Several Pennsylvania dental associations and individual dentists appeal from a summary judgment dismissing their antitrust and state law claims brought against the Medical Service Association of Pennsylvania, doing business as Pennsylvania Blue Shield. Appellants argue that Blue Shield engaged in a price-fixing conspiracy and a group boycott in violation of § 1 of the Sherman Act, 15 U.S.C.A. § 1, attempted to monopolize and monopolized in violation of § 2 of the Act, 15 U.S.C.A. § 2, and that the district court abused its discretion in refusing to certify a subclass of cooperating dentists for treble damages purposes. We conclude that appellants' contentions are without merit, and therefore affirm the judgment of the district court.

The question for decision is whether appellant would be placed in double jeopardy in violation of the fifth amendment were he to be prosecuted in the Western District of Pennsylvania on a charge of conspiracy to distribute and possess marijuana following a plea of guilty and subsequent sentence in the Northern District of Florida on a similar charge. Appellant argues that the Florida and Pennsylvania activities were part of the same conspiracy; the government argues otherwise. The district court agreed with the government and denied appellant's double jeopardy motion to dismiss the indictment. 592 F.Supp. 172. This appeal followed. Although the question is close, we are persuaded that the government failed to meet its burden of proving the existence of two distinct conspiracies.

Section 6

THE STUDY OF REASONS IN JUDICIAL OPINIONS

The study of reasons judges give for their decisions is the study of law. It is necessary to examine the anatomy of judicial reasoning in order to avoid the cynical observation that reasons can be as plentiful as blackberries after a decision is made. "It is on the question of what shall amount to a justification," Holmes once wrote, "and more especially on the nature of the considerations which really determine or ought to determine the answer to that question, that judicial reasoning seems ... often to be inadequate." [1] Lon Fuller emphasized that a rational decision "must be based on some rule, principle or standard. If this rule, principle or standard is to make any appeal to the parties it must be something that pre-existed the decision. An explanation in terms of a principle created *ad hoc* to explain the decision it purports to govern lacks the persuasive power necessary to make adjudication effective." [2]

Professor Robert S. Summers has made a valuable study of reasons given in common law cases, identifying genuine reasons as authority, factual, interpretational, critical, and what he describes as "substantive." [3] Authority reasons are appeals to precedent. Factual reasons are those that support findings of fact. Interpretational reasons are analyses of the importance accorded to the author of the text and the role played by the language of the text in determining intention, as we have discussed in part in Chapter II. And "a critical reason merely formulates a criticism of some element or aspect of a given autonomous reason," [4] usually found in a dissenting or concurring opinion, but also at times in majority opinions. But Summers devotes the bulk of his analysis to what he describes as a substantive reason, "one that derives its justificatory force from a moral, economic, political, institutional, or other social consideration." [5] These may be goal, rightness or institutional reasons.

A goal reason, in Summers' formulation, may derive its force from the fact that, at the time it is given, the decision can be predicted to have effects that serve a good social objective, such as general safety, community welfare, facilitation of democracy, public health or promotion of family harmony. All such reasons are future-regarding and stand in conflict with the notion that goal-oriented reasons should be embraced by legislative law-makers and not the judiciary.

A rightness reason draws its force from the way in which the decision accords with a socio-moral norm of rightness as applied to a

1. Vegelahn v. Gunther, 167 Mass. 92, 44 N.E. 1077, 1080 (1896) (dissenting opinion).

2. H. Hart & A. Sacks, The Legal Process 421 (tent. ed. 1958).

3. R. Summers, *Two Types of Substantive Reasons: The Core of a Theory of Common-Law Justification*, 63 Cornell L.Rev. 707 (1978).

4. Id. at 726.

5. Id. at 716-727.

party's actions or to a state of affairs resulting from those actions. Because the decision it supports accords with a sound rightness norm applicable to a party's past action, it differs from a decision that is predicted to serve a good social goal. Rightness reasons include conscionability, punitive dessert, justified reliance, restitution for unjust enrichment, comparative blame, due care, relational duty, fittingness or proportionality of remedy. Two main types loom large—"culpability" and "mere fairness" reasons.

Finally, an institutional reason, according to Summers, is a goal reason or rightness reason that is tied to a specific institutional role or process, deriving its force from the way in which the projected decision would serve goals or accord with a norm of rightness applicable to the actions of participants, including officials. Institutional reasons include decisions suggesting that law change should come from the legislature, that additional facts are necessary, that the issue is moot, that a claimant was denied a full and fair hearing, that it is impossible to measure damages, or that because the court cannot supervise the decree an injunction is denied. Although confined to common law decisions, Professor Summers' pioneer and taxonomic efforts should prove valuable in assessing the adequacy of judicial reasoning, and, of course, the reasoning contained in critical commentary of judicial opinions.

Important in any aspect of the process of justification, interpretation becomes especially important in our jurisprudential era in which the bulk of controlling legal precepts are statutory or constitutional in origin. The judge constantly is torn between the "original intent" theory and the "ongoing history" theory of interpretation. Certainly, where it is preferred to have stability, predictability, and reckonability in the law, it may be expected that the intent of the drafters be ascertained and held to be controlling. But in constitutional law, interpretation is more likely to be influenced by current moral, political and social ideas. Often a judge's troubled quest for the rational outcome of a difficult case brings him or her to the juncture, described by Roger Traynor:

> [W]here he feels bound to commit himself to one value judgment or another, [and] the intellectual quest merges with a yearning for something more than the mere orderly disposition of problems, a yearning often approximately defined as a sense of justice and culminating in what Edmond Cahn calls *The Moral Decision*. There can be little question that such a decision, deeply reflected as it is, stands to make law of a higher quality than the amoral decision. We should be aware of how difficult it is to come by. As Harry Jones sensitively observes, "just decision requires both an intellect that perceives the good and a will that resolutely preserves in the good course intellectually perceived." The old proverb that when there's a will there's a way must be reversed. The judge must first find the

way and then summon the will.[6]

Consider the opinions of Judge Cardozo and Chief Judge Bartlett again from the standpoint of materials discussed in this chapter. What is the flash point of controversy between the two viewpoints? Finding or Choosing the Law? Interpreting it? Applying it to the facts? Do you detect Conceptual Jurisprudence? Considerations of Social Welfare? Apply Professor Jones' thesis "Reason is But Choosing," ante at 620. Are the opinions influenced by what Pound described as "current moral, political, and social ideas, especially fixed pictures of the end of law?"

MacPHERSON v. BUICK MOTOR CO.

Court of Appeals of New York, 1916.
217 N.Y. 382, 111 N.E. 1050.

See ante at 354

DONOGHUE v. STEVENSON

House of Lords, 1932.
[1932] A.C. 562.

[This was the leading United Kingdom case in which the House of Lords addressed in 1932 the same question that the New York Court of Appeals decided in the 1916 case of MacPherson v. Buick Motor Co. Given the modern emphasis on products liability, at first blush this case seems extremely outdated. By a 3–2 vote, the House of Lords decided that a manufacturer could be held negligent by an ultimate consumer of a product even through the consumer was not in privity with the defendant. The holding of this case is no longer important today. The law in this field has developed in heroic dimensions since the Thirties. For a student of the judicial process, however, the five speeches (opinions) are a rich treasure trove of the common law tradition on how courts decide cases.]

Read the major speeches of Lords Buckmaster and Atkin, and those that follow from Lords Tomlin, Thankerton and Macmillan from the perspective of materials already covered in this book. Were their Lordships discovering or creating law? Were the various conclusions

---

6. R. Traynor, *LaRude Vita, La Dolce Giustizia; or Hard Cases Can Make Good Law,* 29 U.Chi.L.Rev. 223, 235 (1962).

rationally reached? Logically reached? If so, by inductive or deductive reasoning, or how? Were they influenced by rules of law or by principles? In the sense of Pound? Hart? Did they practice "mechanical" or "conceptual" jurisprudence or interested in social welfare or public policy? What values did they place on the method of Analogy? History? Custom or Tradition? Public policy and social welfare? Evaluate the several treatments of MacPherson v. Buick Motor Co.

1932. May 26. LORD BUCKMASTER.

My Lords, the facts of this case are simple. On August 26, 1928, the appellant drank a bottle of ginger-beer, manufactured by the respondent, which a friend had bought from a retailer and given to her. The bottle contained the decomposed remains of a snail which were not, and could not be, detected until the greater part of the contents of the bottle had been consumed. As a result she alleged, and at this stage her allegations must be accepted as true, that she suffered from shock and severe gastro-enteritis. She accordingly instituted the proceedings against the manufacturer which have given rise to this appeal.

The foundation of her case is that the respondent, as the manufacturer of an article intended for consumption and contained in a receptacle which prevented inspection, owed a duty to her as consumer of the article to take care that there was no noxious element in the goods, that he neglected such duty and is consequently liable for any damage caused by such neglect. After certain amendments, which are now immaterial, the case came before the Lord Ordinary, who rejected the plea in law of the respondent and allowed a proof. His interlocutor was recalled by the Second Division of the Court of Session, from whose judgment this appeal has been brought.

Before examining the merits two comments are desirable: (1.) That the appellant's case rests solely on the ground of a tort based not on fraud but on negligence; and (2.) that throughout the appeal the case has been argued on the basis, undisputed by the Second Division and never questioned by counsel for the appellant or by any of your Lordships, that the English and the Scots law on the subject are identical. It is therefore upon the English law alone that I have considered the matter, and in my opinion it is on the English law alone that in the circumstances we ought to proceed.

The law applicable is the common law, and, though its principles are capable of application to meet new conditions not contemplated when the law was laid down, these principles cannot be changed nor can additions be made to them because any particular meritorious case seems outside their ambit.

Now the common law must be sought in law books by writers of authority and in judgments of the judges entrusted with its administration. The law books give no assistance, because the work of living authors, however deservedly eminent, cannot be used as authority, though the opinions they express may demand attention; and the ancient books do not assist. I turn, therefore, to the decided cases to see if they can be construed so as to support the appellant's case ...

. . .

The general principle of these cases is stated ... in these terms: "The breach of the defendant's contract with A. to use care and skill in and about the manufacture or repair of an article does not of itself give any cause of action to B. when he is injured by reason of the article proving to be defective."

From this general rule there are two well known exceptions: (1.) In the case of an article dangerous in itself; and (2.) where the article not in itself dangerous is in fact dangerous, by reason of some defect or for any other reason, and this is known to the manufacturer. Until the case of George v. Skivington [L.R. 5 Ex 1] I know of no further modification of the general rule.

As to (1.), in the case of things dangerous in themselves, there is, in the words of Lord Dunedin, "a peculiar duty to take precaution imposed upon those who send forth or install such articles when it is necessarily the case that other parties will come within their proximity".... And as to (2.), this depends on the fact that the knowledge of the danger creates the obligation to warn, and its concealment is in the nature of fraud. In this case no one can suggest that ginger-beer was an article dangerous in itself, and the words of Lord Dunedin show that the duty attaches only to such articles, for I read the words "a peculiar duty" as meaning a duty peculiar to the special class of subject mentioned.

. . .

I do not propose to follow the fortunes of George v. Skivington; few cases can have lived so dangerously and lived so long. Lord Sumner ... said that he could not presume to say that it was wrong, but he declined to follow it on the ground which is, I think, firm, that it was in conflict with Winterbottom v. Wright [10 M & W 109].

. . .

The dicta of Brett M.R. in Heaven v. Pender [11 Q.B.D. 503, 509] are rightly relied on by the appellant. The material passage is as follows: "The proposition which these recognized cases suggest, and which is, therefore, to be deduced from them, is that whenever one person is by circumstances placed in such a position with regard to another that every one of ordinary sense who did think would at once recognize that if he did not use ordinary care and skill in his own conduct with regard to those circumstances he would cause danger of injury to the person or property of the other, a duty arises to use ordinary care and skill to avoid such danger...."

. . .

So far, therefore, as the case of George v. Skivington and the dicta in Heaven v. Pender are concerned, it is in my opinion better that they should be buried so securely that their perturbed spirits shall no longer vex the law.

One further case mentioned in argument may be referred to, certainly not by way of authority, but to gain assistance by considering how similar cases are dealt with by eminent judges of the United States. That such cases can have no close application and no authority is clear, for though the source of the law in the two countries may be the same, its current may well flow in different channels. The case referred to is that of Thomas v. Winchester. [6 N.Y. 397 (1852)]. There a chemist issued poison in answer to a request for a harmless drug, and he was held responsible to a third party injured by his neglect. It appears to me that the decision might well rest on the principle that he, in fact, sold a drug dangerous in itself, none the less so because he was asked to sell something else, and on this view the case does not advance the matter.

In another case of MacPherson v. Buick Motor Co., [*post,* p. 849], where a manufacturer of a defective motor-car was held liable for damages at the instance of a third party, the learned judge appears to base his judgment on the view that a motor-car might reasonably be regarded as a dangerous article.

In my view, therefore, the authorities are against the appellant's contention, and, apart from authority, it is difficult to see how any common law proposition can be formulated to support her claim.

The principle contended for must be this: that the manufacturer, or indeed the repairer, of any article, apart entirely from contract, owes a duty to any person by whom the article is lawfully used to see that it has been carefully constructed. All rights in contract must be excluded from consideration of this principle; such contractual rights as may exist in successive steps from the original manufacturer down to the ultimate purchaser are ex hypothesi immaterial. Nor can the doctrine be confined to cases where inspection is difficult or impossible to introduce. This conception is simply to misapply to tort doctrine applicable to sale and purchase.

The principle of tort lies completely outside the region where such considerations apply, and the duty, if it exists, must extend to every person who, in lawful circumstances, uses the article made. There can be no special duty attaching to the manufacture of food apart from that implied by contract or imposed by statute. If such a duty exists, it seems to me it must cover the construction of every article, and I cannot see any reason why it should not apply to the construction of a house. If one step, why not fifty? Yet if a house be, as it sometimes is, negligently built, and in consequence of that negligence the ceiling falls and injures the occupier or any one else, no action against the builder exists according to the English law, although I believe such a right did exist according to the laws of Babylon. Were such a principle known and recognized, it seems to me impossible, having regard to the numerous cases that must have arisen to persons injured by its disregard, that, with the exception of George v. Skivington no case directly involving the principle has ever succeeded in the Courts, and, were it well known and accepted, much of the discussion of the earlier cases would have been waste of time, and the distinction as to articles dangerous in themselves or known to be dangerous to the vendor would be meaningless.

. . .

... I am of opinion that this appeal should be dismissed, and I beg to move your Lordships accordingly.

LORD ATKIN. My Lords, the sole question for determination in this case is legal: Do the averments made by the pursuer in her pleading, if true, disclose a cause of action? I need not restate the particular facts. The question is whether the manufacturer of an article of drink sold by him to a distributor, in circumstances which prevent the distributor or the ultimate purchaser or consumer from discovering by inspection any defect, is under any legal duty to the ultimate purchaser or consumer to take reasonable care that the article is free from defect likely to cause injury to health.... The case has to be determined in accordance with Scots law; ... I speak with little authority on this point, but my own research, such as it is, satisfies me that the principles of the law of Scotland on such a question as the present are identical with those of English law; and I discuss the issue on that footing. The law of both countries appears to be that in order to support an action for damages for negligence the complainant has to show that he has been injured by the breach of a duty owed to him in the circumstances by the defendant to take reasonable care to avoid such injury. In the present case we are not concerned with the breach of the duty; if a duty exists, that would be a question of fact which is sufficiently averred and for present purposes must be assumed. We are solely concerned with the question whether, as a matter of law in the circumstances alleged, the defender owed any duty to the pursuer to take care.

It is remarkable how difficult it is to find in the English authorities statements of general application defining the relations between parties that give rise to the duty. The Courts are concerned with the particular relations which come before them in actual litigation, and it is sufficient to say whether the duty exists in those circumstances. The result is that the Courts have been engaged upon an elaborate classification of duties as they exist in respect of property, whether real or personal, with further divisions as to ownership, occupation or control, and distinctions based on the particular relations of the one side or the other, whether manufacturer, salesman or landlord, customer, tenant, stranger, and so on. In this way it can be ascertained at any time whether the law recognizes a duty, but only where the case can be referred to some particular species which has been examined and classified. And yet the duty which is common to all the cases where liability is established must logically be based upon some element common to the cases where it is found to exist. To seek a complete logical definition of the general principle is probably to go beyond the function of the judge, for the more general the definition the more likely it is to omit essentials or to introduce non-essentials....

At present I content myself with pointing out that in English law there must be, and is, some general conception of relations giving rise to a duty of care, of which the particular cases found in the books are but instances. The liability for negligence, whether you style it such or treat it as in other systems as a species of "culpa," is no doubt based upon a general public sentiment of moral wrongdoing for which the offender must pay. But acts or omissions which any moral code would censure cannot in a practical world be treated so as to give a right to every person injured by them to demand relief. In this way rules of law arise which limit the range of complainants and the extent of their remedy. The rule that you are to love your neighbour becomes in law, you must not injure your neighbour; and the lawyer's question, Who is my neighbour? receives a restricted reply. You must take reasonable care to avoid acts or omissions which you can reasonably foresee would be likely to injure your neighbour. Who, then, in law is my neighbour? The answer seems to be—persons who are so closely and directly affected by my act that I ought reasonably to have them in contemplation as being so affected when I am directing my mind to the acts or omissions which are called in question. ... So A.L. Smith L.J.: "The decision of Heaven v. Pender was founded upon the principle, that a duty to take due care did arise when the person or property of one was in such proximity to the person or property of another that, if due care was not taken, damage might be done by the one to the other." I think that this sufficiently states the truth if proximity be not confined to mere physical proximity, but be used, as I think it was intended, to extend to such close and direct relations that the act complained of directly affects a person whom the person alleged to be bound to take care would know would be directly affected by his careless act....

> . . .

... Hamilton, J. recognizes that George v. Skivington was a decision which, if it remained an authority, bound him. He says that, without presuming to say it was wrong, he cannot follow it, because it is in conflict with Winterbottom v. Wright. I find this very difficult to understand, for George v. Skivington was based upon a duty in the manufacturer to take care independently of contract, while Winterbottom v. Wright was decided on demurrer in a case where the alleged duty was based solely on breach of a contractual duty to keep in repair, and no negligence was alleged....

That this is the sense in which nearness of "proximity" was intended by Lord Esher is obvious from his own illustration in Heaven v. Pender [3] of the application of his doctrine to the sale of goods. "This" (i.e., the rule he has just formulated) "includes the case of goods, etc., supplied to be used immediately by a particular person or persons, or one

3. 11 Q.B.D. 503, 510.

of a class of persons, where it would be obvious to the person supplying, if he thought, that the goods would in all probability be used at once by such persons before a reasonable opportunity for discovering any defect which might exist, and where the thing supplied would be of such a nature that a neglect of ordinary care or skill as to its condition or the manner of supplying it would probably cause danger to the person or property of the person for whose use it was supplied, and who was about to use it. It would exclude a case in which the goods are supplied under circumstances in which it would be a chance by whom they would be used or whether they would be used or not, or whether they would be used before there would probably be means of observing any defect, or where the goods would be of such a nature that a want of care or skill as to their condition or the manner of supplying them would not probably produce danger of injury to person or property." I draw particular attention to the fact that Lord Esher emphasizes the necessity of goods having to be "used immediately" and "used at once before a reasonable opportunity of inspection." This is obviously to exclude the possibility of goods having their condition altered by lapse of time, and to call attention to the proximate relationship, which may be too remote where inspection even of the person using, certainly of an intermediate person, may reasonably be interposed. With this necessary qualification of proximate relationship as explained in Le Lievre v. Gould [1], I think the judgment of Lord Esher expresses the law of England; without the qualification, I think the majority of the Court in Heaven v. Pender [2] were justified in thinking the principle was expressed in too general terms. There will no doubt arise cases where it will be difficult to determine whether the contemplated relationship is so close that the duty arises. But in the class of case now before the Court I cannot conceive any difficulty to arise. A manufacturer puts up an article of food in a container which he knows will be opened by the actual consumer. There can be no inspection by any purchaser and no reasonable preliminary inspection by the consumer. Negligently, in the course of preparation, he allows the contents to be mixed with poison. It is said that the law of England and Scotland is that the poisoned consumer has no remedy against the negligent manufacturer. If this were the result of the authorities, I should consider the result a grave defect in the law, and so contrary to principle that I should hesitate long before following any decision to that effect which had not the authority of this House. I would point out that, in the assumed state of the authorities, not only would the consumer have no remedy against the circumstances alleged, there would be no evidence of negligence against any one other than the manufacturer; and, except in the case of a consumer who was also a purchaser, no contract and no warranty of fitness, and in the case of the purchase of a specific article under its patent or trade name, which might well be the case in the purchase of some articles of food or drink, no warranty protecting even the purchaser-consumer. There are other instances than of articles of food and drink where goods are sold

1. [1893] 1 Q.B. 491.   2. 11 Q.B.D. 503.

intended to be used immediately by the consumer, such as many forms of goods sold for cleaning purposes, where the same liability must exist. The doctrine supported by the decision below would not only deny a remedy to the consumer who was injured by consuming bottled beer or chocolates poisoned by the negligence of the manufacturer, but also to the user of what should be a harmless proprietary medicine, an ointment, a soap, a cleaning fluid or cleaning powder. I confine myself to articles of common household use, where every one, including the manufacturer, knows that the articles will be used by other persons than the actual ultimate purchaser—namely, by members of his family and his servants, and in some cases his guests. I do not think so ill of our jurisprudence as to suppose that its principles are so remote from the ordinary needs of civilized society and the ordinary claims it makes upon its members as to deny a legal remedy where there is so obviously a social wrong.

It is always a satisfaction to an English lawyer to be able to test his application of fundamental principles of the common law by the development of the same doctrines by the lawyers of the Courts of the United States. In that country I find that the law appears to be well established in the sense in which I have indicated. The mouse had emerged from the ginger-beer bottle in the United States before it appeared in Scotland, but there it brought a liability upon the manufacturer. I must not in this long judgment do more than refer to the illuminating judgment of Cardozo J. in MacPherson v. Buick Motor Co. in the New York Court of Appeals, in which he states the principles of the law as I should desire to state them, and reviews the authorities in other States than his own. Whether the principle he affirms would apply to the particular facts of that case in this country would be a question for consideration if the case arose. It might be that the course of business, by giving opportunities of examination to the immediate purchaser or otherwise, prevented the relation between manufacturer and the user of the car being so close as to create a duty. But the American decision would undoubtedly lead to a decision in favour of the pursuer in the present case.

My Lords, if your Lordships accept the view that this pleading discloses a relevant cause of action you will be affirming the proposition that by Scots and English law alike a manufacturer of products, which he sells in such a form as to show that he intends them to reach the ultimate consumer in the form in which they left him with no reasonable possibility of intermediate examination, and with the knowledge that the absence of reasonable care in the preparation or putting up of the products will result in an injury to the consumer's life or property, owes a duty to the consumer to take that reasonable care.

It is a proposition which I venture to say no one in Scotland or England who was not a lawyer would for one moment doubt. It will be an advantage to make it clear that the law in this matter, as in most others, is in accordance with sound common sense. I think that this appeal should be allowed.

LORD TOMLIN. My Lords, I have had an opportunity of considering the opinion ... prepared by my noble and learned friend, Lord Buckmaster. . . .

. . .

I will only add to what has been already said by my noble and learned friend, Lord Buckmaster, with regard to the decisions and dicta relied upon by the appellant and the other relevant reported cases, that I am unable to explain how the cases of dangerous articles can have been treated as "exceptions" if the appellant's contention is well founded. Upon the view which I take of the matter the reported cases—some directly, others impliedly—negative the existence as part of the common law of England of any principle affording support to the appellant's claim, and therefore there is, in my opinion, no material from which it is legitimate for your Lordships' House to deduce such a principle.

LORD THANKERTON. The special circumstances from which the appellant claims that such a relationship of duty should be inferred may, I think be stated thus—namely, that the respondent, in placing his manufactured article of drink upon the market, has intentionally so excluded interference with, or examination of, the article by any intermediate handler of the goods between himself and the consumer that he has, of his own accord, brought himself into direct relationship with the consumer, with the result that the consumer is entitled to rely upon the exercise of diligence by the manufacturer to secure that the article shall not be harmful to the consumer. If that contention be sound, the consumer, on her showing that the article has reached her intact and that she has been injured by the harmful nature of the article, owing to the failure of the manufacturer to take reasonable care in its preparation prior to its enclosure in the sealed vessel, will be entitled to reparation from the manufacturer.

In my opinion, the existence of a legal duty under such circumstances is in conformity with the principles of both the law of Scotland and of the law of England. The English cases demonstrate how impossible it is to catalogue finally, amid the ever varying types of human relationships, those relationships in which a duty to exercise care arises apart from contract, and each of these cases relates to its own set of circumstances, out of which it was claimed that the duty had arisen. In none of these cases were the circumstances identical with the present case as regards that which I regard as the essential element in this case—namely, the manufacturer's own action in bringing himself into direct relationship with the party injured. I have had the privilege of considering the discussion of these authorities by my noble and learned friend, Lord Atkin, in the judgment which he has just delivered, and I so entirely agree with it that I cannot usefully add anything to it.

. . .

I am therefore of opinion that the appeal should be allowed and the case should be remitted for proof, as the pursuer did not ask for an issue.

LORD MACMILLAN.

It humbly appears to me that the diversity of view ... is explained by the fact that in the discussion of the topic which now engages your Lordships' attention two rival principles of the law find a meeting place where each has contended for supremacy. On the one hand, there is the well established principle that no one other than a party to a contract can complain of a breach of that contract. On the other hand, there is the equally well established doctrine that negligence apart from contract gives a right of action to the party injured by that negligence—and here I use the term negligence, of course, in its technical legal sense, implying a duty owed and neglected. The fact that there is a contractual relationship between the parties which may give rise to an action for breach of contract, does not exclude the co-existence of a right of action founded on negligence as between the same parties, independently of the contract, though arising out of the relationship in fact brought about by the contract. Of this the best illustration is the right of the injured railway passenger to sue the railway company either for breach of the contract of safe carriage or for negligence in carrying him. And there is no reason why the same set of facts should not give one person a right of action in contract and another person a right of action in tort....

Where, as in cases like the present, so much depends upon the avenue of approach to the question, it is very easy to take the wrong turning. If you begin with the sale by the manufacturer to the retail dealer, then the consumer who purchases from the retailer is at once seen to be a stranger to the contract between the retailer and the manufacturer and so disentitled to sue upon it. There is no contractual relation between the manufacturer and the consumer; and thus the plaintiff, if he is to succeed, is driven to try to bring himself within one or other of the exceptional cases where the strictness of the rule that none but a party to a contract can found on a breach of that contract has been mitigated in the public interest, as it has been in the case of a person who issues a chattel which is inherently dangerous or which he knows to be in a dangerous condition. If, on the other hand, you disregard the fact that the circumstances of the case at one stage include the existence of a contract of sale between the manufacturer and the retailer, and approach the question by asking whether there is evidence of carelessness on the part of the manufacturer, and whether he owed a duty to be careful in a question with the party who has been injured in consequence of his want of care, the circumstance that the injured party was not a party to the incidental contract of sale becomes irrelevant, and his title to sue the manufacturer is unaffected by that circumstance. The appellant in the present instance asks that her case be approached as a case of delict, not as a case of breach of contract....

. . .

The law takes no cognizance of carelessness in the abstract. It concerns itself with carelessness only where there is a duty to take care and where failure in that duty has caused damage. In such circumstances carelessness assumes the legal quality of negligence and entails the consequences in law of negligence. What, then, are the circumstances which give rise to this duty to take care? In the daily contacts of social and business life human beings are thrown into, or place themselves in, an infinite variety of relations with their fellows; and the law can refer only to the standards of the reasonable man in order to determine whether any particular relation gives rise to a duty to take care as between those who stand in that relation to each other. The grounds of action may be as various and manifold as human errancy; and the conception of legal responsibility may develop in adaptation to altering social conditions and standards. The criterion of judgment must adjust and adapt itself to the changing circumstances of life. The categories of negligence are never closed. The cardinal principle of liability is that the party complained of should owe to the party complaining a duty to take care, and that the party complaining should be able to prove that he has suffered damage in consequence of a breach of that duty. Where there is room for diversity of view, it is in determining what circumstances will establish such a relationship between the parties as to give rise, on the one side, to a duty to take care, and on the other side to a right to have care taken.

To descend from these generalities to the circumstances of the present case, I do not think that any reasonable man or any twelve reasonable men would hesitate to hold that, if the appellant establishes her allegations, the respondent has exhibited carelessness in the conduct of his business. For a manufacturer of aerated water to store his empty bottles in a place where snails can get access to them, and to fill his bottles without taking any adequate precautions by inspection or otherwise to ensure that they contain no deleterious foreign matter may reasonably be characterized as carelessness without applying too exacting a standard....

. . .

The burden of proof must always be upon the injured party to establish that the defect which caused the injury was present in the article when it left the hands of the party whom he sues, that the defect was occasioned by the carelessness of that party, and that the circumstances are such as to cast upon the defender a duty to take care not to injure the pursuer. There is no presumption of negligence in such a case as the present, nor is there any justification for applying the maxim, res ipsa loquitur. Negligence must be both averred and proved. The appellant accepts this burden of proof, and in my opinion she is entitled to have an opportunity of discharging it if she can. I am accordingly of opinion that this appeal should be allowed, the judgment of the Second Division of the Court of Sessions reversed, and the judgment of the Lord Ordinary restored.

NOTE

Was the cleavage in the 3–2 decision based on different choices of legal precepts? Different interpretations of the chosen legal precept? Or different applications of the legal precept to the cause? What values did the several judges place on precedent? American precedent? Obiter dictum? Evaluate these opinions and compare them with similar opinions in our state and federal courts.

Chapter VII

EXERCISING THE JUDICIAL FUNCTION

Section 1

OVERVIEW

Everyone is entitled to "a day in court". Access to tiers of appellate review notwithstanding, more often than not, this means only one hearing or a trial, for it is at that proceeding (the pre-trial procedure or trial or hearing, lumped together in the shorthand expression "day in court") that the trial court exercises discretion or makes rulings of law or the fact finder determines the facts from the evidence. Where facts are not in dispute, the court decides the matter without live witnesses and often on papers without oral argument. For the most part these initial determinations are final and binding, irrespective of impressive appellate briefs, thick volumes of records or eloquent oral argument. This aspect of the judicial process is lost on most people. Yet the reality is that most trial court decisions are set in a jurisprudential cement which hardens quickly and will be subject to an extremely limited scope of appellate review.

When the controversy is one of fact, findings ordinarily are permanent. Practical and philosophical impediments prevent displacing the fact finder's resolution of conflicting evidence. Furthermore, it is a popular misconception that all legal determinations, unlike facts, may be reversed on appeal. Though reviewable, a legal ruling, even though erroneous, may not be sufficient grounds for reversing. When the trial court is vested with the right to exercise discretion, the appellate court may not properly substitute its views for those of the trial court. Rather, the appellate function is limited to discovering and defining the perimeters of allowable discretion and interfering only when convinced that the use of discretion has exceeded those limitations. The reviewing court calls such a transgression an "abuse" or, more accurately, a "misuse" of the exercise of proper discretion.

"A defendant is entitled to a fair trial but not a perfect one." [1] Although the trial court may err in some of its rulings, whether the judgment should be reopened turns on whether the error is "reversible" or "harmless." To recognize these distinctions and to accommodate this awareness to the cause at hand is the hallmark of the expert appellate advocate.

---

1. Lutwak v. United States, 344 U.S. 604, 619 (1953).

676

MAURICE ROSENBERG, JUDICIAL DISCRETION OF
THE TRIAL COURT, VIEWED FROM ABOVE *

Whatever reasons there are for non-reviewability of wrong trial court decisions, shortage of judicial machinery is apparently not a significant one. We have plenty of appellate courts, waiting (and Lord Devlin has humorously suggested, hoping) for mistaken calls by trial judges. Their whole reason for existence, it might be argued, is to reverse erroneous decisions by lower courts. Why should they abstain from their duty? To understand why they accept, announce and at times additionally restrict their own review powers in many areas of law, we need a larger perspective on the review functions of appellate courts.

A good place to start is with the worm's-eye view of the trial judge. From his perspective all appellate Gaul is divided into three parts for review purposes: questions of fact, of law and of discretion. Well-accepted principles surround the first two matters:

(1) In reviewing findings of fact, the first issue of consequence is whether the facts were found by a judge or a jury, for that will determine the scope and depth of the appellate court's scrutiny. A reviewing court does not disturb a jury verdict if on any rational view of the evidence after resolving all issues of credibility in favor of the winner, it was "reasonable." It was reasonable if it could have been arrived at by a process of reasoning from the evidence. By contrast, if the facts were found by a judge alone, his findings need somewhat stronger underpinning. The test of sufficiency is typically phrased in terms of whether the supporting evidence is "substantial." A non-jury finding may be more open to reversal if it rests on documentary evidence rather than on the testimony of live witnesses.[1]

(2) In reviewing questions of law, appellate courts usually follow an approach that is brutally simple or simply brutal (depending on whether the process is being evaluated by the trial judge or an observer less intimately concerned). The appellate courts merely ask themselves whether they agree with the trial judge's resolution of the legal issue. If not, they reverse him quick as a flash—unless they determine that the error made was harmless, or waived.

(3) Finally, there are questions of discretion. This is the area in which appellate courts have adopted the remarkably tolerant, generous and permissive attitude.... By doing this, they limit their prerogatives of review by their own act, without prompting or command by the legislature and even when they are not constrained by the inhibitions on review of facts which were described above. This magnanimity and toleration of lower court decisions they disagree with is not limited to certain courts or modern times.

* 22 Syracuse L.Rev. 635, 645–46 (1971). Reprinted by permission.

1. Ed. Note: By a 1985 amendment to Rule 52(a), Federal Rules of Civil Procedure, the distinction between oral and documentary evidence has been eliminated.

Section 2

FACT FINDING

OVERVIEW

Fact finding is the province of the trial tribunal, be it a court or an administrative agency. The skill of a trial advocate is measured by an ability to persuade the fact finder to convert a congeries of testimony and evidence into adjudicative facts. The fact finder may be a jury, a judge, or a hearing examiner or administrative law judge and the board to which he or she reports. Trial advocacy, which deals with fact-based persuasion, calls for skills completely different from appellate advocacy requiring legal persuasion in questions of law.

The fact finder is the sole judge of credibility and is free to accept or reject even uncontradicted oral testimony. Without regard to the number of rungs an appellant may climb up the appellate ladder, if minimal evidentiary quanta have been satisfied, the American tradition generally does not permit a reviewing court to disturb findings of fact.

Three Categories of Facts

For a proper understanding of the jurisprudence of fact finding review, it is necessary to segregate three distinct and fundamental concepts—basic facts, inferred facts and ultimate facts. The importance of distinguishing these three types is reflected in the various standards of judicial review. When the court sitting as fact finder identifies the basic facts and the facts permissibly inferred therefrom, neither may be disturbed on review unless they are deemed clearly erroneous.[1] "[A] review of ultimate facts," on the other hand, "entails an examination for legal error of the legal components of those findings." [2]

Basic and Inferred Facts

Although writers and judges are not uniform in the labels placed on various types of facts, "basic facts" are best understood as historical and narrative accounts elicited from the evidence presented by eye- or earwitnesses at trial, or admitted by stipulation or not denied in responsive pleadings. In 1937 Justice Frankfurter described these as "primary, evidentiary or circumstantial facts." [3] Evidence that is inferred from eye- or ear witness testimony rather than being direct is often called circumstantial. Inferences of fact are permitted only when, and to the extent that, logic and human experience indicate a probability that

1. Fed.R.Civ.P. 52(a); see United States v. United States Gypsum Co., 333 U.S. 364, 394 (1948).

2. Smith v. Harris, 644 F.2d 985, 990 (3d Cir.1981) (Aldisert, J., concurring); see also Universal Minerals, Inc. v. C.A. Hughes & Co., 669 F.2d 98, 102–03 (3d Cir.1981) (an extensive discussion of the distinction between review of basic and inferred facts and ultimate facts.)

3. Helvering v. Tex–Penn Co., 300 U.S. 481, 491 (1936).

certain consequences can and do follow from the basic events or conditions.[4] No legal precept is implicated in drawing permissible factual inferences.

Mixed Questions of Law and Fact

It is important to distinguish an inferred fact (circumstantial evidence) from a mixed question of law and fact, which we refer to here as an "ultimate fact" or "ultimate finding." So perceived, an ultimate fact is a mixture of fact and legal precept. An ultimate fact usually is expressed in the language of a standard enunciated by case law or by statute, e.g., an actor's conduct was negligent or the injury occurred in the course of employment or the rate is reasonable or the company has refused to bargain collectively. "The ultimate finding is a conclusion of law or at least a determination of a mixed question of law and fact."[5]

Fact Finding: Who Does It, and Under What Conditions?

It is the responsibility of the fact finder—jury, judge or administrative agency—to find the narrative or historical facts and to draw proper inferences therefrom. Often the fact finder must go further and determine the ultimate fact as well, on the basis of the court's instruction in a jury case or of a proper application of a legal precept in a non-jury trial or agency hearing. The fact finder always operates within the acknowledged limitations of any judicial process.

Narrative or historical data are at best imperfect reenactments of the actual events. They are constructed from the perceptions of witnesses. The most one can hope for is that the witnesses be not only honest but reasonably accurate in both perception and recollection, and that the fact finder also be honest and both intelligent and fair in evaluating the evidence presented. What the judicial process affords is a time-tested mechanism that seeks to fashion a courtroom reconstruction of what actually occurred. It is not perfection in all cases, but it does serve as a reasonable facsimile in most cases.

For a proper understanding of fact finding review procedures, it is necessary to separate the distinct concepts involved in the review of judicial findings. The difference in these concepts—basic facts (both direct and inferred) and ultimate facts (mixture of law and fact)—is fundamental in the review process.

Once basic facts have been found, they are seldom dislodged. The trial lawyer's skill often is measured by an ability to persuade the fact finder to find favorable basic facts. The appellate advocate's skill, however, is measured in part by an ability to convince the reviewing court that a given "fact" is not a "basic" fact, but rather an "ultimate" fact. This is because the appellate court, and indeed the trial court in a post-trial context, may review only abuses of discretion or an erroneous legal interpretation given in the court's instructions to the jury, or a

---

4. See, e.g., Edward J. Sweeney & Sons, Inc. v. Texaco, Inc., 637 F.2d 105, 116 (3d Cir.1980), cert. denied, 451 U.S. 911 (1981).

5. Helvering v. Tex–Penn Oil Co., 300 U.S. 481, 491 (1937).

legal error by the fact finder in bench trials. Legal error review is limited to the finding or choosing the law, interpreting it and applying the legal precept to the facts found by the fact finder.

Where facts have not been found by a jury, a reviewer of an ultimate fact may not disturb its basic fact component in this mixed question of law and fact unless there is clear error. It is fair, however, for an appellate court to review *de novo* the "law" segment of the ultimate fact.[6] This means that review is available when there is insufficient evidence to sustain the requirements of the legal precept upon which the ultimate fact is premised. For example, in a review of a finding of negligence in an automobile case, the evidence of speed, location of vehicles and direction of travel is historical or narrative. This is the "basic" fact component of the "ultimate" fact of negligence.

The basic fact component is not reviewable in jury trials[7] and is subject to extremely limited review in bench trials.

EDWARD J. SWEENEY & SONS, INC. v. TEXACO, INC.

United States Court of Appeals, Third Circuit, 1980.
637 F.2d 105.

Before: ALDISERT and SLOVITER, Circuit Judges, and RAMBO, District Judge.

ALDISERT, CIRCUIT JUDGE.

The teachings of the Supreme Court are clear on when a matter may be submitted to the jury:

> The matter is essentially one to be worked out in particular situations and for particular types of cases. Whatever may be the general formulation, the essential requirement is that mere speculation not be allowed to do duty for probative facts, after making due allowance for all reasonably possible inferences favoring the party whose case is attacked.

Galloway v. United States, 319 U.S. 372, 395, 63 S.Ct. 1077, 1089, 87 L.Ed. 1458 (1943). A reviewing court applies the same standard to a decision by a trial judge granting a motion for directed verdict. The appellate court must consider the record as a whole and in the light most favorable to the non-moving party, drawing all reasonable inferences to support its contentions. If no reasonable resolution of the conflicting evidence and inferences therefrom could result in a judgment for the non-moving party, the appellate court must affirm the lower court's decision. *See* Columbia Metal Culvert Co., Inc. v. Kaiser Aluminum and

------

6. See, e.g., Universal Minerals, Inc. v. C.A. Hughes & Co., 669 F.2d 98, 102–103 (3d Cir.1981).

7. Basic facts are not reviewable in jury trials except in the intermediate appellate court of Louisiana, hearkening back to Napoleonic Code origins.

Chemical Corp., 579 F.2d 20 (3d Cir.), *cert. denied,* 439 U.S. 876, 99 S.Ct. 214, 58 L.Ed.2d 190 (1979).

The jury's role in our legal tradition probably represents modern America's unique characteristic in the trial of civil cases. Its role cannot be minimized, nor its importance dissipated one iota. Yet the limits of the jury's role must always be recognized. The jury translates as found fact a congeries of relevant evidence on controverted factual issues. The jury does not engage in the final stage of this process until the court makes the critical legal decision that there is sufficient evidence to submit to the jury for the purpose of resolving conflicts in the evidence or inferences permissibly drawn from the evidence, or both. In removing a case from the jury, the court undertakes the vital task of "protecting neutral principles of law from powerful forces outside the scope of the law—compassion and prejudice." Rutherford v. Illinois Central R.R., 278 F.2d 310, 312 (5th Cir.), *cert. denied,* 364 U.S. 922, 81 S.Ct. 288, 5 L.Ed.2d 261 (1960).

The court's role is especially crucial when as here, the plaintiff's case, and therefore the defendant's liability, is based solely on circumstantial evidence. The illegal action must be inferred from the facts shown at trial. Inferred factual conclusions based on circumstantial evidence are permitted only when, and to the extent that, human experience indicates a probability that certain consequences can and do follow from the basic circumstantial facts. The inferences that the court permits the jury to educe in a courtroom do not differ significantly from inferences that rational beings reach daily in informally accepting a probability or arriving at a conclusion when presented with some hard, or basic evidence. A court permits the jury to draw inferences because of this shared experience in human endeavors. *See generally,* McCormick, Handbook of the Law of Evidence 289–96 (2d edition 1972). Perhaps the only distinction between extracting factual conclusions from circumstantial evidence in daily life and in the courtroom is that a jury's act of drawing or not drawing an inference is preceded by a judge's instruction. The instruction serves to guide the jury through some process of ordered consideration. The court informs the jury that it must weigh the narrative or historical evidence presented, making credibility findings when appropriate, and then draw only those inferences that are reasonable in reaching a verdict.

When a trial court grants a directed verdict in a circumstantial evidence case, the court makes a legal determination that the narrative or historical matters in evidence allow no permissible inference of the ultimate fact urged by the opposing party. It decides that no reasonable person could reach the suggested conclusion on the basis of the hard evidence without resorting to guesswork or conjecture. To permit a jury to draw an inference of the ultimate fact under these circumstances is to substitute the experience of logical probability for what the courts describe as "mere speculation." Galloway v. United States, 319 U.S. at 395, 63 S.Ct. at 1089; Columbia Metal Culvert Co. v. Kaiser Aluminum & Chemical Corp., 579 F.2d at 25.

Logicians describe one process of reaching an ultimate fact from insufficient basic facts as the *false cause* or *post hoc* fallacy. The fallacy consists of reasoning from sequence to consequence, that is, assuming a causal connection between two events merely because one follows the other. For this reason the fallacy is often referred to as that of *post hoc ergo propter hoc* (after this and therefore in consequence of this), an expression which itself explains the nature of the error.

Here, the district court properly concluded that the basic facts adduced at trial were insufficient to allow the jury to find for appellants. The basic record facts were that some of Sweeney's competitors complained that Sweeney's stations undersold them by one to three cents per gallon, that Rodden did not know but "guessed" Texaco acted to terminate Sweeney because of these complaints, that Murray surmised Texaco was evaluating Sweeney's ability to get long hauling allowances for short deliveries, and that certain consequences of Sweeney's marketing strategy not directly related to Sweeney's competitive position figured into Doherty's decision to terminate Sweeney. Faced with this scanty record, the district court properly removed the issue of concerted action from the jury. It determined that insufficient narrative or historical evidence had been submitted to permit the conclusion that Texaco's decision was a reaction to the specific complaints received. Moreover, the record was devoid of proof of concerted action among Sweeney's competitors and Texaco. The court concluded that the jury could not infer this ultimate fact from the basic facts in evidence without engaging in pure *post hoc* guesswork. We will not fault the court for these determinations.

A. AT TRIAL OR HEARING

UNITED STATES v. GAUDIN

Supreme Court of the United States, 1995.
__ U.S. __, 115 S.Ct. 2310, 132 L.Ed.2d 444.

JUSTICE SCALIA delivered the opinion of the Court.

In the trial at issue here, respondent was convicted of making material false statements in a matter within the jurisdiction of a federal agency, in violation of 18 U.S.C. § 1001. The question presented is whether it was constitutional for the trial judge to refuse to submit the question of "materiality" to the jury.

I

In the 1980s, respondent engaged in a number of real estate transactions financed by loans insured by the Federal Housing Administration (FHA), an agency within the Department of Housing and Urban Development (HUD). Respondent would purchase rental housing, renovate it, obtain an inflated appraisal, and sell it to a "strawbuyer" (a friend or relative), for whom respondent would arrange an FHA-insured mortgage loan. Then, as prearranged, respondent would repurchase the property (at a small profit to the strawbuyer) and assume the mortgage loan. Twenty-nine of these ventures went into default.

Respondent was charged by federal indictment with, among other things, multiple counts of making false statements on federal loan documents in violation of 18 U.S.C. § 1001. Two of these counts charged that respondent had made false statements on HUD/FHA form 92800–5 by knowingly inflating the appraised value of the mortgaged property. The other false-statement counts charged that respondent had made misrepresentations on HUD/FHA form HUD–1, the settlement form used in closing the sales of the properties. Line 303 of this form requires disclosure of the closing costs to be paid or received by the borrower/buyer and the seller. The forms executed by respondent showed that the buyer was to pay some of the closing costs, whereas in fact he, the seller, had arranged to pay all of them. To prove the materiality of these false statements, the Government offered the testimony of several persons charged with administering FHA/HUD programs, who explained why the requested information was important. At the close of the evidence, the United States District Court for the District of Montana instructed the jury that, to convict respondent, the Government was required to prove, *inter alia,* that the alleged false statements were material to the activities and decisions of HUD. But, the court further instructed, "[t]he issue of materiality ... is not submitted to you for your decision but rather is a matter for the decision of the court. You are instructed that the statements charged in the indictment are material statements." App. 24, 29. The jury convicted respondent of the § 1001 charges.

A panel of the Court of Appeals for the Ninth Circuit reversed these convictions because Circuit precedent dictated that materiality in a § 1001 prosecution be decided by the jury. 997 F.2d 1267 (1993). On rehearing en banc, the Court of Appeals stood by this precedent. It held that taking the question of materiality from the jury denied respondent a right guaranteed by the Fifth and Sixth Amendments to the United States Constitution. 28 F.3d 943 (1994). We granted certiorari. 513 U.S. ___ (1995).

II

Section 1001 of Title 18 provides:

"Whoever, in any matter within the jurisdiction of any department or agency of the United States knowingly and wilfully falsifies, conceals or covers up by any trick, scheme, or device a material fact, or makes any false, fictitious or fraudulent statements or representations, or makes or uses any false writing or document knowing the same to contain any false, fictitious or fraudulent statement or entry, shall be fined not more than $10,000 or imprisoned not more than five years, or both."

It is uncontested that conviction under this provision requires that the statements be "material" to the Government inquiry, and that "materiality" is an element of the offense that the Government must prove. The parties also agree on the definition of "materiality": the statement must have "a natural tendency to influence, or [be] capable of influencing, the decision of the decisionmaking body to which it was addressed." Kungys v. United States, 485 U.S. 759, 770 (1988) (internal quotation marks omitted). The question for our resolution is whether respondent was entitled to have this element of the crime determined by the jury.

The Fifth Amendment to the United States Constitution guarantees that no one will be deprived of liberty without "due process of law"; and the Sixth, that "[i]n all criminal prosecutions, the accused shall enjoy the right to a speedy and public trial, by an impartial jury." We have held that these provisions require criminal convictions to rest upon a jury determination that the defendant is guilty of every element of the crime with which he is charged, beyond a reasonable doubt. Sullivan v. Louisiana, 508 U.S. ___, ___ (1993) (slip op., at 2–3). The right to have a jury make the ultimate determination of guilt has an impressive pedigree. Blackstone described "trial by jury" as requiring that *"the truth of every accusation,* whether preferred in the shape of indictment, information, or appeal, should afterwards be confirmed by the unanimous suffrage of twelve of [the defendant's] equals and neighbors...."* 4 W. Blackstone, Commentaries on the Laws of England 343 (1769) (emphasis added). Justice Story wrote that the "trial by jury" guaranteed by the Constitution was "generally understood to mean ... a trial by a jury of twelve men, impartially selected, who must unanimously *concur in the guilt of the accused before a legal conviction can be had."* 2 J. Story, Commentaries on the Constitution of the United States 541, n. 2 (4th ed. 1873) (emphasis added and deleted). This right was designed "to guard against a spirit of oppression and tyranny on the part of rulers," and "was from very early times insisted on by our ancestors in the parent country, as the great bulwark of their civil and political liberties." *Id.,* at 540–541. See also Duncan v. Louisiana, 391 U.S. 145, 151–154 (1968) (tracing the history of trial by jury).

III

Thus far, the resolution of the question before us seems simple. The Constitution gives a criminal defendant the right to demand that a jury find him guilty of all the elements of the crime with which he is charged; one of the elements in the present case is materiality; respondent therefore had a right to have the jury decide materiality. To escape the force of this logic, the Government offers essentially three arguments. Having conceded the minor premise—that materiality is an element of the offense—the Government argues first, that the major premise is flawed; second, that (essentially) a page of history is worth a volume of logic, and uniform practice simply excludes the element of materiality from the syllogism; and third, that *stare decisis* requires the judgment here to be reversed.

A

As to the first, the Government's position is that "materiality," whether as a matter of logic or history, is a "legal" question, and that although we have sometimes spoken of "requiring the jury to decide 'all the elements of a criminal offense,' *e.g.*, Estelle v. McGuire, [502 U.S. 62, 69] [1991]; see Victor v. Nebraska, [511 U.S. ___, ___ (slip op., at 1)] (1994); Patterson v. New York, 432 U.S. 197, 210 (1977), the principle actually applies to *only the factual components* of the essential elements."

The Government claims that this understanding of the jury's role dates back to Sparf & Hansen v. United States, 156 U.S. 51 (1895), and is reaffirmed by recent decisions of this Court.

By limiting the jury's constitutionally prescribed role to "the factual components of the essential elements" the Government surely does not mean to concede that the jury must pass upon all elements that contain *some* factual component, for that test is amply met here. Deciding whether a statement is "material" requires the determination of at least two subsidiary questions of purely historical fact: (a) "what statement was made?"; and (b) "what decision was the agency trying to make?". The ultimate question: (c) "whether the statement was material to the decision," requires applying the legal standard of materiality (quoted above) to these historical facts. What the Government apparently argues is that the Constitution requires only that (a) and (b) be determined by the jury, and that (c) may be determined by the judge. We see two difficulties with this. First, the application-of-legal-standard-to-fact sort of question posed by (c), commonly called a "mixed question of law and fact," has typically been resolved by juries. See J. Thayer, A Preliminary Treatise on Evidence at Common Law 194, 249–250 (1898). Indeed, our cases have recognized in other contexts that the materiality inquiry, involving as it does "delicate assessments of the inferences a 'reasonable [decisionmaker]' would draw from a given set of facts and the significance of those inferences to him ... [is] peculiarly on[e] for the trier of fact." TSC Industries, Inc. v. Northway, Inc., 426 U.S. 438, 450 (1976) (securities fraud); McLanahan v. Universal Ins. Co., 1 Pet. 170, 188–189, 191 (1828) (materiality of false statements in insurance applications).

The second difficulty with the Government's position is that it has absolutely no historical support. If it were true, the law books would be full of cases, regarding materiality and innumerable other "mixed-law-and-fact" issues, in which the criminal jury was required to come forth with "findings of fact" pertaining to each of the essential elements, leaving it to the judge to apply the law to those facts and render the ultimate verdict of "guilty" or "not guilty." We know of no such case. Juries at the time of the framing could not be forced to produce mere "factual findings," but were entitled to deliver a general verdict pronouncing the defendant's guilt or innocence. Morgan, A Brief History of Special Verdicts and Special Interrogatories, 32 Yale L.J. 575, 591

(1922). See also G. Clementson, Special Verdicts and Special Findings by Juries 49 (1905); Alschuler & Deiss, A Brief History of the Criminal Jury in the United States, 61 U.Chi.L.Rev. 867, 912–913 (1994). Justice Chase's defense to one of the charges in his 1805 impeachment trial was that "he well knows that it is the right of juries in criminal cases, to give a general verdict of acquittal, which cannot be set aside on account of its being contrary to law, and that hence results the power of juries, to decide on the law as well as on the facts, in all criminal cases. This power he holds to be a sacred part of our legal privileges...." 1 S. Smith & T. Lloyd, Trial of Samuel Chase 34 (1805).

Sparf & Hansen, supra, the case on which the Government relies, had nothing to do with the issue before us here. The question there was whether the jury could be deprived of the power to determine, not only historical facts, not only mixed questions of fact and law, *but pure questions of law* in a criminal case. As the foregoing quotation from Justice Chase suggests, many thought the jury had such power. See generally Alschuler & Deiss, *supra,* at 902–916. We decided that it did not. In criminal cases, as in civil, we held, the judge must be permitted to instruct the jury on the law and to insist that the jury follow his instructions. 156 U.S., at 105–106. But our decision in no way undermined the historical and constitutionally guaranteed right of criminal defendants to demand that the jury decide guilt or innocence on every issue, which includes application of the law to the facts. To the contrary, Justice Harlan, writing for the Court, explained the many judicial assertions of the jury's right to determine both law and fact as expressions of "the principle, that when the question is *compounded of law and fact,* a general verdict, *ex necessitate,* disposes of the case in hand, both as to law and fact." *Id.,* at 90 (emphasis in original). He gave as an example the 1807 treason trial of Aaron Burr in which Chief Justice Marshall charged the jury that " 'levying war is an act *compounded of law and fact;* of which the jury, aided by the court must judge.... [And] hav[ing] now heard the opinion of the court on the law of the case[,] [t]hey *will apply that law to the facts,* and will find a verdict of guilty or not guilty as their own consciences may direct.' " *Id.,* at 67 (quoting 2 Burr's Trial 548, 550 (D. Robertson ed. 1875)) (emphasis in original). Other expressions of the same principle abound. See United States v. Battiste, 24 F.Cas. 1042, 1043 (No. 14,545) (CC Mass.1835) (Story, J., sitting as Circuit Justice) (the jury's general verdict is "necessarily compounded of [both] law and fact"). As Thayer wrote at the end of the 19th century: "From the beginning ... it was perceived that any general verdict, such as ... not guilty, involved a conclusion of law, and that the jury did, in a sense, in such cases answer a question of law." Thayer, *supra,* at 253.

The more modern authorities the Government cites also do not support its concept of the criminal jury as mere factfinder. Although each contains language discussing the jury's role as factfinder, see Sullivan v. Louisiana, 508 U.S. ___ (1993); County Court of Ulster Cty. v. Allen, 442 U.S. 140, 156 (1979); Patterson v. New York, 432 U.S. 197,

206 (1977); In re Winship, 397 U.S. 358, 364 (1970), each also confirms that the jury's constitutional responsibility is not merely to determine the facts, but to apply the law to those facts and draw the ultimate conclusion of guilt or innocence. The point is put with unmistakable clarity in *Allen,* which involved the constitutionality of statutory inferences and presumptions. Such devices, *Allen* said, can help "the trier of fact to determine the existence of an element of the crime—that is, an 'ultimate' or 'elemental' fact—from the existence of one or more 'evidentiary' or 'basic' facts. . . . Nonetheless, in criminal cases, the ultimate test of any device's constitutional validity in a given case remains constant: the device must not undermine the fact-finder's responsibility at trial, based on evidence adduced by the State, to find the *ultimate* facts beyond a reasonable doubt." *Allen, supra,* at 156.

See also *Sullivan, supra,* at ___ (slip op., at 2) ("The right [to jury trial] includes, of course, as its most important element, the right to have the jury, rather than the judge, reach the requisite finding of 'guilty' "); *Patterson, supra,* at 204; *Winship, supra,* at 361, 363.

B

The Government next argues that, even if the jury is generally entitled to pass on all elements of a crime, there is a historical exception for materiality determinations in perjury prosecutions. We do not doubt that historical practice is relevant to what the Constitution means by such concepts as trial by jury, see Murray's Lessee v. Hoboken Land & Improvement Co., 18 How. 272, 276–277 (1856); Holland v. Illinois, 493 U.S. 474, 481 (1990), and it is precisely historical practice that we have relied on in concluding that the jury must find all the elements. The existence of a unique historical exception to this principle—and an exception that reduces the power of the jury precisely when it is most important, *i.e.,* in a prosecution not for harming another individual, but for offending against the Government itself—would be so extraordinary that the evidence for it would have to be convincing indeed. It is not so.

Even assuming, however, that all the Government's last-half-of-the-19th-century cases fully stand for the proposition that the defendant has no right to jury determination of materiality, there are cases that support the other view. At most there had developed a division of authority on the point, as the treatise writers of the period amply demonstrate. Bishop in 1872 took the position that "[p]ractically, . . . the whole subject is to be passed upon by the jury, under instructions from the judge, as involving, like most other cases, mixed questions of law and of fact." 2 J. Bishop, Commentaries on Law of Criminal Procedure § 935, p. 508 (2d ed.). May's 1881 treatise reported that "[w]hether materiality is a question of law for the court or of fact for a jury, is a point upon which the authorities are about equally divided." J. May, Law of Crimes § 188, p. 205. Greenleaf, writing in 1883, sided with Bishop ("It seems that the materiality of the matter assigned is a question for the jury"), 3 S. Greenleaf, Law of Evidence § 195, p. 189, n. (b) (14th ed.)—but two editions later, in 1899, said that the question was one for the judge, 3 S. Greenleaf, Law of Evidence § 195, p. 196, n. 2 (16th ed.).

In sum, we find nothing like a consistent historical tradition supporting the proposition that the element of materiality in perjury prosecutions is to be decided by the judge. Since that proposition is contrary to the uniform general understanding (and we think the only understanding consistent with principle) that the Fifth and Sixth Amendments require conviction by a jury of *all* elements of the crime, we must reject those cases that have embraced it. Though uniform postratification practice can shed light upon the meaning of an ambiguous constitutional provision, the practice here is not uniform, and the core meaning of the constitutional guarantees is unambiguous.

C

The Government's final argument is that the principle of *stare decisis* requires that we deny petitioner's constitutional claim, citing our decision in Sinclair v. United States, 279 U.S. 263 (1929).

But the reasoning of *Sinclair* has already been repudiated in a number of respects. The opinion rested upon the assumption that "pertinency" is a pure question of law—that is, it does "not depend upon the probative value of evidence." *Ibid.* We contradicted that assumption in Deutch v. United States, 367 U.S. 456 (1961), reversing a conviction under § 192 because "the Government at the trial failed to carry its burden of proving the pertinence of the questions." *Id.,* at 469. Though it had introduced documentary and testimonial evidence "to show the subject of the subcommittee's inquiry," it had failed to provide evidence to support the conclusion that the petitioner's false statement was pertinent to that subject.

That leaves as the sole prop for *Sinclair* its reliance upon the unexamined proposition, never before endorsed by this Court, that materiality in perjury cases (which is analogous to pertinence in contempt cases) is a question of law for the judge. But just as there is nothing to support *Sinclair* except that proposition, there is, as we have seen, nothing to support that proposition except *Sinclair*. While this perfect circularity has a certain aesthetic appeal, it has no logic. We do not minimize the role that *stare decisis* plays in our jurisprudence. See Patterson v. McLean Credit Union, 491 U.S. 164, 172 (1989). That role is somewhat reduced, however, in the case of a procedural rule such as this, which does not serve as a guide to lawful behavior. See Payne v. Tennessee, 501 U.S. 808, 828 (1991). It is reduced all the more when the rule is not only procedural but rests upon an interpretation of the Constitution. See *ibid.* And we think *stare decisis* cannot possibly be controlling when, in addition to those factors, the decision in question has been proved manifestly erroneous, and its underpinnings eroded, by subsequent decisions of this Court. Rodriguez de Quijas v. Shearson/American Express, Inc., 490 U.S. 477, 480–481 (1989); Andrews v. Louisville & Nashville R. Co., 406 U.S. 320 (1972).

. . .

The Constitution gives a criminal defendant the right to have a jury determine, beyond a reasonable doubt, his guilt of every element of the crime with which he is charged. The trial judge's refusal to allow the jury to pass on the "materiality" of Gaudin's false statements infringed that right. The judgment of the Court of Appeals is affirmed.

It is so ordered.

CHIEF JUSTICE REHNQUIST, with whom JUSTICE O'CONNOR and JUSTICE BREYER join, concurring.

I join the Court's opinion. "A person when first charged with a crime is entitled to a presumption of innocence, and may insist that his guilt be established beyond a reasonable doubt. In re Winship, 397 U.S. 358 (1970)." Herrera v. Collins, 506 U.S. ___, ___ (1993). As a result, "[t]he prosecution bears the burden of proving all elements of the offense charged and must persuade the factfinder 'beyond a reasonable doubt' of the facts necessary to establish each of those elements." Sullivan v. Louisiana, 508 U.S. ___, ___ (1993) (citations omitted); see also Estelle v. McGuire, 502 U.S. 62, 69 (1991) ("[T]he prosecution must prove all the elements of a criminal offense beyond a reasonable doubt"). The Government has conceded that 18 U.S.C. § 1001 requires that the false statements made by respondent be "material" to the Government inquiry, and that "materiality" is an element of the offense that the Government must prove in order to sustain a conviction. *Ante,* at 3. The Government also has not challenged the Court of Appeals' determination that the error it identified was structural and plain. See *id.,* at 8, n. 5; see also 28 F.3d 943, 951–952 (CA9 1994). In light of these concessions, I agree that "[t]he trial judge's refusal to allow the jury to pass on the 'materiality' of Gaudin's false statements infringed" his "right to have a jury determine, beyond a reasonable doubt, his guilt of every element of the crime with which he [was] charged." *Ante,* at 17.

I write separately to point out that there are issues in this area of the law which, though similar to those decided in the Court's opinion, are not disposed of by the Court today. There is a certain syllogistic neatness about what we do decide: every element of an offense charged must be proven to the satisfaction of the jury beyond a reasonable doubt; "materiality" is an element of the offense charged under § 1001; therefore, the jury, not the Court, must decide the issue of materiality. But the Government's concessions have made this case a much easier one than it might otherwise have been.

———

ADDINGTON v. TEXAS

Supreme Court of the United States, 1979.
441 U.S. 418, 99 S.Ct. 1804, 60 L.Ed.2d 323.

MR. CHIEF JUSTICE BURGER delivered the opinion of the Court.

The function of a standard of proof, as that concept is embodied in the Due Process Clause and in the realm of factfinding, is to "instruct the factfinder concerning the degree of confidence our society thinks he should have in the correctness of factual conclusions for a particular type of adjudication." In re Winship, 397 U.S. 358, 370 (1970) (Harlan, J., concurring). The standard serves to allocate the risk of error between the litigants and to indicate the relative importance attached to the ultimate decision.

Generally speaking, the evolution of this area of the law has produced across a continuum three standards or levels of proof for different types of cases. At one end of the spectrum is the typical civil case involving a monetary dispute between private parties. Since society has a minimal concern with the outcome of such private suits, plaintiff's burden of proof is a mere preponderance of the evidence. The litigants thus share the risk of error in roughly equal fashion.

In a criminal case, on the other hand, the interests of the defendant are of such magnitude that historically and without any explicit constitutional requirement they have been protected by standards of proof designed to exclude as nearly as possible the likelihood of an erroneous judgment.[2] In the administration of criminal justice, our society imposes almost the entire risk of error upon itself. This is accomplished by requiring under the Due Process Clause that the state prove the guilt of an accused beyond a reasonable doubt. In re Winship, supra.

The intermediate standard, which usually employs some combination of the words "clear," "cogent," "unequivocal," and "convincing," is less commonly used, but nonetheless "is no stranger to the civil law." Woodby v. INS, 385 U.S. 276, 285, 87 S.Ct. 483, 488, 17 L.Ed.2d 362 (1966). See also McCormick, Evidence § 320 (1954); 9 J. Wigmore, Evidence § 2498 (3d ed. 1940). One typical use of the standard is in civil cases involving allegations of fraud or some other quasi-criminal wrongdoing by the defendant.

---

2. Compare Morano, A Reexamination of the Development of the Reasonable Doubt Rule, 55 B.U.L.Rev. 507 (1975) (reasonable doubt represented a less strict standard than previous common-law rules), with May, Some Rules of Evidence, 10 Am. L.Rev. 642 (1875) (reasonable doubt constituted a stricter rule than previous ones). See generally Underwood, The Thumb on the Scales of Justice: Burdens of Persuasion in Criminal Cases, 86 Yale L.J. 1299 (1977).

J.P. McBAINE, BURDEN OF PROOF:
DEGREES OF BELIEF *

No lawsuit can be decided, rationally, without the application of the commonplace concept of burden of proof [1]—the duty to persuade—or as is sometimes otherwise stated the risk of non-persuasion. Nor can any legal system be praised for practicability if there exists vagueness, uncertainty or confusion as to the scope or extent of the burden, or if the language commonly employed to describe its scope or extent is not easily comprehensible to those whose duty it is to determine whether the burden has been sustained.

. . .

Generally speaking the prevailing attitude is that the courts recognize three types of burdens of persuasion which must be borne by litigants in civil actions and in criminal prosecutions. The courts commonly say that in most civil actions the party who has the burden of proof must prove the existence of the facts upon which he relies by a preponderance of the evidence. The courts also commonly state that as to some issues of fact in civil cases the litigant who asserts their existence must prove them by clear and convincing evidence, or they use similar expressions. In criminal prosecutions it is commonly asserted that the burden is upon the prosecution to prove beyond a reasonable doubt all elements of the crime of which the defendant is accused. This heavy burden also is sometimes imposed in civil actions. It seems quite sensible that the courts should recognize the wisdom and fairness of degrees of persuasion and belief although difficulty may be involved in determining in the civil cases what degree of persuasion should be required as to various issues. We should not, however, it is strongly believed, have uncertainty, conflict and confusion in our legal system as to what are these three degrees of persuasion and belief or how they should be adequately expressed in instructions for a jury.

The only sound and defensible hypotheses are that the trier, or triers, of facts can find what (a) *probably* has happened, or (b) what *highly probably* has happened, or (c) what *almost certainly* has happened. No other hypotheses are defensible or can be justified by experience and knowledge.

NOTE

Is there a difference between "preponderance of the evidence" and a finding that something "probably has happened"; between "clear and convincing evidence" and "highly probable"; between "proof beyond a reasonable doubt" and "almost certain"?

* 32 Calif.L.Rev. 242, 242, 245–247 (1944). Copyright © 1944, California Law Review, Inc. Reprinted by permission.

1. The term "burden of proof" in the texts and judicial decisions is used in two senses. Primarily it is used to describe the duty of a litigant to persuade the judge or the jury that the facts he asserts exist or have existed. The term is also sometimes used to describe the duty of a litigant to produce evidence of an asserted fact. 9 Wigmore, Evidence (3d ed. 1940) §§ 2485, 2487.... In this essay the term is used in former or primary sense.

Jerome Frank makes reference to Professor Walter Wheeler Cook, described as a "leading rule skeptic", reporting that Cook concludes that "facts are the product first of abstraction from the concreteness [of the] 'brute, raw event,' [and] then of interpretation of the elements abstracted." Frank suggests that "facts", as solemnized by the courts, come about through a rather sophisticated process: "There are three steps in the selection: (a) First the witnesses make their selections from the 'brute, raw event' of the past about which they testify. What they pick out depends not only on their individual capacities for seeing, nearing, touching or smelling, but also on each witness' individual emotional condition at the time when he 'selects'; similar factors, plus bias or lying, affect the witnesses' 'selections' when asked to recollect what they originally observed, and again when they testify. (b) Second, when the testimony is oral and the witnesses tell differing stories, the trial court (omitting, for the moment, its gestalt) makes a 'selection'; it chooses to believe some and to disbelieve other testimony. (c) Only after the completion of this second step does there occur the kind of selection ["interpretation"] which Cook describes. The trial court must now, from the previously selected facts, cull out those facts which are 'relevant,' i.e., those which fit into some well-settled rule or some new rule the court contrives." J. Frank, Courts on Trial 318 (1950).

ROGER J. TRAYNOR, *Fact Skepticism and the Judicial Process,* 106 U.Pa.L.Rev. 635, 636 (1958) *: "The problem is that the facts are forever gone and no scientific method of inquiry can ever be devised to produce facsimiles that bring the past to life. The judicial process deals with probabilities, not facts, and we must therefore be on guard against making fact skepticism our main preoccupation. However skillfully, however sensitively we arrange a reproduction of the past, the arrangement is still that of the theater. We acknowledge as much when we speak of re-enacting the crime or the accident or perhaps some everyday event; we know better than to speak of reliving it. The most we can hope for is that witnesses will be honest and reasonably accurate in their perception and recollection, that triers of fact will be honest and intelligent in their reasoning, and that appellate courts will frame opinions with enough perspective to guide others in comparable fact situations and preclude their disputes from festering into litigation."

B. ON REVIEW

OVERVIEW

The first issue of consequence in reviewing findings of fact is whether the facts were found by a judge or a jury. The nature of the fact finder will determine the scope of the appellate court's scrutiny.

* Reprinted by permission.

The Seventh Amendment controls in federal jury cases: "In Suits at common law, where the value in controversy shall exceed twenty dollars, the right of trial by jury shall be preserved, and no fact tried by a jury shall be otherwise re-examined in any Court of the United States, than according to the rules of the common law." Most state constitutions have similar provisions.[1] So long as there is some evidence from which the jury could arrive at the finding by a process of reasoning, the jury's finding of fact will not be disturbed. This, of course, is a different issue than the quantum of evidence necessary to sustain the various burdens of proof in civil and criminal cases.[2]

Facts found by a judge alone require a stronger evidentiary base. The findings, under federal rules and in those states adhering to Rule 52(a) of the Federal Rules of Civil Procedure, shall not be set aside "unless clearly erroneous, and due regard shall be given to the opportunity of the trial court to judge of the credibility of the witnesses." "Clearly erroneous" has been interpreted to mean that a reviewing court can upset a finding of fact, even if there is some evidence to support the finding, only if the court is left with "the definite and firm conviction that a mistake has been committed."[3] This means the appellate court must accept the factual determination of the fact finder unless that determination "either (1) is completely devoid of minimum evidentiary support displaying some hue of credibility, or (2) bears no rational relationship to the supportive evidentiary data."[4]

Because the fact finder is given an opportunity to observe the demeanor of witnesses, generally "a fact finder's determination of credibility is not subject to appellate review."[5] Conversely, in cases in which the trial judge decides a fact issue on written or documentary evidence, some reviewing courts previously adopted the view that "we are as able as [the judge] to determine credibility, and so we may disregard his finding."[6] Many courts and thoughtful commentators, however, thought otherwise.[7] The question finally was resolved by Congressional approval of the amendment to Rule 52(a) Fed.R.Civ.P. suggested by the Federal Advisory Committee on Civil Rules. Since 1985, the rule reads that "[f]indings of fact, whether based on oral or documentary evidence, shall not be set aside unless clearly erroneous, and due regard shall be given to the opportunity of the trial court to judge the credibility of the witnesses."

Fact Finding: Jury or Judge?

Reviewing courts must understand the strictures that deny or severely limit their authority to disturb (1) narrative or historical facts

1. See, e.g., Pa. Const. art. I, § 6; N.J. Const. art. I, § 9; Del. Const. art. I, § 4.

2. See, e.g., Jackson v. Virginia, 443 U.S. 307 (1979).

3. United States v. United States Gypsum Co., 333 U.S. 364, 395 (1948).

4. Krasnov v. Dinan, 465 F.2d 1298, 1302 (3d Cir.1972).

5. See, e.g., Government of the Virgin Islands v. Gereau, 502 F.2d 914, 921 (3d Cir.1974), cert. denied, 424 U.S. 917 (1976).

6. Orvis v. Higgins, 180 F.2d 537, 539 (2d Cir.1950).

7. See, e.g., Lundgren v. Freeman, 307 F.2d 104 (9th Cir.1962); C.A. Wright, *The Doubtful Omniscience of Appellate Courts,* 41 Minn.L.Rev. 751 (1957).

and (2) permissible inferred facts. Thus, as we have observed, when the jury has found such facts, no review generally is available. Although a reviewing court may re-examine a determination of an ultimate fact, its review is limited to the legal component of that ultimate fact; the part of the ultimate fact consisting of historical or narrative facts, or inferences therefrom, is subject either to no review or to limited review. For example, in Universal Minerals, Inc. v. C.A. Hughes & Co.,[8] the question was whether there had been an abandonment of a pile of culm (refuse from a coal mine). The court explained that abandonment is not a question of narrative or historical fact, but an ultimate fact, a legal concept with a factual component, a conclusion of law or at least a determination of a mixed question of law and fact. The court explained:

> In reviewing the ultimate determination of abandonment, as an appellate court, we are therefore not limited by the "clearly erroneous" standard, ... but must employ a mixed standard of review. We must accept the trial court's findings of historical or narrative facts unless they are clearly erroneous, but we must exercise a plenary review of the trial court's choice and interpretation of legal precepts and its application of those precepts to the historical facts. Thus we separate the distinct factual and legal elements of the trial court's determination of an ultimate fact and apply the appropriate standard to each component.[9]

The same approach is used when reviewing a jury's findings on a mixed question, but the distinction is more easily understood in that context because of the strict division of competence between the jury and the trial court and because of the intercession of the Seventh Amendment. If, for example, a jury finds that a party has abandoned an interest in property, the appellate court reviews the lower court's jury instructions to determine whether it erred in its explanation of the law; if there is no error, the record is examined in order to determine whether the evidence was sufficient to justify someone of reasonable mind in drawing the factual inferences underlying the conclusion.

Fact Finding: Administrative Agencies

A reviewing court may not set aside the findings of administrative agencies unless they are "unsupported by substantial evidence" in light of the whole record.[10] What, however, is substantial evidence? For some time, recourse has been made to a Supreme Court statement by Chief Justice Hughes: "Substantial evidence is more than a mere scintilla. It means such relevant evidence as a reasonable mind might accept as adequate to support a conclusion." [11] A later statement supposedly clarified further: Substantial evidence was defined as "evi-

---

8. 669 F.2d 98 (3d Cir.1981).

9. Id. at 103.

10. 5 U.S.C.A. § 706(2)(E); see Beth Israel Hospital v. NLRB, 437 U.S. 483 (1978); Universal Camera Corp. v. NLRB, 340 U.S.

474 (1951); 4 K. Davis, Administrative Law chs. 29–30 (1958 & Supp.1970).

11. Consolidated Edison Co. v. NLRB, 305 U.S. 197, 229 (1938).

dence which is substantial, that is, affording a substantial basis of fact from which the fact in issue can be reasonably infer.... [I]t must be enough to justify, if the trial were to a jury, a refusal to direct a verdict when the conclusion sought to be drawn from it is one of fact for the jury." [12] A half century later, the Supreme Court redefined its definition:

> Judicial review of agency action, the field at issue here, regularly proceeds under the rubric of "substantial evidence" set forth in the Administrative Procedure Act, 5 U.S.C. § 706(2)(E). That phrase does not mean a large or considerable amount of evidence, but rather "such relevant evidence as a reasonable mind might accept as adequate to support a conclusion." [13]

In the review of administrative agency proceedings, as in the review of judicial fact finding, the question of credibility is for the agency to determine.[14] This conflict may have an important bearing on whether there is substantial evidence where the agency has not accepted the credibility findings of the administrative law judge who has had the opportunity to listen to the live witnesses and observe their comportment and demeanor.

A Comparison: Common Law and Civil Law Traditions

The nonreviewability of facts found by a court of the first instance or an administrative agency is peculiar to the common law tradition. Civil law tradition permits review of facts through the courts of the second instance. Thus, new evidence can be taken and the evidence below re-examined in the various appeals courts, e.g., the French *cour d'appel,* the German and Austrian *landesgerichthof,* and the Italian *corte d'appello.* Beyond the court of the second instance, the appeal to the final court is restricted to matters of law only—in France, a *pourvoi en cassation;* in Germany and Austria, a *Revision,* and in Italy, an *appello.*[15] Similarly, there is generous review of facts in appeals from administrative agencies to the specialized courts. In civil cases in Louisiana, the sole jurisdiction in the United States to follow the civil law tradition, the state's courts of appeal (the courts of second instance) may review

---

12. NLRB v. Columbian Enameling & Stamping Co., 306 U.S. 292, 299–300 (1939).

13. Pierce v. Underwood, 487 U.S. 552, 564–65 (1988) (quoting Consolidated Edison Co. v. NLRB, 305 U.S. 197, 229 (1938)).

14. Thus, in NLRB v. Lewisburg Chair & Furniture Co., 230 F.2d 155, 157 (3d Cir.1956): "Questions of credibility of witnesses have to be resolved in litigation but in labor cases this court is not the place where such resolving takes place." Under the substantial evidence standard, a reviewing court does not reweigh the evidence, resolve testimonial conflicts or "displace

the Board's choice between two fairly conflicting views, even though the court would justifiably have made a different choice had the matter been before it *de novo.*" Universal Camera Corp. v. NLRB, 340 U.S. 474, 488 (1951). The Court does not pass on the credibility of the witnesses, reweigh the evidence or reject reasonable Board inferences simply because other inferences might also reasonably be drawn. See NLRB v. Walton Mfg. Co., 369 U.S. 404, 405 (1962).

15. See R.J. Aldisert, *Rambling Through Continental Legal Systems,* 31 U.Pitt.L.Rev. 1 (1982).

facts.[16]

AYLETT v. SECRETARY, H.U.D.

United States Court of Appeals, Tenth Circuit, 1995.
54 F.3d 1560, 1566.

Before SEYMOUR, ALDISERT and BALDOCK, Circuit Judges.

ALDISERT, CIRCUIT JUDGE:

We must sustain an administrative agency's decision if it is supported by "substantial evidence," which is "such relevant evidence as a reasonable mind might accept as adequate to support a conclusion." Fierro v. Brown, 798 F.2d 1351, 1355 (10th Cir.1986). However, "where the Secretary ... overturns a decision of the ALJ ... and, in doing so, differs with the ALJ's assessment of witness credibility, the Secretary should fully articulate his reasons for so doing, and then, with heightened scrutiny, we must decide whether such reasons find support in the record." Id.

In many administrative agencies, reviews of ALJ decisions are considered by a multi-person board or commission. See, e.g., 20 C.F.R. 404.900(a)(4) (in disputes arising under the Social Security Act, the Appeals Council is the final administrative decision-making body); 20 C.F.R. § 725.481 (in disputes arising under the Federal Coal Mine Health & Safety Act, parties may appeal ALJ decision to Benefits Review Board); 29 C.F.R. § 101.12 (in labor disputes, the National Labor Relations Board reviews decisions of the ALJ). This is similar to federal court practices where three circuit judges on the U.S. Courts of Appeals review judgments entered by district judges. The practice in the U.S. Department of Housing and Urban Development is different. A single person considers the appeals. See, e.g., 24 C.F.R. §§ 24.314(c), 26.25(c), 104.930(a) (hearing officer's determination final unless Secretary or designee decides as a matter of discretion to review finding). In this case, the "Secretarial Designee," constituted a one-person reviewing tribunal.

In accordance with the Fair Housing Act, 42 U.S.C. § 3216(h) and pursuant to 24 C.F.R. § 104.930(a), "[t]he Secretary of HUD may review

---

16. Under Article 10(b) of the Louisiana Constitution of 1974: "Except as limited to questions of law by this constitution, or as provided by law in the review of administrative agency determinations, appellate jurisdiction of a court of appeal extends to law and facts." In the case of Arceneaux v. Dominque, 365 So.2d 1330 (La.1978), the Louisiana Supreme Court explained: "Manifestly erroneous in its simplest terms means clearly wrong ... Therefore, the appellate review of facts is not completed by reading so much of the record as will reveal a reasonable factual basis for the finding of the trial court; there must be a further determination that the record establishes that the finding is not clearly wrong." See also Brown v. Avondale Shipyards Inc., 413 So.2d 183 (La.C.A. 4th Cir.1982). Yet, generally speaking, in Louisiana, the trial court's findings of fact, particularly when they are dependent upon credibility of witnesses, are entitled to great weight and will not be disturbed on appeal in absence of manifest error. See, e.g., Echizenya v. Armenio, 354 So.2d 682 (La.Ct.App.1978), writ refused, 356 So.2d 1006 (La.1978).

any finding of fact, conclusion of law, or order contained in the initial decision of the administrative judge and issue a final decision in the proceeding. The Secretary may affirm, modify or set aside, in whole or in part, the initial decision or remand the initial decision for further proceedings."

It is useful to trace the jurisprudence of our court's "heightened scrutiny" test of Fierro in order to understand how to apply it:

> [W]here the Secretary, acting through the Appeals Council, overturns a decision of the ALJ granting benefits, and, in so doing, differs with the ALJ's assessment of witness credibility, the Secretary should fully articulate his reasons for so doing, and then, with heightened scrutiny, we must decide whether such reasons find support in the record. Webber v. Secretary, 784 F.2d 293, 296 (8th Cir.1986); Howard v. Heckler, 782 F.2d [1484,] 1487 [(9th Cir.1986)]; Lopez–Cardona v. Secretary, 747 F.2d [1081,] 1084 [(1st Cir.1984)].

798 F.2d at 1355.

In Webber, 784 F.2d at 296–297, we are told that "[t]he rationale behind this heightened scrutiny is that 'evidence supporting a conclusion may be less substantial when [an agency reaches a decision contrary to that reached by] an impartial, experienced examiner who has observed the witnesses and lived with the case.' Universal Camera Corp. v. NLRB, 340 U.S. 474, 496 (1951)." See also Howard, 782 F.2d at 1487 and cases collected in Eastern Engineering & Elevator Co., Inc. v. NLRB, 637 F.2d 191, 197 n. 8 (3d Cir.1980). Chief Judge Wallace of the Court of Appeals for the Ninth Circuit observed that these decisions often distinguish credibility determinations based on demeanor, sometimes referred to as "testimonial inferences," and inferences drawn from the evidence itself, sometimes referred to as "derivative inferences." Penasquitos Village, Inc. v. NLRB, 565 F.2d 1074, 1078 (9th Cir.1977) (Wallace, J. opinion announcing the judgment of the court). Weight is given the ALJ's determinations of credibility because only the ALJ "sees the witnesses and hears them testify, while the Board and the reviewing court look only at cold records." NLRB v. Walton Manufacturing Co., 369 U.S. 404, 408, (1962) (per curiam).

The Court also teaches:

As we said in the Universal Camera case:

> "... The findings of the examiner are to be considered along with the consistency and inherent probability of testimony. The significance of his [or her] report, of course, depends largely on the importance of credibility in the particular case." 340 U.S., at 496.

For the demeanor of a witness

> "... may satisfy the tribunal, not only that the witness' testimony is not true, but that the truth is the opposite of his story; for the denial of one, who has a motive to deny,

> may be uttered with such hesitation, discomfort, arrogance or defiance, as to give assurance that he is fabricating, and that, if he is, there is no alternative but to assume the truth of what he denies." Dyer v. MacDougall, 201 F.2d 265, 269 [(2d Cir.1952)].

Walton Mfg. Co., 369 U.S. at 408. In the context of reviewing facts found by a trial judge:

> If ... the witness testified orally (i.e., in the trial judge's presence) then the trial judge's "testimonial" or "primary" inference must usually be accepted by the upper court. That is the usual rule because of the importance attached to the witnesses' demeanor in estimating credibility; the demeanor is regarded as a sort of "real evidence." Absent documentary evidence ... his discretion in making "testimonial" or "primary" inferences is virtually unreviewable.

Wabash Corp. v. Ross Elec. Corp., 187 F.2d 577, 601 (2d Cir.1951) (Appendix to dissenting opinion of Frank, J.), cert. denied, 342 U.S. 820 (1951). Although Judge Frank's explanation comes in the context of judicial review of a trial judge's findings and not that of an administrative agency, we deem it relevant to our foregoing reference to the Court's discussion of demeanor in the context of an agency's fact finding. See Walton Mfg. Co., 369 U.S. at 408.

MILLER v. FENTON

Supreme Court of the United States, 1985.
474 U.S. 104, 106 S.Ct. 445, 88 L.Ed.2d 405.

JUSTICE O'CONNOR delivered the Opinion of the Court.

The Court of Appeals recognized that treating the voluntariness of a confession as an issue of fact was difficult to square with "fifty years of caselaw" in this Court. 741 F.2d, at 1462. It believed, however, that this substantial body of contrary precedent was not controlling in light of our more recent decisions addressing the scope of the § 2254(d) presumption of correctness. See Wainwright v. Witt, 469 U.S. 412, 429 (1985) (trial court's determination that a prospective juror in a capital case was properly excluded for cause entitled to presumption); Patton v. Yount, 467 U.S. 1025 (1984) (impartiality of an individual juror); Rushen v. Spain, 464 U.S. 114 (1983) *(per curiam)* (effect of *ex parte* communication on impartiality of individual juror); Maggio v. Fulford, 462 U.S. 111 (1983) *(per curiam)* (competency to stand trial); Marshall v. Lonberger, 459 U.S. 422, 431–437 (1983) (determination that defendant received and understood sufficient notice of charges against him to render guilty plea voluntary). We acknowledge that the Court has not charted an entirely clear course in this area. We reject, however, the Court of Appeals' conclusion that these case-specific holdings tacitly overturned the longstanding rule that the voluntariness of a confession is a matter for independent federal determination.

In the § 2254(d) context, as elsewhere, the appropriate methodology for distinguishing questions of fact from questions of law has been, to say the least, elusive. See Bose Corp. v. Consumers Union of United States, Inc., 466 U.S. 485 (1984); Baumgartner v. United States, 322 U.S. 665, 671 (1944). A few principles, however, are by now well established. For example, that an issue involves an inquiry into state of mind is not at all inconsistent with treating it as a question of fact. See, e.g., Maggio v. Fulford, *supra.* Equally clearly, an issue does not lose its factual character merely because its resolution is dispositive of the ultimate constitutional question. See Dayton Board of Education v. Brinkman, 443 U.S. 526, 534 (1979) (finding of intent to discriminate subject to "clearly erroneous" standard of review). But beyond these elemental propositions, negative in form, the Court has yet to arrive at "a rule or principle that will unerringly distinguish a factual finding from a legal conclusion." Pullman–Standard v. Swint, 456 U.S. 273, 288 (1982).

Perhaps much of the difficulty in this area stems from the practical truth that the decision to label an issue a "question of law," a "question of fact," or a "mixed question of law and fact" is sometimes as much a matter of allocation as it is of analysis. See Monaghan, Constitutional Fact Review, 85 Colum.L.Rev. 229, 237 (1985). At least in those instances in which Congress has not spoken and in which the issue falls somewhere between a pristine legal standard and a simple historical fact, the fact/law distinction at times has turned on a determination that, as a matter of the sound administration of justice, one judicial actor is better positioned than another to decide the issue in question. Where, for example, as with proof of actual malice in First Amendment libel cases, the relevant legal principle can be given meaning only through its application to the particular circumstances of a case, the Court has been reluctant to give the trier of fact's conclusions presumptive force and, in so doing, strip a federal appellate court of its primary function as an expositor of law. See Bose Corp. v. Consumers Union of United States, Inc., 466 U.S., at 503. Similarly, on rare occasions in years past the Court has justified independent federal or appellate review as a means of compensating for "perceived shortcomings of the trier of fact by way of bias or some other factor...." Id., at 518 (Rehnquist, J., dissenting). See e.g., Haynes v. Washington, 373 U.S., at 516; Watts v. Indiana, 338 U.S. 49, 52 (1949) (opinion of Frankfurter, J.). Cf. Norris v. Alabama, 294 U.S. 587 (1935).

In contrast, other considerations often suggest the appropriateness of resolving close questions concerning the status of an issue as one of "law" or "fact" in favor of extending deference to the trial court. When, for example, the issue involves the credibility of witnesses and therefore turns largely on an evaluation of demeanor, there are compelling and familiar justifications for leaving the process of applying law to fact to the trial court and according its determinations presumptive weight. Patton v. Yount, *supra,* and Wainwright v. Witt, *supra,* are illustrative. There the Court stressed that the state trial judge is in a position to assess juror bias that is far superior to that of federal judges reviewing an application for a writ of habeas corpus. Principally for that reason, the decisions held, juror bias merits treatment as a "factual issue" within the meaning of § 2254(d) notwithstanding the intimate connection between such determinations and the constitutional guarantee of an impartial jury.

ROGER J. TRAYNOR, LA RUDE VITA, LA DOLCE GIUSTIZIA; OR HARD CASES CAN MAKE GOOD LAW *

The terrible question in any hard case is whether the court has the whole truth before it. It can hardly assume adversaries so evenly matched that whatever errors they may have made will have cancelled out and whatever strategies they may have devised will have been countered by like strategies. It can hardly assume adversaries so generous as to have become intelligence agents for one another. It can hardly assume adversaries so dedicated to the public interest as to have volunteered all possible enlightenment to the court even at the risk of an outcome adverse to their clients. However the briefs help a court make its way from outer darkness, they afford it no assurance that it now stands in the innermost circle of light. It may be *in medias res* and still far from the heart of the matter. As Justice Walter Schaefer has noted: "The record must be adequate to raise the issue. But even a record which is technically correct may not cast light on all the aspects of the problem."

Once the adversary shouting has died down and the court is left with the echoes and the pro briefs and the con briefs, it is unhappily mindful of the maxim that solemnly places it above the battle in which it is about to become the deciding factor. A judge assigned to write the opinion in a hard case looks up one morning from his desk to receive the record. Often it closes in on him in gigantesque bundles. Once in a while it is encased in a deceptively slender fagot of papers that slides onto his desk without casting a shadow beforehand. Perforce he looks from the instant case to the calendar and reckons how best to budget for it from finite time and resources.

He wagers time for the latest intruder against the relentlessly moving clock, knowing that he must work with intense concentration against it to absorb the record as well as the briefs of lawyers who have deliberated the selected facts. He can only hope that the adversaries have been of sufficiently high mind to assemble enough pieces of the complicated puzzle in enough order to enable him to perceive something of its contours and inner patterns. However perceptively he puts the puzzle together, he will be constrained by the number and arrangement of the pieces that each adversary has litigated in the trial court.

* 29 U.Chi.L.Rev. 223, 225–27 (1962).
Reprinted by permission.

Aware though he is of the duality of fact and law, the judge must nevertheless put first things first and begin with rough matters of fact. It is no easy matter-of-fact job. We are wont to attribute adequacy as well as transcendent neutrality to the findings of fact, however inadequate or slanted the disparate presentations of plaintiff and defendant may have been. The very term *findings of fact* misleads us into taking it at face value, when actually it signifies only findings of probability. We tend to forget how unscientific is the reconstruction of a factual situation by lawyers concerned primarily with persuading rather than enlightening the trier of fact....

For all the semantic confusion in representing probabilities as facts, one can nevertheless recognize the common sense in a distribution of responsibility that normally precludes an appellate court from reassessing probabilities that the triers of fact have assessed at close range. The prevailing rule is that it must uphold the trier of fact, given a conflict in the evidence, if there is substantial evidence to support the findings.

. . .

Hence the widespread amplification that there must be substantial evidence to support the findings in the light of the whole record. Unfortunately even this rule lends itself to a superficial interpretation that equates substantial evidence in all cases with evidence that merely supports a finding as more probable than not. Unfortunately courts apply it indiscriminately not only when the burden in the trial court was merely to prove the facts by a preponderance of the evidence, but also when the burden was to prove the facts by clear and convincing evidence, as in fraud cases, or beyond a reasonable doubt, as in criminal cases.

Such distorted applications of the substantial evidence rule frustrate the very distribution of responsibility that the rule is designed to insure. When it is the responsibility of the trier of fact to make a finding on clear and convincing evidence or beyond a reasonable doubt, it becomes the responsibility of the appellate court to test the finding accordingly. In reviewing the evidence it should do more than determine simply whether the trier of fact could reasonably conclude that the alleged fact was more probable than not, as in the ordinary civil case. What the appellate court should determine is whether the trier of fact could reasonably conclude that the alleged fact was highly probable or was, in criminal cases, almost certain. Appellate courts should not absolve themselves of such review even though it requires the most painstaking examination of the evidence and the most subtle reflection as to the probabilities of its persuasiveness to a reasonable trier of fact. Were they to undertake such review there would be hope that a significant number of hard cases would make good law.

NOTE

Abandonment is not a question of narrative or historical fact but an ultimate fact, a legal concept with a factual component. It is "a conclusion of law or at least a determination of a mixed question of law and fact," Helvering v. Tex–Penn Oil Co., 300 U.S. 481, 491, 57 S.Ct. 569, 573, 81 L.Ed. 755 (1937), requiring "the application of a legal standard to the historical-fact determinations," Townsend v. Sain, 372 U.S. 293, 309 n. 6, 83 S.Ct. 745, 755 n. 6, 9 L.Ed.2d 770 (1963). In reviewing the ultimate determination of abandonment, as an appellate court, we are therefore not limited by the "clearly erroneous" standard, Fleer Corp. v. Topps Chewing Gum, Inc., 658 F.2d 139, 154 (3d Cir.1981), but must employ a mixed standard of review. We must accept the trial court's findings of historical or narrative facts unless they are clearly erroneous, but we must exercise a plenary review of the trial court's choice and interpretation of legal precepts and its application of those precepts to the historical facts. Cf. Cuyler v. Sullivan, 446 U.S. 335, 341–42, 100 S.Ct. 1708, 1714–15, 64 L.Ed.2d 333 (1980) (review of mixed determinations of fact and law on federal habeas corpus). Thus we separate the distinct factual and legal elements of the trial court's determination of an ultimate fact and apply the appropriate standard to each component.

Universal Minerals, Inc. v. C.A. Hughes & Co., 669 F.2d 98 (3d Cir. 1981).

What we have referred to as "basic facts" have been described by the Supreme Court in 1937 as "primary, evidentiary or circumstantial facts" in the context of a mixed question of law and fact. Helvering v. Tex–Penn Oil Co., 300 U.S. 481, 491 (1937). In the same context in 1982 the Court described these as "subsidiary" facts. Pullman–Standard v. Swint, 456 U.S. 273, 287 (1982). The result is the same. Thus, in Helvering the Court stated:

The foregoing includes the substance of all the findings of circumstantial facts material to the question under consideration. They must be taken as established if supported by substantial evidence. Helvering v. Rankin, 295 U.S. 123, 131. Old Mission Cement Co. v. Helvering, 293 U.S. 289, 294. Burnet v. Leininger, 285 U.S. 136, 138–139. Phillips v. Commissioner, 283 U.S. 589, 600. Old Colony Trust Co. v. Commissioner, 279 U.S. 716. There is no suggestion that they are not amply sustained. In addition to and presumably upon the basis of these findings, the board made its "ultimate finding." And upon that determination it ruled that the transaction was not within the non-recognition provisions of § 202(b). The ultimate finding is a conclusion of law or at least a determination of a mixed question of law and fact. It is to be distinguished from the findings of primary, evidentiary or circumstantial facts. It is subject to judicial review and, on such review, the court may substitute its judgment for that of the Board. Helvering v. Rankin, ubi supra.

300 U.S. at 491.

In Pullman–Standard, the Court explained:

> There is some indication in the opinions of the Court of Appeals for the Fifth Circuit ... that the Circuit rule with respect to "ultimate facts" is only another way of stating a standard of review with respect to mixed questions of law and fact—the ultimate "fact" is the statutory, legally determinative consideration (here, intentional discrimination) which is or is not satisfied by subsidiary facts admitted or found by the trier of fact. As indicated in the text, however, the question of intentional discrimination under § 703(h) is a pure question of fact. Furthermore, the Court of Appeals' opinion in this case appears to address the issue as a question of fact unmixed with legal considerations.

> At the same time, this Court has on occasion itself indicated that findings on "ultimate facts" are independently reviewable. In Baumgartner v. United States, 322 U.S. 665 (1944), the issue was whether or not the findings of the two lower courts satisfied the clear-and-convincing standard of proof necessary to sustain a denaturalization decree.

> Whatever Baumgartner may have meant by its discussion of "ultimate facts," it surely did not mean that whenever the result in a case turns on a factual finding, an appellate court need not remain within the constraints of Rule 52(a). Baumgartner's discussion of "ultimate facts" referred not to pure findings of act—as we find discriminatory intent to be in this context—but to findings that "clearly impl[y] the application of standards of law." 322 U.S. at 671.

> Rule 52(a) broadly requires that findings of fact not be set aside unless clearly erroneous. It does not make exceptions or purport to exclude certain categories of factual findings from the obligation of a court of appeals to accept a district court's findings unless clearly erroneous. It does not divide facts into categories; in particular, it does not divide findings of fact into those that deal with "ultimate" and those that deal with "subsidiary" facts.

> The Rule does not apply to conclusions of law. The Court of Appeals, therefore, was quite right in saying that if a district court's findings rest on an erroneous view of the law, they may be set aside on that basis. But here the District Court was not faulted for misunderstanding or applying an erroneous definition of intentional discrimination. It was reversed for arriving at what the Court of Appeals thought was an erroneous finding as to whether the differential impact of the seniority system reflected an intent to discriminate on account of race. That question, as we see it, is a pure question of fact, subject to Rule

52(a)'s clearly-erroneous standard. It is not a question of law and not a mixed question of law and fact.

356 U.S. at 286–288.

Section 3

DISCRETION

A.　EXERCISING DISCRETION

It is unfortunate that in our jurisprudence, several distinct meanings have been attributed to the term discretion. When today's judges and the members of the legal profession discuss discretion they are referring to what Hart and Sacks described as "the power to choose between two or more courses of action each of which is thought of as permissible." [1]

Jurisprudents have given other meanings to the term, all of which utilize a broad concept of choice but not in the narrower sense we use today. They speak of "strong" or "primary" discretion to describe the freedom to choose a legal norm, in the sense of choosing a legal precept as the starting point of legal reasoning. In this sense, this would describe a judge's exercise of a value judgment.

The English legal philosophers seem to use the expression to describe a circumstance in which there is an option to choose a legal precept as distinguished from a circumstance controlled unerringly by principles or rules. Ronald M. Dworkin admits that "[w]ords like 'discretion' and 'choice' have different senses, and it is conceivable that some who say that judges have discretion mean simply that judges have decisions to make, not already made by others for them, or that judges must reason or make judgments of one sort or another in making these decisions." [2] Nevertheless, he describes the process in which a judge chooses a solution as an exercise of judicial discretion. Moreover, Dean Pound has used it as something distinguished from "law": "Before the law we have justice without law; and after the law and during the evolution of law we still have it under the name of discretion, or natural justice, or equity and good conscience, as an anti-legal element." [3]

With all the available words in the English language it is unfortunate that the same word is used to describe completely different aspects of the judicial process. Some jurisprudents are using the word discretion as the power to expand or curtail ruling case law, or to fashion new precepts to meet new situations. For our purpose, we prefer not to affix the nomenclature, discretion, to these aspects of traditional judicial power and authority and proceed on the more popular (and modern)

---

1. H. Hart and A. Sacks, The Legal Process 162 (tent. ed. 1958).

2. Dworkin, Judicial Discretion 60 J.Phil. 624, 625 (1963).

3. Quoted by Jerome Frank, Selections from Law and the Modern Mind 141 (1963).

concept that discretion means the power of our court to choose between two or more courses of action. Thus, it is our preference to ignore, even if set forth in the following materials, references to discretion in the "strong" or "primary" sense. We do this not to overlook these concepts, but solely to suggest that they are mislabelled and have been treated elsewhere in this book with other names.

Sophisticated analyses of discretion in the sense we have limited it have proliferated recently here and in England. The unspoken motivation for the studies probably is a dissatisfaction both with the exercise of discretion by trial courts, administrative agencies, and representatives of the executive branch of government, and with review of the exercise. Indeed, the dissatisfaction may be justified, because courts and legislative bodies have been content with the generic words "discretion" and "discretionary power", without defining the contours of the exercise, other than occasionally attaching the adjective "broad".[4] Knowing simply that one is invested with discretion does not tell much. The crucial inquiry, necessarily, is the extent of the discretionary power conferred.

NOTE

Dworkin, in *The Model of Rules,* 35 U.Chi.L.Rev. 14, 32–33 (1967), delineates two "weak" senses of discretion and one "stronger sense". At one end of the hierarchy is a conferring of discretion because "for some reason the standards an official must apply cannot be applied mechanically but demand use of judgment." Probably at the same level is a conferring of discretion because "some official has final authority to make a decision and cannot be reviewed and reversed by any other official." Dworkin calls both of these senses "weak" to distinguish a discretion in which the official "is simply not bound by standards set by the authority in question." Consider the distinctions in the following: A sergeant is told to pick his five best men to go on patrol. He is told to pick his five fastest runners to go on patrol. He is told to pick any five men to go on patrol. Evaluate the discretion conferred in each instance. *See also* Raz, *Legal Principles and the Limits of Law,* 81 Yale L.J. 823, 843 (1972).

In law school, the student learns that trial judges are vested with discretion in a wide number of areas. Using Dworkin's definitional framework, what kind of discretion is involved:

—in permitting or restricting discovery? Cf. Rodgers v. United States Steel Corp., 508 F.2d 152 (3d Cir.1975), noted in 43 Fordham L.Rev. 1086 (1975) and 88 Harv.L.Rev. 1911 (1975).

—in certifying under F.R.Civ.P. 54(b) that there is "no just reason [to] delay" an appeal of an order that is final as to fewer than all of

---

4. The Supreme Court has agreed that although a district court had discretion under the old doctrine of *forum non conveniens,* it "had a broader discretion in the application of the [change of venue] statute." 28 U.S.C.A. § 1404. Norwood v. Kirkpatrick, 349 U.S. 29, 30 (1955).

multiple parties or claims? *See* Allis–Chalmers Corp. v. Philadelphia Electric Co., 521 F.2d 360 (3d Cir.1975).

—in granting a new trial under F.R.Civ.P. 59 or 60? *See* Stradley v. Cortez, 518 F.2d 488 (3d Cir.1975).

Have you derived certain impressions from answering the foregoing questions?

MAURICE ROSENBERG, TWO MEANINGS AND USES OF JUDICIAL DISCRETION *

If the word discretion conveys to legal minds any solid core of meaning, one central idea above all others, it is the idea of *choice*. To say that a court has discretion in a given area of law is to say that it is not bound to decide the question one way rather than another. In this sense, the term suggests that there is no wrong answer to the questions posed—at least, there is no *officially* wrong answer.

Lawyers are instinctively drawn to this meaning of discretion, which is correct as far as it goes. But it is incomplete and, besides, it conceals a confusing duality by lumping together two distinct types of judicial discretion. They can usefully be referred to as *primary* and *secondary*.

When an adjudicator has the primary type, he has decision-making discretion, a wide range of choice as to what he decides, free from the constraints which characteristically attach whenever legal rules enter the decision process. When the law accords primary discretion in the highest degree in a particular area, it says in effect that the court is free to render the decision it chooses; that decision-constraining rules do not exist here; and that even looser principles or guidelines have not been formulated. In such an area, the court can do no wrong, legally speaking, for there is no officially right or wrong answer.

The other type of discretion, the secondary form, has to do with hierarchical relations among judges. It enters the picture when the system tries to prescribe the degree of finality and authority a lower court's decision enjoys in the higher courts. Specifically, it comes into full play when the rules of review accord the lower court's decision an unusual amount of insulation from appellate revision. In this sense, discretion is a review-restraining concept. It gives the trial judge a right to be wrong without incurring reversal.

A pointed example of this self-denying principle in action occurred in Napolitano v. Compania Sud Americana de Vapores, [421 F.2d 382 (2d Cir.1970),] a longshoreman's suit against a shipowner for unseaworthiness damages. The trial judge flayed the defense lawyer on back-to-back occasions with remarks the appellate court called "unkind," indicative of

---

* *Judicial Discretion of the Trial Court, Viewed from Above*, 22 Syracuse L.Rev. 635, 636–38, 641–43 (1971). Reprinted by permission.

"harsh overreaction," "unnecessary sarcastic comments" and a "tongue-lashing" of counsel. Among other lapses, the court of appeals judges thought the district judge had wrongly denied defendant's reasonable request for a luncheon recess. They declared:

> Had any one of us been in a position to exercise the discretion committed to a trial judge when such a request is made, we have no hesitancy in stating that the decision would have been otherwise; but as appellate judges we cannot find that the action of the district judge was so unreasonable or so arbitrary as to amount to a prejudicial abuse of the discretion necessary to repose in trial judges during the conduct of a trial....

One source of confusion in treating the subject is that courts tend to use the two types of discretion indiscriminately, interchangeably and without marking the distinction. Here is a quotation from the Supreme Court of Alabama that begins by defining discretion in its primary sense and then adds on its secondary meaning as if they were compound and as inseparable as heart-and-soul:

> A judicial act is said to lie in discretion when there are no fixed principles by which its correctness may be determined. [S]uch determinations are not subject to review on appeal....

That casual conjunction of the two meanings of the concept impedes analysis. Courts at every level of the system are given scope for exercise of primary discretion. For instance, when a statute declares that a decree or order in respect to a particular matter (such as award of counsel fees) may be made "in the discretion of the court" and this language is construed as applying to each court in the appellate hierarchy, we have an example of primary discretion. Precise norms are not laid down, decision is intended to pivot on the circumstances of the particular case, and each court along the route is free to reach an independent conclusion as to the result called for by its own sound exercise of discretion. Primary discretion bestows *decision-liberating* choice.

By contrast, secondary discretion is, for practical purposes, confided solely to trial courts, and is essentially a *review-limiting* concept....

. . .

Where secondary discretion exists, neither party may successfully urge before an appellate tribunal that he is entitled to an opposite or different decision, or to a "correct" decision. Even if the appellate tribunal concedes that by its lights the wrong decision has been made, as in the *Napolitano* case, it will not reverse. A trial court determination that is discretionary in this sense has a status or authority that makes it either unchallengeable, or challengeable to only a restricted degree. This form of review-limiting discretion therefore gives the trial judge a right to be wrong without incurring reversal—a limited and variable right, we shall see.

This remarkably tolerant, generous and self-limiting attitude comes chiefly from the appellate courts themselves. Statutes rarely make any attempt to enjoin the normal prerogative of upper courts to give rein to their birthright by indulging in *joie de revision*. The Supreme Court of Delaware many years ago put into words the effect of this remarkable doctrine when it said that "[a]n exercise of discretion by a trial court may be erroneous but still be legal."

Laymen can be excused if they register bafflement at that concept. How can the attributes of being "erroneous" and "legal" co-exist in a judicial decision, considering that one word means *wrong* and the other supposedly means *right*? That sort of anomaly is all right for football commissioners—where absurdities are always in season—but how can judges indulge in such nonsense?

Unexpected it may be, but is it undesirable to bestow unreviewable decisional power on the trial judge? After all, some court has to have the last word. Why not the trial court, the one closest to the evidence, to the witnesses and the jury? Why prefer decisions that are made by distant, upper-court judges from a cold and lifeless printed record?

One argument for doing so is found in history rather than in reason. A right to appeal has been traditional in this country's judicial process, even though the Constitution does not spell out an obligation to grant appeals. Even if constitutional, unreviewable discretion offends a deep sense of fitness in our view of the administration of justice. We are committed to the practice of affording a two-tiered or three-tiered court system, so that a losing litigant may obtain at least one chance for review of each significant ruling made at the trial-court level.

Besides, since most trial courts are manned by a single judge and appellate courts are collegial, our fondness for appellate review may also reflect a feeling that there is safety in numbers. The idea that incantations about discretion can invest a single judge with the final say in important cases makes many people restless.

Finally, and probably more important than either history or the safety-in-numbers reason, is a spillover of anxiety about entrusting power of decision without sufficient assurance that principles of the law will be faithfully followed. It is the same sort of disquiet that primary discretion at times produces. The thought that in some areas of law judges are liberated from legal rules and can take their choice in deciding goes down hard. Throughout history it has made discretion a four-letter word in many legal circles.

Lord Camden called discretion the law of tyrants. He said that "in the best it is oftentimes caprice"; and in the worst, "every vice, folly and passion to which human nature can be liable." Discretion has been said to promote a government of men, not laws. These and other strictures have been summed up in an acrid epigram which asserts: "That system of law is best which confides as little as possible to the discretion of the judge...."

Of course, nothing so roundly villified could be all bad. The element of flexibility and choice in the process of adjudicating is precisely what justice requires in many cases. Flexibility permits more compassionate and more sensitive responses to differences which ought to count in applying legal norms, but which get buried in the gross and rounded-off language of rules that are directed at wholesale problems instead of particular disputes. Discretion in this sense allows the individualization of law and permits justice at times to be hand-made instead of mass-produced.

In urging that discretion is the "effective individualizing agent of the law," Dean Pound pointed out that

> in proceedings for custody of children, where compelling consideration[s] cannot be reduced to rules, ... determination must be left, to no small extent, to the disciplined but personal feeling of the judge for what justice demands.

Of course, a judge's total freedom to follow his own desires in deciding issues would raise the risk of a government of men if he were not under any constraints at all. But he is under at least one bond that, struggle as he will, he cannot break. It is, as Lord Mansfield observed in John Wilkes' case, the constraint of consistency: "We must act alike in all cases of like nature."

On this side of the ocean, the Supreme Court of Vermont stated the point very emphatically in 1904: "It is the essence of all law that when the facts are the same, the result is the same...."

That unwritten command binds the common law judge even in areas where the existence of discretionary power seemingly gives him choice. "Act in your considered judgment, with a resolve to decide in the same way if the issue arises again." That is the unspoken but inescapable silent command of our judicial system. To the extent that judges hear and obey this command, the potential for abuse of discretionary decisional power is tempered.

The dilemma is how judges can be at the same time sensible to the need for even-handedness and constancy in their behavior and sensitive to the value on wielding judicial power flexibly. Is it realistic to suppose they can be made captives of a law-minded tradition that constrains them to decide in one way, when the insistent voice of their discretionary power impels them to decide in another way? Very probably only the slow process of absorbing year after year the common law's values and ideals can produce the subtle blend of power and restraint they need. Perhaps the law school is the place where the seed of the tradition is first planted and has its best chance to root.

NOTE

Consider Rosenberg's statement: "[Discretion] suggests that there is no wrong answer to the questions posed—at least, there is no *officially* wrong answer." Do you agree?

If we are to accept Holmes' assertion, *ante,* 264 that the courts must play the game according to the rules—and irrespective of whether those "rules" are "rules" of Mechanical or Sociological jurisprudence—can it ever be said that a court has "primary" discretion, that it is "free to render the decision it chooses"?

Do you prefer the definitional schema of Dworkin or Rosenberg? Which strikes you as more realistic? Manageable? In your reading of the case law on the exercise and abuse of discretion, do you find courts articulating any such distinctions?

Do you hear the courts playing a Swan Song over "secondary" discretion? If so, is it a popular tune? What would Wright say?

Having read Rosenberg's article, do you feel that the exercise of discretion is "just"? Does your answer reflect considerations of reckonability, so that it may vary from the context of a state judiciary, with elected judges, to that of the federal judiciary? Is the constraint of "consistency" sufficient? Are you satisfied that *your* law school training has adequately implanted the "seed of tradition"?

CHARLES M. YABLON, JUSTIFYING THE JUDGE'S HUNCH: AN ESSAY ON DISCRETION *

Ronald Dworkin distinguishes strong discretion from two weaker senses of discretion, termed "discretion as judgment" and "discretion as finality," which are found in judicial decisionmaking. "Discretion as judgment" occurs when a judge, in order to apply the rule, must utilize her own evaluative powers and judgment. Dworkin's example is a sergeant ordered to take his five most experienced soldiers on patrol. Obviously, the sergeant must make an evaluation of his soldiers in terms of the somewhat nebulous concept of "experience," and different sergeants may select somewhat different groups. Nonetheless (and this is of key importance to Dworkin) such a decisionmaker is still following a rule, though a somewhat vague and "open textured" one, because the decisionmaker still seeks to conform his conduct to the authoritative norm of "experience." [40]

With Dworkin, the debate moves much closer to a prescriptive theory of judging. His theory provides a basis for critiquing not just judicial outcomes but judicial methodologies. Dworkin tells us that the

---

* C. Yablon, *Justifying the Judge's Hunch: An Essay on Discretion,* 41 Hastings L.J. 231 (1990). Reprinted by permission.

40. In this weaker sense of discretion, however, Dworkin seems to have revived the Realist notion that there is a uniquely judicial form of decisionmaking, neither as constrained as formalist jurisprudence indicates nor as free as a legislator. The difference between Dworkin's judicial judgment and Frank's judicial hunch is Dworkin's presupposition that the judge perceives and consciously attempts to apply the preexisting legal norm. Frank's judicial hunch, by contrast, presumes an unmediated perception of the appropriate legal response.

appropriate role of the judge is to consider various potentially applicable norms in reaching her decision. Indications that no such consideration was given are sufficient grounds for criticizing the decision, even if the same result would have been reached after such consideration. Because Dworkin operates at the same theoretical level as Hart, and asks the same primary question (what is appropriate to say about judging?) the fact that judges actually may not decide cases in the way he suggests has little effect on his theory. Kent Greenawalt [44] has criticized Dworkin's notion of discretion as judgment, pointing out that as the rules become more vague, judgment appears to collapse into strong discretion. Suppose that instead of being asked to pick the "five most experienced soldiers" Dworkin's sergeant was asked to pick "the five best soldiers for the job." He might still pick the five most experienced, but he might also, while still following that "rule," appropriately select other people (perhaps a new recruit with excellent night vision). If he were told to "pick five soldiers in a fair way," the sergeant might decide that the fairest way (in terms of the welfare of the entire group) is to send the most experienced; or he might decide, utilizing the same "fairness" criterion, to send the least experienced (since that would help equalize the amount each had been exposed to danger); or he might decide that fairness mandated random selection by lot. In short, if the rule is sufficiently open textured, the sergeant's selection of any five people may be justified in accordance with the rule. At that point, however, the judge seems to be exercising discretion in Dworkin's "strong sense."

Dworkin may still reply that it matters that the judge is seeking to conform her behavior to such nebulous concepts as "fairness," "the interests of justice," or other vague terms. At that point, however, his theory would be only a psychological theory of judging, a reliance on judicial openness and outcome, since any result is justifiable under the rules so long as the appropriate incantations of general norms are cited.

Dworkin might also escape the problem by denying that such vague rules are actually the rules applied by judges. Certainly, it is not uncommon to see doctrinal formulations such as "fairness" or "reasonableness," but perhaps the rules as actually perceived by the judges are narrower and more constraining. In much the same way, Dworkin's sergeant might well be subject to discipline for sending the five newest recruits out on a dangerous patrol, even though his actions could be justified as "fair" on certain ethical theories. But to explore the implications of these arguments concerning actual legal practice requires a level of specificity and attention to context that the theoretical debate has tended to avoid....

Kenneth Culp Davis' book, Discretionary Justice: A Preliminary Inquiry,[56] was, in a sense, a look at the legal world that Arnold, and others like him, had created. Davis, author of the major treatise on

---

44. Greenawalt, *Discretion and Judicial Decision: The Elusive Quest for the Fetters that Bind Judges,* 75 Colum.L.Rev. 359 (1975).

56. K. Davis, Discretionary Justice: A Preliminary Inquiry (1969).

administrative law,[57] was intimately familiar with the decisionmaking process at various levels in the legal system. His conclusion, simply put, is that there is too much "unnecessary" discretion in the system.

Davis' definition of discretion is interesting. While seeming to agree with Hart that discretion is what occurs when the law runs out, his operational definition has nothing to do with the guidance imparted by the rules to the decisionmaker, but solely with power relationships. He states: "A public officer has discretion whenever the effective limits on his power leave him free to make a choice among possible courses of action or inaction."

Davis carefully notes that, under his definition, discretion can exist to perform illegal acts, if the actions, even though prohibited by authoritative legal materials, are not effectively limited by institutional power arrangements.

Davis believes that the primary problem with the American legal system is that there is too much unnecessary discretion. This leads to disparate treatment of similar cases and, therefore, to injustice. He illustrates his thesis empirically, spending much of the book detailing specific instances in which administrative power, often unchecked and unreviewed, is used to treat individuals unjustly. The emphasis on illustrative examples is both the strength and weakness of the book. Many of the examples of discretionary power abuses are quite convincing. Davis' vast experience with, and study of, administrative decisionmaking leads one to accept his conclusion that, in many areas of the law, there is too much discretion, that it is often unnecessary, and that discretionary decisions are not subject to appropriate review.

The problem is that Davis' methodology requires us to accept his conclusion because he never sets forth criteria as to when there is "too much" discretion or proposes a jurisprudential theory that would enable us to distinguish necessary from unnecessary discretion. Davis seems to rely on his own (and our) intuitive notions of justice, which is somewhat ironic in a book that seeks to constrain intuitive judgments by public officials.

Davis' proposed solution to the problem of too much discretion is, in effect, better rules. He would like to see more rules promulgated, particularly at the agency level, that constrain and limit the discretion of decisionmakers. Davis notes that such rules need not always be written in general terms, but may sometimes function, like precedents, to adjudicate a paradigmatic case, thereby providing guidance in future cases. Some of Davis' previous statements about discretion, however, raise questions about his proposed solutions. Davis already has stated that some discretionary actions are "illegal." Can new and better rules constrain in the absence of changes in power relationships? But Davis also has indicated that such constraints, in the form of administrative or judicial review, may simply move discretion to a different level of the

57. K. Davis, Administrative Law Treatise (2d ed. 1978).

process. If so, the question becomes not how much discretion, but whose discretion is appropriate?

Davis is well aware that a change in the form of the rules would not be a panacea and that rules can often be bent or ignored. Operating under a clearer and more explicit set of rules, however, would nonetheless change the attitudes administrative decisionmakers have toward their role and the decisions they are called upon to make, leading to greater responsibility and equality of treatment. Davis is making the other side of Thurman Arnold's argument. Whereas Arnold thought that describing the judicial process in terms of practical matters of procedure would lead to a more flexible and discretionary attitude on the part of judges, Davis believes that describing the administrative process in terms of clear and explicit rules would shift the attitude of administrators toward greater consistency and equal treatment.

Though both arguments are valid, they rely on a particular set of assumptions about the relationship of decisionmakers to legal language and rules—relationships that are assumed but never delineated. Indeed, Davis' book reveals the difficulties of analyzing and critiquing discretion as a matter of process, without the theoretical framework of the jurisprudes. His call for an end to "unnecessary" discretion invites discussion of the role of law in society and what it means to say that a certain legal arrangement is "necessary." His description of certain discretionary decisions as illegal, despite the fact that they are permitted by the institutional power arrangements, calls for a discussion defining the "law." Most importantly, the notion that it is sometimes desirable to move discretion to different levels in the system points out the need for a theory of institutional competence, an account of why certain decisionmakers are most appropriate to make certain decisions.

The beginnings of such an institutional competence theory are found in Maurice Rosenberg's article, Judicial Discretion of the Trial Court, Viewed From Above.[71] Rosenberg's emphasis is on trial and appellate procedure, particularly the discretion of trial judges, rather than administrators. Nonetheless, his work builds on Davis' and seeks to supply some of the theoretical framework that Davis lacks.

Rosenberg, strongly influenced by Hart, begins with a distinction between "primary" and "secondary" forms of discretion. Primary discretion is the freedom of the individual decisionmaker to act in any way she chooses. Closely corresponding to Hart's internal perspective, a judge exercises primary discretion when "decision-constraining rules do not exist." As Rosenberg says, "In such an area, the court can do no wrong, legally speaking, for there is no officially right or wrong answer." Primary discretion then, corresponds roughly to Hart's discussion of decisionmaking when the law runs out. It is the freedom of the legislator.

71. Rosenberg, *Judicial Discretion of the Trial Court, Viewed From Above,* 22 Syracuse L.Rev. 635 (1971).

Rosenberg recognizes, and is ultimately more interested in, secondary discretion. Secondary discretion involves an external perspective and "has to do with hierarchical relations among judges." It occurs when "the rules of review accord the lower court's decision an unusual amount of insulation from appellate revision. In this sense, discretion is a review-restraining concept."

Hart had argued, in the scorer's discretion example, that a judge might have institutional power to decide any way she wanted, without fear of reversal, yet still internally be obliged to follow and apply the rules. In Rosenberg's terms, such a judge has secondary but not primary discretion. But Rosenberg points out that discretion, as lawyers commonly use it, often refers to the instances when trial courts, not appellate courts, have the final say, when trial judges may "be wrong without incurring reversal."

Discretion for Rosenberg, at least in its "secondary" form, is a matter of institutional arrangements and power relationships. Accordingly, it is permitted to the extent that appellate courts are willing to restrain their reviewing power.

Yet, like Hart, Rosenberg's strong separation of internal and external perspectives of decisionmaking leads him to miss certain problems in his analysis. As an example of a very strong form of trial court discretion, Rosenberg cites a case in which Judge Jerome Frank vigorously criticized a trial judge for failing to grant defendant's request for special verdicts, yet affirmed the verdict on the ground that the Federal Rules gave the trial court "full, uncontrolled discretion" in this matter. Was the trial judge in this example "wrong without incurring reversal?" How can it be "wrong" when the Rules, Frank tells us, expressly permit it? But if it is not legally wrong, on what basis is Frank criticizing it? On the same basis one criticizes a legislator who has passed an unwise law? Frank seems to be saying that the trial judge's decision was not just unwise, but failed to follow some kind of rule for the proper conduct of trials. Rosenberg cannot answer these questions, which imply that one's external role can affect one's internal perception of the right answer, because Rosenberg describes the realms of internal decisionmaking and external constraint as separate.

Rosenberg's article is a first step toward a theory of institutional competence, and he sets forth criteria for determining when trial judges, rather than appellate courts, should receive deference in the decision-making process. Yet, while his criteria are clearer and more theoretically grounded than Davis' criteria, they still rest on vague and sometimes dubious jurisprudential assumptions. Rosenberg provides three grounds for conferring discretion on the trial judge: (1) when it is "impracticable" to formulate a rule of decision; (2) when the issue before the court is new or unsettled; and, (3) when circumstances critical to the decision are "imperfectly conveyed" by the record on appeal. But because of Rosenberg's purely external, institutional perspective, he fails to deal with the internal jurisprudential issues raised by his criteria. For example, is there a correct response to a discretionary decision when it is impracticable to formulate a rule of decision or when the issue is new or unsettled?　There would not seem to be, yet if that is the case, then how can they be reviewed for "abuse of discretion?"　Nonetheless, Rosenberg's article represents an important first step in the attempt to combine jurisprudential and institutional perspectives on discretion.

UNITED STATES v. McCOY

United States Court of Appeals, Seventh Circuit, 1975.
517 F.2d 41.

Before FAIRCHILD, CHIEF JUDGE, and STEVENS and TONE, CIRCUIT JUDGES.

STEVENS, CIRCUIT JUDGE.

Appellant was convicted of passing a counterfeit $20 bill in violation of 18 U.S.C.A. § 472.　He challenges [*inter alia*] the failure of the trial judge to exercise his discretion to read a part of the trial transcript to the jury pursuant to a request by the foreman.　We affirm.

.　.　.

During its deliberations, the jury sent a note to the trial judge stating "would like to read or have read to us the testimony of Mary," the employee to whom McCoy had tendered the counterfeit bill.　Without consulting counsel, the court responded: "I have your request that the testimony of Mary Sleiziz be reread to you.　I regret that this is not permissible.　You will be required to proceed on the basis of your best recollection concerning her testimony."

Appellant correctly argues that the trial judge, in his discretion, could have compiled with the jury's request.　Relying on the judge's statement "that this is not permissible," he contends that the judge erroneously failed to exercise that discretion and thereby committed an error requiring reversal, or at least a remand directing that the district judge state on the record whether his ruling reflected an exercise of his discretion or a mistaken view of the law.

Quite different reasons may justify committing a given matter to the discretion of the trial judge.　There are some matters—such as the particular ritual to be observed at the opening of court—for which the judge may fashion his own rules, provided always that his deviation from tradition is not so extraordinary as to call for supervisory review.　In such matters, neither strict adherence by the district judge to a given procedure, nor even his failure to realize that other choices are available, will be held to constitute error.

There are other matters—such as the sentencing decision—in which the choice of alternatives is left to the trial judge, not because the decision is of little importance, but rather because the factors which may properly influence his decision are so numerous, variable and subtle that the fashioning of rigid rules would be more likely to impair his ability to deal fairly with a particular problem than to lead to a just result. In such situations, it may be important that the record demonstrate that the judge has made an informed choice—that is to say, that he both understood the range of his discretion and considered the relevant factors bearing on the individual situation before him. . . .

This case is surely not in the latter category, though admittedly it is not at the other extreme either. It is in an area in which we do not consider it essential for the record to disclose the basis for the judge's decision. Despite the form of his response to the jury's request, we are confident that the judge was fully aware of his authority to read excerpts from the transcript to the jury. But even if we were to make the unlikely assumption that he was not, we believe a judge could properly adopt and follow a routine practice of declining such requests unless supported by some extraordinary showing of need. No such showing is reflected on this record.

B. REVIEW OF DISCRETION

OVERVIEW

Appellate review of a trial court's exercise of discretion follows uncharted seas. In our serious and rule-minded regime, discretion is a jurisprudential oddity. At best, it is an elusive concept; at worst, a device used by appellate courts either to avoid a decision on difficult and sensitive issues or to invade a domain traditionally regarded as the exclusive turf of the trial tribunal.

Bouvier's Dictionary defines discretion as "that part of the judicial function which decides questions arising in the trial of a cause, according to the particular circumstances of each case, and as to which the judgment of the court is uncontrolled by fixed rules of law. The power exercised by courts to determine questions to which no strict rule of law is applicable but which, from their nature, and the circumstances of the case, are controlled by the personal judgment of the court." As we have emphasized, we are reviewing discretion here as the "power to choose between two or more courses of action each of which is thought of as permissible."

Analyses of discretion have revealed much dissatisfaction with both the exercise of discretion by tribunals of the first instance and appellate review of the exercise. The dissatisfaction may be justified, because courts and legislative bodies have been content with the generic words "discretion" and "discretionary power," without defining the boundaries of the discretion except to attach, on occasion, the adjective "broad." To know simply that a court is invested with discretion does not provide much guidance. The crucial inquiry, necessarily, is the extent of the discretionary power conferred. Thus, while recent commentators have outlined sophisticated nuances, it remains for the courts to calibrate its full measure.

Review of discretion is one of the most troublesome aspects of the judicial process. The scope of review ranges from rigid limitations, similar to the limited scrutiny of fact finding determinations, to the extensive review permitted in the review of legal precepts. Language used by appellate courts in review of discretion is unfortunate; often there is sheer hypocrisy in the process. This is best illustrated when an appellate court pontificates that it cannot substitute its discretion for that of the trial court, then proceeds immediately to do just that. Byron comes to mind. "And whispering 'I will ne'er consent'—consented." [1]

If one starts with an understanding of discretion as encompassing the power of choice among several courses of action, each of which is considered permissible, it would seem difficult, if not conceptually impossible, to disturb discretionary choice on review. Nonetheless, appellate courts continue to do so, couching their actions in language which disclaims a substitution of choices for those of the trial courts. This type of review generates tension between trial and appellate courts. When it results in reversal, the successful trial court litigant justifiably is surprised and irate. Notwithstanding lengthy opinions with detailed evaluations of facts, the *rationes decidendi* that support reversals in the guise of finding an improper use of discretion generally are unsatisfactory. Even the omnipresent term "abuse" is unfortunate, meaning as it does "offense; fault; a corrupt practice or custom." To describe an improper or incorrect exercise of discretion, "misuse" would be a more appropriate word. [2]

One answer to the quandary appellate courts face in reviewing exercises of discretion is to formulate legal limits for such action. Absent precise formulations, the solution must come from the conferrer of the right to exercise discretion, which should define with some specificity the outer permissible limits of the discretion intended, thus providing guidance to both the exerciser and the reviewer of discretion. Concomitantly, the exerciser of discretion should explain its choice. When the choice is so reinforced, an appellate court may, more easily and more fairly, review the exercise of discretion for the presence or absence of arbitrary action.

Even the most rudimentary understanding of the contours of proper exercise of discretion is difficult unless proper ground rules are established for the review of this exercise. Until the specific limitations, or lack thereof, are imposed on the exerciser of discretion, no single litmus test is available to determine when the exercise of discretion has exceeded proper bounds. Ronald Dworkin suggests that discretion, like the hole in the doughnut, does not exist except as an area left open by a surrounding belt of restriction. [3] One reviewing the following exercises of discretion would surely use different standards in order to determine

1. Byron, Don Juan, Canto I, St. 117.

2. But see, e.g., Federal Administrative Procedure Act, 5 U.S.C.A. § 706(2)(A), in which a reviewing court may set aside an agency's action if found to be "arbitrary, capricious, an abuse of discretion, or otherwise not in accordance with law."

3. R. Dworkin, Taking Rights Seriously 31 (1977).

when the exerciser's authority was exceeded: A police lieutenant is told by his superiors to pick his five best police officers to handle a case; he is told to pick his five strongest officers; his five most senior officers; his five fastest officers; any five men; any five officers. It would seem that he had unfettered choice in the last instance, unfettered choice among his male officers in the next to last instance, and comparatively restricted choice in all other instances.

Professor Maurice Rosenberg's analysis of discretion [4] deserves special attention. He offers the thesis that there should be no single measure for the review of discretion, but rather various gradations depending upon the presence or absence of special circumstances relating to the superiority of the trial judge's "nether position." Thus, when the appellate court can conclude that the matter is not truly reflected by a cold record, deference should be paid to trial judges because they were there and "smelled the smoke of battle."

Although as an abstract proposition the concept seems cumbersome, the examples cited by Rosenberg demonstrate his point. At the bottom of the scale would be Grade A discretion, almost unshackled trial court discretion with virtually no appellate review. An example would be the refusal of a federal district judge to submit special instructions to a jury in a relatively simple personal injuries case.[5] Grade B discretion, manifesting substantial discretion of the court with modest appellate review, is illustrated in a Ohio case involving a head-on automobile collision. The jury returned a verdict with a statement, "We believe there was negligence on the part of both parties to the accident." Notwithstanding the jury's statement, the trial judge granted plaintiff's motion for a new trial saying he believed that only the defendant was at fault. The Ohio Supreme Court sustained the action of the trial judge, declaring that the question of a new trial was addressed to the trial court's special discretion.[6] Grade C confers both moderate discretion and moderate review. An example is where plaintiff lost an eye in a railroad accident. During final arguments to the jury a blind man entered the courtroom, said a few words to plaintiff's counsel and seated himself in the courtroom in full view of the jury. In summation, plaintiff's counsel said: "The railroad's negligence took away one of my client's eyes. Another and he will be totally blind." The trial judge refused to grant a motion for mistrial. The appellate court reversed.[7] Grade D is a narrowing of trial court discretion and a broadening of appellate review. Rosenberg cites as the classic case a complaint for a declaratory judgment in which the trial court refuses to grant the judgment, either way, on the ground that there is an adequate remedy at law. The appellate court ruled that the trial court had little discretion to refuse to act; that it had the obligation to declare in favor or against

4. M. Rosenberg, *Judicial Discretion of the Trial Court, Viewed from Above,* 22 Syracuse L.Rev. 635 (1971).

5. Skidmore v. Baltimore & Ohio Railway Co., 167 F.2d 54 (2d Cir.1948).

6. Poske v. Mergl, 169 Ohio St. 70, 157 N.E.2d 344 (1959).

7. Fitzpatrick v. St. Louis–.S.F. Ry., 327 S.W.2d 801 (Mo.1959).

the plaintiff.[8] An example of Grade E discretion is a refusal to grant a new trial under the following circumstances: The defendant in a personal injuries action was superintendent of the county's poor farm. At the midday recess on the first day of trial, a juror approached the defendant and said he had always wanted to visit the farm. The defendant obligingly offered the juror a ride to the farm, showed it off, offered him lunch, returned him to the courthouse. Both parties admitted these events but denied that they had discussed the case, and the juror swore that he had not been influenced by his visit with the defendant.[9] The trial judge's refusal to grant a new trial was reversed because the appellate court recognized that although the issue of granting a new trial is normally committed to the trial court's discretion, as in the Grade B discretion example, here the impartiality of the jury had to be above suspicion.

How, then, can court ascertain whether their discretion is to be Grade A or E? Clearly, the best method would be to have the authority that confers the discretion in the first instance set forth appropriate and meaningful guidelines, something more than the amorphous "abuse of discretion." Although the word "discretion" appears in the Federal Rules of Civil Procedure a mere ten times, if one reads the decisions of the U.S. Courts of Appeals and reads the major treatises, Professor Rosenberg reports, "one finds at least forty procedural situations in which the courts of appeals have construed a rule to grant discretion to the district court." [10] In the 30 additional judicially created circumstances, it would have been infinitely preferable for the power-conferring appellate courts to have explained the exact nature and extent of the discretionary power being granted to the district judges.

WILTON v. SEVEN FALLS CO.

Supreme Court of the United States, 1995.
___ U.S. ___, 115 S.Ct. 2137, 132 L.Ed.2d 214.

JUSTICE O'CONNOR delivered the Opinion of the Court

Since its inception, the Declaratory Judgment Act has been understood to confer on federal courts unique and substantial discretion in deciding whether to declare the rights of litigants. The statute's textual commitment to discretion, and the breadth of leeway we have always understood it to suggest, distinguish the declaratory judgment context from other areas of the law in which the concepts of discretion surface. We have repeatedly characterized the Declaratory Judgment Act as "an enabling Act, which confers discretion on the courts rather than an

---

8. New York Foreign Trade Zone Operators, Inc. v. State Liquor Authority, 285 N.Y. 272, 34 N.E.2d 316 (1941).

9. Lynch v. Kleindolph, 204 Iowa 762, 216 N.W. 2 (1927).

10. M. Rosenberg, Appellate Review of Trial Court Discretion 4 (Federal Judicial Center 1977).

absolute right upon the litigant." Public Serv. Comm'n v. Wycoff Co., 344 U.S. 237, 241 (1952). When all is said and done, we have concluded, "the propriety of declaratory relief in a particular case will depend upon a circumspect sense of its fitness informed by the teachings and experience concerning the functions and extent of judicial power."

Acknowledging, as they must, the unique breadth of this discretion to decline to enter a declaratory judgment, London Underwriters nevertheless contend that district courts lack discretion to decline to hear a declaratory judgment suit at the outset. See Brief for Petitioners 22 ("District courts *must* hear declaratory judgment cases absent exceptional circumstances; district courts *may* decline to enter the requested relief following full trial on the merits, if no beneficial purpose is thereby served or if equity otherwise counsels"). We are not persuaded by this distinction. London Underwriters' argument depends on the untenable proposition that a district court, knowing at the commencement of litigation that it will exercise its broad statutory discretion to decline declaratory relief, must nonetheless go through the futile exercise of hearing a case on the merits first. Nothing in the language of the Declaratory Judgment Act recommends London Underwriters' reading, and we are unwilling to impute to Congress an intention to require such a wasteful expenditure of judicial resources. If a district court, in the sound exercise of its judgment, determines after a complaint is filed that a declaratory judgment will serve no useful purpose, it cannot be incumbent upon that court to proceed to the merits before staying or dismissing the action.

We agree, for all practical purposes, with Professor Borchard, who observed half a century ago that "[t]here is ... nothing automatic or obligatory about the assumption of 'jurisdiction' by a federal court" to hear a declaratory judgment action. Borchard, Declaratory Judgments, at 313. By the Declaratory Judgment Act, Congress sought to place a remedial arrow in the district court's quiver; it created an opportunity, rather than a duty, to grant a new form of relief to qualifying litigants. Consistent with the nonobligatory nature of the remedy, a district court is authorized, in the sound exercise of its discretion, to stay or to dismiss an action seeking a declaratory judgment before trial or after all arguments have drawn to a close. In the declaratory judgment context, the normal principle that federal courts should adjudicate claims within their jurisdiction yields to considerations of practicality and wise judicial administration.

III

As Judge Friendly observed, the Declaratory Judgment Act "does not speak," on its face, to the question whether discretion to entertain declaratory judgment actions is vested in district courts alone or in the entire judicial system. Friendly, Indiscretion about Discretion, 31 Emory L.J. 747, 778 (1982). The Court of Appeals reviewed the District Court's decision to stay London Underwriters' action for abuse of discretion, and found none. London Underwriters urge us to follow those other Courts of Appeals that review decisions to grant (or to refrain from granting) declaratory relief *de novo*. See, *e.g.*, Genentech, Inc. v. Eli Lilly & Co., 998 F.2d at 936; Cincinnati Ins. Co. v. Holbrook, 867 F.2d at 1333. We decline this invitation. We believe it more consistent with the statute to vest district courts with discretion in the first instance, because facts bearing on the usefulness of the declaratory judgment remedy, and the fitness of the case for resolution, are peculiarly within their grasp. Cf. First Options of Chicago, Inc. v. Kaplan, 514 U.S. ___, ___ (1995) (slip op., at 10) ("[T]he reviewing attitude that a court of appeals takes toward a district court decision should depend upon 'the respective institutional advantages of trial and appellate courts' ") (citation omitted); Miller v. Fenton, 474 U.S. 104, 114 (1985) ("[T]he fact/law distinction at times has turned on a determination that, as a matter of the sound administration of justice, one judicial actor is better positioned than another to decide the issue in question"). While it may be true that sound administration of the Declaratory Judgment Act calls for the exercise of "judicial discretion, hardened by experience into rule," Borchard, Declaratory Judgments, at 293, proper application of the abuse of discretion standard on appellate review can, we think, provide appropriate guidance to district courts. In this regard, we reject London Underwriters' suggestion, that review for abuse of discretion "is tantamount to no review" at all.

IV

In sum, we conclude that Brillhart v. Excess Ins. Co., 316 U.S. 491 (1942), governs this declaratory judgment action and that district courts' decisions about the propriety of hearing declaratory judgment actions, which are necessarily bound up with their decisions about the propriety of granting declaratory relief, should be reviewed for abuse of discretion. We do not attempt at this time to delineate the outer boundaries of that discretion in other cases, for example, cases raising issues of federal law or cases in which there are no parallel state proceedings. Like the Court of Appeals, we conclude only that the District Court acted within its bounds in staying this action for declaratory relief where parallel proceedings, presenting opportunity for ventilation of the same state law issues, were underway in state court.

————

SNYDER v. JEFFERSON COUNTY SCHOOL DISTRICT

Supreme Court of Colorado, 1992.
842 P.2d 624.

JUSTICE KIRSHBAUM delivered the Opinion of the Court.

The following facts are essentially undisputed. From 1969 until 1983, Snyder was employed by respondent, Jefferson County School District R–1 (the district), as a male teacher named Gerald Max Snyder. In 1975, Snyder began medical treatments in order to appear feminine.

By the end of the 1982–83 school year, after a year of therapy with a psychotherapist experienced in dealing with transsexual patients, Snyder had decided to undergo sex-reassignment surgery. As part of the pre-surgery procedure, Snyder moved to California for one year after the 1982–83 school year to engage in the role of a female in a test to confirm the decision to undergo the contemplated surgery.

In June 1983, the district sent a letter stating that the teaching certificate held by Snyder was due to expire on December 30, 1983. On August 15, 1983, Snyder sent a letter to the district stating that Snyder would not return to teach in the fall because of health reasons. Snyder was subsequently granted leave with pay.

On September 4, 1984, Snyder sent a letter to the district, signed "Michelle Marie Snyder formerly Gerald Max Snyder," requesting continued leave without pay for personal health reasons and stating that she intended to return to her teaching position in January 1985. Snyder's communication contained a letter from two therapists briefly describing Snyder's past medical treatments, indicating that Snyder intended to pursue sex-reassignment surgery, stating that the surgery would be completed in the fall of 1984, and opining that Snyder would be able to resume teaching in January of 1985. This letter constituted Snyder's first notification to the district that she was assuming a new sexual role.

On November 6, 1984, sex-reassignment surgery was performed on Snyder. On November 8, 1984, the district's assistant superintendent of personnel services, Charles E. Rufien, wrote a letter to Snyder containing the following statements:

> The School District cannot employ or pay teachers who lack proper licensing and certification. I request, therefore, that you meet with me no later than Friday, November 16, 1984, to present evidence that you possess a valid Colorado teaching certificate. If the certificate is not presented by that date, I will assume that you have not been recertified as indicated in the records of the Department of Education and your employment in the District will, therefore, be terminated effective October 9, 1984.

Rufien and Snyder ultimately met on November 26, 1984. At the meeting, Rufien asked Snyder whether she held a valid teaching certificate. Snyder said she did not. The next day, November 27, 1984, Rufien sent a letter to Snyder stating that her teaching position with the district was terminated effective October 9, 1984.

The Court of Appeals affirmed the school board's order of dismissal, but reversed its denial of Snyder's request for back pay. The Court of Appeals concluded that in view of the ALJ's factual finding that Snyder did not have a valid teaching certificate and was not on medical leave when she failed to report to the school to which she had been assigned, the school board's conclusion that the lapse in her teaching certificate constituted other good and just cause for dismissal was warranted. Because of this conclusion, the court did not address Snyder's arguments regarding the school board's reliance on the grounds of incompetency and insubordination to support its order of dismissal.

As an initial matter, we must determine the proper standard of appellate review applicable to the school board's order. At the time of Snyder's tenure teacher dismissal proceeding, the 1967 Act directed the Court of Appeals to apply the standard of review embodied in the State Administrative Procedure Act when considering a teacher's appeal of a school board. § 22–63–117(11), 9 C.R.S. (1988). The Court of Appeals applied that standard of review in affirming the school board's ruling here.

A school board by necessity exercises broad discretion in placing and implementing educational programs for its community, including authority to define the grounds for dismissal of tenure teachers. Ricci v. Davis, 627 P.2d 1111, 1118 (Colo.1981). Accord Board of Educ. v. Pico, 457 U.S. 853, 863, 102 S.Ct. 2799, 2806, 73 L.Ed.2d 435 (1982). While a school board's exercise of its discretion to define grounds for dismissal is subject to judicial review, a reviewing court may not freely substitute its judgment for a school board's appraisal of the harm inflicted on the school community by particular instances of teacher conduct. Ricci, 627 P.2d at 1118. See also Blair v. Lovett, 196 Colo. 118, 124, 582 P.2d 668, 672–73 (1978).

The 1967 Act provides a two-stage process for consideration of charges of dismissal. The first stage includes a hearing before an administrative law judge to determine whether allegations of specified grounds for dismissal of a tenure teacher can be established by a district. § 22–63–117(5), 9 C.R.S. (1988). The administrative law judge must review the evidence, assess the credibility of witnesses, weigh conflicting evidence, draw reasonable inferences from the facts, make written findings of both evidentiary and ultimate fact, and make a recommendation that the teacher either be dismissed or retained. § 22–63–117(8), 9 C.R.S. (1988); Blaine, 748 P.2d at 1286–87. A finding of evidentiary fact "involve[s] the raw, historical data underlying the controversy and represent[s] a determination of what the teacher actually did or did not do during the incident in question." Blaine, 748 P.2d at 1287. A finding of ultimate fact "involves a conclusion of law or at least a determination of a mixed question of law and fact and settles the rights and liabilities of the parties." Id.

However, in view of the broad discretion retained by school boards to determine grounds for dismissal and the ultimate authority of school boards to determine whether a tenure teacher should be retained or dismissed, a school board may reject a hearing officer's findings of ultimate fact, enter new findings of ultimate fact and order dismissal of a tenure teacher, so long as the new ultimate findings are fully warranted by the evidentiary findings of the hearing officer and the school board states the reasons for its conclusions. Id. at 1290. See also Lovett, 196 Colo. at 124, 582 P.2d at 672 ("we must also take care not to unduly restrict the board's ultimate authority, for there is no indication of a legislative intent to delegate that authority to the [administrative law judge]").

The second stage in the process requires a school board to review the administrative law judge's findings of evidentiary and ultimate fact and recommendation. § 22–63–117(10), 9 C.R.S. (1988). After conducting such review, a school board may dismiss the teacher, retain the teacher, or place the teacher on one-year probation. Id. If the administrative law judge's findings of evidentiary facts are supported by substantial evidence, the school board must base its ultimate determination only upon those findings and not on some other evidentiary basis. Blaine, 748 P.2d at 1288.

The Court of Appeals concluded that under all of the circumstances here present, the school board's determination that the lapse in Snyder's teaching certificate constituted other good and just cause warranting her dismissal is fully warranted by the record. That court applied the appropriate standard of review and, in our view, did not err in its conclusion.

ALMQUIST v. ALMQUIST

Supreme Court of Kansas, 1974.
214 Kan. 788, 522 P.2d 383.

FOTH, COMMISSIONER.

Mrs. Almquist's . . . complaint goes to the fact that in making the property division the trial court apparently first set aside to her husband the home place and his interest in his mother's estate, and apportioned only the balance. In so doing, she says, the trial court abused its discretion.

The rules applicable to our review in such a case are easy to state but difficult to apply. "The district court is vested with wide discretion in adjusting the financial obligations of the parties in a divorce action and its exercise of that discretion will not be disturbed on appeal in the absence of a showing of clear abuse." (Stayton v. Stayton, 211 Kan. 560, 506 P.2d 1172, Syl. ¶ 1.) One seeking to establish an abuse of discretion assumes a heavy burden, for "If reasonable men could differ as to the propriety of the action taken by the trial court then it cannot be said that the trial court abused its discretion." (Id., p. 562, 506 P.2d, p. 1175.) On the other hand, "The discretion vested in the trial court must be exercised in whole-hearted good faith and be guided by the statutes, not by the court's private opinion of what the statute ought to be. Where the exercise of discretion is arbitrary and not judicial, and the judgment is inequitable, it will be set aside." (St. Clair v. St. Clair, 211 Kan. 468, 507 P.2d 206, Syl. ¶ 6.)

NOTE

"We review a district court's decision to grant a motion to strike unscheduled supplementary material for abuse of discretion. Admiralty Fund v. Hugh Johnson & Co., 677 F.2d 1301, 1314 (9th Cir.1982); see also Carpenter v. Universal Star Shipping, S.A., 924 F.2d 1539, 1547 (9th Cir.1991), cert. denied, ___ U.S. ___, 113 S.Ct. 413, 121 L.Ed.2d 337 (1992) (court's refusal to entertain untimely material in support of a motion for summary judgment reviewed for abuse of discretion). Discretion is abused when the judicial action is 'arbitrary, fanciful or unreasonable' or 'where no reasonable man [or woman] would take the view adopted by the trial court.' Delno v. Market St.Ry.Co., 124 F.2d 965, 967 (9th Cir.1942)."

Golden Gate Hotel Ass'n v. San Francisco, 18 F.3d 1482, 1485 (9th Cir.1994).

"Although the Commissioner's discretion is not unbridled and may not be arbitrary, we sustain his exercise of discretion here, for in this case the write-down was plainly inconsistent with the governing regulations which the taxpayer, on its part, has not challenged . . .

"Section 166(c) states that a deduction for an addition to a bad debt reserve is to be allowed 'in the discretion of the' Commissioner. Consistent with this statutory language, the courts uniformly have held that the Commissioner's determination of a 'reasonable' (and hence deductible) addition must be sustained unless the Commissioner abused his discretion. The taxpayer is said to bear a 'heavy burden' in this respect. He must show not only that his own computation is reasonable; he must also show that the Commissioner's computation is unreasonable and arbitrary."

Thor Power Tool Co. v. C.I.R., 439 U.S. 522, 547 (1979).

MAURICE ROSENBERG, THE EXERCISE OF DISCRETION: REVIEWED *

A federal court of appeals in 1954 hit upon one of the most curious standards in the books. The trial judge had refused in the exercise of his discretion, to set aside a default judgment. The appellate court reversed, saying the trial judge's discretion had to be measured in light of the strong policy favoring trial on the merits instead of defaults. In consequence, it held that a "slight abuse of discretion" was "sufficient to justify a reversal of the order." Contracting a slight case of pregnancy must be another example of a slight abuse of discretion—a nonjudicious type, of course.

. . .

* *Judicial Discretion of the Trial Court, Viewed from Above,* 22 Syracuse L.Rev. 635, 652–653, 659–665 (1971). Reprinted by permission.

After trial, the most important occasions for possible discretionary authority, relate to setting aside verdicts and judgments and granting or denying new trials.

These are admittedly difficult matters to attempt to regulate according to precise rules. My difficulty with the rules which are sometimes drafted or announced is not that they do or do not bestow discretionary authority in particular areas, but rather that they do not say what grade of discretion they are intending to invest in the trial judge. Nor do they set any limits or offer any indicia for the guidance of either the trial court's exercise of the discretion or the appellate court's review of it. Unfortunately, the appeals courts do not tend to fill the gap by the opinions they write.

Instead, most opinions of the appellate courts have indulged in a form of automated verbiage or knee-jerk terminology which has very little idea content. The prime example of this is the phrase "abuse of discretion," which is used to convey the appellate court's disagreement with what the trial court has done, but does nothing by way of offering reasons or guidance for the future. The phrase "abuse of discretion" does not communicate meaning. It is a form of ill-tempered appellate grunting and should be dispensed with.

A constructive avenue is open to appellate courts if they are intent on revising discretionary trial court rulings; that is, to specify the factors that the trial judge should have taken into account but apparently did not in the exercise of his authority....

Appellate courts ... go along with restricted review of decisions wrapped in trial court discretion; acknowledge that discretionary power varies in force from the virtually irresistible to the virtually meaningless; and act as if no magic words will either guarantee or repel recognition of discretion in the trial judge. They do not respond unanimously and on all occasions to the foregoing principles and they do not express themselves clearly or consistently when they do, but the unmistakable direction of their decisions is along the lines ... sketched. The question is: Why?

It is clear that discretion has been widely feared and mistrusted in the common law. It flies in the face of deep principles, such as that announced rules, not unspoken fancies, should shape trial court decisions and that a disappointed litigant should be given a chance to present his claim to a multi-judge court at an appellate level. Why, then, is a sole judge on the lowest rung of the judicial ladder given unreviewable power? Five reasons can be identified from the decisions, three of which are not particularly impressive or substantial, and two of which make good sense. First, the lesser reasons.

One is the plain urge to economize on judicial energies. Appeal courts would be swamped to the point of capsizing if every ruling by a trial judge could be presented for appellate review.... The argument for economizing appellate energies does not help us identify the issues that should be committed to trial judges for final or presumptively final determination. It advances a persuasive reason for often making the first court effectively the court of last resort, but is undiscriminating in selecting the issues that are to be unreviewable. Is an order granting or denying a new trial in that category? Requiring special verdicts? Enlarging time? Allowing or refusing tardy applications for amendment, jury trial, discovery, etc.? Giving the *nisi prius* judge the last word would save time in all these areas of decision, yet obviously not all have an equal claim to restricted appellate review.

A second reason is maintaining morale. A trial judge might become dispirited if he had the sense that every rapid-fire ruling he makes at trial is to be fully reviewable by a clutch of appellate judges who can study, reflect, hear and read carefully assembled arguments, consult their law clerks, debate among themselves and, after close analysis, overturn his ruling. He would have an oppressive sense that appellate Big Brothers were ever watching, peering over the trial bench, waiting for the harried and hurried trial judge to lapse into mortal fallibility.

This realization led the late Judge Calvert Magruder of the United States Court of Appeals for the First Circuit to comment understandingly:

> As to the trial judges, we must always bear in mind that they may be as good lawyers as we are or better. They are under the disadvantage of often having to make rulings off the cuff ... in the press and urgency of a trial.... Hence, we should approach our task of judicial review with a certain genuine humility. We should never unnecessarily try to make a monkey of the judge in the court below or to trespass on his feelings or dignity and self-respect.[51]

That reason, worthy and compassionate as it is, again falls short of telling which of the rapid-fire trial rulings are to be immune from review and which not. An issue of privileged communication may suddenly arise during testimony in a jury trial. Is the trial court's "wrong" ruling (in appellate eyes) to be unassailable or not? The Magruder call for charity toward trial brethren is fine as far as it goes, but, like the call for economy of appellate energies, it does not help discriminate among the innumerable situations it might apply to.

The third reason for hands-off review is finality. The more reverse-proof the trial judge's rulings, the less likely the losing attorney is to test them on appeal and the sooner the first adjudication becomes accepted and the dispute tranquilized. Delay would surely result, and injustice might result, if every trial court order could be dragged up the appellate ladder with some fair hope of reversal. Except where restrained by the final judgment principle, the party with the deeper pocket might try to wear down his adversary by challenging every uncongenial ruling, whether made in the pleading, discovery, trial or post-trial phases of the

51. Magruder, *The Trials and Tribulations of an Intermediate Appellate Court,* 44 Cornell L.Q. 1, 3 (1958).

litigation. Conferring near-finality on trial court orders by restrictive review practices dampens the possibility of that sort of abuse. But once again, the reason is nonselective....

The common vice of the first three reasons—economy, morale uplift, and finality—is their failure to provide clear clues as to which trial court rulings are cloaked with discretionary immunity of some strength, and which are not. Remaining for consideration are two reasons that escape this criticism.

One of the "good" reasons for conferring discretion on the trial judge is the sheer impracticability of formulating a rule of decision for the matter in issue. Many questions that arise in litigation are not amenable to regulation by rule because they involve multifarious, fleeting, special, narrow facts that utterly resist generalization—at least, for the time being. Whether a witness may be called out of regular sequence, the scope of cross-examination in many circumstances, enlarging time, ordering special hearings, requiring special memoranda, and a host of other trial administration issues, are obviously unamenable to hard and fast legal rules. When the ruling under attack is one that does not seem to admit of control by a rule that can be formulated or criteria that can be indicated, prudence and necessity agree it should be left in the control of the judge at the trial level. That is true when the circumstances which rationally deserve attention are so infinitely variable that it is hopeless to try to cover them by general propositions.

On occasion, the difficulty is the novelty of the situation rather than the multifarious minuteness of its circumstances. When the problem arises in a context so new and unsettled that the rule-makers do not yet know what factors should shape the result, the case may be a good one to leave to lower court discretion. Actually, this may be a form of primary or free-form discretion, but the point is that it permits experience to accumulate at the lowest court level before the appellate judges commit themselves to a prescribed rule. By according the trial judge discretionary power, the appeal courts have a chance to bide their time until they see more clearly what factors are important to decision and how to take them into account. Their position might be put as follows: This is an area in which the trial judge must decide by guess and we accept his guess unless it is too wild.

The final reason—and probably the most pointed and helpful one—for bestowing discretion on the trial judge as to many matters is, paradoxically, the superiority of his nether position. It is not that he knows more than his loftier brothers; rather, he sees more and senses more. In the dialogue between the appellate judges and the trial judge, the former often seem to be saying: "You were there. We do not think we would have done what you did, but we were not present and we may be unaware of significant matters, for the record does not adequately convey to us all that went on at the trial. Therefore, we defer to you."

A classic example is Atchison, Topeka & Sante Fe Railway Co. v. Barrett.[52] Barrett brought an action against the Atchison, etc., for head injuries he received while working on the railroad. He claimed his injury was manifested by a sporadic jerking or twitching of his head—a spasmodic torticollis. This started three months after the accident, happened every few seconds, and was uncontrollable and permanent—so he claimed.

Although he had not lost time from work and had not sought medical care until a month after the accident and although one of his doctors had an unhealthy reputation—he was convicted on multiple counts of false claiming, perjury and forgery—the jury awarded Barrett $12,500.

After the trial, plaintiff was placed under surveillance by the railway's under-cover operatives, who took movies showing the twitching had stopped for a two-hour period, at least. When Barrett learned he was being tailed, his twitching started again and continued until the railway's time for a new trial expired. Then, movies again showed he apparently had recovered.

The defendant moved to vacate the judgment for fraud and produced the movies and affidavits about the doctor. The trial judge agreed there were "some strange things" in the case, but denied the motion to vacate the judgment. The court of appeals affirmed, saying: "We are frank to state that had the able trial judge determined that fraud or other misconduct existed to grant appellant relief ... we would not have disturbed that conclusion, on the record before us."

The court of appeals wrote that the decision on the motion was "peculiarly" in the trial judge's discretion:

> The trial judge saw and heard the plaintiff; saw his twitchings, what they were and what they were not, as did the jury. He saw or heard the other matters relied on by appellant; he felt the 'climate' of the trial. The trial judge found no fraud nor misrepresentation.... The Court of Appeals should not and will not substitute its judgment for that of the trial court, nor reverse the lower court's determination save for an abuse of discretion.

The "you are there" reasoning conveyed by that quotation is in my opinion the chief and most helpful reason for appellate court deference to trial court rulings. As one trial judge pungently phrased it, he "smells the smoke of battle" and can get a sense of the interpersonal dynamics between the lawyers and the jury. Not even the televised recordation of trial proceedings ... can capture all the sensory perceptions that presence on the scene conveys. That is a sound and proper reason for conferring a substantial measure of respect to the trial judge's ruling *whenever it is based on facts or circumstances that are critical to decision and that the record imperfectly conveys.* This reason is a

52. 246 F.2d 846 (9th Cir.1957).

discriminating one, for it helps identify the subject matter as to which an appellate court should defer to the trial judge, and suggests the measure of finality or presumptive validity that should be accorded.

In Noonan v. Cunard Steamship Co., [375 F.2d 69, 71 (2d Cir.1967),] Judge Friendly analyzed with characteristic perceptiveness and stated with remarkable succinctness the criteria comprising the "appropriate test" of discretion:

> [T]he fact that dismissal under Rule 41(a)(2) [at the plaintiff's own insistence] usually rests on the judge's discretion does not mean that this is always so. Several of the most important reasons for deferring to the trial judge's exercise of discretion—his observation of the witnesses, his superior opportunity to get "the feel of the case," see Cone v. West Virginia Pulp & Paper Co., 320 U.S. 212, 216, 67 S.Ct. 752, 91 L.Ed. 849 (1947), and the impracticability of framing a rule of decision where many disparate factors must be weighed, see Atchison, T. & S.F. Ry. v. Barrett, 246 F.2d 846 (9 Cir.1957)—are inapposite when a question arising in advance of trial can be stated in a form susceptible of a yes-or-no answer applicable to all cases.

NOTE

Does Professor Rosenberg's explanation of the first "good reason" for conferring discretion on trial courts comport with Holmes' basic definition of the law? Does your answer depend on whether the appellate court ultimately approves of the trial court's accumulation of experience?

Do you find his explanation of the fifth justification for conferring discretionary authority on trial judges persuasive? Does it make a difference if the trial judge shares the responsibility for the inadequacy of the record in conveying what went on at trial to the appellate bench? If so, then does the appellate court exercise an unreviewable discretion of its own in deciding whether or not to defer to the trial judge?

LEVENTHAL, J., in *Greater Boston Television Corp. v. FCC*, 444 F.2d 841, 851 (D.C.Cir.1970): "Assuming consistency with law and the legislative mandate, the agency has latitude not merely to find facts and make judgments, but also to select the policies deemed in the public interest. The function of the court is to assure that the agency has given reasoned consideration to all the material facts and issues. This calls for insistence that the agency articulate with reasonable clarity its reasons for decision, and identify the significance of the crucial facts, a course that tends to assure that the agency's policies effectuate general standards, applied without unreasonable discrimination. As for the particular subject of comparative hearings, the findings must cover all the substantial differences between the applicants and the ultimate conclusion must be based on a composite consideration of the findings as to each applicant.

"Its supervisory function calls on the court to intervene not merely in case of procedural inadequacies, or bypassing of the mandate in the legislative charter, but more broadly if the court becomes aware, especially from a combination of danger signals, that the agency has not really taken a hard look at the salient problems, and has not genuinely engaged in reasoned decision-making. If the agency has not shirked this fundamental task, however, the court exercises restraint and affirms the agency's action even though the court would on its own account have made different findings or adopted different standards. Nor will the court upset a decision because of errors that are not material, there being room for the doctrine of harmless error. If satisfied that the agency has taken a hard look at the issues with the use of reasons and standards, the court will uphold its findings, though of less than ideal clarity, if the agency's path may reasonably be discerned, though of course the court must not be left to guess as to the agency's findings or reasons."

Section 4

PLENARY OR DE NOVO REVIEW: QUESTIONS OF LAW

A. GENERAL

OVERVIEW

When it comes to the review of the trial court's determination of the appropriate legal precept, the appellate courts are given the freest of reins. If review of fact finding is at the nadir of the appellate function, the examination of the trial court's selection and interpretation of legal precepts is the zenith. On a legal question, the appellate court is not restricted by the division of judicial labors which protects findings of fact in the common law tradition and under the constitutions of the various sovereignties or the limited review of discretion. Generally speaking, the appellate court is free to examine *de novo* all aspects of legal precepts—the choice of the controlling precept by the trial tribunal, the interpretation thereof and the application of the precept as chosen and interpreted to the findings of fact.

A reviewing court's function is to determine whether a trial court committed a mistake of sufficient magnitude to require that its judgment be reversed or vacated. Putting aside those jurisdictions in which appellate courts must search the record for error, the reviewing court's role is inexorably intertwined with the performance of the advocates. An appellate court may, under certain conditions, consider matters *sua sponte* but, generally, when an appellate court considers questions raised by an appellant alleging error, it relies upon the issues and legal arguments set forth by the advocates.

In 1877 a reviewing court stated, "The court erred in some of the legal propositions announced to the jury; but all the errors were harmless. Wrong directions which do not put the traveler out of his way furnish no reason for repeating the journey." [1] Roger J. Traynor regarded this as a literary epigram but not as a legal principle, for the question whether wrong directions do or do not put the traveler out of his way is a troublesome one. The difficult question is to decide whether trial error becomes reversible error. Recognizing the doctrine that one is not entitled to a perfect trial, but only to a fair one, it becomes necessary to fashion a method of ascertaining the circumstances under which the results of admittedly imperfect trials will be disturbed.

We cannot draw any line in the sand to determine when run-of-the mill trial mistakes transform themselves into reversible error. When asked, even the most experienced appellate judges will respond, "It depends." For the most part, lapses by the trial court that are not deemed reversible errors relate to trial management, reception of evidence, jury instructions and reasons stating for summary judgments or dismissals based on pleadings. Specific passages in a set of jury instructions are appraised against the instructions as a whole. Stated reasons for certain rulings on pre-trial dispositions are evaluated in the context of alternative unstated but legitimate reasons for the determinations. The line is crossed to reversible error when the collective judgment of a multi-judge reviewing panel believes that the mistake seriously infected the truth-finding process, or when judgment has been rendered on uncontroverted facts, the party against whom the ruling was made could possibly have been entitled to relief.

In the context we have discussed, "non-reversible error" constitutes an act or condition of imprudent deviation from an accepted norm. In lay terms, it is an error. In jurisprudence, however, it does not rise to a quality or magnitude that would require reversing or vacating the judgment of the trial court or granting a petition for review of an agency final order. It is, therefore, not described as an error. In this respect, however, it must not be confused with the doctrine of "harmless error," which has become a term of art.

The doctrine of harmless error differs in two important respects. First, the breach, omission or mistake candidly is described as "error." Second, defining the precise perimeters of the doctrine in both constitutional and non-constitutional cases has occupied the attention of state and federal courts from the seminal *Kotteakos* case in 1946 to refinements as recent as 1995.

Many questions which may spell the difference between affirmance and reversal abide in the law and continue to swell the dockets of appellate courts. In examining the materials, readers should consider how they would urge, or oppose, the underlying contentions in the following questions: When does a verdict shock a court's collective conscience? When will a court find a verdict contrary to the weight of the evidence? When may a court deem a non-jury finding of fact clearly erroneous? When will it? When is a jury's finding based on a prepon-

1. Cherry v. Davis, 59 Ga. 454, 456 (1877).

derance of the evidence? Clear and convincing evidence? Evidence beyond a reasonable doubt? Did the trial court err in instructing the jury? Is it an error of law or abuse of discretion? Was a proper objection timely made? Did the party meet its burden of proof? Did the party meet its burden of going forward with the evidence? Did the court err in granting or refusing judgment n.o.v.?

SALVE REGINA COLLEGE v. RUSSELL

Supreme Court of the United States, 1991.
499 U.S. 225, 111 S.Ct. 1217, 113 L.Ed.2d 190.

JUSTICE BLACKMUN delivered the Opinion of the Court

We conclude that a court of appeals should review *de novo* a district court's determination of state law. As a general matter, of course, the courts of appeals are vested with plenary appellate authority over final decisions of district courts. See 28 U.S.C. § 1291. The obligation of responsible appellate jurisdiction implies the requisite authority to review independently a lower court's determinations.

Independent appellate review of legal issues best serves the dual goals of doctrinal coherence and economy of judicial administration. District judges preside alone over fast-paced trials: Of necessity they devote much of their energy and resources to hearing witnesses and reviewing evidence. Similarly, the logistical burdens of trial advocacy limit the extent to which trial counsel is able to supplement the district judge's legal research with memoranda and briefs. Thus, trial judges often must resolve complicated legal questions without benefit of "extended reflection [or] extensive information." Coenen, To Defer or Not to Defer: a Study of Federal Circuit Court Deference to District Court Rulings on State Law, 73 Minn.L.Rev. 899, 923 (1989).

Courts of appeals, on the other hand, are structurally suited to the collaborative juridical process that promotes decisional accuracy. With the record having been constructed below and settled for purposes of the appeal, appellate judges are able to devote their primary attention to legal issues. As questions of law become the focus of appellate review, it can be expected that the parties' briefs will be refined to bring to bear on the legal issues more information and more comprehensive analysis than was provided for the district judge. Perhaps most important, courts of appeals employ multijudge panels, see 28 U.S.C. §§ 46(b) and (c), that permit reflective dialogue and collective judgment. Over 30 years ago, Justice Frankfurter accurately observed:

"Without adequate study there cannot be adequate reflection; without adequate reflection there cannot be adequate discussion; without adequate discussion there cannot be that fruitful interchange of minds which is indispensable to thoughtful, unhurried decision and its formulation in learned and impressive opinions." Dick v. New York Life Ins. Co., 359 U.S. 437, 458–459 (1959) (dissenting opinion).

Independent appellate review necessarily entails a careful consideration of the district court's legal analysis, and an efficient and sensitive appellate court at least will naturally consider this analysis in undertaking its review. Petitioner readily acknowledges the importance of a district court's reasoning to the appellate court's review.

Any expertise possessed by the district court will inform the structure and content of its conclusions of law and thereby become evident to the reviewing court. If the court of appeals finds that the district court's analytical sophistication and research have exhausted the state-law inquiry, little more need be said in the appellate opinion. Independent review, however, does not admit of unreflective reliance on a lower court's inarticulable intuitions. Thus, an appropriately respectful application of *de novo* review should encourage a district court to explicate with care the basis for its legal conclusions. See Fed.Rule Civ.Proc. 52(a) (requiring the district court to "state separately its conclusions of law").

Those circumstances in which Congress or this Court has articulated a standard of deference for appellate review of district-court determinations reflect an accommodation of the respective institutional advantages of trial and appellate courts. In deference to the unchallenged superiority of the district court's factfinding ability, Rule 52(a) commands that a trial court's findings of fact "shall not be set aside unless clearly erroneous, and due regard shall be given to the opportunity of the trial court to judge the credibility of the witnesses." In addition, it is "especially common" for issues involving supervision of litigation to be reviewed for abuse of discretion. See Pierce v. Underwood, 487 U.S. 552, 558, n. 1 (1988). Finally, we have held that deferential review of mixed questions of law and fact is warranted when it appears that the district court is "better positioned" than the appellate court to decide the issue in question or that probing appellate scrutiny will not contribute to the clarity of legal doctrine. Miller v. Fenton, 474 U.S. 104, 114 (1985); see also Cooter & Gell v. Hartmarx Corp., 496 U.S. 384, 402 (1990) ("[T]he district court is better situated than the court of appeals to marshal the pertinent facts and apply the fact-dependent legal standard mandated by Rule 11"); *Pierce,* 487 U.S., at 562 ("[T]he question whether the Government's litigating position has been 'substantially justified' is … a multifarious and novel question, little susceptible, for the time being at least, of useful generalization").

CHARLES ALAN WRIGHT, THE DOUBTFUL OMNISCIENCE OF APPELLATE COURTS*

For a good many years my colleague, Leon Green, has been pointing out that:

> Probably the strangest chapter in American legal history is how in the short period of the last fifty or seventy-five years, the same period during which trial courts were losing most of their power, the appellate courts have drawn unto themselves practically all the power of the judicial system.

In a recent statement of his views Dean Green has observed, with much justification:

> The trial judge is not much more than a trial examiner, while the jury simply satisfies the public and professional craving for ceremonial—the necessity for dealing with simple matters as though they were freighted with great significance.

The principal means by which appellate courts have obtained such complete control of litigation has been the transmutation of specific circumstances into questions of law. Subtle rules about presumptions and burden of proof, elaborate concepts of causation and consideration and the rest, have been devised in such a way that unless the appellate judge handling the case is a dullard, some doctrine is always at hand to achieve the ends of justice, as they appear to the appellate court.

Dean Green's analysis seems to me unanswerable. The purpose of the present article is to call attention to certain recent developments which add further support to his thesis. Within the last decade the appellate judges have become bolder. No longer do they hide their assumption of power beneath an elaborate doctrinal superstructure. Instead today's appellate courts are inventing new procedural devices by which their mastery of the litigation process can be made direct rather than devious.

Such devices [include:] review by the appellate court of the size of verdicts; orders for a new trial where the verdict is thought to be contrary to the clear weight of the evidence; and expanded use of the extraordinary writs of mandamus and prohibition to control the trial court in its discretionary actions as to the procedure by which a case is to be handled....

. . .

... The appraisal by trial judge and jury of the damages suffered by an injured person is now subject to review by appellate courts; a decade ago it could not have been reviewed. The determination by the trial judge that the verdict is not contrary to the clear weight of the evidence

* 41 Minn.L.Rev. 751, 751–52, 778–82 (1957). Reprinted by permission of the author and the Minnesota Law Review.

is now said, by at least one appellate court, to be within its power to reverse; heretofore the precedents have been uniform that such a determination was not subject to reversal. Many appellate courts now believe that they need not give any weight to findings of fact of a trial judge sitting without a jury where these findings are based on documentary evidence; both the language and intent of Federal Rule 52(a), adopted by the Supreme Court only 19 years ago, are explicit that such findings can only be set aside when clearly erroneous. Finally discretionary decisions by the trial judge on interlocutory procedural matters may now be vacated in the exercise of a supervisory power of appellate courts, contrary to what the Supreme Court said as recently as 1956. Thus the centralization of legal power in the appellate courts, which Dean Green detected more than a quarter century ago, proceeds at an accelerating pace.

But now we must venture some views as to whether this development is good or bad for the cause of justice to which all are devoted. It would be irresponsible even to suggest that these changes have taken place merely because appellate courts are power-mad. The obvious truth, which must be readily admitted by anyone familiar with appellate judges, is that these recent developments in the law, these departures from what had seemed fairly clear lines of precedent, have come only because the judges who have voted for them sincerely believe that they are needed and justified by the highest public interests.

This leads us to the philosophical question which underlies all these specific issues: what is the proper function of an appellate court? Everyone agrees, so far as I know, that one function of an appellate court is to discover and declare—or to make—the law. From the earliest times appellate courts have been empowered to reverse for errors of law, to announce the rules which are to be applied, and to ensure uniformity in the rules applied by various inferior tribunals.

The controversial question is whether appellate courts have a second function, that of ensuring that justice is done in a particular case. In each of the situations considered the motivating force in the appellate court's mind has been the desire to "do justice." Thus the appellate court is unwilling to let an award of damages stand which seems to it so excessive as to be unjust, it refuses to put its approval on a verdict which it deems contrary to the clear weight of the evidence, it will not affirm a judgment based on findings it thinks wrong when it is as well able to interpret documentary evidence and make the finding in question as was the trial court, and it will not let a trial judge's mistaken conception of what is an "exceptional condition" result in exposing parties to the delay and expense of reference to a master.

If it is the function of appellate courts to do justice in individual cases, then each of the developments we have canvassed was sound and desirable, since each has made it easier for the appellate court to enforce its concept of justice in a particular case. The notion that appellate courts should undertake to "do justice" is so attractive on its face that it is difficult to disagree with it. And it enjoys the weighty support of such famous students of the judicial process as Roscoe Pound, Edson Sunderland, Wirt Blume and James Wm. Moore. Nevertheless, with deference to these great men, I think we should refrain from agreeing that appellate courts are to do justice until we have seen the price we must pay for this concept.

The principal consequences of broadening appellate review are two. Such a course impairs the confidence of litigants and the public in the decisions of the trial courts, and it multiplies the number of appeals. Until recently if a defendant thought an award of damages was excessive, he nevertheless had no choice but to pay it, for no appellate court would listen to his attack on it. Now, in similar circumstances, he will appeal. Until recently if a lawyer was dissatisfied when his case was referred to a master, he appeared before the master nevertheless, for an attempted appeal from the order of reference would have been dismissed out of hand. Now he files a petition for a writ of mandamus. We may be sure that the broadened scope of appellate review we have seen will mean an increase in the number of appeals.[118] Is this desirable? We need not worry too much that an increase in appeals will mean overwork for appellate judges; they, after all, have invited the increase. But we should worry about the consequences of more numerous appeals for the litigants and the public. Appeals are always expensive and time-consuming. When they are successful, and lead to a new trial, they add to the burden on already-crowded trial courts. Interlocutory review, as by writ of mandamus, delays the case interminably while the lawyers go off to the appellate court to argue the propriety of the challenged order by the trial judge. It is literally marvelous that, at a time when the entire profession is seeking ways to minimize congestion and delay in the courts, we should set on a course which inevitably must increase congestion and delay.

But we have courts in order to do justice. If better justice can be obtained by broadening the scope of appellate review, then even congestion, delay and expense are not too high a price to pay. Do we really get better justice by augmenting the power of the appellate courts? In some fairly obvious senses I feel quite sure that we do not. If in two similar cases the person rich enough to afford an appeal gets a reversal, however just, while the person of insufficient means to risk an appeal is forced to live with the judgment of the trial court, has justice really been improved? And what of the injured person who settles his claim for less than the amount awarded him by the jury and approved by the trial court rather than wait a year or more until an appellate court has agreed that the verdict is not excessive? Broader appellate review has led to injustice for him.

---

118. A usual means of reducing congestion in the appellate courts has been to narrow the scope of review. For an excellent historical account, see Frankfurter and Landis, *The Supreme Court at October Term, 1929,* 44 Harv.L.Rev. 1, 26–35 (1930).

Further, it may well be, as Blackstone says, that "next to doing right, the great object in the administration of public justice should be to give public satisfaction." It is hard to believe that there has been any great public dissatisfaction with the restricted appellate review which was traditional in this country. Very early in our history Chief Justice Ellsworth observed:

> But, surely, it cannot be deemed a denial of justice, that a man shall not be permitted to try his case two or three times over.

Yet increased review is likely to lead to quite tangible public dissatisfaction. Every time a trial judge is reversed, every time the belief is reiterated that appellate courts are better qualified than trial judges to decide what justice requires, the confidence of litigants and the public in the trial courts will be further impaired. Under any feasible or conceivable system, our trial courts must always have the last word in the great bulk of cases. I doubt whether there will be much satisfaction with the judgments of trial courts among a public which is educated to believe that only appellate judges are trustworthy ministers of justice.

Finally, to come to the very heart of the issue, is there any reason to suppose that the result an appellate court reaches on the kinds of issues discussed is more likely to be "just" than was the opposite result reached by the trial court? Judge Chase's observation ... is in point here:

> Though trial judges may at times be mistaken as to facts, appellate judges are not always omniscient.

Most of our examples have come from the federal courts, and federal district judges are generally believed to be men of much ability, rightly entitled to the greatest respect. In some of the states, it is true, trial judges are not so highly regarded. But this is wrong, regardless of the scope of appellate review. I think there is wide agreement that trial judges should be picked with the same care as appellate judges, and that it probably would be desirable to give them the same conditions of salary and tenure as are given appellate judges.

If trial judges are carefully selected, as in the federal system, it is hard to think of any reason why they are more likely to make errors of judgment than are appellate judges. Where the question is whether an award of damages is excessive or a verdict against the clear weight of the evidence, the trial judge has the vast advantage of having been present in the courtroom and heard the witnesses. Where the question is as to the procedure to be followed in a pending case, the trial judge has the advantage of having lived with the case, and thus should be better able than the appellate judges to gauge its complexity and its procedural needs.

There is no way to know for sure whether trial courts or appellate courts are more often right. But in the absence of a clear showing that broadened appellate review leads to better justice, a showing which I think has not been made and probably cannot be made, the cost of increased appellate review, in terms of time and expense to the parties, in terms of lessened confidence in the trial judge, and in terms of positive injustice to those who cannot appeal, seems to me clearly exorbitant.

I do not wish to speak critically of the appellate courts which have recently announced broader powers of appellate review. Only the most insensitive observer could fail to sympathize with their problem. When a judge upholds the constitutionality of a statute he believes unwise, he has at least all the tradition of deference to a coordinate and popularly responsible branch of government to sustain self-restraint when he is passing on the work of his constitutional inferiors within the judiciary. It must be hard, indeed, for a judge to approve a judgment below he considers to be unjust when he knows that he has the power to set it aside and achieve justice as he sees it. Our hope must be that in those hard moments the judge will remember Justice Jackson's caution that "we are not final because we are infallible, but we are infallible only because we are final," and that, remembering, he may believe that the best way to do justice in the long run is to confine to a minimum appellate tampering with the work of the trial courts.

NOTE

Do you believe that prior service as a trial judge makes any difference in an appellate judge's view of the appellate review function? Given the assumption of greater review powers by appellate courts, with the consequent increased number of appeals, is not the recurring complaint by appellate judges over swollen appellate dockets the result of "self-inflicted wounds"?

Study the philosophies of your state appellate court and of your U.S. Court of Appeals relating to (1) review of the size of jury verdicts and (2) review of orders for new trials where the verdict is challenged as contrary to the clear weight of the evidence. Would the results of your analysis influence you in the choice of a forum in a diversity case?

In the 1968 court year each U.S. Circuit Judge read carefully the briefs in 93 cases. By 1994 the judge was required to read some 446 cases in addition to reviewing opinions by panels of which he was not a member. Is it realistic to expect that each circuit judge reads the record in each on which he or she sits?

Assume a state supreme court of five to seven members which does not sit in divisions or panels. Assume further a case load that is two or three times greater than a U.S. Court of Appeals. Is it realistic to expect that each judge on such a court would read the record in each case on which he or she sits?

Consider again Professor Wright's observations set forth in the previous article. Are not McBaine, and Justice Traynor really defining the evidence rules at trial as follows:

	Case Type	Commonly Expressed Standard Of Proof	Means "Fact" Or Result Is
1.	Most civil cases	Preponderance of evidence; substantial evidence	More probable than not
2.	Civil fraud-type case	Clear and convincing evidence	Highly probable
3.	Criminal case	Proof beyond a reasonable doubt	Almost certain

Assume the viability of these definitions, and an express use of them by the *trial* court. How would you formulate the scope of *appellate* review? Should there be more than one? May the appellate court substitute its views of "more probable than not", "highly probable" or "almost certain"? May any court—trial or appellate—substitute its views for the fact finder who has been expressly directed to find facts in accordance with these definitions?

B.   ISSUE PRESERVATION FOR REVIEW AND THE PLAIN ERROR EXCEPTION

An early-warning flag cautions the appellate court against unnecessary consideration of the merits of the appeal. As a preliminary matter, the court always determines whether the issue now presented on appeal was first presented to the trial or hearing tribunal for a ruling in order to preserve the issue for appeal. This is the essence of the common law tradition that requires questions and objections to be presented timely at the trial or hearing in order to permit the adversary to respond by testimony or argument. This permits the trial court or administrative agency the opportunity to make appropriate rulings in the context of a trial setting. Appellate determination of reversible error is based on the presence of specific interrelated circumstances:

> ● matters contained in specific oral or written motions, pleadings or objections brought to the attention of the trial or hearing tribunal by a party or counsel requesting a particular course of action;

> ● which result in specific rulings, acts or omissions by that tribunal constituting error.

When these elements are present, the issue has been preserved for review.

Generally speaking, if the issue was not first presented to the trial judge or administrative agency, the reviewing court will not notice or consider it. There are, of course, exceptional cases in particular circumstances that will prompt a reviewing appellate court to consider questions of law, *sua sponte,* that were not pressed upon the court or administrative agency standing below it. In these cases, unless the reviewing court noted the issue on appeal, blatant injustice might result. Such cases, however, are rare and come under the category of "plain error." Justice Hugo Black explained the purpose of the general rule:

> Ordinarily an appellate court does not consider issues not raised below, for our procedural scheme contemplates that parties shall come to issue in the trial forum vested with authority to determine questions of fact. This is essential in order that parties may have the opportunity to offer all the evidence they believe relevant to the issues that the trial tribunal alone is competent to decide; it is equally essential in order that litigants may not be surprised on appeal by final decision there of issues upon which they have had no opportunity to introduce evidence. The basic reasons that support this general principle applicable to trial courts make it equally desirable that parties should have an opportunity to offer evidence on the general issues involved in the less formal proceedings before administrative agencies that have been entrusted with the responsibility of fact finding.[1]

For there to be plain error: (1) there must be an "error" in fact; there can be no error noticeable on review if an objection is waived rather than forfeited, (2) the error must be "plain" (synonymous with "obvious") and (3) the plain error must "affect substantial rights" ("affected the outcome of the District Court proceedings", unlike harmless error, however, the defendant bears the burden of persuasion with respect to prejudice).[2]

"Plain errors" may be noticed by the reviewing court although they were not brought to the attention of the trial court. Fed.R.Crim.P. 52(b); Fed.R.Evid. 103(d). This is a matter of the reviewing court's discretion, however, and plain error should not result in a reversal unless the error "seriously affects the fairness, integrity, or public reputation of judicial proceedings."[3]

UNITED STATES v. YOUNG

Supreme Court of the United States, 1985.
470 U.S. 1, 105 S.Ct. 1038, 84 L.Ed.2d 1.

CHIEF JUSTICE BURGER delivered the opinion of the Court.

We granted certiorari to review the reversal of respondent's conviction because of prosecutorial comments responding to defense counsel's closing argument impugning the prosecution's integrity and belief in the Government's case.

1. Hormel v. Helvering, 312 U.S. 552, 556 (1941).

2. United States v. Olano, 113 S.Ct. 1770, 1776 (1993).

3. Id. at 1779.

The plain-error doctrine of Federal Rule of Criminal Procedure 52(b) tempers the blow of a rigid application of the contemporaneous-objection requirement. The Rule authorizes the Courts of Appeals to correct only "particularly egregious errors," United States v. Frady, 456 U.S. 152, 163 (1982), those errors that "seriously affect the fairness, integrity or public reputation of judicial proceedings," United States v. Atkinson, 297 U.S., at 160. In other words, the plain-error exception to the contemporaneous-objection rule is to be "used sparingly, solely in those circumstances in which a miscarriage of justice would otherwise result." United States v. Frady, 456 U.S., at 163, n. 14. Any unwarranted extension of this exacting definition of plain error would skew the Rule's "careful balancing of our need to encourage all trial participants to seek a fair and accurate trial the first time around against our insistence that obvious injustice be promptly redressed." *Id.*, at 163 (footnote omitted). Reviewing courts are not to use the plain-error doctrine to consider trial court errors not meriting appellate review absent timely objection—a practice which we have criticized as "extravagant protection." Henderson v. Kibbe, 431 U.S. 145, 154, n. 12 (1977); Namet v. United States, 373 U.S. 179, 190 (1963).

Especially when addressing plain error, a reviewing court cannot properly evaluate a case except by viewing such a claim against the entire record. We have been reminded:

> "In reviewing criminal cases, it is particularly important for appellate courts to relive the whole trial imaginatively and not to extract from episodes in isolation abstract questions of evidence and procedure. To turn a criminal trial into a quest for error no more promotes the ends of justice than to acquiesce in low standards of criminal prosecution." Johnson v. United States, 318 U.S. 189, 202 (1943) (Frankfurter, J., concurring).

It is simply not possible for an appellate court to assess the seriousness of the claimed error by any other means. As the Court stated in United States v. Socony–Vacuum Oil Co., 310 U.S., at 240, "each case necessarily turns on its own facts."

When reviewed with these principles in mind, the prosecutor's remarks cannot be said to rise to the level of plain error. Viewed in context, the prosecutor's statements, although inappropriate and amounting to error, were not such as to undermine the fundamental fairness of the trial and contribute to a miscarriage of justice. See United States v. Frady, *supra,* at 163; United States v. Atkinson, *supra,* at 160.

UNITED STATES v. SIMMONDS

United States Court of Appeals, Tenth Circuit, 1991.
931 F.2d 685.

MOORE, ALDISERT, and McWILLIAMS, CIRCUIT JUDGES.

ALDISERT, CIRCUIT JUDGE.

This case requires us to decide whether the district court committed plain error by failing to instruct the jury on a defense of diminished capacity in a prosecution of an inmate for assaulting correctional officers. A federal jury convicted Christopher Simmonds, an inmate in a federal penitentiary, of assaulting two correctional officers with razor blades and of possessing the blades with the intent to use them as a weapon. Although Simmonds relied solely on a theory of self-defense at trial, he argues for the first time on appeal that the district court should have inferred from the evidence that Simmonds lacked the capacity to form the requisite specific intent to commit these crimes and instructed the jury sua sponte on a defense of diminished capacity. We conclude that the district court did not commit plain error and affirm the judgment of conviction.

When the defendant fails to object to the jury instructions at the time of trial, we employ a plain error standard of review if the instructions are the basis of the appeal. F.R.Crim.P. 52(b); United States v. Glick, 710 F.2d 639, 643 (10th Cir.1983), *cert. denied,* 465 U.S. 1005, 104 S.Ct. 995, 79 L.Ed.2d 229 (1984). An error is plain if it is obvious or " 'otherwise seriously affect[s] the fairness, integrity or public reputation of judicial proceedings.' " United States v. Devous, 764 F.2d 1349, 1353 (10th Cir.1985) (quoting United States v. Atkinson, 297 U.S. 157, 160, 56 S.Ct. 391, 392, 80 L.Ed. 555 (1936)). The error must be so "plain" that " 'the trial judge and prosecutor were derelict in countenancing it, even absent the defendant's timely assistance in detecting it.' " *Id.* (quoting United States v. Frady, 456 U.S. 152, 163, 102 S.Ct. 1584, 1592, 71 L.Ed.2d 816 (1982)).

At best, plain error is strong medicine. The Supreme Court instructs us to use it "sparingly, solely in those circumstances in which a miscarriage of justice would otherwise result." United States v. Young, 470 U.S. 1, 15–16, 105 S.Ct. 1038, 1046, 84 L.Ed.2d 1 (1985) (quoting *Frady,* 456 U.S. at 163 n. 14, 102 S.Ct. at 1592 n. 14).

We seldom invoke the plain error doctrine because our function on appeal is to examine, within the statement of issues presented for consideration, the legal theories advanced by the parties at trial, and to determine whether the trial court ruled properly on the issues before it. The general precept that we do not notice questions that the parties have failed to present at trial—except under the most unusual circumstances—is based on the common law tradition that the parties must offer all the evidence they believe relevant to the issues that the trial court alone is competent to decide. This requirement also bades fealty to the adversary system: It insures that litigants will not be surprised on appeal of issues upon which they had no opportunity to introduce evidence at trial. *See* Hormel v. Helvering, 312 U.S. 552, 556, 61 S.Ct. 719, 721, 85 L.Ed. 1037 (1941). Our strong hesitation to notice such issues recognizes that it is conceptually impossible to fault a trial court for failing to rule on an issue that had not been presented to it. To be sure, Simmonds is unable to cite any authority supporting his notion that when evidence introduced at trial has the capability of supporting a defense of diminished capacity, notwithstanding the failure of counsel to raise the issue, a trial court has the responsibility of somehow discerning or discovering the defense and then supplanting counsel by gratuitously instructing the jury sua sponte on the unsolicited theory of defense.

DILLIPLAINE v. LEHIGH VALLEY TRUST CO.

Supreme Court of Pennsylvania, 1974.
457 Pa. 255, 322 A.2d 114.

Before JONES, C.J., and EAGEN, O'BRIEN, ROBERTS, POMEROY, NIX and MANDERINO, JJ.

OPINION OF THE COURT

ROBERTS, JUSTICE.

On April 23, 1966, automobiles driven by Wayne F. Dilliplaine and James A. Burdette collided. Subsequently Burdette died of causes unrelated to the accident. Dilliplaine then brought this trespass action against the executor of Burdette's estate, Lehigh Valley Trust Company, for injuries suffered in the accident.

The jury found for defendant and Dilliplaine's motion for a new trial was denied. The Superior Court affirmed. We granted the petition for allowance of appeal. The sole issue is whether the trial court erred by instructing the jury that the deceased was presumed to have exercised due care at the time the accident occurred.

Appellant Dilliplaine frankly concedes that he neither offered a point for charge nor took specific exception to the due care instruction actually given. In his motion for a new trial and again on appeal, he argued that in giving the presumption of due care instruction the trial judge committed basic and fundamental error.

Appellant espouses the theory that an appellate court must consider trial errors claimed to be basic and fundamental despite the absence of any objection or specific exception at trial. Millili v. Alan Wood Steel Co., 418 Pa. 154, 156–157, 209 A.2d 817, 818 (1965); Patterson v. Pittsburgh Rys., 322 Pa. 125, 128, 185 A. 283, 284 (1936). This theory has been applied primarily to asserted infirmities in a trial court's instructions to the jury.

We believe that two practical problems with basic and fundamental error make it an unworkable appellate procedure. Initially, appellate court recognition of alleged errors not called to the trial court's attention has a deleterious effect on the trial and appellate process. Also, despite its repeated articulation, the theory has never developed into a principled test, but has remained essentially a vehicle for reversal when the predilections of a majority of an appellate court are offended.

Appellate court consideration of issues not raised in the trial court results in the trial becoming merely a dress rehearsal. This process removes the professional necessity for trial counsel to be prepared to litigate the case fully at trial and to create a record adequate for appellate review. The ill-prepared advocate's hope is that an appellate court will come to his aid after the fact and afford him relief despite his failure at trial to object to an alleged error. The diligent and prepared trial lawyer—and his client—are penalized when an entire case is retried because an appellate court reverses on the basis of an error opposing counsel failed to call to the trial court's attention. Failure to interpose a timely objection at trial denies the trial court the chance to hear argument on the issue and an opportunity to correct error. It also tends to postpone unnecessarily disposition of other cases not yet tried for the first time. See Pa.R.C.P. 214(d), 12 P.S.Appendix.

The notion of basic and fundamental error not only erodes the finality of the trial court holdings, but also encourages unnecessary appeals and thereby further burdens the decisional capacity of our appellate courts. Trial counsel, though he may not have claimed error at trial, is inspired after trial and an adverse verdict by the thought that an appellate court may seize upon a previously unclaimed error and afford relief on a ground not called to the trial court's attention.

Perhaps at an earlier stage of our jurisprudential development this practice could be justified. Today, however, there is no excuse for and appellate courts should not encourage less than alert professional representation at trial. Virtually all active practitioners at our bar have had a formal legal education at a law school accredited by the American Bar Association.[5] The Pennsylvania Bar Institute, Pennsylvania Trial Lawyers Association, and local bar associations as well as the American Bar Association and the American Law Institute provide programs of continuing legal education for members of the bar.[7]

Requiring a timely specific objection to be taken in the trial court will ensure that the trial judge has a chance to correct alleged trial errors. This opportunity to correct alleged errors at trial advances the orderly and efficient use of our judicial resources. First, appellate courts

---

5. See Pa.Sup.Ct.R. 8, subd. C(2); See Spiegelberg, Forward to A. Levin & H. Cramer, Trial Advocacy, Problems and Materials at xiii (1968).

"A hundred years ago over eighty-five per cent of the lawyers in this country became lawyers by reading law in an office.

Today the figure is less than ten per cent and in some of the more populous states practically negligible."

7. See, e.g., Joint Committee on Continuing Legal Education of the ALI and the ABA, in American Law Institute, 1973 Annual Report.

will not be required to expend time and energy reviewing points on which no trial ruling has been made. Second, the trial court may promptly correct the asserted error. With the issue properly presented the trial court is more likely to reach a satisfactory result, thus obviating the need for appellate review on this issue. Or if a new trial is necessary, it may be granted by the trial court without subjecting both the litigants and the courts to the expense and delay inherent in appellate review. Third, appellate courts will be free to more expeditiously dispose of the issues properly preserved for appeal.[8] Finally, the exception requirement will remove the advantage formerly enjoyed by the unprepared trial lawyer who looked to the appellate court to compensate for his trial omissions.[9]

The other major weakness of the basic and fundamental error theory is its ad hoc nature. The theory has been formulated in terms of what a particular majority of an appellate court considers basic or fundamental.[10] Such a test is unworkable when neither the test itself nor the case law applying it develop a predictable, neutrally-applied standard.

We conclude that basic and fundamental error has no place in our modern system of jurisprudence. This doctrine, which may in the past have been acceptable, has become an impediment to the efficient administration of our judicial system. Basic and fundamental error will therefore no longer be recognized as a ground for consideration on appeal of allegedly erroneous jury instructions; a specific exception must be taken.

Because appellant failed to specifically object to the trial court's instruction on presumption of due care, we will not consider this allegation of error. The order of the Superior Court is affirmed.

O'Brien, J., concurs in the result.

Manderino, Justice (concurring).

I join in the majority opinion by Mr. Justice Roberts holding that the rule of basic and fundamental error is a rule without specific standards and should be abolished. The abolition of the rule, I should like to add, does not leave an aggrieved party without a remedy.

Issues not raised in the trial court because of ineffective assistance of counsel may be reviewable on appeal in a criminal case. Commonwealth ex rel. Washington v. Maroney, 427 P. 599, 235 A.2d 349 (1967),

---

8. When only properly preserved issues are considered on appeal, a full transcript of the trial will often be unnecessary. The trial court on post-trial motions (and the appellate court) will require transcripts of only those portions of the trial which are in issue. Reduction of the number of complete transcripts required for appeal will minimize both the expenses and delay which now make an appeal so costly.

9. See ABA Code of Professional Responsibility, DR 6–101(A)(2) (1971).

"(A) A lawyer shall not:

... (2) Handle a legal matter without preparation adequate in the circumstances."

10. See Leech v. Jones, 421 Pa. 1, 218 A.2d 722 (1966); Millili v. Alan Wood Steel Co., 418 Pa. 154, 209 A.2d 817 (1965); Enfield v. Stout, 400 Pa. 6, 161 A.2d 22 (1960); Patterson v. Pittsburgh Rys., 322 Pa. 125, 185 A. 283 (1936).

sets forth specific standards which are applicable in determining whether counsel was effective in a criminal case.

An aggrieved party in a civil case, involving only private litigants unlike a defendant in a criminal case, does not have a constitutional right to the effective assistance of counsel. The remedy in a civil case, in which chosen counsel is negligent, is an action for malpractice.

POMEROY, JUSTICE (concurring and dissenting).

While I concur in the result reached by the majority in the case before us, I cannot agree that the time has come to discard the doctrine of basic and fundamental error as it applies to erroneous jury instructions. However limited its scope and rare the occasions for its application, I believe the doctrine has a useful role to play in protecting the constitutional rights of litigants in our courts.

The doctrine of basic and fundamental error has been long established in this and other jurisdictions.[1] The doctrine is not confined to errors in jury instructions but can embrace any trial error which deprives a litigant of his fundamental right to a fair and impartial trial. This right is an integral part of due process of law, guaranteed to all litigants by the Fifth and Fourteenth Amendments. Obviously it is only an unusual trial error that will amount to a denial of due process, and in my view, the doctrine should be available to remedy only those trial errors so contrary to fundamental fairness as to reach the dimensions of a constitutional violation. . . .

I am not persuaded that the doctrine of basic and fundamental error encourages careless or cynical disregard of orderly trial procedure by trial lawyers. The very uncertainty, indeed the unlikelihood, of the doctrine's application argues against any such consequence. Attorneys have everything to gain and nothing to lose from timely objection to errors at trial. We have applied the doctrine so sparingly that surely it is a rare lawyer indeed who would risk a charge of malpractice or incompetence on the speculation that an appellate court will find a particular error to be basic and fundamental.

The majority suggests that, whatever justification may once have existed for the fundamental error concept, it may now be safely discarded in view of the high quality of formal education which most trial attorneys receive today, and the various opportunities for continuing legal education. This complacency is not shared by other observers of the workings of our legal system. As Chief Justice Warren E. Burger has remarked but recently:

---

1. Although Federal Rule of Civil Procedure 51 provides that "[n]o party may assign as error the giving or the failure to give an instruction unless he objects thereto before the jury retires to consider its verdict, stating distinctly the matter to which he objects and the grounds of his objection", the federal courts recognize the doctrine of basic and fundamental error as an exception to the rule's requirements. *See* King v. Laborers Local 818, 443 F.2d 273 (6th Cir.1971); Arteiro v. Coca Cola Bottling, Midwest, Inc., 47 F.R.D. 186, 188 (D.Minn.1969) and cases cited.

As to other jurisdictions which recognize the doctrine, *see generally* 5 Am.Jur.2d, Appeal and Error, § 549.

"Many judges in general jurisdiction trial courts have stated to me that fewer than 25 percent of the lawyers appearing before them are genuinely qualified; other judges go as high as 75 percent. I draw this from conversations extending over the past twelve to fifteen years at judicial meetings and seminars, with literally hundreds of judges and experienced lawyers. It would be safer to pick a middle ground and accept as a working hypothesis that from one-third to one-half of the lawyers who appear in the serious cases are not really qualified to render fully adequate representation." W.E. Burger, The Special Skills of Advocacy: Are Specialized Training and Certification of Advocates Essential to Our System of Justice? 42 Ford L.Rev. 227, 234 (1973) (footnotes omitted).

While in Pennsylvania we have what I consider a generally high degree of competence in the trial bar, the fact remains that there has been in recent decades, here as elsewhere, phenomenal change in both substantive and procedural law, accompanied by a tremendous increase in the volume of litigation.[2] As Chief Justice Burger suggests, there is evidence that, at the same time, the quality of trial advocacy in our nation's courts has been declining. We must strive to reverse this trend, to be sure, but I do not think we should do so at the expense of litigants who are not to blame for their attorneys' shortcomings. There are other, more direct and less costly ways of raising standards of trial advocacy than discarding the doctrine of basic and fundamental error.

Nor do I believe that the fundamental error doctrine adds significantly to admittedly overcrowded appellate dockets. It is the nature of humankind to be ever hopeful in the face of the most discouraging odds, and I fear that as long as there are appellate courts there will be litigants pursuing frivolous appeals. This is particularly true in the area of criminal law, where most defendants receive legal representation at no personal cost, and where all state remedies must be exhausted to pave the way for possible relief in the federal courts. A truly egregious criminal trial error which we decline to consider on appeal because not preserved below is almost certain to resurface in a post-conviction proceeding in the form of a charge of ineffectiveness of counsel. Considerations of judicial economy argue in favor of dealing with errors of this sort on direct appeal from the judgment of sentence. . . .

Finally, it bears emphasizing that the rule now being discarded has existed not for the benefit of lazy and incompetent lawyers, but for the protection of litigants who may have been denied the essential elements of a fair and impartial trial. The considerations of judicial convenience and efficiency cited by the majority, important as they are, should give way in the rare situation where basic rights of this sort are in the balance. . . . I believe that, in repudiating the doctrine as it applies to

2. *See generally* The Courts, the Public,   1965).
and the Law Explosion (H.W. Jones, ed.

erroneous jury instructions, the majority has taken a step which is both unnecessary and unwise.

EAGEN, J., joins in this opinion.

C.   HARMLESS ERROR

Unlike the plain error rule, the harmless error rule governs non-forfeited, non-waived error. If this type of error was properly preserved at the trial level, the reviewing court must determine if it was "harmless." The standard is similar to plain error in that this error in question must affect "substantial rights." It is dissimilar to plain error in that the burden of persuasion falls not upon the objecting party but rather on the party seeking to hold the error harmless, unless the error is raised on collateral review. The precise harmless error review standard depends on whether the error in question is of a constitutional or non-constitutional nature.

1.   Constitutional Harmless Error

The standard of review in determining the harmlessness of constitutional error is whether the error is "harmless beyond a reasonable doubt." The non-objecting party, generally the Government in criminal cases, bears the burden of proving that the error is harmless beyond a reasonable doubt. The standard for determining harmlessness of constitutional errors does not appear to differ depending on whether the action is civil or criminal.[1]

Certain constitutional errors may not be deemed harmless, and therefore require reversal. For example, a criminal defendant has an absolute right to counsel, a right to an impartial judge and a right not to have a constitutionally deficient instruction on the reasonable doubt standard. Other errors are amenable to harmless error analysis, including the admission of an involuntary confession, most deficient jury charges (assuming they do not impinge on the basic tenets of the criminal justice system), the denial of an opportunity to be present at trial or to impeach a witness for bias, the admission of an improper comment on a defendant's refusal to testify and the admission of evidence in violation of a defendant's Fourth Amendment rights.

2.   Non-constitutional Harmless Error

Non-constitutional error is not harmless unless it is "highly probable that the error did not contribute to the judgment."[2] "High probability" requires that the court have a "sure conviction that the error did not prejudice" the defendant; the court need not disprove every "reasonable probability" of prejudice.[3] As in the *Chapman* analysis, the party seeking to hold the error harmless has the burden of proving it so.

---

1. See, e.g., McQueeney v. Wilmington Trust Co., 779 F.2d 916, 928 (3d Cir.1985).

2. Id. at 924.

3. See United States v. Jannotti, 729 F.2d 213, 219–20 (3d Cir.1984).

3. Error Raised in Collateral Review Proceedings

The standard in this circumstance is whether, in light of the record as a whole, the error resulted in "actual prejudice" to the defendant. Actual prejudice occurs when the constitutional error "had substantial and injurious effect or influence in determining the jury's verdict." [4] As in the plain error analysis, the burden of proving the error falls on the party asserting the error.

KOTTEAKOS v. UNITED STATES

Supreme Court of the United States, 1946.
328 U.S. 750, 66 S.Ct. 1239, 90 L.Ed. 1557.

MR. JUSTICE RUTLEDGE delivered the opinion of the Court.

The only question is whether petitioners have suffered substantial prejudice from being convicted of a single general conspiracy by evidence which the Government admits proved not one conspiracy but some eight or more different ones of the same sort executed through a common key figure, Simon Brown. Petitioners were convicted under the general conspiracy section of the Criminal Code ... of conspiring to violate the provisions of the National Housing Act....

The indictment named thirty-two defendants, including the petitioners. The gist of the conspiracy, as alleged, was that the defendants had sought to induce various financial institutions to grant credit, with the intent that the loans or advances would then be offered to the Federal Housing Administration for insurance upon applications containing false and fraudulent information.

[The evidence disclosed that one Simon Brown was the key figure in all the transactions proven. He acted as broker in placing loans under the National Housing Act knowing that the proceeds would not be used for the housing modernization purposes set forth in the applications. Brown made out applications for petitioners Lekacos and Kotteakos containing false statements.]

The evidence against the other defendants whose cases were submitted to the jury was similar in character. They too had transacted business with Brown relating to National Housing Act loans. But no connection was shown between them and petitioners, other than that Brown had been the instrument in each instance for obtaining the loans. In many cases the other defendants did not have any relationship with one another, other than Brown's connection with each transaction. As the Circuit Court of Appeals said, there were "at least eight, and perhaps more, separate and independent groups, none of which had any connection with any other, though all dealt independently with Brown as their agent." ... As the Government puts it, the pattern was "that of

---

4. Brecht v. Abrahamson, 113 S.Ct. 1710, 1722 (1993).

separate spokes meeting in a common center," though, we may add, without the rim of the wheel to enclose the spokes.

The proof therefore admittedly made out a case, not of a single conspiracy, but of several, notwithstanding only one was charged in the indictment.... The Court of Appeals aptly drew analogy in the comment, "Thieves who dispose of their loot to a single receiver—a single 'fence'—do not by that fact alone become confederates: they may, but it takes more than knowledge that he is a 'fence' to make them such." ... It stated that the trial judge "was plainly wrong in supposing that upon the evidence there could be a single conspiracy; and in the view which he took of the law, he should have dismissed the indictment." ... Nevertheless the appellate court held the error not prejudicial, saying among other things that "especially since guilt was so manifest, it was 'proper' to join the conspiracies," and "to reverse the conviction would be a miscarriage of justice." This is indeed the Government's entire position. It does not now contend that there was no variance in proof from the single conspiracy charged in the indictment. Admitting that separate and distinct conspiracies were shown, it urges that the variance was not prejudicial to the petitioners.

In Berger v. United States, 295 U.S. 78, this Court held that in the circumstances presented the variance was not fatal where one conspiracy was charged and two were proved, relating to contemporaneous transactions involving counterfeit money. One of the conspiracies had two participants; the other had three; and one defendant, Katz, was common to each. "The true inquiry," said the Court, "is not whether there has been a variance in proof, but whether there has been such a variance as to 'affect the substantial rights' of the accused." ...

The Court held the variance not fatal, resting its ruling on what has become known as "the harmless error statute," § 269 of the Judicial Code, as amended, 28 U.S.C.A. § 391, which is controlling in this case and provides: "On the hearing of any appeal, certiorari, writ of error, or motion for a new trial, in any case, civil or criminal, the court shall give judgment after an examination of the entire record before the court, without regard to technical errors, defects, or exceptions which do not affect the substantial rights of the parties." [9]

9. Both the Federal Rules of Civil Procedure, 28 U.S.C.A. following § 723(c), Rule 61, and the Federal Rules of Criminal Procedure, effective March 21, 1946, Rule 52(a), contain "harmless error" sections. With respect to the latter it is said, "This rule is a restatement of existing law, ..." with citation of 28 U.S.C.A. § 391 and 18 U.S.C.A. § 556. Notes to the Rules of Criminal Procedure for the District Courts of the United States, as prepared under the direction of the Advisory Committee on Rules of Criminal Procedure (1945) 43. See also Preliminary Draft of the Federal Rules of Criminal Procedure (1943) 197; Second Preliminary Draft of the Federal Rules of Criminal Procedure (1944) 185.

[Ed.: The rule of 28 U.S.C.A. § 391 is currently codified as 28 U.S.C.A. § 2111. "Harmless error. On the hearing of any appeal or writ of certiorari in any case, the court shall give judgment after an examination of the record without regard to errors or defects which do not affect the substantial rights of the parties. Added May 24, 1949, c. 139, § 110, 63 Stat. 105."

Rule 61, F.R.Civ.P., provides: Harmless Error. "No error in either the admission or the exclusion of evidence and no error or defect in any ruling or order or in anything

Applying that section, the Court likened the situation to one where the four persons implicated in the two conspiracies had been charged as conspirators in separate counts, but with a failure in the proof to connect one of them (Berger) with one of the conspiracies, and a resulting conviction under one count and acquittal under the other. In that event, the Court said, "Plainly enough, his substantial rights would not have been affected." The situation supposed and the one actually presented, the opinion stated, though differing greatly in form, were not different in substance. The proof relating to the conspiracy with which Berger had not been connected could be regarded as incompetent as to him. But nothing in the facts, it was concluded, could reasonably be said to show that prejudice or surprise resulted; and the court went on to say, "Certainly the fact that the proof disclosed two conspiracies instead of one, each within the words of the indictment, cannot prejudice his defense of former acquittal of the one or former conviction of the other, if he should again be prosecuted." ...

The question we have to determine is whether the same ruling may be extended to a situation in which one conspiracy only is charged and at least eight having separate, though similar objects, are made out by the evidence, if believed; and in which the more numerous participants in the different schemes were, on the whole, except for one, different persons who did not know or have anything to do with one another.

The salutary policy embodied in § 269 was adopted by the Congress in 1919 ... after long agitation under distinguished professional sponsorship, and after thorough consideration of various proposals designed to enact the policy in successive Congresses from the Sixtieth to the Sixty-fifth. It is not necessary to review in detail the history of the abuses which led to the agitation or of the progress of the legislation through the various sessions to final enactment without debate.... But anyone familiar with it knows that § 269 and similar state legislation grew out of widespread and deep conviction over the general course of appellate review in American criminal causes. This was shortly, as one trial judge put it after § 269 had become law, that courts of review, "tower above the trials of criminal cases as impregnable citadels of technicality." So great was the threat of reversal, in many jurisdictions, that criminal trial became a game for sowing reversible error in the record, only to have repeated the same matching of wits when a new trial had been thus obtained.

In the broad attack on this system great legal names were mobilized, among them Taft, Wigmore, Pound and Hadley, to mention only four.[14]

done or omitted by the court or by any of the parties is ground for granting a new trial or for setting aside a verdict or for vacating, modifying or otherwise disturbing a judgment or order, unless refusal to take such action appears to the court inconsistent with substantial justice. The court at every stage of the proceeding must disregard any error or defect in the proceeding which does not affect the substantial rights of the parties."

Rule 52(a), F.R.Crim.P., provides: "(a) Harmless Error. Any error, defect, irregularity or variance which does not affect substantial rights shall be disregarded."]

14. See Hadley, Criminal Justice in America (1925) 11 A.B.A.J. 674; Hadley, Outline of Code of Criminal Procedure

The general object was simple, to substitute judgment for automatic application of rules; to preserve review as a check upon arbitrary action and essential unfairness in trials, but at the same time to make the process perform that function without giving men fairly convicted the multiplicity of loopholes which any highly rigid and minutely detailed scheme of errors, especially in relation to procedure, will engender and reflect in a printed record.

The task was too big, too various in detail, for particularized treatment.... The effort at revision therefore took the form of the essentially simple command of § 269. It comes down on its face to a very plain admonition: "Do not be technical, where technicality does not really hurt the party whose rights in the trial and in its outcome the technicality affects." It is also important to note that the purpose of the bill in its final form was stated authoritatively to be "to cast upon the party seeking a new trial the burden of showing that any technical errors that he may complain of have affected his substantial rights, otherwise they are to be disregarded." H.R.Rep. No. 913, 65th Cong., 3d Sess., 1. But that this burden does not extend to all errors appears from the statement which follows immediately. "The proposed legislation affects only technical errors. If the error is of such a character that its natural effect is to prejudice a litigant's substantial rights, the burden of sustaining a verdict will, notwithstanding this legislation, rest upon the one who claims under it." Ibid; Bruno v. United States, *supra*, 308 U.S. [287] at page 294, 60 S.Ct. at page 200; Weiler v. United States, 323 U.S. 606, 611, 65 S.Ct. 548, 551, 89 L.Ed. 495, 156 A.L.R. 496.

Easier was the command to make than it has been always to observe. This, in part because it is general; but in part also because the discrimination it requires is one of judgment transcending confinement by formula or precise rule. United States v. Socony–Vacuum Oil Co., 310 U.S. 150, 240, 60 S.Ct. 811, 852, 84 L.Ed. 1129. That faculty cannot

(1926) 12 A.B.A.J. 690; Taft, Administration of Criminal Law, in Present Day Problems, A Collection of Addresses (1908) 333; and cf. Hicks, William Howard Taft (1945) 68, 69; Wigmore, Criminal Procedure— "Good" Reversals and "Bad" Reversals (1909) 4 Ill.Rev. 352; Wigmore, Evidence (1904) § 21.

Perhaps the most notable instance of hypertechnicality in a court's assignment of a reason for its decision, arising in the early part of the period of agitation, is to be found in State v. Campbell, 210 Mo. 202, 203, 109 S.W. 706, 14 Ann.Cas. 403. See also State v. Warner, 220 Mo. 23, 119 S.W. 399. The ruling was reversed in State v. Adkins, 284 Mo. 680, 695, 225 S.W. 981, 985.

[Ed.: In State v. Campbell, the court reversed and remanded a rape conviction, holding that the indictment was invalid, under the state constitution, because it concluded, "against the peace and dignity of state," instead of, "against the peace and dignity of the state." Missouri, however, was not alone in demanding technically perfect indictments. See, e.g., Williams v. State, 27 Wis. 402 (1871) (reversed because indictment stated offense was "against the peace of the State" instead of "against the peace and dignity of the State"); Gragg v. State, 148 Tex.Crim. 267, 186 S.W.2d 243 (1945) (defendant convicted under an indictment that charged him with killing "Flora Gragg, by then and there drowning the said Flora Gragg"; reversed because indictment did not allege the "means by which the drowning" was accomplished); Northern v. State, 150 Tex.Crim. 511, 203 S.W.2d 206 (1947) (defendant convicted under indictment charging him with killing "Fannie McHenry by then and there kicking and stomping the said Fannie McHenry"; reversed because indictment failed "to charge the means by which the alleged murder was committed.").]

ever be wholly imprisoned in words, much less upon such a criterion as what are only technical, what substantial rights; and what really affects the latter hurtfully. Judgment, the play of impression and conviction along with intelligence, varies with judges and also with circumstance. What may be technical for one is substantial for another; what minor and unimportant in one setting crucial in another.

Moreover, lawyers know, if others do not, that what may seem technical may embody a great tradition of justice, Weiler v. United States, supra, or a necessity for drawing lines somewhere between great areas of law; that, in other words, one cannot always segregate the technique from the substance or the form from the reality. It is of course highly technical to confer full legal status upon one who has just attained his majority, but deny it to another a day, a week or a month younger. Yet that narrow line, and many others like it, must be drawn. The "hearsay" rule is often grossly artificial. Again in a different context it may be the very essence of justice, keeping out gossip, rumor, unfounded report, second, third, or further hand stories.

All this hardly needs to be said again. But it must be comprehended and administered every day. The task is not simple, although the admonition is. Neither is it impossible. By its very nature no standard of perfection can be attained. But one of fair approximation can be achieved. Essentially the matter is one for experience to work out. For, as with all lines which must be drawn between positive and negative fields of law, the precise border may be indistinct, but case by case determination of particular points adds up in time to discernible direction.

In the final analysis judgment in each case must be influenced by conviction resulting from examination of the proceedings in their entirety, tempered but not governed in any rigid sense of stare decisis by what has been done in similar situations.... Necessarily the character of the proceeding, what is at stake upon its outcome, and the relation of the error asserted to casting the balance for decision on the case as a whole, are material factors in judgment.

The statute in terms makes no distinction between civil and criminal causes. But this does not mean that the same criteria shall always be applied regardless of this difference. Indeed the legislative history shows that the proposed legislation went through many revisions, largely at the instance of the Senate, because there was fear of too easy relaxation of historic securities thrown around the citizen charged with crime. Although the final form of the legislation was designed, and frequently has been effective, to avoid some of the absurdities by which skilful manipulation of procedural rules had enabled the guilty to escape just punishment, § 269 did not make irrelevant the fact that a person is on trial for his life or his liberty. It did not require the same judgment in such a case as in one involving only some question of civil liability. There was no purpose, for instance, to abolish the historic difference between civil and criminal causes relating to the burden of proof placed in the one upon the plaintiff and in the other on the prosecution. Nor does § 269 mean that an error in receiving or excluding evidence has identical effects, for purposes of applying its policy, regardless of whether the evidence in other respects is evenly balanced or one-sided. Errors of this sort in criminal causes conceivably may be altogether harmless in the face of other clear evidence, although the same error might turn scales otherwise level, as constantly appears in the application of the policy of § 269 to questions of the admission of cumulative evidence. So it is with errors in instructions to the jury....

Some aids to right judgment may be stated more safely in negative than in affirmative form. Thus, it is not the appellate court's function to determine guilt or innocence.... Nor is it to speculate upon probable reconviction and decide according to how the speculation comes out. Appellate judges cannot escape such impressions. But they may not make them sole criteria for reversal or affirmance. Those judgments are exclusively for the jury, given always the necessary minimum evidence legally sufficient to sustain the conviction unaffected by the error....

But this does not mean that the appellate court can escape altogether taking account of the outcome. To weigh the error's effect against the entire setting of the record without relation to the verdict or judgment would be almost to work in a vacuum.... In criminal causes that outcome is conviction. This is different, or may be, from guilt in fact. It is guilt in law, established by the judgment of laymen. And the question is, not were they right in their judgment, regardless of the error or its effect upon the verdict. It is rather what effect the error had or reasonably may be taken to have had upon the jury's decision. The crucial thing is the impact of the thing done wrong on the minds of other men, not on one's own, in the total setting....

This must take account of what the error meant to them, not singled out and standing alone, but in relation to all else that happened. And one must judge others' reactions not by his own, but with allowance for how others might react and not be regarded generally as acting without reason. This is the important difference, but one easy to ignore when the sense of guilt comes strongly from the record.

If, when all is said and done, the conviction is sure that the error did not influence the jury, or had but very slight effect, the verdict and the judgment should stand, except perhaps where the departure is from a constitutional norm or a specific command of Congress. Bruno v. United States, supra, 308 U.S. at page 294, 60 S.Ct. at page 200. But if one cannot say, with fair assurance, after pondering all that happened without stripping the erroneous action from the whole, that the judgment was not substantially swayed by the error, it is impossible to conclude that substantial rights were not affected. The inquiry cannot be merely whether there was enough to support the result, apart from the phase affected by the error. It is rather, even so, whether the error itself had substantial influence. If so, or if one is left in grave doubt, the conviction cannot stand.

. . .

It follows that the Berger case is not controlling of this one, notwithstanding that, abstractly considered, the errors in variance and instructions were identical in character. The Berger opinion indeed expressly declared: "We do not mean to say that a variance such as that here dealt with might not be material in a different case. We simply hold, following the view of the court below, that, applying section 269 of the Judicial Code, as amended, to the circumstances of this case the variance was not prejudicial and hence not fatal." 295 U.S. at page 83, 55 S.Ct. at page 631.

On the face of things it is one thing to hold harmless the admission of evidence which took place in the Berger case, where only two conspiracies involving four persons all told were proved, and an entirely different thing to apply the same rule where, as here, only one conspiracy was charged, but eight separate ones were proved, involving at the outset thirty-two defendants. The essential difference is not overcome by the fact that the thirty-two were reduced, by severance, dismissal or pleas of guilty, to nineteen when the trial began and to thirteen by the time the cases went to the jury. The sheer difference in numbers, both of defendants and of conspiracies proven, distinguishes the situation. Obviously the burden of defense to a defendant, connected with one or a few of so many distinct transactions, is vastly different not only in preparation for trial, but also in looking out for and securing safeguard against evidence affecting other defendants, to prevent its transference as "harmless error" or by psychological effect, in spite of instructions for keeping separate transactions separate.

The Government's theory seems to be, in ultimate logical reach, that the error presented by the variance is insubstantial and harmless, if the evidence offered specifically and properly to convict each defendant would be sufficient to sustain his conviction, if submitted in a separate trial. For reasons we have stated and in view of the authorities cited, this is not and cannot be the test under § 269. . . .

. . .

Accordingly the judgments are reversed and the causes are remanded for further proceedings in conformity with this opinion.

Reversed.

NOTE

Had you been on the Court of Appeals for the Second Circuit in 1946 when *Kotteakos* was remanded, how would you have reacted to the Court's opinion?

Relate the adoption of the "harmless error" rule to the demise of Mechanical Jurisprudence and the advent of Sociological Jurisprudence. Is there any coincidence other than the chronological one?

———

STATE OF WISCONSIN v. DYESS

Supreme Court of Wisconsin, 1985.
124 Wis.2d 525, 370 N.W.2d 222.

HEFFERNAN, CHIEF JUSTICE.

This is a review of a decision of the court of appeals which affirmed the conviction of Johrie Dyess for homicide by the negligent use of a motor vehicle.

The trial judge, had he followed the directions of sec. 903.03(3), Stats., would have informed the jury that, if it found as a matter of fact that Dyess was exceeding the posted speed limit of 30 miles per hour, it could regard that fact as sufficient evidence of negligence to make that finding but it was not required to do so.

Here the trial judge told the jury that, "Any speed in excess of that [30 miles per hour] limit would be negligent speed regardless of other conditions." He then went on to tell the jury that, were they to find that the speed was under 30 miles per hour, they could nevertheless determine whether the speed was negligent. The jury was mandatorily directed to find negligence if speed in excess of 30 miles per hour was proved. Discretion to permissibly draw an inference from the facts was vested in the jurors only if they found the speed to be less than that posted.

Here the judge required the jury to find the presumed fact on the evidence of the basic facts. This was in violation of the rule:

> ". . . the judge shall give an instruction that the law declares that the jury may regard the basic facts as sufficient evidence of the presumed fact but does not require it to do so." Sec. 903.03(3), Stats.

No language in the judge's charge permitted the jury to conclude that it was permitted but not required to use the evidence of speeding as proof of negligence.

The instruction given was violative of sec. 903.03(3), Stats. This finding of error requires us to consider whether the error was harmless.

We conclude that the error was not harmless and the judgment must be reversed.

This court for years has been struggling with methodology to rationalize upholding a conviction despite the acknowledgment that error has been committed. Certainly, many errors in the course of trial are of a trivial nature and affect the final result not one whit. Hence, it is reasonable, in accordance with public policy and judicial economy, to affirm convictions unless it is apparent that the procedure has been unfair, rights have been subverted, or an injustice has been done. Most errors are truly harmless. Nevertheless, the great virtue of our legal system—at least its great objective—is that only the guilty be convicted and even the guilty be convicted only by due process of law after guilt has been demonstrated beyond a reasonable doubt. Hence, when error is committed, a court should be sure that the error did not affect the result or had only a slight effect. While our numerous efforts to adopt an ad hoc "harmless error" methodology cannot be said to have resulted in a course of injustice, they do not reveal a coherent articulable philosophy consistent with the elementary principles stated above. When it is clear that error has been committed, we should be sure that the error did not work an injustice. The only reasonable test to assure this result is to hold that, where error is present, the reviewing court must set aside the verdict unless it is sure that the error did not influence the jury or had such slight effect as to be de minimus. This test has been adopted in State v. Poh, 116 Wis.2d 510, 529, 343 N.W.2d 108 (1984); State v. Burton, 112 Wis.2d 560, 571, 334 N.W.2d 263 (1983); State v. Billings, 110 Wis.2d 661, 667, 329 N.W.2d 192 (1983).

* * * We conclude that, in view of the gradual merger of this court's collective thinking in respect to harmless versus prejudicial error, whether of omission or commission, whether of constitutional proportions or not, the test should be whether there is a reasonable possibility that the error contributed to the conviction. If it did, reversal and a new trial must result. The burden of proving no prejudice is on the beneficiary of the error, here the state. Billings, 110 Wis.2d at 667, 329 N.W.2d 192. The state's burden, then, is to establish that there is no reasonable possibility that the error contributed to the conviction.

O'NEAL v. McANINCH

Supreme Court of the United States, 1995.
__ U.S. __, 115 S.Ct. 992, 130 L.Ed.2d 947.

JUSTICE BREYER delivered the opinion of the Court.

Reviewing courts normally disregard trial errors that are harmless. This case asks us to decide whether a federal habeas court should consider a trial error harmless when the court (1) reviews a state-court judgment from a criminal trial, (2) finds a constitutional error, and (3) is in grave doubt about whether or not that error is harmless. We recognize that this last mentioned circumstance, "grave doubt," is unusual. Normally a record review will permit a judge to make up his or her mind about the matter. And indeed a judge has an obligation to do so. But, we consider here the legal rule that governs the special circumstance in which record review leaves the conscientious judge in grave doubt about the likely effect of an error on the jury's verdict. (By "grave doubt" we mean that, in the judge's mind, the matter is so evenly balanced that he feels himself in virtual equipoise as to the harmlessness of the error.) We conclude that the uncertain judge should treat the error, not as if it were harmless, but as if it affected the verdict (i.e., as if it had a "substantial and injurious effect or influence in determining the jury's verdict").

* * *

II

As an initial matter, we note that we deliberately phrase the issue in this case in terms of a judge's grave doubt, instead of in terms of "burden of proof." The case before us does not involve a judge who shifts a "burden" to help control the presentation of evidence at a trial, but rather involves judges who apply a legal standard (harmlessness) to a record that the presentation of evidence is no longer likely to affect. In such a case, we think it conceptually clearer for the judge to ask directly, "Do I, the judge, think that the error substantially influenced the jury's decision?" than for the judge to try to put the same question in terms of proof burdens (e.g., "Do I believe the party has borne its burden of showing ...?"). As Chief Justice Traynor said:

> "Whether or not counsel are helpful, it is still the responsibility of the ... court, once it concludes there was error, to determine whether the error affected the judgment. It must do so without benefit of such aids as presumptions or allocated burdens of proof that expedite fact-finding at the trial." R. Traynor, The Riddle of Harmless Error 26 (1970) (hereinafter Traynor).

The case may sometimes arise, however, where the record is so evenly balanced that a conscientious judge is in grave doubt as to the harmlessness of an error. This is the narrow circumstance we address here.

III

Our legal conclusion—that in cases of grave doubt as to harmlessness the petitioner must win—rests upon three considerations. First, precedent supports our conclusion. As this Court has stated, "the original common-law harmless-error rule put the burden on the beneficiary of the error [here, the State] ... to prove that there was no injury...." Chapman v. California, 386 U.S. 18, 24, 87 S.Ct. 824, 828, 17 L.Ed.2d 705 (1967) (citing 1 J. Wigmore, Evidence § 21 (3d ed. 1940)). When this Court considered the doubt-as-to-harmlessness question in the context of direct review of a nonconstitutional trial error, it applied the same rule. In Kotteakos v. United States, the Court wrote:

> "If, when all is said and done, the [court's] conviction is sure that the error did not influence the jury, or had but very slight effect, the verdict and the judgment should stand.... But if one cannot say, with fair assurance, after pondering all that happened without stripping the erroneous action from the whole, that the judgment was not substantially swayed by the

error, it is impossible to conclude that substantial rights were not affected. The inquiry cannot be merely whether there was enough to support the result, apart from the phase affected by the error. It is rather, even so, whether the error itself had substantial influence. If so, or if one is left in grave doubt, the conviction cannot stand." 328 U.S., at 764–765, 66 S.Ct., at 1248 (emphasis added).

Id., at 776, 66 S.Ct., at 1248–49 (holding that error is not harmless if it had "substantial and injurious effect or influence" upon the jury). That is to say, if a judge has "grave doubt" about whether an error affected a jury in this way, the judge must treat the error as if it did so. See also United States v. Olano, 507 U.S. ___, ___, 113 S.Ct. 1770, ___, 123 L.Ed.2d 508 (1993) (stating that under Federal Rule of Criminal Procedure 52(a) the Government bears the "burden of showing the absence of prejudice"); United States v. Lane, 474 U.S. 438, 449, 106 S.Ct. 725, 732, 88 L.Ed.2d 814 (1986) (quoting Kotteakos as providing the proper harmless-error standard in cases of misjoinder and quoting " 'grave doubt' " language).

When this Court considered the same question in the context of direct review of a constitutional trial error, it applied the same rule. See Chapman, 386 U.S., at 24, 87 S.Ct., at 828 (holding that error is harmless only if "harmless beyond a reasonable doubt"). Indeed, the Chapman Court wrote that "constitutional error . . . casts on someone other than the person prejudiced by it a burden to show that it was harmless." Ibid.

We must concede that in Brecht v. Abrahamson this Court, in the course of holding that the more lenient Kotteakos harmless-error standard, rather than the stricter Chapman standard, normally governs cases of habeas review of constitutional trial errors, stated that habeas petitioners "are not entitled to habeas relief based on trial error unless they can establish that it resulted in 'actual prejudice.' " Brecht, 507 U.S., at ___, 113 S.Ct., at 1721 (emphasis added). This language, however, is not determinative. The issue in Brecht involved a choice of substantive harmless-error standards: the stricter Chapman, or the less strict Kotteakos, measure of harmlessness. Both of those cases had resolved the issue now before us the same way, placing the risk of doubt on the State. Moreover, the sentence from Brecht quoted above appears in a paragraph that adopts the very Kotteakos standard that we now apply. That paragraph does not explain why the Court would make an exception to the "grave doubt" portion of the Kotteakos standard.

* * *

JUSTICE THOMAS, with whom CHIEF JUSTICE REHNQUIST and JUSTICE SCALIA join, dissenting.

In my view, a federal habeas court may not upset the results of a criminal trial unless it concludes both that the trial was marred by a violation of the Constitution or a federal statute and that this error was harmful. Because the Court concludes otherwise, I respectfully dissent.

I

Though the majority begins with an examination of precedent construing the federal harmless-error statute, 28 U.S.C. § 2111, the proper place to begin is with the statute governing habeas relief for prisoners in state custody. After all, the petitioner does not seek relief under the harmless-error statute.

* * *

III

Fortunately, the rule announced today will affect only a minuscule fraction of cases. Even when there is a close question about whether an error was harmful, the conscientious judge ordinarily should make a ruling as to harm. The Court's rule is not a means for judges to escape difficult decisions; it applies only in that "special circumstance" in which a judge, after a thorough review of the record, remains in equipoise.

The rule has such limited application that it most likely will have no effect on this case. The majority suggests that O'Neal "might have lost in the Court of Appeals, not because the judges concluded that [any supposed] error was harmless, but because the record of the trial left them in grave doubt about the effect of the error." Id., at 994. The Sixth Circuit did observe that "[t]he habeas petitioner bears the burden of establishing ... prejudice." O'Neal v. Morris, 3 F.3d 143, 145 (1993). But the Court of Appeals did not refer again to this burden and did not appear to rely on it in reaching a decision. See id., at 147. That we chose this case to establish a "grave doubt" rule is telling: cases in which habeas courts are in equipoise on the issue of harmlessness are astonishingly rare.

Though the question that the Court decides today will have very limited application, I believe that the Court gives the wrong answer to that question.

Accordingly, I respectfully dissent.

————

CHAPMAN v. CALIFORNIA

Supreme Court of the United States, 1967.
386 U.S. 18, 87 S.Ct. 824, 17 L.Ed.2d 705.

Mr. Justice Black delivered the opinion of the Court.

Petitioners, Ruth Elizabeth Chapman and Thomas LeRoy Teale, were convicted in a California state court upon a charge that they robbed, kidnaped, and murdered a bartender. She was sentenced to life imprisonment and he to death. At the time of the trial, Art. I, § 13, of the State's Constitution provided that "in any criminal case, whether the defendant testifies or not, his failure to explain or to deny by his testimony any evidence or facts in the case against him may be commented upon by the court and by counsel, and may be considered by the court or the jury." Both petitioners in this case chose not to testify at their trial, and the State's attorney prosecuting them took full advantage of his right under the State Constitution to comment upon their failure to testify, filling his argument to the jury from beginning to end with numerous references to their silence and inferences of their guilt resulting therefrom. The trial court also charged the jury that it could draw adverse inferences from petitioners' failure to testify. Shortly after the trial, but before petitioners' cases had been considered on appeal by the California Supreme Court, this Court decided Griffin v. California, 380 U.S. 609, in which we held California's constitutional provision and practice invalid on the ground that they put a penalty on the exercise of a person's right not to be compelled to be a witness against himself, guaranteed by the Fifth Amendment to the United States Constitution and made applicable to California and the other States by the Fourteenth Amendment. See Malloy v. Hogan, 378 U.S. 1. On appeal, the State Supreme Court, 63 Cal.2d 178, 404 P.2d 209, admitting that petitioners had been denied a federal constitutional right by the comments on their silence, nevertheless affirmed, applying the State Constitution's harmless-error provision, which forbids reversal unless "the court shall be of the opinion that the error complained of has resulted in a miscarriage of justice."

In fashioning a harmless-constitutional-error rule, we must recognize that harmless-error rules can work very unfair and mischievous results when, for example, highly important and persuasive evidence, or argument, though legally forbidden, finds its way into a trial in which the question of guilt or innocence is a close one. What harmless-error rules all aim at is a rule that will save the good in harmless-error practices while avoiding the bad, so far as possible.

The federal rule emphasizes "substantial rights" as do most others. The California constitutional rule emphasizes "a miscarriage of justice," but the California courts have neutralized this to some extent by emphasis, and perhaps overemphasis, upon the court's view of "overwhelming evidence." We prefer the approach of this Court in deciding what was harmless error in our recent case of Fahy v. Connecticut, 375 U.S. 85. There we said: "The question is whether there is a reasonable possibility that the evidence complained of might have contributed to the conviction." *Id.*, at 86–87. Although our prior cases have indicated that there are some constitutional rights so basic to a fair trial that their infraction can never be treated as harmless error, this statement in *Fahy* itself belies any belief that all trial errors which violate the Constitution automatically call for reversal. At the same time, however, like the federal harmless-error statute, it emphasizes an intention not to treat as harmless those constitutional errors that "affect substantial rights" of a party. An error in admitting plainly relevant evidence which possibly influenced the jury adversely to a litigant cannot, under *Fahy,* be conceived.

NOTE

In Chapman v. California, 386 U.S. 18, 24 (1967), we held that the standard for determining whether a conviction must be set aside because of federal constitutional error is whether the error "was harmless beyond a reasonable doubt." In this case we must decide whether the *Chapman* harmless-error standard applies in determining whether the prosecution's use for impeachment purposes of petitioner's post–*Miranda* silence, in violation of due process under Doyle v. Ohio, 426 U.S. 610 (1976), entitles petitioner to habeas corpus relief. We hold that it does not. Instead, the standard for determining whether habeas relief must be granted is whether the *Doyle* error "had substantial and injurious effect or influence in determining the jury's verdict." Kotteakos v. United States, 328 U.S. 750, 776 (1946). The *Kotteakos* harmless-error standard is better tailored to the nature and purpose of collateral review than the *Chapman* standard, and application of a less onerous harmless-error standard on habeas promotes the considerations underlying our habeas jurisprudence. Applying this standard, we conclude that petitioner is not entitled to habeas relief.

Brecht v. Abrahamson, 113 S.Ct. 1710, 1713–14 (1993).

NOTE ON HARMLESS ERROR

Until modern times, any mistake recognized as trial error called for a reversal. Thus, one California decision reversed a judgment because the robbery indictment failed to recite that the property taken from the victim by threats and force did not belong to the defendant. More recently, however, the law has grown to encompass a rule tolerating "harmless error". As appellate courts have struggled with the concept, several definitional attempts have been forthcoming. See generally R. Traynor, What Makes Error Harmless, The Riddle of Harmless Error (1970).

The so-called orthodox rule, embodying a "sufficiency of the evidence" test and a "correct result" test, is found in Doe v. Tyler, 6 Bing. 561, 563, 130 Eng.Rep. 1397, 1398 (C.P.1830):

It has been contended, that we are to analyze the evidence by a difficult process, and to discriminate the precise effect produced on the mind of the jury on each portion of the proof: but we have a much plainer course; and that is, to hear the report of the trial, and *to sustain the verdict, if we are satisfied that there is enough to warrant the finding of the jury independently of the evidence objected to* ... [sufficiency-of-the-evidence test] *and we cannot send the cause to a new trial when the jury are right upon that portion of the evidence which is unimpeached.* [Correct-result test] (emphasis added).

This rule gave way to a more rigorous "English rule", requiring to a near certainty that the error not have contributed to the judgment. As the House of Lords has said:

> A perverse jury might conceivably announce a verdict of acquittal in the teeth of all the evidence, but the provision that the Court of Criminal Appeal may dismiss the appeal if they consider that no substantial miscarriage of justice has actually occurred in convicting the accused assumes a situation where a reasonable jury, after being properly directed, would, on the evidence properly admissible, *without doubt convict.*

Stirland v. Director of Public Prosecutions, [1944] A.C. 315, 321 (emphasis added).

Former Chief Justice Traynor of the California Supreme Court stated the test in terms of the probability that the error affected the judgment. He admitted that such a standard could be variously drawn so that the appellate court would affirm if it were (a) more probable than not that the error did not affect the judgment, (b) highly probable that the error did not contribute to the judgment or (c) almost certain that the error did not taint the judgment. Traynor chose the middle ground:

> Any test less stringent entails too great a risk of affirming a judgment that was influenced by an error. Moreover, a less stringent test may fail to deter an appellate judge from focusing his inquiry on the correctness of the result and then holding an error harmless whenever he equated the result with his own predilections.
>
> There are objections also to the two tests that are more stringent than that of *high probability.* If the test were the mere presence of error, appellate courts could reverse, as many did in the nineteenth century, for any error, no matter how trivial. The end result was public disaffection with the judicial process.

R. Traynor, The Riddle of Harmless Error 35.* Traynor also criticized the "almost certain" test, which he said was prescribed by the United States Supreme Court when the error is of constitutional dimension and which he noted was supported by Jerome Frank in his dialogue with Learned Hand on harmless error:

> Advocates of the test contend that it is an impossible task to determine whether error influenced the trier of fact. The argument runs that a judge, purporting to evaluate the influence of error as he reviews the record, is realistically driven to evaluate instead the correctness of the judgment, perforce act-

ing as trial judge or jury. Hence the only safe course, whenever the record would support a judgment either way, is to hold the error prejudicial.

Such reasoning springs, not from an abundance of caution, but from a deficiency of will to confront an appellate judge's most difficult task. Concededly, once he undertakes to evaluate error, he is driven to reviewing the whole record, even to weighing the evidence. Nevertheless I believe that in the process it is possible for him deliberately to put aside the question of the correctness of the judgment. Given the will, he finds intuition and reasoning working as one to keep his inquiry in focus on the degree of probability that error influenced the result. In that focus the usual errors—misconduct, erroneous rulings on admissibility of evidence, erroneous instructions— take on a new aspect. Some appear tentatively prejudicial at the outset by their very magnitude, and unquestionably so when the evidence supporting the result lacks the magnitude to dissipate them. Some, not of themselves clearly prejudicial or clearly harmless, cast a cloud on the result that compels an inference of prejudice unless they are likewise so dissipated. Some are dissipated by a record so overwhelmingly supporting the result that any other, even though tenable, is reduced to a mere possibility.

Id. at 35–36.

Under fundamental principles of our legal system, the provinces of the jury and the judge are functionally distinct. Accordingly, in reviewing a case for reversible error, the appellate court should not invade the province of the jury. Consider each of the above described tests in light of the foregoing principle. *See* Crease v. Barrett, 1 C.M. & R. 919, 933, 149 Eng.Rep. 1353, 1359 (Ex.1835):

But we cannot help thinking that the rule is there [Doe v. Tyler] laid down much too generally; and it is obvious that if it were acted upon to that extent, the *Court would in a degree assume the province of the jury;* and besides its frequent application would cause the rules of evidence to be less carefully considered; and the litigant parties would in all probability have on most occasions recourse to bills of exceptions for the rejection or reception of improper evidence: a course productive of great delay and inconvenience. (Emphasis added).

In asserting that the United States Supreme Court had prescribed the "almost certain" test for cases of constitutional error, Traynor referred to Chapman v. United States, 386 U.S. 18 (1967). There, the Court held "that before a federal constitutional error can be held harmless, the court must be able to declare a belief that it is harmless beyond a reasonable doubt." Ibid. at 24. Reconsider Traynor's assertion in light of the Court's discussion and cases reviewed in O'Neal v. McAninch, 115 S.Ct. 992 (1995).

Do you think that an appellate court's approach to "harmless error" differs as the caseload increases? If so, in what area do you think this would be likely to occur—civil cases involving little money, petty criminal cases, interpretation of constitutional principles?

In discussing the equation "correct result = justice", is Traynor using a capital or a small "j"? Recall Hand's anecdote about telling Holmes to "Do Justice", Ante, Chapter II, Sec. 3 at 264. Is it not a significant part of the appellate court's duty to see that the game is played according to the rules? What "rules"? Those of *stare decisis?* Those of Sociological Jurisprudence? In light of Justice Traynor's discussion, re-evaluate your answers to the ultimate questions: What is Justice? Is Justice fair?

PEARSON v. MOTOR DIVISION

Court of Appeals of Arizona, 1995.
181 Ariz. 235, 889 P.2d 28.

OPINION

VOSS, JUDGE.

On the night of December 30, 1992, an Arizona Department of Public Safety officer observed Appellant's vehicle fail to yield the right of way when pulling out of a parking lot, causing other vehicles to take evasive action. The vehicle then proceeded down the street, weaving in traffic. This prompted the officer to make a traffic stop. Once Appellant's vehicle was stopped, the officer observed Appellant and the passenger lean forward inside the vehicle. The officer approached Appellant and asked what he was doing while leaning forward. Appellant responded that he was hiding the beer. The officer smelled liquor on Appellant's breath and Appellant admitted having consumed between eight and ten drinks. After Appellant stepped out of the vehicle, the officer observed Appellant to be unsteady on his feet. Appellant then refused to take a field sobriety test, and he was arrested and transported to the East Valley Task Force DUI command post.

At the command post, the officer read the DUI Implied Consent Affidavit to Appellant and then asked him to take a breath intoxilyzer test. Appellant refused. The officer informed him that refusing to take the test would result in a suspension of his driver's license for twelve months. Appellant still refused to take the breath intoxilyzer test.

As a result, the officer suspended Appellant's driver's license and required him to surrender it. The officer then filled out a certified report, which later was filed with ADOT, stating:

On [December 30, 1992, at 10:55 p.m.] ... I had reasonable grounds to believe the person named had been driving or was in actual physical control of a motor vehicle while under the influence of intoxicating liquor or drugs. Among the actions which led me to that belief were: failed to yield from a private drive, weaving from left to right in traffic.

The report gave Appellant notice that he could request a hearing within fifteen days. Appellant timely requested a hearing.

At the hearing, Appellant challenged the suspension of his license. He argued that the report did not comply with A.R.S. section 28–691(D) (1989) because it failed to set forth reasonable grounds to believe that Appellant was driving under the influence of intoxicating liquor. The hearing officer rejected Appellant's argument and concluded that the observations contained in the report and presented in the hearing constituted reasonable grounds to believe that Appellant was driving under the influence of liquor. The suspension of Appellant's driver's license was affirmed.

Appellant filed a Petition for Judicial Review of Final Administrative Decision to superior court, which affirmed the suspension. On appeal to this court, Appellant argues that the superior court misinterpreted and incorrectly applied A.R.S. section 28–691(D).

Appellant argues that because the report described observations concerning only the vehicle and not about Appellant's condition, it did not contain reasonable grounds to believe that he was operating a vehicle under the influence of intoxicating liquor or drugs. Therefore, Appellant concludes that the report did not comply with the requirements of A.R.S. section 28–691(D). We agree.

Here, no observations about Appellant's condition were included in the report. It merely contained the officer's description of the vehicle—that it failed to yield to traffic, and that it weaved while driving down the street. Alone, these observations are insufficient evidence to demonstrate the probability of Appellant's intoxication to a reasonable person; indeed, they could just as easily indicate the probability of fatigue, a medical problem, or even a driver's inattention. Therefore, we hold that a description or reference to a driver's condition is required to establish reasonable grounds to believe that a person was driving under the influence of liquor or drugs. Because no such description or reference was included in the officer's report, the report erroneously failed to state reasonable grounds in violation of A.R.S. section 28–691(D).

We now examine the effect of such an error. Although Appellant argues that this error is jurisdictional, he offers no authority for such a proposition and we have found none. Therefore, we consider whether this error was reversible or harmless.

The Arizona Supreme Court has held that driver's license "suspension proceedings are civil in nature and are therefore governed by the rules of civil procedure." Campbell v. Superior Court, 106 Ariz. 542, 550, 479 P.2d 685, 693 (1971). Rule 61, Arizona Rules of Civil Procedure, defines harmless error and provides:

No error or defect . . . in anything done or omitted by . . . any of the parties is ground[s] . . . for vacating, modifying or otherwise disturbing a judgment or order, unless refusal to take such action appears to the court inconsistent with substantial justice. The court at every stage of the proceeding must disregard any error or defect in the proceeding which does not affect the substantial rights of the parties.

Rule 61 is consistent with Article 6, section 27 of the Arizona Constitution, which provides in pertinent part: "[n]o cause shall be reversed for technical error in pleadings or proceedings when upon the whole case it shall appear that substantial justice has been done."

Here, Appellant was not prejudiced and substantial justice was done, despite the error in the report. First, we note that A.R.S. section 28–691(D) does not require that the report containing reasonable grounds be given to the driver. Rather, it only requires that the report to be sent to ADOT. Moreover, if a driver requests a hearing, the scope of the hearing is not whether the report listed the officer's reasonable grounds, but rather whether the officer had reasonable grounds. A.R.S. § 28–691(G). Within this statutory scheme, a technical error in a report prepared solely for the purposes of ADOT is hardly prejudicial to a driver, especially when a driver can, and does, challenge the reasonable grounds in a hearing.

Second, the evidence produced at the hearing demonstrated that the officer had reasonable grounds to believe that Appellant was driving under the influence of intoxicating liquor. The officer testified that he smelled liquor on Appellant's breath, that Appellant admitted having between eight and ten drinks, and that Appellant swayed slightly while standing. Moreover, Appellant had the opportunity to cross-examine the officer and to present witnesses to refute the officer's testimony. Erroneously failing to list these reasonable grounds in the report did not prejudice Appellant. Accordingly, such error was harmless.

Finally, we note that our conclusion today furthers the policies underlying A.R.S. section 28–691: to remove from Arizona highways those drivers who may be a menace to themselves and others because of intoxication; to assure prompt revocation of the licenses of dangerous drivers; and to increase the certainty that impaired drivers are penalized even if they refuse to provide evidence of intoxication. Schade, 175 Ariz. at 462, 857 P.2d at 1316; see also Minutes of Arizona State Senate Committee on the Judiciary, H.B. 2273, at 14–16 (April 7, 1987); Campbell, 106 Ariz. at 546, 479 P.2d at 689.

Although the report violated A.R.S. section 28–691(D) because it did not contain the officer's reasonable grounds to believe that Appellant was driving under the influence of intoxicating liquor, the violation here was harmless error. Accordingly, we affirm the trial court's judgment affirming ADOT's suspension of Appellant's driver's license.

D. SUA SPONTE CONSIDERATION ON REVIEW

ALBERT TATE, JR., SUA SPONTE CONSIDERATION ON APPEAL *

Should an appellate court decide an appeal for reasons not raised by the parties themselves? When an appeals tribunal does so *sua sponte*— i.e., of its own motion—should the parties receive prior notice and opportunity to argue the court-raised matter before decision is rendered? Is there any difference in considering *sua sponte* authorities not cited, grounds of decision not argued, or a new issue not raised by counsel?

In several notable instances in our legal history, a high court announced far-reaching changes in law-application upon *sua sponte* notice of an issue. For instance, in Erie R. Co. v. Tompkins, 304 U.S. 64 (1938), the Supreme Court held that in diversity cases the substantive law of the state of trial must be applied, not any federal common law on the subject. This overruled one hundred years of jurisprudence. The dissent pointed out that the issue had not been raised by the parties before either the lower courts or the Supreme Court. Again, in Kilberg v. Northeast Airlines, 172 N.E.2d 526 (1961), the state high court announced that, in conflict-of-law cases, New York would no longer follow the law-of-the-place-of-the-tort rule. The side-opinions stressed that the contention was not before the court and that, in fact, it related to a cause of action technically not before it.

Critical comment emphasized that, aside from the merits of the change, the parties themselves had not had the chance to brief and argue the issue. Yet, in each instance the majority reached out to decide the appeal on an issue not remotely suggested by the parties. Why?

The probable reason for so doing lies in reasons of general law-development and judicial administration. A strong majority felt that the new principle announced was the correct law. It should therefore be applied to multitudes of pending cases and unfiled claims, as well as to the present litigation. To fail to apply the right principle now, approving by inference the wrong or former one—simply because present counsel failed to recognize the issue—might cause injustice not only to present litigants, but also to numerous others erroneously relying upon the principle which the court was about to overrule. To decide the issue now would also avoid the necessity of doing so by reversal in many other pending matters to be tried and then appealed.

In the day-to-day operation of appellate courts—even in the minority of jurisdictions in which appellate courts may not consider an issue not specified by the parties—the courts regularly and frequently consider *sua sponte* authorities not cited and grounds of decision not raised. This

* 9 The Judges J. 68 (1970). Reprinted by permission of the American Bar Association and the National College of the State Judiciary, an activity of the Judicial Administration Division of the American Bar Association.

results in part from the oft-noted poor quality of appellate briefs. The great majority of general practitioners perform their appellate practice on the run, devoting most of their time and energy to the demands of their office and trial practice. Further, the principle at issue may be far more important to the jurisprudence than the litigation is to the parties, and the individual case and fee may not justify the time and expense of thorough briefing. Counsel feel, correctly in my opinion, that the result is determined primarily by the law in the books and the facts at the trial, rather than by their efforts on appeal.

The responsibility of the courts to decide cases in accordance with the law is not diluted by counsel's oversights, lack of research, failure to specify issues or to site relevant authorities. Also, the appellate court is far more readily familiar with the body of its precedent on an issue than counsel (with limited time to devote research to the question) normally can be. Finally, the function of appellate tribunals includes law-announcing and judicial administration. Deciding a case wrongly because counsel did not raise relevant issues or produce relevant data does not prejudice a party to the case alone. Many other persons and the law of the future may be prejudiced if a court fails *sua sponte* to notice a relevant factor of decision and therefore produces a faulty precedent. Therefore, an appellate court routinely bases upon its independent research the *grounds of decision* of an issue (as distinguished from an issue not raised), rather than only upon authorities cited in brief.

ALLAN D. VESTAL, SUA SPONTE CONSIDERATION IN APPELLATE REVIEW*

To say that appellate courts must decide between two constructions proffered by the parties ... would be to render automatons of judges, forcing them merely to register their reactions to the arguments of counsel at the trial level.[1]

An appellate court decides only the issues presented by the parties.[2]

These apparently inconsistent statements suggest a very challenging problem which faces appellate courts. With some frequency a reviewing court in considering a case will discover an unargued legal issue which the court feels is decisive of the case. The failure to argue the point to the appellate court may be a matter of either inadvertence or intention.

* 27 Fordham L.Rev. 477, 477, 487, 498, 503, 504, 506, 508–12 (1959). Reprinted by permission of copyright holder from Fordham Law Review, Vol. 27, pp. 477–512. © 1959 by Fordham University Press.

1. Rentways, Inc. v. O'Neill Milk & Cream Co., 308 N.Y. 342, 349, 126 N.E.2d 271, 274 (1955).

2. Hampton v. Superior Court, 38 Cal.2d 652, 656, 242 P.2d 1, 3 (1952).

"This Court will not perform the duties of counsel; it will not examine a record to see if it can find any errors upon which to reverse a judgment. If the appellant's counsel does not choose, in some form, to call the attention of the Court to the points, provisions of the statute, and the authorities upon which he relies, the judgment will be affirmed." Edmondson v. Alameda County, 24 Cal. 349–50 (1864).

The court must then decide, either consciously or unconsciously, whether it will be restricted to the issues posed by the litigants. The court must decide whether it will view the controversy in the terms and issues posed by counsel or whether it will independently analyze the case in terms and issues of its own making.

. . .

A number of arguments and rationalizations have been urged for the general rule that an appellate court will not consider sua sponte a legal argument not presented and urged by the litigants. These might be summarized as follows: (1) the litigants have a right to control the litigation, therefore the court should decide only those questions raised by the parties; (2) no error requiring rectification has been committed by the lower court since the lower court has—by definition—not ruled on the matter if the question is raised for the first time by the appellate court sua sponte; (3) in some cases this last concept has been enlarged into a fundamental, jurisdictional limitation which foreclosed the consideration of a question not raised in the lower court; and finally (4) the losing party has had no opportunity to rebut the argument accepted by the court, which may in fact be erroneous, and the court has received no assistance in deciding the question from the litigants who are well informed in the matter. . . .

. . .

Some courts of review operate within a framework which specifically authorizes the consideration of issues not raised by the parties.[86] One example of this is found in the Rules of the Supreme Court of the United States wherein it is provided that "errors not specified according to this rule will be disregarded, save as the court, at its option, may notice a plain error not assigned or specified."[87] The Federal Rules of Criminal Procedure provide: "Plain errors or defects affecting substantial rights may be noticed although they were not brought to the attention of the court."[88] Another example of this is found in a statute of Wisconsin which provides: "In any action or proceeding brought to the supreme court by an appeal or writ of error, if it shall appear to that court from the record, that the real controversy has not been fully tried, or that it is probable that justice has for any reason miscarried, the supreme court may in its discretion reverse the judgment or order appealed from,

---

86. "The defendant did not raise in the trial court or in this court the questions which we shall hereafter discuss. However, under the provisions of section 793.18 . . . we are directed, in our consideration of an appeal in a criminal case, to '. . . examine the record, without regard to technical errors or defects which do not affect the substantial rights of the parties, and render such judgment on the record as the law demands; . . .'" State v. Cusick, 84 N.W.2d 554, 555 (Iowa 1957). See also Mo.Sup.Ct.R. 3.27, "Plain errors affecting substantial rights may be considered . . . on appeal, in the discretion of the court, though not raised in the trial court or preserved for review, or defectively raised or preserved, when the court deems that manifest injustice or miscarriage of justice has resulted therefrom." 2 Neb.Rev.Stat. § 25–1919 (1956). "The Supreme Court may, at its option, consider a plain error not specified in appellant's brief."

87. Rules of the Supreme Court of the United States 27(6).

88. Fed.R.Crim.P. 52(b).

regardless of the question whether proper motions, objections or exception appear in the record or not...." [89] Such provisions in statutes or rules, although not establishing definite rules governing the area, certainly indicate an attitude which should be reflected in the decisions of the court. Such provisions, since they make discretionary the consideration of matters sua sponte, can be nothing more than signposts; the applicable rules must be ascertained by an examination of the decided cases....

    . . .

Without attempting to circumscribe the area covered, courts have occasionally stated that fundamental error can be considered sua sponte. As one court stated recently: "We shall not undertake to give an all-inclusive definition of fundamental error; but ... we do hold that an error which directly and adversely affects the interest of the public generally, as that interest is declared in the statutes or Constitution of this state, is a fundamental error." [110] This court has suggested that if a matter is fundamental error, it will be considered even though it is not properly before the appellate court.[111]

    . . .

... [C]ourt rules or statutes giving appellate courts the power to consider matter sua sponte probably do not add to the power of the courts in this area, but such statutes and rules do suggest the nature of the power of the courts....

    . . .

Some courts have used consideration of matters sua sponte to do substantial justice.... The rationale is cast in terms of affirming a correct judgment. For example, "reviewing courts were concerned with the result and not with the reason, and that if a trial court makes a correct ruling but assigns an incorrect reason its judgment will not be reversed." Another court adopted the same position, using the following language: "[A] judgment correct in ultimate effect will not be disturbed on review although the authority below relied upon erroneous reasoning...." In a surprisingly large number of cases in a number of jurisdictions this doctrine has been articulated and followed.[125] The

---

89. Wis.Stat.Ann. § 251.09 (West 1957).

110. Ramsey v. Dunlop, 146 Tex. 196, 202, 205 S.W.2d 979, 983 (1947) (right to consider errors assigned and errors which are fundamental and which appear on the face of the record).

111. Although there may be some question about the matter, the failure to allege a cause of action is not such a fundamental error that it should serve as the grounds for a reversal. A litigant should not be able to wait until an appellate hearing to raise such a question, and an appellate court should not rest a decision on a matter which the litigant has, in the nature of things, waived. Heiman v. Felder, 178 Iowa 740, 160 N.W. 234 (1916); Berly v. Sias, 152 Tex. 176, 255 S.W.2d 505 (1953) (citing a number of Texas cases). Compare Fed.R.Civ.P. 12(h); Iowa R.Civ.P. 110; and Kipp v. Lichtenstein, 79 Ill. 358 (1875); Sargent Co. v. Baublis, 215 Ill. 428, 74 N.E. 455 (1905) (citing a number of Illinois cases). See also Wines, Establishing the Basis for Appellate Review, Ill.L.Forum 135, 142 (1952).

125. Helvering v. Gowran, 302 U.S. 238 (1937); Burgert v. Union Pac. R.R., 240 F.2d 207 (8th Cir.1957); Bullen v. De

courts seem to be willing to affirm on unargued reasoning but seem less willing to reverse on matters not considered by the lower court....

. . .

The generally applicable rule seems to be that appellate courts are reluctant to interfere with the course of litigation determined by the attorneys for the parties, and that generally the courts will allow the parties to determine the nature of the question presented to the courts. The heavy workload of most appellate courts makes impossible any other course as a general policy; most reviewing courts simply do not have the time to do original research into every case coming before the court. Moreover, there seems to be a feeling that deference to the lower court precludes examination in terms other than those in which the case was presented to the lower courts, and this reduces sua sponte consideration of issues by reviewing courts. However, it must be recognized that there are exceptions to the general rule against sua sponte consideration of legal issues.

Courts are generally reluctant to cast these exceptions in absolutes; rather they seem to want to maintain freedom of action, so that the exceptions are articulated in terms of "grace" and "discretion" with no rigid rules established.... Without a doubt the courts refuse to allow the litigants absolute control of the course of litigation, and the actions of the courts do fall into rough categories so that some predictive analysis is possible.

Appellate courts have consistently stated that the question of the jurisdiction of either the trial court or the appellate court can be raised sua sponte by the appellate court. There is a strong thread running through present-day procedure which allows the question of jurisdiction of the subject matter to be raised anytime prior to the final decision of the case....

[T]he area of sua sponte consideration is not limited to jurisdictional matters. Other questions are raised and considered by courts on their own motion. Occasionally an appellate court will consider a matter sua sponte because of the demands of justice. This is a reflection of one of the purposes of appellate review—justice for the parties. Such a decision to probe into the case apparently reflects a number of different factors. Among those considered are whether great additional work is involved and whether the matter to be considered sua sponte is clear and overwhelming in its impact. When the matter involves more than just

Bretteville, 239 F.2d 824 (9th Cir.1956); Ginsburg v. Black, 237 F.2d 790 (7th Cir. 1956); Kithcart v. Metropolitan Life Ins. Co., 150 F.2d 997 (8th Cir.1945); Lautenbach v. Meredith, 240 Iowa 166, 35 N.W.2d 870 (1949); Merkel v. Merkel, 247 Iowa 495, 73 N.W.2d 75 (1955) (citing Iowa Code § 619.16); McManus v. Park, 287 Mo. 109, 229 S.W. 211 (1921). See also Bailey v. O'Fallon, 30 Colo. 419, 70 P. 755 (1902) and In re Smith's Will, 245 Iowa 38, 60 N.W.2d 866 (1953). See also Justice Garfield dissenting in Dickinson v. Porter, 31 N.W.2d 110, 125 (1948); substituted opinion, 240 Iowa 393, 35 N.W.2d 66 (1948).

the individuals, and involves a reflection on the courts and the judicial system, there is more willingness to consider it sua sponte.

. . .

Since the establishing of the corpus juris is of primary importance in appellate review, absolute control by the litigants is somewhat anomalous. There have been a number of occasions when extremely important questions have come before appellate courts where there was some reason to believe that there was lack of adequate representation on one side. Where only private rights are involved, then perhaps there is no reason for overriding the control of the parties. But where public rights are involved or where law of wide application is being established through stare decisis for the public at large, the interest of the public should control.... It would seem appropriate for the court to be free in deciding what the legal question is in such a case. Any other conclusion would seriously circumscribe the appellate court in its very vital, jurisprudential function of establishing the law.

Since case-by-case adjudication affords a very imperfect vehicle for the articulation of the corpus juris of a jurisdiction, judges are occasionally forced to use cases to present a particular ruling when the litigants have not asked for it. When there is a pressing need for a statement of a point of law, the court may be forced to go outside the issues posed by the litigants.... This approach is understandable when one considers the limited opportunity the courts have to present their ideas in a given field. The courts cannot give an advisory opinion gratuitously, rather they must wait until some litigant wishes to raise the question. Since this may occur only infrequently—particularly where the matter is well established—the courts understandably may go somewhat afield in seeking a vehicle for their pronouncement....

Occasionally a court, considering the matter of the corpus juris, may be unwilling to rule on a particular point because of the unsettled or unsettling nature of the problem. The court then may use an unargued point as decisive of the case. So the sua sponte consideration is a two-edged sword which can be used either to pronounce new doctrine or to avoid the making of new law.

NOTE

Putting aside the question of lack of jurisdiction, is there any situation in which an appellate court should consider an issue not presented to the trial court and reverse the trial court judgment? If so, where was the trial error? Is there any situation where the appellate court should not at least afford counsel the opportunity to brief the *sua sponte* issue, either before or after oral argument? Assuming that this opportunity can be readily afforded, is there ever any justification for a reviewing court to decide an appeal on the basis of an issue not raised by the parties without affording an opportunity for the parties to be heard?

AFTERWORD

This book has attempted to assemble and review in one volume teachings from the masters of the American legal tradition. Surely at least one great lesson emerges from this exegesis: our judicial process is remarkably healthy and robust. Indeed, in the relatively short period of its history, the American judicial tradition has developed sophisticated and broadly applicable methods of dispute settlement.

We inherited common law precepts and the common law tradition of adjudication from England, and we have adapted these to suit our exuberant, evolving society. Hence the masters of our judicial tradition have been willing both to establish original techniques and to assimilate teachings from other systems. For example, American appellate courts could always overrule precedent, while this practice was not authorized in Great Britain until 1966. And if the pure common law tradition we inherited was almost exclusively the work of the practitioner, we have not hesitated to borrow from Continental judicial systems the convention of inviting active participation from the academy. The "smell of the lamp" is very much with us: we have welcomed treatises in the law and we frequently cite them as authority.

However, ominous clouds loom on the horizon of judicial scholarship. First, overwhelming case loads deplete the time and energies of state and federal appellate judges, making it difficult for them to provide the high quality of judicial scholarship that has characterized the great American tradition. Next, our formerly untroubled commitment to inductive and deductive reasoning has given way to a penchant for unrestricted citations and overzealous argument. Unfettered citation often obscures, in even our most important cases, the crucial distinction between rational judicial deliberation and personal value judgment. Consequently, many judicial opinions lack the caliber of reasoned elaboration to which we aspire. Indeed, the proliferation of unnecessary citations, confusing jargon and burdensome footnotes makes many of today's opinions resemble tentative law review meanderings (perhaps evidence of excessive reliance on law clerks) instead of "performative utterances" designed to explain clearly why the decisions were reached and how they might guide future adjudication. As the care with which we justify specific decisions has suffered, has not our capacity to make those decisions suffered as well?

As the judicial workload has become almost unmanageable and judicial scholarship less compelling, we have seen a concomitant decline in the intellectual quality of scholarly output from the legal academy. In describing this "new academy," Professor Mary Ann Glendon, Learned

Hand Professor of Law at Harvard, observes a marked trend away from traditional, objective scholarship:

> Many legal scholars, of course, write in hopes of furthering definite practical or political objectives. But advocacy scholarship, as that term is understood among law professors, openly or covertly abandons the traditional obligation to deal with significant contrary evidence or arguments. In fact, advocacy scholarship is not scholarship at all, for its research is not conducted with an open mind and its results are not presented with a view toward advancing knowledge about the subject treated. Ironically, it was a paragon of romantic judging who was one of the first people to call attention to the sudden increase of partisan legal literature in the 1960s. Many writers of law review articles, Justice William O. Douglas complained, were failing to disclose that they were "people with axes to grind." [1]

What Glendon calls "advocacy scholarship" often reduces the academic landscape to a partisan battle over what is intellectually fashionable. Such zealous, either/or thinking ignores critical exploration of other perspectives and bodies of knowledge. It embraces a kind of precious discourse as divisive as it is single-minded, a form of conversation more likely to engender a coercive sectarian atmosphere than a heightened search for enlightenment.

Yet notwithstanding the threat that this myopic academic ideology poses to genuine pluralistic dialogue, academic advocacy, as Professor Glendon points out, has emerged in much of the legal academy:

> What is novel in recent years is the degree to which one-sided advocacy in the guise of scholarship has gained respectability. In many schools, hiring and promotion committees, the gatekeepers of academic standards, no longer insist strictly on a candidate's duty to master important contributions by others in the field or to fairly appraise the pros and cons of the positions he or she takes. The scholarly enterprise has thus been transformed. Although many legal writers, and especially the authors of widely used treatises, still try conscientiously to deal with all relevant information and points of view, a reader can no longer take that for granted.[2]

By ignoring our established critical traditions, we risk losing the hard-earned lessons that those traditions have bestowed upon us. As the great securities scholar Louis Loss has remarked, "[t]here are people on this faculty who scorn treatise writing and liken legal treatises to battleships—prime, prestigious stuff in their time, but not really worth their keep in the contemporary world. They prefer to write about the

---

1. M. Glendon, A Nation Under Law-   2. Id.
yers 208 (1994).

sex lives of caterpillars. But what they don't realize is that these books have shaped the law." [3]

But these are only clouds, still distant; they need not comprise a permanent weather front. Thoughtful people are already at work studying solutions to the inundation of appellate dockets, and we are confident that their ingenuity will help us resolve this critical problem. And although of a dramatically different and less important relation to the judicial process, the difficulties of the "new academy" will find like solution. This may mean a shift of law school curricular direction, or even one of university administration. But however it happens, those who ultimately control our institutions of higher learning will recognize that benchmarks of quality teaching and meaningful learning—candid, open-minded scholarship and thoughtful, open-ended dialogue—must eventually take precedence over other interests, for the importance of the legal academy cannot be overstated. It is there where great instruction abides—a grand tutelage that extends far beyond students enrolled in formal classes and intimately embraces lawyers and judges as well.

Meanwhile, a stalwart judicial process is at work, in part following directions from masters of generations past, thoughtful students of the judicial process who paused to analyze a complex whole and to divide it into its constituent elements. Faced with infinitely more complicated societal and economic issues than pure "lawyer's law," those who followed have made important and necessary adjustments to the system. The impress and imprint of what we have inherited is still there to behold and admire. Nevertheless, the common law tradition today continues to reach beyond what has gone before, most often advancing cautiously, hugging shores like mariners of old, but at times, willing to launch bold, jet-powered excursions to meet "the unrestrained tendency to take to the courts the most explosive issues of society—and present them with explosive forces of advocacy." [4]

3. S. Labaton, "Profile, Louis Loss," *New York Times,* September 26, 1993.

4. M. Rosenberg, *Devising Procedures That Are Civil to Promote Justice That Is Civilized* 69 Mich.L.Rev. 787, 810 (1971).

*

INDEX

References are to Pages

†